Personnel and
Human Resource Management

Personnel and Human Resource Management

Third Edition

Randall S. Schuler
New York University

West Publishing Company
St. Paul ■ New York ■ Los Angeles ■ San Francisco

Copyediting   Joan Torkildson
Design   Paula Shuhert
Composition   Carlisle Graphics
Cover   Photo © Everett C. Johnson/Frozen Images

Library of Congress Cataloging-in-Publication Data

Schuler, Randall S.
    Personnel and human resource management.

    Includes bibliographical references and indexes.
    1. Personnel management.   I. Title.
HF5549.S249   1987   658.3   86–15804
ISBN 0–314–25471–4

Dedicated to: Susan, John, Bob, Stu, Henry, Mac, and Bill—Coaches, Counselors, and Supporters Par Excellence

Contents

13
Occupational Safety and Health / 474

SECTION
VI
Establishing And Maintaining Effective Work Relationships / 509

14
Employee Rights / 510

SECTION
VII
International PHRM and Research / 609

17
International Personnel and Human Resource Management / 610

18
Personnel Research / 641

Summary Case / 685

Appendixes / 693

A
Legislation, Court, and NLRB Decisions Affecting Personnel and Human Resource Management / 694

B
**Personnel and Human Resource
Management Information / 705**

C
Career Management / 713

Preface

Organizations today are confronted with challenges in raising productivity, enhancing innovation, improving product and service quality, and meeting the intense level of international competition never before seen. At the same time, organizations are being asked to provide an increased quality of work life and to comply with laws, guidelines, and court decisions that govern the utilization of human resources. And because people are of the essence in these issues of importance and challenge to organizations, these issues are the heart of personnel and human resource management today. Consequently, personnel and human resource management has an opportunity to enable organizations to survive, grow, be competitive and profitable. It can do this by effectively utilizing the human resources of the organizations. It can be effective by having the appropriate knowledge related to personnel and human resource management and by being able to implement this knowledge in organizations. This third edition of *Personnel and Human Resource Management* has been written to provide that knowledge and assist in implementing it as effectively as possible. To provide this knowledge and assistance, several features are incorporated into this new edition.

As in the second edition of *Personnel and Human Resource Management*, this edition contains the feature entitled "PHRM in the News." As in the second edition, this real-life feature is taken from sources such as *Business Week, The Wall Street Journal, Fair Employment Report,* and *Bulletin to Management.* This feature illustrates the current realities and applications of personnel and human resource management. In contrast to the second edition, the "PHRM in the News" feature is used at the start of each chapter and within the chapter. Used within the chapter it replaces the previous feature "Slice of Life." This change was made for consistency because the features are essentially the same.

Another feature of this edition are cases that appear at the end of most all chapters and at the end of the text. The cases in this edition are like those in the second edition; they offer true-to-life personnel and human resource issues and challenges. As in the second edition, these cases are based upon real-life events, although the names and places have been disguised. While the cases at the end of each chapter are intended to relate to just that one chapter, the case at the end of the text is intended to be related to many chapters in the text. Because this third edition highlights the systemic nature of personnel and human resource management activities, this longer, end-of-text case is meant to require the application of material from several chapters rather than just one chapter in providing an effective solution to the issues and challenges posed. All cases in this third edition are new.

In addition to these features incorporated to provide knowledge and assistance in implementation, this third edition of *Personnel and Human Resource Management* has several other important characteristics. Each chapter contains an extensive set of up-to-date, important references. These are provided in the notes at the end of each chapter, along with commentary to expand on material in the chapter. Thus, these notes are a valuable source of information in themselves, and in locating information that supplements topics presented in the chapter. The references reflect many of the best research and theoretical works as well as many of the most current articles on personnel and human resource management application. In keeping with contemporary practices, only the initials of the authors' first names are used.

Each chapter also contains a discussion of the purposes and importance of the activity being discussed, its important relationships with other personnel and human resource management activities, the internal and external environment, and the legal considerations relevant to that activity. These characteristics are included because they reflect current thinking in personnel and human resource management (PHRM) and the reality of a dynamic, international, and highly competitive environment. Another feature included for the same reason is the section on trends located near the end of each chapter. Within this section there are three topics of increasing importance to the field of PHRM. These topics include: (a) techniques for assessing the effectiveness of each activity; (b) human resource information system needs and computer technology applications in PHRM; and (c) how each PHRM activity can be used more strategically in organizations. A new feature of this third edition is the PC project located at the end of chapters 2–14 and 16–18. Each project is presented only briefly and as an option. Full description of the project and actual PC application is contained in our companion book, *Personnel Computer (PC) Projects for Personnel and Human Resource Management*.

The organization of the chapters in this third edition is similar to that in the second edition. There are, however, several significant changes. First of all, each chapter begins with only one "PHRM in the News" feature. Typically the theme found in each of these features is how PHRM activities can be used to help an organization improve its bottom line; that is, its profitability, competitiveness, survival and/or growth. Replacing the "Slice of Life" feature found in the second edition, are other "PHRM in the News" features. These features illustrate real-world applications of the PHRM activities. A second change is the use of only one selection and placement chapter rather than two. This makes for a tighter presentation of selection and placement. The material removed is the discussion of validation strategies. Because these are important to know, they are a part of the new chapter on personnel research, Chapter 18. In addition, this new chapter contains discussion of organizational surveys and methods to cost out the dollar-and-cents benefits of PHRM activities. Another change is the deletion of "equal employment opportunity" from the titles of the recruitment and selection chapters. This reflects that these considerations are now part-and-parcel of these activities rather than something that is just tacked on at the end. Also, a new feature is the chapter on international personnel and human resource management (Chapter 17). This addition is consistent with the desire to reflect what's happening in the real world of PHRM. There is little doubt that the world market is far more critical and competitive for the United States than ever before. Also added is the PC project component at the end of each chapter. Because PCs are becoming more prevalent in the work place and can benefit tremendously doing PHRM activities, they are introduced here. These, however, are an optional part of this book. The appendixes have been trimmed back to three from the previous eight. This has been done, however, at no loss of information because the deleted material has been weaved into the chapters where it is discussed.

For those who are interested in material to supplement this text, we have three books available:

Readings in Personnel and Human Resource Management, 3d ed., by Randall S. Schuler, Stuart A. Youngblood, and Vandra Huber
Case Problems in Personnel and Human Resource Management by Randall S. Schuler and Stuart A. Youngblood

In summary, this third edition of *Personnel and Human Resource Management* represents a substantial change from the second edition. The third edition is meant to be more extensive, more current, more challenging and useful, and much more readable. I hope that these intentions have been attained.

Acknowledgments

As with the second edition, many people were of critical importance in the completion of this third edition. Stuart Youngblood at Texas A&M and Nick Beutell at Seton Hall University played particularly noteworthy roles. Stuart wrote the excellent case studies that appear at the end of most all chapters and provided extensive substantive comments on each chapter. Nick was the prime mover of the PC projects component found in most all chapters and our companion book, *Personnel Computer (PC) Projects for Personnel and Human Resource Management.*

Also providing important contributions to this third edition were Jeff Lenn at George Washington University, Robert Kerr at the University of Windsor, Mike Burke at New York University, Robert Faley at Kent State University, Peter Dowling at the University of Melbourne, and Robert Davies at New York University. Jeff wrote the integrative case found at the end of this book and Robert Davies, Peter and Robert Kerr contributed parts to the chapter on international personnel and human resource management. Robert Faley and Mike Burke provided several helpful comments on the content and organization of Chapters 3–5. In addition, Mike contributed the new chapter on personnel research.

The following individuals also provided many good ideas and suggestions in their roles as reviewers and evaluators of the third edition:

Karen Dill Bowerman
California State University—Fresno

James A. Breaugh
University of Missouri—St. Louis

Michael J. Burke
New York University

Robert Faley
Kent State University

Vandra Huber
University of Utah

Ki Hee Kim
William Paterson College

Janina C. Latack
Ohio State University

Sheldon Montgomery
University of Redlands

Marilyn Morgan
University of Virginia

Peter D. Nugent
Rockhurst College

James R. Terborg
University of Oregon

Jo Ann Verdin
University of Illinois—Chicago

Several personnel and human resource practitioners and practicing managers also provide many good practical examples. These individuals include Mary Miner, Suzanne Forsyth, Jim Marsh, Wes Baynes, Jim Handlon, Jim Wilkins, Catherine Downes Bower, and Gary Turner.

The support and encouragement of William Guth, chair of the Department of Management at New York University, and Dick West, Dean of the Graduate School of Business at New York University, are sincerely appreciated. Also appreciated is the fine secretarial support at New York University. This support made the preparation of this manuscript a great deal easier. Those who provided the assistance are: Alicia Serino and Belle Gonong.

Special thanks go to Eddie Roberts who typed the bulk of the manuscript quickly and without error. They also include several outstanding people at

West. They are Richard T. Fenton, acquisitions editor, Esther W. Craig, developmental editor, and Pamela Barnard, assistant production editor. Without their professional dedication and competence this book would not have been possible. I also wish to thank Gilbert R. Whitaker, Jr., Dean of the School of Business Administration of The University of Michigan, for the support provided during the completion of this revision while I was a visiting faculty member.

Randall S. Schuler
Ann Arbor
January 1987

Personnel and
Human Resource Management

Introduction to Personnel and Human Resource Management

CHAPTER 1

Personnel and Human Resource Management

CHAPTER

1

Personnel and Human Resource Management

For Personnel, Bigger Role Plus a Fancier Name

Once relegated to the bottom of the corporate barrel, human resources—the business of managing a company's work force—is gaining in importance. "It used to be that the people in charge of personnel hired you, fired you and made sure the watermelon and beer was kept cold at the company picnic," said Cate Bower, vice president of communications at the American Society for Personnel Administration. "Now the human-resource field is far more complex and sophisticated."

Up until about five years ago, the field was referred to mainly as personnel or employee relations, but as companies face increased competition at home and abroad, as new legislation affects the hiring process and as employees take a more active role in guiding the actions of their employers, the term "human-resource management" has come into play.

"In the old definition, personnel was a rigid job classification," said Theodore Hawryluk, director of employee assistance in the human resources department of Philip Morris Inc. "It involved basic record-keeping, mechanical job evaluations and automatic merit increases. But today there is an increasing realization that the way employees feel—physically and emotionally—will significantly affect how much work they produce."

That realization is leading to more cooperative ventures between workers and senior management, said John Sturges, senior vice president for corporate human resources at the Marine Midland Bank in New York. "The evolution of human resources has gone from an administrative function to a more productive role," Mr. Sturges said. "Years ago, for example, companies would set up suggestion boxes which mainly focused on employees' complaints. Now human-resource personnel help set up employee-advisory boards and quality circles, where employees and senior management get together to solve problems."

Many new regulations

The revised job description for human resources results partly from a host of new Federal and state regulations. Hiring and promotion practices are now governed by laws that prohibit discrimination on the basis of age, sex and race. At the same time, the Government is regulating the welfare of the work force. As human-resource personnel assume responsibility for the safety and health of company employees, they are becoming involved in projects that range from monitoring the use of industrial chemicals to establishing incentives for workers to stop smoking.

"We have to be much more aware of what the laws are and how they are changing," Mr. Sturges said. "Tax laws, for instance, change all the time and force us to make changes in compensation and benefit plans."

As the field grows and develops, human-resource personnel say they find themselves becoming more involved in day-to-day company operations. "People in personnel are perceived as not knowing the numbers, not knowing how to read a profit-and-loss statement or how much it costs to run a business," said Dave Wietsha, a human-resource manager with the American Hospital Supply Corporation in Atlanta. "But that picture is totally inaccurate. We are involved in key business decisions the company makes, and the management team here tends to bounce ideas off us."

Career opportunities in the burgeoning human-resource field involve many different areas. While human-resource managers still handle traditional jobs such as recruiting new staff members and negotiating wages, they may also be involved in other important aspects of developing and training personnel. These days, managers may help coordinate mentor programs between junior and senior staff members. They may find themselves in a debate over whether to give lie-detector tests to prospective employees. Or they may help employees find housing if they are forced to move to another city.

"The days when you went to work at a company and expected to be in the same job for 25 years are gone," said Dr. Robert F. Rizley, chairman of the department of personnel and human-resource studies at Cornell University. "Technology is continually changing. The pace has doubled. And companies are forced to train, develop and relocate people quickly and efficiently."

In 1982, the last year for which figures are available, the Federal Bureau of Labor Statistics found that 202,900 people were employed in the personnel and labor-relations field. By 1995, the bureau predicts, that figure will have grown by 23 percent.

Training for careers in human resources begins at the college level. According to the 1985 edition of "The Chronicle Four-Year College Data Book," a directory of major courses of study offered by four-year colleges, 148 universities offer majors in personnel management and 56 have majors in human-resource development. The average starting salary for college graduates entering the field with a bachelor of arts degree is $20,160, up 11.3 percent from last year's salary of $18,108, according to the College Placement Council, a national nonprofit organization that charts the annual salaries of college graduates.

As the field becomes increasingly diversified, many schools are updating their curriculums. At Cornell, one popular new course focuses on "Women at Work," and covers company-sponsored day-care centers and the development of "flex time" for working mothers. Michigan State University recently added a course on the ways in which unions use the media and another on "The Quality of Work Life," which looks at how employees are becoming more autonomous.

Two paths for graduates

There are two paths open for college graduates who are interested in a career in human resources. One is to try to focus on a particular specialty, such as compensation analysis or computerized information systems.

A recent study by Fox-Morris Associates, a Philadelphia-based executive-recruiting company for human-resource personnel, found that the demand was highest for technical recruiters. The second most desired specialists are corporate recruiters; followed by employee-relations representatives and compensation and benefit managers.

"We receive a lot of specialty requests," said Richard R. Wilson, senior vice president of Fox-Morris. "The compensation area is strong right now and when companies request senior compensation managers, they usually require that they have additional specialized computer skills."

The other path, more frequently taken, is to become a generalist, with a broad background in several different areas. Mr. Wietsha, of the American Hospital Supply Corporation, took the generalist route. Besides being responsible, in his job, for calculating the wages and benefits of 500 people in 10 locations throughout the Southeast, he also travels around the nation scouting out new recruits. And he conducts training sessions and motivational classes for personnel ranging from truck drivers to middle managers. A series of seminars he gave recently on how to manage time more effectively focused on the notion that 20 percent of the workday may produce 80 percent of the work.

"The entire field is becoming more respected and more visible," said Richard Schillenbach, a recruiting consultant at Pitney Bowes, a New York-based accounting company. "Companies are realizing that if you manage people properly, the rest will just fall into place."

The preceding "PHRM in the News" reflects on several significant areas: (1) organizations are more concerned than ever about managing human resources effectively; (2) personnel and human resource management (PHRM) is seen as the department that has the expertise in managing human resources effectively; (3) personnel and human resource management is critical to organizations because of the importance of productivity and the vital link between using human resources effectively—the essence of effective PHRM—and productivity improvement; (4) the PHRM profession is growing, and PHRM's importance and contribution to organizations is increasing; and (5) PHRM minimizes fines and penalties that can result from violating the numerous federal, state, and local laws regarding the use of human resources in organizations.

Together, these areas help organizations to be more competitive and profitable as well as to survive and grow. PHRM also enables organizations to enhance the quality of work life for their employees, because effective PHRM is based on respect and concern for individuals' rights and preferences. This area and the first five are expanded in this chapter and throughout the text because they make PHRM essential to organizations today.

Personnel and human resource management is the recognition of the importance of an organization's work force as vital human resources contributing to the organization's goals, and the use of several functions and activities to ensure that human resources are used effectively and fairly for the benefit of the individual, the organization, and society. Although some organizations still use the term *personnel* to refer to the department that deals with activities such as recruitment, selection, compensation, and training, the phrase "personnel and human resource management" is rapidly supplanting it. This change recognizes the vital role that human resources play in an organization, the challenges in managing human resources effectively, and the growing body of knowledge and professionalism surrounding PHRM.[1] In return for this recognition, PHRM departments in organizations must successfully address the areas listed earlier. Nonetheless, effective PHRM is still implemented through numerous functions and activities.[2]

PHRM Functions and Activities

This book describes five PHRM functions and activities, which generally include all of the functions and activities that PHRM departments in organizations actually perform. (The specific jobs found in these departments and their salaries are described later in this chapter.) These functions are as follows:

- Planning for human resource needs
- Staffing the organization's personnel needs
- Appraising and compensating employee behavior
- Improving employees and the work environment
- Establishing and maintaining effective working relationships

Although the PHRM departments of many organizations may not be currently performing all these functions, the trend is clearly moving in that direction. Consequently, describing them here is useful.

Planning for Human Resource Needs

The function of planning for human resource needs involves two major activities: (1) planning and forecasting the organization's short- and long-term human resource requirements and (2) analyzing the jobs in the organization to determine their duties and purposes and the skills, knowledge, and abilities that are needed. These two activities are essential for effectively performing many other personnel and human resource management activities. For example, they help indicate the organization's present and future needs regarding numbers and types of employees. They also help to determine how the employees will be obtained (e.g., from outside recruiting or by internal transfers and promotions) and the training needs that the organization will have. These two activities can be viewed as the major factors influencing the staffing and development functions of the entire organization.

Although these activities are vital in the management of human resources, most organizations have only recently incorporated them into personnel departments. Today, in nearly all of the Fortune 500 companies, personnel managers are responsible for human resource planning; this was true for only a handful of companies five years ago. Now, organizations are increasingly relating human resource planning to corporate goals or strategies.[3] Typical of the trend is Tenneco's requirement that vice-presidents submit five-year "executive resources" plans along with five-year business plans. If a division is planning to shift orientations (e.g., from marketing to production), the vice-president of PHRM must make certain that the vice-president of that division has a human resource plan to help implement the proposed shift.

Staffing the Organization's Personnel Needs

Once the organization's human resource needs have been determined, they have to be filled. Thus, staffing activities become necessary. These include (1) recruiting job applicants (candidates) and (2) selecting from among the job applicants those most appropriate for the available jobs.

To ensure a full and fair search for job candidates, the organization must cast a wide net for potential employees:

Time was when the organization could rely on "walk-ins" to provide the major source of supply for nonexempt employees; it could choose exempt employees from traditional sources. If a comer was spotted, the organization might carefully tailor the job description so that the requisite experience fit him—and probably only him—to the job. Now, however, the organization must prepare job descriptions and specify requisite experience and training with care and publicize its openings.[4]

These recruiting procedures apply to external candidates (those not currently employed by the organization) as well as to internal candidates (those who are currently employed by the organization). After the candidates have been identified, they must be selected. Common procedures used in selection include obtaining completed application forms or resumes; interviewing the candidates; checking education, background, experience, and references; and various forms of testing. Regardless of the exact procedures used, however, they must be related to the job to serve equal employment opportunity (EEO) laws and regulations. In other words, selection procedures must result in a match between a candidate's abilities and the abilities that the job requires.

Appraising and Compensating Employee Behavior

After employees are on the job, determining how well they are doing and rewarding them accordingly become necessary. If they are not doing well, the reasons must be determined. This determination may indicate that the reward structure needs to be changed, that employee training is necessary, or that some type of motivation should be provided. To these ends, this function incorporates several activities associated with appraising and several associated with compensating. Those associated with appraising include (1) appraising and evaluating employee behavior and (2) analyzing and motivating employee behavior.

Although performance appraisal can be painful for both supervisor and employee, it is a critically important activity, especially because legal compliance dictates that employment decisions be made on the basis of performance. For example, if someone is to be selected for a promotion, the decision should be based on an evaluation of that employee's performance.

Not all employees are good performers. Some may be continually absent or late to work, and some may be chemically dependent. With the rise of employee rights, greater social responsibility, and the cost of replacing employees, however, organizations may prefer to assist employees in correcting their undesired behavior and motivate them to perform as well as they can rather than to terminate them.

Employees are generally rewarded on the basis of the job's value rather than on the employee's performance level. Rewards—namely, indirect benefits—provided just for being a member of the organization, however, are rapidly increasing.

Which form of compensation is most fair? Which form is most effective for the organization? By what methods can jobs be evaluated fairly to determine their value? These concerns and others are part of the compensating activity, which includes (1) administering direct compensation on the basis of job evaluation, (2) providing performance-based pay, and (3) administering indirect compensation benefits to employees in the organization.

None of these activities is easy, but all must be done to ensure the effective use of human resources. They must be done not only to get employees to join the organization, to participate, and to perform but also to determine possible training and development needs.

Improving Employees and the Work Environment

In recent years, PHRM interest has grown in three areas: (1) determining, designing, and implementing employee training and development programs to increase employee ability and performance; (2) improving the work environment, especially regarding the quality of work life and productivity improvement programs; and (3) improving the physical work environment to maximize employee safety and health.

Training and development activities include training employees, developing management, and helping to develop careers. These activities are designed to increase employees' abilities in order to facilitate employee performance. Whereas these programs are designed to be used with many employees for many purposes, organizations also offer more specialized training programs, tailored to the topic or group being served (e.g., career management). Making career information and alternatives available to employees can result in high employee satisfaction and retention rates. Concern for employees' careers extends from the organization to the employees themselves.

The primary purpose of improving the physical and sociopsychological work environment is to benefit the employee and the organization, whereas the primary purpose of training and development activities is to improve employee performance. In practice as well as in theory, however, some overlap occurs. For example, in many programs designed to improve the work environment, employee performance may increase along with satisfaction, responsibility, and self-control. One program that is aimed at improving both the quality of work life and productivity is the quality circle effort, one of many programs now being used to increase productivity. This program is one of several discussed in Chapter 12.

In addition to providing training and development programs to improve conditions, organizations also provide PHRM programs for improvements in safety and health and in productivity and quality of life. The federal regulations specified in the Occupational Safety and Health Act of 1970 have special influence in improving employees' work environments. These improvements directly and positively influence employees' physical safety and security as well as their sociopsychological well-being (and thus their productivity and quality of work life).

Establishing and Maintaining Effective Working Relationships

When the organization has obtained the employees it needs, it must take care to bring them into the organization, compensate them, and provide conditions that will make it attractive for them to stay. As a part of this function, organizations must establish and maintain effective working relationships with employees. Although this is formally required for union employees, establishing and maintaining effective working relationships with nonunion employees is also useful. Regarding all employees, this function involves five activities: (1) recognizing and respecting employee rights, (2) understanding the reasons and methods that employees use in organizing, (3) bargaining and settling grievances with employees and the organizations representing them, (4) understanding and learning from PHRM activities in other countries, and (5) conducting research in PHRM activities.

Because employees are increasingly gaining more rights, employment decisions such as discharges, layoffs, and demotions must be made with care and evidence. The managers of the organization must be aware of their employees' rights. The PHRM manager is in an excellent position to inform line managers of these rights.

A union contract often protects unionized employees' rights. PHRM must become familiar with that contract and the issues related to how employees organize themselves in dealing with the organization and how the organization bargains and negotiates with its organized employees. Familiarity with the formal union-management relationship is necessary because, on the one hand, the relationship can effectively define the extent to which other PHRM functions can be applied to the work force. On the other hand, the union-management relationship can be instrumental in developing new PHRM programs (e.g., programs to improve compensation or productivity and quality of life).

Aiding the development of programs for improving productivity and quality of life is an understanding of the PHRM activities in other countries. For this reason and several others, awareness of how organizations in other countries manage their human resources is useful. This information is particularly useful for multinational organizations and U.S. organizations recruiting job applicants in other countries.

Just as the international dimension of PHRM is growing, so is the activity of personnel and human resource management research. Consequently, awareness and understanding of research techniques and issues relevant to managing human resources are critical. The final chapter describes the techniques and issues in personnel research that are relevant to almost all of the other chapters in this book.

Objectives and Purposes of PHRM Functions and Activities

The five separate PHRM functions and their related activities are important in organizations because they fulfill several objectives and purposes.

Objectives of PHRM

The three major objectives of PHRM are to attract potentially qualified job applicants, retain desirable employees, and motivate employees. PHRM functions and activities are important because they serve to attract, retain, and motivate employees. Their growing importance in organizations is also attributed to the recognition that PHRM can and does have an impact on the bottom line of the organization. The term *bottom line* refers to the organization's survival, growth, profitability, and competitiveness. In the case of nonprofit and governmental organizations, the term refers to survival and the ability to do more with the same or fewer resources.[5] Focusing on the bottom line is a key way in which PHRM can gain recognition and respect in organizations. The following "PHRM in the News" describes specific ways in which PHRM can influence the bottom line. General ways of influencing the bottom line are through improved productivity, improved quality of work life, and legal compliance—the purposes of PHRM.

Purposes of PHRM

The three purposes of PHRM are improved productivity, improved quality of work life, and legal compliance. Although the several PHRM functions and activities may serve the three objectives, each may also serve these three purposes and thus the bottom line of the organization.

Productivity.   Without a doubt, productivity is an important goal of organizations. PHRM can do many things to improve productivity. The most pro-

---

PHRM in the News

Human Resources Managers Must Remember the Bottom Line

Today's human resource managers— whether located at corporate headquarters, at a manufacturing plant or a research and development facility— must remember the bottom-line if they are to earn their board and keep.

Although they are indeed in the people business, the end result of their efforts should always be to help the business generate a profit.

It must be recognized, however, that the HRM function *does* contribute significantly to corporate profit by reducing, containing and avoiding costs. Dollars saved through effective human resources management move directly to the bottom line.

Let's look at a typical profit-and-loss statement (P&L)—the businessman's report card.

The cost of products sold

Each personnel manager must look first to the beginning of every company's outlay: the cost of products sold. That category can be broken down into three subcategories.

- *Factory inventory costs (FIC).* The second line of the statement usually shows factory inventory costs (FIC). Human resource managers can make their biggest contribution in this area.

- *Plant burden or overhead.* HR managers can play an important role in another major factor that affects the P&L drastically, that of keeping plants fully utilized and overhead (or burden) positive instead of negative. It's a fact that the higher the production rate, the lower the overhead cost.

■ *Factory cost adjustments (FCA).* Yet another line on the P&L form is that of factory cost adjustments. FCA is, in short, things that have gone wrong—scrap, cost variances, loss of raw material and product inventories, and off-spec products.

If human resource managers direct their efforts toward improving the productivity and efficiency of employees, promoting a dedication to quality work, eliminating waste and scrap, increasing throughput and eliminating attitudes which lead to mistakes, they can minimize this drain on sales dollars and profitability.

Operating expenses

The second major area of concern is operating expenses. Quite a few items fall under the operating expense heading on the P&L. These include:

■ *Distribution.* Distribution expenses cover the cost of freight and warehousing. The proper management and use of warehouse people, assisted by human resource managers, can help keep these costs down.

■ *Selling.* Selling costs include salary, commission, entertainment, travel, incentives and product sample costs incurred by the sales force in the field, at the company's various sales offices and at the corporate office.

   These costs increase if products are not of top, competitive quality, or are not available in sufficient quantity.

■ *Advertising and promotion.* This line shows what the company spends to advertise and promote its products. If profits would permit it, most firms would increase advertising. It's all tied together; when human resource

managers help improve the bottom line they help generate more funds for advertising, which in turn produces more sales volume.

■ *Product service.* The amounts entered on the product service line also subtract from the bottom line. These costs refer to repair, service and maintenance of the company's products once they are sold to customers—particularly during a warranty period.

■ *Research and development.* If a company is to maintain quality products, be competitive in the market place, and produce new products, research and development costs are a must.

   Human resource managers can help hire and retain the kind of R&D people needed to justify these costs, thereby increasing the flow of new and improved products necessary to maintain sales volume at a profit.

■ *Administrative and general.* The expenses shown under the administrative and general heading on the P&L form reflect the cost of top administrative salaries and the cost of doing business. This category encompasses staff charges, bad debts, and the like.

Even here human resource managers can be of service. By having the right people, do the right job, at the right time, the HRM professional is helping top management solve many important problems.

   Now it's time to total it all up. The complete "operating expenses" are subtracted from the "gross profit" line. From this we get the actual "operating profit" of the company. This is the vital "profit before taxes" line on the P&L— the famous bottom line.

   So there you have it. The sales, costs and expenses of a company are directly related to the management of its human resources—blue collar and white collar.

Source: J. F. Gow, *Personnel Journal* (April 1985): 30–32. Reprinted with permission of *Personnel Journal*, Costa Mesa, California, all rights reserved.

ductive organizations in America know this and treat their PHRM departments in ways that are different from less productive organizations.
Recently, A. T. Kearney examined how highly productive American corporations are run. In comparing well-run corporations with those less well run in
the same industries, Kearney found that the leaders in productivity had a
unique set of personnel and human resource management practices. In particular:

- They define the human resource role according to its level of participation
  in business decisions that implement business strategies.
- They focus the current resources devoted to the human resource function
  on important problems before they add new programs or seek additional
  resources.
- Their human resource staffs initiate programs and communication with
  line management.
- The line management share the responsibility for human resource programs.
- The corporate staffs share responsibility for human resource policy formation and program administration across organizational levels.[6]

Thus, PHRM has a unique and timely opportunity for improving productivity.[7]

Quality of Work Life.   The dissatisfying nature of industrial—or clerical—
work is no longer disputed. Many of today's employees prefer a greater level
of involvement in their jobs than was previously assumed. Many desire more
self-control and a chance to make a greater contribution to the organization.
Apparently many employers are equally convinced of the importance of improved quality of work life, particularly the importance of greater worker involvement through employee participation in work place decisions. Communicating with employees and encouraging them to communicate their ideas
is second only to productivity as a major role that chief executive officers desire to see their PHRM managers play.[8]

Legal Compliance.   In managing their employees, organizations must comply with many laws, executive orders, guidelines, and court decisions. A
summary listing of some of these rules is found in Exhibit 1.1. A more extensive listing is found in Appendix A. These laws and regulations affect almost
all of the functions and activities that PHRM uses. Thus, PHRM's constant
concern is compliance with current laws and regulations, and court decisions
such as *County of Washington* v. *Gunther* (1981) or *Connecticut* v. *Teal*
(1982). Additionally, PHRM must be familiar with the actions of the Occupational Safety and Health Administration, the Equal Employment Opportunity Commission, the Office of Federal Contract Compliance Programs, and
the various state and city equal employment commissions and human or civil rights commissions.

 If PHRM fails to maintain awareness of current laws and regulations, organizations may find themselves burdened with costly lawsuits and large
fines. Fortunately, PHRM departments and their managers can avoid these

Selected Sources of Rules That Affect PHRM   *Exhibit 1.1*

Legislation Provisions

Fair Labor Standards Act (1938) and subsequent amendments—FLSA

Minimum Wage Law (1977)

Equal Pay Act (1963 amendment to the FLSA)

Prevailing wage laws—
1. Davis-Bacon Act (1931) and 2. Walsh-Healey Act (1935).

Legally required fringe benefits—
1. OASDHI (1935 and amendments)
2. Unemployment compensation (1935)
3. Worker's compensation (dates differ from state to state)

Employee Retirement Income Security Act (1974)—ERISA

Occupational Safety and Health Act (1970)—OSHA

Title VII Civil Rights Act (1964) (Amended by EEOA 1972)

Equal Employment Opportunity Act (1972)—EEOA

The Pregnancy Discrimination Act of 1978 (1978 Civil Rights Act Amendment to Title VII)

Civil Rights Act of 1866 Section 1981

Civil Rights Act of 1871 Section 1983

Vietnam Era Veterans Readjustment Act (1974)

Age Discrimination in Employment Act (1967)—Revised 1978

Vocational Rehabilitation Act (1973) as amended 1980

Privacy Act of 1974 (Public Law 93-579)

Railway Labor Act (1926)—RLA

Norris-LaGuardia Act (1932)

National Labor Relations Act (1935)—Wagner Act

Labor-Management Relations Act (1947)—Taft-Hartley

Labor Management Reporting and Disclosure Act (1959)—Landrum-Griffin

Amendments to Taft-Hartley Act (1974)

Civil Service Reform Act Title VII (1978)

Constitutional Provisions

The First Amendment, U.S. Constitution

The Fifth Amendment

The Fourteenth Amendment

Executive Order Provisions

Executive Order 11246 (1965) as amended by Executive Order 11375 (1966)

Revised Order Number 4 (1971)

Executive Order 11478 (1969)

Executive Order 10988 (1962)

Executive Orders 11616 (1971) 11838 (1975)

Agency Provisions

Uniform Guidelines on Employee Selection Procedures (1978)

Guidelines on Sexual Harassment (1980)

National Labor Relations Board Rulings

continued

Exhibit 1.1
continued

Exhibit 1.1 continued	Selected Sources of Rules That Affect PHRM

Judicial Provisions

Griggs v. *Duke Power* (1971)	*Bakke* v. *Regents of The University of California* (1978)	*County of Washington* v. *Gunther* (1981)
Diaz v. *Pan American World Airways, Inc.* (1971)	*Marshall* v. *Barlow's Inc.* (1979)	*Connecticut* v. *Teal* (1982)
Spurlock v. *United Airlines* (1972)	*Marshall* v. *Whirlpool* (1980)	*NLRB* v. *Transportation Management* (1983)
Richardson v. *Hotel Corporation of America*	*Texas Department of Community Affairs* v. *Joyce Ann Burdine* (1981)	*Newport News Shipbuilding and Dry Dock Co.* v. *EEOC* (1983)
Brito v. *Zia Company* (1973)	*Northwest Airlines, Inc.* v. *Transport Workers* (1981)	*Arizona Governing Committee* v. *Norris* (1983)
Hodgson v. *Greyhound Lines, Inc.* (1974)	*Lehman* v. *Yellow Freight System* (1981)	*AFSCME* v. *State of Washington* (1983)
Albemarle v. *Moody* (1975)	*First National Maintenance* v. *NLRB* (1981)	*Firefighters Local Union 1784* v. *Stotts* (1984)
International Brotherhood of Teamsters v. *United States* (1977)		*Wygant* v. *Jackson Board of Education* (1986)

costs by constantly monitoring the legal environment for any changes, by complying with those changes, and by practicing effective personnel and human resource management. Throughout this text are many examples of costly lawsuits and effective personnel practices to avoid them. All of these examples highlight just one of many reasons why PHRM is so important in organizations and why PHRM departments are gaining recognition in organizations today.

Relationships Influencing PHRM Functions and Activities

As shown in Exhibit 1.2, PHRM functions and activities do not exist in a vacuum. Indeed, many aspects of the external and internal environment influence the five PHRM functions. Presented later in this chapter are discussions of those who are responsible for PHRM and the levels at which PHRM is practiced. Discussions of relevant aspects of the internal and external environment are also presented in the remaining chapters. These discussions indicate the multitude of forces and events that help shape an organization's PHRM functions and activities. Although stating precise relationships among aspects of the environment and PHRM activities is impossible, statements of general tendencies can be offered. Familiarity with these tendencies is important in understanding how PHRM is practiced in organizations today and how it might be practiced in the future.

Relationships and Aspects of PHRM Functions and Activities

Exhibit 1.2

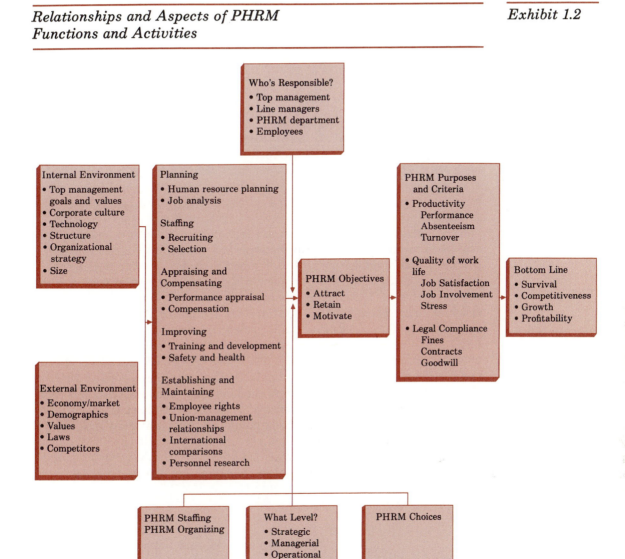

Relationships among the Functions and Activities

Although each PHRM function and activity is discussed in separate chapters, each is highly related to the others. That is, the way in which one activity is done often influences the way in which another is done. Each activity varies in the exact manner in which it relates to other PHRM activities. Because of this variation, a section in each chapter describes the most extensive and important relationships of each activity. The chapter sections also describe the critical relationships that each PHRM activity has with the internal and external environment. This is done to reflect the complex set of conditions that influence and that are influenced by each PHRM activity.

Relationships with the Internal Environment

Several features within organizations influence PHRM, including top management, organizational strategy, technology, structure, culture, and size. Although these features are described here separately, they often influence each other. For example, top management's values help shape corporate culture, and strategy helps determine organizational structure.[9] The key focus here, however, is how these features influence the PHRM functions and activities.

Top management determines how effective human resource management will be in organizations. If top management minimizes the importance of people to the organization's overall success, so will the line managers. In turn, those in the PHRM department will perform the most routine personnel activities. A likely consequence will be minimally effective human resource management.[10] Organizations are increasingly linking PHRM to corporate strategy. Corporate strategy determines which general characteristics organizations need from employees.[11] An example of some of these characteristics is shown in Exhibit 1.3. These characteristics contrast with the specific skills, knowledge, and abilities that employees need to perform their jobs—elements that are determined more by technology, organizational structure, and size than by strategy.[12] Because PHRM activities are capable of fostering and facilitating these employee characteristics, once a strat-

---

| Exhibit 1.3 | General Employee Characteristics to Complement an Organization's Strategy |

Repetitive, Predictable Behavior	—	Creative, Innovative Behavior
Short-term Focus	—	Long-term Focus
Cooperative, Interdependent Behavior	—	Independent, Autonomous Behavior
Low Concern for High Quantity	—	High Concern for High Quantity
Low Concern for Quality	—	High Concern for Quality
Low Risk Orientation	—	High Risk Orientation
Concern for Process	—	Concern for Results
Preference to Avoid Responsibility	—	Preference to Assume Responsibility
Inflexible to Change	—	Flexible to Change
Low Task Orientation	—	High Task Orientation
Low Organizational Identification	—	High Organizational Identification
Focus on Efficiency	—	Focus on Effectiveness

Source: R. S. Schuler, "Personnel and Human Resource Management Choices and Organizational Strategy," in *Readings in Personnel and Human Resource Management*, 3d ed., ed. R. S. Schuler, S. A. Youngblood, and V. Huber (St. Paul: West, 1987).

egy is selected, PHRM activities are influenced. The nature of this influence is described later in this chapter under "Strategic Involvement" and is also described at the end of the remaining chapters.

Organizational or corporate culture represents the organization's value system.[13] Strongly influenced by top management, corporate culture identifies the value of people to the organization, the assumptions made about people, and in turn how the people are to be treated. The impact of corporate culture on employees can be significant:

> S. C. Allyn, a retired chairman of the board, likes to tell a story about his company—the National Cash Register Corporation. It was August 1945, and Allyn was among the first allied civilians to enter Germany at the end of the war. He had gone to find out what had happened to an NCR factory built just before the war but promptly confiscated by the German military command and put to work on the war effort. He arrived via military plane and traveled through burned-out buildings, rubble, and utter desolation until he reached what was left of the factory. Picking his way through bricks, cement, and old timbers, Allyn came upon two NCR employees whom he hadn't seen for six years. Their clothes were torn and their faces grimy and blackened by smoke, but they were busy clearing out the rubble. As he came closer, one of the men looked up and said, "We knew you'd come!" Allyn joined them in their work and together the three men began cleaning out the debris and rebuilding the factory from the devastation of war.
>
> A few days later, as the clearing continued, Allyn and his co-workers were startled as an American tank rumbled up to the site. A grinning GI was at its helm. "Hi," he said, "I'm NCR, Omaha. Did you guys make your quota this month?" Allyn and the GI embraced each other. The war may have devastated everything around them, but NCR's hard driving, sales-oriented culture was still intact.[14]

The impact of corporate culture on PHRM functions and activities is similarly significant because PHRM activities articulate corporate culture. The way in which the PHRM activities are done is determined by the PHRM practices selected from some of the available choices, described later in this chapter.

Organizational size is also an important factor in PHRM activities. Although exceptions exist, generally the larger the organization, the more developed its internal labor market and the lesser the reliance on the external labor market.[15] In contrast, the smaller the organization, the less developed its internal labor market and the greater the reliance on the external labor market. The term **labor market** refers to PHRM policies, practices, and procedures that determine decisions such as who is to be promoted, how much people are to be paid, who can enter a training program, who will have job security, who will have grievance and due process rights, and what types of career opportunities employees will be provided. As more reliance is placed on the internal labor market, the organization relies more on itself in determining how to decide the issues just mentioned. For example, in deciding how much to pay people, job evaluation, job classifications, and internal equity would be used. In contrast, as more reliance is placed on the external labor market, the organization relies less on itself. In deciding how much to pay people, the rates that other organizations are paying and external equity would be used.[16]

Relationships with the External Environment

Major components of the external environment influencing PHRM functions and activities include the economy, demographics, social values, laws, and competitors. Because the last four components are major events contributing to the growing importance of PHRM, they are described in the following section and in Chapter 2.

The national, state, and local economy can have a significant impact on PHRM. A strong economy tends to lower the unemployment rate, increase wage rates, make recruitment more necessary and more difficult, and increase the desirability of training current employees. By contrast, a weak economy tends to increase the unemployment rate, diminish wage increase demands and even result in wage concessions, make recruitment less necessary and easier, and reduce the need for training and developing current employees.[17] Although a weak economy may tend to diminish PHRM's importance, other events in the external environment act to increase its importance.

PHRM's Growing Importance

As the first "PHRM in the News" suggests, PHRM's growing importance is largely due to several events in society as well as to the recognition that PHRM can significantly influence the bottom line of organizations.

Events Influencing PHRM's Importance

Four major events influencing the importance of PHRM are (1) increased competition and, therefore, the need to be competitive; (2) the costs and benefits associated with human resource utilization; (3) the increasing pace and complexity of social, cultural, legal, demographic, and educational changes; and (4) the symptoms of change in the work place.

Increased Competition.   "The most important characteristic of today's business environment—and therefore the yardstick against which managerial techniques must be measured—is the new competition."[18] The new competition is from abroad and from within America. Imports of shoes, textiles, and electronics represent an ever-increasing share of the U.S. market. Less than ten years ago, American companies dominated the office copier business in the United States. Today their share is approximately 50 percent. All this is occurring because of low-priced products or inventive marketing techniques (or both). In China and India, for example, total compensation per employee is estimated at twenty-five to thirty cents per hour. The wage disparity between these countries and the United States is likely to continue, given the fact that between now and the year 2000, 750 million more people will enter the labor force—nine-tenths of them outside the industrialized countries. As a consequence:

The challenge to management in this country has never been greater. Speaking about foreign competition in March 1984, John Young, Chairman of Hewlett-Packard Company and Chairman of the President's Commission on Industrial Competitiveness, commented: "Some competitive disadvantages we'll probably have to accept as 'givens.' With our high standard of living, the human resource cost is one of those. That means we'll have to find ways to make our labor worth what it's paid."[19]

Competition within the United States has increased, in part because of government deregulation in industries such as communications, financial, airlines, trucking and railroads, bus service, and public construction. In addition, venture capital has facilitated the rapid growth of new companies and with them, 20 million new jobs since the mid-1970s. New technology and companies' drive for diversification have also enhanced domestic competition. As a consequence, organizations like IBM, General Electric, and Hewlett-Packard are using their human resource activities as a weapon in competitive strategy.[20]

Human Resource Costs.   Today, with payroll costs running anywhere between 30 and 80 percent of total expenses, corporations realize that it pays to be concerned with how they manage their human resources. For example, organizations now know that their important assets are not just financial resources but also include having the right people at the right time who can effectively manage an organization. Walter Wriston (former chairman and CEO of Citicorp) captured the essence of this point quite well:

> I believe the only game in town is the personnel game. . . . My theory is if you have the right person in the right place, you don't have to do anything else. If you have the wrong person in the job, there's no management system known to man that can save you.[21]

Other benefits from PHRM activities designed to manage and develop human resources effectively are significant reductions in accidents, absenteeism, and error rates and significant increases in morale and in the quality of the product or service, with productivity and profits, their important by-products. For example:

> After running several surveys to measure employee attitudes and morale, Ruben Krigsman, manager of personnel research at Union Carbide Corporation, instituted several new training programs and reorganized the workplace which gave the blue-collar workers more responsibility. The result? In just three months, productivity soared by 25%; the amount of finished goods passing inspection jumped from 50% to 80% and absenteeism dropped 5% to 3%.[22]

The Pace and Complexity of Change.   Several ongoing changes in the cultural and educational levels and the social order of the United States have contributed to PHRM concerns. For example, because midlife career changes are becoming more common and most occupations require increased knowledge, training and development programs for all employees have developed rapidly. During the 1980s, the number of workers in the eighteen to twenty-four age group is declining, while the number in the thirty to forty-four age group is rising. The result is too few needed young workers and too many middle-aged workers with potentially frustrated career ambitions.

The current work force is generally becoming more knowledgeable and better informed. Whereas in 1970 only one of every eight workers had a college degree, in 1980 one of every four workers who entered the labor force had one. These high-quality human resources are potentially more productive. This situation however, presents a paradox to organizations because as society is becoming better informed, it is also becoming more critical and cynical and less accepting of authority. Young workers appear particularly cynical about decisions that supervisors make and correspondingly more resistant to authority. Older workers, however, still tend to reflect earlier societal values and are therefore more inclined to be organization people, to accept authority, and to seek the satisfaction of lower-level needs primarily at work. Thus, effective human resources management requires knowing not only how to manage and channel young workers' skills but also how to manage a work force with a mixed set of values. Other work force characteristics and their impact for human resource planning are described in Chapter 2.

Symptoms of Change in the Work Place.   Rapid social change has been accompanied by changes in the relationship between workers and their jobs. Some of the changes in the work place involve worker alienation and attitudes toward the organization, which are often associated with decreasing motivation, increasing counterproductive behavior, and more worker demands. Although these symptoms can be found in most work places—whether factories or offices, public or private organizations—the extent to which these symptoms are reported to exist varies greatly. In a recent study:

> Fewer than half of today's clerical and hourly employees rate their companies as "one of the best" or "above average"—down sharply since the 1970s. Although not as negative as the clerical and hourly workers, professionals, supervisors, and managers have lowered their regard for their companies and their employers as able managers. Only 53 percent of professionals rate their companies favorably today, in contrast to the 66 percent favorable a decade ago. The study also reports on trends reflecting:
>
> - Downturns in ratings of the quality of supervision.
> - Critical ratings of organizational communication practices.
> - Criticism of the effectiveness of performance appraisals.
> - A widespread feeling that effective job performance is often not rewarded in today's companies.
> - A first-line supervisory workforce that says the respect it receives and the authority it has are eroding.
> - A clerical workforce quite susceptible to unionization.[23]

Another symptom of change in the work place is the desire for a more explicit statement of employee rights. Among the rights that employees desire is the right to work, to know what one's job and its requirements are, to participate in decisions, to be appraised fairly and against objective performance criteria, to be accountable, and to be able to take risks and make mistakes.

Trends in PHRM

Several major trends in PHRM are (1) assessment of PHRM to determine effectiveness, (2) use of computer technology and creation of human resource information systems, and (3) strategic involvement of PHRM in the organization.

Assessment of PHRM

PHRM is often considered not vital to organizations because it fails to demonstrate its effectiveness. That is, PHRM sometimes fails to show how it relates to the three objectives and the three purposes shown in Exhibit 1.2. Recognizing this, PHRM managers are starting to demonstrate their effectiveness just as other managers do: by assessing the costs of PHRM activities against the benefits resulting from those activities. The PHRM manager demonstrates effectiveness by comparing the costs of the PHRM activities against the changes in the benefit criteria that are associated with, or said to result from, the PHRM activities. Thus, PHRM effectiveness initially rests with assessment (i.e., determining the appropriate or relevant cost and benefit criteria).[24]

Benefit Criteria. **Benefit criteria** for PHRM are those indicators against which comparisons can be made to demonstrate value or benefit to the organization. Three indicators used as benefit criteria are the purposes of PHRM. The indicators and their specific components (and indicated direction for demonstrating effectiveness) are as follows:

Productivity
- Increased performance
- Reduced absenteeism
- Reduced turnover

Quality of Work Life
- Increased job involvement
- Increased satisfaction
- Reduced stress
- Reduced accidents and illnesses

Legal Compliance
- Reduced or eliminated costs of fines
- Reduced or eliminated costs of lost contracts
- Enhanced community goodwill and general reputation

In general, productivity represents the efficiency with which an organization uses its work force, capital, material, and energy resources to produce its product. Other things being equal, reducing the work force but getting the same output improves productivity.[25] Similarly, if each employee's performance (quality or quantity) increases, total output increases and so does productivity. Reducing absenteeism is also a way to increase productivity, as is the reduction in turnover of good employees.[26] Improving the quality of work life may result in increased performance and reduced absenteeism and turnover, but the results can also be measured in other ways.[27] For example, the more the organization meets individuals' preferences and interests, the more likely the work force will be more involved with their jobs; register higher satisfaction with their jobs, supervisors, and co-workers; suffer less from stress; and have fewer accidents and better health.

As shown in Appendix A, organizations must comply with many laws and regulations. Failure to comply can result in significant settlement costs, such as the recent $400 million settlement between the U.S. Postal Service and its current and former employees. Other effects include cancellation of future contracts with the federal, state, and local governments. In addition, individual employees can bring suit against the company for violations of some laws and regulations.[28] Finally, goodwill with potential job applicants and the community can be significantly diminished if a company chooses not to comply with laws and regulations.

Cost Criteria.   **Cost criteria** for PHRM are those indicators against which benefit criteria can be compared to determine PHRM effectiveness. Whereas benefit criteria generally apply to all the PHRM activities, cost criteria are more specific to each activity. For example, cost criteria appropriate for the safety and health PHRM activity may be supervisory training, the addition of newer, safer equipment, the removal of hazards and waste materials, and job redesign. Cost criteria for recruitment may be advertising, training, and recruiters' payroll expense.

After determining the appropriate cost criteria (based on the specific PHRM activity of interest) and the appropriate benefit criteria (not all benefit criteria are equally relevant to each PHRM activity), these costs and benefits are compared. This comparison is increasingly being made on the basis of dollars and cents. Thus, the dollars-and-cents value of the cost criteria and benefit criteria is determined. Whereas the value of the cost criteria is more specific to each PHRM activity, the value of the benefit criteria is more general.

Valuation of the benefit criteria in dollars and cents is most feasible for productivity and legal compliance. It is less feasible for quality of work life because of the difficulty in attaching a dollars-and-cents value to intangibles such as job involvement or satisfaction. A more appropriate approach may be relating quality of work life to the organization's ability to survive and adapt, rather than relating it to profitability. Evaluating the quality of work life is sometimes possible, however, because the dollars-and-cents costs of accidents and illnesses can readily be determined. These and related issues are discussed in the assessment sections at the end of the following chapters. Although determining the value of productivity is feasible, it is not necessarily easy. In Chapter 18 are examples of how the value of performance, turnover, and absenteeism can be determined in dollars and cents.

Once the dollars-and-cents value of the benefit and cost criteria are established, PHRM can demonstrate its effectiveness. First, it can demonstrate that the values of the cost criteria are no greater than, or perhaps are even less than, those in other organizations (similar or different). Second, it can enhance the value of those comparisons by including relevant information on benefit criteria. Although it may be neither feasible to obtain nor valid to use dollars-and-cents valuation of the turnover of other organizations, it may be useful to compare *rates* of turnover or absenteeism. Thus, PHRM could show the organization that the costs for managing its human resources are producing more benefits (using only a comparison of turnover rates) than in other organizations.

PHRM can also demonstrate its effectiveness by comparing changes in benefit criteria levels with specific PHRM activities. The valuation of the benefit criteria changes can then be compared with the valuation of the cost criteria associated with the specific PHRM activities. For example, if a new recruitment program is implemented and the absenteeism rate of the new employees recruited with the new program declines 2 percent, the dollar costs of the program can be compared with the dollar gains obtained from reducing absenteeism for those employees by 2 percent. Although this type of comparison can be useful in demonstrating the effectiveness of PHRM, attributing certain changes (e.g., in absenteeism) to a particular program is not always possible. For example, at the time the program was implemented, the national economy may have turned down and thus become the real cause of the reduced absenteeism, rather than the recruitment program. To help prevent erroneous conclusions or false inferences from being drawn, the PHRM manager needs to be aware of varying types of research evaluation designs. These are presented in Chapter 11 on training and development. Other research and statistical issues useful for PHRM are presented in Chapter 18 on personnel research. Aiding the assessment of PHRM are computer technology and human resource information systems.

Computer Technology and HRIS

Effective PHRM requires a great deal of information. Computer technology enables organizations to combine human resource information into a single data base. A common computer-oriented information system used in the management of human resources is often referred to as a **human resource information system** (HRIS):

> Any human resource information system is logically an inventory of the positions and skills extant in a given organization. However, HRIS is more than a simple aggregation mechanism for inventory control and accounting; it is the foundation for a set of management tools enabling managers to establish objectives for the use of their organization's human resources and to measure the extent to which those objectives have been achieved.[29]

Many larger organizations have an HRIS, including Nationwide Life Insurance, Frito-Lay, IBM, Xerox, AMAX, and the U.S. State Department.

Among the many advantages to be gained from using computer technology and the HRIS are four key advantages. First, the computer enables the personnel department to take a more active role in organization planning. Forecasting techniques are feasible that would require a significant time investment without the use of computer technology. Second, the computer integrates and stores in a single data base all personnel information previously filed in separate physical locations. Thus, the personnel department can take a global view of its human resource stock and interpret it in more meaningful ways. For example, data on career interests may be more easily matched with career advancement and training opportunities by creating a simple coding system that automatically identifies candidates. The personnel data that the U.S. State Department gathers include employees' personal preferences, education and training, and experience and skill. The position and personnel data in the HRIS can then be used to make more effective internal selection and placement decisions and career development decisions that are beneficial for both the organization and the individual. Third, the computer speeds the process of comparing costs and benefits in PHRM assessment. Fourth, an HRIS and computer technology facilitate the easy storage and access of personnel records that are vital for organizations.

To comply with federal equal employment laws, organizations must follow several personnel record requirements. Title VII of the 1964 Civil Rights Act says that organizations must keep all employment records for at least six months. The Equal Pay Act and the Age Discrimination in Employment Act say that organizations must keep records for three years. Three years, however, isn't always the limit. If an employee or a government agency lodges a charge against a firm, the firm should hold on to all of its records until the claim is settled. The organization must keep all records regarding the person making the complaint and records on all other employees in similar positions. The organization must also keep records on seniority, benefit, merit, and incentive plans until at least one year after the plans end.

Besides keeping records, organizations have to fill out reports. Employers of one hundred or more workers must annually file EEO-1 forms. Multiestablishment employers need only file separate EEO-1 forms for each establishment employing fifty or more workers. Organizations with government contracts must fill out affirmative action reports that the Office of Federal Contract Compliance Programs (OFCCP) sends. Government contractors required to fill out Standardized Affirmative Action Formats (SAAFs) for the OFCCP can propose one SAAF to cover all its establishments as long as its personnel practices are homogeneous. Also, employers with $10,000 or more in federal contracts must report annually to the secretary of labor the number of Vietnam veterans or special disabled veterans employed, as well as the number hired during the reporting period compared to the total number of new employees.

Failure to send in any of these reports will raise suspicions in the agencies that issue them. Equally important is the posting of job bias posters that the Equal Employment Opportunity Commission and state and local agencies issue. These posters must be displayed in conspicuous places—places where employees, union members, and job applicants will see them. Failure to display them violates the law, can raise suspicions in the agencies that issue them, and can lead courts to extend time limits for suing parties as well as impose fines on offending employers. The following "PHRM in the News" describes further uses and needs of an HRIS and computer technology.

Other potential uses and benefits of the computer in personnel applications are introduced in relation to the central topics in each of the following chapters. Additional ways in which computer technology can be applied, es-

HR's Move Toward Micros

The use of microcomputers is mushrooming in personnel departments as more and more micro-based software designed for human resources applications becomes available. Following is a look at how personnel managers are using their new computers, along with some tips that can help you select the best system for your needs.

Functional files

Microcomputers programmed with appropriate human resources software can be one of the most useful information-management and decision-support tools at a personnel manager's disposal. A PC can save you hours of digging through files by providing immediate access to the exact information you need. It also can help ensure that employment practices comply with the broad range of legal requirements affecting today's workplace. HR software packages also can remind you when to conduct performance reviews or schedule employee medical exams by issuing "action notices" triggered by "tickler" dates. Uses of micro-based HR systems include:

- *Building personnel databases*—PCs can help you maintain and update basic information about every employee on the payroll. A diversity of information, including an employee's name, address, age, sex, race, education and skills, job position, salary, and benefits, can be entered, manipulated, and analyzed in dozens of ways.
- *Monitoring pay policies and practices*—Some programs can review your pay scales for equity and consistency or monitor all the variables affecting payroll costs. Others can create new salary

structures, analyze salary surveys, track performance reviews, calculate job values, and compare salaries between departments, within departments, or for a given job group.

- *Compliance reporting*—HR software programs can produce comprehensive pension, equal employment opportunity, or affirmative action reports in the standardized formats required by the state or federal government.
- *Benefits administration*—Software packages are available that can track pension plan earnings, contributions, and withdrawals; calculate social security or disability benefits; monitor and control employee health care costs; produce benefits statements; administer employee loan programs; and assist retirement planning.
- *HR planning*—Stored data on promotions, retirements, transfers, layoffs, and turnover can be used for succession planning, filling key position vacancies, or forecasting general manpower needs to meet corporate goals.

Micro software also can be purchased featuring education and training modules that analyze training costs, medical modules designed to track and help control health care expenditures, and safety modules that classify and monitor job-related accidents, injuries, and illnesses.

Buyer's guide

While HR packages can help a personnel department do a better job of managing its responsibilities, they do have limitations. Most micros have a relatively small memory capacity, and few can handle a comprehensive range of information involving hundreds of employees. Microsystems, for example, usually can't process an organization's weekly payroll. Many systems lack such desirable features as report generation and formatting, sorting, multi-file access, ability to catalogue, error-trapping, and single-record access. This leads to the first rule for prospective purchasers: Resist the temptation to buy whatever's available. Instead, conduct a needs analysis that identifies the kinds of information you need and the specific problems you want the system to solve. Then shop around and compare systems in terms of capabilities and costs. Other points to consider when buying a micro include:

- *Security*—Personnel data generally are confidential, so access should be limited to authorized users only. Many micros use operator passwords or codes that allow only approved

users to access the system. Some systems allow users at different security levels to only read certain data, but not modify or print out information; still others "blank out" sensitive data, or prevent its appearance on the screen entirely.

- *Costs*—Installation, maintenance, training, and optional features, such as color graphics, spreadsheets, or word processing capability, can add to the costs of a basic software system.

- *Software interface*—Some packages let you use specific system components alone or in combination, thus increasing production and efficiency. Such linkages can eliminate duplicative data collection, processing, and storage.

Source: Bulletin to Management, April 1985, p. 8. Reprinted by permission from *Bulletin to Management*, copyright 1985, by The Bureau of National Affairs, Inc., Washington, D.C.

pecially using a personal computer (PC), are provided in the PC Projects at the end of most chapters. These PC Projects are to be used with the *PC Projects for Personnel and Human Resource Management* as optional exercises.[30]

Strategic Involvement

For many PHRM departments, a relatively limited involvement in the total organization's affairs and goals was consistent with its limited role. Managers in PHRM were often concerned only with making staffing plans, providing specific job training programs, or running annual performance appraisal programs (the results of which were put in personnel files, never to be used). Consequently, managers in PHRM were concerned only with the short-term operational and managerial—perhaps day-to-day—human resource needs. It would have been unusual for these managers to be concerned with demonstrating their departments' effectiveness or even that of the organizations.

Now, because of the extensive relationships among PHRM activities and the internal and external environment, managers in PHRM are becoming more involved in the total organization—where it's going, where it should be going—and are helping it to get there.[31] As a consequence, they and their departments are playing many more roles and utilizing the PHRM functions and activities on a long-term basis as well as the more typical medium- and short-term bases. In utilizing PHRM functions and activities in these three distinct time horizons, PHRM departments are really operating at three organizational levels: strategic, managerial, and operational.

At the operational (short-term) level, PHRM departments make staffing and recruitment plans, set up day-to-day monitoring systems, administer wage and salary programs, administer benefits packages, set up annual or less frequent appraisal systems, set up day-to-day control systems, provide for specific job skill training, provide on-the-job training, fit individuals to specific jobs, and plan career moves.

At the managerial (medium-term) level, PHRM departments do longitudinal validation of selection criteria, develop recruitment marketing plans and new recruiting markets, set up five-year compensation plans for individuals, set up cafeteria benefits packages, set up validated systems that relate current conditions and future potential, set up assessment centers for development, establish general management development programs, provide for organizational development, foster self-development, identify career paths, and provide career development services.

At the strategic (long-term) level, PHRM departments are now just starting to seek ways in which organizations can gain competitive advantage—that is, beat their competitors—and to link their practices (functions and activities) to their organizations' strategies. Because the use of PHRM at the strategic level in organizations is just beginning and is so critical in effectively managing human resources, it is explicitly introduced and described in this chapter and at the end of those to follow. PHRM at the operational and managerial levels is more well established in organizations and is described throughout the remaining chapters.

Gaining Competitive Advantage.   One of the two major ways of using PHRM at the strategic level is to gain competitive advantage.[32] Organizations use one or more PHRM activities to become the lowest-cost producer through increased efficiency or to differentiate their products from the competition. Lincoln Electric is an organization using its PHRM practices (particularly compensation) to increase production efficiency and thereby lower the cost of their electric motors and arc welders. Delco-Remy uses its PHRM practices to produce a higher-quality product, thereby differentiating itself from its competitors. When Delco-Remy trained its employees in participative management, it succeeded in differentiating itself from all competitors in the eyes of Honda and others. Delco's Keith W. Wander describes the success of this training and the resultant competitive advantage:

> Honda of America was seeking an American battery manufacturer as a supplier to its auto plant in Maryville, Ohio. Honda wanted a plant which had a participative system of management and a reputation for producing a quality product at a competitive price. After a contact from the Delco-Remy Sales Department, two American representatives from Honda visited the Delco-Remy plant in Fitzgerald, Georgia. This visit was followed by a second one with Mr. Hoshita, President of Honda, in the group.
>
> During the second visit, plant tours were conducted by Operating Team (hourly employees) members. The tours were followed by Operating Team members explaining to Mr. Hoshita how people were involved in the Fitzgerald business, how Fitzgerald and Honda could be mutual resources to each other because of their

participative systems, and why a Delco battery was the best-built battery in the world.

Mr. Hoshita returned several months later to ask more questions of the Support team (salaried employees) and Operating Teams. Shortly afterward, Honda of America announced Delco-Remy, Fitzgerald, as its sole supplier of batteries, based upon its (1) culture; (2) quality; and (3) price, in that order.

To date, Honda has had zero returns of batteries and zero complaints on quality or delivery.[33]

Gaining competitive advantage through PHRM activities is extremely advantageous for organizations. A major reason is that a response from competitors is likely to be slow in coming because of two major inertia barriers. The first inertia barrier is lack of commitment. Changing human resource practices consumes vast amounts of time and energy; merely attaining consistency requires a great deal of analysis, even under the best of circumstances; and even more is required to meet the needs-matching challenge. This combined with any past failures to change human resource practices makes it difficult to get organizational commitment to any more changes, starting at the top of the firm and working down. Yet, commitment must begin at the top. It begins there with the top-level manager demonstrating concern, confidence, and excitement for the product and for the people. In turn, the rest of management and the employees begin to show the same concern and excitement for their jobs and products and confidence in themselves.

Lee Iacocca has done exactly this at Chrysler Corporation. The results there have been astounding. Workers at the Smyrna, Tennessee, plant of Nissan Motor Manufacturing Corporation USA are producing trucks of measurably higher quality than their Japanese counterparts, largely because of Marvin T. Runyon, president of the firm. Runyon walks the plant floor to demonstrate his concern for and confidence in the workers. He also lets the workers make decisions. According to Runyon, decisions should be made at the lowest possible level.

Because the time horizon is so critical, it is regarded here as a second major inertia barrier. The estimate is that it may take as much as seven years for managers to install, adjust to, and reap the benefits of major changes in human resource management practices; weed out unproductive employees; and create the new generation of employees.[34] Accepting the changes may take the employees equally as long, because "effective relationships between individuals and companies rest on employees' trust that the goals (of the individuals and companies) are connected. But developing trust often requires overcoming years of bad experience and many employees' belief that companies exploit people."[35] Since many managers are rewarded for short-term performance, the time horizon in changing human resource practices becomes perhaps the more significant inertia barrier.

Because gaining competitive advantage is so useful for organizations, the following chapters of this book describe how it can be done using specific PHRM practices. The chapters also describe how the PHRM practices can be linked with organizational strategy.

Linking with Organizational Strategy.   PHRM functions and activities (practices) are increasingly being linked to the organization's strategy. As mentioned under the section entitled "Relationships with the Internal Environment," organizations are recognizing that different employee characteristics are needed with different strategies. As a result, they are using their PHRM practices in different ways, depending upon the types of general characteristics (such as those shown in Exhibit 1.3) that they need from employees.[36] This suggests that the PHRM activities have major alternatives (choices) and that some may be more appropriate than others for a given strategy. Note that there are many choices in PHRM practices; however, many are not relevant to organizational strategy. Only those few relevant to organizational strategy are discussed here. As a result, they may be referred to as strategic choices in PHRM practices. These are illustrated in Exhibit 1.4, along with five organizational strategies and the needed employee characteristics described earlier. Exhibit 1.4 suggests that organizational strategy, in part, determines needed employee characteristics, which in turn determine choices in PHRM activities. This determination is made because certain

PHRM Practices—Organizational Strategy Matches and Needed Employee Characteristics   *Exhibit 1.4*

Organizational Strategy	Needed Employee Characteristics	HRM Practice Choices
Entrepreneurial: Projects with high financial risk are undertaken, minimal policies and procedures are in place, resources are insufficient to satisfy all customer demands, and multiple priorities must be satisfied. The focus here is on the short run and getting the operation off the ground.	To varying degrees, employees need to be innovative, cooperative, longer-term oriented, risk taking, and willing to assume responsibility. It is critical that key employees remain.	(1) Planning—formal, tight, implicit, broad, integrative, high participation. (2) Staffing—broad paths, multiple ladders, open, implicit criteria. (3) Appraising—loosely integrated, results; longer term, high participation. (4) Compensation—external equity, flexible, high participation. (5) Training—broad application, informal and high participation.
Dynamic Growth Strategy: Risk taking on projects is more modest. The constant dilemma is between doing current work and building support for the future. Policies and procedures are starting to be written, as the need is for more control and structure for an ever-expanding operation.	Employees need to have high organizational identification, be flexible to change, have a high task orientation, and work in close cooperation with others.	(1) Planning—broad, informal, integrative. (2) Staffing—broad, open, implicit. (3) Appraising—employee participation; combination of individual and group criteria and short- and long-term focus. (4) Compensation—employee participation, short- and long-term rewards; internal and external equity. (5) Training—broad application; productivity and quality emphasis, some participation.

continued

*Exhibit 1.4
continued*

PHRM Practices—Organizational Strategy Matches and Needed Employee Characteristics

Organizational Strategy	Needed Employee Characteristics	HRM Practice Choices
Extract Profit/ Rationalization Strategy: The focus is on maintaining existing profit levels. Modest cost-cutting efforts and employee terminations may be occurring. Control systems and structure are well developed along with an extensive set of policies and procedures.	The focus is on quantity and efficiency, the short term, and results with a relatively low level of risk and a minimal level of organizational identification.	(1) Planning—formal, narrow, explicit job descriptions, low involvement. (2) Staffing—narrow, closed, explicit criteria, little socialization. (3) Appraising—results criteria, maintenance purposes, individual evaluation. (4) Compensation—short term, internal equity, low participation. (5) Training—narrow application, low participation, productivity focus.
Liquidation/Divestiture Strategy: The focus involves selling off assets, cutting further losses, and reducing the work force as much as possible. Little or no thought is given to trying to save the operation, as declining profits are likely to continue.	Employees need a short-term, narrow orientation, low organizational commitment, a low need to remain, and a limited focus on high quantity.	(1) Planning—formal, segmental, narrow, explicit. (2) Staffing—narrow paths, explicit criteria, limited socialization, closed procedures. (3) Appraising—remedial purposes, behavioral criteria, low participation. (4) Compensation—low participation, few perks, fixed package, no incentives. (5) Training—unplanned, narrow application.
Turnaround Strategy: The focus is to save the operation. Although cost-cutting efforts and employee reductions are made, they are short-term programs for long-run survival. Worker morale may be somewhat depressed.	Employees need to be flexible to change, have a high task orientation, have a longer-term focus, and engage in some nonrepetitive behavior.	(1) Planning—informal, loose, high employee involvement. (2) Staffing—extensive socialization, openness, informal, implicit criteria. (3) Appraising—results criteria, group criteria, high participation. (4) Compensation—short- and long-term incentives, high participation. (5) Training—broad focus, high participation, productivity emphasis.

Source: R. S. Schuler, "Personnel and Human Resource Management Choices and Organizational Strategy," in *Readings in Personnel and Human Resource Management*, 3d ed., ed. R. S. Schuler, S. A. Youngblood, and V. Huber (St. Paul: West, 1987).

PHRM practices in each PHRM activity foster and facilitate certain needed employee characteristics. Because of this, the selection of PHRM practices to match strategy reflects a need for a consistent set of stimuli and reinforcements to be provided or sent to employees. Ideally, then, all PHRM practices are working together to stimulate and reinforce the characteristics that organizations need from their employees to facilitate their strategies.

Although systematic research in this area of matching PHRM practices with strategy is just beginning, a description of it seems warranted, based on actual organizational practice. Consequently, a short description of matching practices with strategy is presented at the end of the remaining chapters. In those chapters, the strategic choices shown in Exhibit 1.4 are described so that readers can understand the linkages made between the organizational strategy and the PHRM practice choices. Nonetheless, keep in mind that other aspects of an organization's internal and external environment, as shown in Exhibit 1.2, can influence the final selection of an organization's actual PHRM practices.

Organizing the PHRM Department

Based on our discussion thus far, organizations can apparently benefit the most by allowing their PHRM departments to become proactive and open, to engage in the several functions and activities at each of the three levels (strategic, management, and operational), and to demonstrate their effectiveness. Organizations, however, can also benefit by allowing their PHRM departments to address several issues associated with organizing the department:

- The number of roles that PHRM plays
- The need for the PHRM staff to be where the action is and to identify with the organization
- The need for a fair and consistent application of personnel policies, regardless of how small or large or diversified the organization
- The need for the PHRM department's views to be an integral part of personnel policy
- The need for the PHRM department to have sufficient power and authority to help ensure that personnel policies will be implemented legally, affirmatively, and without discrimination
- The need for the PHRM department not just to react to personnel crises but also to be active and innovative in dealing with human resource management

These issues, which are the essence of the roles that PHRM departments can play, affect the organization of personnel and human resources. For example, the personnel and human resource department can be organized so that it effectively plays only one of the four roles. Or it can be organized so that it plays two or more roles. The number of roles played often depends on the way top management views personnel activities and on what it is willing to let the PHRM department do. A key indicator of how top management views personnel is what status it is given in the hierarchy and the size of its budget.

Personnel and Human Resource Roles

Personnel can play several roles in an organization.[37] The more roles it plays, the more likely it will be effective in improving the organization's productivity, enhancing the quality of work life in the organization, and complying with all the necessary laws and regulations related to human resource utilization.

The Policy Formulator Role.   One role the personnel department can play is that of providing information for top management's use (at the strategic level). The specific types of information can include employee concerns, the external environment's impact, and how PHRM activities can be used to gain competitive advantage.

The PHRM staff can also advise in the process of policy formulation. The chief executive may still make policy statements, but these could be regarded as drafts of policy. Formal adoption of a final policy can then take place after other executives, such as the personnel manager and line managers, have had a chance to comment. Honeywell has an executive employee relations committee, composed of five operating group vice-presidents and five staff vice-presidents, which is the senior policy board for employee relations issues. This committee not only helps ensure extensive informational input into personnel policies but also increases the input's likelihood of being accepted. This enhanced role for the PHRM department appears to be typical of what is happening in companies, as described in the first "PHRM in the News."

The Provider and Delegator Role.   In reality, PHRM programs succeed because line managers (at managerial and operational levels) make them succeed. The PHRM department's bread-and-butter job, therefore, is to enable line managers to make things happen. Thus, in the more traditional personnel activities, such as selecting, interviewing, training, evaluating, rewarding, counseling, promoting, and firing, the personnel department is basically providing a service to line managers. In addition, the personnel department administers direct and indirect compensation programs. Since the line managers are ultimately responsible for their employees, many of them see these services as useful. The personnel department can also assist line managers by providing information about, and interpretation of, equal employment opportunity legislation and safety and health standards.

The PHRM department's responsibilities are to provide the services that the line managers need on a day-to-day basis, to keep them informed of regulations and legislation regarding human resource management, and to provide an adequate supply of job candidates for the line managers to select from. To fulfill these responsibilities, however, the PHRM department must be accessible, or the PHRM manager will lose touch with the line manager's needs. The personnel staff should be as close to where the people and the problems are as possible. Because bringing the personnel staff close to the action is an organizing concern, this is discussed in the section on departmental organizing later in the chapter.

The Auditor Role.   Although personnel may delegate much of the implementation of personnel activities to line managers, personnel is still responsible for seeing that activities are implemented fairly and consistently. This is especially true today because of fair employment legislation. Various state and federal regulations are making increasingly sophisticated demands on organizations. Responses to these regulations can best be made by a central group supplied with accurate information, the needed expertise, and the blessing of top management.

Expertise is also needed for implementing many personnel activities, such as distributing employee benefits. And since having personnel experts is costly, organizations hire as few as possible and centralize them. Their expertise then filters to other areas of the organization.

In organizations that have several locations and several divisions or units, tension often exists between the need for decentralization and the need for having the expertise necessary to comply with complex regulations and advise the best methods for personnel activities. The audit and control role is discussed at greater length in the section on organizing the PHRM department.

The Innovator Role.   An important and ever-expanding role for the PHRM department is that of providing up-to-date application of current techniques and developing and exploring innovative approaches to personnel problems and concerns.

> Naturally, the innovative role must be in tune with the times and the set of issues confronting a particular company. In periods of rising inflation and escalating wage and salary demands, the emphasis may be on compensation issues. In times of retrenchment and falling profits, creative work sharing and lay-off plans may be needed.[38]

Today, the personnel-related issues demanding innovative approaches and solutions center on how to improve productivity and the quality of work life while complying with the law in an environment of high uncertainty, energy conservation, and intense international competition. How effective an organization is in addressing these issues depends on how well it organizes and staffs the PHRM department.

PHRM in the Organization

The importance that an organization assigns to PHRM is reflected in PHRM's status in the hierarchy. This in turn helps determine the number of roles that PHRM plays and the levels at which they are played.

PHRM in the Hierarchy.   To effectively fulfill the four personnel roles, the top manager of the PHRM department should also be at the top of the organizational hierarchy. According to a Heidrick and Struggles survey of nearly three hundred human resource executives in Fortune 1000 service and industrial firms:

- Twenty-eight percent of the respondents say that they are now more likely to be a part of the top management team, while 21 percent report that they are more bottom-line oriented than five years ago; and
- Eighty-nine percent of the largest companies designate a chief HR executive at the corporate level, and 46 percent of these HR officials report directly to the chief executive officer.[39]

Being at the top allows the PHRM manager to play a part in personnel policy formulation and to have the power necessary for its fair and consistent implementation. When PHRM has this much importance, it is likely to be performing all three levels of personnel activity. Yet being at the top of the hierarchy does not address the need for PHRM to be where the action is.

Centralization Versus Decentralization

The organizing concept of centralization versus decentralization relates to the balance between getting personnel to where the action is and fairly and consistently applying personnel policies. It is also related to the balance between the benefits of having personnel generalists and of having personnel specialists. **Centralization** means that essential decision making and policy formulation are done at one location (at headquarters); **decentralization** means that the essential decision making and policy formulation are done at several locations (in the divisions or departments of the organization).

With the recent increases in regulatory requirements for use of human resources and the increased expertise necessary to deal with complex personnel functions, organizations are moving away from personnel generalists and toward personnel specialists. And at the same time, organizations—especially larger ones—are moving personnel staff into the organization's divisions. As a result, the trend is to centralize some aspects of personnel and human resources and to decentralize others.

For the personnel activities that require expertise, organizations generally hire specialists. But because of the expense, as few specialists as possible are hired. If an organization is large and has several plants or offices or divisions, the specialists are located in one place (at corporate headquarters) but serve all the divisions. The PHRM activities requiring less specialized expertise are staffed by people at the divisional level, thereby increasing the divisions' autonomy. Thus, in a large, multidivisional organization (which describes most of the largest industrial, retailing, and financial organizations), there is generally a corporate personnel and human resource department staffed largely with specialists and several divisional personnel departments staffed largely with generalists. The PHRM department at headquarters, then, has two purposes: (1) to develop and coordinate PHRM policy for the personnel staff in all locations, including headquarters, and (2) to execute the PHRM functions and activities for all the employees at headquarters. As the divisions grow, they begin to hire their own specialists and to administer almost all their own personnel functions and activities. The result is almost a complete personnel and human resource department, similar to what would be found in most organizations without divisions. These specialists help ensure some fairness and consistency in the administration of personnel activities in all of the divisions.

Who Is Responsible for PHRM?

Everyone should be responsible for PHRM, and as organizations demonstrate more openness and mutuality in their human resources policies and practices, everyone is.[40]

The Managers.   PHRM management is the task of individuals who have specialized in, and are primarily responsible for, personnel management (personnel managers). It is also the task of individuals not specialized in but often responsible for the day-to-day implementation of personnel functions and activities (line supervisors and line managers). This is not meant to imply that the PHRM manager never implements personnel functions and activities or that the line manager does not get involved in their development and administration. Indeed, these two managers are interdependent in the effective management of human resources. But the effective management of human resources cannot occur without top management's support and direction. Top management influences the number and execution of personnel functions and activities in an organization. This influence is best shown by the roles that top management allows the PHRM manager and department to play in the organization.

The Employees.   Employees are increasingly taking a role in personnel and human resource management. For example, employees may be asked to appraise their own performance or that of their colleagues. Employees may also help determine their own performance standards and goals. It is no longer uncommon for employees to write their own job descriptions. Perhaps most significantly, employees are taking a more active role in managing their own careers, assessing their own needs and values, and designing their own jobs. Nonetheless, personnel must help guide this process. Thus, the PHRM department must be staffed with qualified individuals.

Several terms are used throughout this text. Note that the term **personnel manager** (or executive) or **personnel and human resource manager** refers to the person heading the PHRM department. In organizations, this position may also be called the vice-president of personnel or the vice-president of employee relations.

The term **personnel and human resource department** (or PHRM) can be used interchangeably with the term **personnel department** or just **personnel**. Different names are used in different organizations. Nevertheless, all the functions and activities of personnel and human resource management relate to any of the terms. The term **staff** or **personnel staff** refers to the employees in the personnel department (either generalists or specialists) working for the PHRM manager.

Line manager (or **supervisor**) refers to the person in charge of the employees who are working directly on the product that the organization produces. The terms **individual, person,** and **worker** or **work force** refer to anyone in the organization. The term **employee** generally refers to the person who works for the line manager or the personnel manager; this person may also be called a nonmanagerial employee. Use of the term **subordinate** is avoided, except in Chapters 6 and 7, where the terms **subordinate** and **superior** are used.

PHRM Budgets

The amount of money that organizations allocate to their PHRM departments continues to rise each year. For example, the per-employee personnel costs rose from $385 in 1980 to a median $433 in 1981. In 1985 they were approximately $582 per employee. The ratio of the number of people in personnel versus the total number of employees is about 1:90. This ratio increases with the size of the employer, such that for companies with over ten thousand employees, the ratio is 1:182.[41]

Staffing the PHRM Department

Perhaps the most effective person who can head the PHRM department is an outstanding performer (a superstar) from the line organization. Since attracting the superstar means paying a higher salary than the person has been receiving, the superstar's acceptance of the position increases the personnel department's credibility and prestige in the organization. Even if the person is not a superstar, however, line experience gives the personnel manager influence over the other line managers. To understand just how far some companies have gone in this area, consider IBM's policy of assigning line managers to work in the corporate personnel department for two or three years as a part of their career development.

In addition, the well-trained personnel specialist often gains influence by becoming a personnel generalist through training and experience. The personnel specialist who wants to reach the top may benefit greatly by rotating through a line job in order to increase his or her ability to understand and deal with the entire organization.

Qualities of the PHRM Manager and Staff

How effectively an organization's human resources are managed depends in large part upon the quality of the people in the PHRM department.

The PHRM Manager.   PHRM managers need to be effective. They must be able to identify problems, develop alternative solutions, and then select and implement the most effective one. In addition, they must develop and maintain an integrated and effective management information system to help identify problems and implement policy. They must be innovative, aggressive, and willing to take the risks incurred by serving as the organization's conscience. Furthermore, they must be effective at selecting, building, and developing an entire personnel staff to carry out the five PHRM functions.

PHRM Generalists.   Line positions are one important source for the rest of the PHRM staff. A brief tour in a personnel position by a line supervisor, usually as a personnel generalist, can convey to the personnel department the knowledge, language, needs, and requirements of the line. As a result, the PHRM department can more effectively fill its service role. Another source of personnel talent is current nonmanagerial employees. In many organizations, personnel positions are staffed with former hourly employees. Like line managers, these people bring with them information about employee needs and attitudes. In many cases, they are particularly effective in their PHRM positions.

Personnel generalists should possess many of the same qualities as personnel specialists, but the level of expertise in a personnel specialty generally need not be at the same depth. The generalist, however, needs to have a moderate level of expertise in many personnel activities and must be able to get more specialized knowledge when it is needed.

PHRM Specialists.   Personnel staff specialists should have skills related to the specialty, an awareness of the relationship of that specialty to other PHRM activities, and a knowledge of the organization and where the personnel and human resource department fits. Individuals joining an organization for the first time should also have an appreciation for the political realities of organizations. Individuals in personnel should guard against the development of "them" and "us" situations and should remember that they are not in business to promote the latest fads—and companies are not in business to perpetuate PHRM departments. Universities are an important source of personnel specialists. Since specialists may work at almost any personnel activity, qualified applicants can come from specialized programs in law, personnel psychology, labor and industrial relations, personnel management, counseling, organizational development, and medical and health science.

PHRM Jobs

PHRM as a field of employment is becoming very attractive. In it are many different types of jobs, many well paying. In addition, a high level of professionalism is associated with the field.

How Much Do They Pay?

The results of a recent survey, along with the types of jobs in a personnel department, are shown in Exhibit 1.5. In that survey, salaries were generally higher for those individuals in larger organizations, for those with more experience, and for those with more education. In addition, salaries were higher in New York City, Los Angeles, and the states in the South and Southwest.[42]

Although the opportunities in PHRM are attractive and expanding, they are better for those with a college degree who enter personnel after gaining experience in a line position.[43]

Exhibit 1.5   *Average Salaries in Human Resource Management*

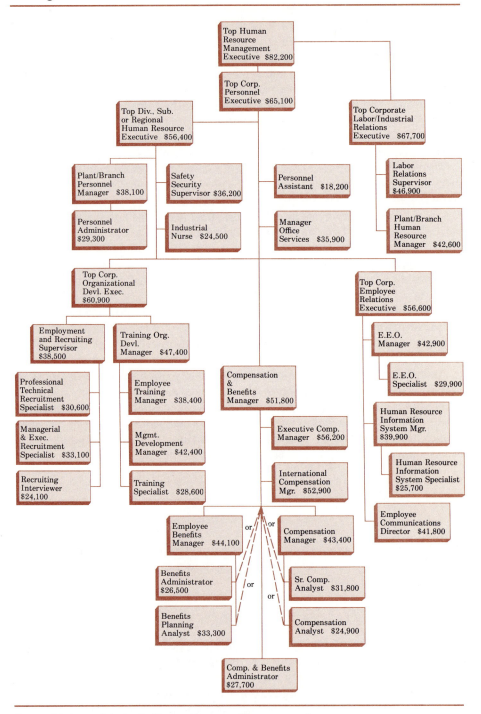

Source: "Average Salaries in Human Resource Management,"
Bulletin to Management, 11 September 1986, 304–305. Reprinted
by permission from *Bulletin to Management,* copyright © 1986
by The Bureau of National Affairs, Inc., Washington, D.C. 1986
ASPA/HANSEN Human Resource Management Compensation
Survey.

In fact, it may be that those persons with a few months or years of background and experience in line positions may be well ahead of those who do not have this perspective. In other words, while it may not be possible for graduating students to go directly into personnel administration, it also may not be wise for them to go directly into the field even if they have the opportunity.[44]

The background in a line position is helpful because it provides you with a better understanding of the organization. It will also give you more credibility with other line managers when you are in personnel trying to work with them. In addition, since many more line jobs than personnel jobs are available, getting a line job and demonstrating your skills and abilities there will be easier. Transferring into a personnel department will then be much easier. See Exhibit 1.5 for a sample of the job titles likely to be found in the PHRM department.

Professionalism in Personnel

Like any profession, PHRM follows a code of professional ethics and has an accreditation institute and certification procedures.[45] All professions share the code of ethics that personnel follows:

1. The practitioner must regard the obligation to implement public objectives and protect the public interest as more important than blind loyalty to an employer's preferences.
2. In daily practice, the professional must thoroughly understand the problems assigned and must undertake whatever study and research are required to assure continuing competence and the best of professional attention.
3. The practitioner must maintain a high standard of personal honesty and integrity in every phase of daily practice.
4. The professional must give thoughtful consideration to the personal interest, welfare, and dignity of all employees who are affected by his/her prescriptions, recommendations, and actions.
5. Professionals must make very sure that the organizations that represent them maintain a high regard and respect for the public interest and that they never overlook the importance of the personal interests and dignity of employees.[46]

Professional Certification

In 1976, the American Society for Personnel Administration (ASPA) helped establish an independent group called the ASPA Accreditation Institute (AAI).[47] Its purposes are as follows:

1. To provide college and universities with guidelines for curricular development
2. To help students select courses related to various career objectives
3. To help senior practitioners keep up-to-date and demonstrate competence in their field

4. To help young practitioners establish career goals and development plans
5. To help employers identify qualified practitioners

The AAI has established two major categories of personnel practitioners: *generalists* and *specialists*. It accredits only active practitioners as generalists. Specialists include active practitioners, educators, and consultants, to name a few. One need not be a member of the ASPA to be accredited; about one in four of those accredited are not ASPA members.

Specialists may be accredited (certified) in six functional areas: (1) employment, placement, and personnel planning; (2) training and development; (3) compensation and benefits; (4) health, safety, and security; (5) employee and labor relations; and (6) personnel research. For each of these areas there are functional standards committees consisting of experts who define the knowledge required for each function and develop bibliographies and examination questions. The accreditation exams are conducted and evaluated by The Psychological Corporation.

Specialists are awarded two types of accreditation: *APS* (Accredited Personnel Specialist) and *APD* (Accredited Personnel Diplomate). The combination of education and experience must amount to six years for the APS and ten years for the APD. A bachelor's degree is counted as four years, and a master's degree counts as five years toward the total six-year (APS) and ten-year (APD) requirements.

Generalists are also awarded two types of accreditation: APM (Accredited Personnel Manager) and AEP (Accredited Executive in Personnel). The APM has a six-year requirement, and the AEP has a ten-year requirement.[48]

An addition to these aspects of the personnel profession are a large number of specialized associations, such as the American Compensation Association, to which practitioners can belong. Also available are many research-oriented and practitioner-oriented journals and magazines of interest to the teacher as well as to the practitioner of personnel. The names and addresses for many of these journals are found in Appendix B.

Plan of This Book

This book is intended to serve readers by fulfilling several specific purposes and by maintaining several themes throughout each of the chapters.

Purposes

The specific purposes are as follows:

- To increase your expertise in the functions and activities of personnel and human resource management
- To assist you in being an effective manager of human resources
- To present the complexities, challenges, and trade-offs involved in being an effective manager of human resources

- To instill a concern and an excitement for effective personnel and human resource management
- To assist you in being a more effective line manager

Themes

The three major themes in this book are (1) applications and challenges, (2) practical realities, and (3) theory and research. Each of these themes is integral in illustrating PHRM's importance and in demonstrating how PHRM can help organizations effectively use their human resources.

Applications and Practical Realities.   Examples from organizations and PHRM managers are used throughout the book to illustrate the challenges and practical realities of the personnel activities being examined. Each chapter begins with a real-life scenario or quotation called "PHRM in the News." Additional real-life scenarios and quotations appear throughout each chapter. Cases are included at the end of Chapters 2–18 and at the end of the book to provide you with a firsthand opportunity to deal with the challenges and practical realities.

Theory and Research.   Another major theme of this book is to provide the most current and useful information related to personnel and human resource management. Thus, the book extensively uses current research and theory related to the effective use and management of human resources. You will receive not only an extensive description of all the current PHRM functions and activities but also an understanding of why PHRM functions and activities should work and how they actually do work. With this knowledge, you can decide how to make the PHRM functions and activities work better; the section on assessment at the end of each chapter will assist you in this area. This section suggests what data to gather in order to make assessments and, therefore, improvements on each activity.

For Whom Is This Book Written?

This book is written for those who are now working or who will one day work in organizations. Knowledge of effective PHRM functions and activities is vital for anyone working in organizations, particularly line managers and especially personnel staff (specialists or generalists) and managers. This is true whether the organization is private or public, large or small, slow growing or fast growing. Although the type and size of the organization may influence the size of the personnel department, the functions and activities that it performs, and even the roles that it plays, every organization usually has a personnel department—and effective management of human resources is always necessary. This is not to say, however, that human resources are managed in the same way in different types and sizes of organizations. Differences exist among organizations, as this chapter has already suggested. Other differences are highlighted in the next chapter, along with a discussion of environmental influences on PHRM.

Summary

This chapter examines the growing importance of the functions and activities of personnel and human resource management, defines what PHRM is, and lists its purposes. Because of the increasing complexity of PHRM, nearly all organizations have established a personnel department. Not all of these departments, however, perform all of the personnel functions and activities discussed in this chapter. A department's functions and activities, and the way it performs them, depend greatly on the roles that the department plays in the organization. A PHRM department can play four roles. Organizations that are most concerned with effective personnel and human resource management allow their PHRM departments to play all four roles. When this occurs, the PHRM departments have most likely demonstrated their value to their organizations by showing how the several PHRM functions and activities influence productivity, quality of work life, and legal compliance—all purposes associated with the organization's bottom-line criteria. In addition, the PHRM departments are likely to be operating at all three levels in the organization: operational, managerial, and strategic. Furthermore, they are probably doing this in a proactive manner rather than waiting for the organization to tell them what to do. If a PHRM department is not doing this, it should be. A PHRM department should demonstrate its effectiveness, perform all four roles and operate at all three levels in the organization, and help the organization to attain its goals.

This book is for everyone who is or will be working in an organization, especially those who are responsible for the management and use of human resources: line managers and personnel managers and their staffs. Three major themes are used to make this book as useful and enjoyable as possible: why PHRM functions and activities work, how they work in practice, and how they can be made to work even better.

The remaining chapters provide a great deal of information about each PHRM activity. Many references are provided to enable you to examine in greater detail many of the topics discussed. These references are contained in the notes at the end of each chapter, along with points of clarification or explanation. Consider the chapter notes as an additional source of useful information.

Discussion Questions

1. What is the bottom line of an organization, and how can PHRM have a significant impact on the organization's bottom line?
2. What trends and crises are presently influencing PHRM's importance in organizations?
3. How can managers in PHRM become proactive in demonstrating their effectiveness?
4. What are some key issues related to the organization of an effective PHRM department?

5. What is the difference between personnel generalists and personnel specialists?

6. Why have the top managers of organizations attributed greater importance to the personnel and human resource management function? How will trends in the future influence these perceptions?

7. Briefly summarize the five major functions that PHRM serves.

8. What are some concrete ways in which the PHRM department can demonstrate its effectiveness to the organization?

9. What roles does PHRM serve in an organization? How are basic functions and activities related to these roles?

10. Why are some PHRM functions centralized while others are decentralized?

Notes

1. Although the term *personnel* is still used in reference to PHRM departments in organizations, the trend is toward use of the term *PHRM.* For a more complete description of this trend, see S. J. Carroll and R. S. Schuler, eds., *Human Resource Management in the 1980s* (Washington, D.C.: Bureau of National Affairs, 1983); M. A. Devanna, D. Fombrun, and N. Tichy, "Human Resources Management: A Strategic Perspective," *Organizational Dynamics* (Winter 1981): 51–67; and K. M. Rowland and G. R. Ferris, eds. *Personnel Management* (Boston: Allyn & Bacon, 1982).

2. Effective PHRM implies that whatever PHRM is doing, it is doing it as well as possible, (i.e., to attain the maximum benefit possible for individuals, the organization, and society). Thus, just because a PHRM activity is being done does not mean that the human resources are being used effectively. Only when the activity is done effectively is there effective PHRM. In this book, each activity is described, including its strengths and shortcomings. Based on this, you should in actual practice be able to play to the strengths of each activity and reduce the shortcomings, thus practicing effective PHRM.

3. "TRW Leads a Revolution in Managing Technology," *Business Week,* 15 Nov. 1982, pp. 124–30; J. G. Milkovich, L. D. Dyer, and T. A. Mahoney, "Human Resource Planning," in *Human Resource Management in the 1980s,* ed. (Washington, D.C.: Bureau of National Affairs, 1983); R. S. Schuler and I. C. MacMillan, "Gaining a Competitive Advantage through Human Resource Management Practices," *Human Resource Management* (Fall 1984): 241–56; "Personnel Widens Its Franchise," *Business Week,* 26 Feb. 1979, p. 116.

4. J. Farley, *Affirmative Action and the Woman Worker* (New York: AMACOM, 1979), p. 33.

5. Or anything else important to the total organization (e.g., employee participation). See K. S. Cameron and D. A. Whetten, *Organization Effectiveness: A Comparison of Multiple Models* (New York: Academic Press, 1983); D. R. Denison, "Bringing Corporate Culture to the Bottom Line," *Organizational Dynamics* (Autumn 1984): 4–22.

6. K. F. Misa and T. Stein, "Strategic HRM and the Bottom Line," *Personnel Administrator* (Oct. 1983): 27–30. See also T. Peters and B. Waterman, *In Search of Excellence* (New York: Warner Books, 1982); T. Peters and N. Austin, *Passion For Excellence* (New York: Warner Books, 1985); M. J. Piore and C. F. Sabel, *The Second Industrial Divide* (New York: Basic Books, 1984).

7. E. K. Burton, "Productivity: A Plan for Personnel," *Personnel Administrator* (Sept. 1981): 85–92; J. D. Hodgson, "An Impertinent Suggestion for Personnel," *Personnel Administrator* (Sept. 1981): 85–92; Y. K. Shety, "Improving Productivity: Management's Role in Declining Productivity," *California Management Review* (Fall 1982): 33–47; H. C. White, "Personnel Administration and Organizational Productivity: An Employee View," *Personnel Administrator* (Aug. 1981): 37–48; R. A. Katzell, P. Beinstock, and P. H. Faerstein, *A Guide to Worker Productivity Experiments in the United States 1971–75* (New York: New York University Press, 1977); R. Guzzo and J. S. Bondy, *A Guide to Worker Productivity Experiments in the United States 1976–81* (Elmsford, N.Y.: Pergamon, 1983); R. A. Katzell and R. A. Guzzo, "Psychological Approaches to Productivity Improvements," *American Psychologist* (Apr. 1983): 468–72.

8. The entire issue of *Personnel Administrator* (Sept. 1982) is developed around the roles that PHRM should play in organizations.

9. T. E. Deal and A. A. Kennedy, *Corporate Cultures* (Reading, Mass.: Addison-Wesley, 1982); R. Pascale, "Fitting New Employees into the Company Culture,"

Fortune, 28 May 1984, pp. 28–40; A. L. Wilkins, "The Culture Audit: A Tool for Understanding Organizations," *Organizational Dynamics* (Autumn 1983): 24–38; V. Sathe, "Some Action Implications of Corporate Culture: A Manager's Guide to Action," *Organizational Dynamics* (Autumn 1983): 4–23; E. J. Koprowski, "Cultural Myths: Clues to Effective Management," *Organizational Dynamics* (Autumn 1983): 39–51; J. Martin and C. Siehl, "Organizational Culture and Counterculture: An Uneasy Symbiosis," *Organizational Dynamics* (Autumn 1983): 52–64.

10. R. K. Swanson, "Personnel Management: A View from the Top," *Personnel Journal* (Sept. 1984): 112; G. R. Ferris, D. S. Cook, and J. Butler, "Strategy and Human Resource Management," in *Readings in Personnel and Human Resource Management,* 3d ed., ed. R. S. Schuler, S. A. Youngblood, and V. Huber (St. Paul: West, 1987).

11. N. Tichy, J. Fombrun, and M. Devanna, "Strategic Human Resource Management," in *Readings in Personnel and Human Resource Management,* 2d ed., ed. R. S. Schuler and S. A. Youngblood (St. Paul: West, 1984).

12. D. C. Funder, "On Assessing Social Psychological Theories through the Study of Individual Differences: Template Matching and Forced Compliance," *Journal of Personality and Social Psychology* 43 (1982): 100–110; B. Schneider, "Organizational Behavior," *Annual Review of Psychology* 36 (1985): 573–611; D. L. Bem and D. C. Funder, "Predicting More of the People More of the Time: Assessing the Personality of Situations," *Psychological Review* 85 (1978): 485–501.

13. Deal and Kennedy, *Corporate Cultures.*

14. Ibid., p. 3.

15. P. B. Doeringer and M. J. Piore, *Internal Labor Markets and Manpower Analysis* (Lexington, Mass.: D. C. Heath, 1971); P. Osterman, ed., *Internal Labor Markets* (Cambridge, Mass.: London, 1984).

16. Ibid.

17. H. R. Northrup, "Labor Market Trends and Policies in the 1980s," in *Readings in Personnel and Human Resource Management,* 2d ed., ed. R. S. Schuler and S. A. Youngblood (St. Paul: West, 1984).

18. D. Q. Mills, *The New Competitors* (New York: Wiley, 1985), p. 19.

19. Ibid., p. 23.

20. Schuler and MacMillan, "Gaining Competitive Advantage"; I. C. MacMillan and R. S. Schuler, "Gaining a Competitive Edge through Human Resources," *Personnel* (Apr. 1985): 24–29.

21. Schuler and MacMillan, "Gaining Competitive Advantage," p. 244.

22. "Personnel Widens Its Franchise," p. 121. Reprinted from the 26 Feb. 1979 issue of *Business Week,* Copyright © 1979 by McGraw-Hill Inc., 1221 Avenue of the Americas, New York, N.Y. 10020. All rights reserved.

23. Bureau of National Affairs, *Bulletin to Management,* 11 Oct. 1984, p. 1; T. F. O'Bogle, "Loyalty Ebbs at Many Companies as Employees Grow Disillusioned," *Wall Street Journal,* 11 July 1985, p. 27; "Human Resource Managers Aren't Corporate Nobodies Anymore," *Business Week,* 2 Dec. 1985, pp. 58–59.

24. J. Fitz-enz, *How to Measure Human Resources Management* (New York: McGraw-Hill, 1984); A. S. Tsui, "Personnel Department Effectiveness: A Tripartite Approach," *Industrial Relations* (Spring 1984): 184–97; J. A. Hooper, "A Strategy for Increasing the Human Resource Department's Effectiveness," *Personnel Administrator* (June 1984): 141–48; J. Fitz-enz, "Quantifying the Human Resources Function," *Personnel,* (March/April 1980): 41–52. For an extensive discussion, see D. R. Dalton, "Absenteeism and Turnover: Measures of Personnel Effectiveness," in *Applied Readings in Personnel and Human Resource Management,* ed. R. S. Schuler, J. M. McFillen, and D. R. Dalton (St. Paul: West, 1981), pp. 20–38; R. S. Schuler, "Occupational Health in Organizations: A Measure of Personnel Effectiveness," in *Applied Readings,* ed. Schuler, McFillen, and Dalton, pp. 39–53; P. M. Podsakoff, "Satisfaction and Performance: Measures of Personnel Effectiveness," in *Applied Readings,* ed. Schuler, McFillen, and Dalton, pp. 3–19; D. R. Dalton, "Legal Compliance: A Measure of Personnel Effectiveness," in *Applied Readings,* ed. Schuler, McFillen, and Dalton, pp. 54–70. This topic is also discussed in terms of utility. For an excellent overview, see F. L. Schmidt, J. E. Hunter, and K. Pearlman, "Assessing the Economic Impact of Personnel Programs on Workforce Productivity," *Personnel Psychology* (Summer 1982): 333–48; C. R. Day, Jr., "Solving the Mystery of Productivity Measurement," *Industry Week,* 26 Jan. 1981, pp. 61–66; F. J. Landy, J. L. Farr, and R. R. Jacobs, "Utility Concepts in Performance Measurements," *Organizational Behavior and Human Performance* 30 (1982): 15–40; W. F. Cascio, *Costing Human Resources: The Financial Impact of Behavior in Organizations* (Reading, Mass.: Addison-Wesley, 1982); J. C. Pingpank, "Preventing and Defending EEO Charges," *Personnel Administrator* (Feb. 1983): 35–40; L. J. Cronbach and G. C. Gleser, *Psychological Tests and Personnel Decisions* (Urbana, Ill.: University of Illinois Press, 1965); H. E. Brogden and E. K. Taylor, "The Dollar Criterion: Applying the Cost Accounting Concept to Criterion Construction," *Personnel Psychology* 3 (1950): 133–54; H. C. Taylor and J. T. Russell, "The Relationship of Validity Coefficients to the Practical Effectiveness of Tests in Selection: Discussion and Tables," *Journal of Applied Psychology* 23 (1939): 565–78; F. Krgystofiak and J. Newman, "Evaluating Employment Outcomes: Availability Models and Measures," *Industrial Relations* 21 (1982): 277–92; R. A. Katzell and R. A. Guzzo, "Psychological Approaches to Productivity Improvement," *American Psychologist* (Apr. 1983): 468–72; J. E. Hunter and F. L. Schmidt, "Quantifying the Effects of Psychological Interventions on Employee

Job Performance and Work-Force Productivity," *American Psychologist* (Apr. 1983): 473–78; R. R. West and D. E. Logue, "The False Doctrine of Productivity," *New York Times,* 9 Jan. 1983, p. F3; J. E. Ross, *Productivity, People, and Profits* (Reston, Va.: Reston, 1981); A. P. Brief and Associates, *Productivity Research in the Behavioral and Social Sciences* (New York: Praeger, 1984).

25. S. B. Henrici, "How Not to Measure Productivity," *New York Times,* 7 Mar. 1982, p. 2F.

26. For extensive discussion of these issues, see D. R. Dalton and W. D. Todor, "Turnover: A Lucrative Hard Dollar Phenomenon," *Academy of Management Review* 7 (1982): 212–218; T. E. Hall, "How to Estimate Employee Turnover Costs," *Personnel* (July/Aug. 1981): 43–52, 212–18; W. Mobley, *Turnover* (Reading, Mass.: Addison-Wesley, 1982); F. E. Kuzmits, "How Much Is Absenteeism Costing Your Organization?" *Personnel Administrator* (June 1979): 29–32.

27. "The New Industrial Relations," *Business Week,* 11 May, 1981, pp. 85–93; P. H. Mirvis and E. E. Lawler III, "Measuring the Financial Impact of Employee Attitudes," *Journal of Applied Psychology* 62 (1977): 1–8.

28. M. D. Levin-Epstein, *Primer on Equal Employment Opportunity,* 3d ed. (Washington, D.C.: Bureau of National Affairs, 1984); B. R. Ellig, "The Impact of Legislation on the Personnel Function," *Personnel* (Sept./Oct. 1980): 49–53.

29. G. Milkovich, L. Dyer, and T. Mahoney, "The State of Practice and Research in Human Resource Planning," in *Human Resource Management in the 1980s,* ed. S. J. Carroll and R. S. Schuler (Washington, D.C.: Bureau of National Affairs, 1983); E. H. Burack and N. J. Mathys, *Human Resource Planning: A Pragmatic Approach to Manpower Staffing and Development* (Lake Forest, Ill.: Brace-Park, 1979); E. C. Smith, "Strategic Business Planning and Human Resources: Part I," *Personnel Journal* (Aug. 1982): 606–10; E. C. Smith, "Strategic Business Planning and Human Resources: Part II," *Personnel Journal* (Sept. 1982): 680–82; L. J. Stybel, "Linking Strategic Planning and Management Manpower Planning," *California Management Review* (Fall 1982): 48–56; L. Dyer, "Human Resource Planning," in *Personnel Management,* ed. K. M. Rowland and G. R. Ferris (Boston: Allyn & Bacon, 1982), pp. 52–77.

30. N. Beutell and R. S. Schuler, *PC Projects for Personnel and Human Resource Management* (St. Paul: West, 1987). For further discussion on the role and importance of PC technology and measurement of PHRM activities, see J. Fitz-enz, *How to Measure Human Resource Management* (New York: McGraw-Hill, 1984); M. Kustoff, "Assembling a Micro-based HRIS: A Beginner's Guide," *Personnel Administrator* (Dec. 1985): 29–36; J. Fitz-enz "HR Measurement: Formulas for Success," *Personnel Journal* (Oct. 1985): 53–60; R. L. Wilson, "A Worksheet for HRIS Management," *Personnel Journal* (Oct. 1985): 44–52;

P. F. Salipante, K. A. Golden, and F. P. Buck, "A Partnership for Deriving Meaning from HR Data," *Personnel Administrator* (Dec. 1985): 55–64, 110; S. Rosenberg, "Flexibility in Installing a Large Scale HRIS: New York City's Experience," *Personnel Administrator* (Dec. 1985): 39–46.

31. A. K. Gupta, "Contingency Linkages between Strategy and General Manager Characteristics: A Conceptual Examination," *Academy of Management Review* 9 (1984): 399–412; J. Lynch and D. Orne, "Managing in the Belly of the Cow," *Management Review* (June 1985): 46–48; M. A. Maidique and R. H. Hayes, "The Art of High Technology Management," *Sloan Management Review* (Winter 1984): 17–31; J. L. Kerr, "Assigning Managers on the Basis of the Life Cycle," *Journal of Business Strategy,* 2, no. 4 (1982): 58–65; J. L. Kerr, "Diversification Strategies and Managerial Rewards: An Empirical Study," *Academy of Management Journal* 28 (1985): 155–79; G. R. Ferris, D. A. Schallenberg, and R. F. Zammuto, "Human Resources Management Strategies in Declining Industries," *Human Resource Management* (Winter 1985): 381–94; P. F. Drucker, *Innovation and Entrepreneurship* (New York: Harper & Row, 1985).

32. R. S. Schuler, "Personnel and Human Resource Management Choices and Organizational Strategy," in *Readings in Personnel and Human Resource Management,* 3d ed., ed. R. S. Schuler, S. A. Youngblood, and V. Huber (St. Paul: West, 1987); J. W. Slocum, W. L. Cron, R. W. Hansen, and S. Rawlings, "Business Strategy and the Management of Plateaued Employees," *Academy of Management Journal* 28 (1985): 133–54; C. C. Snow and L. G. Hrebiniak, "Strategy, Distinctive Competence, and Organizational Performance," *Administrative Science Quarterly* 25 (1980): 307–35; J. H. Song, "Diversification Strategies and the Experience of Top Executives of Large Firms," *Strategic Management Journal* (1982): 377–80; R. E. Miles and C. C. Snow, "Designing Strategic Human Resource Systems," *Organizational Dynamics* Fall (1984): 36–52; R. E. Miles and C. C. Snow, "Fit, Failure, and the Hall of Fame," *California Management Review* 26 (1984): 10–28; A. R. McGill, "Practical Considerations: A Case Study of General Motors," in *Strategic Human Resource Management,* ed. C. Fombrun, N. M. Tichy, and M. A. Devanna (New York: Wiley, 1984), pp. 149–58; T. A. Kochan and P. Cappelli, "The Transformation of the Industrial Relations/Human Resource Function," in *Internal Labor Markets,* ed. P. Osterman (Cambridge: MIT Press, 1983), pp. 133–62; T. A. Kochan, R. B. McKersie, and P. Cappelli, "Strategic Choice and Industrial Relations Theory," *Industrial Relations* 23 (1984): 16–39; A. K. Gupta and V. Govindarajan, "Build, Hold, Harvest: Converting Strategic Intentions into Reality," *Journal of Business Strategy* 4 (1984): 34–47; A. K. Gupta and V. Govindarajan, "Business Unit Strategy, Managerial Characteristics, and Business Unit Effectiveness at Strategy Implementation," *Academy of Management Journal* 9 (1984): 25–41.

33. Schuler and MacMillan, "Gaining Competitive Advantage," p. 248.

34. W. Skinner, "Big Hat, No Cattle: Managing Human Resources," *Harvard Business Review* (Sept./Oct. 1981): 106–14.

35. Ibid., p. 114.

36. R. S. Schuler, I. C. MacMillan, and J. J. Martocchio, "Strategy Execution and Human Resource Management," in *Handbook of Business Strategy—1985/1986 Yearbook*, ed. W. D. Guth (New York: Warren, Gorham & Lamont, 1985); M. E. Porter, *Competitive Strategy* (New York: Free Press, 1980); M. E. Porter, *Competitive Advantage* (New York: Free Press, 1985); R. H. Price and T. D'Aunno, "Managing Work Force Reduction," *Human Resource Management* 22 (1984): 413–30; E. B. Roberts and A. R. Fusfeld, "Staffing the Innovative Technology-Based Organization," *Sloan Management Review* (Spring 1981): 19–34; D. T. Hall, "Human Resource Development and Organizational Effectiveness," in *Strategic Human Resource Management*, ed. C. Fombrun, N. M. Tichy, and M. A. Devanna (New York: Wiley, 1984), pp. 159–82; A. D. Szilagyi and D. M. Schweiger, "Matching Managers to Strategies: A Review and Suggested Framework," *Academy of Management Review* 9 (1984): 626–37; L. L. Cummings, "Compensation, Culture, and Motivation: A Systems Perspective," *Organizational Dynamics* (Winter 1984): 33–43; T. A. Kochan and J. Chalykoff, "Human Resource Management and Business Life Cycles: Some Preliminary Propositions," paper presented at conference on Human Resources and Industrial Relations in High Technology Firms at UCLA, 1985; E. E. Lawler III, "The Strategic Design of Reward Systems," in *Readings in Personnel and Human Resource Management*, 2d., ed. R. S. Schuler and S. A. Youngblood (St. Paul: West, 1984), pp. 253–69; E. E. Lawler III and J. A. Drexler, Jr., "The Corporate Entrepreneur," working paper, Center for Effective Organizations, University of Southern California, 1984; P. Lorange and D. Murphy, "Strategy and Human Resources: Concepts and Practice," *Human Resource Management* 22 (1983): 111–35; P. Lorange and D. Murphy, "Bringing Human Resources into Strategic Planning: Systems Design and Considerations," in *Strategic Human Resource Management*, ed. C. Fombrun, N. M. Tichy, and M. A. Devanna (New York: Wiley, 1984), pp. 275–96; M. Gerstein and H. Reisman, "Strategic Selection: Matching Executives to Business Conditions," *Sloan Management Review* (Winter 1983): 33–49; R. Giles and C. Landauer, "Setting Specific Standards for Appraising Creative Staffs," *Personnel Administrator* 29 (1984): 35–47; J. P. Goodman and W. R. Sandberg, "A Contingency Approach to Labor Relations," *Academy of Management Review* 6 (1981): 145–54; J. D. Olian and S. L. Rynes, "Organizational Staffing: Integrating Practice with Strategy," *Industrial Relations* 23 (1984):

170–83; S. A. Stumpf and N. M. Hanrahan, "Designing Organizational Career Management Practices to Fit Strategic Management Objectives," in *Readings in Personnel and Human Resource Management*, 2d ed., ed. R. S. Schuler and S. A. Youngblood (St. Paul: West, 1984).

37. J. W. English, "The Road Ahead for the Human Resources Function," *Personnel* (Mar./Apr. 1980): 35–39; P. C. Gordon, "'Magnetic' Management: The Real Role of Personnel," *Personnel Journal* (June 1980): 485–87, 500; D. R. Hugar, AEP, "The Personnel Professional in the Small Organization," *Personnel Administrator* (Apr. 1981): 41; T. W. Peters and E. A. Mabry, "The Personnel Officer as Internal Consultant," *Personnel Administrator* (Apr. 1981): 29–32; H. C. White, APD, and M. N. Wolfe, "The Role Desired for Personnel Administration," *Personnel Administrator* (June 1980): 87–97.

38. F. K. Foulkes, "The Expanding Role of the Personnel Function," *Harvard Business Review* (Mar./Apr. 1975): 147.

39. *Bulletin to Management* (Washington, D.C.: Bureau of National Affairs, 1 Jan. 1985), p. 1, referring to a study done by Heidrick and Struggles, 125 S. Wacker, Suite 2800, Chicago, Ill. 60606.

40. M. Beer, B. Spector, P. R. Lawrence, D. Q. Mills, and R. Walton, *Managing Human Assets* (New York: Free Press, 1984).

41. Bureau of National Affairs, "ASPA-BNA Survey No. 48: Personnel Activities, Budgets, and Staffs: 1984–1985," *Bulletin to Management*, 23 May 1985.

42. Bureau of National Affairs, "Personnel and Industrial Relations Survey," *Bulletin to Management*, 5 July 1984, pp. 3–4; S. Langer, "Personnel Salaries," *Personnel Journal* (Jan. 1985): 69–75; S. Langer, "Where the Dollars Are: Annual Salary Survey Results," *Personnel Journal* (Feb. 1986): 92–94.

43. T. J. Bergmann and M. J. Close, "Preparing for Entry Level Human Resource Management Positions," *Personnel Administrator* (Apr. 1984): 95–99; V. R. Lindquist and F. S. Endicott, "The 1984 Northwestern Endicott Report," *Personnel Administrator* (May 1984): 76–77.

44. D. A. Greenwell, "Starting a Career in Personnel Administration," p. 16. Reprinted with permission from the September 1981 issue of the *Personnel Administrator*. Copyright 1981, The American Society for Personnel Administration, 30 Park Dr., Berea, Ohio 44017.

45. S. H. Appelbaum, APD, "The Personnel Professional and Organization Development: Conflict and Synthesis," *Personnel Administrator* (July 1980): 44–49; G. F. Brady, "Assessing the Personnel Manager's Power Base," *Personnel Administrator* (July 1980): 57–61; F. R. Edney, "The Greening of the Profession," *Personnel Administrator* (July 1980): 27–30, 42; F. R. Edney, "Human Resources Managers Aren't Corporate Nobodies Anymore," *Business Week*, 2 Dec.

1985, pp. 58–59; L. B. Prewitt, "The Emerging Field of Human Resources Management," *Personnel Administrator* (May 1982): 81–87.

46. D. Yoder and H. Heneman, Jr., *PAIR Jobs. Qualifications, and Careers, ASPA Handbook of Personnel and Industrial Relations,* (Washington, D.C.: Bureau of National Affairs, 1978) p. 18.

47. W. W. Tornow, "The Codification Project and Its Importance to Professionalism," *Personnel Administrator* (June 1984): 84–100; C. Haigley, "Professionalism in Personnel," *Personnel Administrator* (June 1984): 103–6.

48. G. B. Hansen, "Professional Education for Careers in Human Resource Administration," *Personnel Administrator* (Jan. 1984): 69–80; J. F. Parry, "Accredited Professionals Are Better Prepared," *Personnel Administrator* (Dec. 1985): 48–52.

Planning

2

Human Resource Planning

Planning with People

Human resources managers who make sure that the "people factor" is integrated into strategic business plans can help the company make more cost-effective and productive decisions, declares John O'Brien, vice-president of human resources planning at Digital Equipment Corp. Addressing the American Management Associations' 55th Annual Human Resources Conference, O'Brien says personnel managers have a responsibility to convince corporate business planners that "human resources represent a major competitive advantage" and are every bit as important as the time, money, and material expended to increase profits.

Personnel's tasks

At DEC, O'Brien observes, personnel officers strive to influence the firm's business directions from a "people dimension" and "work at being initiators of change rather than reactors to change." In effect, he says, their goal is to ensure that the personnel department has a role and voice in the key business issues and policies affecting both the company and its workers.

A basic ingredient of an integrated HR-business planning process, O'Brien notes, is personnel managers working side by side with line managers to solve the organization's business and people problems. Jointly, the personnel and line managers strive to:

- Develop business plan strategies for the company's various operating divisions and analyze each unit's strategies to determine what human resources will be needed;
- Collect detailed information on the current workforce and analyze the organization's workforce profile in terms of its future business strategies;
- Identify current and emerging HR issues, and review these with the management committees of units most likely to be affected by changes in the work environment; and
- Develop plans and programs that address the identified issues in support of the business direction.

Tools of the trade

The tools personnel managers can use to carry out their planning responsibilities include:

- Environmental scans—These consist of analyses of trends affecting the workforce or business direction, such as: workforce demographics (workforce growth, aging, education, etc.) and social trends (worker attitudes, work ethics, job satisfaction); geographic factors (relocation incentives, regional growth); economic considerations (interest rates, inflation, unemployment); political, legal, regulatory, or judicial issues (unjust dismissal, plant closings, comparable worth); and productivity (compensation and labor costs, R&D expenditures, foreign competition).
- HR data analyses—Personnel managers, O'Brien says, should prepare workforce profiles that indicate how trends in such areas as technology, population, workforce mobility, compensation, and training, could affect such issues as employee turnover, job design, career advancement, productivity, and salary structures.

The preceding "PHRM in the News" highlights several important aspects of human resource planning. One is that planning with people can lead to a major competitive advantage for an organization. Another is that line managers and PHRM managers share the responsibility for effective human resource planning. A third aspect is that the external environment has to be analyzed and incorporated into an organization's human resource planning. Because these are such critical aspects of human resource planning, they and other aspects are described in this chapter.

In general terms, **human resource planning** is the base upon which effective PHRM is constructed. More specifically, human resource planning involves forecasting human resource needs for the organization and planning the steps necessary to meet these needs. Human resource planning consists of developing and implementing plans and programs to ensure that the right number and type of individuals are available at the right time and place to fulfill organizational needs. As such, human resource planning is directly tied to strategic business planning.[1] Because of the trend toward more strategic involvement by PHRM, discussed in Chapter 1, human resource planning is one of the fastest growing and most important areas in PHRM. Human resource planning helps ensure that organizations fulfill their business plans—plans that chart the organization's future regarding financial objectives, output goals, product mix, technologies, and resource requirements.[2] Once their business plans are determined, often with the assistance of the PHRM department, "the human resource planner assists in developing workable organizational structures and in determining the numbers and types of employees that will be required to meet financial and output goals."[3] After workable structures and the requirements for needed individuals are identified, the human resource planner develops personnel and human resource programs to implement the structure and to obtain the individuals. Line managers and supervisors, however, are responsible for providing the necessary information for human resource planning, and for working with the PHRM manager to ensure that the organization's human resources are used as effectively as possible and that its human resource needs are provided for—important aspects in the four phases of human resource planning. These four phases are described later in the chapter.

Purposes and Importance of Human Resource Planning

The general purpose of human resource planning is to identify future organizational demands and supplies of human resources and to develop programs to eliminate any discrepancies, all in the best interests of the individual and the organization. More specifically, the purposes of human resource planning are as follows:

- Reduce personnel costs by helping management to anticipate shortages or surpluses of human resources and to correct these imbalances before they become unmanageable and expensive

- Provide a better basis for planning employee development that makes optimum use of workers' attitudes
- Improve the overall business planning process
- Provide more opportunities for women and minority groups in future growth plans and identify the specific skills available
- Promote greater awareness of the importance of sound human resource management throughout all levels of the organization
- Provide a tool for evaluating the effect of alternative human resource actions and policies[4]

All of these purposes are now more easily attained than ever before, thanks to computer technology. This technology allows vast job-related records to be maintained on each employee, in essence creating a human resource information system. These records, which include information on employee job preferences, work experiences, and performance evaluations, provide a job history of each employee in an organization and a complete set of information on the jobs and positions in the organization. This in turn can be used to facilitate the purposes of human resource planning in the interests of the individual as well as the organization.

All of these purposes partly explain the recent and growing importance of human resource planning. A large number of environmental and organizational changes also explain the importance of human resource planning and PHRM. These changes are pushing personnel and human resource management into a future-oriented, comprehensive, and integrative perspective that has a number of fundamental attributes: (1) it considers human resource costs an investment rather than an uncontrollable expense; (2) it is proactive rather than reactive or passive in its approach to developing human resource policies and resolving human resource problems; (3) it is characterized by a change in role perspective from an emphasis on the completion of personnel transactions toward a future-oriented approach in which the PHRM department acts as a controller of the organization's human resources; (4) it recognizes that an explicit link must exist between human resource planning and other organizational functions, such as strategic planning, economic and market forecasting, and investment and facilities planning; (5) it recognizes that such PHRM activities as recruitment, selection, labor relations, compensation and benefits, training, organizational planning, and career management must be visualized as dynamic interconnecting activities rather than as a series of separate and nonintegrated functions; and (6) it focuses on approaches that further both organizational and individual goals.[5]

One organizational change that is making human resource planning more important is the growing recognition of the extensive set of relationships that human resource planning has with other personnel and human resource activities. Human resource planning helps establish the organization's staffing needs and provides the basis for meeting those needs.

An important environmental change is the growing shortage of human resources to fill certain jobs. Currently predicted are shortages in blue-collar occupations and entry-level white-collar occupations, such as tool and die makers, bricklayers and other skilled crafts workers. In addition, shortages currently exist for shipbuilders, legal secretaries, engineers, robotics engineers, machinists, and mechanics.[6]

Yet while there are shortages of certain types of individuals, there is a growing abundance of another—those in the thirty-five to forty-four-year-old age category. As discussed later in this chapter, the number of people entering this age group is increasing faster than the number of jobs available for them. Consequently, many of these people can probably anticipate relatively static income and rivalry with older workers for some period of time.

The increasing potential for managerial obsolescence is another critical change. Rapid changes in knowledge are making it difficult for professionals, engineers, and managers to remain adept at their jobs. Consequently, they must be provided with the opportunity for continued training. However, organizations are not sure what to do, nor do they always recognize the potential for obsolescence. Nevertheless, "the unsolved problem of professional obsolescence posed by the production of knowledge is a threat to the growth potential of organizations and society as a whole."[7]

Another change is the growing resistance of employees to change and to relocate. Emphasis on self-evaluation and on evaluation of loyalty and dedication to the organization is also growing. All these changes are making it more difficult for the organization to assume it can move its employees around anywhere and anytime it wants, thus increasing the importance and necessity of planning ahead.

Because all of these changes are increasing PHRM's importance, their implications for planning and program development are described later in the chapter.

Relationships Influencing Human Resource Planning

As the initial "PHRM in the News" suggests, human resource planning has an extensive set of relationships with aspects of the internal and external environment. Because these aspects are critical in human resource planning, a description of them here is useful. First the relationships of planning with other PHRM activities are presented. All these relationships are summarized in Exhibit 2.1.

Relationships with Other PHRM Activities

Human resource planning influences almost all other PHRM activities. As shown in Exhibit 2.1, four of these activities are especially important.

Job Analysis.   Essential in human resource planning is an analysis of an organization's current capabilities. Specifically, an organization needs to know if the current employees are qualified to do the current jobs. To answer this, job requirements and employee qualifications need to be determined—the essence of job analysis as described in Chapter 3.

Aspects and Relationships of Human   *Exhibit 2.1*
Resource Planning

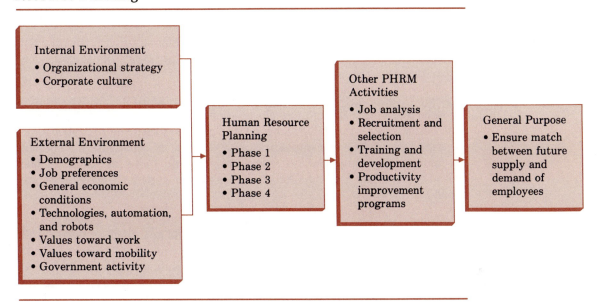

Recruitment and Selection.   Human resource planning helps determine the
human resource staffing needs of an organization. In conjunction with job
analysis, it indicates how many and what types of people need to be recruited. Recruitment influences the pool of available job applicants, which in turn
influences the needs for selection and placement. Thus, human resource
planning can be viewed as a major input into an organization's staffing function. This relationship is highlighted in Chapters 4 and 5.

Training and Development.   Human resource planning helps training and development programs aid an organization in retaining valued employees and
in keeping them from becoming obsolete. Thus, these programs can play an
important role in determining an organization's supply of human resources
and, ultimately, its needs. For example, if career management programs for
employees can help reduce employee turnover and absenteeism, the organization can plan on a larger supply of qualified human resources and, therefore, a smaller need for additional human resources. Training and development programs can also help an organization fulfill its staffing needs by
enabling it to hire job applicants not fully qualified but at least potentially
qualifiable. These uses of training and development are discussed further in
Chapter 11.

Productivity Improvement Programs. With increased competition and
changing demographic characteristics, the traditional ways of structuring
work and organizations are being questioned. New, more flexible structures
are increasingly being tried. Employees are being brought into the decision-
making process more than ever before. The Saturn project of General Mo-

tors is unprecedented in the auto industry in its degree of employee involvement and work force flexibility.

Relationships with the Internal Environment

Human resource planning has two important relationships with the internal environment: the relationship with organizational strategy and the relationship with corporate culture.

Organizational Strategy.   As the initial "PHRM in the News" states, human resource planning is being more closely tied to organizational strategy than ever before.[8] By linking human resource planning into the organizational strategy formulation and implementation phases, an organization increases its chances of having the right people at the right place and time. It also eases the potential hardships on employees when work force reductions are needed.

Corporate Culture.   As Chapter 1 stated, corporate culture reflects the assumptions an organization makes about people and how they are to be treated. Consequently, the nature of the corporate culture influences how PHRM activities are practiced. The growing trend is to shift away from traditional assumptions (people are motivated exclusively by self-interest, people are expendable to organizations, people need to be controlled, and people want to avoid work) and to move toward newer assumptions (people are interested in work, people are capable of self-motivated behavior, and people are an asset to organizations). A more complete illustration of these assumptions and their implications for PHRM practices is shown in Exhibit 2.2.

Relationships with the External Environment

As shown in Exhibit 2.1, many aspects of the external environment impact human resource planning.

Exhibit 2.2	*The Shifting Human Resource Management Model*

Old Assumptions	New Assumptions and Practices
Reactive, piecemeal interventions in response to specific problems	Proactive, systemwide interventions with emphasis on fit • Linking human resource management with strategic planning • Cultural change • Prescreening, placement, promotions, layoffs based on how individuals will *fit* with desired new culture • Coordinating people and structural changes (semiautonomous work groups and business units)

continued

Old Assumptions	New Assumptions and Practices
People as variable cost	People are social capital capable of development • Increasing power to developmental HRM functions • Forming work groups, using skill-based pay to broaden employees' competencies • Heavy emphasis on training • More open communication, greater participation to develop people's commitment • More concern about employment security
Self-interests dominate, conflicts of interests between stakeholders	Coincidence of interests between stakeholders can be developed • Joint union-management efforts based on improving both quality of work life and organizational effectiveness • Emphasis on employee self-esteem with positive human and business outcomes
Seeks power advantages for bargaining and confrontation	Seeks power equalization for trust and collaboration • Joint union-management committees • De-emphasis on status symbols • All salaried work force
Control of information flow to enhance efficiency, power	Open channels of communication to build trust, commitment • Greater sharing of information on business with unions, work groups, organizational units • Greater communication about design and administration of pay system
Relationship orientation	Goal orientation • Setting explicit goals for work groups • Involving organizational subunits in establishing goals
Control from top	Participation and informed choice • Participative management style • Labor-management participation teams • Employee involvement programs • Greater employee control over career choices • Diagonal task forces, problem-solving teams

Source: M. Beer and B. Spector, "Corporate-Wide Transformations in HRM," for the Harvard Business School 75th Anniversary Colloquium on Human Resource Futures, 9–11 May 1984. Reprinted by permission.

Demographics.   American industry is currently faced with a shrinking supply of young workers. After more than two decades of growth, the nation's population between the ages of sixteen and twenty-four has peaked. This has led to problems for organizations:

> A declining number of youths makes it difficult to attract and keep employees who work at or near minimum wage rates. The number of young workers peaked in 1980 at 37 million and will drop to 24 million by 1990, according to the National Commission for Employment Policy. Most of the decline will be white youths. By 1995, by one estimate, young workers will comprise only 16% of the work force, down from 24% in 1979.
>
> Popeye's Fried Chicken in New York and Teaneck, N.J., begins a worker-of-the-month program with bonuses, plaques, and other benefits. The Westport, Conn., Burger King, whose 35-worker staff turns over five times a year, pays up to $4.50 an hour, $1.13 above minimum wage in the state. Paco's Tacos, Boston, raises pay after four months.
>
> Horn & Hardart, New York, says the labor pool is much bigger there. Also, high turnover keeps costs down. But productivity slips, too.[9]

As shown in Exhibit 2.3, the 16–24 age group will continue to decline as a percentage of the total labor force and population. In the meantime, the 25–54 age group (especially the 35–44 segment) will continue to rise. The 35–44 age group is expected to increase 42 percent between 1980 and 1990, from 25.4 million to 36.1 million. This will cause bottlenecks in the promotion paths for that age group for the next several years, because the number of middle manager jobs for the 35–44 age group is expected to increase only 19.1 percent, from 8.8 million to 10.5 million. The consequences of the bottlenecks may be increased militancy and dissatisfaction among the employees, and greater selection opportunities for them as well. Employers, however, may have to accommodate these employees by making their present jobs more challenging and even redefining success (in essence, changing the

---

Exhibit 2.3   *Labor Force Age Group Distribution Percentages*

Age Group	Actual			Projected	
	1975	*1979*	*1985*	*1990*	*1995*
16–24	24.1	24.5	21.3	18.8	17.2
16–19	9.4	5.1	7.5	6.9	6.7
20–24	14.5	14.8	13.8	11.7	10.5
25–54	60.7	61.6	65.8	70.2	72.4
25–34	24.1	26.1	28.4	28.5	25.9
35–44	18.2	28.9	22.5	25.7	27.7
45–54	18.3	16.3	14.8	15.9	18.9
55 and over	15.2	13.9	12.9	10.9	10.2
55–64	12.2	11.3	10.3	8.7	8.3
65 and over	3.2	2.4	2.7	2.4	1.9

Source: H. N. Fullerton, "The 1995 Labor Force: A First Look,"
Monthly Labor Review 103 (December 1980): 15.

outcomes provided) by removing its association with upward promotions. Coincident with these bottlenecks, however, are some changing work force interests and preferences that are moderating possible militancy and dissatisfaction. General Electric and AT&T report that the 35–44 age groups in their companies are still relatively satisfied because of increased interest in family and personal life and a greater reluctance to transfer.[10]

A look at the distribution of sex and race in these same age categories shows several other interesting changes.[11] The total number of men in the labor force will continue to diminish, while the number of blacks and women will continue to increase. Currently, approximately 80 percent of all men eligible to work are now in the work force. Although this number is not expected to change much in the next fifteen years, the percentage of women eligible to work and in the work force is expected to reach 60 percent by 1990. Consequently, of the expected 19.6 million additional employees in the work force by 1990, 11 million are expected to be women.

Other population changes expected to occur in the 1980s include an increase in life expectancy for men (from 69.5 years in 1978 to over 70 years) and women (from 77.2 years in 1978 to 80 years), continued movement of the population to the southern and western portions of the United States, and international migration adding almost 1 million people a year to the U.S. population.[12] Extending projections even further indicates that the first decade of the twenty-first century marks the graying of the work force, with a 42 percent increase in the 55–64 age category between 2000 and 2010. The population of persons aged 45–64 is expected to increase from 43.6 million in 1980 to 72.9 million in 2010, and the population aged 65 and over is expected to increase from 24.5 million in 1980 to 42.8 million in 2020.[13]

All of these population and work force trends are expected to present major challenges for human resource planning. A general challenge affecting all of society is: What jobs will be available for these people? What will their job preferences be?

Job Preferences.   Currently, the occupational makeup of the civilian labor force reflects much higher percentages of women than men in clerical positions, and higher percentages of men than women in managerial and administrative jobs and employed as crafts workers. The distribution of men and women in the nine major occupational categories maintained by the U.S. Department of Labor is shown in Exhibit 2.4. Although these data indicate that 16 percent of the women occupy professional and technical positions, most of those are in the nursing and teaching professions. Thus, a majority of the female work force are in service, clerical (secretarial), nursing, and teaching jobs. The majority of men, on the other hand, are in semiskilled (operative), skilled (crafts workers), managerial and administrative, and professional and technical jobs. This distribution has, in part, resulted from the notion of **job sex-typing**. That is, a job takes on the image of being appropriate only for the sex that dominates the job. Consequently, once a job becomes sex-typed, it attracts only those of that sex. Job sex-typing, combined with **sex-role stereotyping,** has traditionally restricted perceived job choices and preferences of both men and women. Whereas job sex-typing refers to the labeling of jobs as either "men's jobs" or "women's jobs," sex-role stereotyp-

Exhibit 2.4   *Occupational Makeup of the Civilian*
Labor Force

Occupational Group	Percentage of Total Labor Force	Percentage of Male Workers	Percentage of Female Workers
Professional and technical	14	14	16
Managerial and administrative	11	14	7
Sales	6	6	7
Clerical	18	6	34
Crafts workers	14	21	2
Operatives	15	17	11
Laborers	6	9	1
Service workers	14	10	21
Farm workers	2	3	1

Source: Adapted from U.S. Department of Labor, Bureau of
Labor Statistics, *Employment and Earnings,* vol. 27, no. 3
(Washington, D.C.: Government Printing Office, March 1980).

ing refers to labels, characteristics, or attributes that become attached to men and women solely because they are members of their respective sexes.

Evidence now indicates that the range of perceived choices and preferences is expanding for both men and women. This trend has been facilitated in part by the gradual reduction of sex-role stereotyping in our society. In addition, some of the job sex-typing has been reduced through sex-neutral job titles and through legal mandates that encourage employers to hire females for previously male-dominated jobs, and vice versa.[14]

These changes in job preferences and choices will provide both challenges and opportunities for PHRM planning practitioners. The challenges will center on the social impact of men and women entering nontraditional jobs. The opportunities are in developing well-planned programs to help ensure that employees will remain in these nontraditional jobs.

Job Openings.   According to the Bureau of Labor Statistics, 23.4 to 28.6 million new wage and salary jobs will be created by 1995. Of these, between 1.0 and 4.6 million will be in high-technology industries:

> All traditional jobs are not going to die, of course. The United States Bureau of Labor Statistics projected that between 1978 and 1990 there will be more than 600,000 jobs for janitors and sextons compared to 200,000 new jobs for computer system analysts; 800,000 jobs for fast food workers and kitchen helpers, compared to 88,000 jobs for computer operators.[15]

Thus, a substantial number of new jobs will be in industries other than high technology. The industries that will have the greatest number of new jobs by 1995 are shown in Exhibit 2.5.

General Economic Conditions.   One trend that will affect human resource planning is the relative stagnation in the rate of productivity. Presently the rate of inflation is at a moderate level and is not a major consideration in hu-

Industries with the Greatest Number of New Jobs by 1995			*Exhibit 2.5*

Industry	Number of New Jobs	Percentage of All New Jobs
Retail trade	3,089,000	12.2
Business services	2,440,000	9.7
New construction	1,976,000	7.8
Eating and drinking places	1,583,000	6.3
Hospitals	1,461,000	5.8
Wholesale trade	1,149,000	4.6
Other medical services	1,024,000	4.1
Professional services	857,000	3.4
Education services (private)	514,000	2.0
Doctors' and dentists' services	502,000	2.0

Source: V. Personick, "The Job Outlook through 1995: Industry Output and Employment Projections," *Monthly Labor Review* (November 1984).

man resource planning. Yet if inflation were to increase slightly—say, to 7 percent—the cost of most goods sold would double in about ten years. Similarly, wages and salaries would double to keep up with inflation. High inflation would also influence the cost of employer-paid fringe benefits and would further enhance the need for productivity gains and better work force utilization. Consequently, faced with stagnating productivity rates, the possible renewal of high inflation, and continued intense international competition, organizations are concerned with increasing productivity. This concern has significantly increased the use of automation, robots, and advanced technologies in both white- and blue-collar occupations.

Advanced Technologies, Automation, and Robots.   The U.S. technologies that are advancing most rapidly and which have the most potential for enhancing productivity and work force utilization are microelectronics, artificial intelligence, materials research, material surfaces, biotechnology, and geology.[16] A significant application of microelectronics results in increased use of automation, computerization, and robots. Although using these technologies dramatically increases productivity, it also has a profound effect on the size of the needed work force and employee pride and self-esteem. When use of robots is considered, the organization's human resource planning needs must be altered.

Values toward Work.   Stagnating productivity rates are often related to the decline or disappearance of the work ethic. According to some, however, "The work ethic has not disappeared. People today are willing to work hard at 'good' jobs, providing they have the freedom to influence the nature of their jobs and to pursue their own lifestyles."[17] People still value work, but the type of work that interests them has changed. They want challenging jobs that provide them with freedom to make decisions. Generally, people do not seek or desire rapid promotions, especially when they involve geographic transfers, but they do seek influence and control.

Changing values toward work may make it necessary to analyze employees' personalities, interests, and preferences, as well as their skills, knowledge, and abilities, and match them with the organizational structures (i.e., with job and organizational characteristics). Organizations with new, alternative structures may result. Organizations may also have to fit structure with the environment. If structure cannot be changed, individuals may need to be selected for the existing type of structure. In either case, however, the result sought is a fit between the structure and the person.

Values toward Mobility.   Employees' values toward work significantly affect their values toward geographic relocation. Like work values, mobility values will continue to significantly impact PHRM, especially in recruiting, training, promoting, and motivating managers and professionals. Large companies like Boeing, General Electric, Norton, Georgia-Pacific, Bell Telephone, and IBM are having a difficult time getting their employees to move. This growing reluctance, however, may not be all bad for companies. According to the Employee Relocation Council in Washington, D.C., in the past five years, the average company cost of moving a home-owning employee has tripled.

Government Activity.   The influence of government activity on the human resource function in organizations is greater than ever. In some respects, the requirements of federal and state legislation have shaped the modern corporate personnel department. (Appendix A contains many laws and regulations that impose requirements on human resource management.) The remaining chapters will make clear how legislation and regulation (referred to as legal considerations) will continue to influence all PHRM functions and activities.

Changes in these aspects of the external environment are likely to significantly impact human resources management. Familiarity with these changes will aid managers in PHRM to more effectively manage their organizations' work forces. Personnel managers must use this knowledge in developing and implementing effective personnel planning programs. Once implemented, these programs need to be evaluated and revised, then implemented and evaluated again. Only through these continual practices will personnel and human resource management be effective.

Four Phases of Human Resource Planning

As the following "PHRM in the News" illustrates, determining an organization's human resource needs lies at the base of human resource planning. The two major components of this determination are identifying the human resource supply and identifying the human resource demand—the first phase in human resource planning. Although these determinations are critical, organizations have, until recently, avoided making them. Indeed, organizations have avoided or at least resisted engaging in any of the four phases of human resource planning.[18] Some still resist, as Professor Mills describes in the following "PHRM in the News." These roadblocks to effective human resource planning are described later in the chapter.

Human resource planning is generally accomplished in four phases:

1. a. Gathering, analyzing, and forecasting data to develop a human resource supply forecast (and create a human resource information system)

   b. Gathering, analyzing, and forecasting data to develop a human resource demand forecast (and add to the human resource information system)

2. Establishing human resource objectives and policies and gaining top management's approval and support

3. Designing and implementing plans and action programs in areas such as recruitment, training, and promotion that will enable the organization to achieve its human resource objectives

4. Controlling and evaluating personnel plans and programs to facilitate progress toward human resource objectives[19]

PHRM in the News

People-Planning Questions and Answers

Are companies that engage in "people planning" responding to occupational shortages and anticipated business changes? Do they plan because they perceive planning as useful? Are they more successful than organizations that do not consider human resources needs? These and other questions are addressed in a survey conducted by D. Quinn Mills, a professor at Harvard Business School.

Who plans and why

Of the 291 companies surveyed by Mills, 40 percent reported that they include a human resources component in their long-term business plans. Just under 50 percent of the respondents draw up a formal management succession plan, and approximately the same percentage prepare training and development plans for managerial employees. Only 15 percent of the surveyed firms do no people planning at all, Mills finds.

Most of the respondents that engage in people planning do so because they believe it "makes their company more flexible and entrepreneurial, not because the environment forces it on them," Mills says. Of the survey respondents that practice people planning, 72 percent emphasized that it improves profitability, and 39 percent insisted that they can "measure the difference on the bottom line." Those companies that resist human resources planning do so because they believe it is costly and ineffective, Mills finds, adding that these firms also often associate planning with bureaucracy and red tape. Admitting that too much bureaucracy can be a bad thing, Mills says that the successful people planners in his survey avoid the problem by keeping the planning process as informal as possible and putting it in the hands of line managers.

The planning process

To study the evolution of people-planning processes, Mills grouped the sample companies into five stages according to three criteria: the number of people-planning elements used, the degree to which human resources plans are integrated into the business plan, and the amount of expressed commitment to planning. Comparison of the different stages shows that there is a steady evolutionary progression, Mills says. Stage 1 companies, for example, have no long-term business plans, tend to be run paternalistically, and do little or no people-planning, while Stage 2 firms have long-term business plans, but are skeptical of human resources planning. Companies in Stage 3 have several people-planning components and also engage in longer-term staff forecasting; firms in Stage 4 do a great deal of people planning; and Stage 5 companies make human resources planning an integral part of their long-term business plan. Further comparison of the stages reveals that:

- Stage 1 and Stage 2 companies tend to hire or retrain people only when immediate vacancies occur, while Stage 4 and Stage 5 firms often look ahead three to six years.
- Succession planning—the identification of employees to fill key administrative positions as they become vacant—is most often done by Stage 4 and Stage 5 companies.
- Only one company in 10 integrates a succession plan into the long-term strategic plan.

Successful people plans

"People planning has many sources and takes various forms, as companies develop distinctive ways to meet their needs, experience, and business strategies," Mills notes, adding that there are some activities in which all successful people planners participate, including:

- *Thinking ahead*—For people planning to succeed, managers must be able to determine how many employees and what kinds of skills are needed for specific jobs. They also must be able to determine whether their human resources needs can be met by hiring new people or by retraining and reassigning current employees.

- *Motivating workers*—While forecasting staffing and skill needs is common, Mills says, a more important aspect of people planning is developing activities to improve employee morale and stimulate productivity.

- *Linking objectives and people plans*—To ensure profitability, Mills say, business objectives must be linked to people-planning activities. If the right people are unavailable or if performance goals cannot be met, business objectives may have to be revised, Mills observes, adding that "astute managers no longer assume that every plan is doable." (*Harvard Business Review,* Vol. 85, No. 4, Harvard Graduate School of Business Admin., Boston, Mass. 02163)

Source: Bulletin to Management, 8 August, 1985, p. 48. Reprinted by permission from *Bulletin to Management,* copyright 1985, by The Bureau of National Affairs, Inc., Washington, D.C.

Phase 1: Gathering, Analyzing, and Forecasting Supply and Demand Data

The first phase of human resource planning involves developing data that can be used to determine corporate objectives, policies, and plans as well as human resource objectives and policies. The data developed in Phase 1 represent information retrieved from the past, observed in the present, and forecasted for the future. Obtaining data from the past may be difficult because of inadequate or nonexistent records, and forecasting data with reliability and accuracy may be difficult because of uncertainties. Nevertheless, this data should be provided, however tentatively. The more tentative the data, the more flexible and subject to revision they should be. Contingencies causing uncertainties in the forecasts should be incorporated, perhaps in the form of estimated ranges. Organizations in unstable, complex environments are faced with many more contingencies than organizations in stable, simple environments.

Exhibit 2.6 shows the four steps in Phase 1. Each is important for the success of human resource planning and programming. Step 1 consists of an analysis of the human resource situation in an organization. As Exhibit 2.6 indicates, this step consists of four aspects.

Analysis.   One aspect of a human resource analysis is an inventory of the current work force and the current jobs in the organization. Both elements are necessary if the organization is to determine its capability to meet current and future human resource needs. Knowing the current work force's skills, abilities, interests, and preferences is only half of the inventory. The other half consists of knowing the current jobs' characteristics and the skills required to perform them. An updated job analysis program facilitates this half of the inventory and the matching of employees and jobs.

Use of computers makes compiling inventories much more efficient and allows for a more dynamic, integrative human resource program. Through computers, employees in separate divisions and in different geographic areas find it easier to participate in the organization's network for matching jobs and employees. A common computer-oriented information system used in human resources management is the human resource information system (HRIS) described in Chapter 1.

A second aspect of human resource analysis is analyzing the probable future composition of the society's work force. This analysis is often based on wage, occupational, and industrial groups. Historical data on work force composition, along with current demographic and economic data, are used to make human resource projections. These employment projections are not specific to any single organization, but they can often provide an organization with useful information for its human resource plans, particularly for long-term needs.

Another aspect of human resource analysis is determining labor productivity and probable productivity in the future. Organizations can use their HRIS's to measure performance for evaluating the productivity of specific programs, offices, or positions. Related measures are projections of employee turnover and absenteeism. These influence an organization's work force productivity at any one time and, thus, its future human resource needs. These projections might also suggest a need to analyze the reasons for turnover and absenteeism, and then form the basis for strategies to deal with them. Note, however, that at some times and for some employees, increased turnover is desirable. For example, if an organization suddenly finds itself with too many employees, increased turnover—especially among poor performers—might be welcomed.[20]

Exhibit 2.6   **Procedures and Steps for Human Resource Planning and Programming**

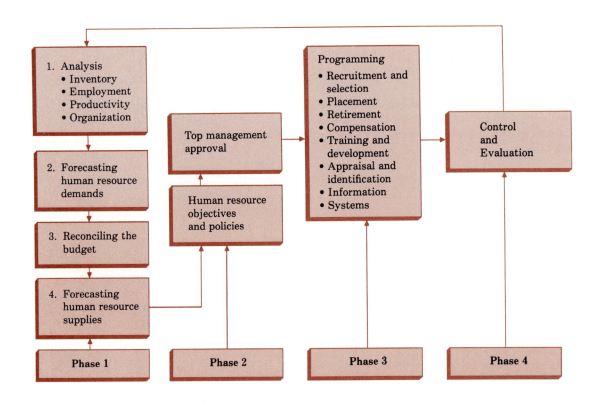

Source: Adapted from E. W. Vetter, *Manpower Planning for High Talent Personnel* (Ann Arbor, Mich.: Bureau of Industrial Relations, Graduate School of Business, University of Michigan, 1967), p. 34.

The final aspect of the first step is examining and projecting organizational structure. This helps determine the probable size of the top, middle, and lower levels of the organization, for both managers and nonmanagers. In addition, it provides information about changes in the organization's human resource needs and about specific activities or functional areas that can be expected to experience particularly severe growth or contraction.

The type of organization is a major factor determining both structure and the amount and intensity of changes. As organizations become more technologically complex and face more complex and dynamic environments, their structures will become more complex—with more departments and a greater variety of occupations—and they will face more changes in the environment.[21]

Forecasting Human Resource Demands.   A variety of forecasting methods—some simple, some complex—can determine an organization's demand for human resources. The type of forecast used depends on the time frame and the type of organization, its size and dispersion, and the accuracy and certainty of available information. The time frame used in forecasting the organization's demand for human resources frequently parallels that used in forecasting the potential supply of human resources. Comparison of the demand and supply forecasts then determines the organization's short-, intermediate-, and long-term needs. These needs form the basis for human resource programming.

Forecasting results in approximations—not absolutes or certainties. The forecast quality depends on the accuracy of information and the predictability of events. The shorter the time horizon, the more predictable events are and the more accurate the information. For example, organizations are generally able to predict how many MBAs they may need for the coming year but are less able to predict their needs for the next five years.

Two classes of forecasting techniques are frequently used to determine the organization's projected demand for human resources. These are **judgmental forecast** and **conventional statistical projections**.

The most common method of the judgmental forecast is the **Delphi technique**. At a Delphi meeting, a large number of experts take turns at presenting a forecast statement and assumptions. An intermediary passes each expert's forecast and assumptions to the others, who then make revisions in their own forecasts. This process continues until a viable composite forecast emerges. The composite may represent specific projections or a range of projections, depending on the experts' positions.

The Delphi technique has been shown to produce better one-year forecasts in comparison with linear regression analysis. But it does have some limitations. Difficulties may arise, for example, in integrating the experts' opinions. This technique, however, appears to be particularly useful in generating insights into highly unstructured or undeveloped subject areas, such as human resource planning.

A related method is the **nominal grouping technique.** Several people sit at a conference table and independently list their ideas on a sheet of paper.[22] The ideas presented are recorded on larger sheets of paper so that everyone can see all the ideas and refer to them in later parts of the session.

Although the two techniques are similar in process, the Delphi technique is more frequently used to generate predictions, and the nominal grouping technique is used more for identifying current organizational problems and solutions to those problems. Another judgmental forecast is called **managerial estimate.** Estimates of staffing needs are made by the organization's top managers (top-down communication) or by lower-level managers who make estimates and pass them up for further revisions (bottom-up communication) to form an overall demand forecast.[23]

Although all of these judgmental forecasts are less complex and rely on less data than those based on the statistical methods discussed next, these forecasts tend to dominate in practice.[24] The most common statistical procedures are simple linear regression and multiple linear regression analyses. In

simple linear regression analysis, a projection of future demand is based on a past relationship between the organization's employment level and a variable related to employment, such as sales. If a relationship can be established between the level of sales and the level of employment, predictions of future sales can be used to make predictions of future employment. Although a relationship may exist between sales and employment, it is often influenced by an organizational learning phenomenon. For example, the level of sales may double, but the level of employment necessary to meet this increase may be less than double. And if sales double again, the amount of employment necessary to meet this new doubling may be even less than that necessary to meet the first doubling of sales. An organizational learning curve can usually be determined by logarithmic calculations. Once the learning curve has been determined, more accurate projections of future employment levels can be established. See Chapter 18 for a more complete description of regression analysis.

Multiple linear regression analysis is an extension of simple linear regression analysis. Instead of relating employment to one other variable related to employment, several variables are used. For example, instead of using only sales to predict employment demand, productivity data and equipment-use data may also be used. Because it incorporates several variables related to employment, multiple regression analysis may produce more accurate demand forecasts than linear regression analysis. Apparently, however, only relatively large organizations use multiple regression analysis.[25]

In addition to these two regression techniques, several other statistical techniques are used to forecast staffing needs. Such techniques include productivity ratios,[26] personnel ratios,[27] time series analysis,[28] and stochastic analysis.[29] Currently, little research exists regarding the use of these techniques for human resource planning.[30] These techniques and a brief description of each are presented in Exhibit 2.7. Although most of these techniques are used for forecasting the total organization's human resource demand, parts of the organization use an additional technique. The **unit demand forecasting** technique relies on labor estimates that the unit or functional area managers provide. This technique may produce forecasts of demands that, when added up for all unit managers, are discrepant with the total organization's forecasted demands. However, it encourages unit managers to be more aware of their employees' skills, abilities, and desires. Such an awareness may also produce a higher-quality forecast. Each unit may also use the same statistical techniques that are used for the total organization.

Since the use of unit demand forecasting often produces discrepant forecasts, reconciliation of the differences is necessary before planning can be undertaken. The discrepancies, however, can often provide a useful basis for questioning and examining each unit's contributions as compared with their demands.

Reconciling the Budget. The third aspect in the first phase of human resource planning and programming puts the whole activity into economic perspective. The human resource forecast must be expressed in dollars, and this figure must be compatible with the organization's profit objectives and budget limitations.[31] The budget reconciliation process may also point up

Exhibit 2.7

Statistical Techniques Used to Project Staffing Demand Needs

Name	Description
Regression analysis	Past levels of various work load indicators, such as sales, production levels, and value added, are examined for statistical relationships with staffing levels. Where sufficiently strong relationships are found, a regression (or multiple regression) model is derived. Forecasted levels of the retained indicator(s) are entered into the resulting model and used to calculate the associated level of human resource requirements.
Productivity ratios	Historical data are used to examine past levels of a productivity index (P): $$P = \frac{\text{Work load}}{\text{Number of people}}$$ Where constant, or systematic, relationships are found, human resource requirements can be computed by dividing predicted work loads by P.
Personnel ratios	Past personnel data are examined to determine historical relationships among the employees in various jobs or job categories. Regression analysis or productivity ratios are then used to project either total or key group human resource requirements, and personnel ratios are used to allocate total requirements to various job categories or to estimate requirements for non-key groups.
Time series analysis	Past staffing levels (instead of work load indicators) are used to project future human resource requirements. Past staffing levels are examined to isolate seasonal and cyclical variations, long-term trends, and random movement. Long-term trends are then extrapolated or projected using a moving average, exponential smoothing, or regression technique.
Stochastic analysis	The likelihood of landing a series of contracts is combined with the personnel requirements of each contract to estimate expected staffing requirements. Potential applications in government contractors and construction industries.

Source: Adapted from L. Dyer, "Human Resource Planning," in
Personnel Management, ed. K. Rowland and G. Ferris (Boston:
Allyn & Bacon, 1982). Used with permission.

the importance of adjusting the budget to accommodate the human resource plan. This reconciliation stage also provides an opportunity to align the objectives and policies of the organization with those of the personnel department.

Forecasting Human Resource Supplies.   Although forecasted supply can be derived from both internal and external sources of information, the internal source is generally most crucial and most available. As with forecasting demand, two basic techniques help forecast internal labor supply: judgmental and statistical. Once made, the supply forecast can then be compared with the human resource demand forecast to help determine, among other things, action programming for identifying human resource talent and balancing supply and demand forecasts. However, most current forecasting of labor supply and demand is short-range and for the purposes of budgeting and controlling costs. Forecasts for over a five-year period are used in planning corporate strategy, planning facilities, and identifying managerial replacements.[32]

Two judgmental techniques that organizations use to make supply forecasts are replacement planning and succession planning. **Replacement planning** uses replacement charts, a sample of which is shown in Exhibit 2.8. These charts are developed to show the names of the current occupants of positions in the organization and the names of likely replacements. Replacement charts make potential vacancies readily apparent and indicate what types of positions most urgently need to be filled. Present performance levels of current employees can be used to estimate potential vacancies. These may occur in those jobs in which the incumbents are not outstanding performers. On the replacement chart in Exhibit 2.8, the incumbents are listed directly under the job title. Those individuals likely to fill the potential vacancies are listed directly under the incumbent. Such a listing can provide the organization with a good estimate of what jobs are likely to become vacant and indicates if anyone will be ready to fill the vacancy. Note that individuals' ages are omitted from the replacement chart so that age will not be used in making the promotion decision; that would be in violation of the Age Discrimination in Employment Act of 1967 and as amended in 1978. However, knowing the ages of individuals may be important for planning, replacement, and training purposes. Care must be exercised in serving these purposes to avoid using age as the only basis for an employment decision. In addition to omitting employees' ages from replacement charts or succession plans, the organization must refrain from using age-related terms in describing its management philosophy and PHRM policies. Heublein Corporation was found guilty of practicing age discrimination because it maintained a promotion policy that essentially conveyed a youth-oriented theme. Because younger rather than older candidates fitted this theme, the policy was used in promotion decisions. Heublein's cost for this practice was a court-rendered fine of approximately $500,000 (*Goodman* v. *Heublein*, 1981).

Succession planning is similar to replacement planning except that succession planning tends to be longer term and more developmental and tends to offer greater flexibility.[33] Other contrasts are shown in Exhibit 2.9. Although succession planning is widely practiced, many employers using it tend to emphasize the characteristics of the managers and downplay the characteristics of the positions to which these managers may eventually be promoted.[34]

Less common than the judgmental techniques in forecasting supply are the statistical techniques. These techniques are not widely used in practice because of inadequate data bases, lack of software computer programs and shortages of trained professionals to use them, and the restrictive conditions under which the models are applicable.[35] A sample of the more common

Sample Employee Replacement Chart   *Exhibit 2.8*

President

Vice-President, Personnel

■	K. Addison	▲
	C. Huser	▲
	S. French	▲

Executive Vice-President

▲	H. Grady	●
	D. Snow	■
	E. Farley	▲

Vice-President, Marketing

▲	S. Morrow	■
	M. Murray	▲
	F. Goland	▲

Vice-President, Finance

▲	G. Sleight	▲
	C. Hood	■

HOUSEHOLD FANS DIVISION   INDUSTRIAL FANS DIVISION   (Proposed new division)

Manager, House Fans

■	D. Snow	■
	J. James	■
	R. Jarvis	■

Manager, Industrial Fans

▲	E. Farley	▲
	R. Jarvis	■
	F. Goland	▲

Manager, Air Conditioners

▲		
	R. Jarvis	■

Manager, Personnel

▲	C. Huser	▲
	A. Kyte	■

Manager, Accounting

▲	C. Hood	■
	W. Wicks	■
	H. Ross	▲

Manager, Personnel

▲	S. French	▲
	T. Smith	■
	J. Jones	▲

Manager, Accounting

●	M. Piper	●

Manager, Production

▲	J. James	■
	W. Long	■
	G. Fritz	▲

Manager, Sales

■	M. Murray	■
	E. Renfrew	■
	B. Storey	▲

Manager, Production

■	R. Jarvis	■
	C. Pitts	■
	C. Combs	▲

Manager, Sales

▲	F. Goland	▲
	S. Ramos	▲

PRESENT PERFORMANCE

Outstanding	▲
Satisfactory	▲
Needs improvement	●

PROMOTION POTENTIAL

Ready now	■
Needs further training	▲
Questionable	●

Source: Adapted from *The Expanded Personnel Function,*
Studies in Personnel Policy 203 (New York: National Industrial
Conference Board, 1966).

Exhibit 2.9   Contrasts between Replacement and
Succession Planning

Variable	Replacement Planning	Succession Planning
Time frame	0–12 months	12–36 months
Readiness	Best candidate available	Candidate with best development potential
Commitment level	Designated preferred replacement candidate	Merely possibilities until vacancies occur
Focus of planning	Vertical lines of succession within units or functions	Development of a pool of talent; candidates with capability to take any of several assignments
Developmental action planning	Usually informal; merely a status report	Usually extensive: specific plans and goals set for each person
Flexibility	Limited by the structure of the plans, but in practice, decisions reflect a great deal of flexibility	Plans are conceived as flexible: intended to promote development and thinking about alternatives
Experience base applied	Each manager's best judgment based on personal observation and experience	Plans are the result of inputs and discussion from multiple managers
How candidates are evaluated	Observation of performance on the job over time; demonstrated competence: progress through the function	Multiple evaluations by different managers of the candidates on varied job assignments; testing and broadening early in careers

Source: James A. Walker, *Human Resources Planning* (New York:
McGraw-Hill, 1980), p. 285. Reprinted with permission.

(in research) statistical techniques is provided in Exhibit 2.10, which briefly describes Markov analysis,[36] simulation (based on Markov analysis),[37] renewal analysis,[38] and goal programming.[39]

Phase 2: Establishing Human Resource Objectives and Policies

As shown in Exhibit 2.6, Phase 2 in the human resource planning process is setting human resource objectives and policies. These objectives and policies are directly related to corporate objectives and policies.[40] The impact of the organization's objectives, policies, and plans on human resource planning seems difficult to deny, but according to a recent survey, only about 25 percent of organizations achieve a substantial link between their general institutional planning and their human resource planning. An additional 45 percent reported only some link, while 20 percent had no link at all.[41]

Some discrepancy appears to exist between the ideal link of corporate and human resource objectives and policies and what many organizations actual-

Exhibit 2.10

Statistical Techniques Used to Project Future Human Resource Supply Availability

Name	Description
Markov analysis	Projects future flows to obtain availability through a straightforward application of historical transition rates. Historical transition rates are derived from analyses of personnel data concerning losses, promotions, transfers, demotions, and perhaps, recruitment.
Simulation (based on Markov analysis)	Alternative (rather than historical) flows are examined for effects on future human resource availabilities. Alternative flows reflect the anticipated results of policy or program changes concerning voluntary and involuntary turnover, retirement, promotion, etc.
Renewal analysis	Estimates future flows and availabilities by calculating: (1) vacancies as created by organizational growth, personnel losses, and internal movements out of states and (2) the results of decision rules governing the filling of vacancies. Alternative models may assess the effects of changes in growth estimates, turnover, promotions, or decision rules.
Goal programming	Optimizes goals—in this case a desired staffing pattern—given a set of constraints concerning such things as the upper limits on flows, the percentage of new recruits permitted in each state, and total salary budgets.

Source: Adapted from L. Dyer, "Human Resource Planning," in *Personnel Management,* ed. K. Rowland and G. Ferris (Boston: Allyn & Bacon, 1982). Used with permission.

ly practice. One study found that 85 percent of the organizations surveyed were using an HRIS, but about one-third were operating at the departmental or divisional level rather than organization-wide. In addition, most HRIS's were used for payroll processing, personnel listings, placement, and, less often, for forecasting and human resource development planning.[42]

Human resource planning may seem to be divorced from the organization's mainstream operations, but the preceding "PHRM in the News" items should indicate the growing importance of human resource planning in determining an organization's goals, plans, and objectives. The relationship works both ways. Ideally, organizational policies, plans, and objectives influence the personnel inventory and forecasting analyses, and these in turn influence organizational policies, plans, and objectives by permitting the effective use of human resources in attaining the organization's goals.

Phase 3: Human Resource Programming

The third phase in human resource planning, human resource programming, is an extremely important extension. After the assessment of an organization's human resource needs, action programming must be developed to serve those needs. These action programs may be designed to increase the supply of the right employees in the organization (e.g., if the forecasts in Phase 1 showed that demand exceeded supply) or to decrease the number of current employees (e.g., if the forecasts showed that supply exceeded demand). Although many alternative programs could be proposed and evaluated to address these purposes, only two are presented here: to increase the supply of the right employees and to decrease the supply of current employees.

Attraction: New Organizational Structures.   As indicated earlier, the human resource planner assists in developing workable organizational structure. Workable structures are those that can serve PHRM's objectives (i.e., to attract, retain, and motivate individuals).[43] Present organizational structures, however, may not be as workable as they once were: "Changes in our society, particularly in the values of the workforce, have seriously undermined the traditional relationship between organizations and their members. This has led to a crisis for organizations that may only be resolved by the evolution of new organizational forms."[44] Some apparent results of this crisis have been the decline in productivity, especially quality of performance, and increases in absenteeism. Consequently, organizations have been losing their ability to effectively use the human resources available to them.

In general, present organizational structures can be characterized by supervisory control, minimal employee participation in work place decisions, top-down communications, an emphasis on extrinsic rewards to attract, retain, and motivate employees (such as pay, promotion, and status symbols), narrowly designed jobs with narrow job descriptions and a primary concern for productivity and fitting people to jobs. These characteristics reflect the traditional assumptions about people shown in Exhibit 2.2. These primary concerns result in selecting and placing people solely on the basis of their skills, knowledge, and abilities to meet the job demands. This practice is called **Match 1**.

Sensing that these organizational structure characteristics are no longer appropriate for attracting, retaining, and motivating individuals, some organizations, such as Honeywell, Control Data, Romac Industries, and Westinghouse, are engaging in alternative structures. These structures can be characterized by greater employee self-control, more employee participation in work place decisions, bottom-up as well as top-down communications, recognition of employee rights, an emphasis on intrinsic rewards (such as responsibility, meaningfulness, and achievement) and extrinsic rewards, more broadly designed jobs allowing for more worker discretion (see Chapter 12), and primary concerns for quality of work life, productivity, and fitting jobs to people. These characteristics reflect the new assumptions about people shown in Exhibit 2.2. These primary concerns result in selecting and placing people on the basis of their personality, interests, and preferences to match job and organization characteristics. This practice is called **Match 2**.[45]

Because a growing number of organizations are currently using alternative structures to improve their effectiveness, they apparently offer human resource planners a way of providing workable structures to serve employees. As described more extensively in Chapter 12, alternative structures are proving effective in some organizations. And, as described in the remaining chapters, alternative structure concerns are being reflected in almost every PHRM function and activity.[46]

Reduction: Dealing with Job Loss.   With the need for massive layoffs in the past few years (because of economic or technological conditions), organizations have become increasingly sensitive in dealing with the effects of layoffs on employees and are trying to either minimize these effects or eliminate the necessity for layoffs. Attempts to minimize these effects are reflected in redundancy planning. **Redundancy planning** is essentially human resource planning associated with the process of laying off employees who are no longer needed (i.e., they are redundant). Involved in this planning may be outplacement counseling, buy-outs, job skill retraining opportunities, and job transfer opportunities.[47] The following "PHRM in the News" provides an example of redundancy planning. Although redundancy planning has been limited to companies in a few industries, some suggest that this effort be done in all industries:

> Since it is obvious that automation is here to stay, company and/or industry committees might be set up in all industries to discuss the problem of redundancy. These committees could each include, along with representatives from government and industry, several redundant workers, so that a better understanding of the more human effects of redundancy can be obtained. It is important that such committees not be limited to industries that are currently experiencing the impacts of automation. To be most effective, the planning for redundancy must begin well before the problems occur.[48]

PHRM in the News

A Happy Ending In Connecticut

Plant closing hailed as model program for other corporations

Greenwich, CT is not a place which evokes images of industrial activity, even less so now that it's lost its only remaining factory.

On May 31 of this year, the Electrolux Corporation closed its red-brick mill where, since 1933, 830 employees had assembled millions of vacuum cleaners. Because of foreign competition and the need to automate, executives at Electrolux said they were forced to close the firm's original plant.

While plant closings are sad occasions and increasingly prove to be "black eyes" for the corporations forced to such actions, the end of Greenwich's factory era proves how a well-planned outplacement program can ease the pain of such a transition for both employees and companies.

Back in November of 1984,

Electrolux officials—led by Roger Loeffelbein, group vice president of human resources—gave employees six months' notice of the plant's closing. In announcing the closing, C. Steve McMillan, chairman and chief executive officer of the firm, pledged that Electrolux would implement one of the most in-depth employee re-employment programs ever offered anywhere.

Best of all, his pledge has become reality.

Through a $4 million outplacement strategy, about half of the Greenwich employees either have found new jobs or retired, and more are still being helped through the firm's re-employment efforts.

To begin work on its outplacement program, the company first formed a Community Action Team to work with local and state officials and agencies. The agencies involved included the State of Connecticut Office of Policy and Management, the United Labor Agency,

Connecticut Job Service, Stamford Economic Assistance Corporation, Connecticut Business Industries Association and the Southwestern Area Commerce and Industry Association. The team identified where re-employment efforts had to be directed to assist employees.

In addition to the action team, a Steering Committee—comprised of leading area employers—was formed, to contact potential employers and to spell out specific employment and training needs.

Plant tours, interviews arranged

A telephone action line staffed by Electrolux management was set up, to answer employee questions. An employee-management committee also was instituted to provide two-way communication between the firm and workers.

While a small staff was to be retained at the plant after plant operations ceased, transfers were offered to other Electrolux sites, including a new technical center in Trumbull. In all, 115 individuals relocated to the Trumbull center, and others moved to various company plants and states. A moving assistance program located housing and provided answers to employees' questions about their new job sites.

Working with the Steering Committee and other SACIA members, a meeting and plant tour were conducted April 25. More than 100 Connecticut employers attended. Job profiles of available people were distributed and 75 specific job requests were submitted to Electrolux personnel that day.

Many firms also left application forms to be filled out by interested employees.

The Connecticut Job Service began accepting on-site job applications, which were fed into the Service's computer bank. The bank is accessible to area employers.

Job resource center

At the beginning of May, Electrolux opened a Job Resource Center to provide telephones, job postings and reference materials. More than 650 jobs have been posted to date and 25 people have been placed because of those ads.

Jobs wanted ads were also placed in consecutive Sunday editions of several area newspapers, to advise employers of experienced workers that were available. Area churches were contacted to assist in providing personal planning.

For those individuals who decided to retire, a six-session pre-retirement planning seminar was offered. There were 80 employees and 49 spouses who completed the program.

An Outplacement Training Program saw 95 percent of all employees. Severance pay and insurance conversion plans were explained in this series of workshops held on-site. Sessions on resume writing were conducted. Paid time off for job interviews was granted.

Luncheons hosted at the factory allowed prospective employers to meet people.

All this attention earned Electrolux praise from state and local officials as a possible model for future closings in a state where the battle over regulating plant closings continues.

In an editorial praising the firm's program, *The Gazette* noted Electrolux has provided "a potentially powerful argument against the need for state legislation that would force companies to take similar steps."

Source: "A Happy Ending in Connecticut," pp. 1, 6, 11. Reprinted from the August issue of *Resource*, copyright © 1985, the American Society for Personnel Administration, 606 North Washington Street, Alexandria, VA 22314.

Employees also play a role in employers' efforts at redundancy planning. Contrary to public belief, many workers laid off because of structural or technological changes manage to find new jobs fairly quickly.[49] Thus, only a minority of redundant workers may need to be trained and placed. The majority of them may need only counseling and placement. A special type of counseling that may be particularly beneficial to redundancy planning and which is becoming more common in organizations is **preretirement counseling**.[50]

> Retirement planning offered by employers for senior workers is growing. In the past five years, several employers, including Abbott Laboratories, IC Industries, FMC, and CalFed, have begun pre-retirement seminars that help workers with benefits, money management, use of leisure time, and estate planning. Hackensack Water plans to begin a program this fall. "We have a lot of workaholics and the program will help them avoid being at loose ends," an official says.
>
> Allied, which began a program four years ago, uses one of its six counseling sessions to discuss medical and psychological concerns of retirement. Lockheed has two counselors and an administrator. It holds eight sessions, offers a newsletter and counsels 1,500 workers annually.[51]

Preretirement counseling can facilitate an employee's transition from work to nonwork and, by doing so, can encourage employee retirement. PHRM may help an organization reduce employee bottlenecks as well as avoid or reduce the number of redundant workers by making sure that counseling programs are provided and that potentially redundant employees are identified and made aware of the counseling. However, organizations should ensure that employees do not see these counseling efforts as ways to eliminate older workers. Also important is ensuring that employees do not view layoffs—nor should layoffs be used—as ways to eliminate older workers.

Regardless of the human resource program implemented, it must be monitored and evaluated. This allows for controlling how well the program is being implemented and revising it as appropriate. Thus, the necessary fourth phase in human resource planning comprises control and evaluation.

Phase 4: Human Resource Planning— Control and Evaluation

Control and evaluation of human resource plans and programs are essential to effectively managing human resources. Efforts in this area are clearly aimed at quantifying the value of human resources. These efforts recognize human resources as an asset to the organization.

An HRIS facilitates program control and evaluation by allowing for more rapid and frequent collection of data to back up the forecast. This data collection is important not only as a means of control but also as a method for evaluating plans and programs and making adjustments. Data collection should be formalized to occur at the end of each year and at fixed intervals during the year. The evaluation should occur at the same time to hasten revisions of existing forecasts and programs. Revisions will likely influence short-term, intermediate, and long-term forecasts.

Evaluation of human resource plans and programs is an important process not only for determining the effectiveness of human resource planning but also for demonstrating the significance of both human resource planning and the PHRM department in the organization as a whole.

Possible criteria for evaluating human resource planning include the following:

- Actual staffing levels against established staffing requirements
- Productivity levels against established goals
- Actual personnel flow rates against desired rates
- Programs implemented against action plans
- Program results against expected outcomes (e.g., improved applicant flows, reduced quit rates, improved replacement ratios)
- Labor and program costs against budgets
- Ratios of program results (benefits) to program costs[52]

An important aspect related to evaluation, revisions, and adjustments is the issue of cause and effect. The PHRM model presented in Chapter 1 is based on the notion of integrated, related activities. For example, if the recruiting program is not working well, an invalid conclusion is that the program needs revision. Perhaps the salaries offered to recruits were too low and not competitive with other organizations. Also possible is that despite the best recruiting efforts, few acceptable applicants applied.

The integrated approach makes the evaluation of any single program not only complex but necessary on the basis of the total program. Indeed, evaluation of planning and programming activities may need to consider only the bottom line—the composite results of a set of activities rather than separate results for each activity. But because many of the program activities for implementing human resource plans are developed by separate units or individuals, developing standards and controls for separate activities while recognizing the interdependence among units is still necessary. The PHRM department can then use the bottom-line evaluation to assess the performance of the total PHRM activity.

Regardless of whether PHRM *should* establish preretirement counseling programs, new organizational structures, or redundancy planning programs, little doubt exists that PHRM will need to consider these and other human resource programs. The many significant changes occurring in society will continue to severely impact human resource needs and supplies as well as the entire organization's operation. Since human resource needs and supplies are PHRM's responsibility, personnel must be knowledgeable about the important changes likely to influence effective personnel and human resource planning. PHRM must also be knowledgeable about the roadblocks to human resource planning.

Roadblocks to Human Resource Planning

A key roadblock to developing human resource planning is the lack of top management support. This roadblock also prevents the PHRM department from playing all the major personnel roles discussed in Chapter 1. PHRM can help remove this roadblock with data and bottom-line facts that demonstrate the effectiveness of human resource planning and PHRM. Another roadblock is the difficulty in obtaining integration with other personnel activities—a necessary step if human resource planning is to work. A challenge for managers in PHRM is to create a personnel system in which all the functions and activities discussed in Chapter 1 are integrated and coordinated in conjunction with the organization's business plan. This not only will help remove a personnel planning roadblock but also will enhance all the PHRM activities' effectiveness.

A third roadblock is line managers' lack of involvement. Failure to involve line management in the design, development, and implementation of a human resource planning system is a common oversight for first-time planners. Personnel and human resource managers are often tempted to develop or adopt highly quantitative approaches to planning, which often have little pragmatic value for line managers' problems, such as reducing excessive turnover, identifying and training replacements for key positions, and forecasting staffing needs. To be effective, personnel planning must be useful. An integral part of being useful is serving line managers' needs. With this important point in mind, personnel can begin developing human resource plans and programs.

Trends in Human Resource Planning

Because of their relevance for the entire area of PHRM, the four major trends introduced in Chapter 1 are also relevant to human resource planning.

Assessing Human Resource Planning

Human resource planning can make or break an organization, especially over the long term. Without effective human resource planning, an organization may find itself with a plant or an office without the people to run it. Organizations can no longer assume that the right number of appropriately qualified people will be ready when and where the organization wants them. On a broad level, then, human resource planning can be assessed on the basis of whether the organization has the people it needs (i.e., the right people at the right place, at the right time, and at the right salary).

At more specific levels, human resource planning activities can be assessed by how effectively they, along with recruitment, attract new employees, deal with job loss, and adapt to the changing characteristics of the environment. Since an important part of human resource planning is forecasting, human resource planning can be assessed by how well its forecasts (whether of specific personnel needs or of specific environmental trends) compare with reality. Accuracy here can be crucial, since human resource planning can not likely do well on a broad level if it fails to do well in forecasting. Several other criteria against which human resource planning can be assessed are those presented earlier under the section on human resource planning control and evaluation.

Computer Technology and HRIS in Human Resource Planning

As described earlier in this chapter, fast and effective human resource planning rests on using computer technology and an accurate, up-to-date human resource information system. Computer technology enables organizations to more rapidly make human resource supply and demand forecasts.

Strategic Involvement of Human Resource Planning

Gaining Competitive Advantage.   Increasingly, companies are being forced to think about using human resource planning to gain competitive advantage. Companies are taking note of recent census data—those data indicate that the number of young workers in the labor force peaked at 37 million in 1980 and will drop to 24 million by 1990. Meanwhile, each year 2.3 million 17-year-olds are added to the ranks of the functionally illiterate. In anticipation of a desperate need for literate young workers at all levels, companies such as Texas Instruments and New York Telephone are getting into secondary and primary education to help increase the literacy rate in the reduced supply of labor force entrants in the 1980s. Without such action, the very ability of some companies to survive is in jeopardy. According to Robert Feagles (senior vice president of Travelers Insurance Company), "The issue of functional illiteracy has coiled at the center of our unemployment problems and it threatens this country's ultimate ability to succeed in the world market."

Another aspect of planning that companies are addressing is rather opposite to the one already described. It is that of the baby boom bulge (people aged 25–54) that is moving through the work force. This is creating a rapid expansion of potential managers with a narrowing base of managerial jobs. Added to this situation is the desire by many of those in this age category to be promoted and be successful. Meanwhile these changes are occurring in an environment that is becoming more turbulent and more demanding of change by the organization.

The intersection of these events is producing a company need for flexibility and current, up-to-date skills. Companies such as AT&T, Bank America Corporation, Sun Company, and Eastman Kodak Company are trying to gain this flexibility and skill currency by offering attractive early retirement packages for carefully selected groups of employees. Since it seems as if all the current demographic, economic, and technological trends will continue, it is reasonable to assume that the companies that most systematically plan with their human resources in mind will be most likely to gain a competitive advantage by having "the right people at the right place at the right time" to produce quality products efficiently.[53]

Linking with Organizational Strategy.   As introduced in Chapter 1, there are several strategic planning choices. The linkage of these choices with a given organizational strategy is shown in Exhibit 1.4. Some of the choices in human resource planning are as follows:

Informal———Formal

Loose———Tight

Short Term———Long Term

Low Employee Involvement———High Employee Involvement

The first choice in the planning menu is the extent or degree of formalization—ranging from informal to formal. The more formal the planning activity becomes, the more attention and concern shown to explicit planning procedures and activities for human resource management. One result of more formal planning is Hewlett-Packard's willingness and ability to state and support its human resource policy of not being a "hire and fire company." An advantage of this type of formalized planning is that it enables a company to provide employees with job security—a facet of human resource management critical to the success of such companies as IBM, Dana, and Delta, in addition to HP.[54]

Other examples of more formal planning include designing jobs to attract and retain the best people and to maximize their performance contribution to the organization, designing organizational structures to match the product needs of the organization, and developing organizational climates that cultivate trust and openness.[55]

A second choice in the planning menu is the degree of tightness. Establishing a tight rather than a loose link between human resource planning and corporate planning is necessary to the implementation and success of a more formal planning policy. This necessity is most evident in the recent discussions of corporate strategic management and human resource management.[56] However, since organizations can choose not to have a tight link between corporate planning and human resource planning, the degree of tightness of this linkage is another critical choice in planning.

A third choice is the time horizon of the planning. As such, organizations can choose to plan only for short-term human resource needs or to extend themselves much farther into the future. However, organizations apparently need to have a longer-term time horizon, since an organization's human resource characteristics are so slow in changing.[57] Nevertheless, since an organization's environment may be volatile, the organization's short-term responses and adjustments may be required. Thus, organizations may benefit from some long-range planning considerations with shorter-range flexibility.

A final choice, and one common to all the PHRM activities, is the degree of employee involvement in the planning activity. Organizations can choose to allow employees involvement ranging from extensive to relatively limited. Extensive involvement can include line managers providing the PHRM department with human resource demand forecasts, employees analyzing their own jobs, and employees participating in the design of programs to attract needed job applicants.

These four practices in human resource planning offer organizations variety in how they want to do planning. The choices to make are likely to depend on several aspects of the environment shown in Exhibit 1.2, such as top management, corporate culture, and organizational strategy. Exhibit 1.4 illustrates how choices might be made based upon organizational strategy and needed employee characteristics.

Summary

Nothing can be done about the performance of past management or the qualifications of today's management. But tomorrow's management can be as good as today's managers make it, which points up the need for human resource planning and programming, at least for managerial employees. Human resource planning must also be implemented for entry-level, nonmanagerial, technical, and professional employees. This is especially true because of societal changes: (1) changes in population and labor force characteristics, such as age, sex, and race composition, job preferences, and job openings; (2) changes in general economic conditions and the increased use of automation and robots; (3) changing social values, especially those toward work, mobility, and retirement; and (4) changing legislation and level of government activity. These changes are making human resource planning more critical and complex. This is enhanced by the growing recognition of how closely human resource planning must be tied to an organization's overall business plan in order for the organization to be effective.

These changes mean that PHRM departments must develop strategic and operational plans for all phases associated with using human resources. These strategic plans describe the broad-range, long-term goals of personnel and human resource management, which should be tied into the strategic plans of the rest of the organization. The operational plans specify how the strategic goals are to be attained. By moving PHRM into a more vital position in total organization management, PHRM can begin to play the several roles described in Chapter 1, one of which is policy formulation. Policy formulation can help ensure that PHRM is seen as a vital and useful department in the organization. It can also ensure that the organization's human resources are used as effectively as possible.

The PHRM department must pay careful attention to accomplishing each of the four phases of human resource planning. The first phase determines present and future resources to develop a forecast of human resource needs. The second phase ensures that PHRM objectives and policies are compatible with the organization's overall objectives. Action programs must be developed and implemented in the third phase. To help ensure the programs' effectiveness, the fourth phase controls and evaluates each program. Based on the results of the evaluation, the programs can then be modified as necessary.

Each phase of the planning and programming activity has several potential problems, but an alert PHRM department can minimize them. One major roadblock to doing all four phases of human resource planning is the lack of top management support. This support, however, can be gained by showing top management the potential benefits of human resource planning: reduced personnel costs, better employee development, improved overall organizational planning, more opportunities for a better-balanced and more integrated work force, greater awareness of the importance of human resource management in the total organization, and tools to evaluate the effectiveness of alternative human resource actions and policies.

Once top management support for human resource planning has been gained, the PHRM department can move into the next important activity in planning for human resources: job design and analysis. Whereas human resource planning may be thought of as dealing with broader issues, job analysis may be thought of as dealing with more narrow issues, which are presented in the next chapter.

Discussion Questions

1. If human resource planning is so difficult, why do some companies still engage in it?
2. Why is planning difficult? As we increase the planning horizon from one year to five years, why does planning become even more difficult?
3. What are the major changes in the demographic, occupational, industrial, and geographic mix of the U.S. labor force? What impact could these changes have on specific human resource functions?
4. What is the difference between judgmental and statistical forecasting? Give examples of how both techniques could be used to forecast human resource demand and supply for an organization.
5. Choose an organization where you work or have previously worked. Assume that you have been given a personal computer and told to create an HRIS. What information would you put into your system? How would you use this information? How could you keep this information current? Would your HRIS make you a better planner? How?
6. What is the essential goal of human resource planning?
7. Aside from identifying future organizational personnel and human resource needs and establishing programs for eliminating discrepancies while balancing individual and organizational interests, what other specific purposes of human resource planning are there?
8. Discuss the roadblocks to human resource planning and how each might be removed.
9. Provide a step-by-step overview of the four phases of human resource planning.
10. In what ways can an organization increase its ability to attract and retain valued employees?

PC Project

Organizations face dynamic environments that can change rapidly and unpredictably. There are, however, many forecasting tools that can help personnel specialists to predict personnel and human resource needs. This PC Project examines a model for predicting staffing requirements for managerial employees. The following questions will be considered: How many employees will the company need to hire today in order to have eighty-five managers in three years? How many employees will be needed in a given future year (e.g., 1990)? This computer project can be used to test many forecasting scenarios.

C   A   S   E   S   T   U   D   Y

Down-sizing: Anathema to Corporate Loyalty?

Jim Daniels suspected things could be worse, but nonetheless he was unprepared for the dilemma facing Defense Systems, Inc. Jim, vice-president for human resources for DSI, joined the company one year ago when he was pirated away from one of DSI's major competitors. DSI manufactures electronic components used in weapons supplied to the air force and navy. In addition, DSI makes semiconductors used in many of the weapons systems as well as in personal computers and automotive computers.

When Jim joined DSI, a major drive was undertaken to staff up in engineering in anticipation of a major upturn in the semiconductor market. Unfortunately, and contrary to industry analysts' optimistic projections, the semiconductor market failed to pick up. DSI had recently completed an aggressive hiring policy at the major universities around the United States. DSI had selected one thousand engineers who were among the cream of the crop with an average GPA of 3.4. Without the pickup in business, however, DSI was confronted with some fairly unpleasant alternatives.

From one point of view, potential cutbacks at DSI were only part of an overall pattern of cutbacks, restructuring, and down-sizing of major U.S. companies during the past few years. The motives among firms who have trimmed their work forces vary—some to please Wall Street and the stockholders, to keep pace with foreign competitors, or to shrink an unwieldy organizational structure. To Jim the DSI layoffs or terminations were poor alternatives to dealing with a turbulent environment.

The major problem, as Jim saw it, was to preserve as many as these jobs as possible until business picked up. To terminate these new hires would irreparably harm DSI's future recruitment efforts. On the other hand, underemploying these talented recruits for very long was bound to lead to major dissatisfaction. Although terminations would improve the balance sheet in the short run, Jim worried about the impact of such a move on corporate loyalty, a fragile commodity at other major firms

who have cut their white-collar work force by as much as 20 percent.

Jim was scheduled to meet with the executive committee of DSI in three days to discuss the overstaffing problem and to generate alternatives. In preparation for this meeting, Jim tried to draw on his experience with his past employer to generate some ideas. A number of differences between DSI and Jim's old employer, though, made comparisons difficult.

For one, DSI does not employ nearly the number of temporaries or student interns as his old employer did. Nor does DSI rely on subcontractors to produce parts needed in its assembly operation. Because of extra capacity, DSI can currently produce 50 percent of the parts it purchases, whereas Jim's ex-employer could produce only 5 percent.

Another major difference was the degree of training provided by DSI. At Jim's old employer, each employee could expect a minimum of forty hours of additional training a year. At DSI, training consisted of about ten hours per year, most of that being orientation training.

Jim wondered if perhaps there might be some additional ways to remove all possible slack from the system but at the same time preserve as many jobs as possible. For example, overtime hours were still being paid to quite a few technicians. Would the engineers be willing to assume some of these duties in the interim until business picked up? Some older employees had accumulated several weeks of unused vacation. Even still, some employees could be encouraged to take unpaid leaves of absence. Perhaps yet another approach would be to offer early retirement incentives to make room for some of the young, bright engineers. DSI also has fourteen other geographic locations, some in need of additional workers.

As Jim ruminated on these options, one thing was clear: he would need to organize and prioritize these ideas into a concise form if he was going to be prepared for his upcoming executive committee meeting.

Notes

1. L. Dyer, "Strategic Human Resources Management and Planning," *Research in Personnel and Human Resources Management* 3, (Greenwich, Conn.: JAI Press, 1985) pp. 1–30; for a set of excellent articles, see the entire Spring/Summer 1983 issue of *Human Resource Management;* G. Milkovich, L. Dyer, and T. Mahoney, "The State of Practice and Research in Human Resource Planning," in *Human Resource Management in the 1980s,* ed. S. J. Carroll and R. S. Schuler (Washington, D.C.: Bureau of National Affairs, 1983); E. H. Burack and N. J. Mathys, *Human Resource Planning: A Pragmatic Approach to Manpower Staffing and Development* (Lake Forest, Ill.: Brace-Park, 1979); E. C. Smith, "Strategic Business Planning and Human Resources: Part I," *Personnel Journal* (Aug. 1982): 606–10; E. C. Smith, "Strategic Business Planning and Human Resources: Part II," *Personnel Journal* (Sept. 1982): 680–82; L. J. Stybel, "Linking Strategic Planning and Management Manpower Planning," *California Management Review* (Fall 1982): 48–56; L. Dyer, "Human Resource Planning," in *Personnel Management,* ed. K. M. Rowland and G. R. Ferris (Boston: Allyn & Bacon, 1982), pp. 52–77.

2. J. W. Walker, *Human Resource Planning* (New York: McGraw-Hill, 1980), uses the term *business plan.* It is used here to refer to those plans for the total organization (whether government, nonprofit, or profit oriented) that help drive the long- and short-range planning needs for human resource planning. See also D. Ulrich, "Strategic Human Resource Management Planning," in *Readings in Personnel and Human Resource Management,* 3d ed., ed. R. S. Schuler, S. A. Youngblood, and V. Huber (St. Paul: West, 1987); E. H. Burack, "Linking Corporate Business and Human Resource Planning: Strategic Issues and Concerns," *Human Resource Planning* 8 (1985): 133–46; R. M. Kanter, "Frontiers For Strategic Human Resource Planning and Management," *Human Resource Management* 22 (1983): 9–21.

3. Dyer, "Human Resource Planning," pp. 57–58.

4. E. W. Vetter, *Manpower Planning for High Talent Personnel* (Ann Arbor, Mich.: Bureau of Industrial Relations, Graduate School of Business, University of Michigan, 1967); D. B. Gehrman, "Objective-Based Human Resource Planning," *Personnel Administrator* (Dec. 1982): 71–75.

5. J. Laurie, "Gaining Acceptance for Your HRD Plan," *Personnel* (Dec. 1982): 896–97; J. P. Muczyk, "Comprehensive Manpower Planning," *Managerial Planning* (Nov./Dec. 1981): 36–41; E. H. Burack and T. J. McNichols, *Human Resources Planning, Technology, Policy Change* (Kent, Ohio: Comparative Administration Research Institute, 1973); C. F. Russ, Jr., "Manpower Planning Systems: Part I," *Personnel Journal* (Jan. 1982): 40–45; C. F. Russ, Jr., "Manpower Planning Systems: Part II," *Personnel Journal* (Feb. 1982): 119–23.

6. A. Etzioni and P. Jargonwsky, "High Tech, Basic Industry, and the Future of the American Economy," *Human Resource Management* (Fall 1984): 229–40; P. H. Mirvis, "Formulating and Implementing Human Resource Strategy: A Model of How to Do It, Two Examples of How Its Done," *Human Resource Management* (Winter 1985): 385–412.

7. Vetter, "Manpower Planning," p. 118.

8. D. Q. Mills, "Planning with People in Mind," *Harvard Business Review* (July–August 1985): 97–105; M. Leshner, "The Case of the Missing HRP," *Personnel Journal* (April 1985): 57–64; M. Froham and A. I. Frohman, "Organizational Adaptation: A Personnel Responsibility," *Personnel Administrator* (Jan. 1984): 45–47, 88; R. O'Connor, *Facing Strategic Issues: New Planning Guides and Practices* (New York: Conference Board, 1985).

9. *Wall Street Journal,* 21 Feb. 1984, p. 1. Reprinted by permission of *The Wall Street Journal.* Copyright © Dow Jones & Company, Inc., 1984. All rights reserved.

10. E. C. Gottschalk, Jr., "Promotions Grow Few as 'Baby Boom' Group Eyes Managers' Jobs," *Wall Street Journal,* 22 Oct. 1981, p. 1; A. Howard and D. W. Bray, "Career Motivation in Mid-Life Managers," paper presented at American Psychological Association, Montreal, Canada, Sept. 1980.

11. V. P. Barabba, "Demographic Change and the Public Work Force," Proceedings of the Second Public Management Research Conference, 17–18 Nov., pp. 29–41; E. Hartzell and R. Lewis, "Soothsayers and Parables: The Workforce Now and Tomorrow," *Personnel Journal* (June 1981): 444–48; D. Lunda, AEP, "Personnel Management: What's Ahead?" *Personnel Administrator* (Apr. 1981): 51–60; D. E. Pursell, "Planning for Tomorrow's Personnel Problems," *Personnel Journal* (July 1981): 559–61; R. R. Wingard, "Our Real Corporate Responsibility," *Personnel Journal* (Aug. 1980): 620; H. N. Fullerton, "The 1995 Labor Force: A First Look," *Monthly Labor Review* (Dec. 1980): 12–20.

12. "Study Sees Major Population Changes During This Decade but Few Surprises," *Wall Street Journal,* 16 June 1982, p. 19; *American Demographics* (Ithaca, N.Y.: American Demographics, 1982, P.O. Box 68, Ithaca, NY 14850).

13. For discussion of these data, projections, and implications in Japan and the United States, see "An Aging Work Force Strains Japan's Traditions," *Business Week,* 20 Apr. 1981, pp. 72–85; "A Changing Work Force Poses Challenges," *Business Week,* 14 Dec. 1981, pp. 116–120; "When Retirees Go Back on

the Payroll," *Business Week,* 22 Nov. 1982, pp. 112, 116; M. Doering, S. R. Rhodes, and M. Schuster, *The Aging Worker: A Compilation and Analysis of the Literature* (New York: Sage, 1983); J. Lindroth, "How to Beat the Coming Labor Shortage," *Personnel Journal* (Apr. 1982): 268–72; B. Rosen and T. H. Jerdee, "Management of Older Employees," unpublished manuscript, University of North Carolina, 1982.

14. For a discussion of these data and issues, see C. Hymowitz, "More Men Infiltrating Professions Historically Dominated by Women," *Wall Street Journal,* 25 Feb. 1981, p. 23; P. F. Drucker, "Working Women: Unmaking the Nineteenth Century," *Wall Street Journal,* 6 July 1981, p. 12; N. R. Brumer, "Blue Collar Women," *Personnel Journal* (Apr. 1981): 279–82; "The Lasting Changes Brought by Women Workers," *Business Week,* 15 Mar. 1982, pp. 59, 62, 67; H. N. Fullerton, Jr., "The 1995 Work Force: A First Look," *Monthly Labor Review* (Dec. 1980): 11–21; "A Look at the Workers You'll Boss in the 80's," *Industry Week,* 26 June 1978, pp. 24–26; K. A. Kovach, "Women in the Labor Force: A Socio-Economic Analysis," *Public Personnel Management Journal* 9 (1980): 318–26; P. Somers, C. Poulton-Callahan, and R. Bartlett, "Women in the Workforce: A Structural Approach to Equality," *Personnel Administrator* (Oct. 1981): 61–64.

15. A. Feingold, "The Future in Employment and Jobs," *Personnel Administrator* (Dec. 1983): 88; for a review of these projections and predictions, see *New York Times,* 9 June 1985, p. 28; A. L. Malabre, "Service Jobs Keep Expanding in Recessions, Make Up Ever Larger Share of Work Force," *Wall Street Journal,* 15 Jan. 1982, p. 44; W. Williams, "The Jobs That Won't Come Back," *New York Times,* 6 Dec. 1981; F. and V. A. Personick, "Industry Output and Employment: BLS Projects to 1990," *Monthly Labor Review* (Apr. 1979): 47–56. "The 1990 Worker: A Profile of the Future," *Trends,* Theodore Barry & Associates, 1981; J. Main, "Work Won't Be the Same Again," *Fortune,* 28 June 1982, pp. 58–65; R. W. Rumberger, "The Changing Skill Requirements of Jobs in the U.S. Economy," *Industrial and Labor Relations Review* (July 1981): 578–90.

16. "Technologies for the '80s," *Business Week,* 6 July 1981, p. 48; C. Norman, "How Microelectronics May Change the Workplace," *The Futurist* (Feb. 1981): 43–46, (published by the World Future Society, 4916 Elmo Avenue, Washington, D.C. 20014); see also "Artificial Intelligence: The Second Computer Age Begins," *Business Week,* 8 Mar. 1982, pp. 66–75; "Employment Outlook in High Technology, *New York Times,* 28 Mar. 1982, sec. 12; "Robots Create Changes in Work Force," *Ann Arbor Business-to-Business* (Oct. 1985): 9.

17. "Expectations That Can No Longer Be Met," *Business Week,* 30 June 1980, p. 84; see also J. Andrew,

"In High School Today, Youths Are Absorbed with Material Goals," *Wall Street Journal,* 3 June 1981, pp. 1, 22; A. Cherns, "Work and Values: Shifting Patterns in Industrial Society," *International Social Science Journal* 32 (1980): 427–41; R. M. Kanter, "Work in a New America," *Daedalus, Journal of the American Academy of Arts and Sciences* 107 (1978): 47–77; P. C. Grant, "Why Employee Motivation Has Declined in America," *Personnel Journal* (Dec. 1982): 905–9; R. J. Erickson, "The Changing Workplace and Workforce," *Training and Development Journal* (Jan. 1980): 62–65; P. Parrish, "PAIR Potpourri," *Personnel Administrator* (July 1981): 15–16; J. Holt, "Growing Up Engaged," *Psychology Today,* July 1980, pp. 14–16, 23–24; M. Sinetar, "Management in the New Age: An Exploration of Changing Work Value," *Personnel Journal* (Sept. 1980): 749–55; W. H. Schmidt and B. Z. Posner, *Managerial Values and Expectations* (New York: AMACOM, 1982); R. L. Hannah, "The Work Ethics of Coal Miners," *Personnel Journal* (Oct. 1982): 746–51; K. E. Debats, "The Continuing Personnel Challenge," *Personnel Journal* (May 1982): 332–44; D. Yankelovich, "New Rules in American Life: Searching for Self-fulfillment in a World Turned Upside Down," *Psychology Today,* April 1981, pp. 35–91; R. Dubin, "Industrial Workers," *Social Problems* 3 (1956): 131–42; R. Dubin and J. E. Chapoux, "Workers' Central Life Interests and Job Performance," *Sociology of Work and Occupation* 1 (1974): 313–26; R. Dubin, R. J. E. Champoux, and L. W. Porter, "Central Life Interests and Organizational Commitment of Blue-Collar and Clerical Workers," *Administrative Science Quarterly* 20 (1975): 411–21; J. W. Walker, "Training and Development," in *Human Resource Management in the 1980s* ed. S. J. Carroll and R. S. Schuler (Washington, D.C.: Bureau of National Affairs, 1983); G. L. Staines and R. D. Quinn, *The 1977 Quality of Employment Survey* (Ann Arbor, Mich.: Survey Research Center, University of Michigan, 1977); G. S. Odiorne, "HRM Policy and Program Management—A New Look in the Eighties," in *Human Resource Management in the 1980s,* ed. S. J. Carroll and R. S. Schuler (Washington, D.C.: Bureau of National Affairs, 1983).

18. C. Mackey, "Human Resource Planning: A Four-Phased Approach," *Management Review* (May 1981): 17–22.

19. For an extensive description of each of these phases, see J. J. Leach, "Merging the Two Faces of Personnel: A Challenge for the 1980's," *Personnel* (Jan./Feb. 1980): 52–57; "Manpower Planning and Corporate Objectives: Two Points of View," *Management Review* (Aug. 1981): 55–61; E. L. Miller and E. H. Burack, "A Status Report on Human Resource Planning from the Perspective of Human Resource Planners," *Human Resource Planning* (1981): 33–40; S. M. Nkomo, "Stage Three in Personnel Administration: Strategic Human Resource Management," *Personnel*

(July/Aug. 1980): 69–77; G. S. Odiorne, "Developing a Human Resource Strategy," *Personnel Journal* (July 1981): 534–36; J. A. Sheridan, "The Relatedness of Change: A Comprehensive Approach to Human Resource Planning for the Eighties," *Human Resource Planning* (1979): 123–33; L. Dyer, "Studying Human Resource Strategy: An Approach and an Agenda," *Industrial and Labor Relations Review* 23 (1984): 156–69; L. Dyer and N. D. Heyer, "Human Resource Planning at IBM," *Human Resource Planning,* 7 (3) (1984): 111–26; N. M. Tichy and C. K. Barnett, "Profiles in Change: Revitalizing the Automotive Industry," *Human Resource Management* (Winter 1985): 467–502.

20. Note that turnover is not always undesirable, especially when the poorer performers leave the organization. For a discussion, see D. R. Dalton, "Absenteeism and Turnover in Organizations," in *Applied Readings in Personnel and Human Resource Management,* ed. R. S. Schuler, J. M. McFillen, and D. R. Dalton (St. Paul: West, 1980).

21. For a discussion of the structure-environment fit and the relationship of this fit with individual preferences and motivations, see J. R. Gallbraith, *Organization Design* (Reading, Mass.: Addison-Wesley, 1977); R. H. Miles, *Macro Organizational Behavior* (Santa Monica, Calif.: Goodyear, 1980); M. J. Gannon, *Organizational Behavior* (Boston: Little, Brown, 1979), p. 97; "Forecasters Turn to Group Guesswork," *Business Week,* 14 Mar. 1970, p. 130.

22. For a more extensive discussion of group techniques, including the nominal group technique, see A. C. Delbecq, A. H. Van deVen, and D. H. Gustafson, *Group Technique for Program Planning* (Glenview, Ill.: Scott, Foresman, 1977); J. K. Murnigham, "Group Decision Making: What Strategy Should You Use?" *Management Review* (Feb. 1981): 56–60; J. Lee, "An Alternative to the Nominal Group Technique Final Vote Procedure," *Appalachian Business Review* (Winter 1979): 2–5; D. H. Gustafson, R. K. Shukla, A. Delbecq, and G. W. Walster, "A Comparative Study of Differences in Subjective Likelihood Estimates Made by Individuals, Interacting Groups, Delphi Groups, and Nominal Groups," *Organizational Behavior and Human Performance* 9 (1973): 280–91.

23. For a description of managerial estimates, see Walker, *Human Resource Planning,* 1980.

24. H. Kahalas, H. L. Pazer, J. S. Hoagland, and A. Leavitt, "Human Resource Planning Activities in U.S. Firms," *Human Resource Planning* 3 (1980): 53–66.

25. G. Milkovich and T. Mahoney, "Human Resources Planning and PAIR Policy," in *PAIR Handbook* vol. 4, ed. D. Yoder and H. Heneman (Berea, Ohio: American Society of Personnel Administration, 1976); Milkovich, Dyer, and Mahoney, "The State of Practice"; D. M. Atwater, E. S. Bress, R. J. Neihaus, and J. A. Sheridan, "An Application of Integrated Human Resource Planning Supply-Demand Model," *Human*

Resources Planning 5 (1982): 1–15; E. P. Bloom, "Creating an Employee Information System," *Personnel Administrator* (Nov. 1982): 67–75; B. W. Holz and J. M. Wroth, "Improving Strengths Forecasts: Support for Army Manpower Management," *Interfaces* 10 (1980): 37–52.

26. S. Makridakis and S. C. Wheelwright, eds., *Forecasting* (New York: North-Holland, 1979).

27. Ibid.; J. R. Hinrichs and R. F. Morrison, "Human Resource Planning in Support of Research and Development," *Human Resources Planning* 3 (1980): 201–10.

28. Burack and Mathys, *Human Resource Planning,* pp. 155–57.

29. N. K. Kwak, W. A. Garrett, Jr., and S. Barone, "A Stochastic Model of Demand Forecasting for Technical Manpower Training," *Management Science* 23 (1977): 1089–98.

30. Milkovich, Dyer, and Mahoney, "The State of Practice."

31. Vetter, "Manpower Planning," p. 35; P. S. Bender, W. D. Northup, and J. F. Shapiro, "Practical Modeling for Resource Management," *Harvard Business Review* (Mar./Apr. 1981): 163–75.

32. "Resource Planning: Forecasting Manpower Needs," *Personnel Journal* (Nov. 1981): 850–57; N. Scarborough and T. W. Zimmerer, "Human Resources e-casting: Why and Where to Begin," *Personnel Administrator* (May 1982): 55–61.

33. Walker, *Human Resource Planning,* 1980; J. W. Walker and R. Armes, "Implementing Management Succession Planning in Diversified Companies," *Human Resource Planning* 2 (1979): 123–33.

34. Milkovich, Dyer, and Mahoney, "The State of Practice"; Dyer, "Strategic Human Resources"; J. Carnazza, *Succession Replacement Planning: Programs and Practices* (New York: Center for Research in Career Development, Columbia Business School, 1982).

35. G. T. Milkovich and T. A. Mahoney, "Human Resources Planning Models: A Perspective," *Human Resources Planning Journal* (1979): 19–30.

36. See, for example, S. H. Zanski and M. W. Maret, "A Markov Application to Manpower Supply Planning," *Journal of the Operational Research Society* 31 (1980): 1095–1102; J. F. Gillespie, W. G. Leininger, and H. Kahalas, "A Human Resource Planning and Validation Model," *Academy of Management Journal* 19 (1976): 650–55.

37. G. T. Milkovich and F. Krzystofiak, "Simulation and Affirmative Action Planning," *Human Resource Planning* 2 (1979): 71–80.

38. W. G. Piskor and R. C. Dudding, "A Computer Assisted Manpower Planning Mode," in *Manpower Planning and Organization Design,* ed. D. T. Bryant and R. J. Niehaus (New York: Plenum, 1978), pp. 145–54.

39. E. S. Bres, D. Burns, A. Charnes, and W. W. Cooper, "A Goal Programming Model for Planning Officer Accessions," *Management Science* 26 (1980): 773–82.

40. D. B. Gehrman, "Objective Based Human Resources Planning," *Personnel Journal* (Dec. 1981): 942–46.

41. Burack and Gutteridge, "Institutional Manpower Planning," p. 18.

42. Burack and Gutteridge in "Institutional Manpower Planning," cite a 1971 survey, *Corporate Manpower Planning,* conducted by Towers, Perrin, Foster, and Crosby (TPF&C).

43. Note that in this section, concern is for the structure-person fit, not the structure-environment fit. For a discussion of the latter, see Galbraith, *Organizational Design* and Miles, *Organizational Theory.* For a discussion of the former, see L. Porter, E. E. Lawler III, and J. R. Hackman, *Behavior in Organizations* (New York: McGraw-Hill, 1975); D. Hellriegel, J. W. Slocum, Jr., and R. Woodman, *Organizational Behavior,* 4th ed. (West, 1986); L. F. Schoenfeldt, "Utilization of Manpower: Development and Evaluation of an Assessment-Classification Model for Matching Individuals with Jobs," *Journal of Applied Psychology* 59 (1974): 583–95.

44. Vetter, "Manpower Planning," p. 67; L. E. Davis, "Individuals and the Organization," *California Management Review* (Spring 1980): 5.

45. For a discussion of the concerns and issues related to Match 1 and Match 2 (i.e., matching people on the basis of their abilities and preferences), see N. Schmidt and B. Schneider, "Current Issues in Personnel Selection," in *Research in Personnel and Human Resource Management*, ed. K. M. Rowland and G. D. Ferris (Greenwich, Conn.: JAI Press, 1983). Note that although the terms *individual skills, knowledge,* and *abilities* are used, this can also include other characteristics as well. For example, aptitudes can be included, since organizations do select on the basis of aptitudes and since some aptitudes may be job related, as discussed in Chapter 5.

46. Organizations are becoming aware of the importance of matching job rewards with individuals' personalities, interests, and preferences, particularly the latter two. This is because of the growing recognition that an individual behaves in an organization on the basis of ability and motivation. Consequently, organizations need to be concerned with both of these bases. They have been concerned with ability, and now they are becoming concerned with motivation, because employees do not always exhibit desirable behaviors (probably partly because individuals' interests and preferences have changed). These changes influence behavior because they influence motivation. How they do this can be explained by expectancy and reinforcement theory concepts. Since these are presented in Chapters 7 and 11, only brief mention is made herein.

Essentially, people do what's rewarded, assuming they believe that they can do what is required to get the rewards. Consequently, if an organization wants its employees to come to work on time, it should reward them for doing so. If the employees believe they can get to work on time, they will try, but only if what the company gives them is really a reward. Organizations give outcomes (e.g., pay). Whether an outcome is rewarding or not depends upon the employees' interests and preferences. If they prefer (value) and thus show interest in the outcome, then it is a reward. Today, organizations are disturbed because some employees are not exhibiting desired behaviors. From a motivation perspective, this may be happening because the outcomes that organizations offer (e.g., pay, promotion, and status) are not seen as rewards or as rewarding by as many employees as they once were. Thus, although they were rewarding before (organizations did not need to be as concerned about employee motivation), they are not today for employees whose preferences and values have changed. Organizations concerned with employees' personalities, interests, and preferences are consequently offering different outcomes, such as participation, job control, and job enrichment (all elements of alternative structures). Although this appears to be working with some employees now, organizations will need to continually think of alternative structures offering different outcomes that will be rewarding to employees with new personalities, interests, and preferences.

See also J. R. Gordon, "Using the People/Problem Management Dichotomy," *Personnel Administrator* (Mar. 1983): 51–57.

47. P. F. Drucker, "Planning for Redundant Workers," *Personnel Administrator* (Jan. 1980): 32; "The Rise in Worker Buy-Outs," *New York Times,* 23 Feb. 1983, pp. D1, D16; Bureau of National Affairs, *Bulletin to Management,* 14 Feb. 1985, p. 1, May 2, 1985, p. 1.

48. Gilchrist and Shenki, 'The Impact of Computers on Employment," p. 49.

49. G. H. Cauble, "Alternatives to a Reduction in Force," *Personnel Journal* (June 1982): 424–25; A. L. Otten, "Many Swedes 60 and Older Cut Working Hours Before Retirement Under Government Program," *Wall Street Journal,* 6 July 1982, p. 46; J. S. Lublin, "More Managers Are Working Part-Time; Some Like It, but Others Have No Choice," *Wall Street Journal,* 2 June 1982, p. 50; N. R. Kleinfield, "A Human Resource at Allied Corp.," *New York Times,* 6 June 1982, p. 4F; "Casting Executives as Consultants," *Business Week,* 30 Aug. 1982, pp. 46, 51; D. Henriksen, "Outplacement: Program Guidelines that Ensure Success," *Personnel Journal* (Aug. 1982): 583–88; J. P. Bucalo, Jr., "Administering a Salaried Reduction-in-Force . . . Effectively," *Personnel Administrator* (Apr. 1982): 79–89; K. B. Noble, "Study Finds 60% of 11 Million Who Lost Jobs Got New Ones," *New York Times,* 7 Feb. 1986, pp. 1, 11.

50. "Helping Employees through a Major Life Transition," *Behavioral Sciences Newsletter,* 26 Feb. 1981; W. Armone, "Preretirement Planning: An Employee Benefit That Has Come of Age," *Personnel Journal* (Oct. 1982); 760–62; B. Rosen, T. H. Jerdee, and R. O.

Lunn, "Retirement Policies and Management Decisions," *Aging and Work* (Fall 1980): 239–46; J. L. Wall and H. M. Shatshat, "Controversy over the Issue of Mandatory Retirement," *Personnel Administrator* (Oct. 1981): 25–30, 45; R. Jud, *The Retirement Decision* (New York: AMACOM, 1981); M. Lyons, "The Older Employee as a Resource Issue for Personnel," *Personnel Journal* (Mar. 1981): 178–86; T. McCarroll, "Rehiring Retirees," *New York Times,* 22 Nov. 1981, sec. F., p. 8; M. Zippo, "Roundup," *Personnel* (Jan.–Feb. 1980): 65–70; F. H. Cassell, "The Increasing Complexity of Retirement Decisions," *MSU Business Topics* (Winter 1978): 15–24; P. Farish, "PAIR Potpourri," *Personnel Administrator* (Dec. 1980): 18–20; P. F. Hagstrom, "The Older Worker: A Travelers Insurance Companies' Case Study," *Personnel Administrator* (Oct. 1981): 41–44; M. H. Morrison, "Retirement and Human Resource Planning for the Aging Work Force," *Personnel Administrator* (June 1984): 151–59; R. C. Ford and M. D. Fottler, "Flexible Retirement: Slowing Early Retirement of Productive Older Employees," *Human Resource Planning* 8 (1985): 147–56; T. A. Beehr, "The Process of Retirement: A Review and Recommendations for Future Investigation," *Personnel Psychology* (in press); J. Mervis, "The Psychological Route to Cutting Cuts," *New York Times,* 24 Nov. 1985, p. 12-F.

51. *Wall Street Journal,* 5 June 1984, p. 1. Reprinted by permission of *The Wall Street Journal.* Copyright © Dow Jones & Company, Inc., 1984. All rights reserved.

52. Dyer "Strategic Human Resources. . ." in Rowland and Ferris, p. 72; H. L. Dahl and K. S. Morgan, "Return on Investment in Human Resources" (Upjohn Company, unpublished manuscript, 1982), cited by Milkovich, Dyer, and Mahoney "The State of Practice" in Carroll and Schuler. For a discussion of the human resource accounting concept, see J. B. Paperman and D. D. Martin, "Human Resource Accounting: A Managerial Tool?" *Personnel* (Mar./Apr. 1977): 41–50; Milkovich, Dyer and Mahoney, "The State of Practice."

53. *Business Week,* 9 May 1984, p. 81.

54. F. K. Foulkes and A. Whitman, "Marketing Strategies to Maintain Full Employment," *Harvard Business Review* (July–Aug. 1985): 30–35.

55. H. G. Angle, C. C. Manz, and A. H. Van de Ven, "Integrating Human Resource Management and Corporate Strategy: A Preview of the 3M Story," *Human Resource Management* (Spring 1985): 51–68.

56. G. Milkovich, L. Dyer, and T. Mahoney, "The State of Practice and Research in Human Resource Planning," in *Human Resource Management in the 1980s,* ed. S. J. Carroll and R. S. Schuler (Washington, D.C.: Bureau of National Affairs, 1983).

57. W. Skinner, "Big Hat, No Cattle: Managing Human Resources," *Harvard Business Review* (Sept./Oct. 1981): 106–14; R. M. Kanter, *The Change Masters* (New York: Simon & Schuster, 1983).

3

Job Analysis

Job Analysis and the *Uniform Guidelines* of 1978

Job analysis in general

The enforcement agencies will take into account the fact that a thorough job analysis was conducted.

(Sec. 9B, p. 38299)

Any validity study should be based upon a review of information about the job for which the selection procedure is to be used. The review should include a job analysis. . . . Any method of job analysis may be used if it provides the information required for the specific validation strategy used.

(Sec. 14A, p. 38300)

Job analysis for criterion-related validity

Evidence of the validity of a test or other selection procedure by a criterion-related validity study should consist of empirical data demonstrating that the selection procedure is predictive of or significantly correlated with important elements of job performance.

(Sec. 5B, p. 38298)

Where appropriate, jobs with substantially the same major work behaviors may be grouped together for validity studies, in order to obtain an adequate sample.

[Sec. 14B(1), p. 38300]

There should be a review of job information to determine measures of work behavior(s) or performance that are relevant to the job or group of jobs in question. These measures or criteria are relevant to the extent that they represent critical or important job duties, work behaviors or work outcomes as developed from the review of job information.

Sec. 14B(2), p. 38300

Job analysis for content validity

Evidence of the validity of a test or other selection procedure by a content validity study should consist of data showing that the content of the selection procedure is representative of important aspects of performance on the job for which the candidates are to be evaluated.

(Sec. 5B,p. 38298)

Job analysis for construct validity

Evidence of the validity of a test or other selection procedure through a construct validity study should consist of data showing that the procedure measures the degree to which candidates have identifiable characteristics which have been determined to be important in successful performance in the job for which the candidates are to be evaluated.

(Sec. 5B, p. 38298)

The preceding "PHRM in the News" from the *Uniform Guidelines* of 1978 illustrates the role and legal importance of job analysis in organizations.[1] Job analysis is the foundation for many PHRM functions and activities and is essentially a legal requirement where selection decisions, performance appraisal, training program admission decisions, and layoff or termination decisions are made. As such, job analysis is described in detail in this chapter and is mentioned in several of the subsequent chapters.

Job analysis is the process of describing and recording aspects of jobs. Typically described and recorded are the purposes of a job, its major duties or activities, and the conditions under which the job is performed. These three components form the essential parts of a job description. On the basis of the job description, job specifications are written. These detail the skills, knowledge, and abilities that individuals need to perform the job. Job descriptions could, but do not typically, include information about performance standards, task design characteristics (as described in Chapter 12), and employee characteristics such as those shown in Exhibit 1.3. Additionally, job specifications could include information about individual personality, interests, and preferences likely to be compatible with the job or satisfied during the job's performance. These two modifications of traditional job descriptions and specifications are in keeping with the concern for attaining two of the three major purposes of PHRM: high productivity and high quality of work life. The other major purpose of PHRM, complying with legal regulations, is served by doing the typical job description and job specifications.[2]

Purposes and Importance of Job Analysis

As shown in Exhibit 3.1, job analysis is the basis of job descriptions and specifications. Job analysis is necessary for legally validating methods used in making employment decisions, such as selection, promotion, and performance appraisal, and is also important because it serves several other purposes:

- Determining jobs' relative worth, which is necessary to maintain external and internal pay equity
- Ensuring that companies do not violate the equal pay for equal work provision of the Equal Pay Act of 1963
- Aiding the supervisor and employee in defining each employee's duties and responsibilities
- Providing a justification for the existence of the job and where it fits into the rest of the organization
- Determining the recruitment needs (when used together with the human resource planning needs discussed in Chapter 2) and the information necessary to make employment decisions
- Serving as the basis for establishing career development programs and paths for employees
- Serving as a means by which to convey to potential job applicants what will be expected of them, the general working conditions, and the types of individual preferences that the job may satisfy[3]

An extensive set of relationships also makes job analysis important.

Relationships Influencing Job Analysis

Job analysis has extensive relationships with other PHRM activities and the internal environment.[4] These relationships are illustrated in Exhibit 3.1.

Relationships and Aspects of Job Analysis   *Exhibit 3.1*

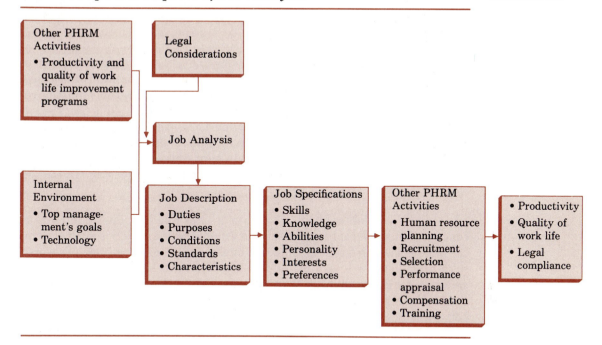

Relationships with Other PHRM Activities

Almost all PHRM activities are critically related to job analysis. The following describes some of the most critical activities.

Human Resource Planning, Recruitment, and Selection.   On the basis of job analysis and in conjunction with human resource planning, the organization knows whom to recruit. Without human resource planning and job analysis, the organization would be unable to specify what types of job applicants it needs and when and where it needs them. This in turn can have negative consequences for organizational productivity and the validity of its selection procedures and decisions. Only with job analysis information can an organization show that its selection procedures are job related, a point that the U.S. Supreme Court clearly articulated in *Albemarle Paper Company* v. *Moody* (1975):

> In *Griggs* v. *Duke Power Co.,* this Court unanimously held that Title VII forbids the use of employment tests that are discriminatory in effect unless the employer meets "the burden of showing that any given requirement (has) . . . a manifest relation to the employment in question." This burden arises, of course, only after the complaining party or class has made out a *prima facie* case of discrimination—has shown that the tests in question select applicants for hire or promotion in a racial pattern significantly different from that of the pool of applicants. . . . If an employer does then meet the burden of proving that its tests are "job related," it remains open to the complaining party to show that other tests or selection devices, with-

out a similarly undesirable racial effect, would also serve the employer's legitimate interest in "efficient and trustworthy workmanship." Such a showing would be evidence that the employer was using its tests merely as a "pretext for discrimination."

Performance Appraisal and Training and Development.   To effectively evaluate employee performance, the appraisal method used must reflect the job's important duties. Additionally, selection into training programs must be related to the job's important duties. Only by examining the skills that the job requires (as defined in the job specifications) can the organization train and promote employees in conjunction with its human resource needs defined by the human resource planning activity. In turn, this enables an organization to structure career paths for employees based on ever-increasing but related skills, knowledge, and abilities.

Compensation.   Job analysis also plays a vital role in a highly important concern of individuals in organizations: compensation. A job is evaluated on the basis of the job analysis. Since job evaluation determines the job's worth to the organization, it is often used to help determine how much an employee gets paid for doing that job. Job analysis is also important in ensuring that the pay level for a job is fair in relation to other jobs. That is, job analysis helps ensure that employees in jobs of equal worth receive the same pay as prescribed by the Equal Pay Act—just one of many legal considerations in job analysis. It can also be used to provide insights into comparable worth considerations discussed in Chapter 8.

Productivity and Quality of Work Life. Improvement Programs.   Programs to improve organizations often involve changing the design of jobs (see Chapter 12). Regardless of the nature of the resulting job design, the new duties, purposes, and conditions have to be analyzed. Although analyzing is relatively straightforward for individually designed jobs, analyzing group- or team-designed jobs is more complex. When the focus of doing work switches from a narrowly defined set of tasks to a more broadly defined set of tasks related to a major portion of a final product, analyzing each individual's duties and necessary skills, knowledge, and abilities becomes more difficult.[5] One consequence is to go from job evaluation and pay grades for specific jobs to skill evaluation and pay for knowledge that employees possess. This is described in more detail in Chapter 8.

Relationships with the Internal Environment

Two aspects of the internal environment that are relevant to job analysis are top management's goals and the technology used to pursue those goals.

Top Management's Goals.   Because they are created by organizations, jobs are top management's explicit statements of what they believe are the most appropriate means for accomplishing their goals. Furthermore, if workers' thoughts and beliefs about their organizations help determine their behavior, then the stated goals and the subsequent standards of excellence that an

organization establishes give clear cues to employees about what is important and where their efforts are required. Since goals help determine organizations' products and environments, they also help determine the criteria
against which workers will be evaluated—hence, their behaviors. The criteria and goals in turn also determine the kinds of individuals who will be attracted to the organization, evaluated highly, and promoted. Thus, organizational goals can help establish the reasons for jobs, the organization's
expectations for workers, and even the legitimacy of the job demands. Goals
have several other consequences through their relationship with the organization's structure, which is in turn related to the design and redesign of
jobs.[6]

Technology.   The type of technology available to and used by an organization is also critical because it determines what types of job designs are possible and what types of jobs are appropriate for various organizational designs. For example, U.S. automobile manufacturers, with huge investments
in plants and machinery to make cars on assembly lines, find it almost impossible to convert their car-making technology so that groups of workers
make the cars. The result is that most assembly jobs are fairly segmented
and repetitive and remain that way. Furthermore, assembly-line technology
determines the structure or design of the organization and in turn the most
appropriate types of job design. Over time, however, these relationships are
less fixed. The current Saturn project of General Motors is an example in
which top management (of the company and the union) has determined that
a new technology for car making is more appropriate than the assembly
line.[7]

Legal Considerations in Job Analysis

In addition to an extensive set of relationships with other PHRM activities
and aspects of the organization, job analysis faces several legal considerations and constraints, largely because it serves as the basis for selection decisions, performance appraisals, and training determinations. The *Uniform
Guidelines* of 1978 and several court decisions have articulated these considerations and constraints. For example, Section 14.C.2 of the *Uniform Guidelines* states: "There shall be a job analysis which includes an analysis of the
important work behaviors required for successful performance. . . . Any job
analysis should focus on work behavior(s) and the tasks associated with
them."[8]

Where job analysis has not been performed, the validity of selection instruments has been successfully challenged (*Kirkland* v. *New York Department of Correctional Services,* 1974; *Albemarle Paper Company* v. *Moody,*
1975). Numerous court decisions regarding job analysis and promotion and
performance appraisal also exist. For example, in *Brito* v. *Zia Company*
(1973), the court stated that the performance appraisal system of an organization is a selection procedure and therefore must be validated—that is, it

must be anchored in job analysis. And in *Rowe* v. *General Motors* (1972), the court ruled that to prevent discriminatory practices in promotion decisions, a company should have written objective standards for promotion. Job analysis can determine these objective standards. In *U.S.A.* v. *City of Chicago* (1978), the court stated that in addition to having objective standards for promotion, the standards should describe the job to which the person is being considered for promotion. These standards can be determined through job analysis.[9]

The emphasis that the *Uniform Guidelines* put on job analysis is highlighted in the initial "PHRM in the News." The *Uniform Guidelines* acknowledge some of the different purposes of job analysis and consequently establish job analysis requirements. For example, when an **empirical relationship** between a selection instrument and job performance is being determined, the job performance measure must be anchored in job analysis that identifies the important job "elements," "work behavior(s)," "duties," or "work outcomes."[10] When a **content relationship** between the selection instrument and the job content is being sought, the job content can be determined by a job analysis that identifies the work behaviors or the observed work products. Finally, when a **construct relationship** is being determined (between the selection instrument and the job), and analysis must clearly describe the constructs believed to underlie successful performance.[11] These three types of relationships are described more extensively in Chapter 18. Keep in mind that according to the *Uniform Guidelines* (Section 14A), "Any method of job analysis may be used if it provides the information required for the specific validation strategy used."

The Vocational Rehabilitation Act of 1973 requires organizations with federal government contracts worth more than $2,500 to make "reasonable accommodation" to hire and promote disabled individuals. Although this act has broad implications for recruitment and selection (as discussed in Chapters 4 and 5), it has specific implications for job analysis:

> Above all, says Sy DuBow, a lawyer at the National Center for Law and the Deaf in Washington, "reasonable accommodation" means more than applying technology. It means, he says, "restructuring jobs to reassign marginal tasks." A company cannot refuse to hire a deaf applicant as a file clerk simply because the previous clerk occasionally helped out at the switchboard. And it means rewriting job descriptions when they include, for no clearly defined reason, phrases such as "good communications ability."[12]

Aspects of Job Analysis

Renewed interest in job analysis has occurred, spurred in part by organizational efforts to become more competitive and profitable and to comply with the *Uniform Guidelines*.[13] Interest has also grown because job analysis serves many purposes and has an extensive set of system relationships in organizations. As a consequence, organizations want to know about all aspects of job analysis, starting with collecting job analysis information.

Collecting Job Analysis Information

As defined earlier, job analysis is the process of describing and recording many aspects of jobs. These aspects vary greatly, often depending on the purposes to be served. Exhibit 3.2 illustrates possible job aspects that can be described. Since gathering information on these aspects is necessary to comply with the *Uniform Guidelines,* one must know who collects the information and how it is collected.

Types of Information Obtained through Job Analysis

Exhibit 3.2

Work Activities

Job-oriented activities (usually expressed in terms of what is accomplished; sometimes indicating how, why, and when a worker performs the activity)
  Work activities/processes
  Procedures used
  Activity records (films, etc.)
  Personal accountability/responsibility
Worker-oriented activities
  Human behaviors performed in work (sensing, decision making, performing physical actions, communicating, etc.)
  Elemental motions (such as those used in methods analysis)
  Personal job demands (energy expenditure, etc.)

Machines, Tools, Equipment, and Work Aids Used

Job-related Tangibles and Intangibles
Materials processed
Products made
Knowledge dealt with or applied (such as law or chemistry)
Services rendered (such as laundering or repairing)

Work Performance
Work measurement (time taken)
Work standards
Error analysis
Other aspects

Job Context
Physical working conditions
Work schedule
Organizational context
Social context
Incentives (financial and nonfinancial)

Personnel Requirements
Job-related knowledge/skills (education, training, work experience, etc.)
Personal attributes (aptitudes, physical characteristics, personality, interests, etc.)

Source: Adapted from E. J. McCormick, "Job and Task Analysis," in *Handbook of Industrial and Organizational Psychology,* ed. M. D. Dunnette. Copyright © 1976 by Rand McNally College Publishing Company, p. 653.

Who Collects the Information?

Typically, someone in the PHRM department, along with a supervisor, collects the job information. Increasingly common is for the incumbent (the person in the job) to also provide job information. Often a combination of the three is used. The exact combination, the information each person provides, how it is used, and who has the final responsibility may depend upon whether the jobs and individuals are exempt or nonexempt (these terms are further described and defined in Chapter 8). For example:

> The procedure at Bunker Ramo Corporation (Oak Brook, Illinois) usually involves the incumbent, the supervisor, and an analyst, says Manager of Compensation Donald C. Kraft. He sent in two position responsibility questionnaires—one for exempt employees and one for nonexempt employees.
>
> Another procedure that involves incumbents is the one from W. R. Sturgeon, senior vice-president and director of Personnel, Indian Head Bank (Nashua, New Hampshire): "A questionnaire is completed by employees. The analyst writes the position description and the supervisor and employee agree (the supervisor has the last word). The job analysis committee reviews it and decides on level."[14]

Joseph Springer, personnel manager at Cook Electric Division, Northern Telecom (Morton Grove, Illinois), describes the process at his company:

> For hourly production and maintenance jobs, the information is collected and the writing-up done by a personnel representative, with review by a personnel representative, with review by two levels of line management; the top line manager has veto power concerning content while the personnel manager has veto power in matters of job analysis. For exempt salaried positions, the incumbent writes up the information in coordination with Personnel; veto power is held by the line function director or vice-president.[15]

Methods of Gathering.   The method by which information is gathered is as extensive as the number of possible aspects. The methods include (1) interviews with job incumbents, (2) conferences with job analysts/experts, (3) observations by job analysts, (4) diaries kept by job incumbents, (5) structured and unstructured questionnaires filled out by incumbents or by observers such as supervisors or job analysts, (6) critical incidents written by incumbents or others who know the jobs, and (7) mechanical devices such as stopwatches, counters, and films.[16] From the data gathered in the job analysis, two major outputs result: job descriptions and job specifications. On the basis of the job descriptions, performance appraisal forms can be developed and job classification systems can be established for job evaluation and compensation purposes. On the basis of the job specifications, recruitment and selection procedures can be devised and training and development programs can be designed.

Job Descriptions and Job Specifications

Although the actual job descriptions used in many organizations contain information on job specifications, describing jobs and identifying the job specifications for those jobs are two different activities. Because these activities are so closely related, however, most of the job analysis techniques described later are used to gather information on both activities. Typically, a single document is written describing or at least listing the job's important aspects, along with the necessary skills, knowledge, and abilities. The final job analysis document should likely include the following:

- Job or payroll title
- Job number and group to which the job belongs (as a result of job evaluation and for compensation purposes)
- Department or division (or both) where the job is located
- Name of the incumbent (optional) and name of the job analyst
- Primary function or summary of the job
- Description of the job's major duties and responsibilities, sometimes with a percentage of time for each duty
- Description of the skills, knowledge, and abilities (physical and mental)
- Relationships of the job to other jobs

Job descriptions should employ a terse, direct writing style, using present tense and active verbs. Each sentence should reflect an objective, either specifically stated or strongly implied.

Any words that impart unnecessary information should be omitted. Care should be taken to use words that have only one connotation and that specifically describe how the work is accomplished. Task descriptions should reflect the assigned work performed and worker traits ratings.[17]

Keep in mind that the job should be described in enough detail so that the reader can understand (1) what is to be done (the domains, behaviors, results, and duties), (2) what products are to be generated (the job's purposes), (3) what work standards are applied (e.g., quality and quantity), (4) under what conditions the job is performed, and (5) the job's design characteristics. Design characteristics are included so that individuals might select and be placed on jobs that match or suit their personalities, interests, and preferences.[18] Nevertheless, organizations generally do not include job design characteristics in their job descriptions. Exhibit 3.3 is an example of a typical job analysis document for a corporate loan assistant. This job description does not provide information on performance standards, design characteristics, or the job's purposes and conditions. The introductory section, however, implies the job's purposes. Performance standards are typically not specified in job descriptions but are, however, increasingly being included. Organizations sometimes prefer to retain flexibility and include standards in the performance appraisal form. Information on task characteristics, such as task identity and amount of skill variety, is rarely included in job descriptions. Chapter 12 provides further discussion of design characteristics and the reasons for possible inclusion in job descriptions. Also typically missing from job descriptions is information on employee characteristics, such as degree of risk taking and emphasis on the shorter term or longer term as presented in Chapter 1.

Job Analysis Techniques

Organizations can choose among many procedures to determine what job information to collect, how to collect it, from whom to collect it, and how to or-

Exhibit 3.3   *Job Analysis Document*

FUNCTIONAL TITLE: Corporate Loan Assistant   DEPARTMENT:
FUNCTION CODE: Corporate Banking
INCUMBENT: DIVISION:
                                                  LOCATION: Head Office
                                                  DATE: June 1986

NOTE: Statements included in this description are intended to reflect in general the
      duties and responsibilities of this classification and are not to be interpreted
      as being all-inclusive.

RELATIONSHIPS:

Reports to: Corporate Account Officer A or AA; or Sr.
                                   Corporate Account Officer B or BB

Subordinate staff: None
Other internal contacts: Various levels of management within the
                                   Corporate Banking Department
External Contacts: Major Bank Customers

SUMMARY STATEMENT:

Assist in the administration of commercial accounts, to ensure maintenance of
profitable Bank relationships.

DOMAINS:
A. Credit Analysis (Weekly)

   Under the direction of a supervising loan officer: Analyze a customer company's
   history, industry position, present condition, accounting procedures, and debt
   requirements. Review credit reports, summarizing analysis and recommending
   course of action for potential borrowers; review and summarize performance of
   existing borrowers. Prepare and follow up on credit communications and reports
   and Loan Agreement Compliance sheets.

B. Operations (Weekly)

   Help customers with banking problems and needs. Give out customer credit
   information to valid inquirers. Analyze account profitability and compliance
   with balance arrangements; distribute to customer. Direct Corporate Loan Note
   Department in receiving and disbursing funds and in booking loans. Correct
   internal errors.

C. Loan Documentation (Weekly)

   Develop required loan documentation. Help customer complete loan documents.
   Review loan documents immediately after a loan closing for completeness and
   accuracy.

D. Report/Information System (Weekly)

   Prepare credit reports, describing and analyzing customer relationship and loan
   commitments; prepare for input into Information System. Monitor credit
   reports for accuracy.

E. Customer/Internal Relations (Weekly)

   Build rapport with customers by becoming familiar with their products,
   facilities, and industry. Communicate with customers and other banks to obtain
   loan-related information and answer questions. Prepare reports on customer and
   prospect contacts and follow up. Write memos on significant events affecting
   customers and prospects.

continued

F. Assistance to Officers (Monthly)

Assist assigned officers by preparing credit support information, summarizing customer relationship, and accompanying on calls or making independent calls. Monitor accounts and review and maintain credit files. Coordinate paper flow to banks participating in loans. Respond to customer questions or requests in absence of assigned officer.

G. Assistance to Division (Monthly)

Represent Bank at industry activities. Follow industry/area developments. Help Division Manager plan division approach and prospect for new business. Interview loan assistant applicants. Provide divisional back-up in absence of assigned officer.

H. Knowledges and Skills

Oral communication skills, including listening and questioning. Intermediate accounting skills. Writing skills. Researching/reading skills to understand legal financial documents. Organizational/analytical skills. Social skills to represent the Bank and strengthen its image. Sales skills. Knowledge of Bank credit policy and services. Skill to use Bank computer terminal. Knowledge of bank-related legal terminology. Independent work skills. Work efficiently under pressure. Courtesy and tactfulness. Interfacing skills. Knowledge of basic business (corporate) finance. Skill to interpret economic/political events.

I. Physical Characteristics

See to read fine print and numbers. Hear speaker 20 feet away. Speak to address a group of five. Mobility to tour customer facilities (may include climbing stairs). Use of hands and fingers to write, operate a calculator.

J. Other Characteristics

Driver's license. Willing to: work overtime and weekends occasionally; travel out of state every three months/locally weekly; attend activities after work hours; wear clean, neat business-like attire.

Typical Line of Promotion:

From:

To: Corporate Account Officer

_____		_____	_____
Analyst		Incumbent	Date
		_____	_____
		Superior	Date

Source: Used by permission of Biddle and Associates.

ganize and present it in job descriptions. Most of the procedures are structured: fixed forms and procedures are used to gather the job analysis data. When organizations use similarly structured methods to analyze jobs, they can exchange compensation information and develop more valid methods of recruitment, selection, and performance appraisal.[19]

Structured techniques tend to divide into two types: those focusing on job aspects (job focused) and those focusing on an individual's aspects (person focused).[20] Typical job-focused techniques include Functional Job Analysis (FJA), the Management Position Description Questionnaire (MPDQ), the Hay Plan, methods analyses, and task inventories.[21] Person-focused techniques include the Position Analysis Questionnaire (PAQ), Physical Abilities Analysis (PAA), the Critical Incidents Technique (CIT), Extended CIT, and Guidelines-oriented Job Analysis (GOJA).

Job-focused Techniques

The several job-focused techniques described here are a testimony to this.

Functional Job Analysis (FJA).   The U.S. Training and Employment Service (USTES) developed functional job analysis to describe concerns (people, data, and things) and to develop job summaries, job descriptions, and employee specifications.[22] FJA was designed to improve job placement and counseling for workers registering at local state employment offices. Today, a number of private and public organizations use many aspects of FJA.[23]

FJA is both a conceptual system for defining the worker activity dimensions and a method of measuring worker activity levels. Its fundamental premises are as follows:

- A fundamental distinction must be made between what gets done and what workers do to get things done. Bus drivers do not carry passengers; they drive vehicles and collect fares.
- Jobs are concerned with data, people, and things.
- In relation to things, workers draw on physical resources; in relation to data, on mental resources; and in relation to people, on interpersonal resources.
- All jobs require workers to relate to data, people, and things to some degree.
- Although workers' behavior or the tasks they perform can apparently be described in an infinite number of ways, only a few definitive functions are involved. Thus, in interacting with machines, workers feed, tend, operate, and set up; in the case of vehicles or related machines, they drive or control them. Although these functions vary in difficulty and content, each draws on a relatively narrow and specific range of worker characteristics and qualifications for effective performance.
- The functions appropriate to dealing with data, people, or things are hierarchical and ordinal, proceeding from the complex to the simple. Thus, to indicate that a particular function—say, compiling data—reflects the job requirements is to say that it also includes lower-function requirements, such as comparing, and excludes higher-function requirements, such as analyzing.[24]

Exhibit 3.4 lists the worker functions associated with data, people, and things. The USTES has used these worker functions as a basis for describing over thirty thousand job titles in the *Dictionary of Occupational Titles* and for creating job families (groupings of jobs) based on similar data, people, and things.

A PHRM manager who has to prepare job descriptions and specifications might start with the *Dictionary of Occupational Titles* to determine general job analysis information. The *Handbook for Analyzing Jobs* is used for more

Functions Associated with Data, People, and Things		*Exhibit 3.4*

Data	People	Things
0 synthesizing	0 mentoring	0 setting up
1 coordinating	1 negotiating	1 precision working
2 analyzing	2 instructing	2 operating-controlling
3 compiling	3 supervising	3 driving-operating
4 computing	4 diverting	4 manipulating
5 copying	5 persuading	5 tending
6 comparing	6 speaking-signaling	6 feeding-offbearing
	7 serving	7 handling
	8 taking instructions-helping	

Source: Adapted from U.S. Department of Labor, Employment Service, Training and Development Administration, *Handbook for Analyzing Jobs* (Washington, D.C.: Government Printing Office, 1972), p. 73.

specific resource planning, recruitment, selection, placement, performance evaluation, training, and job design.

Management Position Description Questionnaire (MPDQ).   Although the FJA approach is complete, using it well requires considerable training, and its nature is quite narrative. The narrative portions tend to be less reliable than more quantitative techniques, such as the Management Position Description Questionnaire.[25] The MPDQ relies on the checklist method to analyze jobs. It contains 197 items related to managers' concerns, responsibilities, demands, restrictions, and miscellaneous characteristics. These 197 items have been condensed into the following 13 job factors:

- Product, market, and financial planning
- Coordination of other organizational units and personnel
- Internal business control
- Products and services responsibility
- Public and customer relations
- Advanced consulting
- Autonomy of action
- Approval of financial commitments
- Staff service
- Supervision
- Complexity and stress
- Advanced financial responsibility
- Broad personnel responsibility

The MPDQ is designed for managerial positions, but responses to the items vary by managerial level in any organization and also in different organizations. The MPDQ is appropriate for determining the training needs of employees moving into managerial jobs, evaluating managerial jobs, creating job families and placing new managerial jobs into the right job family, compensating managerial jobs, and developing selection procedures and performance appraisal forms.

The Hay Plan.   Another method of analyzing managerial jobs is the Hay Plan, which a large number of organizations use. Although less structured than the MPDQ and PAQ, it is systematically tied into a job evaluation and compensation system. Thus, use of the Hay Plan allows an organization to maintain consistency not only in how it describes managerial jobs but also in how it rewards them. The Hay Plan's purposes are management development, placement, and recruitment; job evaluation; measurement of the execution of a job against specific standards of accountability; and organization analysis.

The Hay Plan is based on an interview between the job analyst and the job incumbent. The information gathered relates to four aspects of the incumbent's job: objectives, dimensions, nature and scope of the position, and accountability objectives. Information about objectives shows why the job exists in the organization and for what reason it is paid. Information about dimensions conveys how big a "show" the incumbent runs and the magnitude of the end results affected by his or her actions.

The heart of the Hay Plan, information about the nature and scope of the position, covers five crucial aspects:

- How the position fits into the organization, including reference to significant organizational and outside relationships.
- The general composition of supporting staff. This includes a thumbnail sketch of each major function of any staff under the incumbent's position—size, type, and the reason for its existence.
- The general nature of the technical, managerial, and human relationship know-how required.
- The nature of the problem solving required: What are the key problems that must be solved by this job, and how variable are they?
- The nature and source of control or the freedom to solve problems and act, whether supervisory, procedural, vocational, or professional.

Information about accountability objectives tells what end results the job exists to achieve and the incumbent is held accountable for. The four areas of accountability are organization (including staffing, developing, and maintaining the organization); strategic planning; tactical planning, execution, and directing the attainment of objectives; and review and control.

Because the Hay Plan is based on information gathered in an interview (as opposed to the checklist method in the MPDQ), the plan's success depends on the interviewer's skills. Interviewers can be trained, however, enabling the information to be used for job descriptions, job evaluation, and compensation. The Hay Plan results in one organization can be compared with those in other organizations to ensure external pay comparability. This plan is discussed further in Chapter 8.

Methods Analyses.   Conventional job analysis procedures and structured procedures generally focus on describing the job and its general duties, the conditions under which the duties are performed, and the levels of authority, accountability, and know-how required. Equally important, however, is a description of how to do the job as efficiently and effectively as possible—the purpose of methods analyses. Although methods analysis could be used for many jobs, it is more frequently applied to nonmanagerial jobs, where individual activity units can often be more readily identified.

Methods analysis, or motion study, had its origins in industrial engineering. The following are some of the principles on which it is based:

- The movements of the two hands should be balanced and the two hands should begin and end their motions simultaneously.
- The hands should be doing productive work and should not be idle at the same time except during rest periods.
- Motions of the hands should be made in opposite and symmetrical directions and at the same time.
- The work should be arranged to permit it to be performed with an easy and natural rhythm.
- Momentum and ballistic-type movements should be employed wherever possible to reduce muscular effort.
- All tools and materials should have definite location, and they should be located in front of and close to the worker.
- Bins or other devices should be used to deliver the materials close to the point of use.
- The work place should be designed to ensure adequate illumination, proper work place height, and provision for alternated standing and sitting by the operator.
- Wherever possible, jigs, fixtures, or other mechanical devices should be used to relieve the hands of unnecessary work.
- Tools should be pre-positioned wherever possible in order to facilitate grasping them.[26]

According to industrial engineers, proper application of these principles results in greater motion economy and working efficiency.

One form of methods analysis is **work measurement** or **time study.** In essence, work measurement determines standard times for all units of work activity in a given task or job. Combining these times gives a standard time for the entire job. These standard times can be used as a basis for wage incentive plans (incentives are generally given for work performance that takes less than the standard time), cost determination, cost estimates for new products, and balancing production lines and work crews.[27] Establishing standard times is a challenge of some consequence, since the time it takes to do a job can be influenced as much by the individual doing the job as by the nature of the job itself. Consequently, determining standard times often requires measurement of the "actual effort" the individual is exerting and the "real effort" required. This process often involves trying to outguess someone else.

Common methods of collecting time data and determining standard times include the stopwatch time studies, standard data, predetermined time systems, and work sampling for determining standard time.

Work sampling is not only a technique for determining standard times but also another form of methods analysis. "Work sampling is the process of taking instantaneous samples of the work activities of individuals or groups of individuals."[28] The activities from these observations are timed and classified into predetermined categories. The result is a description of the activities by classification of a job and the percentage of time for each activity.

Work sampling can be done in several ways: The job analyst can observe the incumbent at predetermined times; a camera can be set to take photographs at predetermined times; or at a given signal, all incumbents can record their activity at that moment.

Task Inventories.   In contrast to the multiple methods that are used in work sampling to gather job data, the task inventories method of job analysis is based solely on a structured questionnaire. As such, task inventories are a listing of tasks for the occupations (jobs) being analyzed, with a provision for some type of response scale for each task listed. Using such a questionnaire, the job incumbent, supervisor, or job analyst performs the job analysis by checking the appropriate scale responses for each task listed. Suppose a specific secretarial job were to be analyzed using a task inventory using only three tasks. A part of the questionnaire might look like what follows in Exhibit 3.5. Because the task inventory method is based on a structured questionnaire, it is easy and quick to score and analyze. The results can be readily processed by computer and used for recruitment, selection, and compensation.[29]

Exhibit 3.5   *Sample of a Task Inventory Questionnaire*

	Is Task Done?	Importance	Time Spent
	1. Yes 2. No	1. Extremely unimportant 2. Very unimportant 3. Unimportant 4. About medium importance 5. Important 6. Very important 7. Extremely important	1. Very much below average 2. Below average 3. Slightly below average 4. About average 5. Slightly above average 6. Above average 7. Very much above average
Prioritize typing requirements	①②	①②③④⑤⑥⑦	①②③④⑤⑥⑦
Type address labels	①②	①②③④⑤⑥⑦	①②③④⑤⑥⑦
Type business correspondence	①②	①②③④⑤⑥⑦	①②③④⑤⑥⑦

Person-focused Techniques

Person-focused, or behavior-focused, techniques are behavioral statements resulting in the definition of the person-oriented content of jobs. The job analysis document in Exhibit 3.3 is person focused.

Position Analysis Questionnaire (PAQ).   The PAQ is a structured questionnaire containing 187 job elements and 7 additional items relating to amount of pay that are for research purposes only. The PAQ is organized into six divisions; each division contains some of the 187 job elements. The divisions and a sample of elements include the following:

- Information input: Where and how does the worker get the information used in performing the job? Examples are the use of written materials and near-visual differentiation.
- Mental processes: What reasoning, decision-making, planning, and information-processing activities are involved in performing the job? Examples are the level of reasoning in problem solving and coding/decoding.
- Work output: What physical activities does the worker perform, and what tools or devices are used? Examples are the use of keyboard devices and assembling/disassembling.
- Relationships with other people: What relationships with other people are required in performing the job? Examples are instructing and contacts with the public or customers.
- Job context: In what physical or social contexts is the work performed? Examples are high temperature and interpersonal conflict situations.
- Other job characteristics: What other activities, conditions, or characteristics are relevant to the job?[30]

Each element is also rated on one of six rating scales: (1) extent of use, (2) importance to the job, (3) amount of time, (4) possibility of occurrence, (5) applicability, and (6) other.

Using these six divisions and six rating scales, the nature of jobs is essentially determined in terms of communication, decision making, and social responsibilities; performance of skilled activities; physical activity and related environmental conditions; operation of vehicles and equipment; and processing of information. Using these five dimensions, jobs can be compared and clustered. The job clusters can then be used for staffing decisions and developing job descriptions and specifications.

The PAQ's reliance on person-oriented traits allows it to be applied to a variety of jobs and organizations without modification. This allows organizations to more easily compare their job analyses with those of other organizations.[31]

Physical Abilities Analysis (PAA).   A special subset of abilities and job demands used to analyze jobs is physical proficiency. In analyzing jobs with the PAA, seven-point scales are used to determine the extent to which each job requires each of nine abilities (from maximum performance to minimum performance). The abilities are as follows:

- Dynamic strength—defined as the ability to exert muscular force repeatedly or continuously over time

- Trunk strength—a derivative of the dynamic strength factor; characterized by resistance of trunk muscles to fatigue over repeated use
- Static strength—the force that an individual exerts in lifting, pushing, pulling, or carrying external objects
- Explosive strength—characterized by the ability to expend a maximum of energy in one or a series of maximum thrusts
- Extent flexibility—involves the ability to extend the trunk, arms, or legs (or all of these) through a range of motion in either the frontal, sagittal, or transverse planes
- Dynamic flexibility—contrasts with extent flexibility in that it involves the capacity to make rapid, repeated flexing movements, in which the resilience of the muscles in recovering from distention is critical
- Gross body coordination—the ability to coordinate the simultaneous actions of different parts of the body or body limbs while the body is in movement; frequently referenced as agility
- Gross body equilibrium—the ability to maintain balance in either an unstable position or when opposing forces are pulling
- Stamina—synonymous with cardiovascular endurance; enables the performance of prolonged bouts of aerobic work without experiencing fatigue or exhaustion[32]

With the presence of the Vocational Rehabilitation Act and other affirmative action program requirements, the need for organizations to know the precise physical requirements for jobs is increasing. Thus, the information from the PAA can be instrumental, along with job design, in accommodating more workers to jobs. Other job analysis techniques that help organizations to comply with legal requirements in hiring are the Critical Incidents Technique (CIT), the Extended CIT, and Guidelines-oriented Job Analysis (GOJA).

Critical Incidents Technique (CIT).   A frequently used job analysis technique for developing behavioral criteria is the Critical Incidents Technique (CIT).[33] The CIT requires those knowledgeable about a job to describe to a job analyst the critical job incidents (i.e., those incidents observed over the past six to twelve months that represent effective and ineffective performance). Sometimes the job analyst needs to prompt those describing the incidents by asking them to write down five key things an incumbent must be good at in the job to be analyzed, or to identify the most effective job incumbent and describe that person's behavior.[34]

Those describing the incidents are also asked to describe what led up to the incidents, what the consequences of the behavior were, and whether the behavior was under the incumbent's control. After the critical incidents (often several hundred for each job) have been gathered and described, they are rated by frequency of occurrence, importance, and the extent of ability required to perform them. Then the critical incidents and their characteristics can be clustered into job dimensions. These dimensions, which may often use only a subset of all the critical incidents obtained, can then be used to describe the job.[35] They can also be used to develop performance appraisal forms, particularly Behavioral Anchored Rating Scales (described in Chapter 6). These in turn can be useful for appraising performance and spotting training needs. As with this job analysis method and those to follow, the major disadvantages are the time required to gather the incidents and the difficulty of identifying average performance, since these methods often solicit performance extremes (e.g., ineffective or effective, or very bad or very good) and omit examples of average performance. This disadvantage, however, can be overcome by obtaining examples of all three levels of performance. This is what the Extended CIT does.

Extended CIT.   Instead of beginning by having incumbents or others knowledgeable about the jobs list examples of effective and ineffective behaviors, the Extended CIT begins by having incumbents identify *job domains*.[36] These domains (described further in the discussion of Guidelines-oriented Job Analysis) are essentially representations or umbrellas under which many specific tasks can be included. For example, a job domain for a manager may be *training*. Specific tasks that can be placed under this domain include informally and formally teaching employees to learn new job skills, engaging in self-study on and off the job, and orienting new employees to the job and the organization.

The specific tasks that come under a given domain may vary from organization to organization. Consequently, after the job domains have been identified (often between ten to twenty per job) and defined, the job analyst lists the task statements that represent each domain. The analyst writes these tasks by asking the incumbents to write examples or scenarios that reflect three different levels of performance for each domain. In describing these scenarios, the incumbents list what the main event is, the behaviors of the people in the scenario, and the consequences of those behaviors. Exhibit 3.6 shows an example of a scenario depicting excellent performance for a manager in one domain.

Using scenarios collected from the incumbents, the analyst writes task statements. Each statement is essentially an example of one behavior (or several) in a domain that is described in the scenarios. After these task statements are constructed, the incumbents (generally a different group from those writing the scenarios) indicate if they actually perform the tasks, how frequently, the difficulty in doing so, and the task's importance.

With the information obtained thus far, job descriptions can be written. By adding another step, however, the Extended CIT can be used to develop performance appraisal forms to appraise performance and spot training needs. The step added to attain these benefits includes having the incumbents (a different group to ensure validity) estimate the level of performance each task statement represents and place it in one of the domains that a previous group of incumbents initially identified.

By next having the incumbents describe the abilities (physical and mental) necessary to perform the tasks in each domain, selection procedures can be developed. In this step, the incumbents are presented with a list of abilities with short definitions and asked to indicate the amount needed to satisfactorily perform the tasks in each domain. In addition to being useful in developing selection procedures, the identification of these abilities can be used to write the job specifications on a job analysis document.

Exhibit 3.6   **An Example of Excellent Performance for a
Manager in One Job Domain**

Domain: Management and Supervision of Personnel Resources
Performance Level: Excellent

Once a year, Mary completes the performance evaluations for her six clerical staff members. These evaluations are used to make decisions about promotions and merit increases. They are also used to provide feedback to the workers. Recognizing the importance of these evaluations, Mary considers the behavior of each staff member carefully and tries to identify both the strengths and weaknesses of their performance. Mary is careful not to rely on global impressions when completing her evaluations. Instead, she provides examples of the behaviors that indicate a worker's performance level. Mary then uses these evaluations to provide feedback to members of her staff. She recommends improvements when they are needed and she acknowledges good performance as well. Thus, Mary's evaluations help improve the effectiveness of her unit.

Why is this a useful scenario?

1. Because it describes:
   Who: Mary, 6 staff members
   Main event: Performance evaluations done once a year
   Surrounding circumstances: Evaluations are used to make decisions about promotion, merit increases, and for feedback
   Behaviors: Identifies strengths and weaknesses, does not rely on global impressions, provides examples of behaviors that indicate performance levels, provides feedback, recommends needed improvements, acknowledges good performance.
   Consequences: Improves effectiveness of unit.

The CIT method takes time to develop, but Extended CIT takes even more time. The extended method, however, gathers a great deal more information from the incumbents, such as the jobs' needed abilities, performance levels, and domains. In contrast to the CIT, the Extended CIT goes through several additional development steps. Both, however, are based on identifying job behaviors, and as such, both are useful in performance appraisal and training. The same is true for the next job analysis method.

Guidelines-oriented Job Analysis (GOJA).   Another behavior-focused job analysis technique is the GOJA. GOJA was developed in response to the Uniform Guidelines—hence its name.[37] The several steps in GOJA each involve the job incumbents. Before any of these steps begin, the incumbents indicate their names, length of time on the job, experience, and the location of the current job. In the first step, incumbents list their job domains. Related duties in a job often fall into broad categories. A category with related duties is called a domain. For example, a secretary may type letters, contracts, and memos. Since these duties are related, they are put into the same domain—call it typing. Jobs typically have several domains. In the job description shown in Exhibit 3.3, the job of corporate loan assistant has ten domains.

After the domains are identified, the incumbents list the critical duties typically performed for successful job performance in each domain. Duties are observable work behaviors and something that incumbents are expected to perform. Often each domain contains several duties. The several duties relevant for each of the ten domains for the corporate loan assistant are shown in Exhibit 3.3.

Once the critical duties are identified, the incumbents indicate how frequently the duties are performed. Then each duty's degree of importance is determined.

The fourth step is the incumbents' determination of the skills and knowledge required to perform each duty. Only those skills and knowledge that cannot be learned or acquired in eight hours or less are included. This is consistent with the *Uniform Guidelines.* Not selecting an applicant who could have learned the necessary skills in less than eight hours is not a defensible (job-related) practice. This is discussed further in Chapter 5.

The fifth step is determining the physical characteristics that incumbents needed to perform their job duties. Here the incumbents respond to five open-ended statements, each related to a physical characteristic.

The sixth and final step is a description of other characteristics necessary to perform the job, such as a listing of any legally required licenses or degrees. It may also inquire about the necessity to work overtime and travel, and if so, when, where, and how frequently.

The results of the six GOJA steps are a job description such as the one shown in Exhibit 3.3, a set of individual skills, knowledge, and abilities needed to perform the job, and a basis for developing job-related selection procedures and performance appraisal forms. As with the Extended CIT and the CIT, GOJA, because it focuses on behaviors, is useful for developing performance appraisal forms and spotting training needs.[38] In addition, since skills (physical and mental) and knowledge are identified, selection procedures can also be developed as described in Chapter 5. As with the CIT and the Extended CIT, GOJA enhances employee understanding and validity of the job analysis, since job incumbents are involved in the process. This involvement, however, takes time.

Development of Job Families

The initial results of job analyses are typically many separate and unique job descriptions and employee specifications—as many as there are unique jobs. Oftentimes, however, these unique jobs are not greatly different from each other. That is, employees who perform one job can most likely easily perform several others. Those jobs are also likely to be of similar value to the organization. This is why organizations group jobs into families or classes. Jobs are placed in the same family to the extent that they require similar job specifications or have similar tasks and are of similar value to the organization (as determined by a job evaluation study as described in Chapter 8).[39]

The use of job families provides many benefits. Many organizations use them in designing their compensation programs: justifying paying jobs differently is sometimes difficult when the jobs are nearly identical. Job families can also be used to break down the walls between similar jobs and facilitate the employee movement from job to job. This, coupled with employee agreement to job assignment flexibility, is critical to organizations offering employment security to employees as described in Chapter 12. It also enables organizations to minimize overall staffing levels. Additionally, job families enable organizations to be more efficient in their recruitment, selection, performance appraisal, and training and development activities. For example, instead of developing several selection tests for several different jobs, designing only one or two may be necessary. Because job families can provide so many benefits, they are discussed again in the following chapters.

Assessing Job Analysis Methods

When one is confronted with several alternative job analysis methods, the question is: Which is the best method to use? The appropriateness of a specific job analysis method depends upon two major sets of considerations.[40] The first set represents the purposes that job analysis serves, and the second set represents several practical concerns.[41]

Purposes of Job Analysis

Exhibit 3.7 shows an assessment of how well each job analysis method serves the purposes of job analysis. Methods assessment is unique to each purpose:

■ Job descriptions and specifications: Each method is assessed by the extent to which it can be used to describe the job's range of duties, the work-

Exhibit 3.7   *Assessment of Job Analysis Methods against Job Analysis Purposes*

Purposes	FJA	MPDQ	Hay Plan	PAQ	CIT	Extended CIT	GOJA
Job descriptions	5	4	5	4	3	3	4
Job classification and evaluation	5	4	5	5	2	3	3
Recruitment and selection	4	4	4	4	4	5	5
Performance appraisal	3	3	4	3	4	5	5
Training and development	4	3	3	3	4	5	5
Human resource planning	4	4	3	4	4	4	4

1: Serves this purpose inadequately
2: Serves this purpose somewhat inadequately
3: Serves this purpose adequately
4: Serves this purpose very adequately
5: Serves this purpose extremely adequately

er requirements necessary to perform them, and the conditions under which they are performed.

- Job classification and evaluation: Each method is assessed by how easily and directly the job information collected can be used to establish job classes and families, and by how well internal equity distinctions are identified in using the method for job evaluation.

- Performance appraisal: Each method is assessed by how well it provides behavioral examples of performance and identifies the quality of those examples.

- Training and development: Each method is assessed in relation to how clearly behavioral examples of performance, and the skills and abilities required for those behaviors, are identified. This allows an evaluation of individuals against those requirements.

- Human resource planning needs: Each method is assessed by how well it facilitates a needs analysis (see Chapter 11)—an analysis that can be used to identify specific current and future human resource training needs and the skills needed for future jobs.[42]

Practical Concerns

As with job analysis purposes, several practical concerns are useful in assessing each job analysis method. Exhibit 3.8 presents the assessment of each job analysis method using these practical concerns.[43] In assessing each method against these concerns, the following definitions are used:

- Versatility and suitability: The method's appropriateness for analyzing a variety of jobs.

- Standardization: The extent to which the method yields norms that allow comparisons with different sources of job analysis data collection and at different times.

- User acceptability: The user's acceptance of the method, including its forms.

- User understandability and involvement: The extent to which those who are using the method, or are affected by its results, know what the method is about and are involved in collecting job analysis information.

- Training required: The degree of training needed by those involved in using the method.

- Readiness to use: The extent to which the method is ready to be used for a job.

- Time to completion: Time required for the method to be implemented and the results obtained.

- Reliability and validity: The consistency of the results obtained with the method and their accuracy in describing the duties, their importance, and the skills and abilities required to do the duties.

- Purposes served: The number of purposes listed earlier that the method serves.

- Utility: The amount of overall benefit or value to be gained by the organization in using the method in relation to the costs incurred in its use.

Exhibit 3.8   *Assessment of Job Analysis Methods against Several Practical Concerns*

Practical Concern	FJA	MPDQ	Hay Plan	PAQ	CIT	Extended CIT	GOJA
Versatility and suitability	5	4	4	4	5	5	5
Standardization	5	5	5	5	3	3	3
User acceptability	4	4	4	4	4	4	4
User understand-ability and involvement	4	4	5	4	5	5	5
Training required	3	3	3	3	4	5	5
Readiness to use	5	5	5	5	3	3	3
Time to completion	4	4	4	4	3	3	3
Reliability and validity	4	4	4	4	3	5	5
Purposes served	4	3	3	4	3	4	4
Utility	4	4	4	4	3	4	4

1: Served to a very limited extent
2: Served to a limited extent
3: Served to an average extent
4: Served to an above-average extent
5: Served to a great extent

The assessment of the job analysis methods presented in Exhibits 3.7 and 3.8 suggests that overall, no method is clearly superior to others. In analyzing jobs, several considerations must be weighed and any potential constraints identified. However, if the organization desires to use job analysis as a critical base for developing and directing the remaining PHRM activities, job analysis techniques providing extensive person-focused information, such as the Extended CIT or GOJA, may be most useful.

Trends in Job Analysis

Major trends in job analysis focus on assessment and the use of computer technology and human resource information systems.

Assessing Job Analysis

The assessment of job analysis can be done on the basis of how well it facilitates the organization's staffing needs and whether it results in valid staffing procedures to avoid equal employment fines and penalties. Without job descriptions and worker specifications, potentially qualified job applicants cannot be identified and valid section measures cannot be developed. The result may be rather expensive recruiting efforts and noncompliance with equal employment regulations. As such, these two measures can be used to assess the effectiveness of job analysis. More specifically, the number of qualified applicants to total applicants can be determined and the cost of equal employment violations can be calculated. The dollars-and-cents benefit of these can then be compared with the dollars-and-cents cost of the job analysis method. Because some methods may be less expensive and more appropriate, doing this assessment of job analysis is important. The result may be a search for even more appropriate and less expensive methods to analyze jobs.

Computer Technology and HRIS in Job Analysis

A vast amount of personnel information in job analysis can become part of a human resource information system. This information in turn is critical for effective personnel management. For example, changing organizational requirements for particular blends of skills, knowledge, and abilities and personality, interests, and preferences can result in job descriptions and job specifications that do not accurately reflect current organizational needs.

Computer technology can be instrumental in avoiding mismatches between organizational needs regarding skills, knowledge, and abilities and personality, interests, and preferences. Job description and job specification information crucial to job analysis components may be stored on the computer system and then used to match people with jobs.

The maintenance of timely job descriptions and specifications is also useful in determining the worth of jobs to the organization. By identifying compensable factors (job aspects to which monetary value is assigned), organizations may accurately develop the equitable pay structures discussed in Chapter 8. This process can be greatly aided by the creation of job families that can be more readily constructed with computer technology.

Summary

Job analysis significantly impacts the rest of the PHRM activities and the organization's equal employment considerations. Although job analysis cannot be done perfectly, it can and must be done. The challenge is finding the best or most appropriate way to analyze jobs. Because jobs can be analyzed in so many ways, first identifying what purposes are to be served becomes important. This knowledge is useful, since the different ways to analyze jobs serve different purposes, such as helping to develop tests for selection, criteria for performance appraisal, and needs for training programs. Once the purposes are decided, the possible ways can be narrowed down. A final selection can then be made with the consideration of several practical concerns. Once the selection is made, the organization can start to establish its human resource needs and general staffing requirements. The organization can use these to determine its recruitment, selection, and placement needs, which are discussed in the next two chapters.

Discussion Questions

1. What other areas of personnel management are related to job analysis?
2. List several purposes of job analysis.
3. How does state and federal legislation affect job analysis?
4. Discuss and review the important considerations in selecting job analysis methods.
5. Briefly, how might job analysis activities be assessed according to their importance to organizations?
6. Are jobs static? That is, will a job change over time? If so, what might cause the job to change? What implications does this have for job analysis?
7. Distinguish *job description* from *job specification.*
8. Do you think the existence of job analysis might make a personnel function (such as recruitment, performance appraisal, or compensation) less legally vulnerable? Explain.
9. Why are job analysis techniques structured? Distinguish between person-focused and job-focused approaches. Would you use the same approach for managerial and nonmanagerial workers? Why?
10. Can the reliability of job analysis information be compromised by who provides it? For example, would it make a difference in the type of job description obtained if the job incumbent rather than a personnel specialist provided the description? Could the age, sex, or race of the person providing the job analysis information influence its reliability? Explain.

PC Project

Jobs can be analyzed and described according to functions involving data, people, and things. This PC Project is based on a technique called functional job analysis. Your preferences for various activities will be compared (using graphs) with other occupational groups such as accountants, bankers, and supervisors. This analysis will give you a better understanding of functional job analysis as well as your similarity to different occupational groups. Finally, you can review the job description from the *Dictionary of Occupational Titles* that is most consistent with your profile.

C	A	S	E	S	T	U	D	Y

———————— Job Analysis Fiasco ————————

Joe MacIntosh was excited to learn that he had been selected by Professor Cindy Ferrell for one of the limited student internships at Northwest University. Joe enrolled in Northwest's Master of Science program in the College of Business Administration so that he could concentrate his study in personnel and human resource management. With an undergraduate degree in industrial psychology, Joe believed that an M.S. in management was the best way to "punch his ticket."

Joe had just completed his second semester in the program when Professor Ferrell gave him the intern assignment. Joe felt confident that the survey course in personnel he completed during this past semester would give him the information he needed to successfully complete his intern assignment. Although Joe had no previous full-time work experience, he believed the numerous summer jobs he held while working his way through school were a good exposure to the world of work.

Joe was instructed to call Bruce Johnson, personnel manager at IRC, and set up a meeting to discuss his two-month summer intern assignment. IRC manufactures small computer systems to process insurance claims. IRC has carved out a niche by not only making the hardware but also writing the software for processing claims and assisting in the installation of both the hardware and software. IRC employs one hundred people in their manufacturing division where Bruce Johnson is assigned.

At their first meeting, Bruce explained to Joe what he wanted Joe to accomplish for his internship. Bruce had joined IRC fifteen months earlier and had set out to begin formalizing personnel policies. In Bruce's estimation, a major shortcoming in IRC's personnel system was the absence of any type of job analysis. Bruce had attended a local personnel association meeting the previous month, where the guest speaker spoke on the legal consequences of not having job descriptions when personnel practices were challenged. Bruce's goal was to assemble job descriptions for each of the twenty distinct job positions at IRC.

At their second meeting, Bruce gave Joe the fifty-cent tour of the plant to familiarize Joe with their operations. Bruce made it clear that Joe would be given autonomy to interview both supervisors and employees. Bruce explained to Joe that he was giving him the "ball to run with" and would support him in whatever way possible. Joe sensed that Bruce had a number of other responsibilities and deadlines to meet and that although Bruce expressed the importance of the job analysis, he did not have much time to give to the project. That's fine, Joe thought. This will give me an opportunity to prove myself.

Bruce sent a memo to all of the supervisors, explaining who Joe was and the goal of completing a job analysis for each of the positions they supervised. Bruce asked for their full cooperation and requested they call him if there were any questions. After the memo was circulated, Joe began lining up interviews with the supervisors. Joe thought the supervisors would be the best source for job data in writing up the job descriptions and job specifications. Joe had decided to develop a narrative format similar to a sample job description illustrated in his personnel textbook used for the survey course. As a final step in collecting the job information, Joe decided to interview at least one employee in each of the twenty positions being studied.

After three weeks, Joe became discouraged over the progress he was making on what he believed to be a straightforward project. With only five weeks to go, he had managed to interview only seven of the twenty supervisors. The supervisors seemed unwilling to cooperate with Joe. They often canceled interview meetings with Joe and dragged their feet in rescheduling meetings. Joe didn't want to complain to Bruce or even suggest that he could not get the job done. Although Joe had planned to talk with all the supervisors first, the delay in setting up the interviews prompted him to begin interviewing job incumbents.

After only a few interviews with employees, Joe became concerned about the quality of information he was obtaining for writing the job descriptions and specifications. The employees, for whom he had previously interviewed their supervisors, were giving him conflicting information on their job duties and the necessary skills needed to complete the job. In general, the employees saw their jobs as more demanding, requiring more duties, and requiring more skills than what the supervisors had told Joe. Despite these conflicts, Joe decided to push ahead so that he could submit the completed descriptions and specifications to Bruce by their agreed-upon deadline.

At the end of eight weeks and several long nights, Joe proudly presented a packet of descriptions and specifications to Bruce. Despite the obstacles, Joe believed that he had achieved Bruce's objectives. Bruce thanked Joe for his efforts and reported to Professor Ferrell that Joe had success-fully completed the requirements of his internship. As the summer melded into the fall, Joe began his classes and once again immersed himself in his studies. Four months after he completed his internship, while at a local movie theater, Joe ran into one of the secretaries that worked in Bruce Johnson's personnel department. Joe asked what happened to the job analysis he had completed for IRC. "Oh," replied the secretary, "we filed them in our personnel records, but other than that, we don't see much of them. A couple of the supervisors, though, did come by to discuss with Bruce some discussions they had with their subordinates regarding differences in opinions over their job duties."

Notes

1. The essence of Title VII of the Civil Rights Act of 1964, the Equal Opportunity in Employment Act of 1972, and various court decisions is that employment decisions be made on the basis of whether the individual will be able to perform the job. To determine this, organizations should conduct job analyses to help them determine what skills, knowledge, and abilities individuals need to perform the jobs. Once this is known, selection procedures can be developed. Chapters 4 and 5 expand on the job relatedness of selection procedures.

2. More traditional definitions of job analyses are found in C. P. Sparks, "Job Analysis," in *Personnel Management,* ed. K. M. Rowland and G. R. Ferris (Boston: Allyn & Bacon, 1982), pp. 78–100; C. P. Sparks, "Job Analysis," in *Readings in Personnel and Human Resource Management*, 3d ed., ed. R. S. Schuler, S. A. Youngblood, and V. Huber (St. Paul: West, 1987); S. Gael, *Job Analysis* (San Francisco: Jossey-Bass, 1983); S. E. Bemis, A. H. Belenky, and D. A. Soder, *Job Analysis* (Washington, D.C.: BNA Books, 1983); E. J. McCormick, "Job and Task Analysis," in *Handbook of Industrial and Organizational Psychology,* ed. M. D. Dunnette (Chicago: Rand McNally, 1976), pp. 651–96; E. J. McCormick, *Job Analysis: Methods and Applications* (New York: AMACOM, 1979); J. Chorpade and T. J. Atchison, "The Concept of Job Analysis: A Review and Some Suggestions," *Public Personnel Management* 9 (1980): 134–44. In these sources, job analysis is the process of determining, either by structured or unstructured methods, the characteristics of work, often according to a set of prescribed dimensions, for the purpose of producing a job description.

3. For more discussion on the purposes of job analysis, see E. Prien, "Multi-Domain Job Analysis," paper presented at the National I-O and OB Graduate Student Convention, 23–25 April 1982, University of Maryland; R. A. Ash and E. L. Levine, "A Frame-work for Evaluating Job Analysis Methods," *Personnel* (Nov.–Dec. 1980): 53–39; P. van Rijin, *Job Analysis for Selection: An Overview* (U.S. Office of Personnel Management, Examination Services Branch, Aug. 1979); McCormick "Job and Task Analysis," in Dunnette, p. 683. Sparks, "Job Analysis and Design," pp. 81–88.

4. See L. E. Albright, "Staffing Practices in the 1980s," in *Human Resource Management for the 1980s,* ed. S. J. Carroll and R. S. Schuler (Washington, D.C.: Bureau of National Affairs, 1983); Gael, *Job Analysis;* Sparks, "Job Analysis."

5. In changing technologies, the issue of group versus individual performance arises. For a good discussion of our knowledge of this issue, see D. Ilgen, "Small Groups and Teams in Large Organizations: Some Barriers to Their Success," in *Personnel and Human Resource Management,* 3d ed. (St. Paul: West, 1987).

6. See N. M. Tichy and C. K. Barnett, "Profiles in Change: Revitalizing the Automotive Industry," *Human Resource Management,* (Winter 1985): 467–502.

7. See R. J. Aldag and A. P. Brief, *Task Design* (Glenview, Ill.: Scott, Foresman, 1979); J. R. Hackman and G. R. Oldham, *Work Redesign* (Reading, Mass.: Addison-Wesley, 1980); R. W. Griffin, *Task Design* (Glenview, Ill.: Scott, Foresman, 1982); T. Rendero, "Job Analysis Practices," *Personnel* (Jan.–Feb. 1981): 4–12; J. W. Slocum, Jr., and H. P. Sims, Jr., "A Typology for Integrating Technology, Organization, and Job Design," *Human Relations* 33 (1980): 193–212; J. R. Hackman, "The Design of Work in the 1980s," *Organizational Dynamics* (Summer 1979): 3–17; J. L. Pierce, "Job Design in Perspective," *Personnel Administrator* (Dec. 1980): 67–74; J. R. Hackman, "Work Design," in *Improving Life and Work,* ed. J. R. Hackman and J. L. Suttle (Santa Monica, Calif.: Goodyear, 1977).

8. Sec. 14.C.2. of the 1978 *Uniform Guidelines on Employee Selection Procedures.* For more legal review,

see D. E. Thompson and T. A. Thompson, "Court Standards for Job Analysis in Test Validation," *Personnel Psychology* 35 (1982): 865–74.

9. See W. F. Cascio and H. Bernardin, "Implications of Performance Appraisal Litigation for Personnel Decisions," *Personnel Psychology* 34 (1981): 211–26; D. W. Myers, "The Impact of a Selected Provision in the Federal Guidelines on Job Analysis and Training," *Personnel Administrator* (July 1981): 41–45.

10. Measures of the results or outcomes of work behaviors such as production rate or error rate may be used without a full job analysis where a review of the job information shows that these criteria are important to the user's employment situation. Similarly, measures such as turnover or absenteeism and tardiness may be used without a full job analysis if a review of job information shows these behaviors to be important in the specific situation (EEOC's *Affirmative Action Guidelines,* 1979, p. 2319).

11. These three examples are descriptions of procedures to determine empirical, content, and construct validity, respectively. They correspond in the same order to those statements in the initial "PHRM in the News." These validities are described in more detail in Chapter 18.

12. "Technology is Opening More Jobs for the Deaf," *Business Week,* 9 May, 1983, pp. 134, 138.

13. See Sparks, "Job Analysis"; Gael, *Job Analysis;* Bemis, Belenky, and Soder, *Job Analysis.*

14. Reprinted by permission of the publisher, from "Job Analysis Practices," *Personnel* (Jan.–Feb. 1981) (New York: AMACOM, a division of American Management Associations), p. 9.

    The Fair Labor Standards Act defines exempt employees as those to whom the company does not have to pay overtime, generally after forty hours per week. These employers are often managers, technical workers, and professionals. Nonexempt employees are those who are required to receive overtime pay from the organization for time in excess of forty hours per week. These employees are generally nonmanagers, blue-collar workers, and clerical employees. These classifications are used again in Chapter 9.

15. Rendero, "Job Analysis Practices," p. 7.

16. See McCormick, "Job and Task Analysis," in Dunnette for an extensive description of these methods.

17. See McCormick, *Job Analysis,* 1979, p. 64; see also M. A. Jones, "Job Descriptions Made Easy," *Personnel Journal* (May 1984): 31–34; *How to Analyze Jobs* (Stamford, Conn.: Bureau of Law & Business, 1982); *How to Write Job Descriptions the Right Way* (Stamford, Conn.: Bureau of Law & Business, 1982). These last two sources are excellent guides in how to do job analysis.

18. Only information related to selecting people on the basis of their abilities to do the job is legally needed. Information on employee interests and preferences is suggested here in order to facilitate better selection decisions and enhance employees' quality of work life.

19. "Job Analysis," *Employee Relations Law Journal* (1981): 586–87.

20. G. P. Latham and K. N. Wexley, *Increasing Productivity through Performance Appraisal* (Reading, Mass.: Addison-Wesley, 1981).

21. Other forms include the Occupation Analysis Inventory (OAI), Job Elements Method, Task Inventory paired with CODAP, Work Elements Inventory, and the Time Span of Discretion. For a description of these, see Sparks; "Job Analysis," pp. 88–91; E. J. McCormick, *Job Analysis: Methods and Applications* (New York: AMACOM, 1979); E. Jacques, *Time-Span Handbook* (London: Heineman, 1964); E. Jacques, *Measurement of Responsibility* (New York: Wiley, 1972); J. W. Cunningham, R. R. Boese, R. W. Webb, and J. J. Pass, "Systematically Derived Work Dimensions: Factor Analysis Inventory," *Journal of Applied Psychology* 68 (1983): 232–52. In addition to the use of these forms, job analysis can also be conducted by direct observation without any checklist.

22. McCormick, *Job Analysis,* 1979.

23. McCormick, "Job and Task Analysis," 1976, p. 111.

24. S. A. Fine,"Functional Job Analysis: An Approach to a Technology for Manpower Planning," *Personnel Journal* (Nov. 1974): 813–18. See also Department of Labor, *Dictionary of Occupational Titles,* vol. 2, 3d ed. (Washington, D.C.: Government Printing Office, 1965); Department of Labor, Manpower Administration, *Handbook for Analyzing Jobs* (Washington, D.C.: Government Printing Office, 1972); Department of Labor, *Task Analysis Inventories: A Method of Collecting Job Information* (Washington, D.C.: Government Printing Office, 1973); J. Markowitz, "Four Methods of Job Analysis," *Training and Development Journal* (Sept. 1981): 112–21.

25. W. W. Tornow and P. R. Pinto, "The Development of a Managerial Job Taxonomy: A System for Describing, Classifying, and Evaluating Executive Positions," *Journal of Applied Psychology* 61 (1976): 410–18. See also W. F. Cascio, *Applied Psychology in Personnel Management,* 2d ed. (Reston, Va.: Reston, 1982), p. 61.

26. H. T. Amrine, J. Ritchey, and D. S. Hulley, *Manufacturing Organization and Management,* 3d ed. (Englewood Cliffs, N.J.: Prentice-Hall, 1975); p. 130. Reprinted by permission of Prentice-Hall, Inc.

27. McCormick, *Job Analysis,* 1979, pp. 77, 79.

28. McCormick, *Job Analysis,* 1979, p. 83.

29. McCormick, *Job Analysis,* 1979, pp. 117–135.

30. E. J. McCormick and J. Tiffin, *Industrial Psychology,* 6th ed. (Englewood Cliffs, N.J.: Prentice-Hall, 1974), p. 53. Reprinted by permission of Prentice-Hall, Inc. The Position Analysis Questionnaire (PAQ) is copyrighted by the Purdue Research Foundation. The PAQ and related materials are available through the University Book Store, 360 West State Street, West Lafayette, Ind. 47906. Further information regarding the PAQ is available through PAQ Services, Inc., P.O. Box 3337 Logan, Utah 84321. Computer

processing of PAQ data is available through the PAQ Data Processing Division at that address.

For a description of the validation of a short form of the PAQ, see S. M. Colarelli, S. A. Stumpf, and S. J. Wall, "Cross-Validation of a Short Form of the Position Analysis Questionnaire," *Educational and Psychological Measurement* 42 (1982): 1279–83. The PAQ has been adopted for professional and managerial jobs; for a description, see J. C. Mitchell and E. J. McCormick, "Development of the PMPQ: A Structural Job Analysis Questionnaire for the Study of Professional and Managerial Positions" (Purdue Research Foundation, Purdue University, PMPQ Report 1, 1979).

31. For discussion of the PAQ, see E. T. Cornelius III, A. S. DeNisi, and A. G. Blencoe, "Expert and Naive Raters Using the PAQ: Does It Matter?" *Personnel Psychology* (Autumn 1984): 453–64; J. B. Shaw and J. H. Riskind, "Predicting Job Stress Using Data from the Position Analysis Questionnaire," *Journal of Applied Psychology* (May 1983): 253–61.

32. Sparks, "Job Analysis," p. 92. These physical proficiencies are taken from the extensive work of E. A. Fleishmann, in *Structure and Measurement of Physical Fitness* (Englewood Cliffs, N.J.: Prentice-Hall, 1964); "Toward a Taxonomy of Human Performance," *American Psychologist* 30 (1975): 1017–32; "Evaluating Physical Abilities Required by Jobs," *Personnel Administrator* 42 (1979): 82–92.

33. J. C. Flanagan, "The Critical Incident Technique," *Psychology Bulletin* 51 (1954): 327–58.

34. Latham and Wexley, *Increasing Productivity*, pp. 49–51.

35. These incidents can be used to form the basis for Behavioral Anchored Rating Scales (BARS) (see Chapter 6), in which case many incidents are generally deleted. See Latham and Wexley, *Increasing Productivity*, p. 54. The job description developed may not contain examples of average performance, just very good and very bad.

36. Extended CIT, named for use in this chapter, was developed and is described by S. Zedeck, S. J. Jackson, and A. Adelman in *Selection Procedures Reference Manual* (Berkeley, Calif.: University of California, 1980).

37. GOJA is a specific technique developed by a consulting firm, just as is the Hay Plan. GOJA is from Biddle and Associates and is described here with their permission. Although GOJA was developed in response to the *Uniform Guidelines,* this does not mean it is the only technique that complies with the guidelines. According to the guidelines (sec. 14A), "Any method of job analysis may be used if it provides the information required for the specific validation strategy used" (i.e., content, construct, or empirical). See also G. A. Kesselman and F. E. Lopez, "The Impact of Job Analysis on Employment Test Validity for Minority and Non Minority Accounting Personnel,"

Personnel Psychology (Spring 1979): 91–108; L. S. Kleiman and R. H. Faley, "Assessing Content Validity: Standards Set by the Court," *Personnel Psychology* (Fall 1978): 701–13.

38. When job analysis techniques are used for more than just job descriptions and employee specifications, they are often referred to as integrated techniques. The Guidelines-oriented Job Analysis, for example, is an integrated technique.

39. For an excellent description of issues related to job family or classes, see K. Pearlman, "Job Families: A Review and Discussion of Their Implications for Personnel Selection," *Psychological Bulletin* 87 (1980): 1–28. There is no one best way to construct job families or classes; the work in job evaluation is testimony to this. One newer way to do so, however, is through the job competency framework, which is based on identifying the competencies that individuals need to perform jobs. Jobs requiring similar competencies can be grouped into the same job family. Other ways to construct families can include all the ways of job analysis described in this chapter.

40. Much of the following discussion of assessing job analysis methods is based on the extremely thorough work reported by R. A. Ash and E. L. Levine in "Evaluation of Seven Job Analyses," unpublished monograph, University of South Florida, 17 July 1981. See also E. L. Levine, R. A. Ash, and N. Bennett, "Exploratory Comparative Study of Four Job Analysis Methods," *Journal of Applied Psychology* 65 (1980): 524–35; R. A. Ash and E. L. Levine, "A Framework for Evaluating Job Analysis Methods," *Personnel* (Nov.–Dec. 1980): 53–59; Sparks, "Job Analysis"; Latham and Wexley, *Increasing Productivity.*

41. The assessment of job analysis methods here is meant to be suggestive, not exhaustive and definitive. Readers are urged to review the references in note 43.

42. In addition, part of the assessment of each method for compensation includes how well Equal Pay Act provisions would be served. The assessment of each method for recruitment and selection incorporates how well the method serves the equal opportunity validity requirement (i.e. content, construct, and empirical validity showing for selection methods used). In respect to performance appraisal, the assessment incorporates how well the method serves in developing job-related appraisal forms.

43. The assessments of the several job analysis methods presented in Exhibits 3.7 and 3.8 represent extrapolation from several sources, including job analysts (the Ash and Levine study), academic researchers (Sparks, "Job Analysis"), and by an evaluation of the written documents describing each method. For a more extensive discussion, see L. Fogli, "Job Analysis and Organizational Effectiveness" (Ph.D. diss., University of California, Berkeley, 1978).

III

Staffing

4

Recruitment

Break the Habits of Mass Production

A few years back, America woke up to the fact that something was seriously wrong with its manufacturing. The response from industry has been determined and energetic. The familiar battle cry of "productivity" has been raised across the industrial heartland, spurring companies to establish productivity committees (or even czars), technology labs and control systems. Similarly, the President's Commission on Industrial Competitiveness made productivity its principal focus.

But after five or six years of attempts at industrial revitalization, the effectiveness of this emphasis is questionable, with annual productivity increases that were the hallmark of our economy for so long still lagging and imports of manufactured products pouring into our ports at an unprecedented rate. And our market shares worldwide have continued to drop. Evidently, industrialists need to re-examine their strategies for making manufacturing a formidable competitive weapon once again.

The fact is that when Asian manufacturers can ship a product into the United States at 30 percent less than what it costs American companies to make it (and that percentage of excess is typical), no amount of cutting, skimping and efficiency is going to eliminate such a gap.

Different technology and new industrial competition have changed manufacturing, so that maintaining or increasing market shares these days can seldom be accomplished by using the old productivity tools. Becoming a successful competitor today demands more than just being "efficient" and "productive." The new game requires players to use manufacturing to create powerful competitive advantages. Such advantages can be built on outstanding customer service, extremely short

deliveries, the best lead times in introducing new products or superior quality and product reliability.

Although a number of American companies, among them TRW Inc. and certain divisions of General Electric, have adopted this strategy and thus stemmed or reversed the tide, they are the exceptions. Most companies continue to flail away at cutting costs and trying to become more "efficient."

The reason for this, case research suggests, is simple and in fact not very surprising: cost-cutting, productivity and efficiency are what manufacturing managers have been trained to do, are regularly rewarded for doing and instinctively seize upon in times of crisis. It reflects their value system, the way they evaluate themselves and their subordinates. They seem enslaved by the old rules of production managers developed by Frederick W. Taylor in the early part of this century—the idea that worker productivity is the key to manufacturing success. In the new competitive world, however, a productivity mindset is just as obsolete as a counting room mentality would be in corporate finance.

To reorganize and retool our factories to compete successfully using our still-expensive American labor demands a more flexible mentality. It requires a new approach to the management of people and technology. Instead of focusing on cost reduction, we need to compete in other ways, such as producing new products more quickly, improving quality and speeding deliveries. The overall object is to be more responsive to the market. This approach requires managing inventories, scheduling, work flows, vendors and procurement in brand new ways.

This new game requires new players, or at least players who can play differently from those in the past. But finding and developing such people is a major problem. At present, the three principal sources of factory managers are workers, college graduates who like the bustle and pace of the factory and engineers who see their strength in administration. All three are reasonable sources in the abstract, but present management recruiting and development practices are turning out very few "comers" who combine imaginative, conceptual "systems thinking" with technological understanding and leadership skills.

This is perhaps the single greatest factor blocking the rebuilding of American industry. Part of the problem is that to succeed in the factory, today's young manager must be excellent in handling details and the short-term pressures of meeting daily and weekly delivery schedules and budgets. This training produces managers strong in tactical details but lacking the breadth and insights to lead in the design of new production systems and technology, our

chief hope in restoring a competitive edge.

If American industry is to regain a competitive position, it needs to pay more attention to producing a new breed of managers. The few companies that have recognized this have begun to develop people who can cope with a game of rapid movement rather than the brute power of the old mass-production factories. They are placing their best intellects in production; organizing management-development programs at top and middle levels; transferring bright young managers from marketing, finance and personnel into production, and promoting technologically oriented managers.

Technology and global competition have changed the rules of manufacturing, leaving behind outworn concepts and outdated managers. To get back in the game with the other world-class competitors, we need not only new ideas but also a substantial supply of new players.

Source: W. Skinner, *New York Times,* 25 August 1985. Copyright © 1985 by the New York Times Company. Reprinted by permission.

The preceding "PHRM in the News" highlights the environment's impact on PHRM in general and on recruitment in particular. It describes how new technologies and the increased levels of international competition are re-shaping organizations' people needs. Although the feature focuses on manu-facturing, changes are happening in the service industries as well. Conse-quently, recruitment's growing importance is highlighted here because of its ability to help organizations recapture and maintain their competitive posi-tion. Because recruitment is important in human resource management, this chapter thoroughly discusses the purposes of recruitment and its relation-ship to other personnel activities and functions, internal and external sources of job applicants, legal issues related to recruitment, and assess-ment of the recruitment activity.

Recruitment is generally defined as searching for and obtaining enough potentially qualified job candidates so that the organization can select the most appropriate people for its job needs. The recruitment activity should also be concerned with meeting job candidates' needs. In this way, recruit-ment not only attracts individuals to the organization but also increases the chance of retaining individuals once they are hired. Additionally, the recruit-ment activity must comply with an extensive set of rules and legal regulations. Specifically, then, **recruitment** is the set of activities and processes used to legally obtain a sufficient number of qualified people at the right place and time so that the people and the organization can select each other in their own best short- and long-run interests. Reflecting all these aspects of recruitment is the fact that it serves several purposes in organizations.

Purposes and Importance of Recruitment

The general purpose of recruitment is to provide an organization with a pool of potentially qualified job candidates. The specific purposes of recruitment are as follows:

- To determine the organization's present and future recruitment needs in conjunction with human resource planning and job analysis
- To increase the pool of job applicants with minimum cost
- To help increase the success rate of the selection process by reducing the number of obviously underqualified or overqualified job applicants
- To help reduce the probability that job applicants, once recruited and selected, will leave the organization after only a short period of time
- To meet the organization's responsibility for affirmative action programs and other legal and social obligations regarding work force composition
- To start identifying and preparing potential job applicants who will be appropriate candidates
- To increase organizational and individual effectiveness in the short and long term
- To evaluate the effectiveness of various techniques and locations of recruiting for all types of job applicants[1]

Several important activities are part of recruitment, including determining the organization's short- and long-range needs by job title and level in the organization, staying informed of job market conditions, developing effective recruiting materials, developing a systematic and integrated recruitment program in conjunction with other personnel activities and with line managers' cooperation, obtaining a pool of qualified job applicants, recording the number and quality of job applicants produced by the various sources and methods of recruiting, and following up on applicants, those hired and not hired, to evaluate the effectiveness of the recruiting effort. In addition, all of these activities must be done within a legal context, which may affect an organization's recruitment and selection policies and procedures.

Effectively meeting all these purposes enables the organization to avoid costly legal battles and settlements and to select only those applicants who are qualified and will thus be productive. Because the recruiting activity is as much concerned with retaining selected individuals as it is with getting an initial pool of potentially qualified job applicants, a higher quality of work life should result. In essence, effective recruiting helps an organization attain the three general purposes of PHRM discussed in Chapter 1: productivity, quality of work life, and legal compliance. An extensive set of relationships influences the attainment of these general purposes.

Relationships Influencing Recruitment

As the initial "PHRM in the News" feature illustrates, recruitment is influenced by many relationships with other PHRM activities and with the external environment. The most important of these relationships are described next.

Relationships with Other PHRM Activities

Recognizing the relationships that recruitment has with other PHRM activities is necessary for effective human resource management. Three critical relationships are those involving human resource planning, job analysis, and training and development (see Exhibit 4.1). In essence, these relationships determine who are appropriate job candidates.

Human Resource Planning.   Recruiting programs are developed around three components of planning: strategic business planning, job/role planning, and human resource planning. Strategic business planning determines the organization's goals, future products and services, growth rate, location, legal environment, and structure. Job/role planning, which follows strategic business planning, specifies what needs to be done at all levels in order to meet the strategic business plans. Human resource planning determines what types of jobs the organization needs (and will need) to fill and thus de-

Exhibit 4.1   Relationships and Aspects of the Recruitment Activity

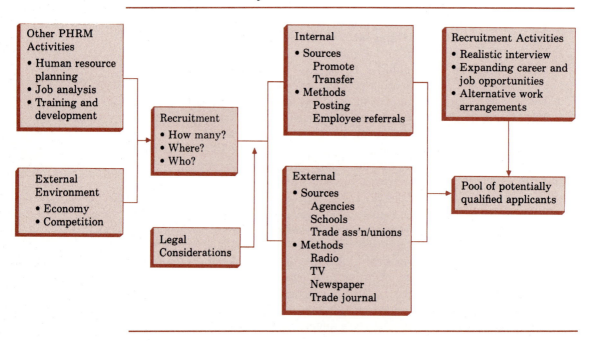

termines the skills, knowledge, and abilities that job applicants need. As part of human resource planning, programs are established in close coordination with recruiting to indicate where and how the individuals with the needed skills, knowledge, and abilities will be found. Results of past recruiting efforts can be used to determine where particular types of individuals may be located again.[2] Caution must be used here, however, because use of past sources may result in the organization's inability to fulfill its legal considerations, such as its affirmative action programs for minorities, women, and the handicapped.

Job Analysis.   Although human resource planning identifies the organization's needs for jobs, the job analysis activity is essential for identifying the necessary skills, knowledge, and abilities and the appropriate individual preferences, interests, and personality traits for each job type in each organizational setting.

> It is very difficult, if not impossible, to do effective recruiting unless the job qualifications are defined, preferably upon initiation of the employment requisition. No internal or external recruiting should begin until there is a clear and concise statement of the education, skills and experience requirements and the salary range for the job. In larger organizations, this information is readily available in job descriptions and salary structures. Yet numerous hours and dollars are spent in recruiting, particularly recruiting advertising, where the applicant is required to play a "guessing game" about the job qualifications required.[3]

Recruitment based on job analysis helps ensure that the people who are hired have the ability to do the job.

Training and Development.   If recruiting activities produce a large pool of qualified job applicants, the need for employee training may be minimal. But recruiting activities may produce only a large, potentially unqualified pool of job applicants. At this point, the organization may weigh the costs of selection versus those of training. If the costs of selection are deemed greater than those associated with training, the organization may hire all needed applicants and train them.

Developing training programs can also be a critical way in which organizations can accommodate handicapped job applicants, thus making it easier to recruit and retain disabled individuals. For example, AT&T has developed a training program for managers who supervise disabled people; Sears, Roebuck & Company has been conducting an affirmative action program for the disabled since 1947; Control Data Corporation provides suddenly disabled employees with computer training to help them get back on the job; and IBM has a program to train and place severely physically handicapped people in entry-level computer jobs. The result of all these companies' training efforts is to make employment easier for handicapped employees and to encourage those employees to stay on the job.[4] These training efforts help the companies meet equal opportunity employment goals as well.

Relationships with the External Environment

The type of employees an organization needs often depends upon the external environment. For example, the current shortage of skilled workers has presented organizations with a real challenge as the organization attempts to recruit skilled workers in sufficient numbers.[5] In times of national economic recession, while most executives worry about job security, chief financial officers and others who can cut costs still get calls from recruiters.[6] In times of intense international competition and change, organizations are faced with the need to recruit a new breed of managers to run manufacturing plants, as described in the initial "PHRM in the News."

Other factors in the external environment also affect recruitment. Consider the results produced by the threatened nationwide boycott of Coca-Cola in July 1981 by the People United to Save Humanity (PUSH). Under the "moral convenant" announced by PUSH founder the Reverend Jesse Jackson and Coca-Cola president Donald R. Keough, Coca-Cola promised to more actively recruit black applicants and promote them into management and to expand the pool of black-owned company distributors.[7]

An extensive set of legal considerations also influences an organization's recruitment activity.

Legal Considerations in Recruitment

Legal considerations, obligations, and requirements play a critical role in the recruitment of most American companies. Although much of the legal framework facing PHRM is directed at employment decisions, such as hiring, firing, health and safety, and compensation, it essentially begins with the organization's search for job applicants, whether conducted inside the organization or outside. Although the equal employment opportunity laws and acts in reference to staffing decisions (e.g., hiring, firing, demoting, transferring, and training) specifically apply only to selection, they have such a direct impact on recruitment that some of them are discussed here. Other equal employment opportunity laws and acts applicable to staffing are discussed in this chapter and the next. The legal considerations discussed here are relevant to an organization's recruitment activity because they essentially help identify who will be selected and, therefore, who should be recruited. Thus, the legal considerations discussed here are those resulting from affirmative action programs. Discussing these considerations in some detail is important, because even if affirmative action programs were not legally required, many organizations would apparently still support them:

> **Affirmative-action goals are favored by several big companies.**
> A draft proposal to remove affirmative-action goals and timetables from government rules for federal contractors will come up for review by the Reagan administration, probably this month. But many firms support flexible goals and want to continue using them. General Electric, AT&T and IBM find the system a useful way of tracking hiring and promotion progress and will continue it.
> Hewlett-Packard says the goals-and-time-tables method helped it measure the rise in minority and female employment, to 18% and 42%, respectively, of its 49,000-member work force (from 7% and 39% in 1966). But many construction contractors support changes, saying goals too often become equated with fixed quotas.

PepsiCo, which isn't a federal contractor, says goals are "not a real-world tool." It uses other methods.[8]

As this quotation suggests, however, many of the legal considerations described here may not last forever.[9]

Affirmative Action Programs and Recruiting

Federal contractors are required to "take affirmative action to employ and advance in employment qualified handicapped individuals at all levels of employment" (Section 503 of the Vocational Rehabilitation Act of 1973). This includes the executive level. A "handicap" is nebulously defined in the rules set by the enforcing agency—the Office of Federal Contract Compliance Programs (OFCCP)—as any "impairment which substantially limits one or more of a person's major life activities." Whatever else this definition may mean, one thing is certain: employment is a "major life activity." Under the OFCCP rules, a "qualified handicapped" is one who is "capable of performing a job's essential functions."[10]

The rules further provide that employers with fifty or more employees who hold federal contracts totaling $50,000 or more must prepare written affirmative action programs for handicapped workers in each of their establishments—for example, in each plant or field office. This condition must be met within 120 days after the contractor receives the federal contract. Those who hold contracts or subcontracts of less than $2,500 are not covered by this act. Those with federal contracts that range from $2,500 to $50,000 are required to include an affirmative action clause in their contracts, but they do not have to have a written affirmative action plan.[11]

Organizations must also engage in affirmative action programs for protected group members. These programs, as well as those for the handicapped, are designed to ensure proportional representation (or to correct underutilization) of women and minorities in each organization's work force. In essence, affirmative action programs (AAPs) may encompass an extensive set of recruiting programs. These programs are designed to facilitate an organization's commitment to provide and achieve proportional representation or parity (or to correct underutilization) in its work force with the relevant labor market of protected group members (defined by Title VII to include women, blacks, Hispanics, American Indians, and Asian-Pacific Islanders).

With the exception of the AAP provisions for handicapped individuals just noted, affirmative action programs generally arise from three different conditions:

1. If a company has a federal contract greater than $50,000 and fifty employees, it is required to file with the Office of Federal Contract Compliance Programs an affirmative action plan outlining steps to be taken for correcting "underutilization" in places where it has been identified. Goals and quotas are a critical part of these plans.

2. A federal court may require an AAP if a discrimination suit brought against the organization through the Equal Employment Opportunity Commission (EEOC) has found evidence of past discrimination. An AAP

under these conditions is generally part of a consent decree, a statement indicating the specific affirmative action steps an organization will take.

3. The organization may voluntarily decide to establish certain goals for hiring and promoting women, members of minority groups, and handicapped individuals. The exact content of AAPs depends on the organization, the area it is located in, and the extent to which various minorities are underrepresented.

The following discusses each of these three conditions in more detail.

Federal Contractors' AAPs

The specific components of an AAP for a federal contractor are specified by the Department of Labor in the Office of Federal Contract Compliance Programs. The AAPs are currently enforced by the OFCCP and EEOC through Executive Order (EO) 11246.

AAPs often contain several important components, including **utilization** and **availability analyses, goals**, and **timetables**.

> An acceptable affirmative action program must include an analysis of areas within which the contractor is deficient in the utilization of minority groups and women, and further, goals, and timetables to which the contractor's good-faith efforts must be directed to correct the deficiencies.[12]

A **utilization analysis** determines the number of minorities and women employed in different jobs within an organization. An **availability analysis** measures how many minorities and women are available to work in the relevant labor market of an organization. If an organization is employing fewer minorities and women than are available, a state of **underutilization** exists.

After the completion of the utilization and availability analyses, **goals** and **timetables** are written to specify how an organization plans to correct any underutilization. Because goals and timetables become the organization's commitment to equal employment, they must be realistic and attainable. An example of a utilization plan for one job group in an organization is shown in Exhibit 4.2.[13]

To aid an organization's efforts to attain the specified goals and timetables, it is also important for the organization to make sure its employment policies, practices, and procedures are operating to facilitate goal attainment. This generally requires an assessment of its current policies, practices, and procedures. The assessment may reveal policies, practices, and procedures that are not operating to facilitate goal attainment if underutilization exists. If so, the policies, practices, and procedures need to be modified.

Consent Decrees

A famous affirmative action program resulting from a consent decree involved American Telephone and Telegraph (AT&T), which the EEOC found to be discriminating against women. Although AT&T did not admit nor was required to admit any act of discrimination, it entered into a consent decree

Utilization, Goals, and Timetables   *Exhibit 4.2*

Job Group: ABC
As of: 2/14/86

Current Utilization

	Male	Female	White	Black	Hisp.	Asian	A. Ind.	Min.	Total
Employees (#)	193	7	186	4	3	6	1	14	200
Employees (%)	96.5	3.5	93.0	2.0	1.5	3.0	.5	7.0	###
Availability (%)	88.0	12.0	66.0	15.0	14.0	4.0	1.0	34.0	100.0
Underutilized ?	No	Yes	No	Yes	Yes	Yes	Yes	Yes	###

Based on expansion of 36

Goals

	Male	Female	White	Black	Hisp.	Asian	A. Ind.	Min.	Total
Long-range goal (%)		15.0		15.5	14.5	4.0	1.0	35.0	100.0
Long-range goal (#)		35		37	34	9	2	82	236
Annual Placement (%)		22.5		21.0	19.7	7.2	1.8	49.7	###

Timetables

If 12 openings (5.1% turnover)—Empl. opportunities 1st yr. 48

	Male	Female	White	Black	Hisp.	Asian	A. Ind.	Min.	Total
Years to Goal (#)		14		15	15	1	3	15	###
Hired first year		11		10	9	3	<1	24	###
Hired 2nd year on		3		3	2		<1	6	###

If 24 openings (10.2% turnover)—Empl. opportunities 1st yr. 60

	Male	Female	White	Black	Hisp.	Asian	A. Ind.	Min.	Total
Years to goal (#)		7		11	10	1	2	9	###
Hired first year		14		13	12	4	1	30	###
Hired 2nd year on		5		5	5		<1	12	###

If 47 openings (19.9% turnover)—Empl. opportunities 1st yr. 83

	Male	Female	White	Black	Hisp.	Asian	A. Ind.	Min.	Total
Years to goal (#)		4		5	5	1	1	4	###
Hired first year		19		17	16	6	2	41	###
Hired 2nd year on		11		10	9			23	###

Projected openings 18 (7.6% turnover)—Empl. opportunities 1st yr. 54

	Male	Female	White	Black	Hisp.	Asian	A. Ind.	Min.	Total
Years to goal (#)		10		14	14	1	2	11	###
Hired first year		12		11	11	4	<1	27	###
Hired 2nd year on		4		4	4		<1	9	###

Utilization Analysis

	Male	Female	White	Black	Hisp.	Asian	A. Ind.	Total
Employees (#)	193	7	186	4	3	6	1	200
Employees (%)	96.5	3.5	93.0	2.0	1.5	3.0	.5	###
Availability (%)	88.0	12.0	66.0	15.0	14.0	4.0	1.0	100.0
Should have (#)	176	24	132	30	28	8	2	###
Underutilized ?	No	Yes	No	Yes	Yes	Yes	Yes	###
Calculation type		Z		Z	Z	Z	P	###
Statistical value		3.59		5.05	4.99	.54	.73	###
Z or probability		0.00		0.00	0.00	.59	.36	###
Significant ?	No	Yes	No	Yes	Yes	No	No	###
Additional needed		8		16	15			###

after the EEOC opposed its application for a rate increase. The first five-year cost of this settlement (1973–1978) is estimated to have been more than $75 million.[14] In a more recent settlement, the U.S. district court in Birmingham, Alabama, required the city of Birmingham and Jefferson County to enter into a $300,000 consent decree. In addition to the dollar payments the city must make, it must also try to reach certain percentage goals of qualified blacks and women in various job categories. Although these goals, as well as those which are a part of the federal contractor's AAP, only specify percentages, in essence they are often seen as establishing **quotas.** That is, the goals establish that an organization must hire a certain number of blacks or minorities to correct underutilization or past discrimination in employment. Although these quotas may result, according to some, in a violation of the Fourteenth Amendment, as well as Title VII protection against all employment discrimination (e.g., white males may not be hired because an organization has a quota to meet), the courts have generally held in favor of quotas and goals as the only way to reverse previous practices of discrimination (*Detroit Police Officers Association* v. *Coleman Young,* 1979; *Charles L. Maehren* v. *City of Seattle,* 1979; and *City of St. Louis* v. *U.S.A.,* 1980). Nevertheless, the issue of reverse discrimination is being heard more frequently, as evidenced by a 1985 reverse discrimination case in Washington, D.C.:

> Eight white District of Columbia firefighters have won a reverse discrimination suit against the city. U.S. District Court Judge Joyce Green has ruled that the firefighters are eligible for back pay and retroactive pensions estimated to be worth about $160,000 (*Edward Dougherty* v. *Marion Barry, Jr.,* Civil Action Nos. 82–1687 and 83–0314). The eight are now retired.
>
> Green found that the white firefighters all had more experience and better "objective credentials" than the two blacks who were appointed as deputy fire chiefs in 1980. "Based on the evidence, one conclusion is clear: race was a substantial, significant, determinative factor" in the promotion of the blacks, Green concluded.[15]

In a related case, the Court ruled that federal courts could not ignore a seniority-based layoff policy and modify a consent decree to prevent the layoff of black workers (*Firefighters Local Union 1784* v. *Stotts,* 1984).

Since this issue relates more directly to selection, it is addressed in more detail in Chapter 5. Reverse discrimination as it relates to recruitment is discussed here as an issue in organizations establishing voluntary AAPs.

Voluntary AAPs

Organizations may establish their own voluntary affirmative action programs without pressure from the EEOC or OFCCP. In fact, organizations may benefit from using EEOC guidelines that support voluntary AAPs. By doing so, however, they may still run the risk of being charged with reverse discrimination.[16] The key considerations in an organization's establishment of a legal voluntary AAP are that it be remedial in purpose, limited in its duration, restricted in its reverse discrimination impact—that is, it does not operate as an absolute ban on nonminorities—and flexible in implementation. When an organization's voluntary AAP has these characteristics, the risk of losing a reverse discrimination suit may be minimized.

A Matter of Commitment

Although equal employment guidelines, goals, and quotas are usually established for the organizations by the EEOC, the OFCCP, or the courts, the actual implementation of these efforts is in the hands of organizations' managers. As with many other personnel techniques, having them is one thing and using or abiding by them is another. If organizations are to fulfill the spirit as well as the letter of the law, managers must be committed to implementing goals.[17] The following are six important characteristics of equal employment opportunities EEO efforts that increase managerial commitment:

- Government influence on goals, policies, and practices
- Clarity of goals
- Top management support for implementing goals
- Managerial accountability for implementing goals
- Managerial participation in setting goals and policies
- Amount of training managers receive for implementing goals[18]

The government not only establishes goals, policies, and practices for EEO but also furnishes technical assistance to organizations trying to comply. Knowledge of these laws and regulations is an important first step in developing an effective EEO program and an AAP. Although doing these steps requires a great deal of time and effort, the results of affirmative action programs are measurable. The following "PHRM in the News" feature provides the results of some measurements.

Now that we are aware of the legal considerations of organizations in recruitment, an appropriate step is to examine the sources of potentially qualified job applicants and the methods used to recruit them. First examined are the internal sources and methods, followed by the external sources and methods.

Obtaining Job Applicants: Sources and Methods

Internal Sources

Internal sources include present employees, friends of employees, former employees, and former applicants. Promotions, demotions, and transfers can also provide applicants for departments or divisions within the organization.[19] Current employees are a source of job applicants in two respects: they can refer friends to the organization, and they can also become applicants themselves by potential promotion transfer.

Promotions.   The case for promotion from within rests on several sound arguments. One is that internal employees are better qualified. "Even jobs that do not seem unique require familiarity with the people, procedures, policies, and special characteristics of the organization in which they are performed."[20] Another is that employees are likely to feel more secure and to identify their long-term interests with the organization that provides them

Affirmative Action: Its Future and Its Effects

Affirmative action efforts have played an important role in improving job opportunities for minorities and women, according to a study conducted by the Potomac Institute, a Washington, D.C., research organization. "There can be no doubt that much of the change in employment patterns" during the 1970s "is attributable to affirmative action," the study notes.

The study, which was based on a statistical analysis of EEO-1 forms filed between 1970 and 1979, credits the improvements to affirmative action requirements imposed on federal contractors, an "intensive educational program" by the National Association of Manufacturers, and "systemic changes" in American industry. The job-related gains made by women and minorities, the study observes, include:

- Blacks' overall share of the private job market rose from 10.1 percent in 1970 to 11.6 percent in 1980. In specific EEO-1 categories, black representation among managers rose from 1.9 percent to 4.0 percent, among professionals from 2.5 percent to 4.3 percent, office and clerical from 7.2 percent to 11.2 percent, and skilled craft workers from 5.6 percent to 8.4 percent.
- Women's share of the private job market rose from 34.4 percent to 41 percent, with the biggest increase in the top three white-collar categories: officials and managers (10.2 percent to 18.5 percent), professionals (24.6

percent to 37.7 percent), and technicians (26.4 percent to 40.2 percent).

- Hispanics' share jumped from 3.6 percent to 5.4 percent, representing a substantial increase in the Hispanic working population. Hispanic representation among managers increased from 1 percent to 2.2 percent, among professionals from 1.1 percent to 1.9 percent, office and clericals from 2.6 percent to 4.6 percent, and among craft workers from 3.0 to 5.2 percent.

The employment gains achieved by minorities and women during the 1970s—a period marked by contractions in economic growth and high unemployment—are evidence of the effectiveness of affirmative action, the study says. "This positive evidence," it adds, "comes at a time when the critics of affirmative action—including the President, the Attorney General, and other high government officials—are waging a campaign to strip the program of its basic elements." Affirmative action is a program developed "to remedy discrimination in employment, not poverty or inadequate education," it stresses, concluding that "it is fair to assume that the success of affirmative action would have been greater had those factors not been present." ("A Decade of New Opportunity: Affirmative Action in the 1970s," Potomac Institute, 1501 18th Street, N.W., Washington, D.C., 20036; $6)

Source: Fair Employment Practices, 4 April 1984, p. 4. Reprinted by permission from Fair Employment Practices Service, copyright 1985 by The Bureau of National Affairs, Inc., Washington, D.C.

the first choice of job opportunities. Availability of promotions within an organization can also motivate employees to perform, and internal promotion can be much less expensive to the organization in both time and money. Luring applicants from outside the organization can be an expensive process. Often the new recruit is brought in at a salary higher than those currently in similar positions in the organization, and the costs to the company of relocating the new recruit and his or her family may range from $10,000 to $50,000. Soon other employees learn of this new recruit. The result, especially if the new recruit fails to contribute as expected, is dissatisfaction among the current employees. In addition, the incentive value of promotions diminishes.[21]

Disadvantages of a **promotion-from-within** policy may include an inability to find the best-qualified person. Also, infighting, inbreeding, and lack of varied perspectives and interests may result. If an organization has a policy of promotion from within, it must identify, select, and pressure candidates for the promotions. When done during times of rapid organizational growth, almost all employees may be identified and selected as promotable because the organization faces a managerial shortage. During growth times, these individuals, regardless of qualifications, are promoted. The rapid growth of the company covers whatever managerial deficiencies they possess. Then when the company's growth rate abates, the company is faced with excessive managers whose poor performance cannot be covered.[22]

Considering these advantages and disadvantages, it is not surprising to find organizations doing some internal promoting while obtaining some applicants from external sources. In addition, organizations tend to obtain particular types of employees from particular sources. For example, many organizations are more likely to hire highly trained professionals and high-level managers from the outside than to promote from within.[23] Further discussion of what sources are used for what applicants is presented later in this chapter. But whether internal or external sources of promotion are used, promotion considerations must incorporate affirmative action and equal employment concerns.

Transfers.   Another critical way to recruit internally is by transferring current employees without promotion. Transfers are often important in providing employees with the more broad-based view of the organization that is necessary for future promotions. Consequently, providing transfers can be a way of getting job applicants from outside the organization as well as inside. But just as promotions require consideration of affirmative action and equal employment, so do transfers. Thus, the first step in deciding to use promotions or transfers is often consideration of affirmative action and equal employment requirements. Once this consideration is accounted for, the criteria used to select the candidates for promotion or transfer must be decided.

A major issue in promoting or transferring candidates from within is seniority versus performance or merit. Unions seem to prefer promotion and transfer based on seniority, and some organizations prefer promotion or transfer based on ability. When seniority systems exist, promotion or transfer decisions can be made on the basis of seniority even if the results may appear contrary to affirmative action and equal employment (*California Brew-*

ers Association v. *Bryant*, 1980; *International Brotherhood of Teamsters* v. *United States*, 1977).

Occasionally the criterion for promotion is personal judgment. This is particularly true for middle- and upper-level managerial positions. Again, this criterion is difficult to defend under legal guidelines, so many organizations have had to reconsider their methods for promotion. The use of test results from managerial assessment centers appears to be one alternative to personal judgments and impressions.[24] Since assessment centers are used more frequently as a selection device than as a recruiting device, they are discussed more extensively in Chapter 5. In addition, the value of the assessment center for predicting future job performance and progression is examined in Chapter 18.

Once the criteria or criterion is established, the candidates are identified through several internal methods of recruitment.

Internal Methods

Job vacancies can be located by a notice on the bulletin board, word of mouth, company personnel records, promotion lists based on performance, potential ratings obtained from assessment activities, seniority lists, and lists generated by the skills inventory in an organization's HRIS. The most frequently used methods include **job posting** and informal contracts, particularly **employee referral programs (ERPs).**

Job Posting.   Job posting, a method of prominently displaying current job openings, extends an open invitation to all employees in an organization. It serves the following purposes:

- Provides opportunities for employee growth and development
- Provides equal opportunity for advancement to all employees
- Creates a greater openness in the organization by making opportunities known to all employees
- Increases staff awareness of salary grades, job descriptions, general promotion and transfer procedures, and what constitutes effective job performance
- Communicates organization goals and objectives and allows each individual the opportunity to find a personal fit in the organization job structure.[25]

Although job postings are usually found on bulletin boards, they also appear in company newsletters and are announced at staff meetings. Generally, except for management positions, all openings are posted. Sometimes specific salary information is included, but job grade and pay range are more typical. Job posting is beneficial for organizations because it improves morale, provides employees with the opportunity for job variety, facilitates a better matching of employee skills and needs, and fills positions at a low cost.[26]

These benefits are not always realized. Conflicts are sometimes created if an "heir apparent" in the department is passed over in favor of an outside candidate. Conversely, the system may lose credibility if the successful candidate within the department has apparently been identified in advance and the manager is merely going through the motions in considering outsiders. In addition, the morale of the unsuccessful candidates may suffer if feedback is not carefully handled. Finally, choices can be more difficult for the selecting manager if two or three equally qualified candidates are encountered.

Employee Referral Programs.   Employee referral programs (ERPs) are word-of-mouth advertisements whereby employees are rewarded for referring skilled applicants to organizations.[27] This method is a low-cost-per-hire way of recruiting, even though in many cases the candidates come from outside the organization. This method is useful for finding applicants in short supply and managerial candidates. For successful referrals, employees may receive five hundred dollars, especially if they refer someone with a critical skill or an occupation much in demand, like a robotics engineer. A major concern with ERPs is that the referred individuals are likely to be similar in type (e.g., race and sex) to those currently in the organization. Although this may not necessarily preclude fulfilling AAP obligations, the potential exists.[28]

External Sources

Recruiting internally does not always produce enough qualified job applicants, especially for organizations that are growing rapidly or that have a large demand for high-talent professional, skilled, and managerial employees. Therefore, organizations need to recruit from external sources. Recruiting from the outside has a number of advantages, including bringing in people with new ideas. Hiring an already trained professional or skilled employee is often cheaper and easier, particularly when the organization has an immediate demand for scarce labor skills and talents. External sources can also supply temporary employees, who provide the organization with much more flexibility than permanent employees. A list of external sources including employee referrals is shown in Exhibit 4.3.

Walk-ins.   As illustrated in Exhibit 4.3, the use of walk-ins in recruiting is especially prevalent for clerical and plant/service job applicants. In the walk-in method, individuals become applicants by walking into an organization's employment office. This method, like employee referrals, is relatively informal and inexpensive and is almost as effective as employee referrals in retaining applicants once hired.[29] Unlike referrals, nonreferred applicants may know less about the specific jobs available and may come without the implicit recommendation of a current employee. This may be a disadvantage in comparison to referrals, since current employees may be reluctant to refer or recommend unsatisfactory applicants.[30]

Although walk-ins may be a relatively inexpensive source of applicants, the walk-in method is not used extensively by managerial, professional, and sales applicants. Furthermore, it tends to be a passive source and thus may not provide sufficient numbers of applicants to help fulfill affirmative action and equal employment considerations. These aspects may be reduced by attracting walk-ins through open house events, which can attract all types of applicants from the nearby community.[31] Open houses, however, may not be

Exhibit 4.3   *Organizational Recruiting Methods*
by Occupation

	Occupation*				
Source	*Office/ Clerical*	*Plant/ Service*	*Sales*	*Professional/ Technical*	*Management*
Employee referrals	92	94	74	68	65
Walk-ins	87	92	46	46	40
Newspaper advertising	68	88	75	89	82
Local high schools or trade schools	66	61	6	27	7
U.S. Employment Service (USES)	63	72	34	41	27
Community agencies	55	57	22	34	28
Private employment agencies	44	11	63	71	75
(company pays fee)	(31)	(5)	(49)	(48)	(65)
Career conferences/ job fairs	19	16	19	37	17
Colleges/universities	17	9	48	74	50
Advertising in special publications	12	6	43	75	57
Professional societies	5	19	17	52	36
Radio-TV advertising	5	8	2	7	4
Search firms	1	2	2	31	54
Unions	1	12	0	3	0

**Note:* Figures are percentages of companies providing data for each employee group.

Source: Reprinted by special permission from *Personnel Policies Forum,* Survey No. 126, Recruiting Policies & Practice, pp. 4–5. Copyright © 1979, by the Bureau of National Affairs Inc., Washington, D.C.

appropriate for every organization, and even if they are, sufficient numbers of some applicants can be attained only by using other sources, such as employment agencies.

Employment Agencies.   Employment agencies are a good source of temporary employees—and an excellent source of permanent employees. Employment agencies may be public or private. The **public employment agencies** in the United States are under the umbrella of the U.S. Training and Employment Service (USTES). The USTES sets national policies and oversees the operations of state employment services, which have branch offices in many cities. The Social Security Act in general provides that any worker who has been laid off from a job must register with the state employment agency in order to be eligible for unemployment benefits. The agencies then have a roster of potential applicants to assist organizations looking for job applicants.

State employment agencies provide a wide range of services. Most of these services are supported by employer contributions to the state unemployment funds. The agencies offer counseling, testing, and placement services to everyone. They provide special services to individuals, military veterans, minority groups, and college, technical, and professional people. The state agencies also make up a nationwide network of job information and applicant information in the form of job banks. These job banks have one drawback, however: USTES and its state agencies do not actually recruit people but passively assist those who come to them, and often those who do come in may be untrained or only marginally qualified for most jobs.

Private employment agencies tend to serve two groups of job applicants: professional or managerial and unskilled. The agencies dealing with the unskilled group often provide job candidates that employers would otherwise have a difficult time finding. Many of the employers looking for unskilled workers do not have the resources to do their own recruiting or have only temporary or seasonal demands for them.

Private agencies play a major role in recruiting professional and managerial candidates. These agencies supply services for applicants of all ages; most, however, have had some work experience beyond college. During the past ten years, the executive recruiting industry has grown phenomenally. The fees that these agencies charge range up to one-third of the first year's total salary and bonus package for the job to be filled. Yes, the search firm may get this money whether or not it is successful in finding someone for the job.[32]

Even if it is successful, the cost to the organization may be much greater than the fees charged. In the prescreening process, for example, the search firm may have erred in rejecting a candidate who would have done well, or by identifying a candidate who will not do well. These errors, discussed in Chapter 5, pose additional costs to the organization.[33] The organization can help minimize these costs, however, by closely monitoring the search firm's activities. Note also that these agencies may prescreen applicants who are already working with other organizations. Consequently, in addition to the expense, this method of dealing with a potential candidate is apt to be secretive and counter to the openness that is desirable in an organization's employment process.

Temporary Help Agencies.   At the same time that private recruiting agencies provide applicants for full-time positions, temporary help agencies represent a $3 billion business. Over three thousand temporary help offices annually employ more than 2.5 million people.[34] Their use is growing as skilled and semi-skilled individuals find it preferable to work less than a forty-hour week or on a schedule of their own choosing. Temporary employees (or temps) also have the chance to work in a variety of organizations; consequently, they can satisfy preferences for schedule flexibility and work place variety. Furthermore, temps may receive higher direct compensation than the organization's permanent staff, although they also generally forgo indirect benefits (these benefits are discussed in Chapter 10).

Organizations are using temporary help agencies more than ever, because some hard-to-get skills are available nowhere else (this is especially true for small companies who aren't highly visible or can't spend the time to recruit). In addition, many organizations need people only for a short time. Getting employees without an extensive search while retaining the flexibility to reduce the work force without costly layoffs and potential unemployment compensation payments is an obvious advantage. These advantages must be weighed against the higher direct compensation rate, since both the agency and the temp must be paid.

Trade Associations and Unions.   Unions for the building trades and maritime workers assume responsibility for supplying employers with skilled labor. This practice takes many labor decisions, such as job assignment, out of company hands. However, the Taft-Hartley Act restricts these "hiring hall" practices to a limited number of industries (see Chapter 16).

Trade and professional associations are also important sources for recruiting. Their newsletters and annual meetings often provide notice of employment opportunities. Annual meetings can also offer employers and potential job applicants an opportunity to meet. Communities and schools have adopted this idea and now bring together large numbers of employers and job seekers at **job fairs**. With only a limited time for interviews, such fairs serve only as an initial step in the recruitment process. Nevertheless, they provide an effective means for both employers and individuals.

Schools.   Schools can be categorized into three types: high schools, vocational and technical schools, and colleges and universities. All are important sources of recruits for most organizations, although their importance varies depending on the type of applicant sought.[35] For example, if an organization is recruiting for managerial, technical, or professional applicants, then colleges and universities are the most important source, as illustrated in the following "PHRM in the News" feature. This is currently the case with teachers as well:

> **Teacher shortages force school districts to recruit aggressively.**
> "You have to be innovative nowadays with so few people going into teaching," says an official in Florida's Broward County School District. Its six recruiters visited 60 colleges last year. In May it will host an open house to lure 250 job-hunting teachers to the district. Austin, Texas, and Birmingham, Mich., school officials hit the college circuit looking for teachers. Birmingham hasn't done so since 1973.
> The National Center for Education Statistics predicts a shortage of 28,000 teachers by 1987. Meanwhile, the teacher "burnout" rate is high; many others are retiring. Columbia University Teachers College offers a program jointly with Kenyon College of Ohio to lure liberal arts majors into teaching.
> "I'm telling our graduating teachers there hasn't been a better time to look for a job," says a Wayne State University placement official.[36]

Colleges, however, become less important when an organization is seeking plant/service and clerical employees, as shown in Exhibit 4.3.

Recruiting at colleges and universities is often an expensive process, even if the recruiting visit eventually produces job offers and acceptances. Approximately 30 percent of the applicants hired from college leave the organization within the first five years of their employment. This rate of turnover is even higher for graduate management students.

Recruiting: Getting People You Want

There is no best way to recruit new employees, asserts Robert K. Armstrong, manager of professional staffing at DuPont Company. While emphasizing that recruiting should change as the company changes, Armstrong maintains that well-thought-out, long-term programs must be developed to "generate candidates to meet organizational needs" for technical/professional and administrative personnel.

At DuPont, this need is met principally through college recruitment programs, which, Armstrong declares, are essential, given the fierce competition for college and university graduates trained as scientists and engineers. An effective college recruitment effort, he adds, should encompass a series of programs designed to develop a positive image for the firm among faculty, administrators, and students. DuPont's effort, for example, includes:

- Summer student programs—Summer student programs are highly attractive because they produce a "greater yield of prospective hirees in a shorter time," Armstrong says. DuPont's summer programs are specifically designed to identify well before graduation students whom the company might consider for employment, evaluate for regular employment those students who work as summer interns, and attract the most qualified interns to the company. DuPont also sponsors an annual Summer Symposium to expose prospective employees to the variety of career opportunities available within the company.

- Faculty/administration visitation programs—DuPont conducts two-day visitation programs for college department heads, minority coordinators, and placement directors. The objective of these sessions, Armstrong says, is to enable the company to develop a close relationship with the people who can influence students' career and employment choices. Visitation programs, he adds, increase college administrators' exposure to high technology and make them more aware of the "many challenging careers" awaiting graduates who choose the company.

- Educational aid programs—DuPont has supported colleges for many years and uses financial aid to "market" the company. It provides unrestricted grants to university departments in which it has a particular interest.

Armstrong adds that DuPont also maintains a strong advertising program that produces a mass of recruiting literature, placement manuals, and inserts for college newspapers and magazines. The company also has an "aggressive follow-up" policy of campus and site visits conducted by former employees, such as retirees, who volunteer their time to talk to students. These "roving ambassadors," Armstrong observes, have contributed significantly to the success of the company's recruitment efforts.

Source: Bulletin to Management, 19 July 1984, p. 3. Reprinted by permission from *Bulletin to Management,* copyright 1984, by the Bureau of National Affairs, Inc., Washington, D.C.

Nevertheless, college placement services are helpful to an organization recruiting in particular fields, such as engineering and microelectronics, and to those seeking highly talented and qualified minorities and women. In addition, organizations are making campus visits to recruit college alumni, not just those about to graduate. College and university outreach programs that provide placement services for their alumni enhance campus attractiveness to employers, who benefit by having a broader and more experienced pool of applicants from which to recruit.

Aliens.   As indicated in Chapter 2, real shortages of some job applicants exist, including professionals such as chemical engineers, nurses, and geologists. As a result, employers seek to recruit aliens—often overseas or in college placement offices.[37] Currently, between 50,000 and 75,000 aliens are permitted to come into the United States each year under immigration totals for workers who have skills not available in the U.S. job market. In response to this "skills crisis," the paperwork necessary to bring these aliens into the country has been made easier and faster. Getting an organization's requests processed by the U.S. Labor Department, the Immigration and Naturalization Service, and the Department of State used to take up to one year but can now take as little as three months.[38]

Although aliens provide a source of needed skilled workers in the United States, they are also a source of less-needed unskilled workers. An estimated 550,000 persons illegally enter the country each year. This huge pool of unskilled alien workers has had repercussions for the current U.S. labor force and economy.[39]

In general, organizations need to use both internal and external sources of recruitment. A summary list of the advantages and disadvantages of each is provided in Exhibit 4.4.

External Methods

Many organizations looking for applicants of all types engage in extensive advertising on radio and television, in the local paper, and in national newspapers such as the *Wall Street Journal.*

Radio and Television.   Of the approximately $2 billion spent annually on recruitment advertising, only a tiny percentage is spent on radio and television.[40] Companies are reluctant to use these media because they fear that the advertising is too expensive, will make the company look desperate, or will damage the firm's conservative image. Yet, organizations are desperate to reach certain types of job applicants, such as skilled workers. In reality, using radio or television to advertise is not a desperate measure. Rather, the level of desperation implied depends upon what is said and how it is delivered. Recognizing this, organizations are increasing their recruitment expenditures for radio and television advertisements, with favorable results.

Newspapers and Trade Journals.   Newspapers have traditionally been the most common method of external recruiting.[41] They reach a large number of potential applicants at a relatively low cost per hire. Newspaper ads are used

| *Sources of Job Applicants* | *Exhibit 4.4* |

Internal

Advantages	*Disadvantages*
Morale of promotee	Inbreeding
Better assessment of abilities	Possible morale problems of those not
Lower cost for some jobs	promoted
Motivator for good performance	"Political" infighting for promotions
Have to hire only at entry level	Need strong management
	development program

External

Advantages	*Disadvantages*
"New blood," new perspectives	May not select someone who will "fit"
Cheaper than training a professional	May cause morale problems for those
No group of political supporters in	internal candidates
organization already	Longer "adjustment" or orientation
May bring competitors' secrets, new	time
insights	May bring in an attitude of "This is
Helps meet EEO needs	the way we used to do it at XYZ
	Company."

Source: R. L. Mathis and J. H. Jackson, *Personnel:
Contemporary Perspectives and Applications,* 4th ed. (St. Paul,
Minn.: West Publishing Co., © 1986). Reproduced by permission.
All rights reserved.

to recruit for all types of positions, from the most unskilled to the most highly skilled and top managerial positions. The ads range from the most matter-of-fact type to the most creative type.[42]

Trade journals enable organizations to aim at a much more specific group of potential applicants. Ads in trade journals are often more creative and of a higher quality than that of newspapers, and the paper stock quality is better than newsprint. Unfortunately, long lead times are required and the ads can thus become dated.

Computerized Services.   A newer and much less common external method (it does not appear in Exhibit 4.3) is the computerized recruiting service. This service works as a place to both list job openings and locate job applicants.

> Personnel officers using a Job/Net terminal "can find people in fifteen minutes that it would take eight hours to find going through paper resumes," says Janice Kempf, a vice-president and cofounder. M/A-Com, a microwave and telecommunications company in Burlington, Massachusetts, recently hired a $30,000 quality-control engineer through Job/Net. "If we had paid an agency fee, it would have been $6,500 to $7,000," says Richard L. Bove, the staffing and development manager. He adds that the service lets him see more resumes of qualified people and lets him choose people who don't require expensive relocation.[43]

Acquisitions and Mergers.   Employees can also be obtained through acquisitions and mergers (not included in Exhibit 4.3 because of their recency as external recruiting methods). A significant result of the merger or acquisition process is a large pool of employees, some of whom may no longer be necessary in the new organization. Consequently, the new organization potentially has a large number of job applicants (although they are current employees) who are already qualified. As a result of the merger or acquisition, however, new jobs may be created in addition to the retention of old jobs. For these new jobs, the pool of employees becomes the pool of potentially qualified applicants. For the old jobs (those unchanged), the pool of employees becomes the pool from which the most qualified people can be identified and selected.

In contrast to the other external methods, acquisitions and mergers may play an immediate role in facilitating an organization's strategic plan by enabling it to quickly obtain a large pool of highly qualified individuals. This pool may enable an organization to pursue a strategic business plan (e.g., entering a new product line that would otherwise be unavailable using other recruiting methods). What these other methods do not present that mergers and acquisitions do, however, is the need to displace excess employees and to quickly integrate a large number of employees into a new organization. Consequently, recruiting via acquisitions and mergers needs to be closely tied in with human resource planning and selection.[44]

Assessing Recruiting Methods

Which of the many recruiting methods identified is best for recruiting each occupational group shown in Exhibit 4.3? Based on a survey of personnel executives conducted by the Bureau of National Affairs, the best methods—or those most effective—varied across occupations.[45] For example, as shown in Exhibit 4.5, private employment agencies were most effective for applicants in sales, professional and technical positions, and management, whereas walk-ins were most effective for office/clerical and plant/service applicants.

Although the results in Exhibit 4.5 are informative, they are the executives' perceptions of effectiveness, and not necessarily those that would be found if a cost-benefit analysis were done on each method. Such an analysis would require measuring the costs involved in using a method of recruiting (e.g., travel, hotel, and salary expenses incurred by a recruiter visiting a college campus). Then the benefits from the college recruiting would be determined. Although measuring the costs here may be relatively easy, determining the benefits (especially in dollar amounts) can be very difficult. Is the length of time an applicant stays on the job once hired a benefit from recruiting? If it is, how is the value of this benefit determined? Can it be translated into dollars and cents? Presently, determining the benefits of recruiting methods in dollars and cents is possible though difficult.[46] More feasible perhaps (using this example of length of time on job) is to record the length of time hired applicants acquired by each recruiting method stay on the job, and then compare the results. These comparisons can then be compared with the costs of each method.

Another way the utility of each method can be determined is by comparing the number of potentially qualified applicants hired by each method for

Organizational Judgments of Most Effective   *Exhibit 4.5*
Recruiting Sources by Occupation

	Occupation*				
Source	*Office/ Clerical*	*Plant/ Service*	*Sales*	*Professional/ Technical*	*Management*
Newspaper advertising	39	30	30	38	35
Walk-ins	24	37	5	7	2
Employee referrals	20	5	17	7	7
Private employment agencies	10	2	23	25	27
U.S. Employment Service (USES)	5	6	0	1	1
Local high schools or trade schools	2	2	0	0	0
Colleges/universities	1	1	8	15	2
Community agencies	1	3	0	1	2
Unions	0	2	0	0	0
Career conferences/ job fairs	0	1	2	2	1
Professional societies	0	1	1	0	2
Search firms	0	0	2	5	17
Radio-TV advertising	0	1	0	0	1
Advertising in special publications	0	0	3	5	8

Note: Figures are percentages of companies providing data for each employee group as indicated in Exhibit 4.3. Columns may add to more than 100 percent because of multiple responses or less than 100 percent because of nonresponses. These percentages are votes for effectiveness.

Source: Reprinted by special permission from *Personnel Policies Forum*, Survey No. 126, Recruiting Policies & Practice, pp. 4–5. Copyright © 1979, by the Bureau of National Affairs Inc., Washington, D.C.

each occupational group. The methods resulting in the most qualified applicants eventually hired in each occupational group may be determined the most effective, if not perhaps the least expensive.

Increasing the Pool of Potentially Qualified Applicants

Although organizations may use both external and internal sources of recruitment, they may not always obtain a sufficient or desired number of the applicants they want, or retain those employees of most value to the organization. This is especially true in highly competitive markets and for highly skilled individuals.[47] But the organization can enhance recruitment through the enticements it offers, such as relocation assistance, or through its efforts to establish programs such as career development or child care to facilitate working in the organization. Organizations are doing several things to increase their pools of potentially qualified job applicants. As an added benefit, many things that companies are doing to increase applicant pools also increase the probability that once hired, the applicant-employee will stay.

Before looking at what the organization can do to attract potentially qualified applicants, looking first at the applicants is useful. That is, if organizations want to attract candidates, they need to know *what* attracts and *how* candidates are attracted.[48] In essence, knowing how candidates are attracted is an understanding of where they get their information regarding job availability. As discussed in the previous section on assessing recruiting methods, different types of candidates learn about job availability through different sources. Consequently, to attract larger pools of candidates, the methods described in Exhibit 4.3 should be used on those applicants for whom they are deemed most effective.[49]

Knowing what attracts candidates involves knowing what makes the organization attractive to the individuals.[50] Essentially, what helps make the organization attractive includes the nature of the job and what it offers or provides the individual. The duties, purposes, characteristics, and performance standards discussed in Chapter 3 describe the nature of the job. What the organization offers or provides includes traditional direct and indirect compensation and several newer forms of indirect compensation that help facilitate an individual's ability to work. Although an organization may become attractive by offering high initial levels of traditional direct and indirect compensation, this may be too costly for an organization and may not be attractive to all individuals. Thus, it is important to discuss new forms of indirect compensation as a means to increase the applicant pool. The traditional forms of direct and indirect compensation are discussed more extensively in Chapters 8, 9, and 10.

Although an individual may learn of job availability through one of the several sources shown in Exhibit 4.3, the individual still needs to learn about the nature of the job and the organization's compensation (enticements). For some individuals, other employees may be the source of this information, while for others it is the organization itself. Because advertisements, pamphlets, and recruiting agencies are generally unable to convey all this information, the organization often needs to rely upon the recruitment interview. This is especially appropriate for external candidates, where knowledge of the job and compensation need to be conveyed. For internal candidates, job information may be more critical; thus, a job-matching program may be more appropriate.

Conveying Job and Organizational Information

The traditional approach to recruiting is concerned with matching the job applicant's abilities with the skills that the job requires. The more recent approach to recruiting, although still concerned with matching skills, knowledge, and abilities, is also concerned with matching the job applicant's personality, interests, and preferences with the job and organizational characteristics. For effective PHRM, getting job applicants to stay is as important as recruiting job applicants who can do the job. Two components of the newer approach to recruiting focus on the **job interview** and **job-matching programs**.

Job Interview.   A vital aspect of the recruitment process is the interview. A good interview provides the applicant with a realistic preview of what the job will be like. It can definitely be an enticement for an applicant to join an organization, just as a bad interview can turn away many applicants.

The quality of the interview is just one aspect of the recruitment process. Other things being equal, the chances of a person's accepting a job offer increase when interviewers show interest and concern for the applicant. In addition, college students feel most positive toward the recruitment interview when they can take at least half of the interview time to ask the interviewer questions and when the interviewer does not embarrass them or put them on the spot.

The content of the recruitment interview is also important. Organizations often assume that it is in their best interests to tell a job applicant only the positive aspects of the organization. But studies by the life insurance industry have reported that providing realistic (positive and negative) information actually increases the number of eventual recruits. In addition, those who receive realistic job information may be less likely to quit once they accept the job.[51]

Assuming that job applicants pass an initial screening, they should be given the opportunity to interview with a potential supervisor and even with co-workers. The interview with the potential supervisor is crucial, for this is the person who often makes the final decision.

Job Matching.   Job matching is a systematic effort to identify people's skills, knowledge, and abilities and their personalities, interests, and preferences and match them to the job openings. Increasing pressure on organizations to maintain effective recruitment, selection, and placement of new and current employees may make an automated job-matching system worthwhile. For example, Citibank's job-matching system for nonprofessional employees evolved from an automated system designed to monitor requisition and internal placement processes. The system is currently used to identify suitable positions for staff members who wish to transfer or who are seeking another job because of technological displacement or reorganization. The system also ensures that suitable internal candidates won't be overlooked before recruiting begins outside the organization. Thus, the system appears not only to help recruit people and ensure that they stay but also to provide a firm basis for job-related recruitment and selection procedures (job relatedness is an important part of legal compliance and is discussed in Chapter 5).

The two major components in a job-matching system are **job profiles** and **candidate profiles**.[52] The job profiles at Citibank were developed from prior job-family studies conducted at Citibank using the U.S. Department of Labor's *Handbook for Analyzing Jobs* and such job analysis instruments as the Position Analysis Questionnaire (see Chapter 3). Thus, the job profiles are elaborate job descriptions and specifications. The candidate profiles contain information regarding candidates' experience or skills related to specific jobs. These jobs are the same ones described in the job profiles. Candidate profiles also list candidates' job preferences and interests. With these profiles, the organization can identify many more potentially qualified job applicants for specific jobs than ever before.

Expanding Career and Job Opportunities

By providing new career opportunities and child-care assistance, organizations can enhance their attractiveness while increasing their applicant pools.

Career Opportunities.   The decision to provide career opportunities involves several choices for the organization. First, should the organization have an active policy of promotion from within? Second, should the organization be committed to a training and development program to provide sufficient candidates for internal promotion? If the answers to these questions are yes, then the organization must identify career ladders consistent with organizational and job requirements and employee skills and preferences, such as Citibank has done with its job-matching program.

An organization may identify several career paths for different groups or types of employees. This concept is based on the premise that an organization cannot afford to recruit applicants for jobs at the lower rungs of the ladder when they already possess those skills necessary for jobs at the higher rungs. This actually occurs, however, with many people recruited from college. Although they are essentially overqualified for their first jobs, the organization hires them for more difficult "future" jobs. This approach is partially to blame for the higher turnover rate of new college graduates and is also a cause for concern regarding legal compliance. Employers may claim that a college degree is necessary for an entry-level managerial job when they may actually consider the degree necessary for the second or third job. Such a policy can lead to discriminatory barriers for recruitment and promotion.

One way to reduce the possibility of discriminatory barriers is for an organization to establish career ladders and paths.[53] When organizations have career ladders and paths with clearly specified requirements anchored in sound job analyses, they can present better legal defenses for their recruitment policies. In essence, organizations establish a case of long-term job relatedness. Organizations with clearly defined career ladders may also have an easier time attracting and recruiting qualified job applicants and a better chance of keeping employees.

Child-care Assistance.   Along with society and technology, the percentage of wage-earning women in America is rapidly changing. Between 1960 and 1980, for example, the percentage of married women with children under six who work outside the home jumped from 19 percent to 46 percent. Today more than one child in five lives with a single parent. Presently about 7.2 million children are in need of day-care services. The forecast for 1990 is that 50 percent of all preschool children will have mothers in the work force, increasing the number of children needing day care of 10.4 million.

Today, more companies than ever before are providing some kind of child-care services for their employees. The benefits of providing such services include reduced turnover, tardiness, and absenteeism, and improved recruiting success, morale, productivity, public relations, and product quality.[54] Organizations can choose from a wide spectrum of child-care services to meet the needs of wage-earning parents. The possibilities include the following:

- *Support existing facilities.* Employers can help lower program costs for participants while improving the delivery of child-care services by contributing funds or products or by donating in-kind assistance.
- *Set up information and referral systems.* To help eliminate some of the worries of being a wage-earning parent, the personnel department can keep a current list, fee schedules, and eligibility requirements of child-care centers.
- *Subsidize employees' child-care costs.* Providing vouchers and "subletting" center slots are the two most common ways of underwriting child-care expenses. In the former, the employer issues a voucher for use at any participating center, which then bills the company for the amount of the subsidy. Under the latter arrangement, management reserves a number of slots in a center and then passes along to employees the savings associated with the group rate.
- *Establish a child-care center.* Where community services are deficient, management can set up its own child-care program for workers or even join with other area employers to form a community center.[55]

Although providing these types of programs is expensive, it is probably less so than the expenses due to less effective recruitment, absenteeism, and turnover from not having these programs. To help keep costs in line and to provide the most appropriate assistance, however, a careful analysis of the organization's needs for this type of service and a careful review of what's available in the community should be the personnel department's responsibility.

Trends in Recruitment

Key trends in recruitment include assessment and computer technology applications. Although some issues of strategic involvement are emerging, they are closely tied in with selection and consequently are described in the next chapter.

Assessing Recruitment

The recruitment activity is supposed to attract the right people at the right time within legal limits so that people and organizations can select each other in their best short- and long-run interests. Likewise, this is how recruitment should be assessed. More specific criteria for assessing recruitment are shown in Exhibit 4.6, grouped by the stage of the recruitment process in which they are most applicable.

Recruitment is not just concerned with attracting people. It is also concerned with attracting those whose personalities, interests, and preferences will most likely be matched by the organization and who have the skills, knowledge, and abilities to perform adequately. Only by matching personalities, interests, and preferences and skills, knowledge, and abilities with the organization's needs will the recruitment activity result in productive employees who will remain with the organization. Thus, as shown in Exhibit 4.6, job performance and turnover are benefit criteria for recruitment whose value should be assessed.[56]

Another benefit criterion by which to assess recruiting is legal compliance. Job applicants must be recruited fairly and without discrimination. During the entry and post-entry stages, they must also receive fair and affirmative opportunities to be matched to appropriate jobs and to perform to their maximum abilities. Thus, the value of the costs saved (benefits gained) from not paying fines should be assessed (as it should be for selection).

In addition to assessing each benefit criterion of recruitment, each method or source of recruitment can be valuated, or "costed out." For example, for each method, such as radio advertising or employee referrals, the cost per applicant and cost per hire can be determined. Then the value of the benefit criteria can be determined for each method, such as the average length of time the newly hired employee stays and the average level of performance of each employee. All these costs and benefits of each method can then be compared. On the basis of this comparison, some methods may be used more, some dropped, or some just modified to reduce their costs. Similarly, recruiting sources can be assessed. Those providing the best benefit-cost ratio can be identified and their use enhanced if appropriate.[57]

Exhibit 4.6   *Some Criteria for Assessing Recruitment*

Stage of Entry	Type of Criteria
Pre-entry	Ability of the organization to recruit newcomers
Entry	Initial expectations of newcomers
	Choice of organization by the individual (needs being matched with climate)
Post-entry	Initial job attitudes, such as
	• satisfaction with one's job
	• commitment to the organization
	• descriptive statements about the job (to be compared with the expectations held as an outsider)
	• thoughts about quitting
	Job performance
	Job survival and voluntary turnover rates

Source: From J. P. Wanous, *Organizational Entry.* Copyright ©
1980, Addison-Wesley Publishing Company, Inc., p. 62.

Computer Technology and HRIS in Recruitment

Computer technology can aid recruitment immensely.[58] The legal obligations to which most organizations are subject, stemming from laws such as Title VII of the Civil Rights Act of 1964, may be more easily fulfilled using computer technology. For example, affirmative action plans require a utilization analysis by particular job categories. These calculations, while mathematically basic, require the organization of much data. The computer can also be used on the operational level to conduct these analyses as well as to plan future outcomes that depend upon organization recruitment policies and external availability of candidates. In short, by projecting alternative anticipated conditions, estimates of various employment needs may be forecasted. Used together, recruitment information and computer technology can enable an organization to develop effective recruitment selection policies consistent with legal requirements.

Through the use of computer technology, the personnel department can manage recruiting effectively and contribute to legal compliance and operation efficiency. The computer can track the historical trends of recruiting sources in a variety of ways. For example, personnel can determine the greatest source of candidates for any position or department as well as note the percentage of candidates hired from a particular source. Compliance is enhanced by ensuring that recruiting sources help achieve any legally determined utilization of protected class members. From the fiscal perspective, recruiting costs can be reduced by avoiding those sources that provide significant numbers of unqualified candidates.

Summary

Recruiting is a major activity in an organization's program to manage its human resources. After human resource needs have been established and job requirements have been identified through job analysis, a program of recruitment can be established to produce a pool of job applicants. These applicants can be obtained from internal or external sources.

For recruiting to be effective, it must consider not only the needs of the organization but also those of society and the individual as well. Society's needs are most explicitly defined by various federal and state regulations in the name of equal employment opportunity. Individuals' needs figure prominently in two aspects of recruiting: attracting candidates and retaining desirable employees. The legal commitments and obligations that influence an organization's recruitment activity most significantly are those associated with affirmative action programs. Such programs result from an organization being a federal contractor, from entering into a consent decree, or from a voluntary action to provide greater equal employment opportunity. Although not legally imposing upon recruitment, they directly influence recruitment through establishing and defining the organization's selection requirements.

Once legal considerations are established, the organizations must recruit sufficient numbers of potentially qualified applicants so that the individuals selected are adequately matched to jobs. This matching will help ensure that the individuals will perform effectively and not leave the organization. Organizations can attract and retain these job applicants by numerous methods and through various sources. Although some methods and sources are more effective than others, the ones chosen are often necessarily determined by the type of applicant sought.

As with other PHRM activities, recruitment assessment is essential. Recruitment can be assessed by evaluating the associated benefit and cost criteria. For example, the benefits of reduced turnover or enhanced performance can be assessed and compared with the costs of the programs to recruit job applicants. Costs of sources and methods can also be assessed and weighed against the benefits, such as the ease of recruiting or the number of qualified applicants obtained. After these assessments are made, recruiting methods and sources can be revised as appropriate. The revision, however, as with the recruitment activity assessment, should be done with consideration for selection, the other half of the staffing function. This is necessary because the two activities are interdependent, as is made more apparent in the next chapter.

Discussion Questions

1. What are the purposes of recruitment, and how do those purposes affect other organizational activities?
2. Discuss why the cost of employee training and development is so closely tied to recruitment programs.
3. How does personnel planning contribute to effective recruitment? What are the roles of the line and personnel manager in each of these activities?
4. Just-in-time inventory is a concept that enables manufacturers to assemble products from parts that are delivered as needed rather than kept in inventory (which is costly). Could this concept be applied to the recruitment function and human resources? Explain.
5. What is an affirmative action program? Why might a company develop an AAP?
6. Describe and explain the meaning of *utilization and availability analyses, goals,* and *timetables.*
7. Why do some organizations use an external search, whereas others use an internal search? Can each be best for that particular organization? Explain.
8. The search for job applicants involves finding not only the right number but also the right kind. Are some recruitment sources richer than others—that is, do they yield more information about the kind of applicant needed? Can you give examples?

9. Assessment of recruitment activities requires an estimate of costs as well as benefits. Choose an organization you are familiar with and describe how you would measure and compare the costs and benefits of the recruitment methods in this organization.

10. What are the best methods of recruiting potentially qualified applicants?

PC Project

Equal employment opportunity laws play a critical role in the recruitment strategies of most companies. This computer project generates a utilization and availability analysis indicating the representation of women and minority managers. The human resource data base includes employee name, age, sex, EEO code, length of service, salary, educational level, and performance appraisal scores. Is there an adequate representation of women and minorities? What groups are underutilized? "What-if" recruitment scenarios can be tested in this project.

C	A	S	E	S	T	U	D	Y

Invisible Ceilings Versus Doors?

Southwestern State University prides itself on its rapid growth and expansion of facilities during the decade of the seventies. Now, in the decade of the eighties, many see Southwestern State poised to become, as college presidents are wont to say, a preeminent university. A traditional land grant university with an emphasis on agriculture, Southwestern State currently boasts one of the largest schools of business and engineering in the country.

John DeNisi, an employee relations specialist in the personnel department at Southwestern, has witnessed firsthand the proud growth and transformation of Southwestern during his eleven-year tenure in university administration at Southwestern. John is less sanguine about the future, though. Growth will continue but at a considerably reduced rate given projected population trends for the region. Moreover, John, like others, is worried about Southwestern's stance toward minority recruitment.

Three years ago, John served on a university-wide committee that examined the status of minorities at Southwestern in staff, faculty, and student areas. The final report his committee delivered to the president was not optimistic, to say the least. Southwestern is predictably underrepresented in all areas with regard to both blacks and Hispanics. Potentially, Southwestern stands to lose federal funds unless the university undertakes significant moves to attract and retain more minorities in the future. Accordingly, the committee's report recommended renewed efforts to recruit aggressively in all areas, to set aside money for minority recruitment, and to set up minority scholarships to attract more students.

Recently, though, John wondered what impact the current administration policy from Washington would have on Southwestern's step toward affirmative action. John had followed closely reports in the *Chronicle of Higher Education* and the College and University Personnel Association newsletter of the battle in Washington over the status of voluntary affirmative action plans. Although professional groups such as the National Association of Manufacturers and the American Society for Personnel Administration support affirmative action as "good business policy," the Department of Justice and the Equal Employment Opportunity Commission (EEOC) seem to have taken a major retreat from earlier administration positions on affirmative action.

The Department of Labor, though, seems to be at odds with the Justice Department and the EEOC by supporting goals and timetables in its enforcement of affirmative action plans for federal contractors. Moreover, the Supreme Court appears to support voluntary affirmative action plans in several recent decisions dealing specifically with such plans. Vocal critics of the new administration stand on affirmative action argue that without affirmative action, minorities will merely bump up against the "invisible ceiling." John wondered what implications these developments could have for Southwestern's stance for the future. If Southwestern initiated such a plan, and then the Department of Justice successfully challenged the constitutionality of affirmative action plans, the university could strap itself with discrimination and reverse discrimination suits well into the twenty-first century.

John's ruminations were abruptly interrupted by a call from the front office informing John that an applicant had requested a meeting. Usually this meant that a disgruntled applicant was unhappy with the impersonal treatment received from the front office. John would then spend a few minutes with the applicant, try to smooth ruffled feathers, and, when necessary, reprimand office staff for rude or discourteous behavior. More often than not,

though, John encountered an obnoxious faculty spouse that not only expected immediate employment but also demanded it publicly in a crowded front office.

As John girded himself, he was introduced at the door to Alma Fisher, a well-dressed and attractive black woman. Alma did not beat around the bush. "Mr. DeNisi," Alma blurted out, "this university doesn't want to hire blacks, and I want to know what you're going to do about it!" After a few minutes of discussion, John learned that Alma had previously worked at the university as a secretary and had left two years ago on maternity. Upon reentering the labor force, Alma had visited the university employment office, taken the clerical tests, and qualified, based on her performance, for a senior secretary position, the highest-paid clerical position at the university.

John's office had matched Alma's qualifications to a position request submitted by the Medical College and referred Alma to the dean of the Medical School for an interview. According to Alma, during the interview the dean asked Alma if she had children and how she supported herself. The straw that broke the camel's back, though, came when the dean asked Alma if she was on welfare. At that point, Alma suggested to the dean that his line of questioning was "inappropriate" and asked the dean to stick to job-related questions concerning her qualifications to do the job. "You know, Mr. DeNisi," asserted Alma, "I did not tell the dean that my previous position with the university was as a secretary to the affirmative action officer. I could sue this university based on his behavior!"

John was struck by the irony of this moment. Why worry about invisible ceilings at Southwestern, he thought, when the invisible doors aren't open?

Notes

1. B. Schneider, *Staffing Organizations* (Santa Monica, Calif.: Goodyear, 1976); E. H. Schein, "Increasing Organizational Effectiveness through Better Human Resource Planning and Development," *Sloan Management Review* (Fall 1977): 1–20.

2. R. Stoops, "Are You Ready for the Coming Recruitment Boom?" *Personnel Journal* (July 1982): 490, 492; R. Stoops, "Recruitment Strategy," *Personnel Journal* (Feb. 1982): 102.

3. H. A. Acuff, "Improving the Employment Function," *Personnel Journal* (June 1982): 407. Reprinted with the permission of *Personnel Journal*, Costa Mesa, Calif. All rights reserved.

4. Bureau of National Affairs, *Bulletin to Management*, 24 Sept. 1981, p. 3. In a U.S. Labor Department survey in 1982, the costs to employers in accommodating employees were reported to be rather low. Fewer than 8 percent of their surveyed firms spend more

than $2,000 on any single accommodation. For a copy of the survey, write Employment Standards Administration, DOL, Room C-3313, 200 Constitution Ave., N.W., Washington, D.C. 20210.

5. L. C. Thurow, "Wanted: More Skilled Workers," *New York Times,* 3 May 1981; *Basic Skills in the U.S. Work Force* (New York: Center for Public Resources, 1983).

6. H. Klein, "Financial Officers Often in Demand As Companies Seek Cost-Cutters," *Wall Street Journal,* 22 Nov. 1982, p. 33; "When the Slump Helps Service Firms Prosper," *Business Week,* 10 May 1982, p. 42.

7. *Fair Employment Report,* 17 Aug. 1981, p. 3.

8. *Wall Street Journal,* 3 Sept. 1985, p. 1. See also A. B. Fisher, "Business Likes to Hire by the Numbers," *Fortune,* 16 Sept. 1985, pp. 26–30.

9. "Draft Order Undermines 1965 Contractor Hiring Goals," *Resource* (Sept. 1985): 1, 7; L. Z. Lorber, "Employers Should Not Take Precipitous Action in Affirmative Action Cases," *Personnel Administrator* (Sept. 1984): 101–2; L. P. Britt II, "Affirmative Action: Is There Life After Stotts?" *Personnel Administrator* (Sept. 1984): 96–100; D. F. Seaver, "The Stotts Decision: Is It the Death Knell for Seniority Systems?" *Employee Relations Law Journal* (Winter 1984/85): 497–504. Note that approximately one-quarter of the work force is employed by organizations with federal contracts.

10. Under an earlier ruling of the OFCCP, the qualified handicapped was one "who is capable of performing a particular job."

11. D. Peterson, "Paving the Way for Hiring the Handicapped," *Personnel* (Mar.–Apr. 1981): 43–44. Note also that affirmative action statements need to be written for Vietnam-era veterans, according to the Vietnam Era Veterans Readjustment Act of 1974.

12. D. A. Brookmire and A. A. Burton, "A Format for Packaging Your Affirmative Action Program," *Personnel Journal* (June 1978): 295. Reprinted with permission of Personnel Journal, Costa Mesa, Calif. All rights reserved.

13. The steps in a utilization and availability analysis are based on the eight-factor analysis (used in Exhibit 4.2). For a description, see R. S. Schuler, *Personnel and Human Resource Management,* 2d ed. (St. Paul: West, 1984), pp. 130–31 and Biddle and Associates, 903 Enterprise Drive, Suite 1, Sacramento, Calif. 95825.

14. AT&T has now gone beyond that consent decree and is operating under a new plan that is even more far-reaching than the old (see *Personnel Administrator* (Oct. 1982): 20, 23).

15. *Fair Employment Report,* 15 May 1985, p. 76.

16. Both voluntary and required AAPs have the potential for preventing white males from obtaining employment opportunity. Although the courts have ruled this to be fair, this is true only when white male interests are not trampled upon or when reverse discrimination is apparent (*Dale H. Jurgens* v. *EEOC,* 1982).

17. J. A. Belohlav and E. Ayton, "Equal Opportunity Laws: Some Common Problems," *Personnel Journal* (Apr. 1982): 282–85; F. S. Hall and S. A. Meier, "Developing Managerial Commitment to EEO," *Personnel Administrator* (May 1977): 36–39; D. Seligman, "Affirmative Action Is Here to Stay," *Fortune,* 19 Apr. 1982, pp. 143–62; B. Rosen, T. H. Jerdee, and J. Huonker, "Are Older Workers Hurt by Affirmative Action?" *Business Horizons* (Sept./Oct. 1982): 67–70.

18. Hall and Meier, "Developing Managerial Commitment." Reprinted with permission from the May 1977 issue of the *Personnel Administrator.* Copyright © 1977, The American Society for Personnel Administration, 30 Park Drive, Berea, Ohio 44107.

19. Only promotion and transfers are considered as internal sources for recruitment. Recruiting by demotions is done infrequently. Demotions are discussed in Chapter 7 and in the section on employee rights in Chapter 14.

20. L. R. Sayles and G. Strauss, *Managing Human Resources* (Englewood Cliffs, N.J.: Prentice-Hall, 1977), p. 147.

21. See A. Patton, "When Executives Bail Out to Move Up," *Business Week,* 13 Sept. 1982, pp. 13, 15, 17, 19. For a review of the costs of relocations see H. Z. Levine, "Relocation Practices," *Personnel* (Jan.–Feb. 1982): 4–10.

22. H. Klein, "Fast Promotions Haunt Some in a Recession," *Wall Street Journal,* 19 Mar. 1982, p. 29.

23. J. P. Campbell, M. D. Dunnette, E. E. Lawler III, and K. E. Weick, Jr., *Managerial Behavior, Performance, and Effectiveness* (New York: McGraw-Hill, 1970).

24. D. Q. Mills, *The New Competitors* (New York: Free Press, 1985).

25. T. Rendero, "Consensus," *Personnel* (Sept.–Oct. 1980): 5.

26. J. R. Garcia, "Job Posting for Professional Staff," *Personnel Journal* (Mar. 1981): 189–92; G. A. Wallropp, "Job Posting for Nonexempt Employees: A Sample Program," *Personnel Journal* (Oct. 1981): 796–98; L. S. Kleiman and K. L. Clark, "An Effective Job Posting System," *Personnel Journal* (Feb. 1984): 20–25; H. Z. Levine, "Job Posting Practices," *Personnel* (Nov.–Dec. 1984): 48–52.

27. B. Stoops, "Employee Referral Programs: Part I," *Personnel Journal* (Feb. 1981): 98, and "Part II" (Mar. 1981): 172–73.

28. "Recruiting Workers," *FEP Guidelines,* #223(2), 1984.

29. P. J. Decker and E. T. Cornelius, "A Note on Recruiting Sources and Job Survival Rates," *Journal of Applied Psychology* 64 (1974): 463–64; D. P. Schwab, "Recruiting and Organizational Participation," in *Personnel Management,* ed. K. M. Rowland and

G. R. Ferris (Boston: Allyn and Bacon, 1982), pp. 103–28.

30. Mangum, "Recruitment and Job Search," p. 99.

31. R. Kenney, "Open House Complements Recruitment Strategies," *Personnel Administrator* (Mar. 1982): 27–32.

32. R. Ricklefs, "Executive Recruiters Start Raising Fees, Prompting Some Companies to Go It Alone," *Wall Street Journal*, 4 Aug. 1981, p. 23; S. Bronstein, "What's New in Executive Recruiting," *New York Times*, 25 Aug. 1985, p. F13; G. P. Craighead, "Are Executive Recruiters Paid Too Much?" *Personnel Journal* (May 1985): 90–94.

33. For a good discussion of the false negatives and positives, see S. Rubenfeld and M. Crino, "Are Employment Agencies Jeopardizing Your Selection Process?" *Personnel* (Sept.–Oct. 1981): 70–78. The selection chapter in this text discusses these decisions also. See also W. J. Bjerregaard and M. E. Gold, "Employment Agencies and Executive Recruiters: A Practical Approach," *Personnel Administrator* (May 1981): 127–31, 135; W. J. Bjerregaard and M. E. Gold, "Executive Utilization of Search Consultants," *Personnel Administrator* (Dec. 1980): 35–39; R. J. Cronin, "Executive Recruiters: Are They Necessary?" *Personnel Administrator* (Feb. 1980): 31–34; B. Horovitz, "Where Headhunters Hunt," *Industry Week*, 9 Feb. 1981, pp. 43–47; C. E. Kur and P. G. Sone, "An Untapped Source of Consulting Help," *Personnel Administrator* (Dec. 1980): 29–33.

34. D. Diamond, "For Rent: Nomadic Engineer (Expensive)," *New York Times*, 27 Sept. 1981, p. F6; G. T. Huddleston, Jr., "One Way To Reduce Temporary Help Costs," *Personnel Administrator* (Jan. 1985): 10–11; See also T. R. Ostrach, "A Second Look at Temporaries," *Personnel Journal* (June 1981):440–42; C. W. L. Deale, "How to Choose a Temporary Help Service: A Guide to Quality Supplemental Staffing," *Personnel Administrator* (Dec. 1980): 55–57; B. E. Rosenthal, "What's New in Temporary Employment," *New York Times*, 16 Dec. 1984, p. F15; "Part-Time Workers: Rising Numbers; Rising Discord," *Business Week*, 1 Apr. 1985, pp. 62–63.

35. D. L. Chicci and C. L. Krapp, "College Recruitment From Start to Finish," *Personnel Journal* (Aug. 1980): 653–57; T. Rendero, "Consensus," *Personnel* (May–June 1980): 4–10; A. E. Marshall, "Recruiting Alumni on College Campuses," *Personnel Journal* (Apr. 1982): 264–66; L. D. Foxman and W. L. Polsky, "What Are the Best Employment Sources?" *Personnel Journal* (Nov. 1984): 26–27.

36. *Wall Street Journal*, 5 Feb. 1985, p. 1. Reprinted by permission of the *Wall Street Journal*. Copyright © Dow Jones & Company, Inc., 1985. All rights reserved.

37. C. E. Morrissey, "Utilizing U.S. Educated Foreign Nationals," *Personnel Journal* (Nov. 1983): 862–66.

38. Ibid.; "A Warmer Welcome for Foreign Technicians," *Business Week*, 17 Aug. 1981, pp. 31–32.

39. R. E. Taylor, "New Fight on Illegal Aliens Planned Amid Signs Opposition Is Softening," *Wall Street Journal*, 10 Mar. 1982; J. G. Minarcini, "Illegal Aliens: Employment Restrictions and Responses," *Personnel Administrator* (Mar. 1980): 71–78; R. Pear, "The Institutionalization of the Illegal Alien," *New York Times*, 29 Sept. 1985, p. E5; "Illegal Immigrants Are Backbone of Economy of States in Southwest," *Wall Street Journal*, 7 May 1985, pp. 1, 10.

40. J. Bredwell, "The Use of Broadcast Advertising for Recruitment," *Personnel Administrator* (Feb. 1981): 45–49; R. Stoops, "Radio Advertising as an Effective Recruitment Device," *Personnel Journal* (Jan. 1981): 21. R. Stoops, "Radio Recruitment Advertising: Part II," *Personnel Journal* (July 1981): 532; "Affirmative Action in the 1980s: What Can We Expect?" *Management Review* (May 1981): 4–5; R. Stoops, "Television Advertising," *Personnel Journal* (Nov. 1981): 838.

41. R. Stoops, "Advertising in Trade Journals," *Personnel Journal* (Sept. 1981): 678; R. Stoops, "A Marketing Approach to Recruitment," *Personnel Journal* (Aug. 1981): 608. An extension of newspapers and journals is direct mail advertising. For a description, see R. Stoops, "More on Direct Mail Advertising," *Personnel Journal* (Mar. 1982): 184.

42. M. Magnus, "Recruitment Ads at Work," *Personnel Journal* (Aug. 1985): 42–63; A. Halcrow, "Anatomy of a Recruitment Ad," *Personnel Journal* (Aug. 1985): 64–65; R. Stoops, "Creative Ad Concepts Are Not Accidents," *Personnel Journal* (Nov. 1984): 86–88.

43. *Wall Street Journal*, 8 Feb. 1983, p. 35. Reprinted by permission of the *Wall Street Journal*. Copyright © Dow Jones & Company, Inc., 1983. All rights reserved.

44. D. L. Schweiger and J. M. Ivancevich, "Human Resources: The Forgotten Factor in Mergers and Acquisitions," *Personnel Administrator* (Nov. 1985): 47–61; D. Robino and K. DeMeuse, "Corporate Mergers and Acquisitions: Their Impact on HRM," *Personnel Administrator* (Nov. 1985): 33–44; J. R. Kimberly and R. E. Quinn, eds., *New Futures: The Challenge of Managing Corporate Transitions* (New York: Dow Jones—Irwin, 1984); L. E. Miller and R. A. Lindsay, "Mergers and Acquisitions: Labor Relations Considerations," *Employee Relations Law Journal* (Winter 1983–84): 427–43.

45. Relatively little work has been done on assessing recruitment method effectiveness. See Schwab, "Recruiting and Organizational Participation," pp. 111–13, for a review of what's been done. See also D. Dennis, "Are Recruitment Efforts Designed to Fail?" *Personnel Journal* (Sept. 1984): 60–67; M. S. Taylor and D. W. Schmidt, "A Process-Oriented Investigation of Recruitment Source Effectiveness," *Personnel Psychology* (Summer 1983): 343–54; D. F. Caldwell and W. A. Spivey; "The Relationship between Recruiting Source and Employee Success: An Analysis by Race," *Personnel Psychology* (Spring 1983): 67–72; M. London and S. A. Stumpf, "Effects of Candidate

Characteristics on Management Promotion Decisions: An Experimental Study," *Personnel Psychology* (Summer 1983): 241–60.

46. J. W. Boudreau and S. L. Rynes, "Role of Recruitment in Staffing Utility Analysis," *Journal of Applied Psychology* (May 1985): 354–66; P. Farish, "Cost Per Hire," *Personnel Administrator* (Jan. 1985): 16.

47. For a good review, see Schwab, "Recruiting and Organizational Participation." See also J. Ullman, "Interfirm Differences in the Cost of Search for Clerical Workers," *Journal of Business* 41 (1968): 153–65; G. J. Stigler, "Information in the Labor Market," *Journal of Political Economy* (1962): 94–105; A. Rees, "Information Networks in Labor Markets," *American Economic Review* (1966): 559–66.

48. Note that information on the general effectiveness of these methods is limited, so each organization should do its own analysis. For example, see V. V. Buzachers and M. Parker, "Sound Recruiting with BMC Soundsheets," *Personnel Administrator* (May 1984): 116–17; D. B. Balkin and S. Groeneman, "The Effect of Incentive Compensation on Recruitment: The Case of the Military," *Personnel Administrator* (Jan. 1985): 29–34.

49. J. H. Greenhaus and O. C. Brenner, "How Do Job Candidates Size Up Prospective Employees?" *Personnel Administrator* (March 1982): 21–25; "Summer Internships Receive High Marks from College Students," *Wall Street Journal,* 27 Aug. 1981, pp. 1, 20; "Firms Providing Business Internships Lure Middle-Aged Women Looking for Careers," *Wall Street Journal,* 2 Sept. 1981, p. 23; R. L. Lattimer, "Developing Career Awareness Among Minority Youths: A Case Example," *Personnel Journal* (Jan. 1981): 17; R. S. Greenberger, "An Oversupply of College Graduates Forces Some into Lower-Level Jobs," *Wall Street Journal,* 25 Feb. 1982, p. 27.

50. K. R. Davis, Jr., W. F. Giles, and H. S. Field, Jr., "Compensation and Fringe Benefits: How Recruiters View New College Graduates' Preferences," *Personnel Administrator* (Jan. 1985): 43–50.

51. For a good discussion of the relevant issues, see J. A. Breaugh, "Realistic Job Previews: A Critical Appraisal and Future Research Directions," *Academy of Management Review* (Oct. 1983): 612–23; S. L. Rynes and H. E. Miller, "Recruiter and Job Influences on Candidates for Employment," *Journal of*

Applied Psychology (Feb. 1983): 147–56; G. N. Powell, "Effects of Job Attributes and Recruiting Practices on Applicant Decisions: A Comparison," *Personnel Psychology* (Winter 1984): 721–32; J. P. Wanous, *Organizational Entry* (Reading, Mass.: Addison-Wesley, 1980); M. D. Hakel, "Employment Interviewing," in *Personnel Management,* ed. K. M. Rowland and G. R. Ferris (Boston: Allyn and Bacon, 1982), pp. 153–54; R. R. Reilly, B. Brown, M. R. Blood, and C. Z. Malatesta, "The Effects of Realistic Previews: A Study and Discussion of the Literature," *Personnel Psychology* (1981), (34): 823–34; R. D. Arvey and J. G. Campion, "The Employment Interview: A Summary and Review of the Recent Literature," *Personnel Psychology* (1982) (35) 281–322; R. R. Reilly, B. Brown, M. R. Blood, and C. Z. Malatesta, "The Effects of Realistic Previews: A Study and Discussion of the Literature," *Personnel Psychology* (1981) (34): 823–34. See also R. A. Dean and J. P. Wanous, "Effects of Realistic Job Previews on Hiring Bank Tellers," *Journal of Applied Psychology* (Feb. 1984): 61–68; D. W. Naffziger, "BARS, RJPs, and Recruiting," *Personnel Administrator* (Aug. 1985): 85–95.

52. P. Sheibar, "A Simple Selection System Called Jobmatch," *Personnel Journal* (Jan. 1979): 26–29, 53. See also L. Albright, "Staffing Policies and Procedures," in *Human Resource Management in the 1980s,* ed. S. J. Carroll and R. S. Schuler (Washington, D.C.: Bureau of National Affairs, 1983).

53. H. L. Wellbank, D. T. Hall, M. A. Morgan, and W. C. Hammer, "Planning Job Progression for Effective Career Development and Human Resources Management," *Personnel* (Mar.–Apr. 1978): 54–64.

54. "Child Care: Larger Number, Positive Effects," *Bulletin to Management,* 25 Nov. 1982, p. 7.

55. "Child Care Programs: Advantages and Approaches," *Bulletin to Management,* 28 Feb. 1985, pp. 1–2.

56. D. L. Dennis, "Evaluating Corporate Recruitment Efforts," *Personnel Administrator* (Jan. 1985): 21–26.

57. Boudreau and Rynes, "Role of Recruitment in Staffing Utility Analysis"; Farish, "Cost Per Hire."

58. R. E. Casper, "On-Line Recruitment," *Personnel Journal* (Apr. 1985): 50–55; W. M. Bulkeley, "The Fast Track: Computers Help Firms Decide Whom to Promote," *Wall Street Journal,* 18 Sept. 1985, p. 33.

5

Selection and Placement

A Fresh Interest in Personality Tests

Last summer, H. Parker Sharpe, Inc. administered the Berkman Method—a widely used personality questionnaire—to Larry Lagerhausen to see if it should hire him as an insurance salesman. At his former job Mr. Lagerhausen had sold only $260,000 worth of insurance in six months. But the Berkman test indicated that he would thrive if closely supervised and recognized for his achievements.

"So Mr. Sharpe put me in a plush office and treated me like a million-dollar producer," recalled Mr. Lagerhausen. In his first six months with Sharpe, Mr. Lagerhausen sold $2.2 million worth of insurance.

Like Sharpe, many companies are finding that judicious use of written tests can be valuable, not only for employee selection but also as a tool for getting the most out of employees. This discovery is one of several trends fueling the current boom in psychological testing—a field consisting of personality, aptitude, and interest tests.

Mark Kleinschmidt, marketing manager at National Computer Systems, a leading test distributor, estimates that the company's commercial testing business has grown more than 30 percent in each of the last two years. He says that United States companies are spending about $50 million annually on such testing, and that the amount is growing each year.

This rapid growth, evident at both entry level and upper management ends of the employment spectrum, comes after a decade of flat sales for the testing business. The slump stemmed from the many equal employment regulations enacted throughout the 1970's. These require companies that use testing to conduct expensive validity studies proving a strict correlation between the qualities measured by testing instruments to those demanded by the job at hand. Many companies stopped using tests as a result.

But many others started seeking bias-free tests. For example, in 1978, members of the Edison Electric Institute, a trade association of power companies, began a project to design and validate industrywide assessment tools for positions in several job categories. By analyzing job requirements, developing and administering experimental tests, and correlating the results with performance appraisals by supervisors, the institute created tests measuring, for example, decision-making capability and electrical knowledge for systems operators, mechanical comprehension for maintenance workers, and language skills for clerical employees.

By last fall, many utility companies across the country had adopted all of the tests. "If every company in our industry did a separate validity study, it would have cost at least 10 times as much," said David Kleinke, manager of psychological services at Edison. Mr. Kleinke estimates that by improving employee selection procedures, the tests should save utility companies at least $20 million this year in operating costs.

Computerization has also spurred the use of testing. Scoring services used to require as much as two weeks to give test results; now, scores are frequently available within 24 hours, a boon to employers juggling several applicants.

This winter, National Computer started marketing its Microtest Assessment System, a package including an I.B.M. PC, the company's own scanner for scoring, and test software. The $7,000 system is among the first designed exclusively for administering and scoring tests on site.

"If a company loses one good applicant because of delays associated with mailing the results, this system will more than pay for itself," said Mr. Kleinschmidt.

The preceding "PHRM in the News" highlights many aspects of selection, a major one being the amount of money that organizations can save by making better selection decisions (e.g., $20 million for Edison Electric Institute). Related to this aspect are several other aspects, including (1) how to collect information on job applicants, (2) how to make selection and placement decisions, (3) how to validate tests used in making selection decisions, and (4) how to make the entire set of selection and placement procedures more useful. These concerns, along with the extensive legal environment of selection decisions, are the essence of selection and placement and equal employment opportunity.

Selection is the process of gathering information for evaluating and deciding who should be hired, under legal guidelines, for the short- and long-term interests of the individual and the organization.[1] **Placement** is concerned with ensuring that job demands and job and organizational characteristics match individual skills, knowledge, and abilities and preferences, interests, and personalities. Traditionally, selection and placement have primarily been concerned with evaluating and matching employee skills, knowledge, and abilities with job demands.[2] Current emphasis is also on matching employee personalities, interests, and preferences with job and organizational characteristics.[3] Concern here for both matches is consistent with our emphasis on serving individuals as well as organizations. Thus, discussion of selection and placement is consistent with and builds on the emphasis prescribed in recruitment and job analysis. Our focus in this chapter, however, is on selection because the equal employment laws apply only to selection, and the information relevant to placement is relatively limited.[4] Continuing to refer to both selection and placement is useful, however, since they share many qualities. Both use information on the characteristics and qualities of the organization, the job, and the individual. They also share many of the same purposes and goals.

Line managers play an important role in the selection and placement activity. They help identify the need for staffing through the organization's human resource planning activity. They help with job analysis and evaluate employee performance. Most likely, however, they lack the time or desire to do an effective and efficient job of selection and placement. Notable exceptions do exist. For example:

> In the 40 or so years during which he ran General Motors, Alfred P. Sloan, Jr., picked every GM executive—down to the manufacturing managers, controllers, engineering managers, and master merchants at even the smallest accessory division. By today's standards, Sloan's vision and values may seem narrow. They were. He was concerned only with performance in and for GM. Nonetheless, his long-term performance in placing people in the right jobs was flawless.[5]

The PHRM department should be responsible for gathering information and should arrange interviews between job applicants and managers. It can then coordinate the information necessary to make a decision to hire, reject, or hold. Letting the PHRM department coordinate selection and placement activities involves several advantages. Applicants have only one place to go to apply for a job and have a better chance of being considered for a greater variety of jobs. Outside sources of applicants can clear employment issues through one central location. Operating managers can concentrate on their operating responsibilities—especially helpful during peak hiring periods. Further, because hiring is done by specialists trained in staffing techniques, selection is often better. Hiring costs may thus be cut because duplication of effort is avoided. Finally, with increased government regulations of selection, it is important that people who know about these rules handle a major part of the hiring process.

Purposes and Importance of Selection and Placement

Selection and placement procedures provide the essence of organizations—their human resources. Largely by effective selection and placement, organizations can obtain and retain the human resources most likely to serve their needs. Since productivity differences are likely to exist between employees, selecting only those employees likely to perform well may result in substantial productivity gains. For example, in a study of budget analysts, the dollar value of the superior performers' (top 15 percent) productivity was $23,000 per year *greater* than that of low performers (bottom 15 percent). In another study of computer programmers, the dollar value difference was $20,000 per year.[6]

Large dollar losses can also be avoided by effective and valid selection and placement procedures. For example, in 1984, U.S. Judge George Leighton, Chicago, signed off on the $60.5 million settlement between Burlington Northern Railroad, thirteen unions, and a group of black workers. The company agreed to hire fifteen thousand blacks within the next six years, using $50.5 million for training, hiring, and promotion. Charges originated after Amtrack took over Burlington passenger service. The workers said they were promised comparable jobs, but instead were given the option of inferior employment or quitting. Suit was filed by two men as well as the Equal Employment Opportunity Commission. Settlement took place shortly before trial was to begin.

Effective selection and placement are critical to any organization. Serving organizations' needs and being effective with selection and placement mean attaining several purposes:

- To contribute to the organization's bottom line
- To fairly, legally, and nondiscriminatorily evaluate and hire potentially qualified job applicants
- To help fulfill hiring goals and timetables specified in affirmative action programs
- To evaluate, hire, and place job applicants in the best interests of both organization and individual

- To engage in selection and placement activities that are useful for initial hiring as well as future selection and placement decisions for the individual (for example, in promotions or transfers)
- To make selection and placement decisions with consideration for the uniqueness of the individual, the job, the organization, and the environment, even to the extent of adapting the job or organization to the individual[7]

To serve these purposes effectively, selection and placement activities must be integrated with several other PHRM activities. Integration is necessary because selection and placement have an extensive set of relationships with other personnel and human resource activities and the internal environment.

Relationships Influencing Selection and Placement

As Exhibit 5.1 illustrates, the success of an organization's selection and placement procedures depends on their relationships with several other personnel and human resource activities and the internal environment.

Relationships with Other PHRM Activities

Selection and placement are associated with human resource planning, job analysis, recruitment, and performance appraisal.

Human Resource Planning.   Human resource planning can facilitate the organization's selection decisions by projecting when and how many such decisions will need to be made. If staffing needs for new jobs are identified, the PHRM department may need to anticipate new selection procedures and job-relatedness studies. Human resource planning can also facilitate selection decisions by ensuring that the maximum number of potential job applicants (especially those within the organization) are identified (especially for promotion decisions). This can be done with an extensive, up-to-date HRIS, described in Chapter 2. An HRIS can be used to store extensive banks of data on employees and jobs, which can be readily matched when job openings are identified.

Job Analysis.   Selection and placement decisions should be made to benefit both individual and organization. To do this, the qualities of the jobs to be filled must clearly be identified. When the essential job dimensions and worker qualifications are known, selection procedures can be developed. Selection procedures developed on the basis of a job analysis are more likely to be job related—and therefore more effective and more likely to serve legal considerations.

Selection procedures based on job analysis information tend to focus on workers' skills, knowledge, and abilities to do the jobs (Match 1). Also necessary is using information about job and organizational characteristics so

*Relationships and Aspects of Selection
and Placement*   *Exhibit 5.1*

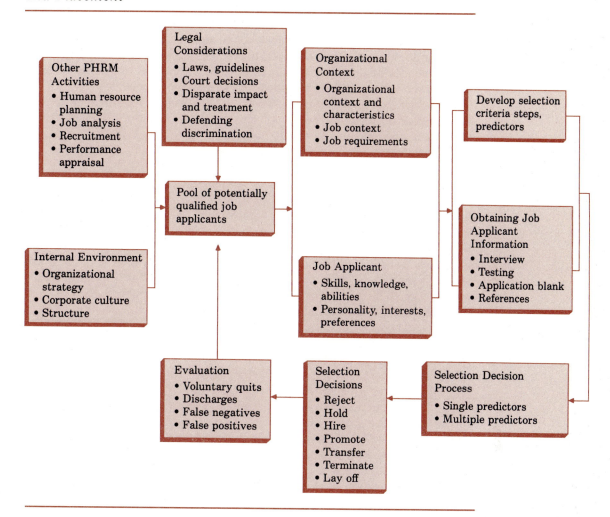

that job applicants can be placed in jobs that match their preferences, interests, and personalities (Match 2). As noted in Chapters 3 and 4, serving these two matches helps ensure that the short- and long-run interests of both individual and organization are served.[8]

Recruitment.   The success of selection and placement procedures depends on the effectiveness of the recruiting activity. If recruiting does not provide a large pool of potentially qualified job applicants, the organization has difficulty selecting and placing individuals who will perform well and not quit. Even if recruitment does provide some applicants, if the pool is small, the potential effectiveness of the selection and placement procedures is lessened because the selection ratio tends to become large.

Performance Appraisal. Selection and placement depend on performance appraisals as a source of feedback to show that the selection devices indeed predict performance. If the criteria used in performance appraisal are not job related (e.g., the appraisals are not built on job analysis (see Chapters 3 and 6) or the criteria are not communicated, the organization has difficulty developing and using selection devices to predict meaningful employee performance. In other words, performance appraisals serve as criteria for evaluating the predictive and economic utility of selection procedures.

These critical relationships with other PHRM activities should be considered in selection and placement procedures. Relationships with the internal environment should also be considered.

Relationships with the Internal Environment

Effective selection and placement procedures enable organizations to select job applicants on the basis of skills, knowledge, and abilities to do the jobs. Although this is consistent with our discussion of Match 1, more information is sometimes necessary. According to Spencer Stuart, president of a large New York–based recruiting firm: "You usually try to test to see if the person is going to fit in with the corporate culture."[9] That is, organizations usually try to fit individuals' characteristics with similar organizational characteristics. Characteristics of individuals include their willingness to take risks, their degree of flexibility to change, their time orientation (short term versus long term), and other qualities listed in Exhibit 1.3. As described in Chapter 1 and shown in Exhibit 1.4, organizations may also gather information on these characteristics to match them with organizational strategy. In making selection decisions, organizations may direct their efforts at matching individuals to jobs and to the organization's strategy and corporate culture. In essence, organizations may select individuals on the basis of their skills, knowledge, and abilities; their personalities, interests and preferences; and other general characteristics, such as general mental ability and leadership skills.

As an organization expands and begins to structure itself, different parts of its structure may develop different cultures and even different strategies. Large organizations such as Kodak, Campbell Soup, 3M, General Electric, and IBM have many different divisions and many different products. These products require different technologies, serve vastly different types of customers, and are in different stages of their life cycles. To select effectively, these organizations must analyze not only the jobs but also the cultures and strategies of their many divisions or strategic business units. As organizations become larger, selection and placement become more complex. Selection and placement are always important, however, no matter what size the organization.

Legal Considerations in Selection and Placement

The legal environment for most organizations is growing so complex that it is a major consideration in making employment decisions. Knowing what impact the legislation has on the selection and placement decision process is a second consideration. Both of these considerations rest on managers in the PHRM.[10]

Acts, Orders, and Guidelines Affecting Selection and Placement

Determining an organization's specific equal employment obligations is made complex by an extensive web of federal acts, federal and state constitutions, state and local legislation, court decisions, executive orders, guidelines, quasi-judicial bodies—such as the Equal Employment Opportunity Commission (EEOC) and the Office of Federal Contract Compliance Programs (OFCCP)—and state equal employment opportunity (EEO) or civil rights agencies. Before the 1960s, acts and guidelines that required equal opportunity in the field of employment were much less extensive. Appendix A lists the many equal employment laws that have been enacted since 1960.

Congressional Acts.   The most significant federal acts related to selection and placement decisions are the Civil Rights Act of 1866, Section 1981, the Civil Rights Act of 1871, Section 1983, the Title VII of the Civil Rights Act of 1964, the Age Discrimination in Employment Act of 1967 and the 1978 amendment, the Vietnam Era Veterans Readjustment Act of 1974, the Equal Employment Opportunity Act of 1972 (an amendment to the 1964 Civil Rights Act), the Equal Pay Act of 1963, and the Rehabilitation Act of 1973.[11]

The Civil Rights Act of 1866, Section 1981, prohibits employment discrimination based on race, color, or national origin. The Civil Rights Act of 1871, Section 1983, enforces the Fourteenth Amendment, which provides for "equal protection of the laws" and prohibits discrimination based on race, color, national origin, religion, sex, or age. The Equal Pay Act of 1963 prohibits discrimination between employees on the basis of sex by paying a wage rate higher for one sex than another for jobs that are equal in skill, effort, responsibility, and working conditions. The Age Discrimination in Employment Act of 1967 (ADEA), as amended in 1978, prohibits discrimination against employees and applicants for employment between the ages of forty and seventy years. The Equal Employment Opportunity Act of 1972 amended the Civil Rights Act of 1964, which created the EEOC. This 1972 amendment expanded the coverage of Title VII to include public and private employers with fifteen or more employees, labor organizations with fifteen or more members, and public and private employment agencies. Elected officials and their appointees are excluded from Title VII coverage but are still covered under the Fourteenth Amendment to the Constitution and the Civil Rights Acts of 1866 and 1871. The 1972 amendment also identified exceptions or exemptions to Title VII, discussed later, including bona fide occupational qualifications, seniority systems, pre-employment inquiries (as long as they are not used in making discriminatory selection decisions), use of job-related tests for selection, national security interests, and veterans' preference rights. Descriptions of how some of these have been interpreted are provided in a later discussion of the Civil Rights Act of 1964.

The Vocational Rehabilitation Act of 1973 prohibits discrimination against persons with physical or mental handicaps that substantially limit one or more major life activities or have a history of impairment or are visible to others. The Vietnam Era Veterans Readjustment Act of 1974 protects disabled veterans and veterans of the Vietnam era in seeking employment opportunities. In addition, both the Vocational Rehabilitation Act and the Vietnam Era Veterans Readjustment Act provide for affirmative action plans as described in Chapter 4. More details of these two acts and the other acts are provided in Appendix A. These are only the major federal acts pertaining to equal employment opportunity. State and local governments also have their own laws and acts, which employers in those states should know.

The Civil Rights Act of 1964 was passed by Congress with the intention of prohibiting employment discrimination against any individual. According to the language in Title VII of that act:

> It shall be an unlawful employment practice for an employer: (1) to fail or refuse to hire or to discharge any individual, or otherwise to discriminate against any individual with respect to his compensation, terms, conditions, or privileges or employment because of such individual's race, color, religion, sex, or national origin; or (2) to limit, segregate, or classify his employees or applicants for employment in any way which would deprive or tend to deprive any individual of employment opportunities or to otherwise adversely affect his status as an employee, because of such individual's race, color, religion, sex, or national origin.

Although the act explicitly states that discrimination against individuals is protected, the courts have generally heard discrimination cases involving an entire group or class of employees. Today cases can be brought by either individuals or classes. When brought by individuals, they are often referred to as **disparate treatment cases.** When brought by classes, they are often referred to as **disparate impact cases.**[12]

Executive Orders.   Executive Order (EO) 11246 of 1965 prohibits discrimination on the basis of race, color, religion, or national origin by federal agencies, contractors, and subcontractors. In 1966, EO 11375 was signed to prohibit discrimination in these same organizations on the basis of sex. EO 11478 prescribes that employment policies of the federal government be based on merit and that the head of each agency establish and maintain a program of equal employment opportunity. Although EO 11478 extended Part I of EO 11246, it left intact Part II of EO 11246, which regulates all federal contractors and subcontractors with federal contracts of $50,000 or more and fifty or more employees. They must submit to the OFCCP the affirmative action programs described in Chapter 4 and detailed in Revised Order Number 4 (1971).

Guidelines.   Several sets of guidelines on equal employment procedures have also had a major impact. The first set was issued in 1970 by the EEOC; the second set was promulgated in 1976 by three other agencies charged with equal employment responsibility: the OFCCP, the Department of Labor, and the Justice Department. These guidelines became the *Federal Executive Agency Guidelines on Employee Selection Procedures* (the *FEA*

Guidelines.) The EEOC did not sign the *FEA Guidelines.* In 1978, however, the EEOC joined these three agencies to adopt what is known as the *Uniform Guidelines on Employee Selection Procedures* (often referred to as the *Uniform Guidelines*), a fourteen-thousand-word catalog of do's and don'ts for hiring and promotion.[13] Among the many provisions in the *Uniform Guidelines* are guidelines in judging how to determine the job relatedness of a selection procedure. Although these guidelines have had substantial impact,

> the recent judicial opinions appear to have placed less reliance on the *Uniform Guidelines* in determining whether a given testing device had adverse impact and in assessing its job-relatedness or any validation efforts. Only two recent decisions found the *Uniform Guidelines* entitled to "great deference," and none applied them rigidly. Indeed, a few of the recent cases resolved the testing issues without reference to the *Uniform Guidelines* at all.[14]

The EEOC has recently published other guidelines in addition to those of 1970, 1976, and 1978. On 10 November 1980, the EEOC issued *Guidelines on Discrimination Because of Sex* (sexual harassment), and on 29 December 1980, it issued the *Guidelines on Discrimination Because of National Origin.* (Sexual harassment is discussed further in Chapter 14.) The national origin guidelines extended earlier versions of this protection by defining national origin as a *place* rather than as a *country* of origin.

In an attempt to clarify the extent of an employer's duty to undertake religious accommodation, the EEOC issued its current *Guidelines on Discrimination Because of Religion.*[15] In essence, an employer is obliged to accommodate the religious differences of current and prospective employees unless the employer demonstrates undue hardship. Apparently, however, if employers show "reasonable attempts to accommodate," the courts may be satisfied that no religious discrimination occurred (*State Division of Human Rights* v. *Rochester Housing Authority,* 1980).

Bases for Illegal Discrimination

Generally, a *prima facie* ("on their face") case of illegal discrimination can be established in four ways, three related to disparate impact and one related to disparate treatment.[16]

Disparate Impact.   Cases of disparate impact can be established through (1) comparative statistics, (2) demographic statistics, and (3) concentration statistics. The argument using comparative statistics is that the rates (or ratios) of hiring, firing, promoting, transferring, and demoting should be approximately the same for all groups of employees. A typical example of this argument is referred to as the **80 percent rule,** or the **bottom-line criterion.** It is also referred to as the **4/5 rule.** If, for example, a company hires 50 percent of all white male applicants who apply in a particular job category, then it must hire at least 40 percent (80 percent × 50 percent) of all blacks who apply and 40 percent of all women and other protected groups. Originally this bottom-line criterion was aimed at identifying disparate impact only for an entire set of selection procedures rather than for any single part of the procedures. This aim, however, has now been modified to apply to each part of the selection procedures as well as to the entire set (*Connecticut* v. *Teal,* 1982).

In contrast, the argument using demographic statistics centers on a comparison of an organization's work force to the population at large. This argument is rooted in the Civil Rights Act of 1964. For example, an employer's selection procedures could be shown as discriminatory (*prima facie*) if the employer's work force failed to reflect parity with the race or sex composition of the **general labor market** (*Griggs* v. *Duke Power Company,* 1971; *Castaneda* v. *Partida,* 1977). Historically, then, Title VII reflected an egalitarian presumption (i.e., that all individuals are equally qualified for all jobs).[17] Today, however, the comparison of the employer's work force has tended to become the **relevant labor market**. In essence, the egalitarian presumption has been set aside, particularly when special qualifications are required to fill particular jobs. In that condition, "comparison to the general population (rather than to the smaller group of individuals who possess the necessary qualifications) may have little probative value" (*International Brotherhood of Teamsters* v. *United States,* 1977). This notion that *prima facie* evidence of discrimination must be based upon the relevant (i.e., that of equally qualified individuals) labor market comparisons rather than those with the general labor market was also reflected in *Hazelwood School District* v. *U.S.* (1977) and *EEOC* v. *United Virginia Bank* (1980). Thus an employer's work force should reflect the percentages of groups in the relevant labor market. What the relevant labor market is, however, means different things to different people:

> For some, it refers to a given geographic location: i.e., the Richmond, Virginia labor market, the Cleveland, Ohio labor market, etc. In economics, the concept of a labor market is more rigorously defined as the area in which buyers and sellers of labor are in sufficiently close communication that wages tend to be equalized. Equating a labor market with a given geographic area is sometimes a convenient simplification, but it is not accurate. Any given area is composed of a large number of submarkets (partially overlapping but essentially noncompeting) which shade gradually into one another. The more highly trained and paid the workers in a market are, the wider the geographic area of the market will tend to be.[18]

As suggested in Chapter 4 in the discussion of affirmative action programs (AAPs) and utilization analysis, organizations may determine their relevant labor market in several ways. One is by identifying where 85 percent of current employees and job applicants reside. As in determining the relevant labor market for AAPs, in determining the relevant labor market to avoid *prima facie* evidence of discrimination, organizations may choose to identify only the labor market from which they generally select applicants that have the necessary skills, knowledge, and abilities. The EEOC, however, may suggest that organizations expand their labor market, geographically or according to the extent to which individuals are able to do the jobs the organizations are seeking to fill. As a consequence of this possible scenario between organizations and the EEOC, determining the relevant labor market is often an art rather than a science. In addition, once the relevant labor market has been determined, it is subject to revisions because of changing demographic characteristics of the U.S. labor force. Organizations are witnessing dramatic demographic changes based on the comparisons of the 1970 and 1980 national censuses. As a result of these comparisons, organizations are having to redetermine their relevant labor markets to successfully defend AAPs and cases of *prima facie* evidence of discrimination, based on comparisons of the representativeness of an organization's work force with the percentages of protected group members in the relevant labor market. *Prima facie* cases of this type are likely to be successfully defended to the extent that parity is attained (i.e., the extent to which the proportions of protected group members in an organization's work force mirror the proportions in the relevant labor market).

The third basis for establishing a case of disparate impact is use of concentration statistics. The argument here is that a *prima facie* case of illegal discrimination exists to the extent that protected group members are all located in one particular area or job category in the organization. For example, equal numbers of male and female employees may be in entry-level jobs in the organization, but the females may be predominantly in secretarial jobs. Such a situation provides a case of disparate impact.

Disparate Treatment. Illegal discrimination against an individual is referred to as disparate treatment. In contrast to the cases of disparate impact, a *prima facie* case of disparate treatment exists to the extent that an individual can demonstrate the following:

- The individual belongs to a minority.
- The individual applied for a job for which the employer was seeking applicants.
- Despite the individual's qualifications, he or she was rejected.
- After the individual's rejection, the employer kept looking for people with applicant's qualifications.

These three conditions were set forth in *McDonnell Douglas Corp.* v. *Green* (1973). Once a *prima facie* case of illegal discrimination has been established by any one of the four ways, the employer must be given the opportunity to defend itself.

Bases for Defending Illegal Discrimination

If an organization is accused by the EEOC of illegal discrimination, it may be able to successfully defend its employment practices by showing the following:

- Job relatedness
- Business necessity
- Bona fide occupational qualifications (BFOQs)
- Bona fide seniority systems (BFSSs)
- Voluntary affirmative action programs (AAPs)
- Alternative procedures

The employer or defendant need only demonstrate that one of these legitimate explanations exists. The plaintiff must then show that the organization's defense is really a pretext for illegal discrimination or that alternative procedures exist that would yield less adverse impact (disparate impact or disparate treatment). Because each of these defenses is legitimate, it is appropriate to discuss them before examining the procedures by which employers obtain information about job applicants.[19]

Job Relatedness.   Employers are interested in measuring employee qualifications and establishing predictions of how well employees who possess the qualifications will "do on the job."[20] Although egalitarianism may have been behind the Civil Rights Act initially, the Tower amendment attached to it permits employers to use tests to measure applicants in selection decisions so long as the tests are not designed, intended, or used to discriminate because of race, sex, color, religion, or national origin. Thus, even though a test is used in making selection decisions that result in adverse impact, if the test is shown to be job related, the adverse impact can be defended (*Griggs* v. *Duke Power Company,* 1971). To demonstrate **job relatedness**, the company must show that its selection and placement procedures (predictors) are related to an employee's being successful on the job.

Showing the job relatedness of a selection procedure is desirable but may not always be possible. Recognizing this situation, some courts have allowed companies to defend their selection procedures by showing business necessity.

Business Necessity.   Business necessity, along with job relatedness, can be used as a basis for defending adverse impact.[21] Whereas the job-relatedness defense often requires a demonstration of actual predictor-criterion relationships, business necessity does not. The case of *Levin* v. *Delta Air Lines, Inc.* (1984), described in the following "PHRM in the News," was decided on the fact that pregnancy was not shown to impact the essence of the business (safe air travel)—not that it failed to impact the ability of a flight attendant to provide service to the air travelers. Thus, business necessity can justify adverse impact. In cases where business necessity clearly is high, demonstrating that a specific selection procedure is job related is not necessary (see *Spurlock* v. *United Airlines,* 1972, and *Hodgson* v. *Greyhound Lines, Inc.,* 1974, in Appendix A).

Bona Fide Occupational Qualifications and Seniority Systems.   Another defense for adverse impact is **bona fide occupational qualifications** (BFOQs). For example, requiring that labor and delivery nurses in the obstetrics and gynecology department in a hospital be female is a BFOQ according to the U.S. District Court for the Eastern District of Arkansas (*Backus* v. *Baptist Medical Center,* 1981). Hiring only males to play male roles in plays and theater productions has been judged a BFOQ. Race and color have been judged to never be a valid BFOQ. Requiring commercial pilots to retire as pilots at age sixty was also a BFOQ as determined by the Federal Aviation Administration. In the summer of 1985 the U.S. Supreme Court, however, struck down this requirement as arbitrary and not sufficiently job related.

A final base of defense for a *prima facie* case of illegal discrimination is the existence of a **bona fide seniority system** (BFSS). As long as a company has

Pregnancy Policy Protected

An airline that transferred flight attendants to ground duty as soon as it learned of their pregnancies did not violate Title VII, the U.S. Court of Appeals at New Orleans holds. Although the policy discriminated against female employees, the court finds that valid safety concerns justify the policy as a business necessity essential to the safe operation of the carrier.

The airline has never allowed flight attendants to continue working on commercial flights once their pregnancy was disclosed. In 1974, the airline adopted its present policy of transferring flight attendants to ground duty when they reported their pregnancies. EEOC and a class of flight attendants filed suit, contending that the policy violated Title VII because it subjected female workers to disparate treatment on the basis of sex. The airline, however, maintained that pregnant flight attendants are subject to illnesses, such as morning sickness, spontaneous abortion, and fatigue, that would render a worker unable to provide assistance to passengers in emergency situations.

The inability to predict in advance which flight attendants will be overcome by fatigue, nausea, or spontaneous abortion and the airline's commitment to safety justify the transfer policy, the court finds. "To pass muster under Title VII, a discriminatory policy must be addressed to the 'essence' of the business operation," the court states, stressing that if the employer's "pregnancy policy can be shown to reduce substantially the risks attending air travel, its policy should be upheld against Title VII challenge." (Levin v. Delta Air Lines, Inc.)

Source: Fair Employment Practices, 17 May 1984, p. 1. Reprinted by permission from *Fair Employment Practices,* copyright 1984, by The Bureau of National Affairs, Inc., Washington, D.C.

established and maintained a seniority system without the intent to illegally discriminate, it is considered bona fide (*International Brotherhood of Teamsters* v. *United States,* 1977; *United States* v. *Trucking Management, Inc.,* 1981; *American Tobacco* v. *Patterson,* 1982). Thus, promotion and job assignment decisions can be made on the basis of seniority.[22] In a recent major decision, the Supreme Court ruled that seniority can also be used in the determination of layoffs, even if by doing so the effects of affirmative action hiring are reversed (*Firefighters Local Union 1784* v. *Stotts,* 1984).

Voluntary Affirmative Action Programs (AAPs). As described in Chapter 4, organizations may establish affirmative action programs without pressure from the EEOC or the OFCCP. For them to be a defense against illegal discrimination, however, they need to be remedial in purpose, limited in duration, restricted in impact, flexible in implementation, and minimal in harm to innocent parties. While charges of reverse discrimination have resulted from the implementation of voluntary AAPs, the courts appear to be sympathetic to these AAPs, particularly if their impact is on the hiring of new employees, rather than the layoff of current employees (*Wygant* v. *Jackson Board of Education,* 1986). The courts are also sympathetic to the defense of AAPs established by consent decrees (Local 93 of the *International Association of Firefighters* v. *City of Cleveland,* 1986).

Alternative Procedures.   Even when a valid defense can be shown to exist for using selection methods with adverse impact, a company may also be required to demonstrate that *no other* procedures would have been as effective in screening out unsuitable candidates and at the same time have less adverse impact. This is called the **alternative procedures requirement.** Critics of this requirement have labeled it the **"cosmic search"** requirement of employers. It was first contained in the 1970 guidelines, but the *Uniform Guidelines* (1978) shifted the burden of meeting from the individual (plaintiff) to the organization (defendant). The courts, however, have indicated that the burden of showing that alternative procedures exist remains on the plaintiff rather than on the defendant (*Texas Department of Community Affairs* v. *Joyce Ann Burdine,* 1981).

With these legal considerations in perspective, we can now examine how they specifically influence the obtaining of selection and placement information.

Selection and Placement Information

Although much selection and placement information is gathered by the organization about the job applicant, the job applicant should also obtain information about the organization. As discussed in Chapter 4, it is appropriate and even desirable for organizations to convey information about the job and organization to the applicant, especially regarding realistic information about the job's context and qualities. First we discuss information about the organizational context, followed by ways of gaining information about the job applicant.

Organizational and Job Context

As shown in Exhibit 5.1, organizations can convey to job applicants information about organizational characteristics and job context and requirements. These three categories of information enable applicants to determine if their skills, knowledge, and abilities match the available jobs and if their personalities, interests, and preferences (or their characteristics) match the characteristics of the organization and job. These categories of information also enable the organization to make the same assessments. Better selection decisions should result when both parties are actively involved in the decision.

Organizational Characteristics.   As discussed in Chapter 1 and at the beginning of this chapter, organizations look for applicants who can do the job and who can fit the organization's corporate culture and strategy. Organizations are aware that different types of people (those with different employee characteristics) are required for different types of organizations. Though this may be more true for managers, all employees are influenced by organizational characteristics such as corporate strategy and culture. As such, these characteristics should be conveyed to job applicants by describing the organization's strategy and culture and how these appear to fit with employee characteristics. Job applicants must also know the context in which a job is performed.

Job Context.   Both the applicant and the organization should be aware of the physical conditions that the applicant will confront on the job. This is particularly true since the 1980 court decision that permits employees to decline a job assignment if they believe danger to life or limb is imminent (*Whirlpool Corporation* v. *Ray Marshall, Secretary of Labor*). Other aspects of the job context include the hours of work, the time pressures under which it is done, where it is performed, the quality of the supervision, and norms and standards of work.

Job Requirements.   Information about job requirements and specifications is obtained from the job analysis and is needed to match individual skills, knowledge, and abilities with job demands. In addition, job design information should also be provided so that the job's characteristics are known. This is critical in helping job applicants determine if the job characteristics can satisfy their personalities, interests, and preferences. As discussed in Chapter 12, the job design characteristics and individual personalities, interests, and preferences information can also be used in redesigning jobs and in placing applicants in more appropriate jobs. To further aid applicants in choosing jobs and in performing them well, standards of performance and other job-related expectations, such as absenteeism, should be passed along from the job analysis.

Information about organizational and job context is only about half of the information needed for effective selection and placement. Job applicant information makes up the other half.

Information from Job Applicants

The specific types of information often obtained from a job applicant are skills, knowledge, and abilities, and personality, interests, and preferences.[23] This information is discussed more fully later in the chapter. This information, along with that about the organization and job, is the basis for predicting how successfully the applicant will perform the job criteria. Appropriately, these pieces of information are often called *predictors*. When they are used to make selection decisions, they are called *tests*.

According to the *Uniform Guidelines,*

> [a] test is defined as any paper-and-pencil or performance measure used as a basis for any employment decision. The guidelines in this part apply, for example, to ability tests that are designed to measure eligibility for hire, transfer, promotion, membership, training, referral, or retention. This definition includes, but is not restricted to, measures of general intelligence, mental ability and learning ability; specific intellectual abilities; mechanical, clerical, and other aptitudes; dexterity and coordination; knowledge and proficiency; occupational and other interests;

and attitudes, personality, or temperament. The term "test" includes all formal, scored, quantified, or standardized techniques of assessing job suitability including, in addition to the above, specific qualifying or disqualifying personal history or background requirements, specific educational or work history requirements, scored interviews, biographical information blanks, interviewers' rating scales, scored application forms, etc.

Although *Uniform Guidelines* defines the word *test* to include all forms by which information to make selection decisions is gathered, in this chapter *test* refers exclusively to written tests.

Gathering predictor information from job applicants is critical in selection and placement. When used in conjunction with criteria information, it is the essence of making selection and placement decisions.

Predictors and Criteria in Selection and Placement Decisions

Predictors for Selection and Placement Decisions.   Selection decisions in organizations are generally made on the basis of job applicants' predictor scores. These scores predict how well the applicants, if hired, will perform according to the job performance criteria. Typically, selection decisions are made using scores from several predictors that are administered to the job applicants sequentially. Likewise, selection decisions are also made in steps. Exhibit 5.2 shows a typical example of the steps in the selection process. Before proceeding with these steps, managers in PHRM must determine the criteria that will be used for selection and placement decisions.

Criteria for Selection and Placement Decisions.   The criteria selected must be critical to the job the organization wants to fill. For example, in the corporate loan assistant's job (Chapter 3), the criterion of making sure loan applicants have a good loan history and are credit-worthy is probably more critical (that is, relevant, reliable, valid, and practical) than making sure loan applicants' desks are always clean and organized. According to the corporate loan assistant job description in Chapter 3, other criteria are also critical to the job. Establishing the exact criteria and their relative importance is critical to developing valid predictors and having a valid performance appraisal system (see Chapter 6).

The exact criteria are also important because they help determine the type of information that should be obtained from job applicants and, to some extent, the method used to gather the information. For example, if absenteeism is an appropriate criterion, a check of references on employment history or a preference test may be used. If quantity of performance is identified as a criterion, a written test measuring an applicant's skills, knowledge, and abilities may be used.[24]

As described in Chapter 3, the job analysis is at the base of determining appropriate, relevant, and important criteria. Compare the relationship between the job dimensions of the corporate loan assistant in Exhibit 3.3 and the knowledge and skills necessary to perform the job duties in Exhibit 5.3. The job incumbents identified the skills, knowledge, and abilities and the job

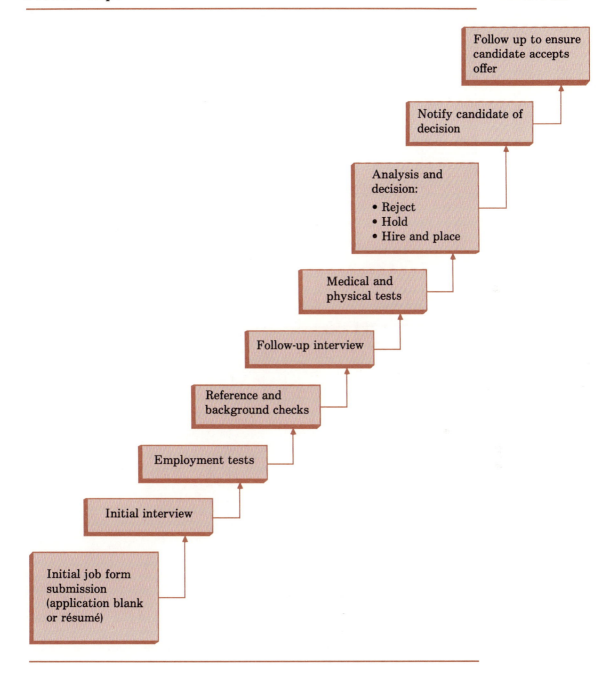

Exhibit 5.3   **Selection Plan Matrix**

FOR: ___CORPORATE LOAN ASSISTANT___   DATE: _____

Practices, Procedures, and Tests Used in Selection

1		2	3	4	5	6	7	8	9	10	11	12	13
Coding			**R =**								**BI/**		
A	**B**	**Short Title**	**Rank**		**SAF**					**DAI**	**REF√**		**PAF**
		Knowledges/Skills											
MQ		1. Communication	R		X					X	X		X
MQ		2. Math			X					X	X		X
MQ		3. Writing			X					X	X		X
MQ		4. Reading			X					X	X		X
MQ		5. Researching			X					X	X		X
MQ		6. Organizing	R		X					X	X		X
MQ		7. Listening	R		X					X	X		X
MQ		8. Social skills			X					X	X		X
MT	B	9. Sales	R		X					X	X		X
MQ		10. Interpret	R		X					X	X		X
WT		11. Bank policy											X
MT	C	12. Bank services	R		X					X	X		X
WT		13. Computer											X
WT		14. Credit report											X

Notes: MQ = Minimum Qualification. *MT* = May be Trained or acquired on the job (desirable). Preference may be given to those who possess this knowledge/skill. When used on a physical characteristic, MT means a reasonable accommodation can be made. WT = Will be Trained or acquired on the job. Not evaluated in the selection process. *WT* = Will be Trained or acquired on the job because it can be learned in a brief orientation (i.e., eight hours or less). Not evaluated in the selection process. *MQ/MT* = Lower level is Minimum Qualification: higher level May be Trained or acquired on the job (desirable). *MQ/WT* = Lower level is minimum Qualification; higher level Will be Trained or acquired on the job. WT part is not measured in the selection process. *MT/WT* = Lower level May be Trained or acquired on the job; higher level Will be Trained or acquired on the job. WT part is not measured in the selection process. *R* = Rank. Applicants may be ranked by how much they possess. This is differentiating among those who possess more and who will probably perform the duties better. Not all the differentiating knowledges, skills, physical characteristics, and "other characteristics" are ranked. *SAF* = Supplemental Application Form. *WKT* = Written Knowledge Test. *ST* = Skills Test. *PCD* = Physical Capability Demonstration. *SOI* = Structured Oral Interview. *DAI* = Departmental Appointment Interview. *BI/REF/√* = Background Investigation/Reference Check. *ME* = Medical Examination. *PAF* = Performance Appraisal Form.

Source: Biddle & Associates, Inc. Used with permission.

dimensions as discussed in Chapter 3 in the discussion of GOJA. Since those job dimensions were identified as the essence of the job, they are essentially the job criteria. (These criteria are behaviors rather than outcomes such as quantity of output or absenteeism, the distinctions between which are clarified in Chapter 6.) The skills, knowledge, and abilities necessary to perform those behaviors (job dimensions criteria) are then determined to be measured or not measured (depending on whether individuals can learn them quickly or whether they will be trained on the job). The method by which each knowledge and behavior is to be measured is indicated in Exhibit 5.3. Note that several measures are used for some knowledge and skills (e.g., bank services). Whether or not several measures are used, these measures, in essence, become the predictors of how well the applicant will perform the job dimensions criteria.

After the important criteria are identified, predictors must be chosen to assess how well an applicant will perform on those criteria. This process is neither easy or inexpensive. If done correctly, however, it results in selection and placement decisions that are effective and serve the legal considerations. Also needed for effective selection and placement decisions is job applicant information. The following discusses the various types of job applicant information and techniques for obtaining it.

Types of Job Applicant Information

Information for selection and placement decisions is obtained from interviews, written tests, application blanks, references, and physical tests. Using these procedures, organizations can gather a great deal of applicant information related to the following:

- Skills, knowledge, and abilities
- Personality, interests, and preferences
- Other characteristics

Skills, Knowledge, Abilities; Personality, Interests, Preferences

Gathering and using information on the individual, particularly to predict performance, generally represents concern for only the match between job demands and an individual's skills, knowledge, and abilities (Match 1). This match appears most subject to legal constraints and traditionally has been of major interest to organizations because it is aimed at predicting how well the individual is likely to perform on the job. However, information about individual personality, interests, and preferences (Match 2) should also be gathered. When used appropriately in combination with information about job rewards and organizational characteristics, this information can increase employee satisfaction and reduce absenteeism and voluntary turnover. It may also enhance the quality of employee performance, because of increased job involvement and motivation resulting from the match between employee personality, interests, and preferences, job rewards, and organizational characteristics. Regardless of the type of information gathered, however, its relationship with the job performance criteria must be demonstrated, not merely assumed.[25]

Although demonstrating job relatedness may be easiest with information about skills, knowledge, and abilities, those that can be learned in less than eight hours or taught on the job should not be used to make selection decisions. Furthermore, if job applicants need only a specified minimum level of a knowledge, skill, or ability, then the only information that should be obtained is whether the applicants meet the minimum levels. If having more of a skill, knowledge, or ability is likely to result in better performance, then information about how much above the minimum a person is should be obtained so that the applicant can be ranked. When making decisions in the areas of firing, demotion, layoff (where a bona fide seniority system does not exist), or discipline, a more appropriate measure is of employees' task or job performance rather than their skills, knowledge, and abilities. If physical abilities are being measured, consideration must be made for job accommodation. If reasonable accommodation cannot be made to a handicap that interferes with performing the essential duties of the job, the applicant can be rejected.

Information on the type of education and experience is often gathered to measure skills, knowledge, and abilities. Evaluation of a candidate's *type* of education or experience is a useful way of ensuring that the candidate for hire, transfer, training, or promotion does have the necessary knowledge and skills required for the job. Evaluation of the content of the education or experience, however, should be done as it relates to the job-required skills, knowledge, and abilities. One should not fall into the trap of evaluating the *number* of years of education or experience a candidate has as proof of specific knowledge and skills.[26]

Other Characteristics

Other characteristics include aptitude, intelligence, general mental ability, general knowledge (not task-specific knowledge), leadership, judgment, dexterity, and common sense. Demonstrating the job relatedness of this information may be difficult, but the attempt should be made if it is to be gathered and used.

Employers can also gather information about other characteristics, such as terms and conditions of employment. This includes licenses required by law; willingness to travel or work split shifts, weekends, or under adverse conditions such as confined facilities and high noise levels; uniform requirements; business-related grooming codes; tools required on the job and not provided by the employer; required training to be taken on the job; and driver's licenses. These characteristics are usually required as minimum qualifications for a job and are rarely used to rank applicants. Applicants either possess them or do not. Although these characteristics do not indicate how candidates will do on the job, candidates can be disqualified for consideration if they are unwilling to comply with them. Information that should not be gathered (primarily because it is discriminatory) for making selection decisions is noted in the following discussion of techniques for gathering information.

Techniques for Obtaining Job Applicant Information

Application Blank

The application blank is shown as the first step in the selection process in Exhibit 5.2. For many professional and managerial jobs, applicant-prepared résumés replace application blanks as a means of gathering data for selection purposes. Unfortunately, these résumés, like references indicated on application blanks, are increasingly less likely to reflect reality and should therefore be used only in conjunction with other information.[27] The **application blank** is a form seeking information about the job applicant's background and present status (including current address and telephone number). Although application blanks in the past requested a great deal of information, often including a photograph, legal challenges have substantially reduced the data required.

Because of the potential for producing adverse impact and the difficulty in demonstrating job relatedness, certain information should not be requested in an application blank. (If it is requested, it should not be used in making selection decisions unless a BFOQ applies). This includes information about the following:

- Clergy as references
- Number of children and who will care for them
- Height and weight unless job related
- Marital status
- Education level or degree
- Arrest record
- Conviction record unless strongly related to job
- Nature of military discharge
- Citizenship
- Credit questions
- Relatives and friends working for the employer
- Questions about age, sex, religion, and national origin

Discretion must be used not only in gathering information on application blanks but also in their use.[28] For example, special codes indicating the acceptability of an applicant should not be put on the application blank.

Even with these prohibitions, application blanks can still yield a great deal of useful information. To make this information as job related as possible, organizations sometimes weight it, or give some information more importance as a predictor of criteria. This procedure produces a **weighted application blank (WAB)**.[29] WABs can be extremely effective in predicting criteria such as turnover and are often developed using multiple regression analysis. Based on the results of the analysis, the relative importance (or weight) of the information on the application blank can be determined and used in selection decisions.

In addition to the application blank, or even as a substitute for it, employers may administer a **biographical information blank (BIB)**. A BIB generally requests more information from the applicant than does an application blank. For example, in addition to requesting information about name, present address, references and skills, and type of education, the BIB may request the applicant to indicate a degree of preference for such things as working split shifts, being transferred, working on weekends, or working alone. Exactly which items are asked should be based on the nature of the job. If the job does require split-shift working, a BIB item that indicates any preference for split shifts may be a good predictor of turnover.[30]

Other information often asked for in a BIB relates to an applicant's work and prework history. For example, an applicant may be asked to indicate whether he or she worked or had a car in high school. This kind of biographical background is gathered on the assumption that past experiences may be important predictors of future behaviors, particularly job performance. Whether they are can be determined by various validation strategies discussed in the next chapter. BIBs in general, however, can be useful ways to collect information predictive of job performance. The following "PHRM in the News" demonstrates the potential usefulness of BIBs.

Selection and Placement Interview

Although aptitude, achievement, personality, interests, and preferences are more reliably assessed by written tests or carefully developed situational tests, the interview remains the most popular method of obtaining information.[31] However, although it appears to be a good procedure for gathering factual background, it is not a particularly good one for making assessments because it is too subjective.[32] Nevertheless, employers continue to use the interview for both data gathering and decision making. This is paradoxical given the pressure on organizations by agencies such as EEOC to use more objective methods of gathering information.[33] These agencies are concerned about interviews because their results can be unreliable (for example, two people interviewing the same applicant can come to different conclusions). They can also be used to obtain discriminatory information, such as that listed in regard to the application blank.

The discussion that follows focuses on the use of interviews and how the information obtained from them can be made more reliable. Information obtained from interviews is more likely to be job related if the prohibitions listed for application blanks are carefully observed.

As shown in Exhibit 5.2, the interview process is important at both the beginning and end of the selection procedure. The way the interview is conducted depends on the type of job being filled. For middle- and upper-level managerial and executive jobs, individuals often submit résumés (by mail or through a placement or job search firm) to organizations. An initial interview is made over the phone if the organization wants to gather more information from the applicant. For lower-level management and nonmanagement jobs, an individual may see a job advertised in the newspaper or posted on the organization's bulletin board and fill out an application. The initial in-

Biographically-based Selections

Obtaining biographical information from job applicants about a wide range of personal and work experiences is an effective selection technique, asserts Robert Means, president of Occidental Consulting Group, Lafayette, Calif. Often referred to as "biodata"—a term Means describes as "misleading"— biographical information can help an employer determine which candidates are best suited to particular jobs. The straightforward background and experience data obtained through such a biographically-based selection process, Means says, can prove to be the best predictors of an applicant's future job performance.

Biodata are obtained from the applicants themselves, who fill out a questionnaire that requires them to provide details about their educational, extracurricular, and job experiences, as well as more personal information in such areas as self-concepts. The questionnaire usually contains 150–170 items in a multiple choice format, Means notes. The responses are statistically compared with those of successful performers on the job to determine the likelihood of each applicant's success or failure in the position. Unlike the traditional selection interview, whose results can be influenced by the subjective variables and biases of interviewers, a biodata-based process provides objective background and experience information, Means contends, adding that the technique is easy and creates no stress. Means also emphasizes that the methodology is a nonbiased, "perfectly fair instrument that will cause no adverse impact." Other benefits cited by Means include:

- Productivity increases of up to 15 percent;

- Reduced costs for hiring, training, and terminating people who should not have been hired;

- Reduced turnover (at least 10 percent for clericals, for example);

- A reduction in interviewing time; and

- Better evaluation of recruiting sources in terms of their ability to produce qualified applicants.

Source: Bulletin to Management, 20 June 1985, pp. 3–4. Reprinted by permission from *Bulletin to Management,* copyright 1985, by The Bureau of National Affairs, Inc., Washington, D.C.

terview may follow. Because of the increased legal necessity to keep records of applicants who have been hired, organizations should document that information before beginning the interview.[34]

Frequently, several individuals interview the applicant, especially if the job is a middle- or upper-level managerial or executive position. Often these interviews ask for in-depth information about motivation, attitudes, and experience in order to make assessments, not just gather information. Even the initial interview has an assessment component, because a reject or pass decision could be made at that stage. Therefore, both interview stages are crucial.

Types of Interviews. Interviews can be categorized according to the techniques and format used. One common interview is the **depth interview**. The interviewer has only a general outline of topics to be covered and often pursues them in an unstructured fashion. The interviewee may be allowed to expand greatly on any question asked. Because the quality of this interview often depends on the interviewer's skill, organizations often use a **patterned** or **structured interview** instead. To ensure consistency, this interview resembles an oral questionnaire. But because it is structured, validation studies indicate that the patterned interview can be effective in predicting job success. A patterned interview may include the following steps:

Conduct a skills analysis—Study the job description of the position in question and review the kinds of skills the job may require, such as typing, scheduling, or negotiating. This step is useful in identifying the skills most important in the job and can tell you what to look for in job candidates. During this process, two kinds of skills should be considered: performance skills, which tell the interviewer how a worker goes about doing a job, and technical/job skills, which represent what needs to be done on the job.

Select skill dimensions—Skill dimensions describe a set of behaviors that may be required in a job, such as ability to cope with deadline pressures or make decisions on available information. Precisely defined skill dimensions help the interviewer to know what qualities to look for in a job candidate and are useful in formulating interview questions.

Prepare interview questions—Once skills are established, prepare "tailormade" questions for the job to maximize your chances of obtaining information about the selected skills. Interviewees should be asked to provide examples of past work that illustrate how a specific skill was used.

Conduct the interview—Try to make the applicant comfortable at the beginning by asking "rapport-building" questions. Take notes throughout the interview, obtaining specific names, dates, and locations.

Evaluate behavior—Before rating a candidate, read over the skills and skill dimensions needed for the job, as well as any interview notes. Determine which of the individual's skills are strongest and which are weakest, and then consider how these strengths and weaknesses correspond to the demands of the job as defined by the skills analysis.[35]

When several individuals interview one applicant, it is called a **panel interview.** Because of its cost, it is usually reserved for managerial job applicants. Another type of interview used for certain types of managerial positions is called the **stress interview,** which is used for jobs where remaining calm and composed under pressure is important. In the stress interview, the interviewer may intentionally annoy, embarrass, or frustrate applicants to see how they react. Although this may be a good format for certain types of jobs, such as those in law enforcement and the military, it appears to be less useful or job related in most organizations.

Common Interview Problems.   Regardless of the format, several problems are inherent with interviews.[36] Personnel can play a key role by making sure that interviewers are aware of the problems, are trained in how to avoid them, and are reinforced for conducting interviews correctly.[37]

Potential problems relating to the interview as a procedure for gathering and assessing information include the following:[38]

■ Managers (as interviewers) may not seek applicant information dimensions needed for successful job performance (or success by any other criteria). Often the interviewers do not have a complete job description or an accurate appraisal of the critical job requirements. In addition, the interviewer often does not know the conditions under which the job is performed. Nevertheless, for performance and legal reasons, all the information obtained must be job related.

■ Especially with several interviewers, managers sometimes overlap in their coverage of some job-related questions and miss others entirely. An applicant may not have four interviews but one interview four times, during which all managers ask the same questions and are provided the same information.

■ Managers may make snap judgments early in the interview and consequently block out further potentially useful information.

■ Managers may permit one trait or job-related attribute to influence their evaluation of the applicant's remaining qualities. This process, called the **halo effect,** occurs when an interviewer judges an applicant's entire potential for job performance on the basis of a single characteristic, such as how well the applicant dresses or talks.

■ Managers may not have organized the various selection elements into a system. Exhibit 5.2 depicts an order in the selection activities, but in practice these activities are often not done in an organized manner. Key references may not be checked ahead of time, resulting in interviews with unqualified applicants. Occasionally, applicants are treated differently, some given certain tests and others not. However innocent such mistakes might be, the result is unfair and discriminatory selection practices.

■ Interviewers sometimes have a tendency to be swayed by negative information.

■ Information from applicant interviews may not be integrated and discussed systematically. If several interviewers share information on an applicant, they may do so in a haphazard manner. They may not identify job-related information or seek to examine any conflicting information. This casual approach to decision making may save time and confrontation— but only in the short run. In the long run, everyone in the organization will pay for poor hiring decisions.

■ Managers' judgments are often affected by the pressure to fill the position and lower their standards. If this leads to a bad decision, managers can always claim an excuse. Managers may also hire an applicant because of the price (salary demands). Personnel managers can reduce this possibility by not revealing salary demands to the line managers responsible for hiring. The best philosophy is to first select the best person for the job and then be concerned with the cost.

■ Managers' judgments regarding an applicant are often affected by the available applicants. First, a good person looks better in contrast to a group of average or below-average people (**contrast effect**). An average person looks below-average or poor in contrast to a group of excellent people. Second, two important **order effects** can occur. At times a first impression (**primacy effect**) becomes lasting; the first person remains the standard used to evaluate the quality of all the other people. But an interviewer, especially at the end of a long day of interviewing, may be more likely to remember the last person better than the other people (**recency effect**). Applicants should be aware of these effects and should avoid being victimized by them.[39]

Overcoming Potential Interview Problems.   The following are essentially ways to increase the validity and reliability of the interview (its job relatedness, the scope of qualifications measured, and the consistency and objectivity of the information gathered):

- *Gather only job-related information.* Be sure to use only information from job-related questions as predictors of future performance. This requires a job analysis on the jobs to be filled and, if possible, validation results for the predictors used. Job relatedness can also be increased by structuring the interview and using multiple interviewers. This procedure improves the reliability of the interview results.

- *Use past behavior to predict future behavior.* Concentrate on obtaining information about the applicant's past job behavior. This background can be conveniently gathered in the initial interview. However, getting specific examples of performance-related experiences and the events surrounding them is preferable.

- *Coordinate the initial and succeeding interviews with each other and with other information-gathering procedures.* The information should be combined in an objective, systematic, job-related manner. This can help reduce quick decisions, bias, and the use of stereotypes in selection.

- *Involve several managers in interviewing and in the final decision.* This can be done as a group or individually. Although the final decision may be made by only one person, several should be involved in gathering and assessing the information.

Nonverbal Cues in Interviews.   Another critical aspect of the interview is the unspoken or nonverbal component. Body movements, gestures, handshakes, eye contact, and physical appearance are all **nonverbal cues.** Often interviewers put more stock in these cues than in what is said:

> It has been estimated that, at most, only 30 to 35 percent of the meaning conveyed in a message is verbal; the remainder is nonverbal. Similarly, in terms of attitudes or feelings, one estimate is that merely 7 percent of what is communicated is verbal, while nonverbal factors account for the remaining 93 percent.[40]

Therefore, it is important to be aware of nonverbal cues: "In fact, one of the reasons that nonverbal cues are so powerful is that, in most cases, interviewers are not aware of them as possible causal agents of impression formation."[41]

What to Ask.   Interviewers may ask anything that, when combined with other information about the job applicant, can be a useful predictor of how well the applicant will perform once hired. Useful questions include the following:

- Has the applicant performed in a similar capacity before?
- How does the applicant feel about the present job qualities and organizational context?
- If the applicant is changing jobs, why is a change being made?
- What are the applicant's career objectives?
- Does the applicant like working closely with other people?
- How has the applicant performed considering the environment of that performance?[42]

Improper questions for an interview are the same as those discussed for the application blank.

Written Tests

Testing is another important procedure for gathering, transmitting, and assessing information about an applicant's aptitudes, experiences, and motivations. The most common types of written tests measure aptitude, achievement, and personality, interests, and preferences (PIPs).

The validity and reliability of written tests are of utmost importance for both the organization and the job applicant because they help ensure that an applicant will perform at a certain level. They also provide the job applicant with a sense of fairness and legality in the selection procedure. However, no component of staffing has generated more controversy and criticism since the early 1960s than the use of written or paper-and-pencil testing.[43] Controversy and criticism center on questions of test fairness (or cultural bias), validity, and test item characteristics such as vagueness and irrelevancy.

The extent of controversy and criticism appears to be out of proportion to the extent that employment tests are actually used, especially among private employers. As reflected by the initial "PHRM in the News," however, the use of ability testing appears to be increasing. This trend may be positive, since many tests typically used for employment decisions are valid predictors of job criteria such as performance for many jobs in a variety of organizations.[44] This trend may also be beneficial, given the alternative selection procedures (e.g., interviews, application blanks, and references). Consequently, understanding which tests are most frequently used in selection is useful. The following examples represent just some of the tests that can be used to measure individuals' skills, knowledge and abilities and personalities, interests, and preferences. If these tests are given but are not used in making selection decisions, the equal-employment-opportunity legal considerations do not apply. For example, PIP measures may be given to help place new employees in the appropriate job context (i.e., on the basis of matching personalities, interests, and preferences with the job and organizational characteristics) *after* the hiring decision is made. However, even though the legal considerations are not as applicable in these placement decisions, the decisions should still be made consistent with the legal considerations (i.e., to positively influence job criteria, at the same time satisfying individuals' personalities, interests, and preferences).

Aptitude Tests.   **Aptitude tests** measure the potential of individuals to perform. Measures of general aptitude, often referred to as general intelligence tests, include the Wechsler Adult Intelligence Scale and the Stanford-Binet test. These tests are primarily used to predict academic success in a traditional setting. Several multidimensional aptitude tests were developed for organizations, including Differential Aptitude Tests, the Flanagan Aptitude Classification Test, the General Aptitude Test Battery, and the Employee Aptitude Survey. Because they are standardized, however, they are not specific to any particular job. But they are reliable and general enough to be used in job situations, especially for indicating the contribution that more specific tests can make.[45]

Another group of aptitude tests, called **psychomotor tests,** combine the mental and the physical. Two of the more widely used psychomotor tests are the MacQuarrie Test for Mechanical Ability and the O'Connor Finger and Tweezer Dexterity Tests. The MacQuarrie test measures skills in tracing, tapping, dotting, copying, locating, arranging blocks, and pursuing. This test seems to be a valid predictor for such occupations as aviation mechanic and stenographer. The O'Connor test is a valid predictor for power sewing machine operators, dental students, and other workers requiring manipulative skills.[46]

A final group of aptitude tests relates to personal and interpersonal competence. One test of **personal competence,** the Career Maturity Inventory, measures whether individuals know how to make appropriate and timely decisions for themselves and whether they put forth the effort to do so. It includes five competence tests related to problems, planning, occupational information, self-knowledge, and goal selection. The better the score on these five competency tests, the more likely an individual is to make career decisions resulting in higher satisfaction and performance.[47]

Interpersonal competence tests have been designed to measure social intelligence. These include aspects of intelligence related to

information, non-verbal, which is involved in human interactions where awareness of attention, perceptions, thoughts, desires, feelings, moods, emotions, intentions, and actions of other persons and of ourselves is important.[48]

Achievement Tests.   **Achievement tests** predict an individual's performance on the basis of what he or she knows. Validation is required of any test used by an organization, but validating achievement tests is a straightforward process. The achievement tests almost become samples of the job to be performed. However, hiring on the basis of achievement tests may exclude applicants who have not had equal access to the opportunities to acquire the skills. Note that not all achievement tests are samples of the job; some are less job related than others.

Paper-and-pencil achievement tests tend to be less job related because they measure the applicant's knowledge of facts and principles—not the actual use of them. For example, you could take a paper-and-pencil test measuring your knowledge of tennis and pass with flying colors and yet play the game poorly. Although this is a serious deficiency, paper-and-pencil achievement tests continue to be used in many areas because of their widespread applicability. For example, admission to the legal profession is through the bar exam, and the medical profession is entered through medical boards. Paper-and-pencil tests are used in these cases because they are related to or are assumed related to performance in the actual job. Job relatedness can be a necessary legal defense for the use of paper-and-pencil tests (as well as all other tests).

The **recognition test** is often used in advertising and modeling to select applicants. The applicants bring portfolios to the job interview—samples of the work they have done. However, portfolios contain no clues to the conditions or circumstances under which they were done. Some organizations may insist on seeing written samples from schoolwork for jobs where written expression may be important.

Recognition tests are examples of past behavior; **simulation tests** are used to see how applicants perform now. Only the task itself—not the situation in which the task is performed—is recreated. Even so, simulation can be extremely useful as a training and practice device.

Some achievement tests overcome the artificiality of simulations by using the actual task and working conditions. These are called **work sample tests.** Work sample tests are frequently given to applicants for secretarial jobs. Applicants may be asked to type a letter in the office where they would be working. Work sample tests are still somewhat artificial, however, because the selection process itself tends to promote anxiety and tension. Nevertheless, work samples are used extensively because of their applicability and validity.[49]

Anxiety and tension may not be artificial for certain jobs, such as a managerial job under time pressure. A work sample test referred to as the **in-basket exercise** has been created for that type of job. Its objective is to create a realistic situation that will elicit typical on-the-job behaviors. Situations and problems encountered in the job are written on individual sheets of paper and set in the in basket. The applicant is asked to arrange the papers by priority. Occasionally the applicant may need to write an action response on the piece of paper. The problems or situations described to the applicant involve different groups of people—peers, subordinates, and those outside the organization. The applicant is usually given a set time limit to take the test but is often interrupted by phone calls meant to create more tension and pressure. Other work sample tests used in managerial selection are the **leaderless group discussion** (LGD) and **business games.**[50] In the LGD a group of individuals are asked to discuss a topic for a given period of time. Business games are living cases. That is, individuals must make decisions and live with them similar to what they do in the in-basket exercise. Because in baskets, LGDs, and business games tend to be useful in managerial selection, they are often used together in an assessment center.

In an **assessment center,** job applicants or current employees are evaluated as to how well they might perform in a managerial or higher-level position. Over twenty thousand companies use this method; its use grows each year because of its validity in predicting which job applicants will be successful and which will be unsuccessful.[51]

An assessment center is usually composed of a half dozen to a dozen people who have chosen or have been chosen to attend the center. The center is usually run by the organization, for one to three days, but off the premises. Attendees' performance is usually determined by managers in the organization who are trained accessors. An excellent example of the use of an assessment center is General Motors' *Manufacturing Supervisors Assessment Program.* The purpose of the assessment program and the exercises and tests is to help determine potential promotability of applicants to the first-line supervisor's job.

The General Motors assessment center program measures eight areas of qualifications identified through job analyses and other research as being essential to good performance in manufacturing supervision. These are:

- Organizing and Planning
- Analyzing
- Decision Making
- Controlling
- Oral Communications
- Interpersonal Relations
- Influencing
- Flexibility

The program also provides an overall evaluation of each candidate's qualifications.

The program content includes a wide range of evaluation techniques, such as group problems, interviews, in-baskets, tests, videotape exercises, and questionnaires. These are designed to simulate the situations and problems that manufacturing supervisors regularly encounter on their jobs. As candidates go through these exercises, their performance is observed by a specially trained team of observers/evaluators (assessors) drawn from the local management group. The assessors then meet after the candidates have finished the program to discuss the candidates and prepare evaluations, based on the combined judgments of all of the assessors, of the candidates in the areas of performance listed above.[52]

The composite performance in the exercises and tests is often used to determine an assessment center attendee's future promotability and the organization's human resource planning requirements and training needs, as well as to make current selection and placement decisions. The composite performance evaluation is generally shared with the attendee, who in turn can use this information for his or her own personal career planning purposes.

PIP Tests.   Designed to assess an individual's personality, interests, and preferences, PIPs may focus on specific jobs in the organization. Tests of individual traits or characteristics are sometimes referred to as **personality inventories.** Unlike tests, personality inventories have no right or wrong answers. Several common multidimensional tests of personality are the Edwards Personal Preference Schedule, the California Psychological Inventory, the Gordon Personal Profile, the Thurstone Temperament Survey, and the Minnesota Multiphasic Personality Inventory. These personality inventories are useful for predicting the performance of salesclerks, clerical workers, and the like.

Companies can save a great deal of money by using valid personality tests for selection decisions. Additionally, once a selection decision is made, personality tests may be useful for placement and career counseling. This is also true for personality measures such as those measuring tolerance for ambiguity and locus of control. If the open job is set in a context of change and uncertainty, selecting individuals with a high tolerance for ambiguity may prove effective.

In light of these factors, and as the initial "PHRM in the News" describes, the use of personality tests is on the rise, particularly in organizations that have a participatory culture:

> The trend is most prevalent at companies that are espousing so-called participatory management, giving workers more responsibility in running operations. And companies like financial service and insurance firms, forced to improve service in the face of increased competition, say they are searching harder for employees with greater "people" skills—empathy, ability to communicate and an overall motivation to please others.[53]

Placement and career counseling decisions can also be facilitated by **interest tests.** Two major interest tests are the Strong Vocational Interest Blank and the Kuder Preference Records. Both are essentially inventories of interests. Although generally not predictive of performance on the job, they can predict which occupation will be more in tune with an individual's interests. Records are grouped into ten vocational categories—outdoor, musical, computational, scientific, persuasive, artistic, literary, musical, social service, and clerical. Specific jobs can be identified within each of the ten groupings. Both of these interest tests should be used with caution. They could not likely predict performance in a job, nor are they always valid for predicting the specific type of job one will choose within a vocational or occupational grouping.

Preference tests are also useful in assessing employee characteristics for matching with organizational characteristics, such as corporate strategy and culture. As with personality tests, however, their focus can also be on specific jobs. Exhibit 5.4 shows an example of a scale to measure employee preferences for certain job characteristics. The results from this scale can be used to assess how individuals will respond to job redesign efforts (described in Chapter 12).

Reference Verification and Background Checks

Another way of gathering information is by **reference verification.** Although Exhibit 5.2 lists this as the fourth step in the selection process, it may be done earlier. The recent trend, however, is to rely less on this form of verification because providing references can result in violation of Title VII of the Civil Rights Act.[54]

In addition, reference verification involves conflicting values—liberty and privacy. On the one hand, employers should be free to discriminate among job applicants, especially when seeking performance-related information about them. On the other hand, liberty for the organization often leads to infringement of an individual's privacy. Currently, this conflict has

Exhibit 5.4   *Sample Preference Test from the Job Diagnostic Survey*

Listed below are a number of characteristics that could be present on any job. People differ about how much they would like to have each one present in their own jobs. We are interested in learning *how much you personally would like* to have each one present in your job.

Using the scale below, please indicate the *degree* to which you would like to have each characteristic present in your job.

Would mildly like having this		Would strongly like having this		Would very strongly like having this		
1	2	3	4	5	6	7

_____ 1. High respect and fair treatment from my supervisor
_____ 2. Stimulating and challenging work
_____ 3. Chances to exercise independent thought and action in my job
_____ 4. Great job security
_____ 5. Very friendly co-workers
_____ 6. Opportunities to learn new things from my work
_____ 7. High salary and good fringe benefits
_____ 8. Opportunities to be creative and imaginative in my work
_____ 9. Quick promotions
_____ 10. Opportunities for personal growth and development in my job
_____ 11. A sense of worthwhile accomplishment in my work

Source: From J. R. Hackman and G. R. Oldham, *Task Design* (Reading, Mass.: Addison-Wesley, 1980), p. 136. Reprinted by permission of the authors.

led to several lawsuits. The result has been several state and federal laws regarding the use of personal information for employee decisions. Today about thirty-five states, up from two in 1977, limit the right of companies to disclose information (discussed in Chapter 14).

As the following "PHRM in the News" suggests, some job applicants falsify their past and current qualifications.[55] As a consequence, employers are turning to outside investigators and more seriously checking past employers used as references. Some are also turning to the use of lie detector testing.

Lie Detector Tests and Honesty Tests.   Increasing numbers of organizations routinely ask job applicants to submit to a **lie detector,** or **polygraph, test** or to take a **paper-and-pencil honesty test** as part of the selection procedures.[56] This is particularly true where the applicant is being considered for a fiduciary position or has access to pharmaceuticals or any small consumer item with resale value.

More 'Honesty' Tests Used To Gauge Workers' Morale

In a corporate whodunit, psychological testing can be a better sleuth than the police.

Last year, for instance, a foreman at a large company almost died after someone poisoned his coffee. Local law enforcement officials were stumped, and the union protested the use of lie-detector tests. But a battery of written tests reduced the number of suspects from 38 to one, who later confessed to police.

Increasingly, such paper-and-pencil tests are being used not just to solve specific crimes but also to screen employees before they are hired and to gauge morale and loyalty on the job. A record 2.3 million employment applicants were given "honesty" tests last year, up from one million in 1981, estimates James Walls, a marketing vice president at Stanton Corp., a psychological testing concern.

Employee theft

Stanton's own evaluations underscore why employers are using the tests more frequently. Thirty-two percent of the employment applicants the company screened last year admitted on signed statements that they had stolen from a previous employer, up from 12% two decades ago. Similarly, a recent survey of 9,000 employees by the Justice Department found that one-third admitted stealing from their current or previous employers.

"More and more employees today have a negative attitude toward their employers," says E. John Keller, a security consultant at Arthur Andersen & Co., the accounting firm. "There's a direct correlation between low morale and high theft."

Such disenchantment isn't confined to hourly workers. At one large retailing company, 35 senior executives were recently given a Stanton honesty test that guaranteed their anonymity. Twenty-two admitted having falsified expense vouchers.

"I've seen senior vice presidents, making $200,000 a year, who committed corporate espionage," says Mr. Keller. He recently investigated a corporate theft ring that involved 18 senior officials—including a division president. "You can have a lot of responsibility and still feel disaffected," he says.

Detecting hostilities

Most honesty tests are designed to probe for disaffection before it becomes a problem. Questions carefully crafted by psychologists and criminologists can often detect smoldering hostilities. For instance, someone taking the Stanton Inventory—a test designed to assess employee attitudes—is asked 96 questions, most of them requiring written responses.

Some are straightforward ("How would you rate this company as a place of employment?"); others allow employees to reveal their feelings indirectly ("How does your nearest loved one feel about you working here?"). In the Stanton test, employees aren't asked to identify themselves, though, curiously, most do.

Sometimes simply giving a test can help solve a company's problems. A convenience food-store chain recently gave an honesty test to a few hundred employees, who were given instructions on how to correct the test themselves. Their exposure to the test and the process of self-correction, according to Mr. Keller, prompted an immediate two-thirds reduction in inventory theft.

Although applicants cannot be forced to take a polygraph test in order to be hired or promoted in most states (no federal law exists in this regard), many companies may ask applicants to sign a release indicating they are taking the test voluntarily. Job applicants should answer questions honestly, especially pertaining to what is on their application blanks. Refusal to answer questions about religion, sexual activity, political leanings, and other nonjob issues is appropriate. Applicants may, however, want to discuss this with the employer after the exam. Typically, organizations hire outside polygraph examiners; but because of the costs and problems associated with their use, companies are beginning to use paper-and-pencil tests to predict individuals who are likely to lie or steal.[57] The following "PHRM in the News" describes the state of honesty testing.

Medical and Physical Tests

Although not all organizations require medical exams or physical tests, they are being given in increasing numbers. One consequence is a concern about genetic screening as a part of the physical examination process.

Physical Examination.   The physical or medical examination is often one of the final steps in the selection process. Many employers give common physical exams to all job applicants, whereas special exams are given to only a subset of all the applicants. For example, production job applicants may receive back X-rays, while office job applicants may not. According to the *Uniform Guidelines*, physical examinations should be used to screen out applicants only when the results indicate that job performance would be adversely affected.

Physical exams can be used in conjunction with physical ability tests to help ensure that proper job accommodation is made and to provide a record for the employer to prevent employees from filing workers compensation claims for preexisting injuries.[58] A more recent use of the physical exam is to screen applicants based upon their genetic makeup. **Genetic screening** is based on the premise that some individuals may be more sensitive to work place elements, such as chemicals.[59] The screening is based on an analysis of an applicant's blood sample. Although genetic screening is still relatively new, its use may continue to grow. At the same time, it may prove to be more appropriately used as information for placement rather than selection. If all applicants are shown to have equal sensitivity to a work place chemical, genetic screening information may be used for work place modification. If applicants are shown to have different sensitivities to a work place chemical, the concern is that the screening may be used to select only certain people and not modify the environment. But because relatively little is known about genetic screening, harm could occur to those selected and unfair discrimination to those not selected. Similar comments are made regarding testing for drug use and AIDS.[60]

Physical Ability Tests.   In Chapter 3, nine physical abilities are discussed, including such things as dynamic, trunk, and static strength. Although these attributes help analyze the physical requirements of tasks, they can also be used as a basis for selecting job applicants. Used in conjunction with the Physical Abilities Analysis in Chapter 3, job-related physical ability tests can be developed and utilized in selection. Ensuring that physical ability tests are job related is important because they are covered by the *Uniform Guidelines.* If shown to result in adverse impact (as in the case of strength tests that exclude females), physical ability tests must prove themselves relevant.

Through the process of attempting to demonstrate the job relatedness of physical ability tests, such as those for dynamic strength, potentially non-job-related tests may be identified and either modified or replaced. This process may also suggest job modifications that can provide more equal employment opportunity, especially for women and handicapped individuals (reasonable accommodation here is a necessity anyway), while maintaining the integrity of the job. With these considerations in mind, the use of physical ability tests can be both a valid and fair means to select applicants.[61]

Summary of Information-gathering Techniques

In general, employment tests for achievement, physical ability tests, interviews, and weighted application blanks are appropriate (i.e., can be shown to be related to job criteria, especially performance) for measuring skills, knowledge, and abilities. Although employment tests for aptitude may be demonstrated to be associated with job criteria, the association is indirect, and thus it may be more difficult to establish job relatedness.

Suggested here as measures of personality, interests, and preferences are the employment tests for personality, interests, and preferences, BIBs, and interviews. Although their association with job criteria may generally be more difficult to demonstrate than with appropriate skills, knowledge, and abilities measures, their association with some specific job criteria (e.g., absenteeism) may not be. Nevertheless, measures of personality, interests, and preferences may be more appropriate for matching employee characteristics with organizational characteristics formed by corporate strategy and culture. Although research is just beginning in this area, organizations are apparently taking these steps now and will continue to do so because they are recognizing that it takes different types of people (i.e., those with different characteristics and not necessarily skills) to run organizations with different types of strategies and cultures.

For gathering information about other characteristics, employment aptitude tests and interviews are used. Interviews are included here as well as in measuring skills, knowledge, and abilities. This versatility may suggest in part why employers use them so frequently.

Job applicant information must also be gathered on characteristics such as work preferences, special licenses, physical condition of the applicant, and even current residence information. The most effective ways of obtaining this information appear to be physical examinations, application blanks, reference checks, and lie detector tests.

After having gathered so much information, how do organizations use it?

Methods for Using Information in Selection and Placement Decisions

Generally, one method can be used alone in making selection and placement decisions (the single predictor approach) or several methods can be combined (the multiple predictors approach).

The Single Predictor Approach

When managers in PHRM use only one piece of information or one method for selecting an applicant, they are taking the **single predictor approach**. Many organizations use single predictors to select employees, especially when they can readily be validated. This occurs most frequently when a single predictor captures the essence or the major dimension of the job, thereby making it easy to validate:

> A few hiring tests are easy enough to validate, especially those in which the candidate actually performs a task he/she will have to perform on the job. It makes obvious good sense, for example, to require a candidate for a secretarial job to pass a typing test, and generally the equal-opportunity establishment accepts such tests.[62]

But for many jobs, a single predictor (test) cannot be used, nor can a single dimension (duty), such as typing, be used to explain the essence of the job. Many jobs can be explained only with several job dimensions, as illustrated in the job description in Chapter 3. For such jobs, several predictors, such as written tests and application blanks, are used in making the selection and placement decisions.

The Multiple Predictors Approach

When several sources of information are combined, selection and placement decisions are made with a **multiple predictors approach**. Information from different sources can be combined in several ways. The type of job typically influences what information is gathered and how it is combined. Generally the information is combined using a noncompensatory approach, a compensatory approach, or a combination of these two approaches.[63]

Noncompensatory Approach to Multiple Predictors.   Two major models are used in making predictions for selection decisions based on a noncompensatory approach. One is the **multiple cutoff** model, and the other is the **multiple hurdle** model. Both models are based on the idea that the job to be performed has several dimensions, and thus several predictors are appropriate in making the selection decision.

In the multiple cutoff approach, an applicant must exceed fixed levels of proficiency on all the predictors in order to be accepted. A score lower than the fixed level cannot be compensated for by a higher-than-necessary score on another predictor. Failing on one predictor cannot be compensated for by doing extremely well on another one. For example, an applicant for an air traffic controller job cannot compensate for failure on a visual recognition test.

The multiple hurdle approach is similar to the multiple cutoff approach except that decisions are made sequentially. In the multiple cutoff approach, selection is made only from the applicants who score at or above the required fixed levels of proficiency on each of the measures being used as predictors. In contrast, when a multiple hurdle approach is used, applicants must first pass one hurdle (a test) before they go on to the next hurdle. For example, they may need to first pass a paper-and-pencil test before they are asked in for an interview.

In the multiple hurdle approach, an applicant may not need to attain or exceed a minimum score on each predictor in order to be selected. Sometimes low scores on a predictor prompt a provisional acceptance of the applicant. This provisional acceptance enables the organization to assess how the applicant performs on the job. If the applicant performs well on those dimensions on which he or she had low scores, the applicant, now an employee, may be granted full acceptance. Although this multiple hurdle approach or model helps ensure higher success rate for the final acceptance decisions, it necessitates hiring applicants who otherwise may not have been hired (e.g., under a multiple cutoff approach) and who may not make it beyond provisional acceptance. Thus, some cost is involved in using multiple hurdles, although it may bring a more sufficient number of applicants who turn out to be successful.[64]

Compensatory Approach to Multiple Predictors.   Assumed by both of the prior models is that doing well on one predictor cannot compensate for doing poorly on another one (i.e., the approaches are **noncompensatory**). When this assumption is not applicable, the multiple regression approach is used. This is a **compensatory** approach that assumes that good performance on one predictor can compensate for poor performance on another predictor (e.g., a low score on ability can be compensated for by a high score on motivation). Based on this assumption, the statistical analysis of multiple regression can then be used to combine predictors to predict job criteria.

Combined Approach to Multiple Predictors.   Many organizations use the combined approach, often beginning with recruitment. The combined approach may use aspects of both the multiple cutoff and compensatory approaches. Generally, the multiple cutoff approach (or part of it) is used first: "You have to get through the door before we'll consider (interview) you." Once in (the interview), the compensatory approach applies. For example, an organization may establish one minimum requirement—an undergraduate degree in accounting *or* a high grade point average—in order to be hired. Thus, when organizations decide to use multiple predictors, they need to assess the characteristics of the jobs to determine the appropriate number of predictors and the extent to which predictor scores can compensate for each other.

Organizations must also demonstrate that each predictor used meets the 4/5 criterion, as discussed earlier. Previously, the bottom-line criterion referred to using the 4/5 rule to assess the results of only the decisions at the very end of the selection process. Now, however, the 4/5 rule must be met for decisions at each step (for each predictor) in the total selection process (*Connecticut* v. *Teal*, 1982). Regardless of whether the 4/5 rule is applied to each step in the selection process or to the final decision of the entire process, employers need only demonstrate predictor validity when challenged (i.e., when an adverse impact charge has been made by the employee, the job candidate, governmental agencies such as the EEOC, or the courts). Until a challenge occurs, however, the employer legally does not have to demonstrate validity or defend predictors used. In general, to defend (if so decided) employment decisions, an employer should be able to show the decision was job related, that it was based on job-related information, and that documentation exists to support the decision.

Issues related to demonstrating the validity of single and multiple predictor strategies are presented in Chapter 18.

Trends in Selection and Placement

The trends in selection and placement include assessment of decisions, computer technology and HRIS usage, and strategic involvement.

Assessing Selection and Placement Decisions

The quality and effectiveness of selection and placement decisions depend on whether the organization hires applicants who turn out to be good performers. If the organization can select and place applicants who turn out to perform well, organizational productivity will benefit. In addition, if the organization does not select and place applicants who would have performed poorly, organizational productivity will also benefit. The critical point is that when an organization makes selection and placement decisions based on activities that benefit organizational productivity, it is making decisions using predictors that are valid and serve its legal considerations. Using predictors that do not result in selection and placement decisions that benefit productivity are counterproductive and generally are not consistent with legal considerations. Consequently, organizations must use valid predictors.[65]

Because developing valid predictors is a critical activity in personnel research, strategies to validate single and multiple predictors are described in Chapter 18. But obtaining and using predictors that are valid is only part of making effective selection and placement decisions. The other parts include base rate, selection rate, the selection ratio, and the overall dollar costs and benefits of the decisions. These are also described in Chapter 18.

Computer Technology and HRIS in Selection and Placement

On any given day, a personnel department will likely evaluate a number of candidates for a variety of positions. Deciding which predictors are relevant (valid) for a particular case and administering a multitude of predictors (tests) makes personnel's work challenging. Effective management of predictors is critical in the face of extensive laws and regulations. Doing all of these effectively requires a great deal of information. Computer technology can enhance personnel's ability to coordinate the scheduling, administration, and evaluation of predictors by processing this information in a variety of ways.

For example, personnel could quickly do a validation study by correlating the current job performance data with any of several predictors, if these data were stored in a human resource information system and analyzed by computer. With an HRIS and computers, the determination of utilization rates for affirmative action programs, as discussed in Chapter 4, can also be done quickly and easily. Results of tests to measure job applicants' skills, knowledge, and abilities and personalities, interests, and preferences can be stored in an HRIS and used together with job analysis data (also in the HRIS) to make better selection and placement decisions. This same information can then be used to help plot career paths for employees when they are hired.

Strategic Involvement of Selection and Placement

Organizations are increasingly realizing that people make a difference and that different types of people are required to run different types of organizations:

> As stated by Reginald H. Jones, former chairman and CEO of the General Electric Company: "When we classified . . . [our] . . . businesses, and when we realized that they were going to have quite different missions, we also realized we had to have quite different people running them. That was where we began to see the need to meld our human resources planning and management with the strategic planning we were doing.[66]

This quote typifies what is beginning to appear in organizations: a growing awareness for the importance of linking staffing concerns with the business.[67]

Recently, Data General changed its managerial structure. For Data General to successfully implement its new structure requiring professional managers rather than entrepreneurs, it has slowly replaced many of its homegrown managers with more experienced ones from outside. To ensure the success of this staffing practice, Edson de Castro, president, and Herbert J. Richman, executive vice-president, spent a vast amount of personal time on hiring only those managers whose styles and interests fit with Data General. The styles and interests that seem to fit best with Data General now are those reflecting a desire for organization, long-range strategic planning, and more stable and methodical growth patterns.

Gaining Competitive Advantage.   Also growing is the awareness of how staffing can be used for competitive advantage. For example, the American Productivity Center in Houston utilizes its staffing practices to gain a competitive advantage. Furthermore, it supports its staffing practices with consistent training practices. According to Stu Winby at the center:

> In hiring consultants we specifically look for the generalist; an individual who has high propensity to learn other areas in the productivity domain; an individual whose appreciation system and skills span both the qualitative and quantitative aspects of productivity and organizational effectiveness. A value of the organization is placed on organizational integration. We promote cross-training and a multi-disciplinary approach to consulting engagements. The competitive advantage is that most members of the consulting staff can "sell" any of the other speciality areas but can also be reasonably effective in the delivery of those specific services.
>
> Against consulting firms that are more specialized and do not seem to have this broad perspective emphasis on hiring generalists and promoting internal integration among consultants has provided competitive advantage.[68]

The Baltimore Orioles also attain differentiation and competitive advantage through their staffing practices, this time with their suppliers. Its farm clubs combine a selection policy emphasizing internal promotion and support this with an extensive training system (the farm clubs). Of these two PHRM practices, the internal promotion is apparently more critical to their overall success. The result of both these practices, however, is a product that is clearly differentiated from other teams in the industry: a consistency at winning, yet retaining key employees at compensation levels far below many competitors despite the lucrative bidding that goes on for top players.[69]

Linking with Organizational Strategy.   Based on our discussion, several strategic staffing choices reflect the recruitment and selection practices. The linkage of all these choices with a given organizational strategy is shown in Exhibit 1.4. The choices include the following:

Internal Sources———External Sources
Narrow Paths———Broad Paths
Single Ladder———Multiple Ladders
Explicit Criteria———Implicit Criteria
Closed Procedures———Open Procedures

The first choice from the staffing menu is choosing the source from which to recruit applicants. At one extreme, companies can choose to use internal sources exclusively (e.g., other departments in the company and other levels in the organizational hierarchy). At the other extreme, they can use external sources exclusively. Although this choice may be limited for entry-level jobs, it is a highly important one for most other jobs. Recruiting internally essentially means a policy of promotion from within. Although this policy can serve as an effective reward, it commits a company to providing training and career development opportunities if the promoted employees are to perform well.

Associated with this first choice is the second choice of establishing broad or narrow career paths.[70] The broader the paths that are established, the greater the opportunity for employees to acquire skills relevant to many functional areas, and the greater the opportunity to gain more exposure and visibility in more parts of the organization. Both of these aspects resulting from broader career paths enhance an employee's skill acquisition and opportunities for promotion within the organization. The time frame for this process of acquiring many skills, however, is likely to be much longer than that required for acquiring a more limited skill base. Thus, promotion may be quicker under a policy of narrow career paths, although an employee's career opportunities may be more limited over the long run.

Another staffing choice to be made is whether to establish one or several promotion ladders. The decision to establish several ladders enlarges the opportunities for employees to be promoted and yet stay within a given technical specialty, without having to necessarily assume managerial responsibilities. Establishing just one promotion ladder enhances the relative value of a promotion and increases the competition in getting it.

Part of a promotion system are the criteria used in deciding who to promote. The choice here is the degree to which the criteria for promotion are explicit. The criteria can vary from very explicit to very implicit. The more explicit the criteria, the less adaptable the promotion system is to exceptions and changing circumstances. What the company loses in flexibility, however, the individual may gain in clarity. This clarity, however, may be beneficial only for those who exactly fulfill the criteria. The more implicit the criteria, the greater the flexibility to move employees around and develop them more broadly.[71]

A final choice is the degree of openness in the staffing procedures. The more open the procedures, the more likely there is to be job posting for internal recruitment, self-nomination for promotion, and self-nomination and involvement in assessment centers for promotion. The less open and more secret the procedures, the more limited employee involvement in selection decisions, but the faster the decisions can be made. To facilitate a policy of openness, however, companies need to make the relevant information accessible and available to the employees. Such a policy, however, is worthwhile, since it allows individuals to select themselves into entrepreneurial jobs, a critical aspect of successful entrepreneurship.[72]

Summary

This chapter examines what selection and placement procedures are and how they relate to other personnel activities. It also examines in detail the legal considerations in making selection and placement decisions, such as BFOQs, business necessity, job relatedness, and bases for illegal discrimination. Organizations want to ensure that they hire job applicants with the abilities to meet job demands. Increasingly, they also want to ensure that job applicants will not only perform well but stay with the organization. Thus, organizations may want to attain a match between job applicants' needs and the rewards that the job qualities and organizational context offer.

To match individual skills, knowledge, and abilities to job demands and individual personalities, interests, and preferences to job and organizational characteristics, organizations need to gather information about job applicants. The three most common methods—interviewing, testing, and application blanks—must operate within legal regulations. These legal regulations are not intended to discourage the use of these methods but rather to ensure that information is collected, retained, and used in recognition of an individual's rights to privacy and an organization's right to select individuals on the basis of legal considerations. Consequently, the types of information and the methods used to obtain information for selection vary according to the type of job for which the applicants are being selected. For example, assessment centers are apt to be used for managerial jobs, and physical ability tests are apt to be used for manufacturing and public health and safety jobs. Exactly how many predictors are used may depend in part on the type of job, but is also likely to depend on the selection ratio, the costs associated with the selection tests in comparison to their benefits, and the degree of validity and reliability of the predictors being used. Because these are important concerns in personnel research, they are described in more detail in Chapter 18.

Discussion Questions

1. Once an organization has had a *prima facie* case of discrimination or adverse impact brought against it, what course does the organization have to defend itself?

2. Where does selection and placement information come from, and what is it used for?

3. Although the interview is still the primary method used in selection and placement, what problems arise from its use?

4. What is the bottom line in gathering and assessing information from the job applicant with respect to future selection and placement in the organization?

5. Distinguish selection from placement in the context of the Match 1 and Match 2 concepts. Who assumes responsibility for Match 1 and Match 2—the employer or the applicant?

6. A frequent diagnosis of an observed performance problem in an organization is, "Joe was a selection mistake." What are the short- and long-term consequences of these so-called selection mistakes? Can you relate this question to your own experience with organizations?

7. How is an achievement test distinguished from an aptitude test? Is the Graduate Management Admissions Test (GMAT) that many schools use to select applicants for Master of Business Administration (MBA) programs an achievement test or an aptitude test?

8. Given all of the weaknesses identified with the interview, why is it a popular selection device? How could you improve the interview to overcome some of these weaknesses?

9. What is genetic screening? Is this a means to assess the applicant's skills, knowledge, and abilities, or the applicant's personality, interests, and preferences? How might the employer's rights conflict with the indi-

vidual's rights when genetic screening is used for selection and placement decisions? How would you resolve this conflict?

10. Successful selection and placement decisions are dependent on other personnel functions. Identify these functions and their relationships to selection and placement.

PC Project

The discriminatory effects of selection procedures can be examined using statistical evidence. Inspection of selection rates is the typical mechanism for determining the existence of adverse impact. As noted in the chapter, the 80 percent rule is used to compare selection ratios for minority and nonminority groups. This PC Project gives you the opportunity to examine the adverse impact of the selection procedures used by a large company. If adverse impact is revealed, what should the company do?

C   A   S   E   S   T   U   D   Y

Equal Opportunity Selection

Karen Daft was looking forward to the monthly executive committee meeting at Commerce Bank. Commerce is a small-town bank (fifty-four employees) located in Winnsboro, South Carolina. Karen, the personnel officer of Commerce Bank, was going to make a proposal to the executive committee to change the way selection of hourly or nonexempt employees was conducted at Commerce. In the two years that Karen had worked at Commerce, this would be the first major initiative she would take. Karen's strategy up to now was to lie low, learn the ropes, and not make any waves.

Karen was promoted to assistant vice-president of personnel, the first female to obtain this rank during the forty-year history at Commerce. She began as a clerk in the personnel department and got her chance at an administrative position when her predecessor was promoted to vice-president in charge of trusts. Commerce was built by Melvin Hitt shortly after World War II and passed along to his two sons, Ronald and Donald, shortly before his death ten years ago. Ronald, the older brother, earned both an MBA and a CPA and was groomed

by the elder Hitt to assume the reins at the bank. Donald, while earning an undergraduate degree in business, had pursued no further education but was secure in his position as president of Commerce while brother Ron served as CEO.

The executive committee of the bank consisted of brothers Ron and Don and four other male vice-presidents for each of the areas of commercial/consumer loans, marketing, operations, and trusts. Karen and others at the bank frequently referred to this group as the "big six" who ultimately made policy and set the tone and direction of the bank. Karen knew that if she was to be successful in implementing new selection procedures, she would have to sell them to the big six first.

Karen had worked hard during the past year to systematize the selection system she inherited from her predecessor. The basic problem with the old system was the failure to follow an orderly process for hiring. In addition, few if any records were kept to document the hiring process. Karen had written a policy and procedures manual that she hoped the big six would adopt.

In the policy and procedures manual, Karen spelled out a five-step process for hiring tellers. Briefly, the process called for taking an application, conducting an interview, administering a paper-and-pencil test, referring the applicant to the area manager if the applicant successfully jumped all the hurdles at this step, and finally, doing a reference check if the area manager recommended a hire decision. In practice, Karen often screened applicants after the interview based on poorly completed applications or admissions during the interview that the applicant had had problems with the law, particularly shoplifting. Karen and her assistant, though, began to have second thoughts about the test they were administering at step three.

It seemed that many of the applicants, particularly minorities, who Karen though would make excellent employees were screened at this stage. Moreover, Karen questioned whether the test was relevant to the type of work done at the bank. The 1961 copyright on the test did not bolster Karen's confidence in the test, either. Karen could sympathize with applicants who missed the cutoff for the test because of arithmetic errors committed on the math section. Karen wasn't strong in arithmetic, either, and reasoned that the widespread use of calculators reduced the criticalness of this skill.

Karen recalled from her personnel course that test manufacturers often produce evidence of test validity during the development process of the test. On a hunch, she decided to call the test company in Chicago and inquire about the existence of criterion validity for the test. The company representative informed Karen that the test had been validated and offered to send Karen a copy of a validity study done for the test. The following Monday, she received the study as promised. To her chagrin but not surprise, the study had been conducted over twenty-five years ago and only with two Chicago banks. The bottom line for Karen was that this test would be hard to defend at Commerce, especially given its history of screening a disproportionate number of minorities.

The following Monday, the executive committee met and Karen presented her proposal for systematizing the selection process. After considerable discussion, much of it focused on the use of the test, the committee elected to table Karen's recommendation for further consideration. When Karen arrived home that evening, she was met by her husband, Jim, who warmly greeted her with, "Hi, do you want to hear about my day?" only to be abruptly cut off by Karen's reply, "No! But let me tell you about mine!" After Karen had set the scene for Jim, she got to the point of her anger and frustration. "Do you know what that jerk Donald proposed? He suggested that we administer the test only to applicants we don't know. Given that I wasn't raised in this community and a few other considerations, how am I supposed to implement such an asinine policy anyway?"

Notes

1. For a more inclusive definition of selection and placement, see N. Schmitt and B. Schneider, "Current Issues in Personnel Selection," in *Research in Personnel and Human Resource Management*, ed. K. M. Rowland and G. D. Ferris (Greenwich, Conn.: JAI Press, 1983). See also L. E. Albright, "Staffing Issues," in *Human Resource Management in the 1980s*, ed. S. J. Carroll and R. S. Schuler (Washington, D.C.: Bureau of National Affairs, 1983); M. D. Hakel, "Personnel Selection and Placement," *Annual Review of Psychology* 37 (1986): 351–80.

2. This traditional concern with selection and placement is consistent with the legal environment. That is, the equal employment laws are directed to ensuring that all individuals are selected on the basis of job-related (i.e., performance-related) predictors. Ensuring that employee preferences are matched with job and organizational characteristics is not a legal concern.

3. B. Schneider and N. Schmitt, *Staffing Organizations* (Reading, Mass.: Addison-Wesley, 1986); B. Schneider, *Staffing Organizations* (Pacific Palisades, Calif.: Goodyear, 1976); B. Schneider, A. E. Reichers, and T. M. Mitchell, "A Note on Some Relationships between the Aptitude Requirements and Reward Attribute of Tasks," *Academy of Management Journal* 25 (1982): 567–74, where the case is made for being concerned with both matches. Whereas selection deals with matching individuals and jobs by choosing only a few of many individuals, placement deals with taking all individuals and matching them (generally after the selection is made). Also, much of the work on quality of work life is concerned with the worker preference-job characteristic match. This is highlighted again in Chapter 12.

4. Nevertheless, some work is being done on placement as described by Schmitt and Schneider, "Current Issues." See also S. Zedeck and W. Cascio, "Psycho-

logical Issues in Personnel Decisions," *Annual Review of Psychology* (1984), in which the authors suggest that selection addresses hiring applicants for specific jobs (thus, they are automatically placed), and placement addresses where to put applicants after they are already hired. Placement might be most applicable to organizations who hire a group of MBAs each year and then decide exactly where to place them. In the placement decision, the concern is with the fit between the organizational and characteristics and individual personality, interests, and preferences, because the match between job demands and skills, knowledge, and abilities has basically already been determined in the selection of the individuals.

5. P. Drucker, "How to Make People Decisions," *Harvard Business Review* (July–Aug. 1985): 22–26.

6. For a description of these results and calculation of dollar costs and benefits, see F. L. Schmidt and J. E. Hunter, "Research Findings in Personnel Selection: Myths Meet Realities in the 1980s," *Public Personnel Administration: Policies and Procedures for Personnel* (New York: Prentice-Hall, 1981). See also F. L. Schmidt, J. E. Hunter, and K. Pearlman, "Assessing the Economic Impact of Personnel Programs on Productivity," *Personnel Psychology* (Summer 1982): 238–48.

7. S. T. Rickard, "Effective Staff Selection," *Personnel Journal* (June 1981): 475–78.

8. F. A. Malinowski, "Job Selection Using Task Analysis," *Personnel Journal* (Apr. 1981): 288–91.

9. *Wall Street Journal*, 5 Nov. 1985, p. 1. For a more extensive discussion of matching or fitting people to organizations, see B. Schneider, "Organizational Behavior," *Annual Review of Psychology* 36 (1985): 573–611; D. C. Funder, "On Assessing Social Psychological Theories through the Study of Individual Differences: Template Matching and Forced Compliance," *Journal of Personality and Social Psychology* 43 (1982): 100–10.

10. B. J. Baroni, "Age Discrimination in Employment: Some Guidelines for Employers," *Personnel Administrator* (May 1981): 97–101; R. Marr and J. Schneider, "Self-Assessment Test for the 1978 Uniform Guidelines on Employee Selection Procedures," *Personnel Administrator* (May 1981): 103–8; C. F. Schanie and W. L. Holley, "An Interpretive Review of the Federal Uniform Guidelines on Employee Selection Procedures," *Personnel Administrator* (June 1980): 44–48; J. L. Wall and H. M. Shatshat, "Controversy over the Issue of Mandatory Retirement," *Personnel Administrator* (Oct. 1981): 25–30, 46.

11. F. S. Hills, "Job Relatedness vs. Adverse Impact in Personnel Decision Making," *Personnel Journal* (Mar. 1980): 211–15, 229. Although the Civil Rights Acts of 1866 and 1871 are less frequently discussed, they are important because they permit individuals to win substantial monetary remedies above and beyond back pay awards granted under Title VII. Consequently, they are discussed again in Chapter 13. See also B. L. Schlei and P. Grossman, *Employment Discrimination Law* (Washington, D.C.: Bureau of National Affairs, 1983); K. L. Sovereign, *Personnel Law* (Reston, Va.: Reston, 1984); J. Ledvinka, *Federal Regulation of Personnel and Human Resource Management* (Boston: Kent, 1982); J. Bernardin, and W. Cascio, *Annotated Bibliography of Court Cases Relevant To Employment Decisions 1980-1984*; M. D. Levin-Epstein, *Primer of Equal Employment Opportunity*, 3d ed. (Washington, D.C.: Bureau of National Affairs, 1984); H. McCarthy, ed., *Complete Guide to Employing Persons with Disabilities* (Albertson, N.Y.: National Center on Employment of the Handicapped at Human Resources Center, 1985).

12. *Employment Coordinator*, 17 Dec. 1984, p. 98, 601.

13. For an excellent overview of the guidelines, see J. A. Belohlav and E. Ayton, "Equal Opportunity Laws: Some Common Problems," *Personnel Journal* (Apr. 1982): 282–85. See also C. F. Schanie and W. L. Holley, "An Interpretive Review of the Federal Uniform Guidelines on Employee Selection Procedures," *Personnel Administrator* (June 1980): 44–48; R. Marr and J. Schneider, "Self-Assessment Test for the 1978 Uniform Guidelines of Employee Selection Procedures," *Personnel Administrator* (May 1981): 103–8; T. H. Curry II, "A Common-Sense Management Approach to Employee Selection and EEO Compliance for the Smaller Employer," *Personnel Administrator* (Apr. 1981): 35–38. For more tips employers can use in selecting employees legally, see K. J. McCulloch, *Selecting Employees Safely under the Law* (Englewood Cliffs, N.J.: Prentice-Hall, 1981).

14. Schlei and Grossman, *Employment Discrimination Law*.

15. Supplementary Information on Guidelines on Discrimination Because of Religion in CCH Employment Practices 715172. See also C. J. Hollon and T. L Bright, "Avoiding Religious Discrimination in the Workplace," *Personnel Journal* (Aug. 1982): 590–94.

16. The author wishes to thank Robert Faley and Mike Burke for their excellent comments and suggestions related to the content and organization of this section.

17. For an excellent description of the historical development here, see J. C. Sharf, "Personnel Testing and the Law" in *Personnel Management*, ed. K. M. Rowland and G. R. Ferris (Boston: Allyn & Bacon, 1982), pp. 156–83. From Sharf:

The well-intended, but critical flaw to Title VII *prima facie* reasoning was the simplistic, egalitarian assumption that all people are equally qualified for all jobs. This very prescription was noted by David Corpus (1975), former Director of National Programs Division at the EEOC and lead attorney on the AT&T

case for the government: "The most widely-known and well established principle of Title VII law as first laid down by the Supreme Court in *Griggs* . . . [and] most frequently applied when an employer or union attempts to explain the absence of women or minorities from certain jobs by claiming that few if any women or minorities possess the skills, abilities, or other qualifications which are required for the job. In order to sustain such a claim of differential distribution of qualifications, the employer or union must shoulder the 'heavy burden' of proving that there is, in fact, 'a fit between the qualifications and the job'. . . . In short, absent compelling proof to the contrary from the defendant, Title VII assumes that Anglo males, females, and minorities are equally qualified for all jobs. The implication of this conclusion for statistical proofs is immense." (Sharf, "Personnel Testing," p. 159, quoting from D. Corpus, "The Numbers Game is the Only Game in Town: Statistical Proofs and Title VII of the Civil Rights Act of 1964," unpublished paper, 1975).

18. H. R. Bloch and R. L. Pennington, "Labor Market Analysis as a Test of Discrimination, *Personnel Journal* (Aug. 1980): 650. Reprinted with permission of *Personnel Journal,* Costa Mesa, Calif. All rights reserved.

19. Defenses against disparate treatment cases (those brought by individuals) are slightly different from disparate impact cases (those brought by classes). In disparate treatment cases, the employer must show some legitimate, nondiscriminatory motive for its action; in the disparate impact cases, the employer need only show business necessity, a lesser burden (from *Employment Coordinator,* 17 Dec. 1984, pp. 98, 602).

20. The phrase "do on the job" is used instead of "performance" to highlight the notion that job relatedness or validity refers to the relationship between the predictor(s) and the criterion or criteria. Just as there can be several measures or indicators predicting how well an individual may do, there are several bases on which an individual can do well. One of those bases may be performance quality, another performance quantity, and another attendance. Here are three criteria, only two of which contain the word *performance.* To say that job relatedness refers to how well predictors will predict performance may be misleading. This may be avoided, however, by thinking of performance as a generic label to include "desirable behaviors and outputs" on a job. Doing this facilitates the use of the term *performance* or *criteria* when describing or discussing job relatedness and validity and even performance appraisal in Chapters 6 and 7.

21. For current application of business necessity, see J. C. Sharf's discussion of *Segar* v. *Smith* (1985) in *TIP,* Dec. 1985, pp. 29–33. For an excellent discussion of the impact and interpretation of the *Uniform Guidelines* and many other issues related to selection and testing, see the special issue of the *American Psychologist* (Oct. 1981), in particular F. L. Schmidt and J. E. Hunter, "Employment Testing: Old Theories and New Research Findings," pp. 1128–37. Schmidt and Hunter refute the usefulness of the need to test for differential validity and instead discuss almost the opposite concept: validity generalization. For a further discussion, see N. Schmitt and B. Schneider, "Current Issues in Personnel Selection, in *Research in Personnel and Human Resource Management,* ed. K. M. Rowland and G. D. Ferris (Greenwich, Conn.: JAI Press, 1983); and D. D. Baker and D. E. Terpstra, "Employee Selection: Must Every Job Test Be Validated?" *Personnel Journal* (Aug. 1982): 602–4. Another issue of importance here is test fairness. For a discussion, see W. F. Cascio, *Applied Psychology in Personnel Management* (Reston, Va.: Reston), pp. 163–76. See also the testimony by B. Schneider before the U.S. House of Representatives, 18 July 1985, as reported in *TIP,* Dec. 1985, pp. 34–36.

22. T. C. McKinney, "The Management of Seniority: The Supreme Court and the California Brewers Case," *Personnel Administrator* (Feb. 1984): 8–14.

23. Schmitt and Schneider in "Current Issues" also use personality, interests, and preferences. Many organizations use measures of PIPs for selection decisions, especially for managers. When used, these measures enable employers to predict how well an individual will fit in, stay on the job, interact with others (essential for managers), and perform (most of which is interacting). Schmitt and Schneider suggest using PIPs to also predict satisfaction and absenteeism, which is consistent with the use here.

24. For an excellent discussion about criteria for selection and placement decisions, see Schmitt and Schneider, "Current Issues. . . ." Important concepts about criteria are contamination, deficiency, sensitivity, discriminability, relevance, and practicality.

25. The basis for the statements and suggestions here include R. Merritt-Haston and K. N. Wexley, "Educational Requirements: Legality and Validity," *Personnel Psychology* (Winter 1983): 743–59; "Educational Requirements," *FEP Guidelines,* no. 243(10), 1985; R. H. Faley, L. S. Kleiman, and M. L. Lengnick-Hall, "Age Discrimination and Personnel Psychology: A Review and Synthesis of the Legal Literature with Implications for Future Research," *Personnel Psychology* (Summer 1984): 327–50; "Educational Requirements," *FEP Guidelines,* no. 186(1); "Experience Required," *FEP Guidelines,* no. 206(9), 1982; "Nepotism," *FEP Guidelines,* no. 190(5), 1981; "Arrest Records," *FEP Guidelines,* no. 190(5), 1981; "The Importance of Record Keeping," *FEP Guidelines,* no. 185(12), 1980; "Personnel Guidelines for Managers and Supervisors," Biddle & Associates, 1982.

26. "Personnel Guidelines for Managers and Supervisors," Biddle & Associates, 1982.

27. K. Johnson, "Rise of the Resume Sleuth," *New York Times,* 9 Jan. 1983, p. 12F; R. Richlefs, "Resume Flood Posing Problems in Job Market," *Wall Street Journal,* 24 Feb. 1981, p. 21; J. Andrew, "Resume Liars Are Abundant, Experts Assert," *Wall Street Journal,* 24 Apr. 1981, p. 35. In a related matter, be careful what you do with the unsolicited résumé. Common practice in many offices is to open any résumé received in the mail and give it a quick review—often before tossing it in the trash. The practice, however, can create potential EEO liability.

   "Unsolicited résumés that are read—even though they may be considered junk mail—represent potential job applicants and potential discriminatees who may become EEO plaintiffs," says David A. Copus, a partner in the law firm of Seyfarth, Shaw, Fairweather & Geraldson. "If they can show the résumé was reviewed by a person with authority to hire, it can be claimed that they were not hired for unlawful reasons."

   To avoid the problem, résumés could be screened at an administrative level with only those containing specific qualifications being passed on to the person with hiring power for review, notes Mr. Copus (ASPA Conference, June 1985).

28. For more information on application blanks, see "Job Application Forms," *FEP Guidelines,* no. 208(11), 1982; C. M. Koen, Jr., "The Pre-Employment Inquiry Guide," *Personnel Journal* (Oct. 1980): 825–29; E. C. Miller, "An EEO Examination of Employment Applications," *Personnel Administrator* (Mar. 1980): 63–69, 81; C. Sewell, "Pre-Employment Investigations: The Key to Security in Hiring," *Personnel Journal* (May 1981): 376–79. See also D. L. Harper and J. A. Breaugh, "EEO in the Courtroom," paper presented at the APA, 1985, Los Angeles.

29. D. G. Lawrence, B. L. Salsburg, J. G. Dawson, and Z. D. Fasmen, "Design and Use of Weighted Application Blanks," *Personnel Administrator* (Mar. 1982): 47–53, 101.

30. Schneider, *Staffing Organizations,* pp. 200–5. For good discussions on preferences and other background data for prediction, see also W. A. Owens, "Background Data," in *Handbook of Industrial and Organizational Psychology,* ed. M. D. Dunnette (Chicago: Rand McNally, 1976), pp. 609–44; J. L. Holland, "Vocational Preferences," in *Handbook,* ed. M. D. Dunnette, pp. 521–70.

31. This is so even though getting reliable information from an interview may be more difficult than other means, such as paper-and-pencil tests. See Scharf, "Personnel Testing," p. 172.

32. For an excellent discussion of interviewing, see M. D. Hakel, "Employment Interviewing," in *Personnel Management,* ed. K. M. Rowland and G. R. Ferris (Boston: Allyn & Bacon, 1982), pp. 129–55; "Interview Guide for Supervisors," College and University Personnel Association, Washington, D.C., 1981; S. G. Ginsburg, "Preparing for Executive Position Interviews: Questions the Interviewer Might Ask—Or Be Asked," *Personnel* (July–Aug. 1980): 31–36; "Editor to Reader," *Personnel Journal* (Feb. 1981): 82–87; R. D. Arvey and J. E. Campion, "The Employment Interview: A Summary and Review of Recent Literature," *Personnel Psychology* 35 (1982): 281–322; "Reader to Editor," *Personnel Journal* (Aug. 1980): 618; J. D. Latterell, "Planning for the Selection Interview," *Personnel Journal* (July 1979): 466–67; T. J. Neff, "How to Interview Candidates for Top Management Positions," *Business Horizons* (Oct. 1980): 47–52; E. D. Pursell, M. A. Campion, and S. R. Gaylord, "Structured Interviewing: Avoiding Selection Problems," *Personnel Journal* (Nov. 1980): 907–12; W. T. Wolz, "How to Interview Supervisory Candidates from the Ranks," *Personnel* (Sept.–Oct. 1980): 31–39; N. Schmitt, "Social and Situational Determinants of Interview Decisions: Implications for the Employment Interview," *Personnel Psychology* 29 (1976): 79–101; R. A. Fear, *The Evaluation Interview,* 3d ed. (New York: McGraw-Hill, 1984); S. P. James, I. M. Campbell, and S. A. Lovegrove, "Personality Differentiation in a Police-Selection Interview," *Journal of Applied Psychology* (Feb. 1984): 129–34; R. L. Dipboye, G. A. Fontenelle, and K. Garner, "Effects of Previewing the Application on Interview Process and Outcomes," *Journal of Applied Psychology* (Feb. 1984): 118–28; G. P. Latham and L. M. Saari, "Do People Do What They Say? Further Studies on the Situational Interview," *Journal of Applied Psychology* (Nov. 1984): 569–73; S. Zedeck, A. Tziner, and S. E. Middlestadt, "Interviewer Validity and Reliability: An Individual Analysis Approach," *Personnel Psychology* (Summer 1983): 355–69.

33. This is true despite its low reliability and its fallibility, confirmed in L. Ulrich and D. Trumbo, "The Selection Interview Since 1949," *Psychological Bulletin* 63 (1965): 100–16; Hakel, "Employment Interviewing," p. 131. See also M. D. Dunnette and W. C. Borman, "Personal Selection and Classification Systems," *Annual Review of Psychology* 30 (1979): 477–525.

34. Each user should maintain and have available for inspection records or other information which will disclose the impact which its tests and other selection procedures have upon employment opportunities . . . (on the basis of) sex and the following races and ethnic groups: Blacks, American Indians (including Alaskan Natives), Asians (including Pacific Islanders), East Indians, Hispanic (including persons of Mexican, Puerto Rican, Cuban, Central or South American, or other Spanish origin or culture regardless of race), Whites (Caucasians) other than Hispanic, and totals. This is to be included in the employer's EEO-1 report (Biddle & Associates, Inc.).

35. Bureau of National Affairs, *Bulletin to Management,* 20 June 1985, p. 3. Reprinted by permission from *Bulletin to Management,* copyright 1985, by The Bureau of National Affairs, Inc., Washington, D.C.

36. W. C. Byham, "Common Selection Problems Can Be Overcome," *Personnel Administrator* (Aug. 1978): 42–47; "The Ten Most Common Interviewing Mistakes," *Personnel Journal* (June 1984): 10–12.

37. Evidence that training helps is reported in A. P. Goldstein and M. Sorcher, *Changing Supervisory Behavior* (New York: Pergamon, 1974); Hakel, "Employment Interviewing," p. 154.

38. Since 1976 much research on interviewing has gone from the validity type to the judgmental processes taking place in the interview, especially by the interviewer; however, little research has been done on the validity of interviews with information gained from the judgmental research. See Schmitt and Schneider, "Current Issues"; and Hakel, "Employment Interviewing."

39. For an excellent discussion of issues involved in people processing information for personnel decisions, see S. J. Motowidlo, "Information Processing in Personnel Decisions," in *Research in Personnel and Human Resources Management*, vol. 4, ed. K. M. Rowland and G. R. Ferris (Greenwich, Conn.: JAI Press, 1986); M. K. Denis, "Subjective Decision Making: Does It Have a Place in the Employment Process?" *Employee Relations Law Journal* (Autumn 1985): 269–90.

40. J. D. Hatfield and R. D. Gatewood, "Nonverbal Cues in the Selection Interview," p. 35. Reprinted with the permission from the Jan. 1978 issue of the *Personnel Administrator*. Copyright © 1978.

41. Hatfield and Gatewood, "Nonverbal Cues in the Selection Interview," p. 37.

42. Albright in Carroll and Schuler, *Human Resource Management*. Part of the criticism in testing is the issue of privacy invasion versus the issue of liberty. Consequently, the recommendation is that organizations inform job applicants of the procedures used in gathering information, particularly from paper-and-pencil tests. The Life Insurance Marketing and Research Association also recommends that organizations using tests inform those taking tests of the following:

■ That the test is only one step in the hiring process
■ What the test measures and that it does so with validity and reliability
■ Why it is being used
■ What passing or failing means to them and about them

Life Insurance Marketing and Research Association, *Recruitment, Selection, Training, and Supervision in Life Insurance* (Hartford, Conn.: Life Insurance Marketing and Research Association, 1966). See also "The Interview," *FEP Guidelines*, no. 202(5), 1982; T. J. Hanson, "An Alternative to Interviews," *Personnel Journal* (June 1985): 114–22; R. P. Lookatch, "Alternatives to Formal Employment Testing," *Personnel Administrator* (Sept. 1984): 111–16;

A. Brown, "Employment Tests: Issues without Clear Answers," *Personnel Administrator* (Sept. 1985): 43–56.

43. See Albright in Carroll and Schuler, *Human Resource Management* on the use of tests. See also M. L. Tenopyr, "The Realities of Employment Testing," *American Psychologist* 36 (1981): 1120–27, which suggests that even if tests were dropped, the impact on women and minorities could be minimal. For an excellent review and overview of testing, see A. K. Wigdor and W. R. Garner, eds., *Ability Testing: Uses, Consequences, and Controversies*, pts. I and II (Washington, D.C.: National Academy Press, 1982). For an evaluation of the current state of testing, see M. D. Dunnette and W. C. Borman, "Personnel Selection and Classification Systems," *Annual Review of Psychology* 30 (1979): 477–525; and Schneider and Schmitt, *Staffing Organizations*.

44. See Schmidt and Hunter in "Research Findings" on validity generalization. See also R. R. Reilly and G. A. Chao, "Validity and Fairness of Some Alternative Employee Selection Procedures," *Personnel Psychology* 35 (1982): 1–62; M. J. Burke and N. S. Raju, "An Overview of Validity Generalization Methods," in *Readings in Personnel and Human Resource Management*, 3d, eds. R. S. Schuler, S. A. Youngblood, and V. Huber (St. Paul: West Publishing, 1987).

45. Schneider, *Staffing Organizations*.

46. J. B. Miner and M. G. Miner, *Personnel and Industrial Relations*, 3d ed. (New York: Macmillan, 1977). See also R. R. Reilly, S. Zedeck, and M. L. Tenopyr, "Validity and Fairness of Physical Ability Tests for Predicting Performance in Craft Jobs," *Journal of Applied Psychology* 64 (1979): 262–74; J. D. Arnold, J. M. Rauschenberger, W. G. Soubel, and R. M. Guion, "Validation and Utility of a Strength Test for Selecting Steelworkers," *Journal of Applied Psychology* 67 (1982): 588–604.

47. D. Goleman, "The New Competency Tests: Matching the Right Jobs," *Psychology Today*, Jan. 1981, pp. 35–46. See also L. M. Hough, "Development and Evaluation of the 'Accomplishment Record' Method of Selecting and Promoting Professionals," *Journal of Applied Psychology* (Feb. 1984): 135–46; B. D. Whelchel, "Use Performance Tests to Select Craft Apprentices," *Personnel Journal* (July 1985): 65–69.

48. J. P. Guilford, *The Nature of Human Intelligence* (New York: McGraw-Hill, 1967), p. 77.

49. For an extensive review and guide of these tests, see L. B. Plumke, "A Short Guide to the Development of Work Sample and Performance Tests," 2d ed., pamphlet from the U.S. Office of Personnel Management, Washington, D.C., Feb. 1980. Note the interchangeability of the words *work sample* and *performance tests*. See also R. M. Guion, *Personnel Testing* (New York: McGraw-Hill, 1965); J. J. Asher and J. A. Sciarrino, "Realistic Work Sample Tests: A Review," *Personnnel Psychology* 27 (1974): 549–33; Whelchel, "Use Performance Tests."

50. For the LGD, see M. M. Petty, "A Multivariate Analysis of the Effects of Experience and Training upon Performance in a Leaderless Group Discussion," *Personnel Psychology* 27 (1974): 271–82. For business games, see B. M. Bass and G. V. Barnett, *People, Work, and Organizations,* 2d ed. (Boston: Allyn & Bacon, 1981).

51. S. L. Cohen, "Pre-Packaged vs. Tailor-Made: The Assessment Center Debate," *Personnel Journal* (Dec. 1980); 989–95; L. A. Digman, "How Well-Managed Organizations Develop Their Executives," *Organizational Dynamics* (Autumn 1978): 65–66; L. C. Nichols and J. Hudson, "Dual-Role Assessment Center: Selection and Development," *Personnel Journal* (May 1981): 350–86; T. C. Parker, "Assessment Centers: A Statistical Study," *Personnel Administrator* (Feb. 1980): 65–67; J. C. Quick, W. A. Fisher, L. L. Schkade, and G. W. Ayers, "Developing Administrative Personnel through the Assessment Center Technique," *Personnel Administrator* (Feb. 1980): 44–46, 62; J. D. Ross, "A Current Review of Public Sector Assessment Centers: Cause for Concern," *Public Personnel Management* (Jan.–Feb. 1979): 41–46.

52. Used by courtesy of General Motors Corporation. For more excellent discussion on assessment centers, see Sharf, "Employment Testing"; V. R. Boehm, "Assessment Centers and Management Development," in *Personnel Management*, ed. K. M. Rowland and G. R. Ferris (Boston: Allyn & Bacon, 1982), pp. 327–62; F. D. Frank and J. R. Preston, "The Validity of the Assessment Center Approach and Related Issues," *Personnel Administrator* (June 1982): 87–94; R. B. Finkle, "Managerial Assessment Centers," in *Handbook of Industrial and Organizational Psychology*, ed. M. D. Dunnette (Chicago: Rand McNally, 1976); S. D. Norton, "The Empirical and Content Validity of Assessment Centers vs. Traditional Methods for Predicting Managerial Excess," *Academy of Management Review* 2 (1977): 353–61; R. J. Klimoski and W. J. Strictland, "Assessment Centers Valid or Merely Prescient," *Personnel Psychology* 30 (1977): 353–61; G. F. Dreher and P. R. Sackett, "Some Problems with Applying Content Validity Evidence to Assessment Center Procedures," *Academy of Management Review* 6 (1981): 461–566; P. R. Sackett and G. F. Dreher, "Some Misconceptions about Content-oriented Validation: A Rejoinder to Norton," *Academy of Management Review* 6 (1981): 567–68; W. F. Cascio and V. Silbey, "Utility of the Assessment Center as a Selection Device," *Journal of Applied Psychology* 64 (1979): 107–18; M. R. Edwards and J. R. Sproull, "Team Talent Assessment: Optimizing Assessee Visibility," *Human Resource Planning* 8 (1985): 157–71.

53. L. Reibstein, "More Firms Use Personality Tests for Entry-Level, Blue-Collar Jobs," *Wall Street Journal,* 16 Jan. 1986, p. 31.

54. Nonetheless, according to the ASPA-BNA Survey No. 45, "Employee Selection Procedures," 5 May 1983, approximately 97 percent of firms (in their study) use reference and record checks to screen outside applicants. Approximately 81 percent use unstructured interviews for the same purpose. For a discussion of some legal aspects of reference checking, see "Reference Letters," *Wall Street Journal,* 3 Nov. 1981, p. 1; E. L. Levine, "Legal Aspects of Reference Checking for Personnel Selection," *Personnel Administrator* (Nov. 1977): 14–16, 28.

55. "The Boom in Digging into a Job Applicant's Past," *Business Week,* 11 June 1984, 68E–68H. See also B. D. Wonder and K. S. Keleman, "Increasing the Value of Reference Information," *Personnel Administrator* (Mar. 1984): 98–103; W. Yu, "Firms Tighten Resume Checks of Applicants," *Wall Street Journal,* 20 Aug. 1985, p.31; "Rooting Out Ringers," *Bulletin to Management,* 28 Mar. 1985, p. 8; *Wall Street Journal,* 4 Oct. 1984, p. 1.

56. "Personal Business," *Business Week,* 27 July 1981, pp. 85–86; J. A. Belt, "The Polygraph: A Questionable Personnel Tool," *Personnel Administrator* (Aug. 1983): 65–69, 91; P. R. Lewis, "Legal Trends," *Personnel Administrator* (Nov. 1983): 6–7; B. S. Murphy, W. E. Barlow, and D. D. Hatch, "Polygraph Tests: Lie Detector or Truth Distorter?" *Personnel Journal* (June 1985): 33–44; G. H. Barlard, "The Case for the Polygraph in Employment Screening," *Personnel Administrator* (Sept. 1985): 58, 61–65; D. T. Lykken, "The Case against the Polygraph in Employment Screening," *Personnel Administrator* (Sept. 1985): 59, 61–65.

57. T. F. O'Boyle, "More Honesty Tests Used to Gauge Workers' Morale," *Wall Street Journal,* 11 July 1985, p. 27; P. R. Sackett, "Honesty Testing for Personnel Selection," *Personnel Administrator* (Sept. 1985): 67–72, 121; P. R. Sackett and M. M. Harris, "Honesty Testing for Personnel Selection: A Review and Critique," *Personnel Psychology* (Summer 1984): 221–46.

58. The role of the medical doctor in providing the physical exam is an important one. With it, however, is attached responsibility to the employer rather than the employee, although this is contrary to the traditional doctor-patient relationship. The responsibility of the doctor to the employer has been subject to extensive litigation. The impact of this is discussed in M. S. Novit, "Physical Examinations and Company Liability: A Legal Update," *Personnel Journal* (Jan. 1981): 47–52.

59. For an extensive discussion of critical issues here, see G. Carmean, "Preplacement Medical Screenings," *Personnel Journal* (June 1985): 124–32; D. Tuller, "What's New in Employment Testing," *New York Times,* 24 Feb. 1985, p. 24F; "Companies Are Starting to Sniff Out Cocaine Users," *Business Week,* 18 Feb. 1985, p. 37; T. F. O'Boyle, "More Firms Require Employee Drug Tests," *Wall Street Journal,* 8 Aug. 1985, p. 6; I. Dave, "Fear and Loathing in the Workplace: What Managers Can Do about AIDs."

Business Week, 25 Nov. 1985, p. 126; T. E. Geidt, "Drug and Alcohol Abuse in the Work Place: Balancing Employer and Employee Rights," *Employee Relations Law Journal* (Autumn 1985): 188–205.

60. J. D. Olian, "Genetic Screening for Employment Purposes," *Personnel Psychology* (Autumn 1984): 423–38; M. Rothstein, "Medical Screening: Protection for Workers or a Discriminatory Tool?" *Personnel Administrator* (Oct. 1985): 48–52, 124; "Medical Screening: Programs and Problems," *Fair Employment Practice,* 9 Aug. 1984, p. 3; T. Roth, "Many Firms Fire AIDS Victims, Citing Health Risk to Co-Workers," *Wall Street Journal,* 12 Aug. 1985, p. 21; "AIDS: To Test or Not to Test," *Fair Employment Practices,* 3 Oct. 1985, pp. 37–38; R. T. Angarola, "Drug Testing in the Workplace: Is It Legal?" *Personnel Administrator* (Sept. 1985): 79–89; T. H. Murray, "Genetic Testing at Work: How Should It Be Used?" *Personnel Administrator* (Sept. 1985): 91–102.

61. M. A. Jones and E. P. Prien, "A Valid Procedure for Testing the Physical Abilities of Job Applicants," *Personnel Administrator* (Sept. 1979): 33–38; M. A. Campion, "Personnel Selection for Physically Demanding Jobs: Review and Recommendations," *Personnel Psychology* (Autumn 1983): 527–38.

62. L. Smith, "Equal Opportunity Rules Are Getting Tougher," *Fortune,* June 1978, p. 154.

63. Most typically the several predictors of success would be determined using a multiple regression model, which combines and weighs the relative importance of the predictors. For greater detail on multiple regression in selection decisions, see W. F. Cascio, *Applied Psychology in Personnel Management,* 2d ed. (Reston, Va.: Reston, 1982), p. 210.

64. For a discussion of the multiple hurdle approach, see L. J. Cronbach and G. C. Gleser, *Psychological Tests and Personnel Decisions,* 2d ed. (Urbana, Ill.: University of Illinois Press, 1965). For multiple cutoffs, see L. S. Buck, *Guide to the Setting of Appropriate Cutting Scores for Written Tests: A Summary of the Concerns and Procedures* (Washington, D.C.: U.S. Office of Personnel Management, 1977). For a discussion of the multiple regression approach, see J. Cohen, "Multiple Regression as a General Data Analytic System," *Psychological Bulletin* 70 (1968): 426–43; A. K. Korman, *Industrial and Organizational Psychology,* (Englewood Cliffs, N.J.: Prentice-Hall, 1971).

65. L. A. Hough, M. A. Keyes, and M. D. Dunnette, "An Evaluation of Three Alternative Selection Procedures," *Personnel Psychology* 36 (1983): 261–76; M. J. Burke and J. T. Frederick, "A Comparison of Economic Utility Estimates for Alternative SDy Estimation Procedures," *Journal of Applied Psychology* 71(2) (1986): 334–39; R. A. Bolda, "Utility: A Productivity Planning Tool," *Human Resource Planning* 8 (1985): 111–32; J. W. Boudreau and C. J. Berger, "Decision-Theoretic Utility Analysis Applied to Employee Separations and Acquisitions," *Journal of Applied Psychology* 70 (1985): 581–612.

66. C. Fombrun, "An Interview with Reginald Jones," *Organizational Dynamics,* (Winter 1982): 46.

67. L. Dyer and N. D. Heyer, "Human Resource Planning at IBM," *Human Resource Planning* 7(3) (1984); G. R. Ferris, D. A. Schallenberg, and R. F. Zammuto, "Human Resources Management Strategies in Declining Industries," *Human Resource Management* (Winter 1985); C. R. Greer, "Counter-Cyclical Hiring as a Staffing Strategy for Managerial and Professional Personnel: Some Considerations and Issues," *Academy of Management Review* (Apr. 1984): 334–46; C. Fombrun, N. M. Tichy, and M. A. Devanna, *Strategic Human Resource Management* (New York: Wiley, 1984); J. L. Kerr, "Assigning Managers on the Basis of the Life Cycle," *Journal of Business Strategy* (1982): 58–65.

68. R. S. Schuler and I. C. MacMillan, "Gaining Competitive Advantage through Human Resource Management Practices," *Human Resource Management* (Fall 1984): 246.

69. Schuler and MacMillan, "Gaining Competitive Advantage."

70. M. London and S. A. Stumpf, *Managing Careers* (Reading, Mass.: Addison-Wesley, 1982).

71. L. L. Cummings, "Compensation, Culture, and Motivation: A Systems Perspective," *Organizational Dynamics* (Winter 1984): 33–43.

72. G. Pinchot III, "Intrapreneurship: How to Top Corporate Creative Energies," *The Mainstream* 1(2) (1984).

Appraising and Compensating

6

Performance Appraisal

Why Ebasco Assesses Potential Instead of Past Performance

The use of performance appraisals for identifying talent is central to organizational and management development in companies. And yet, little is being done to measure individuals' capacity or to predict the future performance of individuals.

The problem can be attributed, at least in part, to the failure of companies to distinguish between appraisal of a manager's performance and appraisal of his potential.

At Ebasco, "potential appraisals" of individuals have been carried out quite separately from their performance appraisals. Evaluation of potential is an attempt to predict the ultimate capabilities of individuals. Their past record and degree of success in past assignments are evidence of their potential, of course, but they do not form the basis of any evaluation of potential. Performance appraisals and potential appraisals are based on quite different sets of criteria.

Performance appraisals are generally useful as a means of measuring accomplishments. As such they of necessity must focus on the past. Appraisals of potential, on the other hand, must look to the future and are primarily concerned with the process a manager uses to achieve results.

This identification of process is crucial, because it provides insight into the behavior and application of skills that have led to the achievement of certain results. Furthermore, a knowledge of the process used helps avoid assuming that behavior used successfully in a certain environment or position will necessarily be appropriate in another environment or job situation.

Dubious pasts

Pragmatic, hard-nosed managers who look only at the bottom line will insist that the only meaningful criterion for evaluating potential is a manager's ability to get things done. At best, this is a myopic view of what it takes to be a good manager. It is all too easy to be seduced by simple solutions for complex problems.

Many "successful" managers build their careers on their ability to get things done. These managers gain a reputation as tough, no-nonsense people who are only interested in results. They act as trouble shooters and are considered ideal in trouble spots that require "straightening out." They achieve desired results in a relatively short time.

Upon closer scrutiny, however, it is not uncommon to find that these "successful" managers go through an organization or department like Attila the Hun, terrorizing and destroying people's careers to achieve the short-term results that make them look so good to top management. In fact, they take pride in being known as SOBs. They can afford to do so, because they normally stay in one place for only a short time. Top management perceives that it would be a waste of talent to leave such good managers to maintain things in an area after it's been straightened out. So they are given new assignments elsewhere.

The tragedy is that those succeeding them come into departments or units that have been left demoralized and in shambles. Unless the successor happens to be an exceptional manager, chances are that he or she will not survive the consequences of the predecessor's steam roller tactics. Ironically, their failure frequently serves to enhance the reputation of these tough, results-oriented managers.

That is why it is so necessary to know *how* a manager gets results.

Potential appraisals

Potential appraisals are concerned with examining the process individuals use to achieve results, as well as their ability to lead, their intellectual capacity, maturity, and potential growth according to sound criteria.

If, during the performance of a job, a particular process proves successful, the employee is rewarded accordingly. But it does not follow that the same process would be appropriate for a different job or higher level position.

This distinction is important because when the employee moves on to a different assignment, the results of past achievements remain behind. They do not accompany the employee to the new job.

What is transferable is the process that the employee uses to accomplish results. It can be hoped that the process is suited to the new situation.

For this reason, the planned growth of an individual must take place in an organized and systematic way. The characteristics of the ultimate position an individual is being groomed for should be specified, for instance. This can be achieved through a formal career planning program that specifies future goals and development requirements of individuals.

Source: Reprinted, by permission of the publisher, from "Why Ebasco Assesses Potential Instead of Past Performance," by Andrew O. Manzini, MANAGEMENT REVIEW, "AMA Forum," September 1984, pp. 29–30 © 1984 AMA Membership Publications Division, American Management Associations, New York. All rights reserved.

The preceding "PHRM in the News" generally suggests how important performance appraisal and the entire performance appraisal system (PAS) are in helping an organization identify needed human resource talent, establish a constructive dialogue between management and its employees, translate its goals into the goals of each employee, understand its own strengths, and develop an identity and knowledge of what it must do to be effective. Effective performance appraisal requires an understanding of numerous components of the entire setting in which it takes place—that is, the performance appraisal system.[1] Because of the many PAS components, two chapters are devoted to performance appraisal. This chapter discusses the components or aspects related to *gathering* the appraisal information. The chapter also describes the importance and purposes of performance appraisal, its relationships with other PHRM activities, and the relevant legal environment. Chapter 7 discusses the components associated with *using* the appraisal information, especially the performance appraisal interview. Then the chapter examines the use of performance appraisal data to identify discrepancies in performance and develops strategies to eliminate them. Also described are the elements in diagnosing and assessing how effectively an organization is conducting performance appraisal. Before these components are presented performance appraisal and the performance appraisal system are defined.

Although employees may learn about how well they are performing through informal means, such as favorable comments from co-workers or superiors, **performance appraisal** is defined here as a formal, structured system of measuring, evaluating, and influencing an employee's job-related attributes, behaviors, and outcomes, as well as level of absenteeism, to discover how productive the employee is and whether he or she can perform as or more effectively in the future so that the employee, the organization, and society all benefit.[2]

To account for all of the factors that affect this formal, structured system of measuring and evaluating performance, the term **performance appraisal system (PAS)** is used. In essence, the performance appraisal system involves (1) the form or method used to gather the appraisal data, (2) the job analysis conducted to identify the appropriate criteria against which to establish standards for evaluating the appraisal data, (3) establishing the validity and reliability of the method(s) used, (4) the characteristics of the rater and ratee influencing the appraisal and the appraisal feedback and interview processes, (5) the processes involved in using the appraisal information for development and evaluation, and (6) the evaluation of how well performance appraisal is doing in relation to its stated objectives. In this chapter, the terms *supervisor* and *manager* are generally discarded, because both the appraiser and the appraisee may be managers or supervisors. Instead, the term *superior* or *rater* is used to denote the person doing the appraising, and the term *subordinate* or *ratee* is used to refer to the employee whose performance is being appraised. The terms *superior* and *subordinate* are used in this chapter only for clarity; they are not meant to imply positions of superiority or inferiority.

Purposes and Importance of Performance Appraisal

As indicated in Chapter 1, productivity improvement is of concern to almost all organizations. Although the productivity of most organizations is a function of technological, capital, *and* human resources, many organizations have not sought to increase productivity through improving the performance of their human resources.[3] Nevertheless, what employees do or don't do influences the productivity of organizations.

Employee performance (or lack thereof) can be measured and evaluated, particularly those critical aspects of productivity identified in Chapter 1: job performance (e.g., the quality and quantity levels of what an employee does) and absenteeism. In other words, employee **job performance** (or simply performance) describes how well an employee performs his or her job, while **absenteeism** refers to whether the employee is in attendance to perform his or her job. Although employee job performance and absenteeism are often discussed separately, this chapter and the next discuss them together. This chapter places emphasis on job performance, since performance appraisal forms are generally developed to measure job performance, although absenteeism is occasionally included on the form. Thus, performance appraisal refers to appraising both job performance and absenteeism. Furthermore, job performance can be measured by an employee's job-related **attributes** (e.g., extent of cooperativeness or initiative), **behavior** (e.g., making a loan), or **outcomes** (e.g., quantity of output). The conditions under which each of these criteria are appropriate are discussed later in the chapter.[4] Discussed in Chapter 12 are ways to reduce undesired turnover as well as absenteeism.

An effectively designed performance appraisal form serves as a *contract* between the organization and the employee. This contract helps act as a control and evaluation system that enables performance appraisal to better serve a multitude of purposes, including the following:

- *Management development:* It provides a framework for future employee development by identifying and preparing individuals for increased responsibilities.
- *Performance measurement:* It establishes the relative value of an individual's contribution to the company and helps evaluate individual accomplishments.
- *Performance improvement:* It encourages continued successful performance and strengthens individual weaknesses to make employees more effective and productive.
- *Compensation:* It helps determine appropriate pay for performance and equitable salary and bonus incentives based on merit or results.
- *Identification of potential:* It identifies candidates for promotion.
- *Feedback:* It outlines what is expected from employees against actual performance levels.
- *Human resource planning:* It audits management talent to evaluate the present supply of human resources for replacement planning.
- *Research on legal compliance:* It helps establish the validity of employment decisions made on the basis of performance-based information. It in turn can minimize the financial losses due to unsuccessful courtroom defense resulting from lack of valid selection techniques.
- *Communications:* It provides a format for dialogue between superior and subordinate and improves understanding of personal goals and concerns. This can also increase the trust between the rater and ratee.

Other purposes of performance appraisal are demotions, terminations, internal recruitment, and research.[5] These many purposes are often condensed into two general categories: evaluative and developmental. The **evaluative purposes** include decisions on pay, promotion, demotion, layoff, and termination. The **developmental purposes** include research, feedback, management and career development, human resource planning, performance improvement, and communications. Generally, these two categories are used in this chapter and the next when referring to the purposes that different performance appraisal methods serve. But whether using the two categories or listing the numerous separate purposes, all these uses of performance appraisal indicate not only how important the activity is but also how extensive its relationships are with other PHRM activities.

Relationships Influencing Performance Appraisal

As Exhibit 6.1 shows, performance appraisal is associated with several aspects of other PHRM activities and the internal and external environment. The text highlights the most important of these relationships.

Relationships, Processes, and Procedures of   *Exhibit 6.1*
Appraising Employee Performance

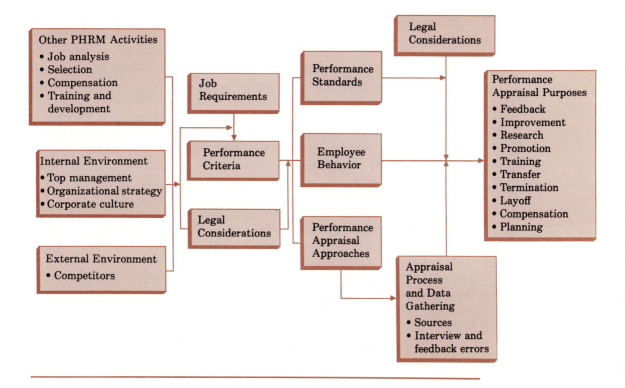

Relationships with Other PHRM Activities

Some of performance appraisal's most critical relationships are with job
analysis, selection, compensation, and training and development.

Job Analysis.   The foundation in the development of the performance appraisal form is the job analysis. According to the *Uniform Guidelines,*

> there shall be a job analysis which includes an analysis of the important work be-
> haviors required for successful performance.... Any job analysis should focus on
> work behavior(s) and the tasks associated with them. Sec. 14. (2)

If a formal job analysis has not been conducted on which to base claims for
the validity of the performance appraisal form, and thus the job relatedness
of a selection procedure, the courts may deny the validity claim (*Kirkland* v.
New York Department of Correctional Services, 1974).[6]

Selection.   To help increase the likelihood that those selected from the job
applicant pool will perform well on the job, organizations use valid selection
tests as discussed in Chapter 5. Since empirical validation of a selection test
is the correlation between test scores and performance scores, having perfor-

mance appraisal results is necessary because performance scores cannot be established without them. When performance appraisal is used in this way, it is particularly important that the appraisal forms are based on job analysis. This job analysis helps produce a job-related performance appraisal form that can increase the likelihood of selecting a good performer and can meet the legal requirements (*Albemarle Paper Company* v. *Moody,* 1975).

Compensation.　　One purpose of performance appraisal is to motivate employees. One way in which performance appraisal can be used to motivate employee performance is by serving as a basis upon which to distribute compensation. A valid appraisal of employee performance is necessary for an organization to provide contingent rewards (those based on performance).[7] As discussed in Chapters 8 and 9, performance appraisal information can be used to determine pay increments under merit pay and performance-based pay plans.

Training and Development.　　Because employee performance is partly determined by employee ability, employee motivation, and the situation, training can improve employee performance by enhancing employee ability. To provide the appropriate training, however, the organization must know the employee's current level of performance and on what aspects of performance the employee is performing at an undesirable level. Also necessary is knowing if the undesirable performance is caused by ability or rather by motivation or the situation. (A process to help determine the reasons for performance deficiencies is discussed in the next chapter.) To gain this knowledge, performance appraisal is necessary. Used in conjunction with job analysis, performance appraisal is also necessary to establish and implement effective pre-employment training programs.

Relationships with the Internal Environment

Aspects of top management, organizational strategy, and corporate culture have important relationships with performance appraisal.[8] In addition to influencing how much time and attention is paid to performance appraisal and keeping employees informed as to where they stand, the internal environment influences how performance appraisal is done. For example, if top management and the corporate culture emphasize employee participation, employees will be likely to become involved in performance appraisal through self-appraisal and appraisal of others. Additionally, if top management decides to use product quality and employee performance as ways to gain competitive advantage for the organization, performance appraisal may be used to help shape organizational strategy. The organization's strategy, however, may also influence the way performance appraisal is done. Short-term criteria may be used in performance appraisal in organizations pursuing a stable, extract profit strategy. Longer-term criteria may be used in organizations pursuing a growth strategy as shown in Exhibit 1.4. Further discussion of these internal relationships appears at the end of Chapter 7.

Relationships with the External Environment

Because the intensity of domestic and international competition is making it more difficult and yet more necessary for organizations to survive, grow, and be profitable, organizations are seeking many ways to improve. Improving employee performance is among the most critical methods of improvement. Measuring employee performance and seeking reasons for any performance deficiencies can facilitate the process. Because this is the essence of gathering and using performance appraisal data, the entire performance appraisal system takes on greater importance in organizations. This will continue to happen in organizations as long as competition remains such a significant part of the external environment.

In addition to the relationships with other PHRM activities and the internal and external environment, performance appraisal can be viewed and analyzed as a system filled with several important processes and legal considerations.

Legal Considerations in Performance Appraisal

As Exhibit 6.1 illustrates, the organization must pay attention to legal considerations at three general points in the process of employee performance appraisal. These considerations may become less of a legal concern to an organization if it does not make employment decisions that result in a *prima facie* case of illegal discrimination.[9] Exhibit 6.2 shows a summary of the characteristics of a legally defensible appraisal system (described later).

Establishing Valid Performance Criteria and Standards

Developing performance appraisals that reflect critical job criteria (job components for performance appraisal) is necessary if the appraisals are to be considered valid. The U.S. Circuit Court in *Brito* v. *Zia Company* (1973) found that Zia Company was in violation of Title VII when a disproportionate number of employees of a protected group were laid off because of low performance scores. The critical point was that performance scores were not based on evaluation of the criteria related to the employees' jobs. Zia essentially laid off employees using performance information based on supervisors' best judgments and opinions, not on important components of doing the job. When companies make performance-based decisions on the basis of appraisals, they are using the appraisals as employment tests; thus, they must be based upon identifiable job-related criteria (*Stringfellow* v. *Monsanto Corp.* [1970]; *U.S.A.* v. *City of Chicago* [1978]). Apparently the best way to determine whether the appraisal criteria are job-related is to do a job analysis (*Albemarle Paper Company* v. *Moody* [1975]).[10] Using a job analysis (see Chapter 3) to develop performance criteria can help ensure that the crite-

Exhibit 6.2	*Prescriptions for Legally Defensible Appraisal Systems*

1. Procedures for personnel decisions must not differ as a function of the race, sex, national origin, religion, or age of those affected by such decisions.
2. Objective-type, non-rated, and uncontaminated data should be used whenever it is available.
3. A formal system of review or appeal should be available for appraisal disagreements.
4. More than one independent evaluator of performance should be used.
5. A formal, standardized system for the personnel decision should be used.
6. Evaluators should have ample opportunity to observe ratee performance (if ratings must be made).
7. Ratings on traits such as dependability, drive, aptitude, or attitude should be avoided.
8. Performance appraisal data should be empirically validated.
9. Specific performance standards should be communicated to employees.
10. Raters should be provided with written instructions on how to complete the performance evaluations.
11. Employees should be evaluated on specific work dimensions rather than a single overall or global measure.
12. Behavioral documentation should be required for extreme ratings (e.g., critical incidents).
13. The content of the appraisal form should be based on a job analysis.
14. Employees should be provided with an opportunity to review their appraisals.
15. Personnel decision makers should be trained on laws regarding discrimination.

Source: J. Bernardin and W. Cascio, "Performance Appraisal and the Law," in R. S. Schuler, S. A. Youngblood, and V. Huber (eds.) *Readings in Personnel and Human Resource Management*, 3d ed. (St. Paul: West, 1987).

ria capture the essence of job performance and are not related to aspects irrelevant to the job.

Once the appropriate job criteria are established, levels or standards marking the degree of desirability or acceptability of employee performance on each job criterion are established. To ensure that the essence of job performance is captured, several criteria may be required. In turn, a standard needs to be established for each criterion. These standards can be established in various ways. For example, methods analysis (see Chapter 3) can establish the number of units of output for acceptable job performance. For many jobs where units of output may not be as relevant a criterion, standards may also be established through managerial dictate or definition, historical records, comparisons with other jobs, comparisons with similar jobs in other companies, and by profitability (relevant for managers of profit centers). Other topics relevant to setting standards and identifying criteria are discussed later in the chapter.

Using Valid Performance Appraisal Forms

Once the critical job components (criteria) are established, the forms used must measure or relate to those job components. For example, if *quantity of output* is a critical job criterion, having a supervisor mark on an appraisal form his or her general impressions of how personable and valuable the employee is may lead to an inappropriate appraisal. If used for an employment decision, it may lead to a *prima facie* case of adverse impact or discrimination. Appraisal forms on which the rater indicates by a check mark ($\sqrt{}$) his or her evaluation of an employee on things such as leadership, attitude toward people, and loyalty (attributes) are often referred to as **subjective forms.**[11] Appraisals in which the evaluation is done against specifically defined behaviors, level of output, level of specific goal attainment, or number of days absent (behaviors and outcomes) are often called **objective forms,** or at least, less subjective forms. Although the courts will allow a company to use a subjective form (*Roger* v. *International Paper Co.* [1975]), they generally frown upon their use (*Albemarle Paper Company* v. *Moody* [1975]; *Oshiver* v. *Court of Common Pleas* [1979]; *Baxter* v. *Savannah Sugar Refining Corp.* [1974]; and *Rowe* v. *General Motors* [1972]), since they may not produce fair or accurate evaluations. Keep in mind, however, three important points:

1. Many companies still use subjective forms.
2. The courts have suggested that a company can make subjective forms more objective by demonstrating that the company performs and relies on a thorough appraisal process (system), which is used fairly and accurately (*Mastie* v. *Great Lakes Steel Corp.* [1976]).
3. The company has the burden of demonstrating that the appraisal form is job related (i.e., valid) and serves a legitimate employment need (*Wade* v. *Mississippi Cooperative Extension Service* [1974]) if a *prima facie* case of illegal discrimination results from the use of the appraisal form.[12]

Once performance criteria and standards are identified and the appropriate appraisal forms developed, the next step is to communicate them to the employees.

Communicating Performance Criteria and Standards

Once performance criteria and standards have been identified, it is only fair that the employees be told what they are. Unfortunately, many employees indicate that they do not know on what basis they are being evaluated. The courts, however, have clearly stated that if performance evaluation is used for any of the purposes shown in Exhibit 6.1, performance criteria and standards must be communicated to the employee (*Patterson* v. *American Tobacco Co.* [1976, 1978, 1982]; *Sledge* v. *J. P. Stevens and Co.* [1978]; *Donald* v. *Pillsbury Co.* [1977]).

Passage of the Civil Service Reform Act of 1978 greatly affected the way in which federal agencies communicate and develop performance criteria and standards.

Civil Service Reform Act of 1978 (CSRA)

The Civil Service Reform Act of 1978 (CSRA) abolished the old Civil Service Commission, created the Office of Personnel Management, and instituted several basic changes in human resource management in the federal government. With respect to performance appraisal, the act did away with the former government-wide requirement for the use of subjective, adjectival ratings of outstanding, satisfactory, and unsatisfactory, and gave each federal agency considerable flexibility in developing its own performance appraisal system. The act requires agencies to do the following in establishing new appraisal systems:

- Encourage employee participation in establishing performance standards
- Set performance standards that permit accurate evaluation of job performance on the basis of job-related criteria
- Provide periodic appraisals of job performance
- Use appraisal results as a basis for developing, rewarding, assigning, promoting, demoting, and retaining or separating employees

The act also requires that agencies communicate to employees their relevant performance standards and performance criteria.[13]

Performance appraisal takes place within this setting of extensive legal considerations for private and government employers. The discussion in the rest of this chapter views performance appraisal as a system of processes and procedures.

Performance Appraisal as a System of Processes and Procedures

Criteria and Standards

To serve the organization's purposes and meet legal challenges, a performance appraisal system must appraise current employee performance. If the appraisal system is to uncover employees' potential for greater responsibilities and promotion, it must also provide accurate data about such potential. In addition, the system must yield consistent (reliable) data about what it is supposed to measure (i.e., the data must be valid).[14]

A reliable performance appraisal system produces the same appraisal of a subordinate regardless of who is doing the appraising at any one point in time. Over different periods of time, a reliable performance appraisal system produces the same results from the same rater if the actual performance of the subordinate has not changed. As described later in this chapter, however, a performance appraisal system may be unreliable because of numerous rating errors.

A valid performance appraisal system must specify **performance criteria** that are job related and important—criteria that can most easily be determined through job analysis. Employees' contributions to the organization can then be evaluated based on the degree to which they perform the criteria and attain the results specified in the job analysis. For example, if selling one hundred units per month is the only important result of an employee's job, then the appraisal system should measure only the number of units sold. In this case, there is only one performance criterion.

Generally, job analysis identifies several performance criteria that reflect employees' contributions. For example, selling one hundred units per month may be accompanied by such criteria as "effects of remarks to customers," "consistency in attendance," and even "effects on co-workers." If the job analysis finds all these performance criteria to be important, they should all be measured by the performance appraisal.

If the form used to appraise employee performance lacks the job behaviors and results important and relevant to the job, the form is said to be **deficient**. If the form includes appraisal of anything either unimportant or irrelevant to the job, it is **contaminated**. Many performance appraisal forms actually used in organizations measure some attributes and behaviors of employees unrelated to the employee's job. These forms are contaminated and are in many cases also deficient.[15]

Single, Multiple, and Composite Criteria.   To avoid performance appraisal deficiency, using more than a single criterion to appraise performance may be necessary. Then the issue is to determine which criteria to combine and how to best combine them.

Although the use of multiple criteria recognizes individual differences and that most job performance is multidimensional, it also presents the problem of how to combine the criteria into a single index that permits comparisons across people. Two major ways to combine the criteria are (1) to set equal weights for each criterion and (2) to set relative or differential weights for each criterion based on subjectively determined weights or dollar value to the organization.[16] Once done, performance comparisons can be made more easily.

Standards.   In addition to determining the performance criteria and deciding how they are combined, standards must be identified to evaluate how well employees are performing. By using standards, performance criteria take on a range of values. For example, selling one hundred units per month may be defined as excellent performance, and selling eighty units may be defined as average. Organizations often use historical records of how well employees have done before (essentially to determine what is really possible) to establish what constitutes average or excellent performance. Standards can also be established by time and motion studies and work sampling (described in Chapter 3). Whereas these methods are often used for blue-collar, nonmanagerial jobs, many organizations evaluate how well their managers do by how well or how many goals are attained. Often these goals are part of an entire performance appraisal method called management by objectives, to be discussed shortly. Increasingly, managers are also being evaluated against standards of profitability, revenues, or costs.

Although the standards used are determined partly by the job's nature, they may also be influenced by the way employee performance is measured. That is, if employee performance is appraised by management by objectives, then the level of goal attainment can be used as a standard. Keep in mind that the direction of this relationship could be reversed, as you read the following discussion of the various ways by which employee performance can be appraised.

Performance Appraisal Approaches

The four major approaches to performance appraisal are (1) comparative standards, (2) absolute standards (quantitative and qualitative), (3) objectives-based approaches, and (4) direct or objective indexes. Within each of these approaches are a variety of appraisal forms.

Comparative Standards.   All **comparative standards** of evaluation compare one subordinate to the others. In **straight ranking**, the superior lists the subordinates in order from best to worst, usually on the basis of overall performance. The first step in **alternative ranking** is to put the best subordinate at the head of the list and the worst subordinate at the bottom. The superior then selects the best and worst from the remaining subordinates; the best is placed second on the list, the worst next to last. The superior continues to choose the best and worst until all subordinates are ranked. The middle position on the list is the last to be filled by this method.

Two other comparative methods are more time-consuming but may provide better information. In the **paired comparison method,** each subordinate is compared to every other subordinate, two at a time, on a single standard or criterion, such as overall performance. The subordinate with the second-greatest number of favorable comparisons is ranked second, and so on.

The three comparative methods discussed so far give each person a unique rank. This suggests that no two subordinates perform exactly alike. Although this may be true, many superiors say that subordinates' performances are too close to differentiate. The fourth method—the **forced distribution method**—was designed to overcome this complaint and to incorporate several factors or dimensions (rather than a single factor) into the ranking of subordinates. The term *forced distribution* is used because the superior must assign only a certain proportion of subordinates to each of several categories on each factor. A common forced distribution scale may be divided into five categories. A fixed percentage of all subordinates in the group fall within each of these categories. A problem with this method is that a group of subordinates may not conform to the fixed percentage. All four comparative methods assume that good and bad performers are in all groups. You may know from experience, however, of situations in which all the people in a group perform identically. If you encountered such a situation, how would you evaluate these people?

Regardless of the specific comparative approach, all are based on the assumption that performance is best captured or measured by one criterion: overall performance. Since this single criterion is a global measure and is not anchored in any objective index, such as units sold, the results can be influenced by ratee subjectivity. As a consequence, the rankings lack behavioral specificity and may be subject to legal challenge.[17] Peer comparisons were used in the *Albemarle Paper Company* v. *Moody, Watkins* v. *Scott Paper Company* (1976), and *Brito* v. *Zia Company* cases. The court ruled against the company in all three decisions, saying that the comparisons were not based on objective performance criteria (or the companies failed to establish that they were).

Absolute Standards.   In the comparative approach to performance evaluation, the superior is forced to evaluate each subordinate in relationship to the other subordinates, often based on a single overall dimension. In contrast, the absolute standard approach allows superiors to evaluate each subordinate's performance independent of the other subordinates and often on several dimensions of performance.

One of the simplest absolute standards forms is the **narrative essay**. In this form the rater can describe, generally in sentences, the ratee's strengths and weaknesses and what could be done to improve the ratee. Since these essays are unstructured, they often vary in their length and detail. Consequently, comparisons of ratees within a department or across departments in a company are difficult. Furthermore, the essay form provides only qualitative data. Thus, these appraisals are not easily used in making zero-sum decisions (i.e., salary increases, promotions, and layoffs). This also applies to several other qualitative forms of appraisal, however, including critical incidents, behavioral checklists, and forced-choice forms.

In the **critical incidents** form, the superior observes and records things that subordinates do that are particularly effective or ineffective in accomplishing their jobs.[18] These incidents generally provide descriptions of the ratee's behaviors and the situation in which those behaviors occurred. Then, when the superior gives feedback to the subordinate, it is based on specific behaviors rather than on personal characteristics or traits, such as dependabililty, forcefulness, or loyalty. This feature of the critical incidents form can increase the chances that the subordinate will improve, since he or she learns more specifically what is expected. Drawbacks of the critical incidents technique include: (1) keeping records on each subordinate is time-consuming for the superior, (2) the technique is nonquantitative, (3) the incidents are not differentiated in their importance to job performance, and (4) comparing subordinates is difficult because the incidents recorded for each one can be quite different.

The **weighted checklist** technique eliminates some of the drawbacks of the critical incidents technique. It can be developed using the critical incidents technique. After several critical incidents of subordinate behaviors are gathered from several superiors or expert raters knowledgeable of the job, they can be used to construct checklists of weighted incidents. An example is shown in Exhibit 6.3. Raters using the form are unaware that each of the incidents has been weighted (i.e., its relative importance to job performance has been determined by the expert raters). The rater merely has to check the incidents that each subordinate performs. Alternatively, the form may be designed to include frequency response categories (e.g., "always," "very often," and "infrequently"). The rater then checks the frequency category for each incident for each subordinate. Nevertheless, the rater does not know the relative importance of each incident, making feedback more difficult for the rater to give. This technique does save the rater time, however, and is based on behaviors rather than on personal attributes and can yield a summary score.

Exhibit 6.3   *Sample Weighted Checklist for Bakeshop Managers*

Item	Scale Value
_____ Occasionally buys some of the competitor's products	6.8
_____ Never consults with the head salesperson when making a bake order	1.4
_____ Belongs to a local merchants' association	4.9
_____ Criticizes employees unnecessarily	0.8
_____ Window display is usually just fair	3.1
_____ Enjoys contacting customers personally	7.4
_____ Does not know how to figure costs of products	0.6
_____ Lacks a long-range viewpoint	3.5
_____ Products are of uniformly high quality	8.5
_____ Expects too much of employees	2.2
_____ Weekly and monthly reports are sometimes inaccurate	4.2
_____ Does not always give enough thought to bake orders	1.6
_____ Occasionally runs a selling contest among salespeople	6.8
_____ Baking in the shop continues until 2:00 P.M. or later	8.2
_____ Has originated one or more workable new formulas	6.4
_____ Sometimes has an unreasonably large inventory of certain items	3.3
_____ Employees enjoy working for the manager	7.6
_____ Does not delegate enough responsibility to others	2.8
_____ Has accurately figured the costs of most of the products	7.8
_____ Wishes he or she were just a baker	0.8
_____ Shop is about average in cleanliness	4.4
_____ Is tardy in making minor repairs in the salesroom	1.9
_____ Periodically samples all of the products for quality	8.1

Source: E. B. Knauft, "Construction and Use of Weighted Checklist Ratings Scales for Two Industrial Situations," *Journal of Applied Psychology* 32 (1948): 63–70. Copyright © 1948 by the American Psychological Association. Reproduced by permission.

To reduce the potential for leniency rating error (discussed later) and to establish a form with more objective standards for comparison of ratees, the **forced-choice form** was developed. The forced-choice method differs from the weighted checklist because it forces superiors to evaluate each subordinate by choosing which of two items in a pair better describes the subordinate. The two items in a pair are matched to be equal in **desirability** but of differential relevance to job performance (**discriminability**). The degrees of desirability and discriminability are established by individuals familiar with the jobs. A sample form is shown in Exhibit 6.4. As a consequence of this format, leniency error is minimized, and validity and reliability may be enhanced. Although the forced-choice scale can be highly useful, the raters are essentially unaware of how their ratings of their subordinates are interpreted. This not only makes feedback difficult but also reduces the rater's trust in the organization.[19]

In addition to these qualitative forms are several **quantitative** forms. Quantitative forms differ from the qualitative forms by generally requiring

---

Forced-Choice Pairs with Equal Desirability
and Differential Discriminability for Corporate
Loan Assistant

Exhibit 6.4

Prepares Credit Reports Accurately	Likes the Customers		Analyzes Credit Histories Thoroughly	Makes Friends with Others Quickly
Desirability Index			Desirability Index	
4.30	4.45		4.39	4.48
Discrimination Index			Discrimination Index	
4.70	1.15		4.15	1.65

the rater to assign or check a specific numerical value to a personal attribute (trait) or behavior shown by the ratee, rather than simply indicate whether or not a ratee has ever exhibited the attribute or behavior. The three quantitative forms are the conventional or graphic rating scale, the behaviorally anchored rating scale (BARS), and the behavioral observation scale (BOS).

The **conventional rating scale** is the most widely used form of performance evaluation (see Exhibit 6.5).[20] Conventional forms vary in the number of dimensions of performance they measure. The term *performance* is used advisedly here because many conventional forms use personality characteristics or traits rather than actual behaviors as indicators of performance. Frequently used traits are aggressiveness, independence, maturity, and sense of responsibility. Many conventional forms also use indicators of output, such as quantity and quality of performance. Conventional forms vary in the number of traits and indicators of output they incorporate. They also vary in the range of choices (only one of which is to be checked) for each dimension and the extent to which each dimension is described.

Conventional forms are used extensively because they are relatively easy to develop, permit quantitative results that allow comparisons across ratees and departments, and include several dimensions or criteria of performance. But because the rater has complete control in the use of the forms, they are subject to several types of error, including leniency, strictness, central tendency, and halo (discussed later). Nevertheless, they have been shown to be as reliable and valid as more complicated forms, such as forced-choice form.[21]

In addition to their potential for errors, conventional forms are criticized because they can't be used for developmental purposes (e.g., they fail to tell a subordinate how to improve and are not useful for the subordinate's career development needs). Consequently, organizations often modify the conventional form and add space for short essays so that the appraisal results can be used for developmental as well as evaluative purposes. Exhibit 6.6 shows an example of how one company modified the conventional form in Exhibit 6.5. Exhibit 6.6 is the reverse side of Exhibit 6.5.

Even when essays are added to the conventional forms, however, the results are still subject to the errors of the conventional forms and the essay

Exhibit 6.5   ## Conventional Form Employee Performance Appraisal

NAME

PRESENT JOB TITLE   CONVERSION CODE

	☐	☐
Quality of Work General excellence of output with consideration to accuracy, thoroughness, and dependability—without close supervision.	Exceptionally high quality. Consistently accurate, precise, quick to detect errors in own and others' work.	Work sometimes superior but usually accurate. Negligible amount needs to be redone. Work regularly meets standards.
Quantity of Work Consider the amount of useful work over the period of time since the last appraisal. Compare the output of work to the standard you have set for the job.	Output consistently exceeds standard. Unusually fast worker. Exceptional amount of output.	Maintains a high rate of production. Frequently exceeds standard. More than normal effort.
Cooperation Consider the employee's attitude toward the work, the employee's fellow workers, and supervisors. Does the employee appreciate the need to understand and help solve problems of others?	Always congenial and cooperative. Enthusiastic and cheerfully helpful in emergencies. Well liked by associates.	Cooperates well. Understands and complies with all rules. Usually demonstrates a good attitude. Liked by associates.
Knowledge of the Job The degree to which the employee has learned and understands the various procedures of the job and their objectives.	Exceptional understanding of all phases. Demonstrates unusual desire to acquire information.	Thorough knowledge in most phases. Has interest and potential toward personal growth.
Dependability The reliability of the employee in performing assigned tasks accurately and within the allotted time.	Exceptional. Can be left on own and will establish priorities to meet deadlines.	Very reliable. Minimal supervision required to complete assignments.
Attendance and Punctuality Consider the employee's record, reliability, and ability to conduct the job within the unit's work rules.	Unusual compliance and understanding of work discipline. Routine usually exceeds normal.	Excellent. Complete conformity with rules but cheerfully volunteers time during peak loads.
Knowledge of Company Policy and Objectives Acceptance, understanding, and promotion of company policies and objectives in the area of the employee's job responsibilities.	Thorough appreciation and implementation of all policies. Extraordinary ability to project objectively.	Reflects knowledge of almost all policies related to this position.
Initiative and Judgment The ability and interest to suggest and develop new ideas and methods; the degree to which these suggestions and normal decisions and actions are sound.	Ingenious self-starter. Superior ability to think intelligently.	Very resourceful. Clear thinker—usually makes thoughtful decisions.
Supervisory or Technical Potential Consider the employee's ability to teach and increase skills of others, to motivate and lead, to organize and assign work, and to communicate ideas and instructions.	An accomplished leader who earns their respect and can inspire others to perform. An articulate and artful communicator, planner, and organizer.	Has the ability to teach and will lead by example rather than technique. Speaks and writes well and can organize and plan with help.

		DATE COMPLETED	
DATE OF BIRTH	DATE OF EMPLOYMENT	OFFICE LOCATION BRANCH DEPARTMENTAL	DEPARTMENT
YEARS IN PRESENT POSITION	SO. SEC. NO.	EDUCATION	

☐	☐	☐
A careful worker. A small amount of work needs to be redone. Corrections made in reasonable time. Usually meets normal standards.	Work frequently below acceptable quality. Inclined to be careless. Moderate amount of work needs to be redone. Excessive time to correct.	Work often almost worthless. Seldom meets normal standards. Excessive amount needs to be redone.
☐	☐	☐
Output is regular. Meets standard consistently. Works at steady, average speed.	Frequently turns out less than normal amount of work. A low producer.	A consistently low producer. Excessively slow worker. Unacceptable output.
☐	☐	☐
Usually courteous and cooperative. Follows orders but at times needs reminding. Gets along well with associates.	Does only what is specifically requested. Sometimes complains about following instructions. Reluctant to help others.	Unfriendly and uncooperative. Refuses to help others.
☐	☐	☐
Adequate knowledge for normal performance. Will not voluntarily seek development.	Insufficient knowledge of job. Resists criticism and instruction.	No comprehension of the requirements of job.
☐	☐	☐
Dependable in most assignments. Normal supervision required. A profitable worker.	Needs frequent follow-up. Excessive prodding necessary.	Chronic procrastinator. Control required is out of proportion.
☐	☐	☐
Normally dependable. Rarely needs reminding of accepted rules.	Needs close supervision in this area. Inclined to backslide without strict discipline.	Unreliable. Resists normal rules. Frequently wants special privileges.
☐	☐	☐
Acceptable but fairly superficial understanding of job objectives.	Limited insight into job or company goals. Mentally restricted.	Not enough information or understanding to permit minimum efficiency.
☐	☐	☐
Fairly progressive, with normal sense. Often needs to be motivated.	Rarely makes suggestions. Decisions need to be checked before implementation.	Needs detailed instructions and close supervision. Tendency to assume and misinterpret.
☐	☐	☐
Fairly well informed on job-related subjects but has some difficulty communicating with others. Nothing distinctive about spoken or written word.	Little ability to interpret or implement. Seems uninterested in teaching or helping others. Careless speech and writing habits.	Unable to be objective or reason logically. Inarticulate and stilted in expression.

Exhibit 6.6   *Modification of the Conventional Form Shown in Exhibit 6.5*

A. Summary of Current Performance:
1. Employee's strongest points
2. Employee's weakest points
3. What steps have been taken to modify weak points?
4. Is employee properly placed in present job? Explain.

B. Employee's Potential:
1. In what significant ways has this employee demonstrated improvement in last twelve months?

2. Have you made any suggestions for the employee's   Yes ☐ No ☐
   self-development?
   a) If yes, (1) What was the suggestion?
                (2) How did the employee react?
   b) If no, what was your reasoning?

3. In your opinion, is the employee limited to the work in   Yes ☐ No ☐
   present job?

4. a) If your answer to 3 is no, what have you considered as a possibility to improve the employee's position in our company?
   b) What has been done about it?

5. If your answer to 3 is yes, please explain.

C. Employee's Reactions: Enter reactions or comments after you have discussed this appraisal with the employee. Are there any changes in your evaluation as a result of your interview?

Supervisor's Signature	Date

Reviewed

Department Head ☐	
	Date
Supv. Officer ☐	
	Date
Personnel Dept. ☐	
	Date

forms described earlier. Thus, even the modified form is not the most appropriate for giving feedback and improving subordinates' performance.

The **behaviorally anchored rating scale (BARS)** was developed to provide results that subordinates could use to improve performance. They were also designed to allow superiors to be more comfortable in giving feedback. The development of a BARS generally corresponds to the first steps in the critical incidents method of job analysis (i.e., incidents describing competent, average, and incompetent behavior for each job category are collected). These incidents are then categorized into broad overall categories or dimensions of performance (e.g., administrative ability, interpersonal skill). Each

Sample Behaviorally Anchored Rating Scale   *Exhibit 6.7*
for One Dimension of the Work Performance of
Corporate Loan Assistant

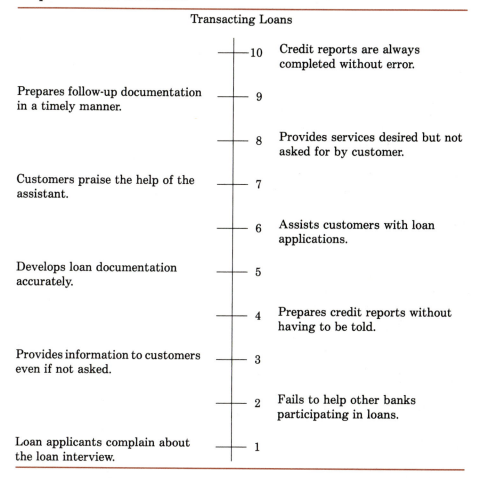

Transacting Loans

- 10 — Credit reports are always completed without error.

Prepares follow-up documentation in a timely manner. — 9

- 8 — Provides services desired but not asked for by customer.

Customers praise the help of the assistant. — 7

- 6 — Assists customers with loan applications.

Develops loan documentation accurately. — 5

- 4 — Prepares credit reports without having to be told.

Provides information to customers even if not asked. — 3

- 2 — Fails to help other banks participating in loans.

Loan applicants complain about the loan interview. — 1

dimension serves as one criterion in evaluating subordinates. Using these categories, another group of individuals lists the critical incidents pertinent to each category. Exhibit 6.7 shows an example of one such criterion or category, transacting loans, and the critical incidents listed as pertinent to it.[22] This exhibit also shows the next step: the assignment of a numerical value (weight) to each incident in relation to its contribution to the criterion.

Armed with a set of criteria with behaviorally anchored and weighted choices, the superiors rate their subordinates with a form that is relatively unambiguous in meaning, understandable, justifiable, and relatively easy to use.[23] Yet, the form has its limitations. Since most BARS forms use a limited number of performance criteria, (e.g., seven), many of the critical incidents generated in the job analysis stage may not be used. Thus, the raters may not find appropriate categories to describe the behaviors—the critical incidents—of their subordinates.[24] Similarly, even if the relevant incidents are observed, they may not be worded in exactly the same way on the dimension; the rater may thus be unable to match the observed behaviors with the dimension and anchors. A procedure that overcomes these and other limitations but retains the BARS form's advantages is called the **behavioral observation scale (BOS).**[25]

The BOS is essentially the same as BARS except in the development of the scales or dimensions, the scale format, and scoring procedures. But they are even similar in this area to the extent that expert raters or judges rate the incidents from the job analysis according to the degree to which each incident represents effective job behavior. BOS and BARS are most different in their scale development in the use of statistical analysis to select items for building each dimension of performance. For BOS, statistical analysis is used to identify those behaviors or critical incidents that most clearly differentiate effective from ineffective performers. For BARS, expert raters perform this function. The major ways in which BOS differs from BARS are the rating scale format and summated scoring procedure used for each dimension. Exhibit 6.8 is based on the critical incidents from the job description of the corporate loan assistant (Exhibit 3.3).

The several advantages of BOS include: (1) like BARS, it is based on a systematic job analysis; (2) its items and behavioral anchors are clearly stated; (3) in contrast to many other methods, it allows participation of employees in the development of the dimensions (through the identification of critical incidents in the job analysis), which facilitates understanding and acceptance; (4) it is useful for performance feedback and improvement, since specific goals can be tied to numerical scores (ratings) on the relevant behavioral anchor (critical incident) for the relevant performance criterion or dimension; and (5) BOS appears to satisfy the *Uniform Guidelines* in validity (relevance) and reliability.[26]

The limitations of BOS are connected with some of its advantages, especially the time and cost for its development as compared with forms such as the conventional rating. A BOS is developed and used across several job categories. This cost may be greater than all of the benefits. Furthermore, several dimensions that are essentially behaviors may miss the real essence of many jobs, especially managerial and highly routinized jobs where the job's essence may be the actual outputs produced regardless of the behaviors used to obtain them. When these conditions exist, some argue that a better method is one that is goal oriented or that appraises performance against output measures.

Objectives-based Approaches.   The two most common types of output performance measuring systems for managerial employees are management by objectives (MBO) and responsibility centers. Another approach similar to MBO is the work standards approach.

Management by objectives (MBO) is probably the most popular method used to evaluate managers.[27] Its popularity apparently results from its identity with commonly held personal values, especially the philosophy that rewarding people for what they accomplish is important. MBO is also popular because it can attain greater individual-organizational goal congruence and reduce the likelihood that managers will be working on things unrelated to the objectives and purposes of the organization (goal displacement).[28]

Sample BOS Items for Corporate Loan Assistant Illustrating Both Effective and Ineffective Performance	*Exhibit 6.8*

Effective Performance

1. The corporate loan assistant prepares credit reports accurately.

Almost Never				Almost Always
1	2	3	4	5

2. The corporate loan assistant is friendly when interviewing loan applicants.

Almost Never				Almost Always
1	2	3	4	5

3. The corporate loan assistant is effective when interviewing job applicants.

Almost Never				Almost Always
1	2	3	4	5

Ineffective Performance

1. The corporate loan assistant fails to prepare follow-up documentation.

Almost Never				Almost Always
1	2	3	4	5

2. The corporate loan assistant does not help customers with loan applications.

Almost Never				Almost Always
1	2	3	4	5

3. The corporate loan assistant needs to be told to prepare credit reports.

Almost Never				Almost Always
1	2	3	4	5

Note: On an actual form, the items would neither be grouped nor identified as effective and ineffective performance.

MBO works in four steps. The first step is to establish the goals each subordinate is to attain. In some organizations, superiors and subordinates work together to establish goals; in others, superiors establish goals for subordinates. The **goals** can refer to desired outcomes to be achieved, means (activities) for achieving the outcomes, or both.

The second step involves the subordinates' performance in a previously arranged time period. As subordinates perform, they know fairly well what there is to do, what has been done, and what remains to be done.

The third step is a comparison of the actual level of goal attainment against the agreed-on goals. The evaluator explores reasons for the goals not being met and for goals being exceeded. This step helps determine possible training needs. It also alerts the superior to conditions in the organization that may affect a subordinate's performance but over which the subordinate has no control.

The final step is to decide on new goals and possible new strategies for goals not previously attained. At this point, subordinate and superior involvement in goal setting may change. Subordinates who successfully reach the established goals may be allowed to participate more in the goal-setting process the next time.[29]

Although the use of goals in evaluating managers is effective in motivating their performance, capturing all the important dimensions of a job in terms of output is not always possible. How the job is done (i.e., job behaviors) may be as critical as the outcomes. For example, it may be detrimental to an organization if a manager meets a personal selling goal by unethical or illegal means. But even if output measures accurately describe the job, the concern still exists to establish goals that are of equal difficulty for all managers and that are sufficiently difficult to be challenging. Other concerns about the use of MBO are described in the following "PHRM in the News."

To help avoid some of the problems encountered in establishing goals in the MBO approach, some organizations have implemented the use of responsibility centers. These centers appear to be most relevant in appraising managers' performance. Under the **responsibility centers** approach, profit, cost, or revenues centers are established (and become criteria), and the performance of the managers of those centers is evaluated in relation to one or a combination of those criteria. To develop these centers, an organization essentially creates many little independent suborganizations.

To the extent that real independence cannot be created, however, the responsibility center approach becomes a less appropriate form by which to evaluate managerial performance. And lack of real independence seems to be more typical of departments in organizations than otherwise. For example, suppose an organization has three departments: production, sales, and finance. One would assume that setting standards for appraising these divisions would be straightforward. For the production department, quantity, quality, time, and cost can be considered. The sales department is concerned with total sales. The finance department can be evaluated on the amount lost to bad debts and the like.

The difficulty here is that the performances of these departments are not independent. For example, the production department could operate most efficiently with a limited product line that varies little in size or color. The sales department wants as much variety as possible, and these are mutually exclusive needs. Similarly, the sales department could, through large sales, overtax the production department, which would increase equipment fatigue, increase overtime payments, and so on. To be effective, the finance department requires sound fiscal policies. So for large sales, finance would request a relatively high down payment and a reasonably accelerated pay-

PHRM in the News

Alcan's Integration of Management Techniques Raises Their Effectiveness

In addition to job descriptions, and the organalysis process, Alcan's integrated Communications System has three other parts; a modified management by objectives process, zero-based budgeting, and, most critical of all, a short- and long-term planning process.

From my discussions with other senior managers who question the value of MBO and our own efforts to develop an effective MBO program, I suspect that there are two calamitous pitfalls in the implementation of MBO.

The first is an overemphasis on technicalities. In the early stages of developing an MBO program, it is easy to become mesmerized by the complex technicalities of measurement. How do you set objectives so an individual's performance in achieving them can be fairly measured? How do you differentiate between the providential factors and those over which an individual has some degree of influence? And how do you account for an individual's performance in achieving an objective when his ability to do so is partially dependent on others?

Our experience also has convinced us that it is critical to limit the number of objectives. In *In Search of Excellence*, Thomas J. Peters and Robert H. Waterman contend that the number of objectives should be only three or four. Our experience suggests an MBO system, if properly designed, can cope with up to ten.

Also, from the top down, a rigorous effort should be made to assure there is a satisfactory balance between long- and short-term objectives. At Alcan, we compensate for the ramifications of including longer-term objectives in an individual's annual performance evaluation by limiting their attainment of objectives to 50 percent of a person's annual rating. The other half depends on how the person has carried out his or her principal accountabilities or performed overall.

Source: Reprinted, by permission of the publisher, from "Alcan's Integration of Management Techniques Raises Their Effectiveness," by Roy A. Gentles, MANAGEMENT REVIEW, "AMA Forum," April 1984, p. 31 © 1984 AMA Membership Publications Division, American Management Associations, New York. All rights reserved.

back period. The sales department, on the other hand, would prefer to sell at a dollar per week forever.

The point is that appraising the performance of just one department may undermine the efforts of another. The performance of all divisions, departments, and groups must be reasonably congruent. And appraisal systems must tap the performance of individuals and groups without encouraging behaviors and attitudes that are dysfunctional to the organization as a whole. These considerations are a major concern and a serious challenge for higher-level management. If independence can be established, however, responsibility centers are a useful way to evaluate and motivate managers. The center concept gives each manager a great deal of freedom—to succeed or fail.

The **work standards approach,** which is similar to MBO, uses more direct measures of performance and is usually applied to nonmanagerial employees. Instead of asking subordinates to set their own performance standards or goals as in MBO, organizations determine them through past experience (e.g., what's been done on this job before), time study data, and work sampling. Data are collected pertaining to how long it takes a worker to do a certain task under particular circumstances to produce time study data (for example, how long it takes a secretary to type a business letter in an office setting with only normal interruptions from the telephone and visitors). If job circumstances can be ignored, more standard data can be used to establish standards and goals. Although the standard data approach is more efficient than time study because each job does not have to be examined, if job circumstances are important, the standard data may produce inapplicable results. Time study and standard data are useful on jobs that are relatively repetitive and noncomplex. With jobs that are less repetitive and more complex, the work sampling technique is more appropriate. This technique determines how workers allocate their time among various job activities.

The disadvantages of these work standards are that they require time, money, and cooperation to develop. Often cooperation of the job incumbents is necessary; the inherent problems are presented in Chapter 3. Without the cooperation, however, the data are neither reliable nor valid. What workers do—a necessary ingredient in work sampling—may reflect what tasks they like and dislike instead of the importance of the tasks and what they should do.[30] As with MBO, the essence of job performance may not be captured entirely by set standards and goals. Consequently, important job behaviors may be ignored in the evaluation process. And although set standards may provide clear direction to the employees and the goals may be motivating, they may also induce undesirable competition among employees to attain their standards and goals. If this competition does not lead to undesirable consequences, and if the employees do not want to participate in the standard-and goal-setting process, this method can be highly motivating.

Direct Index Approach.   The direct index approach differs from the first three approaches primarily in how performance is measured. Except for the objectives-based approach, the first three approaches depend on a superior evaluating a subordinate's performance. These cases contain a certain amount of subjective evaluation. However, the **direct index approach** measures subordinate performance by objective, impersonal criteria, such as productivity, absenteeism, and turnover. For example, a manager's performance may be evaluated by the number of manager's employees who quit or by the employees' absenteeism rate. For nonmanagers, measures of productivity may be more appropriate. Measures of productivity can be broken into measures of quality and measures of quantity. Quality measures include scrap rates, customer complaints, and number of defective units or parts produced. Quantity measures include units of output per hour, new customer orders, and sales volume.

Assessing Performance Appraisal Forms: Which is Best?

Although the appraisal form or method is just one component of performance appraisal, the performance appraisal system often centers on the form. Attention is therefore often focused on assessing the available appraisal forms to enable organizations to choose the best one. This chapter discusses appraisal form assessment and discussion of PAS assessment appears in the next chapter.[31]

Criteria for Assessment.   Determining the best appraisal form prompts a question: What criteria or criterion of assessment is the appraisal form going to use? The criteria include the purposes of performance appraisal—namely, evaluation and development—but an effective appraisal form should also be free from error, be reliable and valid, and allow comparisons across subordinates and departments in an organization. Each of these goals can be used as a criterion. Each form should also be evaluated by its influence on the superior-subordinate relationship. Does the form encourage superiors to watch their subordinates to collect valid data for evaluation and developmental purposes, and does it facilitate the appraisal interview? (Appraisal review is discussed in Chapter 7.) All of these criteria must be counterbalanced by one other major criterion: economics. The costs of developing and implementing a form must be compared against its benefits, or how well it does on the other criteria. The costs and benefits of all forms should be compared to arrive at an estimate of the utility of each form. This is described in more detail in Chapter 18.[32]

Which Form Is Best?   Research on the question of which form is best is limited. It does, however, reinforce the necessity of first identifying the purposes the organization wants to serve with performance appraisal.[33] Each form can then be assessed in relation to the following criteria:

- *Developmental:* Motivating subordinates to do well, providing feedback, and aiding in human resource planning and career development
- *Evaluational:* Promotion, discharge, layoff, pay, and transfer decisions and, therefore, the ability to make comparisons across subordinates and departments
- *Economic:* Cost in the development, implementation, and use
- *Freedom from error:* Halo, leniency, and central tendency and the extent of reliability and validity
- *Interpersonal:* The extent to which superiors can gather useful and valid appraisal data that facilitate the appraisal interview

Exhibit 6.9 shows an assessment of the appraisal forms in relation to each of these criteria.

Analysis of Potential Performance

The various performance appraisal approaches appraise current performance. As the initial "PHRM in the News" illustrates, being able to appraise how employees would perform on a future job (generally, one to which they would be promoted) is occasionally necessary and useful. The **assessment center method,** used to determine managers' performance potential, is a set of activities for assessment, rather than a single appraisal approach. The method evaluates individuals on a large number of activities, is conducted in

Exhibit 6.9   *Evaluation of Performance Appraisal Forms*

Criteria for Evaluation	Comparative Approach		Absolute Approach		
	Straight Ranking	Forced Distribution	Critical Incidents	Weighted Checklist	Forced-Choice
Developmental[a]	1	1	2	2	1
Evaluational[b]	3	2	1	1	2
Economic[c]	3	3	2	1	1
Freedom from Error[d]	3	3	1	2	2
Interpersonal[e]	1	2	2	2	1

Note: 1 = low level; 2 = medium level; 3 = high level.
a. Extent to which subordinates are motivated to improve performance and can develop their careers.
b. Extent to which the form enables the company to make decisions such as for promotions, salary increases, and layoffs.
c. Extent to which the costs, time, and ease in development and use of form are minimized.
d. Extent to which errors in evaluation such as halo, leniency, low validity, and reliability are minimized.
e. Extent to which form facilitates supervision.

a relatively isolated environment, and is designed to measure managerial skills and abilities. In a typical assessment center, a manager may spend two or three days going through a series of activities, which may include management games, leaderless group discussions, peer evaluations, and in-basket exercises. An example of the performance criteria against which organizations evaluate how well employees may perform in a future job is shown in GM's assessment center in Chapter 5.

Advantages of the assessment center include its validity and its ability to open up an organization's identification of future managers, thus giving more employees a chance to have their potential tested and identified.[34] Occasionally, employees get placed in jobs or parts of the organization that are not as visible to top management as some other jobs or parts. This, combined with having a supervisor who fails to make fair evaluations of present performance, may bury some employees in the organization. Having an assessment center program where employees can volunteer to attend helps reduce the possibility of overlooking employee potential.

Potential limitations of the assessment center method are its cost, its focus on competition rather than on cooperation, and its creation of "crown princes and princesses."[35] The creation of a special class of employees is less likely, however, under a program where employees can either be nominated

Conventional	BARS	BOS	Objectives-based Approach		Direct Indexes	
			MBO	Work Standards	Output	Absenteeism
1	2	2	3	2	1	1
2	2	2	3	3	3	3
3	1	1	1	1	3	3
1	2	2	2	2	2	2
1	3	3	2	2	2	2

by their supervisors or volunteer on their own initiative. The nature of the activities in the center and hence the degree of cooperativeness or competitiveness established can be regulated to match the needs of the organization and its environment. The relatively high cost of the assessment approach suggests that the organization, to justify its use of the center, must clearly identify the benefits, such as those gained from a better and bigger pool of potential managers.

Two more narrowly focused approaches for the analysis of potential performance are the job-focus and person-focus approaches. In the **job-focus approach,** the nature of the work performed in the jobs or roles to which employees may be promoted is assessed. For example, managerial functions (such as planning, organizing, coordinating, and controlling) or managerial roles (such as interpersonal, informational, and decisional) can be identified and translated into specific job requirements (essentially, a job analysis procedure).[36] Then the extent to which the employees meet or can meet these requirements is determined.

In the **person-focus approach,** current job incumbents are categorized according to their levels of effectiveness. These incumbents are then administered tests, such as objective personality inventories, interest inventories, projective tests, and simulation tests. Differences found on these tests between the more effective and less effective job incumbents can then be used to predict success rates for other employees. Other employees are then tested to determine the extent to which they possess characteristics most like the effective incumbents.

Regardless of method or approach used, once performance potential is identified, organizations can establish management inventory systems to facilitate a human resource planning activity (see Chapter 2). Using the same information, organizations can also establish career planning and training programs to eliminate any qualification gaps between current possessed and needed skills (see Chapter 11). Before proceeding, however, organizations must understand the context within which performance appraisal occurs.

The Context of Performance Appraisal

Regardless of the form or method used to gather performance appraisal data, the validity and reliability of the data and even the feasibility of gathering the data may be influenced by the superior-subordinate relationship, the nature of the job, and organizational conditions.[37]

Superior-Subordinate Relationships. Important aspects of the superior-subordinate relationship are personal characteristics of the superior, characteristics of the superior in relation to those of the subordinate, the superior's knowledge of the subordinate and the job, and the subordinate's knowledge of the job. For ease of discussion, these can be grouped into problems with the superior and problems with the subordinate.

Generally, four problems with the superior may arise. The first is that superiors may not know what employees are doing or may not understand their work well enough to appraise it fairly. This particular problem occurs more frequently when a manager has a large span of control—a large number of responsibilities and possibly a large number of employees working in different areas. This problem also occurs when the tasks of the employees are varied and technically complex or changing.

The second problem is that even when superiors understand and know how much work subordinates do, they may not have performance standards for evaluating that work. As a result, subordinates may receive unfair (invalid) evaluations because of variability in standards and ratings. This unfairness may be particularly obvious when comparing the evaluations of subordinates working for different superiors. This problem can occur in any organization, regardless of size, complexity, or the amount of change going on.

The third problem is that superiors may use inappropriate standards. They may allow personal values, needs, or biases to replace organizational values and standards. The general result is any one of several errors in evaluation. The most common errors occur when superiors rate an employee or group of subordinates on several dimensions of performance. Frequently a superior will evaluate a subordinate similarly on all dimensions of performance, based on the evaluation of only one dimension—the one perhaps perceived as most important. This effect is the **halo error.** When superiors tend to give all their subordinates favorable ratings, they are said to be committing an **error of leniency.** An **error of strictness** is just the opposite. An **error of central tendency** represents a tendency to evaluate all subordinates as average. A **recency-of-events error** is a tendency to evaluate total performance on the last or most recent part of the subordinate's performance. This error can have serious consequences for a subordinate who performs well for six months or a year but then makes a serious or costly error in the last week or two before evaluations are made.[38]

These errors may occur intentionally or unintentionally. Some superiors, for example, may intentionally evaluate their best performers as slightly less than excellent to prevent them from being promoted out of the superior's group. On the other hand, some superiors may unintentionally evaluate certain subordinates less favorably than others merely because of the superior's perception. A female subordinate, for instance, may be perceived by a male superior as having traditional female qualities, such as dependence, passiveness, and kindness—in unfortunate contrast to the qualities he perceives as required to be a good performer, such as independence, initiative, and impersonalism. Thus, this superior may evaluate this subordinate less favorably. A supervisor may also incorrectly evaluate a subordinate because of personal likes or dislikes the superior has for the subordinate.

Even the most valid and reliable appraisal forms cannot be effective when superiors commit these all-too-common errors. But many of these errors can be minimized if the following are observed:

- Each performance dimension addresses a single job activity rather than a group of activities.
- The rater on a regular basis can observe the behavior of the ratee while the job is being accomplished.
- Terms like *average* are not used on a rating scale, since different raters have various reactions to such a term.
- The rater does not have to evaluate large groups of employees.
- Raters are trained to avoid errors such as leniency, strictness, halo, central tendency, and recency of events.
- The dimensions being evaluated are meaningful, clearly stated, and important.[39]

The last major problem related to the superior, although important in itself, is also important because it often leads to some of the preceding errors, particularly the halo and leniency errors: Superiors do not like, and where possible resist, making ratings, especially ones that need to be defended or justified in writing. Other reasons for resisting making evaluations center on the inherent conflicts between organizational and individual goals in performance appraisals (discussed in Chapter 7). The result is often inadequate or inaccurate evaluations. Superiors may consider performance appraisals a time conflict. For example, they may perceive that appraisals take time away from their "real job." Also, superiors may fail to see how performance appraisals fit into the mainstream of knowledge about the behavior of people in organizations. Halo and leniency errors are easy to make when superiors do not want to take time to consider each performance criterion separately for each subordinate. Superiors often commit leniency errors because giving negative feedback is difficult for them, especially when sufficient justification is lacking.

The problems for superiors in performance appraisal are difficult indeed. However, subordinates also present problems. First, they may not know what's expected of them. They may have the ability but don't know how to apply it. This occurs regardless of the level of difficulty in their jobs and whether they work in hospitals, government agencies, or private organizations.

The second problem is that subordinates may not be able to do what's expected. This may be corrected by training or job matching. Spotting performance inabilities is not always easy, however. The personnel and human resource manager can play an important role in these cases, working with superiors to spot reasons for performance deficiences. Using the performance appraisal to spot and remove performance deficiencies is discussed in Chapter 7.

The Nature of the Job.   "To a considerable extent, the potential value of any performance appraisal system is dependent upon the nature of the subordinate's job."[40] On many jobs, the quality or quantity of performance may be outside the subordinate's control. This is particularly true on routine jobs and where machines control the pace of the jobs. When jobs are highly interdependent, separating the individual's performance from that of the group is difficult.

Organizational Conditions.   Organizational conditions over which subordinates may have little control but are likely to influence their performance (more often negatively than positively) include tools, equipment and supplies availability, and heat, light, and noise levels.[41] If only the subordinates' outcomes, not their behaviors, are appraised, and if organizational conditions are adversely affecting performance, the subordinates are likely to either quit the job or lower their commitment.[42] A condition that may not so much inhibit performance as the use of performance appraisal is whether the subordinates are unionized. If employees are unionized, performance appraisals may not even be used. Unions have traditionally favored the use of seniority to determine wage increases, promotions, transfers, and demotions.

In addition to the performance appraisal form and the context in which appraisal occurs, the determination of who gathers the performance appraisal data must be considered.

Gathering Performance Appraisal Data

Many sources can be used to gather performance appraisal data. Appraisal can be done by superiors, through self-appraisal, by peers, by subordinates (if the ratee is a manager or supervisor), and by computer monitoring.

Appraisal by Superiors.   The superior is the immediate boss of the subordinate being evaluated. The assumption is that the superior knows the subordinate's job and performance better than anyone else. But appraisal by the superior has drawbacks. First, since the superior may have reward and punishment power, the subordinate may feel threatened. Second, evaluation is often a one-way process that makes the subordinate feel defensive. Thus, little coaching takes place; justification of actions prevails. Third, the superior may not have the necessary interpersonal skills to give good feedback. Fourth, the superior may have an ethical bias against "playing God." Finally, the superior, by giving punishments, may alienate the subordinate.

Because of the potential liabilities, organizations may invite other people to share the appraisal process, even giving the subordinate greater input. Allowing other people to gather performance appraisal data creates a greater openness in the PAS, thus helping to enhance the quality of the superior-subordinate relationship.

Self-appraisal.   The use of self-appraisal, particularly through subordinate participation in setting goals, was made popular as an important component of MBO. Subordinates who participate in the evaluation process may become more involved and committed to the goals. Subordinate participation may apparently also help clarify employees' roles and reduce role conflict.[43]

At this time, self-appraisals are effective tools for programs focusing on self-development, personal growth, and goal commitment. However, self-appraisals are also subject to systematic biases and distortions when used for evaluative purposes. Nevertheless, more employers adopt self-evaluation of job performance:

> "There is a clear trend toward self-evaluation," says Edward Morse of Hay Management Consultants' Dallas office. The idea is to get employees to participate in their job reviews and create more of a dialogue with the boss. Handleman Co. is testing an annual self-evaluation system with 30 managers. Employees first rate themselves on a form, then supervisors make ratings and the two evaluations are compared.
>
> Ryder Systems Inc. says, "Employees have greater expectations about (appraisals) being a two-way process." It is developing a program to help managers improve evaluation skills. Dennison Manufacturing Co. added sections to its appraisal forms to stimulate discussion of employee goals, projects and training.[44]

Peer Appraisal.   Peer appraisals appear to be useful predictors of subordinate performance.[45] They are particularly useful when superiors lack access to some aspects of subordinates' performance. However, the validity of peer appraisals is reduced somewhat if the organizational reward system is based on performance and is highly competitive, and if the level of trust among subordinates is low.[46] They are also useful when teamwork and participation are part of the organizational culture:

> Standard performance appraisals, conducted on an individual basis, do not contribute to the team building efforts that are such an important element in today's participative management style.
>
> Individual appraisals can, however, be supplemented with a periodic group appraisal process that yields a wealth of valuable information for the supervisor in a supportive coaching position, and provides a method for resolving those interpersonal conflicts that prevent groups from functioning as effective teams.[47]

Electronic Eye on Employee Performance

Computer monitoring—the electronic tracking of a worker's speed, efficiency, and accuracy—is being used by an increasing number of employers to keep tabs on employee productivity. In many cases, employers are using new computerized job analysis techniques to set and closely monitor performance standards for their workers. While management praises the computer-tracked standards as a valuable tool in the drive to increase productivity, employees charge that the electronic performance monitoring often is intrusive, stressful, and based on unrealistically high expectations.

Who's measuring what?

Time-and-motion studies are nothing new to the U.S. workplace, with stopwatch measurements of workers' activities dating from the late 19th century. However, the computer has far surpassed the stopwatch in terms of heightening management's ability to track individual workers' productivity in minute detail. Today's efficiency experts electronically dissect work processes and employee movements, using standards like TMUs (time measurement units), each of which equals 0.00001 hour, or 0.036 second. Armed with this knowledge, they can determine the appropriate amount of time, down to the millisecond, needed for a worker to complete an assigned task.

Office workers, telephone operators, bank tellers, cashiers, hotel employees—even some managers and supervisors—are finding themselves linked to computerized performance measurement systems that can time virtually every job-related movement, down to the number of keystrokes per hour hit by a typist. Some systems can track how often and how long an employee is away from a work station

and how much time is actually spent working.

Employers using computer monitoring include:

- The Equitable Life Assurance Society, whose supervisors use computerized performance reports to monitor employee compliance with a standard of processing a simple claim—or "work unit"—in 6.5 minutes.

- The Social Security Administration, where 1,000 workers at a regional center in Wilkes-Barre, Pa., are monitored to check their compliance with data-entry performance standards. Agency officials say more than 40 percent of the facility's workforce received better-than-satisfactory performance ratings last year.

Productive or counterproductive?

Employers claim that computer monitoring systems can improve productivity because they allow supervisors to keep better track of a worker's speed and accuracy and take steps to improve a subpar performance—either by providing an employee with help to correct problems or by disciplining a poor performer if such assistance fails. Employers also contend that computer-monitored performance standards provide an objective measure of efficiency that many workers welcome, especially if the system is used as a basis for rewards such as merit pay.

Monitoring can backfire, however, with a host of counterproductive side effects, such as increased stress and resentment among workers. While management views computer-monitoring as a useful tool, workers often see it as a threat, claiming that they feel "violated" because they never know when they are"being watched." Computer monitoring of employee performance also can cause tension-related illnesses which could heighten the risk of heart disease, according to National Institute of Occupational Safety and Health officials.

Tracking tips

Employee demoralization problems are much more likely to develop when computer tracking is misused by "unenlightened management looking for short-term profit and not long-term performance," emphasizes James O'Brien, of the management consulting firm MTM Association. Employers that do not provide workers with sufficient training or an opportunity for input and participation when a system is installed, O'Brien notes, leave themselves open to charges of setting up a "sweatshop" in which "Big Brother" is constantly overseeing performance. Vico Henriques, president of the Computer and Business Equipment Manufacturers Association, maintains that managers who set reasonable standards, use discipline fairly, and offer some form of incentive will elicit employee cooperation despite initial resistance to computers, while those who design repressive monitoring systems will encounter trouble.

Source: Bulletin to Management, 20 September, 1984, p. 8. Reprinted by permission from *Bulletin to Management,* copyright 1984, by The Bureau of National Affairs, Inc., Washington, D.C.

Appraisal by Subordinates.   Perhaps many of you, particularly as students, have had the chance to evaluate an instructor. How useful do you think this evaluation process is? A significant advantage of appraisal by students is that many instructors are unaware of how their students perceive them. They may not realize that students fail to understand some of their instructions. The same is true in a work setting: Subordinates' appraisals can make superiors more aware of their impact on their subordinates.

Sometimes, however, subordinates may evaluate their superiors solely on the basis of personality or serving subordinates' needs rather than those of the organization. At times, subordinates may inflate the evaluation of the superiors, particularly if they feel threatened by them and have no anonymity.[48]

Computer Monitoring.   A more recent event in performance appraisal is the gathering of performance data by computers. Although this method may be fast and seemingly objective, it has raised a number of critical issues in the management and use of human resources. The above "PHRM in the News" describes these issues and where computer monitoring is being used most extensively.

Summary

This chapter examines performance appraisal, a critical PHRM activity, as a set of processes and procedures consisting of developing reliable and valid standards, criteria, and performance appraisal forms. A discussion of who gathers the performance appraisal data is also provided. To ensure the effectiveness of performance appraisal, PHRM managers must be concerned with implementing and monitoring all these aspects of the performance appraisal system with awareness of legal considerations.

Although a substantial amount of organizational experience and research with performance appraisal exists, not all the questions have been answered sufficiently. For example, the advantages of the BOS have not been uncritically accepted by all, nor have all of the criticisms of BOS been resolved. Additionally, the answer to the question, "What is the best performance appraisal form?" remains unanswered.

We do know, however, that the effectiveness of performance appraisal depends on several components of appraisal, not on just one, such as the appraisal form. Recognition of the importance and role of the *system* in performance appraisal has helped focus attention on components of appraisal such as the superior-subordinate relationship, job qualities, and organizational conditions. Another important quality of the system are the raters themselves, particularly how the raters process appraisal information and make evaluation decisions. Because this is a critical quality, it is examined in more detail in Chapter 7.

Now that the several ways of gathering performance appraisal information have been described, an appropriate step is to examine how that information is used, in particular, the process of feeding back performance appraisal information to the subordinates and how the performance appraisal information can be used to help spot performance deficiencies. These descriptions are provided in Chapter 7, along with strategies to improve individual performance. That chapter concludes with an assessment of the entire performance appraisal system.

Discussion Questions

1. How can performance appraisal forms be developed so that supervisory errors in performance appraisal can be minimized?

2. Why does employee performance vary even after employees have successfully passed rigorous organizational selection and placement procedures? How can a performance appraisal system address this performance variability?

3. Assume the identity of each of the following persons: a subordinate, a superior, a personnel professional. Then answer this question: What purpose can a performance appraisal system serve for you? Are the purposes served by the PAS for each of these three people congruent or conflicting? Explain.

4. Why is job analysis essential for the development of a performance appraisal system?

5. Managers often complain that a performance appraisal system puts them in a bind. On the one hand, they are supposed to give the subordinate feedback to help improve future performance; on the other hand,

they are supposed to use the PAS to allocate rewards (pay raises or promotions). How would you respond to this complaint?

6. What are the four major approaches to performance appraisal? Can you give an example of each approach?

7. What is BARS? BOS? What advantages are offered by each of these performance appraisal approaches? Disadvantages?

8. Performance appraisal approaches often differ based on whether behavior or the results of behavior are evaluated. Can you cite examples from organizations with which you are familiar where one approach might be preferred over the other? Explain why.

9. Teachers often complain that students should not be used to evaluate teacher performance. Argue the position that students should be used. What potential rater errors are students likely to commit? How can these be minimized? Are the rater errors that students might commit similar to the type of rater errors that teachers might commit when evaluating student performance?

10. For legal considerations, a well-developed performance appraisal system can provide measurable criteria of job success, which can then be used as a test to validate selection procedures. Under what circumstances could the criterion—in this instance, the performance appraisal—be an actual test, or a predictor of future job success? How would you validate this test?

PC Project

Performance appraisal data can be gathered from many sources. These sources include an employee's supervisor, subordinates (if the ratee is a manager or supervisor), peers, and the employee him- or herself. This PC Project provides performance appraisal data from supervisors, peers, and self. How does the "who rates" question influence performance appraisals? Which set of ratings is the highest (lowest)? Is there any evidence of rating errors (e.g., leniency, central tendency)?

C   A   S   E   S   T   U   D   Y

A Few Good Teachers, Please

The crisis in teaching is here, according to the Carnegie Forum on Education and the Economy report released in 1986. In view of international competition and the fundamental shift in the American economy to "knowledge work," the continued economic strength of the United States is predicated on a strong educational system. Can the United States prepare teachers for the twenty-first century? Consider the following facts cited by the report:

- SAT scores of students with teaching majors have fallen faster in the past decade than the average for all college-bound students.
- Half of the students enrolling in teacher education come from nonacademic high school programs.
- The academic rigor of some undergraduate education programs does not match the level of difficulty of programs typically completed by students expecting to become doctors, lawyers, architects, or engineers.
- Only 6.2 percent of all college freshmen express an interest in a career in education.
- One-half of the new teacher cohort will leave the profession within seven years.
- Between 1976 and 1984, the number of teachers thirty-four years old or younger fell to 37 percent of all teachers from 53 percent.
- Between 1986 and 1992, 1.3 million teachers will be hired.

A number of states have enacted legislation to create "career ladders" to reward outstanding teachers and certification examinations such as the

Texas Educators and Current Administrators Test (TECAT) to ensure that teachers meet minimum competency requirements. A fundamental issue behind all of these measures, though, is what kind of teacher is needed for the education system of the future? Are these measures merely Band-Aids for a mortal flaw in the current system?

According to the Carnegie report, dramatic improvements for teachers are needed such that future teachers can clearly meet higher standards of preparation and skill. Tomorrow's teachers will be true professionals with specific expertise, a command of needed knowledge, and the ability to apply it. The task force suggests that successful teachers must be assessed for their mastery of the subjects they teach, their knowledge of good teaching practices in general, and the techniques required to teach specific subjects. Moreover, teachers must demonstrate the capacity to reach, motivate, and support the learning of students from a variety of backgrounds.

The bottom line of the task force report is that to achieve these objectives, a new method of assessment will be needed. Educators will "have to employ state-of-the-art techniques of formal examination as well as rely in part on the observations of highly trained and experienced teachers of candidates' actual teaching." Can current performance appraisal methods meet these state-of-the-art demands?

Notes

1. S. J. Carroll, Jr. and C. E. Schneier, *Performance Appraisal and Review (PAR) Systems* (Glenview, Ill.: Scott, Foresman, 1982); G. Latham and K. Wexley, *Increasing Productivity through Performance Appraisal* (Reading, Mass.: Addison-Wesley, 1981). Both of these sources present excellent detail on performance appraisal as a system, and as a single form or technique. See also H. J. Bernardin and L. A. Klatt, "Managerial Appraisal Systems: Has Practice Caught Up to the State of the Art?" *Personnel Administrator* (Nov. 1985): 79–86; K. N. Wexley and R. Klimoski, "Performance Appraisal: An Update," in *Research in Personnel and Human Resources Management*, 2d ed., ed. K. M. Rowland and G. D. Ferris (Greenwich, Conn.: JAI Press, 1984).
2. For slight variations of this definition, including that it is a dynamic, multidimensional construct, see Latham and Wexley, *Increasing Productivity*, p. 4. Carroll and Schneier, *Performance Appraisal*, pp. 2–3; M. J. Kavanagh, "Evaluating Performance" in *Per-*

sonnel Management, ed. K. M. Rowland and G. R. Ferris (Boston: Allyn & Bacon, 1982), pp. 187–225. "More generally, however, note that the performance evaluation (PE) can be anything from a printed form your company has all supervisors and managers use to rate all employees periodically, to an offhand remark you made to another supervisor about an employee at the water cooler. Your appraisal of an employee's work when asked to give it in court is also a PA. The point is, anytime you evaluate an employee's performance, you're making, breaking, or leaving untouched that employee's ability to win promotion, higher wages or salary, transfer, or even to keep the job. Don't do it lightly, no matter how informal the circumstances. If you are wrong, or your judgment is somewhat clouded by some lurking stereotyped feelings you were hardly conscious of having, your words might come back to haunt you—once the employee catches on and decides to do something about the way your words have been haunting him or her."

From *FEP Guidelines,* no. 210. (1), 1983, p. 3. Used with permission.

3. Latham and Wexley, *Increasing Productivity,* p. 2.

4. E. J. O'Connor, L. H. Peters, A. Pooyan, J. Weekley, B. Frank, and B. Erenkrantz, "Situational Constraint Effects on Performance, Affective Reactions, and Turnover: A Field Replication and Extension," *Journal of Applied Psychology* (Nov. 1984): 663–70; D. R. Dalton, "Absenteeism and Turnover: Measures of Personnel Effectiveness," in *Applied Readings in Personnel and Human Resource Management,* ed. R. S. Schuler, J. M. McFillen, and D. R. Dalton (St. Paul: West, 1981), pp. 20–38; L. W. Porter and R. M. Steers, "Organizational, Work, and Personal Factors in Employee Turnover and Absenteeism," *Psychological Bulletin* 80 (1973): 151–76; R. M. Steers and S. R. Rhodes, "Major Influences on Employee Attendance: A Process Model," *Journal of Applied Psychology* 63 (1975): 391–407.

5. For other descriptions of these purposes, see L. L. Cummings and D. P. Schwab, *Performance in Organizations: Determinants and Appraisal* (Glenview, Ill.: Scott, Foresman, 1973); M. Beer, "Performance Appraisal: Dilemmas and Possibilities," *Organizational Dynamics* (Winter 1981): 24–36; Carroll and Schneier, *Performance Appraisal.*

6. "Measures of the results or outcomes of work behaviors such as production rate or error rate may be used without a full job analysis where a review of the information about the job shows that these criteria are important to the employment situation of the user. Similarly, measures such as absenteeism and tardiness or turnover, may be used without a full job analysis if these behaviors are shown by a review of information about the job to be important in the specific situation" (EEOC, 1979, pp. 2319). See also C. G. Banks and L. Roberson, "Performance Appraisers as Test Developers," *Academy of Management Review* (Jan. 1985): 128–42.

7. For a description of the impact of contingent rewards on performance behavior, see G. P. Latham, L. L. Cummings, and T. R. Mitchell, "Behavioral Strategies to Improve Productivity," *Organizational Dynamics* (Winter 1981): 4–23; P. J. Stonich, "The Performance Measurement and Reward System: Critical to Strategic Management," *Organizational Dynamics* (Winter 1984): 45–57; D. B. Gehrman, "Beyond Today's Compensation and Performance Appraisal Systems," *Personnel Administrator* (March 1984): 21–33; E. E. Lawler, A. M. Mohrman, Jr., and S. M. Resnick, "Performance Appraisal Revisited," *Organizational Dynamics* (Summer 1984): 20–42.

8. R. Serpa, "Why Many Organizations—Despite Good Intentions—Often Fail to Give Employees Fair and Useful Performance Reviews," *Management Review* (July 1984): 41–46; C. A. Smith, D. W. Organ, and J. P. Near, "Organizational Citizenship Behavior: Its Nature and Antecedents," *Journal of Applied Psychology* (Nov. 1983): 653–63.

9. A *prima facie* case of adverse impact or of discrimination can be established by the 80 percent rule, population comparisons, and deliberate denial of equal opportunity and any of the nine bases presented in Chapter 5. In addition, *prima facie* evidence for individual discrimination suits can be established by the *McDonnell Douglas Corp.* v. *Green* criteria.

For a good review of the legal impact of court decisions on performance appraisal, see *FEP Guidelines,* no. 210(1) 1983, and W. F. Casio and H. J. Bernardin, "Implications of Performance Appraisal Litigation for Personnel Decisions," *Personnel Psychology* 34 (1981): 211–26; M. H. Schuster and C. S. Miller, "Performance Appraisal and the Age Discrimination in Employment Act," *Personnel Administrator* (Mar. 1984): 48–57; H. J. Bernardin and W. F. Cascio, *An Annotated Bibliography of Court Cases Relevant to Employment Decisions (1980–1984),* unpublished paper, Boca Raton, Fla.: Florida Atlantic University.

10. R. Klasson, D. E. Thompson, and G. L. Luben, "How Defensible Is Your Performance Appraisal System?" *Personnel Administrator* (Dec. 1980): 77–83; R. B. McAfee, "Performance Appraisal: Whose Function?" *Personnel Journal* (Apr. 1981): 298–99; C. O. Colvin, "Everything You Always Wanted to Know about Appraisal Discrimination," *Personnel Journal* (Oct. 1981): 758–59; P. Linenberger and T. J. Keaveny, "Performance Appraisal Standards Used by the Courts," *Personnel Administrator* (May 1981): 89–94; M. H. Schuster and C. S. Miller, "Performance Evaluations as Evidence in ADEA Cases," *Employee Relations Law Journal* 6 (4) (1981): 561–83; W. L. Kandel, "Current Developments in EEO," *Employee Relations Law Journal* 6 (3) (1981): 476–83.

For an excellent discussion of the criteria used to evaluate the entire performance appraisal system (in contrast to the criteria used to evaluate employee performance), see J. S. Kane and E. E. Lawler III, "Performance Appraisal Effectiveness: Assessment and Determinants," in *Research in Organizational Behavior,* vol. 1, ed. B. M. Staw (Greenwich, Conn.: JAI Press, 1979), pp. 425–78; P. C. Smith, "Behavior, Results, and Organizational Effectiveness," in *Handbook of Industrial and Organizational Psychology,* ed. M. Dunnette (Chicago: Rand McNally, 1976), pp. 745–76; M. K. Distefano, Jr., W. Pryer, and R. C. Erffmeyer, "Application of Content Validity Methods to the Development of a Job-related Performance Rating Criterion," *Personnel Psychology* (Autumn 1983): 621–32; R. Giles and C. Landauer, "Setting Specific Standards for Appraising Creative Staffs," *Personnel Administrator* (Mar. 1984): 35–47; C. J. Hobson and F. W. Gibson, "Policy Capturing as an Approach to Understanding and Improving Performance Appraisal: A Review of the Literature," *Academy of Management Review* (Oct. 1983): 640–49; C. J. Hobson and F. W. Gibson, "Capturing Supervisor Rating Policies: A Way to Improve Performance Appraisal Effectiveness," *Personnel Administrator*

(Mar. 1984): 59–68; H. J. Bernardin and W. Cascio, "Performance Appraisal and the Law," in *Readings in Personnel and Human Resource Management*, 3d ed., eds. R. S. Schuler, S. A. Youngblood, and V. Huber (St. Paul: West Publishing, 1987).

11. *Wade* v. *Mississippi Cooperative Extension Service* (1974). See also Kancel, for a good discussion; *Brito* v. *Zia Company*, 478 F.2d. 1200 (1973); *Albemarle Paper Company* v. *Moody*, U.S. Supreme Court nos. 74-389 and 74-428, 10 FEB Cases 1181 (1975); *Rowe* v. *General Motors Corporation* 457 F.2d 358 (1972); *Baxter* v. *Savannah Sugar Refining Corporation*, 350 F.Supp. 139 (1972); *Hill* v. *Western Electric Co.*, U.S. District Court (Eastern District of Virginia) no. 75-375-A, 12 FEP Cases 1175 (1976); *Watkins* v. *Scott Paper Co.*, Fifth Circuit Court of Appeals, no. 74-1001, 12 FEP Cases 1191 (1976).

12. Adverse impact, however, can be defended on the basis of job relatedness, but then a search for alternative procedures must be considered. See also Carroll and Schneier, *Performance Appraisal*, L. S. Kleiman and R. L. Durham, "Performance Appraisal; Promotion and the Courts: A Critical Review," *Personnel Psychology* 34 (1981): 103–21.

13. *Manager's Handbook: A Handbook for Federal Managers* (Washington, D.C.: U.S. Office of Personnel Management, Office of Public Affairs, 1979); R. G. Pajer, "Performance Appraisal: A New Era for Federal Government Managers," *Personnel Administrator* (Mar. 1984): 81–89.

14. R. I. Lazer and W. S. Wikstrom, *Appraising Managerial Performance: Current Practice and Future Directions* (New York: Conference Board, 1977). The reliability should be obtained with the same rater across time and at the same time across raters (Latham and Wexley, *Improving Productivity*, p. 65).

15. For extensive discussions of deficiency and contamination, see Cummings and Schwab, *Performance in Organizations;* Carroll and Schneier, *Performance Appraisal.*

16. For a discussion on dynamic versus static criteria, proximal versus distal criteria, and composite versus multiple criteria, see Cascio and Bernardin, "Implications of Performance Appraisal"; Schmitt and Schneider, "Current Issues." The point here is to be aware of the many dimensions of criteria.

17. Cascio and Bernardin, "Implications of Performance Appraisal."

18. J. C. Flanagan, "The Critical Incident Technique," *Psychological Bulletin* 51 (1954): 327–58.

19. P. J. McGuire, "Why Performance Appraisals Fail," *Personnel Journal* (Sept. 1980): 744–46, 762; M. Beer, "Performance Appraisal: Dilemmas and Possibilities," *Organizational Dynamics* (Winter 1981): 24–36; Carroll and Schneier; *Performance Appraisal.* See also the entire issue of *Personnel Administrator* (Mar. 1984).

20. F. J. Landy and D. A. Trumbo, *Psychology of Work Behavior,* rev. ed. (Homewood, Ill.: Dorsey, 1980); W. F. Cascio, *Applied Psychology in Personnel Management,* 2d ed. (Reston, Va.: Reston, 1982).

21. L. M. King, J. E. Hunter, and F. L. Schmidt, "Halo in a Multi-dimensional Forced Choice Performance Evaluation Scale," *Journal of Applied Psychology* 65 (1980): 507–16; R. Jacobs and S. W. J. Kozlowski, "A Closer Look at Halo Error in Performance Rataings." *Academy of Management Journal* (Mar. 1985): 201–12.

22. In Exhibit 6.7 the anchors are stated as actual behaviors. In some forms of BARS, the anchors are stated as expected behaviors (e.g., the person could be expected to develop loan documentation accurately. When expected behaviors are included, the BARS form is more appropriately labeled BES—a Behavioral Expectation Scale. For further discussion, see Landy and Farr, "Performance Rating," *Psychological Bulletin* (Jan. 1980): 72–107; S. Zedeck, "Behavioral Based Performance Appraisals," *Aging and Work* 4 (1981): 89–100.

23. Latham and Wexley, *Improving Productivity.*

24. Latham and Wexley, *Improving Productivity.*

25. G. Latham and K. Wexley, "Behavioral Observation Scales for Performance Appraisal Purposes," *Personnel Psychology* 30 (1977): 255–68; M. Loar, S. Mohrman, and J. R. Stock, "Development of a Behaviorally Based Performance Appraisal System," *Personnel Psychology* (Spring 1982): 75–88.

26. Latham and Wexley, *Improving Productivity,* 1981, p. 63. For a less supportive view of BOS, see J. S. Kane and H. J. Bernardin, "Behavioral Observation Scales and the Evaluation of Performance Appraisal Effectiveness," *Personnel Psychology* 35 (1982): 635–42; K. R. Murphy, C. Martin, and M. Garcia, "Do Behavioral Observation Scales Measure Observation?" *Journal of Applied Psychology* 67 (1982): 562–67.

27. As reported in Carroll and Schneier, *Performance Appraisal,* p. 39, 60 percent of the organizations use MBO to evaluate managers.

28. Carroll and Schneier, *Performance Appraisal,* p. 141. For arguments for and against MBO, see S. J. Carroll and H. L. Tosi, "Goal Characteristics and Personality Factors in a Management by Objectives Program," *Administrative Science Quarterly* 15 (1970): 295–305; J. P. Muczyk, "A Controlled Field Experiment Measuring the Impact of MBO on Performance Data," *Journal of Management Sudies* 15 (1978): 318–39; A. P. Raia, *Managing by Objectives* (Glenview, Ill.: Scott, Foresman, 1974); H. L. Tosi, J. R. Rizzo, and S. J. Carroll, "Setting Goals in Management by Objectives," *California Management Review* 12 (1970): 20–78.

29. L. Olivas, "Adding a Different Dimension to Goal Setting Processes," *Personnel Administrator* (Oct. 1981): 75–78.

30. E. A. Locke, "Toward a Theory of Task Motivation and Incentives," *Organizational Behavior and Human Performance* 3 (1968): 157–89.

31. B. McAfee and B. Green, "Selecting a Performance Appraisal Method," *Personnel Administrator* (June 1977): 61-64; M. E. Schick, "The Refined Performance Evaluation Monitoring System: Best of Both Worlds," *Personnel Journal* (Jan. 1980): 47-50; "Appraising the Performance Appraisal," *Business Week*, 19 May, 1980, pp. 153-54; P. C. Grant, "How to Manage Employee Job Performance," *Personnel Administrator* (Aug. 1981): 59-65; W. J. Birch, "Performance Appraisal: One Company's Experience," *Personnel Journal* (June 1981): 456-60; E. Yager, "A Critique of Performance Appraisal Systems," *Personnel Journal* (Feb. 1981): 129-33.

32. F. L. Schmidt, J. E. Hunter, and K. Pearlman, "Assessing the Economic Impact of Personnel Programs on Workforce Productivity," *Personnel Psychology* (Summer 1982): 333-48; F. Krgystofiak and J. Newman, "Evaluating Employment Outcomes; Availability Models and Measures," *Industrial Relations* 21 (1982): 277-92; F. J. Landy, J. L. Farr, and R. R. Jacobs, "Utility Concepts in Performance Measurement," *Organizational Behavior and Human Performance* 30 (1982): 15-40.

33. For a discussion of the importance of selecting purposes first, since the appropriate forms vary by the purposes, see Kavangh, "Evaluating Appraisal." 1982, Cummings and Schwab, *Performance in Organizations*, 1973. This is my assessment of the appropriateness of the appraisal form–purposes match, based in part on the references in note 31.

34. A. Howard, "An Assessment of Assessment Centers," *Academy of Management Journal* 17 (1974): 115-34; B. M. Cohen, J. L. Moses, and W. C. Byham, "The Validity of Assessment Centers," *Journal of Industrial and Organizational Psychology* 10 (1973): 1-43; R. J. Klimoski and W. J. Strickland, "Assessment Center: Valid or Merely Prescient," *Personnel Psychology* 20 (1977): 354; N. Schmitt, A. Noe, R. Meritt, and M. P. Fitzgerald, "Validity of Assessment Center Ratings for the Prediction of Performance Ratings and School Climate of School Administrators," *Journal of Applied Psychology* (May 1984): 207-13; P. R. Sackett and G. F. Dreher, "Situation Specificity of Behavior and Assessment Center Validation Strategies: A Rejoinder to Neidig and Neidig," *Journal of Applied Psychology* (Feb. 1984): 187-90.

35. Carroll and Schneier, *Performance Appraisal*, p. 205. W. F. Cascio and V. Silbey, "Utility of the Assessment Center as a Selection Device," *Journal of Applied Psychology* 64 (1979): 107-18.

36. Carroll and Schneier, *Performance Appraisal*, pp. 192-95, have an extensive discussion of the job-focus and person-focus approaches.

37. R. E. Lefton, V. R. Buzzotta, M. Scerberg, and B. L. Karraker, *Effective Motivation through Performance Appraisal* (New York: Wiley, 1977); Bureau of National Affairs, "Employee Performance, Evaluation, and Control," *Personnel Policies Forum*, no. 108, Feb. 1975; K. J. Lacho, G. K. Stearns, and M. F. Villere, "A Study of Employee Appraisal Systems of Major Cities in the United States," *Public Personnel Management* (Mar./Apr.1979): 111-24; R. I. Lazer and W. S. Wikstrom, *Appraising Managerial Performance: Current Practice and Future Directions* (New York: Conference Board, 1977); A. H. Locher and K. S. Teel, "Performance Appraisal: A Survey of Current Practices," *Personnel Journal* (May 1977): 245-47; *Personnel Practices in Factory and Office Manufacturing, Studies in Personnel Policy* 194 (New York: National Industrial Conference Boards, 1964); R. Katerberg and G. J. Blau, "An Examination of Level and Direction of Effort and Job Performance," *Academy of Management Journal* (June 1983): 249-52; D. R. Ilgen and J. L. Favero, "Limits in Generalization from Psychological Research to Performance Appraisal Process," *Academy of Management Review* (Apr. 1985): 311-21.

38. W. H. Cooper, "Internal Homogeneity, Descriptiveness, and Halo: Resurrecting Some Answers and Questions about the Structure of Job Performance Rating Categories," *Personal Psychology* (Autumn 1983): 489-502; K. Kraiger and J. K. Ford, "A Meta-Analysis of Ratee Race Effects in Performance Ratings," *Journal of Applied Psychology* (Feb. 1985): 56-65; K. N. Wexley and E. D. Pulakos, "The Effects of Perceptual Congruence and Sex on Subordinates; Performance Appraisals of Their Managers," *Academy of Management Journal* (Dec. 1983): 666-76; R. L. Heneman and K. N. Wexley, "The Effects of Time Delay in Rating and Amount of Information Observed on Performance Rating Accuracy," *Academy of Management Journal* (Dec. 1983): 677-86; M. E. Heilman and M. H. Stopeck, "Being Attractive, Advantage or Disadvantage: Performance-based Evaluations and Recommended Personnel Actions as a Function of Appearance, Sex, and Job Type," *Organizational Behavior and Human Decision Processes* 35 (1985): 202-15; M. H. Bazerman, R. I. Beekun, and F. D. Schoorman, "Performance Evaluation in a Dynamic Context: A Laboratory Study of the Impact of a Prior Commitment to the Ratee," *Journal of Applied Psychology* (Dec. 1982): 873-76.

39. J. L. Gibson, J. J. Ivancevich, and J. H. Donnelly, *Organizations: Behavior, Structure, Processes*, 3d ed. (Dallas, Tex.: Business Publications, 1979), p. 361; B. R. Nathan and R. A. Alexander, "The Role of Inferential Accuracy in Performance Rating," *Academy of Management Review* (Jan. 1985): 109-17; R. L. Dipboye, "Some Neglected Variables in Research on Discrimination in Appraisals," *Academy of Management Review* (Jan. 1985): 118-25; M. R. Edwards and J. R. Sproull, "Rating the Raters Improves Performance Appraisals," *Personnel Administrator* (Aug. 1983): 77-82; R. M. McIntyre, D. E. Smith, and C. E. Hassett, "Accuracy of Performance Ratings as Affected by Rater Training and Perceived Purpose of Rating," *Journal of Applied Psychology* (Feb. 1984): 147-56.

40. K. N. Wexley, "Performance Appraisal and Feed-back," in *Organizational Behavior,* ed. S. Kerr (Columbus, Ohio: Grid, 1979), p. 256; C. Lee, "Increasing Performance Appraisal Effectiveness: Matching Task Types, Appraisal Process, and Rater Training," *Academy of Management Review* (Apr. 1985): 322–31; C. H. Fay and G. P. Latham, "Effects of Training and Rating Scales on Rating Errors," *Personnel Psychology* (Spring 1982): 105–16.

41. L. H. Peters and E. J. O'Connor, "Situational Constraints and Work Outcomes: The Influence of a Frequently Overlooked Construct," *Academy of Management Review* 5 (1980): 391–97.

42. For a discussion of constraint on performance, see Latham and Wexley, *Improving Performance,* 1980, pp. 42–44.

43. R. S. Schuler, "A Role and Expectancy Perception Model of Participation in Decision Making," *Academy of Management Journal* (June 1980): 338; J. S. Kim, "Effect of Behavior Plus Outcome Goal Setting and Feedback on Employee Satisfaction and Performance," *Academy of Management Journal* (Mar. 1984): 139–48; G. P. Latham and T. P. Steele, "The Motivational Effects of Participation Versus Goal Setting on Performance," *Academy of Management Journal* (Sept. 1983): 406–17; H. J. Bernardin and J. Abbott, "Predicting (and Preventing) Differences between Self and Supervisory Appraisals," *Personnel Administrator* (June 1985): 151–57.

44. *Wall Street Journal,* 25 June 1985, p. 1. Reprinted by permission of *The Wall Street Journal,* © Dow Jones & Company, Inc., 1985. All Rights Reserved.

45. J. S. Kane and E. E. Lawler III, "Methods of Peer Assessment," *Psychological Bulletin* 3 (1978): 555–86; J. D. Coombe, "Peer Review: The Emerging Successful Application," *Employee Relations Law Journal* (Spring 1984): 659–71.

46. Cummings and Schwab, *Performance in Organizations,* 1973, p. 105.

47. P. Lanza, "Team Appraisals," *Personnel Journal* (Mar. 1985): 47–50.

48. A. S. DeNisi and G. E. Stevens, "Profiles of Performance Evaluations, and Personnel Decisions," *Academy of Management Journal* (Sept. 1981): 592–602; G. W. Bush and J. W. Stinson, "A Different Use of Performance Appraisal: Evaluating the Boss," *Management Review* (Nov. 1980): 14–17.

Utilizing the Performance Appraisal

Performance Appraisal: Manager as Judge and Jury

Why are performance reviews a part of the management system of most organizations? And why do we review the performance of our subordinates? I posed both questions to a group of middle managers and got the following responses:

- To assess the subordinate's work
- To improve performance
- To motivate
- To provide feedback to a subordinate
- To justify raises
- To reward performance
- To provide discipline
- To provide work direction
- To reinforce the company culture

Next, I asked the group to imagine themselves to be a supervisor giving a review to a subordinate, and asked them what their feelings were. Some of the answers:

- Pride
- Anger
- Anxiety
- Discomfort
- Guilt
- Empathy/concern
- Embarrassment
- Frustration

Finally, I asked the same group to think back to some of the performance reviews they had received and asked what, if anything, was wrong with them. Their answers were quick and many:

- Review comments too general
- Mixed messages (inconsistent with rating or dollar raise)
- No indication of how to improve
- Negatives avoided
- Supervisor didn't know my work
- Only recent performance considered
- Surprises

This should tell you that giving performance reviews is a very complicated and difficult business and that we, managers, don't do an especially good job at it.

The fact is that giving such reviews is the single most important form of task-relevant feedback we as supervisors can provide. It is how we assess our subordinates' level of performance and how we deliver that assessment to them individually. It is also how we allocate the rewards—promotions, dollars, stock options, or whatever we may use. As we saw earlier, the review will influence a subordinate's performance—positively or negatively—for a long time, which makes the appraisal one of the manager's highest-leverage activities. In short, the review is an extremely powerful mechanism, and it is little wonder that opinions and feelings about it are strong and diverse.

But what is its fundamental purpose? Though all of the responses given to my questions are correct, there is one that is more important than any of the others: it is to improve the subordinate's performance. The review is usually dedicated to two things: first, the skill level of the subordinate, to determine what skills are missing and to find ways to remedy that lack; and second, to intensify the subordinate's motivation in order to get him on a higher performance curve for the same skill level.

Source: A. S. Grove, *High Output Management* (New York: Random House, 1983), pp. 181–83. Used by permission.

The preceding "PHRM in the News" illustrates important aspects of using performance appraisal information. First, most managers find giving a performance appraisal review (giving feedback) an emotional experience. According to Andrew Grove, president of Intel, the review triggers emotions of pride, anger, guilt, and discomfort. At the same time, as Grove points out, the review is the "single most important form of task-relevant feedback" supervisors can give. Without it, employee job performance cannot improve, and absenteeism cannot be controlled. Supervisors can even use the feedback to make the tough decision to fire employees and make the decision stick. The feature also suggests that managers not only must give feedback but also can learn how to do it without the usual mental anguish. This chapter discusses issues and potential solutions associated with providing subordinates feedback in the performance appraisal interview. It also presents issues associated with improving performance, including a paradigm for diagnosing causes of performance gaps. It concludes by assessing the effectiveness of the entire performance appraisal system an organization may use and by discussing the trends in performance appraisal.

Major Uses of Performance Appraisal

Utilizing the performance appraisal means to use the appraisal data for their intended purposes: evaluation (salary, promotion, demotion, and layoff decisions) and development (counseling, coaching, improving, and career planning decisions). The major way organizations utilize the performance appraisal is through the interview between the superior and subordinate. Although the performance appraisal interview may be used to gather additional performance data, its major use as discussed here is to feed back performance appraisal data to the subordinate. Based on this feedback, the intended purposes of performance appraisal are served. How effectively they are served depends on how the appraisal system is designed and how the interview or interviews are conducted. An understanding of the inherent conflicts in performance appraisal is useful in discussing the design of the system and the conduct of the interview.

Inherent Conflicts in Performance Appraisal

Performance appraisals draw poor reviews from employees, employers, and experts alike:

> About 30% of employees believe that their performance appraisals weren't effective, says a poll by Opinion Research Corp., of Princeton, N.J. And only 10% of managers say their companies have improved production levels by using performance-appraisal results, says Drake Beam Morin, consultants, in a study of about 260 large industrial firms. Although 75% of the senior executives use the data to plan for the company, experts say all data is underused.
>
> In a study, "Supervision in the '80s: Trends in Corporate America," Opinion Research says first-line supervisors and middle managers haven't developed skills to

supervise others. Few communicate effectively. The result: Inquisitive workers aren't getting answers from their bosses and are losing confidence in their employers.[1]

With the cost of doing performance appraisals so high, why are they not done well? Part of the answer lies in several inherent conflicts in performance appraisal.

The several purposes of performance appraisal presented at the beginning of Chapter 6 can be categorized as either evaluative or developmental. Although the PAS should serve both sets of purposes for organizations, doing so often creates inherent conflicts.[2] These conflicts center on the organization's goals for performance appraisal and those of the individual. Although the organization's goals have already been identified, those of the individual have not. Individuals' goals are to obtain feedback so they know where they stand with their supervisor and the organization, to learn how to improve their performance, and to obtain important rewards in the organization, such as pay and promotions. Additionally, individuals want to affirm their self-image as being competent.[3]

Conflicts in Organizational and Individual Goals.   From organizational and individual goals come three sets of conflicts. One is between the organization's evaluative and developmental goals. When pursuing the evaluative goal, superiors have to make judgments affecting their subordinates' careers and immediate rewards. Communicating these judgments can lead to the creation of an adversarial, low-trust relationship between superior and subordinate. This in turn precludes the superior from performing a problem-solving, helper role that is essential if the organization wants to serve the developmental goal. A second set of conflicts arises from the various goals of the individual being evaluated. On the one hand, individuals want valid feedback that gives them information about how to improve and where they stand in the organization. On the other hand, they want to verify their self-image and obtain valued rewards. In essence, the goals of individuals imply a necessity to be open (to give valid feedback for improvement) yet to be protective (to maintain a positive self-image and obtain rewards).

The third set of conflicts arises between the individual's goals and those of the organization. One conflict is between the organization's evaluation goal and the individual's goal of obtaining rewards. Another conflict is between the organization's developmental goal and the individual's goal of maintaining self-image. Exhibit 7.1 shows the nature of these conflicts.

Consequences of Inherent Conflicts.   Among the several consequences of the inherent conflicts just described are ambivalence, avoidance, defensiveness, and resistance.[4] Some of these consequences and the inherent conflicts are implicit in the discussion of the contextual impact on performance appraisal data gathering, particularly that of the superior-subordinate relationship in Chapter 6.

Ambivalence is a consequence for both superiors and subordinates. Superiors are ambivalent because they must act as judge and jury in telling subordinates where they stand, both because the organization demands it and

Conflicts in Performance Appraisal   *Exhibit 7.1*

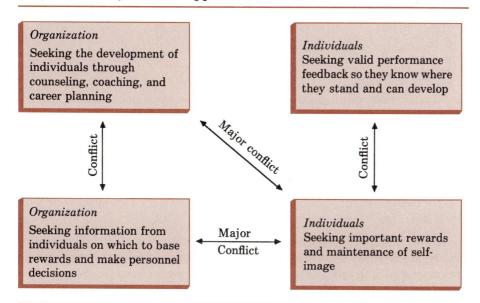

Source: M. Beer, "Performance Appraisal: Dilemmas and
Possibilities," *Organizational Dynamics* (Winter 1981) (New
York: AMACOM, a division of American Management
Associations), p. 27.

because the subordinates want it. Yet, they are uncertain about their judgments and how the subordinates will react to negative feedback. This feeling
is intensified when superiors are not trained in giving feedback. Subordinates are equally ambivalent because they want honest feedback yet want to
receive rewards and maintain their self-image (that is, they really want only
positive feedback). Additionally, if they are open with their superiors in identifying undeveloped potential, they risk the chance that the superiors may
use this to evaluate them unfavorably.

A consequence of this joint ambivalence is avoidance. To avoid the risks
of negative feedback, subordinates reduce their initiative to seek appraisal
data and, through talk, diminish the importance of performance appraisal
data. Meanwhile, the superiors avoid giving appraisals by implicitly collud-
ing with the subordinates, who would rather not know anyway. This process
has given rise to the term **vanishing performance appraisal.**[5] If organizational demands do not allow superiors to engage in the vanishing performance
appraisal process, and if they must give negative feedback (to support current and future decisions regarding layoff, termination, and demotion), they
may resort to the "sandwich approach." Here the superiors squeeze negative
feedback between two pieces of positive feedback. When this is done, subordinates may report that they never received negative feedback despite superiors' reports that they gave it.

Subordinates and superiors also become defensive in performance appraisals. The subordinate becomes defensive in responding to negative feed-

back that threatens self-image and chances for gaining rewards. A study at General Electric made the following discoveries:

- Criticism has a negative effect on goal achievement.
- Praise has little effect one way or the other.
- The average subordinate reacts defensively to criticism during the appraisal interview.
- Defensiveness resulting from critical appraisal produces inferior performance.
- The disruptive effect of repeated criticism on subsequent performance is greater among those who already have low self-esteem.
- The average G.E. employee's self-estimate of performance before appraisal was at the seventy-seventh percentile.
- Only two out of ninety-two participants in the study estimated their performance to be below average.[6]

Accordingly, subordinates attempt to blame others for their performance, challenge the appraisal form, and demand that their superiors justify their appraisals. Initially at least, subordinates are not inclined to apologize for their behavior and seek ways to improve; in fact, they resist superiors' efforts to engage in problem solving. Consequently, superiors spend most of their time trying to defend their appraisals and resisting subordinates' efforts to have their appraisals altered. Overall, the appraisal process is uncomfortable for both participants, especially when poor performance and negative feedback are involved. The following "PHRM in the News" illustrates this point in detail. Even if good performance is involved, however, superiors still have to make evaluation decisions, and somebody may still end up looking like a poor performer. Because appraisals are uncomfortable yet necessary, seeking ways to make the process better is important. Possible ways include the design of the appraisal system and the characteristics of the performance appraisal interview.

Designing the Appraisal System

Several features can be incorporated into the design of the appraisal process to reduce the likely consequences of the inherent conflicts, in performance appraisal.

Separate Evaluation and Development. Because subordinates react defensively to evaluations that are negative, they initially block out considering ways to improve. Superiors' attempts to engage in developmental activities such as problem solving are thus likely to be futile, since for problem solving to be effective, subordinates have to be open and superiors have to play the role of helper, not judge or defender. If organizations want to serve both the evaluation and development purposes effectively, two appraisal interviews should take place. One interview can focus on evaluation and the other, at a different time of year, on development.[7]

Use Appropriate Performance Data.   Even when there are two interviews, subordinates will still become defensive to negative evaluations. Because that defensiveness makes superiors uncomfortable, they can help minimize it by utilizing performance data that focus on specific behaviors or goals. Performance data that focus on personal attributes or characteristics are likely to prompt more defensiveness because they are more difficult for the superior to justify and because more of the subordinate's self-image is at stake.

As shown in Chapter 6, superiors can facilitate specific performance feedback through their selection and use of the appropriate appraisal forms. Specifically, if superiors want to use performance data on behaviors, a critical incident form or a BOS method would be facilitative, while an MBO or work standards approach may be more facilitative in using performance data on goals. Using these appraisal forms allows the supervisors to manage *what* subordinates are doing as well as *how* they are doing.

Separate Current and Potential Performance Appraisal.   Current performance of subordinates may have little to do with their performance potential. Yet superiors may unconsciously incorporate evaluations of performance potential into evaluations of current performance unless a specific and separate form for appraisal of potential exists. One consequence may be an appraisal of current performance that represents an averaging of current and potential performance appraisal. This can result in unfair appraisals, especially for subordinates who may not be interested in being promoted yet perform adequately on their present jobs. Thus, a separation of the appraisal process for current and potential performance could help eliminate the averaging effect and unfairness that may result for some subordinates. Separation would also allow superiors to avoid appraising the potential performance of subordinates not interested in promotion.[8] Thus, this separation is consistent with the importance of recognizing and incorporating individual differences into the appraisal process.[9]

Multiple Appraisal.   To encourage openness in the performance appraisal and to improve superior-subordinate relationships, subordinates can be allowed to engage in appraisal of their superiors as well as themselves. Upward appraisal can help put into better balance, if not equalize, the power of the superior vis-à-vis the subordinate. Such a balance is useful in reducing the authoritarian character of the superior-subordinate relationship, which contributes much to the defensiveness and avoidance in the performance appraisal.[10]

Organization and superiors facilitate the upward appraisal process by providing forms for subordinates to use and by engaging in other human resource policies and procedures indicative of openness (e.g., allowing employees to participate in deciding their own pay increases) (Chapter 8) or in analyzing their own jobs (Chapter 3). Furthering this openness and power equalization approach in performance appraisal is a policy of self-appraisal. Self-appraisal is likely to result in more information for the superior, a more

Bosses: Don't Be Nasty (and Other Tips For Reviewing a Worker's Performance)

Richard Dugan has learned a lot about appraising an employee's performance since a staff member broke down in tears under his criticism. "I've really botched this," he recalls thinking.

Mr. Dugan, managing partner of Arthur Young & Co.'s Pittsburgh office, says it took a long time for him to learn how to give "helpful criticism without being nasty." Now he says he isn't afraid to tell an unsatisfactory performer, "You'll have to do this and this to succeed here or you should perhaps consider another kind of work." It's my obligation to give guidance. And most employees don't want a nice guy, they want to know where they stand."

A majority of employees believe their bosses botch appraisals of their work, if they give reviews at all. Psychological Associates Inc. of St. Louis, surveying 4,000 employees at 190 companies recently, found that 70% believed review sessions hadn't given them a clear picture of what was expected of them on the job, or where they could advance in the company. Only half said their bosses helped them set job objectives, and only one in five said reviews were followed up during the ensuing year.

Handling fear

"It's a tough job, the equivalent of walking up to a person and saying, 'Here's what I think of your baby,' " says Robert Lefton, president of Psychological Associates, a consulting company that has provided training on how to give reviews to over 100 large companies. "It requires knowing how to handle fear and anger and a gamut of other emotions, which a lot of managers aren't comfortable with," he adds.

Increasingly managers must do a better job of appraising employees—not only to help employees mature but to increase productivity and company loyalty. Comprehensive performance reviews also reduce the chances that a fired employee who has been warned of unsatisfactory performance will sue the company.

Employees have a right to expect a performance review at least once a year, personnel experts say. A manager should listen to an employee's self-appraisal before offering his own evaluation, then give a balanced picture of the employee's strengths and weaknesses, discuss differences and offer specific suggestions on how to improve. And he or she should work with the employee to develop goals.

These guidelines are simple enough and yet often forgotten by managers in the thick of a review. Mr. Lefton of Psychological Associates recalls observing one chief executive who talked nonstop for three hours to a senior manager during a review. Then he turned to Mr. Lefton and said, "Aren't we having a great exchange?"

Before doing reviews, managers must analyze their styles of confrontation, Mr. Lefton believes. Some managers take a "let me tell you approach," imposing their own ideas without regard to subordinates. Others mechanically go through the paces of a review but their underlying message is that discussing performance can't make a difference, and they offer no solid information to employees. And then there are managers who say, "Gee, everything is great," and avoid all problems.

Bosses admit they are often reluctant to criticize an employee's work. "You don't want to inflict pain," says an executive of a Midwestern manufacturing company. She agonized for weeks about what to say to one employee who was "technically excellent but threw temper tantrums and was obnoxious to work with."

Anxious to avoid a fight, she finally gave the employee a choice. "I told him, 'you will have to change the way you behave, or if that's difficult for you or you don't want to change, I'll give you a severance package,' " He chose the severance.

Other managers must tackle employees who won't listen to criticism. When Bob Reass, manager of strategic operations in sales at Monsanto Co., told an employee to better manage his own subordinates, the employee became angry and the review session turned into a screaming match.

Mr. Reass suggested a "cooling-off period," which proved the best solution. When he reconvened the review session several days later, the disgruntled employee apologized.

Marilyn Moats Kennedy, managing partner of Career Strategies, a management-consulting company in Wilmette, Ill, says it's important to critique the behavior of an employee, not the employee himself.

"If you bark, 'You have a bad attitude,' to your receptionists, for example, you'll likely find yourself facing a very defensive employee. You'll probably get better results if you say, 'When someone steps up to your desk, I'd like them to get the distinct impression that you're delighted to see them.' "

Of the outstanding employee who has one minor flaw, such as repeatedly missing staff meetings, experts say don't ignore the problem. Instead, they say, confront the employee in a positive way ("I'm concerned about this"), state the consequences ("The group isn't getting your views") and then ask for help ("What can we do about this?").

Reviews shouldn't contain many surprises, such as springing new standards on employees, says Jerome Abarbanel, manager of organization and management development at General Electric Co.'s Credit Corp. unit. A GE manager in one case planned to give an employee who did outstanding work only a satisfactory performance rating because he asked too many questions. But Mr. Abarbanel says that rating is unfair unless the employee knew in advance how much his boss valued independence.

Personnel experts also have tips for what not to do during a review. Don't try to become a therapist to employees with marital, drinking or other personal problems, they advise managers. Instead, refer those employees to programs within the company or to outside help.

It's also best not to discuss salaries during reviews, they say. For one thing, whether or not an employee gets a raise often depends not only on his performance but on the financial condition of the company and the economy, and wages paid by competitors.

When Monsanto Co. years ago tied compensation to a structured review process in which employees set their own goals, "we found it didn't work," says Mr. Reass. Employees, afraid to set goals they couldn't meet, instead set easy-to-reach goals. "We found we were sealing our own mediocrity," he says.

Often the most helpful advice an employee can receive during a performance appraisal has to do with his personal standing in the company. Mr. Reass at Monsanto says he is still grateful to a boss who criticized his style of speech. A native New Yorker, Mr. Reass says he has "a Brooklyn accent that comes on strong when I'm under pressure or am tired." His boss told him: "Watch that accent of yours. It doesn't go across well in this Midwestern company."

Source: C. Hymowitz, *Wall Street Journal*, 17 January, 1985, p. 35. Reprinted by permission of *The Wall Street Journal*, © Dow Jones & Company, Inc., 1985. All Rights Reserved.

realistic appraisal of the subordinate's performance, and a greater acceptance of the final appraisal by subordinates and superiors.

The Performance Appraisal Interview

To further enhance the effectiveness of the performance appraisal, several considerations should be made regarding the actual performance appraisal interview.

Types of Interviews.   The four major types of interviews are: (1) tell and sell, (2) tell and listen, (3) problem-solving, and (4) mixed.[11] The **tell and sell,** or directive, interview lets subordinates know how well they are doing and sells them on the merits of setting specific goals for improvement (if needed). This efficient interview is effective in improving performance, especially for subordinates with little desire for participation.[12] It may be most appropriate in providing evaluation; however, subordinates may become frustrated in trying to convince their superiors to listen to justifications for their performance levels.

The **tell and listen** interview provides subordinates with the chance to participate and establish a dialogue with their superiors. Its purpose is to communicate supervisors' perceptions of subordinates' strengths and weaknesses and to let subordinates respond to those perceptions. Superiors summarize and paraphrase subordinates' responses but generally fail to establish goals for performance improvement. Consequently, the subordinates may feel better, but their performance may not change.

In the **problem-solving,** or participative problem-solving, interview, an active and open dialogue is established between superior and subordinate. Perceptions are shared and solutions to problems or differences are presented, discussed, and sought. Goals for improvement are also established mutually by superior and subordinate. Because this type of interview is generally more difficult for most superiors to do, training in problem solving is usually necessaary and beneficial.[13]

Conducting a **mixed interview** also requires training because it is a combination of the tell and sell and the problem-solving interviews. Skills are needed for the tell and sell and problem-solving interviews, and to make the transition from one to the other. As explained earlier, a desirable approach is to use the tell and sell interview for evaluation and the problem-solving interview for development. Separate interviews for each purpose, however, may not be feasible. Since corporate policies, time, and expectations may prevent separation of purposes, a single interview must accomplish both purposes. In this single interview, the subordinate may start out listening to the superior provide an appraisal of performance but then take a more active role in determining what and how performance improvements can be made (problem solving), concluding with agreed-upon goals for improvement.

Interview Effectiveness.   Although a mixed interview may prove an effective format by which to structure an interview, it fails to specify all the necessary characteristics for an effective interview. These characteristics include preparation for and aspects of the actual interview, which in turn include the following:

- Scheduling so that subordinate as well as superior are aware of and agree upon an appropriate time for the interview
- Agreeing upon the content of the interview; foremost should be whether the interview is for evaluation, for development, or for both
- Agreeing upon the process (e.g., how differences are to be resolved, how problems are going to be solved, and the topical flow of the interview)
- Selecting and using a neutral location in which the interview can be held, including neither the superior's nor the subordinate's work location.[14]

Aspects necessary to facilitate the effectiveness of the appraisal interview include the following:

- High levels of subordinate participation increase the subordinate's acceptance of the superior's appraisal and enhance satisfaction.[15]
- Superior's support of and trust in the subordinate help increase the interview's openness and the subordinate's acceptance of the appraisal and the superior.[16]
- Open, two-way discussion of performance problems and joint problem solving can increase the subordinate's performance.[17]
- Setting specific and challenging goals to be achieved by the subordinate serves to increase the chances for improved performance.[18]
- Provision for effective feedback rather than criticism can enhance the quality of the subordinate-superior relationship and the subordinate's performance.

Since superiors have the opportunity to provide feedback on an informal, daily basis, as well as in the formal performance appraisal interview, it is useful to examine it more closely, particularly the characteristics of effective feedback.

Effective Feedback.   Whether negative or positive, feedback is not always easy to provide.[19] Fortunately, several characteristics of effective feedback have been determined. First, effective feedback is specific rather than general. Telling someone that he or she is dominating is probably not as useful as saying, "Just now you were not listening to what I said, but I felt I either had to agree with your arguments or face attack from you."

Second, effective feedback is focused on behavior rather than on the person. Referring to what a person does is more important than referring to what that person seems to be. A superior might say that a person talked more than anyone else at a meeting rather than that he or she is a loudmouth. The former allows for the possibility of change; the latter implies a fixed personality trait.

Effective feedback also takes the receiver's needs into account. Feedback can be destructive when it serves only the evaluator's needs and fails to consider the needs of the person on the receiving end. It should be given to help, not to hurt. Too often, feedback makes the evaluator feel better or allows him or her to belittle the receiver.

Effective feedback is directed toward behavior that the receiver can change. Frustration only increases when people are reminded of shortcomings or physical characteristics they can do nothing about.

Feedback is most effective when it is solicited rather than imposed. To get the most benefit, receivers should formulate questions for the evaluator to answer and actively seek feedback.

Effective feedback involves sharing information rather than giving advice. In this way, receivers are free to decide for themselves on the changes to make in accordance with their own needs.

Effective feedback is well timed. In general, immediate feedback is most useful—depending on the person's readiness to hear it, the support available from others, and so on.

Effective feedback also involves the amount of information the receiver can use rather than the amount the evaluator would like to give. Overloading a person with feedback reduces the possibility that he or she will use it effectively. An evaluator who gives more feedback than can be used is most likely satisfying a personal need rather than helping the other person.

Effective feedback concerns what is said or done and how—not why. Telling people what their motivations or intentions are tends to alienate them and contributes to a climate of resentment, suspicion, and distrust; it does not contribute to learning or development. Assuming knowledge of why a person says or does something is dangerous. If evaluators are uncertain of receivers' motives or intent, the uncertainty itself is feedback and should be revealed.

Finally, effective feedback is checked to ensure clear communication. One way is to have the receiver try to rephrase the feedback, to see if it corresponds to what the evaluator had in mind. No matter what the intent, feedback is often threatening and thus subject to considerable distortion or misinterpretation.

Effective feedback characteristics and performance appraisal interviews can improve the PAS but will not eliminate performance problems. The performance appraisal system, however, can be used to spot performance problems and develop strategies to solve them. Because spotting performance problems and developing strategies to solve them are crucial to improving productivity, they are examined in detail in the section on improving performance.

Improving Performance

Improving performance is a process of identifying performance deficiencies or gaps, understanding their causes, and then developing strategies to remove those deficiencies.

Identifying Performance Gaps

As discussed in Chapter 6, employee job performance is appraised in terms of attributes, behaviors, and outcomes or goals. These not only serve to determine performance but also serve to identify performance gaps. To do so, however, they are used somewhat differently. For example, goals can be used to identify performance deficiencies by how well an employee does in relation to the goals set. If an employee had a performance goal of reducing the scrap rate by 10 percent but reduced it only by 5 percent, a performance gap exists. The discrepancy between actual and set goals can thus be used to spot performance gaps. This method is valid as long as the goals are not contradictory and can be quantified in measurable terms, and the subordinate's performance can be measured in the terms in which the goals are set.[20]

Although all three conditions necessary to use goals in a valid way to spot gaps may not always exist, two other ways can still be used. One is by comparing subordinates, units, or departments with one another. Organizations with several divisions often measure the overall performance of each division by comparing it with all other divisions. The divisions that are ranked on the bottom become identified as problem areas (i.e., they have performance gaps). Whether ranking individuals or units, identifying performance gaps by comparisons prevents an effective diagnosis of the cause of the performance gaps.

The final method by which gaps can be identified is by comparisons over time. For example, a manager who sold one thousand record albums last month but only eight hundred albums this month appears to have a performance gap. Although performance has declined, does this gap represent a deficiency that should be or can be corrected? The month in which one thousand albums were sold may have been at the peak of the buying season. During the month in which only eight hundred albums were sold, the employee may have had to attend an important conference vital to longer-run record sales.

Although these three methods to spot performance gaps are plausible ways to describe how managers should and do determine performance deficiencies, in reality managers are likely to use these methods somewhat inappropriately. Incorrect evaluations of performance may then be made, resulting in inappropriate strategies for improvement. Managers use these methods inappropriately because they may have limited and perhaps inaccurate information about subordinates' performance, yet they may not seek out more information because they are satisfied with the information they have. Managers may also make invalid comparisons across individuals, units, or even time because of biases or limited ability to process all of the necessary information. These individual qualities limit the validity of managerial assessments of performance deficiencies, and influence the quality and appropriateness of the strategies a manager develops to resolve the deficiencies. Another individual quality influencing strategy development is the attributional process that managers use in determining the cause of the deficiencies.

Determining the Causes of Performance Deficiencies

To uncover the reasons for performance deficiencies, a number of questions can be asked, based on a model of the determinants of employee behavior in organizations.[21] This model enables the personnel manager to diagnose performance deficiencies and correct them in a systematic way. In general, the model says that employees perform well if the following determinants are present:

- Ability[22]
- Interest in doing the job
- Opportunity to grow and advance
- Clearly defined goals[23]
- Certainty about what's expected[24]
- Feedback on how well they are doing[25]
- Rewards for performing well
- Punishments for performing poorly
- Power to get resources to do the job

Exhibit 7.2 shows these determinants and the specific questions to ask in determining the causes of performance deficiencies. Negative responses indicate that the item is probably a cause. Based on a series of such responses, the likely causes for a performance deficiency can be established.

Understanding the attributional processes influencing how managers decide upon the determinants of performance deficiencies is important, since these processes influence the strategies selected to improve an employee's performance.

Attributional Processes.   The process that people use to explain their behavior and that of others is called the **attribution process**. Individuals attribute their and others' behavior to various causes. Understanding the attributional processes that individuals use facilitates predicting what causes and responses managers are likely to attach to the performance deficiencies they see in their subordinates.

In relation to performance, managers attribute causes of subordinates' deficiencies to either the subordinates (**internal attribution**) or to the subor-

---

Exhibit 7.2	*Diagnosing Performance Deficiencies*

Check which of the following factors affecting an individual's performance or behavior apply to the situation you are analyzing.

	YES	NO
I. *Skills, knowledge, and abilities*		
A. Does the individual have the skills to do as expected?	____	____
B. Has the individual performed as expected before?	____	____
II. *Personality, interests, and preferences*		
A. Does the individual have the personality or interest to perform as expected?	____	____
B. Does the individual clearly perceive what's actually involved in performing as expected?	____	____

continued

III. *Opportunity for the individual*
   A. Does the individual have a chance to grow and use valued skills and abilities?   _____ _____
   B. Does the organization offer career paths to the individual?   _____ _____

IV. *Goals for the individual*
   A. Are there goals established?   _____ _____
   B. Are the goals very specific?   _____ _____
   C. Are the goals clear?   _____ _____
   D. Are the goals difficult?   _____ _____

V. *Uncertainty for the individual*
   A. Is the individual certain about what rewards are available?   _____ _____
   B. Is the individual certain about what to do?   _____ _____
   C. Is the individual certain about what others expect?   _____ _____
   D. Is the individual certain about job responsibilities and levels of authority?   _____ _____

VI. *Feedback to the individual*
   A. Does the employee get information about what is right and wrong (quality or quantity) with performance?   _____ _____
   B. Does the information received tell the employee how to improve performance?   _____ _____
   C. Does the employee get information frequently?   _____ _____
   D. Is there a delay between the time the employee performs and receiving information on that performance?   _____ _____
   E. Can the information be easily interpreted by the employee?   _____ _____

VII. *Consequences to the individual*
   A. Is it punishing to do as expected (immediate)?   _____ _____
   B. Is it punishing to do as expected (long-term)?   _____ _____
   C. Do more positive consequences result from taking alternative action (immediate)?   _____ _____
   D. Do more positive consequences result from taking alternative action (long-term)?   _____ _____
   E. Are there no apparent consequences of performing as desired?   _____ _____
   F. Are there no positive consequences of performing as desired?   _____ _____

VIII. *Power for the individual*
   A. Can the individual mobilize resources to get the job done?   _____ _____
   B. Can the individual influence others to get them to do what is needed?   _____ _____
   C. Is the individual highly visible to others higher up in the organization?   _____ _____

Source: This format is based on R. F. Mager and P. Pipe,
*Analyzing Performance Problems, or "You Really Oughta
Wanna"* (Belmont, Calif.: Fearon Pitman, 1970).

dinates' environment (**external attribution**). Internal attributions include low effort or low ability, and external attributions include task interference, bad luck, or lack of organizational rewards. Managers are more likely to make internal attributions to the extent that the subordinate (1) does not perform poorly on other tasks (**high distinctiveness**), (2) has performed poorly on the same task (**high consistency**), and (3) performs poorly while the other subordinates perform well (**low consensus**).[26] Managers are more likely to make external attributions under the opposite conditions.

Whether the manager makes internal or external attributions influences the strategy for performance improvement likely to be selected by the manager. If internal attributions are made, the manager is more likely to select strategies aimed at changing the subordinate, such as retraining, termination, or reprimands. If external attributions are made, the manager is more likely to select strategies that modify the environment, such as job redesign or job rotation. However, if strategies are already spelled out by the organization for dealing with performance deficiencies, the manager's attributions are essentially irrelevant to strategy selection. They may, however, influence how the manager feels about the subordinate. Regardless, they should be considered in developing strategies to improve performance.

Strategies to Improve Performance

Companies can do many things to improve employee performance. In general, however, they may want to implement programs aimed at the eight sets of determinants shown in Exhibit 7.2. More specific and frequently used strategies include the following approaches:

- Positive reinforcement system
- Positive discipline programs
- Employee assistance programs
- Employee counseling
- Negative behavioral strategies

These approaches can be matched to the model of the determinants of performance deficiencies by the particular aspects of employee behavior that they are influencing. Other strategies to improve performance based on this model are described in Chapters 11 and 12.

Positive Reinforcement System.   The **positive reinforcement system** lets employees know how well they are meeting specific goals and rewards improvements with praise and recognition. In the sense that no money is involved, it is a unique incentive system. This approach to improvement encourages desirable job behaviors by establishing behavioral criteria and setting up reward systems, contingent upon achieving them.[27] Implementing this strategy requires developing accurate behavioral measures of performance. This can be done by using the critical incidents technique of job analysis to identify critical behaviors of effective and ineffective performance (described in Chapter 3). If the organization already uses a behaviorally-based performance appraisal form, such as BARS or BOS, these can be used instead.

Once these behavioral criteria are established, subordinates should be made aware of them. (Using these behavioral criteria should help eliminate many rating errors and improve the validity of the appraisals.) Next, goals can be established for each behavioral dimension and rewards specified for goal attainment. To obtain maximum benefit from the goal-setting process, the goals should be relatively difficult, specific, clear, and acceptable to subordinates.

Like all incentive systems, a basic premise of positive reinforcement is that behavior can be understood and modified by its consequences. That is, performance is elicited because of the consequence of getting rewards. In this case, however, the consequences of behaving well are not monetary.

By recording the attendance of a group of employees on a weekly rather than on a monthly basis, Michigan Bell Telephone's positive reinforcement program reduced absenteeism significantly. Within six weeks the absenteeism rate in the pilot group dropped from 11 to 6.5 percent. The change was effective because previously, employees who were absent early in the month forfeited their chances for recognition for the entire month. With the weekly system, employees who missed a day in the first week still had a chance for recognition the next week.

Another program of rewards used specifically to reduce absenteeism is called **earned time**. Earned time is a new approach to the way paid absence is accumulated and used. Under earned time, employees have more choice and responsibility in the way they use their paid time off. Accumulating earned time depends on each employee's preferences. Rather than divide benefits into specific numbers of days for vacation and personal leave, sick leave, or short-term disability, earned time lumps these days into one package. These days can be used for a variety of purposes, including a cash payment at the time of voluntary termination. Earned time is available for use as soon as it is "earned" on the job and, in effect, is "no-fault absence."[28]

The principle behind the program is that the number of earned-time days for which an employee may receive a cash payment is less than the previous total of sick, vacation, jury, and all other benefit days combined. For example, the combined total may be divided by two, three, or four to get the earned time. This is then available to use without having to meet special requirements. The program's prime advantages are: (1) a reduction in unplanned absences, (2) a reduction in employee-supervisor conflict over legitimacy of absences and individual responsibility, and (3) flexibility to suit individual priorities.

Positive Discipline Programs. As the following "PHRM in the News" shows, some organizations improve performance through the use of positive discipline or nonpunitive discipline.[29] The essential aspects of positive discipline programs include the following:

When disciplinary discussions have failed to produce the desired changes, management places the individual on a one-day, "decision-making leave." The company pays the employee for the day to demonstrate the organization's desire to see him or her remain a member of the organization and to eliminate the resentment and hostility that punitive actions usually produce. But tenure with the organization is conditional on the individual's decision to solve the immediate problem and make a "total performance commitment" to good performance on the job. The employee is instructed to return on the day following the leave with a decision either to change and stay or to quit and find more satisfying work elsewhere.[30]

The following "PHRM in the News" describes the experiences and results of the positive discipline program at Tampa Electric Company.

PHRM in the News

Discipline Without Punishment—At Last

It was a particularly nasty incident involving a foreman that triggered Tampa Electric Company's decision to switch to a nonpunitive approach to discipline. The labor relations manager recalled the 1977 confrontation between the foreman and a lineman this way: "The lineman's confrontational behavior caused the working foreman to grab the lineman by his shirt collar and shake him severely. This is unacceptable behavior for a working foreman, and he was suspended for 13 days. I had no choice under the existing policy but to support that suspension, but I never felt good about it. All I did was penalize an employee and his family; I did not change his behavior in any way. I believe he would have done the same thing again. I forced compliance, but he will still believe the company was wrong."

His prediction was accurate. Five months later another disciplinary situation arose with the same foreman. The previous suspension had proved ineffective in improving behavior.

The labor relations manager's frustration with the company's punitive approach resulted in a search for an alternative. The organization wanted a system that provided consistency, fairness, and lasting corrective measures without resorting to punishment. In September 1979, the production operations and maintenance groups replaced the old approach with a nonpunitive system for a one-year trial period. By January 1981, the new system was in effect companywide. The pilot project, which covered 1,000 employees, grew to include nearly 3,000.

After the program had been in place in production operations and maintenance for about a year, Tampa Electric surveyed the 100 managers and supervisors in the affected departments. All but 2 not only agreed that the program should be continued but also recommended its expansion. "When you get 98 out of 100 managers agreeing on anything," one senior executive commented, "you know you've got something that's very successful." Shortly thereafter, Tampa Electric expanded its nonpunitive approach to all operating, service, and administrative departments.

Since the program was adopted companywide in January 1981, Tampa Electric reports only favorable results: more effective and accepted disciplinary measures, fewer successful unemployment compensation claims after employees have been terminated, less absenteeism, and fewer arbitrations. In fact, in 1982, *no* union grievance proceeded to arbitration.

The decline in absenteeism alone resulted in sizable financial savings for the company. Sick time usage in maintenance and production operations dropped from an average of 66.7 hours in 1977 to 36.6 hours in 1983. In one operating department, the average use of sick time per employee dropped from 58.8 hours to 19.5 hours per year in five years. Based on a 1983 average wage rate of $11.78 per hour, this reduction in sick time use saved the company $439,404, or 1.38% of the 1983 payroll—the equivalent of having 18 additional people on the job.

Tampa Electric's experience with its nonpunitive system was best captured by the words of a long-term supervisor who expressed relief over the elimination of the unpaid suspension. "I've never yet seen a guy come back from an unpaid suspension," he said, "feeling better about his boss, his job, the company, or himself."

Employee Assistance Programs.   **Employee assistance programs (EAPs) are** specifically designed to assist employees with chronic personal problems that hinder their job performance and attendance. EAPs are often used with employees who are alcoholics or who have severe domestic problems. Since the job may be partly responsible for these problems, some employers are taking the lead in establishing EAPs to help affected workers.[31]

A company that establishes an employee assistance program generally thinks that it has a responsibility toward employees and that employees should be given a chance to correct any undesirable job behavior. Helping alcoholic employees also makes good economic sense, because 25 percent of each alcoholic's salary is the average cost to the employer in absenteeism, reduced productivity, accidents in the work place, and use of the company medical plan. Furthermore, the estimate is that 65 to 80 percent of those who receive treatment for chemical dependency return to the work force and do what their supervisors consider a satisfactory job. Nevertheless, employees must also help themselves. If they fail to participate in an EAP or recover through other means, employers may have no choice but to terminate them. The philosophy of most EAPs is to help individuals help themselves within a context of fairness yet firmness.

To be successful, an employee assistance program should possess the following attributes:

- Top management backing
- Union or employee support
- Confidentiality
- Easy access
- Trained supervisors
- Trained union steward, if in a union setting
- Insurance
- Availability of numerous services for assistance and referral
- Skilled, professional leadership
- Systems for monitoring, assessing, and revising

Even though EAPs are designed to provide valuable assistance to employees, many employees in need fail to use the programs unless faced with the alternative of being fired. When so confronted, however, the success rate of those attending EAPs is high. The results can mean substantial gains in employee job performance and reductions in absenteeism.

Employee Counseling.   To change the habits of chronically absent employees, McGraw Edison has devised an innovative counseling program that stresses problem-solving and goal-setting techniques. This individual approach focuses on the "5 to 10 percent of the work force" that has a history of absenteeism. Before beginning the actual counseling with individual employees, supervisors take the following steps:

- Identify the consistently worst offenders. Make a list of all employees who have a record of repeated absences, regardless of the "presumed legitimacy or the underlying reasons" for missing work.
- Centralize the absenteeism data. Records and information should be accumulated, analyzed, and maintained in one central location.
- Collect long-term data. Absenteeism records on individuals should be kept for a sufficiently long period to show that a clear pattern exists.

Once the decision is made to meet with the employee, supervisors should do the following:

- Examine the attendance record with the employee.
- Be sure the employee is aware of the severity of the problem, as well as the organization's attendance standards.
- Prepare a brief, accurate memo at the session's end outlining the problem, noting the reasons given by the employee, and specifying whether or not the employee responded with a desire to improve.

If the first session has not produced a significant change, a second counseling session should be scheduled. Participants in this session should include the worker's supervisor, the employee, a union representative (if applicable), and higher management officials. An upper-level manager should be present to ensure that due process protection (Chapter 14) is provided for the employee. Results of the second counseling session should also be documented.

If the employee shows no improvement after the second session, another session can be held, which should also include an upper-level manager. At this stage the "decision to meet the expected standard of attendance and continuity of employment" should be placed directly on the employee. To dramatize the importance and seriousness of the situation, the employee might be allowed to take off a day with pay to decide whether he or she wishes to resign or to commit to a long-term program of positive improvement. If no sign of improvement is shown after this step, discharging the employee may be necessary.

Whether employee counseling is an appropriate remedy depends upon an analysis of the behavioral determinants, as shown in Exhibit 7.2. This is also true for the other strategies. For example, if the undesirable performance is diagnosed to be caused by a lack of positive consequences for desirable behaviors, supervisor praise, organizational recognition, or monetary compensation attached to these behaviors may produce better results than increased counseling. If employees are not performing well, increased feedback or the establishment of goals may be appropriate, if a diagnosis of the situation suggests that employees do not know how well they are doing.

Negative Behavioral Strategies.   Unlike the strategies described that seek to encourage desirable behavior patterns through systems of reward or counseling, negative strategies seek to discourage unwanted behavior by either punishing it or ignoring it.[32] A negative strategy is commonly used in many organizations because of its ability to achieve relatively immediate results. Its negative effects can be reduced by incorporating several "**hot stove principles**," including the following:

- Provide ample and clear warning. Many organizations have clearly defined disciplinary steps. For example, the first offense might elicit an oral warning; the second offense, a written warning; the third offense, a disciplinary layoff; the fourth offense, discharge.
- Administer the discipline as quickly as possible. If a long time elapses between the ineffective behavior and the discipline, the employee may not know what the discipline is for.
- Administer the same discipline for the same behavior for everyone, every time. Discipline has to be administered fairly and consistently.
- Administer the discipline impersonally. Discipline should be based on a specific behavior, a specific person.

Because the immediate supervisor or manager plays the integral role in administering discipline, the PHRM department and the organization should do the following to increase the discipline's effectiveness:

- Allow managers and supervisors to help select their own employees.
- Educate managers and supervisors about the organization's disciplinary policies and train them to administer the policies.
- Set up standards that are equitable to employees and that managers and supervisors can easily and consistently implement.

Taking these steps not only reduces the likely negative effects generally associated with discipline but also helps ensure that employee rights are respected (discussed further in Chapter 14). This is further ensured with the establishment of fair work rules and work policies consistently applied and enforced.

No organization can operate smoothly, safely, or efficiently without work rules and work policies. The general scenario is that employers make the rules and policies, supervisors enforce them, and employees follow them. But no employer has a completely free hand to establish any rules or policies he or she wishes. Work rules and policies are part of the internal discipline system because rule infractions only sometimes result in some form of discipline.

To be effective, work rules and policies must be reasonably related to appropriate management goals and should also be effectively communicated. The rules and policies promulgated and enforced must not result in unfair adverse impact against any group of employees protected by fair employment laws, and the rules and policies cannot violate several other acts and court decisions defining employee rights to job security (discussed in Chapter 14). Furthermore, these rules and policies should embrace the notion of progressive discipline and respect due process as discussed in Chapter 14. In other words, the rules and policies (1) must apply equally to all employees, regardless of race, religion, national origin, sex, age, or disability; (2) must be clearly stated; (3) must be enforced objectively; and (4) should reflect the information necessary to prove equal application and enforcement of work rules.

When administered accordingly, discipline may be an effective strategy to improve performance.[33]

To help ensure the effectiveness of programs to improve performance, performance gaps and their potential causes should first be identified. Then, alternative programs can be selected and their relative utility or effectiveness assessed. This assessment requires determining the costs of the program and the value of its benefits, including assessing the cost of the current performance gap and the extent to which the program can reduce it. In general, this paradigm for assessing performance improvement programs is also applicable to assessing the entire performance appraisal system.

Trends in Performance Appraisal

A significant trend in performance appraisal is assessing the entire system of performance appraisal. This is much more extensive than the assessment of performance appraisal forms described in Chapter 6. Other significant trends are in computer technology and HRIS, strategic involvement, and the development of choices in performance appraisal.

Assessing the Performance Appraisal System

Chapter 6 categorized the importance and purposes of performance appraisal into evaluation and development. That is, appraisal information is important because it is used as input for making evaluation decisions, such as salary increases or decreases, demotions, layoffs, promotions, and terminations. Appraisal information is also used as input for development intentions, including spotting training needs, motivating employees to improve, providing feedback, counseling employees, and spotting performance deficiencies.

Although all organizations may not desire to use their performance appraisal to serve both of these purposes, all should be concerned with the legal requirements it must meet. When performance appraisal is used to serve evaluation and development purposes and to meet the legal requirements, it is affecting the three organizational human resource goals of productivity, quality of work life, and legal compliance. Assuming that organizations desire to serve both purposes and meet the legal requirements, how can they assess how well their performance appraisal systems are doing?[34]

Overall PAS Assessment.   Before assessing specific aspects of an organization's PAS, performing an overall assessment may be useful. An overall assessment quickly suggests how well the PAS is doing and may provide an added stimulus for a more specific assessment.[35]

Although personnel and human resource managers could ask both managers and nonmanagers about specific aspects of the PAS, this would take time. An alternative is for both supervisors and subordinates to respond to a questionnaire such as the one shown in Exhibit 7.3. As indicated in the scoring of the questionnaire, three subcategories (A + B + C) sum to form an overall PAS assessment score. The three subcategories correspond to the major purposes of appraisal, with categories A and B assessing the developmental purpose and category C assessing the evaluation purpose. Part of the assessment of the evaluation purpose includes administrative features of appraisal, (i.e., whether performance appraisal records are maintained and how accessible they are). These features also facilitate the development purpose of performance appraisal.

This overall PAS assessment questionnaire lets the organization know how well it is doing with its PAS. As a guide, scores on the subcategories of 9 or 10 suggest the purpose is being well served, while scores of 4–8 suggest average service, and 2 or 3 suggest the purpose is not being served at all.[36] Adding the scores on the three subcategories results in an overall assessment of how well the purposes of appraisal are being attained. Scores of 26–30 suggest quite well, scores of 21–25, good, 11–20, average, and less than 11, quite poorly. Scores on the subcategories or overall total that indicate room for improvement (e.g., average scores or less) also suggest that specific areas should be assessed in depth to determine what is contributing to the average or low scores. To help ensure that an overall assessment of the PAS will come out positive, the organization should do the following:

Keep evaluations on all employees, not just the ones whose performance you don't like or those who ask for promotions.

Use only objective judgments whenever possible. When subjective judgments are necessary, use examples that show what you mean.

Let employees review their performance with you and challenge items with which they disagree. Such items can still be left in the record, but with the challenge attached.[37]

Specific PAS Assessment.   The specific assessment of an organization's PAS requires the examination of several aspects of the entire system.[38] The following questions can provide an assessment of the specific components:

■ What purposes does the organization want its performance appraisal system to serve?

■ Do the appraisal forms really elicit the information to serve these purposes? Are these forms compatible with the jobs for which they are being used (i.e., are they job related)? Are the forms based upon behaviors or outcomes that might be included in a critical incidents job analysis?

■ Are the appraisal forms designed to minimize errors and ensure consistency?

| *Exhibit 7.3* | *Organizational Performance Appraisal Questionnaire Evaluation (OPAQUE)* |

Respond to the following six statements by indicating the extent to which you agree (or disagree) that the statements accurately describe performance appraisal in your organization. Some statements refer to your experiences in appraising your subordinates' performance; others refer to your experiences in being appraised yourself. Try to reflect as accurately as you can the current conditions in your organization based on your experiences.

> SA = Strongly Agree   A = Agree   ? = Neither Agree nor Disagree
>   D = Disagree   SD = Strongly Disagree

1. I have found my boss's appraisals to be very helpful in guiding my own career development progress. SA A ? D SD
2. The appraisal system we have here is of no use to me in my efforts toward developing my subordinates to the fullest extent of their capabilities. SA A ? D SD
3. Our performance appraisal system generally leaves me even more uncertain about where I stand after my appraisal than beforehand. SA A ? D SD
4. The appraisal system we use is very useful in helping me to clearly communicate to my subordinates exactly where they stand. SA A ? D SD
5. When higher levels of management around here are making major decisions about management positions and promotions, they have access to and make use of performance appraisal records. SA A ? D SD
6. In making pay, promotion, transfer, and other administrative personnel decisions, I am not able to obtain past performance appraisal records that could help me to make good decisions. SA A ? D SD

continued

As discussed previously, some superiors commit errors in their appraisals of subordinates. For example, two employees may perform identically, but one employee's superior may commit a strictness error, and the other employee's superior may commit a leniency error. This will cause one of the employees to appear to be far less competent than the other. These errors are common in organizations using rating forms. If the organization is to treat all its employees fairly, it must try to reduce these errors, perhaps by monitoring the lack of consistency in the way superiors complete appraisal forms.[39]

- Are the processes of the appraisal effective? For example, are the appraisal interviews done effectively? Are goals established? Are they developed jointly? Do superiors and subordinates accept the appraisal process?
- Are superiors rewarded for correctly evaluating and developing their employees? Are they trained in giving feedback, setting goals, and problem-solving techniques? Are they trained to spot performance deficiencies and correctly identify the causes?

Scoring

Use the following grid to determine point scores for each item by transferring your responses onto the grid. Place the number in the box at the bottom of each column, then add pairs of columns as indicated.

		Statement Number					
		1	2	3	4	5	6
R e s p o n s e	SA	5	1	1	5	5	1
	A	4	2	2	4	4	2
	?	3	3	3	3	3	3
	D	2	4	4	2	2	4
	SD	1	5	5	1	1	5

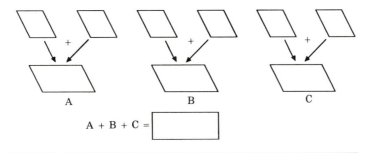

A   B   C

A + B + C = ☐

- Are the evaluation and developmental components separated? Do the superiors vary their interview styles according to the purpose of the interview?
- Are superiors relatively free from task interference in doing performance appraisal?
- Are the appraisals being implemented correctly? What procedures have been set up to ensure that the appraisals are being done correctly? What supporting materials are available to aid superiors in appraising their subordinates?
- Do methods exist for reviewing and evaluating the effectiveness of the total system? Are there goals and objectives for the system? Are there systematic procedures for gathering data to measure how well the goals and objectives are being met?[40]

By addressing these questions and taking corrective action where necessary, an organization's PAS is more likely to serve its purposes and the broader organizational human resource goals of productivity, quality of work life, and legal compliance. For an organization just beginning to implement a PAS, the implications of all these questions should be understood and incorporated into the initial PAS design.[41]

Computer Technology and HRIS in Performance Appraisal

Chapter 6 outlined how performance appraisal is related to other PHRM activities. In particular, computer technology can facilitate the link between performance appraisal and training and selection. By establishing a menu of skills, knowledge, and abilities needed for each position, the results of an employee's review can be used as the basis for determining whether a performance deficiency necessitates training, placement in another position, or a more extreme action like dismissal. Computer technology is not only useful for identifying a training need but also may serve as an indicator of what kind of training is needed. Alternatively, superior performance ratings may signal that employees' skills, knowledge, and abilities are being underutilized in their current positions. This information may serve as a basis for placement in more challenging jobs. Thus, employee dissatisfaction and restlessness may be avoided.

HRIS performance appraisal data is also useful for validating the predictors used in selection. Without valid performance data, however, the validation process is not likely to be fruitful. Thus, accurate, valid performance appraisal information must be gathered and stored in a company's HRIS.

Performance appraisal information is fundamental in serving the purposes of performance appraisal. This information has to be done faster and more easily. The development of strategies to eliminate performance deficiencies is also made easier with the computer.

Strategic Involvement of Performance Appraisal

The strategic use of performance appraisal in organizations is growing rapidly. It is being used to gain competitive advantage and to link with organizational strategy.

Gaining Competitive Advantage.   Organizations are increasingly using performance appraisal to gain competitive advantage. For example, at GTE performance appraisals are viewed as one of the most important tools in the management arsenal. According to GTE chairman Theodore F. Brophy, the GTE appraisal system complements the emergent strategic planning emphasis in all areas of the corporation. The appraisal reviews assist executives in clarifying and articulating objectives and expectations for themselves and their employees. They give GTE a realistic assessment of its strengths, weaknesses, and future requirements. As such, the company is now able to better utilize its human resources than at any time in the past.[42]

Another critical aspect of appraising is correcting poor performance. At Emery Air Freight, the company was losing $1 million annually because employees on the airport loading docks were shipping small packages separately rather than placing those with the same destination in one container that would be carried at lower rates by air carriers. Management also found that the containers were being used 45 percent of the time when they should have been used 90 percent of the time. By establishing a program of positive consequences and feedback, the nearly $1 million annual loss was eliminated. Stories of similar changes in poor performance to good performance and large dollar savings resulting from absenteeism reduction programs and employee assistance programs have been reported by many companies. The result is a tremendous gain in cost reduction and improved efficiency.

Linking with Organizational Strategy.   The choices in performance appraisal are extensive. They provide organizations with the opportunity and ability to match performance appraisal with aspects of the organization such as strategy, as shown in Exhibit 1.4.[43] Some choices organizations have include the following:

Loose, Incomplete Integration———Tight, Complete Integration
Behavioral Criteria———Results Criteria
Purposes:—————·———
DAP   RAP   MAP
Low Employee Participation———High Employee Participation
Short-Term Criteria———Long-Term Criteria
Individual Criteria———Group Criteria

Because performance appraisal is a system with many components, a first choice on the menu is deciding on the degree of integration of these components. This integration includes (1) establishing the link between job analysis and the performance appraisal forms and criteria; (2) identifying who can provide relevant appraisal data on the criteria identified; (3) developing and connecting the types of appraisal forms that can be selected with the purposes to be served; (4) gathering and combining the various sources of performance data as expeditiously as feasible; (5) feeding back the results to the employees in a timely fashion and allowing for appeal; and (6) ensuring that the results are used for their intended purposes, such as compensation, and are still relevant (valid) for the employees and jobs.

The last point brings the process of performance appraisal full circle and suggests that continual monitoring and potential adjustment of the process are necessary. Companies may choose not to engage in this continual monitoring and adjustment, however. Similarly, they may choose not to conceive of performance appraisal in such a systematic manner, or if they do, they may choose not to establish a tight connection between the components. If these choices are made, the company establishes a loose integration. If the opposite choices are made, the integration becomes much tighter.

Another choice in appraising is whether the preference is to appraise and evaluate behaviors or results. Appraisal of behavior focuses on *how* things are done, while appraisal of results focuses on *how many* things are done. Many appraisal forms that organizations can choose to use can be distinguished by their emphasis on behaviors or results. For example, behaviorally anchored rating scales (BARS) focus on behaviors, and management by objectives (MBO) focuses on results. If a company chooses, both types of forms can be used together, and equal emphasis can be given to behavior and results.[44]

A third choice is selecting the general purpose to be served by appraisal. Appraisal can be used to develop employee performance, to maintain it, or to improve it. These three purposes of appraisal are referred to as DAP, MAP, and RAP, respectively.[45] DAP (developmental appraisal purpose) is future-oriented and focuses heavily on spotting employees who are likely to do well on more challenging jobs, and on providing developmental opportunities to help ensure they will do well. In contrast, RAP (remedial appraisal purpose) is more present-oriented and seeks to spot current performance deficiencies, analyze the reasons for them, and then design programs to remove them. MAP (maintenance appraisal purpose) is concerned with maintaining current employee performance levels.

A fourth choice is the degree of employee participation in the entire performance appraisal system. Companies can choose to have employees involved in each of the components of the system, in only some of them, or in none. For example, human resource managers can involve employees in writing their own job descriptions, identifying critical job dimensions, and then identifying examples of effective and ineffective performance on those dimensions. Alternatively, employees could be excluded from actively participating in any of these components.

Another choice for companies is whether to emphasize short- or long-term criteria in appraising and evaluating employees. Although short-term criteria could be included in many performance dimensions, all have in common a twelve-month or less time horizon within which employees demonstrate their ability to perform. Alternatively, many long-term criteria could be used, but all would share a time horizon of more than twelve months, within which employee performance would be appraised.

A final choice in appraising is selecting whether more weight is to be given to individual-determined criteria or to group-determined criteria. On one hand, employees may be appraised individually on criteria over which they collectively have a great deal of ability to influence. If collective action is required to get results, group criteria are more appropriate in appraising individual performance than when collective action is not required.

Summary

Appraising performance is a critical PHRM activity because its results can be used for several evaluational and developmental decisions and actions. Although it is important that the performance appraisal data be collected by effective and appropriate methods, as Chapter 6 describes, without utilizing the data, evaluation and developmental decisions and actions cannot be made. In this chapter, two critical components of utilizing the performance appraisal data are discussed: feeding back the data to the subordinate via the performance appraisal interview, and spotting performance deficiencies and developing strategies for improvement.

In providing effective feedback to subordinates, superiors should use appropriate and specific performance data. The purposes of evaluation and development should be served separately, current and potential performance appraisal discussions should be separated, and multiple appraisals should be used. The effectiveness of the performance appraisal interview session in providing feedback can also be enhanced if the performance appraisals are conducted in a legally defensible way. Doing this involves the organization and the PHRM department in keeping evaluations on all employees, using only objective judgments whenever possible and letting subordinates review their performance appraisals and records.

With effective feedback and legally defensible and therefore valid performance appraisals, engaging in programs of spotting and correcting performance deficiencies is easier. Such programs begin with a model or paradigm for determining the causes of the performance deficiencies. When these deficiencies are traced to employee motivation rather than ability, several programs designed either to control or to prevent the deficiencies can be developed and implemented. In so doing, the full complement of reasons for performance appraisals and performance appraisal systems can be attained.

Facilitating the effectiveness of performance appraisal and performance appraisal systems is the assessment of the entire PAS and its specific components. Such assessments are necessary to help determine how well the evaluational and developmental purposes are being attained and if the legal considerations are being observed. On the basis of such assessments, revisions in current appraisal methods can be made, and more effective strategies for improving performance can be developed and implemented. Once done, an organization has a much better basis on which to make other PHRM decisions, particularly those associated with compensation and training and development, topics addressed in the following chapters.

Discussion Questions

1. Suppose you have decided that an employee is not working out and must be fired. What performance appraisal approach would you want to use to support this decision? Why?

2. An observer of the performance appraisal process once commented that when it comes to appraisal, all organizations experience a "shortage of bastards." What do you suppose this comment means? Does this comment relate to the types of inherent conflict associated with the PAS? Explain.

3. What considerations are there in designing an effective performance appraisal system?

4. To what causes are performance deficiencies associated, and what are the respective strategies used to correct those performance deficits?

5. What are the critical issues in determining the utility of a specific performance appraisal system?

6. From a reward perspective, another observer of the performance appraisal process has argued that effective supervisors should spend appraisal time only with their effective performers. What is the rationale for this strategy? Do you see any potential problems? Explain.

7. Assume you are supervising a group of employees that fall into one of three categories: (1) an effective performer with lots of potential for advancement, (2) an effective performer who lacks motivation or ability (or both) for potential advancement, and (3) a currently ineffective performer. It is performance appraisal time, and you must plan interviews with subordinates from each of these three categories. How will your interviews differ? How will they be similar?

8. Assume you are a professor counseling a student with a grade complaint. Describe how you would conduct this session using: (1) the tell and sell approach, (2) the tell and listen approach, and (3) the problem-solving approach. As a professor, which would you feel most comfortable using? Why? As a student, which would you prefer? Why?

9. If subjective, trait-oriented approaches are legally vulnerable, why do you suppose organizations persist in using them?

10. A common technique for communicating negative feedback is sandwiching. For question 8, describe how the hypothetical professor might use this technique. What are the consequences for the rater and ratee when using it?

PC Project

Performance appraisal data are utilized for evaluative (e.g., salary, promotions) and developmental (e.g., counseling, coaching, improving) purposes. This PC Project utilizes performance data as a basis for providing performance feedback. What might large discrepancies between self and supervisory ratings indicate? Biases and distortions in self-ratings may provide important topics for discussion in the feedback session between subordinate and manager. How might the performance data be used to provide evaluative and developmental feedback?

C A S E   S T U D Y

The "Problem" Employee

I'm sorry, Mr. Gatewood, can you believe I lost your application this morning?" exclaimed Kelly Sherwood. Kelly, an employment intake clerk for the local state employment service, was somewhat flustered over her gaffe but recovered in time with, "Stupid me—I accidentally filed your folder under the *H*'s." To an unassured Mr. Gatewood, Kelly proceeded to explain that she was prone to make mistakes like this, especially on Monday.

Cathy Nuzum, an employment counselor, couldn't help but overhear this exhange from her desk near the front office where walk-ins were processed at the employment office. Cathy had witnessed Kelly's performance for seven months now and was disgusted that Kelly had somehow made it past her six-month probationary period without being fired. More than once Cathy had pointed out to Kelly's supervisor, Flo DiBrito, that Kelly was shirking her office duties.

Kelly and Judy Young both work in the front office as intake clerks. Their jobs have two broad sets of tasks that vary considerably. Their primary duties are to greet walk-ins, take applications, and when necessary, schedule preemployment screening tests such as clerical typing tests of speed and accuracy. The second set of duties requires them to sit at a computer terminal and enter new position openings as well as new applicant information into the computer job bank program. The job bank program enables the employment service to run searches of applicants for specific position openings as well as searches of specific types of available job openings at the request of applicants. As applicants are successfully referred and subsequently hired, the job bank information must be updated.

Although Cathy did not supervise Kelly or Judy, she felt a responsibility toward ensuring that the office was run efficiently and professionally. Cathy was also a good friend of Judy's. This latest episode hardened Cathy's resolve to confront Flo about Kelly's unprofessional behavior. In Cathy's opinion, Kelly was a social butterfly who only wanted to sashay around the front office shooting the breeze and avoiding work.

Judy had complained privately to Cathy about Kelly's behavior, especially the shirking. It seemed that although both Kelly and Judy were supposed to process openings and applicants at the comput-

er terminal, Kelly always found a way to beg off from working at the terminal. Judy, realizing that if the job bank information wasn't current, it couldn't be used, would work at the terminal all afternoon processing the folders into the computer for the next day's use. When Cathy prodded Judy to confront Flo about this inequity, Judy would hesitate and apologetically reply that she "couldn't possibly rat on Kelly."

Next Monday, Cathy once again witnessed a similar display by Kelly. She steamed into Flo's office, closed the door behind her, and demanded that Flo do something about Kelly's shirking. "Flo, you know and everyone else in this office knows that Judy does Kelly's work, and that's not fair!" declared Cathy. After some discussion, Flo agreed to have a "discussion" with Kelly Tuesday morning. With that, Cathy returned to her desk feeling somewhat better.

The next day, Cathy noticed that Kelly was sitting at the terminal entering data into the job bank program. On Thursday, Kelly had been at the terminal for most of the afternoon, but few keystrokes could be heard. Kelly appeared to be spaced out, gazing through the nearby window. Beside her lay a pile of applicant folders for that day, which were clearly not going to make it into the computer by the 5:00 P.M. closing deadline.

On Friday Cathy, once again fed up, confronted Flo behind closed doors. Flo seemed uncomfortable by Cathy's persistent criticism of Kelly. In defense of her own efforts, Flo pointed out to Cathy that within the last three weeks, she had conducted three "discussions" with Kelly regarding her responsibility to perform all of her job duties.

"Flo, Kelly is never going to change, because Judy is conscientious enough to always pitch in and catch up the backlog of work. And your 'discussions' seem to last two days at the most before Kelly reverts to her old behavior patterns," protested Cathy. "I think some stronger measures are about due!"

Notes

1. *Wall Street Journal*, 28 August, 1984, p. 1. Reprinted by permission of *The Wall Street Journal*, © Dow Jones & Company, Inc., 1984. All Rights Reserved.

2. For an extensive discussion of individual and organizational goals and their inherent conflicts, see L. W.

Porter, E. E. Lawler III, and J. R. Hackman, *Behavior in Organizations* (New York: McGraw-Hill, 1975).

3. M. Beer, "Performance Appraisal: Dilemmas and Possibilities," *Organizational Dynamics* (Winter 1981) p. 26. For further discussion of the performance feed-

back effects on self-esteem, see A. Zander, "Research on Self-Esteem, Feedback and Threats to Self-Esteem," in *Performance Appraisals: Effects on Employees and Their Performance,* ed. A. Zander (New York: Foundation for Research in Human Behavior, 1963).

4. Beer, "Performance Appraisal," pp. 27-29.

5. For a discussion of the vanishing performance appraisal and other career issues, see D. T. Hall, *Careers in Organizations* (Glenview, Ill.: Scott, Foresman, 1976).

6. H. H. Meyer, E. Kay, and J. R. P. French, Jr., "Split Roles in Performance Appraisal," *Harvard Business Review* (Jan.-Feb. 1965): 125.

7. R. S. Schuler, "Taking the Pain Out of the Performance Appraisal Interview," *Supervisory Management* (Aug. 1981): 8-13; "Training Managers to Rate Their Employers," *Business Week*, 17 Mar. 1980, pp. 178-79; K. N. Wexley, "Performance Appraisal and Feedback," in *Organizational Behavior*, ed. S. Kerr (Columbus, Ohio: Grid, 1979), pp. 241-62; C. Cammon, D. A. Nadler, and P. H. Mirvis, *The Ongoing Feedback System: A Tool for Improving Organizational Management* (Ann Arbor, Mich.: Survey Research Center, University of Michigan, 1975); T. Rendero, "Consensus," *Personnel* (Nov.-Dec. 1980): 4-12; K. S. Teel, "Performance Appraisals: Current Trends, Persistent Progress," *Personnel Journal* (Apr. 1980): 296-301; R. F. Catalenello and J. A. Hooper, "Managerial Appraisal," *Personnel Administrator* (Sept. 1981): 75-81.

8. Separating the review of past performance and future performance is described by Beer "Performance Appraisal" and also by S. J. Carroll and C. E. Schneier, *Performance Appraisal and Review Systems* (Glenview, Ill.: Scott, Foresman, 1982). For a presentation of why not separate appraisal for development and evaluation, see E. E. Lawler III, A. M. Mohrman, Jr., and S. M. Resnick, "Performance Appraisal Revisited," *Organizational Dynamics* (Summer 1984): 20-42.

9. For more discussion of individual differences in performance appraisal, see Beer, "Performance Appraisal," Carroll, and Schneier, *Performance Appraisal*; M. Kavanagh, "Evaluating Performance," in *Personnel Management*, ed. K. M. Rowland and G. R. Ferris (Boston: Allyn & Bacon, 1982), pp. 187-226.

10. Beer, "Performance Appraisal," p. 31.

11. See these discussed in more detail in N. R. F. Maier, *The Appraisal Interview* (New York: Wiley, 1958); G. P. Latham and K. N. Wexley, *Increasing Productivity through Performance Appraisal* (Reading, Mass.: Addison-Wesley, 1981), pp. 152-54; Carroll and Schneier, *Performance Appraisal*, pp. 160-89.

12. G. P. Latham and L. M. Saari, "The Importance of Supportive Relationships in Goal Setting," *Journal of Applied Psychology* 64 (1979): 163-68; M. Erez, P. C. Earley, and C. L. Hulin, "The Impact of Participation on Goal Acceptance and Performance: A Two-

Step Model," *Academy of Management Journal* (Mar. 1985): 50-66.

13. Latham and Wexley, *Increasing Productivity*, pp. 154-55.

14. For a discussion of these characteristics for an effective appraisal interview, see Beer, "Performance Appraisal," pp. 34-35 and *Bulletin to Management*, 18 Oct. 1984, pp. 2, 7.

15. W. F. Nemeroff and K. N. Wexley, "Relationships between Performance Appraisal Interview Outcomes by Supervisors and Subordinates," paper presented at the Annual Meeting of the National Academy of Management, Orlando, Florida, 1977; K. N. Wexley, J. P. Singh, and G. A. Yukl, "Subordinate Personality as a Moderator of the Effects of Participation in Three Types of Appraisal Interviews," *Journal of Applied Psychlogy* 58 (1973): 54-59; M. K. Mount, "Comparisons of Managerial and Employee Satisfaction with a Performance Appraisal System," *Personnel Psychology* (Spring 1983): 99-110.

16. Latham and Saari, "The Importance of"; M. M. Greller, "Subordinate Participation and Reaction to the Appraisal Interview," *Journal of Applied Psychology* 60 (1975): 544-49; S. B. Silverman and K. N. Wexley, "Reactions of Employees to Performance Appraisal Interviews as a Function of Their Participation in Rating Scale Development," *Personnel Psychology* (Winter 1984): 687-702; D. L. Stone, H. G. Gueutal, and B. McIntosh, "The Effects of Feedback Sequence and Expertise of the Rater on Perceived Feedback Accuracy," *Personnel Psychology* (Autumn 1984): 507-14.

17. Greller, "Subordinate Participation"; Nemeroff and Wexley, "Relationships Between"; Wexley et al., "Subordinate Personality."

18. Meyer, Kay, and French, "Split Roles"; G. P. Latham and G. A. Yukl, "A Review of Research on the Application of Goal Setting in Organizations," *Academy of Management Journal* 18 (1975): 824-45.

19. For an extensive discussion of feedback characteristics, see Carroll and Schneier, *Performance Appraisal*, pp. 160-89. M. Jacobs, A. Jacobs, G. Feldman, and N. Cavior, "Feedback II—The Credibility Gap: Delivery of Positive and Negative and Emotional Behavioral Feedback in Groups," *Journal of Consulting and Clinical Psychology* 41 (1973): 215-23; D. R. Ilgen, C. D. Fisher, and M. S. Taylor, "Consequences of Individual Feedback on Behavior in Organizations," *Journal of Applied Psychology* 64 (1979): 349-71; W. G. Bennis, D. E. Berlew, E. H. Schein, and F. I. Steele, eds., *Interpersonal Dynamics* (Homewood, Ill.: Dorsey, 1973).

20. For a good discussion of the measurement of performance gaps, see G. P. Latham, L. L. Cummings, and T. R. Mitchell, "Behavioral Strategies to Improve Productivity," *Organizational Dynamics* (Winter 1981): 4-23.

21. This section is adapted in part from R. F. Mager and P. Pipe, *Analyzing Performance Problems or "You*

Really Oughta Wanna" (Belmont, Calif.: Fearon Pitman, 1970).

22. Individuals appear to differ on information-processing styles and capacities and on decision-making and problem-solving styles. See I. Mitroff and D. Mitroff, "Personality and Problem Solving: Making the Link Visible," *Journal of Experiential Learning and Simulation* 2 (1980): 111–19; D. Schweiger and A. Jago, "Problem-solving Styles and Participative Decision Making," *Psychological Reports* 50 (1982): 1311–16; S. Kerr and J. W. Slocum, Jr., "Decision-Making Style and Acquisition of Information: Further Exploration of the Myers-Briggs Type Indicator," *Psychological Reports* 49 (1981): 132–34. Although an individual may not be performing well, actual ability may not be the cause but rather perceived ability. Individuals can learn to perceive themselves as not having sufficient ability and consequently give up. This phenomenon is called "learned helplessness." As of now, research is limited on its applications in organizations, but see M. J. Martinko and W. L. Gardner, "Learned Helplessness: An Alternative Explanation for Performance Deficits," *Academy of Management Review* 1 (1982): 195–204.

23. J. M. Ivancevich, J. T. McMahon, J. W. Streidl, and A. D. Szilagyi, Jr., "Goal Setting: The Tenneco Approach to Personnel Development and Management Effectiveness," *Organizational Dynamics* 4 (1978): 58–80; E. A. Locke, K. N. Shaw, L. M. Saari, and G. P. Latham, "Goal Setting and Task Performance: 1969–1980," technical report GS-4, Office of Naval Research (contract no. N10014–79–0680), June 1980; P. K. Mills, "Self-Management: Its Control and Relationship to Other Organizational Properties," *Academy of Management Review* (July 1983): 445–53; M. E. and F. H. Kanfer, "The Role of Goal Acceptance in Goal Setting and Task Performance," *Academy of Management Review* (July 1983): 454–63; J. C. Naylor and D. R. Ilgen, "Goalsetting: A Theoretical Analysis in Motivational Technology," in *Research in Organizational Behavior*, vol. 6, ed. B. M. Staw and L. L. Cummings (Greenwich, Conn.: JAI Press, 1984), pp. 95–140.

24. In addition to the detrimental effects of task conflict and uncertainty are those associated with role conflict and uncertainty (ambiguity). For a review, see M. Van Sell, A. P. Brief, and R. S. Schuler, "Role Conflict and Role Ambiguity: Integration of the Literature and Directions for Future Research," *Human Relations* 34 (1980): 43–72; S. E. Jackson and R. S. Schuler, "A Meta-analysis and Conceptual Critique of Research on Role Ambiguity and Role Conflict in Work Settings," *Organizational Behavior and Human Decision Processes* 36 (1985): 16–78.

25. For more discussion of the relationship between feedback and performance, see "The Components of Effective Performance Appraisal," Special Release No. 5 Copyright © 1977, Life Office Management Association, New York, N.Y. Reprinted with permission. See also R. J. Burke, W. Weitzel, and T. Weir, "Characteristics of Effective Employee Performance Review and Development Interviews: Replications and Extensions," *Personnel Psychology* 4 (1978): 903–19; J. Annett, *Feedback and Human Behavior: The Effects of Knowledge of Results, Incentives, and Reinforcement on Learning and Performance* (Baltimore: Penguin, 1969); C. Camman, D. A. Nadler, and P. H. Mirvis, *The Ongoing Feedback System: A Tool for Improving Organizational Management* (Ann Arbor, Mich.: Survey Research Center, University of Michigan, 1975); T. R. Mitchell, M. Rothman, and R. C. Liden, "Effects of Normative Information on Task Performance," *Journal of Applied Psychology* (Feb. 1985): 66–71; B. L. Davis and M. K. Mount, "Design and Use of a Performance Appraisal Feedback System," *Personnel Administrator* (Mar. 1984): 91–107.

26. For extensive descriptions of attribution theory in performance appraisal, see S. G. Green and T. R. Mitchell, "Attributional Processes of Leaders in Leader-Member Interactions," *Organizational Behavior and Human Performance* 23 (1979): 429–58; T. R. Mitchell, S. G. Green, and R. E. Wood, "An Attributional Model of Leadership and the Poor Performing Subordinate: Development and Validation," in *Research in Organizational Behavior*, vol. 3, ed. L. L. Cummings and B. M. Staw (Greenwich, Conn.: JAI Press, 1981); D. R. Ilegn and J. M. Feldman, "Performance Appraisal: A Process Focus," in *Research in Organizational Behavior*, vol. 5, ed. B. M. Staw and L. L. Cummings (Greenwich, Conn.: JAI Press, 1983); D. N. Campbell, R. L. Fleming, and R. C. Grote, "Discipline Without Punishment at Last," *Harvard Business Review* (July–Aug. 1985): 162–78; D. Cameron, "The When, Why, and How of Discipline," *Personnel Journal* (July 1984): 37–39; R. D. Arvey, G. A. Davis, and S. M. Nelson, "Use of Discipline in an Organization: A Field Study," *Journal of Applied Psychology* (Aug. 1984): 448–60; R. C. Liden and T. R. Mitchell, "Reactions to Feedback: The Role of Attributions," *Academy of Management Journal* (June 1985): 291–304; J. Brockner and J. Guare, "Improving the Performance of Low Self-Esteem Individuals: An Attributional Approach," *Academy of Management Journal* (Dec. 1983): 642–56; D. Tjosvold, "The Effects of Attribution and Social Context on Superiors' Influence and Interaction with Low Performing Subordinates," *Personnel Psychology* (Summer 1985): 361–76.

27. J. E. Belohlav and P. O. Papp, "Making Employee Discipline Work," *Personnel Administrator* (Mar. 1978): 22–24; H. Behrend, "Absence Problems—Are Attendance Bonus Schemes the Answer?" *Management Decisions* 18(4) (1979): 212–16; F. E. Kuzmits, "No Fault: A New Strategy for Absenteeism Control," *Personnel Journal* (May 1981): 387–90; J. M. McDonald, "What Is Your Absenteeism I.Q.?" *Personnel* (May–June 1980): 33–37; M. Cavanagh, "In Search of Motivation," *Personnel Journal* (Mar.

1984): 76–82; R. F. Tyler, "Motivate the Older Employee," *Personnel Journal* (Feb. 1984): 60–61; J. Brewer and C. Dubnicki, "Relighting the Fires with an Employee Revitalization Program," *Personnel Journal* (Oct. 1983): 812–18; S. M. Jacoby, "Progressive Discipline in American Industry: Origins, Development, and Consequences," in *Advances in Industrial and Labor Relations*, vol. 3, ed. D. Lewin and D. B. Lipsky (Greenwich, Conn.: JAI Press, 1986).

28.   Note, however, that many programs to control absenteeism are not effective: D. W. and S. Markham, "Absenteeism Control Methods: A Survey of Practices and Results," *Personnel Administrator* (June 1982): 79. See also the reply to this article: M. Greller, *Personnel Administrator* (Sept. 1982): 8, 10. For general discussion of absenteeism and turnover costs and strategies to deal with them, see F. E. Kuzmits, "The Impact of a Legalistic Control Policy upon Selected Measures of Absenteeism Behavior," paper presented at the Academy of Management Meeting, Eastern Division, May 1981; "Job Absence and Turnover," Bureau of National Affairs Quarterly Report, 2d quarter 1981, Washington, D.C.; D. R. Dalton, "Absenteeism and Turnover: Measures of Personal Effectiveness," in *Applied Readings in Personnel and Human Resource Management*, ed. R. S. Schuler, J. M. McFillen, and D. R. Dalton (St. Paul: West, 1981), pp. 20–38; D. Scott and S. Markham, "Absenteeism Control Methods: A Survey of Results and Practices," *Personnel Administrator* (June 1982): 73–83; L. W. Porter and R. M. Steers, "Organizational, Work, and Personal Factors in Employee Turnover and Absenteeism," *Psychological Bulletin* 80 (1973): 151–76; R. M. Steers and S. R. Rhodes, "Major Influences on Employee Attendance: A Process Model," *Journal of Applied Psychology* 63 (1975): 391–407; C. R. Deitsch and D. A. Dilts, "Getting Absent Workers Back on the Job: The Case of General Motors," *Business Horizons* (Fall 1981): 52–58, G. P. Latham, L. L. Cummings, and T. R. Mitchell, "Behavioral Strategies to Improve Productivity," *Organizational Dynamics* (Winter 1981): 5–23; C. R. Deitsch and D. A. Dilts, "To Cut Casual Absenteeism: Tie Benefits to Hours Worked," *Compensation Review* (First Quarter 1981): 41–46; T. E. Hall, "How to Estimate Employee Turnover Costs," *Personnel* (July–Aug. 1981): 43–52; R. E. Kopelman, G. O. P. Schneller IV, and J. J. Silver, Jr., "Parkinson's Law and Absenteeism: A Program to Rein in Sick Leave Costs," *Personnel Administrator* (May 1981): 57–64; M. Lasder, "Cut Turnover with a Japanese Pattern," *Computer Decisions* (Sept. 1981): 135–40, 144–48; J. S. Piamonte, "An Employee Motivational System that Leads to Excellent Performance," *Personnel* (Sept.–Oct. 1980): 55–66; H. Bekiroglu and T. Gonen, "Labor Turnover: Root, Costs, and Some Potential Solutions," *Personnel Administrator* (July 1981): 67–72; M. Rothman, "Can Alternatives to Sick Pay Plans Reduce Absenteeism?" *Personnel Journal* (Oct.

1981): 788–90; F. Luthans and M. Martinko, "An Organizational Behavior Modification Analysis of Absenteeism," *Human Resource Management* (Fall 1976): 11–18; E. F. Jackofsky and L. H. Peters, "Job Turnover Versus Company Turnover: Reassessment of the March and Simon Participation Hypothesis," *Journal of Applied Psychology* (Aug. 1983): 490–95; E. F. Jackofsky, "Turnover and Job Performance: An Integrated Process Model," *Academy of Management Review* (Jan. 1984): 74–83; G. M. McEvoy and W. F. Cascio, "Strategies for Reducing Employee Turnover: A Meta-Analysis," *Journal of Applied Psychology* (May 1985): 342–56.

29.   L. S. Mosher, "Preventing Poor Past Practices from Becoming Future Policies," *Personnel Administrator* (Mar. 1978): 19–20; W. R. Flynn and W. F. Stratton, "Managing Problem Employees," *Human Resource Management* (Summer 1981): 31; D. A. Nadler and E. E. Lawler, "Motivation—A Diagnostic Approach," in *Perspectives on Behavior in Organizations*, ed. J. R. Hackman, E. E. Lawler, and L. W. Porter (New York: McGraw-Hill, 1977).

30.   D. N. Campbell, R. L. Fleming, and R. C. Grote, "Discipline Without Punishment—at Last," *Harvard Business Review* (July–Aug. 1985): 170.

31.   E. J. Busch, Jr., "Developing an Employee Assistance Program," *Personnel Journal* (Sept. 1981): 708–11; M. Douglass and D. Douglass, "Time Theft," *Personnel Administrator* (Sept. 1981): 13; H. J. Featherston and R. J. Bednarek, "A Positive Demonstration of Concern for Employees," *Personnel Administrator* (Sept. 1981): 43–47; C. A. Filipowicz, "The Troubled Employee: Whose Responsibility?" *Personnel Administrator* (June 1979): 17–22, 33; R. C. Ford and F. S. McLaughlin, "Employee Assistance Programs: A Descriptive Survey of ASPA Members," *Personnel Administrator* (Sept. 1981): 29–35; R. T. Hellan and W. J. Campbell, "Contracting for AEP Services," *Personnel Administrator* (Sept. 1981): 49–51; R. W. Hollman, "Beyond Contemporary Employee Assistance Programs," *Personnel Administrator* (Sept. 1981): 37–41; F. E. Kuzmits and H. E. Hammons II, "Rehabilitating the Troubled Employee," *Personnel Journal* (Apr. 1979): 238–42, 250; H. Z. Levine, "Consensus," *Personnel* (Mar.–Apr. 1981): 4–10; R. Richklefs, "Firms Offer Employees A New Benefit: Help in Personal Problems," *Wall Street Journal* 13 Aug. 1979, pp. 1, 21; L. B. Sager, "The Corporation and the Alcoholic," *Across the Board* (June 1979): 79–82; P. A. Stroberl and M. J. Schneiderjans, "The Ineffective Subordinate: A Management Survey," *Personnel Administrator* (Feb. 1981): 72–76. For a discussion on employee assistance programs, see J. T. Wrich, *Guidelines for Developing an Employee Assistance Program* (New York: American Management Associations, 1982); F. Dickman and W. G. Emener, "Employee Assistance Programs: Basic Concepts, Attributes, and an Evaluation," *Personnel Administrator* (Aug. 1982): 55–66; W. G. Wagner, "Assisting Em-

ployees with Personal Problems," *Personnel Administrator* (Nov. 1982): 59–64; T. Rendero, "Employee Assistance Programs," *Personnel* (July–Aug. 1981): 53–57.

32. For an excellent discussion of the application of discipline in organizations, see R. D. Arvey and J. M. Ivancevich, "Punishment in Organizations: A Review, Propositions, and Research Suggestions," *Academy of Management Review* 5 (1980): 123–32; W. C. Hammer and D. W. Organ, *Organizational Behavior: An Applied Psychological Approach* (Dallas, Tex.: Business Publications, 1978), p. 73–88; R. J. Hart, "Crime and Punishment in the Army," *Journal of Personality and Social Psychology* 36 (1978): 1456–71; J. P. Muczyk, E. B. Schwartz, and E. P. Smith, *First and Second Level Supervision* (Indianapolis: Bobbs-Merrill, 1980); H. P. Sims, Jr., "Further Thought on Punishment in Organizations," *Academy of Management Review* 5 (1980): 133–38; R. J. House and M. L. Baetz, "Leadership: Some Empirical Generalizations and New Research Directions," in *Research in Organizational Behavior*, vol. 2, ed. B. Staw (Greenwich, Conn.: JAI Press, 1980); G. R. Oldham, "The Motivational Strategies Used by Supervisors: Relationships to Effectiveness Indicators," *Organizational Behavior and Human Performance* 15 (1976): 66–86. Additional considerations in dealing with performance problems are presented in Chapter 14, especially the use of termination as a way of correcting performance gaps; P. C. Cairo, "Counseling in Industry: A Selected Review of the Literature," *Personnel Psychology* (Spring 1983): 1–18; C. J. Benfield, "Problem Performers: The Third Party Solution," *Personnel Journal* (Aug. 1985): 96–101; L. A. Schumacher, "How to Help Victims of Domestic Violence," *Personnel Journal* (Aug. 1985): 102–5.

33. "Handling Drug Abuse in the Workplace," *Bulletin to Management*, 29 Aug. 1985, p. 72; R. Discenza and H. L. Smith, "Is Employee Discipline Obsolete?" *Personnel Administrator* (June 1985): 175–86; J. Walls, "Preventing Employee Theft," *Management Review* (Sept. 1985): 48–50.

34. The following assessment discussion relates to aspects of the total PAS generally. Specific parts of the PAS are discussed but not in detail. For a detailed discussion of some parts, see F. Landy and J. Farr, "Performance Ratings," *Psychological Bulletin* 87 (1980): 72–107; F. Landy, J. L. Barnes-Farrell, R. J. Vance, and J. W. Steele, "Statistical Control of Halo Error in Performance Ratings," *Journal of Applied Psychology* 65 (1980): 501–6. See also Chapter 6.

35. M. Sashkin, "Appraising Appraisal: Ten Lessons from Research for Practice," *Organizational Dynamics* (Winter 1981): 37–50.

36. See Sashkin, "Appraising Appraisal," p. 40.

37. *Fair Employment Practices Guidelines*, no. 210 (1), 1983, pp. 3–4.

38. In addition to Sashkin, "Appraising Appraisal," see Kavanagh, "Evaluating Performance," pp. 204–10. See also B. McAfee and B. Green, "Selecting a Performance Appraisal Method," *Personnel Administrator* (June 1977): 61–64; M. E. Schick, "The Refined Performance Evaluation Monitoring System: Best of Both Worlds," *Personnel Journal* (Jan. 1980): 47–50; M. Beer, R. Ruh, J. A. Dawson, B. B. McCaa, and M. J. Kavanagh, "A Performance Management System: Research, Design, Introduction, and Evaluation," *Personnel Psychology* 3 (1978): 505–35; V. R. Buzzotta and R. E. Lefton, "How Healthy Is Your Performance Appraisal?" *Personnel Administrator* (Aug. 1978): 48–51; *Personnel Administrator* (July 1978): 43–46; J. M. McFillen and P. G. Decker, "Building Meaning into Appraisal," *Personnel Administrator* (June 1978): 75–84.

39. Landy, Barnes-Farrell, Vance, and Steele, "Statistical Control of Halo Error."

40. Beer, "Performance Appraisal"; and Kavanagh, "Evaluating Performance"; Carroll and Schneier, *Performance Appraisal.*

41. R. I. Lazar, "Performance Appraisal: What Does the Future Hold?" *Personnel Administrator* (July 1980): 69–73; A. M. Morrison and M. E. Kranz, "The Shape of Performance Appraisal in the Coming Decade," *Personnel* (July-Aug. 1981): 12–22.

42. R. S. Schuler and I. C. MacMillan, "Gaining Competitive Advantage through Human Resource Management Practices," *Human Resource Management* (Autumn 1984): 248–62.

43. R. L. Taylor and R. A. Zawacki, "Trends in Performance Appraisal: Guidelines for Managers," *Personnel Administrator* (Mar. 1984): 71–79; C. G. Banks and K. R. Murphy, "Toward Narrowing the Research-Practice Gap in Performance Appraisal," *Personnel Psychology* (Summer 1985): 335–46.

44. Carroll and Schneier, *Performance Appraisal.*

45. L. L. Cummings, "Compensation, Culture, and Motivation: A Systems Perspective," *Organizational Dynamics* (Winter 1984): 33–43.

8

Total Compensation

Because of their emphasis on short-term financial performance, many high-technology companies have created serious productivity and performance problems for American industry. Many high-technology companies use foreign subcontractors to produce their components, or enter into partnerships with foreign companies to produce items overseas that were designed and marked in the U.S. In some instances, design, engineering, and complete manufacturing operations are being moved overseas. This trend can, and must, be reversed if we are to retain our country's high-technology industry.

Many top managers believe high-technology companies need to emphasize longer-term performance priorities such as efficient and cost-

effective manufacturing, practical and marketable technology, and U.S. production of items designed for use in this country. However, it is also imperative that we change the values and culture of organizations to emphasize sustained high quality, productivity, and profit performance. One important tool will be management compensation programs that are designed to help organizations attain both short-term and long-term performance priorities.

There is solid evidence that the design of management compensation programs is directly related to sustaining the effective financial performance of high-technology organizations.

Source: From J. R. Schuster, "Compensation Plan Design," *Management Review* (May 1985: 21–22).

The preceding "PHRM in the News" illustrates two significant points about total compensation in organizations. The first is that high-technology companies tend to emphasize short-term rather than long-term performance. Many managers believe that this practice is to the companies' detriment. A second point is that this situation can be turned around by changing compensation programs in organizations, because compensation influences organizational survival, profitability, and competitiveness.

Other issues in total compensation are important: How are wages really determined? How do we know when people are paid fairly? How do we decide the wage rate for a given individual? Also to be considered are the legal issues surrounding total compensation, particularly regarding pay for different jobs. One specific issue is whether the Equal Pay Act applies to pay for employees with different yet similar jobs (i.e., jobs of comparable worth). The issue of comparable worth is likely to be a highly visible compensation topic for the rest of the 1980s. This chapter addresses important issues in compensating employees. Other total compensation issues are addressed in the next two chapters.

What is Total Compensation?

Specifically, **total compensation** is the activity by which organizations evaluate employee contributions in order to distribute fairly direct and indirect

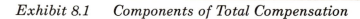

Exhibit 8.1   *Components of Total Compensation*

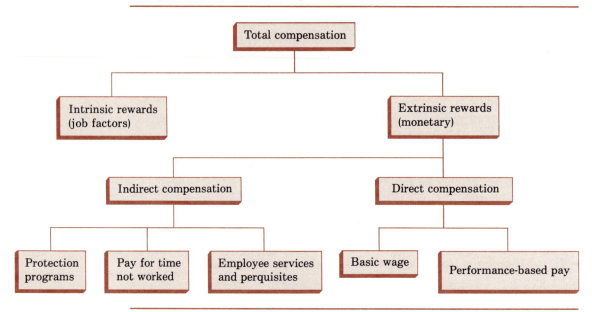

Source: Adapted from J. F. Sullivan, "Indirect Compensation:
The Years Ahead," © 1972 by the Regents of the University of
California. From *California Management Review* vol. XV, no. 2,
p. 65, table 1 by permission of the Regents.

monetary and nonmonetary rewards within the organization's ability to pay
and within legal regulations.[1]

As Exhibit 8.1 indicates, the two categories of **direct compensation** (rewards) are the *basic wage* and *performance-based pay*, and the three categories of **indirect compensation** (rewards) are *protection programs, pay for time
not worked*, and *employee services and perquisites*.[2] This chapter and the
next discuss direct compensation; indirect compensation is discussed in
Chapter 10.

Purposes and Importance of Total Compensation

Total compensation is important because of several major purposes it can
serve:

- *To attract potential job applicants.* In conjunction with the organization's
  recruitment and selection efforts, the total compensation program can
  help assure that pay is sufficient to attract the right people at the right
  time for the right jobs.
- *To retain good employees.* Unless the total compensation program is perceived as internally equitable and externally competitive, good employees
  (those the organization wants to retain) are likely to leave.

- *To motivate employees.* Many employers seek to be productive and have a motivated work force. Total compensation can help produce a motivated work force by tying rewards to performance (i.e., by having an element of productivity incentive).

- *To administer pay within legal regulations.* Because several legal regulations are relevant to total compensation, organizations must be aware of them and avoid violating them in their pay programs.

- *To facilitate organizational strategic objectives.* The organization may want to create a rewarding and competitive climate, or it may want to be an attractive place to work so that it can attract the best applicants. Total compensation can attain these objectives and can also further other organizational objectives, such as rapid growth, survival, and innovation, as shown in the initial "PHRM in the News."[3]

- *To reinforce and define structure.* The compensation system of an organization can help define the organization's structure, status hierarchy, and degree to which people in technical positions can influence those in line positions.

Although serving these purposes is important, the importance of total compensation is highlighted by the fact that approximately 50 percent of an organization's costs are those of compensation. Furthermore, an ever-growing percentage of these compensation costs is going to indirect rather than direct compensation. In addition, failure to abide by the legal regulations can be costly for an organization:

> EEOC said Allstate will pay $5 million to 3,000 women, in addition to changing its system of compensation. "The $5 million in backpay has been placed in a nonrevertible trust fund and will be distributed to women who were employed as sales agents between June 21, 1975, and Oct. 1, 1984, under the old compensation system. The longer the individual worked under the system, the more her share of the backpay will be," EEOC said.[4]

The ability that compensation has in attracting, retaining, and motivating individuals is related to the importance that money has for many people. Money is able to satisfy many employee preferences. Because money, in both direct and indirect forms, has the potential to serve several preferences, and because individuals differ in the importance and type of their preferences, money can take on varying degrees of importance.[5] However, employees are often willing to join an organization and perform in it for reasons other than money alone.[6] They are often willing to perform for nonmonetary rewards that an organization may offer, such as job status and prestige, job security, safety, job responsibility, and variety.[7] As shown in Exhibit 8.2, these are all status symbols, social rewards, or task-self rewards. Although these rewards can be critical, this chapter and the next two chapters primarily discuss monetary rewards, direct and indirect, which are usually regarded as the major part of compensation in most organizations and can be extremely varied, as shown in Exhibit 8.2. Keep in mind the value of nonmonetary rewards, however, especially when the benefits of monetary rewards start to diminish.[8]

Exhibit 8.2   *Organizational Rewards*

Monetary Rewards, Including Fringe Benefits		Status Symbols	Social Rewards	Task-Self Rewards
Pay	Medical plan, including free physical examinations	Office size and location	Friendly greetings	Interesting work
Pay raise				Sense of achievement
Stock options		Office with window	Informal recognition	
Profit sharing	Company auto		Praise	Job or more importance
Bonus plans	Pension contributions	Carpeting	Smile	Job variety
Christmas bonus	Product discount plans	Drapes Paintings	Evaluative feedback	Job-performance feedback
Provision and use of company facilities	Vacation trips	Watches	Compliments	Self-recognition
	Theater and sports tickets	Rings	Nonverbal signals	Self-praise
Deferred compensation, including other tax shelters	Recreation facilities	Formal awards/ recognition	Pat on the back	Opportunities to schedule own work
	Reserved company parking	Wall plaque	Invitations to coffee/lunch	Working hours
Pay and time off for attending work-related training programs and seminars	Work breaks		After-hours social gatherings	Participation in new organizational ventures
	Sabbatical leaves			
	Club memberships and privileges			Choice of geographical location
	Discount purchase privileges			Autonomy in job
	Personal loans at favorable rates			
	Free legal advice			
	Free personal financial planning advice			
	Free home protection—theft insurance			
	Burglar alarms and personal protection			
	Moving expenses			
	Home purchase assistance			

Source: P. M. Podsakoff, C. N. Greene, and J. M. McFillen, "Obstacles to the Effective Use of Reward Systems," in *Readings in Personnel and Human Resource Management*, 3d ed., ed. R. S. Schuler, S. A. Youngblood, and V. Huber (St. Paul: West, 1987).

Relationships Influencing Total Compensation

No other PHRM activity has more relationships with other PHRM activities and the internal and external environment than total compensation. Exhibit 8.3 illustrates these relationships, along with several administrative issues and processes in total compensation.

Relationships, Administrative Issues, and   *Exhibit 8.3*
Processes of Total Compensation

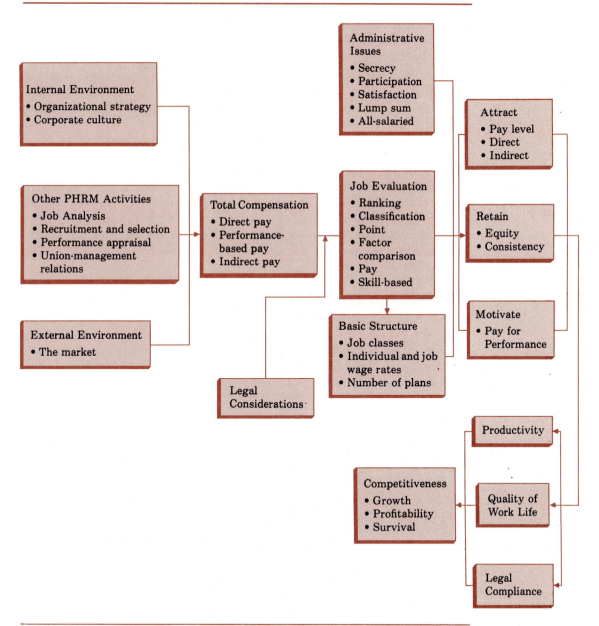

Relationships with Other PHRM Activities

Total compensation relies extensively on other PHRM activities (e.g., job analysis and performance appraisal for input in determining total compensation) and is influenced by other PHRM activities, such as job analysis.

Job Analysis.   Compensation is integrally related to job analysis. The job evaluation process that determines the relative worth of jobs is based largely on how the job is described in the formal job description. Job evaluation influences, along with the job analysis, the basic compensation structure for the organization, including the job classes and individual and job wage rates. Job analysis comes under scrutiny in discussions of the comparable worth issues, as described later in this chapter.

Recruitment and Selection.   Employees differ in the value they put on pay. If PHRM departments can determine how important pay is to individuals, they can recruit people to fill specific jobs with specific pay policy options. Some jobs could be interesting but pay modestly; other jobs could be dull but pay well. Individuals could then be recruited and selected on the basis of their job and pay values. Apparently, however, to attract and retain even the best applicants, maximum pay levels (i.e., the most competitive) need not be offered. Individuals make job choice decisions on the basis of several factors, including the location of the organization, its reputation as a place to work, what friends think of the company, and the nature of the job and the pay level offered. Consequently, rather than taking the job that pays the most, individuals often take the job that satisfies or does as well as possible across all these factors.[9]

Performance Appraisal.   Perhaps the most important relationship for individuals in the organization is that between compensation and performance appraisal. Especially where performance-based pay exists, the results of the performance evaluation are significant. Without the ability to measure performance (based on attributes, behaviors, or outcomes) in a reliable and valid way (see Chapter 6), linking such an important reward as pay to the results may lead to diminished motivation and lowered performance. (Conditions appropriate for performance-based pay are discussed in Chapter 10.) Where promotions are available, the performance evaluation system can have added significance to the extent that promotion is a reward for performance.[10]

Union-Management Relations.   Unions and associations have had a major impact on wage structures, wage levels, and individual wage determinations regardless of whether specific organizations organized. This impact is present from the early stages of job analysis and job evaluation to the final determination of specific wage rates and the selection of the criteria used to set those roles. Although unions generally do not conduct job evaluation programs, in many instances they do help design, negotiate, or modify company programs. Even if union interests are not completely served in the job evaluation process, they can be served at the bargaining table. Serving the interests of members at the bargaining table puts job evaluation into perspective for the union as well as for the management.

Final wage levels are reached on the relative power of the union and management. Individual wage determinations are generally not of concern to the union. The union philosophy is that all employees on the same job are doing essentially the same work and therefore should be paid the same. That philosophy and collective bargaining appear to have paid off for individual members. Unionized employees' wages have generally been higher than the wages of employees without collective bargaining, especially where the unions are strong.[11]

Since 1978 the trend toward higher pay and benefit demands by unions has slowed dramatically, largely because of the serious financial difficulties of organizations and the need to survive. Conditions have become so severe in several industries that workers have voted to take pay cuts as a consequence of take-back negotiations between the union and management. Further discussion of this trend toward productivity and concessionary bargaining is presented in Chapter 16.

Relationships with the Internal Environment

As the initial "PHRM in the News" describes, total compensation is increasingly being influenced by aspects within the organization.

Organizational Strategy.   Compensation can be integral to an organization's strategic planning. A manufacturer of a line of technology-based products developed a new strategic vision of itself as a leader in new technologies. Since accomplishing this goal could have proved disruptive to the current business (located on the East Coast), the company decided to acquire small entrepreneurial companies in the Sun Belt. The parent company quickly realized that these smaller companies required different management styles and a different pay system. Consequently, the general managers' base salary in these small companies compared with the parent company is lower, but the potential size of their annual bonus is four times greater.[12]

An organization may also have a human resource policy that has a direct impact on compensation. For example, it may decide to be the pay leader in an area. If the planning activity identifies shortages of personnel, or at least potential shortages, the compensation level could be adjusted to attract more individuals. Or it may decide to pay below the market (area) average but provide a large package of indirect compensation to increase company loyalty and retention rates of employees. Or it may decide to change the focus of employee performance from the short term to the long term, as described in the initial "PHRM in the News." This change in focus is often made by modifying performance-based pay plans such that long-term rather than short-term criteria are used. Which is better or more appropriate depends on the nature of the business. Where the market conditions dictate short-term concerns for survival, compensation based on short-term criteria should be used. Where market conditions dictate long-term concerns for survival, compensation based on long-term criteria should be used.[13] Naturally, the choices here are not just short-term or long-term criteria. As discussed at the end of the chapter, many choices are involved. As a result, an organization that has several businesses is likely to have several different compensation systems or plans:

> Large banks now employ people not only in regular commercial banking functions but also in managing investments, in handling corporate mergers and acquisitions, on bond and currency trading, and in support functions like data processing. To a degree each of these areas has its own unique character. Facing so much diversity, the banks are having to abandon the effort to have only a single compensation system. A money center bank now is likely to have at least five distinguishable systems: one providing salary alone, another hourly pay, a third pay by work accomplished, a fourth stressing commissions, and a fifth combining limited salary with potentially large bonuses. Employees of the bank earn widely disparate amounts of money, based partly on their functions and partly on the pay system in which they participate.[14]

Corporate Culture. Compensation systems in organizations can influence employee behavior. They can also be used to determine what values, attitudes, and styles are described by the organization. Of these, what and how an organization may choose to influence are in part determined by corporate culture. For example, an organization can use compensation practices to create a human-resource-oriented culture, an entrepreneurial culture, an innovative culture, or a competency-based culture. Because these cultures influence employee values, attitudes, and styles as well as behavior, an organization must be systematic in articulating its compensation practices with its desired culture.[15]

Relationships with the External Environment

The Market. Both union and management base final wage rates and levels on far more than the results of job evaluation and wage surveys, although both often rely on wage surveys. The surveys are used to determine wage rates for comparable work in other sections of the industry and wages paid in the locality or the relevant labor market. Although many organizations use wage survey results to help set pay levels for jobs, organizations should be aware that paying what the market will bear, paying women and minorities less because they are willing to accept less, is no excuse for wage discrimination (*Marshall* v. *Georgia Southwestern College,* 1981). Nonetheless, paying one employee more than another for the same job is not necessarily illegal if market conditions differ for the two employees. An example of such a case is illustrated in the following "PHRM in the News" on *Winkes* v. *Brown University.*

In addition to the market wage levels, other criteria for wage determinations are labor market conditions (the number of people out of work and looking for work), traditions and past history of the organization's wage structure, fringe benefits, indexes of productivity, company profit figures or turnover data, the Consumer Price Index and the Urban Workers' Family Budget figures, both of which help determine cost-of-living increases, and investors. Through their concern for the earnings per share of stocks, investors, particularly pension fund managers buying stocks of corporations,

Pay Raises to Match Competing Bids Do Not Violate the Equal Pay Act

The US Court of Appeals for the First Circuit (Boston) has held that raising the pay of a female professor to match a competing offer made by another university does not violate the Equal Pay Act, even though a male professor in the same department was paid less for performing the same job.

In *Winkes vs. Brown University,* No. 83-1649 (1st Cir. Oct. 26, 1984), Brown University awarded the female professor a $7,000 salary increase, thus matching the competing offer made by another university, while granting the male professor a $1,500 increase.

The court noted that Brown University had a history of matching competing offers, and held that the disparity in pay that resulted in this case was the result of a reasonable decision to try to retain the services of a qualified employee.

Impact: A defense to an Equal Pay Act violation may be raised when the disparity in pay is the result of an attempt to retain an effective employee by matching a competing salary offer.

In the Brown University case, the university had a history of matching such offers in order to retain faculty members. Such a history would be additional evidence that the disparity in pay was due to a factor other than sex.

Of course, when such practices exist, if they are used solely or predominately in favor of retaining male employees and not female employees, the value of the defense will be significantly diminished.

have a significant influence on the short-term versus long-term focus of compensation:

> For nearly two decades, compensation committees measured performance on the basis of earnings per share. Most concerned themselves with keeping salaries competitive, protecting employees from the ravages of inflation, and giving executives the greatest after-tax benefits at the least cost to the corporation. And they used bonuses both to reward performance and to help management cope with the rising cost of living. When the stock market ceased to reflect improved earnings per share and stock incentives became less valuable, committees sought to find new forms of payment schemes, such as performance-unit and performance-share plans. These, too, were largely based on earnings per share, but few challenged the validity of this performance measure.[16]

Today the earnings-per-share criterion for evaluation is coming under close scrutiny. A shift of investor focus away from this criterion could be instrumental in designing compensation plans with a long-term focus, as described in the initial "PHRM in the News."

In determining wage rates, the market can be used directly or indirectly. Used directly, the market provides comparisons for organizations to facilitate their establishing pay rates for benchmark jobs. The rates of these jobs in turn are used to establish pay rates for all other jobs. When used indirectly, organizations first perform a job evaluation on their existing jobs, then establish pay grades and classes (or families) and then go to the market to see what other organizations are paying. Whether used directly or indirectly, however, the market rates are generally not the ones used by an organization. The final rates generally represent a composite of market rate information and answers to pay policy questions such as: Does the organization want to be a pay leader? What can the organization afford? For what does the organization want to pay: job content, seniority, performance, or cost of living?[17] In most organizations, these are usually the central issues in basic wage determination.

Legal Considerations in Total Compensation

As with many of the PHRM activities, several state and federal laws and court decisions are important legal considerations in total compensation.

Davis-Bacon and Walsh-Healey Acts

The federal government has imposed several laws influencing the level of wages that employers may pay, pay structures, and individual wage determinations. The first federal law to protect the amount of pay employees received for their work was the Davis-Bacon Act of 1931, which requires organizations holding construction contracts with federal agencies to pay laborers and mechanics the prevailing wages of the locality in which the work is performed. The Walsh-Healey Public Contracts Act of 1936 extended the Davis-Bacon Act to include all federal contracts exceeding $10,000 and specified that pay levels conform to the industry minimum rather than the area minimum, as specified in Davis-Bacon. This has since been modified so that the area minimum can be used to establish pay levels. The Walsh-Healey Act also established overtime pay at one and one-half times the hourly rate. These wage provisions, however, do not include administrative, professional, office, custodial, and maintenance employees or beginners and handicapped persons.

Fair Labor Standards Act

Partially because Davis-Bacon and Walsh-Healey were limited in their coverage to employees on construction projects, the Fair Labor Standards Act of 1938 (or the Wage and Hour Law) was enacted. The FLSA set minimum wages, maximum hours, child labor standards, and overtime pay provisions for all workers except domestic and government employees. A recent Supreme Court decision, however, extended the coverage of the FLSA to include state and local government employees (*Garcia* v. *San Antonio Metropolitan Transit Authority*, 1985). A 1974 amendment also specified revisions in the minimum wage, which was .25 per hour in 1938 and $3.35 today. By the year 2006 the minimum wage and other wages are likely to be substantially different:

> By the year 2006, just a few years from now, the minimum hourly wage will exceed $12.50. Secretaries will be making $60,000 per year or more. MBAs with little or no experience will start at more than $120,000 per year. MBAs coming straight out of school will start at the 50 percent tax bracket—assuming, of course, that the maximum tax on earned income is not increased. Of course, by then it will cost more than $6 to ride the subway in New York City, and a local telephone call will be $1.50. But the very fact that people are earning more and paying higher taxes is part of the future of the compensation manager.[18]

The overtime pay provisions of the FLSA established who is to be paid overtime for work and who is not. Most employees covered by the FLSA must be paid time and a half for all work exceeding forty hours per week. These are called **nonexempt employees.** Several groups of individuals are exempt from both overtime and minimum wage provisions. These **exempt employees** include employees of firms not involved in interstate commerce, employees in seasonal industries, and outside salespeople. Three other employee groups—executives, administrators, and professionals—are also exempt from overtime pay and minimum wage laws in most organizations. Trainee managers and assistant managers, however, are excluded and should thus be paid overtime.

Failure to abide by these laws can be costly. In 1982 Howard Johnson agreed to pay more than $5 million in back wages to settle a suit brought two years earlier by the Labor Department. The back pay went to manager trainees and assistant managers who, the department charged, had not been paid one and one-half times normal pay for overtime—any hours exceeding forty in one week. The award affects more than five thousand employees in about nine hundred Howard Johnson's and Ground Round restaurants in the United States.

Several state laws also influence wages paid to employees and the hours they can work. Thirty-nine states have minimum wage laws covering intrastate employees and other employees not covered by federal laws. Although many states at one time had laws limiting the number of hours women could work, the number of states with these laws has now declined to about ten.

Wage Deduction Laws

Three other federal laws influence how much employers may deduct from employee paychecks. The Copeland Act of 1934 authorized the secretary of labor to regulate wage deductions for contractors and subcontractors doing work financed in whole or in part by a federal contract. Essentially, the Copeland Act was aimed at illegal deductions. Protection against a more severe threat from an employer with federal contracts was provided in the Anti-Kickback Law of 1948. The Federal Wage Garnishment Law of 1970 also protects employees against deductions to pay for indebtedness. It provides that only 25 percent of one's disposable weekly earnings or thirty times the minimum wage, whichever is less, can be deducted for repayment of indebtedness.

Antidiscrimination Laws

Several federal antidiscrimination laws passed since 1960 also influence individual wage determination. They are the Equal Pay Act of 1963, the Civil Rights Act of 1964, and the Age Discrimination in Employment Act of 1967. Because the Equal Pay Act is administered and enforced by the Equal Employment Opportunity Commission (EEOC), the EEOC has also issued a set of guidelines presenting its interpretation of the Equal Pay Act.[19]

The Equal Pay Act prohibits sex-based compensation discrimination; specifically, it prohibits an employer from discriminating

> between employees on the basis of sex by paying wages to employees . . . at a rate less than the rate at which he pays wages to employees of the opposite sex . . . for equal work on jobs the performance of which requires equal skill, effort and responsibility, and which are performed under similar working conditions.

Four exceptions, however, can be used to legally defend unequal pay for equal work, as specified in the Bennett amendment: the existence and use of a (1) seniority system, (2) merit system, (3) system that measures earnings or quality of production, or (4) any additional factor other than sex. To establish a *prima facie* case of wage discrimination, the plaintiff needs to establish that a disparity in pay exists for employees on equal jobs. If the employer can show the existence of one or more of the four exceptions, however, the differential may be found to be justified.

Based on several cases, the following are some conclusions of how the courts have interpreted the Equal Pay Act:

- *Substantially equal work* is all that's required to invoke the Equal Pay Act. Skills, effort, and responsibilities need not be identical. But skills, effort, and responsibility an employee never exercises on the job don't qualify that employee for higher wages.
- *Titles don't count for much,* either. It's not what you call an employee, it's the nature of the job that matters. Courts will compare work actually done, not the window dressing.
- *Working conditions* are defined as surroundings (fumes, toxic chemicals, etc.) and hazards (physical dangers).
- *Wages include* all the fringe benefits that go into an employee's total compensation.
- *You can't cure an equal pay violation* by freezing or lowering the wages of the higher paid sex. The lower wages must be raised—always.
- *Employees exempt under FLSA* (of which the Equal Pay Act is part) are not necessarily exempt under equal pay law. Don't fall into the trap of thinking your executives, administrators, and professionals aren't covered.
- *Temporary reassignment at a higher rate of pay* is acceptable under the Act, but it begins to look suspicious after about a month. So either reassign the employee permanently or split up the work.
- *Trainees can be paid different wages* only if they participate in a bona fide training program.
- *Only employees in a single "establishment"* must be compared for Equal Pay Act purposes. Different branches, subsidiaries, and so on, can maintain different salary scales for similar positions so long as one establishment is not the exclusive (or nearly exclusive) preserve of one, higher paid sex. But claims of wage

discrimination brought under Title VII are not so limited, according to the Ninth Circuit US Court of Appeals.

- *Don't forget to keep records.* Discussing compliance with fair employment laws and not mentioning recordkeeping would be a serious oversight. To justify differences in wages between men and women, you have to have the written records—job descriptions, job evaluations, and minimum wage and overtime information.
- *Union involvement in wage scales* is another topic that must be mentioned. It's illegal for unions to force on employers wage rates that violate the Equal Pay Act. But bear in mind, it's still you, the employer, who will have to foot the bill for violations, since it is the employer who pays the wages.
- *Back-pay awards can be doubled* if a court finds an employer guilty of intentional discrimination.
- *Men can sue* under the Equal Pay Act, too.[20]

Under Title VII of the Civil Rights Act of 1964 it is an unlawful employment practice for an employer

> to fail or refuse to hire or to discharge any individual, or otherwise to discriminate against any individual with respect to his compensation, terms, conditions or privileges of employment, because of such individual's . . . sex [or to] limit, segregate, or classify his employees or applicants for employment in any way which would deprive or tend to deprive any individual of employment opportunities or otherwise adversely affect his status as an employee because of such individual's . . . sex.

Although Title VII coverage and Equal Pay Act protection appear to overlap, or have the potential to do so, Title VII coverage may be thought of as providing broader protection. An example of this and some other differences between Title VII and the Equal Pay Act is presented in the discussion of comparable worth.

Although both the Equal Pay Act and Title VII are meant to ensure that employees with similar seniority, performance, and background doing the same work are paid the same, regardless of sex, age, race, national origin, or religion, the practice in organizations suggests that employees are still being paid differentially because of sex and race. Several reasons are used to explain this differential. Outright discrimination where women on the same job are paid less than men is one reason. Another reason is that women work in jobs that are valued less (based on job evaluation results) than those jobs in which men work. This notion has given rise to the issues of **comparable worth** and the demand for equal pay for jobs of comparable value. Note that the Equal Pay Act provides legal coverage only for equal pay for equal work unless differences exist in performance, seniority, or other conditions. The Civil Rights Act of 1964, however, provides broader legal coverage for pay discrimination, as demonstrated by *County of Washington, Oregon* v. *Gunther* (1981) and *AFSCME* v. *State of Washington* (1983).

Comparable Worth

Since the topic of comparable worth, or pay equity, is so frequently mentioned and is likely to be a significant compensation issue for the rest of the

1980s, it deserves a separate discussion. The heart of the comparable worth theory is the contention that while the "true worth" of jobs may be similar, some jobs (often held by women) are paid at a lower rate than others (often held by men). The resulting differences in pay that are disproportionate to the differences in the true worth of jobs, therefore, amounts to wage discrimination. Consequently, legal protection should be provided in these cases, according to the comparable worth advocates.[21]

The courts, however, have thus far been reluctant to rule in any consistent way on comparable worth. In *County of Washington, Oregon* v. *Gunther,* the Supreme Court ruled that the women prison guards suffered pay discrimination not because they were being paid less than male prison guards doing the same work but because they were being paid at a rate lower than male guards vis-á-vis the prison's job evaluation results. That is, the job evaluation results indicated that the two guard jobs were different (they were given different point values), but in relation to their separate evaluations, the women were being paid at a lower percentage rate of their job evaluation than the men. The women were being paid at approximately 70 percent of their job evaluation value, while the men were being paid at approximately 90 percent.

The *Gunther* decision meant that the Supreme Court would prefer not to decide if pay discrimination exists based on the notion of comparable worth. The Court indicates that making this decision would require extensive expertise in job evaluation—expertise more likely found in organizations than in the Court. The Court, however, will still rule on pay discrimination cases, and individuals or groups can file discrimination cases under either the Equal Pay Act or Title VII of the Civil Rights Act of 1964. When filing under Title VII, the equal job requirements of the Equal Pay Act needn't be satisfied. That is, pay discrimination can still be determined when different and unequal jobs are being considered, as in *Gunther.* What has to be shown in a Title VII case, however, is proof of *intentional* discrimination. In cases under the Equal Pay Act, only the *effect* (that is, that pay rates differ for the same job) has to be demonstrated.

In *AFSCME* v. *State of Washington,* the district court ruled that the state had systematically paid jobs dominated by females less than the value indicated by the results of job evaluation. A consulting firm had conducted a job evaluation study in the early 1970s, but the state did not entirely follow the results in setting the final wage rates of females and males, as described in the following "PHRM in the News." As a consequence, the court ruled that the state must pay back wages to the victims of the practices. In 1985, however, the circuit court reversed the decision of the district court. In 1986 an out-of-court settlement was reached.

Although the courts have been inconsistent in their rulings on comparable worth, several state and local governments and unions have passed comparable worth or pay equity legislation, as described in the following "PHRM in the News." However, comparable worth plans have made few inroads in the private sector:

> Standard Oil of Indiana monitors its job-evaluation procedures but insists that "we do have pay equity." Wells Fargo & Co. says that "we haven't had any pay-

Comparable Worth: Disaster Or Pay Equality?

Most state governments are expected to consider comparable worth legislation covering their workers in the next two or three years, according to a survey conducted by the Council of State Governments.

The survey notes that four states—Washington, Idaho, New Mexico and Minnesota—have already taken steps to equalize pay levels between predominantly female jobs and comparable male jobs.

In 1983, Minnesota became the first state to adopt a comparable worth plan and has approved a biennial appropriation of $21.8 million for comparable worth raises.

Washington appropriated $1.3 million in fiscal 1984 to begin increasing the salaries of employees whose salary ranges were below the "comparable worth line" in 1982.

Iowa plans to complete its pay equity adjustments by 1987, and New Mexico has increased the salary rate for 23 low-paid, female-dominated jobs through an appropriation measure.

In contrast, four other states—Colorado, Florida, Missouri and Nebraska—defeated comparable worth bills in 1984, and the Pennsylvania legislature tabled a comparable worth bill after public hearings.

The Council's survey further noted that comparable worth studies have been commissioned by 22 states.

In Minnesota, the pay equity system is being implemented over four years and is estimated to cost only 4% of the state's personnel budget. The State of Washington, however, faces potential liability in the hundreds of millions of dollars if a court decision in favor of AFSCME is upheld on appeal.

In *AFSCME vs. State of Washington*, 578 F. Supp. 846 (W.D. Wash. 1983), appeal to Ninth Circuit pending, the district court ruled that the state violated Title VII by paying women employees lower wages than employees in male dominated jobs requiring equivalent skill, effort, and responsibility.

A 1974 comparable worth study commissioned by the State revealed a 20% wage disparity between traditionally male and female job classifications, and the State Civil Service developed a comparable worth wage scale setting the wages the female workers should receive.

In 1983, the State Legislature appropriated $1.5 million to implement the comparable worth wage schedule and pledged to eliminate sex-based wage disparities by 1993.

However, the court held that class members were entitled to immediate relief and rejected the state's argument that an immediate raise and backpay award would impose a crushing financial burden.

The court concluded that the state had failed to rectify an acknowledged discriminatory disparity in compensation and that its budget constraints were an inadequate justification for further delay in implementing the remedy.

Impact: At present, comparable worth remains largely an issue restricted to public sector employment. In addition to Washington, court cases have been brought in Missouri, Michigan and California on behalf of state employees.

Also, national legislation will probably be introduced again this year regarding pay equity for federal government employees. This momentum will likely affect the private sector if comparable worth becomes an accepted means of addressing sex-based wage gaps.

More importantly, employers, whether private or public, should not commission pay studies unless they intend to comply with the results immediately.

Depending on the outcome of the Washington case on appeal, employers face the potential requirement of immediate payment for sex-based wage disparities determined by such pay studies.

Source: B. S. Murphy, W. E. Barlow, and D. D. Hatch, *Personnel Journal,* April 1985, p. 21. Reprinted with the permission of PERSONNEL JOURNAL, Costa Mesa, California; all rights reserved.

related problems." Ralston-Purina tries to keep "abreast of the issue." But San Francisco's Amfac Inc., a diversified concern, hires a pay consultant to make sure that the "french-fry cooker in Portland is paid the same as a sugar-cane worker in Hawaii."

The concept booms in the public sector. More than 30 states are doing job studies or adjusting salaries of mostly female jobs to align them with comparable jobs held by men. But corporations "are looking at it with a jaundiced eye. It would be a horrendous task," says a New York recruiter.

It's controversial: A Deere & Co. spokesman says "we'd prefer not to be involved in a discussion of that issue."[22]

Basic Wage Issues

Among basic wage issues are four that represent most activities in many compensation departments: (1) determination of the value of jobs—job evaluation, (2) determination of job classes, (3) establishment of pay structures, and (4) individual wage determinations.

Job Evaluation

Job evaluation is important when organizations are concerned about establishing internal equity among the different jobs in the organization. The amount paid for a job could be decided on the basis of a manager's impression of what the job should pay or is worth, but to help ensure internal equity, more formal methods are often used.[23] After jobs are formally evaluated, they are grouped into classes, families, or grades. Within each class, jobs are then arranged in order of importance, and ranges of pay are established with the aid of wage surveys. Job evaluation and job classes, then, are critical elements in determining pay structure.

Although organizations offer rewards to individuals on the basis of their job performance and personal contributions, "organizations implicitly recognize job-related contributions by assigning pay in accordance with the difficulty and importance of jobs."[24] To do so, most organizations use some type of formal job evaluation or informal comparisons of job content for determining the relative worth of job-related contributions. However, usually only in the formal job evaluation process are job-related contributions explicitly specified. Job evaluation is the comparison of jobs by the use of formal and systematic procedures to determine their relative worth within the organization.[25]

Job evaluation has four essential steps. The first step is a thorough job analysis (see Chapter 3). This step provides information about the job duties and responsibilities and about employee requirements for successful performance of the job.

The second step is deciding what the organization is paying for—that is, determining which factors will be used to evaluate jobs (although not all methods of job evaluation explicitly use factors). The factors are like yardsticks for measuring the relative importance of jobs. Since these factors help determine what jobs are paid, they are called **compensable factors**. The factors that organizations use vary widely, but they all presumably reflect job-related contributions. Such factors might include accountability, know-how, problem-solving ability, and physical demands. Regardless of the exact factors, the factors chosen should have the following characteristics:

■ Represent all of the major aspects of job content for which the company is willing to pay (compensable factors)—typically skill, effort, responsibility, and working conditions
■ Avoid excessive overlap or duplication
■ Be definable and measurable
■ Be easily understood by employees and administrators
■ Not cause excessive installation or administrative cost
■ Be selected with legal considerations in mind[26]

Since jobs in organizations vary so greatly in their job content, often more than one job evaluation is conducted. Occasionally, the number of job evaluations reflects the number of distinct groups of employees found in the company. These distinct groups often represent operations employees; sales employees; administrative, technical, and supervisory employees; professional employees; management employees; and executives.

After the determination of compensable factors, their relative importance must be decided. The relative importance is reflected by differential points or degrees (weights) assigned to each of the compensable factors. The weights assigned to the factors should be determined by the employer's judgment of the relative importance of the factors to the organization. Exhibit 8.4 provides an illustration of differential weighting.

The third step is to choose and adapt a system for evaluating jobs in the organization according to the compensable factors chosen in the second step. There are many basic methods of job evaluation that organizations can adapt to their own needs. Several job evaluation methods to choose from are discussed next.

Since the fourth step in the process of job evaluation is to decide who will do the job evaluation and use the evaluation methods, examining the operation of job evaluation methods in detail is important. The two common nonquantitative methods of job evaluation are ranking and job classification. The point rating method, Hay Plan, and factor comparison method are more quantifiable.[27] A newer method of job evaluation is called skill-based evaluation.

Since job evaluation is the crux of many of the discussions of equal pay and job comparability, as you read the discussion on job evaluation, think

Exhibit 8.4   *Sample of Point Rating Method*

Compensable Factor	First Degree	Second Degree	Third Degree	Fourth Degree	Fifth Degree
Basic knowledge	15	30	45	60	—
Practical experience	20	40	60	80	—
Complexity and judgment*	15	30	45	60	—
Initiative	5	10	20	40	—
Probable errors	5	10	20	40	—
Contacts with others	5	10	20	40	—
Confidential data	5	10	15	20	25
Attention to functional detail	5	10	15	20	—
Job conditions	5	10	15	—	—

For Supervisory Positions Only

Character of supervision	5	10	20	—	—
Scope of supervision	5	10	20	—	—

*This factor appraises the scope and complexity of the job regarding the consistent variety of functions, their intricacy, and general level of importance. It also appraises the amount of discretion and judgment involved, as measured by the importance of recommendation preliminary or tantamount to decisions. It is frequently referred to as the "headwork" factor.

First Degree: 15 Rating Points

Simple repetitive duties involving little or no choice as to course of action and requiring only commonsense judgment in carrying out detailed instructions.

Second Degree: 30 Rating Points

Routine duties that generally follow a prescribed course of action or involve the application of readily understood rules and procedures. Standard practices restrict independent action and judgment to a limited number of procedural decisions.

Third Degree: 45 Rating Points

Semidiversified work involving a thorough practical knowledge of a restricted field of activity, and involving decisions based on a wide range of procedures and the analysis of facts in situations to determine what action should be taken within the limits of standard practice.

Fourth Degree: 60 Rating Points

Work is diversified and involved. Duties require independent thought and action in working toward general objectives, which in turn may necessitate devising new methods or in modifying or adapting standard principles and practices to new or changed conditions common to administrative, executive, professional, or sales function. Requirement for discretion and judgment in making decisions that in general are based upon precedent or standard operating policies and procedures.

about the issue of true worth and the difficulty in determining it through job evaluation.

Ranking Method.   Job analysis information can be used to construct a hierarchy or ladder of jobs, which reflects their relative difficulty or value to the organization. This is the core of the **ranking method**. Although any number of compensable factors could be used to evaluate jobs, the job analyst often considers the whole job on the basis of just one factor, such as difficulty or value.

This method is convenient when there are only a few jobs to evaluate and when one person is familiar with them all. As the number of jobs increases and the likelihood of one individual knowing all jobs declines, detailed job analysis information becomes more important and ranking is often done by committee. Especially when a large number of jobs are to be ranked, key or benchmark jobs are used for comparison.

One difficulty in the ranking method is that all jobs are forced to be different from each other. Making fine distinctions between similar jobs is often difficult, and thus disagreements arise. One way of avoiding this difficulty is to place jobs into classes or grades.

Job Classification Method.   The **job classification method** is similar to the ranking method, except that classes or grades are established and the jobs are then placed into the classes. Jobs are usually evaluated on the basis of the whole job, often using one factor such as difficulty or an intuitive summary of factors. Again, job analysis information is useful in the classification, and benchmark jobs are frequently established for each class. Within each class or grade, there is no further ranking of the jobs.

Although many organizations use job classification, the largest is the U.S. government, which has eighteen distinct classifications from GS 1 to GS 18 (GS means "general schedule"). The top three classifications are referred to as super grades. GS 11 and above usually denote general management and highly specialized jobs, while GS 5 to GS 10 are assigned to management trainees and lower-level management positions, and GS 1 to GS 4 are for clerical and nonsupervisory personnel.

A particular advantage of this method is that it can be applied to a large number and wide variety of jobs. As the number and variety of jobs in an organization increase, however, the classification of jobs tends to become more subjective. This is particularly true when an organization has a large number of plant or office locations, and thus jobs with the same title may differ in content. Because evaluating each job separately in such cases is difficult, the job title becomes a more important guide to job classification than job content.

A major disadvantage of the job classification method is that the basis of the job evaluations is either one factor or an intuitive summary of many factors. The problem with using one factor, such as difficulty (skill), is that it may not be important on all jobs. Some jobs may require a great deal of skill, but others may require a great deal of responsibility. Does this mean that jobs requiring much responsibility should be placed in a lower classification than jobs requiring much skill? Not necessarily. Perhaps both factors could be considered together. Thus, each factor becomes a compensable factor, valued by the organization. Jobs would be evaluated and classified on the basis of both factors. However, "this balancing of the compensable factors to determine the relative equality of jobs often causes misunderstandings with the employees and the labor leaders."[28] To deal with this disadvantage, many organizations use more quantifiable methods of evaluation.

Point Rating Method.   The most widely used method of job evaluation is the **point rating** or **point factor method,** which consists of assigning point values for previously determined compensable factors and adding them to arrive at a total. The point rating method has several advantages:

1. The point rating plan is widely used throughout industry, permitting comparisons on a similar basis with other firms.
2. The point rating plan is relatively simple to understand and is the simplest of quantitative methods of job evaluation.
3. The point values for each job are easily converted to job and wage classes with a minimum of confusion and distortion.
4. A well-conceived point rating plan has considerable stability: it is applicable to a wide range of jobs over an extended period of time. The greatest assets here are consistency and uniformity and its widespread use throughout industry.
5. The point rating method is a definitive approach requiring several separate and distinct judgment decisions.[29]

The limitations of the point rating method are few, but an especially critical one is the assumption that all jobs can be described with the same factors. Many organizations avoid this limitation by developing separate point rating methods for different groups of employees. Exhibit 8.4 shows eleven compensable factors used by one organization to evaluate the jobs in supervisory, nonsupervisory, and clerical categories. The exhibit also shows a description of what is associated, by degree and points, with one of the factors (complexity and judgment), and sets forth the specifications for the degrees or levels within that factor. Some factors are more important than others, as shown by the different point values. For example, the second degree of practical experience is worth four times as much as the second degree of job conditions. Each job is evaluated only on its compensable factors. The PHRM department determines which degree of a factor is appropriate for the job. Then, the points assigned to each degree of each factor are totaled. Levels of compensation are determined on the basis of the point totals. The description provided on complexity and judgment is similar to that written on all of the compensable factors.

As with other job evaluation plans, the point factor method incorporates the potential subjectivity of the job analyst. As such it has the potential for wage discrimination. Bias or subjectivity can enter (1) in the selection of the compensable factors, (2) in the relative weights (degrees) assigned to factors, and (3) in the assignment of degrees to the jobs being evaluated. At stake here are equal pay and job comparability. To make sure its point factor evaluation system is free from potential bias and is implemented as objectively as possible, an organization may solicit the input of the job incumbent, the supervisor, and job evaluation experts as well as its PHRM department.[30]

Hay Plan.   Exhibit 8.5 shows a method with only three general factors. This method, generally known as the **Hay Plan,** is a widely used method for evaluating managerial and executive positions. The three factors—mental activity, know-how, and accountability—are used because they are assumed to be the most important aspects of managerial and executive positions. Although the Hay Plan appears to use only three factors, in a practical sense there are eight: three subfactors in know-how, two in mental activity, and three in accountability. In deriving the final point profile for any job, however, only the three major factors are assigned point values.

Factor Comparison Method.   The point rating method, regardless of the number of factors and degrees of each factor, derives a point total for each job. Several very different types of jobs can have the same total points. After the total points are determined, jobs are priced—often according to groups or classes, similar to the job classification method. The **factor comparison method** avoids this step between point totaling and pricing by assigning dollar values to factors and comparing the amounts directly to the pay for benchmark jobs. In short, factor comparison is similar to point rating in that both use compensable factors. But the point method uses degrees and points for each factor to measure jobs, whereas factor comparison uses benchmark jobs and money values on factors.

The "price" or wage rates for the benchmark jobs are determined by the market.[31] Although this is a quick method by which to set wage rates, it has the potential to perpetuate the traditional pay differentials between jobs because the wage rates for other jobs are determined against these jobs. Because the process of determining the rates of other jobs is in the hands of the wage and salary analyst, it can be subjective, furthering the potential for wage discrimination.[32] As such, it has come under attack from the job comparability advocates for claims of pay discrimination.

Skill-based Evaluation.   Whereas the first five job evaluation plans "pay for the job," **skill-based evaluation** is based on the idea of "paying for the person." As such, this type of evaluation is concerned with employee skills and in developing training programs to facilitate employee skill acquisition.[33] This type of evaluation is also called "pay for knowledge."

The idea of paying for the person, or at least for the person-job combination rather than for just the job, is not new. Many professional organizations (e.g., universities, law offices, and research and development labs) have been doing this for a long time. What is new, however, is paying for the person in blue-collar jobs:

> Honeywell Inc. and TRW Inc. try "skills-based pay" at some plants. Workers are paid according to the number of skills they master. "The more you know, the more you make," says a TRW boss. Honeywell and Dana Corp. experiment with "gainsharing." At 25 Dana plants, everyone from the plant manager to the floor sweeper share in any savings from productivity increases that lower base costs. The best plans pay bonuses of 22% a month.

Exhibit 8.5   *Hay Plan Compensable Factors*

Mental Activity (Problem Solving)	Know-How	Accountability
The amount of original, self-starting thought required by the job for analysis, evaluation, creation, reasoning, and arriving at conclusions	The sum total of all knowlege and skills, however acquired, needed for satisfactory job performance (evaluates the job, not the person)	The measured effect of the job on company goals

Mental Activity has two dimensions:

- The degree of freedom with which the thinking process is used to achieve job objectives without the guidance of standards, precedents, or direction from others
- The type of mental activity involved; the complexity, abstractness, or originality of thought required

Mental Activity is expressed as a percentage of Know-How for the obvious reason that people think with what they know. The percentage judged to be correct for a job is applied to the Know-How point value; the result is the point value given to Mental Activity.

Know-How has three dimensions:

- The amount of practical, specialized, or technical knowledge required
- Breadth of management, or the ability to make many activities and functions work well together; the job of company president, for example, has greater breadth than that of a department supervisor
- Requirement for skill in motivating people

Using a chart, a number can be assigned to the level of Know-How needed in a job. This number—or point value—indicates the relative importance of Know-How in the job being evaluated.

Accountability has three dimensions:

- Freedom to act, or relative presence of personal or procedural control and guidance; determined by answering the question, How much freedom has the job holder to act independently?—for example, a plant manager has more freedom than a supervisor under his or her control
- Dollar magnitude, a measure of the sales, budget, dollar value of purchases, value added, or any other significant annual dollar figure related to the job
- Impact of the job on dollar magnitude, a determination of whether the job has a primary effect on end results or has instead a sharing, contributory, or remote effect

Accountability is given a point value independent of the other two factors.

Note: The total evaluation of any job is arrived at by adding the points (not shown here) for Mental Activity, Know-How, and Accountability.

Employees at New England Electric System, a Massachusetts utility, will get a 3% bonus this year if certain goals are met. Instead of annual merit raises, some concerns give top workers fat boosts sooner; low performers wait longer and get less, says Towers, Perrin, Forster and Crosby, New York consultant.[34]

Skill-based evaluation plans are based on a starting rate given to all new employees. After coming on board, employees are advanced one pay grade for each job they learn. Jobs can be trained in any order and at any price. Members of each employee's team ensure that the jobs are learned correctly. They decide when the employee has mastered a job. Employees reach the top pay grade in the plant after learning all jobs.

Determining Job Classes

Once the job evaluations are conducted, and before salaries are determined, job classes or families are created. Job families or classes may be created using the results from a single job evaluation or several (if several are used based upon job differences referred to earlier). Determining **job classes** or **job families** means grouping together all jobs that are similar in value—for example, grouping all clerical jobs together or grouping all managerial jobs together. The jobs within the same class may be quite different, but they should be about equal or comparable in value to the organization. All jobs in each class are assigned one salary or range of salaries.

Why group jobs into classes? One reason is efficiency of salary administration. Also, if job classes are not created, justifying the small differences in pay that might exist between jobs can be difficult. Finally, small errors that occur in evaluating the jobs can be eliminated in the classification process. Employees can, however, find fault with the classification results if their jobs are grouped with jobs they believe are less important. Sometimes the jobs that are grouped together are too dissimilar. This may occur because too few classes of jobs are used. Using only a few classes is appropriate, however, if many of the jobs in the organization are of similar value. When a wide range of job value is used, too few job classes may lead to employee complaints of inequity.[35]

Once the job evaluation has been conducted and job families established, the job structure is essentially completed. The last two wage issues are the establishment of the pay structure and individual wage rate determination.

Establishing the Pay Structure

Although job classes are determined for establishing wage rates, job classes are often based on wage rates that have already been established. This practice may seem somewhat bizarre, but it is common in organizations. Most organizations are already paying their employees and thus need to determine job classes only when many new jobs are introduced or if the organization has never had a sound job analysis program. In addition, if the organization has grown and incorporated many more jobs, it may need to group them into classes for salary administration. Alternatively, an organization that is just being established is most likely small, and the price of its jobs would be determined by surveys of what other organizations are paying. Regardless, wage surveys are a critical component in establishing the pay structure.

Wage and Salary Surveys.   As discussed earlier, the market, along with other factors, can influence the wage rates established by the organization. The market exerts this influence when the organization conducts wage and salary surveys.

Wage surveys can be used to develop compensation levels, wage structures, and even payment plans (the amount and kind of direct and indirect compensation). Whereas job evaluation helps ensure internal equity, wage surveys provide information to help ensure external equity. Both types of equity are important if an organization is to be successful in attracting, retaining, and motivating employees. In addition, survey results can also be used to indicate compensation philosophies of competing organizations. For example, a large electronics company may have a policy of paying 15 percent above the market rate (the average of all rates for essentially the same job in an area); a large service organization may choose to pay the market rate; a large bank may decide to pay 5 percent less than the market rate.

Most organizations use wage surveys extensively. Separate surveys are published for different occupational groupings; thus, many larger organizations subscribe to several surveys.[36] For example, there are surveys for clerical workers, professional workers, managers, and executives. Separate surveys are conducted not only because such wide differences exist in skill levels but also because labor markets are so different. An organization surveying clerical workers may need to survey companies only within a ten-mile radius, whereas a survey of managerial salaries may cover the entire country.[37]

Once the survey data are collected, the organization must decide how to use them. The organization needs to decide whether to use only the average wage and salary levels from all the companies in the survey to determine its own wage and salary levels or whether to weight the wage and salary levels of companies by the number of employees.[38] The organization must also decide if it is going to use the wage and salary ranges from all the companies to determine its own wage and salary ranges. After deciding upon the wage and salary information it wants, the organization develops a grade structure with pay rates for job categories.

Grade Structure.   Exhibit 8.6 shows a typical example of a grade structure. This grade structure is based on job evaluation points associated with a point-factor evaluation. The boxes shown are associated with a range of job evaluation points (the job class) and a range of pay (the pay grade).[39] In essence, these **pay grades** are the job families or classes. Consequently, several different jobs may be within one box, but they are similar in job evaluation points, if not in content. The boxes vary in shape but generally ascend from left to right. This reflects increased job worth and associated higher pay levels (shown on the vertical axis) for more valued jobs. The pay levels are established using market information (to help ensure external equity).[40]

The wage rate for each job is then determined by locating its grade and moving over to a point on the vertical axis, as done for Job A in grade II. A pay limit exists for the jobs in each grade. Staying within those limits (the **salary range**) is essential to maintaining internal equity, assuming the job evaluation is valid.[41] For employees to obtain a significant salary increase,

*Establishing a Grade Structure Based on
Job Evaluation*   *Exhibit 8.6*

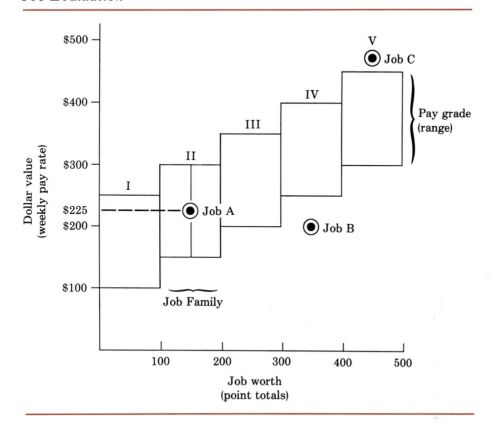

they must move into a job in the next higher grade. However, an employee can also receive a pay raise within a given grade. Generally, each job has a rate range. As shown, Job A has a range from $150 per week to $300 per week. The midpoint of this range is $225.[42] These numbers can become critical. Many organizations would like to have the average salary of employees in a job equal the midpoint. If the average is higher than the midpoint, employees might no longer receive significant salary increases without being promoted.

Occasionally, jobs are found that fall outside the established pay grades (Jobs B and C in Exhibit 8.6). When a job falls *below* the established pay grade, it is circled, and usually a wage adjustment (sweetener) is made to bring the job within the established pay grade. Sometimes, though, a job will be overpaid (Job C in pay grade V). One means of dealing with this is to circle the job. That is, as long as the current incumbent remains in the job, the pay rate remains unchanged. But when the incumbent leaves the job, the rate will be adjusted downward to put the job back in the established grade. Sometimes the entire salary structure has to be adjusted upward to bring jobs within established pay grades, thereby moving the midpoints up for all pay grades. Initially, an employee may start at the bottom of the range and go up. How quickly the employee's wages rise will depend on factors related to individual wage determination.

Individual Wage Determination

Once the job analysis and job evaluation have been completed, the job classes established, and the wage structure determined, the issue of how much to pay each individual arises. For example, consider Ann and John, both of whom work on the same job. The rate range is $1,500 to $2,000 per month; Ann is paid $2,000 and John $1,750. What might account for the pay differential? Although performance contribution is perhaps the logical answer, seniority, market demand, age, experience, and appearance (personal contributions) have also been found to influence individual wages. Age and seniority are frequently perceived as important factors.[43]

In actuality, individual wage determinations are based on both personal contributions and performance. Thus, age and seniority as well as performance probably influence Ann's and John's pay. (Merit pay is discussed in Chapter 9.) Even though managers might argue that pay differences based on performance are more equitable, many Japanese companies, for example, reward seniority more than performance.[44]

But if performance is the criterion, is it past, current, or future performance? Many employees are given raises on the basis of their performance potential; however, athletes are usually paid on the basis of last year's performance (this is not true for certain sports, such as race-car driving, tennis, and horse racing). But several difficulties arise in giving merit raises based on past performance. One difficulty is employees' perceptions of their performance. Ann and John, like many people, are apt to rate their performance in at least the top 50 percent. Using performance as the sole explanation for the pay differential may therefore upset John—unless he has a significantly lower level of performance, knows it, and accepts it. More issues related to paying for performance are discussed in Chapter 9.

The answer to the question of how much to pay Ann and John can be as varied as the number of people answering the question. Compensation managers should also ask questions such as: What does the rest of my compensation program look like? What was the initial understanding or contract with Ann and John? and Can I defend my decisions? Overall, defensibility and consistency are perhaps the two most important aspects of compensation management. Regardless of the method used or the decision reached, criticism from others will always take place. But being able to defend the decision and show that it is consistent with others goes a long way in reducing criticism. With criticism at low levels, compensation managers are then able to consider other issues in wage and salary administration.

Issues in Wage and Salary Administration

Among the several contemporary issues in wage and salary administration are four of particular importance: (1) To what extent should employees be able to participate in choosing their forms of pay and in setting their own wages? (2) What are the advantages and disadvantages of pay secrecy? (3) What is needed for employees to be satisfied with their pay? and (4) Should all employees be salaried? More administration issues are addressed in Chapters 9 and 10.

Participation Policies

For many employees, total compensation generally represents a mixture of direct salary and indirect benefits. These indirect benefits may represent as much as 45 percent of total compensation, but employees generally have no choice as to what indirect benefits they receive. Management defends this policy on the grounds that it ensures that employees have the proper benefits, and a cost advantage is involved in buying the same benefits for all employees.[45] Yet the proliferation of indirect pay arrangements has created a kind of smoked-glass effect through which the recipient's attitudes and desires can be seen only vaguely, if at all. Employees often receive costly benefits they neither want nor need and, in many cases, do not even know about. Even in cases where employees know they are receiving particular forms of compensation, they tend to undervalue the benefits.

What are the alternatives? The popular form of participation for employees is the **flexible compensation approach,** in which individuals select the items they want from a variety of compensation "entrées." Another form incorporates employee-management negotiations on compensation levels and forms.

Because the flexible compensation approach allows individuals to make some pay decisions, employees are more likely to be satisfied with their compensation package. Allowing employees to participate in the compensation package also helps increase their understanding of what they are receiving from the organization. This approach has generally restricted participation to initial decisions on the proportion and type of direct and indirect benefits.

A newer method of employee participation is allowing employees to set their own wage rates. One way of doing this is to let employees vote on who should get a raise. At Romac, a pipe-fitting plant in Seattle, Washington, employees request their pay raises by completing a form that includes information about their current pay level, previous raise, the raise requested, and reasons why they think a raise is deserved. The employee then "goes on board." His or her name, hourly wage, and photograph are posted for six consecutive working days. The employees then vote, and the majority rules. Although top-level managers can't vote, they can veto a raise. This, however, hasn't happened yet, since management has learned that employees can responsibly set their own wages if they trust management and have a sufficient understanding of the "cost of doing business."[46]

Pay Secrecy

According to organizational etiquette, asking others their salaries is generally considered gauche. In a study of E. I. du Pont de Nemours, all employees were asked if the company should disclose more payroll information so that everyone would know everyone else's pay. Only 18 percent voted for an open pay system.

Nevertheless, some companies practice open salary administration because they believe it is right to do so. For example, the Polaroid Corporation has established a pay-level structure for its exempt salaried employees and, in keeping with its policy of openness, involves those employees in making salary decisions. Employees are also involved in the job evaluation process to get a broad understanding of the process by which job value is established.[47]

Satisfaction with Pay

If organizations want to minimize absenteeism and turnover through compensation, they must make sure that employees are satisfied with their pay. Since satisfaction with pay and motivation to perform are not necessarily highly related, organizations must know the determinants of pay satisfaction. With this knowledge, organizations can develop pay practices more likely to result in satisfaction with pay. Three major determinants of satisfaction with pay are pay equity, pay level, and pay administration practices.

Pay Equity.   Pay equity refers to what people believe they deserve to be paid in relation to what others deserve to be paid. The tendency is for people to determine what they and others deserve to be paid by comparing what they give to the organization with what they get out of the organization. In comparing themselves with others, people may decide whether they are being paid fairly. If they regard this comparison as fair or equitable, they are more likely to be satisfied. If they see this comparison as unfair, they are likely to be dissatisfied.

Pay Level.   Pay level is an important determinant of the perceived amount of pay. People use this perception and compare it with what they believe they should receive. The result of the comparison is satisfaction with pay if the "should" level of pay equals the actual level of pay. Pay dissatisfaction results if the actual level is less than the "should" level.

Pay Administration Practices.   What does the preceding discussion suggest for pay administration practices? First, if the employer is to attract new employees and keep them satisfied with their pay, the wages and salaries offered should approximate the wages and salaries paid to other employees in comparable organizations (i.e., external equity must exist).[48]

Second, the pricing of jobs can enhance pay satisfaction when it is perceived as embodying a philosophy of equal work or equal pay for jobs of comparable worth. The determination of equal pay for equal work can be aided by sound job evaluations. But the worth of jobs must be evaluated according to the factors considered most important by the employees and the organization (so that internal equity exists).

Third, pay-for-performance systems must be accompanied by a method for accurately measuring the performance of employees and must be open enough so employees can clearly see the performance-pay relationship.[49] This is expanded further in Chapter 9.

Fourth, compensation rates and pay structures should be continually reviewed and updated if necessary. Over time the content of a job may increase or decrease, thus distorting the relationship between its true worth and its job-evaluated worth.

A final pay administration practice is trust and consistency. Employees must perceive that the organization is looking out for their interests as well as its own. Without trust and consistency, pay satisfaction is low and pay becomes a target for complaints regardless of the real issues.

All-salaried Work Force

Although some evidence indicates that all employees prefer to be salaried rather than paid on an hourly basis, most organizations distinguish their employees by method of pay. That is, salary status is usually reserved (along with a parking space) for management, and nonmanagement employees (except clerical workers) are usually paid on an hourly basis.

Still, some organizations put all their employees on salary. IBM has had an all-salaried work force since the 1930s. Eaton Corporation is using the all-salary concept in its newer plants, along with throwing out the time clocks. Some employees may abuse being on salary (for example, they can come in late or miss a day and still be paid), but overall the all-salary concept awards employees more mature treatment and a sense of trust by management.

Though little hard evidence supports the effectiveness of the all-salaried concept, it appears to be a practical way to increase productivity and quality of work life—two measures by which to assess total compensation.[50]

Trends in Total Compensation

Compensation is a dynamic, challenging, and exciting PHRM activity. It is also a valuable activity for positively influencing the bottom line of organizations as illustrated by the following description of three trends in compensation. Chapters 9 and 10 provide further descriptions of compensation trends.

Assessing Total Compensation

The six major purposes of total compensation should be used to assess how effectively an organization administers its compensation program:

- Attract potentially qualified employees
- Motivate employees
- Retain qualified employees
- Administer pay within legal constraints
- Facilitate organizational strategic objectives
- Reinforce and define structure

To attain these purposes, employees generally need to be satisfied with their pay. This means that the organization's pay levels should be extremely competitive, that employees should perceive internal pay equity, and that the compensation program should be properly administered.[51] It also means that compensation practices must adhere to the various state and federal wage and hour laws. It suggests that the notion of comparable worth be considered in pay administration practices. Consequently, an organization's total compensation can be assessed by comparing its pay levels with other organizations, by analyzing the validity of its job evaluation method, by measuring employee perceptions of pay equity and performance-pay linkages, and by determining individual pay levels within jobs and across jobs. By doing these activities, the strategic objectives of an organization may be facilitated.

Since attracting, motivating, and retaining employees are worthy purposes of total compensation and can facilitate organizational objectives, attaining them at a lower rather than higher cost of total compensation can also facilitate an organization's strategic objectives. This can be done by replacing nondeductible pay expenditures (e.g., expensive perquisites such as cars and club memberships) with deductible pay expenditures, such as contributions to employee stock ownership plans. This replacement must be done with consideration for the differential impact of alternative pay expenditures on attracting, motivating, and retaining employees. These differentials being relatively minimal, replacing nondeductible forms of compensations with deductible forms can increase the effectiveness of the total compensation dollar.

Since total compensation is composed of base pay, performance-based pay and indirect pay, the assessment here of total compensation represents just part of the total assessment. Chapters 9 and 10 are the other two parts necessary for total assessment.

Computer Technology and HRIS in Total Compensation

Computer technology and compensation data in an HRIS can be instrumental in managing total compensation and ensuring equity. The four components of total compensation are direct monetary, indirect monetary, direct nonmonetary, and indirect nonmonetary rewards. In ledger format, personnel can maintain the value of total compensation in several configurations. For example, total compensation can be computed for each employee and the average for each position or department. In addition, specific components of total compensation can be calculated and used for projecting and establishing salary and benefits budgets for appropriate organizational units. In conjunction with job evaluation, the PHRM department can determine whether compensable factors are being assigned monetary values systematically or randomly. This may serve as an initial step in minimizing inequitable compensation.

Performance appraisal information is also related to personnel's compensation function. Based on a particular performance rating, an individual receives a salary increase. Computer technology can link personnel with other departments to facilitate projecting departmental salary budgets. By having each department manager submit projected performance ratings for each employee, personnel can use the computer to project anticipated salary increases associated with performance (assuming salary increases are a function of performance rating). The PHRM department can also estimate salary increases that can be paid on various proposed salary budget increases.[52]

Strategic Involvement of Total Compensation

Gaining Competitive Advantage.   Lincoln Electric is a leader in small motors and arc welders, and has a compensation system tied to the company's profits. This system has resulted in the average Lincoln worker making up to $44,000 a year. In addition to the high motivation to produce, Lincoln workers rarely quit. Their turnover rate is less than 1 percent. The result of Lincoln's compensation system is a cost-efficiency competitive advantage that allows it to price its products below competitors with equal, if not better, quality. Other companies also use their compensation systems strategically. For example, TRW and the Hewlett-Packard Company use compensation to drive their search for innovative products and services.

At Hewlett-Packard, entrepreneurial behavior is stimulated in its project leaders by tying more rewards to their success. Successful project leaders are being given banquets, stock options, and personal computers. At TRW, units or teams are given credit for sales generated in another department in return for helping that department. TRW fosters innovation by stimulating interdependence through its compensation practices. These companies get what they pay for: a steady stream of product and service improvements and enhancements that help them stand alone among their competitors, hence a strong competitive advantage.

Linking with Organizational Strategy.   Many choices are involved in total compensation that link with organizational strategy as shown in Exhibit 1.4. Because of the extensive relationships among the many choices, all are presented here. They include the following:

> Low Base Salaries———High Base Salaries
> Internal Equity———External Equity
> Few Perquisites———Many Perquisites
> Standard, Fixed Package———Flexible Package
> Low Participation———High Participation
> No Incentives———Many Incentives
> Short-term Incentives———Long-term Incentives
> No Employment Security———High Employment Security

One of the first choices is determining the level of base pay, which can range anywhere from low to high. As a part of this choice, companies can choose to pay base pay on an hourly or salary basis. In using an hourly basis, the implication is that employees are not paid for time missed, as they are when paid on a salary basis.

Determining the level of base pay may be influenced in part by another choice for the company: whether to be more concerned with internal equity or with external equity.[53] That is, companies can choose to determine pay rates for jobs that better reflect their relative worth, determined by a company's own internal job evaluation results, or to determine these rates for jobs that better reflect what other companies pay.

Another critical choice is whether to provide few perquisites or many. Though often presented in the context of benefits, companies can also choose to offer varying degrees of flexibility in the total compensation package that employees receive. Companies can choose to offer a standard package of direct and indirect compensation, or they can offer a great deal of variety and flexibility in the mix and value of components in the total compensation package, such as that found in flexible pay programs.

In offering more flexibility in total compensation packages or in just the indirect component, companies are also in part making the choice of how much employee participation to have in compensation. Offering flexibility in compensation is often done so that employees will get what they value. Since employees are the best judge of what they value, having high employee participation along with offering flexibility makes a great deal of sense. Employees can also participate in other aspects of compensation, such as job- or skill-based evaluations and salary increase decisions.[54] Alternatively, companies can choose not to allow any employee participation in compensation. In allowing participation, the company must be ready to provide relevant pay information and abandon any attempts at pay secrecy.

Other compensation choices are whether to provide incentives and, if so, whether they should be short- or long-term based. For example, companies can choose to offer either cash or stock to reward the achievement of short-term goals (less than twelve months) on criteria such as output, sales, or return on capital. Rewards such as incentive stock options (ISOs) or stock appreciation rights (SARs) may be offered for longer-term goal attainment.[55]

A final choice in compensating employees is whether to offer extensive guarantees. This choice is critical but one that excellent companies seem to make in favor of security.[56] Employment security apparently facilitates employee risk taking, longer-term orientations, and greater loyalty and commitment to the company.

Summary

Many pay-related issues are of concern to PHRM managers and others in organizations. One particular issue is comparable worth and its impact on organizations. The notion of comparable worth is that the true value of a job should be used in determining compensation rates. Proponents of comparable worth maintain that compensation rates of jobs presently reflect that men occupy certain jobs and women occupy others. Attaining comparable worth would significantly raise compensation rates and costs but would probably help remove previous wage discrimination. It would also involve some changes in the job evaluation procedures of many organizations.

Although determining a job's true worth is an important concept in comparable worth, it is difficult to measure or determine precisely. True worth can be determined only with great difficulty; using sound job evaluation procedures can enable an organization to move in that direction. Sound procedures, such as using a point factor system, involve (1) using a single set of factors (i.e., just one evaluation system or plan) rather than one for the clerical staff, one for the blue-collar workers, and yet another for the supervisory group; (2) selecting factors that reflect the working environment and the organization's objectives; (3) developing factors and relative weights free of bias; (4) eliminating as much as possible the subjective measurement error in evaluating positions; (5) eliminating bias in the evaluation committee that reviews job evaluation results on jobs; and (6) sustaining an updated system to ensure that factors or evaluations do not become outdated.

Even if true worth is determined precisely, jobs must still be priced. Although job evaluation procedures are important in establishing true worth, they are more relevant to establishing relative job prices than absolute job prices. To help establish absolute job prices, organizations often use market survey data, especially for those jobs that have identical or nearly identical counterparts in the marketplace. Doing market surveys to directly price jobs that are not found in other organizations should be done with caution. It involves subjectivity and therefore is open to potential wage discrimination charges. Organizations should be careful in using market rates to perpetuate wage differentials that are obviously discriminatory. Fair evaluations should be conducted to help reduce that likelihood.

In establishing wages, organizations can rely upon job evaluations and market surveys, and can use inputs from the employees themselves. Apparently, employees can responsibly set their own wages. In the few companies that have tried it, employees have set their own wages without management's having to alter the procedures or change decisions. The method is most successful, however, in organizations where employees and management have mutual trust, and employees are provided with information to help them understand the financial status of the company.

Establishing wages and determining which job evaluation method to use, though important, are only two components of compensation. Other components include selecting the best performance-based pay plan and obtaining benefit from indirect compensation. Chapters 9 and 10 discuss these and other important components of compensation.

Discussion Questions

1. What is the issue of comparable worth, and how is it related to compensation?
2. How can an organization's total compensation package be assessed?
3. How can the true worth of jobs be determined?
4. What is the current dilemma the United States faces regarding export competitiveness and compensation?
5. What forms of pay and rewards make up total compensation?
6. Total compensation is said to be a systemic PHRM function. That is, it has relationships to other functions. Describe and explain the nature of these relationships.

7. Briefly describe the major laws that influence compensation. Could any of these laws conflict with the purposes of total compensation? Explain.

8. What are four basic wage issues that any job evaluation system must address?

9. Assume that you completed a job evaluation for an organization that you are familiar with and you produced an exhibit similar to Exhibit 8.6. How would you answer the following questions about your exhibit: Why have you drawn boxes that rise from left to right? On what basis did you set the bottom and top of the box? Why are there five boxes? Why didn't all of the jobs fall within the boxes? If you decided to give all jobs a ten-dollar per week increase for each of the next twenty-four months, what would happen to your pay structure? Would the structure change if you gave each job a 10 percent increase per week for each of the next twenty-four months? Explain.

10. Designing a total compensation system is one challenge; administering the system is yet another. How do the following issues affect administration: employee participation in the system, pay secrecy, paying for performance versus seniority, perceptions of equity, perceptions of trust and consistency of treatment, and pay satisfaction.

PC Project

Keeping wages and salaries competitive is a critical aspect of total compensation. This PC Project demonstrates the use of market-indexed compensation and the effects of pay compression. A market index represents a company's response to shifts in the labor market and the economy, coupled with the ability to respond to such changes. Pay compression occurs when long-service employees are paid at a level similar to that of new employees. The overall competitiveness of the pay structure is a key element in retaining valued employees. The effects of changes in the pay grade structure can be evaluated.

C	A	S	E	S	T	U	D	Y

Comparable Worth Finds Rockdale

Bill Starbuck was proud to be assigned to the city beat of the *Rockdale Times*. Bill, a newspaper reporter for two years now, was paying his dues at a small-town newspaper, hoping to work his way up to a larger circulation daily. The city beat would mean that Bill could draw on his background in journalism and political science at Wabash College, to write news stories with substance. His prior assignment to the features section of the *Rockdale Times* was interesting but not intellectually stimulating.

Bill's first major assignment was coming up in two days with an invitation to cover a breakfast meeting with the city council. Clyde Langston, Rockdale city manager, would present the revised city budget. Bill prepared for the meeting by calling one of his contacts in the city office for some "inside" information. Bill had been dating Jill Bateman, a secretary to the personnel executive director, and he was confident he could learn something about the breakfast meeting agenda.

As Bill hung up from his call to Jill, he wondered what the rumor of a pay raise for some city employees could mean. If anything, the city was expected to trim its budget because of a slowdown in the local economy and loss of revenues due to the shutdown of two plants in the community within the past year. According to Jill, the rumor was that some of the clerical and administrative staff employees were scheduled for midyear pay adjustments. The figure working the hallways was a 3 percent pay raise, which would come as a pleasant surprise to the ninety-five employees in the administrative-office-clerical positions.

As Bill arrived at the Wednesday morning breakfast meeting, he quickly scanned the room to identify the four city councilmen and one councilwoman. Bill wanted to interview at least three of the members for his story, which was due by 1:00 P.M. After Mayor Jim Earnie arrived, the city council, city manager, and local news reporters finished a quick and cordial breakfast.

Clyde Langston called the group to attention with a rap on his water goblet, and the cordial bantering quickly subsided. Clyde distributed a five-page report of the preliminary budget. Bill quickly scanned the report and noted that $13.7 million total was considerably trimmed down from last year's budget of $16.4 million. Then, as Bill anticipated, Clyde pointed out a $41,000 line item increase in salaries within the pared-down budget.

Clyde proceeded to explain that the city had done an analysis of their 95 administrative-office-clerical positions and their 350 technical-craft positions and decided to make some pay adjustments. All but one of the administrative-office-clerical positions are female, while only 27 of the technical-craft positions are female. The pay range for office workers begins at a low of $5.19 per hour to a high of $11.17 per hour, with an average of $6.30 per hour. The technical-craft jobs begin at $4.83 per hour and max out at $13.85 per hour, with an average of $9.69 per hour. The net effect of the $41,000 increase was to provide about a 3 percent increase to the administrative-office-clerical workers.

Clyde pointed out that a recently conducted job evaluation study had resulted in the merger of the previously separated job families, such that all jobs were to be evaluated on a common set of attributes. Clyde elaborated further that the impetus for this change was to avoid any litigation over the comparable worth issue. After completing the budget review briefing, Clyde offered to answer questions. When the council members sat silently, Jim Earnie thanked the council for their time and adjourned the meeting.

Bill scurried to the door to intercept the council members as they prepared to leave, hoping to get a few reactions to this surprise comparable worth initiative by the city government. Bill caught all five of the city council members and the mayor and proceeded to ask them what they thought of Clyde's proposal for the pay adjustments. Mayor Jim Earnie, along with three of the council members, indicated that they did not understand the rationale for the raises. After Bill questioned them, they even agreed that they thought that the issue deserved some further discussion.

"I did not know we were using that standard," Councilman Jim Maloney said. "If we're applying comparable worth throughout the system, it would be good to know that, and on what basis it's being done."

Councilwoman Marcie Rivera said she was in accord with the approach. "I'm inclined to agree with the way Clyde put it out," she said, "to avoid any problems in discrimination. If that's the concern here, I feel like it's a step in the right direction."

Amazing, thought Bill as he headed to his car with notes in hand. I just attended a city council breakfast meeting to review the upcoming city budget, and comparable worth is proposed by the city manager. And the mayor and city council hardly noticed until after the meeting was adjourned!

Notes

1. Many authors include intrinsic rewards as a part of total compensation. Such rewards, though not monetary, can be successful in attracting, retaining, and motivating employees. For discussions of these issues, see E. E. Lawler III, "The Strategic Design of Reward Systems," in *Readings in Personnel and Hu-*

man *Resource Management* 2d ed., ed. R. S. Schuler and S. A. Youngblood (St. Paul: West, 1984); E. E. Lawler III, *Pay and Organizational Development* (Reading, Mass.: Addison-Wesley, 1981); A. Nash, *Managerial Compensation* (Scarsdale, N.Y.: Working American Institute, 1980); J. R. Hackman and G. R. Oldham, *Work Redesign* (Reading, Mass.: Addison-Wesley, 1980); R. E. Sibson, *Compensation*, rev. ed. (New York: AMACOM, 1981); D. W. Belcher, *Compensation Administration* (Englewood Cliffs, N.J.: Prentice-Hall, 1974); G. T. Milkovich and J. M. Newman, *Compensation* (Plano, Tex.: Business Publications, 1984).

2. The use of divisions is practical because it is then easier to discuss compensation. This is just one way to divide up the components of compensation. For an alternative way, see R. I. Henderson, "Designing a Reward System for Today's Employee," *Business Horizons* (July–Sept. 1982): 2–12; Milkovich and Newman, *Compensation.*

3. For example, see Sibson, *Compensation;* Lawler, "Strategic Design of Reward Systems"; R. M. Tomasko, "Focusing Company Reward Systems to Help Achieve Business Objectives," *Management Review* (Oct. 1982): 8–12; B. R. Ellig, "Gearing Compensation to Market Cycles," *Management Review* (Nov.–Dec. 1982): 17–21; *Elements of Sound Pay Administration* (Berea, Ohio: American Compensation Association and American Society for Personnel Administration, 1981); J. F. Kerr, "Diversification Strategies and Managerial Rewards: An Empirical Study," *Academy of Management Journal* (Mar. 1985): 155–79; G. R. Ungson and R. M. Steers, "Motivation and Politics in Executive Compensation," *Academy of Management Review* (Apr. 1984): 313–24; D. B. Gehrman, "Beyond Today's Compensation and Appraisal Systems," *Personnel Administrator* (Mar. 1984): 21–33. M. A. Von Glinow, "Reward Strategies for Attracting, Evaluating, and Retaining Professionals," *Human Resource Management* (Summer 1985): 191–206; A. Freedman, *The New Look in Wage Policy and Employee Relations* (New York: Conference Board, 1985).

4. *Fair Employment Report,* 8 Oct. 1984, p. 156.

5. Use of the term *preference* implies a conscious selection or indication of what is wanted (but not necessarily needed). V. Vroom, *Work and Motivation* (New York: Wiley, 1964); J. Campbell and R. Pritchard, "Motivation Theory in Industrial and Organizational Psychology," in *Handbook of Industrial and Organizational Psychology,* ed. M. Dunnette (Chicago: Rand McNally, 1976); C. Alderfer, *Existence, Relatedness, and Growth* (New York: Free Press, 1972); W. H. Griggs and S. Manning, "Money Isn't the Best Tool for Motivating Technical Professionals," *Personnel Administrator* (June 1985): 63–78.

6. See Molkovich and Newman, *Compensation.*

7. P. M. Podskoff, C. N. Greene, and J. M. McFillen, "Obstacles to the Effective Use of Reward Systems" in *Readings in Personnel and Human Resource Management,* 3d ed., ed. R. S. Schuler, S. A. Youngblood, and V. Huber (St. Paul: West, 1987).

8. E. E. Lawler III, *Pay and Organizational Effectiveness: A Psychological View* (New York: McGraw-Hill, 1971), p. 35.

9. For a discussion on job choice, see H. A. Simon, "Rational Decision Making in Business Organizations," *American Economic Review* 69 (1979): 493–513; S. Lippman and J. McCall, "The Economies of Job Search: A Survey," *Economic Inquiry* 14 (1976): 155–90; D. P. Schwab, "Recruiting and Organizational Entry," in *Personnel Management,* ed. K. M. Rowland and G. R. Ferris (Boston: Allyn & Bacon, 1982); F. S. Hills and T. Bergmann, "Professional Employees: Unionization Attitudes and Reward Preferences," *Personnel Administrator* (July 1982): 50–54.

10. D. B. Gehrman; "Executive Compensation: Looking to the Long Term Again," *Business Week,* 9 May 1983, pp. 80–83.

11. See Milkovich and Newman, *Compensation;* Sibson, *Compensation;* R. E. Winter, "Pay Raises Start to Shrink, Signaling Possible Long-Term Fall in Inflation," *Wall Street Journal,* 30 June 1982, p. 25.

12. Tomasko, "Focusing Company Rewards," pp. 8–9. See also Lawler, "Strategic Design of Reward Systems"; R. J. Greene and R. G. Roberts, "Strategic Integration of Compensation and Benefits," *Personnel Administrator* (May 1983): 79–86; J. Schuster, *Management Compensation in High Technology Companies* (Lexington, Mass.: Lexington Books, 1984); Lawler, "Strategic Design"; P. Stonich, "The Performance Measurement and Reward System: Critical to Strategic Management," *Organizational Dynamics* (Winter 1984): 45–57; D. B. Balkin and L. R. Gomez-Mejia, "Compensation Practices in High Technology Industries," *Personnel Administrator* (June 1985): 111–23; D. B. Balkin and L. R. Gomez-Mejia, "Determinants of R and D Compensation Strategies in the High Tech Industry," *Personnel Psychology* (Winter 1984): 635–49.

13. D. Q. Mills, *The New Competitors* (New York: Wiley, 1985).

14. Ibid., p. 121.

15. For a more extensive discussion of culture and compensation, see Lawler, "Strategic Design"; J. Kerr and J. W. Slocum, Jr., "Linking Reward Systems and Organizational Cultures," in *Readings in Personnel and Human Resource Management,* 3d ed., ed. R. S. Schuler and S. A. Youngblood (St. Paul: West, 1987); L. L. Cummings, "Compensation, Culture, and Motivation: A Systems Perspective," *Organizational Dynamics* (Winter 1984): 33–44.

16. *Business Week,* 9 May 1983, p. 80.

17. Sibson, *Compensation; Elements of Sound Pay Administration;* B. L. Fielder, "Constructing a Wage and Salary Survey," *Personnel Journal* (Dec. 1982): 879–80.

18. Sibson, *Compensation,* pp. 4–5.

19. 46 Federal Register 43848, 1 Sept. 1981. See also P. S. Greenlaw and J. P. Kohl, "The EEOC's New Equal Pay Act Guidelines," *Personnel Journal* (July 1982): 517–21.

20. *FEP Guidelines*, Jan. 1985, p. 2. This copyrighted material is reprinted with permission of the Bureau of Business Practice, Waterford, CT 06386.

21. For an excellent discussion of Gunther and the entire set of issues in comparable worth, see S. C. Wisniewski, "Achieving Equal Pay for Comparable Worth through Arbitration," *Employee Relations Law Journal* 8 (1982): 236–55; J. S. Lublin, "Big Fight Looms over Gap in Pay for Similar 'Male', 'Female' Jobs," *Wall Street Journal*, 16 Sept. 1982, p. 33; T. Brinks, "The Comparable Worth Issue: A Salary Administration Bombshell," *Personnel Administrator* (Nov. 1983): 37–40; M. F. Carter, "Comparable Worth: An Idea Whose Time Has Come," *Personnel Journal* (Oct. 1981): 792–94; M. Celarier, "The Paycheck Challenge of the Eighties—Comparing Job Worth," *Ms.*, Mar. 1981, pp. 38–44; J. N. Drazin, "Labor Relations," *Personnel Journal* (Sept. 1981): 684; L. N. Gaseway, "Comparable Worth: A Post-Gunther Overview," *Georgetown Law Journal* 69 (1981): 1123–69; B. A. Nelson, E. M. Opton, Jr., and T. E. Wilson, "Wage Discrimination and Title VII in the 1980s: The Case Against 'Comparable Worth'," *Employee Relations Law Journal* (1980): 380–405; D. Thomsen, "Compensation and Benefits," *Personnel Journal* (Apr. 1981): 258–60; "Bias against Jobs Dominated by Women Found by Federal Study on Pay Inequities," *Wall Street Journal*, Sept. 1981, p. 8; *Personnel Administrator* (Apr. 1982); T. A. Mahoney, "Approaches to the Definition of Comparable Worth," *Academy of Management Review* 8 (1983): 14–22; G. G. Milkovich and R. Broderick, "Pay Discrimination: Legal Issues and Implications for Research," *Industrial Relations* 21 (1982): 309–17; *Sex and Salary: A Legal and Personnel Analysis of Comparable Worth* (Alexandria, Va.: American Society for Personnel Administration, 1985); R. Grams and D. P. Schwab, "An Investigation of Systematic Gender-Related Error in Job Evaluation," *Academy of Management Journal* (June 1985): 279–92; D. P. Schwab and D. W. Wichern, "Systematic Bias in Job Evaluation and Market Wages: Implications for the Comparable Worth Debate," *Journal of Applied Psychology* (Feb. 1983): 60–69; R. M. Madigan, "Comparable Worth Judgments: A Measurement Properties Analysis," *Journal of Applied Psychology* (Feb. 1985): 137–47; R. I. Henderson and K. L. Clarke, *Job Pay for Job Worth* (Atlanta, Ga.: Georgia State University, 1985); *Comparable Worth: An Analysis and Recommendation*, A Report of the United States Commission on Civil Rights, June 1985; G. R. Siniscalco and C. L. Remmers, "Comparable Worth in the Aftermath of *AFSCME* v. *State of Washington*," *Employee Relations Law Journal* (Summer 1984): 6–29; W. H. Volz and J. T. Breitenbeck, "Comparable Worth and the Union's Duty of Fair Representation," *Employee Relations Law Journal* (Summer 1984): 30–45; R. Buchele and M. Aldrich, "How Much Difference Would Comparable Worth Make?" *Industrial Relations* (Spring 1985): 222–33.

22. *Wall Street Journal*, 16 Apr. 1985, p. 1. Reprinted by permission of *The Wall Street Journal*, © Dow Jones & Company, Inc., 1985. All Rights Reserved.

23. Much of what is discussed here on pay structures could be abbreviated if an organization chooses to use market comparisons and benchmark jobs to determine wage rates. If it so chooses, it is using the direct process of market comparisons discussed in the preceding section.

24. Belcher, *Compensation Administration*.

25. D. J. Thomsen, "Compensation and Benefits," *Personnel Journal* (May 1981): 348–54; *Elements of Sound Pay Administration*, a publication of the American Society for Personnel Administration, p. 7. The use of the term *job evaluation* here represents a more restricted definition. Some people use the term to include the element of market pricing as well as internal job content analyses.

26. *Elements of Sound Pay Administration*, pp. 7–8.

27. Other methods of job evaluation similar to these include maturity curves, slotting, and scored questionnaires. For a discussion of the frequency of use of different job evaluation methods, see J. W. Steele, *Paying for Performance and Position* (New York: American Management Associations, 1982), pp. 18–19. See also R. C. Mechan, "Quantitative Job Evaluation Using the Position Analysis Questionnaire," *Personnel Administrator* (June 1983): 82–124; D. Doverspike, A. M. Carlisi, G. V. Barrett, and R. A. Alexander, "Generalizability Analysis of a Point-Method Job Evaluation Instrument," *Journal of Applied Psychology* (Aug. 1983): 476–84.

28. R. Snelgar, "The Comparability of Job Evaluation Methods in Supplying Approximately Similar Classifications in Rating One Job Series," *Personnel Psychology* (Summer 1983): 371–80; J. D. Dunn and F. M. Rachel, *Wage and Salary Administration: Total Compensation Systems*, p. 175. Copyright © 1971 by McGraw-Hill Book Company.

29. Dunn and Rachel, *Wage and Salary Administration*, p. 177.

30. S. L. Fraser, S. F. Cronshaw, and R. A. Alexander, "Generalizability Analysis of a Point Method Job Evaluation Instrument: A Field Study," *Journal of Applied Psychology* (Nov. 1984): 643–47; D. Doverspike, "An Internal Bias Analysis of a Job Evaluation Instrument," *Journal of Applied Psychology* (Nov. 1984): 648–50.

31. Benchmark jobs were mentioned earlier (see note 21) as a direct way of using the market in pricing jobs. In that discussion, the benchmark jobs were not necessarily formally evaluated as they are in this discussion.

32. Thomsen, "Compensation and Benefits," May 1981, pp. 348–54.

33. E. E. Lawler, *Pay and Organizational Development* (Reading, Mass.: Addison-Wesley, 1981); H. Tosi and L. Tosi, "Knowledge Based Pay: Some Propositions and Guides to Effective Use," *Organizational Dynamics* (Winter 1986): 52–64

34. *Wall Street Journal,* 22 May 1984, p. 1. Reprinted by permission of *The Wall Street Journal,* © Dow Jones & Company, Inc., 1984. All Rights Reserved.

35. The use of job families or job classes is consistent with our discussion of them in Chapters 3 and 5. In those chapters, however, the focus is on creating job families for the purpose of selection rather than compensation. The assumption there is that jobs in the same family require similar skills and could be tested the same way. The assumption in compensation is that jobs in the same family have similar value to the organization.

36. Sibson, *Compensation,* pp. 17–19. Most organizations often have several salary programs, including a special one for top management. Different salary programs often reflect different job evaluations and different ways of being paid.

37. The types of surveys that organizations use in helping to establish wage rates include several published by associations and consulting firms, such as Hewitt and Associates, Hay Associates, Handy Associates, and Towers, Perrin, Forster, and Crosby. The use of survey pay data has antitrust implications. For a discussion, see G. D. Fisher, "Salary Surveys—An Antitrust Perspective," *Personnel Administrator* (Apr. 1985): 87–97, 154. See also M. Camuso, "Keep Competitive with the Right Salary Survey," *Personnel Journal* (Oct. 1985): 86–92.

38. Pay data from surveys can be analyzed by mathematical or statistical processes, such as histograms, scattergrams, sample variances and standard deviations, least squares, standard error of estimate, correlation coefficients, and coefficients of determination and multiple regression. For a description of these, see any basic compensation text, such as Belcher, *Compensation Administration,* or Dunn and Rachel, "Wage and Salary Administration."

39. These boxes can vary in size and shape. Varying the size and shape as well as number has significant implications for the motivational value of the pay structure. The top of the box represents the top of the salary range, and the bottom represents the bottom of the salary range. Circled rates are those rates currently outside (above or below) the rates in the boxes. For further discussion, see basic compensation texts, such as Belcher, *Compensation Administration;* and Milkovich and Newman, *Compensation.* Occasionally, boxes are not used in the pricing of jobs. This happens in the pay determination of professionals. With professionals, pay is often a function of the years of experience and level of performance. The exact pay rates are determined by maturity curves. See T. A.

Mahoney, "Compensating for Work," in *Personnel Management,* ed. K. M. Rowland and G. R. Ferris (Boston: Allyn & Bacon, 1982), pp. 246–50.

40. *Elements of Sound Pay Administration* (see note 25).

41. For a discussion on the validity of job evaluation systems, see Mahoney, "Compensating for Work," p. 257. For a discussion of salary ranges, see P. Baxter, "Why Does a Company Need Salary Ranges?" *Personnel Administrator* (Apr. 1985): 12; Milkovich and Newman, *Compensation.*

42. These numbers become critical. Many organizations would like the average salary of employees in a job to be equal to the midpoint. If it is higher than the midpoint, this suggests that many people can no longer receive significant salary increases without being promoted. It may also mean that the whole salary structure has to be moved up—in essence, moving the midpoint up.

43. R. J. Greene, "Which Pay Delivery System Is Best for Your Organization?" *Personnel* (May–June 1981): 51–58. See also *Fair Employment Practices Guidelines* 18 (9) (1980): 7–8.

44. Remember, however, that the Equal Pay Act indicates four bases to justify pay differentials on the same job.

45. E. E. Lawler III, "Workers Can Set Their Own Wages Responsibly," *Psychology Today,* Feb. 1977, pp. 109–12.

46. M. Zippo, "Roundup," *Personnel* (Sept.–Oct. 1980): 43–45.

47. M. Zippo, "Roundup," *Personnel* (May–June 1981): 43–50.

48. L. Dyer, D. P. Schwab, and J. A. Fossum, "Impacts of Pay on Employee Behaviors and Attitudes: An Update," *Personnel Administrator* (Jan. 1978): 56.

49. Dyer, Schwab, and Fossum, "Impacts of Pay," p. 56; Mahoney; T. R. Mitchell, "Motivational Strategies," in *Personnel Management,* ed. K. M. Rowland and G. R. Ferris (Boston: Allyn & Bacon, 1982), pp. 263–300.

50. J. C. Toedtman, "A Decade of Rapid Change: The Outlook for Human Resources Management in the '80s", *Personnel Journal* (Jan. 1980): 29–33.

51. A "properly administered" compensation program implies several qualities of total compensation, including: the job evaluation process is valid; pay structures are fairly and objectively derived; pay is administered in a nondiscriminatory way; compensation policies are communicated to be understood; the administrative costs are contained; it has sufficient motivational value; and it is supported by top management. For a discussion of these, see J. D. McMillan and V. C. Williams, "The Elements of Effective Salary Administration Programs," *Personnel Journal* (Nov. 1982): 832–38; M. G. Dertien, "The Accuracy of Job Evaluation Plans," *Personnel Journal* (July 1981): 566–70; S. B. Henrici, "A Tool for Salary Ad-

ministrators: Standard Salary Accounting," *Personnel* (Sept.–Oct. 1980): 14–23; B. Ellig, "Gearing Compensation."

52. J. D. Finch, "Computerized Retrieval of Pay Survey Data," *Personnel Administrator* (July 1985): 31–38.
53. Lawler, "Strategic Design."
54. Lawler, "Strategic Design"; Tosi and Tosi, "Knowledge Based Pay."

55. M. Bentson and J. Schuster, "Pay and Executive Compensation," in *Human Resource Management in the 1980s,* ed. S. J. Carroll and R. S. Schuler (Washington, D.C.: Bureau of National Affairs, 1983).
56. Mills, *The New Competitors,* offers a good discussion of employment security in Chapter 4. See also D. Riggan, "Employment Security Revisited in the '80s," *Personnel Administrator* (Dec. 1985): 67–74.

Performance-based Pay Systems

Giving Workers a Piece of the Action

EMPLOYEES listen closely each quarter when the president of Electro Scientific Industries Inc. in Portland, Ore., reports sales and profits. And there are probably few who don't grasp the subtleties of pretax and aftertax profits.

It's no wonder. The employees collectively are paid 25 percent of the pretax profits each quarter, with a fourth of that going straight into their pockets and the rest into retirement or stock ownership accounts.

It's pretty much the same at the Olga Company, a maker of lingerie and underwear in Van Nuys, Calif. Founders Olga and Jan Erteszek, who fled Poland at the outbreak of World War II, preach "the dignity of man." They also pay between 20 and 25 percent of annual pretax earnings into a profit-sharing plan for all "associates"—employees.

Despite varying philosophies, dozens of the "100 Best" use some form of profit-sharing, usually in an effort to give employees a sense of ownership and a feel for the bottom line.

Raychem, Tektronix, Johnson Wax, Lowe's Companies, Liebert, Hewlett-Packard, Hallmark Cards, Baxter Travenol, Goldman Sachs, Marion Labs, Reader's Digest, J. P. Morgan and Quad/Graphics, among others, all routinely pay out some portion of pretax profits to all employees, either outright or into trusts.

Savings incentives are popular, too. Rainier Bancorp, in Seattle, matches employees' contributions to savings, dollar for dollar, up to 4 percent of their salary. Inland Steel, in Chicago, matches the first 5 percent contributed by salaried workers into a tax-deferred savings plan.

Merck, in Rahway, N.J., the country's largest prescription drug maker, puts up 50 cents for every dollar saved, up to 10 percent of salary. Johnson & Johnson,

which started its plan in 1982, does the same, up to 6 percent of salary.

Shell Oil, in Houston, matches savings up to 10 percent of salary for employees with seven and a half years at the company, up to 5 percent of pay for five-year employees and up to 2½ percent for three-year employees. Better yet, Shell pays the tax on its contribution. "You could walk out of this company with a pile of cash," say the authors of "100 Best."

Not all of the plans survive hard times intact. Deere & Company, the farm-equipment manufacturer based in Moline, Ill., used to add 75 cents to every dollar of earnings that a salaried worker put into the company stock purchase plan. The maximum contribution is 6 percent of pay. In 1982, 87 percent of eligible workers signed up. But when sales plummeted last year, the plan was shelved. It was later reinstated, but only at the 25-cent level.

Generous medical benefits have been a staple at many of the companies, but lately, more attention is being given to keeping people healthy.

The Hospital Corporation of America, for example, which was started by a physician, paid an average of $146 to employees in 1982 for racking up points in its "aerobic challenge"—a smorgasbord of swimming, running, walking, bicycling, aerobic dancing and racquetball.

All nonsmokers at Quad/Graphics, a magazine-grade printing company near Milwaukee, get a $200 bonus each year. Johnson Wax starts off each employee with a $300 deposit in the health plan. Any money left at the end of the year is paid out in cash.

Then there is Tenneco. It spent $11 million on a physical fitness center in its high-rise headquarters in Houston because "we're in a tight labor market in this city and we want to compete for the best people," James L. Ketelsen, chairman, told the "100 Best" authors.

The center has four racquetball courts, exercise rooms with Nautilus equipment, saunas and a one-fifth-mile banked jogging track that circles the eighth floor. About 3,700 employees use the facility regularly, getting monthly computer printouts on their conditioning status. It's no problem if someone forgets to bring workout gear. The center is stocked with necessary clothing, including athletic supporters.

Source: T. C. Hayes, *New York Times,* 6 May 1984, p. F17. Copyright © 1984/85 by The New York Times Company. Reprinted by permission.

The preceding "PHRM in the News" illustrates several important aspects of performance-based pay. One is that organizations like Electro Scientific Industries can use compensation to gain competitive advantage.[1] Another is that many of the best American companies use some form of profit sharing that enhances employee involvement and organizational profitability.[2] A third aspect is that performance-based pay is an effective way to motivate employees and improve organizational profitability, survival, and competitiveness. Before examining these and other aspects of performance-based pay, we need to define the two major types of **performance-based pay systems.**

Types of Performance-based Pay Systems

Performance-based pay systems relate pay to performance. The extent of the relationship and the measure of performance are used to differentiate the two major types of performance-based pay systems: **incentive pay plans** and **merit pay plans.** In incentive pay plans, performance is often, but not always, measured by standards of productivity and direct indexes of individuals, groups, or organizations. By contrast, merit pay plans generally use less direct measures of performance, such as rankings or ratings made by supervisors. Another aspect of many incentive pay plans is that the major portion of an individual's compensation, such as a salesperson on commission, is from incentive pay. Since the level of compensation varies with performance, the level of an individual's compensation can vary greatly. Merit pay plans, however, affect a relatively small percentage of an individual's total salary, because merit pay is generally used only to move an individual's compensation within a rate range (and this adjustment is made only once a year). Traditionally, incentive pay plans have used only money as a reward. More recently, nonmonetary rewards such as praise, participation, and feedback are also being tied to performance.[3]

Merit pay plans are methods of monetary compensation generally related to subjectively evaluated performance that represent only a small percentage increment in an employee's direct compensation. Incentive pay plans are methods of monetary and nonmonetary compensation generally related to direct indexes (e.g., outcomes) of performance for the individual, group, or organization, and generally represent a substantial proportion of an individual's direct compensation.

Although many people are rewarded by performance-based pay, it is primarily under merit pay plans. Consequently, much of the total compensation that people receive is not related to performance but rather to the results of the job evaluation and steps in rate ranges discussed in Chapter 8. Nevertheless, when the conditions are right, performance-based pay systems, especially incentive plans, can get workers to perform at high levels. This describes, in large part, the purposes and importance of performance-based pay systems.

Purposes and Importance of Performance-based Pay

Money can be an extremely powerful motivator of performance. Studies of performance-based pay systems (especially incentive plans) have shown that individual incentive plans can improve performance on an average of almost 30 percent over non-performance-based pay systems. Group incentive plans can increase performance 15 to 20 percent.[4] These figures are impressive given that other PHRM programs, such as goal setting, participation plans, and job enrichment, have less of an impact on productivity.[5]

As the initial "PHRM in the News" illustrates, pay is also important because pay-motivated employee performance can enhance organizational survival and competitiveness.[6] This is true even in areas where performance-based pay has traditionally not been used:

> **Incentive pay plans are growing as the health-care business changes.**
> Health Central Corp., Minneapolis, says senior management incentives help it to focus better on goals as the industry becomes more cost-conscious and competitive. Its top managers may earn bonuses of up to 20% of base pay. Alliance Health System, Norfolk, Va., sets goals early in the year; at year end, bonuses are paid according to progress made by managers individually and by the management team.
>
> Hay Group, a Philadelphia consultant, says 54% of 71 of the nation's largest health-care providers have incentives for senior executives, up from 15% in 1980. The incentives average 30% of base pay, compared to only 8% in 1980. By contrast, industrial concerns pay bonuses averaging 37% of base pay, Hay adds.
>
> Some health-care companies are devising incentives for middle managers, too, notes Korn/Ferry International, New York recruiter.[7]

Performance-based pay is important to organizations because it is extremely effective in positively influencing the bottom line. Performance-based pay systems, however, have some disadvantages. One is that they take time to administer; typically, employees have to work exceptionally hard to earn large incentive bonuses, and occasional conflicts can arise from not rewarding certain behaviors. These advantages and disadvantages of performance-based pay apply only when the appropriate conditions exist for its implementation. When these conditions do not exist, the disadvantages far outweigh the advantages. The conditions are critical in knowing when to use performance-based pay and are described later in this chapter. Also important to consider are the relationships influencing performance-based pay.

Relationships Influencing Performance-based Pay

Although most of the key relationships of performance-based pay are described in Chapter 8, two that are highlighted here are with other PHRM activities.

Relationships with Other PHRM Activities

Two other PHRM activities share a unique relationship with performance-based pay: training and development and the union-management relationship.

Training and Development.   Managers must be trained to be made aware of the effects of contingent (performance-based) rewards on performance, to observe employee performance accurately, and to provide employees with feedback as quickly as possible after the desired behavior, via pay, praise, and other rewards. In addition, employees must be trained to be able to perform as expected. The following "PHRM in the News" illustrates how the relationship between compensation and training can influence the growth and development of a successful business.

Union-Management Relationship.   Chapter 8 described one relationship influencing total compensation that is especially applicable here: union-management relations. Since wages are a bargainable issue, whether an organization has a performance-based pay system may depend on a union's desires. Further, because unions have traditionally opposed performance-based pay systems for several reasons, including safety and the preferences of their members, organizations must convince the union of the benefits of these pay systems. Once shown the benefits and even necessities of such pay systems, some unions seem willing to cooperate and help implement these systems. An example is the recent agreement between the International Woodworkers of America and Crown Zellerbach Corporation:

> The company's 600 loggers in Washington and Oregon agreed in principle in late October to give up their traditional wage scale and to be paid according to how much they produce—in return for more of a say in managing their work. The new system, which also eliminates craft distinctions and restrictive work rules, will be tricky to administer without alienating workers. But if it succeeds, it may provide a model for restructuring the compensation of thousands of other employees at Crown Zellerbach and other forest products companies.[8]

Legal Considerations in Performance-based Pay

As indicated in Chapter 8, Title VII of the Civil Rights Act of 1964 applies not only to selection decisions but also to pay decisions. A supervisor may be

Growing with Style

"Nobody who goes into hairdressing sees it as the business it really can be. Until they see this."

"This" is Visible Changes Inc.—the largest, fastest-growing haircutting chain in any city in the country—and the man leading the tour of this bustling, neon-and-ceramic-tile beauty salon is its president and co-founder, John McCormack. Since its start in 1977, Visible Changes has grown to 15 locations in Houston and Austin, Tex., with expected 1985 revenues of $12 million.

McCormack himself is a relatively new convert to the idea of hairdressing as a growth business. Eight years ago, as an ex-New York City cop-turned-stockbroker, he was looking for a business to run when he took up with Maryanne Warren, a hairdresser who is now his wife and business partner. She saw money to be made in a streamlined approach to hair-cutting that she had developed. McCormack agreed.

They wanted to start a "haircutting company," and their business plan called for a chain of high-volume, no-appointment hair salons located in indoor shopping malls—a new twist at the time. The McCormacks hoped then, as they do today, to take the chain national. What they didn't figure on, however, was the lukewarm reception they got from bankers and mall developers, who considered beauty salons high-turnover, low-margin propositions. While the McCormacks eventually secured the necessary financing and leases, it took all the persuasive power they could muster: "They thought we were going to be just another bunch of yo-yo hairdressers."

John McCormack knew from the beginning that if Visible Changes salons were to grow and multiply, he would have to find ways of assuring quality control, while building managerial bench strength. To him, that meant the development of a strong employee-training program, as well as compensation and promotion policies that encourage and reward achievement. But the real challenge was how to accomplish that in an industry in which most of those in the labor pool are "young, relatively uneducated, and thanks to salaries in this business that average $7,000 a year, almost totally lacking in self-esteem."

The salaries that the McCormacks dangle beneath employees' noses are uncommonly high, stretching into the $30,000 to $60,000 range for managers and assistant managers. Their profit-sharing plan is worth $3 million. And the cream of the employee crop gets a chance to manage million-dollar salons. None of these career-ladder carrots is simply there for the picking, however. Training starts weeks before recruits go to work, and it continues, in weekly installments, long after they are "on the floor." Raises, hikes in commission, bonuses, and promotions all depend on the employees' ability to get customers in and out of the chair in half an hour or less, and to maintain a good request rate—the frequency with which customers ask for them by name.

But, as much as the McCormacks like to grant management responsibility early, they have learned the hard way that training and achievement alone do not a manager make. They have had to fire one manager, along with half of that salon's staff, for condoning the use of marijuana. Others, unable to cope with the stresses of the job—or, in the case of some female managers, uncomfortable with making more money than their spouses or boyfriends—have asked to step down. Now, instead of promoting at age 23, McCormack is holding off until perhaps age 27. He is also mixing the managerial ranks with experienced outside hires.

"A manager is what makes or breaks the salon," McCormack says—and, he might have added, the company. To continue Visible Changes's record of solid, sensible growth—the kind that McCormack wants to see a little more of before he ventures beyond Texas borders—he needs to be able to lean all the more heavily on the people he promotes. After all, he shrugs, "this is a business."

Source: Reprinted with permission, INC. magazine, (June 1985). Copyright © 1985 by INC. Publishing Company, 38 Commercial Wharf, Boston, MA 02110.

charged with unlawful discrimination by an employee (in a protected group) who believes that a pay raise was denied on the basis of factors unrelated to performance. Raises not related to performance, however, can be given legally. Defensible factors influencing merit pay (when they are equally applied to all employees) include the following:

- Performance
- Position in salary range
- Time since last increase
- Size of last increase
- Pay relationships within the company or department
- Pay levels of jobs in other companies
- Salaries of newly hired employees
- Budgetary limits

What is critical is that the same rules of the game are used to give raises fairly and consistently to all employees. The same is true for incentive pay plans.

Tax laws are also important considerations in performance-based pay, particularly where frequent use is made of stocks and stock options to reward executives for performance.[9] Compensation for executives is often designed with the tax laws in mind. For example, the tax rules and regulations of **incentive stock option** (ISO) plans are defined and described by the Economic Recovery Tax Act of 1981 (ERTA) (discussed in Chapter 10). The level of executive compensation is also subject to legal considerations. For example, the Internal Revenue Service (IRS) can claim that executives are paid in excess of what they are worth and that their pay must be reduced. Excessive pay, referred to by the IRS as "unreasonable compensation," is illegal because the federal government receives more money when a company's profits are paid as dividends than it does when they are distributed as wages, and is therefore losing tax dollars. Another form of executive compensation that can be regarded as incentive compensation is the "golden parachute." Because it is really a benefit, it is described in Chapter 10.

In general, incentive pay plans appear to have substantially more motivational value, but merit pay plans remain much more frequent because they tend to be easier to set up and administer. Whereas essentially one type of merit plan exists, there is a wide variety of incentive plans. The range of both types is shown in Exhibit 9.1.

Performance-based Pay Systems by Level   *Exhibit 9.1*

Merit Pay Plans	Incentive Pay Plans	
(one type)	*Individual*	*Group*
	• Piecework plan	• Scanlon plan
	• Standard hour plan	• Rucker plan
	• Measured day work	• Profit-sharing plans
	• Sales incentive plan	
	• Managerial incentive plans	
	• Suggestion systems	

Merit Pay Plans

The results of a recent survey on merit pay plans conducted by the Conference Board indicate that merit pay plans are widely used:

> Pay for performance policies have been widely adopted by employers in an effort to link workers' salaries to job performance, according to a Conference Board study of 557 United States firms. The study finds that in 1982 the merit increase was practically the sole method used by the firms to raise the pay of exempt personnel. It also notes that formal performance appraisal systems existed in a majority of the companies, and that, despite some administrative problems, most employers felt that their pay-for-performance plans were successful to at least some degree.
>
> Merit increase policies were in effect at 95 percent of the firms surveyed, and 96 percent of the organizations actually granted such increases. Other pay-raise vehicles for exempt employees, such as general or cost-of-living adjustments, were relatively infrequent (13 percent and 19 percent, respectively), the study finds. Although merit raises are directly tied to employee performance, the study adds, they do not reflect performance-related factors exclusively. Also considered in pay raise decisions, for example, are "nonperformance" factors such as position in the salary range, time and size of last increase, pay relationships within the unit or with similar jobs in other units, and budgetary limits on salary increases.[10]

In merit pay plans, guidelines must be established for determining the size of merit pay raises, the timing of when they are given, and the relationship between merit pay increments and place in the salary range. Especially during times of high inflation rates, organizations have to address the general relationship between merit pay and cost-of-living adjustments.

Merit Pay Guidelines

Because most large private organizations have some type of merit plan, looking at a specific example of a typical plan may be useful. Exhibit 9.2 shows that the pay increments depend not only on employee performance but also on employee position in the salary range.[11] Position is determined by expressing the employee's current salary as a percentage of the salary that is the midpoint of the range of salaries for that job. The lower the position in

Exhibit 9.2	*Sample Merit Pay Plan*

Performance Rating	Current Position in Salary Range			
	First Quartile	*Second Quartile*	*Third Quartile*	*Fourth Quartile*
Truly outstanding	13–14% increase	11–12% increase	9–10% increase	6–8% increase
Above average	11-12% increase	9–10% increase	7–8% increase	6% increase or less
Good	9–10% increase	7–8% increase	6% increase or less	delay increase
Satisfactory	6–8% increase	6% increase or less	delay increase	no increase
Unsatisfactory	no increase	no increase	no increase	no increase

the range (the first quartile is the lowest), the larger the percentage of the merit raise.

An important component of compensation administration is monitoring the number of people in each quartile. Although the percentage of merit increases is greater in the lower quartiles, the absolute size of increases is often larger in the higher quartiles. The more people in the higher quartiles, the larger the budget necessary for merit increases. Therefore, the compensation manager must monitor the line managers who attempt to get their employees pushed to the top of the ranges in each job as a way to offer more rewards to their employees. The compensation manager ends up playing the role of police officer, especially in a highly centralized operation. Unpleasant as it may be, this role is necessary for budget purposes and to ensure equity for all employees in the organization. Employees who perform equally well on the same job generally should not be paid different salaries and given different merit increases.[12]

Merit Versus Cost-of-Living Adjustments

Many large organizations grant **cost-of-living adjustments** (COLAs) or general (non-performance-related) increases to their employees, especially firms in which unions have written COLAs into their contracts.[13] Neither COLAs nor general increases are based on performance, yet they can take the lion's share of money available for compensation increases. And where unionized workers have COLA guarantees, the pressures are great to provide the same benefits to nonunion, often white-collar, employees. However, many organizations would rather eliminate their COLAs in favor of merit pay plans, primarily because COLAs have no relationship to performance yet can be rather expensive.[14] In addition to not getting performance from pay, COLAs often take some salary control away from the organization and the compensation manager. Since most COLAs are tied to the Consumer Price Index (CPI), all the organization can do is watch salaries increase as the CPI goes up. The more the CPI increases, the more the organization must pay. The more the COLA budget, the smaller the pot for merit increases. Yet, some argue that for merit increases to work, they must be fairly large. Thus, the issue in times of high inflation may be whether to use the entire salary budget for COLAs or for merit increases, rather than how to divide up the budget.

But even when the rate of inflation is low and merit raises are given, the incentive value of the raises tends to be modest. This is due to the relatively small amount that merit increases generally represent and to the relatively small differences (in absolute dollars) between getting the top increase and just an average increase.[15] Consequently, organizations look to incentive pay plans when they desire more motivational value from their compensation dollar.

Incentive Pay Plans

In the United States, most incentive plans are either piecework or standard hour plans. Increasingly, however,

> there are a number of profit-sharing and productivity gainsharing plans, each one using somewhat different measurements and motivational techniques. In addition to various piecework arrangements, there are Improshare Plans, which measure gains in physical productivity; Scanlon plans, which measure labor cost savings; Rucker plans, which track value-adding; and straight cash or deferred profit-sharing plans.[16]

In general, incentive plans will more likely be used if labor costs are large, the market is cost competitive, technology is not advanced, and one employee's output is relatively independent of another employee's.[17] These factors, may influence whether incentive plans are used, as well as which type of plan is used.

The types of incentive plans are numerous. The easiest way to discuss them is by the level at which they are applied: individual, group, or organization. Each type of plan is generally unique to a specific level. Regardless of the level at which a plan is implemented, the intended beneficiaries are always the organization and the individuals covered by the plan.

Individual-level Incentive Plans

The piecework plan is perhaps the most widely known of the several individual-level incentive plans.

Piecework Plan. Piecework is the most common type of incentive pay plan. Under this plan, employees are guaranteed a standard pay rate for each unit of output. The pay rate per unit is frequently determined by time-and-motion studies and the current base pay of the job. For example, if the base pay of a job is twenty dollars per day and the employee can produce at a normal rate twenty units a day, the piece rate may be established at one dollar per unit. The incentive pay rate is based on the standard output and the base wage rate. The "normal" rate is more than what the time-and-motion studies indicate but is supposed to represent 100 percent efficiency. The final rate also reflects the bargaining power of the employees, economic conditions of the organization and community, and what the competition is paying.

Standard Hour Plan.   The standard hour plan is the second most common incentive plan. It is essentially a piecework plan, except that standards are denominated in time per unit of output rather than money per unit of output. Tasks are broken down by the amount of time it takes to complete them. This can be determined by historical records, time-and-motion studies, or a combination of both. The time to perform each task then becomes a "standard time."

Measured Day Work.   An individual-level incentive plan that removes some of the relationship between rates and standards is measured day work. Again, formal production standards are established, and employee performance is judged against these standards. But with measured day work, the typical standards are less precise. For example, standards may be determined by the results of a rating or ranking procedure rather than by an objective index such as units produced.[18]

Sales Incentive Plans.   All the incentive plans discussed thus far share an important characteristic: they are usually applied to blue-collar employees and, in some cases, to office employees. Other employees participate in incentive plans with similar characteristics or incentive values. Many managerial employees and salespeople participate in incentive plans that have large incentive values. Incentive plans for salespeople are referred to as **commissions**. The power of this incentive value can be so high that it elicits unintended behaviors (e.g., churning among stockbrokers).

> Churning, or overtrading, occurs when a broker trades a customer's account excessively to generate commissions, without regard to the customer's financial needs and investment objectives. The compensation system that prevails in the securities industry actually encourages brokers to churn accounts. The only compensation that a brokerage firm receives from its customer is the commission paid by the customer on completed transactions. Furthermore, the only compensation received by a broker employed by the firm is a portion of this commission—averaging about 40%. If the customer doesn't trade, no matter how good his portfolio may be, the broker goes home empty-handed. As a federal judge said recently, "as long as investment brokers have been remunerated on a commission basis, the potential has existed for brokers to excessively trade accounts in an effort to generate fees."[19]

Regardless of the potential for such impact, about two-thirds of all salespeople are paid a salary plus commission. In real estate sales, however, almost 75 percent of the people are paid straight commissions; straight commissions are paid to only 25 percent of all salespeople. As with the individual incentive plans for blue-collar and office employees, few salespeople (11 percent) work without some guaranteed minimum pay.

Managerial Incentive Plans.   Incentive plans for managers generally take the form of cash bonuses for good performance of the department, division, or organization as a whole. Other forms of compensation that can be used as managerial incentives are stock options, performance shares, and junior stock. A **stock option** is an opportunity for a manager to buy stocks of the organization at a later date but at a price established when the option is granted. The idea is that managers will work harder to increase their performance and the profitability of the company (thus increasing the price of the company's stock) if they can share the profits over the long run. If the market price of the stock increases over time, managers can use their options to buy the stock at a lower price and to realize final gain.

Performance shares provide a close connection between individual performance (as reflected in company profitability) and rewards. In this instance, the manager or executive is rewarded only if established goals are met. The goals are usually stated in earnings per share (EPS). Furthermore, if the EPS goal is met, the manager receives shares of stock directly. Usually the manager receives cash (called bonus units) as well as stock in order to pay taxes on the equity (stock) reward. Receipt of the shares alone, however, can result in a substantial reward.[20]

To reduce the tax liability to both company and individual of the stock option and performance share arrangements, the **junior stock** plan is used. This plan has the tax advantages of the incentive stock option (ISO) but eliminates some ISO drawbacks. Yet it also has the pro-company features of performance units, which reward managers only if they fulfill specified requirements. The junior stock plan has several components that make the plan work well:

- *Special issue.* XYZ Corporation issues special "junior," nonvoting common stock paying dividends. The shares can be exchanged by holders for regular XYZ common stock share for share, at a specified date if the holders meet certain conditions.

- *Bargain price.* The junior shares are sold to XYZ executives at a bargain price—for example, twenty dollars—while the regular common stock is trading at thirty dollars. The executives, using a fairly obscure section of the tax code, then "elect" to be currently taxed on their present benefit.

- *Fixed formula.* Certain conditions must be met for the junior shares to be exchanged for common stock. For instance, the executives must complete a five-year term of service with XYZ, and XYZ's earnings per share must rise according to a fixed formula.

- *Tax-free exchange.* At the end of the term, with XYZ common stock trading at perhaps eighty dollars, the executives swap the junior stock for the common in a tax-free exchange. Each executive pays ordinary income taxes on the original price advantage—in this case a ten-dollar price spread. On sale of the common stock, the executive has a tax basis of thirty dollars—the twenty dollars paid for the junior shares plus the ten-dollar price advantage. Thus, a capital gain of fifty dollars per share—eighty dollars less thirty dollars—is taxed at 20 percent.[21]

Although junior stock provides a good incentive, a recent ruling by the Internal Revenue Service has reduced its value. The ruling changed the capital gain tax provision and requires the receiver to pay the higher personal income tax on any gains.

Suggestion Systems.   Suggestion systems reward employees for money-saving or money-producing ideas and are used extensively. They are perhaps unique in that they attempt to increase the number of good ideas rather than output directly. Yet they are similar to other plans in that the rewards are monetary. Approximately 80 percent of the nation's five hundred largest corporations have suggestion systems.[22]

Suggestion systems are also important because they can bestow substantial sums of money. Some organizations allow employees as much as 30 percent of the first year's savings. Since the inception of Eastman Kodak's suggestion system, Kodak employees have submitted over 1.8 million ideas, and approximately 30 percent have been accepted. In 1983, Kodak paid $3.6 million to Kodak employees for their suggestions. The success of quality circles (discussed in Chapter 12) depends on the quality of employee suggestions. Employees make productivity improvement suggestions, which are then collected by supervisors and discussed with top management at monthly meetings.

Suggestion systems generally do not have a favorable reputation, however, often because individual awards are too small. Also, employees sometimes never learn the results of their ideas, and companies often save much more than the individual receives. Occasionally, an individual's suggestion is apparently discarded, only to be put in operation by management later—with no reward to the employee. This increases hostility, resentment, and distrust between management and nonmanagement. In turn, the use of the suggestion system, particularly the suggestion box, may become an object of ridicule and jokes.

Although most suggestion systems elicit and reward individuals' ideas, some are designed for groups of employees. Such a system is incorporated into the Scanlon plan, which is discussed later in the section on group-level incentive plans.

Because of the many incentive plans and the variety of jobs, many organizations use a combination of plans. The following "PHRM in the News" provides an excellent example.

Group-level Incentive Plans

As organizations become more complex, a growing number of jobs become interdependent in either of two senses. Some jobs are part of a sequence of operations, so that performance that precedes and follows them affects their performance; other jobs require joint efforts to achieve results.[23]

In either case, measurement of individual performance is difficult at best and often impossible. Individual-level incentives are not appropriate under

Paddling for Profits

Salespeople get commissions. Everyone else just gets raises. Whether they like it or not, these are facts of life that nonsales employees usually learn to accept.

But at Delta Business Systems Inc., the facts of life have changed.

Delta, a $23-million Orlando company that sells, leases, and services office equipment, offers some 20 different incentive programs to its 315 employees—and a baker's dozen of them apply to the 215 people in nonsales positions. For example:

Secretaries and administrative assistants compete for a $50 award in a monthly contest, judged by managers, for "Most Valuable Associate."

Field-service technicians can add from 3% to 25% to their annual salaries by retaining their customer base—renewing maintenance agreements, persuading customers to recondition machines, or giving salespeople leads.

Each dispatcher can earn up to $40 a month by scheduling preventive-maintenance calls.

Delta's four corporate warehouse workers can divide up to $400 every two months if they function smoothly as a team. They are rewarded for filling orders promptly, filing invoices in time to receive cash discounts, and keeping the facility well stocked, secure, and orderly.

A former educational materials salesman and general manager of an automobile dealership, Delta co-founder and president Bryan King has long been convinced of the power of a bonus. But since starting the privately held company seven years ago, he has taken the concept of pay-for-performance to extremes. King has built an interconnected web of individual and companywide bonus programs, along with an employee stock ownership plan. He has tried to structure Delta so that

managers' salaries are tied to the profitability of their respective divisions. Service department managers' salaries are also based on customer satisfaction surveys. As the staff has grown and sales have climbed (from $1.9 million in 1979), King has continued to expand the options.

"We take the incentive plans down to the lowest level possible," he says, even if there is no way to measure a performance in terms of revenue. "If we can see how fast someone's canoe moves in the water, we provide an incentive."

Often, of course, the payoff to Delta *is* directly measurable. When King wanted to speed up collection of receivables, for instance, he offered staffers up to $200 a quarter to reduce the outstanding bills. Within six months, total long-term receivables had been cut by 50%, a $20,000 annual saving to the business.

"I'm very goal oriented," says collections administrator Carrie Pirrotta, who joined Delta last year partly because she liked the company's incentive system. "The idea of earning a bonus tied to *my* productivity and not to anyone else's appealed to me."

Ironically, employees sometimes resist incentives. Over in the accounts-payable department, clerk Virginia Gant balked at the chance to earn up to $50 a month for taking advantage of prompt-payment discounts. "I didn't like it," she remembers, explaining that she feared she would be penalized for overlooking a possible discount. "I thought they would charge it back to me." It took loads of reassurance from her supervisor, Allan Woodlief—and a few bonus-padded paychecks—before Gant saw the plan's merit.

Talking up the system, says Woodlief, is crucial to its success. "What we are trying to do," he explains, "is convince a group of skeptical people who are used to working their 40 hours and going home . . . that management is sincerely trying to offer equitable incentives."

But all this cheerleading can be wearing—and there are other problems with the bonus programs as well. Just keeping up with the paperwork can be an enormous task. And with managers' bonuses largely dependent on the profitability of their divisions, interdepartmental clashes are common. King says he constantly has to play referee, reminding employees that while

they might have to give up a bonus now, they will recoup it in the form of a year-end bonus based on a percentage of gross sales, equally divided among all employees. He is now writing an employee-policy handbook to spell out the plans more clearly.

Still, King insists, Delta's bonus system has been worth every bit of the effort. It makes employees accountable for their own performance, he says, and "that's important if you want to unleash their entrepreneurial spirit."

Source: Reprinted with permission, INC. magazine, (March 1985). Copyright © 1985 by INC. Publishing Company, 38 Commerical Wharf, Boston, MA 02110.

these conditions because they fail to reward cooperation. Group-level incentives can do this whether at the small group or department level or at the organizational level. Individual-level incentive plans may become less common as changing technologies make jobs even more interdependent and individual performance more difficult to measure.

Although both individual and group-level incentive plans attempt to tie pay to performance by giving employees incentives for increasing output or profit or decreasing costs, the two plans differ significantly. First, incentives are based on group performance, not on individual performance. Second, incentives are usually given on the basis of present profits or cost savings against past accounting data on the same figures. Two popular group plans using cost savings comparisons are the Scanlon plan and the Rucker plan, also referred to as gainsharing plans. Types of group plans based on profit comparisons are referred to as profit-sharing and stock ownership plans, as described in the initial "PHRM in the News."

For group-level incentive systems to effectively motivate performance, they should have an objective measure of performance for the group. The individuals in the group must believe that they can affect the measure by their performance.[24] Also, the system must be perceived as rewarding cooperation as well as group performance. In addition, the culture or core values of the organization need to be congruent with group-level incentive plans. For example, because gainsharing plans operate with a high level of employment involvement, the organizations using them need to value and encourage employee involvement and participation in the organization. When these conditions exist, the results can be favorable.

Scanlon Plan.   The **Scanlon plan** represents as much a philosophy of management-employee relations as it does a companywide incentive system. It emphasizes employer-employee participation and sharing the operations and profitability of the company. As such, Scanlon plans are adaptable to different companies and changing needs.[25] The plan is used in union as well as nonunion plants.

The Scanlon plan reflects that efficiency of operations depends on companywide cooperation and that bonus incentives encourage cooperation. The bonus is determined on the basis of savings in labor costs, which are measured by comparing the payroll to the sales value of production on a monthly or bimonthly basis. Previous months' ratios of payroll to sales value of production help establish expected labor costs. Savings in labor costs are then shared by employees (75 percent) and the employer (25 percent). Because all employees share the savings, one group does not gain at the expense of another. Each employee's bonus is determined by converting the bonus fund to a percentage of the total payroll and applying this percentage to the employee's pay for the month.

Although Scanlon plans can be successful, their real incentive value can be short-lived. This can occur if employees believe they can no longer work smarter or harder and, therefore, believe they cannot improve upon previous months' ratios of payroll to sales value of production. At this point, employee performance levels off, and the Scanlon plan loses its incentive value. This effect is greatly minimized where work methods and products are always changing. Under these conditions, employees are more likely to believe they can always find better ways to work. The Scanlon plan experience at Herman Miller, a furniture manufacturer in Michigan, provides an example:

> Results indicated an average suggestion rate of 84% per year, an average of 11% bonus, and over $6 million in bonuses paid. Over these 30 years of development, the mandate for the organization changed and the gainsharing plan changed with it. The same principles applied but different structures and processes were necessary to apply these principles. This is an excellent example of the need for understanding the processes and methods for fitting structures and processes in a given situation.[26]

Rucker Plan.   The **Rucker plan** is similar to the Scanlon plan, except the basis for determining the size of incentives is more complex. Here a ratio is calculated that determines the value of production required for each dollar of the total payroll costs. For example:

1. Assume accounting records show the company put $0.60 worth of electricity, materials, supplies, and so on into production, to produce $1.00 worth of product. The value added is $0.40 for each $1.00 of sales value. Assume also that records show that 45 percent of the value added was attributable to labor; a productivity ratio (PR) can be allocated from the formula:
2. PR × 45% = 1.00. Solving yields PR = 2.22
3. If the wage bill equals $100,000, the *expected* production value is the wage bill ($100,000) × PR (2.22) = $222,222.22
4. If *actual* production value equals $280,000.00, then the savings (actual production value – expected production value) equals $57,777.78.
5. Since the labor contribution to value added is 45 percent, the bonus to the work force should be .45 × $57,777.78 = $26,000.00.
6. The savings are distributed as an incentive bonus according to a formula identical to the Scanlon formula—75 percent of the bonus is distributed to workers immediately and 25 percent is kept as an emergency fund to cover poor months. Any excess in the emergency fund at the end of the year is then distributed to workers.[27]

This example helps illustrate that incentives are tied to a wide variety of cost savings. In contrast, the Scanlon plan uses only labor cost savings. Nevertheless, both plans can be adapted to best fit an organization's needs and situation.[28]

Profit-sharing Plans.   Group-level incentive plans based on profit comparisons fall into one of three categories: current distribution, deferred distribution, and a combination of current and deferred distribution. Because of provisions in tax laws, deferred distribution plans are the fastest-growing type. Distribution is typically done upon retirement, termination, death, or disability.

Profit-sharing plans, in contrast to gainsharing plans, are based on profit comparisons. Typically, between 14 and 33 percent of profit increases are distributed to employees, making these plans easier to administer than gainsharing plans. Profit-sharing plans are also easier to administer to both large and small organizations. Gainsharing plans tend to be most effective in small organizations. Regardless of size, however, employee involvement is not an aspect of profit-sharing plans. Incentives may be given to employees even when their performance remains the same. They may, however, work harder and receive no incentives if the organization is not profitable. The volatility of organizational profitability is a reason why some organizations use thrift savings plans instead of profit-sharing plans. These plans are described in Chapter 10.

Some conditions, however, limit the potential effectiveness of all incentive plans and also exist for merit pay plans. These conditions can be recognized and dealt with to some extent by the PHRM manager. In so doing, the PHRM manager is addressing a critical administrative issue in performance-based pay.

Administrative Issues in Performance-based Pay

Although performance-based pay systems are capable of substantially improving productivity, many obstacles in their design and implementation may suppress their potential effectiveness. Organizations can identify these obstacles and remove them. The following discussion of the obstacles pertains equally to both merit pay and incentive pay; discussion of the second and third administrative issues pertains primarily to merit pay.

Obstacles to Performance-based Pay System Effectiveness

The many obstacles in the design and implementation of performance-based pay systems can be grouped into three general categories: (1) difficulties in specifying and measuring job performance, (2) problems in identifying valued rewards (pay being one of many rewards), and (3) difficulties in linking rewards to job performance.[29]

Prerequisites to rewarding job performance are specifying what job performance is, determining the relationships between levels of job performance and rewards, and accurately measuring job performance. These activities are often difficult because of the changing nature of work, its multidimensional nature, technological developments, lack of supervisory training, and the manager's value system.

A second set of obstacles applies to monetary and nonmonetary rewards. These obstacles highlight the importance and value of using rewards other than pay to reward desired behaviors. Rewards other than pay may have more motivational value, especially for employees whose pay increments may be largely consumed by increased taxes.[30] Managers must learn which rewards are most valued by employees and contingently administer on a timely basis those that are most reinforcing. This process is filled with potential problems.

The third set of obstacles involves the difficulties in linking rewards to job performance. The causes of these difficulties include creating inappropriate contingencies, using an inaccurate performance appraisal measure, and existing employee opposition. Employee opposition is often a major obstacle in successfully implementing performance-based pay, especially incentive plans, because of many perceptions that employees may have about incentive plans:

- Incentive plans result in work speedup.
- Rates are cut if earnings under the plan increase too much.
- Incentive plans encourage competition among workers and the discharge of slow workers.
- Incentive plans result in unemployment through "working yourself out of a job."
- Incentive plans break down crafts by reducing skill requirements through methods study.
- Workers don't get their share of increased productivity.
- Incentive plans are too complex.
- Standards are set unfairly.
- Industrial engineers are out to rob workers.
- Earnings fluctuate, making it difficult to budget household expenditures and even to obtain home mortgages.
- Incentive plans are used to avoid a deserved pay increase.
- Incentive plans increase strain on workers and may impair their health.
- Incentive plans increase the frequency of methods changes.
- Incentive plans ask workers to do more than a fair day's work.
- Incentive plans imply a lack of trust in workers by management.[31]

The last belief pervades most of the other beliefs as well. Lack of trust has immediate implications for the establishment of rates and standards that incentive systems are based on. Workers may play elaborate charades for the benefit of time-study engineers doing work measurement described in Chapter 3, but these maneuvers do not entirely fool the engineers, who know that workers might try to be misleading. Therefore, they plug in estimates of how much they are being fooled, combining scientific observation and measurement with a guessing game.[32] The result may be inaccurate or unfair rates, which reduce the incentive value of the system, the profitability of the company, or both. The implications for management in removing these causes of difficulties in linking rewards to job performance are shown in Exhibit 9.3.

Exhibit 9.3   *Obstacles to the Design of Effective Reward Systems and Their Implications for Management*

Obstacles	Causes	Implications for Management
A. Difficulties in specifying and measuring performance	1. Changes in the nature of work • Increase in service-oriented jobs • Increase in white-collar, managerial, and professional jobs • Increases in the interdependencies and complexity of work 2. Multidimensional nature of work • Single-item measures of performance are often inadequate • In many jobs today, multiple criteria are necessary to assess performance 3. Technological developments • Technological developments often result in new and untested methods of work • Machine-paced jobs permit little variation in performance 4. Lack of supervisory training • Use of untrained, inexperienced supervisors in the evaluation process • Perceptual biases 5. The manager's value system • Lack of interest in or inability to differentiate among high and low performers • Failure to see long-range outcomes of differential rewarding	1. Develop techniques for specifying desirable behaviors and clarifying the objectives of the organization 2. Utilize evaluation procedures that recognize the multidimensional nature of performance 3. Develop a valid and reliable performance appraisal system based on results and/or behavioral standards 4. Train supervisors to utilize the performance appraisal system appropriately and to understand potential sources of bias 5. Clearly define long-term consequences of performance-contingent and noncontingent reward practices

continued

Obstacles	Causes	Implications for Management

B. Problems in identifying valued rewards	1. Choice of rewards
	  • Choosing a reward that is not reinforcing
	2. Utilizing rewards of insufficient size or magnitude
	  • Lack of resources
	  • Company policy
	3. Poor timing of rewards
	  • Size of organization: bureaucracy
	  • Standardization/ formalization of feedback mechanisms
	  • Complexity of feedback system
		1. Make managers aware of the effects of rewards on employee performance and satisfaction
		2. Train managers to identify rewards for their subordinates
		3. Administer rewards of sufficient magnitude
		4. Administer rewards as quickly after desirable responses as possible

C. Difficulties in linking rewards to performance	1. Failure to create appropriate contingencies between rewards and performance
	  • Lack of knowledge, skill, experience
	  • Belief system
	  • Difficulty of administration
	2. Creating inappropriate contingencies
	  • Rewarding behavior that does not increase performance
	  • Rewarding behavior A, but hoping for B
	3. Nullifying intended contingencies
	  • Using improper performance instrument
	  • Improper use of appraisal instrument
	  • Failure to use information obtained
	  • Inconsistently applied
	4. Employee opposition
	  • Individually: mistrust, lack of fairness, inequity
	  • Socially: restrictions due to fear of loss of work
	  • Outside intervention: union
		1. Train manager to establish appropriate contingencies between rewards and performance
		2. Use information obtained from appraisals of employee performance as basis for reward allocation decisions
		3. Administer the reward system consistently across employees
		4. Obtain employee participation in the design and administration of the pay plan

Source: P. M. Podsakoff, C. N. Greene, and J. M. McFillen, "Obstacles to the Effective Use of Reward Systems," in *Readings in Personnel and Human Resource Management,* 3d ed., ed. R. S. Schuler, S. A. Youngblood, and V. Huber (St. Paul: West, 1987).

Auditing the Merit Pay System

Critical to the success of any merit pay system is administering it so as to maintain its integrity. This suggests that merit pay should be administered accurately across employees, fairly across all units or divisions in a company, and within the pay structure for all salary grades. That is, all employees should know that their merit raise is being determined in the same way regardless of the supervisor and that the determination is based on an accurate measure of job performance. Although ensuring accuracy of appraisals may be effectively addressed by a behavioral-based performance appraisal method such as BARS or BOS (see Chapter 6), ensuring fair and consistent administration (within the pay structure) is done through the use of compra-ratios and performance ratios.

Used together, compra-ratios and performance ratios can highlight pay and job performance relationships by individual employee, by salary grade, by level in the organization, or by department or division in the company. The **compra-ratio** is the measure of an individual's salary in relationship to the midpoint of the range for a salary grade. This ratio is determined by dividing an individual's salary by the midpoint of the salary range and multiplying by 100. A ratio of 110 means that the individual is being paid 10 percent over midpoint. Assuming a normal distribution of job performance or experience levels (or both), the average compra-ratio in any department or division should be close to 100. Ratios higher than 100 may suggest leniency (therefore inaccuracy) in a supervisor's appraisals, and ratios less than 100 may suggest the opposite. Allowed to exist, differential ratios across departments or divisions may indicate inconsistent merit pay administration.

Similar conclusions can be drawn from the use of **performance ratios**. These ratios indicate where the performance rating of any employee stands relative to the other employees. This is done by determining the midpoint of a performance range, dividing that into each employee's performance rating, and multiplying that figure by 100. This process can be facilitated by using a performance appraisal method with points rather than relative rankings. Most performance appraisal methods discussed in Chapter 6, except the relative approach, can thus be used in determining performance ratios. Again, assuming normal performance distributions, the average performance ratio for a department or division should be close to 100. Variations from 100 may suggest and be related to unfair and inconsistent merit pay practices.[33]

Lump-sum Salary Increases

Although merit increases are generally given at the end of a six-month or a one-year interval, the additional pay is given out in only small weekly or monthly portions.[34] Consequently, an individual may receive as much as a 10 percent merit increase but not be very excited about it. Consider an example of an individual with a $50,000 yearly salary. A 10 percent merit increase results in a $5,000 bonus. Assume that the individual is paid every two weeks.

Since this individual is in the 50-percent tax bracket (federal, state, and local taxes combined), he or she takes home approximately $100 more in every check. In times of rapid inflation, the real value of what the individual gets in every check may be much less than $100.

Recognizing that this method may reduce the motivational impact of the salary increase, companies such as B. F. Goodrich, Timex, and Westinghouse have started lump-sum programs. Specifically, they give the employee the choice of receiving salary increases in the traditional way (divided up into parts for each check) or as a lump sum. Although this idea is relatively new, apparently a majority of employees choose the lump-sum payment unless the payment is treated as a loan for one year and interest is charged. When interest is charged, the attractiveness and motivational value of the lump sum decline substantially.

Participation in Performance-based Pay Systems

Employee participation can take place at two critical points in performance-based pay systems: (1) in the design stage and (2) in the administration stage.

Design Stage.   Many pay plans are designed by top management and installed in a fairly authoritative fashion. Apparently, however, employees can do the same things and even more effectively. That is, employees can be responsible in designing the pay plan, as suggested in the previous chapter. Furthermore, they understand and accept the plan more readily because of this involvement. Participation in plan design also helps to reduce the potential resistance to change that accompanies almost any change in an organization. As a consequence of these factors, employees are more motivated to increase performance.

Despite these potential advantages of employee participation in pay plan design, they may not always occur. They fail to occur when management is not truly participative but rather tries to manipulate employees into participation. They also fail to occur when employees prefer not to participate. These reasons for failure also apply to employee participation in the administration of the pay plan.

Administration Stage.   As indicated in Chapter 8, employees can responsibly determine when and if other workers should receive pay increases. This also appears to be true for individuals determining their own pay increases. Nevertheless, employee participation may not work in all cases, nor is it necessarily appropriate under all circumstances. As shown in Exhibit 1.4, employee participation in pay decisions may be appropriate in organizations with entrepreneurial or growth strategies, but they may not be appropriate in organizations with turnaround or liquidation strategies. Other considerations in selecting a high degree of employee participation are mentioned in Chapter 8 in "Trends in Total Compensation."

Trends In Performance-based Pay

Because Chapter 8 discussed the trends in strategic involvement and choices for all aspects of total compensation, only the trends associated with assessing performance-based pay and computer technology and HRIS in performance-based pay are discussed here.

Assessing Performance-based Pay Systems

Regardless of organizational conditions and considerations, performance-based pay systems can be assessed on the basis of three criteria: (1) the relationship between performance and pay—that is, the time between performance and the administration of the pay (the actual time and the time as perceived by employees); (2) how well the plan minimizes the perceived negative consequences of good performance, such as social ostracism; and (3) whether it contributes to the perception that rewards other than pay (such as cooperation and recognition) also stem from good performance.[35] The more the plan minimizes the perceived negative consequences, and the more it contributes to the perception that other good rewards are also tied to performance, the more motivating it is likely to be. Exhibit 9.4 presents an evaluation of individual and group (department and organization) plans based on these three criteria.

Exhibit 9.4 uses three objective measures to determine the level of job performance to be rewarded: sales or units made (productivity), cost effectiveness or savings below budget, and traditional supervisor ratings. As discussed in Chapter 6, the more objective measures generally have higher credibility, are more valid, and are more visible and verifiable than the traditional supervisor ratings. Consequently, the objective measures (productivity and cost effectiveness) are more likely to link pay to job performance than they are to minimize negative side effects. This evaluation is based on the notion that people do what's rewarded. More objective measures tend to clarify what's rewarded and what's not. This may produce more keen competition with other workers, result in more social ostracism, and lead workers to perceive that good job performance may reduce the work available to them.[36]

The overall evaluation of plans suggests that compared with individual-level incentive plans, department and organization-wide incentive plans, although not high in relating individual performance with pay, result in fewer negative side effects (the exception is with intergroup competition) and additional benefits besides pay, such as esteem, respect and social acceptance from other employees.

Considering all three levels of incentive pay plans, there are no clear winners by all criteria. Incentive plans have more incentive value than seniority increases, across-the-board raises, and merit pay plans. Thus, the situation for motivating job performance with pay is favorable. In a study of fifty-four companies with incentive programs, average increase in productivity over their previous nonincentive programs was 22.8 percent. Furthermore, even

Effectiveness of Performance-based
Pay Systems

Exhibit 9.4

	Type of Plan	Performance Measure	Tie Pay to Performance	Minimize Negative Side Effects	Tie Other Rewards to Performance
Merit	Individual	Productivity	+2	0	0
		Cost effectiveness	+1	0	0
		Superiors' rating	+1	0	+1
	Department	Productivity	+1	0	+1
		Cost effectiveness	+1	0	+1
		Superiors' rating	+1	0	+1
	Organization-wide	Productivity	+1	0	+1
		Cost effectiveness	+1	0	+1
		Profit	0	0	+1
Incentive	Individual	Productivity	+3	−2	0
		Cost effectiveness	+2	−1	0
		Superiors' rating	+2	−1	+1
	Department	Productivity	+2	0	+1
		Cost effectiveness	+2	0	+1
		Superiors' rating	+2	0	+1
	Organization-wide	Productivity	+2	0	+1
		Cost effectiveness	+2	0	+1
		Profit	+1	0	+1

Source: E. E. Lawler III, *Pay and Organizational Effectiveness,*
p. 165. Copyright © 1971 by McGraw-Hill Book Company.
Reprinted with permission.

larger gains are apparently possible and more certain to be maintained when the following conditions exist:

■ The plan is clearly communicated.

■ The plan is understood, and bonuses are easy to calculate.

■ The employees have a hand in establishing and administering the plan.

■ The employees believe they are being treated fairly.

■ The employees have an avenue of appeal if they believe they are being treated unfairly.

■ The employees believe they can trust the company; therefore, they believe they have job security.

■ The bonuses are awarded as soon as possible after the desired performance.

Unfortunately, meeting all of these conditions is difficult for many organizations. In addition, as the cost of indirect compensation continues to grow for most organizations, the amount of money left to attain maximum motivational value for the total compensation dollar becomes less. Consequently, organizations look to their indirect compensation to provide some motivational value, as discussed in Chapter 10.

Computer Technology and HRIS in Performance-based Pay

Much of the time spent in compensation planning is lost to pencil pushing and number crunching, not planning. Computer technology can accommodate performance-based pay planning and administration in the following ways. First, administration may be conducted by establishing a merit pay plan grid on a computer system. The computer can be programmed to post the appropriate percentage increases. Second, budget planning is facilitated simply by manipulating the percentage values on the grid, automatically changing each individual's pay. As in total compensation, performance-based planning may be considered by department, position, or other meaningful ways. In addition, these values may be equally useful to top management. Because time is a cost to the organization, the ability to analyze this information with a minimal time investment represents a substantial cost efficiency.

Computer technology facilitates the management and manipulation of data that can be used to formulate projections concerning salary structure proposals, compra-ratios, compensation cost/amount of revenue generated ratios, total cost of selected configurations of benefits packages, and the cost of compensation in the future under different rates of inflation. These calculations may be made on an individual employee, group, or overall organizational basis. Selected information may be further extracted to make summary reports and projections for areas other than the personnel department, such as a budget sheet for the comptroller.

Computer technology can also be applied to compensation planning by analyzing the various monetary components that make up compensation. These include, for example, base salary, performance-based salary, seniority bonus, performance bonus, profit sharing, and cost of benefits.

Summary

Performance-based pay systems (except merit pay) are used in relatively few organizations, but they continue to attract the attention of many PHRM managers, and line managers continue to ask whether pay can be used as a motivator with their employees. Yet their experiences with merit pay convince them that pay cannot motivate. The success of many incentive plans indicates that pay can motivate job performance, although many problems can arise because of the many issues associated with the implementation of incentive plans. Implementation requires an effective performance appraisal program. The more objective the measures of job performance, the more value incentive plans have. But many organizations do not have effective appraisal programs. As a result, pay is not based on job performance (even though some people may be doing more work than others) but rather on nonperformance factors, such as the cost of living or seniority. To retain some appearance of rewarding job performance, some organizations may use merit pay plans. Consequently, most organizations do not or cannot provide the full incentive value of pay. Nevertheless, a few organizations are attempting to remove the obstacles to incentive plans by using plans that allow a great deal of employee participation in implementation and administration, provide employees with a clear understanding of the plan, allow employees to appeal pay decisions, and provide rewards as soon as possible after the job performance.

Yet, despite the potential motivational value of performance-based pay systems, the majority of organizations continue to choose essentially nonperformance-based plans. Some organizations believe that performance-based pay systems are not possible, because of the lack of appropriate conditions or because of the cost. However, if organizations can measure performance, and everyone thinks the system is fair and tied to the objectives of the organization, paying for performance should increase profitability. Increased profitability should enable organizations to pay for the cost of the plan.

Which performance-based pay plan to use must be determined by several factors, such as the level at which job performance can accurately be measured (individual, department, or organization) for given individuals, the extent of cooperation needed between departments, and the level of trust between management and nonmanagement. Several plans can be used together to reward different groups of employees for good job performance. However, there may be limits on a specific organization's decision to use performance-based pay, which may include management's desire to have performance-based pay; management's commitment to take the time to design and implement one or several systems; the extent to which employees influence the output; the extent to which a good performance appraisal system exists; the existence of a union; and the degree of trust in the organization. Whether the organization is public or private influences the decision, too. Generally, only private organizations utilize incentive systems. Both types, however, can and do use merit pay systems.

Which pay system is best depends on many factors. One is the level at which job performance can be measured accurately and objectively. Another is the control a person has over the level of job performance, and another is the extent of cooperation needed between individuals and departments. Another consideration is the degree of negative consequences produced by a system. A final major consideration is the extent to which employees will understand and accept the plan.

Even when organizations adopt some type of incentive plan, they still need to provide employees with indirect compensation, such as pension and retirement benefits, holidays, and other benefits related only to organizational membership and not to performance. The extent and costliness of such benefits are described in Chapter 10.

Discussion Questions

1. Do you believe that an employee's behavior is always influenced by the rewards expected? Is this true for your behavior in this course?
2. Suppose that people don't always do things because of the tangible rewards they can receive in return for their actions. Does this invalidate the theory of performance-based pay? Explain.
3. What conditions are necessary for effective performance-based pay systems (i.e., systems that enhance the organization's strategic goals)?
4. What obstacles are there in specifying and measuring job performance?
5. How can an organization determine whether merit pay is administered accurately across all employees or across all its units and divisions?
6. Describe a performance-based pay system that you have directly experienced. Did the system work? If not, why not?
7. Under what conditions would you expect a performance-based pay system to have the greatest likelihood of success?
8. What other PHRM functions can contribute to the success of a performance-based pay system? Explain how.
9. Debate the following assertion: If selection and placement decisions are done effectively, individual performance should not vary by a great deal; therefore, a performance-based pay system is not needed.
10. How can employees participate in both the design and the administration of a performance-based pay system? In general, will this have positive or negative consequences for the operation of the system?

PC Project

Rewarding performance with pay is an important and controversial aspect of personnel and human resource management. In this PC Project you will allocate merit pay to employees. Since merit pay is based on performance appraisals, the system must be monitored. Compra-ratios and performance ratios will be examined to determine whether there are systematic biases in the compensation system. Employees' perceptions of the relationship between pay and performance will also be studied.

| C | A | S | E | | S | T | U | D | Y |

The Time Clock

Sharon Taylor was feeling good about the new position at Western National Bank. Sharon, a seven-year employee at Western, had come a long way from her starting position as secretary to the personnel director. Sharon was now the personnel director at Western, thanks in many respects to her predecessor, JoAnn Givens.

JoAnn had recently resigned from the bank to take a position with a local computer software company, which had exploded in growth to one hundred employees within the past two years. The company recognized a need to systematize their staffing practices, so when JoAnn learned of the opportunity, she jumped eagerly. JoAnn was frustrated by what she considered conservative and stodgy management at the bank, so a change in scenery was welcome relief.

JoAnn had begun at Western as an assistant to then personnel director Alice Johnson. JoAnn had an MBA degree from a Big Ten university, while Alice had earned an undergraduate degree in business from a small university in the east. JoAnn quickly realized that her technical skills were superior to Alice's, but she admired Alice's street smarts and willingness to battle the president and CEO of the bank over new initiatives in the personnel area. Alice had put in a performance evaluation plan and an absenteeism plan before transferring to the trust department, which was publicly announced as a promotion by Larry Wilson, president of Western.

JoAnn, though, did not see the move as a promotion. In her estimation, Alice had gotten too strong and was creating a lot of waves for the top brass at the bank, who were unwilling to move at the pace Alice set. When Larry asked JoAnn to assume the role of assistant vice-president of personnel, JoAnn welcomed the opportunity to continue the initiatives begun by Alice.

JoAnn decided that she was going to undertake two goals immediately. First, she was going to begin developing Sharon. Alice was too hard on Sharon, in JoAnn's estimation. Although Sharon didn't have a college degree, she had common sense and extremely good people skills. Over the next year, JoAnn progressively increased Sharon's responsibilities by involving her in applicant screening and interviewing and including her on project assignments. Over time, Sharon and JoAnn developed a teamlike approach to their work and learned to rely on each other to keep the personnel office functioning smoothly.

When Sharon learned of JoAnn's departure, she was saddened but not surprised. JoAnn always seemed too liberal and progressive for the upper management of the bank. JoAnn valued people and looked for the best in them. JoAnn, more than the other officers at the bank, seemed genuinely concerned about the welfare of the employees, especially the mostly nonexempt employee work force. Sharon was flabbergasted, though, when Larry Wilson called her into his office and asked her to assume JoAnn's job. Her pay would increase by 150 percent, to say the least. Although the job would mean longer hours and responsibilities, under JoAnn's prior tutelage Sharon felt confident that she could rise to the occasion.

Sharon wanted more than anything to carry through on JoAnn's second goal, which was to try to link the performance evaluation system developed by Alice to the annual pay increases. The bank had entered an era of competition from other banks and savings and loans, so productivity was a major concern for the bank. Besides cutting staff to the minimum, Sharon believed that in the long run, linking pay to effort and performance would encourage productivity among all employees. Sharon believed that Western's staff were hardworking and would welcome the opportunity to see their pay linked to their performance.

Sharon noticed that it was almost 5:00 P.M., and she needed to speak with John Dinkel, VP for operations, regarding her proposed merit plan, which would influence his group the most. As she passed by the elevators, she noticed several employees waiting beside the time clock. It was a common practice for the nonexempts to wait for a seemingly inordinate amount of time for the elevator to arrive on the fifth floor of the bank building. A common practice was to wait until the elevator bell chimed and the doors began to open before clocking out.

As several of the employees hurriedly punched the clock and dashed to the elevator, Larry Wilson appeared behind Sharon. Larry called out to Sharon, who was deep in thought about how to present her merit plan to John Dinkel. "Sharon, did you see that?" questioned Larry. "I'm sorry, Larry, I was lost in thought. What are you talking about?" replied Sharon. As the elevator doors closed, Larry picked up his voice in obvious irritation. "I think those employees would just as soon cheat us if they are charging their wait time on the elevators! How do we know that they're not trying to cheat us in the morning when they clock in or even still, when they return from lunch late and have a co-worker punch them in? Sharon, I want you to investigate this tomorrow, first thing. This kind of fraud has got to stop immediately!" Oh boy, thought Sharon. How am I going to defuse this bomb? As Sharon started back down the hall toward John Dinkel's office, she began to understand the frustration that occasionally leaked through JoAnn's otherwise calm exterior when she occupied Sharon's job.

Notes

1. For additional information on Lincoln Electric, see W. Serrin, "The Way That Works at Lincoln," *New York Times*, 15 Jan. 1984, p. 4F; A. D. Sharplin, "Lincoln Electric's Unique Policies," *Personnel Administrator* (June 1983): 8-9.

2. For a description of the one hundred best companies, see R. Levering, M. Moskowitz, and M. Katz, *The 100 Best Companies to Work for in America* (Reading, Mass.: Addison-Wesley, 1984).

3. Also recall that several excellent nonmonetary rewards (see Exhibit 8.2) could be used with pay and contingent on performance in performance-based pay systems. They could also be used in lieu of pay. As organizations become more cost conscious and learn that not all employees indicate their first preference to be pay, the use and attractiveness of these nonmonetary rewards could become much greater. See P. M. Podsakoff, C. N. Greene, and J. M. McFillen, "Obstacles to the Effective Use of Reward Systems," in *Readings in Personnel and Human Resource Management*, 3d ed., ed. R. S. Schuler, S. A. Youngblood, and V. Huber (St. Paul: West, 1987); E. E. Lawler III, "Pay for Performance: A Motivational Analysis," in *Readings in Personnel and Human Resource Management*, 3d ed., ed. R. S. Schuler, S. A. Youngblood, and V. Huber (St. Paul: West, 1987).

4. K. W. Bennett, "Employee Incentives Plus New Technology Equals Productivity," *Iron Age*, 2 Feb. 1981, pp. 43-45; T. Rendero, "Roundup," *Personnel* (Nov.-Dec. 1979): 57-59; E. E. Lawler III, *Pay and Organizational Development* (Reading, Mass.: Addison-Wesley, 1981); E. E. Lawler III, *Pay and Organizational Effectiveness: A Psychological View* (New York: McGraw-Hill, 1971).

5. Although goal setting and job enrichment programs are ways to increase productivity, incentive compensation appears to be able to produce larger increases in productivity.

6. D. Q. Mills, *The New Competitors* (New York: Wiley, 1985); G. Milkovich and J. Newman, *Compensation* (Plano, Tex.: Business Publications, 1984).

7. *Wall Street Journal*, 9 July 1985, p. 1. Reprinted by permission of *The Wall Street Journal*, © Dow Jones & Company, Inc., 1985. All Rights Reserved.

8. "Loggers Tie Pay to Productivity," *Business Week*, 29 Nov. 1982.

9. For an excellent discussion of the entire area of executive (managerial) compensation tax laws, see M. Bentson and J. Schuster, "Pay and Executive Compensation," in *Human Resource Management in the 1980s*, ed. S. J. Carroll and R. S. Schuler (Washington, D.C.: Bureau of National Affairs, 1983); W. J. Smith, "Executive Compensation after ERTA," *Personnel Administrator* (Feb. 1983): 63-65; G. Klott, "Incentive Stock Options Subject to New Taxes,"

New York Times, 21 Jan. 1984; J. McMillan and S. D. Hickok, "Taking Stock of the Options," *Personnel Journal*, (Apr. 1984): 32-37; and Milkovich and Newman, *Compensation*.

10. Bureau of National Affairs, "A Study of Performance Pay," *Bulletin to Management*, 24 May 1984, P. 8. Reprinted by permission from *Bulletin to Management*, copyright 1984, by The Bureau of National Affairs, Inc., Washington, D.C. See also R. E. Kopelman, "The Case for Merit Rewards," *Personnel Administrator* (Oct. 1983): 60-68; W. L. Mihal, "Merit Pay: A Good Idea But Does It Work?" *Personnel Administrator* (Oct. 1983): 60-68; C. A. Peck, *Compensating Salaried Employees during Inflation: General vs. Merit Increases* (New York: Conference Board, 1981); Lawler, *Pay and Organizational Development*; D. J. Thomsen, "Salary Increases vs. Incentives," *Personnel Journal* (Dec. 1980): 974; H. W. Doyal and J. L. Johnson, "Pay Increase Guidelines with Merit," *Personnel Journal* (June 1985): 46-50.

11. Other factors influencing merit pay that can still be legally defended (when they are equally applied to all employees) include (1) position in salary range, (2) time since last increase, (3) size of last increase, (4) pay relationships within the company or department, (5) pay levels of jobs in other companies, (6) salaries of newly hired employees, and (7) budgetary limits.

12. J. G. Goodale and N. M. Mouser, "Developing and Auditing a Merit Pay System," *Personnel Journal* (May 1981): 391-97.

13. C. R. Deitsch and D. A. Dilts, "The COLA Clause: An Employer Bargaining Weapon?" *Personnel Journal* (Mar. 1982): 220-23.

14. B. L. Metzger, *Profit Sharing in Perspective*, 2d ed. (Evanston, Ill.: Profit Sharing Research Foundation, 1966), p. 45; H. Risher, "Inflation and Salary Administration," *Personnel Administrator* (May 1981): 33-38, 68; J. D. Schwartz, "Maintaining Merit Compensation in a High Inflation Economy," *Personnel Journal* (Feb. 1982): 147-52; Peck. D. J. Thomsen, "Compensation Trends in 1981," *Personnel Journal* (Jan. 1981): 22; Milkovich and Newman, *Compensation*; M. S. Melbinger, "Negotiating a Profit-sharing Plan: A Survey of the Options," *Employee Relations Law Journal* (Spring 1985): 684-701; C. S. Mishkind and D. E. Khorey, "Employee Stock Ownership Plans: Fables and Facts," *Employee Relations Law Journal* (Summer 1985): 89-105; D. R. Brown and B. H. Kleiner, "Employee Ownership: Problems and Prospects," *Personnel Administrator* (Dec. 1985): 75-82.

15. For a discussion of these and other aspects of merit pay administration, see E. J. Brennan, "Merit Pay: Balance the Old Rich and the New Poor," *Personnel Journal* (May 1985): 82-85.

16. Bureau of National Affairs, "Incentive Pay: Popular-

ity Booms," *Bulletin to Management,* 18 Oct. 1984, p. 8.

17. Lawler, *Pay and Organizational Effectiveness.*

18. J. D. Dunn and F. M. Rachel, *Wage and Salary Administration: Total Compensation Systems* (New York: McGraw-Hill, 1971), p. 236.

19. A. R. Pinto and N. Poser, "Brokers Who Trade Too Often," *Wall Street Journal,* 20 May 1985, p. 21. Reprinted by permission of *The Wall Street Journal,* © Dow Jones & Company, Inc., 1985. All Rights Reserved.

20. R. J. Bronsteing, "The Equity Component of the Executive Compensation Package," *California Management Review* (Fall 1980): 64–70. For an excellent discussion of the entire area of executive (managerial) compensation, see M. Bentson and J. Schuster, "Pay and Executive Compensation," in *Human Resource Management in the 1980s,* ed. S. J. Carroll and R. S. Schuler (Washington, D.C.: Bureau of National Affairs, 1983); A. Nash, *Managerial Compensation* (Scarsdale, N.Y.: Work in America Institute, 1980); "After the Qualified Stock Option," *Business Week,* 25 May 1981, pp. 100–102; P. Meyer, "Executive Compensation Must Promote Long-Term Commitment," *Personnel Administrator* (May 1983): 37–44; D. Rankin, "Warm Welcome for Incentive Options," *New York Times,* 13 June 1982, p. F15.

21. "A Plum for Executives and for Companies, Too," *Business Week,* 25 July 1983, p. 42. See also J. McMillan and S. D. Hickok, "Taking Stock of the Options," *Personnel Journal* (Apr. 1984): 32–37.

22. M. A. Tather, "Turning Ideas into Gold," *Management Review* (Mar. 1975): 4–10; V. G. Reuter, "A New Look at Suggestion Systems," *Journal of Systems Management* (Jan. 1976): 6–15; A. W. Bergerson, "Employee Suggestion Plan Still Going Strong at Kodak," *Supervisory Management* (May 1977): 32–33.

23. D. W. Belcher, *Compensation Administration* (Englewood Cliffs, N.J.: Prentice-Hall, 1974), pp. 323–24.

24. K. D. Scott and T. Cotter, "The Team That Works Together Earns Together," *Personnel Journal* (Mar. 1984): 59–67.

25. B. E. Moore and T. L. Ross, *The Scanlon Way to Improved Productivity: A Practical Guide* (New York: Wiley, 1978); A. J. Geare, "Productivity from Scanlon-Type Plans," *Academy of Management Review* (July 1976): 99–108; R. J. Schulhof, "Five Years with a Scanlon Plan" *Personnel Administrator* (June 1979): 55–63; L. S. Tyler and B. Fisher, "The Scanlon Concept: A Philosophy as Much as a System," *Personnel Administrator* (July 1983): 33–37.

26. R. J. Bullock and E. E. Lawler, "Gainsharing: A Few Questions, and Fewer Answers," *Human Resource Management* (Spring 1984): 23–40.

27. George T. Milkovich and Jerry M. Newman, Business Publications, Inc., Plano, Tx., COMPENSATION © 1984.

28. Milkovich and Newman, *Compensation.*

29. These have been identified and discussed by Podsakoff, Greene, and McFillen. See also R. I. Henderson, "Designing a Reward System for Today's Employee," *Business Horizons* (July–Sept. 1982): 2–12.

30. This is particularly true for individuals in high tax brackets. When taxes are significant, individuals may prefer the same size (in dollar value equivalence) reward as an indirect benefit (e.g., the use of a car, club membership, and other possibilities listed in Chapter 10). See also "Pay at the Top Mirrors Inflation," *Business Week,* 11 May 1981, pp. 58–59; "Surge in Executive Job Contracts," *Dunn's Business Month* (Oct. 1981): 86–88; K. E. Foster, "Does Executive Pay Make Sense?" *Business Horizons* (Sept.–Oct. 1981): 47–58; D. B. Thompson, "Are CEOs Worth What They're Paid?" *Industry Week,* 4 May 1981, pp. 65–74.

31. S. Barkin, "Labor's Attitude toward Wage Incentive Plans," *Industrial and Labor Relations Review* (July 1984): 553–72. See also Milkovich and Newman, *Compensation.*

32. W. F. Whyte, "Skinnerian Theory in Organizations," *Psychology Today,* Apr. 1972.

33. Goodale and Mouser, "Developing and Auditing," pp. 394–95. See also J. D. McMillan and V. C. Williams, "The Elements of Effective Salary Administration Programs," *Personnel Journal* (Nov. 1982): 832–38; T. A. Mahoney, "Compensating for Work," in *Personnel Management,* ed. K. N. Rowland and G. R. Ferris (Boston: Allyn & Bacon, 1982), pp. 227–62.

34. N. B. Winstanley, "Are Merit Increases Really Effective?" *Personnel Administrator* (Apr. 1982): 37–41.

35. Lawler, *Pay and Organizational Effectiveness.*

36. S. R. Collings, "Incentive Programs: Pros and Cons," *Personnel Journal* (July 1981): 571–75; R. B. Goettinger, "Compensation and Benefits," *Personnel Journal* (Nov. 1981): 840–42. For a case study illustration of merit pay assessment issues, see S. C. Freedman, "Performance-Based Pay: A Convenience Store Case Study," *Personnel Journal* (July 1985): 30–34; J. R. Terborg and G. R. Ungson, "Group Administered Bonus Pay and Retail Store Performance: A Two-Year Study of Management Compensation," *Journal of Retailing* (Spring 1985): 63–77.

10

Indirect Compensation

Shifts in Coverage Dramatic: Survey Benefits Growth

Driven by pressures for cost containment and greater responsiveness to employee needs, benefits programs have changed dramatically over the past few years. A recent study of benefits conducted by Hewitt Associates showed that, over the past two years, significant changes have been made—particularly among medical and retirement benefits.

401(k) growth

According to the sampling of 250 large employers, growth in the number of 401(k) plans continues at a fast pace. In 1982, less than two percent of companies provided employees the opportunity to contribute to a savings or profit sharing plan on a before-tax basis. In 1983, 43 percent of companies offered salary reduction plans.

And last year, nearly three-quarters of the survey companies permitted 401(k) salary reduction contributions.

Also last year, medical plans with front-end deductibles outnumbered "first dollars" medical benefits for the first time. As recently as three years ago, less than one out of five firms required employees to pay a front-end deductible for medical expenses. In 1983, about a third did. By last year, front-end deductibles were required by 52 percent of the companies surveyed.

Deductibles are on the rise, too. Most plans—85 percent—until 1982 had a deductible of $100 or less. By 1984, that percentage had shrunk to 51 percent and the deductible climbed to $150 or more.

In conjunction with front-end deductibles, cost sharing is on the rise at most firms. Six years ago, nine out of 10 firms provided full reimbursement for hospital costs. That number has continued to shrink, reaching 50 percent last year.

Similarly, the number of companies paying 80 percent of hospital costs increased from five percent in 1979 to 26 percent in 1984.

Employers are also including new plan requirements in policies to help educate their employees about the high costs associated with medical care. About half of the firms cover hospice care at the same or higher rate than traditional hospital care; about one out of every two firms gives employees an incentive to have surgery done on an outpatient basis.

More firms are requiring second opinions when surgery is called for. In 1984, more than a third required it. Also, one-third encouraged employees to have any necessary testing done before entering the hospital.

Dental plan coverage

Although the rate of growth has slowed, the prevalence of dental plans continued to increase in 1984. The most significant growth in dental coverage occurred from 1979 to 1981, when dental plans increased from 70 percent to 85 percent of survey companies. By last year, the number of plans had increased to 91 percent.

Most firms continue medical coverage to retirees after age 65. In 1979, 88 percent of firms provided post-65 coverage. By 1982, the number had increased to 94 percent, where it remained stable through last year.

Pensions

Retirement security has held ground as a top benefit priority among those firms surveyed.

The number of companies providing pensions during the last six years has remained steady at 98 percent. In addition more companies offered one or more defined contribution plans. In 1979, 10 percent of the firms had no accumulation plans versus only three percent last year.

The preceding "PHRM in the News" highlights several critical aspects of indirect compensation. One is the magnitude of indirect compensation costs; in some cases, they are nearly equal to those of direct compensation. At the same time, however, some employers are questioning whether the benefits they receive from providing indirect compensation are worthwhile. Employees now expect employers to provide extensive indirect compensation benefits. Employers are expected to provide these merely to stay competitive with other organizations in attracting job applicants. The most qualified job applicants are likely to go to those organizations that provide the most attractive and flexible indirect compensation. Although the costs of indirect compensation may be high, they may attract and retain highly qualified individuals and provide benefits to the organization as worthwhile as those from direct compensation.

The initial "PHRM in the News" also illustrates the dynamic nature of indirect compensation activity. As employees preferences and the legal environment change, organizations adapt by changing the benefits offered or the way they are provided.

As with direct compensation, many employees are vitally concerned with indirect compensation. Aside from its high value, this is a form of compensation on which employees generally do not have to pay income taxes. But as the cost of indirect benefits in proportion to the total payroll cost grows, organizations are becoming more concerned about how they do or can provide benefits, what they must do to satisfy employees, and how to keep the cost of these benefits down.

What Is Indirect Compensation?

Almost all organizations offer some form of indirect compensation. For some of these organizations, indirect compensation may make up as much as 50 percent of the cost of total compensation.[1] Furthermore, the percentage of total compensation devoted to indirect compensation is expected to increase. Since the costs of indirect compensation are becoming so significant, organizations question whether the costs are worthwhile. The answer depends on the purposes or objectives of indirect compensation and what it is (i.e., how it is defined). **Indirect compensation** is defined here as those rewards provided by the organization to employees for their membership or participation (attendance) in the organization. Indirect compensation is divided into three categories:[2]

- Protection programs
  Public
  Private
- Pay for time not worked
  On the job
  Off the job
- Employee services and perquisites
  General
  Limited

Although several of these categories are mandated by federal and state governments and must therefore be administered within the boundaries of laws and regulations, many others are provided voluntarily by organizations.[3] In part because indirect compensation categories are so diverse and employees' preferences are so varied, not all indirect compensation is always valued or seen as a reward by all employees. When indirect compensation is matched with employee preferences, however, many of the purposes of indirect compensation can be attained.

Purposes and Importance of Indirect Compensation

The average cost of employer-paid benefits to hourly rate employees in 1983 rose by approximately 5.5 percent to $7,582 per year per employee or $3.69 per payroll hour, according to the latest annual survey of employers conducted by the U.S. Chamber of Commerce. Benefits in 1983 came to 36.6 percent of total payroll, down from a peak of 37.3 percent in 1981.

The total price tag to employers for all benefits in 1983 amounted to $550 billion, up from $510 billion in 1982, the study reports. According to James R. Morris, director of the Chamber's Survey Research Section, total benefit costs for 1984 and 1985 are estimated at $595 billion and $645 billion respectively.

Costs in manufacturing industries are estimated at $148 billion, or 37.4 percent of the $395.2 billion paid in wages and salaries. Service industry benefits are estimated at $79 billion, or 26 percent of the $303.4 billion in wages and salaries. Benefits in wholesale and retail trade are estimated at $81 billion; finance, insurance, and real estate at $43 billion; construction at $23 billion; transportation at $24.8 billion; utilities and communication at $25.5 billion; mining at $11.3 billion; agriculture at $2.4 billion; and federal, state and local government benefits at $112 billion.

Employee benefit payments as percent of payroll varied widely from industry to industry. The primary metal industries paid 47.1 percent, followed by the transportation equipment industry paying 40.9 percent, and the petroleum industry paying 40.7 percent. Wholesale and retail trade (other than department stores) paid 29.0 percent, and both department stores and hospitals paid 31.8 percent.

Benefit payments also varied with region. For all industries, payments averaged 38.2 percent of payroll in the East North Central region, followed by 38.1 percent in the Northeast region. The Western region averaged 35.9 percent, and the Southeast region averaged 33.9 percent.[4]

Indirect compensation costs as a percentage of payroll or salary also differ by level of employee in the organization. The percentage of indirect benefits is greatest at the lowest salary levels. Indirect compensation costs also differ in the private sector organizations versus the federal government. Whereas the benefits received by federal employees used to be inferior to those received by private employees, the federal benefits package is now estimated at approximately 5 percent ahead or more valuable. The most significant difference in benefits between the two sectors is in retirement benefits. Federal retirement benefits total 28.2 percent of pay (only the employers' contributions), while private retirement benefits, including social security, total only 16.7 percent.[5] Regardless of salary level or sector of the economy, however, the cost of benefits to organizations is enormous.

In return for these benefits, organizations seek to attain several purposes:

- Attracting good employees
- Increasing employee morale
- Reducing turnover
- Increasing job satisfaction
- Motivating employees
- Enhancing the organization's image among employees
- Making better use of compensation dollars[6]

Only rarely are all these purposes attained. "There is ample research to demonstrate that these purposes are not being attained, largely because of inadequate communication."[7] The argument can be made, however, that some of these purposes cannot be attained with indirect compensation. For example, employees can be motivated with incentives because the rewards are tied closely to performance, but the rewards of indirect compensation are tied only to organizational membership. Thus there is no direct reason why employees should be more motivated to perform because of increased indirect compensation. Because of this, organizations have been recommended to tie indirect compensation to performance.[8]

Another important reason why some of the purposes of indirect compensation are not attained is that employees may regard compensation benefits not as rewards but as conditions (rights) of employment. They may also think of indirect benefits as safeguards against insecurity provided by the organization as a social responsibility because they are not provided by society.[9]

Even when indirect compensation is regarded as a reward, its importance relative to other aspects of the organization (e.g., opportunity for advancement, salary, geographic location, job responsibilities, and prestige on the job) may be low. Employees also differ with respect to the importance of the same indirect benefits. Consequently, organizations are offering benefit flexibility to employees. The following "PHRM in the News" shows how American Can derives benefits from giving employees benefit flexibility.

Relationships Influencing Indirect Compensation

Although the many relationships of total compensation that are described in Chapter 8 are applicable here, highlighting a few that apply to indirect compensation is appropriate. The relationships between indirect compensation and other PHRM activities are particularly influential.

Relationships with Other PHRM Activities

Indirect compensation has important relationships with recruitment and selection, direct compensation, and safety and health.

The American Can Experience

In 1978, American Can introduced a sophisticated flexible benefits program that even today provides its employees with the greatest degree of choice of any work force in the country. The American Can program was the first to make use of "flexible credits," pre-tax employer-provided money which employees could use to purchase benefits. It was also the most comprehensive program yet offered, providing a wide range of options in all five of the major benefit areas: Medical, life, vacation, disability and capital accumulation/retirement. Since 1978, the program has been expanded to include a 401(k) CODA, dependent care, a financial planning option and coverage for adoptions.

Experience indicates that this program has proven to be extremely cost effective, with per capital medical costs for the "flex-eligible" population rising only one-third as fast as the costs for the non-flex group, and less quickly than the U.S. medical CPI. The key reason for this slow rate of increase can be traced to the flex-eligible population becoming better consumers over the years. In 1979, 71 percent of the eligible population purchased one of the two most expensive health care plans offered. By 1984, only 31 percent of employees made this choice. Employees purchased less expensive coverage in order to spend their flexible credits on other benefit areas which were of greater value because of their unique individual needs.

At the same time the company was saving money, employee satisfaction with benefits was remarkably high. This was demonstrated in a study conducted by Yankelovich, Skelly and White in which satisfaction levels of American Can's flexible employees were 50 to 100 percent higher than a national sample of employees in traditional benefits plans.

Source: J. A. Haslinger, "Flexible Compensation: Getting a Return on Benefit Dollars," p. 41. Reprinted from the June issue of *Personnel Administrator,* Copyright © 1985, The American Society for Personnel Administration, 606 North Washington Street, Alexandria, Va. 22314.

Recruitment and Selection.   As individuals demand more of indirect compensation, the organization must offer more to attract a pool of potentially qualified job applicants. Without providing benefits comparable to those offered by others in the same industry or same area, an organization may lose qualified individuals to other employers.[10] Oftentimes, however, an individual may not learn of an employer's indirect compensation package until after being recruited. If this is the case, recruitment may not be as negatively affected as selection. That is, a job applicant may go through several expensive selection steps described in Chapter 5, only to reject the job offer because of an inadequate indirect compensation package.

But just as an organization's recruitment and selection can be adversely affected by its indirect compensation, they can also be favorably affected. Organizations such as American Can Company, TRW, and IBM are attractive to potential job candidates partly because of their indirect compensation. Their benefit packages are not only extensive but also flexible. Thus, employees can have what they want within broad parameters, and the employers can recruit and select from the most highly qualified job applicants.[11]

Direct Compensation.   Indirect compensation can have an immediate impact on direct compensation, especially when organizations strive to hold total payroll costs constant. In this situation, as organizations find themselves offering more indirect benefits (to be able to recruit and select effectively), they are forced to restrain the pressure to increase direct compensation.[12] This in turn makes it more difficult for direct compensation to be used to attract, retain, and motivate employees. Under this pressure, and the desire to hold payroll costs relatively constant, some organizations lay off employees rather than reduce either direct or indirect compensation. This appears to happen even in the basic industries, such as steel, automobiles, and rubber, where total compensation is relatively high.[13]

Safety and Health.   As the rates of safety and health in organizations decline, the level of worker compensation rates often increases. This in turn increases the cost of indirect compensation to organizations. In addition, even if indirect compensation costs do not increase, larger costs in damage suits against the employer could result, effectively increasing total compensation costs. This is explored further in the discussion of workers' compensation insurance.

In addition to these important relationships influencing compensation is an extensive set of acts, laws, and court decisions. These legal considerations influence several aspects of indirect compensation, especially the issue of which individuals receive certain benefits.

Legal Considerations in Indirect Compensation

Although indirect benefits occurred before 1930, their rapid growth took place in the mid-1930s. In 1929, indirect benefits were less than 5 percent of the cost of total compensation—a dramatic contrast to the average 35-40 percent today. The depression of the 1930s gave the necessary impetus for the beginning of the legal impact on indirect benefits. It prompted the passage of the Social Security Act and the Wagner Act. The Social Security Act, passed in 1935, provided old age, disability, survivors', and health benefits, and was the basis for federal and state unemployment programs. The Wagner Act, or the National Labor Relations Act of 1935 (NLRA), helped ensure their growth by strengthening the union movement in the United States (see Chapter 15). Both of these acts continue to play a significant role in the administration of benefits.

After World War II, the legal environment further stimulated indirect benefits. Two court cases helped to expand benefit coverage by declaring that pension and insurance provisions were bargainable issues in union and management relations. The right to bargain over pensions was decided in *Inland Steel* v. *National Labor Relations Board* (1948), and the right to bargain over insurance was decided in *W. W. Cross* v. *National Labor Relations*

Board (1949). In the 1960s the legal environment became more complex with the passage of several acts by Congress.

Equal Pay Act of 1963

The Equal Pay Act, described in Chapter 8, mandates that employees who have identical jobs be paid equally except for differences in seniority, merit, or other conditions unrelated to sex. Included in the term *paid equally* is direct as well as indirect compensation. For example, women and men on the same job, other factors being equal, must receive the same level of direct and indirect compensation. However, actuarial data indicate that women live approximately seven years longer than men. Therefore, on the average, women will receive a greater total level of retirement benefits than men. Is this equal indirect compensation? Would it be equal if women contributed more? In *Los Angeles Department of Water* v. *Manhart* (1981), the Court ruled against the department's policy of having female employees contribute more to their retirement than the male employees because women on the average live longer than men. In *Spirit* v. *Teachers Insurance and Annuity Association and College Retirement Equities Fund* (1982), the Second U.S. Court of Appeals ruled that retirement annuities must be equal regardless of sex. More recently, however, the Supreme Court ruled that pension benefits paid out to males and females must be equal (*Arizona Governing Committee* v. *Norris,* 1983). Additional guarantees for equal pension benefit treatment to surviving spouses, male and female, are contained in the Retirement Equity Act of 1984.

Pregnancy Discrimination Act of 1978

In recent years, the trend was to treat pregnancy as a disability. Opponents of this trend argued that pregnancy is a voluntary condition, not an involuntary sickness, and therefore should not be covered by disability benefits. The Pregnancy Discrimination Act of 1978, however, states that pregnancy is a disability and must receive the same benefits as any other disability. Thus, a state appeals court in Michigan ruled that a labor contract between the General Motors Corporation and the United Auto Workers that provided sickness and accident benefits of up to fifty-two weeks but limited childbearing disability to six weeks was illegal.[14]

A more recent issue in this area is whether companies have to offer the same pregnancy benefit program to the wives of male employees as it does to the husbands of female employees. The Equal Employment Opportunity Commission (EEOC) says they must, but the Ninth U.S. Court of Appeals rules against the EEOC in *EEOC* v. *Lockheed Missiles and Space Co., Inc.* (1982). This decision, however, is contrary to that rendered by the Fourth U.S. Circuit in *Newport News Shipbuilding and Dry Dock Co.* v. *EEOC* (1982) and the decision by the U.S. Supreme Couut in an appeal of the *Newport News* case (1983). In that case, the Supreme Court ruled that employers who provide health care insurance to spouses of employees that includes complete coverage for all disabilities except pregnancy are violating Title VII of the Civil Rights Act. In essence, then, employers must provide equal benefit coverage for all spouses.

Age Discrimination in Employment Act of 1967

Although the Social Security Act allows women to retire earlier than men (at age sixty-two as opposed to age sixty-five), the U.S. Supreme Court, by refusing to hear a lower-court ruling, affirmed the provisions of the Age Discrimination in Employment Act (ADEA) that it is illegal to require women to retire earlier than men. On the issue of mandatory retirement, neither men nor women can now be forced to retire before the age of seventy if they are working for a private business with at least twenty persons on the payroll. Exceptions are top-level executives who can be retired at age sixty-five and others such as airplane pilots who must retire at age sixty by Federal Aviation Administration law. These provisions are contained in a 1978 amendment to the 1967 Age Discrimination in Employment Act and took effect 1 January 1979. Employees may still choose to retire at age sixty-five and receive full benefits, however. But because Social Security is facing financial difficulties, some congressional representatives now want to increase the age at which full Social Security benefits can start to sixty-eight. Although this has not been done yet, Congress has attempted to reduce some of the burden on Social Security through a provision in the Tax Equity and Fiscal Responsibility Act of 1982. According to that act, employers of twenty or more workers must include those between the ages of sixty-five and sixty-nine in their group health plans unless the employees specifically choose to continue Medicare, funded by Social Security, as their primary coverage.[15] Nonetheless, employers may still freeze pension contributions and plans for employees at sixty-five.

ERISA and Private Employees' Pensions

The Employees' Retirement Income Security Act (ERISA) was enacted in 1974 to protect employees covered by private pension programs. A significant aspect of this protection is to ensure that companies adequately fund their pension programs to pay retirement benefits. In addition, if employees are due pension benefits upon retirement (this means they are **vested** in the company's pension program), they will receive them even if their company chooses to terminate its pension program. ERISA has established the Pension Benefit Guarantee Corporation to take over defunct pension programs and assume their liabilities. If a plan goes defunct, individuals receiving retirement benefits continue to receive them, and those still working are guaranteed their pension benefits.[16]

Another aspect of ERISA relates to the responsibility of the **fiduciaries**—that is, those responsible for managing the money in the pension fund. Generally, the money in the pension fund is invested to gain interest and increase the size of the fund. To help guide the behavior of the fiduciaries, ERISA contains a provision, called the "prudent man" rule, stating that the investment decisions made by the fiduciaries must be similar to those a prudent person would make. To help ensure that prudent fiduciaries have money to invest, ERISA also requires that newly created pension programs be **funded.** That is, the money for the pension fund has to be earmarked for retirees (whether paid in part by the employee, as in **contributory programs,** or solely by the employer, as in **noncontributory programs**). This rule essentially prohibits the use of **unfunded** pension programs that rely upon the goodwill of the employer to pay retirement benefits out of current operating funds on an as-needed basis.

Although ERISA has helped many individuals, many are still unprotected or unprovided for when it comes to private pension plans. On the tenth anniversary of ERISA, only half of the American work force was covered by a private pension plan, and only half of those were vested. Congress passed the Retirement Equity or Pay Equity Act of 1984, which amends ERISA. A major intent of this act is to provide more adequate and extensive private pension program coverage.[17]

Multiemployer Pension Plans

Because ERISA did not address problems unique to multiemployer plans, Congress found it necessary to amend its provisions with the Multiemployer Pension Plan Amendments Act (MEPPAA) of 1980. This act is important for personnel departments because, for the first time, it forces them to become involved in fixing multiemployer plan benefit levels and paying those benefits. Whereas ERISA covers only single pension plans funded and administered by one company, MEPPAA addresses plans covering employees in many different companies. Because multiemployer plans are generally collectively bargained, they are considered "union" plans. Currently, multiemployer pension plans provide retirement benefits to about 8 million Americans in trucking, construction, coal, food-retailing, and other industries.[18]

Tax Acts and the Internal Revenue Service

Almost yearly, Congress passes a tax act that influences indirect compensation programs—either the benefits themselves or how they are administered. For example, in 1981 Congress passed the Economic Recovery Tax Act (ERTA) of 1981. A major provision of ERTA enables employees to make tax-deductible contributions of up to $2,000 to an employer's pension, profit-sharing, or savings plan or to an individual's retirement account (IRA) outside the employer's plan. Another provision is that employers can deduct the cost of the child-care benefits they offer. ERTA also makes it possible for employers to provide company stock to employees and pay for it with tax credits. This aspect of ERISA established the payroll-based stock ownership plan (PAYSOP). PAYSOP facilitates employee stock ownership of organizations. This purpose, however, is not new. The Tax Reduction Act of 1975 created the employee stock ownership plan (ESOP) referred to as TRASOP (Tax Reduction Act Employee Stock Ownership Plan). Since ERTA, the Deficit Reduction Act of 1984 amended PAYSOPs to make them more attractive. As a consequence of these tax acts and the provision of employee stock ownership plans, the concept of worker as owner is spreading from an enclave in small business to the giant corporation. Millions of employees are gaining direct ownership of stock in their own companies—thus getting a foot in a door that has historically been shut to all but the wealthy few. At that pace, 25 percent or more of all U.S. workers will own part or all of their companies by the year 2000.

Seven thousand companies have already enrolled nearly 10 million workers in employee stock ownership plans—up from fewer than 500,000 a decade ago. The number of new plans is currently increasing at a 10 percent annual rate. Although many regard them as excellent vehicles for deferred savings or deferred profit sharing, ESOPs have been questioned by some as schemes for organizations to benefit at the expense of employees.[19]

In 1982, Congress passed the Tax Equity and Fiscal Responsibility Act of 1982 (TEFRA), which sharply cut the maximum benefit and contribution limits for **qualified pension plans** (i.e., those covered under ERISA) and set limits for loans from such plans. Previously, the IRS limited the maximum annual benefits for pension plans to individuals to $136,425. TEFRA reduced that limit to $90,000. Maximum annual contributions by employers for employees' pension programs was reduced from $45,475 to $30,000. Because these changes influenced the pension plans for higher-paid employees, employers have had to provide other protection programs, such as **nonqualified pension plans** or other forms of indirect compensation, as discussed under protection programs. Qualified plans come under the purview of ERISA, the employer's contribution is tax deductible, and the employee is not taxed on the contributions until payments commence. The opposite is true of nonqualified plans.

In addition to the tax acts passed by Congress, indirect compensation has been influenced by tax rulings rendered by the Internal Revenue Service. These rulings can sometimes relate to tax acts. For example, Section 401K of the Internal Revenue Code was adopted in 1979. The amount of tax-deferred savings that employers can provide for employees was established by TEFRA. They are extremely popular with employers and employees as a method of tax-deferred savings. **401(k) plans** are also referred to as **CODAs (cash-or-deferred arrangements)**. These and employee stock ownership plans are described in the following "PHRM in the News."

Because of the Deficit Reduction Act of 1984 and IRS rulings, some benefits, particularly flexible spending plans, are now taxed. Flexible spending plans come in several forms. In one form employees are given the opportunity to choose nontaxable benefits in return for reduced pay. In another, money is set aside initially for benefits, and if employees don't use the benefit by the end of the year, they receive the money. In still another form, no money is set aside initially, but employees are reimbursed for some expenses as they occur. This arrangement is called a **zero-balance reimbursement account,** or **zebra plan**. Because of the tax changes, these plans are soon likely to become obsolete.

In the area of taxing other benefits, the IRS, Congress, and the president share a concern. Essentially, indirect compensation provided to employees is nontaxable. By law this is true for some benefits like employer-paid health and life insurance premiums. By practice this is true for other benefits. Facing the IRS, Congress, and the president is the dilemma of whether to tax any or all of these benefits, including those classified as protection programs.[20]

Timely Trends

Cash-or-deferred arrangements and employee stock ownership plans are compensation and benefit programs that are well-suited to most organizations, according to speakers at a BNA-sponsored executive benefits conference held in Washington, D.C.

CODAs considered

Qualified cash-or-deferred arrangements—also known as 401(k) plans—can be adapted to most employment situations and should be adopted by the majority of employers, according to Louis H. Diamond, a partner in the Washington, D.C., law firm of Finley, Kumble, Wagner, Heine, Underberg & Casey. Employers can achieve a number of "very desirable objectives simultaneously" by establishing a CODA, Diamond maintains.

Under a CODA (see *Compensation* 343:452), employees are allowed to divert otherwise taxable income into a tax-free growth account for use at a future date, Diamond explains. CODAs also can be an integral part of an overall flexible compensation package that provides employees with a wide range of benefit choices at little or no cost to the company. Additionally, when offered with, or in lieu of, other qualified plans, CODAs can help the organization achieve a number of desirable results with respect to its highly-paid employees. Diamond warns, however, that since some benefits, such as group life insurance and pensions, are based on an employee's salary, they potentially could be reduced under a CODA. To prevent this, plans should define "compensation" to include any employee deferrals.

Employers have several options when it comes to structuring a CODA, Diamond notes. These include:

- CODAs funded solely by employee deferrals—In this form of CODA, the organization permits employees to save on a tax-deductible basis, and the employer does not incur any additional outlay to provide fringe benefits. Although these CODAs are subject to certain maximum contribution limitations, they enable employees to set aside amounts that are potentially much greater than the $2,000 annual ceiling imposed on individual retirement arrangements.

- Cash-or-deferred thrift plans — Employers can convert an existing thrift plan or establish a new plan that utilizes a cash-or-deferred approach. These plans allow employees to make contributions on a pre-tax basis.

- Cash-or-deferred employee stock ownership plans—Employee salary deferrals also can be used to purchase employer stock on a tax-deductible basis for the worker. This type of arrangement has the advantage of generating capital for the employer.

- Profit-sharing plan with maximum discrimination—When properly structured, a CODA can provide what would otherwise be a discriminatorily high level of benefits for employees in the top one-third income category.

ESOP offerings

Employee stock ownership plans are an "exceptionally attractive" compensation vehicle that can accomplish "interesting and different objectives" for employers, Diamond declares, adding that "anything that is good for a company is good for its executives." Enabling employees to acquire company stock, which is the principal objective of an ESOP (see *Compensation* 343:541), provides several benefits to the employer, Diamond maintains, including substantial tax deductions, enhanced corporate liquidity without using any of the company's own assets, flexibility in corporate stock transactions, a strengthened market for the company's stock, and the creation of a significant employee incentive. Additionally, he notes, ESOPs can be used to finance new capital, spin off a subsidiary or division, resist corporate takeovers, and implement a wage reduction program.

Payroll-based ESOPS, called PAYSOPs, are an "absolutely wonderful arrangement" because they enable employers to receive a tax credit for their contributions, based on a percentage of payroll, Diamond explains. While PAYSOPs are becoming increasingly popular, Diamond observes, like ESOPs in general, they require careful planning. He recommends that an employer's decision to adopt an ESOP be based on a comprehensive evaluation of the company's economic stability, the availability of sufficient taxable income and payroll, a valuation of the firm's stock, projected corporate profitability, and the future composition of the workforce.

Source: Bulletin to Management, 22 March 1984, p. 8. Reprinted by permission from *Bulletin to Management,* copyright 1984, by The Bureau of National Affairs, Inc., Washington, D.C.

Protection Programs

Protection programs of indirect compensation are designed to protect the employee and family if and when the employee's income (direct compensation) is terminated, and to protect the employee and family against the burden of health-care expenses.[21] Protection programs required by federal and state governments are referred to as **public programs,** and those voluntarily offered by organizations are called **private programs.** An outline of typical private and public protection programs appears in Exhibit 10.1.

Public Protection Programs

Many public protection programs are, for the most part, direct products of the Social Security Act of 1935. The protection programs of Social Security were initially funded by old age, survivors', and disability insurance. The act initially set up systems for retirement benefits, disability, and unemployment insurance. Health insurance, particularly Medicare, was added in 1966 to provide hospital insurance to almost everyone age sixty-five and older.

The Social Security System.   Funding of the Social Security system is provided by equal contributions from employee and employer. Employees' contributions are deducted from paychecks under the terms of the Federal Insurance Contribution Act (FICA). Initially, employee and employer each paid 1 percent of the employee's income up to $3,000. Currently, the employee and employer pay Social Security tax on the first $42,500 of the employee's income at a rate of 7.15 percent. Although the funding of the Social Security system was in doubt in the early 1980s, recent reforms by the

---

Protection Programs   *Exhibit 10.1*

Hazard	Private Plans	Public Plans
Old age	• Pensions • Deferred profit sharing • Thrift plans	• Social Security old age benefits
Death	• Group term life insurance (including accidental death and travel insurance) • Payouts from profit-sharing, pension, and/or thrift plans • Dependent survivors' benefits	• Social Security survivors' benefits • Workers' compensation
Disability	• Short-term accident and sickness insurance • Long-term disability insurance	• Workers' compensation • Social Security disability benefits • State disability benefits
Unemployment	• Supplemental unemployment benefits and/or severance pay	• Unemployment benefits
Medical/dental expenses	• Hospital/surgical insurance • Other medical insurance • Dental insurance	• Workers' compensation • Medicare

Source: Adapted from J. S. Sullivan, "Indirect Compensation: The Decade Ahead," *California Management Review* 15 (Winter 1972): 65.

National Commission on Social Security Reform, approved by Congress and the president, appear to have diminished this concern.[22]

Social Security Pension Benefits.   The average pension a Social Security beneficiary now receives is about $5,400 per year. In 1972, Congress passed a law providing that increases in pension benefits be determined by an inflation escalator clause. As a result, recipients receive increases in benefits greater than the inflation rate of the preceding year. Consequently, the maximum benefits from Social Security are now approximately $700 per month plus 50 percent for an aged dependent spouse. In addition, individuals over age sixty-five receiving pension benefits can now earn up to $7,320. When they reach age seventy, they can earn unlimited amounts. Presently, private sector, some state, self-employed individuals, and federal employees hired starting in 1984 are eligible.

Unemployment Compensation Benefits.   To control the pension benefits of Social Security, the unemployment provisions dictate that compensation be determined jointly through federal and state cooperation. As a result, employer costs and employee benefits can vary from state to state. The unemployment compensation fund is supported solely by employers, except in Alabama, Alaska, and New Jersey, where employees also contribute. The base rate for employer contributions varies depending on the number of unemployed people an organization (turnover) has drawing from the state's unemployment fund. Thus, it pays for an organization to maintain relatively stable employment and to avoid layoffs.[23] The Federal Unemployment Tax Act (FUTA) now requires all profit-making organizations to pay a tax on the first $7,000 of wages paid to each employee. The average rate of this tax was 3.4 percent in 1983 and 4.2 in 1984.

The purpose of unemployment compensation is to provide income to an individual who is employed but not currently working (indefinite layoff) or who is seeking a job. To be eligible for benefits, an employee must first have worked a minimum number of weeks (set by the state), currently be without a job, and be willing to accept an appropriate job offered through the state unemployment compensation commission. Although the typical period of time a person may receive unemployment benefits is twenty-five weeks, the period has often been extended, especially when unemployment is high. Employees are also covered if they are unable to work because of a lockout by the employer *(Abrendts* v. *Ohio Valley Hospital Association,* 1985).

Disability and Workers' Compensation Benefits.   Disability and workers' compensation benefits are provided in public programs by the Social Security system and by state systems. At both the state and federal level, **workers' compensation** benefits are administered to assist workers who cannot work because of occupational injury or ailment. Totally disabled employees can receive payments from Social Security until retirement. Usually these payments are minimal (less than $100), but state compensation benefits can increase them substantially. State compensation benefits are usually paid for permanent partial, temporary, or total disability.[24]

The exact benefits received depend on the state the individual works in, the individual's earnings, and the number of dependents. Payment for total disability is generally in the form of weekly or monthly payments. Permanent partial disability payments are often predetermined lump sums—for example, $10,000 for the loss of an eye or a leg. Payments are also made for medical and hospital costs resulting from a work-related injury or illness and for survivor benefits in the case of death.

Workers' compensation insurance, although provided by the state and federal government, is paid for by the employer. Although these payments are additional costs to employers, their obligations have been limited by the Workers' Compensation Act of 1911, which generally prohibits the injured worker from suing the employer. A recent trend, however, has employees disregarding workers' compensation and directly suing the employer. Recently an award of $600,000 was granted to an employee for a suit that ordinarily would have been taken care of by workers' compensation insurance *(William* v. *International Paper Co.,* 1982).[25]

Medical and Hospital Benefits.   The major public program providing medical and hospital benefits is Medicare. This program is now funded by Social Security, although the recommendation of the Social Security Council is to fund it separately. Such a move, however, may increase an organization's total contributions for the support of public programs. If the proposed recommendation is adopted by Congress, each organization would continue to pay its Social Security contributions for every employee, although at a lower rate, and pay an additional tax for Medicare.

Medicare applies only to people over sixty-five, but the Health Maintenance Organization Act of 1973 is an attempt to provide medical and hospital benefits for younger people as well. It establishes and regulates **health maintenance organizations (HMOs)**, which incorporate the services of hospitals, clinics, doctors, nurses, and technicians at a single monthly rate. This act also requires employers of at least twenty-five persons to offer an HMO plan option if they offer traditional health benefits. If HMOs organized for both group and individual practice operate in an employer's area, the employer is required to offer enrollment in both types.

Private Protection Programs

Private protection programs are those offered by organizations (private and public) that are not required by law, although their administration may be regulated by law. The programs provide benefits for health care, income after retirement, and insurance against loss of life and limb. Almost all employers provide them for their employees. In contrast, only about 2 million employees, or about 2 percent of the work force, are covered by programs providing income before retirement in the form of supplemental unemployment benefits and guaranteed pay and work programs.

Retirement Benefits.   About 78 percent of all plant workers and 85 percent of all office workers are covered by private pension programs, none of which are required by law. Although these percentages may appear to be high, only about one-half of the entire American work force is covered. This proportion, however, does represent a significant gain in coverage since the 1940s, when pension programs became a bargainable issue *(Inland Steel* v. *National Labor Relations Board).* In addition, pension coverage varies widely by type of industry, size of firm, and whether the employees are unionized. In 80 percent of the plans, employees are fully vested after ten years; 58 percent of them are integrated with Social Security benefits, and in 76 percent of them, employees must be sixty-five years old to collect full pension benefits.

Most private pension programs are noncontributory, except those covering public employees. Public employees contribute about 7 percent of wages or salary to the retirement fund. As a result, pension benefits for public employees are one-third greater than those for private employees.

With the passage of ERTA, TEFRA, and ERISA, as well as the provisions for 401(k) plans, the traditional approach to providing retirement benefits is changing. More typical of retirement benefit plans now is that they are "multisystem plans." As such, they are likely to be made up of the following:

■ Worker contribution-intensive plans, such as 401(k) and thrift plans, which benefit the employer by being cost effective and benefit the employee by providing a tax break

- Company stock plans, which increase the employer's capital, reduce costs, and guard against corporate takeovers
- PAYSOPs, which provide a tax credit for employers

Another trend in the area of retirement is to offer early retirement to employees. This makes it possible for more senior employees to retire early and for the company to promote younger employees. Although this helps make room for the baby boom generation, companies such as Polaroid and Kodak have discovered that it can remove talented employees. Consequently, employers need to use their human resource information system to anticipate who will be trained and available to fill slots when they are vacated by employees exercising early retirement.[26]

Insurance Benefits.   Three major types of insurance programs are provided by most organizations: life, health, and disability. Because the cost is far below what employees would pay to buy their own insurance, they represent considerable benefits, although employees do not always recognize this fact. Nevertheless, these programs have grown substantially, both in the dollar amount of benefits and the percentage of employees covered.

Life insurance programs cover almost all employees. For managerial employees, the benefits are equal to about two years' income. After retirement the benefits continue for most employees, but they may be reduced by as much as two-thirds. A majority of the life insurance programs offered by organizations are noncontributory. The trend is toward more noncontributory programs, even though a trend exists to provide more coverage, especially to family members. Despite the cost, organizations are doing this to keep up with other organizations.

Because of the rapidly rising costs of health care, however, a different philosophy dictates the offering of private health insurance programs. Companies are increasingly asking employees to pay for some of their own health care. Where not asked to pay, employees are being asked to make a choice among different forms of health-care delivery. For example, employees can choose (1) to join a regular health maintenance organization, (2) to join a preferee-provider organization, or (3) to stay with a regular private medical plan with an individual doctor approved by the organization. Organizations are also requiring a second opinion for elective surgery and increasing the deductibles.[27] Chrysler Corporation initiated a program to reduce health-care costs. In addition to incorporating the methods already listed, Chrysler rewarded employees for not using health care. The result of this program was a $58 million savings in 1984. Instead of paying $460 million for health insurance premiums, they paid only $402 million.[28]

Health insurance programs generally cover short-term absences from work because of sickness, whereas short-term absences because of disability are covered by short-term disability insurance offered by the employer. Longer-term absences due to sickness or disability are covered by long-term sickness and disability insurance. Both types of disability insurance generally supplement state and federal disability programs. These programs are discussed under "Disability and Workers' Compensation Benefits." However, short-term disability protection is generally offered by more organizations than long-term protection. About 70 percent of all organizations provide long-term coverage.[29] Long-term sickness and disability coverage for non-managerial employees is often a set sum, such as $10,000; for managerial employees, reimbursement is often a percentage of salary and therefore increases with the level of manager. Another form of payment is reimbursement for a fixed percentage of the expenses caused by sickness or disability.

Supplemental Unemployment Benefits.   A small number of organizations offer employees protection against loss of income and loss of work before retirement. **Supplemental unemployment benefits (SUB)** are for people laid off from work. When SUB benefits are combined with unemployment compensation benefits, laid-off employees can receive as much as 95 percent of their average income. The size of these benefits makes it easier for employees with more years of service to accept layoffs, thus allowing employees with less service, often younger, to continue working. SUB programs exist in a limited number of industries, and all are the production of labor-management contracts. They are found in the automotive, steel, rubber, glass, ceramic, and women's garment industries.

Pay for Time Not Worked

Pay for time not worked is not as complex to administer as benefits from protection programs but is almost as costly to the organization. In general, pay for time not worked continues to grow in amount as well as in kind. For example, in 1955 the average number of paid holidays per year was approximately six; in 1978 it was ten. During the same period, the average number of weeks of paid vacation went from three to four. Recently, however, the effects of concessionary bargaining between union and management have meant fewer, not more, paid vacation days and holidays.

The two major categories of pay for time not worked are time not worked off the job (holidays and vacations) and time not worked on the job.

Off the Job

Payments for time not worked (and other off-the-job benefits) constitute a major portion of the total cost of indirect compensation. These account for about 10 percent of the total payroll costs. By comparison, the largest portion of indirect compensation relative to total compensation, approximately 15 percent, goes primarily for pension and insurance payments. The most common paid off-the-job components are vacations, sick leave, holidays, and personal days.

On the Job

Paid benefits for time not worked on the job include rest periods, lunch periods, wash-up time, and clothes-change and get-ready times. Together these benefits are the fifth most expensive indirect compensation benefit. Another benefit growing in popularity is paid time for physical fitness. This is clearly pay for time not worked, but organizations often offer it because of its on-the-job benefits.

Physical Fitness Benefits.   With increased awareness of the relationship between job stress and coronary heart disease and other physical and mental disabilities, organizations have become more concerned with finding ways to alleviate stress whenever possible. People who are in good physical condition can often deal with stress better and suffer fewer negative symptoms. In addition, physical exercise is a good way to cope with stress and reduce its effects. By providing athletic facilities on company premises, organizations are encouraging their employees to be physically fit and to engage in exercise. These facilities are essentially a service to employees. An example of an extensive corporate program is the Xerox managerial health program. Xerox is one of many organizations that has learned the cost benefits of offering corporate "wellness" programs:

> **Health care costs can drop because of corporate "wellness" programs.**
> Tenneco Inc. reports that insurance claims for exercising women workers in 1983 averaged less than half those of women who didn't exercise. The same was generally true about male workers. Absenteeism for men and women who exercised was far less than for those who didn't, Tenneco adds. Besides a drop in health-care costs, the company says, productivity rose. In Houston, Tenneco has a fitness center.
>
> Shell Oil says its programs are "cost effective" for the company. USAA, an insurance company, says its exercise programs have significantly cut health-care costs. But some others say the saving is difficult to figure. "I don't know if companies will ever be able to do that," says a Rockwell International Corp. official.
>
> Xerox Corp. says the benefits from its health programs are so "apparent," but proving it would be costly.[30]

Employee Services and Perquisites

The third and final component of indirect compensation is employee services and perquisites (perks), which may consist of food service costs or losses; employee discounts; day-care centers; employer-sponsored scholarships (or tuition assistance) for employees and their dependents; employee counseling and advisory services (legal, tax, and personal problems); low-cost loans; company-leased or -owned vehicles for business and personal use; and service/suggestion awards. Primarily for top executives are perquisites such as annual company-paid physical examinations; company-paid memberships in country, athletic, and social clubs; use of company expense accounts to cover personal travel, meals, and entertainment; business and personal use of corporate aircraft; and relocation costs.

> BMC Industries, a St. Paul, Minn., electronics products concern, offers officers a menu of flexible perks worth up to 10% of base pay—including spousal travel, day care, a personal-computer lease, a home security system, an athletic club membership, financial counseling and legal services. That's in addition to standard perks like health-care expenses and office parking.
>
> Other companies give loans to finance college tuition and offer to help lower house payments; some outfit executive homes with physical fitness equipment. To lure new executives, 20th Century Fox Film Co. recently offered first-class travel to spouses on trips over five days, low-interest loans up to $1 million, screening-room gear and choice of cars.[31]

Although services and perquisites represent the smallest percentage of indirect compensation, they are rewarding as well as necessary for many employees.[32] To some, they represent an important element in the status system of the organization; to others, they represent a means by which working is made possible. For example, day-care centers make it more practicable for some individuals to start working and more feasible for them to continue working with less absenteeism.[33]

Many of the services and perquisites listed earlier have been provided by organizations for many years, but a few have been recent additions. Some are so recent that many organizations have still not included them in their compensation programs. In addition, a few services and perquisites formerly offered only to managers are now also available to nonmanagers.

Counseling and Assistance Services

Although counseling in organizations is not new, the types of services provided are. Employee counseling services now include advice and information regarding legal concerns, tax matters, and more personal problems such as drinking and absenteeism.

Discussion and recognition, especially of personal problems, have been combined with action-oriented programs to help employees rehabilitate themselves. These programs recognize that an employee's problem is also the organization's problem, whether the organization caused it or not. Employees are considered a valuable resource to the organization, and organizations have a social responsibility to assist their employees in dealing with problems related to their performance.

Golden Employment Practices

Although many counseling and assistance services are provided to almost all employees, golden employment practices are provided only to those most indispensable to the organization. They are, however, sometimes provided at great cost.

Golden Parachutes.   A recent development in executive compensation is the **golden parachute** arrangement. These arrangements generally provide financial protection for top corporate executives in the event of a change in control in the company. This protection is either in the form of guaranteed employment or severance pay upon termination or resignation. The need for golden parachutes came about with the rapid flurry of mergers and acquisitions in the early 1980s. Because mergers or acquisitions can financially help some companies and shareholders, the parachutes were devised to soften top-management resistance to takeover attempts. Top managers who might be replaced as the result of a takeover would still be financially well off. Many golden parachute arrangements actually left top managers better off than before. For example, when Allied merged with Bendix in 1981, William Agee, the head of Bendix, was paid $825,000 annually to depart. In other words, the golden parachute he used to float safely to the ground was worth approximately $5 million! Although attractive to some individuals, golden parachutes have been adversely affected by the 1984 Deficit Reduction Act.[34]

Golden Handcuffs.   In contrast to the golden parachutes that ease an executive's departure from an organization are the **golden handcuffs**. These handcuffs, which make it too costly for an executive to leave an organization, can be composed of many types of compensation, but stock options and retirement packages are the major inducements. By leaving, the executive forfeits these financially attractive benefits. A wise use of golden handcuffs can help keep valued employees.

Administrative Issues in Indirect Compensation

Although organizations tend to view indirect compensation as a reward, recipients do not always see it that way. This causes organizations to become concerned with their package of indirect compensation benefits and how they are administered.

Determining the Benefits Package

The benefits package should be selected on the basis of what's good for the employee as well as the employer. Knowing employee preferences can often help determine what benefits should be offered. Indirect compensation programs and benefits are often provided, however, without any specific knowledge of what employees want or prefer. Employees nevertheless have indicated strong preferences for certain benefits over others, regardless of cost considerations. Employees in one company indicated a strong preference for dental insurance over life insurance, even though dental insurance was only one-fourth the cost to the company. The most desired benefit appears to be time off from work in large chunks. As workers get older, the desire for higher pension benefits steadily increases. This is also the case for employees with rising incomes. Employees with children prefer greater hospitalization benefits than those without. These instances argue strongly for providing benefit flexibility.

Providing Benefit Flexibility

When employees can design their own benefits packages, both they and the company benefit.[35] At least that's the experience at companies such as American Can, Ex-Cello, TRW, the Educational Testing Service (ETS), and Morgan Stanley.[36] At ETS, the company provides a core package of benefits to all employees, covering basic needs such as personal medical care, dental care, disability, vacation, and retirement. In addition, each individual can choose, cafeteria-style, from optional benefits or increase those in the core package. Employees are allowed to change their packages once a year. At ETS the entire benefit package represents 37.8 percent of total payroll costs; 49 percent of this is the cost of providing the flexibility.

At Morgan Stanley, about two-thirds of its eligible employees elected their own benefit package over the standard no-choice plan. The options themselves were developed by the employees working in small-group discussions.

That providing benefit flexibility is so effective is not surprising. What is surprising is that so few organizations provide such flexibility, considering the results of a recent benefits survey:

- More than six in 10 employees would be willing to modify their coverage if there were options in the benefit program, and only 25 percent of the workers were not sure if they would make changes.
- Workers want to choose how to pay for their benefits. For example, most employees would be willing to increase premium payments to retain their medical coverage.
- Nearly half of the employees would be willing to voluntarily contribute more of their own paychecks to improve their benefits, with about four in 10 willing to contribute an additional $5 or less monthly, two in 10 willing to pay an additional $10 monthly, and three in 10 willing to pay an additional $20 or more monthly.
- In contrast, just over half of the surveyed employees would not trade more of their salary for additional benefits, and two in 10 were undecided.
- Almost half of the employees surveyed would participate in a flexible spending account, one-fourth were undecided, and just over two in 10 said they would not participate. Flexible spending accounts are used to reimburse out-of-pocket expenses for medical, dental, legal, and day care services and are financed by tax-free employee allotments from salary.
- The new benefits most preferred by employees were preventive medical care, wellness programs, vision care, and Section 401(k) cash or deferred compensation plans.
- Concerning specific trade-offs employees would make in a flexible benefits program, one-third of the surveyed employees would improve their medical and dental benefits at the expense of other benefits. Over four in 10 employees would maintain their existing medical and dental coverages.
- Employees would decrease voluntary accident insurance and company-sponsored events for improvements in more desirable benefits. Benefits employees want maintained at present levels included educational assistance, short- and long-term disability, vacations, sick-leave days, and holidays.
- Approximately 80 percent of the surveyed employees favored cost-effective health care alternatives, such as second surgical opinions and out-patient surgery. The majority would give up certain kinds of insurance and perquisites to obtain more desirable medical and dental coverage.[37]

Communicating the Benefits Package

Providing benefit flexibility is a good idea not only because it gives employees what they are more likely to want but also because it makes employees aware of what benefits they are gaining and increases their morale.[38]

Many employees are unaware of the costs of the benefits they are receiving and of which benefits they are receiving. If employees have no knowledge of their benefits, then there is little reason to believe that the organization's benefit program objectives will be attained. Many organizations indicate that they assign a high priority to telling employees about their benefits, although a majority spend only a small amount per employee per year doing this. The average benefits package, however, costs over $5,000 per employee.

Considering that most benefits program objectives are not currently attained, assessment of communication effectiveness would likely produce unfavorable results. This may be partly due to the communication techniques used. Almost all organizations use impersonal, passive booklets and brochures to convey benefits information; only a few use more personal, active media, such as slide presentations and regular employee meetings. An especially good technique is one that communicates the total compensation components every day. This can be done through giving employees calendars. Each month of the calendar shows a company employee receiving a compensation benefit. For example, one month may feature a photo of an employee building a new home made possible through the company's incentive program and savings plan. Another month may feature the usefulness of the company's medical plan.

Through communicating the benefits package and providing employees with benefit flexibility, the positive impact of indirect compensation may be increased. Whether communicating improves the positive impact of indirect compensation programs can be determined by using some of the components contained in the next section on assessing the benefits of indirect compensation.

Trends in Indirect Compensation

Major trends in indirect compensation focus on reducing indirect compensation costs. The trends of assessing indirect compensation plans and using computer technology to aid this assessment enable organizations to contain, if not reduce, indirect compensation costs. This is also true for the trend toward the strategic involvement of indirect compensation. Since these three trends of developing choices in indirect compensation can also reduce or contain costs, they are covered in Chapter 8.

Assessing Indirect Compensation

Listed at the beginning of this chapter are several purposes of indirect compensation. The impact of the indirect benefits on these purposes is one-half of the way to measure the effectiveness of the benefits package. The other half is by determining the costs. Another way is to determine the effectiveness of the indirect benefit program and then compare the costs and benefits.

An organization can determine the dollar value of the costs of indirect compensation in four ways:

- Total cost of benefits annually for all employees
- Cost per employee per year divided by the number of hours worked
- Percentage of payroll divided by annual payroll
- Cost per employee per hour divided by employee hours worked[39]

These costs can then be compared with the benefits, such as reduced turnover, absenteeism, or an enhanced company image among employees. The dollar value of these benefits (e.g., reduced absenteeism) can then be determined, thus enabling the organization to directly compare its dollar costs of benefits against its dollar savings of benefits.

After the company determines these cost-benefit ratios, it can further assess the benefits of its indirect compensation by doing the following:

- Examining the internal cost to the company of all benefits and services, by payroll classification, by divison or profit center, or for each benefit. This information also helps monitor benefit costs and helps ensure some degree of uniformity in their costs across levels and divisions in the organization. Thus, this information serves a role similar to that served by compra-ratios and performance ratios discussed in Chapter 9. Such a role (of assessing and monitoring) is also served by the next point.
- Comparing the company's costs for benefits to external norms. For example, the company can compare its costs to average costs, averages by industry, and so on, as reported in surveys such as those conducted by the chamber of commerce, for the package as a whole, and for each benefit. These data can help ensure that a company is not spending more than it needs to attract and retain individuals. It can also help determine how much the company needs to spend if it wants to do better than other companies.
- Analyzing the costs of the program to employees. Determine what each employee is paying for benefits, totally and by benefit.
- Comparing the data in the previous step with external data such as chamber of commerce data.
- Analyzing how satisfied the employees are with the organization's current program—and as compared with competitors' programs.

These methods focus on assessing the current benefits provided by an organization. Two other methods focus on assessing the alternatives available:

- Exploring the costs and benefits of alternative benefit possibilities such as those associated with providing flexible or cafeteria benefit plans. Costs in this case involve those associated with the benefits themselves as well as the administrative costs. Administrative costs are especially critical in flexible benefit plans.[40]

- Comparing these costs and benefits of alternative benefit possibilities with those associated with the current benefit program. Although the current benefits program may be providing benefits at high costs, the costs of the benefits from alternative programs may be even greater and therefore less affordable.

Computer Technology and HRIS in Indirect Compensation

Computer technology can be applied to indirect compensation planning by analyzing its various components. These include items such as health and medical benefits, vacation time, sick time, pensions, and profit sharing. The key here is planning. Given budgeted values for salary and bonuses, projections of spending and allocation may be determined with regard to budget restrictions. In addition, including information about actual benefit usage may reveal that a significant amount of money is being spent on one that is not widely used. Thus, personnel may maximize the value of limited funds by offering employees only the most relevant benefits.

With an HRIS and computer technology, an organization can more easily implement and administer a flexible or cafeteria-style benefit package. The computer can quickly cost out different benefit combinations that employees may select. As a consequence, equity can be more easily attained across employees. The costs of indirect compensation can be more strictly controlled and even reduced with compensation information in an HRIS.[41]

Strategic Involvement of Indirect Compensation

Gaining Competitive Advantage.   A trend in indirect compensation is to use it to gain competitive advantage for the organization. This ranges from using pension funds to fend off corporate takeovers to taking steps to engage in strategic planning for compensation.[42] According to Timothy L. Williams, director of human resources planning at Owens-Illinois in Toledo, Ohio, organizations can take several steps in strategic compensation planning:

- Other employers' compensation and benefits programs—Employers should conduct an external survey to determine if their compensation programs are at a level that will attract and retain talented labor. . . . Such surveys could be national, regional, or local industry-related, and could focus on selected jobs or overall pay.
- Current compensation and benefits trends—Employers should consider such trends as containing benefits growth, providing retirees with health care security, offering flexibility in benefits, moving away from blanket benefit coverages, and moving toward benefit equality, regardless of such factors as marital status, age, sex, service, or number of dependents. . . .
- The firm's strategic plans and goals—A complete understanding of corporate direction is important in strategic planning for total compensation. . . .
- The financial impact of designs— . . . It is important to understand not only plan design, but alternative, tax effective methods of financing.

■ Employees' perception of the value of their benefits—Internal surveys can help determine the level of employee knowledge about each element of a total compensation plan, the relative value employees place on each element, and the allocation of benefit dollars among benefit options offered under a flexible plan.[43]

Although these steps are designed for the strategic planning of total compensation, most apply solely to indirect compensation. This suggests the importance of indirect compensation to organizations; little evidence indicates this will change. These steps, used in conjunction with the discussion of strategic involvement in Chapter 8, are capable of having dramatic and positive effects on any organization's bottom line by helping organizations gain competitive advantage.

Summary

Chapters 8, 9, and 10 address frequently asked questions in organization orientation programs: How much do I get paid? and When and how long is my vacation? Although most organizations have been responding to both questions with, "More than ever before," the growth in indirect compensation has been double that of direct compensation. This doubling has occurred despite the lack of evidence that indirect compensation helps to attain the purposes of total compensation. Money, job challenge, and opportunities for advancement appear to serve the purposes of compensation as much as, if not more than, pension benefits, disability provisions, and services, especially for employees aspiring to managerial careers.

This is not to say, however, that employees do not desire indirect benefits. Organizations are offering them at such a rapid rate in part because employees desire them. The specific indirect benefits offered by an organization are not always valued by all employees, however, nor do all employees know what benefits are offered. As a result, some organizations solicit employee opinions about their preferences for compensation programs. Organizations are also becoming more concerned with the communication of their benefits programs, partly because of the requirements of ERISA. Current evidence suggests that employees' lack of awareness of the contents and value of their benefit programs may partially explain why the programs are not perceived more favorably.

Increased communication and more employee participation in the benefits packages may increase the likelihood that organizations will receive some benefit from providing indirect compensation. These benefits do not come without costs, although some benefits may be gained at less costs than others. To ensure that an organization is getting the most from its indirect compensation, thorough assessments must be made of what the organization is doing, what other organizations are doing, and what employees prefer to see the organization doing.

To improve the motivational value of indirect compensation, organizations should try to provide what employees want. As with direct compensation, employees apparently will continue to want more benefits like the ones they now have as well as some they presently do not have. For example, employees want greater private retirement benefits, health and insurance coverage, and more time off. Demands for dental coverage, eye care, and legal services will probably increase. Greater educational and career development opportunities are also likely to be demanded by employees.

Although the trend in many benefits is for more, one benefit that may be the most important is job security. As the economy continues to shift and dislocate employees and as international competition increases, job security will continue to take on even greater importance. Further, different people may want different benefits. For example, younger employees may have a stronger preference for insurance benefits, time off, and educational benefits, while older employees may have a greater interest in retirement benefits, and preretirement counseling opportunities.

In addition to providing a wide range of benefits to employees, communicating them, and having employees participate in their formulation and administration to help enhance the effectiveness of indirect compensation, numerous federal and state laws must be taken into account and observed. Federal laws, such as the Pregnancy Discrimination Act, the Equal Pay Act, and the Multiemployer Pension Plan Act, have a significant influence on indirect compensation. Ignoring these federal laws and various state laws may result in fines and penalties, thus reducing the effectiveness of indirect compensation.

But even if indirect as well as direct compensation are administered as effectively as possible, their potential effectiveness vis-à-vis increasing employee performance through enhanced motivation is constrained by employee ability. Since enhancing performance depends on both motivation and ability, an appropriate step is to examine ways to improve employee ability. This is taken up in Chapter 11. Chapter 12 examines programs to improve productivity and quality of work life.

Discussion Questions

1. How are unemployment benefits derived, and what is the status of unemployment compensation?
2. In what sense is indirect compensation "indirect"?
3. How has legislation shaped the total compensation package? How has legislation shifted the balance of direct to indirect compensation? What implications does this shift have for employee performance?
4. If it were possible, why doesn't the government or, for that matter, the employer simply give employees a fixed sum of money and let them purchase whatever mix of benefits are currently mandated by law or voluntarily provided by the employer?
5. How has legislation and the changing nature of the work force created the tremendous Social Security benefit burden that most employers and workers confront when they witness the size of the FICA deduction from their paycheck?

6. How would you rationalize the benefit to the organization of providing a physical fitness facility and program for the work force? How would you assess and compare benefits and costs?

7. For each of the various forms of indirect compensation, describe what incentives the employer and the employee have for minimizing the cost of this benefit.

8. In theory flexible benefit plans sound great. In practice this may not be so. Describe the problems that could be encountered in administering a flexible benefit program.

9. For the moment, imagine that you are a futurist. Describe the work force in the year 2000. How will this work force differ from today's? How will these differences influence preferences for specific indirect compensation?

10. Distinguish between public and private protection programs, and give examples of each.

PC Project

Employees, in many cases, do not have accurate perceptions of their indirect compensation. Yet indirect compensation has been growing as a percentage of total compensation. How much does it cost the company to provide such benefits? This PC Project estimates the costs of different types of indirect compensation. Once these estimates are derived, each benefit category can be reported as a function of total compensation.

C A S E   S T U D Y

Baby Boomers Booming for Child Care?

Consider the following statistics in regard to the American family today:

■ In the 1950s, about 60 percent of American families contained a male breadwinner and a female homemaker. Today only 20 percent of American families fit this profile.

■ Today, in about two-thirds of marriages, both spouses work, regardless of income level.

■ Nearly half of all mothers with children under five work outside the home.

■ By 1995 80 percent of all women in their primary childbearing years are expected to be working.

■ The Census Bureau estimates that nearly half of the nation's new mothers hold jobs or are looking for jobs within a year of the birth of their child.

■ There are currently an estimated 6.5 million "latchkey" children left alone or with slightly older siblings for part of the day while their parents work.

- By 1990 an estimated 14 million preschool children will be cared for by someone other than a parent.

- Employers lose an average of eight working days every year from each employee with a child under age thirteen because of child-care problems.

- Child care ranks as the fourth-largest budget item for families behind housing, food, and taxes.

- In 1981 child care became a nontaxable benefit, but the IRS has hesitated to issue regulations on how benefits packages will be treated.

- Only 1,800 firms out of the nation's nearly 6 million provide some type of child-care assistance.

- The United States is the only major country without a national maternity leave policy, with currently 60 percent of wage-earning mothers without leave rights.

- In 1986 legislation was proposed in the House to provide up to eighteen weeks of unpaid leave for parents of newborn or adopted children and up to twenty-six weeks of unpaid medical leave, and that employers restore the same or equivalent jobs with continued benefits and seniority.

- Although one-third of major companies offer male employees unpaid parental leaves, surveys show that they are rarely used.

Mitch Kapor, software industry tycoon and founder of Lotus Development Corporation, has in 1986, at the age of thirty-five, retired and turned the reins over to his successor, Jim Manzi, age thirty-four. The company has, in its four-year history, lavished attention on its employees (average age thirty-one). High salaries, large stock option and stock purchase plans, and quarterly outings for employees and families are typical. Mitch Kapor, in announcing his retirement from Lotus, stated a desire to spend time with his newborn child and to do something new with his life. Before retiring, though, Kapor announced the expected arrival of his first child with a decree that Lotus will provide day care for *all* employees. Can Lotus afford the hundreds of thousands of dollars on this benefit as its baby boom work force begins families?

Notes

1. The term *indirect compensation* replaces the term *fringe benefits* or *supplemental income*, since the costs of indirect compensation are becoming so great. The term *benefits, fringe, benefits,* or *indirect benefits* is occasionally used in reference to indirect compensation, since many organizations still refer to it as such. For an excellent overview of the current state of benefits, see D. L. Salisbury, ed., *America in Transition: Implications for Employee Benefits* (Washington, D.C.: EBRI, 1982); *Employee Benefits* available from the U.S. Chamber of Commerce, 1615 H Street, N.W., Washington, D.C. 20062; *Salaried Employee Benefits Provided by Major U.S. Employers in 1984* (Lincolnshire, Il.: Hewitt & Associates, 1985).

2. J. F. Sullivan, "Indirect Compensation: The Years Ahead," *California Management Review* (Winter 1972): 65–76; R. I. Henderson, "Designing a Reward System for Today's Employee," *Business Horizons* (July–Sept. 1982): 2–12; G. T. Milkovich and J. M. Newman, *Compensation* (Plano, Tex.: Business Publications, 1984).

3. Employees, however, may still provide benefits not required by law, such as private pensions that must still be administered within federal or state guidelines, as the ERISA does for private pensions. For extensive discussion here, see B. J. Coleman, *Primer on Employee Retirement Income Security Act* (Washington, D.C.: Bureau of National Affairs, 1985); K. D. Gill, ed., *ERISA: The Law and the Code,* 1985 ed. (Washington, D.C.: Bureau of National Affairs, 1985).

4. Bureau of National Affairs, "Employee Benefits—1983," *Bulletin to Management,* 14 Feb. 1985, p. 5. Reprinted by permission from *Bulletin to Management,* copyright 1985, by The Bureau of National Affairs, Inc., Washington, D.C.

5. Other differences between private and federal benefits include .5 percent of pay for life insurance in the private sector versus .3 percent in the federal; $1,045 health insurance value for the private sector versus $760 in the federal; 2,062 hours per year of work in the private sector versus 2,080 in the federal; and 360 hours per year of time off in the private sector versus 367 in the federal. These differences are reported in the *OPM Newsletter,* Aug.–Sept. 1981.

6. Milkovich and Newman, *Compensation.*

7. R. C. Huseman, J. D. Hatfield, and R. W. Driver, "Getting Your Benefit Programs Understood and Appreciated," *Personnel Journal* (Oct. 1978): 560.

8. D. W. Belcher, *Compensation Administration,* (Englewood Cliffs, N.J.: Prentice-Hall, 1974).

9. *Ibid.,* p. 376.

10. For discussion of what attracts individuals to organizations, see D. P. Schwab, "Recruiting and Organizational Participation," in *Personnel Management,* ed. K. M. Rowland and G. R. Ferris (Boston: Allyn & Bacon, 1982), pp. 103–28.

11. For an extensive discussion of flexible or cafeteria benefit programs, see Salisbury, *America in Transition;* Milkovich and Newman, *Compensation.*

12. This is especially relevant when the organization is not able to raise its prices and other expenditures fail to decrease.

13. One might expect that in these industries, workers would choose to have less of both direct and indirect compensation rather than layoffs; this, however, appears to not be the case very consistently.

14. The Pregnancy Discrimination Act (PDA) also has other provisions. For a description of them, see R. Trotter, S. R. Zacur, and W. Greenwood, "The Pregnancy Disability Amendment: What the Law Provides," pt. II, *Personnel Administrator* (Mar. 1982): 55–58. Congress enacted the PDA because the Supreme Court ruled in *General Electric Co.* v. *Gilbert* (1976) that pregnancy-related classifications (provisions) did not on their face constitute discrimination under Title VII. J. S. Lublin, "Big Test Nears on Benefits for Pregnancy," *Wall Street Journal,* 3 Jan. 1983, pp. 25, 31; S. Wermiel, "Sex-Discrimination Suit May Force Big Changes in Retirement Benefits," *Wall Street Journal,* 10 Jan. 1983, p. 21; *Fair Employment Report,* 6 March 1985, p. 37; *Fair Employment Report,* 22 Oct. 1984, p. 165; *Fair Employment Practices,* 6 Sept. 1984, pp. 1–8.

15. J. H. Schechter, "The Deficit Reduction Act of 1984: Some Implications for Employers," *Personnel* (Nov.–Dec. 1984): 31. See also S. P. Kurash and G. F. Fasoldt, "An Outline of Changes Required by the New Retirement Equity Act," *Personnel Journal* (Nov. 1984): 80–84; "Severance Benefits and ADEA," *Fair Employment Practices,* 22 Aug. 1985, pp. 1–2.

16. Bureau of National Affairs, "ERISA's Effects on Pension Plan Administration," *Bulletin to Management,* 9 Aug. 1984, pp. 1–2; Coleman, *Primer on Employee;* Gill, *ERISA.*

17. K. Slater, "Pension-Equity Bill Isn't Seen Requiring Firms to Add Significant Funds to Plans," *Wall Street Journal,* 13 Aug. 1984, p. 6; J. Redeker, "Medicare Has New Rules for Older Workers," *Personnel Administrator* (Feb. 1984): 23–25; D. S. Carpenter, "Beware the New Retirement Equity Act," *Inc.* (Jan. 1985): 104–8; M. E. Segal, "Working Women and Employee Benefits," *Personnel Journal* (Sept. 1985): 73–81.

18. J. A. LoCicero, "How to Cope With the Multiemployer Pension Plan Amendments Act of 1980," *Personnel Administrator* (May 1981): 51–54, 68; J. A. LoCicero, "Multiemployer Pension Plans: A Time Bomb for Employers?" *Personnel Journal* (Nov.

1980): 922–24, 932; P. T. Schultz and H. J. Golden, "Current Developments in Employee Benefits," *Employee Relations Law Journal* 6 (3): 494–97; *Wall Street Journal,* 5 Mar. 1982, p. 50, 12 March 1982, p. 30, 18 Mar. 1982, p. 32; D. S. Bowling III, "The Multiemployer Pension Plan Amendments Act of 1980," *Personnel Journal* (Jan. 1982): 18–20.

19. G. E. Hagerty, "Should You Establish a Qualified Cash or Deferred Arrangement?" *Personnel Journal* (Feb. 1983): 110–14; E. J. Brennan, "Benefits and Liabilities of Deferred Compensation," *Personnel Journal* (June 1984): 26–28; "Pension Equity Bill Signed into Law," *Resource* (Sept. 1984): 1; T. Brambley, "The 401(k) Solution to Retirement Planning," *Personnel Journal* (Dec. 1984): 66–67; U. Gupta, "Sifting through 401(k) Plans," *Venture* (May 1985): 34; P. M. Kelly, ed., *The Economic Recovery Tax Act of 1981* (New York: American Management Association, 1982); *Business Week,* 2 Aug. 1982, p. 78; M. Zippo, "ERTA and Employee Benefits: Mixed Reactions from Benefit Planners," *Personnel* (Jan.–Feb. 1982): 32–33; The Staff of Kwasha Lipton, "Economic Recovery Tax Act: The Impact on Defined Contribution Plans," *Personnel* (Jan.–Feb. 1982): 21–30; M. Lewis and R. Sears, "How Do 401(k) and Traditional Savings Plans Compare?" *Personnel Administrator* (Oct., 1982): 71–76, 92; B. Nolan, "The Advantages of a Payroll Deduction IRA," *Personnel Journal* (July 1982): 488, 492; "Tax and Regulation Update," *Personnel Journal* (Dec. 1981): 924, 926; *Business Week,* 18 Jan. 1982, pp. 118–20.

20. L. Sloane, "Bid to Tax Health Benefits," *New York Times,* 9 July 1983, p. 34; F. H. Stark, "Bring Fair Play to Taxing of Perks," *New York Times,* 18 Sept. 1983, p. 2F.

21. Henderson, "Employees Benefits 1983." For a good description of what the employer should provide to the family, see J. McCroskey, "Work and Families: What Is the Employer's Responsibility?" *Personnel Journal* (Jan. 1982): 30–38.

22. B. Keller, "Another Stab at Pension Reform" *New York Times,* 15 July 1984, p. 4F; R. C. Murphy and R. E. Wallace, "New Directions for the Social Security System," *Personnel Journal* (Feb. 1983): 138–41. For an extensive discussion of Social Security, see "How to Save Social Security," *Business Week,* 29 Nov. 1982; V. Cahan and S. H. Willstrom, "Can Reagan Revolutionize Social Security?" *Business Week,* 25 May 1981, p. 42; "The Battle over Repairing Social Security," *Business Week,* 28 Sept. 1981, pp. 116–20; R. Schulz, P. J. Ferera, and R. C. Keating, "Social Security: Three Points of View," *Personnel Administrator* (May 1981): 45–49; "The Social Security Quagmire," *Business Week,* 20 Aug. 1982, p. 93; "Saying 'No' to Social Security," *Business Week,* 31 May 1982, pp. 72, 74; "How Poor Are the Elderly?" *New York Times,* 19 Dec. 1982, p. 4F; P. G. Peterson, "Social Security: The Coming Crash," *New York Review*

of Books, 26 Nov. 1982; "Excerpts from Final Report of the Commission on Social Security Reform," *New York Times,* 21 Jan. 1983, p. A12.

23. B. DeClark, "Cutting Unemployment Insurance Costs," *Personnel Journal* (Nov. 1983): 868–72. See also "U.S. Penalizes Firms in States Past Due on Jobless Payments," *Wall Street Journal,* 4 Dec. 1984, p. 31; P. S. Saucier and J. A. Roberts, "Unemployment Compensation: A Growing concern for Employers," *Employee Relations Law Journal* (Spring 1984): 594–604.

24. A. Davis, "Workmen's Compensation," in *Handbook of Modern Personnel Management,* ed. J. Famularo (New York: McGraw-Hill, 1972), chap. 51; R. M. McCaffery, *Managing the Employee Benefits Program* (New York: American Management Associations, 1972); H. M. Christman, "Aiding the Disabled," *New York Times,* 6 Sept. 1981, p. 2F; D. Vandergoot and C. Lindberg, "Investing in Rehabilitation," *Personnel Administrator* (June 1981): 71–78. For a detailed look at what states pay, see Bureau of National Affairs, "Workers' Compensation Laws—Income Benefits for Total Disabilities—January 1984," *Bulletin to Management,* 14 June 1984, 4–5.

25. "On-the-Job Injuries: Now, Suits against the Boss," *Business Week,* 25 Jan. 1982, p. 84; E. Johnson, "Fast-Food Chains Act to Hold Down Crime and Prevent Lawsuits." *Wall Street Journal,* 8 Nov. 1984, pp. 1, 25. For more information, write the U.S. Department of Labor, Pension and Benefits Programs, Room N4659, 200 Constitution Ave., Washington, D.C. 20216.

26. R. Alsop, "As Early Retirement Grows in Popularity, Some Have Misgivings," *Wall Street Journal,* 24 Apr. 1984, pp. 1, 17. Characteristics of these plans: in 80 percent of the plans, employees are fully vested after ten years; 58 percent of the plans are integrated with Social Security benefits; in 76 percent of the plans, employees must be sixty-five years old to collect full pension benefits. For more information, write the U.S. Department of Labor, Pension and Benefits Programs, Room N4659, 200 Constitution Ave., Washington, D.C. 20216.

27. D. D. Buss, "GM Proposes Health-Care Plan to Reduce Medical Costs by 10%—UAW is Receptive," *Wall Street Journal,* 16 Aug. 1984, p. 12; K. P. Shapiro, "More Companies Shifting Cost of Medical Care to Employees," *Management Review* (Apr. 1983): 29, 34; M. E. Segal, "Are PPOs the Answer to Rising Health Care Costs?" *Personnel Journal* (June 1984): 84–86; _____, *Controlling Health Care Costs* (Washington, D.C.: Bureau of National Affairs, 1983); N. R. Kleinfield, "When the Boss Becomes Your Doctor," *New York Times,* 5 Jan. 1986, sec. 3, pp. 1, 24.

28. D. E. Rosenbaum, "Chrysler Program Saves Millions in Health Costs," *New York Times,* 29 Apr. 1985, B6. See also K. F. Clarke and L. D. Groves, "Medical Plan Changes: Are You Doing Enough to Contain Costs?" *Personnel Administrator* (Sept. 1985): 115–19; K. Pheban, "Do HMOs Mean Lower Health Care Costs?" *Personnel Journal* (Mar. 1985): 67–71; T. L. Thorkelson, "26 Ways to Reduce Medical Insurance Costs," *Personnel Journal* (Aug. 1984): 29–31; R. Pear, "Companies Tackle Health Costs," *New York Times,* 3 Mar. 1985, p. F11.

29. W. B. Lathan, *Health Care Costs: There Are Solutions* (New York: American Management Associations 1983); _____, *Employee Health and Welfare Benefits,* p. 10; and _____, "Insurance Survey," *Personnel Journal* (July 1981): 525.

30. *Wall Street Journal,* 20 Aug. 1985, p. l. Reprinted by permission of *The Wall Street Journal,* © Dow Jones & Company, Inc., 1985. All Rights Reserved. See also Bureau of National Affairs, "Fitness Centers: Movement Motives," *Bulletin to Management,* 20 Dec. 1984, p. 1; Bureau of National Affairs, "Wellness: A New Health Care Goal," *Bulletin to Management,* 25 Apr. 1985, p. 1; Bureau of National Affairs, "Employee Wellness: Learning through Living," *Bulletin to Management,* 23 May 1985, pp. 1–2.

31. *Wall Street Journal,* 23 Apr. 1985, p. 1. Reprinted by permission of *The Wall Street Journal,* © Dow Jones & Company, Inc., 1985. All Rights Reserved.

32. K. M. Evans, "The Power of Perquisites," *Personnel Administrator* (May 1984): 45–52; M. E. Haskins, "In-House Financial Planning for Everyone," *Personnel Administrator* (Aug. 1985): 99–116; P. Florey, "A Growing Fringe Benefit: Arbitration of Nonunion Employee Grievances," *Personnel Administrator* (July 1985): 14–15.

33. J. Immerwahr, "Building a Consensus on the Child Care Problem," *Personnel Administrator* (Feb. 1984): 31–37; S. A. Youngblood and K. Chambers-Cook, "Child Care Assistance Can Improve Employee Attitudes and Behavior," *Personnel Administrator* (Feb. 1984): 45, 93, 95; R. Y. Magid, *Child Care Assistance Can Improve Employee Attitudes and Behavior, Personnel Administrator* (Feb. 1984): 45, 93, 95; R. Y. Magid, *Child Care Initiatives for Working Parents* (New York: American Management Associations, 1983); K. M. Evans, "The Power of Perquisites," *Personnel Administrator* (May 1984): 45–52; W. Meyers, "Child Care Finds a Champion in the Corporation," *New York Times,* 4 Aug. 1985, Sec. 3, pp. 1, 6.

34. W. J. Karney, "Poking Holes in Golden Parachutes," *Wall Street Journal,* 16 Apr. 1984, p. 32.

35. Bureau of National Affairs, "Flexible Comp Communication Concerns," *Bulletin to Management,* 21 June 1984, p. 2; Bureau of National Affairs, "Flexible Compensation Trends," *Bulletin to Management,* 19 Apr. 1984; pp. 1–2. See also Salisbury, *America in Transition* and J. Lindroth, "Inflation, Taxes, and Perks: How Compensation Is Changing," *Personnel Journal* (Dec. 1981): 934–40; J. H. Foeger, "Compensation and Benefits," *Personnel Journal* (July 1981): 530; J. H. Shea, "Cautions about Cafeteria-Style

Benefit Plans," *Personnel Journal* (Jan. 1981): 36–38, 58; "Flexible Benefits," *Personnel Journal* (Aug. 1981): 602; "More Workers Are Getting a Chance to Choose Benefits Cafeteria-Style," *Wall Street Journal*, 14 July 1981, p. 33; R. B. Cockrum, "Has the Time Come for Employee Cafeteria Plans?" *Personnel Administrator* (July 1982): 66–72.

36. K. H. Loeffler, "Flexible Benefits at Ex-Cello: A Case Study," *Personnel Journal* (June 1985): 106–12; P. W. Stonebraker, "A Three-Tier Plan for Cafeteria Benefits," *Personnel Journal* (Dec. 1984): 51–57.

37. Bureau of National Affairs, "Employees Would Change Benefits If Possible," *Bulletin to Management*, 15 Aug. 1985, pp. 1–2. Reprinted by permission from *Bulletin to Management*, copyright 1985, by The Bureau of National Affairs, Inc., Washington, D.C.

38. Bureau of National Affairs, "Cost, Communication, and Compliance Concerns," *Bulletin to Management*, 21 Mar. 1985, p. 7; "Pay Off," *Wall Street Journal*, 8 July 1982, p. 1; R. Foltz, "Communiqué," *Personnel Administrator* (May 1981): 8; Huseman, Hatfield, and Driver, "Getting Your Benefits Program," pp. 560–66, 578; "How Do You Tell Employees about Benefits?" *Personnel Journal* (Oct. 1980): 798; R. M. McCaffery, "Employee Benefits: Beyond the Fringe?" *Personnel Administrator* (May 1981): 26–30, 66; T. F. Casey, "One-to-One Communication of Employee Benefits," *Personnel Journal* (Aug. 1982): 572–74; Bureau of National Affairs, "Employee Benefits: Attitudes and Reactions," *Bulletin to Management*, 11 Apr. 1985, p. 1.

39. For an excellent model to determine the worth of alternative benefit plans, see R. B. Dunham and R. A. Formisano, "Designing and Evaluating Employee Benefit Systems," *Personnel Administrator* (Apr. 1982): 29–36.

40. For suggestions on redesigning the indirect compensation package for greater motivational value and enhanced productivity, see S. C. Bushardt and A. R. Fowler, "Compensation and Benefits: Today's Dilemma in Motivation," *Personnel Administrator* (Apr. 1982): 23–26; D. L. Salisbury, "Benefit Trends in the '80s," *Personnel Journal* (Feb. 1982): 104–8; R. J. Greene and R. G. Roberts, "Strategic Integration of Compensation and Benefits," *Personnel Administrator* (May 1983): 79–82; P. Kienast, D. MacLachlan, L. McAlister, and D. Sampson, "The Modern Way to Redesign Compensation Packages," *Personnel Administrator* (June 1983): 127–33; J. W. Bracken, "Getting through the Mazes Knowing the Fundamentals of Employee Health Benefit Planning," *Personnel Administrator* (May 1984): 64–74.

41. P. Farish, "Interactive Pension Data," *Personnel Administrator* (July 1985): 10–12; H. D. Spring, "Medical Benefit Plan Costs," *Personnel Administrator* (Dec. 1984): 64–72; "IRS Benefit Regulations Call for Strict Record-Keeping," *Resource* (Feb. 1985): 1, 9; J. L. Krakauer, "Slash Health Care Costs with Claims Automation," *Personnel Journal* (Apr. 1985): 88–91; R. D. Huff, "The Impact of Cafeteria Benefits on the Human Resource Information System," *Personnel Journal* (Apr. 1983): 282–83.

42. R. J. Greene and R. G. Roberts, "Strategic Integration of Compensation and Benefits," *Personnel Administrator* (May 1983): 79–82; "Business Reduces Pension Funding to Cut Costs, Fend Off Takeovers," *Wall Street Journal*, 11 Oct. 1984, p. 35; P. F. Drucker, "Taming the Corporate Takeover," *Wall Street Journal*, 30 Oct. 1984, p. 30; L. Asinof, "Excess Pension Assets Lure Corporate Raiders," *Wall Street Journal*, 11 Sept. 1985, p. 6.

43. Bureau of National Affairs, "Total Compensation Strategies," *Bulletin to Management*, 4 Oct. 1984, p. 8.

Improving

11

Training and Development

Keeping Current at Motorola

On a $500 bet with his brother and the chance to learn something about semiconductors, A. William Wiggenhorn left a job he liked—director of human resources—and a company he had been with for a decade—Xerox Corp.—to come to work for Bob Galvin at Motorola, Inc.

The story goes like this: Bill Wiggenhorn's niche has always been in marketing and training; his brother is an engineer. About the time Bill joined Xerox, his brother started working for Motorola. For the next 10 years, the two argued about which discipline is more vital to an organization's success. When Bill was considering the move to Motorola in 1981, he recalls, "My brother bet me that I could never really start a training function here. I set a goal to be an officer within four years, figuring that would tell him that training was going to stay around."

As for the interest in semiconductors, having an engineer for a brother may have had something to do with that too. Says Bill, "Personally, I wanted to learn the technology. At Motorola, it is centralized in the fact that you're allowed to get into all the components of the business—manufacturing, engineering, etc. That's what really hooked me."

Sibling rivalry aside, Wiggenhorn's decision to take the Motorola job was not an easy one. He went through 22 interviews in six months for the position of director of a new corporate body called the Motorola Training and Education Center (MTEC). The creation of MTEC was CEO Robert Galvin's baby, and Galvin made it very clear that "he was behind the idea 110%," Wiggenhorn says. "Then when I met with the other senior officers of the company, they told me, 'This is the dumbest idea I've ever heard. What a waste of money. If you come here, we're going to watch you like a hawk.' "

"I was impressed with the extreme candor of senior management," he adds in earnest.

He was equally impressed with the company's commitment to training. "The fact that the chairman would interview a candidate for this job amazed me." In addition, Motorola had a five-year training plan based on an in-depth, company-wide study commissioned by Galvin. "I had never seen a five-year plan for training," Wiggenhorn exclaims. "And I've never seen another one since."

Galvin's belief in training translated into a whopping $44 million spent and more than 1 million man-hours of training delivered in 1984, not to mention groundbreaking on a new 96,000-square-foot training facility scheduled to open its doors this coming January. And as if that weren't enough to convince Wiggenhorn's brother that Motorola is serious about training, Bill became a vice president of the company last March.

The preceding "PHRM in the News" illustrates several aspects of training and development. One is that many companies, such as Motorola, believe that training is so critical that the chief executives, such as Robert Galvin, are totally committed supporters of training and development. The Motorola feature also shows how expensive training and development can be. Another aspect is that companies need to do more than spend money to demonstrate their commitment to the importance of training and development. They must also make it part of the organization and reward managers for training their employees.

Because training and development is so important and costly, organizations want to do it as effectively as possible. Effective training and development requires awareness and use of many techniques and programs. This chapter discusses the importance and purposes of training and development, along with training techniques and programs that organizations can provide. Prior to these discussions, training and development is defined, and its several relationships are described.

What Is Training and Development?

Training and development is any attempt to improve current or future employee performance by increasing, through learning, an employee's ability to perform, usually by increasing the employee's skills and knowledge.[1] The need for training and development is determined by the employee's performance deficiency, computed as follows:

> Standard or desired performance (present or future)
> − Actual (present or potential) performance
> = Training and development need[2]

Although this formula is simple, it may be difficult for an organization to determine exactly what performance is desired, especially in the future, and what level of performance employees are currently exhibiting or are likely to exhibit in the future. Nevertheless, organizations that engage in training and development attempt to make these estimates to increase the potential effectiveness of their training and development programs. This is becoming particularly true as the importance and purposes of training and development are recognized.

Because training and development is so essential, it must be done effectively. This requires that someone assume responsibility for these programs. Failure to run effective training and development programs results in part from the "failure to adhere to the principle that it is each *line* manager's responsibility to develop and utilize his human resources to get the results for which he is held directly accountable . . . and that staff [the personnel department] can/should really only assist him in this."[3] Staff specialists can help line managers serve the training and development needs of their employees by conducting interviews with employees and gathering performance data, analyzing performance requirements for each position, comparing employee skill and performance levels with those requirements, recommending and designing training and development programs to improve employee skill levels and to remove any unfavorable discrepancies, and conducting training and development programs where appropriate.[4]

Purposes and Importance of Training and Development

A major purpose of training and development is to remove performance deficiencies, whether current or anticipated, that cause employees to perform at less than the desired level. Training and development thereby enables employees to be much more productive. Training for performance improvements is particularly important to organizations with stagnant or declining rates of productivity. It is also important to organizations that are rapidly incorporating new technologies and consequently increasing the likelihood of employee obsolescence. For example, Xerox spends approximately $125 million a year in training and retraining, much of which is related to dealing with obsolescence. Furthermore:

> **Obsolete workers are more often retrained than replaced by their firms.** When Crown Zellerbach recently modernized a Louisiana pulp mill plant, it set up a training facility nearby and paid workers full wages to learn new skills. Hewlett-Packard is spending $1 million to move 350 workers to new jobs. Boeing enrolled laid-off electronics technicians in college to learn microprocessor skills. The Seattle aircraft maker's goal is to "train or retrain our own people before we go outside."
>
> At General Electric's dishwasher plant in Louisville, assembly-line workers learn how to make sense of computer readouts and monitors. The company runs a $6 million learning center in Pennsylvania and sponsors numerous education programs worldwide. Dresser Industries of Dallas offers workers more than 500 training and development courses.
>
> But ITT Educational Services surveys 322 U.S. companies and finds that nearly half are still replacing workers with outdated skills.[5]

Another purpose of training and development that is especially relevant to organizations that are rapidly incorporating new technologies is that of making the current work force more flexible and adaptable. If an organization can increase the adaptability of its work force through training and development, it can increase the adaptability of the organization itself, thus increasing its potential for survival and profitability.

Training and development can also increase the level of commitment of employees to the organization and increase their perceptions that the organization is a good place to work. Increased commitment can result in less turnover and absenteeism, thus increasing an organization's productivity.[6] Increasingly recognized is that training and development can benefit society by enabling individuals to be productive and contributing members of organizations.[7]

Relationships Influencing Training and Development

As Exhibit 11.1 shows, training and development consists of a large number of procedures and processes that are extensively related to many of the

Exhibit 11.1   *Training and Development Processes,*
Procedures, and Relationships

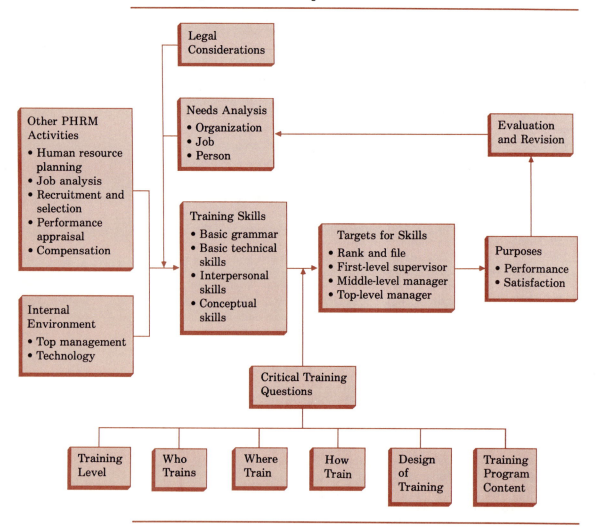

PHRM activities discussed so far. It is also related to two aspects of the internal environment.

Relationships with Other PHRM Activities

The training and development activity has critical relationships with human resource planning, job analysis, performance appraisal, recruitment and selection, and compensation. As with the other PHRM activities, these relationships are critical to the success of training and development.

Human Resource Planning.   Determining the organization's training and development needs often depends initially on its personnel and human resource planning requirements. These requirements, as discussed in Chapter 2, are derived from the organization's overall plans and objectives, its projected human resource needs (by skill, type, and number), and the anticipated supply of human resources to fill these needs. As a result of changing technology, organizations are finding it increasingly difficult to fill some of their human resource needs with already trained employees. As a result, they are finding it increasingly necessary to do more of their own training and to develop talent from within the organization. Human resource planning helps formalize this necessity and articulates management's concern for effectively utilizing its human resources now and in the future. Furthermore, human resource planning serves to integrate changing business needs with other PHRM activities.[8]

Job Analysis and Performance Appraisal.   Whereas human resource planning helps establish the general context within which training and development takes place, job analysis and performance appraisal help identify specific training and development needs (this process may be particularly well facilitated by behaviorally based performance appraisal methods such as BOS or BARS described in Chapter 6). Performance appraisal results may reveal a performance deficiency, and further analysis (such as described in Chapter 7) may indicate the cause as being an individual skill deficiency. This information, used in conjunction with job analysis, can then determine the specific training needs required to remove the deficiency.[9] This entire process, however, may suggest that the supervisor is unable to make valid performance appraisals, and thus training and development programs need to be directed toward removing that deficiency.

Recruitment and Selection.   Although an organization may determine that it needs training and development, it may still choose to recruit trained individuals rather than train its current employees. This may save training and development costs, but when organizations do this for jobs above the entry level, they risk reducing the promotional rewards that could be used as incentives for their current employees. They also risk negatively affecting employee commitment to the organization. Consequently, many organizations have training and development programs both for employees needing skills for future jobs and for those needing skills for current jobs. Occasionally, organizations need a uniquely skilled individual and therefore choose to recruit externally. Even after recruiting externally, whether for uniquely skilled individuals or not, organizations may be unable to find adequately trained job applicants. As a result, organizations may choose to develop and implement pre-employment training programs. With pre-employment training programs, organizations can use the recruitment activity to identify potentially qualifiable as well as potentially qualified job applicants. Potentially qualifiable applicants are then provided the opportunity for pre-employment training. After completing this training, they may be placed in the potentially qualified applicant pool, or they may have been offered a specific job contingent upon the successful completion of the pre-employment training program. The results of such a program may be a substantial reduction in turnover, along with increased product quality and customer satisfaction.

Compensation.   Rewards should be attached to any training and development activity; otherwise an employee may not be interested in performing better if there are no monetary or promotional rewards. For instance, to encourage managers to train their employees, organizations often evaluate managers on how well they perform this function. The use of incentives is important not only for getting employees into training and development programs but also for maintaining the effects of these programs. Employees may revert to the old performance if that is the one that is rewarded.[10]

Relationships with the Internal Environment

As the initial "PHRM in the News" suggested, the roles of top management and changing technology are important in training and development.

Top Management.   Top management support and commitment of the kind provided by Robert Galvin at Motorola are also being provided by Andrew E. Pearson, president of PepsiCo. As a consequence of Pearson's involvement, PepsiCo is emphasizing the importance of training and development in the manner described in the initial "PHRM in the News":

> The company wants to emphasize the value of coaching and training management traits that aren't rewarded now. In the future, promotions and pay will be based partly on how well an executive furthers the development of subordinates.
>
> According to J. Roger King, the new head of personnel, PepsiCo hopes to accomplish all this without sending managers to "sensitivity" training courses. "There are a lot of workshops where you dip people in and bring them up clean," Mr. King says. "I call it the bathtub theory of training. Two hours later they're dirty. It doesn't work because you can't take it to the workplace."
>
> Instead, he favors on-the-job changes that, while slight, may change attitudes and behavior. In the past, for instance, January bonus checks have been distributed with a handshake but few words. This year, the employee's supervisor will review performance and try to explain precisely what determined the size of the bonus.[11]

Without top management support and commitment to training, the major focus of an organization is likely to be on activities other than training. This is particularly true when the focus of attention is on short-term goals and immediate results. This situation allows too little time to wait for the benefits of training and development. Top management at PepsiCo began to emphasize training and development at the same time they began recognizing that they had to develop their people and businesses much more slowly.[12]

Changing Technology.   Changing technology is a significant factor in the increased emphasis on training and development. The skills of today will not be sufficient for the future. Although this applies to both manufacturing and service industries, the pace of complex technological change is perhaps greatest in manufacturing:

> The next generation of manufacturing managers will need to know computer-aided design and computer-aided manufacturing (CAD/CAM), computer-integrated manufacturing (CIM), group technologies, flexible manufacturing, "just-in-time"

inventory control, manufacturing resource planning (MRP), robotics, and a whole litany of other techniques and technologies in manufacturing.

They're going to have to understand systems thinking, as more and more of the major corporations move toward the globalization of their manufacturing to achieve the competitive advantages of economies of scale, vertical integration, and offshore production.

They'll have to develop different perspectives on managing a work force as the concepts of lifestyle employment, worker participation, and job enrichment extend further and further through the American enterprise system.

Perhaps most importantly, they are going to have to have a well-developed understanding of corporate strategies, not only to find those organizations and sub-units of organizations in which they will be most comfortable and successful, but also to be able to take an important role in determining and directing those strategies. The demands on manufacturing managers—on their skills, abilities, and training—are going up, but so too are their status and importance in manufacturing-based industries.[13]

In many organizations today, however, employee skills are insufficient for the current jobs because of recent technological change. Consequently, organizations such as Crown Zellerbach and General Electric are retraining employees. With the pace of technology likely to accelerate, the most reasonable scenario is one of organizations continually retraining current employees and recruiting new employees with unique skills. Changing technology necessitates continual training program formulation and implementation, and employees who are willing to adapt, to be reassigned to different jobs, and to be retrained. To encourage and support employees in these efforts, employers may provide employment security.[14] Because the area of retraining is so vital, unions have become heavily involved, as discussed in Chapter 16.[15] The following "PHRM in the News" provides an excellent illustration of the impact of technology and other forces on training and development.

PHRM in the News

Training for Today and Tomorrow

The rapid pace of technological change in the workplace calls for a "new, more dynamic corporate training strategy— one that anticipates new technologies far in advance and helps employees develop skills, not only for today's technology, but for tomorrow's and the day after's," according to a new report by the Work in America Institute, a not-for-profit research group. The report, part of a three-year national study on training policies, recommends that training be linked directly to an organization's long-term strategy to achieve corporate goals.

The need for dynamic training

While the problems of training employees as technology advances are "as old as industry itself," the rapidity with which new technology becomes old technology is a new issue, the report points out. Where once an organization "could expect reasonable periods of technological stability between waves of change," today, as "one change rapidly follows another," there is "a premium on anticipating new technologies far in advance." Consequently, the report observes, employees must be trained to deal with change "in a proactive, rather than in a defensive, manner." In addition to technological advances, other forces are accelerating change in the workplace and reinforcing the need for a more dynamic training strategy, including:

- *Structural changes in organizations*— The continual reshaping of organizational structures through acquisitions, mergers, and new product development requires that employees be retrained to carry out new responsibilities and duties, the report asserts. If organizations are to "avoid playing catch-up," the report adds, training must be linked to strategic decisions about the company's future.

- *Occupational changes*—While some jobs are becoming obsolete, new ones are emerging to accommodate rapid changes in the economy, the shift from manufacturing to service-producing industries, and the impact of research, development, and technology, the report says. Noting that two of every five workers will have to change occupations every five years, the report asserts that training must be made more flexible to decrease turnover and improve productivity.

- *Workforce attitudes*—"An overwhelming majority of American workers believe they have the right to participate in decisions affecting their work," the report points out, stressing, however, that employee involvement in decision-making is successful only when organizations provide appropriate opportunities for training and self-development.

Meeting the challenge

Some organizations have already begun to make training "part and parcel" of their long-term strategy for growth and development, the report finds. For

example, Travelers Insurance, which is striving to become a preeminent financial services company, has plans to train all employees to use the latest data-processing equipment and to teach supervisors how to manage an organization transformed by new technology. To achieve these training goals, Travelers is building a state-of-the-art training center; has designed, tested, and launched a computer literacy program; and is preparing a management redevelopment program. The report also notes that:

- Investment in training is highest among companies "at the leading edge of technology." The report stresses, however, that, even in low-tech companies, employees need to learn more than "just enough to operate the new technology to which they are assigned." While broader knowledge enables employees to discover profitable applications of technology, it also is "crucial" for workers' personal growth.

- Those organizations that are the most successful in devising long-term training strategies have the support of top management and make training a critical component of their corporate strategy. At Motorola, for example, the chief executive officer sits on a committee that sets the company's technical training policy.

- Involving line managers in training programs can be critical to success. When managers at New England Telephone attended a special course on effective listening techniques and then returned to instruct their subordinates, "impressive" results— including annual cost savings of $2,280,000—were achieved, the report says. (Copies of "Training for New Technology" are available from Work in America Institute, Inc., 700 White Plains Road, Scarsdale, N.Y. 10583.)

Source: Bulletin to Management, 3 October 1985, p. 112. Reprinted by permission from *Bulletin to Management,* copyright 1985, by The Bureau of National Affairs, Inc., Washington, D.C.

Legal Considerations in Training and Development

As mentioned in Chapters 4 and 5, Title VII of the Civil Rights Act of 1964, the Age Discrimination in Employment Act, and the Equal Pay Act pertain to discrimination in many aspects of the employment process. Discriminatory practices in initial selection decisions receive much attention and concern. Similarly, discriminatory practices in training and development decisions, deserve much attention and concern. Both types of decisions are equally covered by Title VII.[16]

Legal considerations are relevant to several aspects of training and development. One aspect is determining the training and development needs of an applicant for a position. Recall from Chapter 5 that an applicant cannot be eliminated from the selection pool if he or she does not possess a skill that can be learned in eight hours. Thus, it is important to determine what skills an individual needs to perform a job, what skills an applicant possesses, which training programs can remove any deficiencies, and the time necessary to complete these programs.

Another legal consideration relevant to training and development is the selection of job applicants on the basis of test scores related to training program performance preceding actual job placement. Even though the test scores, if related to training program performance, may not need to have a demonstrated relationship to actual job performance (*Washington* v. *Davis,* 1976), they should be used only to screen out applicants rather than rank applicants according to the Fifth Circuit Court of Appeals arguments in *Ensley Branch NAACP* v. *Seibels* (1980).

Another legal consideration pertains to providing training and development opportunities for current employees.[17] Here, bans on discrimination extend to on-the-job training and one-day introductions to new jobs or equipment, as well as to affirmative action and formal apprenticeship/training programs. Admission to formal training programs, however, can be limited to those under a certain age, as long as they are not women or minorities who have previously been denied training opportunities. Specific discriminatory training practices can often be determined based upon the responses to the following questions:

- Are minorities or women (or both) given the same training opportunities as white males? Be careful! Advertising and recruiting practices come into play here.
- Are requirements for entry into a training program (i.e., tests, education, experience, and so on) job related, or are they arbitrary?
- Are nearly all machine functions or other specialized duties that require training performed by white or male workers?
- Does one class of trainees tend to get more challenging assignments or other special training opportunities?
- Do supervisors know what constitutes training? It could be almost any learning experience from how to fit a drill bit to a two-week seminar on complex sales procedures.
- Who evaluates the results of instruction or training—only white males?

- Are all trainees given equal facilities for instruction? Are they segregated in any way?
- Do a disproportionate number of females or minorities (or both) fail to pass training courses? If so, find out if it is because they are more often unqualified or because they receive inferior instruction. Adverse impact here is treated the same as it is in recruitment and selection (refer to Chapters 4 and 5 for a brief review of adverse impact).

To defend against charges of discrimination, organizations can provide a reasonable defense by showing that the training programs were conceived and administered without bias. This, however, will be exceedingly difficult to demonstrate unless companies have the foresight to document their training practices. Thus, they should follow these guidelines:

- Register affirmative action training and apprenticeship programs with the Department of Labor. The Department of Labor requires the programs to be in writing. Include the goals, timetables, and criteria for selection and evaluation of trainees. Such a record will help prove job relatedness or that there was no intent to discriminate. It can also be valuable in proving that an organization's program was not used as a pretext to discriminate. This is consistent with the *Weber* decision described in detail in Chapter 4.
- Keep a record of all employees who wish to enroll in your training program. Detail how each trainee was selected. Keep application forms, tests, questionnaires, records of preliminary interviews, and anything else that bears on an employee's selection or rejection for at least two years or as long as training continues.
- Document all management decisions and actions that relate to the administration of training policies.
- Monitor each trainee's progress. Provide progress evaluations and make sure counseling is available. Continue to evaluate the results even after completion of training.

A final legal consideration in training and development is federal and state governmental support. This support can enable organizations to defray some training costs and receive already trained employees. It can also enable employees to obtain training and jobs. Currently, support from the federal government is funneled through block grants to states and through the Office of Federal Contract Compliance Programs under provisions in the Job Training Partnership Act of 1982. Under that act, grants are provided to states that in turn use the money to train economically disadvantaged youths and adults as well as workers whose jobs have been eliminated. In addition, money is to be provided for training individuals to overcome sex stereotyping in occupations traditionally for the other sex. The federal government also supports training by providing funds to 460 private industry councils. These councils are composed primarily of business people who help determine what training programs should be offered and disburse funds to those who provide that training.[18] Determining what training and development programs should be offered is therefore critical. In general, however, it begins with determining training and development needs.

Determining Training and Development Needs

The three major phases of any training and development program are the **assessment phase,** which determines the training and development needs of the organization; the **implementation phase** (actual training and development), in which certain programs and learning methods are used to impart new attitudes, skills, and abilities; and the **evaluation phase.** The relationships among these three phases are shown in Exhibit 11.2.

This section focuses on the assessment phase, which consists of analyzing the organization's needs, the job's needs, and the person's needs.[19]

Organizational Needs Analysis

Organizational needs analysis begins with an examination of the short- and long-term objectives of the organization and the trends that are likely to affect these objectives.[20] According to one expert, "organizational objectives should be the ultimate concern of any training and development effort."[21] In addition to examining the organization's objectives, the organizational needs analysis also consists of human resource analysis and analyses of efficiency indexes and the organizational climate.[22] Although analyses of the efficiency indexes and the organizational climate help to locate training needs, they are primarily useful in the evaluation of training and development programs and therefore are discussed in the last section of this chapter.

Human resource analysis consists of translating the organization's objectives into the demand for human resources, skills required, and programs for supplying the needed skills and human resources. Training and development programs play a vital role in matching the supply of human resources and skills with the demands.

Analysis of efficiency indexes provides information on the current efficiency of work groups and the organization. Efficiency indexes that can be used include costs of labor, quantity of output, quality of output, waste, equipment use, and repairs.[23] The organization can determine standards for these indexes and then analyze them to evaluate the general effectiveness of training programs and to locate training and development needs in the group of organizations.

The analysis of the organizational climate is the final aspect of the organizational needs analysis. Organizational climate is used here to describe the quality of the organization, how the employees feel about it, and how effective they are. Like the analysis of efficiency indexes, it can help identify where training and development programs may be needed and provide criteria against which to evaluate the effectiveness of the programs that are implemented. Measures of the quality of the organizational climate include absenteeism, turnover, grievances, productivity, suggestions, attitude surveys, and accidents.[24]

Although these three aspects of the organizational needs analysis present a broad definition of the organization's need for training and development, they are extremely important in isolating where the training and development programs should be focused and in providing some criteria against

Exhibit 11.2   Model for an Instructional System

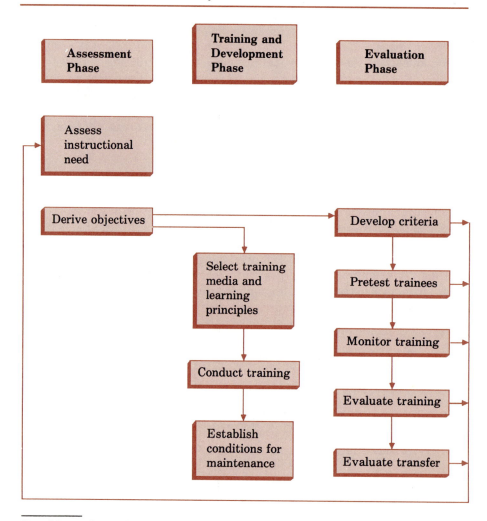

which to evaluate the effectiveness of the programs. Many organizations fail to do this analysis, preferring to jump in and train because everyone else is doing it.

Job Needs Analysis

Just as important as analyzing the organization's needs, and perhaps just as frequently overlooked, is the second phase of any needs analysis. Since the organizational needs analysis is too broad to spot training and development needs for specific jobs, a **job needs analysis** must be conducted.[25] Essentially, this analysis provides information on the tasks to be performed on each job (the basic information contained in job descriptions), the skills necessary to perform those tasks (from the job specifications or qualifications), and the minimum acceptable standards (information that is often not a part of the traditional job analysis).[26] These three pieces of information may be gathered independently from current employees, personnel, or current supervisors. They may also be gathered simultaneously by teams of individuals representing different areas of the organization.[27]

Next, one or more people rank the skills necessary to perform a task, in order of their importance to the task. Only when all the people rating the task agree that the skills are related to an independent measure of performance is the job needs analysis validated.

As an example of job skills identification, consider the three common skills needed for managerial jobs at all levels: managerial and administrative, interpersonal, and technical and professional skills.[28]

- *Managerial and administrative:* Includes understanding the complexities of the organization, being able to set objectives and goals, solving problems, and controlling results
- *Interpersonal:* Includes understanding of motivation, effectiveness of relationships with co-workers, sensitivity, and communication skills
- *Technical and professional:* Covers knowledge of the area of the business the employee works in and its methods and techniques, as well as the ability to use them

After information about the necessary skills and their importance and the minimal acceptable standards of proficiency has been collected, only the person needs analysis remains to be done before the potential training and development needs can be determined.

Person Needs Analysis

The **person needs analysis** can be accomplished in two different ways. Employee performance discrepancies may be identified either by comparing actual performance with the minimum acceptable standards of performance or by comparing an evaluation of employee proficiency on each required skill dimension with the proficiency level required for each skill. The first method is based on the actual, current job performance of an employee; therefore, it can be used to determine training and development needs for the current job. The second method, on the other hand, can be used to identify training and development needs for future jobs.

A relevant training question for the first method is, Can the employee do his or her current job? For the second method, the relevant question is, Can this employee or new job applicant do some job he or she has yet to do? To ensure equal opportunity and affirmative action, the basis for the previous answers must be a validated set of measures that will enable the organization to determine current performance or future performance potential, as described in Chapter 6.[29]

An increasingly used technique to gather information in person needs analysis is self-assessment. Self-assessment, as discussed in Chapter 6 as a source of performance appraisal, can elicit from the individual an appraisal of training needs for his or her present job or those necessary for desired future jobs.[30]

Type of Training and Development Needs Identified

Based on the organizational, job, and person needs analyses, the appropriate type of training can be determined. Although many types of training exist, for ease of discussion they are grouped into four categories that correspond to the skills and abilities being increased by the training:

- *Basic skills of grammar, math, safety, reading, listening, and writing* (**BSG**). These skills are often missing in new employees and are also missing in many executives who have been around a long time. For example:

  Ask most business executives how they would like to improve their reading on the job, and they will probably answer, "I would like to read faster. I can't keep up with all the reading material that comes across my desk."

  Employees have begun to recognize their reading limitations and are now requesting reading improvement courses. Many corporations, such as Scott Paper Company, Provident National Bank, Western Electric Company, and Getty Oil, have appreciated this need and have implemented programs for their employees. The response of industry in general indicates a belief on its part that efficient reading by employees should be a major goal for business.[31]

- *Basic skills of a technical nature to do the specific job* (**BST**). These skills might include how to type, file, or use a personal computer. The personal computer not only is necessitating the training of many employees but also is facilitating the delivery of the training.[32]

- *Interpersonal skills, including communications, human relations, leadership, and labor relations* (**IPS**). Also included are skills related to legal considerations and even skills in how to be better organized and use time more effectively. Perhaps the demand and need for IPS are greatest at the level of the first-time supervisor, although, as shown in Exhibit 11.3, IPS is integral at all levels of management.[33]

- *Broader-based conceptual integrative skills, such as strategic and operational planning, and organizational design and policy skills* (**CIS**). Also included are decision-making skills and skills in adapting to complex and changing environments—often a part of top and middle management, as shown in Exhibit 11.3.

Targeting the Types of Training and Development

After the types of needs have been identified, they need to be matched with those who are most appropriate for them, as determined by the needs assessment.[34] Exhibit 11.3 lists four major groups of employees: (1) rank and file,

Mix of Training Skills and Training Targets by Employee Group

Exhibit 11.3

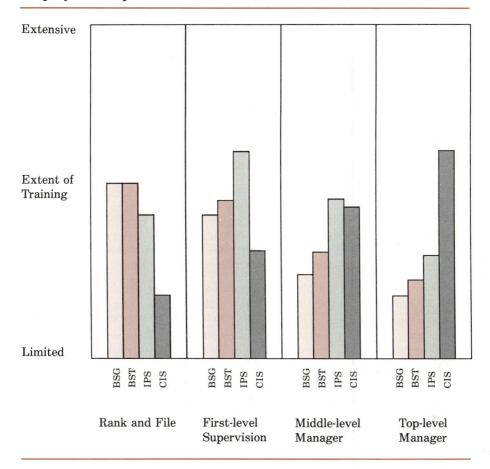

(2) first-level supervisors (managers), (3) middle-level managers, and (4) top-level managers. These groupings are general. Many organizations break down training target groups even further.[35] For example, Chase Manhattan Bank identifies three distinct segments of management:

> (1) the highest potential individuals most capable of development and growth to fill senior executive and business manager positions; (2) individuals identified as having the highest potential for filling senior functional or more individually focused positions (these are jobs calling for strong functional, professional, or specialized experience and capability); and (3) talented and experienced individuals who, though consistently identified as high performers, have little or no potential or interest in higher positions with increased responsibility (this segment includes both managers and nonmanagers whom the organization critically needs to retain and to utilize effectively).[36]

Large retail stores, such as Hecht's in Washington, D.C., may break down target groups by function as well as by level in the function. For example,

Hecht's has training programs for assistant buyers, for buyers, for group managers (sellers), and for department managers.

Regardless of how a specific organization breaks down its target groups, it usually tailors specific programs for those groups only. Exceptions are programs aimed at group or team building. These training efforts are often targeted toward members of several groups to improve the quality of group interaction:

> **Ford Motor classes teach managers and workers how to work together.** Bosses take self-scoring tests to evaluate their management styles and learn how to make group decisions. One group pretends it is lost on Mars and picks the best equipment to escape. During the 3 1/2-day seminar, sealed reviews are opened to reveal what workers think about their bosses. "Managers usually assess themselves more favorably than their subordinates do," says a Ford executive who took the course.
>
> Hourly workers grade themselves and their bosses in shorter sessions. They draw "windows" to rank bosses on collaboration; the best have big squares, the worst get peepholes. Ford says the program improves teamwork; the development of a new transmission went smoother because all involved took the course.
>
> IBM and Kroger use the same "Models for Management" program, which was designed by Teleometrics International of Houston.

Generally, however, each program is unique in that it emphasizes different skills and different proportions of those skills. Training programs for rank-and-file employees generally have more BSG and BST than the programs for supervisors. In turn, programs for supervisors generally have more IPS and CIS than programs for managers.[38] Exhibit 11.3 summarizes these training skills and training target relationships.

Although Exhibit 11.3 matches training program skills with target groups, it fails to identify the specific programs that can be used to provide those skills. Furthermore, it fails to identify several aspects involved in implementing training and development programs. These are discussed next as part of the implementation phase.

Implementing Training and Development Programs

Successful implementation of training and development programs depends on selecting the right programs for the right people under the right conditions. Needs analysis helps identify the right people and the right programs, and several training and development considerations help make the right conditions.[39]

Training and Development Considerations

Each of several considerations associated with implementing training and development programs must be appropriately addressed to increase the chances of the programs being effective.[40] These considerations are as follows:

- Who participates in the program
- Who teaches the program
- What media are used to teach
- What the level of learning is to be
- What learning principles are needed
- Where the program is conducted

With these considerations in mind, the personnel and human resource manager selects a training and development program from among the many available. Effective selection depends upon a knowledge of the programs that are available and the types of skills and level at which the program is best directed.

Who Participates.   Generally, training and development programs are designed specifically to teach particular skills. This is because in most programs, only one target audience is in attendance. At times, however, having two or more target audiences together may be helpful. For example, rank-and-file employees and their supervisors may effectively learn about a new work process or machine together so they have a common understanding about the new process and their respective roles. As stated earlier, bringing several target audiences together may also facilitate group processes such as problem solving and decision making.

Who Teaches the Program.   Training and development programs may be taught by one of several people:

- Immediate supervisors
- Co-workers, as in buddy systems
- Members of the PHRM staff
- Specialists in other parts of the company
- Outside consultants
- Industrial associations
- Faculty members at universities
- Company established universities such as Solectron, as described in the following "PHRM in the News."

Which of these people is selected to teach often depends on where the program is held and which skill is being taught. For example, programs teaching the basic skills are usually done by members of the PHRM staff or specialists in other parts of the company, whereas interpersonal skills and conceptual, integrative skills for management are often taught in universities.[41] However, large organizations such as McDonald's, XEROX, Proctor and Gamble, General Electric, and Phillips Petroleum, who have large numbers of employees seeking management skills, provide their own management and advanced management skills programs.[42] An example of just how critical it can be to an organization to do its own management training is shown in the "PHRM in the News" feature on Solectron. In addition, many

Grow Your Own Managers

Five years ago, Solectron Corp. nearly drowned in its own success. An early leader in the electronic assembly field, the company was bootstrapping its way through 800% revenue growth in its first two years, from $450,000 in 1978 to $3.6 million in 1980. But the young company could not pay enough to attract experienced managers to oversee its 200 to 300 workers in the labor-intensive business. So it opted to do the next best thing: "We decided to produce our own managers internally," says Winston Chen, Solectron's president and CEO.

Chen masterminded Solectron's Entrepreneur University, a series of daily lectures, exams, and role-playing workshops to train Solectron managers in the company's business, corporate philosophy, and employee management and motivation. So far 150 Solectron managers, ranging from shop foremen to general managers, have completed the two-year program, which includes hour-long daily classes beginning at 7 a.m. and approximately 5 hours of homework a week. Almost all of those managers have stayed with the San Jose, Calif., company, says Chen, 43.

Roy Kusumoto, a former director of international operations for Atari Inc., founded Solectron in November, 1977, with $5,000 of his own money. Chen joined the company in 1978 from IBM where he managed tape drive-head development. Solectron grew to nearly $50 million in sales before raising its first venture capital round of $8.2 million in February, 1984, from such investors as Hambro International Venture Fund, New York, and Citicorp Investment Management, New York. Revenues for fiscal 1984 ended Aug. 31 were $54 million with about a 5% profit margin. Sales of $80

million are projected for fiscal 1985.

Solectron now has 2,200 employees and 14 divisions housed in 10 buildings. The company acts somewhat like a manufacturing arm for personal computer companies. Workers place hundreds of minute wires and circuits onto intricately patterned computer boards, and then test each board for faulty connections. "It's the grunt work of the industry," says Kusumoto, 42.

With employees spread over one million sq. ft. of space, Solectron needed entrepreneurial managers who could make difficult decisions on their own. At IBM, Chen's own curiosity had driven him to informally interview close to 200 managers and executives on what was most important to their success. The volumes of notes he kept became the basis for Solectron's curriculum. Now a staff of nine headed by 30-year-old Marjorie Quon manages the program, which is set up like a university but does not offer credit. Speakers include local college professors, consultants, accountants, and entrepreneurs.

Employees attend the sessions on a voluntary basis and are paid for their time. Subjects range from basic financial analysis and strategic planning to motivational psychology and stress management. Danny Lee, who started with Solectron five years ago managing five other employees and is now general manager of Solectron's most profitable machine-assembly division with 350 employees, says the employee motivation sessions were vital to his promotion. "I got to see problems from both sides," says Lee. Chen believes the program is well worth its expense— about $500,000 this year. "These employees get MBA training for free. The entire company benefits," he says.

Source: Reprinted from the April, 1985 issue of VENTURE, The Magazine for Entrepreneurs, by special permission. Copyright 1985 Venture Magazine, Inc., 521 Fifth Ave., New York, N.Y. 10175.

organizations contract out basic skill training for computer literacy and use training.[43]

What Media Are Used to Teach the Program.   There are several ways to learn. In many colleges and universities, the basic ways used are lectures, lecture-discussion combinations, case discussions, and some self-programmed instructions.[44] These are also the ways used in many training and development programs. Some additional training media or techniques are:

- role playing[45]
- behavior modeling[46]
- group participation exercise[47]
- one-on-one counseling[48]
- demonstrations[49]
- videotape recording and playback[50]

Often combinations of these techniques are used as well as the use of more than one trainer.[51] For example, some retail stores are training their department managers by a videotape-modeling combination.[52] Managers in training view a videotape of a manager (really an actor) behaving in an ideal way. Then the managers watching are given a chance to "model" the behavior of the actor on the videotape. By watching they provide themselves their own feedback in addition to that provided by the trainers.

What the Level of Learning Is to Be.   As discussed earlier, four major categories of skills can be taught:

- Basic skills
- Basic job skills
- Interpersonal skills
- Broader-based conceptual skills

In addition to these categories of skills are three basic levels at which these skills can be learned. At the lowest level, the employee or potential employee must develop **fundamental knowledge,** which means developing the basic understanding of a field and getting acquainted with the language, concepts, and relationships involved in it. The goal of the next-highest level is **skill development,** or acquiring the ability to perform in a particular skill area. The highest level aims for increased **operational proficiency,** which means obtaining additional experience and improving skills that have already been developed.[53] Each of the four skill categories can be learned at all three levels. How effectively they are learned depends on several training design principles.

Learning Principles.   Training and development programs are much more likely to be effective when they incorporate the following critical learning principles:

- Employee motivation
- Recognition of individual differences
- Practice opportunities

- Reinforcement
- Knowledge of results (feedback)
- Goals
- Transfer of learning
- Follow-up

Having employees motivated to change and acquire different behavior makes training easier and more successful. Sometimes the knowledge that a new job is available or that a raise is possible is enough to provide employees with sufficient motivation. But training will not be effective if employees have high motivation and no ability. Since ability is a crucial component in determining training effectiveness, the ability level of each individual must be considered. Other individual differences must also be taken into account. Some individuals learn more rapidly than others, some have had more experience than others, and some may be more physically able to exhibit the behaviors resulting from the training.[54]

Regardless of individual differences and whether a trainee is learning a new skill or acquiring knowledge of a given topic, the person should be given the opportunity to practice what is being taught. Practice is also essential after the individual has been successfully trained. Even professional tennis players or pianists, for example, have to practice several hours a day. Practice can be a form of positive reinforcement.

According to the principles of **reinforcement,** people will do what is rewarded and will avoid doing what is not rewarded or is punished.[55] Although learning can be rewarding for its own sake, it is generally regarded as a difficult and distasteful process that must be rewarded extrinsically to ensure its effectiveness. This fact may be useful for training and development programs, because extrinsic rewards are often at the disposal of the organization and the trainer. For example, managers may praise their employees for learning a new skill, and the organization may provide promotional opportunities for those who successfully complete a training and development program. These extrinsic rewards are said to reinforce an individual's behavior (for example, learning a new skill) because they are given on the basis of that behavior. Another term used to describe extrinsic rewards is **contingent rewards,** which can be both positive and negative. Because the principles of reinforcement are so important in learning, the implementation and maintenance of effective training depend in part on the handling of rewards.[56]

Effective management of contingent rewards depends on knowing when to give them. Although reinforcement should be given immediately following the desired behavior, it need not be given after each behavior.[57] Indeed, an individual who is reinforced only after a certain number of desired behaviors will perform vigorously and quickly until the required number of behaviors is achieved. In addition, the behaviors learned under such a **partial reinforcement** schedule are much more resistant to extinction than those learned under conditions of continuous reinforcement.[58] Partial reinforcement is important to managers who want to change the behavior of their employees or maintain a change that has occurred. In addition, partial reinforcement schedules are a benefit because they do not require the manager to observe and administer rewards to employees every time they perform.

Instead, they allow the manager to observe employees' behavior intermittently.[59]

Here are some descriptions and examples of schedules of reinforcement:

- **Continuous schedule:** Rewards are administered after every desired behavior, and punishment is administered after every incorrect behavior. An example is giving praise after every sale that is made.
- **Fixed-interval schedule:** Reinforcement or punishment is provided after a certain fixed period of time. A monthly paycheck is an example of a typical fixed-interval reward.
- **Fixed-ratio schedule:** Reinforcement or punishment is provided after a certain predetermined number of behaviors have been observed. For example, punishment may be administered only after a worker has been absent for five consecutive days.
- **Intermittent or variable-ratio schedule:** Reinforcement or punishment is provided after a number of behaviors have been observed. Unlike the fixed-ratio schedule, however, the number of observed behaviors constantly changes and is therefore not known by the person being observed. For example, a supervisor may give an employee an afternoon off for one excellent report and then not provide one again until three or four more good reports have been submitted. The employee never knows how many good reports will earn an afternoon off.

Although evidence indicates that contingent rewards and punishments are effective if they are administered properly, managers occasionally claim that there are few rewards to give. Yet they often fail to provide what is probably the single most important reinforcement and incentive: **knowledge of results.**[60] In learning a new behavior, people sometimes cannot judge whether they are behaving correctly. Managers can play an important role at this point simply by telling employees how well they are doing. Adding rewards for properly performed behaviors and imposing punishments for improper behaviors accelerates learning considerably.

Goal setting can also accelerate learning, particularly when accompanied by knowledge of results.[61] Individuals generally perform better and learn more quickly when they have goals, particularly if the goals are specific and reasonably difficult. Goals that are too easy or too difficult have little motivational value. Only when people have some chance of reaching the goal can they really become motivated.[62] The motivational value of goal setting may also increase when employees participate in the goal-setting process.[63] When the manager or trainer and the employee work together to set goals, the employee's unique strengths and weaknesses can be identified. Aspects of the training and development program can then be tailored to specific employees, which may increase the effectiveness of the training program.[64]

Learning, however, does not always progress at the same rate during a training program. Differing rates of learning can be described by learning curves and plateaus, which illustrate the relationship between the time an individual spends learning the task for which he or she is being trained and the rate of success in acquiring that skill. Often the skills for complex tasks are acquired at a much slower rate than for simple tasks. Have you noticed that the amount you can learn per hour decreases rapidly the longer you study? That pattern of learning is described as a **decreasing returns curve.** An **increasing returns curve** illustrates a situation in which learning progresses slowly at first and then accelerates dramatically. Another learning curve, the **S-shaped curve,** is a composite of the decreasing and increasing returns curves. "Many psychologists believe that if we could measure a response (successful learning) from the very first stages of learning to the asymptote, we would always come up with an S-shaped curve."[65]

The S-shaped curve is typical of the rate of learning in many situations, but somewhere along the S-shaped curve is generally a **plateau,** a temporary leveling off. Plateaus can occur for several reasons. After the initial excitement of learning, motivation may decline for a while and then pick up again. Or the individual may need to synthesize what has been learned so far, and until synthesis takes place, little new learning may occur. Or the individual may be taking time to sort out and eliminate incorrect learning.[66]

One serious mistake in designing training and development programs is the "failure to provide definite systems, policies and/or follow-up programs to ensure the learners' effective use of their newly acquired skills, knowledge, and attitudes on the job."[67] As a result, what an employee learns in a training program may never be tried in the actual job situation. Or if the newly learned behavior is tried, it may quickly be extinguished because of lack of support. Provisions must therefore be made in training programs for the positive transfer to the job of the behaviors learned in training. This can be done in three ways. One is to have conditions in the training program identical to those in the job situation. The second is to teach principles for applying the behaviors learned in the training program to the job situation, and the third is the contract plan.

A final design principle to remember is **follow-up.** Once a participant leaves the training program, the PHRM manager should provide a means of follow-up to help ensure that the participant will do what was taught. All too often, participants who want to change their current behavior get back to work and slip into the old patterns. This in turn results in a significant loss of effectiveness of the training program. One approach to help prevent this from happening is the **contract plan.** Its simplicity is a key factor in its success. Each participant writes an informal agreement near the end of a training program, stating which aspects of the program he or she believes will have the most beneficial effect back on the job and then agreeing to apply those aspects. Each participant is also asked to choose another participant from the program to whom a copy of the contract is given and who agrees to check up on the participant's progress every few weeks.[68]

Although incorporating these principles of learning is desirable, many training and development programs do not have them or are designed without consideration of individual differences, motivation, learning curves and plateaus, and reinforcement, feedback, and goal setting. Nevertheless, application of these principles of learning can increase the chances of successfully implementing a training and development program. Successful implementation also depends on selecting where the program is conducted.

Where the Program Is Conducted.   The decision on where the training and development program is to be conducted is made from among three choices:

- At the job itself
- On site but not on the job—for example, in a training room in the company
- Off the site, such as in a university or college classroom, a hotel conference center, or the wilderness, such as with the Outward Bound program

Typically, the basic job skills are taught at the job, and the basic grammar skills are taught on site. Much of the IPS and CIS training are done off the site. For purposes of the following discussion, and to be consistent with how training is often discussed in organizations, the term *on the job* encompasses both at-the-job and on-site locations, and the term *off the job* refers to off-the-site locations.

Training and Development Programs

A multitude of training and development programs are available for both managers and nonmanagers. Although other characteristics may be used, these programs are most often distinguished by who participates (for example, managers or nonmanagers); where the programs are conducted (on the job or off the job); and what employee ability is being changed (technical skills and knowledge, interpersonal skills and attitudes, or conceptual skills and knowledge). The abilities gained by the employee in any of these programs can be used to reduce current or future performance deficiencies.

On-the-Job Programs.   As shown in Exhibit 11.4, several programs can be conducted on the job.[69] These programs are often formally developed and implemented by the organization, but some training and development is informal. One such informal method is supervisory assistance, which can be provided for both nonmanagerial and managerial employees.

Generally, organizations use on-the-job training programs because they provide hands-on learning experience that facilitates learning transfer and because they can fit into the organizations' flow of activities. Separate areas for training and development are thus unnecessary, and employees can begin to make a contribution to the organization while still in training.[70] On-the-job training programs, however, are not without their disadvantages. They may result not only in customer dissatisfaction but also in damage to equipment, costly errors, and frustration for both the trainer (most likely a co-worker or supervisor) and the trainee.

The disadvantages of on-the-job training can be minimized by making the training program as systematic and complete as possible. **Job instruction training (JIT)** represents such a systematic technique. JIT was developed "to provide a guide for giving on-the-job skill training to white- and blue-collar employees as well as technicians."[71] Since JIT is a technique rather than a program, it can be adapted to training efforts for all employees in off-the-job as well as on-the-job programs.

JIT consists of four steps: (1) careful selection and preparation of the trainer and the trainee for the learning experience to follow; (2) a full explanation and demonstration by the trainer of the job to be done by the trainee; (3) a trial on-the-job performance by the trainee; and (4) a thorough feedback session between the trainer and trainee to discuss the trainee's performance and the job requirements.[72]

Exhibit 11.4   *Major Training and Development*
Program Availability

On-the-Job Training and Development (OJT)
Job Instruction Training (JIT)
Apprenticeship training*
Internships and assistantships
Job rotation
Personal career planning
Multiple management (junior board)
Supervisory assistance:
• Coaching
• Counseling
• Mentoring

Off-the-Job Training and Development (OFFJT)
Formal course method
• Training by oneself
    Programmed instruction
    Computer-assisted instruction
    Reading
    Correspondence courses
• Training by others
    Lectures
    Classroom courses
Simulation
• Vestibule
• Management games
• Assessment centers
Role playing
Sensitivity training

---

*These programs are actually composed of off-the-job as well as
on-the-job components.

Another method for minimizing the disadvantages of on-the-job training
is combining it with off-the-job training. Apprenticeship training, internships, and assistantships are programs based on this combination. **Apprenticeship training** is mandatory for admission into many of the skilled trades,
such as plumbing, electronics, and carpentry. These programs are formally
defined by the U.S. Department of Labor's Bureau of Apprenticeship and
Training, and involve a written agreement "providing for not less than 4,000
hours of reasonably continuous employment . . . and supplemented by a recommended minimum of 144 hours per year of related classroom instruction."[73] The Equal Employment Opportunity Commission (EEOC) does not
prevent the nation's 48,000 skilled trade (apprentice) training programs
from excluding anyone aged forty to seventy, since apprenticeship programs
are part of the educational system aimed at youth.[74] To be most effective, the
on- and off-the-job components of the apprenticeship program must be well
integrated and appropriately planned, must recognize individual differences

in learning rates and abilities, and must be flexible enough to meet the changing demands and technology of the trades.[75]

Somewhat less formalized and extensive than apprenticeship training are the internship and assistantship programs. **Internships** are often part of an agreement between schools and colleges and local organizations.[76] As with apprenticeship training, individuals in these programs earn while they learn, but at a rate that is less than that paid to full-time employees or master crafts workers. The internships, however, function not only as a source of training but also as a source of exposure to job and organizational conditions. Students on internship programs are often able to see the application of ideas taught in the classroom more readily than students without any work experience. **Assistantships** involve full-time employment and expose an individual to a wide range of jobs. However, since the individual only assists other workers, the learning experience is often vicarious. This disadvantage is eliminated by programs of job or position rotation and multiple management.

Both job rotation and multiple management programs are used to train and expose employees to a variety of jobs and decision-making situations. Although **job rotation** provides employee exposure, the extent of training and long-run benefits it provides may be overstated. This is because the employees are not in a single job for a long enough period to learn very much and are not motivated to work hard because they know that they will move on in the near future.[77] As a personal career planning strategy, you may want to avoid job rotation and opt instead for job assignments that are more fixed but provide a greater challenge.[78]

Because career planning is important to organizations as well as individuals, some organizations offer personal career planning. **Personal career planning** provides individuals an opportunity to indicate to the organization such things as desired jobs and training activities. Exhibit 11.5 shows an example of a career planning form from a large organization. Appendix C contains a more extensive career planning form and discussion that you can personally benefit from doing.[79]

In **multiple management** programs, lower- and middle-level managers participate formally with top management in the planning and administration of corporate affairs. In essence, the top level of management makes decisions with the advice of the middle and lower levels. Using multiple managers provides an opportunity for top management to identify and select top-management candidates. In a sense, it becomes an on-the-job assessment process. Being part of a multiple-management program can be an important step in an individual's career. Because of a relatively limited number of positions in the multiple management program, competition for them can be great, but the potential rewards are even greater. At McCormick, a spice company, the rewards of their multiple management program extend to all employees. This is because the program is seen both as a system of managing and training and as a philosophy of how employees should be treated. As such, McCormick expands the notion of multiple management by including blue-collar, hourly classified employees as well as managers in the decision-making process. The multiple management program provides not only a vehicle by which potential managers can be identified but also a way of enhancing employee participation in the organization.

Exhibit 11.5   *Personal Career Planning Guide*

	Very Low	Low	Average	High	Very High
1. My job satisfaction on my present job is ...	____	____	____	____	____

2. I would like to progress in my work by:

	Yes	No
A. Developing improved performances and results on my present job	____	____
B. Qualifying for the next logical higher position above my present one	____	____
C. Qualifying for a different type of work within another department	____	____
D. Qualifying for several positions above my present one	____	____

3. I consider myself best suited to:

A. Supervision	____	____
B. Supporting staff work	____	____
C. Production or operations management	____	____

4. Goals

A suitable job goal for me is: _____

_____

_____

5. Qualifications

Evaluate your own qualifications based on current standing and what is needed for your job goal.*

6. My Development Balance Sheet

   A. My strong points are: _____

   B. I like to do work that is: _____

   C. My limiting factors are: _____

   D. I dislike work that is: _____

7. Development

If I want to develop either on my present job or to qualify for a different job, I need the following:

   A. More job knowledge in: _____

   B. More skill in: _____

   C. A better attitude or outlook concerning: _____

8. Taking Action to Reach Your Job Goal

List how you can develop greater knowledge, job skills, or personal abilities that will help you reach your career goals.

   A. Formal study of a subject (list seminars, night school, company training program, or correspondence courses that will increase your knowledge of a subject): _____

_____

_____

_____

*When this form is used within the company, space is provided so that an individual is able to write a lengthy response. This is true for items 5–8.

The final and most informal program of training and development is **supervisory assistance**.[80] This method of training is a regular part of the supervisor's job. It includes day-to-day coaching, counseling, and monitoring of workers on how to do the job and how to get along in the organization. The effectiveness of coaching, counseling, and monitoring as a technique for training and development depends in part on whether the supervisor creates feelings of mutual confidence, provides opportunities for growth to employees, and effectively delegates tasks.[81]

Off-the-Job Programs.   Exhibit 11.4 lists four categories of off-the-job training and development programs. The first two—formal courses and simulation—are applicable to both nonmanagerial and managerial employees; the last two are primarily for managerial employees.[82]

The **formal course method** of training and development can be accomplished either by oneself, by programmed instruction, computer-assisted instruction, reading, and correspondence courses, or by others, as in formal classroom courses and lectures. Although many training programs use the lecture method because it efficiently and simultaneously conveys large amounts of information to large groups of people, it does have several drawbacks:

- It perpetuates the authority structure of traditional organizations and hinders performance because the learning process is not self-controlled.[83]
- Except in the area of cognitive knowledge and conceptual principles, there is probably limited transfer from the lecture to the actual skills and abilities required to do the job.
- The high verbal and symbolic requirements of the lecture method may be threatening to people with low verbal or symbolic experience or aptitude.
- The lecture method does not permit individualized training based on individual differences in ability, interests, and personality.[84]

Because of these drawbacks, the lecture method is often complemented by self-training methods based on auto-instructional technologies.

The two predominant auto-instructional methods are the linear programming method and the branch programming method, both of which are types of **programmed instruction (PI)**. In each, the learning material is broken down into "frames." Each frame represents a small component of the entire subject to be learned, and each frame must be learned successfully before going on to the next. To facilitate the learning process, feedback about the correctness of the response to a frame is provided immediately.

The successful use of PI requires that the skills and tasks to be learned be broken down into appropriate frames. Once this is done, the probability of an individual learning by PI is high, because PI allows individuals to determine their own learning pace and to get immediate and impersonal feedback.[85] Nevertheless, many skills and tasks are impossible to break down into appropriate frames. Thus, other methods, such as simulation, are used for off-the-job training and development.

Simulation, a training and development technique that presents participants with situations that are similar to actual job conditions, is used for both managers and nonmanagers. A common technique for nonmanagers is the vestibule method, which simulates the environment of the individual's actual job. Since the environment is not real, it is generally less hectic and safer than the actual environment; as a consequence, the potential exists for adjustment difficulties in going from the simulated training environment to the actual environment. Because of this, some organizations prefer to do the training in the actual job environment. But the arguments for using the simulated environment are compelling: It reduces the possibility of customer dissatisfaction that can result from on-the-job training; it can reduce the frustration of the trainee; and it may save the organization a great deal of money, because fewer training accidents occur. Even though these arguments may seem compelling, not all organizations, even in the same industry, see the situation the same way. Some banks, for example, train their tellers on the job, whereas others train them in a simulated bank environment.

An increasingly popular simulation technique for managers is the **assessment center method**. This is discussed in Chapter 5 as a device for selecting managers. Assessment centers are also especially useful for identifying potential training needs. Whether used for training or selection, they appear to be a valid way to make employment decisions.[86] However, certain aspects of the assessment center, such as the management games and in-basket exercises, are excellent for training and do not have to be confined to these programs.

Regardless of where they are used, management or business games almost always entail various degrees of competition between teams or trainees. In contrast, the **in-basket exercise** is more solitary. The trainee sits at a desk and works through a pile of papers found in the in-basket of a typical manager, prioritizing, recommending solutions to problems, and taking any necessary action in response to their contents.[87]

Although the in-basket exercise tends to be an enjoyable and challenging exercise, the extent to which it improves a manager's ability depends in part on what takes place after the exercise. The analysis of what happened and what should have happened in both the business games and the in-basket exercise, when done by upper-level managers in the organization, should help trainees learn how to perform like managers. The opportunity for improvement may be drastically reduced if the trainees are left to decide what to transfer from the game or exercise to the job.

Whereas the simulation exercises may be useful for developing conceptual and problem-solving skills, two types of **human relations** or process-oriented training are used by organizations. **Role playing** and **sensitivity training** develop managers' "interpersonal insights—awareness of self and of others—for changing attitudes and for practice in human relations skills, such as leadership or the interview."[88]

Role playing generally focuses on emotional (that is, human relations) issues rather than factual ones. The essence of role playing is to create a realistic situation, as in the case discussion method, and then have the trainees assume the parts of specific personalities in the situation. The usefulness of role playing depends heavily on the extent to which the trainees get into the parts they are playing. If you have done any role playing, you know how difficult this can be and how much easier it is to do what amounts to simply reading the part. But when the trainee does get into the role, the result is a greater sensitivity to the feelings and insights that are presented by the role.

A method of training and development that has been quite popular is **sensitivity training,** or laboratory training. Individuals in an unstructured group exchange thoughts and feelings on the "here and now" rather than the "there and then." Although the experience of being in a sensitivity group often gives individuals insight into how and why they and others feel and act the way they do, critics claim that these results may not be beneficial because they are not directly transferable to the job.[89]

Exhibit 11.6 presents a summary of the advantages and disadvantages of all the training and development programs just discussed.

A Summary of the Advantages and Disadvantages of On-the-Job and Off-the-Job Training Programs

Exhibit 11.6

	Advantages	Disadvantages
Job instruction training	Facilitates transfer of learning No need for separate facilities	Interferes with performance Damages equipment
Apprenticeship	No interference with real job performance Provides extensive training	Takes a long time Expensive May not be related to job
Internships Assistantships	Facilitates transfer of learning Gives exposure to real job	Not really a full job Learning is vicarious
Job rotation	Exposure to many jobs Real learning	No sense of full responsibility Too short a stay in a job
Personal career planning	Employees participate in career development Helps succession planning	May create unmet expectations May not be used
Multiple management	Involves high-level responsibility Good experience	Not many positions available May be costly
Supervisory assistance	Informal, integrated into job Inexpensive	Effectiveness rests with supervisor Not all supervisors may do it
Formal courses	Inexpensive for many No interference with job	Require verbal skills Inhibit transfer of learning
Simulation	Helps transfer Creates lifelike situations	Can't always duplicate real situations exactly
Role playing	Good for interpersonal skills Gives insights into others	Can't create real situations exactly—still playing
Sensitivity training	Good for self-awareness Gives insights into others	May not transfer to job May not relate to job

Selecting a Program

A knowledge of the principles of learning, the four categories of skills needed by individuals in organizations, and the methods of training and development available and their advantages and disadvantages provide the necessary information to select the training and development programs that are most appropriate for specific organizations. Program selection is based on the answers to three questions:

- What skills do the employees need to learn?
- At what level do these skills need to be learned?
- What training and development programs are most appropriate for the required skills and level?

Skills Needed.   The answers to the first two questions are determined by the results of the needs analyses. What skills employees need to learn can be answered in part by knowing what types of employees need the training. For example, if performance deficiencies exist among the supervisory and rank-and-file employees, most of the training should be aimed at increasing technical skills. On the other hand, interpersonal skills would be the primary need of middle-management employees, and top-level managers would most be in need of conceptual or managerial and administrative skills.[90] These matches between type of employee and the predominant type of skill training needed are useful guides to training employees for their current jobs and for future jobs they might assume. Knowledge of these matches can be used to facilitate employee career development and the organization's planning of what training and development programs it will need to offer.

Level Needed.   To use these matches for the benefit of the individual and the organization, one must still know the appropriate level of skill training: increased operational proficiency, skill development, or fundamental knowledge. The results of the job and person needs analyses determine the necessary level, particularly for current job training. The levels required for future job training depend on the organizational needs analysis as well as job and person needs analyses.

Program Needed.   The final step is to determine which programs are most appropriate for the skill and level of training needed. A guide for this determination is shown in Exhibit 11.7.[91] For example, apprenticeship training is appropriate for those who need to increase their operational proficiency in basic technical skills, whereas the case discussion method is appropriate for conceptual or managerial and administrative skill training at all three levels.

Unfortunately, selection of the appropriate program does not ensure the success of a training and development effort. Success also depends on effective use of the principles of learning (such as reinforcement and feedback), provisions for learning transfer, well-trained trainers, and systematic and supportive organizational policies for the training and development of employees. Even then, the success of the training and development effort cannot be assumed. The effort must be assessed.

Selecting a Training and Development   *Exhibit 11.7*
Program

		Skills Required		
		BSG/BST	**IPS**	**CIS**
Level of Skill Required	**Fundamental Knowledge**	job rotation multiple management apprenticeship training job instruction training	role playing sensitivity training formal courses	job rotation multiple management simulation case discussion
	Skill Development	job rotation multiple management simulation supervisory assistance	role playing sensitivity training job rotation multiple management simulation	job rotation multiple management simulation case discussion

	Operational Efficiency	job rotation
		multiple management
		apprenticeship training
		job instruction training
		  simulation
		  internship
		  and assistantship
		supervisory assistance
			role playing
			job rotation
			multiple management
			apprenticeship training
			job instruction training
			simulation
				job rotation
				multiple management
				simulation
				case discussion

Source: Adapted from T. J. Von der Embse, "Choosing a
Management Development Program: A Decision Model,"
Personnel Journal (October 1973): 911.

Trends in Training and Development

As with the other PHRM activities described thus far, several important
trends are evident in training and development. One that is particularly important is assessment, because many of the assessment skills relevant to
other PHRM activities are used frequently in training and development. A
more extensive discussion of assessment skills appears in Chapter 18.

Assessing Training and Development Programs

Although the assessment of training and development programs is a necessary and useful activity for PHRM, in practice, assessment is often not conducted. Without assessment, evaluation is not feasible. Recall in Chapter 1 the discussion of the necessity for PHRM to demonstrate its effectiveness and worth to the rest of the organization. Assessment and evaluation are necessary for demonstrating effectiveness. Assessment involves determining what data are relevant for a valid evaluation and then gathering the data, or what in essence are the criteria. Thus far, valid criteria for each PHRM have been presented in the assessment section of each chapter. Although methods by which to gather data have been mentioned (e.g., interviews, tests, performance appraisal results, surveys of other companies), they are discussed further in Chapter 18, where organizational surveys are described.

Once the relevant criteria data are gathered, evaluation is possible. Evaluation is the comparison of two or more sets of criteria. The comparison facilitates a determination of the degree and direction of effectiveness. Without evaluation, the determination of effectiveness is not feasible, yet in many organizations evaluation of training and development programs is absent. Evaluation of employee training and development programs may be lacking for several reasons. Frequently, organizations are willing to accept programs at face value and are unaware of the importance and value of evaluation. Other times, managers are fearful of finding out that the programs are not working. There may also be a lack of understanding of the methods of evaluation and disagreements about the best criteria of effectiveness. The people in the organization may not be totally committed to the support of any training or change. Finally, a general design or framework for planning the evaluation of training and development programs and organizational change programs may be lacking.[92]

Nevertheless, the importance and necessity for evaluating the impact of any program remain. Evaluation is necessary to determine how well a program achieves its goals, the efficiency with which the goals were attained by the program, and the extent to which the changes that occurred were due to the program. Evaluation should therefore be regarded as a necessary aspect of any employee training and development program and of other programs to improve the other PHRM activities. Thus, in addition to suggesting assessment criteria for training and development programs here, also necessary is discussing **evaluation designs** (i.e., ways to evaluate data to determine effectiveness).

Assessment Criteria.   Criteria against which the effectiveness of a training program can be evaluated include productivity, attitude surveys to measure things such as organizational climate, and accidents. The criteria selected to evaluate the training program should depend on what the program is aimed to improve. If it is aimed at increasing employee job skills, then productivity and its dollar savings may be the most appropriate criterion. If it is aimed at

Style

Language is simple, direct, and
   precise.

Tone and style are appropriate for
   decision-making readers, given
   their organizational roles, preferences, and relationships to the
   writer.

Report is free of mechanical and
   grammatical errors.

1------------2------------3----O----+

1------------2------------3-------(+)

1------------2------------3-------(+)

1------------2------------3-----(+)

Overall Rating = _____ **(out of 60)**

Rater: _CB 59.5_
oBamgers

Comments: Write strong points, weak points, and other observations here or on
the draft. Tell the writer your reactions to this report. Does it demonstrate real
progress? What important information does it present? What documentation is
especially impressive? What else do you want to know?

Good report

Problem Context

I. Insufficient Supervision of Stripe Shop

Task {
- inconsistent employee training
- unsatisfied customers
- stock levels not properly maintained.

Research Question & Design

? How can employee training methods be improved?

A - Ask employees
- Consult Personnel text.
- browse ?

? - How to improve customers

A - Ask customers -

? - Can ordering & receiving be improved?

A - Ask employees.

- Consult purchasing dept.

making employees more aware of safety procedures, then accidents may be most appropriate.[93]

Evaluation Designs.   In addition to determining the appropriate criteria to evaluate the program, the PHRM manager must select an evaluation design. Evaluation designs are important because they help the PHRM manager determine if improvements have been made and if the training program caused the improvements. In addition to aiding in the evaluation of training programs, evaluation designs can (1) aid in evaluating any personnel and human resource program to improve productivity and the quality of work life, and (2) aid in evaluating the effectiveness of any personnel and human resource activity. Combining the data collection tools (i.e., organizational surveys) discussed in Chapter 18 with knowledge of evaluation designs can prove essential for PHRM in demonstrating its effectiveness and that of any of its programs and activities to the rest of the organization. Because the combination of data collection and evaluation design is vital for PHRM, evaluation design is discussed in more detail here. Review the assessment sections of all the other chapters to see how these evaluation designs might be used with data collection techniques to help measure personnel and human resource effectiveness.

The three major classes of evaluation designs are pre-experimental, quasi-experimental, and experimental.[94] Although each can be used to evaluate the effectiveness of a PHRM program, it is preferable to use the **experimental design,** which is the most rigorous. Evaluation using the experimental design allows the personnel and human resource manager to be more confident that

- a change has taken place—for example, that employee productivity has increased;
- the change is caused by the program or PHRM activity; and
- a similar change could be expected if the program were done again with other employees.

Because of many organizational constraints, however, the PHRM manager is generally not able to use the experimental and must settle for the moderately rigorous **quasi-experimental design.** Even when quasi-experimental designs are feasible, most evaluations that are done rely on the **pre-experimental design.** This design is used because it is easier and quicker. Unfortunately, this design is a poor one for most purposes. Exhibit 11.8 shows an illustration of all three designs. This exhibit is also used to convey how, using these designs, programs can be evaluated and what is required. In Exhibit 11.8, X indicates that the program was administered. T_1 indicates that a measure of the variable against which the program is to be evaluated is taken (e.g., productivity or the level of accidents). T_2 indicates that a second measure is taken on the same variable. Then the results of T_1 and T_2 are compared. Note that the two designs in the experimental class are different from the other two classes of designs because all of the individuals used in the evaluation are randomly assigned. Thus, if there are differences between T_1

Exhibit 11.8	*The Three Major Classes of Evaluation Designs to Help Determine Program Effectiveness*	

Pre-experimental	Quasi-experimental	Experimental
1. One-shot case study design X T_2	1. Time-series design $T_1 T_2 T_3$ X $T_4 T_5 T_6$	1. Pretest/post-test control group design T_1 X T_2 T_1 T_2
2. One-group pretest/ post-test design T_1 X T_2	2. Nonequivalent control groups T_1 X T_2 T_1 T_2	2. Solomon four-group design T_1 X T_2 T_1 T_2 X T_2 T_2

Source: Based on I. Goldstein, *Training: Program Development and Evaluation*, 2d ed. (Monterey, Calif.: Brooks/Cole Publishing Company, 1986), pp. 49–65.

and T_2, the personnel and human resource manager can be more confident that the changes were due to the program (X) and that the results can be repeated in future programs.

As indicated, although using the experimental design is desirable, many organizations find it difficult to randomly assign employees to training programs. Organizations generally want all employees in a section trained, not just a few who are randomly selected. Consequently, the pre-experimental design is more typical of the type of evaluations that organizations use.

Computer Technology and HRIS Uses and Needs in Training and Development

Each individual possesses a unique blend of skills, knowledge, and abilities and personality, interests, and preferences. It is to an organization's advantage to maximize the utilization and development of its human resources, because employees are more likely to be satisfied and productive as a result. The personnel department can take an active role here through the use of an HRIS and computer technology. Establishing a directory of employee skills, knowledge, and abilities and personality, interests, and preferences as an integral part of an HRIS data base aids personnel in identifying individuals for training opportunities or special assignments necessitating special skills, knowledge, and abilities and personality, interests, and preferences. Maintaining such information not only heightens personnel's awareness of internal candidates for promotion, but also contributes to organizational efficiency, getting the most from its human resources.

Use of an HRIS and computer technology is also helpful to an organization when it wants to spot training needs. An HRIS with performance data can help identify performance deficiencies. Once training and development programs have been run to remove these deficiencies, an HRIS and computer technology make it easy to measure the effectiveness of the programs.

Strategic Involvement of Training and Development

Gaining Competitive Advantage. Organizations can use their training and development activity to gain competitive advantage. For example, Dayton-Hudson Corporation is using training and development skills to create future customers. B. Dalton Bookseller Division has earmarked $3 million over four years for a literacy training program. Their goals are to recruit volunteer tutors and to tell people without basic skills about the free teaching programs available in their communities. As a part of this program, B. Dalton gives grants to local school districts to hire speakers who will persuade teachers to put more emphasis on teaching reading skills.

Texas Instruments is engaged in a similar program. Although the results of both the B. Dalton and TI programs are of immediate benefit to the individuals gaining literacy, the companies broaden their base of potential customers over the long run.[95]

IBM has followed a similar strategy for many years in teaching programming skills to customers' employees—capturing unending loyalty of the firms and the employees to IBM products.

McDonald's uses training to ensure its distributors of a competitive advantage through cost/efficiency. McDonald's uses its intensive training program at Hamburger University to ensure that its franchises or distributors run as efficiently as possible. Although training is also done to attain consistent quality, its competitive advantage from training is attained from a cost/efficiency thrust.[96]

Linking with Organizational Strategy. As with other PHRM activities, the training and development menu also consists of many choices that link with the organizational strategies shown in Exhibit 1.4. They include:

Short Term———Long Term
Narrow Application———Broad Application
Productivity Emphasis———Quality of Work Life Emphasis
Spontaneous, Unplanned, Unsystematic———Planned, Systematic
Individual Orientation———Group Orientation
Low Participation———High Participation

The first choice on this menu is the extent to which training and development focuses on the short-term versus the long-term needs of employees. To the extent that emphasis is given to the short term, there will be more training programs and fewer development programs.

Even though training may be more short-run focused, it can still be offered to improve an employee's skills, knowledge, and abilities to do his or her present job or to enable the employee to learn skills, knowledge, and abilities more relevant for other jobs in the organization. A similar distinction can also be made with development programs. The choice here is to pro vide training and development for a more narrow or a more broad application. To some degree, this choice is also influenced by whether the utilization of human resources focuses primarily on a company's need for improved quality of work life or for productivity. Although those improvements are not mutually exclusive, the primary emphasis constitutes a training and development choice.

Another critical choice is the degree to which the training and development activities are planned, formalized, and systematically linked to the other PHRM activities. At issue is how closely the training and development activities are linked with human resource planning, job analysis, recruitment, selection, performance appraisal, and compensation. Also at issue is whether these activities have been established proactively or merely in reaction to the short-term needs of the company.

Another choice is whether to deliver training and development with an individual or group orientation. The choice here involves the extent to which training and development activities are delivered to individuals as individuals or as members of a cohort group. Being a member of a cohortlike group can facilitate the socialization process as well as the training and development activities. Group membership can also buffer its individual members against the stress and time pressures in the company.

A final choice in training and development is the extent of participation to allow employees. For example, companies can allow employees to identify preferred career paths and goals. They can also allow employees to help identify their own training needs. This type of participation may better enable companies to spot training needs and performance deficiencies, since employees may ordinarily attempt to hide this information from their supervisors.[97] Nevertheless, companies may still choose to allow their employees a relatively limited amount of participation or implementation of their training and development activities.

Summary

The training and development of employees is becoming an increasingly important and necessary activity of personnel and human resource management. Rapidly changing technologies increase the potential obsolescence of employees more quickly today than ever before. As employee training and development becomes more important, it also becomes more necessary that the training and development be done effectively. This requires careful attention to the three phases of training and development: assessment or needs analysis, program development and implementation, and evaluation. The three types of needs analysis discussed in this chapter are a careful and systematic diagnosis of the short- and long-range human resource needs of the organization; a determination of the skills and abilities necessary for specific jobs in the organization; and an analysis of the current and expected performance levels of employees in the organization compared with the performance levels desired of them. This difference between actual and desired employee performance (either present or expected) defines a training and development need. This performance deficiency becomes a training and development need, however, only when it is the result of employee ability.

Effective training and development depends upon a sound needs analysis and on sound selection and implementation of training programs. There is no one best program to train employees, since program effectiveness depends in part on the skills to be learned and the level at which they need to be learned. However, several program design qualities can help make any program much better. Those qualities include providing feedback, reinforcement, follow-up, practice, goals, sufficient employee motivation, and consideration for individual differences. Making sure that these are a part of the program can help ensure that changes in employee behavior will occur.

As the emphasis on productivity increases, organizations will become more concerned about having employee behavior changed that improves productivity. Although programs that increase an employee's awareness or understanding will continue and are useful, behavioral and performance changes that last over time will also be expected. People, however, generally don't change unless they desire to change. Thus, without sufficient employee motivation, training will not work. Sufficient motivation can occur if organizations make their employees dissatisfied with their current levels of performance or make it rewarding for them to exhibit a new or different behavior. The training and development program should offer sufficient time for practice of the new skills, goals, reinforcement, feedback, and follow-up. These help ensure the program will have an immediate and a long-term benefit, regardless of the type of program.

The final question then remaining is, Who should be trained? In general, anyone with an important performance discrepancy should be trained. Once that decision is made, the type of program is determined, which can be made according to the match between type of skills needed and type of employee. After the program is selected, it can be developed and implemented.

The last major phase of training and development is the evaluation phase. This phase compares data to see if a change has occurred and determines if the change is due to the training and development program. Although showing that a training and development program has been solely responsible for producing a change is technically complex, many organizations use a practical method to demonstrate a change due to training. This method takes a baseline measure of what the training and development program should change—for example, competency in math or job performance. Then the program is conducted. After the program, another measure is taken. The results of this measure are then compared with the results of the first measure.

PHRM managers claim success of a training program if the difference between the first and second measures is reasonably large and in the right direction. However, most PHRM managers still do not use this method to determine if their programs are worthwhile. Often they just measure how the participants (the employees) felt about the program, whether they thought it was well done or worthwhile and whether they would send someone else. These measures are taken after the program is conducted. Although they can indicate whether the employees liked the program, they tell the organization nothing about whether the program actually affected job behavior.

A technically more sound approach is to take before and after measures on the group being trained (the experimental group), and do the same for another similar group not being trained (the control group). Ideally, the measures taken should be of actual job behaviors. Unfortunately, the extent to which experimental and control groups are used in organizations is relatively limited. Their use may expand, however, as the emphasis in PHRM increases for demonstrating effectiveness and as the concern increases for implementing specific PHRM programs to improve productivity and the quality of work life, as discussed in the next chapter.

Discussion Questions

1. Reflect for a moment on your own work experience. What benefits were there for your former (or present) employer to train you? Why didn't your employer just hire someone who could perform the job without training?

2. Some employers have been identified as training grounds for a particular industry (e.g., Texas Instruments). Why do these employers continue to invest in training even though some of their employees eventually leave to market their skills at other companies?

3. As a first-line supervisor, what indicators would you need to decide whether a low-performing subordinate was a selection mistake or merely in need of training? Can you illustrate this dilemma with an example from your own organizational experience?

4. What legal considerations influence training and development decisions? How can training and development programs avoid potential legal problems? Explain.

5. What are some design principles that can enhance learning that takes place in training and development programs? Are those present in your course?

6. Suppose that two of your professors are engaged in a heated debate over the best way to teach the PHRM course. One wants to use outside speakers to replace lectures. The other wants to use the basic lecture method only. Propose an evaluation design that would enable the department head to choose between these two approaches. Be specific in proposing your design, and discuss what criteria you would use to judge training effectiveness.

7. What steps are involved in the assessment phase of determining training and development needs?

8. Discuss the four basic categories of training and identify to what types of employees these categories of training are generally related.

9. List and briefly describe several training and development design principles.

10. Why do organizations often overlook or lack proper evaluation of employee training and development programs?

PC Project

Companies spend enormous amounts of money training and developing their employees. Frequently the decision to continue a program is based on its cost effectiveness—is the program paying off? This PC Project involves a cost-benefit analysis of a training program. The training costs will be approximated from historical data, and the benefits will be estimated through productivity gains. Should the training program be continued?

C   A   S   E   S   T   U   D   Y

The Good Guys Wear White Hats

Defense contracting has come under new scrutiny these days, particularly since the release of a General Accounting Office report alleging widespread fraud and waste. Not since the seventies has there been this much attention to ethics in the post-Watergate era of business. From corporate campaign contributions to overseas bribes has come a new era of rapidly changing business conditions that create new problems and ethical dilemmas.

Recent publicity of well-known companies such as General Dynamics and General Electric, charged with defrauding the Pentagon, has led to a new surveillance of defense contractors by the Department of Defense. Corporate executives have become interested in these problems as some of their colleagues head off to federal penitentiaries to serve time for their culpability in such fraudulent practices. Lawsuits, fines, loss of reputation, and perhaps more government regulation are possible consequences for corporations to consider when their employees engage in questionable or unethical decisions.

Where, might you ask, are business schools in this time of need? Can ethics be taught to aspiring students of business? Is it simply that young men or women are not being adequately prepared for the world of business today?

Alternatively, some would argue that there is no way to completely prepare young men and women for the kinds of ethical dilemmas they will face in the business environment. The corporate culture, system of values, and the reward structure are oftentimes more powerful influencers of behavior.

Polly Hilton, a training and development manager at a large electronics firm that receives over $1.5 billion in billings for defense work, is concerned about ethics in her organization. The division manager has come to Polly with a request that her group develop a program to increase ethical awareness and lessen the likelihood that their division will someday wind up in court and on the front page of the *Wall Street Journal.*

Polly is puzzled on how to get started. After all, wouldn't you be a bit defensive if someone challenged your level of ethics? Who is to say that your standard of ethics is the one I should follow? Polly is wondering whether she should even try to publish and circulate a company code of ethics. Perhaps she could develop some posters of the division manager reminding employees to "be good." Or better yet, she could have the instructional materials group put together a video of the top executives discussing ethics as it applies to their company.

The more Polly thought about the problem, the more she thought that perhaps she was getting a little ahead of herself. After all, she doesn't know if her company has an "ethics problem." I wonder, she thought, what kind of ethical dilemmas our engineers, technicians, office workers, or project managers find themselves in anyway? What kinds of factors cause people to commit unethical decisions? Can the organization influence the ability of their employees to make ethical decisions? Perhaps there are some kinds of people we should not hire.

Polly even considered the use of the organizational reward system to encourage ethical behavior. But wait a minute—aren't people supposed to be ethical in the first place? Do you have to reward people for behavior that you expect to be routine, if not automatic, in the first place? On the other hand, is there a difference between good business decisions and good ethical decisions?

Another possibility that occurred to Polly was to invoke sanctions for unethical behavior by em-ployees. Perhaps by catching employees "being bad," the company could make an example of these culprits and encourage ethical behavior. Polly envisioned the use of an organizational hotline or perhaps a company ombudsman to serve as a safety valve for people otherwise hesitant to raise ethical problems in the work place.

Although all of these ideas were thought provoking, they had not moved Polly toward her goal of producing a memorandum outlining a plan of action for the defense group. Polly decided that she was going to have to draw on her staff's expertise in training and development to develop a plan of attack to present to her division manager.

Notes

1. I. L. Goldstein, "Training in Work Organizations," *Annual Review in Psychology* 31 (1980): 229–72; R. J. House, *Management Development: Design Evaluation and Implementation* (Ann Arbor, Mich.: Bureau of Industrial Relations, Graduate School of Business, University of Michigan, 1967); T. Rendero, "Roundup," *Personnel* (July–Aug. 1981): 53–58; K. N. Wexley and G. P. Latham, *Developing and Training Human Resources in Organizations* (Glenview, Ill.: Scott, Foresman, 1981); K. N. Wexley, "Training Human Resources in Organizations," *Annual Review in Psychology* 35 (1984): 519–52; D. W. Lacey, R. J. Lee, and L. J. Wallace, "Training and Development," in *Personnel Management,* ed. K. M. Rowland and G. R. Ferris (Boston: Allyn & Bacon, 1982); J. W. Walker, "Training and Development," in *Human Resource Management in the 1980s,* ed. S. J. Carroll and R. S. Schuler (Washington, D.C.: Bureau of National Affairs, 1983).

2. T. F. Gilbert, "Proxeconomy: A Systematic Approach to Identifying Training Needs," *Management of Personnel Quarterly* (Fall 1967): 20–33; J. R. Hinrichs, "Personnel Training," in *Handbook of Industrial and Organizational Psychology,* ed. M. D. Dunnette (Chicago: Rand McNally, 1976), pp. 829–60; R. F. Mager and P. Pipe, *Analyzing Performance Problems* (Belmont, Calif.: Fearon, 1970); G. S. Odiorne, *Training Objectives: An Economic Approach to Management* (New York: Macmillan, 1970); D. W. Lacey, R. J. Lee, and L. J. Wallace, "Training and Development," in *Personnel Management,* ed. K. M. Rowland and G. R. Ferris (Boston: Allyn & Bacon, 1982); J. W. Walker, "Training and Development," in *Human Resource Management in the 1980s,* ed. S. J. Carroll and R. S. Schuler (Washington, D.C.: Bureau of National Affairs, 1983); H. W. Smith, "Implementing a Management Development Program," *Personnel Administrator* (July 1985): 75–86.

3. "Ten Serious Mistakes in Management Training Development" by J. W. Taylor, pp. 357–362. Reprinted with permission, *Personnel Journal,* Costa Mesa, Calif. Copyright © May 1974; A. S. Grove, "Why Training Is the Boss's Job," *Fortune,* 23 Jan. 1984, pp. 93–96; H. J. Hagedorn, "Training as a Way of Life for Line Managers," *Management Review* (July 1984): 8–13.

4. E. Mandt, "A Basic Model of Manager Development," *Personnel Journal* (June 1979): 395; E. Mandt, "Managing the Knowledge Worker of the Future," *Personnel Journal* (Mar. 1978): 139; Wexley and Latham, *Developing and Training.* As indicated in Chapter 2, most of the new jobs being created are in the service industries; thus, many individuals, previously employed in manufacturing industries, are without the necessary skills. With the apparent lack of relationship between jobs and what's learned in secondary schools, the potential exists for even more unqualified job applicants. For further discussion, see J. D. Dickey, "Training with a Focus on the Individual," *Personnel Administrator* (June 1982): 35–38; Bureau of National Affairs, "Technology and the Workplace," *Bulletin to Management,* 2 Dec. 1982; Wexley and Latham, *Developing and Training;* "Retraining Displaced Workers: Too Little, Too Late?" *Business Week,* 19 July 1982, pp. 178–85.

5. *Wall Street Journal,* 29 May 1984, p. 1. Reprinted by permission of *The Wall Street Journal,* © Dow Jones & Company, Inc., 1984. All Rights Reserved.

6. For a description of the turnover and productivity relationships, see D. R. Dalton, "Absenteeism and Turnover: Measures of Personnel Effectiveness," in *Applied Readings in Personnel and Human Resource Management,* ed. R. S. Schuler, J. M. McFillen, and D. R. Dalton (St. Paul: West, 1981), pp. 20–38; T. R. Horton, "Training: A Key to Productivity Growth," *Management Review* (Sept. 1983): 2–3.

7. H. Z. Levine, "Consensus," *Personnel* (July–Aug. 1981): 4–11; F. X. Mahoney, "Targets, Time, and Transfer: Keys to Management Training Impact," *Personnel* (Nov.-Dec. 1980): 25–34; A. E. Wallach, "System Changes Begin in the Training Department," *Personnel Journal* (Dec. 1979): 846, 872.

8. H. H. Huggins, Jr., "IBM's Retraining Success Based on Long-Term Manpower Planning," *Management Review* (Aug. 1983): 29–30.

9. R. B. McAfee, "Using Performance Appraisals to Enhance Training Programs," *Personnel Administrator* (Nov. 1982): 31–34; S. J. Carroll and C. E. Schneier, *Performance Appraisal and Review Systems* (Glenview, Ill.: Scott, Foresman, 1982); H. J. Bernardin and M. R. Buckley, "A Consideration of Strategies in Rater Training," *Academy of Management Review* 6 (1981): 205–12; H. J. Bernardin, "Effects of Rater Training on Leniency and Halo Errors in Student Ratings of Instructors," *Journal of Applied Psychology* 63 (1978): 301–8; E. D. Pulakos, "A Comparison of Rater Training Programs: Error Training and Accuracy Training," *Journal of Applied Psychology* (Nov. 1985): 581–88.

10. Wexley and Latham, *Developing and Training;* H. P. Sims, Jr., "The Leader as a Manager of Reinforcement Contingencies: An Empirical Example and a Model," in *Leadership: The Cutting Edge,* ed. J. G. Hunt and L. L. Larson (Carbondale, Ill.: Southern Illinois University Press, 1977), pp. 121–37; C. W. Hamner, "Worker Motivation Programs: Importance of Climate, Structure, and Performance Consequences," in *Contemporary Problems in Personnel,* ed. W. C. Hamner and F. L. Schmidt (Chicago: St. Clair Press, 1977); W. C. Hamner and D. W. Organ, *Organizational Behavior: An Applied Psychological Approach* (Dallas, Tex.: Business Publications, 1978), see especially pp. 237–70 for an excellent discussion of maintaining the effects of behavioral changes with rewards.

11. T. Hall, "Demanding PepsiCo Is Attempting to Make Work Nicer for Managers," *Wall Street Journal,* 23 Oct. 1984, P. 31. Reprinted by permission of *The Wall Street Journal,* © Dow Jones & Company, Inc., 1984. All Rights Reserved.

12. Ibid.

13. Reprinted, by permission of the publisher, from "The Next Elite: Manufacturing Supermanagers," by Jeanne Lynch and Dan Orne, MANAGEMENT REVIEW, April 1985, p. 49 © 1985 AMA Membership Publications Division, American Management Association, New York. All rights reserved.

14. D. Q. Mills, *The New Competitors* (New York: Free Press, 1985).

15. "There Really Are Jobs after Retraining," *Business Week,* 28 Jan. 1985, pp. 76–77; Huggins, "IBM's Retraining."

16. Based on C. J. Bartlett, "Equal Opportunity Issues in Training," *Human Factors* 20 (1978): 179–88; C. J. Bartlett, "Equal Opportunity Issues in Training," *Public Personnel Management* (Nov.-Dec. 1979):

398–405; Wexley and Latham, *Developing and Training,* pp. 22–27.

17. "Training for Promotion," *FEP Guidelines,* no. 224(3), 1984, pp. 1–8. For an excellent review of relevant court cases involving training and development, see J. S. Russell, "A Review of Fair Employment Cases in the Field of Training," *Personnel Psychology* (Summer 1984): 261–78.

18. "Job Training Bill Geared to Some Special Interests," *Fair Employment Report,* 6 Dec. 1982, p. 196; "Business Tackles Hard-Core Unemployment," *Business Week,* 20 Sept. 1982, pp. 86–88.

19. I. I. Goldstein, *Training: Program Development and Evaluation,* 2d ed. (Monterey, Calif.: Brooks/Cole, 1986); W. McGehee and P. W. Thayer, *Training in Business and Industry* (New York: Wiley, 1961); M. L. Moore and P. Dutton, "Training Needs Analysis: Review and Critique," *Academy of Management Review* (July 1978): 532–45; Goldstein, *Training,* 1980; Walker "Training and Development" in Carroll and Schuler (eds.); S. D. Truskie, "Getting the Most from Management Development Programs," *Personnel Journal* (Jan. 1982): 66–68; J. Laurie, "Diagnosis Before Prescription: Data Collection, Part I," *Personnel Journal* (July 1982): 494–98; J. Laurie, "Begin at the Beginning: Data Collection, Part II," *Personnel Journal* (Aug. 1982): 568–69; M. S. Mehoff and M. J. Romans, "Needs Assessment as Step One toward Enhancing Productivity," *Personnel Administrator* (May 1982): 35–39.

20. Goldstein, *Training.*

21. T. J. Von der Embse, "Choosing a Management Development Program: A Decision Model," *Personnel Journal* (Oct. 1973): 908. Reprinted with permission Personnel Journal, Costa Mesa, Calif. Copyright © October 1973.

22. McGehee and Thayer, "Training in Business."

23. Moore and Dutton, "Training Needs Analysis."

24. For a good discussion on organizational climate, see B. Schneider, "Organizational Climates: An Essay," *Personnel Psychology* 28 (1975): 447–79; B. Schneider and A. E. Reichers, "On the Etiology of Climates," *Personnel Psychology* 36 (1983): 19–40; B. Schneider, "Organizational Climates: Individual Preferences and Organizational Realities Revisited," *Journal of Applied Psychology* 60 (1975): 459–65; W. F. Joyce and J. W. Slocum, Jr., "Climates in Organizations," in *Organizational Behavior,* ed. S. Kerr (San Francisco: Grid, 1979); W. F. Joyce and J. Slocum, "Climate Discrepancy: Refining the Concepts of Psychological and Organizational Climates," *Human Relations* 35 (1982): 951–72.

25. Walker, "Training"; Goldstein, *Training,* 1980; Wexley and Latham, *Developing and Training.*

26. L. A. Berger, "A DEW Line for Training and Development: The Needs Analysis Survey," *Personnel Administrator* (Nov. 1976): 51–55.

27. F. X. Mahoney, "Team Development, Part I: What is TD? Why Use It?" *Personnel* (Sept.-Oct. 1981): 13–24.

28. E. Mandt, p. 396, "Supervisory Training: HR Issues and Intricacies," *Bulletin to Management,* 26 Apr. 1984, pp. 2, 7; B. J. Middlebrook and F. M. Rachel, "A Survey of Middle Management Training and Development Programs," *Personnel Administrator* (Nov. 1983): 27–31; M. A. Pubich, "Train First-Line Supervisors to Handle Discipline," *Personnel Journal* (Dec. 1983): 980–86.

29. For identification of both current and future performance potential, see Carroll and Schneier, *Performance Appraisal;* G. P. Latham and K. N. Wexley, *Increasing Productivity through Performance Appraisal* (Reading, Mass.: Addison-Wesley, 1981), on the use of behavioral measures such as BOS/BARS to validly measure performance, as discussed in Chapter 7.

30. "Developing First Line Supervisors," *Performance* (Mar. 1981): 1–2; B. E. Box and F. Whellan, "The Evolution of a Staff Development System," *Management Review* (Oct. 1982): 54–60.

31. T. Hornberger and R. Trueblood, "Misused and Underrated: Reading and Listening Skills," *Personnel Journal* (Oct. 1980): 808–12. Reprinted with the permission Personnel Journal, Costa Mesa, Calif. All rights reserved.

32. "AMA Designs Training Programs for Use on Personal Computers," *AMA Forum* (Dec. 1983): 29–30; G. Kearsley, *Computer-Based Training: A Guide to Selection and Implementation* (Reading, Mass.: Addison-Wesley, 1983); V. L. Huber and G. Gray, "Channeling New Technology to Improve Training," *Personnel Administrator* (Feb. 1985): 49–57; S. Schwade, "Is It Time to Consider Computer Based Training?" *Personnel Administrator* (Feb. 1985): 25–35; W. C. Heck, "Computer-Based Training—The Choice Is Yours," *Personnel Administrator* (Feb. 1985): 39–46.

33. "Training Bosses," *Time,* 7 June 1982, p. 61.

34. L. A. Digman, "Management Development: Needs and Practices," *Personnel* (July–Aug. 1980): 45–57; M. Hachey, "A Checklist for In-House Secretarial Training," *Personnel Journal* (Jan. 1980): 59–60; S. D. Truskie, "Guidelines for Conducting In-House Management Development," *Personnel Administrator* (July 1981): 25–32.

35. See Lacey, Lee, and Wallace, "Training." For a desciption of how management could be broken down into apprenticeship, craftsmanship, mentorship, and spokesmanship, see Lacey, Lee, and Wallace, "Training," Bureau of National Affairs, p. 318. See also "Supervisory Training: HR Issues and Intricacies," *Bulletin to Management,* 26 Apr. 1984, pp. 2, 7; D. J. Cirillo, "Helping Middle Managers Manage Office Technology," *Personnel* (Nov.–Dec. 1984): 612; D. L. Kirkpatrick, "Effective Supervisory Training and Development—Part I: Responsibility, Needs, and Objectives," *Personnel* (Nov.–Dec. 1984): 25–30.

36. Reprinted by permission of the publisher, from "Roundup," *Personnel* July–Aug. 1981 (New York: AMACOM, a division of American Management Associations, 1981), p. 54.

37. *Wall Street Journal,* 8 May 1984, p. 1. Reprinted by permission of *The Wall Street Journal,* © Dow Jones & Company, Inc., 1984. All Rights Reserved.

38. These matches between training programs and employee type or level should be regarded as suggestive rather than definitive. See Walker. Wexley and Latham. J. W. Walker, "Work Analysis: A Basis for Planning," in *Human Resource Planning,* ed. J. W. Walker (New York: McGraw-Hill, 1980).

39. E. E. Lawler III, "Education, Management Style, and Organizational Effectiveness," *Personnel Psychology* (Spring 1985): 1–17; M. J. Kruger and G. D. May, "Two Techniques to Ensure that Training Programs Remain Effective," *Personnel Journal* (Oct. 1985): 70–75; M. London and S. Stumpf, "Individual and Organizational Career Development in Changing Times," in *Career Development in Organizations,* ed. D. T. Hahl (San Francisco: Jossey-Bass, 1986).

40. R. F. Reilly, "Corporate Assistance in Professional Development," *Personnel Journal* (Feb. 1981): 124. Wexley and Latham, *Developing and Training.*

41. J. Main, "The Executive Yearn to Learn," *Fortune,* 3 May 1982, pp. 234–48.

42. M. M. Starcevich and J. A. Sykes, "Internal Advanced Management Programs for Executive Development," *Personnel Administrator* (June 1982): 27–34.

43. E. Vogt, "PC Education: Which Road to Take?" *Personnel Administrator* (Feb. 1985): 59–64.

44. J. E. Holbrook, "Here's How to Sell Your Ideas for Audio-Visual Training Programs to Top Management," *Personnel Administrator* (July 1981): 34–39. Wexley and Latham. R. D. Freedman, C. L. Cooper, and S. A. Stumpf, eds., *Management Education* (London: Wiley, 1982).

45. R. J. House, "Experiential Learning: A Social Learning Theory Analysis," in *Management Education.*

46. G. P. Latham and L. M. Saari, "The Application of Social Learning Theory to Training Supervisors through Behavioral Modeling," *Journal of Applied Psychology* 64 (1979): 239–46; F. Luthans and T. R. V. Davis, "Beyond Modeling: Managing Social Learning Processes in Human Resource Training and Development," *Human Resource Management* (Summer 1981): 19–27.

47. W. Dyer, *Team Building: Issues and Alternatives* (Reading, Mass.: Addison-Wesley, 1977); L. J. Cronback and R. E. Snow, *Aptitudes and Instructional Methods* (New York: Irvington, 1977).

48. P. Salipante and P. Goodman, "Training, Counseling, and Retention of Hard-Core Unemployed," *Journal of Applied Psychology* 61 (1976): 1–11; E. F. Huse, *Organization Development and Change,* 2d ed. (St. Paul: West, 1980).

49. W. McGehee and W. L. Tullar, "A Note on Evaluating Behavior Modifications and Behavioral Modeling as Industrial Training Techniques," *Personnel Psychol-*

ogy 31 (1979): 477–84; R. Treadgold, "At Last, a Training Program That Works," *Personnel Journal* (Feb. 1982): 110–12; J. E. Hunter, J. S. Russell, and K. N. Wexley, "Questioning the Effectiveness of Behavior Modeling Training in an Industrial Setting," *Personnel Psychology* (Autumn 1984): 465–77.

50. Holbrook, "Here's how to."
51. J. W. Newstrom, "The Dynamics of Effective Team Teaching," *Personnel Administrator* (July 1981): 55–64.
52. B. L. Rosenbaum, "A New Approach to Changing Supervisory Behavior," *Personnel* (Mar.–Apr. 1978): 37–44; "For Some Managers, Training Program Is Real Obstacle Course," *Wall Street Journal*, 27 July 1981, p. 1.
53. Von der Embse, "Choosing a Management," p. 908.
54. Goldstein, "Training," 1980, pp. 249–50.
55. B. M. Bass and J. A. Vaughan, *Training in Industry: The Management of Learning* (Belmont, Calif.: Wadsworth, 1966), p. 62; Luthans and Davis; Rosenbaum; D. D. White and B. Davis, "Behavioral Contingency Management: A Bottom-Line Alternative for Management Development," *Personnel Administrator* (Apr. 1980): 67–75.
56. W. D. Hamner, "Worker Motivation Program: Importance of Climate, Structure, and Performance Consequences," in W. C. Hamner and F. L. Schmidt, eds., *Contemporary Problems in Personnel* (Chicago: St. Clair Press, 1977).
57. Sims, "The Leader as a Manager."
58. Goldstein, *Training.*
59. Sims, "The Leader as a Manager."
60. B. M. Bass and J. A. Vaughan, *Training in Industry: The Management of Learning* (Belmont, Calif.: Wadsworth, 1966), p. 66.
61. D. R. Ilgen, C. D. Fisher, and M. S. Taylor, "Consequences of Individual Feedback on Behavior in Organizations," *Journal of Applied Psychology* 64 (1979): 349–71; E. A. Locke, "Effects of Knowledge of Results, Feedback in Relation to Standards, and Goals on Reaction-Time Performance," *American Journal of Psychology* 81 (1968): 566–75.
62. Bass and Vaughan, *Training in Industry.*
63. R. Likert, "Motivational Approach to Management Development," *Harvard Business Review* 37 (1959): 75–82.
64. R. Treadgold, "At Last, a Training Program That Works," *Personnel Journal* (Feb. 1982): 110–12.
65. Bass and Vaughan, *Training in Industry*, p. 44.
66. Ibid.
67. Ibid., p. 62.
68. S. R. Siegel, "Improving the Effectiveness of Management Development Programs," *Personnel Journal* (Oct. 1981): 770–73.
69. Wexley and Latham, *Developing and Training*, pp. 101–24.
70. Goldstein, *Training.*
71. Bass and Vaughan, *Training in Industry*, p. 88.
72. P. S. Greenlaw and W. D. Biggs, *Modern Personnel Management* (Philadelphia: Saunders, 1979), pp. 270–72; Goldstein, "Training."
73. Bureau of National Affairs, "Planning the Training Program," *Personnel Management: BNA Policy and Practice Series*, no. 41 (Washington, D.C.: Bureau of National Affairs, 1975), p. 205. Reprinted by special permission from BNA Policy and Practice Series. Copyright © 1975 by The Bureau of National Affairs, Inc., Washington, D.C. See also Bass and Vaughan, *Training in Industry*, pp. 89–90; J. M. Geddes, "Germany Profits by Apprentice System," *Wall Street Journal*, 15 Sept. 1981, p. 33.
74. See the EEOC Guidelines on the Age Discrimination in Employment Act in the *Federal Register.*
75. Bass and Vaughan *Training in Industry;* Goldstein, *Training.*
76. D. T. Hall, *Careers in Organizations* (Santa Monica, Calif.: Goodyear, 1976).
77. J. R. Hinrichs, "Personnel Training," in *Handbook of Industrial and Organizational Psychology*, ed. M. D. Dunnette (Chicago: Rand McNally, 1976), p. 854.
78. Hall, *Careers.*
79. For useful references on career management issues, see L. Baird and K. Kram, "Career Dynamics: Managing the Superior/Subordinate Relationship," *Organizational Dynamics* (Spring 1983): 46–64; R. S. Sims, "Kolb's Experiential Learning Theory: A Framework for Assessing Person-Job Interaction," *Academy of Management Review* (July 1983): 501–8; M. London, "Toward a Theory of Career Motivation," *Academy of Management Review* (Oct. 1983): 620–30; J. F. Veiga, "Mobility Influences during Managerial Career Stages," *Academy of Management Journal* (Mar. 1983): 64–85; K. E. Kram, "Phases of the Mentor Relationship," *Academy of Management Journal* (Dec. 1983): 608–19; J. W. Slocum, Jr., W. L. Cron, R. W. Hansen, and S. Rawlings, "Business Strategy and the Management of Plateaued Employees," *Academy of Management Journal* (Mar. 1985): 133–48; J. F. Kelly, Jr., "Coping with the Career Plateau," *Personnel Administration* (Oct. 1985): 65–76; S. Doerflein, "Directions for Career Planning," *Personnel Administrator* (Oct. 1985): 93–106; M. P. Kleiman, "Retain Valuable Employees with Career Adaptation Counseling," *Personnel Journal* (Sept. 1985): 36–39; P. H. Thompson, K. L. Kirkham, and J. Dixon, "Warning: The Fast Track May Be Hazardous to Organizational Health," *Organizational Dynamics* (Spring 1985): 21–33.
80. T. Delone, "What Do Middle Managers Really Want from First-Line Supervisors?" *Supervisory Management* (Sept. 1977): 8–12; W. E. Sasser, Jr., and F. S. Leonard, "Let First Level Supervisors Do Their Job," *Harvard Business Review* (Mar.–Apr. 1980): 113–21; The Woodlands Group, "Management Development Roles: Coach, Sponsor, and Mentor," *Personnel Journal* (Nov. 1980): 918–21.
81. Kram, "Phases"; Baird and Kram, "Career Dynamics." See also G. S. Odiorne, "Mentoring an Ameri-

can Management Innovation," *Personnel Administrator* (May 1985): 63–70; J. Naisbitt, "Challenge for the 1980s: Retraining Managers," *Management Review* (Apr. 1985): 33–35; R. W. Goddard, "The Pygmalion Effect," *Personnel Journal* (June 1985): 10–16.

82. Greenlaw and Biggs, *Modern Personnel;* Wexley and Latham, *Developing and Training,* pp. 126–207.

83. A. K. Korman, *Industrial and Organizational Psychology* (Englewood Cliffs, N.J.: Prentice-Hall, 1971); S. C. Pressey, "Two Basic Neglected Psychoeducational Problems," *American Psychologist* 20 (1965): 391–95.

84. Hinrichs, "Personnel Training," p. 849.

85. Goldstein, *Training;* Hinrichs, "Personnel Training."

86. For an excellent discussion of assessment centers, see V. R. Boehm, "Assessment Centers and Management Development," in *Personnel Management,* ed. K. M. Rowland and G. R. Ferris (Boston: Allyn & Bacon, 1982), pp. 327–62; R. B. Finkle, "Managerial Assessment Centers," in *Handbook of Industrial and Organizational Psychology,* ed. M. D. Dunnette (Chicago: Rand McNally, 1976), pp. 861–88; D. L. Warmke, "Effects of Accountability Procedures upon the Utility of Peer Ratings of Present Performance," Ph.D. diss., Ohio State University, 1979. See also Chapter 5, notes 53 and 54.

87. S. Carey, "These Days More Managers Play Games, Some Made in Japan, as a Part of Training," *Wall Street Journal,* 7 Oct. 1982, p. 35.

88. Hinrichs, "Personnel Training," p. 885.

89. B. Mezoff, "Human Relations Training: The Tailored Approach," *Personnel* (Mar.–Apr. 1981): 21–27; J. P. Campbell, M. D. Dunnette, E. E. Lawler III, and K. E. Weick, Jr., *Managerial Behavior, Performance, and Effectiveness* (New York: McGraw-Hill, 1970).

90. Mandt, "A Basic Model."

91. Von der Embse suggested a table for the selection of training programs for managerial employees only. I revised the table, adding more training programs and adapting it to cover nonmanagerial as well as managerial employees.

92. For extensive description of training and development assessment, see M. J. Burke and R. R. Day, "A Cumulative Study of the Effectiveness of Managerial Training," *Journal of Applied Psychology* (1986): 232–45; J. K. Ford and S. P. Wroten, "Introducing New Methods for Conducting Training Evaluation and for Linking Training Evaluation to Program Redesign," *Personnel Psychology* (Winter 1984): 651–66; H. H. Meyer and M. S. Raich, "An Objective Evaluation of a Behavior Modeling Training Program," *Personnel Psychology* (Winter 1983): 755–62; P. J. Decker, "The Effects of Rehearsal Group Size and Video Feedback in Behavior Modeling Training," *Personnel Psychology* (Winter 1983): 763–74; P. J. Decker, "Effects of Different Symbolic Coding Stimuli in Behavior Modeling Training," *Personnel Psychology* (Winter 1984): 711–24; J. Lawrie, *Personnel Journal* (Dec. 1984): 64–65; R. Gould, "Conjoint Executive Assessment for Strategic Planning," *Personnel Administrator* (Apr. 1985): 51–56; D. F. Russ-Eft and J. H. Zenger, "Common Mistakes in Evaluating Training Effectiveness," *Personnel Administrator* (Apr. 1985): 57–62; H. W. Smith and C. E. George, "Evaluating Internal Advanced Management Programs," *Personnel Administrator* (Aug. 1984): 118–31; D. L. Kirkpatrick, "Four Steps to Measuring Training Effectiveness," *Personnel Administrator* (Nov. 1983): 19–25; V. S. Kaman and J. D. Mohr, "Training Needs Assessment in the Eighties: Five Guideposts," *Personnel Administrator* (Oct. 1984): 47–53; M. J. Burke and R. B. Day, "A Cumulative Study . . ."

93. For a discussion of four types of criteria that can be used (i.e., reactions, skills, knowledge, and behaviors), see Goldstein, *Training.*

94. For a more extensive presentation of these designs, see Goldstein, *Training.*

95. "How Business is Joining the Fight against Functional Illiteracy," *Business Week,* 16 Apr. 1984, pp. 94, 98.

96. R. S. Schuler and I. C. MacMillan, "Gaining Competitive Advantage through Human Resource Management Practices," *Human Resource Management* (Fall 1984): 248–64; A. Sourwine and A. A. Schindman, "Effective Training-Function Management through a Better Understanding of Its Relationship to the Product Life Cycle," *Management Review* (Jan. 1984): 55–61; J. F. Bolt, "Tailor Executive Development to Strategy," *Harvard Business Review* (Nov.–Dec. 1985): 168–76.

97. M. Beer, "Performance Appraisal: Dilemmas and Possibilities," *Organizational Dynamics* (Winter 1981): 25–33.

Quality of Work Life and Productivity

Participative Management: Recipe for Success

A participative management program can lead to productivity improvements if employees know their jobs are secure and the participative system is coupled with some type of gainsharing plan, according to speakers at a New York City conference, sponsored by Executive Enterprises, Inc., and covered by BNA.

Effectiveness essentials

If management wants employees to strive for participative-based productivity improvements, notes management consultant Henry Conn, it must work to create a "common fate" culture in which employees know their jobs are secure. Management also must communicate to employees that "if you do well, you will share in the benefits," Conn says. In most cases, he adds, an organization with an established culture—particularly an "autocratic" one—will need a "crisis" to change over to a participative management style. Warning that adoption of such changes can be a slow process, Conn says that "if you have an autocratic company, don't even think about moving to teams within two years."

Other points made by conference speakers include:

- The duration and depth of top management's commitment are key factors in a participative program's success. Top management, consultant Lyman Ketchum emphasizes, "must learn the concepts well enough to teach and apply them," and bears the primary responsibility for "getting middle managers to go along" with the program.

- The middle management ranks can be a formidable obstacle to successful introduction of a participative management program. "Typically, participative management is something the top tells the middle to do to the bottom," notes Donald Bartlett, an employee relations manager for the Cleveland Pneumatic Co. "The bottom gets extensive training in it, and the middle managers get a memo. If that middle manager feels isolated, he can either passively acquiesce in the participatory system or subtly oppose it. Either way, it can go down the tubes."

- While introducing a participatory system is easier in a nonunion setting, unions can be worked with if approached properly. Saying that unions often are turned off by such terms as "quality circle" and "brainstorming," Bartlett points out that he got the union at Cleveland Pneumatic involved by setting up a labor-management relations committee. Because the committee included representatives of top management, the union believed that, unlike quality circles, it had the authority to initiate change. Within 10 months, Bartlett says, the situation was transformed from one in which "the union and management simply wouldn't talk to each other" to one marked by a high degree of cooperation, a reduced grievance rate, and measurable increases in operating efficiency.

The preceding "PHRM in the News" highlights several issues. One is the emphasis on employee participation that enhances the quality of work life (QWL) and productivity. Another is the concern for productivity improvement in organizations. Employee participation, however, is just one way to increase productivity. Many PHRM programs are available to improve productivity and QWL. Consequently, this is the time for the PHRM manager to be at the forefront of productivity improvement. The PHRM manager should also assume a proactive posture and play an innovative role in developing techniques to improve the quality of an organization's work life. This chapter discusses many of the multiple approaches to improving productivity and QWL.

Increasing U.S. productivity is a dilemma discussed in executive suites and by almost all PHRM managers. Increasing productivity is a major goal for many organizations. Without increased productivity, the intensity of domestic and international competition will not allow an organization to survive. A key aspect of improving productivity is defining and measuring it. Almost no one challenges productivity's most basic, traditional definition: output divided by input; the debate arises in deciding what is output and what is input.

Organizations are discovering that measures of productivity have to be tailored to each organization and to its goals. Although units of output may be an appropriate measure to determine productivity in one organization, the measurement of each employee's performance against past efforts may be more appropriate in another. Whatever criterion is used, it must be (1) measurable in some way (e.g., by units of output, by valid performance appraisal results, by quality of output or by comparisons of actual costs versus budgeted costs); (2) related to the goals of the organization (e.g., units and quality of output for a manufacturing firm and actual costs versus budgeted costs for a governmental agency); and (3) relevant to each job (e.g., units of output for a production worker and performance appraisal results for a white-collar knowledge worker). Absenteeism and turnover (especially of high-performing employees) tend to reduce productivity because more inputs are needed to produce the same level of output. As absenteeism rates increase, for example, organizations must hire more workers to ensure that they have a given number of workers on any given day.

Although recognizing that each organization must develop its own measures of productivity, **productivity** is defined here as measures or indicators of output of an individual, group, or organization in relation to (divided by) inputs or resources, used by the individual, group, or organization for the creation of the outputs.

Quality of work life, although quite different from the notion of productivity, shares a similar degree of elusiveness in definition and measurement. Nevertheless, QWL is defined here as a process by which all members of the organization, through appropriate and open channels of communication, have some say in decisions that affect their jobs in particular and the work environment in general, resulting in greater work job involvement and satisfaction and reduced levels of stress. In essence, QWL represents an organizational culture or management style in which employees experience feelings of ownership, self-control, responsibility, and self-respect.[1] Exactly what organizations do to produce these employee feelings varies, as do measures of productivity. Generally, however, in an organization characterized as having a high QWL, extensive participation, suggestions, questions, and criticism that might lead to any kind of improvement are encouraged and welcomed. In such a setting, creative discontent is viewed as a manifestation of constructive caring about the organization rather than destructive griping. Management encouragement of such feelings of involvement often leads to ideas and actions for upgrading operational effectiveness and efficiency, as well as environmental enhancement. Increased productivity, measured in work quality and quantity, is thus likely to result as a natural byproduct, as illustrated by the initial "PHRM in the News."[2]

Purposes and Importance of QWL and Productivity

Because the importance and purposes of QWL and productivity are highly related but also unique, they are discussed separately.

Quality of Work Life

The attention being paid to the quality of work life reflects its growing importance and a general concern for Match 2, as discussed in Chapter 2. Workers are beginning to demand improvements in both economic and noneconomic outcomes from their jobs. The importance of noneconomic rewards is increasing relative to that of economic ones, especially among white-collar and highly educated workers.[3] Apparently, there is both a need and considerable room for improvement in the quality of work life of many contemporary American workers.[4]

The importance of QWL is reflected in the effects of its absence.[5] Some people attribute part of the present productivity slowdown and decline in the quality of products in the United States to deficiencies in the quality of work life and to changes in the interests and preferences that employees consider important, as described in Chapter 2. People are demanding greater control and involvement in their jobs. They prefer not to be treated as cogs in a machine. When they are treated with respect and given a chance to voice their opinions and a greater degree of decision making, productivity improves, as indicated by the initial "PHRM in the News." As the next "PHRM in the News" describes, however, many other ways can be used to improve productivity through human resource management.

Productivity

An equal if not greater level of attention is being paid to productivity, since companies and managers are more immediately evaluated on how well they are doing by the level of profitability of the company. Since the level of productivity is generally a major factor in determining profitability or staying within budget, ways to improve productivity are always of interest to companies. This is especially true now, with the current rate of productivity growth in the United States less than that of most other industrialized countries. If the United States increases its productivity, it should become more competitive in the international as well as national markets.[6]

Increasing productivity is also important because more Americans are realizing that their standard of living is declining. If the current trend continues, the present generation will live less well than the previous generation—a first-time occurrence in America.

Interest in the quality of work life and productivity usually focuses on changing aspects of the organization to improve employee satisfaction, job involvement, and performance and to reduce stress, turnover, and absenteeism for enhanced profitability, competitiveness, and survival.

PHRM in the News

Management: The Key to Productivity

Skilled, people-oriented managers are the "key link in the entire productivity chain," declares Robert Ranftl, director of managerial productivity for the Hughes Aircraft Co. Managers play a critical role in the drive to achieve high productivity, Ranftl stresses, citing the findings of a Hughes productivity study of 59 major employers in industry, government, and education, which included surveys of more than 3,500 managers. While acknowledging that productivity levels depend on everyone in the workforce, Ranftl says that the study clearly indicates that it is the "ideas, judgment, direction, and example" of managers that "set the pace for organizational productivity down the line."

Management's effect on productivity

For an organization to achieve and maintain high productivity, Ranftl notes, every manager has to be "highly motivated, positively oriented, and totally committed." Maintaining that employees' productivity rates depend primarily on the attitude and motivation transmitted downward by management, Ranftl points out that "it is management that either gives the challenging assignments or does not; it is management that either establishes equity (fairness) within the organization or fails to do so; it is management that either offers genuine interest, encouragement, appreciation, and equitable incentives and rewards or neglects these essentials."

Ranftl notes that the study has identified the supervisory methods most likely to lead to high productivity. According to Ranftl, these methods include:

- Matching individuals to the jobs for which they are best suited;
- Involving subordinates in decisions that affect them;
- Letting employees demonstrate their capabilities and grow professionally;
- Managing by "expectation," which involves setting high standards and encouraging subordinates to achieve them;
- Keeping subordinates fully, but not excessively, occupied with work;
- Maintaining light pressure on subordinates to produce;
- Being available through an open-door policy;

- Refusing to view all tasks as maximum efforts or special cases and avoiding surprises and unexplained changes;

- Providing feedback on employee performance, citing mistakes fairly and recognizing achievements;

- Making a special effort to help deficient subordinates improve their performance;

- Serving as a buffer to protect subordinates from daily administrative and operational frustrations;

- Maintaining an effective flow of two-way communications;

- Keeping workers informed of the broader aspects of organizational operations;

- Avoiding imposing personal standards on employees and not "oversupervising"; and

- Giving higher management an equitable picture of all subordinates and their work, and allowing, whenever possible, the person who originated a unique idea or did an outstanding job to brief top management.

Source: Bulletin to Management, 28 June 1984, pp. 2, 7. Reprinted by permission from *Bulletin to Management,* copyright 1984, by The Bureau of National Affairs,Inc., Washington, D.C.

Productivity and QWL improvements can be done independently as well as together.[7] The programs to be described are illustrated in Exhibit 12.1. In addition to QWL, many other programs can influence productivity, discussed in the section on productivity improvements. Programs to improve QWL are discussed in a separate section on QWL improvements. Both sets of programs are critical for effective personnel and human resource management.

Relationships Influencing QWL and Productivity Improvement Programs

As Exhibit 12.1 shows, many relationships influence QWL and productivity improvement programs.

Relationships with Other PHRM Activities

QWL and productivity programs have a significant impact on several other PHRM activities. Although the effects of these programs may reduce the necessity for other activities to improve productivity and QWL (all PHRM activities are assessed in part by their impact on productivity and QWL, as discussed in Chapter 1), implementing programs to improve QWL and productivity often requires changes in the other activities. Occasionally, a program to improve QWL and productivity is based almost entirely on a specific PHRM activity, such as pay plan programs.

Recruitment and Selection.   Recruitment and selection activities are often directly affected by QWL and productivity programs that result in lowered absenteeism and turnover. Companies with high absenteeism and turnover

Relationships of and Programs for Quality of　　　*Exhibit 12.1*
Work Life and Productivity Improvements

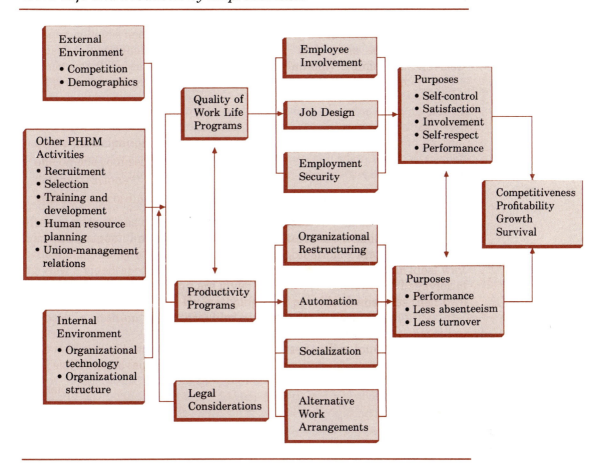

need to recruit and select more job applicants. This may result in organizations having to hire applicants who, in the absence of so many vacant positions, would otherwise not be hired. These employees in turn may be more likely to be absent and quit, thus perpetuating an unwanted cycle. A QWL or productivity program, such as career management, that reduces absenteeism and turnover may improve the staffing efforts (simply by reducing the selection ratio described in Chapter 18) and break the unwanted cycle.

Training and Development and Human Resource Planning.　　QWL projects also influence personnel and human resource planning. Because turnover and absenteeism may be reduced by these projects, human resource needs may also be reduced. However, training needs may increase, at least initially, especially for supervisors who must adjust to a new supervisory role as a consequence of QWL programs. It is often the first-level supervisor whose cooperation is most needed to ensure the success of QWL programs and whose role is most often changed by them.[8] The exception is the middle manager. As described in the initial "PHRM in the News," middle managers may resist participatory management programs, fearing the consequence of job loss.

Union-Management Relations.   Unions can play an important role in QWL and productivity programs.[9] Such programs often involve changing the conditions of employment and therefore are often subject to bargaining between union and management, as described more thoroughly in Chapter 16.[10] But unions can also play a proactive role and push for improvement programs to potentially save jobs as well as enhance the QWL for those who have jobs.[11] Not all unions care to be a party to improvement programs, however, let alone play a proactive role. For some unions, such involvement can mean the blurring of the distinction between the respective roles of management and labor in the work place.[12] It can also mean association with a program that is neither desired by the employees (the rank-and-file union membership) nor successful.[13]

Another influence that unions may have on improvement programs is perhaps less direct that those just described, for it is based more on the absence than on the presence of unions, described later in this chapter in the section on legal considerations.

Relationships with the Internal Environment

Although top management must be behind efforts to improve productivity and QWL, the key relationships of productivity and QWL programs are with the technology and structure of the organization.

Organizational Technology.   The technology of an organization refers to the machines, methods, and materials that are used to produce the organization's product. The type of technology (in the system) can strongly influence the job design approach used. The assembly line is often used as an example of a technology in which the jobs are extremely repetitive and simple. Jobs that skilled workers and some managers perform are generally the opposite of assembly-line jobs. Both skilled workers and managers can control the pace of their work and can often use a variety of skills.

Although technology can strongly influence job design, organizations can sometimes choose the type of technology they want to use to make the same product. For example, in the manufacture of automobiles, General Motors, Ford, and Chrysler have traditionally chosen to use the assembly line. This, however, is not the only way to make cars. Volvo in Sweden is an example in which a nonassembly method was adopted.[14] This switch in technologies represented a significant change and had a major impact on the rest of the organization. The switch represented more than a change in technology, however; it also represented a way of thinking about people as human resources. People no longer were thought of as replaceable parts but rather as irreplaceable components of the organization. In diagnosing the technology, one must consider its impact on job design, the variety of technologies that can be used in making a product, and the organization's philosophy about its human resources.[15] The new Saturn project reflects these considerations by General Motors.

Organizational Structure.   Just as technology can initially limit efforts in improving productivity and QWL by restricting job redesign programs, so can organizational structure. This is particularly true for control structure in the organization. Control structures are also likely to prevent the organization from adopting a new job design or a particular type of design. Control structures include things such as production and quality control reports, scrap reports, supervisors, attendance reports, and time sheets (cards). Because locating who is responsible for problems or errors is important, control structures often specify who is accountable, how things should be done, and from whom to get approval for doing something differently. Although this helps reduce the complexity of each job and the responsibility of each worker, the effect is to set up impersonal boundaries. The boundaries then become critical in the way people behave and what they will not do.

Changing control structures is just as difficult as changing technology. Yet both need to be changed to facilitate job design changes. Furthermore, particular types of job designs are unlikely to be adopted, given the philosophies of key decision makers. For example, if the top management or owners want to retain close control, or if they don't think employees can act responsibly, they will likely choose the scientific approach to job design rather than one of the contemporary approaches discussed later in this chapter.

Relationships with the External Environment

Intense levels of domestic and international competition are forcing organizations to be more productive. As illustrated in the second "PHRM in the News," the more effective management of human resources is seen as a way to help organizations improve their productivity. Because of the nature of work force demographics, many of the efforts to better manage human resources involve some form of employee involvement or participation.[16] This is consistent with the preferences of many individuals in the 35 to 54-year-old age group for greater involvement and a greater say in work place decisions.

Legal Considerations in QWL and Productivity

In considering productivity and especially QWL programs, organizations must consider the Wagner Act of 1935, the basic labor law of the United States, particularly in the absence of unions representing the workers. Section 8(a)(2) of the Wagner Act (the National Labor Relations Act) states that it is an unfair labor practice for an employer to dominate or interfere with the formation or administration of any labor organization or to contribute financial or other support to it. Section 2(5) states further that a "labor organization" is an "organization of any kind or any agency or employee representation committee or plan in which employees participate or which exists for the purpose, in whole or in part, of dealing with employers concerning grievances, labor disputes, wages, rates of pay, hours of employment, or conditions of work."

Although the courts initially interpreted the Wagner Act strictly in the meaning of labor organizations (*NLRB* v. *Cabot Carbon Co.*, 1959; *NLRB* v. *Stow Manufacturing Co.*, 1965), more recent decisions have been more liberal (*General Foods Corp.*, 1977; *Sparks Nugget*, 1977; and *Mercy-Memorial Corp.*, 1977). In those three most recent cases, decided by the National Labor Relations Board (NLRB) and not the courts, the NLRB recognized that not all committee structures established by the employer constitute a "labor organization." Employers can apparently establish QWL programs (or alternative work force arrangements) involving employee committees, communications, and cooperation, especially under conditions where the committees do not serve as a bargaining agent for the employees; where the employer does not dominate the committees; where the employees are not coerced into joining the committees; where the committees serve limited roles; and where the impetus for establishing programs cannot be traced to a union-organizing drive (*Chicago Rawhide Manufacturing Co.* v. *NLRB*, 1955; *NLRB* v. *Northeastern University*, 1979; *Hertzk & Knowles* v. *NLRB*, 1974; and *NLRB* v. *Streamway Division of the Scott and Fetzer Co.*, 1982).

In cases where a union represents the employees, the employer must consider that almost all issues, including the establishment of programs to improve productivity and QWL, must be bargained over with the union. In many cases, however, the employers and unions can cooperatively work together on improvement programs. When this is done, the NLRB states that employers have to provide information to the union when requested for purposes related to the improvement program. If such information is not provided, whether to the union or to the employees, the union and the employees are both uninformed and more likely to resist programs for improvement, such as the ones described in this chapter.

Programs for QWL Improvements

Programs for QWL improvements range from those requiring limited changes to the organization to those requiring extensive changes. All the programs share an orientation of concern and respect for the employee. Typically, the organization begins to reflect more openness, more choice, and greater willingness to invest in programs that benefit the individual as well as the organization.[17] Such programs include (1) employee involvement programs, (2) job design approaches, and (3) employment security.

Employee Involvement Programs

Of the two forms of employee involvement programs, one is narrowly focused, and the other can be extensive. The first is quality circles.

Quality Circles.   Quality circles is an innovative management concept that helped contribute to Japan's dynamic industrial growth. The concept amounts to a targeted philosophy that taps a company's own work force as its most valuable resource because the work force is often the most qualified to identify and solve work-related problems.

Since Honeywell and Lockheed first introduced quality circles in America, more and more corporations have developed similar programs. Among the more than 1,500–2,000 companies running more than 2,500 circles are Bethlehem Steel, Westinghouse, Ford, Solar Turbine, Hughes Aircraft, General Electric, Boeing, Martin Marietta, RCA, Control Data, and General Motors. A great many more are seriously considering installing programs as a means of obtaining greater productivity, quality, and morale.[18]

A quality circle consists of seven to ten people from the same work area who meet regularly to define, analyze, and solve quality and related problems in their area. Membership is strictly voluntary, and meetings are usually held once a week for an hour. During the group's initial meetings, members are trained in problem-solving techniques borrowed from group dynamics, industrial engineering, and quality control. These techniques include brainstorming, Pareto analysis, cause-and-effect analysis, histograms, control charts, stratification, and scatter diagrams.[19]

In principle, unions have not opposed the introduction of quality circles, nor should they in the future. The fact that participation is voluntary helps forestall possible union objections. If participation were mandatory, the union might decide to make quality circles a bargaining issue, reasoning that workers were being ordered to do something that was leading to greater profits for the company. One way the company can get into the union's good graces is to explain quality circles to the union before they are implemented and invite the union to send a representative to a meeting of the steering committee.[20]

In many instances, the first-line supervisor runs the team meeting. In essence, he or she acts as the facilitator. This reinforces the existing organizational authority pattern as well as creates better communication between the supervisor and employees. The team leader undergoes a basic training course (often conducted by PHRM) in group dynamics, problem solving, and other techniques, while members often receive preliminary training on establishing priorities and brainstorming.

Do workers really have the expertise to improve production techniques? In a few spectacular cases, knowledge of day-to-day production intricacies led to decisions that benefited companies enormously. At General Motors' Packard Electric plant in Warren, Ohio, creation of worker-management teams to advise on construction of four factories resulted in a $13.5 million cost reduction and a $4.5 million reduction in inventory of supplies; it also achieved the lowest injury, grievance, and absenteeism rates in the division.

Bethlehem Steel's Los Angeles Works reduced operating costs by $225,000 over two months after worker-management teams identified ways to exploit mill downtime for production. At Westinghouse Electronic Corporation's Defense and Electronic Systems Center near Baltimore, a purchasing department quality circle noticed waste in the way vendors were sending supplies and saved the plant $636,000.[21]

In addition to these productivity improvements, QWL improvements include better communication and enhanced satisfaction, teamwork, and group cohesion.[22] In a recent survey of twenty-four hospitals,

more than half (54.4 percent) of the facilities claimed very positive results for their circles, 38.4 percent reported positive results, and only 5.5 percent reported neutral results. The goals for which the most positive results were reported were improved employee involvement (71.8 percent) and improved communications (63.2 percent).[23]

Not all organizations are suited to quality circles, however, and even those that are may not reap the productivity and improvements described.[24] Negative results may be due to a lack of trust between employees and management; trust appears to be one of several essentials for quality circles.[25] The other essential characteristics for quality circles are as follows:

- The role of the facilitator is the most important aspect of a quality circle program. Whoever fills the function must be able to work with people at all levels of the organization, must be creative and flexible, and must be aware of the political atmosphere of the organization.
- Management must support the quality circle program. If a union is involved, it also should support the program, and its support and views should be solicited.
- The program is voluntary for employees, but management should encourage the establishment of quality circles.
- Within established limits, quality circle members must feel free to work on problems of their choosing.
- Facilitators must keep management informed of what the quality circles are working on and their progress.
- Quality, not quantity, should be the first consideration. The program will expand as success stories spread by word of mouth.
- A successful program must adhere to the concept and principles of the program. One of the facilitator's most crucial tasks is to see that quality circles follow correct procedures. Once the circles forgo using the procedures, they become nonproductive and eventually dissolve.[26]

Although quality circles can result in improved productivity, they generally do not alter the nature of employees' jobs, except for providing the opportunity to make suggestions and decisions on how to improve the product or job on which employees are working. Nevertheless, productivity improvements can be attained by changing the task itself.

Quality circles represent one form of increased participation, but more extensive efforts at increasing employee participation are being undertaken in many companies. For example, at the Carborundum Company plant in Falconer, New York, employees developed a plant redesign that saved almost half of the $7 million cost of a previously proposed design.[27] At Donnelly Mirrors in Holland, Michigan, where the average return on equity over the past twenty years has tripled, employees elect representatives to the committee that makes corporate decisions.[28] These efforts and others aimed at increasing participation improve profits, and workers report a greater sense of control over their work, more satisfaction, better safety, and improved work conditions.[29]

Increased Participation.   One common result of more participation by employees is the elimination of a layer of middle management. Because the employees rather than the managers are making the decisions in companies such as Tandem Computers, Polaroid, and General Foods, some managers become redundant. Consequently, some middle managers resist programs to increase participation, as the initial "PHRM in the News" described. With fewer managers, employees are able to not only make more decisions but also do things their own way and assume more responsibility. At General Motors, as a consequence of programs to increase participation, workers now select their own team leader, who acts in a less directive manner and solicits and listens to employees' ideas. As a result of this practice, absenteeism and grievances have diminished as much as 90 percent, and scrap costs have been cut by 50 percent.[30]

Despite these reported successes at increasing participation, there are limits on the extent to which participation in organizations can be increased. Indeed, there are limits on its effectiveness in organizations.[31] The effectiveness of participation in decision making (such as found in quality circle programs) depends upon several factors: (1) the desire of the employees for participation in decision making; (2) the type and extent of decisions in which employees participate (i.e., whether employees decide issues related only to their jobs or to the total organization); (3) the amount of information the organization is willing to share with employees; (4) the willingness of supervisors and managers to allow their employees to participate; and (5) the availability of problems and situations for which decisions are necessary. Exhibit 12.2 shows other potential factors influencing the appropriateness of participation and the topics in which employees may participate.

Job Design Approaches

Jobs can be designed in many different ways, four of which are discussed here. Other methods of designing jobs are essentially combinations of the four major ways. Regardless, jobs designed differently, differ primarily on the three job design qualities. This will become more apparent as the four

---

Topics Appropriate for Participation and   *Exhibit 12.2*
Potential Constraints on Their Use

Topical Areas

Job analysis	Compensation
Job design	Training and development
Recruitment	Safety
Selection	Employee rights
Performance appraisal	Work schedules

Potential Constraints

Limited change frequency
Extensive rules and procedures
Top management resistance
Middle management resistance
Limited information access and availability
Unwillingness to change
Lack of proactive PHRM department

major job design approaches are discussed: scientific (traditional), individual contemporary, team contemporary, and ergonomics.

Scientific.   Traditionally, job analysis has been used to describe the dimensions of the job to be performed and the required worker specifications. The dimensions of the job described in the analysis are largely determined by job design. Under the **scientific approach**, job analysts (typically, industrial engineers) take special pains to design jobs so that the tasks performed by employees do not exceed their abilities. The jobs designed by scientific management often result in work being partitioned into small, simple segments. These tasks lend themselves well to motion and time studies and to incentive pay systems, each for the purpose of obtaining high productivity. The scientific approach to job design still is an important part of many present organizational structures described in Chapter 2.[32]

Individual Contemporary.   The individual contemporary and team contemporary approaches are job designs that achieve high productivity without incurring the human costs that are sometimes associated with the scientific approach. The three individual contemporary approaches are **job rotation, job enlargement,** and **job enrichment**.

Job rotation does not really change the nature of a specific job. It does, however, often increase the number of duties an employee performs over a period of time. This is because the employee moves from one job to another after a specified period of time. The nature of each job's task characteristics may or may not be varied. A reasonable assumption, however, is that an employee's sense of identity and scope of purpose with what he or she does increase because the employee is performing several jobs.

Job enlargement differs from rotation by adding more duties to a specific job rather than moving an employee around to experience the duties of several jobs. Job enlargement is the opposite of the scientific approach, which seeks to reduce the number of duties, although the characteristics of the duties may be similar.

Job enrichment differs from job enlargement by seeking to vertically rather than horizontally load a job. **Horizontal loading** means adding more duties with the same types of task characteristics. **Vertical loading** in job enrichment means creating a job with duties that have many different characteristics, for example, job identity, job significance, autonomy, feedback, and skill variety. These are defined accordingly:

- **Skill variety:** The degree to which a job requires a variety of different activities in carrying out the work, involving the use of a number of different skills and talents of the person.
- **Job significance:** The degree to which a job has substantial importance on the lives of other people, whether those people are in the immediate organization or in the world at large.
- **Job identity:** The degree to which a job requires completion of a "whole" and identifiable piece of work—that is, doing a job from beginning to end with a visible outcome.

- **Autonomy:** The degree to which a job provides substantial freedom, independence, and discretion to the individual in scheduling the work and in determining the procedures to be used in carrying it out.
- **Feedback:** The degree to which carrying out the work activities required by the job provides the individual with direct and clear information about the effectiveness of his or her performance.

The impact of this job enrichment design is further illustrated in Exhibit 12.3.

Team Contemporary. Whereas the individual contemporary and scientific approaches design jobs for individuals, the **team contemporary approach** designs jobs for teams of individuals.[33] The final designs generally show a concern for the social needs of individuals as well as the constraints of the technology. In the team contemporary approach, teams of workers often rotate jobs and may follow the product they are working on to the last step in the process. If the product is large—for example, an automobile—teams may be designed around sections of the final car. Each group then completes only a section and passes its subproduct to the next team. In the team contemporary design, each worker learns to handle several duties, many requiring different skills. Thus, they can satisfy preferences for achievement and task accomplishment and some preferences for social interaction.

Two other aspects often associated with the team contemporary design are group gain sharing and participation in decision making. When faced with decisions, teams generally try to involve all members. If their decisions and behaviors result in greater output, all team members share the dollar benefits. Although increased participation can also be given to employees working individually, it is less acknowledged a part of the design of those employees' jobs than it is under a team contemporary job design approach.

The Impact of the Core Job Characteristics on   *Exhibit 12.3*
Employee Psychological States

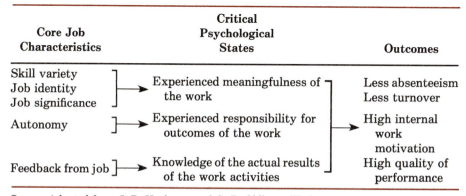

Core Job Characteristics	Critical Psychological States	Outcomes
Skill variety Job identity Job significance	Experienced meaningfulness of the work	Less absenteeism Less turnover
Autonomy	Experienced responsibility for outcomes of the work	High internal work motivation
Feedback from job	Knowledge of the actual results of the work activities	High quality of performance

Source: Adapted from J. R. Hackman and G. R. Oldham, *Work Redesign,* © 1980, Addison-Wesley Publishing Company, Inc., Reading, Mass. Pg. 77, figure 4.2. Reprinted with permission.

Ergonomics.   Ergonomics is concerned with trying to design and shape jobs to fit the physical abilities and characteristics of individuals so they can perform the jobs. The **ergonomic approach** is critical to organizations and is being used to redesign jobs to accommodate women, as well as handicapped individuals. Often this serves equal employment opportunity and affirmative action objectives. This approach is even helping to serve as an alternative to retirement. In addition to helping organizations serve their legal objectives, this approach helps organizations better utilize their work forces. Studies have shown that when jobs are designed along ergonomic principles, worker productivity is greater. In a recent study done by the National Institute for Occupational Safety and Health (NIOSH), two groups of employees working under an incentive pay system were compared. The group working on jobs designed according to ergonomic principles were 25 percent more productive than the group working on the jobs designed without these principles.

NIOSH, along with several unions, is also actively involved in redesigning jobs using ergonomic principles to help reduce the incidence and severity of **carpal tunnel syndrome,** which is characterized by numbness, tingling, soreness, and weakness in the hands and wrists. It is caused or aggravated by jobs requiring repetitive hand motions. Redesigning jobs to eliminate these motions is being done successfully by companies such as Armco, Inc., and Hanes Corporation using ergonomic principles.[34]

Which Design to Use?   Chapters 1 and 2 discussed in detail the concern (some call it a crisis) that many people have for what they see as a decline in the productivity and QWL of American companies. In trying to explain this phenomenon, many people point to the nature (design) of the jobs in organizations, combined with changing work force values. They claim that most jobs are too simple and repetitive, that many workers could do a lot more than they are now doing, and that they could be using more skills. Organizations should resist the temptation to design jobs with more complexity until they have analyzed the appropriateness of each job design approach. The characteristics of both individuals and of organizations should be analyzed. Failure to conduct this analysis may result in the selection of the inappropriate job design.[35] Exhibit 12.4 shows some of the advantages and disadvantages to consider in selecting a job design. The decision of which job design to implement is a complex one and includes the following steps:

1. Recognize a need for a change and gather prechange data for evaluation.
2. Determine that task redesign is the appropriate change.
3. Diagnose the organization, work flow, group processes, and individual needs.
4. Determine how, when, and where to change jobs.
5. Provide for training and support if necessary.
6. Make the job changes.
7. Evaluate the change by comparing postchange data with prechange data.[36]

Employment security is the final area to be considered in our discussion of programs for QWL improvements.

Approach	Advantages	Disadvantages
Scientific	Ensures predictability Provides clarity Fits abilities of many people Can be efficient and productive	May be boring May result in absenteeism, sabotage, and turnover
Individual contemporary	Satisfies needs for responsibility, growth, and knowledge of results Provides growth opportunity Reduces boredom Increases quality and morale Lowers turnover	Some people prefer routine and predictability May need to pay more, since more skills needed Hard to enrich some jobs Not everyone wants to rotate
Team contemporary	Provides social interaction Provides variety Facilitates social support Reduces absenteeism problem	People may not want interaction Requires training in interpersonal skills Group no better than weakest member
Ergonomics	Accommodates jobs to people Breaks down physical barriers Makes more jobs accessible to more people	May be costly to redesign some jobs Structural characteristics of the organization may make job change impossible

A Summary of Some of the Advantages and Disadvantages of the Four Job Design Approaches

Exhibit 12.4

Employment Security

Sony Corporation has had a plant in San Diego for many years. Several years ago the company encountered a sudden decline in sales. Soon the San Diego plant was piling up inventory, and then had to begin reducing production. Where were costs to be cut?

The American managers of the plant requested permission from headquarters in Japan to begin work force reductions. They received a refusal. They renewed the request, pointing out that sales were way down and that significant losses would soon appear on the bottom line.

To this, Akio Morita, the founder of Sony, replied, "Think of the opportunity."

"What opportunity?" the American managers persisted. "We are going to be drowning in red ink."

"Think of the opportunity," Morita repeated. Then he explained. "If we keep the American work force with us through these difficult times, then they will understand that we are really committed to them. And they will be committed to us."

There was no layoff. The company absorbed losses for a while until business recovered. In the next few years the San Diego plant performed very well, in some instances even outperforming the company's plants in Japan—the first foreign facility of Sony to do so.[37]

Other organizations, small as well as large, have also thought of the opportunity from offering employment security. Managers of these organizations know that layoffs are expensive. Costs of layoffs include lower employee involvement and loyalty, severance pay, higher unemployment compensation taxes, continuation of health and other benefits for a period after the layoff, legal and administrative expenses, and the expense of rehiring and training workers when recalled. In addition to these are the costs of lower productivity and the lack of ability to compete in world markets.

Despite the costs of not having employment security, many organizations still fail to offer or even consider offering employment security. At times, however, this may be appropriate. Offering employment security is probably unwise if an organization is already overstaffed. After restructuring is a more appropriate time to offer employment security. Similarly unwise is offering employment security when an organization is in decline and pursuing a strategy of liquidation or disinvestment.

But even when overstaffing is not evident and the organization is pursuing a growth strategy, the economy and patterns of competition are difficult to accurately predict. Because of these conditions, organizations may use a group of permanent part-time employees to complement the regular full-time employees. Employment security is provided only to the regular employees. Found in many Japanese organizations, the permanent part-time employees are referred to as contingent (depending on the organization's need) employees or buffer employees:

> Using contingent employees allows companies to offer the regular workforce greater job security, according to Audrey Freedman, an economist with The Conference Board. Freedman estimates that one out of every four working people is a contingent worker, including freelancers (self-employed persons working for companies on specific projects), temporaries (those who work for temporary help services), business services employees (workers hired by companies that provide services, such as advertising, to other companies), and part-time workers (employees hired by firms to work less than a full schedule).
>
> Contingent employees often are used as a "buffer" workforce that can be quickly reduced or increased to match business needs, Freedman notes. The technique enhances the job security of a core workforce, while reducing the job security of the contingent workforce, Freedman stresses, noting that contingent employees generally receive no pensions, no vacation or holiday pay, and no health benefits. Additionally, there is no obligation to train, promote, or retain contingent employees, whose compensation also is often lower, Freedman observes. This situation is applauded by business strategists concerned with costs because it reduces labor costs per unit of output enormously, Freedman notes.[38]

When organizations decide to adopt employment security, they know that there is no turning back, or at least that it can be done only once. Consequently, they commit themselves to the training and retraining of employees. This is essential because employment security offers the promise of continual employment, not the promise of continued work on the same job (job security). Organizations also commit themselves to linking corporate strategy with human resource planning. This enables organizations to better establish training programs and ensure that the right people with right skills are at the right place at the right time.

In offering employment security, organizations expect in return from employees a commitment to work, assignment flexibility, and a willingness to retrain. This expectation is clearly reflected in the Saturn Division agreement between General Motors and the United Auto Workers. Typical of many organizations considering employment security, General Motors and the United Auto Workers see it as a fundamental component of organizational survival and competitiveness in the United States in the years ahead.[39]

Programs for Productivity Improvements

As with QWL, improvements for productivity can represent the results of a wide range of programs. For example, Citizens and Southern National Bank in Georgia completely turned around its operations with a new top management that emphasized a hard-nosed management by objectives program. Now "all bank officers participate in setting their own goals—and are held accountable for them."[40] Programs clarifying performance expectations, job descriptions, and job duties not only reduce stress, as discussed earlier in this chapter, but also go a long way toward improving productivity.

A less frequently used approach to improving productivity was Intel's "work more hours" solution. Intel Corporation, based in Santa Clara, California, asked its 5,100 professional managers to work fifty hours a week instead of forty for the same pay. Intel's purpose in using this solution was to increase the pace at which new money-making products were produced.[41]

In addition to the programs illustrated in these examples, other programs to improve productivity include (1) organizational restructuring, (2) automation, (3) socialization, and (4) alternative work arrangements.

Organizational Restructuring

Faced with intense competition and a rapidly changing environment, organizations are responding by restructuring themselves. Although this restructuring is done in a variety of ways, two ways involving PHRM are referred to here as down-sizing and stimulating entrepreneurship.

Down-sizing.   **Down-sizing,** or the act of eliminating employees by permanent layoffs, cutbacks, attrition, early retirement, and termination, is proving an effective way of improving productivity:

> When Jack Reichert became chairman of the Brunswick Corporation in 1982, that company was running a $20 million loss from continuing operations. Outside experts told Mr. Reichert to dump poorly performing businesses. Instead, he dumped excess people. He pared a corporate staff of close to 600 down to 200, and got rid of two management layers (chief operating officer and group executives) in the process. Result: Decisions that once took weeks or months are now being made in hours or days, and the red ink of three years back turned into a $94 million profit in 1984.

"Once we reduced the central staff, we found that there weren't so many unnecessary requirements being placed on the divisional staffs," one of Mr. Reichert's executives explains. In fact, Brunswick enjoyed a ripple effect: staff reductions, accompanied by improved executive productivity, at the divisional levels. "The divisions soon found they could handle their tasks with less people on *their* staff," he said.[42]

In essence, down-sizing is done to make organizations "lean and mean." It hits service industries as well as manufacturing. According to W. James Fish, Ford Motor Company's personnel planning manager, "We're looking at a total restructuring of American business."[43] And as the following "PHRM in the News" shows, the middle management layer is particularly hard hit.

Although down-sizing is done because it is easy, saves money quickly, and improves productivity, it can also stimulate entrepreneurial behavior in the remaining employees. This last benefit occurs when the down-sizing results in decentralizing authority and decision making. By **decentralizing**, organizations

> are encouraging their employees to be entrepreneurs, to take risks, to act autonomously—and they are recognizing that the only way to do so is to cut red tape, remove shackles, and let them run with their ideas.
>
> General Motors is setting up its new Saturn division along these lines. I.B.M.'s 18 or so independent business units (one of which developed the PC) operates this way.[44]

Stimulating Entrepreneurship.   By creating an environment in which **entrepreneurial behavior** may operate, General Electric has obtained a new source of financial gain and a way to speed the process of product development through its internal corporate venture groups.[45] Similarly, 3M has spurred product development in its consumer products division by setting up a separate and entrepreneurial-structured marketing group. By allowing this group to operate autonomously, 3M's chairman, Lewis W. Lehr, expects product development to be enhanced, since it is structured into small entre-

---

PHRM in the News

Middle Managers Are Still Sitting Ducks

There's nothing unusual about a company cutting management ranks when times turn sour, and the last recession had its wave of cutbacks in white-collar jobs. But the economy, if not exactly sparkling, is nonetheless growing—and still the squeeze is on. More striking, it's not limited to troubled industries such as oil and steel. Profitable companies are just as eagerly putting middle management on a diet.

The cutbacks seem to know no bounds, hitting service industries as

well as manufacturing. In the past month, companies as diverse as American Telephone & Telegraph, Ford, Union Carbide, and CBS have announced substantial work force reductions through dismissals, early retirement, or voluntary separations. Eugene E. Jennings, a Michigan State University professor who has been studying corporate staffing, found that since 1980, 89 of the 100 largest U.S. companies have reorganized to reduce the number of management levels. And it appears that the trend is here to stay: "There is no turning back," says consultant David M. Richardson. Agrees W. James Fish, Ford Motor Co.'s personnel planning manager: "We're looking at a total restructuring of American business."

More dispensable

The reasons for the ever-tightening grip on executives are as diverse as the companies involved. For companies plagued by financial problems, it's an obvious way to save money. And it's easy, too, since middle managers rarely enjoy the job protection afforded by unions at the blue-collar level or the employment contracts enjoyed by top management. In addition, administrative jobs have little direct impact on output, making them more dispensable than manufacturing positions. Of the 24,000 jobs being eliminated by the end of 1986 at AT&T's troubled Information Services, the lion's share—30%—are in management. Similarly, Texas-based Mostek Corp., United Technologies Corp.'s troubled semiconductor subsidiary, has laid off 2,600 of its 9,800 employees since March, more than 20% of them managers.

Meanwhile, some prosperous companies that suffered through rough times in the early 1980s are nervous about the possibility of a repeat and are keeping a tight lid on costs. Mounting low-cost competition from overseas has made some companies particularly wary. Ford, for example, wants to reduce the white-collar work force in its Ford North American Automotive Operations by 20%, or about 9,600 jobs, over the next five years.

Companies are also paying more attention to shareholder pressure to keep profits up. And a takeover attempt, or even the threat of one, can add even more pressure to slim down operations.

At Union Carbide Corp., a massive restructuring will result in the elimination of 4,000 jobs, or about 15% of the company's white-collar work force. The action came after the company was shaken by accidents at its chemical plants in Bhopal, India, and Institute, W. Va., and as GAF Corp. sought to increase its stake in Carbide to 15% (page 29). CBS Inc., reeling from Ted Turner's unsuccessful assault and facing the cost of buying back more than 20% of its common stock, on Aug. 30 offered 2,000 employees sweetened pension benefits if they would retire by Nov. 29.

'In vogue'

Consultants expect to see even more companies announcing management cuts in the coming months. "These kinds of moves usually only mean good for a company," says David F. Smith of Korn/Ferry International. "It motivates good performers to do better, improves the bottom line, and eliminates nonproductive jobs that can cause morale problems." In addition, companies are becoming more eager to publicize staff reductions because they believe it demonstrates their resolve to keep a short rein on costs. "There was a period when this kind of action was looked upon as very traumatic," says consultant Richardson. Now, "it's in vogue."

Those affected by the cuts can hardly regard them as good news. But while there are fewer positions available and more unemployed managers looking for jobs, the evolution of the corporate world will eventually pick up the slack. Some executives are taking jobs involving customer service; others are becoming consultants. Still others are joining the growing ranks of entrepreneurs. Flexibililty will determine who adjusts and survives— and who doesn't.

Source: Reprinted from the September 16, 1985 issue of *Business Week* by special permission, © 1985 by McGraw-Hill, Inc.

preneurial teams to develop new products that are spun off into separate businesses (intraorganizationally) as they grow. Lehr believes that although this move serves as a test to the flexibility of 3M's management, such decentralization and entrepreneurial structure are major sources of the consumer products division's $500 million in sales for 1983.[46]

Although entrepreneurship is a critical organizational force for survival in the years ahead, only a limited number of large corporations have gotten into entrepreneurship thus far. Apparently, however, all large organizations may need to stimulate entrepreneurship. Rosabeth Moss Kanter, author of *The Change Masters,* "foresees the possibility that sooner or later all U.S. corporations will be forced to develop innovative entrepreneurial structures in order to survive."[47]

Some organizations have been utilizing their PHRM practices to stimulate entrepreneurial behavior.[48] Essentially, they take the PHRM practices that are linked with a corporate entrepreneurial strategy and apply them in the division or unit where entrepreneurial behavior and innovation are desired. Exhibit 12.5 shows the PHRM practices used.[49] These are consistent with and impact upon the discussion in Chapter 1 and Exhibit 1.4. Although all the practices shown in Exhibit 12.5 can stimulate entrepreneurial behavior, one that appears particularly critical is some degree of employment security. This practice is useful in stimulating many productivity improvement efforts.

Exhibit 12.5   *Personnel and Human Resource Management Practices to Foster and Facilitate Entrepreneurship*

PLANNING	STAFFING
Informal	External sources
Tight	Broad paths
Short-term	Multiple ladders
Implicit	Implicit criteria
Broad	Extensive socialization
Integrative	Open procedures
High involvement	

APPRAISING	COMPENSATING
Loose, incomplete integration	High base salary
Results criteria	External equity
High participation	Many perks
Long-term criteria	Flexible benefits package
Group/individual determined criteria	Many incentives
	Employment security

TRAINING AND DEVELOPMENT
Broad application
Quality of work life emphasis
Spontaneous, informal
Group orientation
High participation

Automation

After a decade of decline in the face of low-cost, high-quality imports, U.S. industry is beginning to automate at a pace that will soon change the face of American factories and offices. Computer-controlled systems of robots will continue to replace most humans on plant floors and produce unprecedented gains in productivity. Automated equipment is also being used more in offices. These changes will affect more than 45 million U.S. jobs, many during the next twenty years.[50]

Since automation is so significant and likely to be a major contributor to improving productivity, PHRM must understand it and utilize it to improve productivity and QWL. Automation is especially critical to PHRM, since it has the potential to change the nature of so many jobs and create many new jobs. These changes in turn will impact employee recruitment and selection, performance appraisal, and training.[51]

Factory Automation.   U.S. manufacturing companies are finally in position to leap into total automation, which they are now beginning to do. Although the United States now lags behind Japan and Germany in automation use, many executives predict this will change by 1990.[52] "We are gathering momentum in the U.S. today, and as that momentum builds we are going to make quantum leaps in factory automation," according to Joseph Tulkoff, director of manufacturing technology for Lockheed-Georgia Company.

Accompanying the increase of factory automation is increased use of robots. Annual sales of robots are expected to be twenty thousand units by the end of the century, compared with the current rate of five thousand units. Estimates are that by 1995, robots will displace about 4.3 percent of the work force. Although most employees are expected to remain with their current employers, substantial retraining will be required. The costs of this training will be offset by lower labor costs, enhanced product quality, fewer defects, and a better flow of materials.[53]

Office Automation.   Eventually, almost 80 percent of the white-collar jobs in the United States will be automated, including managers, professionals, and clerical staff. The biggest gains in office productivity are predicted to come from automating the jobs of professionals and managers.[54]

The consulting firm of Booz, Allen, and Hamilton reported that less than half of the $50 billion spent by U.S. business each year for office automation goes for equipment for managers and professionals. Yet the yearly compensation for these two groups is nearly double ($550 billion) that of the clerical group. Consequently, with more office automation for managers and professionals, Booz, Allen, and Hamilton predict that U.S. companies can increase their productivity by 15 percent and save up to $125 billion annually by

- Using automated calendars, tickler files, and other forms of equipment that replace the handwritten lists made by business people to keep track of their time and that of others.
- Using word and image processors that allow managers and professionals to better review and edit their work. Personal computers could reduce the time these individuals spend in making decisions and analyzing data, and

audiovisual conferences could replace the face-to-face meeting—and eliminate the accompanying travel time.

■ Installing retrieval-of-information services and electronic mail (the latter a broad term encompassing facsimile, keyboard, and speech or voice-activated mail) that could increase productivity and help connect other types of automated tools with each other.[55]

Socialization

Socialization represents the process that companies use to expose new employees to their culture and ways of doing things. When done successfully, it results in intensely loyal employees who are dedicated to the company. Companies that have perfected the socialization process include IBM, Procter and Gamble, and Morgan Guaranty Trust. Often the socialization process begins before the employee is hired. At Procter and Gamble, for example, an elite cadre of line managers trained in interviewing skills probes applicants for entry-level positions in brand management for qualities such as the "ability to turn out high volumes of excellent work." Only after successfully completing at least two interviews and a test of general knowledge is the applicant flown to P&G headquarters in Cincinnati, where the applicant confronts a daylong series of interviews. If the applicant passes this extensive screening process, he or she is confronted with a series of rigorous job experiences calculated to induce humility and openness to new ways of doing things. Typically this phase of socialization involves long hours of work at a pressure cooker pace. Throughout this phase and others of the socialization process, the new employee is constantly made aware of transcendent company values and organizational folklore. Such values and folklore include the emphasis on product quality and the dedication and commitment of employees long since past.[56] The results of this intense socialization include increased commitment to the success of the company, willingness to work long hours, and decreased absenteeism and turnover.[57]

Socialization can have a tremendously positive impact for organizations. But socialization can be difficult, especially when organizational values differ from a new employee's existing values. If the organization is not successful in socializing new employees, they may soon leave the organization.[58]

Socialization is concerned with the roles that employees play rather than with the jobs they occupy. Although employees need specific skills to perform their jobs and are trained to perform them, they also need an awareness of the basic goals of the organization, the means to attain those goals, their responsibilities, and the acceptable behavior patterns for the roles they are expected to play.[59] Employees acquire this awareness by being socialized, formally and informally, through continuing contacts and experiences with others. Employees must also be aware of what their jobs are about and what skills are required. But this awareness is generally acquired through job descriptions and job previews, which are predominantly pre-employment activities.[60]

Organizations usually recruit from familiar sources that have supplied good applicants in the past. They may also recruit individuals who are already socialized. But recruitment and selection processes aren't likely to produce new employees who know the values, norms, and behavior patterns of the organization. When this is the case, more extensive socialization efforts must be conducted.[61] Of the several possible formalized methods of socialization, two deserve particular attention: orientation programs and job assignments.

Orientation Programs.   **Orientation programs** are frequently used to brief new employees on benefit programs and options, to advise them of rules and regulations, and to provide them with a folder or handbook of the policies and practices of the organization:

> A first-rate orientation system for new-hires can reduce turnover rates, decrease employee learning time, and improve quality and productivity throughout the organization, according to Edmund McGarrell, Jr., supervisor of special projects at Corning Glass Works. Addressing the American Management Association's 56th Annual Human Resources Conference, which was held in New Orleans and covered by BNA, McGarrell stresses that the company's orientation process is designed to provide new-hires with "red carpet treatment" that will turn them into highly skilled, involved, and committed employees.[62]

Orientation programs require more than folders or handbooks, however. They also usually contain information about equal employment opportunity practices, safety regulations, work times, coffee breaks, the structure and history of the organization, and perhaps the products or services of the organization. Typically, however, the orientation program does not tell employees about the real politics of the organization—for example, that the organization may soon be going out of business, that it may be merging with another company, or even that an extensive layoff may soon occur.[63]

The orientation program conveys some information about the norms, values, attitudes, and behaviors appropriate for new employees, but much of the socialization is left to informal day-to-day interactions among employees. Nevertheless, orientation programs are useful for factual information, and the handbook can be used to tell employees where to get additional information after orientation is over.

Orientation programs are almost always coordinated by the personnel director of the organization. The program is often run by a staff member of the personnel department, with some participation by line managers or representatives from other departments or divisions in the organization.

When organizations are large, orientation programs are often conducted every week. Some organizations even have two orientation sessions one week apart. Typically these programs are run for groups of new employees. Although this is an efficient method, it tends to negate each employee's sense of identity and consequence.[64] Therefore, each employee is often assigned to a trainer or buddy (sometimes the immediate supervisor) who can answer further questions and introduce the new employee to the other employees in the work unit or department.

Orientation programs are usually conducted within a week of an employee's initial employment date. For maximum effectiveness, the earlier the better. Organizations that put off orientation programs run the risk of letting the new employees gain critical information about the company from current employees. This information may be inaccurate and thus not in the best interests of the organization or the new employees.[65]

Orientation programs may last longer than one or two days. The orientation program at Corning Glass Works, for example, lasts fifteen months. Exhibit 12.6 shows the critical components of the program at Corning. Most orientation programs last for only a few hours, though, and are done within the first week or two of employment. Occasionally an orientation follow-up takes place a year or so later. Most employees take longer than just one or two weeks to acquire all the information contained in the orientation program. Because orientation programs do only part of the job of socialization, other methods are also used.

Job Assignments.   The important socializing aspects of job assignments are the characteristics of the initial job, the nature of early experiences on the job, and the first supervisor. The initial job often determines the new employee's future success. The more challenge and responsibility the job offers, the more likely an employee will be successful with the organization.[66] A challenging (but not overwhelming) job assignment implies that the organization believes the employee can do well and that the organization values him or her. Many times, organizations give new employees simple jobs or ro-

---

Exhibit 12.6   *Critical Components of the Orientation*
Program at Corning Glass Works

- Pre-arrival period—The supervisor gets the office ready and, based on discussions with the new-hire, creates a preliminary management-by-objectives list.
- First day—Following breakfast with the supervisor, the new-hire goes through personnel processing, attends a half-day "Corning and You" seminar, tours the facility and meets co-workers.
- First week—This time is set aside for getting settled in the department or office and for one-on-one discussions with the supervisor and co-workers. Performance expectations and other general job-related matters are discussed, and details of the MBO plan are formalized.
- Second through fourth weeks—Regular assignments begin. The new-hire also attends a special employee benefits seminar.
- Second through fifth months—Assignments increase and progress is reviewed biweekly with the supervisor. The employee also attends six two-and-one-half-hour seminars on such topics as quality and productivity and reviews these with the supervisor.
- Sixth month—The new employee reviews the MBO list with the supervisor and receives a performance review.
- Seventh through 15th months—MBO and performance and salary reviews are conducted.

McGarrell says that since initiating the system in 1982, Corning has reduced its turnover rate by 69 percent, shortened employee learning time by one month, and saved more than $500,000 in recruiting and training costs.

Source: Bulletin to Management, 9 May 1985, pp. 1, 2. Reprinted by permission from *Bulletin to Management,* copyright 1985, by The Bureau of National Affairs, Inc., Washington, D.C.

tate them through departments to get a feel for different jobs. But employees may interpret these practices to mean that the organization does not yet trust their abilities or loyalties.[67]

Closely related to the first job are employees' initial experiences, which are often provided by supervisors. These types of experiences help prepare new employees for the acquisition of the appropriate values, norms, attitudes, and behaviors. Supervisors of new employees can serve as role models and set expectations. The positive influence that the supervisor's expectations can have on the new employee is referred to as the **Pygmalion effect**. A supervisor who believes that the new employee will do well will convey this belief to the employee, who will be apt to live up to those expectations.[68]

Alternative Work Arrangements

This may be the decade in which Americans free themselves from the tyranny of the time clock. Already more than 10 million workers have taken advantage of several types of **alternative work arrangements**. The growing number of single-parent families, the high costs of commuting, the desire for larger blocks of personal time, and the desire of older workers to reduce their hours all suggest that this trend will increase. Far from representing a decline in the work ethic, alternative work arrangements seem to strengthen it by reducing the stresses caused by the conflict between job demands, family needs, leisure values, and educational needs. Thus, organizations can expect to reduce absenteeism and turnover by offering alternatives to their standard work arrangements.[69]

Standard Work Schedules.   In the 1860s the average work week was seventy-two hours—twelve hours a day, six days a week. It was fifty-eight hours in 1900 and remains approximately forty hours a week today. Standard work schedules include day, evening, and night sessions as well as overtime, part-time, and shift work over a forty-hour week.

Someone who does shift work might report from 7:00 A.M. to 4:00 P.M. one week and from 4:00 P.M. to midnight the next. Since the end of World War I, shift work systems have become more prevalent in industrialized countries. Currently about 20 percent of all industrial workers in Europe and the United States are on shift-work schedules. The percentage of employees on part-time schedules has also increased steadily—from approximately 15 percent in 1954 to 23 percent today.

All of these standard work schedules have advantages and disadvantages, as Exhibit 12.7 shows, but traditionally they offer little choice to employees. Initially employees may select a given schedule, but after that the days of the week (five) and the hours of the day (eight) are generally fixed. Because employee preferences and interests change over time, what had once been an appropriate work schedule may no longer be so. If alternative arrangements are not provided, the employee may leave the organization. Furthermore, the organization may have a difficult time attracting similar types of employees.[70] As a result, it pays to give employees a choice between a nonstandard and standard schedule, as well as a choice of hours, days, and total number of hours to work per week.

Exhibit 12.7   *Advantages and Disadvantages of Standard Work Schedules*

Type of Schedule	Advantages	Disadvantages
Regular	Allows for standardization, predictability, and ease of administration; consistent application for all employees	Does not fit needs of all employees; not always consistent with preferences of customers
Shift	More effective use of plant and equipment; allows continuous operation and weekend work	Can be stressful, especially if rotating shifts; lower satisfaction and performance
Overtime	Permits more efficient utilization of existing work force; cheaper than alternatives; allows flexibility	Job performance may decline; may not be satisfying and may contribute to employee fatigue
Part-time	Allows scheduling flexibility to the organization, enabling it to staff at peak and unusual times; cheaper than full-time employees	Applicable to only a limited number of jobs; increased costs of training; no promotion opportunities

Source: From "Part-time and Temporary Employees," ASPA-BNA Survey 25, *Bulletin to Management*, 5 December 1974, p. 5. Reprinted by permission from *Bulletin to Management*, copyright 1974 by The Bureau of National Affairs, Inc., Washington, D.C.

Flextime Schedules.   This nonstandard work schedule is popular with organizations because it decreases absenteeism, increases employee morale, induces better labor-management relations, and encourages a high level of employee participation in decision making, self-control, and discretion. Simply stated, **flextime** is a schedule that gives employees daily choice in the timing of work and nonwork activities. Consideration is given to **band width**, or maximum length of the workday. This band (often ranging between ten and sixteen hours) is divided into core time and flexible time. **Core time** is when the employee has to work; **flexible time** allows the employee the freedom to choose the remaining work time. Exhibit 12.8 shows how a twelve-hour band width can be divided into blocks of flexible and core times.

Among the advantages of flextime is its ability to generally increase employee productivity. It also allows organizations to accommodate employee preferences, some of which may be legally protected, such as reasonable religious obligations. On the other hand, flextime forces the supervisor to do more planning, makes communications sometimes difficult between employees (especially with different schedules), and complicates record keeping of employees' hours. Furthermore, most flextime schedules still require employees to work five days a week.

Compressed Work Weeks.   An option for employees who want to work fewer than five days is **compressed work weeks.** By extending the workday beyond

Sample of Flextime Scheduling   *Exhibit 12.8*

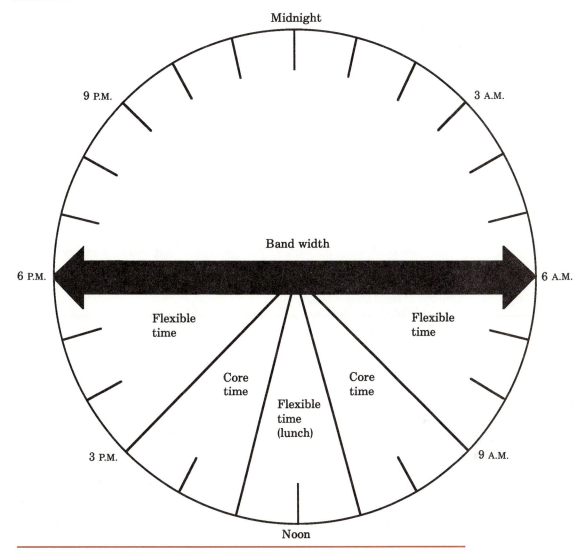

Source: Adapted from A. Cohen and H. Gadon, *Alternative Work
Schedules: Integrating Individual and Organizational Needs,* ©
1978, Addison-Wesley Publishing Company, Inc., Reading, Mass.
Pg. 35 (adapted figure). Reprinted with permission.

the standard eight hours, employees generally need to work only three to
four days to equal a standard forty-hour week.[71] For example, at two General
Tire and Rubber plants, some employees work only two twelve-hour shifts
each weekend and yet are considered full-time employees. Compressed work
weeks are becoming especially popular for certain occupations, such as nursing.

At the same time, compressed work weeks permit an organization to make better use of its equipment and decrease turnover and absenteeism. Scheduling and legal problems may accompany such arrangements, but legal exceptions can be made, and scheduling can become a joint negotiation process between supervisor and employees.

Permanent Part-time and Job Sharing. Traditionally, part-time work has meant filling positions that lasted only for a short time, such as those in retail stores during holiday periods. Now some organizations have designated **permanent part-time (PPT)** positions. A permanent part-time work schedule may be a shortened daily schedule (e.g., from 1:00 to 5:00 P.M.) or an odd-hour shift (e.g., between 5:00 and 9:00 P.M.). Organizations can also use PPT schedules to fill in the remainder of a day composed of two ten-hour shifts (representing a compressed work week).[72]

Job sharing is a particular type of part-time work. In job sharing, two people divide the responsibility for a regular full-time job. Both may work half the job, or one could work more hours than the other. Part-time workers generally receive little or no indirect compensation, but workers on permanent part-time and job-sharing schedules often do. The benefits to these workers are not equal to those of full-time workers but are prorated according to the amount of time they work.

Both PPT and job sharing provide the organization and individuals with opportunities that might not otherwise be available. They offer staffing flexibility that can expand or contract to meet actual demands, using employees who are at least as productive, if not more so, than regular full-time employees. Individuals benefit from being able to enjoy permanent work with less than a full-time commitment to the company.

Industrial and Electronic Cottages. To provide individuals with even more choices in how to arrange their work and work schedules, companies are allowing employees to work at home. Work-at-home arrangements can be made for those with a full-time commitment to the company and for those wanting only part-time employment. Increasingly, individuals are working at home by means of computer terminals linked to the mainframes at their regular office or plant. In essence the employee's home then becomes an **electronic cottage**. Individuals can also take work home that involves assembly, such as small toys. After a batch is done, the worker takes it to the regular plant and turns it in for more parts. In this example, the home becomes an **industrial cottage**.[73]

The use of industrial and electronic cottages is increasing. This arrangement offers workers another choice as well as more freedom. One drawback, however, is the difficulty of protecting the health and safety of the employee at home. Another is ensuring that workers are still paid a fair wage for their work. State and federal laws can also restrict home work. For example, a federal law prohibits commercial knitting at home. These restrictions must be dealt with carefully if such expanding cottages are to remain a viable option.

Trends in QWL and Productivity Improvement

Two major trends are described here: assessing improvement programs, and computer technology and HRIS in improving QWL and productivity. Issues associated with strategic involvement and choices are the essence of this entire chapter.

Assessing Improvement Programs

As Exhibit 12.1 shows, the programs aimed at improving QWL and productivity have several intended purposes. Although the two sets of programs have different purposes, QWL programs can also bring about the intended purposes of the productivity programs. Consequently, QWL programs can be assessed by how well they attain all of the purposes in Exhibit 12.1.

QWL Programs.   As with the other personnel and human resource activities discussed, assessing the benefits of QWL programs solely on the basis of dollars and cents is almost impossible. For example, what dollar value would be gained by increasing employee satisfaction or self-control by 10 percent? It may be difficult to say, but the question is, Do all QWL programs have to be justified on the basis of dollars and cents? Or can they be justified solely on the basis of increasing self-control, satisfaction, involvement, and self-respect (essentially all employee benefits)?[74]

Although corporations think that benefits to the individual are important, many QWL programs are supported by corporations and employees because they also reap benefits to the organization—that is, individual performance and productivity gains. Thus, the difficulty of evaluating QWL in dollars and cents is diminished. Some difficulty remains, however, because the productivity gains (which can be evaluated in dollars and cents) resulting from QWL programs may not occur for several years after the QWL program begins.

But even if the employees' benefits from QWL programs cannot easily be assessed in dollars and cents, they can still be assessed either in relation to the level of benefits alone or by the level to which the benefits are obtained in relation to the cost of the QWL program. For example, Kroger Corporation in Cincinnati, Ohio, implemented a team development program in seven stores and assessed its effectiveness by attitude surveys measuring employee commitment, involvement, and interest in the success of its stores. The program was considered a success in relation to these benefits alone, although the company could have easily assessed the program in costs as well as benefits.

Productivity Programs.   The process of assessing productivity programs is made less complex than that for QWL programs because individual outcomes are much more measurable, as shown in Chapter 18. For example, productivity programs can be assessed by individual job performance, absenteeism, and turnover. Productivity programs at the organizational level can be assessed in profitability, competitiveness, and survival measures.[75] As indicated at the start of this chapter, measuring productivity may be difficult, especially where it has not previously been done. This difficulty appears more related to gaining acceptance that productivity *will* be measured rather than that it *can* be measured. Once the organization accepts that productivity can be assessed, productivity measures can be established in white-collar as well as blue-collar jobs, and the effects of productivity improvement programs can be assessed.

Computer Technology and HRIS in Improving QWL and Productivity

Computer technology can be utilized in two ways to improve QWL. First, it is an invaluable tool for managing information collected by organizational surveys. Data can not only be summarized for the entire organization but also organized in other meaningful ways. For example, the responses for a particular question or group of questions measuring the same dimensions, such as role conflict and role awareness, can be extracted by department, by position, or by particular physical locations. Analyzing the data by category like this is useful when attempting to identify issues involving only certain segments of the organization. Second, the computer can be used as a checklist to determine which surveys have not been returned. This is especially crucial when measuring attitudes about a newly proposed policy that will affect everyone. All the benefits of surveys and computer technology are greatest when an organization maintains an up-to-date HRIS.

Current information in an HRIS can also be helpful in trying to improve productivity. Data such as performance, absenteeism, and turnover can be part of an HRIS and used to measure levels of productivity in different areas of the organization. This information can also be used to determine if programs to improve productivity are successful.

Summary

Faced with increasing international competition, U.S. companies are confronted with a productivity crisis of major proportions. Changing social and individual values have created a similar crisis in quality of work life. Some U.S. companies are responding to these crises by implementing programs for productivity and QWL improvements. Other companies have avoided these crises because they have had productivity and QWL programs for many years. In some cases, faced with crises or not, organizations are engaging in new productivity and QWL programs as they are developed.

This chapter examines only a few of many programs being used by U.S. companies to improve productivity and QWL. Among the many things that can be done to increase productivity, some may not work as well as others in all organizations. A diagnosis must be done to determine what is needed.

Once accomplished, an organization can choose from among several programs, many directly related to their PHRM activities. For example, the total compensation system could be changed to be more performance based. Wholesale adoption of programs because they are popular is not likely to result in success. Regardless of the particular program, employee involvement in program design or implementation (or both) enhances the program's success. Getting such involvement generally implies that the organization shares relevant information with the employees.

Just as many programs can be used to improve QWL. Indeed, some suggest that much of the productivity crisis would be solved if QWL were improved. But many reasons account for the current productivity crisis, such as the way managers are rewarded and promoted, the decline in research and development, and the proportionately larger segment of the U.S. economy not producing goods and services. The increasing age of the capital equipment in the United States and increased international competition are also important in understanding our current productivity crisis.

Although the programs presented in this chapter can improve QWL and productivity, they represent only one major way to improve organizations. Another major way is by designing and implementing programs to improve the health and safety of employees. The importance of and need for such programs, as well as possible programs to implement, are described in the next chapter.

Discussion Questions

1. What are the important factors in considering the effectiveness or utility of increased participation in decision making?
2. What are the essential characteristics of any quality circle effort?
3. Why are the benefits of QWL programs more difficult to ascertain than the benefits associated with productivity programs, if indeed they are?
4. How would you distinguish QWL from productivity issues? How are the two issues related?
5. Some evidence suggests that the quality of your work experience affects your behaviors and attitudes off the job. Can you think of an example to illustrate this? What implications does this phenomenon have for PHRM?
6. Given what you know about the PHRM functions related to selection and placement, job analysis, training and development, and performance appraisal, explain how doing these functions poorly will detract from QWL.
7. How are job enrichment programs different from job enlargement programs of job design?
8. Automation of office systems since the advent of microcomputers has resulted in some companies permitting employees (e.g., computer programmers) to work at home. What are some advantages to this arrangement? Disadvantages? How would you overcome these disadvantages?

9. Suppose that you asked several of your friends to develop career paths with specific timetables, based on their use of a personal career planning model. Five years have passed, and you compare their actual experience against their previously prepared career paths and find little correspondence. Does this result render career planning useless? Explain. Would those same arguments apply to human resource planning described in Chapter 2?

10. Describe in your own words what quality circles, survey feedback programs, and organizational restructuring efforts are. What do these programs have in common? What makes them distinctive?

PC Project

"If you want to know how employees feel, ask them." Surveys can play a highly useful role in measuring the reactions of employees to quality of work life programs and other organizational interventions. However, the survey must be carefully planned and have a specific purpose. This PC Project shows how the computer can be used to analyze the results of an attitude survey. Data-base commands can be used to break down the results according to demographic characteristics of the respondents. Are there differences based on age, sex, and length of service? What type of feedback should be provided?

C   A   S   E   S   T   U   D   Y

We Work Hard and Play Hard

Infotronics was started by Kirby Folterman, now forty-seven, as a small high-tech firm that specializes in making the video recorders used by banks for their automatic teller machines and retail stores. Eventually the company branched out into data recorders used by airlines and audio recorders used in defense security systems. Kirby, the "old" man of the group, has a reputation for being a bit on the unconventional side:

Kirby led an expedition of employees down the Tuolumne River near Yosemite Park, which has people still talking three years after the hairy whitewater adventure.

One October, employees were encouraged to celebrate Halloween by coming to work in costume.

To celebrate the successful completion of a project within a deadline that Kirby bet could not be met, he jumped from a cake nude.

At an after-hours party for employees and their families at a posh country club, Kirby instigated a pool dunk that resulted in everyone being pitched into the pool before the evening was over.

For Don Hillis, personnel director at Infotronics, they don't come any crazier than Kirby. But by the same token, their outfit works pretty hard, too. Kirby's contention is that the stresses of the work place need to be safely released, so a little fun and spontaneity on and off the job help people work together. Secretly, Kirby believes this is why his company's turnover rate is half the industry average.

Don was persuaded by Kirby to quit his job with a large automotive division to head up the personnel division five years ago when Infotronics began a period of rapid growth. At first, Don was apprehensive about working for such an unorthodox entrepreneur and a considerably smaller company. But something inside told him it was right, and he hasn't regretted the decision since his move.

In view of Kirby's lighthearted approach to work, Don was curious how he might respond to an idea Don had been carrying around since his days at the automotive company. The concept simply was to set up physical facilities at the company and to hire an exercise physiologist to work with the 150 current employees to improve their wellness.

The motivation for Don's proposal was due in large part to the escalating costs of health care and the steady increase in the company premiums for the insurance programs that Infotronics provided its employees. Don recalled a similar effort made by the medical director at the automotive com-

pany. His idea was different, though. At the auto company the medical director implemented a rigorous physical screening test that rejected applicants who were overweight, had high blood pressure, or had other physical ailments linked to longer-term health problems. The result was that the company insurance premiums dropped by 20 percent in the first year after the plan was implemented.

Don saw things differently at Infotronics. The work force was stabilized and made up of a cadre of creative, bright individuals selected for their specific expertise. The question was how to retain this group and promote their health and quality of life both on and off the job. Don believed that the philosophy that the employer is responsible for the work place's effect on the employee in an ethical way was consistent with Kirby's fun-oriented approach toward work and play. The key question in Don's mind, though, was whether he could sell the cost-benefit aspects of such a wellness program.

Notes

1. D. A. Nadler and E. E. Lawler III, "Quality of Work Life: Perspectives and Directing,"*Organizational Dynamics* (Winter 1983): 20–30; L. E. Davis and A. B. Cherns, eds., *The Quality of Working Life,* vols. I and II (New York: Free Press, 1975); B. A. Macy, "A Public Sector Experiment to Improve Organizational Effectiveness and Employees' Quality of Work Life: The TVA Case," paper presented at the Forty-first Annual Meeting of the Academy of Management, 2–5 Aug. 1981, San Diego, California; J. R. Hackman and J. L. Suttle, *Improving Life at Work* (Santa Monica, Calif: Goodyear, 1977); J. Rosow, "Quality of Work Life Issues for the 1980's," *Training and Development Journal* (Mar. 1981): 33–37; R. P. Quinn and G. L. Staines, *The Quality of Employment Survey* (Ann Arbor, Mich.: Survey Research Center, Institute for Social Research, University of Michigan, 1979).

2. R. A. Guzzo, R. D. Jette, and R. A. Katzell, "The Effects of Psychologically Based Intervention Programs on Worker Productivity: A Meta-Analysis," *Personnel Psychology* (Summer 1985): 275–93; H. Gorlin and L. Schein, *Innovations in Managing Human Resources* (New York: Conference Board, 1984).

3. D. Yankelovich, *New Rules: Searching for Self-Fulfillment in a World Turned Upside Down* (New York: Random House, 1981); P. C. Grant, "Why Employee Motivation Has Declined in America," *Personnel Journal* (Dec. 1982): 905–9. With the relative importance of noneconomic rewards increasing, the quality

of work life takes increasing importance as a possible reward that organizations can provide their employees. Although the importance of economic rewards and job security remains high, individuals appear to be as concerned about the quality of their work life. See D. Lacey, "What Will Workers Want in Post-Recession America?" *Personnel Administrator* (May 1983): 71–78.

4. Hackman and Suttle, *Improving Life at Work;* F. Herzberg, "The Human Need for Work," *Industry Week,* 24 July 1978, pp. 45–52.

5. The importance of QWL, however, can also be reflected by its many benefits to be discussed throughout this chapter.

6. D. Q. Mills, *The New Competitors* (New York: Free Press, 1985); W. List, "When Workers and Managers Act as a Team," *Report on Business,* October 1985, pp. 60–67.

7. R. R. Blake and J. S. Mouton, "Increasing Productivity through Behavioral Science," *Personnel* (May–June 1981): 59–67; D. S. Cohen, "Why Quality of Work Life Doesn't Always Mean Quality," *Training/HRD* (Oct., 1981): 54–60.

8. L. A. Schlesinger and B. Oshry, "Quality of Work Life and the Manager: Muddle in the Middle," *Organizational Dynamics* (Summer 1984): 4–14; L. M. Apcar, "Middle Managers and Supervisors Resist Moves to More Participating Management," *Wall Street Journal,* 16 Sept. 1985, p. 27.

9. Bureau of National Affairs, "74 Daily Labor Report," 16 Apr. 1982. See also J. P. Swann, Jr., "The Most Effective Employee Committees Are Probably Illegal," *Personnel Journal* (Nov. 1984): 91–92.

10. Z. D. Fasman, "Legal Obstacles to Alternative Work Force Designs," *Employee Relations Law Journal* (Autumn 1982): 256–81; List.

11. Fasman, "Legal Obstacles"; "Support for QWL Programs," *Bulletin to Management,* 16 Dec. 1982, see chaps. 16 and 17.

12. T. Mills, "Europe's Industrial Democracy: An American Response," *Harvard Business Review* (Nov.–Dec. 1978): 148.

13. Not all QWL programs are successful. Further, of the approximately 5 million companies in the United States, perhaps fewer than 3,000 have personnel programs for QWL or productivity improvements. "Stonewalling Plant Democracy" *Business Week,* 28 Mar. 1977, pp. 78, 81–82.

14. P. Gyllhammar, "How Volvo Adapts Work to People," *Harvard Business Review* (July/Aug. 1977): 112; B. Jonsson and A. G. Lank, "Volvo: A Report on the Workshop on Production Technology and Quality of Work Life," *Human Resource Management* (Winter 1985): 455–66.

15. R. Griffin, *Task Design—An Integrative Approach* (Glenview, Ill.: Scott, Foresman, 1982); J. R. Hackman and G. R. Oldham, *Work Redesign* (Reading, Mass.: Addison-Wesley, 1980); R. J. Aldag and A. P. Brief, *Task Design and Employee Motivation* (Glenview, Ill.: Scott, Foresman, 1979); "Boosting Productivity at American Express," *Business Week,* 5 Oct. 1981, pp. 62–66.

16. Mills, *The New Competitors.*

17. Organizations characterized by greater openness and participation are similar to those with System IV characteristics described in R. Likert, *New Patterns of Management* (New York: McGraw-Hill, 1961), and *The Human Organization: Its Management and Value* (New York: McGraw-Hill, 1967).

18. T. Mroczkowski, "Quality Circles, Fines—What Next?" *Personnel Administrator* (June 1984): 173–84; C. P. Alexander, "A Hidden Benefit of Quality Circles," *Personnel Journal* (Feb. 1984): 54–58; D. Gillet, "Better QCs: A Need for More Manager Action," *Management Review* (Jan. 1983): 19–25; Bureau of National Affairs, "Quality Circles: Flying High at McDonnell Douglas," *Bulletin to Management,* 10 May 1984; T. Rendero, "Productivity and Morale Sagging? Try the Quality Circle Approach," *Personnel* (May–June 1980): 43–45; "Quality Circle Boom Part of Growing American Trend," *Supervision* (Sept. 1981): 8–11; G. R. Ferris and J. A. Wagner III, "Quality Circles in the United States: A Conceptual Reevaluation," *Journal of Applied Behavioral Sciences* 21 (1985): 156–67.

19. List, "The United Steel Workers."

20. G. R. Ferris and J. A. Wagner III, "Quality Circles."

21. D. Hage, "Goal Is Improving Work Place," *Minneapolis Star,* 19 Nov. 1981, p. 1C.

22. G. J. Gooduz, Jr., "What Is a Quality Circle?" *BNAC Communicator* (Winter 1982): 3; R. Wood, "Productivity: Quality Circles for Supermarket," *New York Times,* 15 Apr. 1982, p. F19.

23. Bureau of National Affairs, "Health Care: Problems and Prescriptions," *Bulletin to Management,* 21 Mar. 1985, p. 1.

24. Ferris and Wagner III, "Quality Circles."

25. P. Farish, "QC Factor: Trust," *Personnel Administrator* (Aug. 1982): 10.

26. G. W. Meyer and R. G. Scott, "Quality Circles: Panacea or Pandora's Box?" *Organizational Dynamics* (Spring 1985): 34–50; G. Munchus III, "Employer-Employee Based Quality Circles in Japan: Human Resource Policy Implications for American Firms," *Academy of Management Review* (April 1983): 255–61; C. N. Greene and T. A. Matherly, "Quality Circles: A Need for Caution and Evaluation of Alternatives," in *Readings in Personnel and Human Resource Management,* 3d ed., ed. R. S. Schuler, S. A. Youngblood, and V. Huber (St. Paul: West, 1987).

27. J. Simmons and W. J. Mares, "Reforming Work," *New York Times,* 25 Oct. 1982, p. 18.

28. Ibid.

29. M. R. Weisbord, "Participative Work Design: A Personal Odyssey," *Organizational Dynamics* (Spring 1985): 4–20; R. M. Kanter and J. D. Buck, "Reorganizing Part of Honeywell: From Strategy to Structure," *Organizational Dynamics* (Winter 1985): 4–25; S. R. Hinckley, Jr., "A Closer Look at Participation," *Organizational Dynamics* (Winter 1985): 57–67; M. Sashkin, "Participative Management Is an Ethical Imperative," *Organizational Dynamics* (Spring 1984): 4–22; M. Sashkin, "Participative Management Remains an Ethical Imperative," *Organizational Dynamics* (in press).

30. For extensive illustrations of this concept, see L. Rhodes, "The Un-Manager," *Inc.* (Aug. 1982): 34–46; C. Grisanti, "One-Time Harvard Teacher Builds Group of Firms by Leaving His Managers Alone," *Wall Street Journal,* 12 July 1982, p. 21; M. Magnet, "Managing by Mystique at Tandem Computers," *Fortune,* 28 June 1982, pp. 84–91.

31. R. S. Schuler, "A Role and Expectancy Model of Participation in Decision Making," *Academy of Management Journal* 23 (1980): 331–40; E. A. Locke, D. B. Feren, V. M. Caleb, and K. N. Shaw, "The Relative Effectiveness of Four Methods of Motivating Employee Performance," in *Changes in Working Life: Proceedings of the NATO International Conference,* ed. K. Duncan, M. Gruneberg, and D. Wallis (London: Wiley, 1983); S. E. Jackson, "Participation in Decision Making as a Strategy for Reducing Job-related Strain," *Journal of Applied Psychology* (Feb. 1983):

3–19; T. M. Harrison, "Communication and Participative Decision Making: An Exploratory Study," *Personnel Psychology* (Spring 1985): 93–116.

32. R. Ford, *Motivation through Work Itself* (New York: American Management Association, 1969).

33. For an illustration, see A. Nag, "To Build a Small Car GM Tries to Redesign Its Production System," *Wall Street Journal,* 14 May 1984, pp. 1, 16.

34. "Ergonomics Training Eases Man-Machine Interface," *Management Review* (Oct. 1984): 55.

35. For a critique of job design approaches and another recommendation, see R. E. Kopelman, "Job Redesign and Productivity: A Review of the Evidence," *National Productivity Review* (Summer 1985): 237–55. Many ideas in this section reflect those found in Aldag and Brief, *Task Design;* Griffin, *Task Design;* B. Schneider, A. Reichers, and T. M. Mitchell, "A Note on Some Relationships between the Aptitude Requirements and Reward Attributes of Tasks," *Academy of Management Journal* 25 (1982): 567–74; B. Schneider, *Staffing Organizations* (Santa Monica, Calif.: Goodyear, 1976); E. J. McCormick and J. Tiffin, *Industrial Psychology,* 6th ed. (Englewood Cliffs, N.J.: Prentice-Hall, 1974); L. H. Lofquist and R. V. Davis, *Adjustment to Work* (New York: Appleton-Century-Crofts, 1969). This discussion can be extended to an analysis of the question, Should people be selected to fit jobs, or should jobs be made to fit people? For views on this question, see J. R. Hackman, G. R. Oldham, R. Janson, and K. Purdy, "A New Strategy for Job Enrichment," *California Management Review* (Summer 1975): 57–71; J. R. Hackman, J. L. Pearce, and J. C. Wolfe, "Effects of Changes in Job Characteristics on Work Attitudes and Behaviors: A Naturally Occurring Quasi-Experiment," *Organizational Behavior and Human Performance* 21 (1978): 289–304; J. Thomas and R. Griffin, "The Social Information Processing Model of Task Design: A Review of the Literature," *Academy of Management Review* (Oct. 1983): 672–82; M. A. Campion and P. W. Thayer, "Development and Field Evaluation of an Interdisciplinary Measure of Job Design," *Journal of Applied Psychology* (Feb. 1985): 29–43.

36. Adapted from R. Griffin, *Task Design.*

37. Mills, *The New Competitors,* pp. 69–70.

38. Bureau of National Affairs, "Employment Security News and Views," *Bulletin to Management,* 1 Aug. 1985, p. 40. For additional views on employment security, see Mills, *The New Competitors,* 1985; S. Weinig, "Guaranteed Lifetime Employment Pays Off Employee Commitment," *AMA Forum* (Aug. 1984): 29, 34.

39. "How Power Will Be Balanced on Saturn's Shop Floor,"*Business Week,* 5 Aug. 1985, pp. 65–66. See also R. Kuttner, "Sharing Power at Eastern Air Lines," *Harvard Business Review* (Nov.–Dec. 1985): 91–101.

40. "How One Troubled Bank Turned Itself Around," *Business Week,* 24 Aug 1981, pp. 117–22.

41. "Intel's 125% Solution," *Business Week,* 9 Nov. 1981, p. 50; "The Rise of the Productivity Manager," *Dunn's Review* (Jan. 1981): 64, 65, 69; D. P. Garino, "Some Companies Try Fewer Bosses to Cut Costs, Decentralize Power," *Wall Street Journal,* 10 Apr. 1981, sec. 2.

42. T. Peters, "Why Smaller Staffs Do Better," *New York Times,* 21 Apr. 1985, p. F1.

43. "Middle Managers Are Still Sitting Ducks," *Business Week,* 16 Sept. 1985, p. 54.

44. Peters "Why Smaller Staffs Do Better." Also see T. Peters and N. Austin, *A Passion for Excellence* (New York: Warner Books, 1985). For a description of alternative organizational designs and structures, see H. Mintzberg, "Organizational Design: Fashion or Fit?" *Harvard Business Review* (Jan.–Feb. 1981): 103–16; J. Main, "The Recovery Skips Middle Managers," *Fortune,* 6 Feb. 1984, pp. 112–20; M. Langley, "Many Middle Managers Fight Back as More Firms Trim Work Forces," *Wall Street Journal,* 29 Nov. 1984, p. 37.

45. "Big Business Tries to Imitate the Entrepreneurial Spirit," *Business Week,* 18 Apr. 1983, pp. 84–89.

46. "3M's Aggressive New Consumer Drive," *Business Week,* 16 July 1984.

47. R. M. Kanter, *The Change Masters* (New York: Simon & Schuster, 1983).

48. R. M. Kanter, "Change Masters and the Intricate Architecture of Corporate Culture Change," *Management Review* (Oct. 1983): 18–28; R. M. Kanter, "Superstars and Lone Rangers Rescue Dull Enterprises," *Wall Street Journal,* 23 Jan. 1984, p. 22; F. de Chambeau and E. M. Shays, "Harnessing Entrepreneurial Energy within the Corporation," *Management Review* (Sept. 1984): 17–20; P. F. Drucker, "Our Entrepreneurial Economy," *Harvard Business Review* (Jan./Feb. 1984): 59–64; P. F. Drucker, *Innovation and Entrepreneurship* (New York: Harper & Row, 1985); E. E. Lawler III, "The Strategic Design of Reward Systems," in *Readings in Personnel and Human Resource Management,* 3d ed., ed. R. S. Schuler, S. A. Youngblood, and V. Huber (St. Paul: West, 1987), pp. 253–69; R. S. Schuler, "Fostering and Facilitating Entrepreneurship through Organization Structure and Human Resource Management Practices," *Human Resource Management* (Winter, 1986).

49. S. C. Brandt, *Entrepreneuring in Established Companies* (Homewood, Ill.: Dow Jones-Irwin, 1986); R. A. Burgelman, "Corporate Entrepreneurship and Strategic Management: Insights from a Process Study," *Management Science* (Dec. 1983): 1349–64.

50. "The Speedup in Automation," *Business Week,* 3 Aug. 1981, p. 62.

51. C. Brod, "Managing Technostress: Optimizing the Use of Computing Technology," *Personnel Journal*

(Oct. 1982): 753–57; R. Nardoni, "The Personnel Office of the Future Is Available Today," *Personnel Journal* (Feb. 1982): 132–34. See also P. F. Drucker, "Automation Payoffs Are Real," *Wall Street Journal*, 20 Sept. 1985, p. 26.

52. M. Kanabayashi, "A March of the Robots, Japan's Machines Race Ahead of America's," *Wall Street Journal*, 24 Nov. 1981, p. 1.

53. "Robots Create Changes in the Work Force," *Ann Arbor Business-to-Business* (Oct. 1985): 9.

54. See the entire Sept. 1984 issue of the *Personnel Administrator;* D. L. Tarbania, "Automation in the Office: Users Expand Its Role at All Levels," *AMA Forum* (Nov. 1984): 29–30.

55. T. Rendero, "Want to Boost Managerial Productivity and Cut Costs? Try Automation," *Personnel* (Mar.–Apr. 1981) © 1981 by AMACOM, a division of American Management Associations, pp. 39–40. Reprinted by permission of the publisher.

56. R. S. Schuler and I. C. MacMillan, "Gaining Competitive Advantage through HRM Practices," *Human Resource Management* (Fall 1984): 240–52.

57. R. Pascale, "Fitting New Employees into the Company Culture," *Fortune*, 28 May 1984, pp. 28–40; E. J. McGarrell, Jr., "An Orientation System That Builds Productivity," *Personnel Administrator* (Oct. 1984): 75–85.

58. O. G. Brim and S. Wheeler, *Socialization after Childhood* (New York: Wiley, 1966).

59. H. S. Becker, "Personal Stages in Adult Life," *Sociometry* 27 (1954): 40–53.

60. J. A. Clausen, ed., *Socialization and Society* (Boston: Little, Brown, 1968).

61. E. H. Schein, "Organizational Socialization and the Profession of Management," *Sloan Management Review* 9 (1968): 5.

62. Bureau of National Affairs, "Orientation Goals: Better Learning, Reduced Turnover," *Bulletin to Management,* 9 May 1985, pp. 1–2.

63. M. Lubliner, "Employee Orientation," *Personnel Journal* (Apr. 1978): 207–8; J. P. Wanous, *Organizational Entry* (Reading, Mass.: Addison-Wesley, 1980), pp. 167–97. See also J. Van Maanen and E. H. Schein, "Toward a Theory of Organizational Socialization" in *Research in Organizational Behavior*, vol. 1, ed. B. M. Staw (Greenwich, Conn.: JAI Press, 1979), pp. 209–64; D. Feldman, "The Multiple Socialization of Organizational Members," *Academy of Management Journal* (Sept. 1981): 309–18; P. Popovich and J. Wanous, "The Realistic Job Preview as a Persuasive Communication," *Academy of Management Review* 7 (1982): 570–78; M. R. Louis, "Managing Career Transitions: A Missing Link in Career Development," *Organizational Dynamics* (Spring 1982): 68–78.

64. Lubliner, "Employee Orientation," pp. 207–8.

65. Lubliner, "Employee Orientation," pp. 207–8. Schein, "Organizational Socialization," pp. 1–19.

66. D. Berlew and D. T. Hall, "The Socialization of Managers: Effects of Expectations on Performance," *Administrative Science Quarterly* (Sept. 1966): 207–23.

67. Schein, "Organizational Socialization."

68. J. S. Livingston, "Pygmalion in Management," *Harvard Business Review* (July/Aug. 1969): 81–89.

69. T. A. Mahoney, "The Rearranged Workweek: Evaluations of Different Work Schedules," *California Management Review* (Summer 1978): 31–39; A. R. Cohen and H. Gadon, *Alternative Work Schedules: Integrating Individual and Organizational Needs* (Reading, Mass.: Addison-Wesley, 1978); M. Maurice, *Shift Work* (Geneva, Switzerland: Internal Labor Office, 1975); D. L. Tasto and M. J. Collegan, *Shift Work Practices in the United States* (Washington, D.C.: National Institute for Occupational Safety and Health, 1977); M. Goss, "The Thirty-Hour Work Week," *Management Review* (July 1985): 40–42; S. Zedeck, S. E. Jackson and E. Summers, "Shiftwork Schedules and Their Relationship to Health, Adaptation, Satisfaction, and Turnover Intention," *Academy of Management Journal* (June 1983): 297–310; S. E. Jackson, S. Zedeck, and E. Summers, "Family Life Disruptions: Impact of Job-induced Functional and Emotional Interference," *Academy of Management Journal* (Sept. 1985): 574–86; J. A. Breaugh, "The Twelve-Hour Work Day: Differing Employee Reactions," *Personnel Psychology* (Summer 1983): 277–29; G. L. Staines and J. H. Pleck, "Nonstandard Work Schedules and Family Life," *Journal of Applied Psychology* (August 1984): 509–14.

70. S. A. Coltrin and B. Barendse, "Is Your Organization a Good Candidate for Flextime?" *Personnel Journal* (Sept. 1981): 712–15; L. F. Copperman, F. D. Keast, and D. G. Montgomery, "Old Workers and Part-Time Work Schedules," *Personnel Administrator* (Oct. 1981): 35–38; T. E. Curry, Jr., and D. N. Haerer, "The Positive Impact of Flextime on Employee Relations," *Personnel Administrator* (Feb. 1981): 62–66; P. Farish, "PAIR Potpourri," *Personnel Administrator* (June 1981): 10; D. J. Petersen, "Flextime in the United States: The Lessons of Experience," *Personnel* (Jan.–Feb. 1980): 21–31; D. Stetson, "Work Innovation Improving Morale," *New York Times,* 20 Sept. 1981, p. 53; "Why Flextime Is Spreading," *Business Week,* 23 Feb. 1981, pp. 455–60.

71. R. H. Crowder, Jr., "The Four-Day, Ten-Hour Workweek," *Personnel Journal* (Jan. 1982): 26–28; "A Full-Time Job—Weekends Only," *Business Week,* 15 Oct. 1979, pp. 151–52; R. B. Dunham and D. L. Hawk, "The Four-Day/Forty-Hour Week: Who Wants It?" *Academy of Management Journal* 20 (1977): 644–55; M. D. Fottler, "Employee Acceptance of the Four-Day Workweek," *Academy of Management Journal* 20 (1977): 656–68; J. S. Kim and A. F. Campagna, "Effects of Flextime on Productivity: A Field Experiment in a Public Sector Setting," paper presented at

the National Academy of Management, Detroit, Michigan, 1980; V. Schein, E. Maurer, and J. Novak, "Impact of Flexible Working Hours on Productivity," *Journal of Applied Psychology* 62 (1977): 463–65; R. B. Dunham and J. L. Pierce, "The Design and Evaluation of Alternative Work Schedules," *Personnel Administrator* (Apr. 1983): 67–75; A. R. Cohen and H. Gadon, *Alternative Work Schedules: Integrating Individual and Organizational Needs* (Reading, Mass.: Addison-Wesley, 1978); J. C. Latack and L. W. Foster, "Implementation of Compressed Work Schedules: Participation and Job Redesign as Critical Factors for Employee Acceptance," *Personnel Psychology* (Spring 1985) 75–89.

72. S. J. Mahlin, "Peak-Time Pay for Part-Time Work," *Personnel Journal* (Nov. 1984): 60–65; S. R. Sacco, "Are In-House Temporaries Really an Option?" *Personnel Administrator* (May 1985): 20–24.

73. D. Kroll, "Telecommuting: A Revealing Peek Inside Some of Industry's First Electronic Cottages," *Management Review* (Nov. 1984): 18–23.

74. However, for an example of how QWL programs can be evaluated in dollars and cents, see P. H. Mirvis and E. E. Lawler III, "Measuring the Financial Impact of Employee Attitudes," *Journal of Applied Psychology* 62 (1977): 1–8. See also Chapter 18 of this textbook.

75. C. R. Day, Jr., "Solving the Mystery of Productivity Measurement," *Industry Week*, 26 Jan. 1981, pp. 61–66; J. W. Forrester, "More Productivity Will Not Solve Our Problems," *Business and Society Review* (Spring 1981): 10–19; J. W. Boudreau, "Economic Considerations in Estimating the Utility of Human Resource Productivity Improvement Programs," *Personnel Psychology* (Autumn 1983): 551–65; J. W. Boudreau, "Effects of Employee Flows on Utility Analysis of Human Resource Productivity Improvement Programs," *Journal of Applied Psychology* (Aug. 1983): 396–406.

13

Occupational Safety and Health

Health and Safety in the Workplace

Is it possible for a large corporation with assets totaling $2.2 billion, net worth of $1.2 billion, a very healthy cash flow position and an annual income potential of $150 million to file for bankruptcy under Chapter 11? Yes, and this type of action is occurring with increasing frequency due to a very important problem: Safety and health in the workplace.

The safety and health problem has been reduced continually since 1936, a year in which 35,000 deaths were reported. Most professionals agree that with current technology we can and must continue to reduce occupational safety and health problems. In 1970, at the time the Occupational Safety and Health Act was being formulated, an estimated 14,200 American workers died on the job. 2.2 million suffered disabilities, and another 300,000 to 500,000 suffered from occupationally induced illnesses.

Considerable progress has been made in reducing death, injury and illness at the worksite since the passage of the Occupational Safety and Health Act of 1970, but the progress has been painfully slow and the cost of accidents remains staggering. National Safety Council data for calendar year 1983, 12 years after the enactment of the Act, showed 11,200 work-related accidental deaths, approximately 1.9 million disabling work-related injuries and a total work accident cost of at least $32.1 billion.

In addition to the often intense personal suffering and financial loss to the injured worker and family, worker injuries add greatly to a worker's compensation costs. Employee injuries on or off the job disrupt productivity, increase downtime, disrupt production schedules and add to hiring, scheduling and training costs. Further, the bad press which frequently follows a major accident (and sometimes even a minor one) can seriously impair the image of a firm in the community and on the open market. Today, management is open to scrutiny not only from superiors but also from the work force, competitors, governmental agencies, the public, special interest groups and the media. Literally, there is no place to hide when it comes to employee health-related issues.

Since 1971, the National Institute for Occupational Safety and Health has invested approximately $70 million through its training grant program to help ensure an adequate supply of safety and health professionals needed to protect the American worker. NIOSH has expanded its manpower development activities to extend beyond the traditional training of engineers, physicians, nurses and other occupational safety and health professionals to include education for future managers in specialized areas of occupational safety and health.

Managers who make major resource allocation decisions need to be knowledgeable in areas of safety and health. Many technical safety and health professionals say that safety and health is frequently a "hard sell" item to upper management, despite the fact that such training invariably pays high dividends to the safety-minded manager. One reason for ignoring health and safety-related issues is the American manager's emphasis on short-term profits and the "bottom line." A second reason is the lack of academic exposure to health and safety issues. This lack of preparation often leads to poor decision-making regarding health, safety and security issues. These types of decisions can ultimately result in loss of advantage in a competitive market, litigation and possible bankruptcy.

Source: D. S. Thelan, D. Ledgerwood, and C. F. Walters, "Health and Safety in the Workplace: A New Challenge for Business Schools," pp. 37, 38. Reprinted from the October issue of *Personnel Administrator,* copyright © 1985, the American Society for Personnel Administration, 606 North Washington Street, Alexandria, VA 22314.

The preceding "PHRM in the News" highlights several important aspects associated with occupational safety and health. One is the relationship between the two major federal agencies: the Occupational Safety and Health Administration (OSHA) and the National Institute for Occupational Safety and Health (NIOSH). Both agencies were established by the 1970 Occupational Safety and Health Act. OSHA devises and enforces regulations to protect workers from job-related safety and health hazards. NIOSH conducts scientific research on job safety and health hazards and suggests ways to remove or diminish them.

Another aspect is the tremendous cost in lives and human suffering because of work place accidents and work-related diseases. A third aspect is the large dollar cost to organizations resulting from accidents and diseases. These and other aspects of safety and health are discussed throughout this chapter.

With a mandate to be more cost effective and to play a more significant role in the management of human resources, the personnel and human resource manager can benefit greatly from being concerned with occupational health in organizations. Indeed, many PHRM functions and activities are related to occupational health, and a neglect of occupational health can result in substantial costs for the organization. By focusing on occupational health, the personnel and human resource manager has a great chance to demonstrate another area where PHRM can show its effectiveness. The personnel and human resource manager may want to begin by developing an awareness of occupational health in the organization, with strategies for improvements.[1]

Occupational safety and health refers to the physiological, physical, and sociopsychological conditions of an organization's work force resulting from the work environment. An organization that is effective from an occupational safety and health perspective will have fewer employees suffering from harmful physiological, physical, or sociopsychological conditions than will an organization that is less effective.

Common harmful physiological and physical conditions, the essence of occupational diseases and accidents, include loss of life or limb, cardiovascular diseases, death, various forms of cancer (such as of the lungs), emphysema, and arthritis. This set of conditions also includes leukemia, white-lung disease, brown-lung disease, black-lung disease, sterility, central nervous system damage, and chronic bronchitis.

Common harmful sociopsychological conditions, the essence of occupational stress and a low quality of work life, are dissatisfaction, apathy, withdrawal, projection, tunnel vision, forgetfulness, inner confusion about roles or duties, mistrust of others, vacillation in decision making, inattentiveness, irritability, procrastination, and tendency to become distraught from trifles.

From an occupational safety and health perspective, these conditions are often caused by a poor work environment. OSHA inspections are conducted to protect workers against safety and health hazards in the work environment. New policies regarding OSHA inspections are geared toward making OSHA more effective. They also help spread the apparent responsibility for safety and health in organizations from top management, through line and personnel and human resource managers, all the way to the rank-and-file, blue-collar workers. Safety and health should be the concern of everyone in the organization.[2] However, the top management of the organization often has the formal responsibility for ensuring that employees are aware of health and safety, and that the organization meets federal and state health and safety requirements. Indeed, strong management support and extensive communication by top management are essential if safety and health programs, such as those at DuPont or the Nashua Corporation are to succeed.[3]

In large organizations, those with over two thousand employees, the responsibility often shifts to the PHRM department or line managers.[4] Sometimes a safety director or an industrial engineer directly responsible for safety and health reports to the personnel and human resource manager or the plant or office manager. In most organizations, however, the day-to-day enforcement of safety rules falls into the supervisor's hands. The personnel and human resource manager or safety director then plays the role of assisting the supervisor, often by providing administrative research and advice. Although the PHRM department may rely on experts in safety and health, such as those at NIOSH, or on its own specialized staff, it must also rely on its own understanding of the sources of safety and health in developing strategies to make the work place safer.

Purposes and Importance of Improving Occupational Safety and Health

The importance of improving occupational safety and health rests primarily with the costs of the two sets of harmful conditions described earlier. The purposes of improving safety and health rest with reducing these costs and making the work environment better for employees.

Costs

On an average yearly basis in the United States, as many as 10,000 deaths and 6 million lesser injuries result from **occupational accidents**. On the same basis, as many as 400,000 new incidences of **occupational disease** occur, and as many as 100,000 workers die as a result of occupational diseases.[5] The National Safety Council estimates the annual cost of occupational accidents and diseases at $20 billion and $15 billion, respectively. Furthermore, estimates are that because of the failure of the worker compensation system, payments to victims of job-related disease impose a $4 billion drain on Social Security. Because determining the exact cost of occupational accidents and diseases is elusive, these estimates could be regarded as conservative.[6] Other cost data are shown in the initial "PHRM in the News."

In addition, organizations incur enormous costs associated with **organizational stress** and a **low quality of work life**. For example, alcoholism, often exacerbated by job stress and a low quality of work life, costs organizations and society over $43 billion annually. Of this, $20 billion is attributed to lost productivity and the remainder to the direct costs of insurance, hospitalization, and other medical costs.[7] Although perhaps more difficult to quantify, but just as symptomatic of stress and a low quality of work life, is the worker's lack of psychological meaningfulness and involvement in his or her work and the loss in feeling important as an individual.

Attacking the sources of harmful conditions in the organization is a useful approach. The two general sources are the **physical work environment** and the **sociopsychological work environment**. Harmful conditions in these sources are often associated with a lack of organizational effectiveness, such as loss of productivity, absenteeism, turnover, worker compensation claims, and medical costs. All workers do not respond to the same sources and conditions in the same way, however. What is harmful for one may not be for another. Together, the harmful physiological/physical and sociopsychological conditions, their sources, and their outcomes constitute a model of occupational health and safety in organizations. This model is discussed later in the chapter.

Benefits

If organizations can reduce the rates and severity of their occupational accidents, diseases, and stress and improve the quality of work life for their employees, they will be more effective. Fewer incidences of accidents and diseases, a reduced level of occupational stress, and improved QWL result in (1) more productivity due to fewer lost workdays for absenteeism; (2) more efficiency from workers who are more involved with their jobs; (3) reduced medical and insurance costs; (4) lower worker compensation rates and direct payments because of far fewer claims being filed; (5) greater flexibility and adaptability in the work force as a result of increased participation and feeling of ownership in changes from QWL projects; and (6) better selection ratios because of the increased attractiveness of the organization as a place to work.[8] As a consequence of all these factors, companies can increase their profits substantially:

> DuPont and Procter and Gamble are examples that epitomize how, through safety efforts, corporations can reap enormous savings. In its U.S. plants in 1980, Du-Pont had an annual rate of 0.12 accidents per 100 workers, or one-twenty-third the National Safety Council's average rate for all manufacturers for that year. Had DuPont's record been average, the company would have spent more than $26 million on additional compensation and other costs, or 3.6 percent of its profits. To make up the difference, in view of the company's 5.5 percent net return on sales at the time, DuPont would have had to increase sales by nearly $500 million.[9]

Because the costs and benefits of occupational safety and health are so enormous, organizations are concerned about trying to make improvements in this area. They are also concerned because occupational safety and health activities are extensively related to other PHRM activities.

Relationships Influencing Occupational Safety and Health

Although occupational safety and health have relationships with aspects of the internal and external environments, only the most critical relationships—those with the other PHRM activities—are described here. The set of legal considerations in safety and health, however, is extensive.

Relationships with Other PHRM Activities

Exhibit 13.1 provides a summary of the many relationships that safety and health activities have with other PHRM activities.

Recruitment and Selection.   To the extent that an organization can provide a safe, healthy, and comfortable work environment, it may increase its success in staffing and maintaining the human resource needs of the organization. When organizations have high rates of accidents, particularly fatal ones, they need to recruit more employees. If organizations develop reputations

Aspects and Relationships of Safety and   *Exhibit 13.1*
Health in Organizations

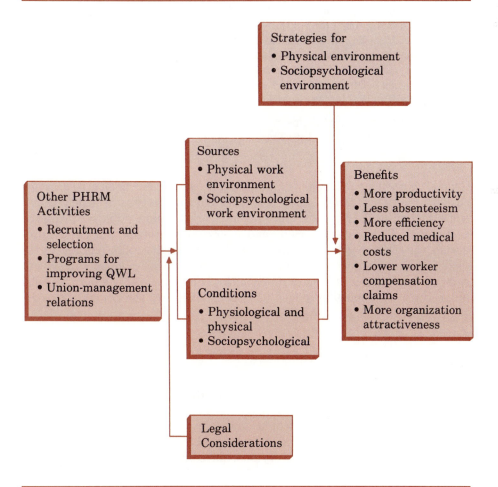

for being unsafe places to work, they will find it more difficult to recruit and select qualified employees.

Programs for Improving QWL.   Since a low QWL is associated with several costly sociopsychological conditions, programs for improving QWL are directly associated with occupational safety and health. Because QWL often depends upon the employees' perceptions of organizational policies and structures, many American companies have commissioned organizational surveys to measure the existing quality of work life. More informal mechanisms to enhance communications are also being implemented. Informal two-way communications, especially through methods like a safety committee or a quality circle, do much to create a concern for improving safety and health and to develop strategies to improve the work environment. As described in Chapter 12, the ways in which jobs are physically designed have an important impact on people's performance. Ergonomic problems, stemming from a failure to properly match people and jobs, also impact work place accidents:

> Most workplace accidents are the result of ergonomic problems stemming from the "most drastic sort of man/machine mismatch," asserts C. G. Drury, an industrial engineering consultant to the National Institute for Occupational Safety and Health. Addressing a NIOSH seminar in Cincinnati, Drury maintains that "changing the nonhuman parts" of an industrial system is a better way to achieve workplace safety than trying to alter worker behavior. For workers under stress, he notes, "the natural way" to do a task is the way they've always done it, regardless of any training they've received to the contrary.[10]

Matching the physical abilities of individuals with those required by the job may mean redesigning the job. These options are described later in the chapter.

Union-Management Relations.   Occupational safety and health is a major concern of unions. Many union contracts have some type of safety provisions, including the right to refuse unsafe work, a union-employer pledge of cooperation in the development and operation of safety and health programs, the right to grieve unsafe work, the right to discipline employees for violating safety rules, regulation of crew size, posting rules of safety, and right of inspection by a joint or union safety committee.[11] The sanctity of the union contract regarding safety has been upheld by the courts (*Irvin H. Whitehouse & Sons Co.* v. *NLRB*, 1981).

Legal Considerations of Occupational Safety and Health

The legal considerations of occupational safety and health can be divided into three major categories: the Occupational Safety and Health Administration, worker compensation programs, and common-law doctrine of torts.

Occupational Safety and Health
Administration (OSHA)

The federal government's main response to the issue of safety and health in the work place has been the Occupational Safety and Health Act of 1970, which prescribes inspections of organizations, regardless of size, for safety and health hazards; record keeping and reporting by employers; investigations of accidents and allegations of hazards; communicating hazards to employees; and establishing standards.[12] Although this act was well-intentioned, it was soon perceived as emphasizing minor safety matters while overlooking major ones and, even more vital, as failing to focus attention on health standards.[13] This perception developed around one of the three organizations established by the act: the Occupational Safety and Health Administration (OSHA). The other two organizations are NIOSH, mentioned earlier, and the Occupational Safety and Health Review Commission (OSHRC). The OSHRC plays the role of reviewer of appeals by organizations that have received citations from OSHA inspectors for alleged safety and health violations.

Inspection.   OSHA was given responsibility for establishing and enforcing occupational safety and health standards, and for inspecting and issuing citations to organizations that violate these standards. But the United States has over 5 million organizations, and the number of OSHA inspectors is limited. Thus, the general agreement is that the approximately 65,000 inspections that OSHA makes annually, affecting less than 2 percent of the 5 million work places, must be aimed more specifically at frequent and flagrant violations of OSHA rules. As a consequence, OSHA inspections now often include the following:

- A targeting system so that companies with injury rates at a certain low level (e.g., six lost workday cases per one hundred workers) can be exempt from inspection
- Fewer immediate inspections in response to worker complaints unless OSHA perceives an imminent danger, and then only if the problem is not corrected after written OSHA notification to the company
- Exemption from inspections for companies with in-plant worker-management committees that respond to worker complaints, conduct monthly inspections, and ensure that hazards are eliminated.[14]

These provisions significantly alter the previous legal privilege of OSHA to conduct inspections but are consistent with *Marshall* v. *Barlow's.* Previously, OSHA inspectors were given the right to enter at reasonable times any factory, plant, establishment, construction site, or other area, work place, or environment where work is performed. However, this inspection mandate was changed by the Supreme Court's decision in *Marshall* v. *Barlow's,* handed down in May 1978. According to this decision, employers are not required to let OSHA inspectors enter their premises unless the inspectors have search warrants.[15] This decision has been clarified and supported by subsequent court decisions (*Weyerhaeuser Co.* v. *Marshall*, 1978; *Cerro Metal Products* v. *Marshall*, 1978; and *Marshall* v. *Gibson's Products*, 1978).

Another court decision also influenced OSHA inspections. In *Chamber of Commerce* v. *OSHA,* the U.S. Court of Appeals for the District of Columbia Circuit struck down the walk-around pay requirement. The requirement had made it mandatory for companies to pay the wages of employees during the time they spent accompanying an OSHA inspector on the tour of the work site.

Record Keeping.   Regardless of whether organizations are inspected, they are required to keep safety and health records so that OSHA can compile accurate statistics on work injuries and illnesses. These include all disabling, serious, or significant injuries and illnesses, whether or not involving loss of time from work, other than minor injuries requiring only first aid treatment and which do not involve medical treatment, loss of consciousness, restriction of work or motion, or transfer to another job.[16] Exhibit 13.2 shows OSHA's guidelines for determining what must be recorded. Falsification of

Exhibit 13.2   *OSHA Guidelines to Recording Cases*

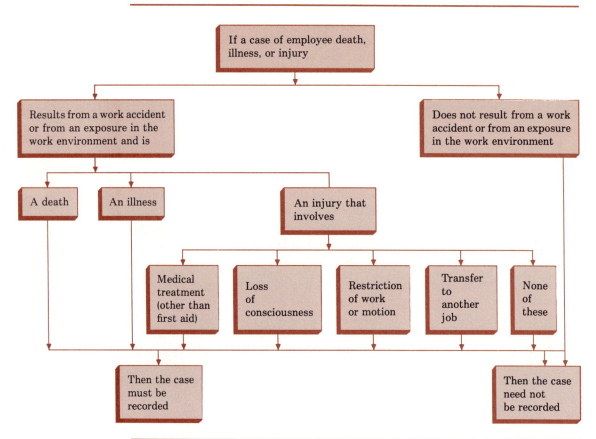

records results in a fine of up to $10,000, imprisonment for up to six months, or both.

Communicating Health and Safety Information.   In addition to keeping records, organizations must now also show or give to employees, their designated representatives, and OSHA, their on-the-job medical records. This is provided for by the Access to Employee Exposure and Medical Records regulation of 1980. This regulation also requires employers to provide access to records that indicate measurement of employee exposure to toxic substances.[17] The employee's right to know has been further strengthened by the Hazard Communication Standard that went into effect in 1986.[18] This standard applies only to manufacturing companies. Meanwhile, some state laws require companies to label chemicals and identify their potential health threats.[19]

Establishing Standards.   As with inspections, the way in which OSHA establishes standards has been changing. It has also been affected by several Supreme Court decisions. Previously, OSHA could set **no-risks** standards. That is, OSHA could tell companies that they had to make a work environment absolutely free of any risk from employee exposure. Now, however, OSHA has the burden of making a threshold assessment that an existing exposure level poses **significant risks** to employee health before it can force companies to adhere to the more stringent no-risk standard (*Industrial Union Department, AFL-CIO* v. *American Petroleum Institute,* 1980). This decision is also referred to as the **benzene standard.** However, if significant risks from exposure are shown to exist, OSHA can demand compliance regardless of the costs (*United Steelworkers of America, AFL-CIO* v. *Marshall,* 1980). This court decision is also known as the **lead standard,** which reaffirmed the same type of decision resulting in the **cotton standard** (*American Textile Institute* v. *Donovan,* 1981).[20]

Whereas OSHA was established to provide workers protection against accidents and diseases, worker compensation was established to provide financial aid for those unable to work because of accidents and diseases.

Worker Compensation Programs

For years worker compensation awards were granted only to workers unable to work because of physical injury or damage (i.e., due to accidents and diseases). Since 1955, however, court decisions have either caused or enticed fifteen states to allow worker compensation payments in job-related cases of anxiety, depression, and mental disorders (essentially from organizational stress and low quality of work life) severe enough to be disabling.[21] These decisions have moved occupational health and safety into a larger arena of concern (i.e., the physical *and* the sociopsychological work environment and for physical *and* sociopsychological manifestation of harm or damage from the work environment). Generally the term *stress* is used to capture the essence of sociopsychological manifestation of harm.[22]

In 1955, the Texas Supreme Court charted this new direction in worker compensation claims by stating that an employee who became terrified and highly anxious and unable to work because of a job-related accident had a compensable claim even though he had no physical injury (*Bailey* v. *American General Insurance Company,* 1955). In a more recent case (*James* v. *State Accident Insurance Fund,* 1980), an Oregon court ruled in favor of a worker's claim for compensation for inability to work due to job stress resulting from conflicting work assignments.

Although coverage for worker injury caused by the physical and sociopsychological environment may be consistent with the intention of worker compensation, inclusion of nonphysical or mental injury claims is putting financial strains on worker compensation funds in many states. A more recent trend is for workers to go outside the state-run worker compensation programs that provide only limited disability income, to seek much larger settlements by suing employers.[23]

Common-Law Doctrine of Torts

Employees can obtain damage awards by suing employers; however, employees must demonstrate that the employer engaged in reckless or intentional infliction designed to degrade or humiliate. Although cases of such a type have been successfully brought against employers (*Alcorn* v. *Ambro Engineering,* 1970; and *Contereras* v. *Crown Zellerbach Corporation,* 1977), they appear to be the exception. Nevertheless, with these precedents established, additional cases against employers are likely. This is particularly likely for cases charging sexual harassment, described in the next chapter.

It is important for organizations to keep all of these legal considerations in mind when deciding on strategies for improvement and in locating the sources of safety and health.

Hazards to Occupational Safety and Health

As Exhibit 13.3 shows, two major aspects of the work environment influence occupational safety and health: the physical and the sociopsychological. Within each of these two aspects are two more sources of health and safety. For the physical, it is occupational diseases and accidents; for the sociopsychological, it is QWL and stress. Though both major aspects of the work environment influence the indicators of poor health and safety, traditionally only the physical environment has received the attention of most companies and OSHA. Increasingly, however, both OSHA (especially through the efforts of NIOSH) and companies are admitting to the impact of the sociopsychological environment on indicators of poor health and safety.[24] Consequently, efforts to improve occupational health and safety must include strategies for both aspects of the work environment. Developing effective strategies depends on knowing about each of the four sources of safety and health in organizations.

Model of Occupational Safety and Health
in Organizations

Exhibit 13.3

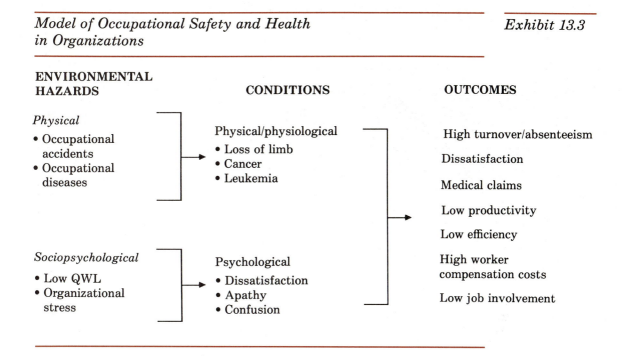

ENVIRONMENTAL
HAZARDS

Physical
- Occupational
  accidents
- Occupational
  diseases

Sociopsychological
- Low QWL
- Organizational
  stress

CONDITIONS

Physical/physiological
- Loss of limb
- Cancer
- Leukemia

Psychological
- Dissatisfaction
- Apathy
- Confusion

OUTCOMES

High turnover/absenteeism

Dissatisfaction

Medical claims

Low productivity

Low efficiency

High worker
compensation costs

Low job involvement

Factors Affecting Occupational Accidents

Certain organizations, and even certain departments within the same organization, have higher accident rates than others. Several factors explain this difference.

Organizational Qualities.   Accident rates vary substantially by industry. For example, firms in the construction and manufacturing industries have higher incidence rates than firms in services, finance, insurance, and real estate. Small and large organizations (those with fewer than one hundred employees and more than one thousand, respectively) have lower incidence rates than medium-sized organizations. This may be because supervisors in small organizations are better able to detect safety hazards and prevent accidents than those in medium-sized organizations. And larger organizations have more resources than medium-sized organizations to hire staff specialists who can devote all their efforts to safety and accidents.[25]

Although data on incidence, severity, and frequency rates by type of industry and size of organization are important, these rates often veil differences between same-size organizations in the same industry. For example, DuPont's accident rate is twenty-eight times lower than the chemical industry and sixty-four times lower than industry as a whole. These differences can partly be attributed to the effectiveness of DuPont's safety programs.[26]

Safety Programs.   Organizations differ in the extent to which they develop techniques, programs, and activities to promote safety and prevent accidents. The effectiveness of these techniques and programs varies by the type of industry and size of organization. For example, in large chemical firms, greater expenditures for off-the-job safety, medical facilities and staff, safety training, and additional supervision are associated with decreased work-injury costs.[27] On the other hand, work-injury costs have actually increased with additional expenditures for correction of unsafe physical conditions for safety staff, for employee orientation, and for safety records if these expenditures are applied ineffectively. As a result, some organizations in the same industry may have higher injury costs per employee than others. This is clearly illustrated by the DuPont statistics cited earlier. Those organizations that have no safety programs generally have higher injury costs than similar companies that have implemented such programs.

The Unsafe Employee?   Although organizational factors play an important role in occupational safety, many experts point to employees as the cause of accidents. Accident rates are affected by the behavior of the person, the degree of hazard in the work environment, pure chance, and the badly informed ambivalent, or frightened employee. The following "PHRM in the News" illustrates the latter source.

The degree to which people contribute to accidents is often regarded as an indicator or proneness to accidents. Accident proneness cannot be considered as a stable set of personal traits that always contribute to accidents; besides, traits that contribute to accidents may differ from one situation to another, since accidents happen in a great variety of ways. Nevertheless, certain psychological and physical characteristics make some people more susceptible to accidents than others. For example, employees who are emotionally low have more accidents than those who are emotionally high, and employees who have had fewer accidents have been found to be more optimistic, trusting, and concerned for others than those who have had more accidents.[28] Employees under greater stress are likely to have more accidents than those under less stress, and those with better vision have fewer accidents than those with poorer vision. Older workers are less likely to be hurt than younger workers.[29] People who are quicker in recognizing differences in visual patterns than in making muscular manipulations are less likely to have accidents than those who are faster in muscular manipulation. Many psychological conditions that may be related to accident proneness—for instance, hostility and emotional immaturity—may be temporary states. Thus, they are difficult to detect until after at least one accident.

Since none of these characteristics is related to accidents in all work environments, and since none is ever-present in employees, selecting and screening job applicants on the basis of accident proneness is difficult. Even if it were possible, however, aspects of the organization, such as its size, technology, management attitudes, safety programs, and quality of supervision, would still be important sources of accidents for those job applicants who are actually hired.

Workers Are Often a Hazard to Themselves

After twelve years working in a Florida battery recycling plant, George Mount has lead coursing through his bloodstream. Doctors have told him that, at age thirty-two, he has serious kidney damage from exposure to the poison.

But when the Federal Occupational Safety and Health Administration ordered him moved to a safer job, Mount did more than resist; he volunteered to participate in a controversial experiment that would have kept him near the vats of molten lead. "Sure, I'm worried about my health," Mount said. "But what am I supposed to do? Just give up everything I worked for and put into that company?"

That attitude is not unique. Advocates of workplace safety sometimes find their toughest enemy is not a malevolent employer or lax regulatory agency, but an ambivalent, frightened, or badly informed work force. Dorothy Nelkin, a Cornell University sociologist whose book, *Workers at Risk* (University of Chicago Press), explores employees' attitudes toward safety said workers often feel confused and powerless when confronted with the issue. They are easily reassured by company experts, she said, especially if the experts suggest that costly safety measures could mean layoffs.

John Miles, OSHA's director of field operations, said workers are often hostile to hard hats and other protective equipment they find uncomfortable to wear. Sheldon W. Samuels, safety director for the Industrial Unions Department of the A.F.L.-C.I.O., noted, too, that where risks are long term, workers are tempted to gamble.

"Workers know the chances they won't get cancer or lung disease are greater than the chances of getting it," he explained. "They say it's not going to

happen to me, and in most cases, that's true." That is why many health experts prefer more expensive engineering controls such as ventilation systems, which automatically clean an area, to apparatus such as respirators, which must be worn to be effective.

The lesson seems to be that employee education is at least as important as Government regulation when it comes to workplace safety. Yet, Congress and the Reagan Administration have cut OSHA's safety training grants from $13.9 million in 1981 to $6.8 million— and at a time when economic uncertainty and technological complexity have made employees particularly ambivalent about safety measures.

Two recent examples involve companies seeking waivers from Federal rules so they can use workers in safety experiments. Both have been cited as indictments of OSHA regulators, who endorsed the experiments and justified their approval in part by saying the workers did not mind being test subjects.

One case is George Mount's. When a check-up found that the level of lead in his blood exceeded Federal standards, OSHA rules required that he be moved from his job supervising lead refining vats to a risk-free area. The non-union employer, Gulf Coast Lead, said it considered Mount indispensible. Apparently, so did Mount, who was the company's strongest ally when it sought its waiver. OSHA acceded to the exemption and helped design an experiment whereby Mount would wear a respirator. The experiment began in April. It was canceled a month later when a medical examination detected his kidney condition.

Mount now does chores at a company-owned apartment complex, a job he considers menial. It also lacks the pay bonuses to which he is accustomed. He may return to his old job if his blood lead count drops below Federal standards.

Meanwhile, Mount said, he resents the company for putting him at risk, OSHA for upsetting his life, and both for keeping him in the dark about the risks of lead and the ramifications of his kidney ailment.

In another case, an experiment proposed by Dan River involves the theory that a bacterium growing in cotton, and not cotton dust, causes byssinosis, or brown lung disease. Instead of installing $7.5 million worth of ventilating equipment in one of its Virginia textile mills, as required by Federal safety rules, the company wants workers to wear respiratory masks.

With OSHA's blessing, Virginia officials have granted the company a temporary waiver, permitting blood tests on about twenty workers. The state will soon decide whether to allow the respirator experiment.

The Dan River proposal has met with protests from scientists, national union officials and newspaper editorials, but silence from Local 248 of the United Textile Workers of America. The U.T.W.A. is a small union with a reputation for timidity. In Danville, where Dan River is the dominant employer, few of the 6,500 company employees pay union dues. It came as no surprise, then, that when the company proposed the byssinosis experiment, the union accepted assurances that workers would not be endangered. Only under prodding from state and national union officials has it expressed some misgivings. Kim Meeks, the local's business agent, said the several hundred affected workers have also been silent. "The key to this thing is they haven't been explained to and don't know what this is all about," Meeks said. Besides, "these people have been pretty much subject to the proposition that, well, if we get too much static here we'll just close this little plant up."

Meeks said that if workers at the textile plant did complain, it would very likely be about wearing the heavy respirators. And that, according to Meeks, is why Dan River officials have been "as liberal as they can be" about not forcing workers to wear the devices.

Source: B. Keller, "Workers Are Often a Hazard to Themselves," *New York Times,* 8 July 1984. Copyright © 1984/85 by The New York Times Company. Reprinted by permission.

Factors Affecting Occupational Diseases

The potential sources of work-related diseases are as distressingly varied as the ways they affect the human organism:

> Typical health hazards include toxic and carcinogenic chemicals and dust, often in combination with noise, heat, and other forms of stress. Other health hazards include physical and biological agents. The interaction of health hazards and the human organism can occur either through the senses, by absorption through the skin, by intake into the digestive tract via the mouth, or by inhalation into the lungs.[30]

Ten major health hazards contributing to worker diseases are arsenic, asbestos, benzene, bischloromethylether (BCME), coal dust, coke-oven emissions, cotton dust, lead, radiation, and vinyl chloride.

Categories of Occupational Diseases.   The fastest-growing category of occupational disease includes illnesses of the respiratory system. "Chronic bronchitis and emphysema are the fastest growing diseases in the country, doubling every five years since World War II, and [they] account for the second highest number of disabilities, under Social Security."[31] Cancer, however, tends to receive the most attention, since it is a leading cause of death in the United States (second after heart disease). Many of the known causes of cancer are physical and chemical agents in the environment. And because physical and chemical agents are theoretically more controllable than human behavior, OSHA places emphasis upon eliminating them from the work place.[32]

OSHA's emphasis on health is not aimed solely at eliminating cancer and respiratory diseases, however. OSHA is concerned with all seven categories of occupational diseases and illnesses about which employers are required to keep records:

- Occupation-related skin diseases and disorders
- Dust diseases of the lungs
- Respiratory conditions due to toxic agents
- Poisoning (systemic effects of toxic materials)
- Disorders due to physical agents
- Disorders associated with repeated trauma
- All other occupational illnesses[33]

Occupational Groups at Risk. Miners, construction and transportation workers, and blue-collar and lower-level supervisory personnel in manufacturing industries experience the bulk of both occupational disease and injury. The least safe occupations are fire fighting, mining, and law enforcement.[34] Large numbers of petrochemical and oil refinery workers, dye users, textile workers, plastic-industry workers, painters, and industrial chemical workers are also particularly susceptible to some of the ten most dangerous health hazards. Interestingly, skin diseases are the most common of all reported occupational diseases, the group most affected being leather workers.[35]

Occupational diseases are not exclusive to the blue-collar workers and manufacturing industries. The "cushy office job" has evolved into a veritable nightmare of physical and psychological ills for white-collar workers in the increasingly growing service industries. Among the common ailments are varicose veins, bad backs, deteriorating eyesight, migraine headaches, hypertension, coronary heart disorders, and respiratory and digestive problems. The causes of these ailments in an office environment include the following:

- Too much noise
- Interior air pollutants such as cigarette smoke and chemical fumes—for example, from the copy machine
- Uncomfortable chairs
- Poor office design
- Chemically treated paper
- New office technology such as video display terminals[36]

Dentists are routinely exposed to radiation, mercury, and anesthetics, and cosmetologists suffer from high rates of cancer and respiratory and cardiac diseases connected with their frequent use of chemicals.

Factors Affecting Low Quality of Work Life

For many workers, a low quality of work life is associated with conditions in the organization that fail to satisfy important preferences and interests, such as feelings or senses of responsibility, challenge, meaningfulness, self-control, recognition, achievement, fairness or justice, security, and certainty.[37]

Some of the conditions that exist in organizations that lead to these preferences and interests not being satisfied include (1) jobs with low significance, variety, identity, autonomy, and feedback (see Chapter 12 for a discussion of these); (2) minimal involvement of employees in decision making and a great deal of one-way communicating with employees; (3) pay systems not based on performance or based on performance that is not objectively measured or under the control of the employee; (4) supervisors, job descriptions, and organizational policies that fail to convey to the employee what's expected and what's rewarded; (5) personnel and human resource policies and practices that are discriminatory and of low validity; and (6) employment conditions that may only be temporary or where employees are dismissed at will (employee rights don't exist).

Many conditions in organizations are associated with low quality of work life. The same is true with organizational stress. Remember, however, that a condition associated with stress or low QWL for one individual may not be so associated for another, because of differing preferences and interests and differing perceptions of the degree of uncertainty.[38]

Sources of Organizational Stress

As Exhibit 13.4 shows, many sources of stress exist in organizations (organizational stressors).[39] Only the more prevalent ones are described here.

The Four S's.   The four S's that are stressful for many employees are (1) supervisor, (2) salary, (3) security, and (4) safety.[40]

The two major stressors that employees associate with the supervisor are petty work rules and relentless pressure for more production. Both deny workers fulfillment of the needs to control the work situation and to be recognized and accepted.

Salary is a stressor when it is perceived as being given unfairly. Many blue-collar workers believe that they are underpaid relative to their white-collar counterparts in the office. Teachers think they are underpaid relative to people with similar education who work in private industry.[41]

Employees experience stress when they are unsure whether they will have their jobs next week, next month, or even next day. For many employees, lack of job security is even more stressful than jobs that are generally unsafe. At least the employees know the jobs are unsafe; with a lack of job security, the employees are always in a state of uncertainty.

Organizational Stressors   *Exhibit 13.4*

Roles   **Job Qualities**
Low role awareness   Quantitative overload/underload
Role conflict   Qualitative overload/underload
Too little management support   Time pressures
Middle-management positions   Responsibility for things/people
                                             Work pace
                                             Lack of security
Relationships
Relationships with supervisors   **Organizational Structure**
Relationships with subordinates   Lack of participation
Relationships with colleagues   No sense of belonging
Inability to delegate   Poor communications
                                             Restrictions on behavior
Physical Environment   Lack of opportunity
Temperature, noise, lights   Inequality in pay and performance evaluation
Spatial arrangements   Work hours
Crowding
Lack of privacy
Lack of safety

Change
Organizational change
Individual change

Source: Adapted from C. L. Cooper and J. Marshall,
"Occupational Sources of Stress: A Review of the Literature
Relating to Coronary Heart Disease and Mental Ill Health,"
Journal of Occupational Psychology 49 (1976): 12.

Organizational Change.   Changes made by organizations are often stressful, because usually they involve something important and are accompanied by uncertainty. Many changes are made without advance warning. Although rumors often circulate that a change is coming, the exact nature of the change is left to speculation. People become concerned about whether the change will affect them, perhaps by displacing them or by causing them to be transferred. The result is that the uncertainty surrounding a change yet to come causes many employees to suffer stress symptoms.

Work Pace.   Work pacing, particularly who or what controls the pace of the work, is an important potential stressor in organizations. Machine pacing gives control over the speed of the operation and the work output to something other than the individual. Employee pacing gives the individual control of the operations. The effects of machine pacing are severe, since the individual is unable to satisfy a crucial need for control of the situation. Workers on machine-paced jobs reportedly feel exhausted at the end of the shift and are unable to relax soon after work because of increased adrenaline secretion on the job.[42] In a study of twenty-three white- and blue-collar occupations, assembly workers reported the highest level of severe stress symptoms.

Work Overload.   Although some employees complain about not having enough to do, others have far too much.[43] Some have so much to do, that the work load exceeds their abilities and capacities:

> Employees in high-stress jobs should be compensated for stress-related disabilities, according to the Rhode Island Supreme Court.
>
> The high court has ruled that the *Pawtucket Evening Times* must compensate the widow of one of its sports writers who died after covering a football game in 1978. He died of a cerebral hemorrhage. The widow of Edward Mulcahey sued the paper, saying job stress aggravated his high blood pressure and diabetes because of the odd hours he worked and the deadlines he was under.[44]

Physical Environment.   Although office automation (discussed in Chapter 12) is a way to improve productivity, it has its stress-related drawbacks. One aspect of office automation with a specific stress-related drawback is the video display terminal (VDT). Currently, the findings are not complete on just how serious an effect VDT screens have on workers, although countries such as Sweden and Norway have taken more steps to deal with VDTs than has the United States. Nevertheless, NIOSH is gathering data on VDTs. Other aspects of the work environment associated with stress are crowding, lack of privacy, and lack of control over being able to change aspects of the environment (e.g., to move the desk or chairs or even to hang pictures in a work area in an effort to personalize it).[45]

Job Burnout.   A special type of organizational stress is called **job burnout**. This stress condition happens when people work in situations in which they have little control over the quality of their performance but feel personally responsible for their success or lack of it. People most susceptible to burnout include police officers, nurses, social workers, and teachers. When people begin to show burnout, they reveal three symptoms: (1) emotional exhaustion, (2) depersonalization, and (3) a sense of low personal accomplishment. Since this condition benefits neither the individual nor the organization, many programs have been designed to help people deal with burnout.[46]

Based on this existing but limited knowledge of the etiology of occupational accidents and diseases, low QWL, and occupational stress, strategies for making improvements in occupational safety and health can be suggested.

Occupational Safety and Health Strategies for Improvement

To improve the occupational health of an organization's work force, the sources of the harmful conditions must be identified. Based on the sources, strategies for improving an organization's occupational safety and health ratings can be developed. Then, to evaluate the success of the strategies, the occupational safety and health rating before a strategy was implemented must be compared with the ratings after the strategy has been in effect. Only by doing this can organizations determine whether their strategies are effective. Organizations should know how to compute occupational safety and health ratings and should be aware of the possible strategies to use. Exhibit 13.5 shows a summary of these strategies as well as the sources of occupational safety and health.

Strategies for Improving Occupational Safety and Health in the Physical Work Environment

Common to improving both accidents and diseases in the physical work environment is the use of records. These records can be used to assess where the organization is regarding current incidences of accidents and diseases, in essence forming a baseline against which to compare and evaluate other specific strategies for work place improvements. Since the process of gathering these data creates an awareness of the safety and health problems, it could be regarded as a strategy for work place improvements as well as a process that helps determine the effectiveness of other strategies.[47] The process of establishing safety and health rates is described first, and then separate strategies for improving accident and disease conditions are presented.

Safety and Health Rates.   Safety and health rates are described in frequency, severity, and incidence. OSHA requires organizations to maintain records of the incidence of accidents and disease (illness) for comparison purposes; many organizations also maintain frequency and severity records of accidents and illnesses. Exhibit 13.2 is an OSHA guide to determining what constitutes an accident or illness that must be recorded. These procedures are not only designed to measure poor health and safety from the physical environment. They can also be adapted to be used for the sociopsychological environment. Since PHRM is generally responsible for safety and health, PHRM must know how to compute safety and health rates.

Summary of Sources and Strategies for Occupational Safety and Health

Exhibit 13.5

Physical Work Environment

Occupational accidents	Redesigning the work environment
	Setting goals and objectives
	Establishing safety committees
	Training
	Providing financial incentives
Occupational diseases	Measuring the work environment
	Setting goals and objectives

Sociopsychological Work Environment

Quality of work life	Redesigning jobs
	Increasing participation in decision making
Organizational stress	Establishing organizational stress programs
	Establishing individual stress strategies

The **incidence rate** is most explicit in combining both illnesses and injuries, as shown by this formula:

$$\text{Incidence rate} = \frac{\text{Number of recordable injuries and illnesses} \times 1 \text{ million}}{\text{Number of employee exposure hours}}$$

Suppose an organization had 10 recorded injuries and illnesses and 500 employees. To get the number of exposure hours, it would multiply the number of employees by 40 hours and by 50 work weeks: $500 \times 40 \times 50 = 1$ million. In this case, the incidence rate would be 10.

The **severity rate** reflects the hours actually lost due to injury or illness. It recognizes that not all injuries and illnesses are equal. Four categories of injuries and illnesses have been established: deaths, permanent total disabilities, permanent partial disabilities, and temporary total disabilities. OSHA assigned each category a specific number of hours to be charged against an organization. The severity rate is calculated by this formula:

$$\text{Severity rate} = \frac{\text{Total hours charged} \times 1 \text{ million}}{\text{Number of employee hours worked}}$$

An organization with the same number of injuries and illnesses as another but with more deaths would have a higher severity rate. However, because OSHA decided the assignment of hours charged for each type of accident and illness was arbitrary, it dropped the idea of using a severity rate.

The **frequency rate** is similar to the incidence rate except that it reflects the number of injuries and illnesses per million hours worked rather than per year:

$$\text{Frequency rate} = \frac{\text{Number of disabling injuries} \times 1 \text{ million}}{\text{Number of employee hours worked}}$$

Occupational Accidents.   This aspect of the physical work environment describes that most closely associated with immediate physical injury to workers. Such injuries include minor cuts and sprains as well as loss of limb or even life.

Designing the work environment to make accidents difficult is perhaps the best way to prevent accidents and increase safety. Among the safety features that can be designed into the physical environment are guards on machines, handrails in stairways, safety goggles and helmets, warning lights, self-correcting mechanisms, and automatic shutoffs. The extent to which these features will actually reduce accidents depends on employee acceptance and use. For example, eye injuries will be reduced by the availability of safety goggles only if employees wear the goggles correctly. The effectiveness of any safety regulation depends on how the regulation is implemented and whether there is a conflict in complying with it. If employees are involved in the decision to make some physical change to improve safety, they are more likely to accept the decision than if they are not part of the decision-making process.

Another way of altering the work environment to improve safety is to make the job itself more comfortable and less fatiguing. This approach is generally referred to as **ergonomics.** Ergonomics considers changes in the job environment in conjunction with the physical and physiological capabilities and limitations of the employees. As a result, employees are less likely to make mistakes due to fatigue and tiredness.[48] Such changes can often be initiated by an ergonomic audit. According to Drury, a noted safety expert,:

> Most companies can upgrade job safety, he says, by initiating an ergonomic audit system that focuses not only on medical records and the workplace as a whole, but also on the productivity and workings of individual departments. Such audits can point the way toward "fairly small changes" that could yield big improvements in job safety, he notes. "When a task demands more than human capabilities can provide, if even for a moment, an accident results," Drury stresses, adding that 50 percent of workplace safety/productivity problems "should be able to be cured on the spot with minimal adjustments" keyed to human capabilities. As an example, he points out that an ergonomic study in a large computer company resulted in the firm's making changes in its employees' seating, lighting, and work benches. Within a year, the changes earned back 4.3 times their cost through increased productivity and savings. They also led to a drop in the number of rejected components from 4 percent to 2 percent, the elimination of repetitive trauma injuries, and a nearly 20 percent boost in the number of workers expressing satisfaction with their jobs.[49]

Whereas ergonomics focuses on the physical and physiological, another approach focuses on the psychological. Job redesign, although not aimed primarily at accident prevention, attempts to increase employee motivation and reduce boredom. The result may be increased alertness and fewer accidents.

Several people-oriented responses to accidents can be made by the personnel department, by supervisors and managers, and by both groups working together. One response that is done by both groups is the recording of accidents. These records can highlight the sources of accidents and their severity and frequency. This information can then be used in the selection of safety strategies and the evaluation of their success. Accident rates determined from these records can be compared with the rates in other organizations, and such a study may point out more effective safety strategies to the organization with the higher rate.

Another strategy for accident prevention is the use of the **safety committee.** The personnel department can serve as the coordinator of a committee composed of several employee representatives. Where unions exist, the committees should have union representation as well. Often organizations have several safety committees at the department level for implementation and administration purposes and one larger committee at the organizational level for the purpose of policy formulation.

The PHRM department can be instrumental in accident prevention by assisting the supervisors in their training efforts and by implementing safety motivation programs, such as contests and communications. Many organizations display signs indicating the number of days or hours worked without an accident, or display posters that read "Safety First." In safety contests, prizes or awards are given to individuals or departments with the best safety record. These programs seem to work best when employees are already safety conscious and when physical conditions of the work environment provide no extreme safety hazards.[50] The following "PHRM in the News" illustrates the benefits of such efforts.

Implementing programs, maintaining records of accidents, and providing feedback to employees can also increase safety. Many organizations have set up management-by-objectives programs to deal with occupational health. The five basic steps of these programs are as follows:

- Awareness and recognition of the hazards of existing harmful conditions. This awareness and recognition can be obtained from the personnel records.

- Based on the personnel records, evaluation of the severity and risk of these hazards can be accomplished.

- Formulation and implementation of appropriate programs to control, prevent, or reduce the possibilities of accidents and setting objectives regarding reduction of accidents.

- After hazardous situations are identified, a system for objectively assessing improvements and giving positive feedback for correct safety procedures needs to be established.

- Monitoring and evaluating the progress of programs against stated goals and objectives and making revisions in the programs as needed.[51]

Although the previous steps for improvement can be successful, they are all people-oriented strategies. One that improves conditions but is non-people-oriented is the use of robots. In many cases, robots can be used to replace employees in dangerous situations. The use of robots, however, can also be a source of employee accidents.[52]

Occupational Diseases.   More harmful and costly to organizations and employees than occupational accidents are occupational diseases. Because the casual relationship between the physical environment and occupational diseases is often far more subtle, developing strategies to reduce their incidence is generally more difficult.[53] Nevertheless, the following strategies can be suggested:

- Record keeping
- Setting objectives
- Recognition
- Educational programs

Organizational approaches to health hazards are often determined by OSHA standards and requirements, unless an organization chooses to ignore them. One OSHA requirement is that organizations measure the chemicals in the work environment and keep records on these measurements. The records must include the date, number of samples taken, length of period over which the sampling was done, procedure used, analytical method, the employees' names, Social Security numbers, job classifications, where the employees work in the organization, and the protective equipment used. Often a physician is involved in the process of gathering this information, but the responsibility for having the information lies with the organization.

Safety Tips from the Pros

Employers should consider adopting a safety incentives program "not only because it works but because it reduces accidents, absenteeism, and workers' compensation costs, and increases productivity," according to speakers at the 64th annual Massachusetts Safety and Health Conference, which was held in Boxborough, Mass., and covered by BNA.

Incentive ideas

Augurias G. Manomaitis, safety director for the Nashua Corporation in Nashua, N.H., cites his company's "safety work order system" as an example of a safety incentive program that works. Under the system, any employee can make out a safety work order that ensures prompt corrective action on any procedure or equipment believed to be hazardous. The goal at each of the locations is to make that facility the safest in the corporation, Manomaitis says. The reward—or incentive—is to win the charity safety award—a two-part reward for completion of 30 consecutive workdays without a lost-time injury. Employees who work at the plant winning the award can name a local charity to receive a $500 donation and also receive free coffee, soft drinks, and pastries for a 24-hour period.

According to Manomaitis, the program has been extremely effective. He notes, for example, that one department that had 10 lost-time injuries in March 1982 went 370 days without a lost-time injury following implementation of the program. After suffering one lost-time injury, the department then went another year without another injury.

Safety, quality, and productivity

Other job-safety points made by conference speakers include:

- Managers must emphasize and support safety to the same degree as quality control and productivity. Once supervisors accept the fact that "every time you have an accident, it affects quality and productivity," conference participants are told, "you start to win the game."

- Safety training should be integrated into an organization's management training programs. This training should be designed to make managers aware of the high indirect costs of safety violations, which include downtime, retraining time, reduced production, and investigation time.

- A charge-back mechanism can make managers more aware of the correlation between poor safety records and profits, and encourage competition between departments for good safety records. However, any incentives program that rewards or penalizes managers on the basis of their department's safety record must be "equitable, easily understood, and budgetable."

Source: Bulletin to Management, 16 May 1985. Reprinted by permission from *Bulletin to Management,* copyright 1985, by The Bureau of National Affairs, Inc., Washington, D.C.

The organization is required to keep this information "for as long a period as is associated with the incubation period of the specific disease—it could be forty years of medical surveillance of the environment."[54] If the organization is sold, the new owner must assume responsibility for storing the old records and continuing to gather the required data. If the organization goes out of business, the administrative director of OSHA must be informed of the whereabouts of the firm's records.

OSHA's purpose in having these records is to contribute to the knowledge of epidemiology to determine how to improve future work environments. Although organizations find this goal commendable, they often only keep these records because they are required to comply with OSHA regulations or because they may have to defend their behavior in negligence suits.

Compliance with OSHA standards and requirements is not the only approach that organizations can take to alleviate occupational health hazards. They can also become more active in the process by which OSHA establishes those standards. OSHA must publish its intent to review or establish standards, and it must hold a hearing. At this hearing, organizations can contribute information regarding what they believe the standard should be.

The second strategy is setting objectives, implementing programs, and maintaining records of diseases. This strategy uses the information collected in the first strategy and follows the same steps as management by objectives programs for reducing occupational accidents. A third strategy is for organizations to recognize the importance of previously neglected ailments and make a committed effort to help workers with those ailments. For example, Burlington Industries has jointly undertaken, with the Arthritis Foundation and the University of North Carolina School of Medicine, a program to assist employees with arthritis. Arthritis is a serious ailment. In an average year, arthritis sufferers lose 27 million working days, and receive over $1 billion in disability payments (about 15 percent of all Social Security disability payments are made to them).[55]

A final strategy is to introduce worker educational and physical fitness programs.[56] Educational programs on arthritis are now being conducted at General Motors, Manville, Western Electric, Sentry Insurance, and Samsonite. A part of educating workers is informing them of clinics across the nation to which they can go for a diagnosis of work place exposures.

Strategies for Improving Occupational Safety and Health in the Sociopsychological Work Environment

Many techniques can be used to improve the sociopsychological work environment, including job redesign, quality circles, and organizational restructuring. Since these are described in Chapter 12, only general programs designed to remove either organizational or individual factors causing stress are discussed here.

Organizational Stress Management Programs.   Specific programs can be designed to improve the aspects of an organization causing stress, such as supervisors, work overload, the physical environment, the salary structure, and employee job security. Although any organization would not likely use all of these programs, many companies are using at least a few of them. In part because of employee demand, general dissatisfaction, and new policies and procedures resulting from federal and state legislation, TRW has implemented the following steps to manage and reduce stress:

- Crisis-counseling training sessions with the industrial relations staff
- Increasing the employees' general awareness of stress and what they can do about it
- Adding stress discussions to the supervisory training program
- Adding a module on stress to middle-management programs
- Offering after-hours programs such as workshops in the use of biofeedback, meditation exercises, and other relaxation techniques[57]

Individual Stress Management Strategies.   Time management can be an effective individual strategy to deal with organizational stress. It is based in large part on initial identification of an individual's personal goals, such as the career development exercise in Appendix C. Other individual strategies that should be part of individual stress management include good diets, regular exercise, monitoring physical health, and building social support groups.

Many large organizations such as Xerox encourage employees to enroll in programs of regular exercise and careful monitoring of their fitness and health.[58] **Wellness tests** include measures of blood pressure, blood cholesterol, high-density cholesterol, skin fold evaluation of diet, life change events, smoking, drinking, and family history of coronary heart disease.

Organizations can offer many activities or programs to improve physical and sociopsychological work conditions. Selecting the most appropriate activity depends on a thorough diagnosis of existing safety and health hazards. It also depends on an assessment of past activities and those used by other organizations.

Trends in Occupational Safety and Health

The two major trends in safety and health described here are those of assessment and computer technology and HRIS. Although organizations can save money with better safety and health rewards, this may be more appropriately viewed as a benefit of improving conditions for employees rather than as a method of gaining strategic advantage. Similarly, although a few choices are available in the ways of doing safety and health activities, a more appropriate approach may be to view them as activities that should be done for the benefit of all employees rather than as a set of choices.

Assessing Occupational Safety and Health Activities

The effectiveness of safety and health activities run by organizations can be assessed using data on the outcomes associated with safety and health shown in Exhibit 13.1. However, assessing strategies or activities for improving safety and health targeted at the physical work environment differs from the evaluation of the strategies targeted at the sociopsychological work environment.

Physical Work Environment Strategies.   The effectiveness of physical work environment strategies is often measured by the effects of a specific strategy on employee absenteeism and turnover, medical claims and worker compensation rates and costs, productivity (quantity and quality), and efficiency. The effects of these strategies can also be seen in the rates of accidents or the incidences of specific diseases—that is, the physical/physiological indicators of safety and health levels in an organization. The relative effectiveness of these strategies can be considered by determining the cost of the program and the relative benefits.[59] For example, work place safety can be increased substantially by correcting person-machine mismatching through ergonomics. Since ergonomic changes are relatively quick and inexpensive, ergonomics may be the most effective strategy to use for physical work environment changes.[60]

Sociopsychological Work Environment Strategies.   In contrast to the physical work environment strategies, the effectiveness of sociopsychological work environment strategies is determined by assessments of the psychological indicators of safety and health levels and employee dissatisfaction and job involvement. In addition, effectiveness can be measured using the same assessments as for determining the effectiveness of physical work environment strategies. Indeed, measuring the effectiveness of stress management strategies against the physical and physiological indicators is highly appropriate.

But even though appropriate, making a cause-and-effect assessment between stress strategies and most physical and physiological indicators is often difficult. To do so requires using measures that are relatively sensitive to stress reduction, such as heart rate. It has also been done successfully by Equitable Life Assurance by demonstrating a significant reduction in time spent not working. Equitable Life did this by comparing the amount of time previously taken up by stress-related visits to the company's dispensary with the amount of time later spent in stress management programs. In addition to demonstrating a reduction in total time off, Equitable costed out the value of the time saved from reduced trips to the dispensary and time off and compared it against the cost of the programs. Substantial benefits per cost were clearly demonstrated.[61] Since evaluating the effectiveness of safety and health strategies against the psychological indicators of dissatisfaction and job involvement raises questions similar to those raised when assessing QWL programs, refer to Chapter 12 for that discussion.[62]

Computer Technology and HRIS in Occupational Safety and Health

Information for improving safety and health can be effectively stored on an HRIS. Accident rates and the types of employee diseases can be gathered and stored in an HRIS to begin evaluating the present conditions. Similar information on other companies may also be gathered and stored. With this initial data base, an organization can determine how good or bad its accident and disease rates are. It can also help determine if particular areas or sections of the organization are worse off than others.

Efforts to minimize employer medical costs due to work-related accidents and diseases include the use of computer technology and an HRIS. In this application, the computer serves two purposes. First, medical costs stored in the HRIS can be tallied and summarized across departments or the organization. Second, with costs systematically coded by the nature of their causes, personnel can begin to identify patterns of similar problems in particular physical locations within the company. This may also serve as the basis for developing action programs to deal with causes of accidents and diseases effectively. In this function, PHRM is directly contributing to improved safety and health, organizational efficiency, and legal compliance.

Summary

The health of employees in organizations will become increasingly important in the years ahead. Employers are becoming more aware of the cost of ill health and the benefits of having a healthy work force. The federal government, through OSHA, is also making it more necessary for employers to be concerned with employee health. The government's current concern is primarily with employee health as related to occupational accidents and diseases, both aspects of the physical environment. However, organizations can choose to become involved in programs dealing with employee health and the workers' sociopsychological environment as well. If organizations choose not to become involved with improving the sociopsychological environment, the government may prescribe mandatory regulations. Thus, it pays for organizations to be concerned with both aspects of the work environment now. Effective programs for both environments can significantly improve both employee health and the effectiveness of the organization.

When adoption of programs for improvement is being considered, employee involvement is important. As with many quality of work life programs being implemented in organizations, employee involvement in improving safety and health is not only a good idea but also one likely to be desired by the employees. Many things can be done to make work environments better. But it is important to distinguish two types of environments: the physical and the sociopsychological. Each is different and has its own unique subparts. Although some improvement strategies may work well for one part of the work environment, they will not work in other parts. Again, a careful diagnosis is required before programs are selected and implemented.

Assuming that a careful diagnosis indicates the need for a stress management program, the challenge is in deciding which program or strategy to select from the many organizational and individual stress management strategies currently available. Programs such as time management or physical exercise could be set up so employees could help themselves cope, or the organization could alter the conditions within the organization that are associated with stress. The latter requires a diagnosis of what is happening, where, and to whom before deciding how to proceed. Because so many possible sources of stress exist, and because not all people react the same way to them, implementing individual stress management strategies may be more efficient. However, if many people are suffering similar stress symptoms in a specific part of the organization, an organizational strategy is more appropriate.

Information regarding many aspects of safety and health is insufficient—either because it does not exist (e.g., knowledge of causes and effect) or because organizations are unwilling to gather or provide it. From a legal as well as humane viewpoint, it is in the best interests of organizations to seek and provide more information so that more effective strategies for improving safety and health can be developed and implemented. Failure to do so may result in costly legal settlements against organizations or further governmental regulation of work place safety and health. These comments apply equally to the next chapter on employee rights.

Discussion Questions

1. In what ways can an organization prevent occupational accidents?
2. How can physical work environment strategies and sociopsychological work environment strategies be assessed?
3. The United States prides itself on freedom, democracy, and free labor markets. If this is true, why not make employees responsible for health and safety? In other words, employers who offer riskier employment will simply pay workers more for bearing the risk (a wage premium), and the workers can in turn buy more insurance coverage to cover this risk. Discuss the advantages and disadvantages of this approach.
4. Who is responsible for work place safety and health? The employer? The employee? The federal government? Judges and juries? Explain.
5. How are physical hazards distinct from sociopsychological hazards? What implications does this have for programs to deal with these hazards?
6. Is there such a thing as an unsafe worker? Assuming that accident-prone workers exist, how can effective personnel functions address this problem?
7. Is accident proneness a reliable trait? If not, does that mean that organizations cannot control it? Explain.
8. What incentives does OSHA provide the employer for promoting work place safety? Explain.

9. How might a company's strategy to prevent occupational accidents differ from a program to prevent occupational disease? In what ways might the program be similar?

10. Distinguish the "no-risk" from the "significant risk" standard. What are the benzene, lead, and cotton standards?

PC Project

Work stress is a by-product of our fast-paced, upwardly mobile society. Stress has been associated with industrial accidents, turnover, absenteeism, and poor job performance. This PC Project examines sources of work- and career-related stress. Your task is to analyze the stress data and make recommendations for reducing stress to manageable levels.

C   A   S   E   S   T   U   D   Y

Which Road for Safety?

Highway 231 was as familiar to John Axtell as the back of his hand. John traveled this road three days a week as a commuter student in the Master's of Science in Industrial Relations program at Purdue University. John and his wife, Mary, live sixty miles south in Greencastle, Indiana, where Mary is completing her undergraduate degree at DePauw University, a small liberal arts college.

On this pleasant spring day in April, John is returning from a full day of classes. During the ride home, John likes to replay the days events and rethink the interesting ideas he has picked up from his classes. John calls his trip the two-cigar ride, since the sixty-mile commute usually gives him enough time to smoke two twenty-five-cent cigars or, if he's feeling extravagant, two imported Creme de Jamaica cigars.

As John reached the southern-most edge of the West Lafayette city limits, he began to pick up speed for the open road. His thoughts today were on the seminar discussion he participated in earlier in his personnel class. The professor had posed an interesting question: "Why can't we reduce traffic fatalities to zero?" John gave this idea more serious consideration as he lit his cigar with the cigarette lighter and glanced down to see the speedometer reading sixty miles per hour.

John eased back down to the double nickel and thought about his own experience on Route 231 this past year. In February he narrowly missed serious injury when his car hydroplaned off the road during a snow blizzard and just missed a major utility pole. Fortunately a six-foot snowdrift snagged his car inches short of the utility pole, and he and his '64 Valiant escaped serious harm. Mary worried a lot about John and urged him to drive slower and give up the cigars. John had reassured her that he would slow down, but he couldn't possibly give up the stogies.

The idea of no fatalities intrigued John. I suppose, he thought, that if we lined Highway 231 with collision barrels, put huge padded bumpers on my car, put airbags and seat-restraint systems in every car, reduced the speed limit to 30 MPH, and strictly enforced the use of all of these systems, I could be virtually assured of an injury-free commute between Greencastle and West Lafayette.

John chuckled as he tried to imagine such a scenario of immensely padded cars traveling down a barrel-lined Highway 231 at thirty miles per hour.

But that was just the point his professor was trying to make. We obtain safety and health at some price. Apparently the United States is willing to live with, if you will, the fifty-thousand-plus traffic fatalities a year given the amount of money expended for highway safety and accident prevention. The work place is no different from Highway 231, thought John, because you have to decide how much safety at what price. The interesting question to John, though, was, how does this system provide incentives for individual workers and employers to be safe?

From his class in employment law, John immediately thought of the court system as a way to provide incentives. For example, there was the judge who found three officials of Film Recovery Systems, Inc., in nearby Chicago guilty of murder last year for the death of a worker who inhaled toxic cyanide fumes. This clearly could serve as an after-the-fact warning to employers to be safe. But would they be safe enough even with the threat of large court fines or jail sentences?

The workers' compensation system, with its experience-based rate structure, might provide another basis for employers to be safe. Presumably, riskier employers would have higher business costs and eventually be driven out of the market by safer employers. Hence, safe business practice would equate to good business practice.

John wondered how his "free market" graduate student friends might argue if workers were given the choice of a safe or risky employer. They would argue that employers are like highways. You could choose to travel the padded Highway 231 and arrive at your destination assured of your life but three hours late to school, or you could take the interstate and arrive in thirty minutes but with a .005 probability that you will also die trying. John remembered his accident this past February and recalled how he had taken his well-traveled road for granted. In theory, employers could provide compensating wage differentials for riskier jobs. John wondered if workers or employers could accurately assess these risks, though.

John recalled yet another source of safety incentives from his seminar discussion. OSHA clearly must play some role in this process. John took a skeptical view of another regulatory agency passing rules and conducting on-site employer inspections for the nation's 4.6 million work places. Moreover, his views were consistent with the Reagan administration views that resulted in a cut in health and safety enforcement in 1981 and a subsequent reduction in health and safety spending by employers.

His professor, however, concluded today's seminar by sharing some recent illness, injury, and death on the job statistics released by the Bureau of Labor Statistics. Since 1974, the deaths per 100,000 employees have been falling from the 1974 rate of 9.8 to a low of 5.6 in 1983. In 1984, though, this rate turned up to a figure of 6.4. Similarly, the number of injury and illness per 100 employees fell from a 1974 rate of 10.3 to a low of 7.6 in 1983, but the rate turned up to 8.0 in 1984. Could there be a connection between public policy regarding the role of OSHA and these occupational statistics? At this moment, John extinguished his cigar as he entered the city limits of Crawfordsville. On the other side of the city limits, he would light his second cigar and ponder this issue for the remaining thirty miles home.

Notes

1. R. S. Schuler, "Occupational Health in Organizations: Strategies for Personnel Effectiveness," *Personnel Administrator* (Jan. 1982): 47–56; R. S. Schuler, "Occupational Health in Organizations: A Measure of Personnel Effectiveness," in *Readings in Personnel and Human Resource Management*, 2d ed., ed. R. S. Schuler and S. A. Youngblood (St. Paul: West, 1984).

2. *The Occupational Safety and Health Act*, Public Law 91–596, 29 Dec. 1970, and *The Occupational Safety and Health Act*, publication no. 149 (Washington D.C.: American Federation of Labor and Congress of Industrial Organizations), Sept. 1971. Companies of all sizes (by number of employees) having an effect on commerce are included under OSHA except state or local government, companies regulated by another federal agency, and to some extent, the federal government.

3. See the entire April 1983 and October 1985 issues of the *Personnel Administrator*.

4. "The Pressure on OSHA to Get Back to Work," *Business Week,* 10 June 1985, pp. 55–56; "The Overhaul That Could Give OSHA Light under Reagan," *Business Week,* 19 Jan. 1981, pp. 88–89; "OSHA Is Now Trying to Help You," *Nation's Business,* Aug. 1981, pp. 20–26; "A Lighter Schedule of OSHA Inspections," *Business Week,* 14 Sept. 1981, p. 38; M. Hinds, "Pressure Grows to Alter Rules on Worker Safety," *New York Times,* 27 Nov. 1982, p. 7L; C. W. Newcom, "Employee Health and Safety Laws," *Labor Law Journal* 35 (1981): 395–406.

5. These figures should be regarded as best estimates because variations can be produced depending on the source used. For example, see H. J. Hilaski, "Understanding Statistics on Occupational Illnesses," *Monthly Labor Review* (Mar. 1981): 25–29; Bureau of National Affairs, "Occupational Injuries and Illnesses, 1980–1981," *Bulletin to Management,* 13 Dec. 1982, pp. 4–6. For other estimates, see L. J. Warshaw, *Stress Management* (Reading, Mass.: Addison-Wesley, 1979); A. A. McLean, *Work Stress* (Reading, Mass.: Addison-Wesley, 1979). Schuler, "Occupational Health."

6. These estimates could be regarded as conservative because they do not include the costs due to stress and low-QWL-associated (caused) health and accident costs.

7. A. J. J. Brennan, "Worksite Health Promotion Can Be Cost Effective," *Personnel Administrator* (Apr. 1983): 39–48; J. G. Nelson, "Health: A New Personnel Imperative," *Personnel Administrator* (Feb. 1980): 69–71.

8. A. P. Brief, R. S. Schuler, and M. Van Sell, *Managing Job Stress* (Boston: Little, Brown, 1980); T. Cox, *Stress* (Baltimore: University Park Press, 1978); C. L. Cooper and R. Payne, eds., *Stress at Work* (New York: Wiley, 1978); T. A. Beehr and R. S. Bhagat, eds., *Stress and Human Cognition* (New York: Wiley, 1984); T. A. Beehr and R. S. Schuler, "Stress in Organizations," in *Personnel Management,* ed. K. M. Rowland and G. R. Ferris (Boston: Allyn & Bacon, 1982); R. S. Schuler and S. E. Jackson, "Managing Stress through PHRM Practices: An Uncertainty Interpretation," in *Research in Personnel and Human Resources Management,* vol. 4, ed. K. M. Rowland and G. R. Ferris (Greenwich, Conn.: JAI Press, 1986).

9. D. S. Thelan, D. Ledgerwood, and C. F. Walters, "Health and Safety in the Workplace: A New Challenge for Business Schools," *Personnel Administrator* (Oct. 1985): 37–46.

10. Bureau of National Affairs, "Safety Roundup," *Bulletin to Management,* 23 Dec. 1982, pp. 1–2.

11. Each year the Bureau of Labor Statistics studies the safety provisions of labor management contracts and publishes them under the title "Characteristics of Major Collective Bargaining Agreements," which are then available from the Superintendent of Document, U.S. Government Printing Office, Washington, D.C. 20402.

12. *The Occupational Safety and Health Act,* Public Law 91–595, 29 Dec. 1970, sec. 2, p. 1.

13. "Now OSHA Must Justify Its Inspection Targets," *Business Week,* 9 Apr. 1979, p. 64; M. Hayes, "What Can You Do When OSHA Calls?" *Personnel Administrator* (Nov. 1982): 65–66; "Has OSHA Become Too Much of a Pussycat?" *Business Week,* 11 Mar. 1985, pp. 82G–82J.

14. *The Occupational Safety and Health Act,* Public Law 91–596, 29 Dec. 1970, sec. 12, p. 6. The Labor Department, in which OSHA is housed, proposed exempting about 474,000 employers from keeping routine records about occupational injuries and illnesses. These are employers in white-collar businesses employing about 19 million people largely in retail, finance, insurance, real estate, and services (low-hazard industries). This provision took effect 1 January 1983.

15. Hayes, "What Can You Do When OSHA Calls?"

16. M. Goozner, "The Battle over Chemical Labeling," *New York Times,* 12 Sept. 1982, p. 8F; Bureau of National Affairs, "OSHA's Final Labelling Standard," *Bulletin to Management,* 1 Dec. 1983, p. 1; B. Meier, "Use of Right-to-Know Rules Is Increasing Public's Scrutiny of Chemical Companies," *Wall Street Journal,* 23 May 1985, p. 10; P. A. Susser, "The OSHA Standard and State "Right-to-Know" Laws: The Preemption Battle Continues," *Employee Relations Law Journal* (Spring 1985): 615–34.

17. N. J. Sullivan, "The Benzene Decision: A Contribution to Regulatory Confusion," *Administrative Law Review* (1981): 351–65; "From the Editor," *Employee Relations Law Journal* 6(3)(1981): 361–63; R. H. Sand, "Current Developments in OSHA," *Employee Relations Law Journal* 6(3)(1981): 484–93; L. Greenhouse, "Court Goes Its Own Way on Key Regulatory Cases," *New York Times,* 21 June 1981, p. 8E; Meier; BNA, "OSHA's Final Labelling Standard."

18. P. A. Susser, "Update on Hazard Communication," *Personnel Administrator* (Oct. 1985): 57–61; M. G. Miner, "Legal Concerns Facing Human Resources Managers: An Overview," in *Readings in Personnel and Human Resource Management,* 3d ed., ed. R. S. Schuler, S. A. Youngblood, and V. Huber (St. Paul: West, 1987).

19. *Wall Street Journal,* 2 Oct. 1984, p. 1; Bureau of National Affairs, "State Right-to-Know Laws: Toxic Substances," *Bulletin to Management,* 22 Nov. 1984, pp. 4–5; "Worker Right to Know," *Chemical Work,* 18 Apr. 1984, pp. 38–44; J. B. Dubeck and P. A. Susser, "Hazard Communications: New Disclosure Burdens on Management," *Personnel Administrator* (May 1984): 79–83; W. E. Stead and J. G. Stead, "OSHA's Cancer Prevention Policy: Where Did It Come From and Where Is It Going?" *Personnel Journal* (Jan. 1983): 54–60; F. Allen, "Battle Building over "Right to Know" Laws Regarding Toxic Items Used by Workers," *Wall Street Journal,* 3 Jan. 1983.

20. N. J. Sullivan, "The Benzene Decision: A Contribution to Regulatory Confusion," *Administrative Law*

Review (1981): 351–65; "From the Editor," *Employee Relations Law Journal* (1981): 361–63; R. H. Sand, "Current Developments in OSHA," *Employee Relations Law Journal* (1981): 484–93; L. Greenhouse, "Court Goes Its Own Way on Key Regulatory Cases," *New York Times*, 21 June 1981.

21. M. Novit, "Mental Distress: Possible Implications for the Future,"; *Personnel Administrator* (Aug. 1982): 47–54. The Civil Rights Act of 1866, Section 1981, prohibits employment discrimination based on race, color, and national origin. The Civil Rights Act of 1871, Section 1983, enforces the Fourteenth Amendment providing for "equal protection of the laws" and prohibits employment discrimination on the basis of race, color, national origin, religion, sex, or age.

22. Determining responsibility is sometimes difficult because determining cause-and-effect relationships is difficult, especially when reactions such as asbestosis or hypertension take so long to develop or occur only in some people working under the same conditions as others. For a discussion, see B. Rice, "Can Companies Kill? Suits That Are Searing Asbestos," *Business Week*, 13 Apr. 1981, pp. 166–69; J. S. Lublin, "Occupational Diseases Receive More Scrutiny Since the Manville Case," *Wall Street Journal*, 20 Dec. 1982, p. 1. For an excellent review of these issues, see J. M. Ivancevich, M. T. Matteson, and E. P. Richards III, "Who's Liable for Stress on the Job?" *Harvard Business Review* (Mar.–Apr. 1985): 60–70.

23. "Safety Sense," *Personnel Administrator* (Jan. 1983): 73.

24. Ivancevich, Matteson, and Richards, "Who's Liable?" See also reports and articles from NICSH, such as B. Wilkes and L. Stammerjohn, "Job Demands and Worker Health in Machine-paced Poultry Inspection," report published by the U.S. Department of Health and Human Services, Cincinnati, Ohio, May 1981; M. J. Colligan and L. R. Murphy, "Mass Psychogenic Illness in Organizations: An Overview," *Journal of Occupational Psychology* 52 (1979): 77–90; M. J. Colligan and M. J. Smith, "A Methodological Approach for Evaluating Outbreaks of Mass Psychogenic Illness in Industry," *Journal of Occupational Medicine* 20 (1978): 401–2.

25. J. V. Grimaldi and R. H. Simonds, *Safety Management* (Homewood, Ill.: Irwin, 1975).

26. P. Farish, "A Religion of Safety," *Personnel Administrator* (Feb. 1981): 23.

27. Ibid.

28. B. Keller, "Workers Are Often a Hazard to Themselves," *New York Times*, 8 July 1984; R. B. Hersey, "Rates of Production and Emotional State," *Personnel Journal* (Apr. 1982): 355–64.

29. N. Root, "Injuries at Work Are Fewer among Older Employees," *Monthly Labor Review* (Mar. 1981): 30–34.

30. N. A. Ashford, "The Nature and Dimension of Occupational Health and Safety Problems" p. 45. Reprint-ed with permission from the Aug. 1977 issue of the *Personnel Administrator*. Copyright © 1977, The American Society for Personnel Administration, 30 Park Drive, Berea, Ohio, 44017; M. Schuster and S. Rhodes, "The Impact of Overtime Work on Industrial Accident Rates," *Industrial Relations* (Spring 1985): 234–46.

31. Ashford, "The Nature and Dimension," p. 48.

32. M. Corn, "An Inside View of OSHA Compliance," *Personnel Administrator* (Nov. 1979): 39–44.

33. C. L. Wang, "Occupational Skin Disease Continues to Plague Industry," *Monthly Labor Review* (Feb. 1979): 17–22.

34. Ashford, "The Nature and Dimension," p. 48.

35. Wang, "Occupational Skin."

36. K. R. Pelletier, "The Hidden Hazards of the Modern Office," *New York Times*, 8 Sept. 1985, p. F.3; J. Hyatt, "Hazardous Effects of VDT Legislation," *Inc.* (Mar. 1985): 27; W. L. Weis, "No Smoking," *Personnel Journal* (Sept. 1984): 53–58; "VDT Study: Safety Charges, Design Changes," *Bulletin to Management*, 21 July 1983; "Office Hazard: Factory Environment Can Boomerang," *Impact*, 22 June 1983, 1; D. C. Kent, M. Schram, and S. Cenci, "Smoking in the Workplace: A Review of Human and Operating Costs," *Personnel Administrator* (Aug. 1982): 29–33, 83; J. B. Hull, "Burned-Up Bosses Snuff Out Prospects of Jobs for Smokers," *Wall Street Journal*, 15 Apr. 1982; T. Yenckel, "Careers: So You Think Your Job is Cushy?" *Washington Post*, 23 Sept. 1981; E. Marshal, "FDA Sees No Radiation Risk in VDT Screens," *Science*, 5 June 1981, 1120–21.

37. For a set of references identifying and discussing each preference or interest listed here, see R. S. Schuler, "Definition and Conceptualization of Stress in Organizations," *Organizational Behavior and Human Performance* 23 (1980): 184–215; R. S. Schuler, "An Integrative Transactional Process Model of Stress in Organizations," *Journal of Occupational Behavior* 3 (1982): 3–10; R. S. Schuler, "Organizational and Occupational Stress and Coping: A Model and Overview," in *Readings in Personnel and Human Resource Management*, 2d ed., ed. R. S. Schuler and S. A. Youngblood (St. Paul: West, 1984); T. Beehr and R. Bhagat, *Human Stress and Cognition* (New York: Wiley, 1985); R. S. Bhagat, S. J. McQuaid, H. Lindholm, and J. Segovis, "Total Life Stress: A Multimethod Validation of the Construct and Its Effects on Organizationally Valued Outcomes and Withdrawal Behaviors," *Journal of Applied Psychology* (Feb. 1985): 202–14.

38. Beehr and Bhagat, *Human Stress and Cognition;* Schuler, "Organizational and Occupational Stress."

39. C. L. Cooper and D. Torrington, "Identifying and Coping with Stress in Organizations: The Personnel Perspective," in *Behavioral Problems in Organizations*, ed. C. L. Cooper (Englewood Cliffs, N.J.: Prentice-Hall, 1979), pp. 183–202; R. Weigel and S. Pinsky, "Managing Stress: A Model for the Human

Resource Staff," *Personnel Administrator* (Feb. 1982): 56–60; M. J. Davidson and C. L. Cooper, "A Model of Occupational Stress," *Journal of Occupational Medicine* (Aug. 1981): 564–74; S. E. Jackson, R. S. Schuler, and D. J. Vredenburgh, "Managing Stress in Turbulent Times," in *Occupational Stress and Organizational Effectiveness,* ed. A. Riley, S. Zaccaro, and R. Rosen (New York: Praeger, 1986).

40. A. B. Shostak, *Blue Collar Stress* (Reading, Mass.: Addison-Wesley, 1980).

41. Ibid.; E. E. Lawler III, *Pay and Organization Development* (Reading, Mass.: Addison-Wesley, 1981); "Reward Systems," in *Improving Life at Work,* ed. J. R. Hackman and J. L. Suttle (Santa Monica, Calif.: Goodyear, 1977).

42. B. Wilkes and L. Stammerjohn, "Job Demands and Worker Health."

43. M. Pesci, "Stress Management: Separating Myth from Reality," *Personnel Administrator* (Jan. 1982): 57–67; M. Frankenhaeuser and B. Gardell, "Underload and Overload in Working Life: Outline of a Multidisciplinary Approach," *Journal of Human Stress* 2 (1976): 35–45. But even if individuals are under heavy work loads and stress, they may not necessarily want to eliminate them. See R. Richlefs, "Many Executives Complain of Stress, but Few Want Less-Pressured Jobs," *Wall Street Journal,* 29 Sept. 1982, p. 35.

44. "Deadline Pressures Aggravate Stress: Court Orders Money for Widow," *Resource* (May 1985): 1.

45. For extensive discussion of office space and physical design issues, see R. S. Schuler, L. R. Ritzman, and V. Davis, "Merging Prescriptive and Behavioral Approaches for Office Layout," *Production and Inventory Management Journal* 3 (1981): 131–42; E. Sundstrom, "Interpersonal Behavior and the Physical Environment," in *Social Psychology,* 2d ed., ed. L. Wrightsman (Monterey, Calif: Brooks/Cole, 1977); F. I. Steele, *Physical Settings and Organizational Development* (Reading, Mass.: Addison-Wesley, 1973); D. D. Umstot, C. H. Bell, and T. R. Mitchell, "The Effects of Job Enrichment and Task Goals on Satisfaction and Productivity: Implications for Job Design," *Journal of Applied Psychology* 61 (1976): 379–94.

46. S. E. Jackson and R. S. Schuler, "Preventing Employee Burnout," *Personnel* (Mar.–Apr. 1983): 58–68.

47. H. M. Taylor, "Occupational Health Management-by-Objectives," *Personnel* (Jan.–Feb. 1980): 58–64; H. J. Hilaski, "Understanding Statistics on Occupational Illnesses," *Monthly Labor Review* (Mar. 1981): 25–29; B. Hopkins, B. Conard, and D. Duellman, *Behavior Management for Occupational Safety and Health* (U.S. Department of Health, Education, and Welfare, 1979); R. A. Reber, J. A. Wallin, and J. S. Chhokar, "Reducing Industrial Accidents: A Behavioral Experiment," *Industrial Relations* (Winter 1984): 119–25.

48. V. Reinhart, "Ergonomic Studies Improving Life on the Job," *Job Safety and Health* (Dec. 1975): 16–21; C. G. Drury, "Most Workplace Accidents Are the Result of Ergonomic Problems," *Bulletin to Management,* 23 Dec. 1982, pp. 1–2. Corn, p. 42.

49. "Safety Roundup," *Bulletin to Management,* 23 Dec. 1982, pp. 1–2.

50. "New OSHA Tack," *Personnel Administrator* (June 1981): 12; A. Czernek and G. Clark, "Incentives for Safety," *Job Safety and Health* (Oct. 1973): 7–11; D. Hampton, "Contests Have Side Effects, Too," *California Management Review* 12 (1970): 86–94.

51. Taylor, "Occupational Health Management-By-Objectives." For the discussion of a method not presented here—the counseling type on an individual basis—see M. D. Glicken, "Managing a Crisis Intervention Program," *Personnel Journal* (Apr. 1982): 292–96; J. B. Chlokar and J. A. Wallin, "A Field Study of the Effect of Feedback Frequency on Performances," *Journal of Applied Psychology* (June 1984): 524–30; "High-Tech Hazard Control," *Bulletin to Management,* June 1984, p. 1.

52. W. M. Buckley, "Manufacturers Seek to Create More Safety-Conscious Robots," *Wall Street Journal,* 4 Oct. 1985, p. 23; "Robot Safety Tips," *Resource* (May 1985): 3.

53. "Dubious Tactics in the War on Cancer," *Business Week,* 14 June 1976, p. 76.

54. Corn, "An Inside View," p. 42.

55. R. E. Dedmon and M. K. Kubiak, "The Medical Director's Role in Industry," *Personnel Administrator* (Sept. 1981): 59–64.

56. J. J. Hoffman, Jr., and C. J. Hobson, "Physical Fitness and Employee Effectiveness," *Personnel Administrator* (Apr. 1984): 101–13; S. W. Hartman and J. Cozzetto, "Wellness in the Workplace," *Personnel Administrator* (Aug. 1984): 108–17; M. T. Matteson and J. M. Ivancevich, "The How, What, and Why of Stress Management Training," *Personnel Journal* (Oct. 1982): 768–74; S. E. Jackson and R. S. Schuler, "Preventing Employee Burnout"; R. W. Driver and R. A. Ratliff, "Employers' Perceptions of Benefits Accrued from Physical Fitness Programs," *Personnel Administrator* (Aug. 1982): 21–26; S. Salmans, "A Fitness Center for Professionals," *New York Times,* 3 Jan. 1985, p. D5; J. N. Kondrasuk, "Corporate Physical Fitness Programs: The Role of the Personnel Department," *Personnel Administrator* (Dec. 1984): 75–80; M. F. Davis, "Worksite Health Promotion," *Personnel Administrator* (Dec. 1984): 45–50.

57. Brief, Schuler, and Van Sell, *Managing Job Stress;* Warshaw, *Stress Management;* A. S. Sethi and R. S. Schuler, *Handbook of Stress Coping Strategies* (Cambridge: Ballinger, 1984).

58. M. T. Matteson and J. M. Ivancevich, "The How, What, and Why of Stress Management Training," *Personnel Journal* (Oct. 1982): 768–74; S. E. Jackson and R. S. Schuler, "Preventing Employee Burnout"; R. W. Driver and R. A. Ratliff, "Employers' Perceptions of Benefits Accrued from Physical Fitness Programs."

59. P. A. Workman, "Using Statistics to Manage a State Safety and Health Program," *Monthly Labor Review*

(Mar. 1981): 42–44. For an example of a program at work, see the description of the one at Kimberly-Clark Corporation in Dedman and Kubiak, "The Medical Director's Role."

60. Reinhart, "Ergonomic Studies." See also the discussion of ergonomics in task design in Chapter 12.

61. These ideas were presented by J. R. Mancuso at the Conference on Occupational Stress, Baltimore, 17 April 1982.

62. For example, see Driver and Ratliff, "Employers' Perceptions."

Forestalling Plant Closings Possible?

Is there an emerging legal war over plant closings? While the handful of plant closing suits filed so far have met with little success, it appears the increase in such complaints could lead to recognition of new community rights when a factory decides to shut down.

The city of Chicago has filed a lawsuit to keep Playskool from closing up shop in that city, claiming that the toy manufacturer is obligated to remain in Chicago for the 20-year term of its $1 million industrial revenue bond negotiated with the city. Playskool maintains its obligation to operate is ended since the firm has long since repaid its debt.

Instead of challenging plant closings as violations of collective bargaining agreements—the traditional charge of unions—state and local government units and community organizations are using public policy arguments to force manufacturers into maintaining operations. The idea that a company must make some type of public accounting to a community is not unlike the changing doctrine of employment at will. That common law principle—that employees can be dismissed for any cause or no cause—has been slowly eroding through court decisions in several states.

A first attempt

The first lawsuit to argue community rights involved the closing of the U.S. Steel mills in Youngstown the company had promised to keep open if employees agreed to wage concessions necessary to make the two operations profitable.

The company later announced it was closing the mills despite the concessions. A coalition of local and state officials, unions, unemployed workers and religous leaders sued to enforce the company's promise. At that time, a preliminary injunction was granted and the plants were forced to remain open. That was in 1980. And that was the only time a federal court has ordered a major corporation to remain running whether or not it wanted to.

That injunction was later reversed and the mills then closed.

A stronger case?

A more recent case—again, involving U.S. Steel—now before the Illinois Supreme Court pits union leaders, workers and community organizations against the company for not going through with its planned $200 million rail mill in Chicago.

The plaintiffs are trying to keep the giant steelmaker from breaching an alleged contract in which the firm would have developed the mill in return for wage concessions from the union and the state repeal of taxes on rails. A lower court issued a temporary restraining order against U.S. Steel and a state appeals court upheld that decision last November.

According to public interest lawyers, an even stronger case is the Playskool closing.

In 1979 the city of Chicago agreed to guarantee an industrial revenue bond on the basis of continued employment promised by Playskool. Chicago is arguing that Playskool must remain open under its agreement, though the firm has moved for dismissal of the charges. It claims repayment of bonds eliminates any obligation to the city.

Whatever the outcome of these cases, it seems clear that courts could be moving toward recognizing a community right to keep operations going, based on the word of executives—whether oral or written.

The preceding "PHRM in the News" describes what is becoming a prominent issue in PHRM: employee rights. Some managers view employee rights as a way in which employees can second-guess management's decisions and begin to take control of the organization. Other managers and many employees view employee rights as a way to help ensure that management decisions are made on a sound, justifiable basis and that employees are protected from arbitrary and vindictive management actions.

These views contrast sharply. Although the differences will not likely be resolved soon, personnel and human resource management requires an appreciation of these differences. The personnel and human resource manager must be current on the legal considerations regarding employee rights and must develop strategies for organizations to use in addressing employee rights.

The initial "PHRM in the News" also describes the issue of the right to plant/office closing notification. Other employee rights not described in "PHRM in the News," but important nonetheless, include (1) the right to privacy, (2) the right to know about work place hazards, (3) the right to work in an environment free of sexual harassment, (4) the right to be provided assistance in correcting ineffective performance and job outplacement, and (5) the right to be exempt from termination or firing solely at the employer's will. This chapter focuses on these key issues, which are likely to remain central to employee rights throughout the rest of the 1980s.

Although much of the current discussion of employee rights addresses the right of employers to "terminate at will," employee rights cover much more, including the employee's right to a job under almost any conditions, and the employee's right to fair, just, and respectable treatment while on the job. Within these two broad areas of employee rights are several more specific issues, including freedom from sexual harassment, the right of plant closing notification, due process treatment in discharge cases, freedom from discriminatory treatment based on sex, race, religion, or national origin, and the right to have personal records remain confidential. Although some of these rights are protected by law or collective bargaining agreements, others are not. If some rights are covered only by collective bargaining agreements, this leaves 80 percent of the nonunionized work force unprotected.[1]

As such, **employee rights** are regarded here as those rights that employees desire regarding the security of their jobs and the treatment administered by their employers while on the job, regardless of whether or not those rights are currently protected by law or collective bargaining agreements. As these employee rights become recognized by employers, the extent of management rights—the prerogatives management has in dealing with its work force, such as discharging at will—diminishes. Thus, employee rights have significant impact on and importance for PHRM. In general, the thrust of the two-way match that underlies much of our discussion of the PHRM activities is expanded by the concern for employee rights. Whereas the two-way match focused on matching (1) job demands and employee skills, knowledge, and abilities and (2) job and organizational characteristics and employee personality, interests, and preferences; concern for employee rights also focuses on matching or balancing (3) management rights and employee rights.

Purposes and Importance of Employee Rights

The earlier discussion of recruitment and selection in Chapters 4 and 5 focused on the considerations of getting job applicants into organizations. This chapter now focuses on the considerations involved in establishing and maintaining relationships with the job applicants who are hired. The previous chapters emphasized the importance of making sure employees (new and old) are informed about what's expected of them and what opportunities are available in the organization. This chapter focuses on the thrust of employee rights: treating employees fairly and with respect while on the job and when terminating their employment.

Treating employees fairly and with respect is important to organizations. Violation of legally protected employee rights (e.g., the right to not be discriminated against in employment decisions) can result in severe penalties and fines:

> Eight women employees of the William Mitchell College of Law in St. Paul, Minnesota, agreed to accept $300,000 to settle their sexual harassment claims, the school said June 27, 1984.
>
> The eight charged in a $3 million suit that they had been touched and subjected to suggestive remarks in forty-six instances over two years, and were retaliated against when they resisted. "In settling the case, the board of trustees recognizes that the plaintiffs asserted their claims of sexual harassment in good faith. The board trusts that the settlement of this lawsuit will restore any loss of compensation, dignity, and reputation which plaintiffs have suffered," the school said.[2]

In another case, one based on age discrimination, U. S. Judge Robert Merhige, Jr., declared that the Liggett and Myers Cigarette Company illegally dismissed 107 white-collar workers between the ages of forty and sixty-five between 1971 and 1973. As a consequence, the judge ordered the company to award back pay to the individuals. Back pay was determined by calculating the amount of salary benefits and raises the workers were entitled to against the amount they earned since the firings until 1982. Since this was an Age Discrimination in Employment Act case and the firings were intentional, the actual awards were double the pay determination.[3]

Becoming as costly to organizations are violations of employee rights that are not explicitly protected—that is, rights for which no acts have been passed and no court decisions rendered that explicitly cover the employee right being violated.[4] For example, in June 1980, the Michigan Supreme Court ruled that Blue Cross/Blue Shield and MASCO Corporation unfairly dismissed one employee each because they had made oral assurances that they would not be fired as long as they performed their jobs. As a consequence, the Blue Cross/Blue Shield employee was awarded a $72,000 settlement, and the employee from MASCO was awarded $300,000. Although the companies said they were merely following the traditionally accepted management right of practicing "termination at will," the court said that it cannot be used where employment contracts (explicit or implied) exist.[5]

Although not respecting employee rights can be costly to organizations as a consequence of back pay awards and fines, it can also be costly because of the increased difficulty in attracting and retaining good employees. Thus, two other important purposes served by respecting employee rights are attracting and retaining good employees, making recruitment and selection more effective and their need less frequent. Additional purposes of respecting employee rights are observed through their extensive relationships with the other PHRM activities.

Relationships Influencing Employee Rights

As Exhibit 14.1 shows, the area of employee rights has extensive relationships with other PHRM activities and the internal environment. Other relationships exist, but Exhibit 14.1 shows some of the more important ones.

Relationships with Other PHRM Activities

The most important relationships between PHRM activities and employee rights are those involving union-management relations, training and development, and performance appraisal.

Exhibit 14.1   Relationships and Aspects of Employee Rights

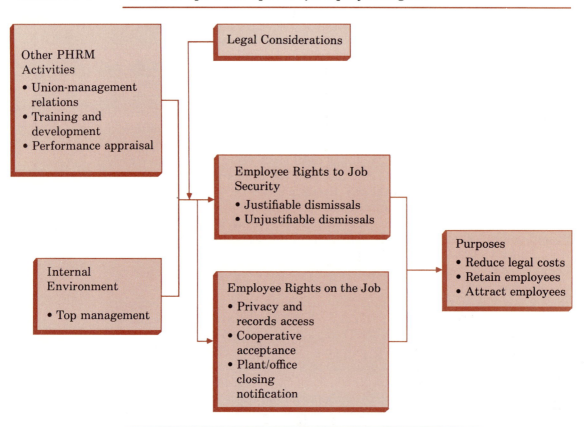

Union-Management Relations.   Where unions exist, employee job security rights are generally protected by the union-management contract. Since less than 25 percent of the labor force is unionized, many workers are left without this protection. However, as more cases similar to those in the Blue Cross/ Blue Shield and MASCO Corporation are settled, the protection afforded the union-management contract becomes relatively less protective. Nevertheless, if job security becomes a major issue, it may stimulate organizing activity, as suggested in Chapter 15.

Training and Development.   Supervisors are more likely to unjustifiably dismiss employees and commit sexual harassment offenses if they have not received effective training on these issues. A frequently suggested approach to the issue of sexual harassment is to develop an organizational policy on it and train all the supervisors and managers in avoiding sexual harassment.[6]

Performance Appraisal.   A frequent ground for dismissal (in addition to the termination-at-will doctrine) that supervisors often use is poor employee performance. When asked by the court to show evidence of such, however, supervisors and PHRM managers are often unable to produce it. Often records of employee performance are either inaccurately maintained or inaccurately used. Sometimes employees are never made aware that they are performing inadequately or never given a chance to respond to charges of poor performance nor to improve (lack of due process). As a consequence of more suits against unjustifiable dismissal being won by the employees, organizations are likely to intensify efforts to train supervisors and managers in good appraisal practices, to maintain accurate PHRM records, and to establish grievance procedures to ensure due process protection.[7]

Relationships with the Internal Environment

Top management shares some of the responsibility for employee rights because they set policy, with input from PHRM, on the treatment of human resources. Although flexibility may be limited in deciding whether or not to respect the legal rights of employees, there is flexibility in deciding whether or not to respect the "humane" rights of employees. Top management's policy regarding these rights is important in shaping some of the PHRM activities and the way the organization's human resources are treated—above and beyond the way they "must" be treated.

Discussion of the purposes and importance of employee rights and the relationships that influence those rights inevitably involves references to legal considerations. This is because numerous legal considerations are relevant to employee rights, including those involving job security and rights on the job.

Legal Considerations in Employee Rights

Because the entire activity of employee rights is filled with legal considerations, this section is much larger than those in previous chapters. This section is followed by suggested PHRM strategies to facilitate employer recognition of all the employee rights discussed in this chapter.

Employee Rights to Job Security

The following "PHRM in the News," which describes the history of the termination-at-will practice, presents several historical and legal considerations that are used to justify termination of an employee at the employer's will, without cause. Although employers have relied on the termination-at-will doctrine over the years, using it today as a justifiable defense is proving less legally defensible because of several recent legal considerations[8]:

- Title VII of the Civil Rights Act of 1964, which prohibits discharge (as well as other employment decisions) because of sex, race, religion, or national origin of the individual or because the individual has made a charge, testified, assisted, or participated in any manner in any investigation, proceeding, or hearing under Title VII.[9]

- The Vocational Rehabilitation Act of 1973 as amended in 1978 and various state fair employment acts, which prohibit employees from being discharged because of handicaps unrelated to the performance of the major duties of the job or when the employer fails to make a reasonable accommodation allowing the employees to perform (*Frito-Lay* v. *Wisconsin Labor and Industry Review Commission*, 1981).[10]

- The Age Discrimination in Employment Act of 1967 (ADEA) as amended in 1978, which prohibits discharge because of age for employees between forty and seventy years (*Cancellier* v. *Federated Department Stores*, 1981).

- The National Labor Relations Act of 1935 (NLRA), which prohibits discharge because of union-organizing activities or for the assertion of rights under a union contract, even if the employee in question had a record of poor performance (*NLRB* v. *Transportation Management*, 1983). The NLRA, which established the National Labor Relations Board (NLRB), created a special situation in relation to discharge by the employer where employees are represented by a union. In this situation, the termination-at-will doctrine essentially does not apply. The union-management contract replaces this doctrine. Although the contract provisions cannot violate statutory law, they can specify (either explicitly or more generally) the conditions under which employees can be fired. Consequently, the Court of Appeals for the Seventh Circuit ruled that a company cannot fire an employee who, because of religious beliefs, refuses to pay union dues and instead contributes the money to charity, even though the company and the union have a collective bargaining agreement stating that a condition of employment is payment of dues (*Nottelson* v. *Smith Steel Workers*, 1981).

- The Occupational Safety and Health Act of 1970, which prohibits discharge for resistance to work under unsafe conditions (*Whirlpool Corp.* v. *Marshall*, 1980).

- Court decisions like *Petermann* v. *International Brotherhood of Teamsters* (1959) and *Ness* v. *Hocks* (1975), which protect employees against

History of the Termination-at-Will Rule

The termination-at-will rule, which was developed in the United States nearly 100 years ago, was explained by one Tennessee court in 1884 in this way: "All may dismiss their employee(s) at will, be they many or few, for good cause, for no cause, or even for cause morally wrong without being thereby guilty of legal wrong [*Payne* v. *Western & A.R.R. Co.*, 81 Tenn. 507 (1884)]. Thereafter, the common law rule became so well established that, in the absence of some explicit contractual provision, every employment was considered to be an employment at will; employers could dismiss employees for any reason or for no reason at all. A century of court rulings provided a variety of justifications for the termination-at-will rule: If an employee can quit for any reason, an employer can discharge for any reason. The employment relationship should not be forced upon either the employer or the employee; seldom do both parties expect an employment relationship to be permanent. Some experts traced the rationale for the termination-at-will rule to those sections of the *Restatement of Agency* that provide that the employee be viewed as an agent of the employer and thus legally bound to obedience and loyalty to the employer. Hence the common law protection of the employer's right to discharge has traditionally been viewed as a protection of the organization's economic activity.

Early in this century many courts were adamant in their strict application of this common law rule. For example, the termination-at-will rule was used in a 1903 case, *Boyer* v. *Western Union Tel. Co.* [124 F 246, CCED Mo. (1903)], in which the court upheld the company's right to discharge its employees for union activities and indicated that the results would be the same if the company's employees had been discharged for being Presbyterians. Later on, in *Lewis* v. *Minnesota Mutual Life Ins. Co.* [37 NW 2d 316 (1949)], the termination-at-will rule was used to uphold the dismissal of the life insurance company's best salesman—even though no apparent cause for dismissal was given and the company had promised the employee lifetime employment in return for his agreement to remain with the company.

Only recently have court decisions and legislative enactments moved the pendulum of protection away from the employer and toward the rights of the individual employee through limitations on the termination-at-will rule.

Source: S. A. Youngblood and G. L. Tidwell, "Termination-at-Will: Some Changes in the Wind," *Personnel,* May–June 1981 (New York: AMACOM, a division of American Management Associations, 1981), p. 24.

discharge for failing to do what the employer ordered or even giving testimony against the employer. However, this protection may not be afforded to employees in states whose laws stipulate that (because of the termination-at-will or employment-at-will doctrine) employees can be fired for any or no reason (*Phillips* v. *Goodyear Tire and Rubber Co.,* 1981).[11]

- Court decisions like those handed down by the Michigan Supreme Court (*Toussaint* v. *Blue Cross/Blue Shield* [1980] and *Ebling* v. *Masco Corporation* [1980]) protecting employees against discharge if there is a *written or implied contractual agreement* between employer and employee, evidence of which may be found in corporate policy statements that state that they are a fair employer (these statements are often found in companies' personnel handbooks).[12]

- Court decisions like *Morge* v. *Beebe Rubber Co. (1974)* and Geary v. *United States Steel Corp.* (1974) and congressional legislation like the Whistleblower's Protection Act, which protect employees from discharge for retaliation or malice that is not in the best interests of our economic system or the public good (*O'Sullivan* v. *Mallon,* 1978; *Harless* v. *First National Bank in Fairmont,* 1978).[13] Although judges have overruled dismissals on these best interest grounds, they are not always willing to do so (*Martin* v. *Platt,* 1979; and *Abrisz* v. *Pulley Freight Line Inc.,* 1978).

- Court decisions like the *Board of Regents of State Colleges* v. *Roth* (1972) and *Perry* v. *Sindermann* (1972), which protect workers from discharge when due process protection has not been given by the employer.

- Various state acts, such as Montana's Maternity Leave Act, which prohibit employers from terminating female employees because of pregnancy or from refusing reasonable leaves of absence for pregnant workers (*Miller-Wohl Co.* v. *Commission of Labor,* 1981).[14]

Based on these many court decisions and laws, discharge is not a legitimate action, under any circumstances, for the following employee actions:

- Whistleblowing (e.g., opposing and publicizing policies or practices that violate laws such as the antitrust, consumer protection, or environmental protection laws)
- Garnishment for any one indebtedness
- Complaining or testifying about equal pay or wage/hour law violations
- Complaining or testifying about safety hazards and/or refusing an assignment because of the belief that the assignment is dangerous
- Engaging in union activities, provided there is no violence or unlawful behavior
- Engaging in concerted activity to protest wages, working conditions, or safety hazards
- Filing a workers' compensation claim
- Filing unfair labor practice charges with the NLRB or a state agency
- Filing discrimination charges with the Equal Employment Opportunity Commission (EEOC) or a state or municipal fair employment agency
- Cooperating in the investigation of a charge
- Reporting Occupational Safety and Health Administration (OSHA) violations[15]

A significant number of laws and acts support an employee's right to job security from being terminated at will (or without cause). Yet, the employer still retains some right to termination without cause. Granted, this right is shrinking and is gradually being taken in the direction of **termination for good cause,** which is similar to **termination for just cause,** found in union-management agreements where workers are unionized.

Although termination for good cause has not been an explicitly accepted doctrine for nonunion organizations, the decisions that courts are rendering suggest the safest (legal) grounds for discharge include the following:

- Incompetence in performance that does not respond to training or to accommodation
- Gross or repeated insubordination
- Too many unexcused absences
- Repeated lateness
- Verbal abuse
- Physical violence
- Falsification of records
- Drunkenness on the job
- Theft

Even in these instances, however, discharge may most effectively be regarded as a last resort. Firing or discharge, even under one of the prior nine conditions, should be the last step in a progressive discipline system such as the one presented in Chapter 8.[16] Furthermore, all evidence and material relevant to each step and even any decision to discharge an employee should be documented. Even though an employer may have the right to fire an employee, the employer may be requested to show evidence indicating that none of the protections against termination at will or for good cause was violated. This evidence, however, may not be required until after the discharged employee establishes a *prima facie* case of such a violation, (e.g., sex discrimination) (*Texas Department of Community Affairs* v. *Burdine*, 1981; *Miller* v. *WFLI Radio, Inc.*, 1982).[17] Thus, if several employees are caught engaged in theft, and the company decides that such behavior is grounds for dismissal, all employees committing the theft must be treated similarly, discharged in this example (*McDonald* v. *Santa Fe Trail Transportation Co.*, 1976), or else there is a *prima facie* case of discrimination.

Adding to the nine grounds for discharge listed earlier is a recent one involving an IBM employee. IBM's discharge of an employee for disclosing confidential pay data was upheld by the National Labor Relations Board. But even though an employer may have the right to fire an employee, the employer may be requested to show evidence indicating that none of the protections against termination-at-will was violated.

Employee Rights on the Job

Of the several employee rights on the job, those examined here include rights to privacy and access to employment records, cooperative acceptance—particularly freedom from sexual harassment—and the right to plant closing notification.[18]

Rights to Privacy and Access to Employment Records.   Several legal considerations are applicable to privacy rights. Recently several lawsuits have been brought on behalf of individuals against organizations for invasion of privacy rights. These lawsuits have been related to or responsible for four federal laws. The encompassing law is the Privacy Act of 1974, which applies only to federal agencies. It pertains to the verification of references in selection and employment decisions. This act allows individuals to determine which records pertaining to them are collected, used, and maintained; to review and amend such records; to prevent unspecified use of such records; and to bring civil suit for damages against those intentionally violating the rights specified in the act.

The second federal privacy law is the Fair Credit and Reporting Act, which permits job applicants to know the nature and content of the credit file on them that is obtained by the organization. The third law is the Family Education Rights and Privacy Act, or the Buckley Amendment. This allows students to inspect their educational records, and prevents educational institutions from supplying information without students' consent. If students do not provide this consent, potential employers are prevented from learning of their educational record. The fourth law is the Freedom of Information Act, which also pertains only to federal agencies. This act allows individuals to see all the material an agency uses in its decision-making processes.

Although these four laws apply primarily to federal agencies, private organizations will most likely face similar federal or state laws in the near future. These laws may establish the right of all individuals to have access to their personnel (personal) files and to be notified of the pending release of information to third parties. Several states have already enacted privacy legislation affecting the privacy of job applicants as well as that of current employees. For example, state legislation enacted in California, Maine, Connecticut, Michigan, Oregon, and Pennsylvania gives employees access to their personnel files and defines which information employees are entitled and not entitled to see, as well as where, when, and under what circumstances the employees may see their files. The provisions of these state laws are similar to some of those recommended by the U.S. Privacy Protection Study Commission in 1977 for private employers to adopt before states intervened.[19]

In addition to these state and federal regulations are the rights of employees, their designated representatives, and OSHA to have access to their on-the-job medical records and records that indicate measurement of employee exposure to toxic substances. These rights are provided for by the Access to Employee Exposure and Medical Records Regulation of 1980 (amending OSHA) and the Hazard Communication Standard, and they are consistent with the employee's right to know, mentioned in Chapter 13.

Rights to Cooperative Acceptance.   The category of cooperative acceptance refers to the right of employees to be treated fairly and with respect regardless of race, sex, national origin, physical disability, age, or religion while on the job (as well as in obtaining a job and maintaining job security). This means that employees not only have the right to not be discriminated against in employment practices and decisions but also have the right to be free of sexual harassment.

Today the right to not be discriminated against is generally protected under Title VII, the Age Discrimination in Employment Act, the Rehabilitation Act, the Vietnam Era Veteran's Readjustment Assistance Act, and numerous court decisions and state and local government laws. Though the right to be free of sexual harassment is found explicitly in fewer laws, it has been made in the 1980 EEOC guidelines stating that sexual harassment is a form of sex discrimination. The equating of sexual harassment as a form of sex discrimination under Title VII is also found in numerous court decisions (*Tomkins* v. *Public Service Electric and Gas Company et al.*, 1977; *William* v. *Saxbe*, 1976; *Barnes* v. *Costle*, 1977; *Heelen* v. *Johns-Manville Corp.*, 1978; *Scott* v. *Sears Roebuck*, 1985; *Horn* v. *Duke Homes*, 1985; *Glasgow* v. *Georgia Pacific Corp.*, 1985; *Meritor Savings Bank* v. *Vinson*, 1986).[20]

Rights to Plant/Office Closing Notification.   The employee's **right to plant/office closing or relocation notification** is an important one.[21] The suicide rate among displaced workers is almost thirty times the national average. The right of employers (where a union represents the workers) to move production facilities is greatly affected by federal labor law under the NLRA, Section 8(a). It has been clearly established that employers must bargain over the *effects* of a plant closing/relocation. The Supreme Court, however, recently ruled against the NLRB, saying that a corporate decision to close a particular location or even a product line is not a subject that must be negotiated in advance with the union as long as it is for solely economic reasons (*First National Maintenance* v. *NLRB*, 1981). In 1984 the NLRB also ruled, in a decision against the United Auto Workers, that Otis Elevator could move operations without bargaining with the union.

Several states have now recognized the importance of plant or office closings and relocations and are considering legislation to control them. Maine and Wisconsin require prenotification and have penalties for employers who move plants without doing so. Massachusetts recently passed plant closing legislation. At the federal level, legislation is still in the formulation stage. Possible acts may require employers to give prenotification of plant closings and relocations and the payment of severance pay to those employees displaced.

In addition to legal considerations in employee rights on the job, more "humane" considerations include outplacement assistance for employees who are no longer needed even though they may be competent performers. Such circumstances may arise if a plant or office is moving or closing, or if it must reduce its work force for economic reasons.[22]

Strategies for Employee Rights

Because of several legal and humane considerations for employers being concerned with employee rights, organizations must develop and implement strategies for recognizing these rights. Effectively implementing the other PHRM activities discussed in this book is one general way to help ensure that many of the legally based employee rights are recognized. In addition, organizations can implement specific programs including employee privacy policies, employee assistance programs, outplacement activities, and sexual harassment prevention training.

Employer Strategies for Employee Job Security Rights

In addition to adhering to all the various legal considerations applying to job security rights mentioned earlier, employers should do several things to ensure just dismissals. **Communicate Expectations and Prohibitions.** Although ignorance is generally no excuse in nonemployment settings, it is in employment settings. Generally, employees may be disciplined only for conduct not in accordance with what he or she knows or reasonably understands is prohibited or required (*Patterson* v. *American Tobacco Co.*, 1976, 1978; *Sledge* v. *J. P. Stevens & Co.*, 1978; and *Donaldson* v. *Pillsbury Co.*, 1977). Employers must therefore ensure that performance expectations are conveyed to employees along with information about what is prohibited. Employers can do this by requiring written policy statements, job descriptions, and performance criteria. Written standards should also exist for promotions (*Rowe* v. *General Motors Corp.*, 1972; and *Robinson* v. *Union Carbide Corp.*, 1976).

Writing policy statements and communicating them is insufficient, however. Just as important is making sure that policy statements are reasonable and related to the essence of the business. Failure to include these in policy statements are likely to lead to results experienced by IBM. The following "PHRM in the News" describes the situation in more detail.

Treat Employees Equally.   If the employer discharges one employee for five unexcused absences, then another employee with five unexcused absences must also be discharged (*McDonald* v. *Santa Fe Trail Transportation Co.*, 1976). Periodic training for supervisors can help ensure that discharge policies are communicated and administered the same way by all supervisors.

Grievance Procedures and Due Process.   Grievance precedures not only should be established to ensure due process for employees but also should be administered consistently and fairly.[23] For example, evidence should be available to employee and employer, and both parties should have the right to call witnesses and refuse to testify against themselves. Furthermore, these grievance procedures should be clearly stated as company policy and communicated to the employees. Exhibit 14.2 shows an example of the contents of a grievance policy. Simultaneous with the existence of a grievance policy should be a progressive discipline policy.

Establish Progressive Discipline Procedures.   For most violations of company rules, firing should be the last step in a carefully regulated system of escalating discipline, often called **progressive discipline**. The steps possible in progressive discipline procedures include the following:

- *Warning* may be oral at first, but should be written, signed by the employee, and a copy kept in the personnel files. Having that as well as the follow-

---

PHRM in the News

Employee Fired for Violating Privacy Policy Wins Damages

A recent decision by the California Court of Appeal emphasizes the need for employers to adhere to established company policies.

In *Rulon-Miller* v. *IBM,* No. AO 16455 (1st Dist. 1984), the employee was awarded $300,000 in damages against her former employer when she was discharged for dating an employee of a competitor.

The plaintiff, a female employee of IBM, began dating a co-employee while they were both assigned to San Francisco. One year later, the male co-employee left IBM to join a competitor and was transferred to Philadelphia.

When he returned to San Francisco following a one-year absence, the plaintiff and he resumed their relationship. The fact that the two were seeing each other was widely known.

Not until one year later was the fact that the plaintiff was dating an employee of a competitor questioned. Because of the "conflict of interest," she was given a choice to stop seeing her former co-employee or to be terminated, and was given between two days and one week to make her decision.

The next day she was terminated. Of major significance in the case was a memorandum signed by a former chairman of IBM to all managers emphasizing the need to respect the right to privacy of IBM employees, and discouraging in no uncertain terms employment decisions based on private activities that have no impact on job performance and that are "not rightfully the company's concern."

Impact: This case emphasized three things of which employers must be aware. First, in drafting personnel policies and procedures some care must be taken not to insert gratuitous, overly broad policies that are not necessary to the efficient operation of the company.

Second, all managers with authority to make employment decisions must be aware of any policy affecting the manner in which such decisions are made, and must be cautioned to act at all times with such policies in mind.

Third, any decision with regard to employment, compensation, discipline, or termination should be based on verifiable job-related criteria.

Source: *Personnel Journal,* February 1985, p. 10. Reprinted with permission of *Personnel Journal,* Costa Mesa, California, all rights reserved.

---

ing information in the personnel files is important when building a case for disciplinary discharge. Unfortunately, the information needed is often missing from the file. The biggest deficiencies in employment records often surface only after an employee challenges the legality of a discharge. Valid personnel files, along with a progressive discipline policy for discharge, can be the best defense for discharge decisions, according to several arbitration decisions regarding discharge for excessive absenteeism (*S. Cabin* v. *Union Carbide Corp.,* 45 LA 195; *C. La Cugna* v. *General Electric Co.,* 32 LA 637; *E. Jones* v. *Lockheed Aircraft Corp.,* 35 LA 725).[24]

- *Reprimand* is official, in writing, and placed in the employee's file.
- *Suspension* can be for as short as part of a day or as long as several months without pay, depending on the seriousness of the employee's offense and the circumstances.

Exhibit 14.2   **A Typical Grievance Procedure**

With good working relations, it is to be expected that supervisory personnel and department heads will recognize and work to resolve employee problems and dissatisfactions at their first appearance and, therefore, that this appeal procedure should have limited usage.

STEP 1:   Discuss the problem or dissatisfaction with your supervisor, who will attempt to resolve it in accordance with established hospital personnel policies within *two working days,* unless there are extenuating circumstances.

STEP 2:   Should the problem remain unresolved, your supervisor will endeavor to make an appointment for you to discuss the matter with your department head within the next *three working days.*

STEP 3:   Should the problem continue to remain unresolved, the employee should present the problem or dissatisfaction in writing (see attached form) and forward it to the director, employee relations, who either will schedule a meeting with all interested parties or will present a recommendation within *five working days* for a resolution of the problem based upon hospital personnel policies and practices.

Most matters of employee concern should be resolved at the conclusion of Step 3. However, for that unusual problem which may not have been resolved to the employee's satisfaction, the employee may request that the matter be brought to the attention of administration for consideration and decision. An administrative decision will be rendered and communicated in writing to all interested parties within *ten working days.* This decision will be final and binding.

Source: T. Rendero, "Grievance Procedures for Nonunionized Employers," *Personnel,* Jan.–Feb. 1980 (New York: AMACOM, a division of American Management Associations, 1980), p. 7.

- *Disciplinary transfer* may take the pressure off a situation that might explode into violence or one in which personality conflict is a part of the disciplinary problem.
- *Demotion* can be a reasonable answer to problems of incompetence or an alternative to layoff for economic reasons.
- *Discharge* is the last resort, used only when all else has failed, although it might be a reasonable immediate response to violence, theft, or falsification of records. But firing can be exceedingly painful even if well organized and planned. Many individuals are capable of effective performance, but only in certain types of situations. Thus, some organizations carefully diagnose performance deficiencies, as discussed in Chapter 7. Such a diagnosis may result in reassigning employees to different parts of the organization and trading top-level managers to other organizations.[25]

Another step in progressive discipline that may be added is the "last chance agreement." Before firing, an employer may be willing to grant an employee one more chance to prove him- or herself, but only with several stipulations. For example, instead of suspending or terminating an employee for excessive absenteeism, the employer may grant the employee one last chance.[26] To support such a program, an organization may use employee assistance programs (EAPs), as described in Chapter 7.[27]

Taking all of these steps, however, does not ensure that the problem will be solved. Termination may still be necessary. The following advice may help in performing this difficult task:

> The termination interview should be brief. Normally, a ten-to-fifteen-minute meeting is sufficient. A longer meeting increases the opportunity for the company representative (in this case, you) to make a mistake. Some mistakes can be costly.
>
> It is best to conduct the termination meeting in that person's office or in some office other than your own. If conducted in your own office, you may be trapped into a lengthy harangue by a disgruntled individual who is using you to vent . . . hostility, anger, and frustration.
>
> Many individuals hear very little after they understand they have lost their job. This is understandable. They often begin to think of their future [or] the anxiety and stress of having no job, and there is a strong concern about their family, especially if the individual is the chief wage earner in the family.
>
> Hence, have a written description of benefits and/or salary continuation, if applicable. Also include how the individual is to be paid.
>
> It is a good idea to role play with someone before you actually do the termination. It is better, yet, if you can video tape the role play(s). Practice can help iron out the bugs and the discomfort and make it easier and less cumbersome in the actual termination meeting.[28]

To help reduce the possibilities of terminated employees successfully bringing suit, organizations are also changing other employment practices:

> **Firing rights are eroded by courts, forcing employers to revise methods.**
>
> The long-held right to fire employees "at will" has been limited by state court decisions. As a result, "you can still fire people" says a New York apparel concern executive, but if companies aren't careful, "you can have some very expensive consequences" if employees sue. Corporate personnel manuals "are getting very detailed" as protection against legal action, says Columbia University professor David Lewin.
>
> Del E. Webb Corp. rewrites its employee manual and job-application forms, eliminating the word "permanent" from employee descriptions. The company mulls hiring a placement firm to handle dismissals. Other companies spend more time negotiating dismissals; severance pay often is given for release from liability.
>
> NAS Insurance Services Inc., Santa Monica, Calif., offers insurance for companies sued by employees for wrongful discharge.[29]

Employer Strategies for Employee Rights on the Job

To protect employee rights on the job, employers must develop effective policies, procedures, and programs in regard to privacy and records access, cooperative acceptance—particularly sexual harassment—and plant or office closings.

Employee Privacy Rights and Records Access.   New since the 1960s is the concern for the privacy of personnel records and employee access to personnel files.[30] As discussed previously, privacy legislation generally does not cover private employer-employee relationships. Nevertheless, many companies, such as General Tire and Chase Manhattan Bank, are moving ahead on their own to establish policies and rules governing employee privacy and access rights.[31] Although a few years ago, employers were only attempting to define employee privacy, today almost 50 percent of the major companies have written policies regarding the privacy of personnel records. In addition, over 85 percent provide employees access to records containing information about themselves.[32]

Employer concerns about employee privacy rights are also influencing pre-employment screening and the use of polygraph tests. Prehire practices are being examined to ensure that only job-related information is collected, because collecting nonjob information is now considered an unnecessary intrusion into the private lives of job applicants. Similar opinions are becoming widespread on the use of polygraph tests as a way of gathering information for selection and placement decisions.[33]

Employee Rights to Cooperative Acceptance.   Although many issues are associated with employee rights to cooperative acceptance, sexual harassment is one that has recently surfaced and is of considerable concern to many employees and employers. The focus here on only sexual harassment in no way diminishes the issues related to the rights to cooperative acceptance on the basis of race, age, disability, national origin, religion, or retaliation.

Where once certain activities between supervisors (or managers) and employees may have been regarded as good-natured fun, today these same activities may constitute sexual harassment.[34] According to the 1980 EEOC guidelines on harassment, certain conduct is sexual harassment if it is verbal and physical conduct of a sexual nature, and if the following apply:

- Submission to such conduct is made either explicitly or implicitly a term or condition of an individual's employment.
- Submission to or rejection of such conduct by an individual is used as the basis for employment decisions affecting such individuals.
- Such conduct has the purpose or effect of substantially interfering with an individual's work performance or creating an intimidating, hostile, or offensive working environment.

Employers need to be particularly concerned with developing strategies to prevent sexual harassment, because employers are responsible for the sexual harassment committed on or by their employees (*Barnes* v. *Costle*, 1977).[35] The following five steps can help form a strategy[36]:

- The PHRM manager should affirmatively raise the issue of harassment and its existence to the rest of the organization and should encourage top management to make it a rule that all discharges must be reviewed by a senior corporate officer or review board.
- Since the employer is liable for sexual harassment except where it can be shown that the organization took immediate and appropriate corrective action (then the offending individual is guilty), it pays to set up reporting (grievance) procedures for those who have been harassed.

■ Procedures for corroborating a sexual harassment charge should be established. That is, the PHRM manager should make sure that the person charged with sexual harassment has a right to respond immediately after charges are made by the alleged victim. Due process must be provided the alleged victim as well as the alleged perpetrator.

■ A set of steps in a framework of progressive discipline for perpetrators of sexual harassment should be specified. These could be the same steps used by the organization as a way of treating any violation of organizational roles and policies (see the progressive discipline procedures discussed earlier).

■ Finally, all employees should be made aware of the company's position on sexual harassment. Support such as training programs for managers and supervisors should be provided.

Although implementing these steps does not guarantee prevention or elimination of sexual harassment, it establishes a clear articulation of company policy on this important area in utilizing human resources. Implementing a policy regarding plant or office closings and employment outplacement does the same.

Employee Rights to Plant/Office Closing Notification. Employees have few legal rights to notification by employers of a facility to be closed down or relocated. As in resisting the right of an employee to a job, employers resist this notification right because they say it limits their flexibility to manage, that it violates their management rights and rights of ownership. But, as important to employees, employers argue that it is better for management to have its rights because this leads to the survival of the company and more jobs.[37]

These arguments, however, are beyond the immediate interest of the employees involved in a potential or actual plant closing as described in the initial "PHRM in the News." Despite their resistance, employers are recognizing the "humane" right of employees to be helped out when facilities are closed. Since this help starts before the facilities are closed, employees are notified in advance of the closing. Although some of this help was initiated by the pressure of unions on management, many nonunion companies are now providing help.[38] The most common form of help is outplacement assistance.

Outplacement assistance is usually offered to individuals who are discharged or displaced, but its major benefits are for entire work forces displaced because of plant or office closings. Outplacement assistance programs typically represent a large number of single components for employees. Since PHRM managers should be at the forefront in putting together these programs, briefly presenting one program and its results is useful.

The American Hospital Supply Corporation needed to close a division, and designed a six-month outplacement program. The single components were as follows:

■ Severance pay
■ Enhanced benefits

- Four-week termination notification period
- Training and development programs to help develop new skills and find other jobs
- Double pay for overtime work needed to get the facility ready to close down
- Retention bonus to encourage employees to stay until the time of actual closing

Results of this six-month wind-down outplacement assistance included the following:

- Zero exempt employee unplanned turnover and less than 5 percent nonexempt employee unplanned turnover during the wind-down period. This compares to 14 percent exempt and 22 percent nonexempt turnover during this six-month period in 1979.
- Approximately 23 percent of the employees were placed in other divisions of the corporation.
- Almost 90 percent of the outplaced employees received similar or superior compensation packages in their position.
- The six-month program was completed two weeks ahead of schedule.
- The outplacement assistance program enhanced the image of American Hospital Supply Corporation as a humane, people-oriented company.[39]

Trends in Employee Rights

The two major trends in employee rights are in assessing and in computer technology and HRIS. The trends in computer technology and HRIS are likely to provoke a great deal of interest and legal activity on the part of employees and employers.

Assessing Employee Rights Activities

When organizations recognize employee rights and establish programs to ensure they are observed, they can fulfill a third match: the match between employee rights and obligations and employer rights and obligation. In serving this third match, both organizations and employees benefit. Organizations benefit from reduced legal costs, since not observing many employee rights is illegal, and their images as good employers increase, resulting in enhanced organizational attractiveness. This in turn makes it easier for the organization to recruit a pool of potentially qualified applicants. Although expanded employee rights, especially job security, may reduce needed management flexibility and thus profitability, it may be an impetus for better planning, resulting in increased profitability.

Increased profitability may also result from the benefits that employees receive when their rights are observed: employees may experience a feeling of being treated fairly and with respect, increased self-esteem, and a heightened sense of job security. Employees who have job security may be more productive and committed to the organization than those without job security. As employees are beginning to see the guarantees of job security as a benefit, organizations are also gaining through reduced wage increase demands and greater flexibility in job assignments. This is happening in many of the traditionally unionized manufacturing industries. In those industries, the question of how employee rights, especially job security, are addressed is now more than a matter of profitability—it's a matter of survival. As discussed in Chapters 15 and 16, it's also a matter of concern for a new era of union-management relations.

An organization's employee rights activities can be assessed many ways, some of which are more appropriate than others, depending on the activity and the right in question. For example, evaluating employee rights activities by the size of legal costs is appropriate in the areas of cooperative acceptance and unjustifiable dismissal. Where employee rights are not legally protected, using legal costs to assess these activities may be less appropriate. If organizations fail to recognize and observe those "humane" rights not now legally protected, however, they may soon find themselves using legal costs to evaluate all their employee rights activities. Many organizations recognize this and are moving to recognize and observe humane rights as well as legal rights. This seems particularly true for employee rights to privacy and access to records and facility closing notification.

Computer Technology and HRIS in Employee Rights

Chapters 1 through 13 have presented computer applications that enable the PHRM department to use information actively in support of personnel planning, evaluation, and development. While pursuing these important goals by means of computer technology, employee rights must be taken into account. With computers and an HRIS, personnel can generate confidential personnel information in a variety of formats in a short time. Thus, many copies of confidential information may exist at any one time, increasing the likelihood that some may be misplaced or even stolen. Information required for a particular decision should be disseminated only to authorized individuals.

If the confidentiality of employee records is respected, an HRIS can be used to improve the process of monitoring employee rights. The computer can assist the PHRM department in maintaining records of employee complaints involving their on-the-job rights. By coding these complaints and storing them in an HRIS, information may be generated by department, by group of individuals working for a particular supervisor, or in other meaningful ways. Identifying patterns of complaints can signal to personnel that legally consistent policies and procedures have not been communicated to employees or perhaps have not been established by the company.

Summary

The entire area of employee rights is gaining considerable attention in our society. Though employees have won many legal rights over the years, the rights of most controversy are those not legally protected or those that may or may not be legally protected. Thus, the courts and the state and federal legislative and executive bodies have a potentially significant role in the future of employee rights. Whether the courts and the legislative and executive bodies move to increase the number of legally protected rights of employees depends to some extent on how employers behave in the area of unprotected employee rights. If they take a proactive position of recognizing many of the unprotected rights as "humane" rights that employees have, the courts and the legislative bodies may be less inclined to legislate employee rights, both job security and on-the-job rights. A great deal of momentum has already gathered to provide some type of legal protection for job security rights. Nevertheless, PHRM managers and employers can still have an impact in shaping the form of such legal protection.

Personnel and human resource managers also have an impact in how their organizations treat their employees in relation to legally protected rights. To help ensure that managers and supervisors treat employees fairly and with respect, PHRM managers must actively make the organization aware of the law and provide training opportunities so its managers and supervisors can implement the law.

Although many employers claim that essentially all their rights have been taken away, they still retain the right to terminate workers for poor performance, excessive absenteeism, unsafe conduct, and generally poor organizational citizenship. However, employers must maintain accurate records of these events for their employees and inform the employees of where they stand. To be safe, employers should also have a grievance process for employees to ensure that due process is respected. These practices are particularly useful in discharge situations that involve members of groups protected by Title VII, ADEA, the Rehabilitation Act, or the Vietnam Era Veterans Act.

Today, keeping objective and orderly PHRM files is more important than ever. They are critical evidence that employers have treated their employees fairly and with respect and have not violated any laws. Without these, organizations may get caught on the short end of a lawsuit. Although several federal laws influence record keeping, they are primarily directed at public employers. Many private employers, however, are moving on their own initiative to give their employees the right to access their personnel files and to prohibit the file information from being given to others without their consent. In addition, employers are casting out of their personnel files any non-job-related information and ending hiring practices that solicit that type of information.

Even when employers have the right to close down a facility without any notification, many employers are notifying their employees in advance of the closing. This is true even in nonunion companies. In addition to giving notification, employers are implementing outplacement assistance programs. These offer employees retraining for new jobs, counseling and aid in finding new jobs or in getting transfers, provisions for severance pay, and even retention bonuses for those who stay until closing time. Closing a facility with notification and with outplacement assistance seems to produce positive results for the organization and minimize the negative effects for the employees.

Finally, in the area of employee rights to cooperative acceptance, employers must prevent sexual harassment. This can be done with top management support, grievance procedures, verification procedures, training for all employees, and performance appraisal and compensation policies that reward those who practice antiharassment behavior and punish those who do not. Where appropriate, developing policies to prevent harassment in cooperation with the union is also useful. Union cooperation, however, should be sought on many issues. The benefits of doing so can be substantial, as discussed in the next two chapters.

Discussion Questions

1. Identify and discuss the four federal laws that have an impact on employee rights to privacy and access of employee records.
2. What is the bottom line in protection offered to employees concerning plant closing/relocation?
3. What is the termination-at-will doctrine? Why do you suppose courts in the late 1880s were more willing to uphold the doctrine than courts today?
4. How would you distinguish a just from an unjust dismissal? Is this distinction easier to make for lower-level jobs than for upper-level or managerial jobs? Explain.
5. The industrial, occupational, and demographical composition of the labor force has shifted over the past twenty years. How might these specific shifts coincide with the heightened interest in employee rights in the 1980s?
6. Due process has been interpreted as the duty to inform an employee of a charge, solicit employee input, and provide the employee with feedback in regard to the employment decision. How can a grievance procedure ensure this type of due process for an employee accused of sexual harassment? How can the grievance procedure protect the victim of the alleged harassment?
7. Develop counterarguments for the following arguments in support of the termination-at-will doctrine:
   a. If the employee can quit for any reason, the employer can fire for any reason.
   b. Because of business cycles, employers must have flexibility to expand and contract their work force.
   c. Discharged employees are always free to find other employment.
   d. Employers have incentives not to unjustly discharge employees; therefore, their power to terminate should not be restricted.
8. What do you suppose are the most common reasons for termination decisions? How can PHRM prevent these causes of termination?
9. What potential employee rights violations could occur with an automated HRIS? How could you protect against these violations?
10. What kinds of behaviors might constitute sexual harassment? How does an organization prevent those types of behaviors from occurring?

PC Project

The area of employee rights has received considerable attention. One important aspect of employee rights is knowledge of the law. This PC Project will assess your knowledge of the legality of various interview questions. You or someone that you know may have been (or will be) asked an illegal question in an employment interview. You can compare your responses with those of graduating business students. In what areas does there seem to be a lack of knowledge of the law? What are the implications for interviewees and interviewers?

C A S E   S T U D Y

Office Romance or Sexual Harassment?

Dick Fenton read the anonymous memorandum slowly, wondering who the author(s) might be. As associate dean of the College of Business at Eastern State College for the past year and a half, he thought he had seen and heard everything. But today was a new day and one that Dick was likely not to forget.

The gist of the memo was an allegation that a married faculty member in the accounting department was having an affair with one of his Ph.D. students and that this was the cause of some unfair and inequitable treatment of other Ph.D. students. To make matters worse, the accused faculty member was also the Ph.D. coordinator for the accounting department Ph.D. program, which currently enrolled twenty-two doctoral students.

Dick, an accountant himself, knew and had worked with this faculty member when he was still in the department prior to his administration days. He had heard some rumors of office romances at cocktail parties but hadn't given them serious attention. Dick believed that although the grapevine was an efficient pipeline of information, its accuracy, based on his prior experience, was of dubious value.

As Dick put the memo down, he recalled an incident involving his predecessor, Bill McDonald, who has since returned to his academic department. Bill had received a similar complaint from some MBA students who believed that a professor

was harassing another MBA student. When Bill confronted the professor with the allegation, the enraged professor told Bill in no uncertain terms to MYOB. Although that professor has since left Eastern, he eventually married the student. Dick could count three faculty marriages within the college currently where the faculty spouse was a former student of the faculty member.

From a college perspective, Dick was upset by the potential liability of the college should the writers of the memo go public with their allegations. Two complaints specifically were that competitive selection to attend professional conferences and preliminary examination procedures were biased in favor of the student engaged in the affair with the professor. If these charges were true, the college would look silly attempting to defend itself.

From yet another perspective, Dick worried about the potential adverse effect a public revelation like this could have on future doctoral student recruitment efforts. The college currently boasted a program of about one hundred students and planned to continue to expand the graduate program while shrinking the undergraduate program. Dick has been successful raising money from Big Eight firms for support of computer equipment and student fellowships. Bad publicity could only jeopardize these efforts.

Then another disturbing scenario began to emerge as Dick processed the ramifications of the anonymous memo. What if the Ph.D. student was not a "willing" party to this office romance? After all, the professor is in a position of power over the student, especially when the professor runs the Ph.D. program. What if the alleged romance cools off and now a bitter Ph.D. student emerges with vindictiveness in her heart?

The inescapable conclusion was that Dick knew he had to do something—but what? In light of his predecessor's experience with these types of allega-

tions, he was hesitant to intervene in any way. Yet, if he did nothing and the charges in the memo were essentially true, a number of constituents could potentially be harmed. Dick believed he had to take the concerns of the other Ph.D. students, the faculty of the department, the college as a whole, and the two people allegedly involved in the office romance in mind before proceeding, regardless of the direction chosen.

Notes

1. "Beyond Unions," *Business Week*, 8 July 1985, pp. 72–77; L. Ingrassia, "Non-Union Workers Are Gaining Status, But So Far the Talk Outweighs the Action," *Wall Street Journal*, 24 July 1980, p. 42; "The Growing Costs of Firing Non-Union Workers," *Business Week*, 6 Apr. 1981, pp. 95–98. Of the remaining 80 percent of the work force, approximately 15 million employees work for the federal, state, and local governments and are protected by civil service procedures or some form of tenure arrangements.

2. *Fair Employment Report*, 2 July 1984, p. 107. Used by permission.

3. For a description of these cases, see *Fair Employment Report*, 11 Oct. 1982, p. 165; *Fair Employment Report*, 8 Nov. 1982, p. 178.

4. *Fair Employment Guidelines*, no. 192, July 1981, pp. 1–8; J. R. Madison, "The Employee's Emerging Right to Sue for Arbitrary or Unfair Discharge," *Employee Relations Law Journal* 6 (3): 422–36; S. A. Youngblood and G. L. Tidwell, "Termination at Will: Some Changes in the Wind," *Personnel* (May–June 1981): 22–33. For an excellent summary of these issues, see S. A. Youngblood and L. Bierman, "Due Process and Employment-at-Will: A Legal and Behavioral Analysis," in *Research in Personnel and Human Resource Management*, vol. 3, ed. K. Rowland and G. R. Ferris (Greenwich, Conn.: JAI Press, 1985), pp. 185–230.

5. C. W. Summers, "Protecting All Employees against Unjust Dismissal," *Harvard Business Review* (Jan.–Feb. 1980): 132–39, 204–10; D. W. Ewing, "Due Process: Will Business Default?" *Harvard Business Review* (Nov.–Dec. 1982): 114–22.

6. G. E. Biles, "A Program Guide for Preventing Sexual Harassment in the Workplace," *Personnel Administrator* (June 1981): 49–56.

7. J. P. Swann, Jr., "Formal Grievance Procedures in Non-Union Plants," *Personnel Administrator* (Aug. 1981): 66–70; S. Brigg, "The Grievance Procedure and Organizational Health," *Personnel Journal* (June 1981): 471–74; "Dispute-Resolution Options: Ombudsmen and Arbitration," *Fair Employment Practices*, 23 Feb. 1984, pp. 3–4.

8. Youngblood and Bierman, "Due Process."; T. H. Williams, "Employment-at-Will," *Personnel Journal* (June 1985): 73–77; J. P. Shapiro and J. F. Tame, "Implied Contract Right to Job Security," *Stanford Law Review* (1974): 26; C. Summers, "Arbitration of Unjust Dismissal: A Preliminary Proposal," *The Future of Labor Arbitration in America* (New York: American Arbitration Association, 1976); C. J. Peck, "Unjust Discharges from Employment: A Necessary Change in the Law," *Ohio State Law Journal* 40 (1979): 1–49; J. Steiber, "The Case for Protection of Unorganized Employees against Unjust Discharge," *Proceedings of the Thirty-Second Annual Meeting*, Industrial Relations Research Association series, Dec. 1979, pp. 155–63; R. L. Hogler, "Employee Discipline and Due Process Rights: Is There an Appropriate Remedy?" *Labor Law Journal* 33 (1982): 783–92; W. M. Bulkeley, "Nuns vs. the Bishop: Teachers' Dismissal Winds Up in Court," *Wall Street Journal*, 13 Sept. 1982, p. 1; W. L. Wall, "Firms See Aid on Avoiding Employee Suits," *Wall Street Journal*, 28 July 1982, p. 23; E. L. Harrison, "Legal Restrictions on the Employers' Authority to Discipline," *Personnel Journal* (Feb. 1982): 136–46; A. T. Oliver, Jr., "The Disappearing Right to Terminate Employees at Will," *Personnel Journal* (Dec. 1982): 910–17. According to Oliver, two recent court decisions in California (*Cleary* v. *American Airlines, Inc.*, 1980; and *Pugh* v. *See's Candies*, 1981) appear to have all but ended termination at will in that state.

9. B. B. Durling, "Retaliation: A Misunderstood Form of Employment Discrimination," *Personnel Journal* (July 1981): 555–58.

10. In this case, the company failed to accommodate to an employee's condition of amblyopia, or "lazy eye." For a description, see *Fair Employment Report*, 9 Nov. 1981, p. 180.

11. For a description of this case, see "Public Policy Pair," *Bulletin to Management*, 10 Sept. 1981, p. 1.

12. "A Fight over the Freedom to Fire," *Business Week*, 20 Sept. 1982, p. 116.

13. "Armor for Whistle-Blowers," *Business Week*, 6 July 1981, pp. 97–98; W. F. Westin, "Michigan's Law to Protect Whistle Blowers," *Wall Street Journal*, 13 Apr. 1981, p. 1.

14. For further description of related cases and issues, see *Yancey* v. *State Personnel Board*, 1985; *Holien* v. *Sears Roebuck*, 1984; "Employment-at-Will Evolves," *Bulletin to Management*, 5 Apr. 1984, pp. 1–2; "Mandatory Retirement," *FEP Guidelines*, no. 225 (H), 1984; B. S. Murphy, W. E. Barlow, and D. D. Hatch, "Constructive Discharge under Title VII," *Personnel Journal* (Feb. 1985): 17; "Another View of Employment-at-Will," *Bulletin to Management*, 12 Sept. 1985, p. 88; B. Keller, "Of Hearth and Home and the Right to Work" *New York Times,* 11 Nov. 1984, p. 8E.

15. "Firing," *FEP Guidelines*, no. 241 (8), 1985, p. 3. See also "Discrimination Denied," *Bulletin to Management*, 13 June 1985, p. 3.

16. However, if a union-management contract exists, an arbitrator may not uphold firing if based on false application information. J. N. Drazin, "Firing over False Applications," *Personnel Journal* (June 1981): 433.

17. For a description of *Miller* v. *WFLI Radio, Inc.*, see *Fair Employment Report*, 27 Sept. 1982, p. 157.

18. Other rights (legal and humane) on the job that could be mentioned here include the right to a safe and quality work environment under OSHA (see Chapter 13); religious accommodation (see *Nottelson* v. *Smith Steel Workers* as an example); protection from retaliation (see *Fair Employment Guidelines*, no. 188, Mar. 1981, p. 1–8; B. B. Durling, "Retaliation: A Misunderstood Form of Employment Discrimination"); the right of an employee to have a co-worker along at an interview for disciplinary action (the Weingarten right, as discussed in *Personnel Administrator*, Nov. 1982, p. 10); the right of employees to smoke-free work areas (see "Office Smokers Feel the Heat," *Business Week*, 29 Nov. 1982, p. 102); and the freedom from national origin harassment (see C. J. Hollon and T. L. Bright, "National Origin Harassment in the Work Place: Recent Guideline Developments from the EEOC," *Employee Relations Law Journal* (Autumn 1982): 282–93).

19. For suggested courses of action, see R. J. Nobile, "Employee Searches in the Workplace: Developing a Realistic Search Policy," *Personnel Administrator* (May 1985): 89–98; J. C. O'Meara, "The Emerging Law of Employees' Right to Privacy," *Personnel Administrator* (June 1985): 159–65; *Employee Access to Records* (Englewood Cliffs, N. J.: Prentice-Hall, 1984).

20. C. K. Behrens, "Co-Worker Sexual Harassment: The Employer's Liability," *Personnel Journal* (May 1984): 12–14; "New Ruling on Sexual Harassment," *Management Review* (June 1985): 5; "Retaliation," *FEP Guidelines*, no. 237 (4), 1985; "Sexual Harassment," *FEP Guidelines*, no. 238 (5), 1985; "Participation Bars Protest," *Fair Employment Practices*," 12 Jan. 1984, p. 1; R. E. Quinn and P. L. Lees, "Attraction and Harassment: Dynamics of Sexual Politics in the Workplace," *Organizational Dynamics* (Autumn 1984): 35–46.

21. G. L. Felsten, "Current Considerations in Plant Shutdowns and Relocations," *Personnel Journal* (May 1981): 369–72; J. N. Draznin, "Closings and Consolidations," *Personnel Journal* (Oct. 1981): 764–65; L. Chavez, When ARCO Left Town," *New York Times*, 25 July 1982, pp. 15; F. J. Solomon, "Citicorp's Big-City Tactics Leave Them Jobless and Angry in Indiana," *Wall Street Journal*, 19 Aug. 1982, p. 19.

22. R. E. Taylor, "Before Closing St. Louis Globe-Democrat Owner Must Consider Offer, Agency Says," *Wall Street Journal*, 9 Nov. 1983, p. 14; J. J. McDonald, Jr., "State Plant Closing Laws: Preempted by the NLRA?" *Employee Relations Law Journal* (Autumn 1984): 241–57; P. R. Lewis, "Plant Closings: Legal Trends," *Personnel Administrator* (Oct. 1983): 21–22, 115–16; P. R. Lewis, "Legal Trends," *Personnel Administrator* (Jan. 1984): 8–12; "Plant Shutdowns: States Take a New Tack," *Business Week*, 24 Oct. 1983; pp. 72–76; A. B. Carroll, "When Business Closes Down: Social Responsibilities and Management Actions," *California Management Review* (Winter 1984): 125–39.

23. R. Folger and J. Greenberg, "Procedural Justice: An Interpretive Analysis of Personnel Systems," in *Research in Personnel and Human Resources Management*, vol. 3, ed. K. M. Rowland and G. R. Ferris (Greenwich, Conn.: JAI Press, 1985); "Improve Employee Relations with a Corporate Ombudsman," *Personnel Journal* (Sept. 1985): 12–13; T. Rendero, "Grievance Procedures for Nonunionized Employees," *Personnel* (Jan.–Feb. 1980): 4–10.

24. *Fair Employment Guidelines*, no. 194, Sept. 1981, pp. 1–8; D. Scotland and S. Markham, "Absenteeism Control Methods: A Survey of Practices and Results," *Personnel Administrator* (June 1982): 73–84.

25. D. N. Adams, Jr., "When Laying Off Employees, the Word is 'Out-Training,' " *Personnel Journal* (Sept. 1980): 719–21.

26. *Fair Employment Guidelines*, no. 192, Aug. 1981; P. Farish, "Pair Potpourri," *Personnel Administrator* (Aug. 1981): 8; H. Z. Levine, "Consensus," *Personnel* (May–June 1981): 4–11.

27. E. J. Busch, Jr., "Developing an Employee Assistance Program," *Personnel Journal* (Sept. 1981): 708–11; M. Douglass and D. Douglass, "Time Theft," *Personnel Administrator* (Sept. 1981): 13; H. J. Featherston and R. J. Bednarek, "A Positive Demonstration of Concern for Employees," *Personnel Administrator* (Sept. 1981): 43–47; D. Quayle, "American Productivity: The Devastating Effect of Alcoholism and Drug Abuse," *American Psychologist* (May 1983): 454–58;

C. A. Filipowicz, "The Troubled Employee: Whose Responsibility?" *Personnel Administrator* (June 1979): 17–22, 33; R. C. Ford and F. S. McLaughlin, "Employee Assistance Programs: A Descriptive Survey of ASPA Members," *Personnel Administrator* (Sept. 1981): 29–35; R. T. Hellan and W. J. Campbell, "Contracting for AEP Services," *Personnel Administrator* (Sept. 1981): 49–51; R. W. Hollman, "Beyond Contemporary Employee Assistance Programs," *Personnel Administrator* (Sept. 1981): 37–41; F. E. Kuzmits and H. E. Hammons II, "Rehabilitating the Troubled Employee," *Personnel Journal* (Apr. 1979): 238–42, 250; H. Z. Levine, "Consensus," *Personnel* (Mar.–Apr. 1981): 4–10; R. Ricklefs, "Firms Offer Employees A New Benefit: Help in Personal Problems," *Wall Street Journal,* 13 Aug. 1979, pp. 1, 21; L. B. Sager, "The Corporation and the Alcoholic," *Across the Board* (June 1979): 79–82, P. A. Stroberl and M. J. Schniederjans, "The Ineffective Subordinate: A Management Survey," *Personnel Administrator* (Feb. 1981): 72–76; Dickman and Emener, p. 56. P. E. Nathan, "Failures in Prevention: Why We Can't Prevent the Devastating Effect of Alcoholism and Drug Abuse," *American Psychologist* (May 1983): 459–67.

28. L. D. Foxman and W. L. Polsky, "Ground Rules for Terminating Workers," *Personnel Journal* (July 1984): 32; G. B. Hansen, "Preventing Layoffs: Developing an Effective Job Security and Economic Adjustment Program," *Employee Relations Law Journal* (Autumn 1985): 239–68.

29. *Wall Street Journal,* 1 Oct. 1985, p. 1. Reprinted by permission of *The Wall Street Journal,* © Dow Jones & Company, Inc., 1985. All Rights Reserved. See also L. Bierman and S. A. Youngblood, "Employment-at-Will and the South Carolina Experiment," *Industrial Relations Law Journal* (in press).

30. D. F. Linowes, "Update on Privacy Protection Safeguards," *Personnel Administrator* (June 1980): 39–42; D. F. Linowes, "Is Business Giving Employees Privacy?" Business and Society Review (Winter 1979–80): 47–49; A. F. Westin, "What Should Be Done about Employee Privacy?" *Personnel Administrator* (Mar. 1980): 27–30.

31. "Respecting Employee Privacy," *Business Week,* 11 Jan. 1982, pp. 130–31.

32. H. X. Levine, "Privacy of Employee Records," *Personnel* (May–June 1981): 4–11; J. A. Gildea, "Safety and Privacy: Are They Compatible?" *Personnel Administrator* (Feb. 1982): 78–83.

33. J. N. Draznin, "Polygraph Tests," *Personnel Journal* (Mar. 1981): 166.

34. E. G. C. Collins and T. B. Blodgett, "Sexual Harassment ... Some Get It ... Some Won't," *Harvard Business Review* (Mar.–Apr. 1981): 77–78; K. A. Thurston, "Sexual Harassment: An Organizational Perspective," *Personnel Administrator* (Dec. 1980): 59–64.

35. See also the rationale behind the employer being responsible for employee behavior under the two common-law doctrines of respondent superior and negligent hiring: M. S. Novit, "Employer Liability for Employee Misconduct: Two Common Law Doctrines," *Personnel* (Jan.–Feb. 1982): 11–18.

36. Biles. O. A. Ornati, "How to Deal with EEOC's Guidelines on Sexual Harassment," *EEO Compliance Manual* (Englewood Cliffs, N. J.: Prentice-Hall, 1980), pp. 377–80; R. H. Faley, "Sexual Harassment: A Critical Review of Legal Cases with General Principles and Practice Measures," *Personnel Psychology* 35 (1982): 583–600; "Sexual Harassment: Prevention Program," *Fair Employment Practices,* 14 June 1984, p. 4; "Sexual Harassment: Investigatory procedures; Alternate Remedies," *Fair Employment Practices,* 6 Sept. 1984, p. 3.

37. P. D. Johnston, "Personnel Planning for a Plant Shutdown," *Personnel Administrator* (Aug. 1981): 53–57.

38. T. Rendero, "Outplacement Practices," *Personnel* (July–Aug. 1980): 4–11; B. H. Millen, "Providing Assistance to Displaced Workers," *Monthly Labor Review* (May 1979): 17–22; "Outplacement Assistance," *Personnel Journal* (Apr. 1981): 250; M. Elleinis, "Tips for Employers Shopping Around for a New Plant Site," *AMA Forum* (July 1982): 34; "Plant Closings: Problems and Panaceas," *Management Review* (July 1982): 55–57. The issue of the employee's right to plant closing notification is also important on an international scale for multinational corporations: R. G. Caborn, "Workers Have a Right to Know More," *New York Times,* 3 Oct. 1982, p. 2F.

39. T. Bailey, "Industrial Outplacement at Goodyear, Part 1: The Company's Position," *Personnel Administrator* (Mar. 1980): 42–48; J. A. Bearak, "Termination made Easier: Is Outplacement Really the Answer?" *Personnel Administrator* (Apr. 1982): 63–71, 99.

Huge Four-Year Losses Renews Union Campaign to Spur Membership

That union membership is dropping is not startling news, but the fact that membership losses amounting to almost three million people in four years—with more losses predicted—indicates that unions have not kept pace with the needs and expectations of workers and have largely ignored the shift from blue-collar to white-collar industries. But don't think unions are going to continue to let their numbers shrink.

Marked acceleration in numbers downward

According to information supplied by the Bureau of Labor Statistics, the percentage of the work force that is unionized fell from 23 percent in 1980 to just over 19 percent last year. In real numbers that decline has amounted to 2.7 million members.

While there has been a gradual decline in union members since World War II, this last four-year period has shown the largest decline in union members ever recorded. Since World War II, the percentage of wage and salary workers who are unionized has fallen by almost half. In 1945, union workers amounted to 35.5 percent of the employee pool of the United States.

Most of the losses in numbers in the last four years can be attributed to the recession: in labor intensive industries, most of the jobs which were lost—and most were lost permanently—were unionized positions. Add to that job losses due to layoffs needed to cut operating costs so firms could remain solvent, and you get roughly three million "lost" jobs.

But also during the last 40 years, the number of nonunion jobs has increased as union jobs were slowly evaporating, so that the loss of union positions cannot be equated to the number of firms closing.

Getting with the program

As their numbers droop, unions increasingly are slapped awake to the political realities of a changing workplace and are planning new ways to capture and retain members, especially in high-tech and information-processing industries.

One of the most telling statements by the AFL-CIO reveals just how crucial it is that unions begin offering employees new and better services, lest they go the way of the horse and buggy. In 1983, the AFL-CIO's Committee on the Evolution of Work issued the first of a three-report series called "The Future of Work." The second report from the Committee was issued just this past February and consists of two parts: "The Changing Situations of Workers and Their Unions" and "Recommendations."

In essence, the recommendations the union has devised recognize that unions have got to work together with management and address productivity and efficiency issues, temper wage expectations and relax work rules. But the recommendations also spell out new ways to bring employers to the bargaining table and step up and improve union organizing tactics.

Because unions have lost so many members and their financial strength is not what it used to be, unions understand they cannot fund as many campaigns at one time. However, the first areas the AFL-CIO is looking at organizing this year include clericals, technicals, and other professional employees.

Union recommendations for member growth

As released by the union, here are the recommendations the AFL-CIO wants implemented to increase member ranks:

- Make new use of the concept of collective bargaining. Unions should tailor "models to the needs and concerns of different groups that provide greater flexibility in the workplace and greater reliance on mediation and arbitration . . . and address new issues of concern to workers"—such as comparable worth and increased worker participation in decision-making.

- Set up new membership categories. While many former union members are now in nonunion positions, they might still be interested in affiliating if costs were not prohibitive and services besides bargaining representation were offered.

- Provide direct services and benefits. The union suggested looking at providing services such as job referrals and supplemental insurance.

- Use "corporate" campaigns to deflect employer interference with attempts to form unions. Increase non-workplace pressure—called "corporate" or "coordinated" campaigns—on employers to allow for union development.

- Improve labor communications. This includes training members to act as representatives to the media to publicize union activity.

- Encourage union mergers.

- Establish organizing committees which would focus attention on a particular industry or region.

Source: "Huge Four-Year Losses Renews Union Campaign to Spur Membership," pp. 1, 5. Reprinted from the April issue of *Resource,* copyright © 1985, the American Society for Personnel Administration, 606 North Washington Street, Alexandria, VA 22314.

The preceding "PHRM in the News" points to many important aspects of the unionization of employees. One is the rapid decline, just in the last thirty years, of the percentage of the work force that is unionized. Concurrent with this percentage decline in unionization has been the decline in union economic and political power. Unions, as well as managements, are having to fight for the survival of the very industries they organized many years ago. Now, instead of getting wage gains in those industries, they are having to take wage cuts.

All is not unfavorable for unionization, however. Some industries still appear ripe for unionization, such as the health-care industry. As union campaigns in the health-care industry continue to succeed, unionization can continue to survive and perhaps even grow. One mild trend that threatens to put a damper on these hopes is decertification. Management, noting this trend, is increasing its efforts to make unionization a less attractive alternative to their employees—either ones currently unionized or still unorganized. In some cases, they are succeeding. Among other things, management's desire to make unions less attractive is a recognition that unions are still a force to be dealt with.

Employers are concerned about issues generally associated with the establishment of unions in their companies and about relationships with unions once they are established. Consequently, these general issues are the focus of our discussion. Because each of these general issues involves numerous specific issues, the discussion of them is presented in two chapters. In this chapter, issues associated with the establishment of unions (i.e., union attraction and organizing) are discussed. Also included in this chapter are the legal considerations for union-management relations, encompassing both the establishment of unions and the relationships with unions once they are established. In the next chapter, the fundamental aspects of collective bargaining, negotiating, contract administration, and conflict resolution are examined.

Unionizing, or **unionization,** is the effort by employees and outside agencies (unions or associations) to band together and act as a single unit when dealing with management over issues related to their work. The most common form into which employees organize is the **union,** an organization with the legal authority to negotiate with the employer on behalf of the employees—over wages, hours, and other conditions of employment—and to administrate the ensuing agreement.[1] In the public sector, employees are sometimes represented by employee organizations often referred to as associations, such as the National Education Association. Although employee associations may not be involved in as many functions as a private-sector union (they may not bargain with the employer, for example), most of the large associations do engage in the same activities and have become similar to private-sector unions. The differences that do exist between private-sector unions and public-sector unions or associations are identified later in this chapter and the next.

Purposes and Importance of Unionization

Unionization has importance for both employers and employees. To employers, unionization assumes importance because the existence of a union, or even the possibility of its existence, can exert a significant influence on the ability of the employer to manage its vital human resources.[2] To employees, unionization assumes importance because unions can help employees get what they want (e.g., high wages and job security) from their employers.[3]

Understanding the unionizing or organizing process, its causes, and its consequences is an important part of personnel and human resource management. Unionization often results in management having less flexibility in hiring, job assignments, and the introduction of new work methods such as automation. Other results are a loss of management control, inefficient work practices, and inflexible job structures. Further, as indicated in Chapter 14 on employee rights, unions get for their members rights that employees without unions do not legally have. This makes organizations with unions consider their employees' reactions to many more decisions than organizations without unions. In some cases, however, employers who are nonunion and who want to remain that way give more consideration and benefits to their employees. Consequently, the claim that it is more expensive for a company to operate with unionized employees than with nonunionized employees is not always true.[4]

Unions are important because through wage concessions or cooperation and assistance in work place joint efforts such as quality circles or Scanlon plans, employers may survive particularly difficult times and even be profitable and competitive. Unions may also assist employers in helping to identify work place hazards and otherwise improve the quality of work life for employees.

Unionization is also important because of its extensive relationships with other PHRM activities and functions.

Relationships Influencing the Unionization of Employees

As Exhibit 15.1 shows, the unionization of employees is related to many other PHRM functions and has an extensive set of legal relationships. Because these legal relationships influence organizing as well as other collective bargaining activities, an entire section in this chapter is devoted to the discussion of the legal considerations for unionization and collective bargaining.

Exhibit 15.1   *Relationships and Aspects of the Unionization of Employees in the Union-Management Relationship*

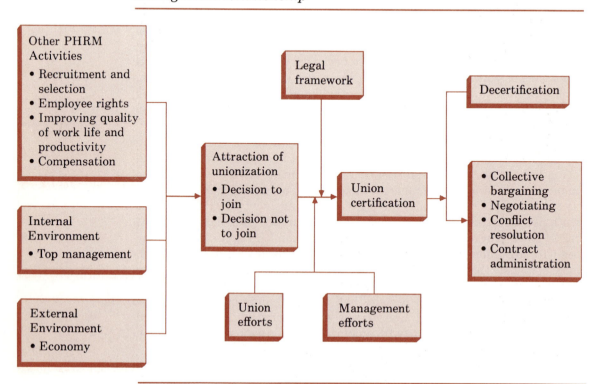

Relationships with Other PHRM Activities

Several other PHRM activities have important relationships with the unionization of employees.

Recruitment and Selection.   Unionization may have a direct impact on who is hired and the conditions under which applicants are hired. In the construction industry, for example, union hiring halls are generally the source of employees for any employer hiring construction workers who are union members. In states with **union shop** provisions (approximately three-fifths of the states), employees must join the union (if the company has one for the particular group of employees) after a set number of days—often sixty or ninety. In the remaining states where **right-to-work** provisions exist, employees do not have to join a union even if one exists.

Unions can also play an important role in deciding who is to be promoted, given a new job assignment, put into training programs, terminated, or laid off. This role is facilitated through the establishment of seniority provisions in union-management contracts. This role is further strengthened by court decisions such as *International Brotherhood of Teamsters* v. *United States* (1977) and *Firefighters Local Union 1784* v. *Stotts* (1984), which recognize the force of seniority provisions if they are part of a bona fide seniority system, as identified in Chapter 4.

Employee Rights.   When employers treat employees with fairness and respect, employees may be more inclined to exhibit loyalty toward their employers. Since treating employees fairly and with respect results from recognizing and observing employee rights, the more rights that employers recognize and observe, the better employees feel.[5] This suggests that an organization that wants to remain union free may choose to observe all the legal rights of employees and to recognize and observe many of the "humane" rights of employees described in Chapter 14. If employers fail to do this, employees may be more likely to unionize. Once unionized, the union will help ensure that many employee rights (legal and humane) are recognized and observed.

Improving Quality of Work Life and Productivity.   As described in Chapter 12, many PHRM programs for QWL and productivity improvement are undertaken jointly by union and management. Although not all unions support the QWL programs, many unions do offer active support and the involvement (generally voluntary) of their members. As indicated in Chapter 12, employers have to be aware of the provisions of the National Labor Relations Act of 1935, such as Sections 8(a)(2) and 2(5). Unions are offering support for work-rule changes to improve productivity.[6]

Compensation.   An important goal of employees is a decent wage and adequate indirect benefits. Since unions are perceived as causing employers to provide them,[7] employees who are not provided these wages and benefits are more likely to find unionization attractive. The threat of possible unionization, however, is often enough to cause employers to provide even more than decent wages and benefits.

Relationships with the Internal Environment

Top management is a major factor in the unionization of employees. If top management desires to remain union free, a great many PHRM activities will be directed to that end. For example, organizations may recruit and select individuals that they judge will be loyal to the company. Top management can direct this to happen. Similarly, compensation levels may be increased so that they are higher than the rest of the industry, as top management directs.

Top management can also set the stage for unionization by creating dissatisfied employees and thus promoting their desire for the protection that unionization offers. Unionization can also be done through the invitation of top management and its belief that managing unionized employees is better than managing nonunionized employees.

Relationships with the External Environment

As illustrated in the initial "PHRM in the News," the state of the economy has a significant influence on unionization. As national and international competition have increased, employers have looked to cutting wage levels as a way to stay competitive. Organizations have threatened to move if wage levels were not reduced. This environment, coupled with relatively high levels of unemployment, has given organizations a relatively strong hand in dealing with the unions. As a consequence, unions have granted wage concessions, and the size of the union movement has been stable at best. Helping to further stabilize and even reduce the size of the union movement has been the decline of manufacturing, a traditional source of union membership. An additional influence has been the legal environment.

Legal Considerations in the Unionization of Employees

The federal government entered the labor scene in an attempt to stabilize the violent and disruptive labor situation in the 1920s and 1930s.[8] Court actions and efforts by employers previous to this time appeared to suppress the rights of workers to act collectively to protect their interest. This, however, was consistent with classical economic theory in which the free operation of the law of supply and demand was considered essential.

> According to this theory, control of wage rates by workers artifically inflated prices, ultimately harming commerce, the community, and even workers themselves, because higher prices discouraged consumption and created unemployment. Therefore, according to many observers, the best prescription for a healthy economy was one free of either government regulation or private regulation via collective action of workers.
>
> Until 1935, application of these restrictive theories of law inherited from England reflected the political assumption that free competition and the sanctity of

contract and property rights of individuals were fundamental values of society that must be protected.[9]

These "fundamental values of society" were protected by declaring attempts by workers to ban together (i.e., form a union) to increase wages a conspiracy condemned by law (*Commonwealth* v. *Pullis*, Philadelphia Cordwainers, Pennsylvania, 1806), although later this outright condemnation was modified to include the necessity of applying a "means test" before condemning the union as an illegal conspiracy (*Commonwealth* v. *Hunt*, 1842). Using the means test (i.e., were the measures or means used by the members to form a union harmful and pernicious?), the courts hampered efforts at unionization. This was reinforced by the replacement of criminal law by civil law, particularly by the use of civil injunctions by the 1880s. The importance of the injunction was that it maintained (and still maintains) the status quo until legal issues can be decided. Thus, if workers attempted to join together and strike for the purpose of attaining higher wages, an injunction could be granted by the courts forcing the workers to return to work until the legality of the strike could be decided. The injunction was also important because it could be granted quickly (to provide an equitable remedy) without the use of juries and other time-consuming legal proceedings.[10] The impact of injunctions on unionization was particularly evident when the Supreme Court ruled that injunctions could be used to enforce **yellow-dog contracts** (i.e., contracts signed by employees agreeing not to join a union) (*Hitchman Coal & Coke* v. *Mitchell*, 1917).

Furthering the protection of the "fundamental values of society" was the Sherman Anti-Trust Act passed by Congress in 1890 to limit the ability of organizations (e.g., unions) to engage in acts (e.g., union mergers) that lessened competition. This act, as applied to unions, was upheld by the Supreme Court in *Loewe* v. *Lawlor* (the Danbury Hatters case of 1908). The meaning and application of the Sherman Anti-Trust Act for unions was reinforced by the Clayton Anti-Trust Act of 1914, *Duplex Printing Co.* v. *Deering*, 1921; *Coronado Coal*, 1925.

Although this protection of the "fundamental values of society" was largely maintained through the 1920s, early legislation in the railway industry (because of the industry's impact on the public welfare) suggested that such protection was not sacrosanct (e.g., see the Arbitration Act of 1888; the Erdman Act of 1898, which outlawed the yellow-dog contracts in the railway industry, and *Adair* v. *United States*, 1921, which upheld the unconstitutionality of the yellow-dog contract). These events in the railway industry were culminated by the Railway Act of 1926 that in turn established the demise of the protection of the "fundamental values of society" for all other industries. Because the act is so important, it is appropriate to discuss it and several other acts that followed and are critical in unionization today.

Private Sector

Although many of the major acts passed by Congress apply only to organizations in the private sector, a few pertain to the public sector. A description of these follows the private sector discussion.

Railway Labor Act.   The Railway Labor Act (RLA) was passed by Congress in 1926 to prevent the serious economic consequences of labor unrest in the railway industry. It has since been expended to include air carrier employees as well.

The RLA was the first act to protect "the fundamental right of workers to engage in labor organizing actively without fear of employer retaliation and discrimination."[11] Other objectives of the act were to avoid service interruptions, to eliminate any restrictions on joining a union, and to provide for prompt settlement of disputes and grievances.[12]

The act specified that employers and employees would maintain an agreement over pay, rules, working conditions, dispute settlement, representation, and grievance settlement. A board of mediation (later called the National Mediation Board) was created to aid in the settlement of disputes through encouragement of, first, negotiation, then arbitration, and finally the president's emergency intervention. A second board—the National Railway Adjustment Board—was created in 1934 to deal with grievances. This board has exclusive jurisdiction over questions relating to grievances or the interpretation of agreements concerning pay, rules, or working conditions; it makes decisions and awards that are binding on both parties.

National Labor Relations Act.   The success of the Railway Labor Act led Congress to enact a comprehensive labor code in 1935. The purpose of the National Labor Relations Act (NLRA), also known as the Wagner Act, was to "restore the equality of bargaining power arising out of employers' general denial to labor of the right to bargain collectively with them."[13] Such employer refusal resulted in poor working conditions, depression of wages, and a general depression of business.

The NLRA affirmed employees' rights to form, join, or assist labor organizations, to bargain collectively, and to choose their own bargaining representative through majority rule. The second significant portion of the act identified, in Section 8, five unfair labor practices on the part of the employers:

- Interference with the efforts of employees to organize
- Domination of the labor organization by the employer
- Discrimination in the hiring or tenure of employees to discourage union affiliation
- Discrimination for filing charges or giving testimony under the act
- Refusal to bargain collectively with a representative of the employees

Court interpretation of these unfair labor practices has made it clear that bribing, spying, blacklisting union sympathizers, moving a business to avoid union activities, and other such employer actions are illegal.[14]

The National Labor Relations Board (NLRB) was established to administer the NLRA. Its major function is to decide all unfair labor practice suits and render decisions consistent with the NLRA. For example, the NLRB recently ruled that labor law isn't necessarily violated when supervisors who support union activities are fired along with workers as part of an employer plan to discourage unions. In this case, however, the board said the employer

NLRB Rules Employers Needn't Bargain With Unions Before Moving Operations

The National Labor Relations Board, overturning an earlier board decision, ruled that employers don't need to bargain with unions before choosing to transfer operations elsewhere.

The decision, which widens the impact of a Supreme Court ruling, is the latest in a recent series of reversals of broad, pro-labor principles by the NLRB's new conservative majority. The decision further erodes unions' ability to negotiate over work transfers as well as a range of other management decisions.

Companies aren't required to bargain over any "decisions which affect the scope, direction, or nature of the business," the NLRB asserted. The board limited employers' bargaining duty to decisions that solely "turn upon a reduction of labor costs."

The case concerned Otis Elevator, a United Technologies unit. In 1977, Otis decided to discontinue its research and development functions at Mahwah, New Jersey, and transfer them to a bigger facility in East Hartford, Connecticut. The United Auto Workers union, which represented about 274 professional and technical employees at Mahwah, contended the company should have bargained over the decision.

In March 1981, the labor board upheld a UAW complaint that Otis's refusal to bargain was an unfair labor practice. But three months later, the Supreme Court ruled that an employer could close part of a business for economic reasons without bargaining with employees over the decision.

The high court specifically said the ruling didn't apply to other decisions, such as selling or relocating a particular plant or subcontracting. But in reversing its stance in the Otis case, the NLRB, in effect, applied the Supreme Court's bargaining limits to a broader range of management decision making.

The board said "the critical factor" is whether the employer's decision "turns upon a change in the nature or direction of the business" and "not its effect on employees nor a union's ability to offer alternatives." Otis Elevator moves the research operations because its technology was dated and its produce wasn't competitive, the NLRB ruling said. "The decision at issue here clearly turned upon a fundamental change in the nature and direction of the business, and thus wasn't amenable to bargaining," the board said.

Stephen Schlossberg, the UAW's Washington counsel, said the NLRB decision "has fairly serious policy ramifications" because it "strikes at the heart of bargaining." Given the chance, the union "could have really done something" about the threatened transfer, he insisted.

Other UAW officials said the union hasn't yet decided to appeal the ruling. The union warned that the Otis case "threatens to unleash a new wave of plant closings, joblessness, and community misery as companies are released from any obligations to bargain with their workers, before transferring or subcontracting work, or even to supply any information relative to the move."

Management attorneys applauded the NLRB move. "It answers the unanswered questions" of the Supreme Court case, said John Irving, a management lawyer. He called the board ruling "a good decision for management" because it no longer has to bargain with unions on "matters having to do with the direction of the enterprise and which are unrelated to labor costs."

must rehire the workers fired for union activities.[15] In 1974, the Supreme Court ruled in *NLRB* v. *J. Weingarten, Inc.,* that a union employee has the right to demand a union representative be present at an investigatory interview that the employee reasonably believes may result in disciplinary action. In 1982 the NLRB ruled in *Materials Research Corporation* that

> unrepresented employees now have the right to demand that a co-worker of their choice be present at an investigatory interview, if the employee reasonably believes that the meeting may result in disciplinary action. As summarized by the NLRB in *Materials Research:* "[W]e conclude that the right enunciated in *Weingarten* applies equally to, [union] represented and unrepresented employees."[16]

Construed as not favoring unions, this decision is consistent with the *Otis Elevator* decision described in the following "PHRM in the News." This is also consistent with the Supreme Court's decision stating that employees may resign from a union at any time, even during a strike or when one is imminent (*Pattern Makers' League* v. *NLRB,* 1985).

Such decisions are only part of organized labor's current dissatisfaction with its own "Magna Carta." Consequently, many unions are now calling for reform of the NLRA.[17] In addition, the NLRB has authority in determining unfair labor practices associated with the phases of the organizing campaign (*General Shoe Co.,* 1984; *Hollywood Ceramics,* 1962; and *Shopping Kart Food Market,* 1977).[18] The phases of the organizing campaign are described in detail later in this chapter.

Labor-Management Relations Act.

Labor-Management Relations Act.   Employer groups criticized the Wagner Act on several grounds. They argued that the act, in addition to being biased toward unions, limited the constitutional right of free speech of employers, did not consider unfair labor practices on the part of unions, and caused employers serious damage when there were jurisdictional disputes.

Congress responded to these criticisms in 1947 by enacting the Labor-Management Relations Act, often called the Taft-Hartley Act, or the Taft Act. This act revised and expanded the Wagner Act to establish a balance between union and management power and to protect the public interest. The following were among the changes it introduced:

- Employees were allowed to refrain from union activity as well as to engage in it.
- The closed shop was outlawed, and written agreement from employees was required for deducting union dues from workers' paychecks.
- Unions composed of supervisors did not need to be recognized.
- Employers were ensured of their right to free speech, and they were given the right to file charges against unfair labor practices. The unfair practices that were identified were coercing workers to join the unions, causing employers to discriminate against those who do not join, refusing to bargain in good faith, requiring excessive or discriminatory fees, and engaging in featherbedding activities.
- Certification elections (voting for union representation) could not be held more frequently than once a year.
- Employees were given the right to initiate decertification elections.[19]

These provisions indicated the philosophy behind the act—as Senator Taft put it, "simply to reduce the special privileges granted labor leaders."

From time to time, amendments are added to the Taft-Hartley Act. For example, the 1980 amendments to the act provided for an identical accommodation for employees with religious objections to union membership or support. Thus, employers and unions must accommodate (within reason) the religious beliefs of employees as protected by Title VII. For example, an employee may, based on religious grounds, contribute to a charity in lieu of paying union dues *(Tooley* v. *Martin-Marietta Corporation,* 1981).

Labor-Management Reporting and Disclosure Act. Although the Taft-Hartley Act included some regulation of internal union activities, abuse of power and the corruption of some union officials led to the passage of a "bill of rights" for union members in 1959. The Labor-Management Reporting and Disclosure Act, or the Landrum-Griffin Act, provided a detailed regulation of internal union affairs. Some of the provisions include the following:

- Equality of rights for union members in nominating and voting in elections
- Controls on increases in dues
- Control of suspension and fining of union members
- Elections every three years for local office and every five for national or international offices
- Restriction of the use of trusteeship to take control of a member group's autonomy for political reasons
- Definition of the type of person who can hold union office
- Filing of yearly reports with the secretary of labor

The intention of this act was to protect employees from corrupt or discriminatory labor unions. By providing detailed provisions for union conduct, much of the flagrant abuse of power was eliminated, and the democratic rights of employees were protected to some degree. The United Mine Workers, for example, held their first election of international officers in 1969. This event would not have been likely to occur even then without the provisions of the Landrum-Griffin Act.

The labor laws described thus far were enacted to govern labor relations in the private sector. In fact, the Wagner Act specifically excludes the U.S. government, government corporations, states, and municipal corporations in its definition of *employer.* As a result, for a long time government employees lacked the legislative protection afforded private-sector workers.

Public Sector

Until recently, federal employee labor relations were controlled by executive orders issued by the president. The government's view of its employees differs from its view of private-sector employees. Several rights of unions in the private sector are not included in public-sector regulations, although the content of these regulations is often lifted from private-sector acts.

Federal Employee Regulations.   The first set of regulations for federal employee labor relations was Executive Order 10988, introduced by President John Kennedy in 1962. This order forbade federal agencies from interfering with employee organizing or unlawful union activity and provided for recognition of employee organizations. Employee organizations were denied the right to strike, however, and economic issues were not part of the bargaining process, since these are fixed by the civil service classification system. Agency heads were made the ultimate authority on grievances, and managers were excluded from the bargaining units.

Executive Order 11491, issued in 1970 and amended in 1971 (EO 11616) and 1975 (EO 11838), addressed some of the difficulties presented by the first executive order. It created the Federal Labor Relations Council to hear appeals from the decisions of agency heads, prescribed regulations and policies, and created a Federal Services Impasses Panel to act on negotiation impasses. The council and the employee representatives could meet and discuss personnel practices and working conditions, but all agreements had to be approved by the council head. Unfair labor practices by both agency management and labor organizations were delineated. The council was restricted from interference, discrimination, and sponsorship of union discipline against an employee for filing a complaint and was required to recognize or deal with a qualified union. Labor organizations were also restrained from interfering, coercing management or employees, discriminating against employees, calling for or engaging in a strike, or denying membership to an employee.

These controls on employers and labor organizations are similar to those found in private-sector legislation. Yet federal employees do not have the same bargaining rights. They lack rights in four areas:

- No provision is made for bargaining on economic issues.
- Although the parties can meet and confer, there is no obligation to do so.
- The ultimate authority is the agency head rather than a neutral party.
- There is no provision for union security through the agency shop, which requires all employees to pay dues but not to join the union.

In 1978 the Federal Service Labor-Management Relations Statute was passed as Title VII of the Civil Service Reform Act, which has been referred to as "the most significant change in federal personnel administration since the passage of the Civil Service Act in 1883."[20] Several significant changes were made by the statute, prime among them, the following:

- Passage of the statute removed the president's ability to change the act through executive order and in general made it more difficult to change the legislation.
- It established the Federal Labor Relations Authority (FLRA), modeled after the NLRB, as an "independent, neutral, full-time, bipartisan agency"[21] created, as President Jimmy Carter said, "to remedy unfair labor practices within the Government." Interpretation of the act is the province of the FLRA and the courts. Agency heads, including the president, cannot define the meaning of the act.

■ An aggrieved person may now seek judicial review of a final order of the FLRA. The FLRA may also seek judicial enforcement of its order.

■ Negotiated grievance procedures, which must be included in all agreements, must provide for arbitration as the final step.

State and Local Employee Regulations.   Employee relations regulations at the state and local level are varied. Not all states have legislation covering municipal employees as well. One widespread regulation can be noted: Collective bargaining is permitted in most states, and it covers wages, hours, and other terms and conditions of employment. The "other terms and conditions" have caused the most difficulty in interpretation. Managerial prerogatives are usually strong, especially for fire fighters, police, and teachers. The requirement to bargain over certain issues in the private sector is not as stringent as it is at the state or local level. In addition, some twenty states have passed "right-to-work" laws, which prohibit union membership as a condition of employment.

Although the rights and privileges of public-sector labor organizations are not as extensive as those in the private sector, the greatest growth in unionization in recent years has come in the public sector. This will become an increasingly important area of labor relations during the rest of the 1980s. Relevant in some cases to both the public and private sector are several court decisions.

Court Decisions

A significant court decision of the 1980s is *First National Maintenance Corp.* v. *NLRB.*[22] In this case, the Supreme Court held that an employer is not obligated to bargain with the union about a decision to close a portion of its business. As discussed in Chapter 14, however, many employers are discussing plant closings and relocation plans with employees and unions. This not only implies a recognition of the employee's right to know but also bodes well for future relationships between the employees and management and for the ease of the facility being closed.[23]

The cornerstone of labor relations, the grievance-arbitration process, was established in *Textile Workers Union* v. *Lincoln Mills* (1957). In that case, the Supreme Court held that the agreement to arbitrate grievances is the *quid pro quo* for an agreement not to strike through the year of the contract. This agreement, however, has been afflicted with the problem of unfair representation by the union of its members.[24] Over the past ten years, cases filed by employees with the NLRB against their unions for unfair representation (breach of duty) have more than tripled to several thousand annually. Although the union's obligation of fair representation is clear, the parameters of the specific duties of this obligation have been left unclear by numerous court decisions, including *Ford Motor Co.* v. *Huffman* (1953); *Vaca* v. *Sipes* (1967); *Hines* v. *Anchor Motor Freight Co.* (1976); *Milstead* v. *Teamsters, Local 957* (1979); and the NLRB ruling in *Miranda Fuel Co.* (1962).[25]

Finally, in the area of seniority systems, the Supreme Court has ruled that "bona fide" seniority systems are protected under Section 703(h) of Title VII of the 1964 Civil Rights Act. Thus, equal employment considerations in general do not replace seniority systems in employment decisions where a seniority system has been in existence for some time or where its intention is not discriminatory (*California Brewers Association* v. *Bryant* [1980] and *International Brotherhood of Teamsters* v. *United States* [1977]), as discussed in Chapter 4. Recently, the sanctity of the seniority system as related to layoff decisions was affirmed in *Firefighters Local Union 1784* v. *Stotts* (1984).

The extensive legal considerations affecting unionization, however, do not ensure union membership. Unions must attract members, or employers must create unfavorable working conditions producing dissatisfaction.[26]

The Attraction of Unionization

To understand the union movement today, we must consider the reasons employees decide either to join or not to join unions.

The Decision to Join a Union

Three separate conditions that have a strong tendency to influence an employee's decision to join a union are dissatisfaction, lack of power, and union instrumentality.

Dissatisfaction. When an individual takes a job, certain conditions of employment (wages, hours, type of work) are specified in the **employment contract**. Employer and employee also have a **psychological contract**, which consists of the unspecified expectations of the employee—about reasonable working conditions, requirements of the work itself, the level of effort that should be expended on the job, and the amount and nature of authority the employer has in directing the employee's work.[27] These expectations are related to the employee's desire to satisfy certain personal preferences in the work place. The degree to which the organization fulfills these preferences determines the employee's level of satisfaction.[28]

Dissatisfaction with either the employment or the psychological contract will lead the employee to attempt to improve the work situation, often through unionization. A major study found a strong relationship between level of satisfaction and the proportion of workers voting for a union. Almost all workers who were highly dissatisfied voted for a union, but almost all workers who were satisfied voted against the union.[29]

If management wants to make unionization less attractive to employees, it may consider making work conditions more satisfying. Management and the PHRM department often contribute to the level of work dissatisfaction through the following actions:

- Giving unrealistic job previews, creating expectations that can't be fulfilled
- Designing jobs that fail to use the skills, knowledge, and abilities of employees and that fail to satisfy their personalities, interests, and preferences

- Practicing day-to-day management and supervisory behaviors, such as poor supervisory practices, unfair treatment, and lack of upward communication

- Failing to tell employees that they would prefer to operate without unions and that they are committed to treating employees with respect[30]

But conditions that create employee dissatisfaction represent only some of the reasons individuals decide to join a union. Another reason is their lack of power.

Lack of Power.   Unionization is seldom the first recourse of employees who are dissatisfied with some aspect of their job. The first attempt to improve the work situation is usually made by an individual acting alone. Someone who has enough power or influence can effect the necessary changes without collaborating with others. The features of a job that determine the amount of power the jobholder has in the organization are **essentiality**, or how important or critical the job is to the overall success of the organization, and **exclusivity**, or how difficult it is to replace the person.[31] Employees with essential tasks who are difficult to replace may be able to force employers to make changes. If, however, the tasks are not critical and the employees can easily be replaced, they are likely to consider other means, including collective action, to increase their power to influence the organization.[32]

In considering whether collective action is appropriate, employees are also likely to consider the likelihood that a union would obtain the aspects of the work environment not now provided by the employer and weigh those benefits against the costs of unionization. In other words, the employees would determine **union instrumentality**.[33]

Union Instrumentality.   Just as employees can be dissatisfied with many aspects of a work environment, such as pay, promotion opportunity, treatment by the supervisor, the job itself, and work rules, employees can also perceive a union as instrumental in obtaining many positive work environment aspects, such as better pay, fairer treatment by the supervisor, and fair work rules. The more that employees perceive the union as likely to obtain positive work aspects, the more instrumental the union is for the employees. The employees then weigh the value of these likely positive work aspects (the benefits to be obtained through unionization). Then the costs of unionization are determined (e.g., the bad feelings with the supervisors and managers, the lengthy organizing campaign, and the bad feelings with other employees who may not want a union). Finally, the employees weigh the costs and benefits with consideration for the likelihood of a union being able to obtain the benefits: the lower the perceived union instrumentality, the less the value of the benefits.[34]

Exhibit 15.2 shows three reasons for deciding to join a union. In general, the expectation that work will satisfy personal preferences may induce satisfaction or dissatisfaction with work. As the level of dissatisfaction increases, individual workers seek to change their work situation. If they fail, and if the positive consequences of unionization seem to outweigh the negative consequences, individuals will be inclined to join the union. This, however, will not always be the case. Employees may choose not to join a union.

Exhibit 15.2   *Processes in the Decision to Organize*

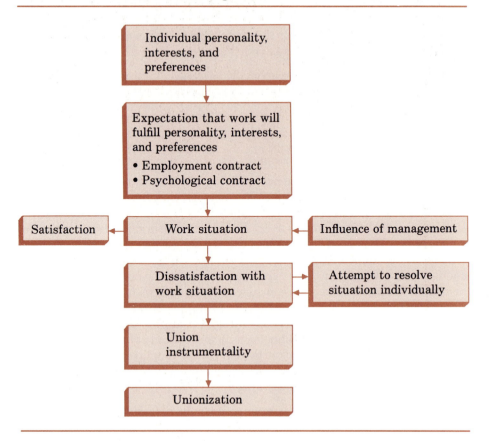

The Decision Not to Join a Union

The question of whether to join a union involves an assessment of the negative consequences of unionization. Employees may have misgivings about how effectively a union can improve unsatisfactory work conditions. Collective bargaining is not always successful; if the union is not strong, it will be unable to make an employer meet its demands. Even if an employer does respond to union demands, the workers may be affected adversely. The employer may not be able to survive when the demands of the union are met, and thus the company may close down, costing employees their jobs. The organization may force the union to strike, inflicting economic hardship on employees who may not be able to afford being out of work, or it may in some cases attempt reprisals against pro-union employees, although this is illegal.[35]

Beyond perceptions of unions as ineffective in the pursuit of personal goals, employees may also resist unionization because of general attitudes toward unions. Employees may identify strongly with the company and have a high level of commitment to it. They would therefore tend to view the union as an adversary and would be receptive to company arguments against unions. Employees may also perceive the goals of the union to be objectionable, intending to harm the company and the free enterprise system in general. They may object to the concept of seniority or even to the political activities of the unions. Moreover, certain employees—for example, engineers or college professors—view themselves as professionals and find collective action to be contrary to such professional ideals as independence and self-control.[36] The decision not to unionize can be influenced by management as well. Employers may influence the employees' decision not to join a union by establishing good management practices; fostering employee participation in planning and decision making, opening channels of communication, setting up processes for handling employee problems and grievances, developing employee trust, and offering competitive wages—all characteristics of PHRM discussed throughout this book.[37]

Along with the many benefits employees may receive from joining a union, however, some employers may perceive that they benefit from their employees unionizing. This is especially so when the union brings some certainty and discipline to the work force. In essence, a union can help management manage the work force.[38] Organizations haven't always seen unions in this way, however; a review of the historical development of unionization in America may even suggest the opposite.

The Development and State of Unionization

The study of labor unions is enhanced a great deal by an appreciation of their historical context.[39] A better understanding of the attitudes and behaviors of both unions and management can also be gained through a knowledge of past labor-management relations. This understanding can be enhanced by matching the legal considerations discussed earlier with this historical presentation.

The Early Days

Labor unions in the United States can be traced back to the successful attempt of journeymen printers to win a wage increase in 1778.[40] By the 1790s, unions of shoemakers, carpenters, and printers had appeared in Boston, Baltimore, New York, and other cities. The Federal Society of Journeymen Cordwainers, for example, was organized in Philadelphia in 1794, primarily to resist employers' attempts to reduce wages. Other issues of concern to these early unions were union shops (companies using only union members) and regulation of apprenticeship to prevent the replacement of journeymen employees.

The early unions had methods and objectives that are still in evidence today. Although there was no collective bargaining, the unions did establish a price below which members would not work. Strikes were used to enforce this rate. These strikes were relatively peaceful and, for the most part, successful.

One negative characteristic of early unions was their susceptibility to depressions. Until the late 1800s, most unions thrived in times of prosperity but died off during depressions. Part of this problem may have been related to the insularity of the unions. Aside from sharing information on strikebreakers or scabs, the unions operated independently.

The work situation at the end of the nineteenth century evidenced several important changes. Transportation systems (canals and turnpikes) expanded the markets for products and increased worker mobility. Increases in capital costs prevented journeymen from reaching the status of master craft worker (that is, from setting up their own businesses), thereby creating a class of skilled workers. Unionism found its start in these skilled occupations, largely because "the skilled worker. . . had mastered his craft and was no longer occupationally mobile" and the alternatives were "to passively accept wage cuts, the competition of nonapprentice labor and the harsh working conditions, or to join in collective action against such employer innovations."[41]

Employers reacted to the unions by forming employers' associations and taking court action. The major legal tool was the conspiracy law, which was used to prosecute workers' organizations as illegal conspiracies in restraint of trade. The Cordwainers of Philadelphia were found guilty of such a conspiracy in 1806, and the courts established a "conspiracy doctrine" that was used against unions in the ensuing decades. This doctrine, along with a depression in 1819, successfully repressed the union movement.

The unions continued to experience highs and lows that were largely tied to economic conditions. Employers took advantage of the depressions to combat unions: In "an all out frontal attack . . . they engaged in frequent lockouts, hired spies . . . summarily discharged labor 'agitators,' and [engaged] the services of strike breakers on a widespread scale."[42] These actions, and the retaliations of unions, established a tenor of violence and lent a strong adversarial nature to union-management relations, the residual of which is in evidence today.

The Recent Days

In recent days, however, some of the adversarial nature of the union-management relationship has been replaced by a more cooperative relationship. This newer relationship is discussed in the next chapter; current trends in union membership, the current distribution of membership, and the structure of the union movement are discussed here.

The Decline in Membership.   In 1984, the number of employees belonging to unions or employee associations was about 17 million. Exhibit 15.3 shows the distribution of these members among unions and employee associations.[43]

The proportion of the labor force represented by unions has been declining steadily since the mid-1960s. In 1984, only 18.8 percent of all workers were represented by unions, the lowest proportion since the mid-1930s and down from 23.0 percent in 1980. In 1970, the percentage of unionized labor force was 24.7 percent. Although the percentage of unionized work force declined

| Union Membership, 1984 | | | *Exhibit 15.3* |

| | Union Membership (in thousands) | | |

Union Members	Total Number of Workers	Members of Unions*	Percentage of Employed in Unions
All private and public wage and salary workers	92,194	17,340	18.8
All private workers	76,361	11,684	15.3
Private goods-producing workers**	27,081	6,508	24.0
Private service-producing workers	49,281	5,176	10.5
Government workers	15,833	5,656	35.7

*Includes members of a labor union or employee association similar to union.
**Includes agricultural workers.

Source: Bureau of Labor Statistics.

between 1970 and 1980, membership in labor organizations increased. Factors that contribute to this decline include the increase in public-sector employment and white-collar jobs—both of which have historically had a low proportion of union members—the decline in employment in industries that are highly unionized and the high levels of unemployment, increased decertification of unions, union leadership, union responsiveness to membership, and management initiatives.[44]

In the future, however, economic conditions and legislation may make unionization more feasible in white-collar and public-sector jobs. Indeed, most organizing activities today are focused on the public-sector services and health care, as described in the initial "PHRM in the News."[45] To gain more organizational ability, power, and financial strength, several unions have recently merged. Between July 1971 and August 1978 there were twenty-one union mergers, and during the first twenty months of 1980–81, there were eight mergers.[46] Although mergers may not automatically increase membership, they can mean more efficiency in union-organizing efforts and an end to costly jurisdictional disputes among unions. Increased organizational strength from mergers may also enable unions to expand the coverage of their membership by unionizing industries and occupations previously underrepresented in union membership.

The Distribution of Membership.   Historically, membership has been concentrated in a small number of large unions.[47] In 1976, sixteen unions represented 60 percent of union membership, and eighty-five unions represented just 2.4 percent. Similarly, the National Education Association accounted for 62 percent of all association members. Many employee associations are small because they are state organizations; their membership potential is therefore limited. Exhibit 15.4 shows the distribution of membership in various

Exhibit 15.4   *Unions Reporting 100,000 Active Members or*
More, Including Canadian Members, 1982

Organization	Members	Organization	Members
Teamsters (IBT) (Ind.)	1,800,000	Electrical Workers (IUE)	190,786
National Education		Letter Carriers (NALC)	175,000
Association (NEA) (Ind.)	1,641,354	Graphic Communication	
Steelworkers (USW)	1,200,000	Workers (GCIU)	165,000
Auto Workers (UAW)	1,140,370	Painters (PAT)	165,000
Food and Commercial		Firefighters (IAFF)	162,792
(UFCW)	1,079,213	United Electrical Workers	
State, County (AFSCME)	950,000	(UE) (Ind.)	162,000
Electrical (IBEW)	883,000	Nurses (ANA) (Ind.)	160,357
Service Employees (SEIU)	700,000	Police (FOP)	160,000
Carpenters (CJA)	679,000	Iron Workers (BSOIW)	155,587
Machinists (IAM)	655,221	Bakery, Tobacco (BCTW)	152,100
Communications Workers		Classified School (AACSE)	
(CWA)	650,000	(Ind.)	150,000
Teachers (AFT)	573,644	Mine Workers (UMW) (Ind.)	150,000
Laborers (LIUNA)	450,442	Sheet Metal Workers	
Clothing and Textile		(SMW)	144,000
Workers (ACTWU)	400,000	Railway Clerks (BRAC)	140,000
Hotel and Restaurant		Oil, Chemical Workers	
(HERE)	375,000	(OCAW)	125,000
Plumbers (PPF)	353,127	Bricklayers (BAC)	120,000
Operating Engineers		Transit Workers (ATU)	120,000
(IUOE)	345,000	Boilermakers (BBF)	117,642
Ladies' Garment Workers		Longshoremen (ILA)	116,000
(ILGWU)	276,000	Transportation (UTU)	115,000
Paperworkers (UPIU)	263,695	Office and Professional	
Musicians (AFM)	260,000	(OPEIU)	112,793
Retail (RWDSU)	250,000	Rubber Workers (URW)	100,175
Postal Workers (APWU)	248,000		
Government Workers			
(AFGE)	210,000		

Note: All organizations not identified as (Ind.) are affiliated with
the AFL-CIO.

Source: Bureau of Labor Statistics.

unions. Unions today are exhibiting a substantial and increasing amount of diversification of membership. For example, in 1958, 73 percent of the unions had at least four-fifths of their members in a single industry; this figure dropped to 55 percent in 1976. The most pronounced diversification has occurred in manufacturing. For example, of the twenty-nine unions that represent workers in chemicals and allied products, twenty-six presently have less than 20 percent of their membership in a single industry.[48]

With this understanding of union history and member characteristics, we can now examine the structure of unionization.

Structure of Unionization in America

The basic unit of labor unions in the United States is the **national union** (or international union), a body that organizes, charters, and controls member **union locals**. The national union develops general policies and procedures by which locals operate and provides assistance to them in such areas as collective bargaining. National unions provide clout for the locals because they control a large number of employees and can influence large organizations through national strikes or slowdown activities.[49]

The major umbrella organization for national unions is the AFL-CIO—the American Federation of Labor and Congress of Industrial Organizations. It represents about 77 percent of the total union membership and contains ninety-nine national unions.[50] Although several major unions are not members, including the biggest (the Teamsters), the AFL-CIO is an important and powerful body.

The AFL-CIO

The American Federation of Labor (AFL) began in 1886 and quickly assumed a leading role in the union movement. Much of its early success can be traced to the pragmatic approach of its president, Samuel Gompers, and to the principles he adopted:

- The national unions were to be autonomous within the AFL.
- Only one national union would be accepted for each trade or craft.
- The AFL would focus on the issues of wages, hours, and working conditions and avoid reformist goals.
- The AFL would avoid permanent political alliances.
- The strike would become a key weapon for achieving union objectives.

The AFL also accepted and endorsed the free enterprise system, choosing to operate within it rather than to change the whole system. The policy of giving national craft unions substantial control over their own affairs successfully attracted these unions and allowed the AFL to grow substantially despite employer campaigns to inhibit growth. Legislation passed in the 1930s made the legal climate more conducive to union growth.

The Congress of Industrial Organizations (CIO) was formed in 1935 as a rival union organization that focused on industrywide unions rather than on craft unions. The competition between the AFL and the CIO intensified unionizing efforts, and by 1941, 10.2 million workers were union members.

Eventually the CIO and the AFL, realizing that their competition was not in the best interests of labor, merged into the AFL-CIO in 1955. The merger of these organizations eliminated jurisdictional squabbles and gave union leaders a stronger voice. The new organization had great expectations for a significant growth in membership.

In spite of these expectations, the AFL-CIO lost membership over the next two decades. Several factors accounted for this decline. The Teamsters and the United Auto Workers left the organization, corruption among unions tarnished their image, and increasingly high wage demands resulted in a lack of public confidence. Changing attitudes among employees and the public also reduced the appeal of labor unions. Membership today continues to grow at a slow pace, and hopes for large-scale unionization seem to be fading. The United Auto Workers, however, have returned to the fold, and the concerns of job security and wages are more important than ever.

Every two years, the AFL-CIO holds a convention to develop policy and amend its constitution. Each national union is represented in proportion to its membership. Between conventions, an executive council (the governing body) and a general board direct the organization's affairs; a president is in charge of day-to-day operations. The executive council's activities include evaluating legislation that affects labor and watching for corruption within the AFL-CIO. Standing committees are appointed to deal with executive, legislative, political, educational, organizing, and other activities. The Department of Organization and Field Services, for instance, focuses its attention on organizing activities. Outside of headquarters, three structures exist to organize the local unions. Many of the craft unions are organized into the Trade Department and the Industrial Department, which represent them to the national union. The remaining locals are organized directly into national unions, which are affiliated with headquarters but retain their independence in dealing with their own union matters.

At the heart of the labor movement are the seventy thousand or so local unions, varying in size up to forty thousand members. The locals represent the workers at the work place, where much of the day-to-day contact with management and the personnel department takes place. Most locals elect a president, a secretary-treasurer, and perhaps one or two other officers from the membership. In the larger locals, a business representative is hired as a full-time employee to handle grievances and contract negotiations. The other important member of the union local is the **steward,** an employee elected by his or her work unit to act as the union representative on the work site and to respond to company actions against employees that may violate the labor agreement. The steward protects workers' rights by filing grievances when the employer has acted improperly.

Operations of Unions

Activities of union locals center on collective bargaining and handling grievances. In addition, locals hold general meetings, publish newsletters, and otherwise keep their members informed. Typically, however, the membership is apathetic about union involvement. Unless a serious problem exists, attendance at meetings is usually low, and often even elections of officers draw votes from less than one-fourth of the membership.

At headquarters, the AFL-CIO is involved in a variety of activities. Staff and committees work on a wide range of issues, including civil rights, community service, economic policy, education, ethical practices, housing, international affairs, legislation, public relations, research, safety, social security, and veterans' affairs. In addition, a publication department produces a variety of literature for members and outsiders. National union headquarters also provide a variety of specialized services to regional and local bodies. Specialists in organizing, strikes, legal matters, public relations, and negotiations are available to individual unions.

Another important role for national unions and the AFL-CIO is in the political arena. Labor maintains a strong lobbying force in Washington, D.C., and is also involved at the state and local level. A recent development is the international political activities of some of the large national unions. For example, the United Auto Workers have held discussions with Japanese car manufacturers concerning the level of imports into the United States and the construction of assembly plants here. They have lobbied in Washington to restrict imports of cars in an attempt to bolster U.S. automakers and increase jobs. Thus, in an attempt to help their membership, unions are expanding their activities on all levels, and in some cases, they work with organizations to attain mutual goals.

Without doubt, times are tough for unions. Recent indications are that the lobbying clout of unions in Washington has diminished substantially when compared with business. Most large unions have always had political action committees in Washington, but the number of business committees has increased tenfold from 1974 to 1981. This increase in activity and the concern for the abuse of influence by big business have encouraged labor, consumer, and public-interest groups to unite to curb the power of business.[51] This adversity, however, is forcing the union movement to also get tough. It is also causing factions of the union movement to band together for political and economic reasons.[52] A consequence may be an enhanced pace of union activity. If this is the result, there will be more organizing campaigns, an extensive process watched over by the NLRB.

The Organizing Campaign

A major function of the National Labor Relations Board is to conduct the selection of unions to represent nongovernment employees. This is accomplished through a certification election to determine if the majority of employees want the union. Under American labor law, the union that is certified to represent a group of employees has sole and exclusive right to bargain for that group.

> The process by which a single union is selected to represent all employees in a particular unit is crucial to the American system of collective bargaining. If a majority vote for union representation, all employees are bound by that choice and the employer is obligated to recognize and bargain with the chosen union.[53]

Because unions may thereby acquire significant power, employers may be anxious to keep them out. To add to this situation of potential union-management conflict, more than one union may be attempting to win certification as representative of a group of employees, creating competition and conflict between unions.

Several stages in the certification process can be identified: (1) a campaign to solicit employee support for union representation, (2) the determination of the appropriate group the union will represent, (3) the pre-election campaign by unions and employers, (4) the election itself, and (5) the certification of a union.[54] These steps are outlined in Exhibit 15.5. The next stage of the organizing process, negotiation of a collective bargaining agreement, is discussed in Chapter 16.

Exhibit 15.5	*Certification Process*

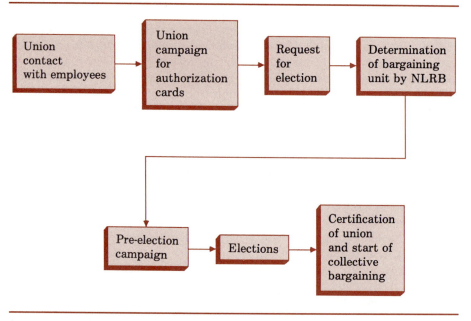

Source: William D. Todor.

The Campaign to Solicit Employee Support

In the campaign to solicit employee support, unions generally attempt to contact the employees, obtain a sufficient number of authorization cards, and request an election from the NLRB.

Establishing Contact between the Union and Employees.   Contact between the union and employees can be initiated by either party. National unions usually initiate contact with employees in industries or occupations that they have an interest in or are traditionally involved in. The United Auto Workers, for example, would be likely to contact nonunion employees in automobile plants and have done so for the new plants that have been built in the South. Another prominent example of union initiative was the attempt by two competing unions—the United Farm Workers and the Teamsters—to organize the agricultural workers in California. Often these unions were aggressive, even violent, during their campaigns for worker support. One consequence of their precertification activities, which included national boycotts of grapes and lettuce, was the California Agricultural Relations Act, passed in 1975. The purpose of this act is to regulate union-management relations in the agriculture industry.

In many cases, the union is approached by employees interested in union representation, and the union is usually happy to oblige. Employees may have strong reasons for desiring union representation—low pay, poor working conditions, and other factors relating to dissatisfaction.[55] Since workers tend to be apathetic toward unions, their concern generally becomes serious before they will take any action.[56]

Authorization Cards and the Request for Elections.   Once contact has been made, the union begins the campaign to get sufficient **authorization cards,** or signatures of employees interested in having union representation. This campaign must be carried out within the constraints set by law. If the union collects cards from 30 percent of an organization's employees, it can petition the National Labor Relations Board for an election. (Procedures in the public sector are similar.) If the NLRB determines that there is sufficient interest, it will schedule an election. If the union gets more than 50 percent of the employees to sign authorization cards, it may petition the employer as the bargaining representative. Usually employers refuse, whereupon the union petitions the NLRB for an election.

The employer usually resists the union's card-signing campaign. For instance, companies usually prohibit solicitation on the premises.[57] However, employers are legally constrained from interfering with an employee's freedom of choice. Union representatives have argued that employers ignore this law because the consequences for doing so are minimal—and they can effectively discourage unionism.[58] During the union campaign and election process, however, the PHRM manager should caution the company against engaging in unfair labor practices. Unfair labor practices, when identified, generally cause the election to be set aside. Severe violations by the employer can result in certification of the union as the bargaining representative, even if it has lost the election. Accordingly, a list of do's and don'ts regarding organizing campaigns are described in the following "PHRM in the News."

Determination of the Bargaining Unit

When the union has gathered sufficient signatures to petition for an election, the NLRB will make a determination of the **bargaining unit,** the group of employees that will be represented by the union. This is a crucial process, for it can determine the quality of labor-management relations in the future:

> At the heart of labor-management relations is the bargaining unit. It is all important that the bargaining unit be truly appropriate and not contain a mix of antagonistic interests or submerge the legitimate interest of a small group of employees in the interest of a larger group.[59]

To assure "the fullest freedom of collective bargaining, there are legal constraints and guidelines in the determination of the unit."[60] Professional and nonprofessional groups cannot be included in the same unit, and a craft unit cannot be placed in a larger unit unless both groups agree to it. Physical location, skill levels, degree of ownership, collective bargaining history, and extent of organization of employees are also guidelines to be considered.

From the union's perspective, the most desirable bargaining unit is one whose members are pro-union, so that they can win certification. The unit must also have sufficient influence over the operations of the employer to give the union some power once it wins representation. Employers generally want a bargaining unit that is least beneficial to the unit; this will help to

Dealing with Organizing: Do's and Don'ts

Faced with a declining membership base and an erosion of bargaining power, organized labor is stepping up its efforts to enlist new members from previously untapped or underrepresented segments of the labor force. Unions are focusing on women and minorities, as well as high-tech and service industry employees, as likely recruits. In planning for a "resurgence" of labor's fortunes (see page 7), unions also are adopting innovative tactics, such as television advertising campaigns, to rebuild their public image. In light of these developments, employers would be well-advised to review the legal ground rules governing what management can and can't do during a representation campaign.

Inadvisable actions

The Taft Act, as enforced by NLRB and the federal courts, places certain restrictions on supervisors' statements and conduct during a union organizing drive. These rules are designed to prevent unfair labor practices that interfere with employees' right to join or support a union. Under the law, for example, supervisors cannot:

- Misrepresent the facts—Any information management provides about a union or its officers must be factual and truthful.

- Threaten employees—It is unlawful to threaten employees with loss of their jobs or transfers to less desirable positions, income reductions, or loss or reduction of benefits and privileges. Use of intimidating language to dissuade employees from joining or supporting a union also is forbidden. In addition, supervisors may not blacklist, lay off, discipline, or discharge any employee because of union activity.

- Promise benefits or rewards— Supervisors may not promise a pay raise, additional overtime or time off, promotions, or other favorable considerations in exchange for an employee's agreement to refrain from joining a union or signing a union card, vote against union representation, or otherwise oppose union activity.

- Make unscheduled changes in wages, hours, benefits, or working conditions—Any such changes are unlawful unless the employer can prove they were initiated before union activity began.

- Conduct surveillance activities— Management is forbidden to spy on or request anti-union workers to spy on employees' union activities, or to make any statements that give workers the impression they are being watched. Supervisors also may not attend union meetings or question employees about a union's internal affairs. They also may not ask employees for their opinions of a union or its officers.

- Interrogate workers—Managers may not require employees to tell them who has signed a union card, voted for union representation, attended a union meeting, or instigated an organization drive.

- Prohibit solicitation—Employees have the right to solicit members on company property during their nonworking hours, provided this activity does not interfere with work being performed, and to distribute union literature in nonwork areas during their free time.

Lawful conduct

It's also important for supervisors to know what they are permitted to do when an organizing drive begins. In addition to expressing their personal opinions about unions and union policies, supervisors may:

- Discuss the history of unions and make factual statements about strikes, violence, or the loss of jobs at plants that have unionized.

- Discuss their own experiences with unions.

- Advise workers about the costs of joining and belonging to unions.

- Remind employees of the company benefits and wages they receive without having to pay union dues.

- Explain that union representation will not protect workers against discharge for cause.

- Point out that the company prefers to deal directly with employees, and not through a third party, in settling complaints about wages, hours, and other employment conditions.

- Tell workers that in negotiating with the union, the company is not obligated to sign a contract or accept all the union's demands, especially those that aren't in its economic interests.

- Advise employees that unions often resort to work stoppages to press their demands and that such tactics can cost them money.

- Inform employees of the company's legal right to hire replacements for workers who go out on strike for economic reasons.

Source: Bulletin to Management, 7 March 1985, p. 8. Reprinted by permission from *Bulletin to Management,* copyright 1985, by The Bureau of National Affairs, Inc., Washington, D.C.

maximize the likelihood of failure in the election and to minimize the power of the unit.[61]

The Pre-election Campaign

After the bargaining unit has been determined, both union and employer embark on a pre-election campaign. Unions claim to provide a strong voice for employees, emphasizing improvement in wages and working conditions and the establishment of a grievance process to ensure fairness. Employers emphasize the costs of unionization—union dues, strikes, and loss of jobs.

The impact of pre-election campaigns is not clear. A study of thirty-one elections showed little change in attitude and voting propensity after the campaign.[62] People who will vote for or against a union before the election campaign generally vote the same way after. Severe violations of the legal constraints on behavior, such as using threats or coercion, could be effective, but the NLRB watches the pre-election activity carefully to prevent such behavior.

Election and Certification

The final steps in the certification process are elections and certification. The NLRB conducts the election and certifies the results. If a majority vote for union representation, the union will be certified. If the union does not get a majority, another election will not be held for at least a year. The NLRB holds about nine thousand elections a year involving about 500,000 employees. Generally, about one-third to one-half of the elections certify a union, with less union success in larger organizations. Once a union has been certified, the employer is required to bargain with that union.

Decertification Elections.   The NLRB also conducts decertification elections, which remove a union from representation. If 30 percent or more of the employees request such an election, it will be held.[63] These decertification elections most frequently occur in the first year of a union's representation, when the union is negotiating its first contract. At this point, union strength has not yet been established, and employees may be discouraged about union behavior.

Trends in the Unionization of Employees

Two trends in the unionization of employees to be described here are those of assessing and computer technology and HRIS. Since trends in strategic involvement relate mostly to union-management relations, they are described in the next chapter.

Assessing the Unionization of Employees

Although on occasion management may desire to have its employees unionized, its general tendency may be to have nonunionized employees.[64] Consequently, the pressure is on the PHRM manager to prevent the employees from becoming dissatisfied and joining a union. In other words, the effectiveness of the personnel and human resource manager here can be determined by how satisfied and involved the employees are with the company. This can be determined through the use of organizational surveys (discussed in Chapter 18).

Since union-management activities are encased in a network of laws, another element of effectiveness is how well the PHRM manager avoids violating any of these laws in maintaining effective relationships with the work force. This element also applies to how effectively the PHRM manager negotiates and administers contracts if the employees are unionized.

Computer Technology and HRIS in the Unionization of Employees

Computer technology and an HRIS can be helpful in determining how attractive a union is to an organization's nonunion employees. Although employers cannot directly ask employees what they think about unions, they can ask how satisfied they are with work and other conditions. This information, gathered by an organizational survey, can be stored in an HRIS and rapidly analyzed by computer to measure employee satisfaction. If an organization wishes to avoid unionization, this measure may suggest that something needs to be done to improve employee satisfaction. This same information can also be used to help measure the results of any programs undertaken to improve satisfaction.

If unionized, a company and the union may wish to gather information on quality of work life and productivity to determine if joint programs for improvement are necessary. Such programs are more critical than ever for the survival of both companies and unions. The QWL and productivity information could also be used to measure the impact of any joint improvement programs.

Summary

Employees are generally attracted to unionization because they are dissatisfied with work conditions and feel powerless to change these conditions. Some major sources of dissatisfaction are inequity in pay administration, poor communications, and poor supervisory practices. By correcting these, or by not allowing them to occur in the first place, organizations help prevent unions from being attractive. However, once a union-organizing campaign begins, a company can't legally stop it unless an unfair labor practice is committed. At this point, the best approach may be to hire a labor attorney familiar with the NLRB and labor law to monitor the practices of the union. But even if a charge is filed with the NLRB, it takes a long time for the charge to be heard. However, other ways can be used to delay the organizing campaign, such as challenging the bargaining unit, challenging the election procedures, and even conducting a campaign telling of the benefits provided by the company.

Organizations can also initially establish conditions that make unions a less attractive alternative. For example, organizations can make sure their compensation package is in good order. Pay should be competitive, and the principles of equal pay for equal work and for comparable worth should be observed. Supervisors should be trained in effective communication styles and methods. Employee rights—both the legally protected rights and the so-called humane rights—must be observed. QWL programs and safety programs are also helpful in establishing a positive, attractive organizational climate.

Some organizations may not bother establishing conditions to make unions a less attractive alternative because their perception may be that unions are useful to have. Unions can bring an element of peace and stability among the workers and help organizations manage. At the same time, unions may cause too much inflexibility and block attempts to make improvements where needed (e.g., in QWL or productivity). Thus, if an organization already has a union, it may prefer to help the employees get rid of it. At this point, an organization may want to contact a consultant who specializes in this area. These people can help ensure that an organization does not violate any labor-management laws and that its chances for success at encouraging its employees to decertify the union are reasonably high. A failure at this effort could be costly. An organization may hope that its employees initiate a decertification election on their own without company encouragement.

Historically, unions and management have operated as adversaries because many of their goals are in conflict. But since conflict is detrimental to both management and unions, effective labor relations have been established to reduce this conflict. For instance, unions and management have begun to cooperate to achieve mutual goals. Although cooperation is not widespread, it may be the style of union-management relations in the future. Its effects are particularly apparent in collective bargaining, contract negotiation, and grievance processing—all topics of the next chapter.

Discussion Questions

1. Briefly state how the legal climate has changed with respect to organized labor since the inception of unions.
2. What are the steps required for employee organizations to establish union certification?
3. What are decertification elections, and how do they affect organized labor and management?
4. Why have unions appealed to workers historically? Are the reasons today different than fifty years ago? Explain.
5. What is the NLRB? How does the NLRB help promote the policy of "free collective bargaining" in the United States?
6. Describe the climate among U.S. workers during 1935 when the Wagner Act was passed. How might the climate have differed in 1947 when Taft-Hartley was passed? Would this explain in part the content of Taft-Hartley? How?
7. How does the Landrum-Griffin Act protect workers from their own unions? Have unions outlived the need for Landrum-Griffin?
8. What is a certification election? A decertification election? Who do you suppose wins the majority of certification elections today? Why has the rate changed over time?
9. Originally, unions sought to organize only skilled trades. Why?
10. What is the structure of unionization in America today?

C A S E   S T U D Y

My Doctor the Unionist

Unions are having a tough time these days. Recent Bureau of Labor Statistics data show a continued decline of membership as a proportion of the labor force. Currently fewer than one out of every five workers belongs to a union, where once that figure was one of every three. The shape of unionism has changed dramatically in the past two decades as workers have become much more "rights" conscious. The demography of the labor force has changed, too, with younger and more female representatives. Industrially, the traditional sectors for unionization (e.g., steel, auto, airlines, mining) have been rocked by international competition and deregulation. Economic times also play havoc with union growth. The recessions of the past decade have weakened the union ranks.

Now, hold on a minute! What's this? Doctors have begun joining unions? Doctors are professionals, highly paid, and their own bosses represented by the American Medical Association (reputed by many to be a union in its own right). Why, you ask, would any doctor choose to join a union?

Typically, workers join unions because of dissatisfaction over wages, hours, and working conditions. Coupled with this is the belief among workers that they are powerless to change their situation for the better. Workers who do not view unions in a negative way (i.e., too powerful or corrupt) and who believe that others whose opinion they respect will support their decision are more likely to support a union.

How, then, could unions possibly succeed in organizing doctors? Consider the following:

The health-care industry has undergone a radical change with profit-oriented hospitals and insurance companies competing to provide quality health care at the lowest possible cost.

The government has changed dramatically the way health care is paid for.

Today 75 percent of all patient-care doctors belong to private practices, yet an increasing number of doctors (about 208,000 currently) work for third-party employers such as government or health maintenance organizations.

The labor market for doctors is increasingly becoming more competitive with an estimated glut of physicians.

For those doctors working for third-party employers, there is a divided loyalty between the employer and the patient. On the one hand, the doctor wants to do what is best for the patient. On the other hand, the doctor wants to comply with his or her employer's concern for cost competitiveness to ensure long-term survival in an increasingly competitive environment. Where doctors confront employers who don't have the patient's best interest in mind, who refuse to permit the doctor to admit patients to a hospital for further tests, and who require doctors to work thirty-six-hour shifts without sleep, unions may offer an alternative for change and control. Is the recent success of a few physician unions merely a flash in the pan? From a public policy perspective, is organized medicine in the best interests and health of our country for the future?

Notes

1. For a more extensive discussion of unionization and the entire union-management relationship, see H. J. Anderson, *Primer of Labor Relations,* 21st ed. (Washington, D.C.: Bureau of National Affairs, 1980); D. C. Bok and J. J. Dunlop, *Labor and the American Community* (New York: Simon & Schuster, 1970); E. F. Beal, E. D. Wickersham, and P. Kienast, *The Practice of Collective Bargaining* (Homewood, Ill.: Irwin, 1972); J. A. Beirne, *Challenge to Labor: New Roles for American Unions* (Englewood Cliffs, N.J.: Prentice-Hall, 1969); T. R. Brooks, *Toil and Trouble: A History of American Labor* (New York: Dell, Delta Books, 1972); J. G. Getman, *Labor Relations: Law, Practice, and Policy* (Mineola, N.Y.: Foundation Press, 1979); R. C. Richardson, *Collective Bargaining by Objectives* (Englewood Cliffs, N.J.: Prentice-Hall, 1977); B. W. Justice, *Unions, Workers, and the Law* (Washington, D.C.: Bureau of National Affairs, 1983); R. N. Block and S. L. Premack, "The Unionization Process: A Review of the Literature," in *Advances in Industrial and Labor Relations,* vol. 1, ed. D. B. Lipsky and J. M. Douglas (Greenwich, Conn.: JAI Press, 1983), pp. 31–70; W. N. Cooke, "Toward a General Theory of Industrial Relations," in *Advances in Industrial and Labor Relations,* vol. 3, ed. D. B. Lipsky and J. M. Douglas (Greenwich, Conn.: JAI Press, 1983), pp. 31–70; P. Cappelli, "Theory Construction in IR and Some Implications for Research," *Industrial Relations* (Winter 1985): 90–112; L. Troy and N. Sheflin, *Union Sourcebook: Membership, Structure, Finance, Directory, 1984 Edition* (West Orange, N.J.: Industrial Relations Data and Information Service, 1984); R. B. Freeman and J. L. Medoff. *What Do Unions Do?* (New York: Basic Books, 1984).

2. C. V. Fukami and E. W. Larson, "Commitment to Company and Union: Parallel Models," *Journal of Applied Psychology* (August 1984): 367–71. For further discussion of these predictions, see J. M. Brett, "Why Employees Want Unions," *Organizational Dynamics* (Spring 1980): 47–56; J. M. Brett, "Behavioral Research on Unions and Union Management Systems," in *Research in Organizational Behavior,* vol. 2, ed. B. M. Staw and L. L. Cummings (Greenwich, Conn.: JAI Press, 1980); J. M. Brett and T. H. Hammer, "Organizational Behavior and Industrial Relations," in *Industrial Relations Research in the 1970s: Review and Appraisal,* ed. T. A. Kochan, D. J. B. Mitchell, and M. S. Lipyer

(Madison: Industrial Relations Research Association Series, 1982); J. Fiorito and C. R. Greer, "Determinants of U.S. Unionism: Past Research and Future Needs," *Industrial Relations* 21 (1982): 1–32; T. A. Kochan, "How American Workers View Labor Unions," *Monthly Labor Review* 102 (1979): 23–31; W. T. Dickens and J. S. Leonard, "Accounting for the Decline in Union Membership 1950–1980," *Industrial and Labor Relations Review* (Apr. 1985): 323–34.

3. "Beyond Unions," *Business Week,* 8 July 1985, pp. 72–77.

4. For a good discussion of this in an actual situation, see W. Brown, "Powder River Basin Mines Try to Best Unions at Benefits Game," *Washington Post,* p. A2. See also S. Briggs, "The Grievance Procedure and Organizational Health," *Personnel Journal* (June 1981): 471–74; "A Creaky System of Collective Bargaining," *Business Week,* 30 June 1980, pp. 82–83; J. F. Rand, "Preventive Maintenance Techniques for Staying Union Free," *Personnel Journal* (June 1980): 497–99.

5. For a review of some of the literature dealing with and managing employees, see H. P. Sims and A. D. Szilagyi, "Leader Reward Behavior and Subordinate Satisfaction and Performance," *Organizational Behavior and Human Performance* 14 (1975): 496–98; L. Ingrassia, "Union Rank and File Talk Bitterly of Their Bosses," *Wall Street Journal,* 12 Apr. 1982, p. 22; P. Hersey and K. H. Blanchard, *Management of Organizational Behavior,* 3d ed. (Englewood Cliffs, N.J.: Prentice-Hall, 1977); E. P. Hollander, *Leadership Dynamics: A Practical Guide to Effective Relationships* (New York: Free Press, 1978); R. J. House, "A Path Goal Theory of Leader Effectiveness,"*Administrative Science Quarterly* 16 (1971): 321–39; R. J. House and J. L. Baetz, "Leadership: Some Empirical Generalizations and New Research Directions," in *Research in Organizational Behavior,* vol. 2, ed. B. Staw (Greenwich, Conn.: JAI Press, 1980); R. J. House and G. Dessler, "The Path Goal Theory of Leadership: Some Post Hoc and A Priori Tests," in *Contingency Approaches to Leadership,* ed. J. G. Hunt and L. L. Larson (Carbondale, Ill.: Southern Illinois Press, 1974); G. A. Yukl, *Leadership in Organizations* (Englewood Cliffs, N.J.: Prentice-Hall, 1981); G. A. Yukl, K. N. Wexley, and J. D. Seymore, "Effectiveness of Pay Incentives under Variable Ratio and Continuous Reinforcement Schedules," *Journal of Applied Psychology* 56 (1972): 19–23; P. M. Podsakoff, "Determinants of a Supervisor's Use of Rewards and Punishments: A Literature Review and Suggestions for Further Research," *Organizational Behavior and Human Performance* 29 (1982): 58–83; P. M. Podsakoff, W. D. Todor, and R. Skov,"Effects of Leader Contingent and Non-Contingent Reward and Punishment Behaviors on Subordinate Performance and Satisfaction," *Academy of Management Journal* 25 (1982): 810–21.

6. The support, however, may be influenced by economic conditions and layoffs in the industry and the specific site where the joint QWL program is being conducted. See "R. L. Starting to Look Rather Shaky," *Wall Street Journal,* 2 June 1982, pp. 1, 19; R. S. Greenberger, "Work-Rule Changes Quietly Spread as Firms Try to Raise Productivity," *Wall Street Journal,* 25 Jan. 1983, p. 35; "How Power Will be Balanced on Saturn's Shop Floor," *Business Week,* 5 Aug. 1985, pp. 65-66; D. Sockell, "The Legality of Employee-Participation Programs in Unionized Firms," *Industrial and Labor Relations Review* (July 1984): 541–56.

7. This is less true today, however, than at any time in the past several years. For a discussion, see "Beyond Unions," *Business Week;* and R. W. Mondy and S. R. Preameaur, "The Labor-Management Power Relationship Revisited," *Personnel Administrator* (May 1985): 51–55.

8. A good discussion of earlier contributions to labor law can be found in D. P. Twomey, *Labor Law and Legislation,* 6th ed. (Cincinnati, Ohio: South-Western, 1980).

9. L. Balliet, *Survey of Labor Relations* (Washington, D.C.: Bureau of National Affairs, 1981), p. 44.

10. Civil law refers to a suit between two parties or between the government and a private party over their respective rights. In a criminal matter of law, the government representing the public interest attempts to punish a party for illegal conduct. (Balliet, *Survey of Labor Relations,* p. 45.)

11. H. B. Frazier II, "Labor Management Relations in the Federal Government," *Labor Law Journal* (Mar. 1979): 131.

12. Twomey, *Labor Law and Legislation.*

13. Twomey, *Labor Law and Legislation,* p. 77.

14. A. Sloan and F. Whitney, *Labor Relations,* 3d ed. (Englewood Cliffs, N.J.: Prentice-Hall, 1977).

15. "Supervisors, Beware!" *Wall Street Journal,* 12 July 1982, p. 2; "Firing Managers," *Wall Street Journal,* 18 Jan. 1983, p. 1.

16. D. Israel, "The Weingarten Case Sets Precedent for Co-Employee Representation," *Personnel Administrator* (Feb. 1983): 23.

17. For further description of the NLRB, see "Bob Hunter: Reagan's 'Point Man' on the NLRB," *Personnel Administrator* (May 1985): 27–32; S. Estreicher, "Workers Still Need Labor Law's Shield," *New York Times,* 21 July 1985, p. 2F; R. A. Epstein, "Abolish the Board, Deregulate Unions," *New York Times,* 21 July 1985, p. 2F; H. E. Gerson and L. P. Britt III, "1984 Labor and EEO Review," *Personnel Administrator* (May 1985): 37–41; F. C. Morris, Jr., and H. N. Turk, "A Labor Board Roundup and Forecast: The Balance Continues to Shift," *Employee Relations Law Journal* (Summer 1985): 32–55; R. Turner, "Impasse in the 'Real World' of Labor Relations: Where Does the Board Stand?" *Employee Relations Law Journal* (Winter 1984–85): 468–95.

18. Sloan and Whitney, *Labor Relations.*

19. J. A. Fossum, *Labor Relations: Development, Structure, Process,* 2d ed. (Dallas, Tex.: Business Publications, 1982).

20. Frazier, "Labor Management Relations." p. 133.

21. Frazier, "Labor Management Relations." p. 133. See also T. J. Krajci, "Labor Relations in the Public Sector," *Personnel Administrator* (May 1985): 43–47.

22. J. N. Draznin, "Labor Relations,"*Personnel Journal* (Oct. 1981): 764–66.

23. These relationships, however, can always change. See P. J. Harkins, "The Fickle Nature of Employment Agreements," *Personnel Journal* (May 1985): 76–80; "Companies Can Void Contracts if 'Burdensome' to Employers," *Resource* (Mar. 1984): 1, 10; B. S. Murphy, W. E. Barlow, and D. D. Hatch, "A Successor Employer's Duty to Bargain," *Personnel Journal* (May 1985): 29–36.

24. G. W. Bohlander, "Fair Representation: Not Just a Union Problem," *Personnel Administrator* (Mar. 1980): 36–40, 82; J. P. Swann, Jr., "Misrepresentation in Labor Union Elections," *Personnel Journal* (Nov. 1980): 925–26.

25. "Unions Are Getting Clobbered in the Courts," *Business Week,* 22 July 1985, p. 106A.

26. For an excellent discussion on what motivates employees generally and in regard to unions specifically, see J. A. Fossum, "Union-Management Relations," in *Personnel Management,* ed. K. M. Rowland and G. R. Ferris (Boston: Allyn & Bacon, 1982), pp. 430–31; T. R. Mitchell, "Motivational Strategies," in *Personnel Management,* pp. 263–300; S. A. Youngblood, A. D. DeNisi, J. Molleston, and W. H. Mobley, "The Impact of Work Attachment, Instrumentality Belief, Perceived Labor Union Image, and Subjective Norms on Union Voting Intentions and Union Membership," *Academy of Management Journal* 27 (1984): 576–90.

27. E. H. Schein, *Organizational Psychology* (Englewood Cliffs, N.J.: Prentice-Hall, 1965).

28. For a discussion of the concept of met expectations and satisfaction, see A. C. Kalleberg, "Work Values and Job Rewards: A Theory of Job Satisfaction," *American Sociological Review* 42 (1977): 124–43; E. A. Locke, "What Is Job Satisfaction?" *Organizational Behavior and Human Performance* 4 (1969): 309–35.

29. J. G. Getman, S. B. Goldberg, and J. B. Herman, *Union Representation Elections: Law and Reality* (New York: Russell Sage, 1976). Employees can be satisfied or dissatisfied (or any point in between) vis-à-vis many aspects of the work environment. For example, employees may be dissatisfied with the following:

- Lack of job security
- Wages
- The company as a place to work
- Unequal treatment by supervisors
- Fringe benefits
- Lack of supervisory recognition
- Chances for promotion
- Petty work rules

The more aspects with which employees are dissatisfied, the more likely they are to favor a union. Not all employees will be dissatisfied with the previous aspects, even if they work in the same company. Those more likely to be dissatisfied and vote for a union are characterized as follows:

- Younger in age
- Belong to a minority
- Have low seniority
- Make very low wages
- Have voted for a union in a previous election
- Are dissatisfied with conditions

30. J. F. Rand, "Preventive Maintenance Techniques for Staying Union Free," *Personnel Journal* (June 1980): 498. A recommended way employers can communicate this preference and commitment is through a policy statement similar to this example:

Our success as a company is founded on the skill and efforts of our employees. Our policy is to deal with employees as effectively as possible, respecting and recognizing each of them as individuals.

In our opinion, unionization would interfere with the individual treatment, respect, and recognition the company offers.

Consequently, we believe a union-free environment is in the employee's best interest, the company's best interest, and the interest of the people served by the corporation.

31. R. Dubin, *The World of Work* (Englewood Cliffs, N.J.: Prentice-Hall, 1958).

32. J. M. Brett, "Behavioral Research on Unions," in *Research in Organizational Behavior,* vol. 2, ed. B. M. Staw and L. L. Cummings (Greenwich, Conn.: JAI Press, 1980); J. M. Brett, "Why Employees Want Unions," *Organizational Dynamics* (Spring 1980): 47–59; W. C. Hamner and F. J. Smith, "Work Attitudes as Predictors of Unionization Activity," *Journal of Applied Psychology* (Aug. 1978): 415–21.

33. See also Fossum, *Labor Relations.*

34. For a good discussion of instrumentality in general, see Mitchell, "Motivational Strategies," and E. E. Lawler, *Pay and Organization Development* (Reading, Mass.: Addison-Wesley, 1982). For a more specific discussion of instrumentality applied to work attachment and union attraction, see S. A. Youngblood, A. D. DeNisi, J. Molleston, and W. H. Mobley, "The Impact of Work Attachment, Instrumentality Beliefs, Perceived Labor Union Image, and Subjective Norms on Union Voting Intentions and Union Membership," in *Readings in Personnel and Human Re-*

source Management, 3d ed., ed. R. S. Schuler, S. A. Youngblood, and V. Huber (St. Paul: West, 1987).

35. Getman, Goldberg, and Herman, *Union Representation Elections.*

36. F. Bairstow, "Professionalism and Unionism: Are They Compatible?" *Industrial Engineering* (Apr. 1974): 40–42; P. Felville and J. Blandin, "Faculty Job Satisfaction and Bargaining Sentiments," *Academy of Management Journal* (Dec. 1974): 678–92; B. Husaini and J. Geschwender, "Some Correlates of Attitudes toward and Membership in White Collar Unions," *Southwestern Social Science Quarterly* (Mar. 1967): 595–601; L. Imundo, "Attitudes of Non-Union White Collar Federal Government Employees toward Unions," *Public Personnel Management* (Jan.–Feb. 1974): 87–92; A. Kleingartner, "Professionalism and Engineering Unionism," *Harvard Business Review* (Mar.–Apr. 1971): 48–54.

37. J. H. Hopkins and R. D. Binderup, "Employee Relations and Union Organizing Campaigns,"*Personnel Administrator* (Mar. 1980): 57–61.

38. Pro-union legislation in the 1920s and 1930s was favored by some pro-management groups because it was seen as a way to bring some degree of certainty and peace to union-management relationships. See Balliet, *Survey of Labor Relations,* pp. 13–68.

39. Interesting discussions of early American labor history can be found in R. B. Morris, "A Bicentennial Look at the Early Days of American Labor," *Monthly Labor Review* (May 1976): 21–26.

40. Fossum, *Labor Relations.*

41. Sloan and Whitney, *Labor Relations,* p. 59.

42. Ibid., p. 64.

43. For an extensive presentation of union membership data, see C. D. Gifford, ed., *Directory of U.S. Labor Organizations, 1984–85 Edition* (Washington, D.C.: Bureau of National Affairs, 1984).

44. "Beyond Unions," *Business Week;* D. Yoder and P. D. Staudohar, *Personnel Management and Industrial Relations,* 7th ed. (Englewood Cliffs, N.J.: Prentice-Hall, 1982); D. Yoder and P. D. Staudohar, "Assessing the Decline of Unions in the U.S.," *Personnel Administrator* (Oct. 1982): 12–15.

45. This forecast is not necessarily shared by all. For multiple views on the outlook for unions, see W. J. Usery, Jr., and D. Henne, "The American Labor Movement in the 1980s," *Employee Relations Law Journal* 7 (1981): 251–59; "Are the Unions Dead or Just Sleeping? *Fortune,* 20 Sept. 1982, pp. 98–110; A. H. Raskin, "Frustrated and Wary, Labor Marks Its Day," *New York Times,* 5 Sept. 1982, pp. 1F, 6F; S. A. Levitan, "Labor: Still Alive," *New York Times,* 12 Sept. 1982, p. 9F; J. S. Lublin, "Pugnacious Companies and Skeptical Workers Cost Unions Members," *Wall Street Journal,* 21 Oct. 1982, pp. 1, 27; F. Carbry, "What Happened to the 'Threat' of White-Collar Unionization?" *Management Review* (Mar. 1985): 52–56; M. W. Miller, "Unions Curtail Organizing in

High Tech," *Wall Street Journal,* 13 Nov. 1984, p. 35; L. M. Apcar and C. Trost, "Realizing Their Power Has Eroded, Unions Try Hard to Change," *Wall Street Journal,* 21 Feb. 1985, pp. 1, 20.

46. U.S. Department of Labor, Bureau of Labor Statistics, "Corrected Data on Labor Organizations, Membership," *News* USDL: 81-466, 18 Sept. 1981, p. 3; C. J. Janus, "Union Mergers in the 1970s: A Look at the Reasons and the Results," *Monthly Labor Review* (Oct. 1979): 13–23; "Labor's Marriages of Convenience," *Business Week,* 22 Nov. 1982, pp. 28–29; "A Push to Unify the News Unions," *Business Week,* 22 Nov. 1982, pp. 93–94; J. A. Fossum, "Labor Relations," in *Human Resource Management in the 1980s,* ed. S. J. Carroll and R. S. Schuler (Washington, D.C.: Bureau of National Affairs, 1983).

47. U.S. Department of Labor, Bureau of Labor Statistics, *Directory of National Unions and Employee Associations, Bulletin No. 2044* (Washington, D.C.: Government Printing Office, 1979), p. 60.

48. C. J. Janus, "Union Mergers in the 1970s: A Look at the Reasons and Results," *Monthly Labor Review* (Oct. 1978): 13–23; "Building Trades Lose Ground," *Business Week,* 9 Nov. 1981, p. 104–6; "A Union Fight That May Explode," *Business Week,* 16 Mar. 1981, pp. 102–4; B. Keller, "Unions' Economic Troubles Are Spurring Merger Trend," *New York Times,* 13 May 1984, pp. 1, 26.

49. Balliet, *Survey of Labor Relations,* pp. 72–105.

50. "Labor's Marriages of Convenience," *Business Week,* 1 Nov. 1982, pp. 28–29. The telephone numbers and addresses for these individuals are found in Gifford, ed., *Directory of U.S. Labor Organizations, 1982–1983 Edition.*

51. "Reagan Is Arousing AFL-CIO Activism," *Business Week,* 5 Oct. 1981, p. 35; "Labor Moves in on the Democrats," *Business Week,* 5 Oct. 1981, p. 143; "A Hard Line on Soviet Trade," *Business Week,* 22 June 1981, p. 143; "Can Labor Recapture Its Political Clout?" *Business Week,* 22 June 1981, p. 123; A. R. Karr, "Airlines, Unions Mount Lobbying Battle as Senate Nears Vote on Bill to Protect Jobs," *Wall Street Journal,* 11 Aug. 1982, p. 46; L. M. Apcar, "Kirkland's Call to Void Law Laws Ignites a Growing National Debate," *Wall Street Journal,* 6 Nov. 1984, p. 31; W. Serrin, "Organized Labor Is Increasingly Less So," *New York Times,* 18 Nov. 1984, p. E3; "The Election Leaves Labor in the Lurch," *Business Week,* 19 Nov. 1984, p. 42.

52. "Can Labor Recapture Its Political Clout?" *Business Week,* 22 June 1981, p. 123.

53. Getman, Goldberg, and Herman, *Union Representation Elections,* p. 1.

54. For an extensive discussion of the organizing campaign, see Fossum, "Union-Management Relations," and W. E. Fulmer, "Step by Step through a Union Campaign," *Harvard Business Review* (July–Aug. 1981): 94–102.

55. Getman, Goldberg, and Herman, *Union Representation Elections.*

56. Fulmer, "Union Campaign."

57. For many examples of managements' resistance tactics, see D. McInnis, "A New Chill on Organizing Efforts," *New York Times,* 30 May 1982, p. 4F; W. Serrin, "An Organizer Beset," *New York Times,* 19 Sept. 1982, p. 6F; M. Z. Sappir, "The Employer's Obligation Not to Bargain When the Issue of Decertification Is Present," *Personnel Administrator* (Feb. 1982): 41–45; S. M. Klein and K. W. Rose, "Formal Policies and Procedures Can Forestall Unionization," *Personnel Journal* (Mar. 1982): 214–19; "Pros Who Try to Help Unions Win," *Business Week,* 23 Aug. 1982, pp. 96–100; E. L. Harrison, D. Johnson, and F. M. Rachel, "The Role of the Supervisor in Representation Elections," *Personnel Administrator* (Sept. 1981): 67–72, 82; K. A. Kovach, "J. P. Stevens and the Struggle for Union Organization," *Labor Law Journal* (May 1978): 307; Twomey, *Labor Law,* p. 137; S. Salmans, "J. P. Stevens: One," *New York Times,* 18 Oct. 1981, sec. F, p. 8.

58. For a limited description of the potential penalties involved in community unfair labor practices, see "Testing a New Weapon against Litton," *Business Week,* 27 Dec. 1982, pp. 32–33.

59. Twomey, *Labor Law,* p. 134.

60. Getman, Goldberg, and Herman, *Union Representation Elections.*

61. W. Bitler, Jr., "Unionization of Security Guards: A Unique Problem," *Personnel Administrator* (June 1981): 79–83; "An Acid Test at DuPont," *Business Week,* 14 Dec. 1981, pp. 123–27.

62. W. Imberman, "How Expensive Is an NLRB Election?" *MSU Business Topics* (Summer 1975): 13–18.

63. For a good overview of the rules of the game here, see J. P. Swann, Jr., "The Decertification of a Union," *Personnel Administrator* (Jan. 1983): 47–51; J. W. Hunt, *The Law of the Workplace* (Washington, D.C.: Bureau of National Affairs, 1984).

64. For a discussion of this point, see D. Q. Mills, *The New Competitors* (New York: Free Press, 1985), pp. 225–42.

Collective Bargaining

Tough Line Pays

A dramatic shift to tougher and more disciplined wage and benefit policies by American companies has been a critical factor in holding down U.S. labor costs, according to The Conference Board's Audrey Freedman. In her latest study, "The New Look in Wage Policy and Employee Relations," which draws on data provided by more than 500 firms, the labor economist says that competitive pressure is cited as the most important influence on management's turnaround in wage-setting practices.

U.S. companies are increasingly basing wage decisions on their own productivity and labor-cost trends rather than industry-wide patterns. This has helped to slow wage hikes throughout the economy. Hourly earnings in manufacturing, Freedman's report notes, have only gone up 4.3 percent per year during the last three years, compared to an average rise of 8.5 percent yearly in 1979 and 1980.

"Management has increasingly gained the upper hand in negotiations. Unions have lost their industry-wide influence over wages," Freedman states, adding: "With competition certain to remain intense, American business is not likely to return to the wage-limitation habits that prevailed in the 1970s."

The report shows that among companies using productivity and labor cost factors to govern their wage decisions, annual wage and benefit gains in their largest bargaining units averaged 4.6 percent a year in the most recent settlement, compared with 5.8 percent a year among companies in which these criteria ranked fourth or lower. Among companies using anticipated profits as their key influence in bargaining, wage and benefit increases averaged four percent, against 5.9 percent in firms where expected profits ranked fourth or lower as a major influence.

Other points in the Freedman study:

■ Despite a toughened bargaining stance by many companies, the management-union climate has improved. Some 76 percent of the unionized firms say their ability to work cooperatively with their major union is "good" or "very good," up from 67 percent in the 1978 survey.

■ Companies which were willing to grant more liberal benefits to unions seven years ago are now demanding and receiving give-backs in nonwage areas. The two areas of greatest concern: Health insurance and time off with pay.

■ The current trend is likely to continue throughout the decade.

Freedman says, "Bargaining power has been greatly altered as a result of the growth of nonunion competition inside the U.S. and abroad. Management's power to administer prices has faded. With this decline in the market power of their employers, unions' ability to affect wage levels within industries has declined."

Source: P. Farish, "Tough Line Pays," p. 12. Reprinted from the June issue of *Personnel Administrator,* copyright © 1985, the American Society for Personnel Administration, 606 North Washington Street, Alexandria, VA 22314.

The preceding "PHRM in the News" highlights two sides of a major trend in the union-management collective bargaining relationship. A major trend is toward union-management activities to make organizations more competitive. In part this has led toward concessionary bargaining, wherein the union generally concedes or gives back previously won wages, benefits, and work rules in exchange for jobs and job security provided by the employer. One perspective on this trend is that it is necessary and vital for both unions and management in order for companies to survive and compete. What's more, this trend provides an opportunity for labor unions to survive and to contribute to the revitalization of U.S. industry. The other side of this trend is that unions and their members are being asked and even coerced to grant concessions while management in return concedes essentially nothing. In other words, enabling companies to survive and compete is at the expense of unions only and not management.

But this major trend has also led to the trend of more union-management cooperation. A consequence is the establishment of training programs to enable workers to retrain for new jobs.

There is, however, more to collective bargaining than these trends. A multitude of issues are associated with negotiating the collective bargaining agreement, resolving conflicts under the agreement, and administering the contract. These issues are described in the definition of collective bargaining.

The core of union-management relations is **collective bargaining**. It generally includes two types of interaction. The first is the negotiation of work conditions that, when written up as the collective agreement (the contract), become the basis for employee-employer relationships on the job. The second is the activity related to interpreting and enforcing the collective agreement (contract administration) and the resolution of any conflicts arising out of it.[1]

This chapter discusses both of these interactions within the collective bargaining process. First, however, the quality of the union-management relationship is discussed, since this has such a powerful influence on the negotiating process, the settlement of grievances, and the rest of the collective bargaining process.

The Collective Bargaining Process

Collective bargaining is a complex process in which union and management negotiators maneuver to win the most advantageous contract.[2] As in any complex process, a variety of issues come into play. How these issues are dealt with and resolved depends upon the following:

- The quality of the union-management relationship
- The processes of bargaining used by labor and management
- Management's strategies in the collective bargaining process
- Union's strategies in the collective bargaining process
- Joint union-management strategies

These critical determinants of the collective bargaining process are described in detail prior to a description of the negotiation process.

Union-Management Relationships

An understanding of union-management relationships is facilitated by seeing them set in a **labor relations sytem**. The labor relations sytem is composed of three subunits—employees, management, and the union—with the government influencing the interaction among the three. Employees may be managers or union members, and some of the union members are part of the union-management system (local union leaders). Each of the three interrelationships in the model is addressed by specific legal regulations: union and management (by the National Labor Relations Act and Title VII of the Civil Rights Act), management and employees (by the National Labor Relations Act and Title VII of the Civil Rights Act), and union and employees (by the Labor-Management Reporting and Disclosure Act and Title VII of the Civil Rights Act). In addition to these legal regulations are numerous other acts and court decisions applicable to both unionization and collective bargaining, as presented in the previous chapter.

Each of the groups identified in the labor relations model has traditionally had different goals.[3] Workers are interested in improved working conditions, due process, wages, and opportunities; unions are interested in their own survival, growth, and acquisition of power, which depend on their ability to maintain the support of the employees by providing for their needs. Management has overall organizational goals (i.e., profit, certainty, market share, growth), and it also seeks to preserve managerial prerogatives (i.e., management rights, to direct the work force, and to attain the personal goals of the managers, such as promotion and achievement). Government is interested in a stable and healthy economy, protection of individual rights, due process, and safety and fairness in the work place.

These sets of goals, particularly those of union and of management, are important because they can play an integral part in the nature of the relationship between union and management. For example, if the goals of union and management are seen as incompatible, an adversarial relationship may exist between the two parties. If the goals are seen as complementary, then a more cooperative relationship may exist. These relationships can also be viewed somewhat differently. For example, by assuming or thinking the union-management relationship to be adversarial, the goals of union and those of management may be seen as incompatible. Determining the nature of this relationship is important in understanding the union-management relationship as well as in changing the nature of the relationship. Therefore, the nature of the possible relationships between union and management are discussed in detail, starting with the adversarial relationship.

The Adversarial Relationship.   In the adversarial relationship, the goals of union and management are generally seen as incompatible. When seen this way, an **adversarial system** emerges, with labor and management attempting to get a bigger cut of the pie while government looks on to protect its interests.

In an adversarial system of union-management relations, the union's role is to gain concessions from management during collective bargaining and to preserve those concessions through the grievance procedure. The union is an outsider and critic.[4]

Historically, unions have adopted an adversarial role in their interactions with management. Their focus has been on wages and working conditions as they have attempted to get "more and better" job conditions from management. This approach works well in economic boom times but becomes difficult when the economy is not healthy. High unemployment and the threat of continued job losses have recently induced unions, as well as management, to revise their relationship. Many unions have begun to enter into new, collaborative efforts with employers. The result of this can be described as a cooperative relationship.

The Cooperative Relationship.   In a **cooperative system,** the union's role is that of a partner, not a critic, and the union becomes jointly responsible with management for reaching a cooperative solution. Thus, a cooperative system requires that union and management engage in problem solving, information sharing, and integration of outcomes.[5] Cooperative systems have not been a major component of labor relations in the United States. Other countries—Sweden, Yugoslavia, and West Germany, for example,—have built a cooperative mechanism (codetermination is discussed in Chapter 17) into the labor system. On occasion, however, American management and labor have worked together to solve a problem. Most changes and job redesign projects undertaken by management need the acceptance of the union to be successful. Active involvement of the union is one of the best ways to gain this acceptance.[6]

An example of what this cooperation can bring is the worker participation and involvement project at Ford Motor's plant in Edison, New Jersey:

> The innovation at Edison—other Ford plants are now installing the stop concept—is only the most visible symbol of a near-revolution in labor-management relations that started five years ago and has since become entrenched. Ford and the United Auto Workers have established what may be the most extensive and successful worker participation process in a major, unionized company. Thousands of teams of workers and supervisors at eighty-six of Ford's ninety-one plants and depots meet weekly to deal with production, quality, and work-environment problems.[7]

Regardless of whether union and management share an adversarial relationship or a cooperative one, they must still engage in processes of bargaining to arrive at a union-management contract. These processes are often influenced by the type of relationship that union and management have. For example, an adversarial relationship is more likely to accommodate a process of distributive bargaining, while a cooperative relationship is more likely to accommodate a process of integrative bargaining. Other accommodations can more readily be made after discussing all the processes of bargaining.

Processes of Bargaining

The most widely used description of the bargaining processes incorporates four types of bargaining in contract negotiations: distributive bargaining, integrative bargaining, attitudinal structuring, and intraorganizational bargaining.[8]

Distributive Bargaining.   **Distributive bargaining** takes place when the parties are in conflict over an issue and the outcome represents a gain for one party and loss for the other. Each party tries to negotiate for the best possible outcome. The process is outlined in Exhibit 16.1.

On any particular issue, union and management negotiators each have three identifiable positions. The union has an **initial demand point**, which is generally more than they expect to get; a target point, which is their realistic assessment of what they may be able to get; and a resistance point, which is

---

Distributive Bargaining Process   *Exhibit 16.1*

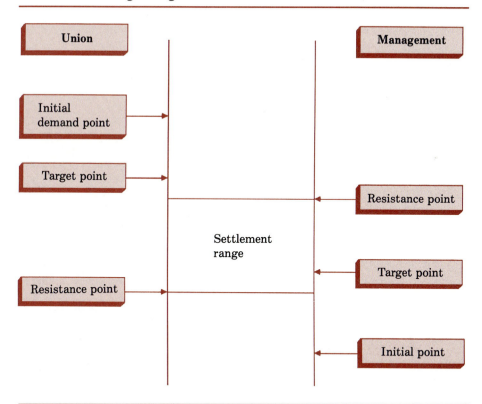

Source: U.S. Department of Labor Bureau of Labor Statistics, *Occupational Safety and Health Statistics Concepts and Methods.* BLS report 438 (Washington, D.C. Bureau of Labor Statistics, 1975), p. 2.

the lowest acceptable level for that issue. Management has three similar points: an **initial offer,** which is usually lower than the expected settlement; a **target point,** which is the point at which it would like to reach agreement; and a **resistance point,** which is its highest acceptable limit. If, as shown in Exhibit 16.1, management's resistance point is greater than the union's resistance point, there is a positive settlement range where negotiation can take place. The exact agreement within this range depends on the bargaining behavior of the negotiators. If, however, management's resistance point is below the union's, there is no common ground for negotiation. In such a situation, there is a negative settlement range, and a bargaining impasse exists.[9]

Using wages as an example, the union may have a resistance point of $8.40 per hour, a target of $8.60, and an initial demand of $8.75. Management may offer $8.20 but have a target of $5.45 and a resistance point of $8.55. The positive settlement range is between $8.40 and $8.55, and this is where the settlement will likely be. However, only the initial wage demand and offer are made public at the beginning of negotiations.

Since many issues are involved in a bargaining session, the process becomes much more complicated. Although each issue may be described by the previous model, in actual negotiations an interaction occurs among issues. Union concessions on one issue may be traded for management concessions on another. The total process is dynamic.

The ritual of the distributive bargaining process is well established, and deviations are often met with suspicion. The following story illustrates this point:

> A labor lawyer tells the story of a young executive who had just taken over the helm of a company. Imbued with idealism, he wanted to end the bickering he had seen take place during past negotiations with labor. To do this, he was ready to give the workers as much as his company could afford. Consequently he asked some members of his staff to study his firm's own wage structure and decide how it compared with other companies, as well as a host of other related matters. He approached the collective bargaining table with a halo of goodness surrounding him. Asking for the floor, he proceeded to describe what he had done and with a big smile on his face made the offer.
>
> Throughout his entire presentation, the union officials stared at him in amazement. He had offered more than they had expected to secure. But no matter, as soon as he finished, they proceeded to lambaste him, denouncing him for trying to destroy collective bargaining and for attempting to buy off labor. They announced that they would not stand for any such unethical maneuvering, and immediately asked for 5 cents more than the idealistic executive had offered.[10]

Integrative Bargaining.   **Integrative bargaining** is the situation in which management and the union work to solve a problem to the benefit of both. For instance, issues of work crew size may be addressed, or union concerns for job security. Most changes in quality of work life involve integrative bargaining. The new work setting will benefit employees as well as the employer. Given the adversarial nature of labor-management relations, integrative bargaining is not common, although the recent interest in cooperative relations may change that.

Examples of integrative bargaining are the Scanlon plan and many of the QWL programs described in Chapter 12.[11] Not all bargaining processes, however, determine who gets how much or whether problems are solved. In some bargaining processes, union or management tries to influence the attitudes of the other. This is referred to as attitudinal structuring.

Attitudinal Structuring.   Here, the relationship between labor and management results in **attitudinal structuring,** or the shaping of attitudes toward one another. Four dimensions of this relationship have been identified: (1) motivational orientation, or tendencies that indicate whether the interaction will be competitive and adversarial or cooperative; (2) beliefs about the legitimacy of the other, or how much a party believes the other has a right to be bargaining; (3) level of trust in conducting affairs, or belief in the integrity and honesty of the other party; and (4) degree of friendliness, or whether the interactions are friendly or hostile.[12] As the bargaining process proceeds, these attitudes may be altered. The attitudes emerging from the negotiations will have a serious impact on the administration of the contract and on future negotiations. They also influence the other processes of bargaining. For example, generating attitudes that give recognition to the other party and farsightedness in work relationships can facilitate a cooperative relationship and an integrative bargaining process.[13]

Occasionally, attitudinal structuring of a different kind is needed. It is the kind that is necessary when union or management leaders need to change the attitudes of their supporters or members when their support is needed.[14] This type of bargaining influence process is referred to as intraorganizational bargaining.

Intraorganizational Bargaining.   During negotiations, the bargaining teams from both sides may have to engage in **intraorganizational bargaining,** or conferring with their constituents over changes in bargaining positions. Management negotiators may have to convince management to change its position on an issue—for instance, to agree to a higher wage settlement. Union negotiators must eventually convince their members to accept the negotiated contract, so they must be sensitive to the demands of the membership as well as realistic. When the membership votes on the proposed package, it will be strongly influenced by the opinions of the union negotiators.

A special form of intraorganizational bargaining, practiced particularly in the public sector, is **multilateral bargaining.** This form of bargaining is a consequence of major conflicts with the management negotiating team resulting from political pressures exerted on elected officials (represented by the management negotiating team) by officials from the unions also party to the negotiations. One result of this pressure is to force the elected officials to tell their negotiators to grant more concessions to the unions than they otherwise may have. Bargaining then becomes a process involving multiple levels.

With all these processes of bargaining, unions and management can engage in a wide variety of actual bargaining behavior. The behaviors and the processes they use are frequently a product of the strategies they choose to pursue, either separately or jointly.

Management Strategies

Prior to the bargaining session, management negotiators prepare by developing the strategies and proposals they will use. Four major areas of preparation have been identified:

- Preparation of specific proposals for changes in contract language
- Determination of the general size of the economic package that the company anticipates offering during the negotiations
- Preparation of statistical displays and supportive data that the company will use during negotiations
- Preparation of a bargaining book for the use of company negotiators, a compilation of information on issues that will be discussed, giving an analysis of the effect of each clause, its use in other companies, and other facts[15]

An important part of this preparation is calculation of the cost of various bargaining issues or demands. The relative cost of pension contributions, pay increases, health benefits, and other provisions should be determined prior to negotiations. Other costs should also be considered. For instance, what is the cost to management, in its ability to do its job, of union demands for changes in grievance and discipline procedures or transfer and promotion provisions? The goal is to be as well prepared as possible by considering the implications and ramifications of the issues that will be discussed and by being able to present a strong argument for the position management takes.

An example of preparation to the extreme is the bargaining practice called **Boulwarism**, in which management presents the union with an offer early in the negotiations and holds firm to that offer. This practice, used successfully by General Electric in the 1960s and early 1970s, involves preparing for negotiations by effecting what company representatives describe as "the steady accumulation of all facts available on matters likely to be discussed." This information will be modified only on the basis of "any additional or different facts" the company is made aware of, either by its unions or from other sources, before or during the negotiations. The company offers at an "appropriate" but invariably early point during the bargaining "what the facts from all sources seem to indicate that we should," and it changes this offer only if confronted with "new facts."[16]

Along with these bargaining strategies, GE engaged in a massive communication program aimed at convincing workers that GE was looking out for their interests. During the 1960 negotiations and subsequent strike, GE sent out 246 written communications to its employees.[17] Using these tactics, GE was able to have its proposal accepted by the International Brotherhood of Electrical Workers. Union leaders protested that these tactics constituted an unfair labor practice because the company refused to bargain.[18] To be sure, this bargaining approach made the union look bad and further weakened its position with union members. (The union had already been relatively weak because of internal problems and conflicts with other unions.)

GE is having less success in getting its offers accepted in recent negotiations, because the union has since become stronger and better prepared.

Other companies have not adopted GE's strategy, since the NLRB declared Boulwarism illegal partly because it represents a lack of good faith bargaining, and partly because they do not want to give up potential gains at the bargaining table or risk higher costs when a strong union responds to this strategy. Since the court upheld the NLRB ruling, GE has also dropped this strategy.

Union Strategies

Like management, unions need to prepare for negotiations by collecting information. More and better information gives the union the ability to be more convincing in negotiations. Since collective bargaining is the major means by which a union can convince its members that it is effective and valuable, this is a critical activity.

Unions collect information in at least three areas:

- The financial situation of the company and its ability to pay
- The attitude of management toward various issues, as reflected in past negotiations or inferred from negotiations in similar companies
- The attitudes and desires of the employees

The first two areas give the union an idea of what demands management is likely to accept. The third area is important but is sometimes overlooked. The union should be aware of the preferences of the membership. For instance, is a pension increase preferred over increased vacation or holiday benefits? The preferences will vary with the characteristics of the workers. Younger workers are more likely to prefer more holidays, shorter work-weeks, and limited overtime, whereas older workers are more interested in pension plans, benefits, and overtime. The union can determine these preferences by using a questionnaire to survey its members (discussed in Chapter 18).

Joint Union-Management Strategies

Consistent with cooperative union-management relationships and integrative bargaining are joint union-management strategies. The three major types of such strategies are productivity bargaining, concessionary bargaining, and continuous bargaining.

Productivity Bargaining. A relatively recent procedure in negotiations is **productivity bargaining,** a special form of integrative bargaining. Labor agrees to scrap old work habits and work rules for new and more effective ones desired by management, and in exchange management returns to labor some of the gains of modernization and increased efficiency in the form of new and better work incentives.[19]

Some unions have been hesitant to agree to this approach because they fear that their members will lose jobs, that the company will require excessive work, or that technological change will eventually eliminate more jobs. Despite this hesitancy, productivity bargaining has been used successfully.

One notable result is that the bargaining process changes from distributive to integrative. Labor and management work together, not only to create the agreement itself, but to create an atmosphere of ongoing cooperation.[20] Another notable result is that significant cost savings are made, enabling company survival and continued jobs for union members.

Concessionary Bargaining.   As the initial "PHRM in the News" suggests, **concessionary bargaining** is prompted by severe economic conditions of employers. Seeking to survive and prosper, employers seek givebacks or concessions from the unions, giving in return promises of job security. During the past few years, this type of bargaining has been particularly prevalent, especially in the smokestack industries, such as automobiles, steel, and rubber, and to some extent in the transportation industry. In these industries, concessions sought by management from the unions include wage freezes, wage reductions, work-rule change or elimination, fringe benefit reductions, delay or elimination of COLAs, and more hours of work for the same pay. A more recent form of wage concessions is the two-tier arrangement. Because of its recency, its effectiveness is yet to be determined, as the next "PHRM in the News" describes.

Although some rank-and-file union members are not pleased with the concessions, and many are rejecting tentative contracts that have concessions, their alternatives seem to be limited.[21] Either concessions can be made, or plants can be closed or moved, or the entire company can declare bankruptcy.[22] For the most part, unions and their members are willing to grant concessions now, with the knowledge that such concessions do not guarantee job security forever.[23] Another alternative available is having the employees buy the company or parts of the company. Such purchases can be facilitated through employee stock ownership plans (ESOPs), described in Chapters 9 and 10.

Continuous Bargaining.   As affirmative action, safety and health requirements, and other government regulations continue to complicate the situation for both unions and employers, and as the rate of change in the environment continues to increase, some labor and management negotiators are turning to **continuous bargaining**. A joint committee meets on a regular basis to explore issues, analyze problems, and solve problems of common interest. These committees have appeared in retail food, over-the-road trucking, nuclear power, and men's garment industries.[24]

Several characteristics of continuous bargaining have been identified:

- Frequent meetings during the life of the contract
- Focus on external events and problem areas rather than on internal problems
- Use of outside experts in decision making
- Use of a problem-solving (integrative) approach[25]

The intention is to develop a union-management structure that is capable of adapting to sudden changes in the environment positively and productively. This continuous bargaining approach is different from, but an extension of, the emergency negotiations that unions have insisted on when inflation or

The Two-Tier Trend

Two-tier wage structures—pay plans setting lower compensation rates for new hires—are being touted as a solution to a central business dilemma: How do you reduce labor costs without riling experienced workers?

Two-tier wage structures allow employers to pay current workers at rates they are accustomed to, or even give them raises, while offering the prospect of reduced compensation costs over the long term. As top-tier workers leave the company, they are replaced by workers paid on the lower-tier schedule. For companies with high turnover rates or those planning to expand their labor force, two-tier wage structures can offer quicker pay-offs because lower-tier workers will make up a larger percentage of the workforce sooner.

Few observers interviewed by BNA, however, see two-tier wage structures, in their pure form, as problem-free, and a number of experts predict that two-tier pay structures will turn out to be more trouble than they are worth. Friction between top-tier and bottom-tier workers is cited by critics as likely if not inevitable. Labor officials say the system can drive a wedge between members, threatening worker solidarity and the hallowed union concept of equal pay for equal work.

In addition, legal problems could arise for both unions and employers. Clyde Summers, labor law specialist and law professor at the University of Pennsylvania says that unions that agree to the dual system may be liable for not representing all members equally under the duty of fair representation. On the other hand, Summers points out that employers whose workforces are comprised predominantly of white males could find themselves in legal hot water if they hired a disproportionate number of minority employees in the lower tier, while allowing the white males to work in the upper tier.

Variety of approaches

A wide variety of two-tier wage structures have emerged. There are, however, two basic formulas around which many of the current structures have been built. They are:

- "Permanent" two-tier systems in which new hires start at lower wages and/or benefits and remain in the lower tier for the life of the contract. The top scale for bottom-tier employees will always be lower than that paid to top-tier workers.

- Two-tier systems that limit benefit coverage or pay for new hires, but allow the new hires to "graduate" to top-tier pay and benefits after a period of time.

Critics of the graduated systems say that they yield very little in terms of long-term labor cost savings, because new employees rise within a matter of months or a few years to regular pay scales. "They only delay the problem," one industry official maintains. On the other hand, critics of the "permanent" two-tier systems claim the systems will produce worker unrest and, possibly, legal problems.

Between the two alternatives there are numerous choices. Some two-tier structures limit pay for new hires; others lower benefits, such as vacation days, pension benefits, and employer-paid health coverage; some lower both wages and benefits.

Food industry experience

In most industries, the effectiveness of these plans has yet to be proven. Two-tier provisions, by and large, are too new to have had any effect. The food industry, however, has had several years' experience with two-tier pay schedules. The rapid expansion of cheaper, non-union facilities and the rapid transformation of food marketing has fueled the development, according to union and employer officials.

As long as unionized grocery workers refuse to take pay cuts and non-union competition flourishes, pressure for two-tier pay schedules is likely to continue in the retail food industry, according to Don Hirsch, vice president for labor relations at the Kroger Co., one of the largest retail food operations in the country. Non-union grocery operations are able to set up shop paying clerks $5 an hour and less—sometimes half the pay unionized workers received in the same locality, Hirsch states. Without

wage relief, the unionized store cannot hope to compete, he observes.

Hirsch regards dual pay scales as both essential to business viability and workable in terms of employee relations. Friction between top and bottom-tier employees is minimal, he declares, in part due to educational efforts. "You've got to do a little talking to new hires," Hirsch maintains, adding that employees are generally receptive to the need to cut costs. "I think people today see those things better than in the past," he concludes.

Source: Bulletin to Management, 5 January 1984, p. 8. Reprinted by permission from *Bulletin to Management,* copyright 1984, by The Bureau of National Affairs, Inc., Washington, D.C.

other factors have substantially changed the acceptability of the existing agreement. Continuous bargaining is a permanent arrangement intended to help avoid the crises that often occur under traditional collective bargaining systems. Although not a formal adoption of continuous bargaining, the re-negotiation of contract terms between the United Auto Workers and Ford, Chrysler, and General Motors in 1982 before contract expiration was done to help avert an even greater crisis in the U.S. automobile industry.

Although the selection and utilization of a bargaining strategy is important in determining the outcomes of collective bargaining, so too is the actual process of negotiation, or negotiating the agreement.

Negotiating the Agreement

Once a union is certified as the representative of a work unit or bargaining unit, it becomes the only party that can negotiate an agreement with the employer for all members of that work unit, whether or not they are union members. This is therefore an important and potent position. The union is responsible to its members to negotiate for what they want, and it has the "duty to represent all employees fairly."[26] The union is a critical link between employees and employer. The quality of its bargaining is an important measure of union effectiveness.

Negotiating Committees

The employer and the union select their own representatives for the negotiating committee. Neither party is required to consider the wishes of the other. Management negotiators, for example, cannot refuse to bargain with representatives of the union because they dislike them or do not think they are appropriate.

Union negotiating teams typically include representatives of the union local, often the president and other executive staff members. In addition, the national union may send a negotiating specialist, who is likely to be a labor lawyer, to work with the team. The negotiators selected by the union do not have to be members of the union or employees of the company. The general goal is to balance bargaining skill and experience with knowledge and information about the specific situation.

At the local level, when a single bargaining unit is negotiating a contract, the company is usually represented by the manager and members of the labor relations or personnel staff. Finance and production managers may also be involved. When the negotiations are critical, either because the size of the bargaining unit is large or because the effect on the company is great, specialists such as labor lawyers may be included on the team.

In national negotiations, top industrial relations or personnel executives frequently head a team made up of specialists from corporate headquarters and perhaps managers from critical divisions or plants within the company. Again, the goal is to have expertise along with specific knowledge about critical situations.

The Negotiating Structure

Most contracts are negotiated by a single union and a single employer. In some situations, however, different arrangements can be agreed on. When a single union negotiates with several similar companies—for instance, the construction industry or supermarkets—the employers may bargain as a group with the union. At the local level, this is called **multiemployer bargaining;** at the national level, it is referred to as **industrywide bargaining.** Industrywide bargaining occurs in the railroad, coal, wallpaper, and men's suits industries.[27] National negotiations result in contracts that settle major issues, such as compensation, whereas issues relating to working conditions are settled locally. This split bargaining style is common in Great Britain and has been used in the auto industry in the United States. When several unions bargain jointly with a single employer, they engage in **coordinated bargaining.** Although not as common as the others, coordinated bargaining appears to be increasing, especially in public-sector bargaining. One consequence of coordinated and industrywide bargaining is often **pattern settlements,** where similar wage rates are imposed on the companies whose employees are represented by the same union within a given industry. Pattern settlements can be detrimental because they ignore differences in the employers' economic condition and ability to pay. The result can be settlements that are tolerable for some companies but cause severe economic trouble for others. As a partial consequence, the incidence of pattern settlements resulting from coordinated and industrywide bargaining has started to decline.[28] Nevertheless, the incentive to use these bargaining structures is usually related to efficiency and the relative strength of union and management. In multiemployer bargaining, the companies negotiate similar contracts to eliminate the time and cost of individual negotiations. Since it, too, will save time and money, the union may be willing to accept this type of bargaining if its own bargaining position is not weakened. Where local conditions vary substantially, there may be a need for splitting the bargaining between the national and local levels—settling the major issues at the national level and leaving specific issues for the local level, where they can be adjusted to meet local needs.

A negotiating structure that exists in the contract construction industry is **wide-area and multicraft bargaining.** This bargaining structure has arisen in response to the need for unionized employers to be more price competitive and have fewer strikes, and the desire by construction trade unions to gain more control at the national level. Consequently, the bargaining is done on a regional (geographic) basis rather than on a local basis, as previously done. In addition, it covers several construction crafts simultaneously instead of one. The common contract negotiations resulting from wide-area and multi-craft bargaining help lessen the occasion for unions to **whipsaw** the employer (i.e., to use one contract settlement as a precedent for the next), which then forces the employer to get all contracts settled so that all the employees will go back to work. A frequent result of whipsawing is an employer agreeing to more favorable settlements on *all* contracts, regardless of the conditions and merits of each contract, just to get all employees back to work.[29]

Issues for Negotiation

The issues that can be discussed in collective bargaining sessions are specified by the Labor Management Relations Act (discussed in Chapter 15). The act differentiates among three categories: mandatory issues, permissive issues, and prohibited issues.[30]

Employers and employee representatives (unions) are obligated to meet and discuss wages, hours, and other terms and conditions of employment. These are the **mandatory issues.** Historically, there has been a debate over what specific topics fall into this category. The Supreme Court's decision in the *Borg Warner* case (1958) suggests that the distinction between mandatory and permissive bargaining issues is based on whether the topic regulates the relations between the employer and its employees.[31] Any issue that changes the nature of the job itself or compensation for work must be discussed in collective bargaining. Mandatory issues therefore include subcontracting work, safety, changes of operations, and other actions management might take that will have an impact on employees' jobs, wages, and economic supplements. With the recent Supreme Court decision in *First National Maintenance,* described in the previous chapter, management's obligation to bargain over plant closings has been substantially reduced.[32]

Permissive issues are those that are not mandatory but are not specifically illegal. They are issues not specifically related to the nature of the job but still of concern to both parties. For example, issues of price, product design, and decisions about new jobs may be subject to bargaining if the parties agree to it. Permissive issues usually develop when both parties see that mutual discussion and agreement will be beneficial, as may be more likely when a cooperative relationship exists between union and management. Management and union negotiators cannot refuse to agree on a contract if they fail to settle a permissive issue.[33]

Prohibited issues are those concerning illegal or outlawed activities, such as the demand that an employer use only union-produced goods or, where it is illegal, that it employ only union members. Such issues may not be discussed in collective bargaining sessions.

Mandatory bargaining issues, therefore, are the critical factors in the bargaining process. They are the issues that may affect management's ability to run the company efficiently or clash with the union's desire to protect jobs and workers' standings in their jobs.[34]

Although the actual issues for negotiation can be expected to vary in different union-management bargainings, the issues for negotiation are likely to be far more extensive than those for the initial organizing campaign, described in the previous chapter. In contrast to organizing, where the critical issues are grievances, economics, job security, and supervision, there are a multitude of mandatory issues for negotiation, not to mention the permissive issues.[35] Most of the issues for negotiation are mandatory.

Wages.   Probably no issues under collective bargaining continue to give rise to more difficult problems than do wage and wage-related subjects. Wage conflicts are the leading cause of strikes. Difficulties here are understandable: A wage increase is a direct cost to the employer, as is a wage decrease to the employee.

The wages that an employee is paid are primarily determined by the basic pay rate for a certain job. This pay may then be increased by several other factors, all of which are subject to collective bargaining. Although management would prefer that basic pay be related only to productivity, this is seldom the case. Three additional standards are frequently used: comparative norm, where rate of pay is influenced by the rates provided for similar jobs in other companies within an industry or even by comparative rates between industries; ability to pay, where the pay rate is influenced by the financial capability of the company and especially the amount of its profit; and standard of living, where changes in the cost of living influence the rate of pay. Recently because of the productivity crisis and increased international competition, firms are having profitability problems. In turn, they are asking unions to hold the line on wage increases and, in some cases, to take a wage reduction.[36] As described in the section on concessionary bargaining, however, when employers ask for wage concessions or wage moderation, unions ask for job security in return. To facilitate being able to provide job security, employers may then provide early retirement incentives to all their employees.

Wages are one general category of payment to employees. The other is **economic supplements,** or fringe benefits. Collective bargaining deliberations may include discussion of how an increase in compensation will be split between these two types of payments. This is an important question, because the cost to the company of wages and fringe benefits may differ.

Economic Supplements.   An increasingly important part of the pay package is the section covering **economic supplements,** or fringe benefits such as vacations, holidays, pensions, and insurance. These benefits run as high as 45 percent of the cost of wages and are now a major factor in collective bargaining.

Provisions written into the bargaining agreement are very difficult to remove. If the union wins a new medical plan, for example, management will not be able to negotiate for its removal at the next bargaining session. Since management has less control over fringe benefits than over wages, it tends to be cautious about agreeing to costly benefits.

The following are some of the more common economic supplements:

- *Pensions:* Once management has decided to provide a pension plan, the conditions of the plan must be determined (when the benefits will be available, how much will be paid, and whether they become available according to age or years of service). Finally, the organization must decide how long employees must work for the company to receive minimum benefits (vesting) and whether the organization will pay the whole cost or whether the employees or the union will be asked to help.

- *Paid vacations:* Most agreements provide for paid vacations. The length of vacation is usually determined by length of service, up to some maximum. The conditions that qualify an individual for a vacation in a given year are also specified. Agreements occasionally specify how the timing of vacations will be determined. For example, employees may be given their choice of vacation time according to seniority.

- *Paid holidays:* Most agreements provide time off with pay on Independence Day, Labor Day, Thanksgiving, Christmas, New Year's Day, and Memorial Day. Several others may also be included.

- *Sick leave:* Unpaid sick leave allows the employee to take time off for sickness without compensation. Paid sick leave is usually accumulated while working. Typically one-half to one and one-half days of paid sick leave are credited for each month of work.

- *Health and life insurance:* The employer may be required to pay some or all of the costs of health and life insurance plans.

- *Dismissal or severance pay:* Occasionally employers agree to pay any employee who is dismissed or laid off because of technological changes or business difficulties.

- *Supplemental unemployment benefits:* In the mid-1950s, the United Auto Workers negotiated a plan to supplement state unemployment benefits and to make up the difference when these state benefits expired. Most contracts with this provision are found in the auto and steel industries, where layoffs are common, but workers in other industries are beginning to negotiate them as well.

Institutional Issues.   Some issues are not directly related to jobs but are nevertheless important to both employees and management. Institutional issues are those that affect the security and success of both parties.

- *Union security:* About 63 percent of the major labor contracts stipulate that employees must join the union after being hired into its bargaining unit. However, twenty states that traditionally have had low levels of unionization have passed "right-to-work" laws outlawing union membership as a condition of employment.

- *Checkoff:* Unions have attempted to arrange for payment of dues through deduction from employees' paychecks. By law, employees must agree to this in writing, but about 86 percent of union contracts contain this provision anyway.

- *Strikes:* The employer may insist that the union agree not to strike during the life of the agreement, typically when a cost-of-living clause has been included. The agreement may be unconditional, allowing no strikes at all, or it may limit strikes to specific circumstances.

- *Managerial prerogatives:* Over half the agreements today stipulate that certain activities are the right of management. In addition, management in most companies argues that it has "residual rights"—that all rights not specifically limited by the agreement belong to management.

Administrative Issues.   The last category of issues is concerned with the treatment of employees at work.

- *Breaks and cleanup time:* Some contracts specify the time and length of coffee breaks and meal breaks for employees. Also, jobs requiring cleanup may have a portion of the work period set aside for this procedure.

- *Employment security and job security:* This is perhaps the issue of most concern to employees and unions. Employers are concerned with restriction of their ability to lay off employees. Changes in technology or attempts to subcontract work are issues that impinge on job security. A typical union response to technological change was the reaction of the International Longshoremen's Association in the late 1960s to the introduction of containerized shipping. The union operated exclusive hiring halls, developed complex work rules, and negotiated a guaranteed annual income for its members. Job security continues to be a primary issue for longshoremen, telephone workers, and automobile workers.

- *Seniority:* Length of service is used as a criterion for many personnel decisions in most collective agreements. Layoffs are usually determined by seniority. "Last hired, first fired" is a common situation. Seniority is also important in transfer and promotion decisions. The method of calculating seniority is usually specified to clarify the relative seniority of employees.

- *Discharge and discipline:* This is a touchy issue, and even when an agreement addresses these problems, many grievances are filed concerning the way employees are disciplined or discharged.

- *Safety and health:* Although the Occupational Safety and Health Act specifically deals with worker safety and health, some contracts have provisions specifying that the company will provide safety equipment, first aid, physical examinations, accident investigations, and safety committees. Hazardous work may be covered by special provisions and pay rates. Often the agreement will contain a general statement that the employer is responsible for the safety of the workers so the union can use the grievance process when any safety issues arise.[37]

- *Production standards:* The level of productivity or performance of employees is a concern of both management and the union. Management is concerned with efficiency, but the union is concerned with the fairness and reasonableness of management's demands.

- *Grievance procedures:* This is a significant part of collective bargaining, and is discussed in more detail later in this chapter.
- *Training:* The design and administration of training and development programs, and the procedure for selecting employees for training, may also be bargaining issues. (The results of including them are described in the following "PHRM in the News.")
- *Duration of the agreement:* Agreements can last for one year or longer, with the most common period being three years.

PHRM in the News

Training Treatments

Training laid-off workers to become video production technicians in Nashville, licensed practical nurses in Detroit, and microwave technologists in California are some of the successes registered by the Employee Development and Training Program (EDTP) chartered under the 1982 UAW-Ford Motor collective bargaining agreement. Marshall Goldberg, a training and reemployment specialist at the jointly sponsored National Development and Training Center, says that the program, which is funded in part by a five-cents per hour worked contractual provision, provides training, retraining, and developmental opportunities for both active and displaced employees.

Training programs currently under way for more than 2,000 active employees include:

- Prepaid tuition training assistance of up to $1,000 per year at educational institutions;
- Personal development assistance covering prepaid courses such as communication skills, computer literacy, and motivation;
- Basic skills education, which provides self-paced training for high school completion and English as a second language; and
- Targeted training, to fit the needs of a geographic area or segment of the workforce.

With 22,000 enrollments, activities for laid-off workers are designed to retrain and reemploy workers outside the auto industry. The training programs, which are geared to local industry opportunities, include:

- Targeted skills retraining in locations with identifiable job prospects;
- Career counseling and guidance through classes and workshops;
- Job search skills training to teach job-hunting and interviewing skills and provide labor market data; and
- Basic skills enhancement to help improve math, language, and communication skills, or complete high school requirements.

Source: Bulletin to Management, 19 July 1984, p. 8. Reprinted by permission from Bulletin to Management, copyright 1984, by The Bureau of National Affairs, Inc., Washington, D.C.

Partly because there are so many issues over which to bargain, agreement and contract settlement are not always attained without conflict. When this occurs, forms of conflict resolution are utilized.

Conflict Resolution

Although the desired outcome of collective bargaining is agreement on the conditions of employment, on many occasions, negotiators are unable to reach such an agreement at the bargaining table. In these situations, several alternatives are used to resolve the impasse. The most visible response is the strike or lockout, but third-party interventions such as mediation and arbitration are also used.

Strikes and Lockouts

When the union is unable to get management to agree to a demand it believes is critical, it may resort to a strike. A **strike** may be defined as the refusal by employees to work at the company. Management may refuse to allow employees to work, which is called a **lockout**. During the 1960s and 1970s, major strikes (those involving more than one thousand employees) averaged 285 per year. In 1983 this number was 81, and in 1984 it was 62.[38]

In order to strike, the union usually holds a strike vote to get its members' approval for a strike if the negotiations are not successful. Strong membership support for a strike stengthens the union negotiators' position. If the strike takes place, union members picket the employer, informing the public about the existence of a labor dispute and preferably, from the union's point of view, convincing them to avoid this company during the strike. A common practice is the refusal of union members to cross the picket line of another striking union. This gives added support to the striking union.

Employers usually attempt to continue operations while the strike is in effect. They either run the company with supervisory personnel and people not in the bargaining unit or hire replacements for the employees. Although the company can legally hire these replacements, the union reacts strongly to the use of "scabs," and they may be a cause of increasingly belligerent labor relations. The success of a strike depends on its ability to cause economic hardship to the employer. Severe hardship usually causes the employer to concede to the union's demands. Thus, from the union's point of view it is paramount that the company not be able to operate successfully during the strike and that the cost of this lack of production be high. The union is therefore very active in trying to prevent replacement employees from working. In addition, the timing of the strike is often critical. The union attempts to hold negotiations just prior to the period when the employer has a peak demand for its product or services, when a strike will have maximum economic impact.

Although strikes are common, they are costly to both the employer, who loses revenue, and the employees, who face loss of income. If the strike is prolonged, the cost to employees will probably never fully be recovered by the benefits gained.[39] Partly because of this, employers are seeking more no-strike guarantees from labor. Because times are tough for labor, especially in manufacturing, labor is increasingly agreeing to this guarantee as a concession for job security.

Moreover, public interest is generally not served by strikes. They are often an inconvenience to the public and can have serious consequences to the economy as a whole. Conflict resolution that avoids work stoppage, which may occur regardless of the existence of no-strike clauses, by interventions such as mediation, arbitration, and injunctions may therefore be desirable from several perspectives.

Mediation

Mediation is a procedure in which "a neutral third party assists the union and management negotiators in reaching voluntary agreement."[40] Having no power to impose a solution, the mediator attempts to facilitate the negotiations between union and management. The mediator may make suggestions and recommendations and perhaps add objectivity to the often emotional negotiations. To have any success, the mediator must have the trust and respect of both parties and have sufficient expertise and neutrality to convince the union and employer that he or she will be fair and equitable. The U.S. government operates the Federal Mediation and Conciliation Service (FMCS) to make experienced mediators available to unions and companies. For situations in which problems frequently reappear, a program is offered by the FMCS to eliminate the causes of recurrent impasses. The program is called Relationships by Objectives, and it utilizes aspects of attitudinal structuring to increase the likelihood of a cooperative relationship between union and management.[41]

Arbitration

Arbitration is a procedure in which a neutral third party studies the bargaining situation, listens to both parties and gathers information, and then makes recommendations that are binding on the parties. The arbitrator, in effect, determines the conditions of the agreement.[42]

Three types of arbitration have developed.[43] The first is an **extension of bargaining,** where the arbitrator attempts to reach a rational and equitable decision acceptable to both parties. The second type is called **final-offer arbitration.** It involves the arbitrator choosing between the final offer of the union and the final offer of the employer. The arbitrator cannot alter these offers but must choose one as it stands.[44] Since the arbitrator chooses the offer that appears most fair, and since losing the arbitration decision means settling for the other's offer, there is pressure to make as good an offer as possible. The intention of final-offer arbitration is to encourage the parties to make their best offer and to reach an agreement before arbitration becomes necessary. This is also true with respect to the use of **closed-offer arbitration,** where the arbitrator receives information on only the parties' original positions without any information on the bargaining progress up to the point.[45]

Once the impasse is resolved, union and management have a contract by which to abide. Abiding by it is the essence of contract administration; however, at times during contract administration, arbitration is again necessary, namely when a grievance is filed. This type of arbitration is referred to as **grievance arbitration.** In contrast, the arbitration process described earlier that deals with the contract terms and conditions is called **interest arbitration.** Although interest arbitration is relatively infrequent in the private sector (e.g., the FMCS reported only 1.3 percent of their arbitrations as interest cases),[46] it is more common in the public sector. In the public sector, interest arbitration is regarded as a necessary *quid pro quo* for forgoing the strike option.[47] Grievance arbitration in the private sector receives the most attention and concern. The role of the grievance arbitrator is considered in Step 4 of the grievance procedures in the discussion of contract administration.

Contract Administration

The collective agreement, once signed, becomes the basic legislation governing the lives of the workers.[48] That is, the daily operation and activities in the organization are subject to the conditions of the agreement. Since it is impossible to write an unambiguous agreement that will anticipate all the situations occurring over its life, disputes will inevitably arise over interpretation and application of the agreement. The most common method of resolving these disputes is a **grievance procedure.** Virtually all agreements negotiated today provide for a grievance process to handle employee complaints.

Grievance Procedures

A grievance is a "charge that the union-management contract has been violated."[49] A grievance may be filed by the union for employees or by employers, although management rarely does so. The grievance process is designed to investigate the charges and to resolve the problem.

Five sources of grievances have been identified:

- Outright violation of the agreement
- Disagreement over facts
- Dispute over the meaning of the agreement
- Dispute over the method of applying the agreement
- Argument over the fairness or reasonableness of actions[50]

In resolving these sources of conflict, the grievance procedure should serve four separate groups: the *employers* and *unions,* by interpreting and adjusting the agreement as conditions require; the *employees,* by protecting their contractual rights and providing a channel of appeal; and *society* at large, by keeping industrial peace and reducing the number of industrial disputes in the courts.[51]

Grievance procedures typically involve several stages. The collective bargaining agreement specifies the maximum length of time that each step may take. For example, it may require the grievance to be filed within five days of the incident that is the subject of dispute. The most common grievance procedure, shown in Exhibit 16.2, involves four steps, with the final step being arbitration.

Step 1.   An employee who believes that the labor contract has been violated usually contacts the union steward, and together they discuss the problem with the supervisor involved.[52] If the problem is simple and straightforward, it is often resolved at this stage. Many contracts require the grievance to be in written form at this first stage. However, some cases may be resolved by informal discussion between the supervisor and the employee, and therefore do not officially enter the grievance process.

Step 2.   If agreement cannot be reached at the supervisor level, or if the employee is not satisfied, the complaint can enter the second step of the grievance procedure. Typically, an industrial relations representative of the company seeks to resolve the grievance.

Exhibit 16.2   *Typical Grievance Procedure*

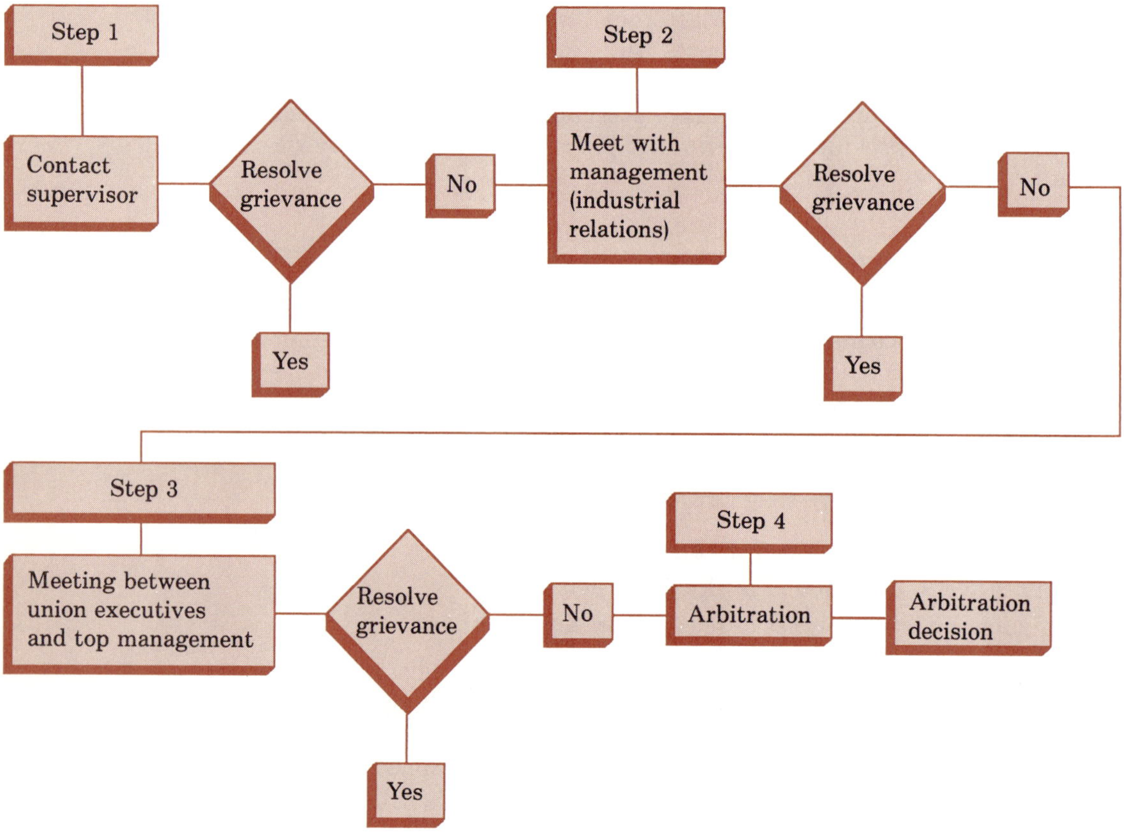

Source: W. D. Todor.

Step 3.   If the grievance is sufficiently important or difficult to resolve, it may be taken to the third step. Although contracts vary, top-level management and union executives are usually involved at this step. These people have the authority to make the major decisions that may be required to resolve the grievance.

Step 4.   If a grievance cannot be resolved at the third step, most agreements require the use of an arbitrator to consider the case and reach a decision. The arbitrator is a neutral, mutually acceptable individual who may be provided by the Federal Mediation and Conciliation Service or some private agency. The arbitrator holds a hearing, reviews the evidence, then rules on the grievance. The decision of the arbitrator is usually binding.

Since the cost of arbitration is shared by the union and employer, there is some incentive to settle the grievance before it goes to arbitration. An added incentive in some cases is the requirement that the loser pay for the arbitration.[53] The expectation is that the parties will screen or evaluate grievances more carefully, because pursuing a weak grievance to arbitration will result in a loss and the costs of arbitration.[54]

Occasionally, the union will call a strike over a grievance in order to resolve it. This may happen when the issue at hand is so important that the union believes it cannot wait for the slower arbitration process, which takes an average of 223 days.[55] This "employee rights" strike may be legal, but if the contract specifically forbids strikes during the tenure of the agreement, it is not legal and is called a **wildcat strike**.[56] Wildcat strikes are not common, however, since most grievances are settled through arbitration.[57] The issues that are resolved through the grievance process can be quite varied.

Grievance Issues

Grievances can be filed over any issue relating to the work place that is subject to the collective agreement, or they can be filed over interpretation and implementation of the agreement itself. The most common type of grievance reaching the arbitration stage is concerned with discipline and discharge, although many grievances are filed over other issues.

Although absenteeism can be grounds for discharge, the critical issue is the determination that the absenteeism in question is excessive. Insubordination usually is either failure to do what the supervisor requests or the more serious problem of outright refusal. If the supervisor's orders are clear and explicit and if the employee is warned of the consequences, discipline for refusal to respond is usually acceptable. The exception is when the employee believes that the work endangers health.

Since seniority is usually used to determine who is laid off, bumped from a job to make way for someone else, or rehired, its calculation is of great concern to employees. Since promotions and transfers also use seniority as one of the criteria to determine eligibility, management must be careful in this area to avoid complaints and grievances.

Compensation for time away from work, vacations, holidays, or sick leave is also a common source for grievances. Holidays cause problems because often special pay arrangements are made for people working on those days.

Wage and work schedules may also lead to grievances. Disagreements often arise over interpretation or application of the agreement relating to issues such as overtime pay, pay for reporting, and scheduling.

Grievances have been filed over the exercise of management rights—that is, its right to introduce technological change, use subcontractors, or change jobs in other ways. This type of behavior may also be the source of charges of unfair labor practices, since these activities may require collective bargaining.

The Taft-Hartley Act gives unions the right to file grievances on their own behalf if they believe their rights have been violated. This act also gives unions access to information necessary to process the grievance or to make sure the agreement is not being violated. In addition, unions may file grievances for violations of union shop or checkoff provisions.

Occasionally other activities prompt grievances. Wildcat strikes or behavior that is considered to be a strike (mass absences from work, for example) may result in a management grievance. The major focus of grievances, however, is in the administration of the conditions of the agreement.

Management Procedures

Management can significantly affect the grievance rate by adopting proper procedures when taking action against an employee. An important area for such procedures is discipline and discharge.[58] Since the issue of just cause and fairness is central to most discipline grievances, employers must ensure that the employee is adequately warned of the consequences, that the rule involved is related to operation of the company, that a thorough investigation is undertaken, and that the penalty is reasonable. The following activities have been identified as being useful in meeting these conditions:

- Explanation of rules to employees
- Consideration of the accusations and facts
- Regular warning procedures, including written records
- Involvement of the union in the case
- Examination of the employee's motives and reasons
- Consideration of the employee's past record
- Familiarization of all management personnel, especially supervisors, with disciplinary procedure and company rules[59]

In areas outside of discipline and discharge, management can avoid some grievance problems by educating supervisors and managers about labor relations and the conditions of the collective agreement. Supervisors with labor knowledge are an important factor in the reduction of grievances.

Union Procedures

The union has an obligation to its members to provide them with fair and adequate representation and to speedily process and investigate grievances brought by its members (*Vaca* v. *Sipes*, 1967; *Hines* v. *Anchor Motor Freight*, 1976; and *Smith* v. *Hussman Refrigerator Co. & Local 13889, United Steel*

Workers of America, 1980). Thus, it should have a grievance-handling procedure that will aid in effectively processing grievances without being guilty of unfair representation.

Unfair representation, according to the National Labor Relations Board, is usually related to one of four types of union behavior:

- *Improper motives or fraud:* The union cannot refuse to process a grievance because of the employee's race or sex or because of the employee's attitude toward the union.

- *Arbitrary conduct:* The union must investigate the merits of the grievance. Unions cannot dismiss a grievance without investigating it.

- *Gross negligence:* The union cannot display a reckless disregard of the employee's interests.

- *Union conduct after filing the grievance:* The union must process the grievance to a reasonable conclusion.[60]

Because the employer can also be cited for unfair representation, management should attempt to maintain a fair grievance process. Company labor relations managers should avoid taking advantage of union errors in handling grievances, lest this action affect fair representation.

Unions may have an additional interest in grievances as a tool in collective negotiation. They may attempt to increase grievance rates to influence management as collective bargaining approaches. Grievances may also be a way to introduce or show concern for an issue in negotiations. In some cases, grievances may be withdrawn by unions in exchange for some management concessions, although this may be dangerous, since it may be an unfair representation of the employee.

An important influence on the grievance process is the union steward. Since the union steward is generally the first person to hear about an employee's grievance, the steward has substantial influence on the grievance process. A steward can encourage an employee to file a grievance, can suggest that the problem is really not a grievance, or can informally resolve the problem outside the grievance procedure. The steward, being in such a key position, can have a profound effect on the situation. Personality characteristics of stewards may even influence the number of grievances filed.[61] Since stewards are selected from the ranks of employees and may have little knowledge of labor relations, the union should provide training to improve their effectiveness. The company, since it may also be liable in a fair representation suit, should support such training.

Public-sector Collective Bargaining

Collective bargaining in the public sector differs somewhat from that in the private sector. Federal employees do not have the right to strike. The recently passed Civil Service Reform Act, however, has changed the situation by creating an independent agency to remedy unfair labor practices. Yet, federal employees still do not have the same collective bargaining rights as private workers. In the federal sector, management must bargain over a limited number of issues.

Arrangements for collective bargaining at the state and local level vary considerably. All but fourteen of the states have collective bargaining provisions. A wide range of coverage exists among states; some include municipal employees, some include state employees, and some include both. Special legislation for police officers, fire fighters, and teachers are also often found.

One distinctive characteristic of public-sector collective bargaining is the tendency to have multilateral bargaining. Governments tend to have so many levels of authority that unions can sometimes go outside the government negotiating team to higher authorities to seek a settlement. However, such actions tend to disrupt the bargaining process and can lead to distrust and difficulties in future negotiations.

The frequency of strikes in the public sector is increasing,[62] partly because the penalty for striking has rarely been enforced in the public sector. The success of strikes or work stoppages in the public sector depends on both the political clout of the union and its ability to impose economic costs. Since many public-sector services are not essential, and strikes can mean a cost savings in unpaid wages to the government involved, strikes of teachers or public employees have a lower success rate than for unions.[63] However, when a strike does have economic and political impact, arbitration is generally used.[64] Arbitration procedures for bargaining impasses have been effective in reducing the incidence of strikes in police and fire fighter negotiations.[65] Mediation and arbitration are becoming common methods for resolving difficulties in the public sector as a whole.

The Civil Service Reform Act requires a grievance procedure with arbitration to be included as the last step in all agreements. Thus, the mechanism for grievance settlement is similar to that in the private sector. However, unlike the private sector, the collective bargaining process in the public sector appears to provide higher wages and greater final benefits to union employees than to nonunion employees. In addition, personnel practices are more formalized, and the discretion of management in discipline, promotion, transfers, and work assignments is reduced.[66]

Trends in Collective Bargaining

Three trends in collective bargaining to be described are assessing, computer technology and HRIS, and strategic involvement. Among these trends, strategic involvement is the most recent and is in the early stages of development.[67]

Assessing the Collective Bargaining Process

The effectiveness of the entire collective bargaining process and the union-management relationship can be measured by the extent to which each party attains its goals. Difficulties are associated with this approach, however. Because goals are incompatible in many cases and can therefore lead to conflicting estimates of effectiveness, a more useful measure of effectiveness may be the quality of the system used to resolve conflict. Conflict is more apparent in the collective bargaining process, where failure to resolve the issues typically leads to strikes. Another measure of effectiveness is the success of the grievance process, or the ability to resolve issues developing out of the bargaining agreement.

Effectiveness of Negotiations.   Since the purpose of negotiations is to achieve an agreement, agreement becomes an overall measure of bargaining effectiveness. A healthy and effective bargaining process encourages the discussion of issues and problems and their subsequent resolution at the bargaining table. In addition, the effort required to reach agreement is a measure of how well the process is working. Some indications of this effort are the duration of negotiations, the outcome of member ratification votes, the frequency and duration of strikes, the use of mediation and arbitration, the need for government intervention, and the resulting quality of union-management relations (whether conflict or cooperation exists). Joint programs for productivity and QWL improvements could be regarded as successes resulting from the quality of union-management relations.[68]

Effectiveness of the Grievance Procedures.   The degree of success of a grievance procedure may be assessed from different perspectives. Management may view the number of grievances filed and the number settled in management's favor as measures of effectiveness. Unions may also consider the number of grievances, but from their point of view, a larger number rather than a smaller number may be considered more successful.

Although the views of management and the union may differ, an overall set of measures to gauge grievance procedure effectiveness may be related to the disagreements between managers and employees. Measures that might be included are frequency of grievances; the level in the grievance procedure at which grievances are usually settled; the frequency of strikes or slowdowns during the term of the labor agreements; the rates of absenteeism, turnover, and sabotage; and the necessity for government intervention.

The success of arbitration is often judged by the acceptability of the decisions, the satisfaction of the parties, innovation, and the absence of biases in either direction. The effectiveness of any third-party intervention rests in part on its ability to reduce or avoid strikes, since the motivation for third-party intervention is the realization that strikes are not a desirable form of conflict resolution.

Computer Technology and HRIS in Collective Bargaining

Computer technology and an HRIS can facilitate decision making in union-management negotiations by maintaining a data base of information about other union settlements in the same or different industries. Relevant data that could be stored in an HRIS include salary and benefit data, productivity figures, and data on general economic conditions and the cost of living. Management could then use these data to establish, compare, and evaluate its offers to the union more quickly and easily. These data could also be used by management in establishing with the union the need for wage concessions or productivity improvements. In turn, the data could be used again to monitor and evaluate the progress or impact of any concessions or productivity improvement programs.[69]

Strategic Involvement of Collective Bargaining

Gaining Competitive Advantage.   Critical to the success of many companies vis-à-vis competitors are their labor costs. In many industries today, companies face possible bankruptcy because of high labor costs. Helping to lower costs are wage reductions reached between unions and management. Recently American Airlines, Greyhound, McDonnell Douglas, Boeing, and Ingersoll-Rand have negotiated two-tiered wage systems to help reduce total costs by reducing labor costs. Without these jointly negotiated systems, these companies would not have survived. Thus, a company's relationship with its union can be critical to its survival, and the better its relationships are, the more likely it is to ever gain a competitive advantage.[70]

Crown Zellerbach Corporation and the International Woodworkers of America demonstrated, however, that a competitive advantage can be gained without reducing total wages. Based on a recent incentive pay plan agreed to by the union and management, workers earn about three dollars more per hour than before on straight wages. Because this incentive system makes the workers more productive, the company in exchange had to give the union greater worker involvement in work-related decisions. Thus, the workers gain in involvement and salary, and the company gains in cost reductions and greater competitiveness.

Ford Motor Company has engaged in a program of more worker involvement and more cooperative labor relations with the United Auto Workers. The results of this program are higher product quality than its competitors and a marketing campaign centered on quality of Job 1. As with the two-tiered wage systems, this program of more worker involvement gains competitive advantage through cost reductions and improved efficiencies. Similar results of high product quality and efficiency have been obtained at Westinghouse Electric Corporation, Warner Gear Division of Borg-Warner Corporation, and the Mass Transportation Authority of Flint, Michigan. In these companies, gains in quality and efficiency have resulted from employee commitment associated with quality circle programs. In addition to increased quality and efficiency, these companies have experienced fewer grievances, reduced absenteeism and turnover, lower design costs, higher engineering productivity, and fewer costly changes in design cycles.

Summary

United States union-management relations are at a critical crossroads today. Global competition and an extended recession into the 1980s have put a greater emphasis on mutual survival. This has resulted in a shift from the traditional adversarial relationship between union and management toward cooperation. New bargaining strategies characterize this altered relationship. Productivity bargaining is an attempt to encourage increased effectiveness in the work place by passing some of the economic savings of modernization or increased efficiency on to the employees. Another innovation is continuous bargaining, where a joint union-management committee meets on a regular basis to deal with problems.

Although obstacles exist to union-management cooperation—a history of adversarial relations, hesitancy on the part of the union to give up the traditional roles of labor, and both parties' fear of losing power—present economic conditions and the threat of an influx of foreign products are prompting many organizations to act for their mutual benefit. In one notable example, the president of the United Auto Workes (UAW) lobbied successfully in both Washington and Japan to reduce auto imports between 1981 and 1985. The success of such cooperative activities can be measured first by the attainment of specific goals and second by the effect they have on labor-management relations in general. The need for cooperation has been recognized by some union leaders, who recommend more decision-making participation with management. The agreement by Chrysler to permit the president of the UAW to assume a position on the board of directors also signals a new era of union-management cooperation. Cooperation may become more common in the future as unions reexamine their roles.

The quality of the union-management relationship can have a strong influence on contract negotiations. Labor and management each select a bargaining committee to negotiate the new agreement. The negotiations may be between a single union and a single company or multiple companies, or between multiple unions and a single company. Bargaining issues are either mandatory, permissive, or prohibited. Mandatory issues must be discussed, permissive issues can be discussed if both parties agree, and prohibited issues cannot be discussed. The issues can be grouped into wage issues, economic supplements issues, institutional issues, and administrative issues.

Almost all labor contracts outline grievance procedures for handling employee complaints. The most common grievance is related to discipline and discharge, although wages, promotions, seniority, vacations, holidays, and management and union rights are also sources of complaints. Management can influence the results of grievances by developing a procedure that ensures their actions are just and fair. Written records of actions taken are useful for potential arbitration. Unions have a legal responsibility to represent the employee fairly in grievances; therefore, they also need a grievance-handling procedure.

The effectiveness of collective bargaining and contract administration is usually assessed by measures of how well the process is working. Bargaining can be evaluated using measures such as the duration of negotiations, the frequency of strikes, use of third-party intervention, and the need for government intervention. The effectiveness of the grievance process can be assessed by number of grievances; level in the grievance process that settlement occurs; frequency of strikes or slowdowns; rate of absenteeism, turnover, and sabotage; and need for government intervention.

Discussion Questions

1. Based on your understanding of U.S. labor legislation, is it consistent with the new theme of labor-management cooperation?
2. Can the distributive bargaining model be used to predict settlements in management-labor negotiations? Why might strikes occur even when a settlement range exists?
3. Rank-and-file workers have increasingly rejected negotiated contracts. Is the failure to ratify a new contract an indicator of ineffective intraorganizational bargaining?
4. To what extent do you think unions would support federal or state legislation to protect employee rights by requiring discharges to be for just cause only?
5. Distinguish unions' mandatory, permissive, and prohibited bargaining issues. How might these distinctions differ between the private sector and the public sector?
6. What kinds of topics would you expect to find in a typical collective bargaining agreement? Assume that you and the other students "organize." For what terms would you negotiate with your professors in your agreement?
7. Distinguish mediation from arbitration. How does grievance arbitration differ from interest arbitration? What is final-offer arbitration?
8. From a public policy perspective, is it necessarily bad for union and management to regularly depend on interest arbitration to resolve conflicts?
9. What are the steps of a typical grievance procedure? Is this process formal or informal?
10. Why does the NLRB concern itself with the duty of fair representation? In what sense is the union steward caught in the middle on the issue of fair representation when representing a grievant?

PC Project

Management negotiators prepare by developing strategies and proposals prior to collective bargaining sessions. An important part of this preparation is calculating the costs of issues or demands. For example, the costs of pension contributions, pay increases, and health benefits must be calculated. This PC Project shows how the computer can be used to specify economic scenarios for the contract negotiation process. The computer greatly facilitates the financial computations and makes "what-if" analyses with lightning speed.

| C | A | S | E | S | T | U | D | Y |

———————— Don't Call Me Sweetheart ————————

Victor Reuther, a retired United Auto Workers (UAW) official and brother of the late Walter P. Reuther, and Reed Larson, president of the National Right to Work Committee (NRTWC) are strange bedfellows these days. They both think a contract signed by the UAW and General Motors' (GM's) Saturn Division stinks. Reuther claims that the agreement is a return to piecework systems where one team is pitted against another. Larson does not like the contract for yet another reason: he claims it is a sweetheart contract between management and the union that denies individual workers the right to choose whether they want a union or not.

In June of 1986, the National Labor Relations Board (NLRB) dismissed charges that the labor agreement between GM and the UAW violated federal labor law. The labor agreement between GM and the UAW is considered an innovative step toward labor-management cooperation. At the heart of the contract is a trade-off. The union has agreed to help management raise productivity in return for lifetime security for workers and union alike. The Saturn contract eliminates work rules and job classifications found in older contracts and gives workers a voice in the operations.

The hitch for management is that in return for these union concessions, GM has agreed to hire "a majority of the initial complement" of Saturn workers from other GM plants. In effect, GM has implicitly recognized the union as its bargaining agent before the slab of the Spring Hill, Tennessee, plant has been poured. The NRTWC has termed this a "sweetheart" contract between top management and top union officials. Federal labor law, beginning with the National Labor Relations Act of 1935, was designed to give workers the right to choose whether they wanted a union or not and if they belonged to a union whether they wanted that union to continue to represent them.

This kind of union-management agreement can have far-reaching consequences for other foreign automotive producers planning to build in the United States. The GM-Toyota joint venture in Freemont, California, signed a similar agreement before workers were hired. Other plants to watch are the Toyota plant planned for Georgetown, Kentucky; the Mazda plant going in near Detroit; and a Mitsubishi-Chrysler plant planned for Bloomington-Normal, Illinois.

For a labor movement that has hit upon hard times recently, the NLRB ruling was a shot in the arm. Even the Department of Labor secretary, William E. Brock III, has supported these new cooperative arrangements between labor and management. But the NRTWC maintains that these kind of agreements are "compulsory unionism," the very thing our legislators sought to avoid in the drafting of our national labor relations policy.

———————————

Notes

1. For a good overview and in-depth discussion of collective bargaining, see A. R. Weber, ed., *The Structure of Collective Bargaining*, (New York: Free Press, 1961); A. Sloane and F. Whitney, *Labor Relations* (Englewood Cliffs, N.J.: Prentice-Hall, 1972); R. C. Richardson, *Collective Bargaining by Objectives* (Englewood Cliffs, N.J.: Prentice-Hall, 1977); L. Balliet, *Survey of Labor Relations* (Washington, D.C.: Bureau of National Affairs, 1981); J. A. Fossum, "Union-Management Relations," in *Personnel Management*, ed. K. M. Rowland and G. R. Ferris (Boston: Allyn & Bacon, 1982), pp. 420–60; J. A. Fossum, "Labor Relations," in *Human Resource Management in the 1980s*, ed. S. J. Carroll and R. S. Schuler (Washington, D.C.: Bureau of National Affairs, 1983); B. F. Beal, E. D. Wickersham, and P. Kienast, *The Practice of Collective Bargaining* (Homewood, Ill.: Irwin, 1976); T. A. Kochan, *Collective Bargaining and Industrial Relations* (Homewood, Ill.: Irwin, 1980); R. B. Freeman and J. L. Medoff, *What Do Unions Do?* (New York: Basic Books, 1984); R. J. Donovan, "Bringing America into the 1980s," *American Psy-*

chologist (Apr. 1984): 429–31; J. Barbash, *The Elements of Industrial Relations* (Madison: University of Wisconsin Press, 1984); N. W. Chamberlain and J. W. Kuhn, *Collective Bargaining,* 3d ed. (New York: McGraw-Hill, 1986).

2. See Balliet, *Labor Relations,* especially pp. 106–48. What is best or most advantageous, however, is not necessarily what is best for only one party, although maximizing for one party may happen in an adversarial relationship. In a cooperative relationship, maximizing for both may be regarded as most advantageous.

3. See J. M. Brett, "Behavioral Research on Unions and Union Management Systems," in *Research in Organizational Behavior,* vol. 2, ed. B. Staw and L. L. Cummings (Greenwich, Conn.: JAI Press, 1980); J. M. Brett, "Why Employees Want Unions," *Organizational Dynamics* 8 (1980): 45–59; W. C. Hamner and F. J. Smith, "Work Attitudes as Predictors of Unionization Activity," *Journal of Applied Psychology* 63 (1978): 415–21; "Unions Are Turning to Polls to Read the Rank and File," *Business Week,* 22 Oct. 1984, pp. 66–67; W. Serrin, "Unions Are Shifting Gears but Not Goals," *New York Times,* 31 Mar. 1985, p. 2E.

4. Brett, "Behavioral Research," p. 200.

5. Ibid.

6. "The New Industrial Relations," *Business Week,* 11 May 1981, pp. 85–98; "A Partnership to Build the New Workplace," *Business Week,* 30 June 1980, pp. 96–101; "Hot UAW Issue: Quality of Work Life," *Business Week,* 17 Sept. 1979, pp. 120–22; "A Try at Steel-Mill Harmony," *Business Week,* 29 June 1981, pp. 132–36; "Quality of Work Life: Catching on," *Business Week,* 21 Sept 1981, pp. 72–80; J. M. Draznin, "Labor Relations," *Personnel Journal* (Oct. 1980): 805; R. E. Steiner, "Labor Relations," *Personnel Journal* (May 1981): 344–46; D. Q. Mills, *The New Competitors* (New York: Free Press, 1985), pp. 225–42; M. Schuster, "The Impact of Union-Management Cooperation on Productivity and Employment," *Industrial and Labor Relations Review* (Apr. 1983): 415–30; H. C. Katz, T. A. Kochan, and K. R. Gobeille, "Industrial Relations Performance, Economic Performance, and QWL Programs: An Interplant Analysis," *Industrial and Labor Relations Review* (Oct. 1983): 3–17; S. M. Jacoby, "Union-Management Cooperation in the United States: Lessons from the 1920s," *Industrial and Labor Relations Review* (Oct. 1983): 18–33; M. Schuster, "A Re-examination of Models of Cooperation and Change in Union Settings," *Industrial Relations* (Fall 1985): 56–68; T. H. Ferguson and J. Goals, "Codetermination: A Fad or a Future in America?" *Employee Relations Law Journal* (Autumn 1984): 176–93; P. V. Simpson, R. M. Patlison, and R. W. Novotny, "Collective Bargaining: Management's Opportunity to Improve Labor

Economies," *Employee Relations Law Journal* (Summer 1985): 72–87.

7. "What's Creating an 'Industrial Miracle' at Ford," *Business Week,* 30 July 1984, p. 80.

8. Interesting discussions of early American labor history can be found in R. B. Morris, "A Bicentennial Look at the Early Days of American Labor," *Monthly Labor Review* (May 1976): 21–26; Kochan, 1980.

9. J. A. Fossum, *Labor Relations: Development, Structure, Process,* 3d ed. (Dallas, Tex.: Business Publications, 1985).

10. Reprinted by permission of the *Harvard Business Review.* Excerpt from "Collective Bargaining: Ritual or Reality?" by A. A. Blum (Nov./Dec. 1961). Copyright © 1961 by the President and Fellows of Harvard College. All rights reserved.

11. For examples of more programs, see E. E. Lawler, *Pay and Organization Development* (Reading, Mass.: Addison-Wesley, 1981); S. E. Seashore, E. E. Lawler III, P. H. Mirvis, and C. Cammann, eds., *Observing and Measuring Organizational Change: A Guide to Field Practice* (New York: Wiley-InterScience, 1980); E. E. Lawler III and S. A. Mohrman, "Unions and the New Management," in *Readings in Personnel and Human Resource Management,* 2d ed., ed. R. S. Schuler and S. A. Youngblood (St. Paul: West, 1984); J. Barbash, "Do We Really Want Labor on the Ropes?" *Harvard Business Review* (July–Aug. 1985): 10–20.

12. For a good description of these, see R. E. Walton and R. B. McKersie, *A Behavioral Theory of Labor Negotiations* (New York: McGraw-Hill, 1965).

13. R. B. Paterson and L. Tracy, "Testing a Behavioral Model of Labor Negotiations," *Industrial Relations* 16 (1977): 35–50.

14. This support is often critical, since union members generally vote on tentative contracts. This arrangement, however, can be altered to increase the control by the top. See, for example, T. F. O'Boyle and J. E. Beazley, "USW Chiefs, Backing Concessionary Pact, Slash Number Eligible to Ratify Contracts," *Wall Street Journal,* 13 Jan. 1983, p. 10.

15. A. Sloan and F. Whitney, *Labor Relations,* 3d ed. (Englewood Cliffs, N.J.: Prentice-Hall, 1977), p. 59.

16. Ibid., p. 64.

17. Ibid., pp. 83–84.

18. A good discussion of earlier contributions to labor law can be found in D. P. Twomey, *Labor Law and Legislation,* 6th ed. (Cincinnati, Ohio: South-Western, 1980).

19. H. B. Frazier II, "Labor Management Relations in the Federal Government," *Labor Law Journal* (Mar. 1979): 131.

20. D. D. Cook, "Labor Faces the Productivity Challenge," *Industry Week,* 9 Mar. 1981, pp. 61–65; Twomey, *Labor Law and Legislation,* p. 77. For an extensive discussion on work-rule changes, see "A Work

Revolution in U.S. Industry," *Business Week,* 16 May 1983, pp. 100–10; L. M. Apcar, "Work-Rule Programs Spread to Union Plants," *Wall Street Journal,* 16 Apr. 1985, p. 6.

21. "Moderation's Chance to Survive," *Business Week,* 19 Apr. 1982, pp. 123–26; "Some Troubled Firms Limit Their Givebacks to Nonunion Workers," *Wall Street Journal,* 5 Mar. 1982, pp. 1, 18; L. Ingrassia, "Factory Workers View Givebacks Indignantly–And Submissively," *Wall Street Journal,* 4 Feb. 1982, pp. 1, 25; W. Serrin, "Unionism Struggles through Middle Age," *New York Times,* 27 Oct. 1985, p. 46.

22. J. S. Lublin, "Unions Try New Kinds of Resistance as Anger Over Plant Closings Grows," *Wall Street Journal,* 21 Jan. 1982, p. 29; A. Nag and T. O'Boyle, "USW's Rejection of a Three-Year Wage Freeze Is Likely to Result in More Plant Closings," *Wall Street Journal,* 2 Aug. 1982, p. 5; J. M. Stenels, "The Remedies Can Be Found at Home," *New York Times,* 2 Jan. 1983, p. 2F.

23. J. F. Falhee, "Concession Bargaining: The Time is Now!" *Personnel Administrator* (Jan. 1983): 27–28; R. F. Garrett, "Reducing the Adversary Relationship," *Personnel Administrator* (Feb. 1982): 31–32; "A Year of Settling for Less and Breaking Old Molds," *Business Week,* 20 Dec. 1982, pp. 72–74; "Concessionary Bargaining," *Business Week,* 14 June 1982, pp. 66–81; "Can GM Change Its Work Rules?" *Business Week,* 26 Apr. 1982, pp. 116, 119; "Give-Backs Highlight Three Major Bargaining Agreements," *Personnel Administrator* (Jan. 1983): 33–35, 75, 77.

24. Sloan and Whitney, *Labor Relations.*

25. Fossum, "Labor Relations," pp. 395–96.

26. *1979 Guidebook to Labor Relations,* 18th ed. (Chicago: Commerce Clearing House, 1978), p. 282. See also H. Raiffa, *The Art and Science of Negotiation* (Cambridge: Harvard University Press, 1982); J. J. Hoover, "Negotiating the Initial Union Contract," *Personnel Journal* (Sept. 1982): 692–97.

27. Fossum, *Labor Relations: Structure, Development and Process.*

28. C. Hymowitz, "Coordinated Steel Talks May Collapse," *Wall Street Journal,* 4 Apr. 1985, p. 6; Fossum, "Labor Relations."

29. P. T. Hartman and W. H. Franke, "The Changing Bargaining Structure in Construction: Wide-Area and Multicraft Bargaining," *Industrial and Labor Relations Review* (Jan. 1980: 170–84.

30. Fossum, "Labor Relations," p. 171.

31. E. Platt, "The Duty to Bargain as Applied to Management Decisions," *Labor Law Journal* (Mar. 1968): 145.

32. Fossum, "Labor Relations."

33. Ibid., p. 173.

34. Platt, "The Duty to Bargain," p. 144.

35. Brett, "Why Employees Want Unions"; T. A. Kochan, "How American Workers View Labor Unions,"

Monthly Labor Review 102 (1979): 23–31; "Beyond Unions," *Business Week,* 8 July 1985, pp. 72–77.

36. "Why the URW Will be More of a Team Player," *Business Week,* 28 Sept. 1981, pp. 97–99; "The Demands Airlines Are Pressing on Labor," *Business Week,* 7 Dec. 1981, p. 37; "Tough Choices for the UAW," *Business Week,* 7 Dec. 1981, p. 105; "Detroit Gets a Break from UAW," *Business Week,* 30 Nov. 1981; "A New Moderation in Rail Talks," *Business Week,* 31 Aug. 1981, p. 50; "The IBT Pact Could be a Model of Moderation," *Business Week,* 28 Sept. 1981, p. 38; M. N. Dodosh, "Companies Increasingly Ask Labor to Give Back Past Contract Gains," *Wall Street Journal,* 27 Nov. 1981, p. 21.

37. T. A. Kochan, *Collective Bargaining.*

38. K. B. Noble, "Big Strikes Found in Decline in U.S." *New York Times,* 12 July 1985, p. 9.

39. D. J. B. Mitchell, "A Note on Strike Propensities and Wage Developments," *Industrial Relations* 20 (1981): 123–27; T. A. Kochan and R. N. Block, "An Inter-Industry Analysis of Bargaining Outcomes: Preliminary Evidence from Two-Digit Industries," *Quarterly Journal of Economics* 91 (1977): 68–76; J. Kennan, "Pareto Optimality and the Economics of Strike Duration," *Journal of Labor Research* 1 (1980): 77–94.

40. T. A. Kochan, "Collective Bargaining in Organizational Research," in *Research in Organizational Behavior,* vol. 2, ed. B. M. Staw and L. L. Cummings (Greenwich, Conn.: JAI Press, 1980); T. A. Kochan and T. A. Jick, "A Theory of the Public Sector Mediation Process," *Journal of Conflict Resolution* 23 (1979): 209–40; H. A. Landsberger, "The Behavior and Personality of the Labor Mediator: The Parties' Perception of Mediator Behavior," *Personnel Psychology* 13 (1960): 329–47.

41. D. T. Hoyer, "A Program for Conflict Management: An Exploratory Approach," *Proceedings of the Industrial Relations Research Association,* (Milwaukee, Wisc.: IRRA, 1980); R. C. Richardson, *Collective Bargaining.*

42. "Judgment Day for Arbitrators," *Business Week,* 19 Apr. 1982, p. 66; R. Johnson, "Interest Arbitration Examined," *Personnel Administrator* (Jan. 1983): 53–59, 73; "More Support for Arbitration," *Business Week,* 5 Oct. 1981, p. 132; J. N. Draznin, "Labor Relations," *Personnel Journal* (Apr. 1981): 256; D. King, "Three Cheers for Conflict!" *Personnel* (Jan.–Feb. 1981): 13–22; J. F. Rand, "Creative Problem-Solving Applied to Grievance Arbitration Procedures," *Personnel Administrator* (Mar. 1980): 50–52; D. Sheane, "When and How to Intervene in Conflict," *Personnel Journal* (June 1980): 515–18; "Arbitration Cases Increase," *Personnel Journal* (Nov. 1981): 832; S. C. Walker, "The Dynamics of Clear Contract Language," *Personnel Journal* (Jan. 1981): 39–41; J. Steiber, R. N. Block, and L. Corbitt, "How Representative Are Published Arbitration Decisions?" *Pro-*

ceedings of the NAA (Chicago, Ill.: NAA, May 1984); J. P. Cain and M. J. Stahl, "Modeling the Policies of Several Labor Arbitrators," *Academy of Management Journal* (Mar. 1983): 140–51.

43. Kochan, "Collective Bargaining in Organizational Research," p. 151.

44. Here the arbitrator is aware of what has transpired thus far in the bargaining process.

45. H. N. Wheeler, " 'Closed Offer' Alternative to Final Offer Selection," *Industrial Relations* 16 (1977): 298–305.

46. Johnson, "Interest Arbitration Examined."

47. Ibid.

48. Fossum, *Labor Relations: Development, Structure and Process.*

49. S. H. Slichter, J. J. Healy, and E. R. Livernash, *The Impact of Collective Bargaining on Management,* (Washington, D.C.: Brookings Institution, 1960), p. 694.

50. Ibid., pp. 694–96.

51. J. N. Draznin, "Labor Relations," *Personnel Journal* (July 1981): 528; J. N. Draznin, "Labor Relations," *Personnel Journal* (Aug. 1980): 625; G. A. Jacobs, "Don't Take 'No' for an Answer," *Industry Week*, 26 Jan. 1981, pp. 38–43; I. Paster, "Collective Bargaining: Warnings for the Novice Negotiator," *Personnel Journal* (Mar. 1981): 203–6.

52. The steward can be a critical person here, since the determination of how cases are resolved may depend on the steward. For an extensive discussion on some characteristics of stewards likely to influence this determination, see D. R. Dalton and W. D. Todor, "Manifest Needs of Stewards: Propensity to File a Grievance," *Journal of Applied Psychology* 64 (1979): 654–59; D. R. Dalton and W. D. Todor, "Union Steward Locus of Control, Job, Union Involvement, and Grievance Behavior," *Journal of Business Research* 10 (1982): 85–101; D. R. Dalton and W. D. Todor, "Antecedents of Grievance Filing Behavior: Attitude, Behavioral Consistency and the Union Steward," *Academy of Management Journal* 25 (1982): 158–69.

53. B. R. Skeleton and P. C. Marett, "Loser Pays Arbitration," *Labor Law Journal* (May 1979): 302–9.

54. D. R. Dalton and W. D. Todor, "Win, Lose, Draw: The Grievance Process in Practice," *Personnel Administrator* (Mar. 1981): 25–32; J. W. Robinson, "Some Modest Proposals for Reducing the Costs and Delay in Grievance Arbitration," *Personnel Administrator* (Feb. 1982): 25–28.

55. G. W. Bolander, "Fair Representation: Not Just a Union Problem," *Personnel Administrator* (Mar. 1980): 39; J. E. Martin, "Employee Characteristics and Represention Election Outcomes," *Industrial and Labor Relations Review* (Apr. 1985): 365–76; W. N. Cooke, "Determinants of the Outcomes of Union Certification Elections," *Industrial and Labor*

Relations Review (Apr. 1983): 402–14; H. G. Heneman III and M. H. Sandver, "Predicting the Outcome of Union Certification Elections: A Review of the Literature," *Industrial and Labor Relations Review* (July 1983): 537–59; F. C. Botta, "The Accretion Clause in the Supermarket Industry: Unit Determinations and Employee Rights," *Employee Relations Law Journal* (Summer 1985): 106–17; J. J. Lawler, "The Influence of Management Consultants on the Outcome of Union Certification Elections," *Industrial and Labor Relations Review* (Oct. 1984): 38–51.

56. G. L. Tidwell, "The Meaning of the No-Strike Clause," *Personnel Administrator* (Nov. 1984): 51–61.

57. For the number and type of these arbitration awards, generally of a closed type, see *Bulletin to Management,* 11 Nov. 1982, and contact the Federal Mediation and Conciliation Service, 2100 K Street NW, Washington, D.C. 20427.

58. S. R. Korshak, "Arbitration, the Termination of a Union Activist," *Personnel Journal* (Jan. 1982): 54–57.

59. Bureau of National Affairs, *Grievance Guide,* 4th ed. (Washington, D.C.: Bureau of National Affairs, 1972), pp. 8–9; A. J. Conti, "Mediation of Work-Place Disputes: A Prescription for Organizational Health," *Employee Relations Law Journal* (Autumn 1985): 291–310; F. Elkouri and E. A. Elkouri, *How Arbitration Works,* 4th ed. (Washington, D.C.: Bureau of National Affairs, 1985); D. A. Peach and E. R. Livernash, *Grievance Initiation and Resolution* (Cambridge: Harvard University Press, 1974); D. Lewin and R. B. Peterson, *The Modern Grievance Procedure in the American Economy: A Theoretical and Empirical Analysis* (Westport, Conn.: Quorum Books, 1986).

60. Memorandum 79-55, National Labor Relations Board, 7 July 1979.

61. Dalton and Todor, "Manifest Needs of Stewards."

62. H. Graham and V. Wallace, "Trends in Public Sector Arbitration," *Personnel Administrator* (Apr. 1982): 73–78; H. R. Northrup, "The Rise and Demise of PATCO," *Industrial and Labor Relations Review* (Jan. 1984): 167–84.

63. L. Ingrassia, "Municipal Officials Getting Tougher in Bargaining with Public Employees," *Wall Street Journal,* 18 Aug. 1981, p. 35.

64. Graham and Wallace, "Public Sector Arbitration."

65. Kochan, "Collective Bargaining in Organizational Research," p. 471.

66. Ibid., p. 472.

67. T. A. Kochan, R. B. McKersie, and P. Cappelli, "Strategic Choice and Industrial Relations Theory," *Industrial Relations* (Winter 1984): 16–38; T. A. Kochan and J. Chalykoff, "Human Resource Management and Business Life Cycles: Some Preliminary Propositions," paper presented at UCLA

Conference on Human Resources and Industrial Relations in High Technology Firms, 21 June 1985; D. Q. Mills, *The New Competitors* (New York: Free Press, 1985), pp. 243–71.

68. J. Usaj and J. Howell, "Potential Issues Audit: New Channels of Communication in a Union Environment," *Personnel Administrator* (Sep. 1985): 40–41; M. F. Payson, "Wooing the Pink Collar Work Force," *Personnel Journal* (Jan. 1984): 48–53.

69. D. O. Cantrell, "Computers Come to the Bargaining Table," *Personnel Journal* (Sept. 1984): 27–30.

70. R. S. Schuler and I. C. MacMillan, "Gaining Competitive Advantage through Human Resource Management Practices," *Human Resource Management* (Fall 1984): 250–62. See also J. P. Goodman and W. R. Sandberg, "A Contingency Approach to Labor Relations Strategies," Academy of Management Review (Jan. 1981): 145–54; J. A. Fossum, "Strategic Issues in Labor Relations," in *Strategic Human Resource Management,* ed. C. Fombrun, N. M. Tichy, and M. A. Devanna (New York: Wiley, 1984), pp. 343–60.

17

International Personnel and Human Resource Management

European Executives Put High Priority On Raising White-Collar Productivity

Improving the productivity of white-collar workers—and particularly middle managers—is a paramount corporate goal for the years ahead, according to a survey of chief executives of more than 200 major European firms.

A panel of corporation heads surveyed for the *Wall Street Journal/Europe* with the assistance of Booz-Allen & Hamilton, the consulting firm, forecasts a radically different European workplace by the year 1990, with the workweek cut to thirty-six hours or less and many more computers in use.

It is assumed that the recent success of West Germany's metalworkers in winning a shortened workweek will put pressure on companies around Europe to make such concessions to their work forces—white-collar as well as blue-

collar. That is going to put a squeeze on profits and a premium on productivity to stay competitive.

Per Wejke, managing director of Atlas Copco Mining & Construction of Stockholm, worries that Western Europe will be at a competitive disadvantage. "I think that we will have to have a lower standard of living in Europe because we work less," he comments. "We can't afford to pay as much."

Kaspar Kielland, president and chief executive officer of Norway's Elken, says "Many (white-collar) workers haven't realized that their benefits have increased beyond what some companies can afford. It is very difficult to make some workers see they may have to put in more effort in the future for less payment."

A Model for Developing Key Expatriate Executives

The experience and training of a manager in the home country do not necessarily prepare him or her for managing subsidiaries in the host country. Premature rate of return of expatriate managers is presently in the range of 25 to 40 percent. The cost of premature return is about $80,000 for a family. The multinational corporation also suffers because some expatriates who are unsuitable or unhappy stick out their assignment with reduced effectiveness. These "brownouts" do not

become statistics, since they do not come home prematurely. However, there are many of them across the world, costing firms dearly in both money and reputation.

The reasons for expatriate failure are to be found in the cultural, political, economic, legal, and other factors in a host country, which are often radically different from the home country and a potential cause for conflict among the major parties interested in international business.

The growing internationalization of the world makes it more important than ever to have some awareness of how other countries utilize their human resources and how their personnel and human resource management practices compare with those in the United States.[1] The preceding "PHRM in the News" features highlight several critical aspects of PHRM in other countries. Interestingly enough, productivity is a major issue in European countries, as it is in the United States. Furthermore, attempts to deal with this issue focus on human resources, particularly as it relates to compensation. Other critical aspects here include the trend to reduced workweeks of thirty-six hours by 1990, increased use of technology to replace expensive human resources, and increased levels of international competition. Finally, one issue that U.S. companies have to specifically deal with because of internationalization is the expatriate employee.

This chapter confines its discussion to America's major trading partners—Japan, Canada, Great Britain, Australia, and some European countries. This brief look at how other countries manage their human resources highlights PHRM practices that have relevance, if only by contrast, to what has been or may someday be done in the United States. Comparisons address activities such as planning, staffing, appraising, compensating, training, and labor-management relations. Finally, this chapter presents the dilemma of multinational corporations in trying to select and train expatriate employees—particularly managers—to operate effectively in foreign countries.

Comparing U.S. PHRM Practices With Other Countries

The same forces described in Chapter 1 that have increased the importance of PHRM are also creating new trends in other nations.[2] Comparing the United States with countries such as Japan, Germany, Great Britain, Sweden, and Canada suggests a broad spectrum of approaches to major PHRM activities, including planning, staffing, compensating, training, and labor-management relations.

Comparisons in Planning for Human Resource Management

The Japanese system of lifetime employment contrasts sharply with human resource management practices in the United States. Less radical, in this sense, are the German modifications of traditional job designs associated with the assembly line.

Japan.   The commitment to lifetime employment is a distinguishing feature of the Japanese labor market. Described as *Shushin Koyo,* or "lifetime employment," the practice comes close to a guarantee that once an employee joins a company, he will stay with it until retirement age. He will not decide halfway through his career to move to another company, nor will the employer decide to dismiss him before retirement, except under extreme circumstances. (In Japan, lifetime employment has not generally applied to women workers, who for the most part have left the company once they were married or pregnant.)

Though not required by law nor formalized by a written contract, lifetime employment is encouraged and endorsed by the ministry of labor and *Nikkeiren*, the Japan Federation of Employers' Associations, and is practiced by all major employers. Lifetime employment does not appear to be practiced within smaller companies, such as vendors and small parts suppliers, although not uncommon is for a major corporation to provide extra benefits to valued employees within vendor companies as a means of encouraging lasting relationships with important suppliers.[3]

With lifetime employment, human resource planning is less flexible, yet at the same time it must be tied even more closely with, and perhaps even guiding, broader corporate objectives. Implications of this lifetime employment practice are discussed further in relation to other PHRM activities.

Germany.   Many German workers perform in "work islands" where they can avoid boredom by rotating jobs, socializing, and working in cycles of up to twenty minutes rather than a few seconds. In assembling electronics products, automobiles, and appliances, the Germans appear to be well ahead of other countries in modifying or reducing the conventional assembly line and its simple, repetitive jobs.[4] This enlightened position in alternative job design utilization is a product of the work humanization movement in Germany, initially funded by the German government in 1974 and maintained by the cooperative relationship between labor and management. Many companies also furnish their own funds for work design innovation projects.

Although each company's project may result in different types of job design, common emphasis is placed upon enlarging assembly jobs by adding more complex tasks. One goal is to increase the job cycle to over one and one-half minutes, the point at which employees have been found to become dissatisfied with the job. As a consequence of the experiments in various companies, three major ways are being used to modify the traditional assembly line and its jobs. In group assembly, workers rotate jobs, as they follow the product from the first to the last step in the assembly process. This is the notion of the "work island," where workers have the opportunity to socialize and are tied together by a group incentive pay plan. With individual work stations, work is done by the individual in a cycle time of ten to fifteen minutes. During this time, the worker assembles a major subcomponent of the total product (e.g., an electric motor for a washing machine). The final way is a modification of the assembly line to make work easier and lighter. Where the assembly line cannot be easily replaced as in automotive assembly, the line has been altered so that the worker stands on platforms moving at the same speed as the car.

Although these alternative job designs do not eliminate problems of worker dissatisfaction and alienation, they do ameliorate some of the worst complaints about the traditional assembly line.

Comparisons in Staffing the Organization's Human Resource Needs

Staffing activities in Japan and Germany present alternatives that could be used in the United States. Canada provides a useful comparison with this country in regard to equal employment and human rights legislation.

Japan.   Because of the lifetime employment policy, recruitment is different from the United States, where hiring emphasis is on skill or job qualifications. In Japan, emphasis is placed on the general attributes of the person being hired. All regular employees of the corporation are hired at one time of the year only (in April, immediately after the end of each academic year) and are recruited from either the high school graduate or college and university graduate level. Employees not hired at this time are considered "nonregular" employees (that is, they may have been employed by other companies earlier in their careers or self-employed; in short, they are hired at times other than the beginning of their occupational careers). In addition to "regular" and "nonregular" employees are temporary employees and part-time workers.

For the most part, company employment policies are directed toward regular employees, and a great competition takes place at the time of the April hiring, both among the companies, which seek to attract the best candidates (tests are given on academic and basic aptitudes), and among the graduates, who wish to align themselves with growth companies.

This division between "regular" employees (estimated to be between 30 to 50 percent of the total national work force) and the nonregular, part-time, and temporary employees makes the lifetime commitment possible despite economic fluctuations. In times of temporary growth or decline, additional temporary workers may be hired or laid off. Alternative solutions for dealing with down cycles that affect the retention of regular workers include shifting employees to new areas of operation or contracting employees out to other companies in more prosperous industries. The transferred employee continues to remain formally affiliated with the original employer in such cases.

In more serious circumstances, temporary layoffs may be required, though according to Japan's labor standards law, workers receive 60 percent of normal salary during this "vacation," or *kyugyo.* However, because Japanese companies pay close attention to the development of long-term trends, they are generally able to predict a leveling off or decline within an industry and adjust their springtime recruitment efforts accordingly.[5] In addition to the impact of lifetime employment on staffing, Japanese companies also have an extensive commitment to hire and accommodate handicapped individuals.

Germany.   An alternative work arrangement not discussed in Chapter 12 is the experimental **flexiyear schedule** in Germany. Under flexiyear, employees base their work schedule thinking on a year rather than on a day or a week, as is generally the case in flextime or compressed workweek arrangements. Actual implementation of such schedules may vary across organizations, but typically, employees indicate how many hours they want to work each month. Then the employer and the employees together reach agreement on the exact days and hours of the day to be worked. As with many alternative work plans in the United States, a critical advantage of flexiyear schedules is the choice it provides employees. The results thus far are extremely favorable: reduced absenteeism, reduced conflict between work and family for many employees, and increased accommodation of employees' desires for more leisure time.[6]

Canada.   In Canada, most companies use techniques of recruiting and selection similar to those in the United States. At the same time, they face significantly different equal employment legislation or, more broadly, human rights legislation.[7] Relatively comprehensive human rights legislation now exists at the federal level and in each of Canada's ten provinces. This legislation follows a common pattern but has specific deviations in each jurisdiction.

The typical Canadian human rights statute prohibits discrimination based on race, color, religion, ancestry, place of origin, marital status, sex, age, or physical handicap, when such discrimination involves employment or trade union membership, services or accommodation that are available to the public, residential or commercial rentals, or public notices.[8] Some of the statutes also prohibit discrimination by occupational or professional associations, employer or business associations, or employment agencies. The statute is enforced by a human rights commission, whose staff investigates and conciliates complaints of statute violations. If the commission staff is unable to conciliate a complaint successfully, an ad hoc tribunal or board of inquiry of one or more members may be appointed to hold a public hearing. The commission normally takes the lead in supporting the complaint at this hearing. If the tribunal finds that discrimination has occurred, it can formulate a remedial order. The legislation varies as to whether the tribunal issues the order or recommends the order to either the human rights commission or a designated cabinet minister, who in turn has the authority to issue it. Normally, the order can be enforced by court proceedings and is appealable to a court. Violations of the statutes are also subject to the ordinary penal process, although consent of either the human rights commission or a designated cabinet minister is usually necessary to commence prosecution.

Some uncertainty exists as to what operations are subject to the federal statute and what operations are subject to the appropriate provincial statute. Federally regulated industries, such as banks and interprovincial transportation and communications, are clearly subject to the federal statute. Unlike most comparable federal legislation, however, nothing in the federal statute expressly limits it to such industries, although tribunals under the statute have held that it is implicitly so limited. All other operations are clearly subject to the provincial statutes. The federally regulated industries have sometimes assumed that they are not subject to the provincial statutes, but some case law indicates that the provincial statutes also apply to federally regulated industries.

The federal statute, in addition to basic human rights, prohibits discrimination on the basis of criminal conviction where the person has been pardoned.[9] In the case of the physically handicapped, employment discrimination is prohibited, but not other forms of discrimination, and employers are not compelled to renovate their premises to accommodate the handicapped. A unique feature of the federal statute in the area of sex discrimination is that employers are required to provide equal pay for work of equal value. This contrasts with the provincial legislation, which does not affect pay differentials between different jobs as long as there is no ongoing practice of denying access to these jobs because of sex. Penal proceedings for discrimination under the federal statute are possible only where a person violates the terms of an agreed settlement of a complaint. Otherwise, enforcement must proceed through the hearing procedure and, if necessary, court enforcement of the resulting decision.

Under the Alberta statute, no provision exists for a penal proceeding to enforce the statute.[10] However, there are provisions for applying to a court for an injunction against continued violation of the statute if the board of inquiry does not make such an order.

In British Columbia, age discrimination is prohibited only in relation to employment, and no express prohibition exists of discrimination based on marital status or physical handicap.[11] On the other hand, discrimination on any basis is prohibited unless there is reasonable cause for it. The statute also expressly prohibits discrimination in employment on the basis of political belief. Another provision prohibits basic discrimination in the sale of property.

The Manitoba statute prohibits discrimination except for reasonable cause, both in respect to public accommodations and services and in respect to residential and commercial rentals.[12] The Manitoba law also prohibits discrimination on the basis of source of income in relation to public notices and rental accommodation and on the basis of political belief in relation to employment. There are specific provisions against discriminatory terms in standard form contracts and discrimination in the sale of property. Apart from the usual enforcement procedure, provision exists in the Manitoba statute for applying directly to court to obtain an injuction against violations of the statute. Elsewhere such relief is available only following proceedings before an ad hoc tribunal or penal proceedings.

New Brunswick law specifically prohibits basic discrimination in the sale of property.[13]

Under the Newfoundland statute, discrimination on the basis of political opinion is covered generally, but age discrimination is covered only in relation to employment, and physical handicaps are not covered at all.[14] The human rights commission is not directly responsible for investigation and conciliation of complaints and may be called upon to conduct a public hearing as an alternative to an ad hoc tribunal.

Although Nova Scotia's provision is ambiguously phrased, age and physical handicap discrimination appear to be covered only in relation to employment.[15] Another provision prohibits basic discrimination in the sale of property.

In Ontario, the statute covers citizenship, family status, record of offenses, and mental handicap in addition to basic human rights.[16] Also, discrimination based on receipt of public assistance is prohibited in relation to accommodations. Sexual harassment is expressly prohibited, although even in the absence of such provisions, such harassment has been held to constitute sexual discrimination. The prohibition against sexual harassment applies against co-workers as well as against employers, and harassment based on any discriminatory ground applies against fellow tenants as well as against landlords. All of the rights against discrimination are worded to apply to infringements by co-workers and consumers, as well as by employers and businesses, but the express provisions in the cases noted may prevent this from being inferred in other cases. Provisions in other legislation nullify discriminatory covenants in property deeds on all the usual bases except age, sex, physical handicap, and marital status, and prohibit discrimination in insurance contracts on grounds of race or religion.[17]

The Prince Edward Island statute covers discrimination based on political belief as long as one's political party is registered under the provincial election law. Basic discrimination in the sale of property is covered by this statute.[18]

Under the Quebec statute, sexual orientation, political convictions, and social conditions are included among the prohibited bases of discrimination, but age is not included, and civil status is listed instead of marital status.[19] Handicaps are covered generally, presumably including mental handicaps, and a general provision exists against discriminatory clauses in legal arrangements. If the commission is unable to settle a complaint of discrimination, it seeks relief directly from a court, without a hearing by an ad hoc tribunal.

Saskatchewan does not cover age discrimination in the case of rental accommodations.[20] Other provisions prohibit discrimination in education and in standard form contracts, but age is not included in the list of prohibited discriminations in either case, and physical disability is not included in the case of contracts. The statute prohibits basic discrimination in the sale of property.

On a national scale, Canadian companies now face affirmative action obligations similar to those in the United States. The basis for such action dates back to 1977 when Canada's federal human rights law was passed. As the legal considerations regarding how organizations use their human resources have grown, so have the image and role of the personnel departments in Canadian companies.[21]

Australia.   The development of equal opportunity in Australia has been a slow process, with community support and awareness remaining at a relatively low level. Early government action in this area was little more than formal endorsement of international standards condemning discrimination, such as the International Labour Organisation Convention III on discrimination, which was ratified in 1973. Following ratification of this convention, the Commonwealth of Australia established national and state committees on discrimination in employment and occupation to investigate complaints of discrimination in employment. These committees do not have a statutory basis, and their power is limited to reporting matters to the Commonwealth minister for employment and industrial relations who, at his discretion, may name discriminatory employers in Parliament.

Not until the South Australian government passed the Sex Discrimination Act 1975 did formal sex discrimination machinery appear in Australia. The impetus for this first act was the personal interest of the then premier and the development of a women's lobby group within the Australian Labor Party (ALP). Two other states enacted equal opportunity legislation shortly after the Sex Discrimination Act: the New South Wales government passed the Anti Discrimination Act 1977, and the Victorian government passed the Equal Opportunity Act 1977. All three state acts are "complaint-based," which enables individuals to place grievances before a special board or tribunal.

Within the trade union movement, various women's groups developed a Working Women's Charter to guide policy development in the area of equal opportunity. This charter was adopted by the Australian Council of Trade Unions (ACTU) Congress in 1977. The aims and objectives of the charter include the following:

- Equal access to education, training, and vocational guidance
- Quality child care controlled by parents and employees
- Elimination of discrimination in conditions of employment
- Flexible working hours
- Adequate paid maternity and paternity leave
- Regular on-the-job medical services for workers
- Increased recruitment, training, and participation of female members in trade unions

As these broad aims and objectives show, the main objective of the charter was to serve as a basis for union activity in the equal opportunity area. A somewhat similar task was undertaken by the tripartite National Labour Consultative Council (NLCC) on this issue. (The NLCC is a consultative forum comprising the Commonwealth government, the ACTU, and the Confederation of Australian Industry.) In 1978, the NLCC issued a booklet titled "Guidelines for Employers—Equal Employment Opportunities for Women," which encouraged employers to adopt equal opportunity practices in their organizations.

By 1980, equal opportunity had emerged as an issue that was "on the agenda" in a number of ways. Three states had equal opportunity legislation and federally established national and state committees on discrimination in employment. On a policy level, the ACTU had endorsed the Working Women's Charter, and the NLCC had endorsed the concept of voluntary acceptance by employers of equal opportunity practices. However, equal opportunity was not a high-profile issue. By and large, the equal opportunity legislation in New South Wales, South Australia, and Victoria emphasized conciliation rather than compulsion, and many private-sector employers simply ignored this legislation. The effectiveness of the legislation was probably further reduced because of the concern of individuals who lodged complaints that they might be later victimized in their employment. Feminist groups within the ALP argued that stronger equal opportunity legislation was required if significant progress was to be made in the area of equal op-

sive," during which many of th
independent, actions in demar
percent of the organized worker
sult of this trend, wage decisior
ence the outcome of other indv
dardized wage increase rates th

A distinguishing feature of t.
a semiannual bonus or wage all
cremental rate. Usually paid w
the bonus amount is determine
related to both the general ecc
Generally, the equivalent of fiv
midsummer and at the end of th

In addition to basic salary,
pensation in the form of housin;
(including transportation, meal
ational benefits, and medical ar
varies according to the size of th
try's 1975 general survey, such
made up about 14 percent of the

Canada. In Canada, the sharp
ing appraisal and compensatior
larly pensions. Yet, even these c
ample, Canada has the Canada
Plan in the province of Quebec,
Security system. CPP is a man
workers. Like the Social Securit
ability pensions, benefits for «
benefits, and pension benefits tc
pension plans, although fewer t
by these plans. The administrat
Benefits Act, which is less ex
plans than the U.S. Employees'

Australia. In Australia, apprai
a powerful labor union moveme
force, and a long-established, c
tem, which plays a central rol«
these two factors make apprais
very different from those in the

The key institution in the A
Australian Conciliation and Arl
statutory basis in the Conciliati
settling industrial disputes, the
by which national wage policy is
do this because approximately §
der awards or agreements mad
ployees is achieved because AC

portunity for women. These views were reflected in the Sex Discrimination Bill, which was introduced into the Commonwealth Parliament in 1983.

The Sex Discrimination Bill 1983 was introduced by the Federal Labor Government and had three objectives:

- To give effect to certain provisions of the United Nations Convention on the Elimination of All forms of Discrimination Against Women
- To eliminate discrimination on the grounds of sex, marital status, or pregnancy in the areas of employment, education, accommodation, the provision of goods, facilities, and services, the disposal of land, the activities of clubs, and the administration of Commonwealth laws and programs, and discrimination involving sexual harassment in the work place and in educational institutions
- To promote recognition and acceptance within the community of the principle of the equality of women

This bill contained no proposals for affirmative action because the government thought that the concept of and proposals for affirmative action would be more appropriate as the subject of public discussion. To this end, it issued a discussion paper, *Affirmative Action for Women*, in mid-1984.

Considerable opposition arose to the 1983 bill. The opposition took two forms:

- Particular objections to wording, the procedure specified for dealing with complaints, the inclusion of certain types of discrimination, and the use of external affairs power of the Australian constitution as the legal basis for the bill
- General objections to the whole concept of equal opportunity legislation

Despite some opposition, an amended form of the bill was passed as the Sex Discrimination Act 1984—the first comprehensive federal equal opportunity legislation that covers the Australian work force.[23] Before the Sex Discrimination Act 1984, equal opportunity was not a high-profile issue. Although antidiscrimination machinery existed before 1983 and the NLCC had issued policy guidelines, the conciliation orientation of the antidiscrimination machinery and the voluntary nature of the policy guidelines effectively put equal opportunity toward the bottom of the issue agenda. Essentially, the policy debate on equal opportunity has just started, with the Sex Discrimination Act serving as the first major stimulus to the policy development process.

Affirmative action remains a politically controversial topic in Australia.[24] The major policy initiative announced in the federal government's affirmative action discussion paper was the implementation of a voluntary pilot program, whereby a number of organizations would set up affirmative action programs with assistance from a special Affirmative Action Resource Unit located in the Office of the Status of Women in the Department of the Prime Minister and Cabinet. The organizations involved in the pilot programs represent both the private and the public sectors.

The results of this pilot program will be monitored by the Working Party on Affirmative Action, comprising government ministers and representa-

tives of busine
ganizations. T
dations to the
cover all priva
ple and all hig

The discus:
federal goverr
ganizations to
sanctions. Bo
the term *goal*
controversy s
However, apa
form future af

Comparisons

Japan's comp
in America, v
country.

Japan.   The J
the Imperial l
which stems f
which determi
this system, a
service length
system has it:
tionship, whic
family (compa
(or company) i
fective workin

During the
given to the a
then those wh
the predomina
corporates bo
increases, whi
amount of the
considers a w
tance is also p
Initially, indiv
employees hir
that, an empl(
system. In ad
job responsibi
ment, now con

In a compa
among the hig
initiated a cor

U.S. system) apply to all employees (union and nonunion) whose employers are respondents before the ACAC. Labor unions ensure that virtually all employers are respondents before the ACAC by serving a log of claims or demands on each employer. Each employer may either agree to the union claim (which is generally highly inflated and represents the opening demand from which the union will bargain) or become a party to the ACAC hearing—usually represented by their relevant employer association. This system is substantially different from U.S. labor relations practice.[27]

Since the early part of this century, a system of quarterly or six monthly national wage hearings has developed where government, employers, and trade unions make submission to the ACAC, which then determines whether a national wage increase is warranted and, if so, by what percentage industrial awards will increase. When a conservative federal government is in power, the government generally favors the employer position, while labor governments usually favor the union position. The ACAC and its permanent staff are legally independent of the government of the day but clearly must seriously consider the government's views; a U.S. analogy would be the relationship between the president and the Federal Reserve. The present labor federal government has signed an accord with the trade unions whereby the government supports the unions' request to the ACAC for quarterly national wage increases to match changes in the Consumer Price Index in return for broad compliance with the government's macroeconomic strategy to reduce inflation and unemployment.[28]

Because labor unions in Australia have tended to oppose individual performance appraisal,[29] most employers must pay all workers performing a similar job the award rate determined by the ACAC, plus any overaward benefits that may have been negotiated between the employer and the unions. A traditional U.S.-style individually oriented appraisal and compensation system appears only with managerial-level employees who are not covered by an industry award.

Comparisons in Training and Improving

In contrast to most companies in the United States, Japanese companies appear to offer far more extensive training for their employees. This also appears to be the case in Germany, particularly regarding apprenticeship training.

Japan.   In most large companies, all job training is done within the company itself. According to a 1973 study of vocational training made by the ministry of labor, 80.4 percent of all business enterprises conduct in-company job training. Broken down according to employee classification, job training is made available to new regular employees in 75.5 percent of all companies, and to nonregular employees in 52.7 percent of them.

If classified according to the size of the firm, 48.7 percent of all firms with thirty to one hundred employees offer job training, 75 percent with one hundred to three hundred employees do so, and 96.7 percent of firms with one thousand to five-thousand employees also provide training. Every firm with more than five thousand employees provides its own training. Vocational training in small to medium-sized companies depends to a greater extent on cooperative centers established through the effort of the government's employment promotion agency, aided by prefectural, municipal, and town agencies.

The in-company form of training is looked upon as the key to each company's productivity and managerial control. Regular employees are hired as either high school or college graduates; they generally have academic training but few, if any, vocational skills. The company looks upon training as a means of orienting the employee to its needs, in the broad sense as well as for specific jobs. Not unusual, for example, is for a new employee to have anywhere from one to six months' training before being integrated into the work force. Supplemental training usually continues throughout the first three years of an employee's career, with additional training provided as needed throughout employment.

Descriptions of training programs generally reveal a greater emphasis on the company as a whole—its role in society (including the community, the nation, and the world), its relationship to the competition, its marketing goals and objectives, what it must do to meet these objectives, its disadvantages in comparison to the competition, and what can be done to remedy these weaknesses. In short, training constantly seeks to develop the individual worker as a fully rounded worker who can not only see the whole picture but also respond to it.

Actual job training teaches workers to apply skills to a variety of situations, thereby permitting worker rotation, which decreases worker boredom and job fatigue and allows the shifting of workers to meet fluctuations in production requirements. All blue-collar workers are expected to be multi-skilled within four to five years after joining the company. Many believe that this orientation toward skills enrichment and labor mobility is a crucial factor in the rapid growth of the Japanese economy.

Among white-collar workers, job rotation—especially during early years of employment—is considered beneficial in giving each employee a better understanding of the company as a whole as well as specific areas of expertise.[30] Generally, a new employee is rotated to a new assignment at three- to six-month intervals. This process, coupled with formal training, continues for the first three to four years of an employee's career. Following that period, individualized training is made available for those who desire development in a specific area. Employees are tested or selected for specialized training, which may be provided through a company's own education center or through university study, either at home or abroad.

The consequence of job rotation, combined with other programs such as quality control circles, is a highly committed and loyal work force that produces high-quality products. Similar results are appearing in U.S. plants that are managed by the Japanese. Such plants include Nissan's truck plant in Tennessee and Sanyo's appliance plant in Arkansas. Interestingly, similar results do not always appear in U.S. plants managed by Americans using some of the Japanese techniques.[31]

The Japanese also differ substantially in how they train today's college graduate to become tomorrow's manager. The two major aspects of this training are preemployment education, or socialization and training given before the first day on the job, and initial managerial education. This training has the following general aims:

- To educate new graduates as members of the company, emphasizing self-discipline and the transition from student to company life
- To teach professionalism and the significance and meaning of work
- To provide background information about the company and to familiarize employees with distinctive management trends
- To familiarize employees with basic company procedures and fundamental business rules and etiquette
- To cultivate a spirit of harmony and teamwork among employees[32]

Preemployment education consists of communications between the company and the future employees who are still in school. Some companies recommend to future employees what they should read before starting work. Future employees are frequently sent a directory of all new recruits, an employee handbook, a booklet on health and nutrition, and even words of encouragement from senior employees. Many companies provide an opportunity for future employees to get to know one another by holding meetings that

> afford an opportunity . . . to learn the company song, to meet senior employees who are graduates of the same university, to visit the factories and see exhibitions of the company's products, and to become familiar with the company's various departments and divisions.[33]

Initial managerial education has three parts: (1) orientation, (2) work experience, and (3) residency. The program of work experience involves starting from the ground up, especially in the area of production. For example, the current president of Matsushita Electric Works spent his first six months carrying and shifting goods in the company's storage area. Most of the present executives of Japan's major companies have also passed through similar on-the-job training programs.

During orientation and the work experience program, new employees live together in company residences. Here they learn social rules, etiquette, human relations, and punctuality—all considered necessary for an effective manager.

An important aspect of this training and development is the evaluation of how well the new employees have done. Mitsubishi and Isetan, for example, administer a quiz, which the recruits must pass, on the essential knowledge for handling the companies' products. Immediate supervisors of these new employees also file reports, which are later used in identifying the work areas new employees should be placed in and the jobs they should be rotated through.[34]

Germany.   A relatively unique feature of training and developing employees in Germany is the extensive and successful apprenticeship system.[35] This system receives financial and organizational support from both labor and management. In contrast to the United States, the German government also contributes financial support to the apprenticeship system.

Apprenticeship training for many German students begins at age fifteen when compulsory schooling ends. At that point, youths select one of several programs that lasts between two and three years. Presently, an apprenticeship is required for 451 jobs in Germany. In total, almost half of the German youths between fifteen and eighteen are enrolled in the almost half-million apprenticeships. The results of this apprenticeship system include training for currently available jobs and an unemployment rate among youths that is far less than that in the United States.

In addition to these comparisons of training and development, Europe offers a comparison of quality of work life (QWL) programs, and Canada provides a comparison in health and safety.

Europe.   The Volvo QWL projects have been implemented in several plants in Sweden, but the most famous is at Volvo's new assembly plant in the city of Kalmar. This plant, in operation since 1972, uses work teams instead of the traditional assembly line and allows employees to design and organize their own work. The plant was built in response to employees' job-hopping, absenteeism, apathetic attitudes, and antagonism. One reason this became necessary was the extremely low level of unemployment in Sweden, which meant the pool of replacement workers was very small.

Volvo's QWL project made substantial improvements by changing the technology for assembling cars. Although changing the technology of an organization is not easy or inexpensive and entails some risk, Volvo proved that it can be done successfully. In fact, changing the technology may be the only way to satisfy the needs and values of employees. As P. G. Gyllenhammar of Volvo reported in the *Harvard Business Review:*

> When we started thinking about reorganizing the way we worked, the first bottleneck seemed to be production and technology. We couldn't really reorganize the work to suit the people unless we also changed the technology that chained people to the assembly line.[36]

Now car assembly is done in work groups of about twenty people. The change in technology has been accompanied by a new climate of cooperation, partnership, participation, and an improved physical working environment.

Employee participation through councils and committees resulted in increased employee involvement and further improvements in the work itself. This participation is implemented in accordance with a 1977 Swedish law calling for full consultation with employees and full participation by their representatives in decision making from board level to the shop floor. Because shop floor workers may not be prepared to serve on boards in Swedish companies, they need to be trained. This training is described in the following "PHRM in the News."

A QWL project has been instituted at Volvo's major plant in Torslanda. Here, participation and autonomous groups are the two dominant techniques, rather than just participation, as at Kalmar. This is mostly because Torslanda has a large-scale assembly line and employs eight thousand workers, compared with six hundred at Kalmar.

A technique used in both plants at the discretion of the workers is job rotation. This is done within the relatively autonomous work groups. Today approximately 70 percent of the assembly workers engage in job rotation. Again, P. G. Gyllenhammar of Volvo observes: "There will always be a few

The Education of Employee Representatives on Company Boards in Sweden

Swedish worker directors receive three one-week periods of training for their board duties. The training, which is scheduled over three years, is sponsored by the trade unions.

The first week starts with background history on how the labor movement in Sweden developed its industrial democracy goals and implemented the legislative and collective bargaining strategy to realize them. Instructors point out that in the past, labor had opposed the concept of worker directors because of the fear that the trade union representatives would be co-opted. The change in trade union opposition is now presented as part of an overall strategy to extend employees' rights to participate in management decision making at the workplace level and eventually to extend employee influence to changes in ownership and control of capital.

The role and responsibilities of worker directors form the core of the first week's course. There is particular concern that communication between the worker directors and the other union members and the union officials may break down.

Participants are instructed to establish a continuing two-way communications process with union members and the unions, to keep them informed of the board's work, and to identify members' problems and recommendations for use in their representation on the board.

Where this is difficult because of the large number of union members represented, it is recommended that a representative reference group be formed in the workplace with whom the worker director can consult. The reference groups also serve to disseminate information from worker directors to members; organize the problems, views, and recommendations of the workers in different departments; and generally support the worker directors in carrying out their mandate.

One of the most effective methods for instilling confidence in worker directors and at the same time develop representation skills is the technique of simulation. From the start, participants engage in extensive role playing of a company board meeting. The instructors act as the employer-directors and the participants take turns in playing their own role. The class then carefully analyzes the strengths and weaknesses of their performances.

Participants are taught how to demand information to be discussed at board meetings in sufficient time so that it can be useful. Participants are advised on what kinds of information, reports, and documents they can expect to receive before the board meetings and what recourse they have in the event the employer does not provide this information.

The second week of the worker-director training course is scheduled about a year after the first, permitting participants to share their experiences as members of company boards. Much time is spent on the specific problems experienced by participants in carrying out their roles.

The second week also provides instruction in skills in analyzing and interpreting company financial reports and planning documents, and in obtaining early access to information on investments, new technology, product and production changes, relocations, sales, costs, and profits. The idea is not to develop financial specialists but rather to develop some degree of competence in raising searching questions on the company budget and its short- and long-range plans.

Economic trends and issues in the national economy and specific industries represented in the class also receive attention.

The third week of training, given to employees after two years as worker directors, focuses on working out alternative company budgets and advising participants on how to propose their "own" short- and long-range plans. Problems encountered in the companies represented are inventoried and examined.

The group also develops proposals to improve working environments, to budget for improved capital equipment, and to distribute profits more equitably. In some classes, considerable emphasis is given to the problems of functioning on the relatively powerless boards of subsidiaries of multinationals and on ways of coordinating the work of representatives on the boards of subsidiaries of conglomerates and holding companies.

Source: Reprinted, by permission of the publisher, from "The Education of Employee Representatives on Company Boards in Sweden," *Management Review,* "AMA Forum," February 1984, p. 38 © 1984 AMA Membership Publications Division, American Management Associations, New York. All rights reserved.

people, however, especially older ones, who don't want to change (jobs) at all."[37] This recognition and acceptance of employee differences, which was also characteristic of GM's Tarrytown program,[38] is an important factor in the long-run success of QWL projects in general. Without allowing for such differences, changes and QWL techniques will probably be resisted, and improvement in QWL is unlikely to occur.

Canada.   Employee health and safety are major concerns in Canada, as they are in the United States. In both nations, safety and health are regulated at the federal level—in Canada by the Canada Labor Code—and at the state or province safety and health agencies. However, whereas the Occupational Safety and Health Act in the United States covers all employees regardless of the type of employer, Canada has a separate health and safety program for federal employees. In Canada the provinces generally exert more authority over health and safety issues than do the states in this country.

Comparisons in Effective Working Relationships

Comparing labor-management relations in Great Britain, Western Europe, Canada, and Japan suggests that unions and employee involvement in organization decision making is no isolated phenomenon. Many countries even appear to have stronger employee organizations than those found in the United States.

Great Britain.   The industrial relations system in Great Britain differs markedly, both from the United States and from other European countries. Traditionally, the framework of labor law in Britain has been noninterventionist, fostering an essentially voluntary system of industrial relations. Under this system, employers have had no general legal duty to recognize and bargain with their employees, while employees have had no legally protected rights to organize themselves in unions. Also, negotiated agreements signed between union and employers are not enforceable as legal contracts. The collective agreements familiar to American managers are more akin to gentleman's agreements in Britain and are based on social rather than on legal sanctions.

As with so many aspects of life in Britain, the explanation for this state of affairs is largely historical. The development of the framework of British labor law has progressed via the granting of immunities from existing restrictive statutes—such as immunity from prosecution for criminal conspiracy—rather than through the legislation of positive rights. Unlike their American counterparts, therefore, British unions have not viewed the law as a positive and protective force guaranteeing their right to existence.

The tradition of legal nonintervention in industrial relations has, however, come under increasing challenge in recent years. Concern over the country's poor economic performance, and a growing international reputation for labor strife, sparked a vigorous debate among the major political parties in Britain during the 1960s and eventually led to the establishment of a royal commission of inquiry (the Donovan Commission). This commission, which reported in 1968, highlighted the growing importance of what it termed Britain's unofficial system of industrial relations. Under this system, terms and conditions of employment were increasingly being negotiated between local managers and informally elected shop stewards, rather than between management and paid full-time union officials.

Rejecting the Donovan Commission's recommendation that reform should be accomplished without destroying the tradition of keeping industrial relations out of the courts, a newly elected Conservative government made an ill-fated attempt in 1971 to reform Britain's voluntary system of industrial relations along American lines. The Industrial Relations Act of 1971 included provisions to formalize the process of union certification through the establishment of bargaining units for which a designated union would be the sole bargaining agent. This reform was intended to replace the practice of voluntary recognition, which led to a complex pattern of multiunionism under which a single local management could find itself negotiating with as many as half a dozen unions at the same work place. Provisions were also included to make collective agreements legally enforceable, unless the parties included a clause to the contrary. (In practice, most negotiators did include such a clause.)

The 1971 legislation also defined and strengthened a number of individual rights, including protection against unfair dismissal. The rationale for this legislation was not merely to redress a perceived inequality in the balance of power between the individual employee and a management able to fire at will. Rather it was an attempt to limit the large number of unofficial "wildcat" strikes that were called, often with some success, to pressure management into reinstating a dismissed employee.

Active union hostility combined with management indifference to the 1971 legislation made it largely unworkable, and the act was repealed by a Labour government in 1974. Between 1974 and 1979, with the support of the unions, the Labour government introduced a number of pieces of legislation that took a significant step in the direction of creating more positive legal rights to protect and support trade union membership. Legislation also entrenched a variety of individual rights, including protection against unfair dismissal and discrimination on the basis of sex or race.

Many observers have seen this legislation as a form of *quid pro quo* for the cooperation of the Trade Union Council (TUC) (the central umbrella organization for Britain's unions) in the Labour government's incomes policy, which was in place between 1975 and 1978. Incomes policies in one form or another have acted as important constraints on management freedom in compensating employees in Britain during most of the 1960s and 1970s, but none has been based on the same degree of union cooperation.

By 1979, union power in Britain, measured by political influence and industrial strength as well as by membership, was undoubtedly at a postwar peak. Since the election of the Thatcher Conservative government in 1979, however, the industrial relations climate has changed dramatically. A process of step-by-step reform, including laws against secondary picketing, restrictions on the operation of the closed shop, and the establishment of secret union ballots before strikes, has effectively shifted the balance of power back toward management. High levels of unemployment have further undermined union bargaining power. Between 1979 and 1985, the percentage of the labor force in unions fell by about one-fifth from its postwar peak of about 55 percent. Despite some highly publicized disputes, which give an unduly inflated impression of Britain's overall strike proneness, strike activity has also fallen to historically low levels.

The full, long-run consequences of these changes are difficult to predict with any certainty. Managers in Britain still face a work force that is highly unionized compared with the United States, where less than 18 percent of the labor force are currently in unions. Managers in many parts of British industry must also negotiate with a multiplicity of unions whose representational boundaries often owe more to craft tradition and the accidents of history than they do to the logic of efficient production. They must also operate on a day-to-day basis without the support of legally enforceable collective agreements. Important developments at the shop floor level do, however, offer some clue to a changed future. On the union side, both the engineering and the electricians' unions have been willing to sign single-union agreements that include no-strike clauses. They have also shown a preference for cooperative over confrontational relations with management. Perhaps significantly, the key movers on the management side of these innovative agreements have often been overseas companies setting up operations in Britain. Japanese companies such as Nissan, Hitachi, and Toshiba are notable examples, but innovative agreements have also been signed with some U.S. firms. This is a useful reminder that the behavior and attitudes of both sides determine the quality of labor-management relationships.

Europe.   The belief that worker interests are best served if employees have a direct say in the management of the company is called **codetermination**. Originally conceived in Germany, this philosophy of labor-management relations now exists in Sweden, the Netherlands, France, Norway, Denmark, Luxembourg, and Austria.

Codetermination means, for example, that unions are given seats on the boards of directors of corporations. In addition, managers are encouraged to consult with unions before making major organizational changes, whether they be mergers, investments, or personnel matters such as plant closings and relocations. If management disagrees with the union position, management prevails. However, unions may veto subcontracts by the company, and they have access to all company information.

Codetermination has also caused unions to propose asset formation. Such proposals seek to place under the control of the union funds provided by the employer. At this time, however, these proposals have been rejected to management.

Although the European ideas of codetermination and union-controlled funds will not likely be applied in the United States in the 1980s, increased cooperation may occur between labor and management on issues of productivity and QWL. An issue on which cooperation, both in Europe and America, has been less evident is that of the thirty-five-hour workweek. The extent of union-management disagreement on this issue is particularly evident in West Germany.[39] In Sweden, however, some progress has been made in hours reduction.[40]

Canada.   Approximately one-third of the Canadian labor force is unionized. About three-fourths of the union members are affiliated with the Canadian Labor Congress (CLC). As in the United States, the union local is the basic labor unit. The CLC is the dominant labor group at the federal level. Its political influence may be compared with that of the AFL-CIO.

Although the labor laws of Canada are similar to those in the United States, noteworthy differences exist. Since 1925, the majority of Canadian workers have been covered by provincial, not federal, labor laws, whereas in the United States over 90 percent of the workers are covered by the National Labor Relations Act. The Canadian Industrial Relations Disputes and Investigation Act of 1973, on the other hand, covers less than 10 percent of the labor force.

Canadian labor laws require frequent intervention by government bodies before a strike can take place. In the United States, such intervention is largely voluntary. Compulsory arbitration is governed by the Public Service Staff Relations Act of 1967. This law also allows nonmanagerial federal employees to join unions and bargain collectively.

The history of labor relations in Canada and the United States is similar because both nations follow British common law, except that Canadian provincial governments, rather than the federal government, have developed most of the labor laws. Since the decision in *Toronto Electric Commissioners* v. *Snider* (1925), Canadian workers have been governed primarily by provincial laws (except for employees working for the federal government and industries under federal coverage, as defined by amendments to the 1973 industrial relations act—for instance longshoring, seafaring, provincial railroads, Crown corporations, and airlines). Many of the features of the U.S. Taft-Hartley Act have been incorporated into the labor laws of the Canadian provinces.

For the union movement as a whole, trends towards concessionary bargaining to avoid layoffs and plant closings appear to be less evident than they are in the United States.[41] At the same time, Canadian labor organizations affiliated with unions dominated by labor organizations in the United States are becoming increasingly autonomous. This trend was recently highlighted when the United Auto Workers in Canada became independent from the same union in this country.

Japan. The third sacred treasure of the Imperial House is what is known as the enterprise union. Unlike the United States and Europe, where unions are organized horizontally and industrywide, almost all trade unions in Japan are formed on a company-by-company, or enterprise, basis. In 1978, as many as 70,868 labor unions could be found in Japan, where one exists in practically every company or plant to conduct labor negotiations at that level. Enterprise unions today account for nearly 90 percent of all Japanese union organizations. Also, four principal industrywide federations of workers serve as coordinators, formulators of unified and reliable standards, and sources of information.

Although the enterprise concept received a fair amount of attention in the United States during the 1920s and 1930s, such employees' unions collapsed, primarily as a result of excessive management involvement and their narrow field of interest. The success of the enterprise union in Japan is attributed to two major differences. The first of these is the allocation of financial responsibility between the enterprise union and the trade or regional organizations, which reflects a difference in the organizational roles of Japanese labor unions. In Western countries, where centralized union control and authority is predominant, the national union receives union dues, decides how they are to be used, and returns a portion to the local unions for expenses. In Japan, the enterprise union controls the dues, passing on 10 percent or, at most, 20 percent to the federation.

As a result of the enterprise union's role, problems in labor-management relationships can be dealt with more directly, without necessarily involving an outside body. The "mixed" union representation of all blue-collar and some white-collar workers also proves valuable in determining more representative concerns. The greater union participation by employees of a given company has resulted in 15.7 percent of Japan's current top management being once active labor union leaders. This should lead to better management understanding of the needs and interests of employees.

The second difference that accounts for the success of the enterprise union system in Japan is the greater company and national loyalty shown by each worker. Accordingly, workers do not look upon the union solely as a negotiating body but use its structure to deal with issues such as industry and technical reforms, new plant and equipment investments, and matters of personnel and productivity development.

Australia. The institutional framework of both U.S. and Australian industrial relations evolved from similar historical circumstances: the need to compel strong employers to meet and deal with a weak labor union movement for collective bargaining purposes.[42] However, the legislative solutions to this situation that were enacted in each country were quite different. American legislation in the 1930s carefully avoided imposing the decisions of a third party on labor and management by providing a detailed legal framework within the parties were compelled to bargain in good faith with each other. In contrast, Australian legislation at the turn of the century provided government machinery for the making and enforcement of industrial awards.

Walker has argued that the principal distinguishing features of the period that led to the establishment of the institutional framework of Australian industrial relations were as follows:[43]

1. The development of a strong and vigorous union movement that achieved industrial power and interunion solidarity earlier than in most countries. Many of the nineteenth-century settlers who arrived in Australia had experienced the "dark Satanic mills" of industrial England, and some had been transported from Britain for participation in labor union activities.
2. The complete defeat of the labor unions following nationwide strikes in the 1890s. This convinced the labor movement of the need for political representation and led to the formation of the Australian Labor Party (ALP), which rapidly became a major political party.
3. The development of a labor movement that, despite its direct involvement in politics, was characterized by a nonrevolutionary and pragmatic ideology.
4. Acceptance by the labor movement of the concept of compulsory arbitration of industrial disputes.

The result of this process was twofold. First, the notion of conciliation and arbitration was written into the Australian Constitution, enacted in 1900. Section 51 (XXXV) of the constitution limits the role of the federal Parliament to making laws "with respect to conciliation and arbitration for the prevention and settlement of industrial disputes extending beyond the limits of any one state." Second, the Conciliation and Arbitration Act of 1904 established the institutional framework of Australian industrial relations, which is still in place today, making this system of conciliation and arbitration the oldest national labor relations mechanism in the Western industrial democracies. The centerpiece of this legislation was the establishment of a federal tribunal, today known as the Australian Conciliation and Arbitration Commission (ACAC).

The constitutional limitation of federal government intervention in industrial relations issues and the emphasis on the role of a federal tribunal in the Conciliation and Arbitration Act combined to quickly give the ACAC a leading role in Australian industrial relations. This system was explicitly designed to encourage union organization, and trade union membership rapidly increased from less than 5 percent to over 50 percent.[44] Employers who operated outside of the system were excluded from tariff protection—a major economic penalty. Faced with a rapidly growing labor movement and a centralized industrial relations system, employers developed strong employer associations to represent their interests before the federal and state tribunals. This remains a distinctive feature of Australian industrial relations.

The Australian industrial relations system is now over eighty years old. Although a strength of the present system is that the role of the ACAC allows for effective macrowage policy implementation, at the microlevel, serious labor market rigidities are apparent—for example, all companies in the industry face the same award regardless of cost structure and market position, and individual companies cannot restructure a federal award through private negotiations with labor unions. The Business Council of Australia has identified labor market failures as perhaps the single most important obstacle to improving the competitiveness of the Australian economy.[45] In recognition of these problems, the present labor federal government commissioned a Committee of Inquiry on industrial relations in Australia (generally referred to as the Hancock Committee in recognition of the chairman, Professor Hancock). The Hancock Committee has recommended a number of changes to the present system (the establishment of a new labor court, extending grievance procedures) but did not recommend total deregulation of the current centralized system.[46] To date, the federal government has not indicated its response to the Hancock report, but it is clearly aware that change is necessary if Australia wishes to successfully compete for a share in the dynamic growth of the Pacific Basin. The recent deregulation of the financial markets by the federal government is an illustration of this awareness.[47] However, given the collectivist and centralist traditions of Australian labor relations, dramatic changes are unlikely, and any assumption of convergence over time to a plant or enterprise collective bargaining system, as in the United States, would be unwarranted. Foreign companies doing business in Australia will still need to consider the industrial relations implications of their business strategy in considerable detail.

Multinational Operations: The Expatriate Employee

Although the number of American **expatriate employees** is relatively small, their importance to companies operating in the international markets is relatively large. Without effective expatriate employees—managers and nonmanagers—U.S. companies are essentially unable to operate abroad successfully. Nevertheless, the ineffectiveness of expatriate employees is alarmingly commonplace. Consequently, American-based multinational companies not only need to obtain candidates for expatriate positions but also must do things to ensure they are effective on the job. Because these activities are the essence of PHRM, it is useful to discuss the key personnel practices—especially selection and development—that can help companies more effectively manage their expatriate employees, particularly managers.

Selecting Expatriate Managers

A key in selecting any employee is knowing what the job entails. In general, six major categories of relations involve expatriate managers. These are shown in Exhibit 17.1.

Expatriate managers perform their daily activities in the context of the parent company's headquarters, the host country's government, the parent company's government, and a local culture that is often quite different from their home culture. In addition, expatriate managers typically operate in a culture with a different language—a major obstacle for many of them.[48] Thus, for expatriate managers to be successful, they need the skills not only to perform the specific type of job but also to perform the general duties required by these six categories. Using these criteria for selection, as well as for structuring a related management development program, can go a long way to increase the likelihood of expatriate managerial success.[49]

Exhibit 17.1	*Major Relations between the Expatriate Manager and Other Parties Interested in International Business*

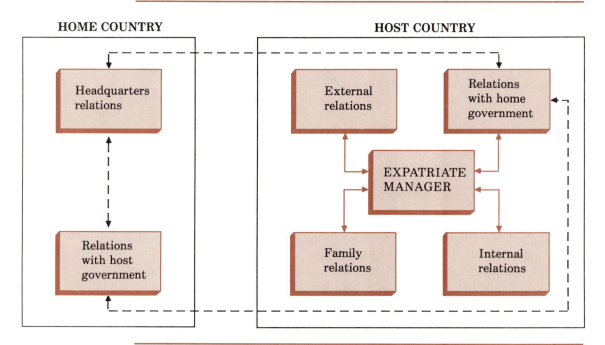

Source: "A Model for Developing Key Expatriate Executives," by Afzalur Rahim, copyright April, 1983. Reprinted with the permission of PERSONNEL JOURNAL, Costa Mesa, California; all rights reserved.

Management Development for Expatriate Managers

Management development of expatriates should take up where selection leaves off. Although only a few companies provide expatriate training, it is critical. The basic aspects of expatriate development include the following:

- Development of expatriates before, during, and after foreign assignments
- Orientation and training of expatriate families before, during, and after foreign assignments
- Development of the headquarters staff responsible for the planning, organization, and control of overseas operations[50]

This range of training is aimed at bringing about attitudinal and behavioral changes in the expatriates, their families, and the staff (here and abroad) responsible for the multinational operations. Exhibit 17.2 gives an idea of how extensive this training must be.

By having such an extensive management development effort for expatriates, multinational companies can help increase the effectiveness of their expatriate managers. Such a program can also increase the likelihood of getting more domestic managers to apply for expatriate positions. To really make expatriate positions attractive, however, multinational companies must also offer commensurate salaries.[51] This in turn makes it expensive for these companies to have expatriate managers. It would currently cost a company, for example, almost $200,000 a year to maintain an expatriate manager in Japan. Such a middle-level manager would earn about $60,000 at home. In addition to providing an attractive salary to expatriate managers, multinationals also need to provide an attractive package of indirect compensation, including things such as 401(k) plans.[52]

Although the selection and development of expatriate managers is a large and expensive undertaking, doing this well can help multinationals operate and compete more effectively abroad. And as the economy of nations becomes more interconnected, it becomes increasingly necessary for companies to operate as multinational firms, especially those in the United States. Hence, the importance of PHRM will continue to grow, for international as well as for national reasons.

Summary

This overview of PHRM practices in other countries was designed to give you an appreciation for their similarity to and divergence from those you have studied in relation to U.S. firms. Although it would be naive to suggest that foreign PHRM practices can easily be transported to America, an understanding of them may enable you to rethink the assumptions that underlie American PHRM practices. QWL efforts, quality circles, and proposed job security protection from unjust discharge are examples of PHRM practices that have been shaped by international comparisons and experimentation.

Exhibit 17.2   *A Model for the Development of*
Multinational Management

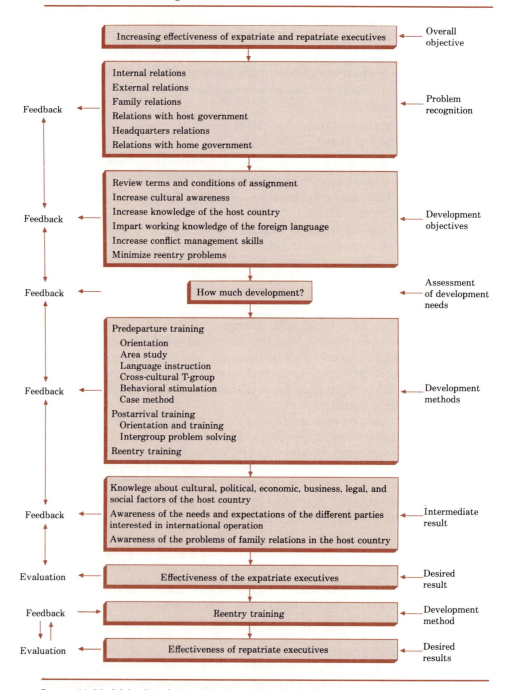

Discussion Questions

1. What is the most salient feature of Germany's training and development efforts?
2. Based on your understanding of PHRM practice abroad, in which country would you most like to be employed? Why?
3. Japanese concern for lifetime employment differs substantially from the career experiences of U.S. workers. What forces could potentially change U.S. employer practices in this direction? Which direction would you expect change to occur: Japanese employment becoming more like U.S. employment, or vice versa?
4. Does the United States employment, have an equivalent to "regular" and "nonregular" employees?
5. Go to the library and research a joint American-foreign investment in the United States (e.g., the GM-Toyota auto plant in California). How have basic assumptions about human resources been challenged by the partnership?
6. If you were to highlight American PHRM practices for other countries, what specific practices deserve mention because of their success here?
7. How do you suppose Japanese managers motivate workers when annual wage increases are so low in comparison to U.S. raises?
8. Compare and contrast collective bargaining in the United States with that in Japan. Would an enterprise union be legal in this country?
9. What can U.S. firms learn about new employee orientation from the Japanese?
10. What is codetermination? Why do you suppose it is possible in European countries? Is it likely to catch on in the United States over the next decade?

PC Project

A multinational company is seeking an internal candidate for promotion. The ideal candidate will speak French, have above-average performance reviews, earn between $35,000 and $55,000, and have been with the company at least twenty-four months. This PC project uses various data-base commands to select U.S.-based managers for foreign assignment. Various data from the human resource data base are provided. Selection criteria can be manipulated to select potential candidates.

| C | A | S | E | S | T | U | D | Y |

Going International

T he Japanese have come to the United States in a big way within the past decade. Perhaps nowhere is their presence felt as greatly as in the automotive industry. With trade protectionist sentiment of the U.S. auto industry waxing strong in the late seventies, and the Japanese yen faring strong against the U.S. dollar in the eighties, the Japanese have a strong incentive to invest offshore.

Much of the fascination of the American press with the Japanese style of management has been shaped by the joint GM-Toyota car venture in Freemont, California. The New United Motor Manufacturing, Inc. (NUMMI), plant has stirred considerable attention given the plant's spotty record under GM supervision. At the time the plant shut down in 1982, laying off five thousand workers, eight hundred grievances were pending and absenteeism rates exceeded 20 percent. Now under "new" management, the plant reports fewer than fifteen grievances and absenteeism rates of 2 to 3 percent.

The NUMMI plant produces 240,000 cars annually with half the work force previously employed by GM. A NUMMI UAW representative says that the Japanese took the same building and technology but applied a different management and production system. By 1990, industry projections show that Japanese investment in auto production will expand current output threefold to 1.6 million vehicles annually. New plants begun in the United States by Toyota, Mitsubishi, Mazda, and Subaru-Isuzu will join plants already operated by Honda, Nissan, and the NUMMI companies.

The question frequently asked is, what is the management style like in a Japanese-run company? The following are some selected comments and observations from workers who have experienced Japanese management both here and abroad. Based on these observations, can you provide an answer to how the Japanese are able to transform moribund U.S. companies into successful enterprises?

American worker views of Japanese:

A NUMMI worker observes that the pre-NUMMI workers were a reflection of the SOBs they worked for.

A current NUMMI employee observes that peer pressure and discipline raise tension: "If someone doesn't show up for work, there's a hardship.

If you want hierarchy, status, and frequent formal feedback, don't go to work for a Japanese company.

The Japanese agree to a plan and stick to it; the Americans abandon the plan as soon as the numbers start looking bad.

There are fewer meetings, since most problems get discussed and solved as they arise; the few meetings held are highly productive.

The Honda president in Marysville, Ohio, has no office; he sits in the same room with a hundred other workers.

Japanese managers elicit cooperation from others by presenting themselves as equals.

Japanese hire foreigners to work oversees, but it is a fad; those that are hired to work in the United States will reach an invisible ceiling.

Japanese managers on Americans:

American managers display more self-confidence.

American managers often make decisions faster than their Japanese counterparts who rely on participation and consensus.

Americans are quick to "pat their own backs while slipping the knives into their colleagues."

Americans are job-hoppers and do not display company loyalty.

Americans display a sense of lightheartedness and fun in comparison to the humorless grind of Japanese workers; Japanese are too serious.

And finally:

For all the intimacy between the Japanese and the Americans, they know so little about each other.

Notes

1. L. Smith, "Cracks in the Japanese Work Ethic," *Fortune*, 14 May 1984, 162–68.

2. For an extensive presentation of the issues and trends projected for PHRM in the 1980s, see S. J. Carroll and R. S. Schuler, eds., *Human Resources Management in the 1980s* (Washington, D.C.: Bureau of National Affairs, 1983).

3. This section and others on Japan are adapted in large part from M. S. O'Connor, *Report on Japanese Employee Relations Practices and Their Relation to Worker Productivity*, a report prepared for the study Mission to Japan, 8–23 Nov. 1980. M. S. O'Connor's permission to reproduce this material is appreciated. See also K. J. Duff, "Japanese and American Labor Law: Structural Similarities and Substantive Differences," *Employee Relations Law Journal* (Spring 1984): 629–41; R. Marsland and M. Beer, "The Evolution of Japanese Management: Lessons for U.S. Managers," *Organizational Dynamics* (Winter 1983): 49–67; E. Zussman, "Learning from the Japanese: Management in a Resource-Scarce World," *Organizational Dynamics* (Winter 1983): 68–76; E. Daspin, "Managing Expatriate Employees," *Management Review* (July 1985): 47–50.

4. "Moving Beyond Assembly Lines," *Business Week*, 27 July 1981, pp.87–88.

5. O'Connor, *Report on Japanese Practices*, pp. 8–9.

6. B. Teriet, "Flexiyear Schedules in Germany," *Personnel Journal* (June 1982): 428–429.

7. A. Templer, "Professional Challenges Parallel National Changes," *Personnel Administrator* (June 1983): 58–63.

8. Some, but not all, of the statutes define *age* so as to limit the effect of this particular ground of discrimination. Such definitions normally have an upper limit at age sixty-five, but the lower limit varies from nineteen to forty-five. This section on human rights in Canada was prepared by Robert J. Kerr, Professor of Law, University of Windsor, for use in this book.

9. "Canadian Human Rights Act," *Statutes of Canada*, 1976–77, chap. 33.

10. "The Individual's Rights Protection Act," *Revised Statutes of Alberta*, 1980, chaps. 1–2.

11. "Human Rights Code of British Columbia," *Revised Statutes of British Columbia*, 1979, chap. 186, as amended.

12. "The Human Rights Act," *Statutes of Manitoba*, 1974, chap. 65, as amended.

13. "Human Rights Code," *Revised Statutes of New Brunswick*, 1973, chap. H–11, as amended.

14. "The Newfoundland Human Rights Code," *Revised Statutes of Newfoundland*, 1970, chap. 262, as amended.

15. "Human Rights Act," *Statutes of Nova Scotia*, 1969, chap. 11, as amended.

16. "Human Rights Code," *Statutes of Ontario*, 1981, chap. 53.

17. "The conveyancing and Law of Property Act," *Revised Statutes of Ontario*, 1980, chap. 90, sect., 22, and "The Insurance Act," *Revised Statutes of Ontario*, 1980, chap. 218, sec. 117.

18. "Human Rights Act," *Statutes of Prince Edward Island*, 1975, chap. 72, as amended.

19. "Charter of Human Rights and Freedoms," *Revised Statutes of Quebec*, 1977, chap. C–12.

20. "The Saskatchewan Human Rights Code," *Statutes of Saskatchewan*, 1979, chap. S–24.1, as amended.

21. Templer, "Professional Challenges."

22. *Affirmative Action for Women*, vols. 1 and 2 (Canberra: Australian Government Publishing Service, 1984).

23. For a detailed description of the Sex Discrimination Act 1984, see C. E. Landau, "Recent Australian Legislation and Case-Law on Sex Equality at Work," *International Labour Review 124* (3) (1985): 335–51.

24. For a discussion of this issue, see B. J. Chapman, "Affirmative Action for Women: Economic Issues," *Australian Bulletin of Labour 11* (1984): 30–38; C. Davis and J. Nieuwenhuysen, *Equal Work Opportunity in Australia: Anti-Discrimination Laws and the Wider Issues*, Committee for Economic Development in Australia, Monograph M75, 1984.

25. O'Connor, *Report on Japanese Practices*, pp. 16–18.

26. For a detailed discussion of wage determination in Australia, see S. Deery and D. Plowman, "National Wage Determination," in *Australian Industrial Relations*, 2d ed. (Sydney: McGraw-Hill, 1985).

27. For a comparison of Australian and U.S industrial relations, see M. Derber, "Reflections on Aspects of the Australian and American Systems of Industrial Relations," in *Perspectives on Australian Industrial Relations*, ed. W. A. Howard (Melbourne: Longman Cheshire, 1984).

28. For a discussion of the advantages and disadvantages of centralized wage systems, see F. Bairstow, "The Trend toward Centralized Bargaining—A Patchwork Quilt of International Diversity," *Columbia Journal of World Business* 20 (1) (1985): 75–83.

29. Many large private-sector and public-sector organizations do have performance appraisal systems, but the emphasis of these systems tends to be on employee development rather than compensation decisions.

30. See also W. Ouchi, "The Broad Career Path of Japanese Executives," *Wall Street Journal*, 6 Apr. 1981.

31. J. Main, "The Trouble with Managing Japanese-Style," *Fortune*, 2 Apr. 1984, pp. 50–56; "The Japanese Manager Meets the American Worker," *Business Week*, 20 Aug. 1984, pp. 128–29; R. Novotny, "Working for the Japanese," *Personnel Administrator* (Feb. 1984): 15–19.

32. H. Tanaka, "The Japanese Method of Preparing To-day's Graduate to Become Tommorrow's Manager," *Personnel Journal* (Feb. 1980): 109–10.

33. Ibid., p. 110.

34. R. R. Rehder, "Education and Training: Have the Japanese Beaten Us Again? *Personnel Journal* (Jan. 1983): 42–47.

35. This section is based on the description by J. M. Geddes, "Germany Profits by Apprentice System," *Wall Street Journal*, 15 Sept. 1981.

36. P. G. Gyllenhammar, "How Volvo Adapts Work to People," *Harvard Business Review* (July–Aug. 1977): 106.

37. Gyllenhhammar, "How Volvo Adapts," p. 110.

38. R. H. Guest, "Quality of Work Life: Learning from Tarrytown," *Harvard Business Review* (July–Aug. 1979); 74–86.

39. J. M. Markham, "German Workers Watch the Clock," *New York Times*, 13 May 1984.

40. P. Revzin, "Swedes Gain Leisure, Not Jobs, by Cutting Hours," *Wall Street Journal*, 7 Jan. 1985.

41. D. J. Schneider, "Canadian and U.S. Brands of Unionism Have Distinctly Different Nationalities," *Management Review* (Oct. 1983): 31–32.

42. This observation was drawn from S. Deery and D. Plowman, *Australian Industrial Relations*, 3d ed. (Sydney: McGraw-Hill, 1985).

43. K. F. Walker, "The Development of Australian Industrial Relations in International Perspective," in *Perspectives on Australian Industrial Relations*, ed. W. A. Howard (Melbourne: Longman Cheshire, 1984).

44. For a comparison of laws governing union security in Australia and the United States, see B. Aaron, "Union Security in Australia and the United States," *Comparative Labor Law 6* (1984): 415–41.

45. "Management Pressures for Change and the Industrial Relations System," Business Council of Australia submission to the Alternatives to the Present Arbitration System Conference, Sydney, October 1984.

46. *Report of the Committee of Review: Australian Industrial Relations Law and Systems* (Canberra: Australian Government Publishing Service, 1985).

47. For an analysis of these changes, see "Australia Vaults Ahead with Free Banking," *Wall Street Journal*, 4 Nov. 1985.

48. D. M. Noer, *Multinational People Management: A Guide for Organizations and Employees* (Washington, D.C.: Bureau of National Affairs, 1975).

49. M. A. Conway, "Reducing Expatriate Failure Rates," *Personnel Administrator* (July 1984): 31–38; J. S. Lublin, "More Spouses Receive Help in Job Searches When Executives Take Positions Overseas," *Wall Street Journal*, 26 Jan. 1984; J. E. Heller, "Criteria for Selecting an International Manager," *Personnel* (May–June 1980): 47–55.

50. A. Rahim, "A Model for Developing Key Expatriate Executives," *Personnel Journal* (Apr. 1983): 315.

51. N. Shahzad, "The American Expatriate Manager," *Personnel Administrator* (July 1984): 23–28; C. G. Howard, "How Best to Integrate Expatriate Managers in the Domestic Organization," *Personnel Administrator* (July 1982): 27–33.

52. J. C. Roberts, "Section 401(k) and the Expatriate Employee," *Personnel Administrator* (July 1984): 18–21.

Personnel Research

———— *PHRM in the News* ————

Human Resources Managers Aren't Corporate Nobodies Anymore

It is the most dramatic change in a managerial function since financial executives rose to power in the 1960's conglomerate era. The trend reflects a more competitive business environment, the growing complexity of sociopolitical problems, and a change in corporate philosophy from asset management to operations management. At a time when companies are constantly acquiring, merging, and spinning off divisions, entering new business, and getting out of old ones, management must base strategic decisions more than ever on HR considerations—matching skills with jobs, keeping key personnel after a merger, and solving the human problems that arise from introducing new technology or closing a plant.

Source: Business Week, 2 December 1985, p. 58.

For PHRM, the trends outlined in the preceding "PHRM in the News" represent challenges and opportunities never before seen. But they also present unresolved questions—questions that managers in PHRM can address through personnel research and through playing the innovative and policy-formulating roles introduced in Chapter 1. These unresolved questions arise from exactly what has made the field so successful: the efforts to understand and improve individual and organizational performance and the demand for PHRM services. To address these unresolved questions, personnel research is often a necessity. Without research, there would be no knowledge to apply to the practical situation on the job. This chapter reviews methods and procedures used in conducting personnel research, discusses areas in which researchers are currently addressing unresolved questions, and describes recent personnel and human resource research findings. Primary emphasis is placed on validation research related to personnel assessments. Such personnel assessments include, but are not limited to, standardized paper-and-pencil ability tests, educational or experience requirements, interest inventories, lie detector tests, assessment center evaluations, scored interviews, performance appraisals, evaluations of advancement potential, training program evaluations, organizational surveys, and other assessment standards.

Conducting Personnel Research

Many of us have beliefs about why people perform as they do on the job. For instance, some managers may believe that providing annual performance feedback is just as effective in improving performance as consistent (e.g.,

*This chapter was prepared by Michael J. Burke, Graduate School of Business Administration, New York University.

daily) performance feedback. An organization may believe that the most important determinant of successful job performance for its salespeople is their level of interpersonal communication skills. Individuals and organizations possess numerous beliefs about why people perform as they do. In many instances, these beliefs may be conflicting. The question in such cases is, which beliefs are true? One way to test our beliefs is to conduct research. Understanding the research process helps individuals to solve personnel and human resource problems in organizations, to understand and apply the research results of others, to assess the accuracy of claims made by others concerning the benefits of new procedures, programs, equipment, and so on, and to evaluate the soundness of a theory relating to the performance of individuals in organizations.[1]

Empirical Research Process

Exhibit 18.1 shows the five basic steps needed to conduct sound empirical research. Initially, the personnel researcher will need to identify or be alerted to a problem and formulate a question or set of questions that will address the problem. At approximately the same time, the researcher will translate the research question into a testable **hypothesis**—a tentative statement about the relationship between two or more variables. Typically in personnel research, one variable—the variable that the personnel researcher has some control over or manipulates—is referred to as the **independent** or **predictor variable**. Examples of predictor variables are scores on selection tests or judgments of interviewers. The predictor variable is often hypothesized to have some effect on or relationship with a **dependent variable** or **criterion**. The criterion is frequently a measure of job performance, such as an accident rate, reject rate, supervisory performance rating, or training score.[2]

The second major step—the design of the research study—focuses on the development of a strategy to examine the validity or truth of the hypothesis. Next, the personnel researcher implements the study and obtains scores (numerical values) on the variables being examined. These scores are then collected and statistically analyzed to determine the observed relationship between the variables. Finally, conclusions are drawn as to whether or not the hypothesized relationships were supported, as well as to the implications of the results. The conclusions derived from the study often provide useful information for formulating new research questions.

A number of research strategies exist for studying personnel and human resource problems.[3] These include the laboratory experiment, field experiment, and field study. The laboratory experiment is characterized by (1) a setting explicitly created by the researcher to study a problem, (2) the researcher having control over the assignment of subjects to the experimental group (the group that receives a treatment, such as the independent variable) and control group (a comparison group that does not receive the independent variable), and (3) the researcher having control over all variables that can influence the dependent variable.

Exhibit 18.1   *The Empirical Research Process*

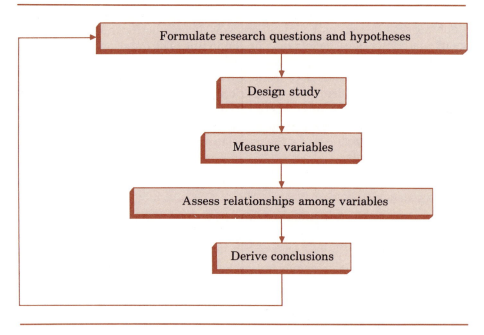

The field experiment is conducted in the actual setting (the organization); however, the researcher still manipulates one or more independent variables while maintaining as much control as possible over the situation. Like the laboratory experiment, the researcher then observes the effects of the manipulations on one or more dependent variables (criteria). Although the laboratory experiment and field experiment permit one to determine whether one variable—the independent variable—causes the dependent variable, these strategies are often costly and do not lend themselves well to studying the broad research questions that frequently confront the personnel researcher.

As noted in Chapter 11, however, these strategies may be useful in determining the effectiveness of certain organizational interventions such as training programs. Consequently, the personnel researcher relies more on strategies such as the field study, which does not involve the manipulation of variables. This type of study does, however, allow the researcher to systematically measure numerous variables and examine the relationships between these variables. In most cases, field studies gather data with questionnaires or through interviews. An important consideration of the personnel researcher employing the field study is to intrude as little as possible on the organization, department, or individuals being studied. The organizational surveys and the personnel test validation studies (to be discussed later) provide examples of different types of field studies.

Once a strategy or study design has been determined, the personnel researcher will need to implement the strategy. In doing so, the personnel researcher may measure variables with one or more of the methods discussed in Chapter 5. These methods could include, but are not limited to, questionnaires, psychological ability and personality tests, interviews, and observations of behavior. Regardless of the method used in measuring the relevant variables, the researcher is interested in the reliability as well as the validity of measurement. **Reliability** refers to the consistency of measurement, whereas **validity** relates to the truth or accuracy of measurement. The concept of correlation is discussed prior to the issues concerning reliability and validity.

Correlation Coefficient

The term *correlation* or observed **correlation coefficient** (denoted by the symbol *r*) is the degree to which two or more sets of measurements vary. A positive correlation exists when high values on one variable (e.g., job knowledge test) are associated with high values on another variable (e.g., high overall ratings of job performance). A negative correlation exists when high values on one variable are associated with low values on another variable. The correlation coefficient, which expresses the degree of linear relationship between two sets of scores, can range from positive to negative. The range is from $+1$ (a perfect positive correlation coefficient) to -1 (a perfect negative correlation coefficient). Illustrations of several linear relationships represented by plotting actual data of personnel selection test–job performance relationships are shown in Exhibit 18.2.

Scatterplots Indicating Possible Relationships between Personnel Selection Test Scores and Job Performance Scores   *Exhibit 18.2*

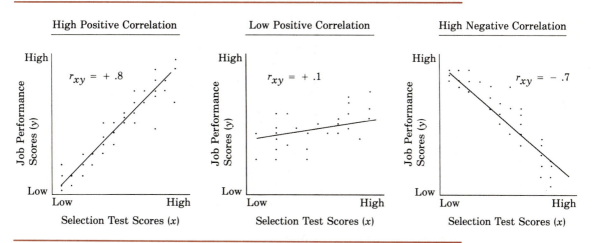

The correlation between scores on a predictor (x) and a criterion (y) is typically expressed for a sample as r_{xy}. If we did not have a sample but were able to compute our correlation on the population of interest, we would express the correlation as ρ_{xy} (where ρ is the Greek letter rho). In almost all cases, researchers do not have access to the population. Therefore, they must estimate the population correlation coefficient based on data from a sample of the population. For instance, an organization may desire to know the correlation between a computer programming ability test (scores on the predictor, x) and job performance (scores on a performance appraisal rating form, y) for all of its computer programmers, but decides it cannot afford to test all computer programmers (i.e., the population of interest). Instead the organization may select a sample of computer programmers and estimate the correlation coefficient in the population (ρ_{xy}) with the observed correlation in the sample (r_{xy}). Different types of correlations are used under various conditions.[4] The type of correlation coefficient computed will depend on how the predictor and criterion variables were measured.

Each scatterplot in Exhibit 18.2 shows a solid line that best describes the linear relationship between the two variables. This line is described by the general equation for a straight line ($y = ax + b$, where a is the slope of the line and b is where the line intercepts the y axis). The importance of this general equation, or **prediction equation**, is that it allows personnel researchers to estimate values of y (the criterion) from knowledge of x (the predictor). For example, we may conduct a study to determine the correlation between sales performance (i.e., dollar sales volume) and a predictor (such as number of years of sales experience) for a group of current job incumbents. Once we have developed a prediction equation, we can then estimate how well a sales applicant might perform on the job. Keep in mind that the correlation would provide an idea of how accurate our prediction equation is.

In many personnel research settings, researchers or decision makers often employ more than one predictor variable. This is noted in Chapter 5 when an organization uses a multiple predictor approach when making personnel selection and placement decisions. Similar to the single predictor approach, the purpose of multiple prediction is the estimation of a criterion (y) from a linear combination of m predictor variables ($\hat{y} = a + b_1x_1 + b_2x_2 + \ldots b_mx_m$).[5] Such an equation provides a **multiple-prediction** or **multiple-regression** equation. The b's are the regression weights applied to the predictor variables. In addition, the relationship between the predicted criterion ($\hat{y}$) and the actual criterion score (y) is referred to as the **multiple-correlation coefficient**. As will be discussed later, this is a common approach for predicting who will be successful employees.

Reliability

As noted earlier, an important component in the use of measures in personnel research—particularly personnel selection tests—is reliability. If a measure such as a personnel selection test is to be useful, it must yield reliable results. There are several ways of defining and interpreting test (i.e., predictor and criterion) reliability. Although the term *test* is traditionally used when discussing different types of reliability, the term as used here refers to either a predictor or criterion measure. Each of these methods, to be discussed later, is based on the notion that observed scores (x) comprise true scores (T) plus some error, or $x = T + E$,[6] where T is the expected score if there were no error in measurement. To the extent that observed scores on a test are correlated with true scores, a test is said to be reliable. That is, if observed and true scores could be obtained for every individual who took a personnel selection test, the squared correlation between observed and true scores in the population (ρ^2_{xT}) would be called the reliability coefficient for that selection test.

Reliability can also be defined as the correlation between observed scores on **parallel tests** (i.e., like tests that produce the same estimate of the true score).[7] If two parallel tests are given to a population of examinees, the correlation between the observed scores ($\rho_{xx'}$), where x and x' are the observed scores on the parallel tests) is the reliability coefficient. $\rho_{xx'}$ will be used to refer to the **population reliability coefficient,** even when parallel tests are not used to define reliability. Since true scores are theoretical and it is not possible to verify that tests are parallel, reliability must be estimated by other methods.

One means of estimating reliability ($\rho_{xx'}$) is **test-retest reliability.** This method is based on testing a sample of individuals twice with the same measure and then correlating the results to produce a reliability estimate, $r_{xx'} = \hat{\rho}_{xx'}$. A potential major problem with the test-retest reliability estimate is the possibility of **carry-over effects** between the testing sessions: the second testing is influenced by the first testing. For instance, some people may improve between testing sessions.

Another means of estimating the reliability of a measure is by correlating scores on alternate forms of the measure. **Alternate test forms** are any two test forms that have been constructed in an effort to make them parallel, and they may have equal (or very similar) observed score means, variances (i.e., a measure of the spread of scores about the means), and correlations with other measures.[8] They are also intended to be similar in content and designed to measure the same traits.[9] The use of alternate or parallel forms, however, does not necessarily eliminate the possibility of carry-over effects related to response styles, moods, or attitudes.

A problem with test-retest reliability and alternate forms reliability is the necessity of testing twice. **Internal consistency reliability,** however, is estimated based on only one administration of a measure. The most common method, **coefficient** α (Greek letter alpha), yields a **split-half reliability** estimate. That is, the measure (e.g., test) is divided into two parts, which are considered alternate forms of each other, and the relationship between these two halves is an estimate of the test's (i.e., the measure's) reliability. The major advantage of internal consistency reliability estimates is that the reliability of a measure can be estimated based on one administration of the measure.

In summary, the personnel researcher is interested in assessing the reliability of measures based on one or more of the previous methods. The researcher must evaluate the reliability of measures, since reliability is a necessary condition for determining validity. We must be able to measure something (an ability) consistently (reliably) before the measure is of any value in relating it to other measures. That is, reliability sets an upper limit on how high a measure can correlate with another measure, since it is highly unlikely that a measure will correlate higher with a different measure than it does with itself.

Validity

As defined in the *Principles for the Validation and Use of Personnel Selection Procedures* (American Psychological Association), validity is the degree to which inferences from scores on tests or assessments are supported by evidence. This definition implies that validity refers to the inferences made from use of a measure, not to the measure itself. Three primary strategies have been identified to gather evidence to support or justify the inferences made from scores on measures: criterion-related, content-oriented, and construct validation strategies.

Criterion-related Strategy.   A criterion-related strategy is an assessment of how well a measure (i.e., predictor) forecasts a criterion such as job performance. The two types of criterion-related validation strategies are concurrent and predictive—shown in Exhibit 18.3.

Concurrent validation evaluates the relationship between a predictor and a job criterion score for all employees in the study at the same time. For example, this strategy could be used to determine the correlation between years of experience and job performance. PHRM would collect from each person in the study information about years of experience and performance scores. All persons in the study would have to be working in similar jobs, generally in the same job family or classification. Then a correlation would be computed between the predictor scores and criterion scores.

Exhibit 18.3	*Criterion-related Validation Strategies*	
	Concurrent Study	
Time 1	*Time 1*	*Time 1*
Test (predictor) scores are gathered	Criterion scores are gathered	Correlation between scores on predictor (x) and criterion (y), r_{xy}, is calculated
	Predictive Study	
Time 1	*Time 2*	*Time 2*
Test (predictor) scores are gathered	Criterion scores are gathered	Correlation between scores on predictor (x) and criterion (y), r_{xy}, is calculated

The steps in determining predictive validity are similar, except that the predictor is measured sometime before the criterion is measured, as shown in Exhibit 18.3. Thus, the **predictive validity** of a predictor could be determined by measuring an existing group of employees on a predictor and waiting to gather their criterion measures later, or by hiring a group of job applicants regardless of their scores on the predictor and measuring them on the criterion later. For either type of criterion-related validation strategy, it is important to demonstrate that the predictors and performance criteria are related to the duties of the job.

The classic example of a predictive validation study is AT&T's Management Progress Study.[10] In that study, personnel researchers at AT&T administered an assessment center, similar to the one described in Chapter 5, to 422 male employees, stored the results, and waited eight years before evaluating their predictions of how far these individuals would progress in AT&T's management hierarchy. For a group of college graduates, the predictions were highly accurate; a correlation of .71 was obtained between the assessment center predictions and level of management achieved. In addition, a twenty-year follow-up of the original predictions showed that the assessment center was still useful in predicting who would reach even higher levels in AT&T's management hierarchy.

An assessment of criterion-related validity is often important for many personnel decisions. In fact, it is the heart of most personnel decisions. The greater the validity coefficient for a test, the more efficient selection and placement decisions will be. And the more efficient these decisions, the more productive the work force will be.

Although the *Uniform Guidelines* require organizations to demonstrate the job relatedness of a selection procedure, they do not specify the actual degree of job relatedness. Thus, an organization can claim its selection procedures are job related or permit valid inferences even though the correlation coefficient between the predictor and criterion is .3 rather than .6 or .7. Although the *Uniform Guidelines* do not specify the magnitude of the correlation necessary to claim job relatedness, they do indicate that the correlation should be statistically significant.

An important aspect of criterion-related validity is the relevance or appropriateness of the criterion being correlated with the predictor. In a criterion-related validity study, the predictors should be shown to correlate with the criteria, and the criteria should be shown relevant and important to the jobs in question. Failure to establish these points was the heart of the Supreme Court's decision in the *Albemarle* case, in which the Court first looked at a validation study:

> The study in this case involved no analysis of the attributes of, or the particular skills needed in, the studied job groups. There is accordingly no basis for concluding that "no significant differences" exist among the lines of progression, or among distinct job groupings within the studied lines of progression.
>
> Albemarle's supervisors were asked to rank employees by a "standard" that was extremely vague and fatally open to divergent interpretations. . . . (T)here simply was no way to determine whether the criteria actually considered were sufficiently related to the Company's legitimate interest in job-specific ability to justify a testing system with a racially discriminatory impact.

The fact that the best of those employees working near the top of a line of progression score well on a test does not necessarily mean that that test, or some particular cut-off score on the test, is a permissible measure of the minimal qualifications of new workers entering lower level jobs.

Albemarle's validation study dealt only with job-experienced white workers; but the tests themselves are given to new job applicants who are younger, largely inexperienced, and in many instances nonwhite.

On many occasions, employers are not able to obtain sufficient empirical data for a criterion-related validity study.[11] Consequently, other methods of validation are helpful in determining the validity of measures used in personnel research.

Content-oriented Strategy.   A **content-oriented validation** strategy differs from a criterion-related strategy in that it estimates or judges the relevance of a predictor as a sample of the relevant situations (e.g., behaviors or tasks) that make up a job. In essence, job relatedness here is an estimation or judgment. According to the *Uniform Guidelines,* "A selection procedure can be supported by a content validity strategy to the extent it is a representative sample of the content of the job." The administration of a typing test (actually a job sample test if used for typists) as a selection device for hiring typists is a classic example of a predictor judged to be content valid.[12] In this case, the predictor is a skill related to a task that is actually part of the job. Thus, to employ a content validation strategy, one must know the duties of the actual job.[13] As discussed in Chapter 3, information about job tasks and duties can be obtained using one or more job analysis procedures.

Job analysis is discussed here as a critical element in content validation. It should be regarded as the starting point and the thread that ties together any basic personnel selection and validation study. It is also a critical activity in determining construct validity.

Construct Strategy.   Instead of showing a direct relationship between a test or other selection information (e.g., education or experience levels) and job criteria, selection methods seek to measure (often by tests) the degree to which an applicant possesses abilities and characteristics (psychological traits) that are deemed necessary for successful job performance. These underlying psychological traits are called **constructs** and include, among many others, intelligence, leadership ability, verbal ability, interpersonal sensitivity, and analytical ability. Constructs deemed necessary for doing well on job criteria are inferred from job behaviors and activities (duties) indicated in the job analysis.

A **construct validation** study attempts to demonstrate that a relationship exists between a selection procedure or test (a measure of the construct) and the psychological trait (construct) it seeks to measure. For example, does a reading comprehension test reliably and accurately measure how well people can read and understand what they read? To demonstrate construct validity, one would need data showing that high scorers on the test actually read more difficult material and are better readers than low scorers on the test, and that reading ability is related to the duties shown in the job description. Other evidence that the test is measuring the relevant construct could be obtained based on its relationship to other measures that assess both similar and unrelated constructs.[14] In essence, construct validity is not established with a single study. Rather, it is assessed based on the cumulation of a body of empirical evidence. This evidence is likely to include information gathered from both criterion-related and content-oriented validation studies.

Personnel Selection

The primary validation strategy employed in personnel research has been the criterion-related validation strategy. The major steps that make up this strategy are shown in Exhibit 18.4. This exhibit underscores the importance of job analysis in the criterion-related validation process. That is, as discussed in Chapters 3 and 5, job analysis provides the necessary information for both identifying and developing predictors and criterion measures.

Once these measures have been developed and administered to a sample, the data are collected, and criterion-related validity coefficients are then computed. Predictors that significantly contribute to the prediction of job performance criteria are typically chosen for operational use in selecting employees. After the final predictor battery has been determined and is in operational use for a period of time, an advantageous step for the organization is to conduct follow-up studies. These follow-up studies might include a reassessment of the predictor-criterion relationship, an evaluation of the usefulness of equations for predicting job performance, an estimation of the economic benefits from the use of a predictor or set of predictors (i.e., a selection battery), and a determination of whether or not the selection program is fair and in compliance with government guidelines. The following sections discuss recent developments in personnel research related to these types of follow-up studies. Assessing compliance with current government guidelines was previously discussed in Chapter 5.

Estimating Population Validity Coefficients

As discussed in the section on correlation coefficients, if we were able to assess the relationship between a predictor and a criterion in a population of interest, with no measurement error, then we would have computed the true (population) correlation or validity coefficient, ρ_{xy}. Since we almost never have the population available and almost always have measurement error, our observed correlation coefficients (validity coefficients in personnel selection) underestimate the population validity coefficients between selection tests and job performance criteria.

Although predictor and criterion reliability have been noted as statistical artifacts that lower predictor-criterion relationships, other factors are also known to lower these estimated true relationships. Two other primary statistical artifacts, which obscure true relationships, are sampling error and range restriction. **Sampling error** refers to the inaccuracy in estimating the true population validity resulting from the use of a sample size that is less than the population when computing the validity coefficient. **Range restric-**

Exhibit 18.4   **Steps for Implementing and Evaluating a**
Personnel Selection Program

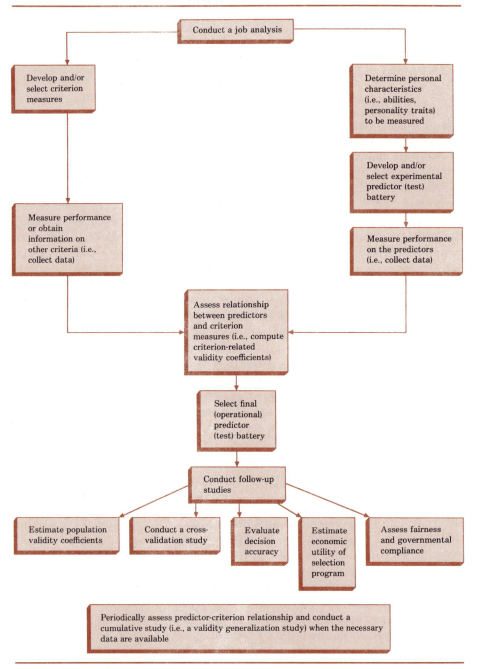

tion relates to computing a correlation or validity coefficient between the predictor and criterion scores for a restricted group of individuals. That is, the validity coefficient in personnel research is typically not computed on the entire range of scores for which the predictor will actually be used. This is evident when validity coefficients are based on a concurrent test validation study where only predictor scores obtained from the restricted group (i.e., current job incumbents as opposed to the entire range, which would include all applicant predictor scores) are used. We simply cannot hire all applicants and then relate their predictor scores to scores on a criterion measure such as a job performance rating. For this latter case, the resulting observed validity coefficient typically underestimates the population validity coefficient.

Formulas have been developed to remove the effects of predictor unreliability, criterion unreliability, and range restriction and for determining sampling error variance. That is, one would use the correction formulas to remove the influence of the previous statistical artifacts and, consequently, obtain a better idea of the predictor-criterion relationship in the relevant population. Recently, a number of studies have been conducted to examine the usefulness of these correction formulas in estimating population validity coefficients. These studies have examined the effects of variations in sample size,[15] range restriction,[16] and reliability[17] on the size and variability of observed validity coefficients. These studies have improved our understanding of how observed validity coefficients are affected by measurement error and factors such as range restriction. As a result, this line of research has assisted the personnel and human resource management field in gaining a better grasp of the true (population) relationships between predictors and criteria. Although this line of research has been helpful, most of the studies examined the impact of correcting observed validity coefficients for only one factor (e.g., range restriction). More recently, personnel researchers have been exploring the effects of correcting correlation coefficients for both range restriction and unreliability of measures.[18] The hope is that continued research in this latter area will yield valuable information concerning the true relationships between our predictors and criteria. As will be discussed later, knowledge of such relationships will greatly enhance our determination of the practical benefits (e.g., economic gains) to be realized from the use of job-related measures.

Validity Generalization

Over the past fifty years, hundreds of validation studies have been conducted in organizations to determine the predictive effectiveness of personnel selection measures (e.g., ability tests) for selecting and placing individuals. Often the validity coefficients for the same or similar predictor-criterion relationship differed substantially from one setting to another. Although personnel researchers were aware that these differences between the same or similar predictor-criterion relationships were affected by the statistical artifacts noted earlier (i.e., range restriction, predictor unreliability, criterion unreliability, and sampling error), only recently were corrections for these statistical artifacts integrated into systematic procedures for estimating to what degree true validity estimates, for the same predictor-criterion relationship, generalize across settings.[19]

A series of studies has applied **validity generalization** procedures to validity coefficient data for clerical jobs, computer programming jobs, petroleum industry jobs, and so on.[20] In general, these investigations showed that the effects of criterion unreliability, predictor unreliability, range restriction, and sample size accounted for most of the observed variance in validity coefficients for the same or similar test-criterion relationship within an occupation (i.e., job grouping or job family). Thus, the estimated true validity coefficients (i.e., ρ_{xy} or corrected validity coefficients) were higher and less variable than when they were left as observed validity coefficients (i.e., $r_{xy}s$ or observed validity coefficient not corrected for unreliability, range restriction, or sample size).

The implications of these findings are that inferences (predictions) from scores on personnel selection tests can be transported across situations for similar jobs. That is, if two similar jobs exist in two parts of an organization or in two different organizations, a given selection test should have approximately the same validity coefficients for both jobs. This assumes, however, that some degree of similarity in jobs and conditions can be first identified. Similarity of jobs and conditions are judged by results of job analyses.[21] If validity generalization can be successfully argued, an organization can save a great deal of time and money developing valid, job-related predictors. In essence, if the inferences from a predictor for a job have already been established, it may be utilized as a predictor in another job, perhaps newly created, that is similar to the original jobs that were part of the validity generalization study.

More recently, the concept of validity generalization (or what is also commonly referred to as meta-analysis),[22] has been applied to other areas of personnel research than just personnel selection.[23] This latter research has assisted the personnel and human resource field in gaining a better understanding of the true effectiveness of interventions such as training programs, goal-setting programs, and performance measurement (appraisal) programs. In addition to determining how well validity generalizes across settings, personnel researchers are interested in how stable their prediction equations are across samples.

Cross-validation

As discussed in the section on correlation coefficients, personnel researchers often develop prediction equations (or regression equations) with multiple predictors. For the prediction equations to be of any practical use, they must produce consistent results. **Cross-validation** is a procedure for determining the amount of capitalization on chance that has affected the prediction equation (the **regression weights**). If the results were not stable, we might have to develop and use a different equation in each new sample or setting. This would be costly and time-consuming for most organizations.

Traditional or empirical cross-validation typically involved holding out some of the data (sample). The equation developed in the initial sample could then be applied to the holdout sample to evaluate its stability. In general,

this latter procedure has been shown to be less precise than formulas for estimating the stability of regression equations. The reason for the increased
precision when using formula-based estimates is that all information (the total sample) is used at once in estimating the original weights.

As is the case in personnel selection, one is interested in how well the regression weights (the *b*'s noted earlier) estimated in a sample will predict the
criterion value of new subjects (e.g., job applicants) not used in the estimation sample.[24] Assume we are interested in determining the criterion-related
validity of three assessment center exercises (in basket, group exercise, and
ability test) for predicting supervisory performance ratings. After collecting
assessment center exercise scores and performance ratings, we may find a
multiple correlation between the measures of .60. We are unsure, however,
how useful the equation for predicting supervisory ratings will be in another
sample. Using a formula to estimate this usefulness, we might find that our
multiple correlation in another sample (based on the regression weights developed in the original sample) drops to around .40. Although lower than .60,
this **population cross-validated multiple correlation** may still have substantial practical utility for the organization.

Decision Accuracy

An important step in determining the practical usefulness of a selection procedure is assessing whether the decisions one reaches by use of the procedure are more accurate than using no predictor. The classical validity approach to assessing the practical utility of a selection procedure considers
only the validity coefficient. The degree of decision accuracy, however, is dependent not only on the validity coefficient but also on the base rate of success. In using valid predictors, an organization knows that they will result in
a greater success rate than not using them (i.e., a greater percentage of predicted successful employees of those hired—**predictor rate**—than the organization could have obtained if the applicants had been selected at random—
base rate.) For example, if the base rate is .5 (half the applicants hired at random turn out to be good performers) and the predictor rate is .8 (80 percent
of the applicants hired by using a particular predictor turn out to be successful), the percentage of correct predictions over and above the base rate is .30.

A series of tables was developed to portray the increase in the percentage
of correct predictions over and above the base rate as the cutting score (i.e.,
the predictor score above which we predict success and below which we predict failure) is raised, given a **selection ratio**[25] (percentage hired) and correlation coefficient.[26] This increase in the percentage of correct predictions can
be illustrated by using Exhibit 18.5. Exhibit 18.5 depicts the possible selection decision outcomes for a population of 500. The base rate of success is .2
or

$$\text{base rate of success} = \frac{A + B}{A + B + C + D} = \frac{70 + 30}{70 + 30 + 270 + 130} = .2$$

That is, 20 percent of the applicants would be successful if we had no valid
selection procedure and hired at random. However, with a validity coeffi-

Exhibit 18.5   **Personnel Selection Decision Outcomes (Based on a Selection Ratio of .4, Base Rate of .2, and a Validity Coefficient of .5)**

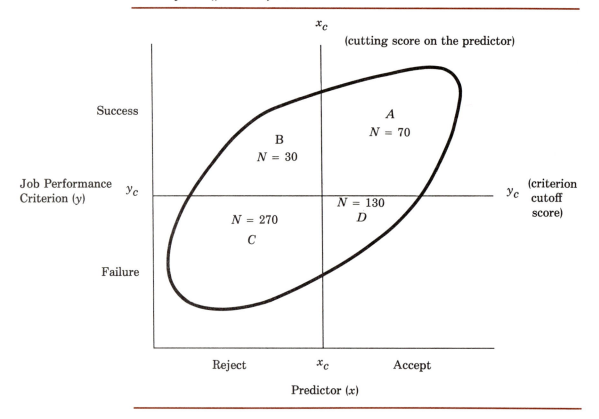

cient for a selection procedure of .5 and a cutting score on the predictor at a value of x_c (so that we end up with a selection ratio of .4), we can see how our prediction accuracy has increased. In fact, our percentage of correct predictions for those selected improves 15 points over the base rate of .2:

$$\% \text{ increase in correct predictions} = \frac{A}{A + D} - \frac{A + B}{A + B + C + D} = .15$$

where the first quantity is our predictor rate and the latter is the base rate. In addition, a more elaborate set of tables, referred to as **expectancy tables** or **expectancy charts**, which convert the correlation coefficient to frequencies of correct predictions have been presented.[27] For these latter tables, the predictor distribution is divided into five equal intervals. Then, for a particular base rate of success and a specified validity coefficient, the percentage of individuals in each quintile (score range) on the predictor who fall in the success category (i.e., above the base rate) is determined. The validity coefficient can be transformed to its equivalent increase in the criterion mean by use of the Naylor-Shine tables.[28]

We have now moved from discussions of predictive validity to that of predictive accuracy. At this point, we might ask the question, does a 15 percent increase in predictive accuracy resulting from the use of any selection procedure always result in the same economic benefit to an organization? As we will see later, the benefit of an increase in predictive accuracy is dependent on the costs to obtain it as well as the payoff associated with the correct predictions.[29] Thus, we now move from a concern with predictive accuracy to a discussion of the practical usefulness of this increase in the accuracy of predictions.

Utility Analysis

As indicated in Exhibit 18.4, follow-up studies can be conducted to evaluate the economic utility of personnel selection programs. This discussion initially focuses on assessing the economic utility of personnel selection programs. A subsequent section discusses how to evaluate the economic impact of training, absenteeism, and turnover. The financial impact of personnel selection programs and other organizational interventions is of particular interest to many human resource professionals.[30] This interest is being spurred by the recent emphasis on evaluating human resource programs via **decision-theoretic utility equations.**[31]

The following is an example of how decision-theoretic utility equations can be used for evaluating the economic impact of alternative personnel selection procedures. Recently, decision-theoretic utility equations were expanded to include economic concepts such as taxes and variable costs that are considered by organizational decision makers.[32] The following equation, which incorporates these economic concepts, can be employed when comparing two alternative personnel selection procedures:

$$\Delta U = N_s \left[\sum_{t=1}^{T} (1/(1 + i)^t) \, SD_y \, (1 + V) \, (1 - TAX) \, (\hat{\rho}_1 - \hat{\rho}_2) \, \bar{z}_s \right] - (C_1 - C_2)(1 - TAX)] \tag{18.1}$$

where

ΔU = total estimated dollar value of replacing one selection procedure (1) with another procedure (2) after variable costs, taxes, and discounting,

N_s = the number of employees selected,

T = the number of future time periods,

t = the time period in which a productivity increase occurs,

i = the discount rate,

SD_y = the standard deviation of job performance in dollars,

V = the proportion of SD_y represented by variable costs,

TAX = the organization's applicable tax rate,

$\hat{\rho}_1$ = the estimated population validity coefficient between scores on one selection procedure and the criterion,

$\hat{\rho}_2$ = the estimated population validity coefficient between scores on an alternative selection procedure and scores on the criterion,

$\bar{z}_s$ = the mean standard score on the selection procedure of those selected (this is assumed to be equal in the equation 18.1 for each selection procedure),

C_1 = the total cost of the first selection procedure, and

C_2 = the total cost of the alternative selection procedure.[33]

For illustration purposes, let us employ a portion of the utility analysis information collected at a large international manufacturing company, which we will call Company A.[34] Company A undertook a utility analysis to obtain an estimate of the economic impact of their current selection procedure for selecting sales managers as compared with their previously used interviewing selection programs. The current selection procedure was a managerial assessment center. Although the assessment center had been in operation for seven years at the time of the utility analysis, a value for T of four years was used, since this was the average time (tenure) for the 29 (N in equation 18.1) sales managers who had been selected from a pool of 132 candidates. A primary objective of the utility analysis at Company A was to compare the estimated dollar value of selecting 29 managers with the assessment center with what the economic gain would have been if 29 sales managers were selected by an interviewing program.

Company A employed an interdisciplinary approach when estimating the various components of equation 18.1. For instance, values of V and TAX were provided by the accounting and tax departments, respectively. These values were $-.05$ for V and .49 for TAX. V was considered the proportion of dollar sales volume as compared with operating costs. Since there was a positive relationship between combined operating costs (e.g., salary, benefits, supplies, automobile operations) and sales volume, a value for V of $-.05$ was used in equation 18.1. In addition, the value for i, .18, was based on examination of corporate financial documentation. The accounting department also provided the figure for C_1 (the total cost of the assessment center), $263,636. Based on 29 selected individuals, the cost of selecting one district sales manager was computed to be about $9,091. The estimated total cost to select 29 sales managers by the previously used one-day interviewing program was $50,485 (i.e., the value for C_2 in equation 18.1). Let us now turn to the final four components of equation 18.1: $\hat{\rho}_1$, $\hat{\rho}_2$, $\bar{z}_s$, and SD_y.

$\hat{\rho}_1$, the estimated population validity coefficient for the assessment center, was obtained by correlating five assessment dimension scores (i.e., scores for planning and organizing, decision making, stress tolerance, sensitivity, and persuasiveness) with an overall performance rating. The multiple correlation between the measures was .61. Next, the population cross-validated multiple correlation was calculated using the formulas mentioned in the section on cross-validation. This resulting value of .41 was finally corrected for range restriction and criterion reliability to yield an estimated value of .59 for $\hat{\rho}_1$.

Since Company A had not conducted a criterion-related validity study for the interviewing selection program, a value was obtained from the validity generalization literature.[35] The value of $\hat{\rho}_2$ for the interviewing program was .16. In addition, the standard score on the predictor ($\bar{z}_s$) was determined to be .872. This value was assumed to be the same for both the assessment center and interviewing program.

The final and traditionally the most difficult component to estimate in equation 18.1 has been SD_y. As indicated earlier, SD_y is an index of the variability of job performance in dollars in the relevant population. The relevant population or group for evaluating a selection procedure is the applicant group. The applicant group is the group with which the selection procedure is used. When evaluating the economic utility of organizational interventions, however, the relevant group is current employees. Since the intervention would be applied to current employees, the appropriate value of SD_y is for this group. In this latter case, if the SD_y were estimated from the applicant group, it could be an overestimate.

A former assumption was that cost-accounting methods could be used to estimate SD_y, but experience has revealed that these methods are extremely difficult and expensive and, in the end, yield estimates of uncertain accuracy.[36] A potential solution to this problem is obtaining a judgment-based estimate of SD_y. A judgment-based method is based on the following reasoning: If performance on the criterion in dollar terms is normally distributed, then the difference between the value of the performance by the average employee and that of an employee at the 85th or 15th percentile is equal to SD_y; and that experienced supervisors can estimate these values. At present, supervisors have provided these estimates for jobs such as sales manager,[37] computer programmer,[38] insurance counselor,[39] and entry-level park ranger.[40] The approximate value for a sales manager, $30,000, will be used for SD_y in the present example.

Placing the previous values into the utility analysis equation would result in a value of approximately $316,460. This value represents the estimated present value, over a four-year time period, to the organization from the use of the assessment center in place of an interviewing program to select 29 sales managers. Although the cost of the interviewing program is only about one-fifth of the assessment center cost, the estimated dollar gain from use of the assessment center instead of the interviewing program is substantial. This result is primarily due to the greater predictive effectiveness (i.e., higher validity coefficient) of the assessment center.

Estimating the Economic Impact of Organizational Interventions, Absenteeism, and Turnover

Organizational Interventions

Although research on the economic utility of personnel selection programs has been enlightening, more recently advances have been made in the utility analysis of organizational interventions.[41] The following is an example of an evaluation of the economic value of a managerial training program.

In illustrating the value of decision-theoretic utility analysis for estimating the dollar worth of a training program, use is made of a hypothetical example. Suppose there are 200 managers of computer programmers in a large data processing company and that half are assigned randomly to a leadership training course while the other 100 managers continue their jobs as usual and serve as a comparison group. The cost of the leadership training course is $500 per manager. Each manager supervises a unit of approximately 10 computer programmers. The outcome variable is the number of error-free computer programs produced by each unit. The t test for the difference between the experimental and comparison groups is statistically significant. The important question is, What is the dollar value of this training program to the data processing company?

Since the t statistic does not provide a direct answer to this question, we must determine the average gain in performance due to the leadership training in standard score units and then convert this statistic to dollars. The following equation permits us to make such an estimation of the economic value of the training program:

$$\Delta U = [\sum_{t=1}^{T} (1/(1 + i)^t) N SD_y d_t (1 + V) (1 - TAX)] - NC (1 - TAX) \tag{18.2}$$

where

ΔU = the dollar value of the training program,

T = the number of years' duration of the training effect on performance,

N = the number trained,

d_t = the true difference in job performance between the average trained and untrained employee in SD units,

SD_y = the standard deviation of job performance in dollars of the untrained group, and

C = the cost of training per trainee.

The other terms are as defined in equation 18.1.

Since we have already discussed how most parameters of this equation can be estimated, let us see how the parameter d_t in equation 18.2 is estimated in our example. The performance mean of the trained group was 55, whereas it was 50 for the untrained group. The standard deviation (SD) of the number of error-free programs for both groups was 10. In cases in which the SD is unequal for the two groups, the control group SD should be used because of the possibility that training may affect the SD of the experimental group.[42] The observed gain in performance in standard score units is:

$$d_t = \frac{55 - 50}{10} = .5$$

Since this difference has not been attenuated by criterion unreliability, we needn't correct for this effect. If the criterion was not measured with perfect reliability, criterion unreliability would result in a biased (conservative) estimate of d_t. Furthermore, let us assume that the effect of training will last 3 years.

Since we are concerned here with a management position and do not have available an estimate of SD_y, we might consider a percentage of mean salary as a conservative estimate of SD_y. Recently, evidence has been provided to support the assertion that SD_y for a given job falls between 40 percent and 70 percent of yearly salary.[43] Thus, with knowledge of the mean annual salary for a group, SD_y can be conservatively estimated to be 40 percent of this value. For our example, a mean computer programming manager salary of $33,000 would yield an SD_y estimate of $13,200. Using this value for SD_y, the previous values for the training components (i.e., .5 for d_t and 3 for T), as well as the previously noted economic values in the selection utility example ($i = .18$, $V = -.05$, and $TAX = .49$), we are now ready to calculate the dollar value of the training program:

$$\Delta U = [\sum_{t=1}^{T} (1/(1 + i)^t) N SD_y d_t (1 + V)(1 - TAX)] - N C (1 - TAX)$$

$$\Delta U = [\sum_{t=1}^{3} (1/(1 + .18)^t) 100 \; 13{,}200 \; .5 \; (1 - .05)(1 - .49)] - 100 \; 500 \; (1 - .49)$$

The expected economic value of the managerial training program is $669,767. If this example is realistic, then the impact of organizational interventions on the bottom line of the company is substantial.

The realism of this example is highly dependent on the assumed d_t value of .5. The important question is whether this value is reasonable for organizational interventions such as managerial training programs. A quantitative review of the managerial training literature has recently indicated the mean true effect size (d corrected for measurement error) across 17 studies (with 118 effects) for human relations or leadership training with respect to subjective behavior criteria (e.g., supervisory ratings) is .44.[44] Thus, the present assumed value is fairly reasonable.

Measuring the Costs of Absenteeism

Let's assume your curiosity has been aroused to the point where you would like to estimate the cost of absenteeism to your organization for a one-year period—1978, for example.[45] As in most research projects, the first step involves gathering information. Assuming your organization regularly computes traditional absence statistics and labor cost data, much of the information you will need should not be too burdensome or time-consuming to gather. Some estimates will involve discussions with other staff and management personnel, but the overall time you spend on this project should be well worth the effort.

As an aid in computing estimates for your organization, we'll provide examples at each step along the way. Using the hypothetical firm Acme International, a medium-sized steel manufacturer employing 1,200 people, our examples should provide a realistic portrayal of the problems and costs related to employee absenteeism. The following is an outline of the data you'll need to collect and compute:

1. *The organization's total worker-hours lost to absenteeism for the period for all employees—blue-collar, clerical, management, and professional.* In-

clude time lost for all reasons except organizationally sanctioned time off, such as vacations, holidays, official "bad weather" days, and so on. Be sure to include both whole-day and part-day absences in computing the total hours lost. Include, for example, absences resulting from illness, accidents, funerals, jury duty, emergencies, personal time off, and doctor's appointments whether "excused" or "unexcused."

In our example, let's assume Acme International's personnel records show 9,792 days, or 78,336 total worker-hours, lost to employee absenteeism for all reasons except vacations and holidays in 1978. This figure represents an absence rate of 3.4 percent for the year—about average for manufacturing firms.

A great deal of confusion exists concerning the computation of absence rates, as a number of different formulas have reportedly been published and used. The formula used here is recommended by the U.S. Department of Labor and also used by the majority of firms responding to absenteeism surveys conducted by the Bureau of National Affairs (see "Employee Absenteeism and Turnover," *Personnel Policies Forum*, survey no. 106, Washington, D.C., Bureau of National Affairs, 1974).

$$\text{Absenteeism rate} = \frac{\text{Number of worker-days lost through job absence during the period}}{\text{Average number of employees} \times \text{number of work days}} \times 100$$

This computation may not be quite as straightforward as it appears. Often, wage earners are not covered under a sick leave plan while salaried employees are. Look closely at your organization's employee benefits program to determine if your estimates should reflect differential absenteeism costs for employee groups who receive sick pay and those who do not. In addition, some organizations have policies that define the kinds of absences for which employees are not paid ("unauthorized" or "unexcused"). Should this be the case in your organization, you will need to segregate absences by "paid" versus "unpaid" and apply the appropriate costs to each category.

2. *The weighted average hourly wage/salary level for the various occupational groups that claimed absenteeism during the period. Note: If your organization does not pay absent workers, skip this step and go directly to Step 3.*

For Acme International, let's assume about 85 percent of all absentees were blue-collar, 13 percent clerical, and 2 percent management and professional. To keep our example simple, we'll also assume all employees were paid for sick days taken under the company's employee benefits program. The average hourly wage rate per absentee is computed by applying the appropriate percentages to the average hourly rate for each major occupational regrouping. The following illustration reflects how this figure is computed:

Occupational Class	Approximate Percentage of Total Absenteeism	Average Hourly Wage	Weighted Average Hourly Wage
Blue-collar	85	$4.25	$3.61
Clerical	13	3.95	.51
Management and professional	2	9.85	.20
			$4.32 Total

3. *The cost of employee benefits per hour per employee.* For most organizations, employee benefits (profit sharing, pensions, health and life insurance, paid vacations and holidays, and so on) represent a sizable portion of total employee compensation—often as much as one-quarter to one-third. One method for computing the cost of employee benefits per hour per employee is to divide the total cost of benefits per employee per week by the number of hours worked per week.

We'll assume Acme International's cost of benefits per employee is $76.00 per week. Using this figure, Acme's cost for this time is computed as follows:

$$\text{Cost of benefits/hour/employee} = \frac{\text{Cost of benefits/week/employee}}{\text{Hours worked/week}} = \frac{\$76.00}{40} = \$1.90$$

4. *The estimated total number of supervisory hours lost to employee absenteeism for the period.* This estimate will be more difficult to make compared with wage and benefits estimates, as existing records seldom provide the information necessary to compute this figure. First, estimate the average number of supervisory hours spent per day rectifying the myriad problems resulting from employee absenteeism. Examples of such problems include time spent solving production problems, instructing replacement employees, checking on the performance of replacements, and counseling and disciplining absentees. Perhaps the most accurate way to develop this estimate is through discussions with a sampling of supervisors. In estimating your average, be sure to take into account typically high-absence days (Monday, Friday, days before and after holidays, day after payday). After estimating this figure, compute the total number of supervisory hours lost to your organization by multiplying three figures: the estimated average number of hours lost per supervisor per day times the total number of supervisors who deal with problems of absenteeism times the number of working days for the period. Include all shifts and weekend work, if any, in your estimate.

In our example, let's assume Acme International's data in these areas are as follows:

- Estimated number of supervisory hours lost per day: one-half hour

- Total number of supervisors who deal with absence problems: 32
- Total number of working days for the year: 240

Acme International's total supervisory hours lost to absenteeism for the year is estimated by multiplying . . . one-half hour per day per supervisor × 32 supervisors × 240 working days = 3,840 total supervisory hours lost to employee absenteeism.

5. *The average hourly wage rate for supervisors, including benefits.* In your estimate, include only the salaries of supervisors who normally deal with problems of absenteeism. Usually the first level of supervision within the manufacturing and clerical areas bears the lion's share of absenteeism problems.

We'll estimate Acme International's cost for the figure as follows:

Average hourly supervisory salary $7.25
Cost of benefits per hour per employee 1.90
Total compensation per hour per supervisor $9.15

6. *The last estimate is a catchall—a conglomerate of costs unique to your organization that were not included in the previous estimates.* Such costs may include temporary help, labor pools for absent workers, overtime premiums, production losses, machine downtime, quality problems, and inefficient materials usage. Like the previous figure, the estimates will be difficult to generate and should be based on discussions with a number of management and staff personnel.

We'll assume Acme International incurred overtime premiums, production losses, and inefficient materials usage problems as a result of absenteeism, and these problems resulted in an estimated financial loss of $38,500 for the year. Having computed all the necessary estimates, the total cost of employee absenteeism is determined by summing the individual cost figures pertaining to wages and salaries, benefits, supervisory salaries, and other costs incidental to absenteeism.

Space has been provided (in Exhibit 18.6) for your figures and we'll also put Acme International's estimates next to your estimates for illustrative purposes. (Remember that Acme International is a hypothetical firm—don't pass judgment on your figures by comparing them with Acme's!)

Are Acme's costs too high? About right? And more important, what about *your* estimates? What do they say about the absenteeism problem your organization may be facing?

Having computed the costs of absenteeism for your organization, the next step is to evaluate the figures against some predetermined cost standard or financial measure of performance. A comparison of the absence costs of your organization to an industry average would provide valuable information in determining whether an absenteeism problem does in fact exist or how significant the problem may be.

Unfortunately, absenteeism cost data are not published on a regular or periodic basis. Unlike traditional cost, revenue, and profit data, where regularly published financial ratios and composite income statements and balance

*Total Estimated Cost of Employee
Absenteeism*

Exhibit 18.6

Item	Acme International	Your Organization
1. Total worker-hours lost to employee absenteeism for the period	78,336	
2. Weighted average wage salary per hour per employee	$4.32	
3. Cost of employee benefits per hour per employee	1.90	
4. Total compensation lost per hour per absent employee a. Absent workers are paid (wage salary plus benefits)	$6.22	
b. If absent workers are not paid (benefits only)		
5. Total compensation lost to absent employees (total worker-hours lost × 4a or 4b, whichever applicable)	$487,250	
6. Total supervisory hours lost on employee absenteeism	3,840	
7. Average hourly supervisory wage, including benefits	$9.15	
8. Total supervisory salaries lost to managing problems of absenteeism (hours lost × average hourly supervisory wage—item 6 × item 7)	$35,136	
9. All other costs incidental to absenteeism not included in the above items	$38,500	
10. Total estimated cost of absenteeism— summation of items 5, 8, and 9.	$560,887	
11. Total estimated cost of absenteeism per employee (Total estimated costs)	$560,886	
(Total number of employees)	1200 $467.41 per employee	

Source: Frank E. Kuzmits, "How Much Is Absenteeism Costing Your Organization?" p. 31. Reprinted with permission from the June 1979 issue of the *Personnel Administrator.* Copyright © 1979, The American Society for Personnel Administration, 606 North Washington Street, Alexandria, VA 22314.

sheets enable one to accurately gauge the financial soundness of an individual organization, little data are available for passing judgment upon the level of dollars and cents lost to employee absenteeism. Although the costs of absenteeism to individual organizations occasionally appear in the literature, these estimates normally result from case studies of individual firms rather than surveys of specific industries.

Without a sound basis for comparing the costs of absenteeism by industry category or other relevant organizational criteria, is it worth the time and effort to undertake a cost analysis of the individual organization? Yes—and at least two compelling reasons exist for doing so. Perhaps the principal reason for computing the economic costs of employee absenteeism is to call management's attention to the severity of the problem. Translating behavioral acts into dollars and cents enables managers to readily grasp the burdens of absenteeism, particularly in a firm suffering from extraordinary absence problems. The spark recognition of a five-, six,- or even seven-figure outlay for absenteeism will likely result in a concentrated effort to combat the problem.

A second reason for computing the cost of employee absenteeism is to create meaningful criteria for evaluating the effectiveness of absence control programs. Comparing the quarterly, semiannual, and annual costs of absenteeism across various departments and supervisory work units provides a valid and reliable information system for measuring the success—or lack of success—of methods and techniques designed to reduce the problem. Organizations with computerized absence reporting systems should find this additional information relatively easy and inexpensive to generate.

How to Estimate Employee Turnover Costs

Employee turnover is a matter of concern not only to the heads of U.S. companies but also to their human resources managers.[46] Many organizations keep track of employee turnover and issue reports on the problem. For example, the Bureau of National Affairs found that employee turnover in companies participating in their 1979 nationwide survey averaged 1.9 percent per month, or 22.8 percent per year. The American Electronics Association, which surveys its member companies annually, reported a turnover rate in 1980 of 35.4 percent.

Employee turnover in the U.S. manufacturing industry is often cited as one of the reasons U.S. industry has failed to compete effectively with foreign industries, particularly that of Japan. Employee turnover is also cited as one of the factors behind the failure of U.S. employee productivity rates to keep pace with those of our competitors. As a result, human resources managers throughout the United States are increasing efforts to calculate turnover within their organizations and take steps toward reducing it.

Unfortunately, though, little effort so far has been made to determine the dollar impact of employee turnover on industry or on individual companies. Some efforts have been made to determine hiring costs per employee on a national or regional basis—but little, if any, effort has been made to establish total turnover cost. This is a serious mistake, because in the typical organization, the human resources department competes with other departments for funds or resources to help the department meet organizational goals. In companies experiencing high turnover rates, resources are desperately needed to solve this problem. If the human resources executive is unable to determine the cost of employee turnover, he or she may have trouble getting necessary funds or resources allocated to reduce such turnover. To justify additional expenditures for turnover reduction, the human resources manager must be in position to identify, on a quantitative basis, the savings for the organization if these expenditures are made—and the necessary quantitative base to establish such savings is the cost of employee turnover to the company.

Another problem facing the human resources department in a high-turnover company is the need to develop line-management commitment to reducing turnover. A commitment from line management to make the best new-hire selections and then to make every effort to retain them and keep them productive is an essential part of any turnover-reduction program. Unfortunately, line managers do not always realize the magnitude of the turnover problem, mainly because human resources managers fail to provide them with quantitative information that measures the dollar impact of employee turnover on the overall organization and on individual departments.

Therefore, a high-turnover company must develop a data base on employee turnover costs. Unfortunately, the typical reaction of the human resources departments to this problem is to indicate that the data aren't available to develop such cost information or that the project is too costly and time-consuming. In an effort to refute this "conventional wisdom," I developed a model for estimating total employee turnover costs that is easy to use and inexpensive.

Developing a Data Base.   The first step in estimating employee turnover costs, establishing a data base, is not as difficult as it may seem. It can be done by establishing the necessary accounts for accumulating data from accounting department records and being ready to make informed estimates of turnover costs if precise data are not available.

Historically, calculation of employee turnover costs—where it has been done—focused on individual occupations or employee groups and typically attempted to apply scientific methods to the data collection. This, however, is a time-consuming and expensive process; most companies are, understandably, unwilling to undertake such a process. A simpler method is to estimate costs where necessary to develop the required data base. Normally, this means keeping track of advertising fees, agency fees, applicant expenses, employment office costs, and so on, as well as costs related to hiring and replacing employees that are incurred by line management. With a little planning, this task can be achieved without major effort in the typical large organization that has computerized accounting and cost reporting.

Turnover Cost Estimation Model.   The turnover cost estimation model (shown in Exhibit 18.8) helps human resources managers develop the turnover cost data. They have only to follow the steps listed to complete the model and determine total estimated turnover costs.

To help readers understand how to complete the forms, we have included data from a sample company on all the forms. This is intended to help you work your way through the various steps involved. For example, in Exhibit 18.7 you will note that we've established a targeted turnover reduction rate of 25 percent for this sample company. This means that if that company is able to achieve a 25 percent reduction in turnover in both nonexempt and exempt classifications, it saves $307,352 in operating costs for the following year.

To distinguish between nonexempt (hourly) job classification turnover costs and exempt (salaried) turnover costs, the model specifies collecting data for them separately. This is important because much greater time, effort, and money is usually spent in recruiting, hiring, and training individuals for exempt positions than for nonexempt positions. Although this may entail additional data-collection effort, the effort pays off for the typical high-turnover company.

Estimating Direct Turnover Costs.   The model also distinguishes between direct and indirect hiring costs. Direct costs are defined as those costs normally incurred in the employment function that are easily identifiable and typically directly associated with the recruitment effort. Indirect costs are the less visible ones; most of them like training and productivity losses, occur after the new employee has been hired (see Exhibit 18.8).

Completing the Model.   Once you have compiled the necessary data, preferably for a one-year period, complete the model (beginning with Exhibit 18.7) as indicated in the following steps. Enter annual costs separately for nonexempt and exempt job classifications and total them in the column to the right. Again, if accurate data are not readily available, complete the model by using informed estimates.

1. *Employment advertising.* Include here all recruitment advertising and related costs.
2. *Agency and search fees.* Include all fees to employment agencies, search firms, and recruitment consultants.
3. *Internal referrals.* Include all costs for bonuses, fees, gifts, and so on, awarded to employees participating in a company-sponsored applicant-referral program.
4. *Applicant expenses.* Include the travel and subsistence costs entailed in bringing an applicant (and spouse) to the place of interview. Also include cost of the spouse's travel, if applicable.
5. *Relocation expenses.* This includes the costs of travel, moving of household effects, subsistence allowances, and all other costs associated with relocation.
6. *Employment staff compensation.* Include all salaries, benefits, and bonuses of the employment staff.
7. *Other employment office expenses.* Include all other expenses that can be attributed to the employment function, such as the cost of facilities, telephones, equipment depreciation, office supplies, printing, physical examinations, consultants, and so on.

Estimation Model for Turnover Costs   *Exhibit 18.7*

Activity	Nonexempt Cost	Exempt Cost	Total
1. Employment advertising	$ 25,000	$ 30,000	$ 55,000
2. Agency and search fees	5,737	25,000	30,737
3. Internal referrals	10,800	3,979	14,779
4. Applicant expenses	500	9,318	9,818
5. Relocation expenses	3,000	79,132	82,132
6. Employment staff compensation	10,200	25,000	35,200
7. Other employment office expenses	1,150	1,150	2,300
8. Recruiters' expenses	3,000	500	3,500
9. Direct hiring costs (sum of 1–8)	$ 59,387	$174,079	$ 233,466
10. Number of hires	278	84	362
11. Direct costs per hire (9 ÷ 10)	$ 214	$ 2,072	$ 645*
12. Indirect costs per hire (from Exhibit 18.8)	3,705	6,180	
13. Total costs per hire (11 + 12)	$ 3,919	$ 8,252	4,840**
14. Number of replacement hires (turnover)	200	54	254
15. Total turnover costs (13 × 14)	$783,800	$445,608	$1,229,408
16. Target percentage reduction	25%	25%	25%
17. Potential savings (15 × 16)	$195,950	$111,402	$ 307,352

*Calculated by dividing total hiring costs (line 9) by the total number of hires (line 10).
**Calculated by dividing the total turnover costs (line 15) by the total number of replacement hires (line 14).

Breakdown of Indirect Turnover Costs   *Exhibit 18.8*

Activity	Nonexempt Cost	Exempt Cost
18. *Cost of management time per hire*—Estimated dollar cost of management time spent orienting new employees (average hourly rate × hours spent per hire)	$ 98	$ 293
19. *Cost of lead employees' time per hire*—Estimated cost of time spent by lead employees in orienting and training new hires (average hourly rate × hours spent per hire)	407	—
20. *Cost of training per hire*—Estimated total training costs allocated to new hires (total training cost ÷ new hires)	203	—
21. *Cost of learning curve labor productivity losses*—Nonproductive labor costs of new employees	2,997	5,887
22. *Total indirect hiring costs per hire*—The sum of lines 18–21.	$3,705	$6,180

8. *Recruiters' expenses.* Include here subsistence allowance and all expenses reimbursed by the company for recruitment trips. Don't forget any extra costs in connection with interviewing an applicant, such as tickets to sports and cultural events, wining and dining, and so on.

9. *Direct hiring costs.* The total of items 1 through 8.

10. *Number of hires.* The total number of permanently hired employees during the year.

11. *Direct costs per hire.* Divide direct hiring (9) by number of hires (10).

12. *Indirect costs per hire.* These figures are obtained from line 22 in Exhibit 18.8.

13. *Total costs per hire.* This is the sum of direct (11) and indirect (12) costs per hire.

14. *Number of replacement hires (turnover).* Enter the number of yearly terminations, not including temporary hires.

15. *Total turnover costs.* Multiply total cost per hire (13) times number of replacement hires (14).

16. *Target percentage reduction.* This is to be used in planning turnover reduction for individual companies.

17. *Potential savings.* This is to be used in estimating dollar savings to the company if the planned turnover reduction is achieved. To obtain this figure, multiply target percentage reduction (16) by total turnover costs (15).

Estimating Indirect Turnover Costs.   As noted previously, indirect turnover costs are less visible than direct costs, and most of them are incurred after the employee has been hired. Collecting data for this portion of the model is more difficult; it will require research and, in some cases, making informed estimates of cost allocation. Exhibit 18.8 depicts the model used to estimate indirect costs of employee turnover.

Developments in Computerized Assessment

Human resource researchers and practitioners are making important progress not only in assessing the economic utility of organizational interventions but also in the application of computer technology. Although developments in computer technology have been previously noted in the chapters on job analysis, recruitment, and selection, one area that deserves further discussion is that of computer-assisted testing. As noted in the following "PHRM in the News," interest in computer-assisted testing has been increasing over the past few years.

One area of computer-assisted testing that is currently receiving increased research attention is that of tailored or adaptive testing. **Tailored or adaptive testing** refers to the situation in which the computer program adjusts the test difficulty to the ability of the individual being tested:

A computer-assisted or adaptive test uses a multi-stage process to estimate a person's ability several times during the course of testing, and the selection of succes-

Interest Rises in Testing by Computer

For decades, computers have graded answers to the standardized tests that serve as rites of passage in American life. Now computers are beginning to pose the questions, too.

Some people already take psychological tests on computer systems that immediately print results. By 1983, the Pentagon plans to administer recruitment tests at computer terminals. And researchers at the Educational Testing Service are hoping to offer computerized college-admission tests by the year 2000.

For the moment, the selling points of computerized tests are mostly convenience and speedy results, but researchers say the computer soon could change the nature of mass testing. In the so-called adaptive tests that are being developed, the computer would weigh previous answers in picking the next suitable question. By quickly honing in on individual aptitude, researchers say, these tests could use more of the allotted testing time to learn such things as whether errors are due to guessing or to a mislearned concept.

Much of the impetus for these ideas comes from the Navy Personnel Research and Development Center, San Diego, Calif. It is leading efforts to computerize the Armed Services Vocational Aptitude Battery, a series of tests given to potential recruits in all branches of the military. The Pentagon wants to start computer testing in three years and eventually make 5,000 to 10,000 computer terminals available for testing.

The new recruitment test is supposed to be adaptive, not just a software copy of its paper predecessor. And the testing format and hardware, says James McBride, a Navy psychologist, will be "custom-designed not to intimidate."

"We are enormously excited about the new assessment opportunities," says ETS researcher Ernest J. Anastasio. Trade and professional tests also are computer candidates. Already, the National Association of Securities Dealers gives computerized tests to securities brokers and commodities dealers.

Source: R. Koenig, *Wall Street Journal,* 18 April 1983, p. 29. Reprinted by permission of *The Wall Street Journal,* © Dow Jones & Company, Inc., 1983. All Rights Reserved.

sive test items based on those ability estimates. The person tested uses an interactive computer terminal to answer a test question. If the answer is correct, the next item will be more difficult; if not, an easier item follows. With each response, a revised and more reliable estimate is made of the person's ability. The test proceeds until the estimate reaches a specified level of reliability. Generally, the results both are more reliable and require fewer items than a paper and pencil test.[47]

A few researchers have examined issues concerning the validity of computer-administered adaptive tests.[48] One interesting study compared the Armed Services Vocational Aptitude Battery (ASVAB), Arithmetic Reasoning, and Word Knowledge subtests with computer-administered adaptive tests as predictors of performance in an air force mechanic training course.[49] The study found that computer-administered adaptive tests one-third to one-half the length of conventional (i.e., paper-and-pencil) ASVAB tests could approximate the criterion-related validity coefficients of these conventional tests. The importance of these findings is even more impressive when one considers that adaptive tests administer different items to different individuals.

Others have pointed out that increased measurement accuracy is not the only benefit of computer-administered adaptive testing.[50] Additional benefits include a reduction in testing time, fatigue, and boredom as well as cost savings in some cases over conventional paper-and-pencil testing.[51] A study conducted within the U.S. Office of Personnel Management placed the cost of adaptive testing at less than that of paper-and-pencil testing.[52] Moreover, a report prepared for the Canadian government estimated that even considering the capital investment in computer equipment, computer-administered adaptive tests could show a savings over conventional paper-and-pencil tests in one year.[53]

Although potential benefits are associated with computerized testing for making employment decisions, this form of assessment will likely be examined by the courts. Based on numerous and significant recent court decisions concerning employment testing,[54] continued legal scrutiny of employment testing is clearly a reality. This fact is amply illustrated in the following "PHRM in the News." To ensure that computerized testing is capable of withstanding legal as well as professional scrutiny, there is an impending necessity for the testing profession—particularly personnel and human resource researchers—to adopt and adhere to a set of standards for computerized testing.[55] The belief is that such standards will be developed and adopted by professionals in the near future.

PHRM in the News

Job-Bias Suits Filed by U.S. Against Three Firms

Washington—The Equal Employment Opportunity Commission, accusing three companies of pervasive job discrimination, filed class-action suits seeking millions of dollars in back pay for the alleged victims.

The commission sued PHH Group Inc., a Hunt Valley, Md.-based conglomerate, and Peterson, Howell & Heather Inc., its vehicle-fleet-leasing subsidiary, in federal court in Baltimore. In a separate case also filed in the Baltimore court, the job-discrimination agency sued Citizens Bank & Trust Co., a major commercial bank owned by Citizens Bancorp. of Riverdale, Md. The third suit, brought in a Chicago federal

court, involves Panduit Corp., a Tinley Park, Ill., maker of electrical wire devices.

The commission charged that all of the concerns have discriminated against blacks and women in recruitment and hiring since the 1970s. In addition, Citizens Bank and Panduit were accused of discriminating against Hispanics and members of other minority groups. The EEOC wants each company to give several million dollars in back pay to several hundred individuals, agency officials said at a news conference.

The cases are the largest ones to accuse companies of widespread job bias since the federal agency adopted a new enforcement policy earlier this year. The commission no longer tries to settle discrimination complaints through hiring and promotion goals and timetables, traditional civil-rights remedies that have been under attack throughout the Reagan administration.

Instead, the commission emphasizes relief for identifiable victims, changes in personnel policies and closer scrutiny of corporations' affirmative-action efforts.

"We have gotten quotas, goals and timetables on the brain to the point that we're overlooking the reality" of discriminatory practices, asserted Clarence Thomas, EEOC chairman, at the news conference. He added, "There are people that don't like women in certain jobs, that don't like blacks in certain jobs. They hide behind this shroud of goals and timetables."

Reacting to biting congressional criticism of the agency's purported lax litigation efforts, Mr. Thomas also predicted that EEOC soon would bring more suits. He said the number "will be substantially higher this year" than the 411 cases approved for filing during fiscal 1985, which ended Sept. 30.

In the PHH case, the commission charged that the corporation "was basically all white," according to Dorothy Mead, director of the EEOC's Baltimore office. PHH and its Peterson Howell unit hired through word-of-mouth and employee referrals, she contended. "The practice itself led to a perpetuation of an all-white work force."

She alleged that Citizens Bank's discriminatory policies "began at the top," affected both entry-level and supervisory positions and resulted in the segregation of its handful of black managers. During the seven-year EEOC investigation, the bank's employment of women and minorities dropped even though it opened 39 branches, noted William A. Webb, a commission member.

In the Panduit case, Mr. Webb asserted, the company excluded minorities by directing recruitment advertising to zip codes of neighborhoods that are predominately white.

"There were a number of instances like that," Mr. Webb said. Other EEOC officials charged that Panduit turned down women and blacks for unskilled blue-collar and skilled factory jobs based on their education and experience—even though the jobs lacked such requirements.

PHH called the EEOC's charges "unsubstantiated" and said "further investigation of the charges will vindicate" the company and its Peterson Howell unit.

The management services concern said that during the past five years, it "has made every effort to ascertain the focus of the charge and to successfully resolve the matter," but it "has been unable to do so."

In Riverdale, Md., Citizens Bank said that "the allegations of the complaint are incorrect and untrue," and that it will "vigorously" defend itself.

The bank said it hadn't received a copy of the EEOC action, the result of an investigation begun in 1978. It said its hiring practices have been reviewed and approved since then by the U.S. Department of Labor's Office of Federal Contract Compliance Programs. The company declined to comment further until it had reviewed the complaint with its lawyers.

In Tinley Park, Ill., an attorney for Panduit said the company last discussed the discrimination charges with the EEOC in March 1984 and at that time considered the case closed.

He called the charges "unfounded" and said he would have no further comment until the company has an opportunity to study the complaint.

Source: J. S. Lublin, *Wall Street Journal,* 13 November 1985, p. 10. Reprinted by permission of *The Wall Street Journal,* © Dow Jones & Company, Inc., 1985. All Rights Reserved.

Communicating with Employees:
Organizational Surveys

Whereas many of the previous issues are concerned with assessing selection and placement decisions, also important is that the good employees stay. In part, this requires assessing the individuals themselves and the socialization process. For instance, we may be interested in measuring employees' satisfaction with work, the extent to which they believe their skills and abilities are being used and their needs satisfied, as well as their level of involvement with the job and organization. Since employee satisfaction, involvement, and skill level can change, personnel managers must continually monitor these changes. Regular, periodic organizational surveys are one method of doing this.

Purposes of an Organizational Survey.   An organizational survey serves several purposes. First, it helps determine the effectiveness of PHRM functions and activities. Second, it measures the quality of the organization's internal environment and, therefore, helps to locate aspects that require improvement. Finally, the survey aids in the development of programs to make the necessary changes, and helps in evaluating the effectiveness of these programs.

What Surveys Measure.   In many of the chapters thus far, the need for PHRM data has frequently been for either measures of job performance itself or predictors of job performance, such as tests and background characteristics.[56] But the PHRM manager often needs other types of data. For example, to develop ways to improve employee job performance, the PHRM manager needs to measure employee perceptions of organizational characteristics, including the consequences of job performance, organizational policies, frequency of feedback, job design qualities, task interference characteristics, aspects of goal setting, role conflict and awareness, and supervisor behaviors. Equally necessary is gathering data on the employee's reactions to the organizational conditions, the quality of work life, and reactions such as satisfaction and job involvement.

In addition to these subjective or reactive measures, also useful is determining the actual or objective (nonreactive measures) qualities of the organizational characteristics.[57] For example, to make improvements in the design of jobs, one may need to know what the actual characteristics of jobs are that the employees perceive as highly repetitive. With this information and information about the employees' reactions, job design changes are more feasible. However, these changes can probably be made effectively only when other organizational characteristics are considered as well.[58]

Other measures or variables that could be used to supplement organizational surveys are objective measures of employee reactions. Many of these reactions can be symptoms of employee stress, which include physiological measures such as blood pressure and heart rate. Since one of the criteria for the effectiveness of personnel and human resource management is employee health, these additional measures of employee reactions may become more

common in organizational surveys.[59] Besides these reactions, employee behaviors to be measured objectively include job performance, absenteeism,
turnover, rates and types of accidents, and incidents of diseases.[60] In summary, organizational surveys are really efforts to systematically gather information on objective and subjective bases about organizational characteristics and employee reactions and behaviors for one or more of the purposes
noted earlier. For instance, the Ford Motor Company is systematically gathering information on its managers to assist in their efforts to change Ford's
corporate culture:[61]

> Ford is putting its managers (2,000 so far) through workshops where they take
> tests to determine their management style and how they cope with change. Each
> person's results are then displayed on his or her name tag. The workshops, which
> started last year, also include a session at which participants confide what it is
> they most admire about one another. "What we're trying to do is make this place
> the most loving, caring group of people in Ford," Joseph Kordick, the general
> manager of parts and service, says of the workshops held in his division.[62]

Steps in an Organizational Survey.   The PHRM manager—or an outside consultant—has several important steps and issues to consider when conducting an organizational survey. These become necessary, however, only after
top management has given its support for the survey.[63]

As the first step, the PHRM manager must consider the following:

- The specific employee perceptions and responses that should be measured
- The methods that will be used to collect the data, including observations,
  questionnaires, interviews, and personnel records
- The reliability and validity of the measures to be used
- The people from whom the data will be collected—all employees, manage-
  rial employees only, a sample of employees, or only certain departments
  within the organization
- The timing of the survey and the way to make the survey part of a longer-
  term effort
- The types of analyses that will be made with the data
- The specific purposes of the data—to determine reasons for the organiza-
  tion's turnover

This last consideration is important, because by identifying the problem, the
PHRM manager can determine which models or theories will be relevant to
the survey. Knowing which model or theory to use tells the PHRM manager
what data are needed and what statistical techniques will be necessary to
analyze the data.

The next step is the actual collection of data. Three areas are important
here: (1) Who will administer the questionnaire—the line manager, someone
from the personnel department, or someone from outside the organization?
(2) Where, when, and in what size groups will the data be collected? Both
these considerations are influenced by the method used to gather the data.
For example, if a questionnaire is used, larger groups are more feasible than
if interviews are conducted. (3) Employee participation in the survey must
be ensured. This can be done by gathering the data during company time

and by providing feedback—for instance, by promising employees that the results of the survey will be made known to them.

The actual feedback process is the third step in the survey. As part of this process, the data are analyzed according to the purposes and problems for which they were collected. The results of the analysis can then be presented by the personnel department to the line managers, who in turn discuss the results with their employees. The feedback sessions can be used to develop solutions to any problems that are identified and to evaluate the effectiveness of programs that may already have been implemented on the basis of results of an earlier survey.

The extent to which employees actually participate in the development of solutions during the feedback process depends on the philosophy of top management. Organizations that are willing to survey their employees to ask how things are going are also usually willing to invite employee participation in deciding to make things better. This willingness allows organizational surveys to be used most effectively.

A Sample Questionnaire.   The most common method of obtaining survey data is the paper-and-pencil questionnaire.[64] Exhibit 18.9 is a questionnaire

---

Exhibit 18.9	*Role Awareness and Role Conflict Questionnaire*

Read each classroom characteristic, and select the scale number that best reflects your opinion.

Definitely not characteristic of this class				**Definitely characteristic of this class**
1	2	3	4	5

1. I know what my responsibilities are.	1	2	3	4	5
2. I receive assignments without the time to complete them.	1	2	3	4	5
3. Part of my grade depends on a group project.	1	2	3	4	5
4. I have to go through all sorts of hassles to find out what's expected of me.	1	2	3	4	5
5. Good work or a good idea is not really recognized by the instructor.	1	2	3	4	5
6. I have been given clearly planned goals and objectives for this class.	1	2	3	4	5
7. I know how to study for this class to do well.	1	2	3	4	5
8. I do things that are apt to be accepted by the instructor at one time but not accepted at another time.	1	2	3	4	5
9. I feel certain about how much I am responsible for.	1	2	3	4	5
10. I know exactly what is expected of me.	1	2	3	4	5
11. I have to do things that can be done in different ways.	1	2	3	4	5
12. Explanations of what has to be done are clear.	1	2	3	4	5
13. I work on unnecessary things.	1	2	3	4	5
14. The amount of work I am expected to do is not fair.	1	2	3	4	5

Source: Adapted from J. R. Rizzo, R. J. House, and S. I. Lirtzman, "Role Conflict and Ambiguity in Complex Organizations," *Administrative Science Quarterly* 15 (1970); 156.

asking students to describe the degree to which they know what's expected of them (role awareness) and how much conflict they face in doing what's expected (role conflict). Measures of role awareness and role conflict have been used extensively in organizational surveys; typical items have been reworded here to apply to a classroom situation. To use this questionnaire, circle the appropriate numbers before reading any further.

Once you have completed the questionnaire, add the numbers you circled in items 1, 6, 7, 9, 10, and 12. This is your *role awareness* score. Now add the remaining numbers you circled to determine your *role conflict* score. Next, in the following display, circle the response that you think best describes your overall level of satisfaction with the class:

	Strongly Disagree	Disagree	Neutral	Agree	Strongly Agree
All in all, I am very satisfied with this class	1	2	3	4	5

How does your score on satisfaction compare with your scores on role conflict and role awareness? Are you high on all three? Low on all three? Do you have a mixed pattern?

What is the importance of these scores? In most organizational surveys, employees are asked for their perceptions of and attitudes toward many aspects of the organization. These surveys generally reveal definite patterns. Satisfaction, for instance, tends to have a negative relationship with role conflict and a positive relationship with role awareness. Role conflict and role awareness are also frequently related to employee performance and stress.[65] Therefore, an employee's role conflict and role awareness scores reveal a great deal about the employee. Other variables—for example, descriptions of the employee's supervisor, the job, and the extent of the employee's perceived participation in decision making—also reveal important information about how the employee is reacting to the organization. Still other variables, such as employee perceptions of and attitudes toward group members, may indicate the quality of group relationships.

Organizational surveys, coupled with knowledge of the practical usefulness of organizational interventions, provide rich information for improving individual and organizational performance. Improvements in survey development will serve to make organizational surveys an increasingly important means for identifying problems as well as a feasible criterion measure for evaluating the effectiveness of organizational interventions.[66] In addition, future improvements in utility analysis as well as continued cumulative research on the effectiveness of alternative organizational interventions will assist the PHRM decision maker in increasing work force productivity and, consequently, increasing the efficiency of personnel decisions.

Summary

This chapter stresses the necessity for conducting personnel research for a variety of purposes aimed at improving individual and organizational effectiveness. Emphasis is placed on describing the usefulness of the empirical research process in PHRM research, assessing the reliability and validity of measurement, evaluating the practical and economic utility of personnel selection and organizational intervention programs, discussing recent developments in computerized assessment, and describing the usefulness of organizational surveys. Recent advancements in PHRM research related to assessing the validity as well as the economic utility of various PHRM activities and programs have helped to improve organizational effectiveness. Continued research efforts will further advance our knowledge of PHRM activities as well as contribute to the steadily increasing importance of the PHRM function.

Discussion Questions

1. Discuss how the empirical research process can assist in finding solutions to organizational problems.
2. Describe three methods for assessing the reliability of measures, and evaluate the practicality of each method.
3. Discuss the importance of criterion-related validity in personnel selection test validation.
4. How should an organization evaluate the predictive effectiveness of a particular personnel selection test battery (i.e., series of tests) in another situation?
5. How does the concept of validity generalization relate to the development of ability-performance relationships?
6. How might one use the Taylor-Russell tables to determine an optimal selection ratio?
7. Discuss the importance of decision-theoretic utility equations for estimating the economic utility of alternative organizational interventions.
8. Discuss some of the major considerations one must take into account when measuring the cost of absenteeism.
9. Discuss the potential benefits of computerized adaptive testing for both the PHRM department and the examinee.
10. How do organizational surveys serve as indicators of problems as well as criteria for evaluating the effectiveness of organizational interventions?

PC Project

Organizations use a variety of selection procedures (i.e., predictors) in making selection decisions. These predictors include paper-and-pencil tests, interviews, application blanks, and work samples. Predictors are used to identify those applicants who will be successful job performers. Thus, the validity of the predictors must be assessed. This PC Project looks at the criterion-referenced validity of an employment test. Next, a linear regression is used to predict job performance for a pool of job applicants. How well does the test predict job performance?

| C | A | S | E | S | T | U | D | Y |

CompuTest, Inc.: The Case of Alternative Personnel Selection Strategies

Fiscal 1985 was a landmark year of development and growth for CompuTest, Inc. As Jerome J. Rosner, president, indicated in a report to the stockholders, "Our company emerged to become a major force in the growing field of computerized psychological testing." It was a year that saw the company transform from 350 employees to over 460 employees. Although a number of personnel were added to the marketing, sales, and research operations, the largest number of employees were selected for clerical and administrative positions.

To date, the company has principally targeted its products at individual mental health practitioners, psychiatric hospitals, and other medical professionals. The company expects these specialized markets to continue to represent a substantial part of their revenue base through 1987. Thereafter, CompuTest expects its sources of revenue to shift as they aggressively enter the vast industrial market. In business and industry, thousands of psychological and ability tests are administered annually. In the past, these tests were given to employees and prospective employees by traditional paper-and-pencil methods—a long, cumbersome, and expensive process. As Paul Lefebre, the company's manager of personnel research states, "CompuTest's current and future testing products have the capability of revolutionizing the area of employee screening with new technologies never before available in the PHRM field."

One of the newest products developed for the industrial market is a comprehensive battery of computer-administered clerical tests. The company, however, does not want to introduce these tests into the market prior to gathering evidence concerning the predictive effectiveness of the tests. Paul Lefebre is currently searching for potential research sites to conduct a criterion-related validity study.

At the present time, Lane Carpenter, the director of human resources, has brought to the attention of President Rosner that many complaints are being raised about the quality of clerical personnel being selected with the company's verbal ability test. Lane has informed President Rosner that although 170 clerical and administrative personnel have been selected with this verbal ability test, the company has not conducted a criterion-related validation study to evaluate its usefulness. Because of the complaints and the need to select additional clerical personnel, President Rosner has called a meeting with Lane Carpenter and Paul Lefebre.

Jerome Rosner: As you both are aware, we are facing a number of complaints about the quality and quantity of clerical job performance throughout our company. In addition, I would like to bring to your attention that we have projected a need of fifty additional clerical personnel in our current job categories by the end of 1987. This situation requires us to closely examine our current clerical selection procedure and possibly consider viable alternatives. Furthermore, I would like us to reconsider the performance appraisal form we are currently using to evaluate clerical personnel. Our performance appraisal system does not seem to incorporate some of the major duties or tasks that our clerical personnel are being asked to perform. Lane, you have expressed some concerns about the currently used verbal ability test for selecting clerical personnel.

Lane Carpenter: Yes, I am concerned not only with how good this test is at screening potentially successful clerical personnel but also with how we would defend such a test if challenged in court. I assume you are aware that this test was developed and adopted only on the basis of a content-oriented validation study.

Jerome Rosner: Yes, Paul has informed me of the strategy used in developing the verbal ability test. Paul, you also mentioned in a previous discussion that we might be able to conduct another type of validation study for this test.

Paul Lefebre: We currently have a sufficient number of clerical personnel with verbal ability test scores and performance ratings to conduct a criterion-related validation study. In addition, since we have just completed a comprehensive job analysis of all clerical positions and expected openings within the company, we have the capability of revising our clerical performance appraisal system to more accurately reflect the tasks that they perform.

Jerome Rosner: Does this job analysis also indicate the necessary abilities to effectively perform these tasks?

Paul Lefebre: Yes, the job analysis clearly identified the required abilities. Furthermore, the job analysis indicated that although the major duties differed across some of our clerical jobs, the entry-level ability requirements for all of our clerical jobs were similar.

Lane Carpenter: If the ability requirements are similar across all clerical jobs, we might be able to conduct a criterion-related validation study for the verbal ability test with our current clerical employees.

Paul Lefebre: That would be a definite possibility. It might also be helpful for us to consider validating our newly developed computerized clerical ability test battery. That is, we could gather some evidence for its predictive effectiveness in our own company prior to marketing it to industry. Of course, my department would have to determine which tests were appropriate or should be considered for a validation study here.

Jerome Rosner: Paul, that sounds like a good idea. If we are going to successfully market our computerized testing products to industry, we should also be willing to use them. An important question related to your suggestion is how our computer-administered clerical test battery would compare with our currently used verbal ability test. Would we be improving our predictions of who will turn out to be successful workers? If we decided to replace our current selection test with a battery of clerical tests, would it be cost beneficial? Paul, I would very much appreciate your preparing a proposal for how we might go about validating our currently used verbal ability test and the computer-administered clerical test battery and how we might compare these alternatives.

Notes

1. For a discussion of reasons for conducting organizational research, see J. E. Stone, *Research Methods in Organizational Behavior* (Santa Monica, Calif.: Goodyear, 1978).
2. American Psychological Association, Division 14, *Principles for the Validation and Use of Personnel Selection Procedures* (Washington, D.C.: APA, 1980).
3. F. J. Landy and D. A. Trumbo, *Psychology of Work Behavior* (Homewood, Ill.: Dorsey, 1980).
4. For a summary of the conditions under which each type of correlation coefficient is used, refer to M. J. Allen and W. M. Yen, *Introduction to Measurement Theory* (Monterey, Calif.: Brooks/Cole, 1979), pp. 36–41.
5. G. V. Glass and J. C. Stanley, *Statistical Methods in Education and Psychology* (Englewood Cliffs, N.J.: Prentice-Hall, 1970).
6. F. M. Lord and M. R. Novick, *Statistical Theories of Mental Test Scores* (Reading, Mass.: Addison-Wesley, 1968).
7. See M. J. Allen and W. M. Yen, *Introduction to Measurement Theory,* pp. 57, 59–60, for a technical introduction to the definition of parallel tests and parallel forms reliability.
8. M. J. Allen and W. M. Yen, *Introduction to Measurement Theory.*
9. E. E. Ghiselli, J. P. Campbell, and S. Zedeck, *Measurement Theory for the Behavioral Sciences* (San Francisco: Freeman, 1981).
10. For a discussion of the AT&T Management Progress Study as well as an overview of assessment centers, see A. Howard, "An Assessment of Assessment Centers," *Academy of Management Journal* 17 (1974): 115–34. A twenty-year follow-up study of AT&T's original Management Progress Study predictions was reported in A. Howard, "Cool at the Top: Personality Characteristics of Successful Executives," paper presented at the Annual Convention of the American Psychological Association, Toronto, Canada, August 1984.
11. An alternative method is a type of empirical validity referred to as synthetic validity. In synthetic validity, a systematic analysis of all jobs is made. Through this analysis, job dimensions common to several jobs

in the total set can be identified. Validity coefficient can then be calculated for separate tests for each of the job dimensions. The validities of the separate tests all relevant to the dimensions in a single job can then be combined to present in essence evidence of quasi-empirical validity. See also J. J. Balma, "The Concept of Synthetic Validity," *Personnel Psychology* 12 (1959): 395-96.

12. R. S. Barrett, "Is the Test Content-Valid: Or, Who Killed Cock Robin?" *Employee Relations Law Journal* 6 (4) (1981): 584-600; R. S. Barrett, "Is the Test Content-Valid: Or, Does it Really Measure Construct?" *Employee Relations Law Journal* 6 (3)(1981): 459-75; S. Wollack, "Content Validity: Its Legal and Psychometric Basis," *Public Personnel Management* (Nov.-Dec. 1976): 397-408; E. P. Prien, "The Function of Job Analysis in Content Validation," *Personnel Psychology* 30 (1977): 167-74; L. S. Kleiman and R. H. Faley, "Assessing Content Validity: Standards Set by the Court," *Personnel Psychology* 31 (1978): 701-13.

13. For a discussion and reconceptualization of the concept of content validity, see R. M. Guion, "Content Validity—The Source of My Discontent," *Applied Psychological Measurement* 1 (1977): 1-10. In this article, Guion proposes five conditions as necessary if one is to accept the use of a measuring instrument as a valid operational definition on the basis of content sampling. In addition, Guion discusses the unifying nature of the three conventionally listed aspects of validity (criterion-related, content-oriented, and construct) in R. M. Guion, "On Trinitarian Doctrines of Validity," *Professional Psychology* 11 (1980): 385-98.

14. A method for assessing construct validity based on correlation coefficients between the relevant construct measure (i.e., the measure being validated) and measures of similar and unrelated constructs is the multitrait-multimethod matrix. This method requires that at least two constructs be measured by minimally two methods. An assessment of construct validity is based on the degree of convergence (i.e., the correlation coefficients between measures of the same construct) and divergence (i.e., judged by higher correlation coefficients between two methods of measuring the same construct than between correlation coefficients of two constructs measured by the same method). For a discussion of the multitrait-multimethod matrix, refer to D. T. Campbell and D. W. Fiske, "Convergent and Discriminant Validation by the Multitrait-Multimethod Matrix," *Psychological Bulletin* 56 (1959): 81-105. A more concise discussion of the multitrait-multimethod matrix is presented in A. Anastasi, *Psychological Testing* (New York: Macmillan, 1976), pp. 156-58.

15. R. L. Linn, D. L. Harnisch, and S. B. Dunbar, "Validity Generalization and Situational Specificity: An Analysis of the Prediction of First-year Grades in Law School," *Applied Psychological Measurement* 5 (1981): 281-89.

16. For studies concerning correcting observed validity coefficients for range restriction, see R. A. Forsyth, "An Empirical Note on Correlation Coefficients Corrected for Range Restriction," *Educational and Psychological Measurement* 31 (1971): 115-23; R. A. Alexander, G. M. Alliger, and P. J. Hanges, "Correcting for Range Restriction When the Population Variance is Unknown," *Applied Psychological Measurement* 8 (1984): 431-37; J. M. Greener and H. G. Osburn, "An Empirical Study of the Accuracy of Corrections for Restriction in Range Due to Explicit Selection," *Applied Psychological Measurement* 3 (1979): 31-41; J. M. Greener and H. G. Osburn, "Accuracy of Corrections for Restriction in Range Due to Explicit Selection in Heteroscedastic and Nonlinear Distributions," *Educational and Psychological Measurement* 40 (1980): 337-46; R. L. Linn, D. L. Harnisch, and S. B. Dunbar, "Corrections for Range Restrictions: An Empirical Investigation of Conditions Resulting in Conservative Corrections," *Journal of Applied Psychology* 66 (1981): 655-63.

17. R. A. Forsyth and L. S. Feldt, "Investigation of Empirical Sampling Distributions and Correlations Corrected for Attenuation," *Educational and Psychological Measurement* 29 (1969): 61-71.

18. P. Bobko, "An Analysis of Correlations Corrected for Attenuation and Range Restriction," *Journal of Applied Psychology* 68 (1983): 584-89; R. Lee, R. Miller, and W. Graham, "Corrections for Restriction of Range and Attenuation in Criterion-Related Validation Studies," *Journal of Applied Psychology* 67 (1982): 637-39.

19. F. L. Schmidt and J. E. Hunter, "Development of a General Solution to the Problem of Validity Generalization," *Journal of Applied Psychology* 62 (1977): 529-40. Alternative validity generalization procedures have been presented in J. C. Callender and H. G. Osburn, "Development and Test of a New Model for Validity Generalization," *Journal of Applied Psychology* 65 (1980): 543-58; N. S. Raju and M. J. Burke, "Two New Procedures for Studying Validity Generalization," *Journal of Applied Psychology* 68 (1983): 382-95.

20. For a review of validity generalization research, see M. J. Burke, "Validity Generalization: A Review and Critique of the Correlation Model," *Personnel Psychology* 37 (1984): 93-115. For a commentary on important questions concerning validity generalization and meta-analysis, see F. L. Schmidt, J. E. Hunter, K. Pearlman, and H. R. Hirsch, "Forty Questions about Validity Generalization and Meta-Analysis"; and P. R. Sackett, N. Schmitt, M. L. Tenopyr, J. Kehoe, and S. Zedick, "Commentary on Forty Questions about Validity Generalization and Meta-Analysis," *Personnel Psychology* 38 (1985): 697-798.

21. For a discussion related to statistical methodologies for resolving the question of whether or not jobs are similar, see R. D. Arvey and K. M. Mossholder, "A Proposed Methodology for Determining Similarities and Differences Among Jobs," *Personnel Psychology* 30 (1977): 363–74; R. M. McIntyre and J. L. Farr, "Comment on Arvey and Mossholder's 'A Proposed Methodology for Determining Similarities and Differences Among Jobs'," *Personnel Psychology* 32 (1979): 507–10. Also, for a comparison of two job classification methods for showing the appropriateness of cognitive tests in settings that were not involved in supplying data for a validity generalization analysis, see E. T. Cornelius, F. L. Schmidt, and T. J. Carron, "Job Classification Approaches and the Implementation of Validity Generalization Results," *Personnel Psychology* 37 (1984): 247–60.

22. G. V. Glass coined the term *meta-analysis* to refer to the statistical analysis of the findings of many individual studies in an article titled "Primary, Secondary, and Meta-Analysis of Research," *Educational Researcher* 5 (1976): 3–8. Although numerous articles and books are beginning to be written on the subject of meta-analysis (of which validity generalization can be considered a subset), two original and frequently cited texts in this area are G. V. Glass, B. McGaw, and M. L. Smith, *Meta-Analysis in Social Research* (Beverly Hills: Sage, 1981); and J. E. Hunter, F. L. Schmidt, and G. Jackson, *Meta-Analysis: Cumulating Research Findings Across Settings* (Beverly Hills: Sage, 1982).

23. For instance, a meta-analysis of realistic job previews was presented in S. L. Premack and J. P. Wanous, "A Meta-Analysis of Realistic Job Preview Experiments," *Journal of Applied Psychology* 70 (1985): 706–19. A more general meta-analytic study comparing alternative organizational interventions was done by R. A. Guzzo, R. D. Jette, and R. A. Katzell, "The Effects of Psychologically Based Intervention Programs on Worker Productivity: A Meta-Analysis," *Personnel Psychology* 38 (1985): 275–91.

24. P. Cattin, "Estimations of the Predictive Power of a Regression Model," *Journal of Applied Psychology* 65 (1980): 407–14. Another important article that stresses that cross-validation may no longer be necessary for certain purposes is J. G. Claudy, "Multiple Regression and Validity Estimation in One Sample," *Applied Psychological Measurement* 2 (1978): 595–607. For a review of general methods of cross-validation, see K. R. Murphy, "Cost-Benefit Considerations in Choosing Among Cross-Validation Methods," *Personnel Psychology* 37 (1984): 15–22. A related topic of interest in PHRM is determining the best procedure for weighting multiple criteria into a composite for administrative decisions. A noteworthy study in this area by Fralicx and Raju compared five weighting methods for combining multiple criteria into a composite with 117 bank tellers. The study found that four out of the five methods (Management Weights, Equal Weights, Unit Weights, and Factor Weights) yielded nearly identical results, whereas the fifth method (Canonical Weights) correlated almost zero with the other methods. See R. D. Fralicx and N. S. Raju, "A Comparison of Five Methods for Combining Multiple Criteria into a Single Composite," *Educational and Psychological Measurement* 42 (1982): 823–27.

25. The selection ratio refers to a population parameter representing the proportion of successful applicants or, more specifically, the proportion of individuals in the population scoring above a cutting score. Typically, the selection ratio is equated with the hiring rate (a sample description), which can lead to errors. For a discussion of the distinction between the terms *selection ratio* and *hiring rate*, see R. A. Alexander, G. V. Barrett, and D. Doverspike, "An Explication of the Selection Ratio and Its Relationship to Hiring Rate," *Journal of Applied Psychology* 68 (1983):342–44.

26. H. C. Taylor and J. T. Russell, "The Relationship of Validity Coefficients to the Practical Validity of Tests in Selection: Discussion and Tables," *Journal of Applied Psychology* 23 (1939): 565–78.

27. J. Tiffin and E. J. McCormick, *Industrial Psychology*, 5th ed. (Englewood Cliffs, N.J.: Prentice-Hall, 1965).

28. M. L. Blum and J. C. Naylor, *Industrial Psychology: Its Theoretical and Social Foundations*, rev. ed. (New York: Harper & Row, 1968).

29. Initial discussions of the value of the correlation coefficient as an index of predictor usefulness were presented by H. E. Brogden in two classic papers: H. E. Brogden, "On the Interpretation of the Correlation Coefficient as a Measure of Predictive Efficiency," *Journal of Educational Psychology* 37 (1946): 65–76; and H. E. Brogden, "When Testing Pays Off," *Personnel Psychology* 2 (1949): 171–83. At a later point, the cost of testing was incorporated into the equations developed by Brogden in L. J. Cronbach and G. Gleser, *Psychological Tests and Personnel Decisions* (Urbana, Ill.: University of Illinois Press, 1965).

30. For a discussion and presentation of equations, based on a decision-theoretic approach, for evaluating employee separations and acquisitions, see J. W. Boudreau and C. J. Berger, "Decision-Theoretic Utility Analysis Applied to Employee Separations and Acquisitions," *Journal of Applied Psychology* 70 (1985): 581–612. W. F. Cascio has also provided a discussion and example of how decision-theoretic utility analysis can be applied to evaluating the economic impact of organizational interventions as well as absenteeism and turnover in *Costing Human Resources: The Financial Impact of Behavior in Organizations* (Boston, Mass.: Kent, 1982). A pragmatic, experimental approach to evaluating organizational interventions as well as absenteeism and turnover is

provided by J. Fitz-enz, *How to Measure Human Resources Management* (New York: McGraw-Hill, 1984).

31. For a review of recent developments in applications of decision theory to a wide range of HRM decisions, see J. W. Boudreau, "Decision Theory Contributions to HRM Research and Practice," *Industrial Relations* 23 (1984): 198–217. Also, discussions of why decision-theoretic utility equations were not widely applied relating to (1) the belief that data did not fit the assumptions of the equations, (2) difficulty in estimating equation components, and (3) the inability to generalize validity coefficients are presented in J. E. Hunter and F. L. Schmidt, "Fitting People to Jobs: The Impact of Personnel Selection on National Productivity," in *Human Performance and Productivity,* vol. 1, *Human Capacity Assessment,* ed. M. D. Dunnette and E. O. Fleishman (Hillsdale, N.J.: Erlbaum, 1982); F. L. Schmidt, J. E. Hunter, R. C. McKenzie, and T. W. Muldrow, "The Impact of Valid Selection Procedures on Work-Force Productivity," *Journal of Applied Psychology* 64 (1979): 609–26.

32. J. W. Boudreau, "Economic Considerations in Estimating the Utility of Human Resource Productivity Improvement Programs," *Personnel Psychology* 36 (1983): 551–76.

33. For more information on the economic components of this equation, see J. W. Boudreau. A study that has employed this full equation and provides useful information for estimating the economic components as well as the true validity coefficients is presented in M. J. Burke and J. T. Frederick, "A Comparison of Economic Utility Estimates for Alternative SD_y Estimation Procedures," *Journal of Applied Psychology,* in press.

34. Burke and Frederick, in press.

35. J. E. Hunter and R. F. Hunter, "Validity and Utility of Alternative Predictors of Job Performance," *Psychological Bulletin* 96 (1984): 72–98.

36. Hunter and Schmidt, "Fitting People to Jobs."

37. M. J. Burke and J. T. Frederick, "Two Modified Procedures for Estimating Standard Deviations in Utility Analysis," *Journal of Applied Psychology* 69 (1984): 482–89.

38. Schmidt, Hunter, McKenzie, and Muldrow, "The Impact of Valid Selection." The estimated SD_y for computer programmers was $10,413.

39. P. Bobko, R. Karren, and J. J. Parkington, "Estimation of Standard Deviations in Utility Analysis: An Empirical Test," *Journal of Applied Psychology* 68 (1983): 170–76.

40. F. L. Schmidt, M. J. Mack, and J. E. Hunter, "Selection Utility in the Occupation of U.S. Park Ranger for Three Modes of Test Use," *Journal of Applied Psychology* 69 (1984): 490–97. The estimated SD_y for forest park rangers was $4,451.

41. F. L. Schmidt, J. E. Hunter, and K. Pearlman, "Assessing the Economic Impact of Personnel Programs on Workforce Productivity," *Personnel Psychology* 35 (1982): 333–47.

42. Ibid.

43. Hunter and Schmidt, "Fitting People to Jobs."

44. M. J. Burke and R. R. Day, "A Cumulative Study of the Effectiveness of Managerial Training," *Journal of Applied Psychology,* in press.

45. This material is graciously provided by F. E. Kuzmits and is reprinted with permission from the June 1979 issue of the *Personnel Administrator.* Copyright © 1979. The American Society for Personnel Administration, 606 N. Washington Street, Alexandria, Virginia, 22314.

46. T. E. Hall, "How to Estimate Employee Turnover Costs," *Personnel* (July–Aug. 1981): 57–61. Used by special permission of T. E. Hall.

47. R. J. Niehaus, *Computer-assisted Human Resources Planning* (New York: Wiley, 1979), 222.

48. For summaries of research related to adaptive testing via the computer, see D. J. Weiss, "Improving Measurement Quality and Efficiency with Adaptive Testing," *Applied Psychological Measurement* 6 (1982): 473–92; and D. J. Weiss, "Adaptive Testing by Computer," *Journal of Consulting and Clinical Psychology,* in press.

49. J. B. Sympson, D. J. Weiss, and M. J. Ree, *Predictive Validity of Conventional and Adaptive Tests in an Air Force Training Environment* (AFHRL 81–40), Brooks Air Force Base, Tex., Manpower and Personnel Division, Air Force Human Relations Laboratory.

50. C. L. Hulin, F. Drasgow, and C. K. Parsons, *Item Response Theory: Application to Psychological Measurement* (Homewood, Ill.: Dorsey, 1983).

51. For a critique of the espoused benefits and problems associated with not only adaptive testing but also computerized psychological testing in general, see M. J. Burke and J. Normand, "Computerized Psychological Testing: An Overview and Critique," *Professional Psychology,* in press.

52. V. W. Urry, "Tailored Testing: A Successful Application of Latent Trait Theory," *Journal of Educational Measurement* 14 (1977): 181–96.

53. D. R. Budgell, "Preliminary Analysis of the Feasibility of Computerized Adaptive Testing and Item Banking in the Public Service," unpublished report, Public Service Commission, Ottawa, Canada, 1982.

54. L. S. Kleiman and R. H. Faley, "The Implications of Professional and Legal Guidelines for Court Decisions Involving Criterion-related Validity: A Review and Analysis," *Personnel Psychology* 38 (1985): 803–33.

55. Burke and Normand, "Computerized Psychological Testing."

56. R. B. Dunham and F. J. Smith, *Organizational Surveys* (Glenview, Ill.: Scott, Foresman, 1979); W. D. Todor, "Organizational Surveys in Human Resource Management," in *Readings in Personnel and Human Resource Management,* 2d ed., ed. R. S. Schuler and

S. Youngblood (St. Paul: West, 1984). For a discussion on legal constraints in the use of surveys, see A. S. Friedson, "The Legality of Employee Attitude Surveys in Union Environments," *Employee Relations Law Journal* (Spring 1983): 648–69.

57. For a discussion of these types of measures, see E. J. Webb, D. T. Campbell, R. D. Schwarts, and L. Sechrest, *Unobstrusive Measures: Nonreactive Research in the Social Sciences* (Chicago: Rand McNally, 1972).

58. G. R. Oldham and J. R. Hackman, "Work Design in the Organizational Context," in *Research in Organizational Behavior,* vol. 2, ed. B. M. Staw and L. L. Cummings (Greenwich, Conn.: JAI Press, 1980), pp. 247–78; and comments by G. R. Oldham at the National Academy of Management Meetings in New York, 1982, symposium entitled "Personnel Programs for Productivity and QWL Improvements."

59. M. T. Matteson and J. M. Ivancevich, "Organizational Stressors and Heart Disease: A Research Model," *Academy of Management Journal* 4 (1979): 347–57; R. S. Schuler, "Definition and Conceptualization of Stress in Organizations," *Organizational Behavior and Human Performance* (Apr. 1980): 184–215.

60. Although categorized here as objective data, performance data can often suffer from many subjective rating errors, as described in Chapters 6 and 7.

61. For a series of articles on corporate cultures, see the special issue of *Personnel Administrator* (January 1986).

62. *Wall Street Journal,* 4 Dec. 1985, p. 25.

63. Dunham and Smith, *Organizational Surveys*; E. J. Bernestin, "Employee Attitude Surveys: Perception vs. Reality," *Personnel Journal* (Apr. 1981): 300–305; W. Martin, "What Management Can Expect from an Employee Attitude Survey," *Personnel Administrator* (July 1981): 75–79, 87.

64. Dunham and Smith, *Organizational Surveys*, p. 13.

65. For an extensive discussion of these relationships, see M. Van Sell, A. P. Brief, and R. S. Schuler, "Role Conflict and Role Ambiguity: Integration of the Literature and Directions for Future Research," *Human Relations* 34 (1980): 43–72; R. S. Schuler, "A Role and Expectancy Perception Model of Participation in Decision Making," *Academy of Management Journal* 23 (1980): 331–50.

66. For a helpful discussion of what a proper, professionally designed survey should look like, as well as a presentation of the functions (e.g., employee development, assessment of change, a management audit) a well-designed survey serves in contributing to the overall planning process, see D. R. York, "Attitude Surveying," *Personnel Journal* (May 1985): 70–73. Some words of caution about misinterpreting attitude survey data are offered in R. C. Ernest and L. B. Baenen, "Analysis of Attitude Survey Results: Getting the Most from the Data," *Personnel Administrator* (May 1985): 71–80.

Summary Case

The Tall Pines Hotel and Conference Center*

Gordon McGregor sorted through his morning mail to find the report from Natalie Sharp about the open house sponsored by the hotel for job applicants. With the sounds of hammering and the smell of fresh paint all around, he was eager to get a picture of his new staff as he neared the opening of the hotel in about two months. He pushed aside samples of carpeting left by a subcontractor this morning to read the five-page report from Natalie.

As hotel manager, Gordon was faced with the last of the major hurdles in getting Tall Pines open—the filling of about 315 positions ranging from bellhops and butchers to clerks and chambermaids. The grand opening scheduled for May first made it imperative to bring his full staff on board and get them trained and operational quickly. He had brought in most of his managerial and supervisory staff over the past six months. Many had come from other hotels in the nationwide chain. Some he had worked with in other parts of the chain in his fifteen years in the system, so there was a sense of excitement about being together as a team to create something brand new. Today marked the beginning of the final phase of his plan to manage his own hotel successfully.

The Tall Pines Hotel

Gordon had been involved in the planning of the hotel for about two years. Corporate management had selected the site four years ago on the basis of a careful study by its market research staff of the southeastern part of the United States. They were interested in launching a new concept in hotels and had chosen the city of Riverton (pop. 95,000), located in the suburbs of Roosevelt City, a major city in the Southeast. The entire metropolitan area had grown dramatically since the early 1960s to a total population of about 1.9 million, with further growth forecast for the next fifteen years before a leveling off would occur.

Riverton comprised about half the area and two-thirds the population of one of counties that surrounded Roosevelt City. Growth in population, wealth, and industry had been concentrated in the suburban counties, although there was new interest in the revitalization of the old downtown area. Riverton had been especially aggressive in its plan to attract new industry with the creation of an economic development committee, which had been successful in enticing a number of high-technology firms to open offices or build small facilities within the city limits. Many offices had moved from

---

*By D. Jeffrey Lenn, School of Government and Business Administration, George Washington University, 1986. This case is based on an actual situation, but the names, location, and other significant data have been altered to provide anonymity. Its purpose is not to focus on effective or ineffective management but to provide a basis for teaching and discussion.

Roosevelt into the suburbs to take advantage of lower taxes, new buildings, and a pool of skilled workers. Shopping centers, restaurants, and housing developments mushroomed to meet the demands of the population shift.

Corporate management saw the opportunity to fill a niche in the suburbs because of lack of hotel and conference space. They purchased an eighteen-acre tract on a major highway that entered Roosevelt City from the south on the west side of Riverton. It was to be developed as a campuslike setting with the preservation of two major pine groves and the expansion of a natural lake. The hotel had been constructed in line with these plans to include 350 rooms, two swimming pools, three restaurants, small shops, and a small exercise and weight room. An outdoor jogging trail was being completed as well. The conference center was built to cater to corporate meetings with secretarial services, teleconferencing facilities, and even access to personal computers. The entire facility was oriented toward comfortable stays of extended periods as well as overnight lodging.

An architect of national reputation had designed the building to become a focal point for the surrounding area. Twin towers jutted through the pines to provide the foundation for a five-story atrium. The glass enclosure provided light and freshness to the restaurants and public space below. The building was striking as viewed from the interstate in both directions, standing boldly against the horizon and rising from the pine groves. Tall Pines was a particularly appropriate name for the entire center, which could act as a comfortable retreat from both city activity and corporate life.

The building had also been controversial. The Riverton Board of Architectural Review was besieged by complaints about the design. But support from the city council and the mayor dissolved the opposition quickly. Projections of a $3.8 million payroll and annual tax bills of $350,000 for the city and $420,000 for the state made the entire project highly appealing. The board voted unanimously to accept the architectural plans.

Natalie Sharp, Director of Personnel

Last November, Gordon had hired Natalie Sharp to become his director of personnel. She had worked for two other hotel chains after college and then been hired three years ago to help with the opening of a new one-hundred-room hotel in the Southwest. She had done an outstanding job of staffing this hotel set in the center of an older city undergoing major renovation. Corporate management was enthusiastic about her potential and had urged Gordon to consider her for the job. Two days of interviews at Tall Pines confirmed this potential as well as the experience he needed in opening a new hotel.

Natalie was given the responsibility for the entire staffing process, although Gordon had made it clear that his department managers had the final authority for those working in their departments. Supervisory personnel were hired with Natalie confirming managerial decisions and working out job descriptions, salaries, and other specifics for each position.

Her major task was the recruitment and hiring program for the bulk of the staff to ready the hotel for opening on May first. She and Gordon had met in the middle of January to review her plan. She had worked closely with the state Department of Employment Services as well as Riverton's Employment Options Office to arrange for a Job Fair on February fifteenth. Held at a local school on a Saturday, the fair was designed to attract candidates and provide a screening session and even some first-round interviews. Tall Pines would provide a good package of benefits on top of a competitive wage:

- Blue Cross/Blue Shield
- Paid vacation (after one year)
- Pension plan (vested after seven years)
- On-site job training
- Educational benefits

Natalie had convinced Gordon that although minimum wage would be the controlling factor for many entry-level positions, the promise of raises in six months was needed as an inducement for retention of good employees.

Natalie believed that the primary pool of candidates would be found in Roosevelt City and Riverton. The figures provided by a local governmental agency supported her belief that a number of people would apply for the various positions to be filled.

LOCAL UNEMPLOYMENT RATES*	
Metropolitan area	3.7%
Roosevelt City	8.1
Riverton	5.0
All suburbs	3.7
*December figures.	

An advertising campaign directed toward the larger metropolitan area, coupled with state and city support, should yield at least double the number of candidates needed for each position. Natalie had shown Gordon a series of articles in the *Metro Star*, the major daily, about a large hotel opening last year in the center of Roosevelt City. Over 11,000 applications were made for 350 positions; the articles included pictures of long lines of people trying to get through the door for interviews. Tall Pines would find an eager group ready to work at its hotel.

The Disappointing Report

The note of optimism of last month was missing from the short report on yesterday's Job Fair. Just over 200 people had applied for the 315 positions. Of these, only 75 had been screened and interviewed. Most had little experience in the hotel business but seemed capable of on-the-job training. The applicants were mostly from the surrounding towns in the county and Riverton, with a few from Roosevelt City.

Natalie had done an informal survey of her small cadre of interviewers late in the afternoon. Applicants had concerns about wage scales and transportation. Unskilled workers with some experience found it difficult to believe that they would start at minimum wage, saying that they could get more at many fast-food chains. Three employees from Big Tex, a regional hamburger chain, had come to the fair together and reported that the chain had just upped starting salaries for counter help to seventy-five cents above minimum wage. Natalie's follow-up call to Big Tex, as well as her conversation with a representative of the county chamber of commerce, had confirmed that many employers were offering hourly wages in excess of minimum wage simply to fill empty positions.

The concerns about transportation were more difficult to bring into focus. Natalie pieced together a picture of Tall Pines being out of the way for most people using public transportation. A few asked about whether the hotel planned to provide bus transportation into Roosevelt City. It had taken them nearly an hour from home with a transfer from a subway stop onto a bus, which dropped them off about three blocks away. Riverton residents indicated that it took thirty minutes to get over from the east side of the city, which meant crossing the interstate because the bus route ended there. Location clearly was a factor in keeping applicants away.

The Stream of Telephone Calls

Gordon's optimism about his gala opening was suddenly deflated by this report. Natalie's conclusion was concisely stated in one sentence:

> I have arranged another Job Fair in ten days with the hope that our results will be better this time.

He wondered whether there would be enough candidates for the remaining positions and whether there would be enough time to train them after all of the necessary personnel paperwork had been completed.

His thoughts were interrupted by a call from his secretary indicating that a reporter was on the line from the *Riverton Telegram*, asking questions about the Job Fair. He directed the call to Natalie's office. A call from the *Metro Star* was also redirected. But he did take a call from the Riverton mayor's office to assure them that the hotel had the hiring situation under control with the opening still set for May first. Later in the afternoon, the director of one of the associations scheduled to hold a conference at the hotel during the first week called to ask about the opening. Bad news travels fast! thought Gordon as he hung up with another set of assurances to the anxious director.

Natalie sailed into the office to report on the two phone calls from the press. Both had received information about the disappointing turnout at the Job Fair and were interested in both the reasons and the impact on the opening. She thought that it would be difficult to assess the impact of the publicity until the morning editions were out. Gordon suggested a breakfast meeting with the hotel's top staff to discuss the problem and work toward a solution.

The Breakfast Staff Meeting

Both papers covered the story with short articles hidden away in the second sections. The *Telegram* headline read:

NEW HOTEL NEEDS 240 WORKERS

It briefly described the low turnout at the Job Fair with a listing of the positions still available. A quote from Natalie indicated that another fair would be held in the near future. The story was done in a generally favorable light with emphasis on new business within Riverton, which the hotel should attract.

The *Star* headline was more critical:

NEW SUBURBAN HOTEL SURPRISED TO
FIND FEW APPLY FOR 315 JOBS

The new twin towers were pictured along with a sheet from the fair that listed the jobs available at the hotel. Natalie was quoted about the continuing search to be carried out as well as the types of benefits offered by Tall Pines. A representative of the Roosevelt City Office of Job Services was quoted: "It's not so much that people here won't look in the suburbs; it's that once you cross over that city line, there is a mental barrier about being away from home. Employers have to offer good jobs, good transportation, and a lot of encouragement to get people to apply." A union office spokesman wondered whether people were discouraged because Tall Pines is a nonunion hotel. A man who had been offered a second interview at the fair indicated that he would rather work close to his home in Roosevelt City, but had been out of work for four months and needed the job.

Gordon and Natalie agreed that neither article gave a negative perspective on hotel management, but questions could be raised about postponement of the opening. Clearly, it was important to follow up with the Riverton mayor's office as well as meeting planners who had scheduled the hotel opening for May and June to assure them that the situation would be under control. Contact with the Roosevelt City Office of Job Services was mandatory now.

At the meeting, Gordon asked Natalie to review her report as well as the press clippings for the assembled department heads. They both answered a number of questions about the Job Fair and the type of applicants at the fair. Gordon suggested that they delay the discussion about the future until later in the meeting so that all of the facts surrounding the problem could be sorted through carefully. It became clear that many departments could operate for the first two weeks in May on a reduced staffing pattern using supervisory personnel to fill in. But a full staff was essential to accommodate the anticipated increase in business.

The meeting then turned to a brainstorming session to help Natalie develop a strategy for attracting people who would be good candidates to fill the remaining positions. The group agreed that four areas merited further consideration:

- *Advertising campaign*
  Directed particularly toward Roosevelt City and Riverton with focus on benefits of working at Tall Pines.
- *Upgrade of wage scale*
  Additions to minimum wage for entry-level jobs in order to be competitive. Necessity for incentive pay to retain good employees.
- *Transportation system*
  Necessity for assistance to workers coming from both Riverton and Roosevelt City in particular because of their reliance on public transportation.
- *Cooperation with public agencies*
  Cultivation of relationships with a number of agencies to identify other applicant pools.

Gordon asked Natalie to make use of these ideas in the development of a plan to fill the 240 remaining positions. He assured the managers that he would call them the next day with a finalized plan to meet the objective of full staffing by May first. In the meantime, he would handle the public relations aspect of the issue through his office. The meeting adjourned with an agreement that any hotel was only as good as its personnel.

Reflections Over Lunch

As manager of Tall Pines, Gordon enjoyed a number of perquisites unavailable in other jobs. Today, he was delighted to initiate one of those—access to the best meals from the hotel kitchens. Jack Sanders, the sales and convention manager, wheeled in a cart of delectable dishes prepared by one of the French chefs interviewing for the position as head chef. Expecting to join Gordon for lunch, he set a small table for two and uncorked a bottle of wine. As he settled into one of the chairs and pulled out his napkin, Gordon interrupted: "Sorry, Jack. This is a working lunch for me with all of this hiring mess on my mind. You're welcome to take a plate back to your office, but I need to be alone to get a handle on this situation." Jack excused himself, a full plate and wineglass in hand, while Gordon settled into his chair.

The meal was excellent, with the wine chosen for its appropriate balance with the food. Gordon thought about his fortunate managerial situation—no fast-food lunches, no traveling throughout the week, and no narrow job responsibilities. All of these were left behind for any hotel manager. There was a sense of excitement about what lay in store for him both here at Tall Pines and within the larger national organization as it expanded.

But the past day had drowned out much of that excitement. What seemed so close to completion was now filled with a number of questions. Could Tall Pines attract a good staff? Could they be trained and on the job by May first? How costly was it going to be to pay a competitive wage? Could he instill within the staff a sense of pride about Tall Pines? Could the hotel open on May first?

The smell of paint, the carpet samples, and even the faint sound of hammers now came into fuller focus as he asked the last question. Where had he gone wrong in the development of his plan to open the hotel? Why didn't he foresee a potential problem about staffing earlier? Getting the right people seemed like the easiest of his plans to implement. Now it looked like an impossible task. With a cup of coffee in hand, he moved back to his desk to begin the process of solving the problem he faced.

Appendixes

Legislation, Court, and NLRB Decisions Affecting Personnel and Human Resource Management

---

Legislation/Basic Provisions

Employment Legislation

Act	*Jurisdiction*	*Basic Provisions*
Fair Labor Standards Act (1938) and subsequent amendments—FLSA	Most interstate employers, certain types of employees are exempt from overtime provisions—executive, administrative, and professional employees and outside salespeople	Establishes a minimum wage; controls hours through premium pay for overtime; controls working hours for children
Minimum Wage Law (1977)	Small businesses	Sets graduated increases in minimum wage rates
Equal Pay Act (1963 amendment to the FLSA)	Same as FLSA except no employees are exempt	Prohibits unequal pay for males and females with equal skills, effort, and responsibility working under similar working conditions
Civil Rights Act (1964) (amended by EEOA 1972)	Employers with fifteen or more employees, employment agencies, and labor unions	Prevents discrimination on the basis of race, color, religion, sex, or national origin; establishes EEOC
Equal Employment Opportunity Act (1972)—EEOA	Adds employees of state and local government and educational institutions; reduced number of employees required to fifteen	Amends Title VII; increases enforcement powers of EEOC

Act	*Jurisdiction*	*Basic Provisions*
Executive Order 11246 (1965) as amended by Executive Order 11375 (1966)	Federal contractors and subcontractors with contracts over $50,000 and fifty or more employees	Prevents discrimination on the basis of race, color, religion, sex or national origin; establishes Office of Federal Contract Compliance (OFCC)
Revised Order Number 4 (1971)	Federal contractors	Defines acceptable affirmative action program
Executive Order 11478 (1969)	Federal agencies	Prevents discrimination on the basis of race, color, religion, sex, or national origin
Age Discrimination in Employment Act (1967)— Revised 1978; 1986	Employers with more than twenty-five employees	Prevents discrimination against persons from age forty and states compulsory retirement for some workers
Vocational Rehabilitation Act (1973) as amended 1980	Government contractors and federal agencies	Prevents discrimination against person with physical and/or mental handicaps and provides for affirmative action
Prevailing wage laws—1. Davis-Bacon Act (1931) and 2. Walsh-Healey Act (1935)	Employers with government construction projects of $2,000 (Davis-Bacon) and government contracts of $10,000 or more	Guarantees prevailing wages to employees of government contractors
Legally required fringe benefits— 1. OASDHI (1935 and amendments)	Virtually all employers	Provides income and health care to retired employees and income to the survivors of employees who have died
2. Unemployment compensation (1935)	Virtually all employers	Provides income to employees who are laid off or fired
3. Workers' compensation (dates differ from state to state)	Virtually all employers	Provides benefits to employees who are injured on the job and to the survivors of employees who are killed on the job
Occupational Safety and Health Act (1970)—OSHA	Most interstate employers	Assures as far as possible every working man and woman in the nation safe and healthful working conditions and to preserve our human resources

Act	*Jurisdiction*	*Basic Provisions*
Employee Retirement Income Security Act (1974)—ERISA	Most interstate employers with pension plans (no employer is required to have such a plan)	Protects employees covered by a pension plan from losses in benefits due to: ■ mismanagement ■ plant closings and bankruptcies ■ job changes
Freedom of Information Act	Federal agencies only	Allows individuals to see all the material used in a decision made about them
The Pregnancy Discrimination Act of 1978 (1978 Civil Rights Act Amendment to Title VII)	Same as Civil Rights Act (1964)	Pregnancy is a disability and, furthermore, must receive the same benefits as any other disability
Privacy Act of 1974 (Public Law 93–579)	Federal agencies only	Allows individuals to review employers' records on them and bring civil damages
Uniform Guidelines on Employee Selection Procedures (1978)	Same as EEOA (1972)	Updates EEOC 1970 guidelines to more clearly define adverse impact and test validation
Guidelines on Sexual Harassment (1980)	Same as EEOA (1972)	Defines standards for what constitutes harassment
Vietnam Era Veterans Readjustment Act (1974)	Government contractors with contracts in excess of $10,000	Provides for affirmative action in the employment of Vietnam era veterans
Civil Rights Act of 1866 Section 1981	All citizens	It gives all persons, regardless of race, alienage, and national origin, the same contractual rights as "white citizens." Does not apply to sex-based discrimination
Civil Rights Act of 1871 Section 1983	All citizens	As the Civil Rights Act of 1866 but does apply to sex-based discrimination
The First Amendment, U.S. Constitution	All citizens	Guarantees freedom of speech and religion
The Fifth Amendment	All citizens	No person shall be deprived of life, liberty, or property without the due process of law
The Fourteenth Amendment	All citizens	Prohibits abridgment of federally conferred privileges by actions of the state

Labor Relations Legislation: Private Sector

Act	*Jurisdiction*	*Basic Provisions*
Railway Labor Act (1926)— RLA	Railroad workers and airline employees	Provides right to organize; provides majority choice of representatives; prohibits "yellow dog" contracts; outlines dispute settlement procedures
Norris-LaGuardia Act (1932)	All employers and labor organizations	No yellow dog contracts; no injunction for nonviolent activity of unions (strikes, picketing, and boycotts); limited union liability
National Labor Relations Act (1935)—Wagner Act	Nonmanagerial employees in private industry not covered by Railway Labor Act (RLA)	Provides right to organize; provides for collective bargaining; requires employers to bargain; unions must represent all members equally
Labor-Management Relations Act (1947)—Taft-Hartley	Nonmanagerial employees in private industry not covered by RLA	Prohibits unfair labor practices of unions; outlaws closed shop; prohibits strikes in national emergencies; requires both parties to bargain in good faith
Labor Management Reporting and Disclosure Act (1959)—Landrum-Griffin	Labor organizations	Outlines procedures for redressing internal union problems
Amendments to Taft-Hartley Act (1974)	Labor organizations	Specifies illegal activities within union

Labor Relations Legislation: Public Sector

Executive Order 10988 (1962)	Federal employees	Recognizes employees' right to join unions and bargain collectively; prohibits strikes. Requires agency to meet and confer with union on policy practices and working conditions
Executive Orders 11616 (1971) 11838 (1975)	Federal employees	Expand EO 11491 to cover labor-management relations: cover disputes of bargaining rights; order elections; consolidate units; limit scope of grievance and arbitration procedures

Act	*Jurisdiction*	*Basic Provisions*
Civil Service Reform Act Title VII (1978)	Federal employees	Defines grievance procedure and requirements for goal-type performance appraisals; establishes Senior Executive Service (SES)

Court and NLRB Decisions/Basic Provisions

Title/Date

Griggs v. *Duke Power* (1971)
Test for hiring cannot be used unless job related. Organization must show evidence of job relatedness. Not necessary to establish intent to discriminate.

Albemarle v. *Moody* (1975)
Need to establish evidence that test related to content of job. Could use job analysis to do so, but not evidence from global performance ratings made by supervisors.

Washington v. *Davis* (1976)
When a test procedure is challenged under constitutional law, intent to discriminate must be established. No need to establish intent if file under Title VII, just show effects. Could use communication test to select applicants for police force.

Dothard v. *Rawlinson* (1977)
Height requirements not valid, therefore constitutes discriminatory practice.

Bakke v. *Regents of the University of California* (1978)
Reverse discrimination not allowed. Race, however, can be used in selection decisions. Affirmative action programs permissible when prior discrimination established.

Brito v. *Zia Company* (1973)
Zia violated Title VII because they laid off a disproportionate number of a protected group on the basis of low performance scores on measures that were not validated.

Marshall v. *Barlow's, Inc.* (1979)
Employers are not required to let OSHA inspectors enter their premises unless they have search warrants.

Marshall v. *Whirlpool* (1980)
Employees have right to refuse job assignment if constitutes clear and present danger to life or limb. Employer, however, not required to pay if, as a result, employee sent home because of no work.

Wade v. *Mississippi Cooperative Extension Service* (1976)
Performance scores used to decide promotions and salary issues not valid because no job analysis.

James v. *Stockman Values and Fittings Company* (1977)
Applicants to apprenticeship program selected by white supervisors without formal guidelines is discriminatory. Need more discrete performance appraisal.

Patterson v. *American Tobacco Company* (1976, 1978)

Sledge v. *J. P. Stevens & Company* (1978)

Donaldson v. *Pillsbury Company* (1977)
All of these three require clear establishment and communication of job requirements and performance standards.

Rowe v. *General Motors Corporation* (1972)

Robinson v. *Union Carbide Corporation* (1976)
These two require written standards for promotion to help prevent discrimination.

Watkins v. *Scott Paper Company* (1976)
Performance data to validate tests that are derived from graphic scales are too vague and easily subject to discrimination.

Gilmore v. *Kansas City Terminal Railway Company* (1975)

Meyer v. *Missouri State Highway Commission* (1977)

United States v. *City of Chicago* (1978)
These three require in promotion cases specific promotion criteria that are related to the job to which being promoted.

Spurlock v. *United Airlines* (1972)
Use of college degree as a selection criterion valid because job related, even though no performance data provided.

Hodgson v. *Greyhound Lines, Inc.* (1974)
Could discriminate without empirical evidence on basis of age. Good faith used to show older people would make less safe drivers.

Richardson v. *Hotel Corporation of America* (1972)
Dismissal on grounds on conviction record resulted in adverse impact. But since conviction record argued (not shown) to be related to business necessity (not job performance) dismissal is okay.

Northwest Airlines, Inc. v. *Transport Workers* (1981)
An employer found guilty of job discrimination cannot force an employee's union to contribute to the damages, even though the union may have negotiated the unequal terms.

Texas Department of Community Affairs v. *Joyce Ann Burdine* (1981)
A defendant in a job discrimination case need only provide a legitimate, nondiscriminatory explanation for not hiring or promoting a woman or minority, and need not prove that the white man hired was better qualified. The burden of proving intentional discrimination rests with the plaintiff.

Fernandez v. *Wynn Oil Company* (1981)
Title VII does not permit employers to use stereotypic impressions of male and female roles as a BFOQ defense to sex discrimination. Employer can't use customer preferences for working with male employees as a defense of discrimination.

EEOC v. *Sandia Corporation* (1980)
Discrimination against employees protected by ADEA in regard to a decision on work force reduction required by budget restraints. Used a subjective (ranking) evaluation form for their scientists, engineers, and technical employees. Statistical impact and informal comments indicated bias.

Weahkee v. *Perry* (1978) and *Weahkee* v. *Norton* (1980)

Use of quotas in performance evaluation not objectively used or enforced so not justified in using if discrimination results. Weahkee was reinstated, but no finding of discrimination.

Flowers v. *Crouch-Walter Corporation* (1977)

Plaintiff established *prima facie* evidence that a discharge was discriminatory and not based on performance.

Diaz v. *Pan American World Airways, Inc.* (1971)

The primary function of an airline is to transport passengers safely from one point to another. Therefore, not hiring males for flight attendants is discriminatory. *Business necessity* is established.

Harper v. *Trans World Airlines, Inc.* (1975)

Smith v. *Mutual Benefit Life Insurance Company* (1976)

Tuck v. *McGraw-Hill, Inc.* (1976)

Yukas v. *Libbey-Owens-Ford* (1977)

All of these against nepotism, especially close relatives and spouses, are nondiscriminatory, especially in same department and/or as in supervisor-subordinate relationship.

Smith v. *Mutual Benefit Life Insurance Company* (1976)

Employer is not discriminating if refusing to hire male appearing to be effeminate.

United Air Lines, Inc. v. *McMann* (1977)

Employer can force retirement before age of sixty-five if has bona fide retirement plan; since AEDA (1978) can't force retirement before age of seventy.

Lehman v. *Yellow Freight System* (1981)

Informal affirmative action not permissible although formal voluntary one such as *Weber* is okay.

Fullilove v. *Klutznick* (1980)

Congress can impose racial quotas in handing out federal money (10 percent) to federal contractors who are minority owned (51 percent).

International Brotherhood of Teamsters v. *United States* (1977)

Bona fide seniority systems maintained without discriminatory intent are exempt from Title VII liability if established before 1964.

American Tobacco v. *Patterson* (1982)

Bona fide seniority systems without discriminating intent are exempt from Title VII liability.

United States v. *Trucking Management, Inc.* (1981)

Same as in prior above *Teamsters* case, but adds exemption from EO 11246 also.

County of Washington, Oregon v. *Gunther* (1981)

It can be illegal (under Title VII and EPA 1963) to pay women unfairly low wages even if not doing same work as men (not a comparable worth case).

First National Maintenance v. *NLRB* (1981)

Management does not have to negotiate with unions in advance over closing plants or dropping lines.

American Textile Manufacturers Institute v. *Donovan* (1981)
OSHA need not do cost benefit analyses before issuing working health standards.

Los Angeles Department of Water v. *Manhart* (1978)
Employer is required to provide equal benefits to employees under both Title VII and EPA.

Tomkins v. *Public Service Electric and Gas Company et al.* (1977)

Heelen v. *Johns-Manville Corporation* (1978)

William v. *Saxbe* (1976)

Barnes v. *Costle* (1977)
All of these state that sexual harassment is a form of sex discrimination under Title VII, Section 703, and employer is responsible if takes no action on learning of events.

Tooley v. *Martin-Marietta Corporation* (1981)
Must be religious accommodation for employees who object to union membership or support (as long as no undue hardship on union).

McDonnell Douglas Corporation v. *Green* (1973)
Employer's test device constitutes *prima facie* case of racial discrimination under four different criteria.

Rogers v. *International Paper Company* (1975)
Subjective criteria are not to be condemned as unlawful per se because some decisions about hiring and promotions in supervisory and managerial jobs cannot be made using objective standards alone. This opinion, however, is somewhat contrary to those in *Albemarle Paper Company* v. *Moody* (1973); *Baxter* v. *Savannah Sugar Refining Corporation* (1974); and *Rowe* v. *General Motors* (1972).

Stringfellow v. *Monsanto Corporation* (1970)
Established the precedent for giving credit to the employer for making performance appraisal–based decisions on the basis of evidence that the appraisal uses definite identifiable criteria based on the quality and quantity of an employee's work.

Mastie v. *Great Lakes Steel Corporation* (1976)
As with *Stringfellow,* the court said that the objectivity of evaluation can be established by demonstrating that the company performed and relied on a thorough evaluation process intended to be used fairly and accurately.

Oshiver v. *Court of Common Pleas* (1979)
Without objective or extrinsic documented evidence of poor performance or evidence not hastily developed, an employment decision is suspect if based on the notion of "poor performance."

Mistretta v. *Sandia Corporation* (1977)
Employment decisions suspect when based on evaluations that reflect only best judgments and opinions of evaluators rather than identifiable criteria based on quality or quantity of work or specific performances that are supported by some kind of record.

Clayton v. *United Auto Workers* (1981)
When a union member feels unfairly represented and only the employer can grant the relief requested, the employee need not exhaust internal union remedies before suing the employer.

NLRB v. *Wright Line, Inc.* (1981)
In cases where an employee is fired for what may appear to be union-related activities, the employer must show (to be vindicated in the dismissal) that the discipline imposed is the same as in other cases where union activity was not an issue.

Connecticut v. *Teal* (1982)
Employers must defend each part of a selection process against adverse impact and not just the end result of the entire process (the bottom line).

Hodgson v. *Robert Hall Clothes, Inc.* (1973)
Pay differentials between salesmen and saleswomen justified on the basis of profitability of area in which employees work.

Corning Glass Works v. *Brennan* (1974)
The Equal Pay Act is violated by paying male inspectors on the night shift a higher base wage than female inspectors on the day shift.

Schultz v. *Wheaton Glass* (1979)
The employer's lower wage rate for women is in violation of the Equal Pay Act when the wage differentials are based on artificially created job classifications that differentiate otherwise equal jobs.

Castaneda v. *Partida* (1977)
Prima facie evidence of discrimination established when evidence of both statistical disparity and discriminatory selection procedures vis-à-vis the gross population figures.

EEOC v. *United Virginia Bank* (1980)
Prima facie evidence of discrimination established on the basis of statistical disparity vis-à-vis the relevant labor market (i.e., comparably qualified individuals).

Phillips v. *Martin Marietta Corp* (1971)
Whether a BFOQ exists is whether it can be shown that the qualification is demonstrably more relevant to job performance for a woman than a man.

General Foods Corp. (1977)
Corporatewide team program of employee-employer cooperation does not violate the National Labor Relations Act because program established to promote efficiency, not forestall unionization.

Kirkland v. *New York Department of Correctional Services* (1975)
The use of quotas was rejected as a method of determining promotions except as an interim measure to be used until nondiscriminatory procedures to determine promotion are established.

Sugarman v. *Dougal* (1973)
The due process and equal protection clauses of the Fifth Amendment also apply to aliens in public employment.

Steelworkers v. *Weber* (1979)
Quota system to admit employees into a training program may supersede seniority provisions as long as the program is a temporary one to correct past employment practices and does not trample the interests of the more senior employees.

Stamps (EEOC) v. *Detroit Edison* (1975)
Title VII does not provide for an award of punitive damages. Back pay and attorney fees are the explicit provisions of Title VII.

Green v. *Missouri Pacific R.R. Co.* (1975)
Applying the lessons from *Griggs* v. *Duke Power*, the court and the EEOC have found it unlawful to refuse to hire job applicants because of their arrest record except for certain circumstances (*Richardson* v. *Hotel Corporation of America*).

State Division of Human Rights v. *Rochester Housing Authority* (1980)
Although religious preferences cannot be used for discrimination, an employer may defend not hiring an applicant because of religion by showing that a reasonable attempt was made to accommodate the applicant.

Backus v. *Baptist Medical Center* (1981)
A defense of bona fide occupational qualifications was extended to permit the hiring and staffing of only female nurses in an obstetrics and gynecology department in a hospital.

Newport News Shipbuilding and Dry Dock Co. v. *EEOC* (1983)
If an employer supplies any level of health benefits to female workers' husbands, the employer must also supply the same level of benefits to male workers' wives, and that includes pregnancy benefits. This, in effect, reverses the Supreme Court's ruling in *General Electric* v. *Gilbert*, where the court said that pregnancy benefits need not be given the same treatment by employers as other health and disability programs.

Arizona Governing Committee v. *Norris* (1983)
Pension pay-outs by employers should be equal for women and men, and past unequal treatment of women must be cured by retroactive funding of pensions. This decision is in essence the other half of the issue. The first half was rendered in the Supreme Court decision of *Los Angeles Department of Water and Power* v. *Manhart*, where the decision was made that requiring larger contributions by females than males into pension programs is discriminatory.

NLRB v. *Transportation Management* (1983)
Employees are protected by the NLRA when helping organize employees. If an employee claims to be fired for trying to organize a union but the employer claims it was poor performance, the employer has the burden of proof. In cases where such "mixed" motives for employer action may exist, the employer must prove the case.

Firefighters Local Union No. 1784 v. *Stotts* (1984)
In this decision, the Supreme Court upheld the bona fide seniority system over an affirmative action consent decree in a situation of layoffs. Thus, the employees most recently hired could be subject to layoff even though this action could compromise the affirmative action efforts.

Pattern Makers' League v. *NLRB* (1985)
Employees may resign from a union at any time, even during a strike or when one is imminent.

Scott v. *Sears Roebuck* (1985)
Woman unsuccessful in sex harassment suit based on acts by co-workers. Woman did not complain to supervisors. Court ruled only responsible for acts of co-workers if they knew or should have known of acts and took no action.

Horn v. *Duke Homes* (1985)
Court endorsed principle that employers have strict liability for sexual harassment by supervisors (company claimed that it was not liable because it was not aware of the behavior). Court supported full back pay (plaintiff had been terminated).

Glasgow v. *Georgia Pacific Corp.* (1985)

Court accepts sexual harassment argument on basis of creating hostile work environment (no *quid pro quo*). Company was found by Court to have made sexually harassing environment a condition of employment because harassment went on for long period of time with organization doing nothing. Court outlined four-point test for sexually harassing work environment.

1. Harassment was unwelcome
2. Harassment was because of sex
3. Harassment affected terms and conditions of employment
4. Knowledge of harassment is "imputed" to employer

Wygant v. *Jackson Board of Education* (1986)

The Court ruled that white teachers were illegally dismissed in order to hire minority teachers in the School Board's efforts to fulfill a voluntary affirmative action program.

Local 28 of the Sheet Metal Workers v. *Equal Employment Opportunity Commission* (1986)

The Court approved a lower court order requiring a New York City sheet metal workers' local to meet a 29 percent minority membership goal by 1987. The Court also held that judges may order racial preferences in union membership and other contexts if necessary to rectify especially "egregious" discrimination.

Local 93 of the International Association of Firefighters v. *City of Cleveland* (1986)

The Court held that lower Federal courts have broad discretion to approve decrees in which employers, over the objections of white employees, settle discrimination suits by agreeing to preferential hiring or promotion of minority-group members. It upheld a decree in which Cleveland agreed to settle a job discrimination suit by black and Hispanic firefighters by temporarily promoting black and Hispanic workers ahead of whites who had more seniority and higher test scores.

Meritor Savings Bank v. *Vinson* (1986)

The Court held that sexual harassment is a form of sex discrimination prohibited by Title VII of the Civil Rights Act and that employers may be liable for condoning a hostile work environment. However, the Court made it clear that employers will not be automatically liable for sexual harassment by supervisors or employees.

---

*This set of court cases is meant to be a sample of all those referenced in the text. For description of these and of the other cases, see J. Ledvinka, *Federal Regulation of Personnel and Human Resource Management* (Boston: Kent, 1983); J. Bernardin and W. Cascio, *Annotated Bibliography of Court Cases Relevant to Employment Decisions 1980–1984* (Boca Raton: Florida Atlantic University, 1984); M. D. Levin-Epstein, *Primer of Equal Employment Opportunity*, 3d ed. (Washington, D.C.: NA, 1984); and M. McCarthy, ed., *Complete Guide to Employing Persons with Disabilities* (Albertson, N.Y.: National Center on Employment of the Handicapped at Human Resources Center, 1985).

B

Personnel and Human Resource Management Information

I. Journals and Associations

Employee Relations Law Journal, published by Executive Enterprises, Inc., 33 West 60th Street, New York, New York 10023. Articles on current personnel topics with the related legal considerations are contained in each quarterly issue.

Fair Employment Practices; Bulletin to Management; the Bulletin on Training, published by the Bureau of National Affairs, 1231 25th Street N.W., Washington, D.C. 20037.

Fair Employment Report, published by Business Publishers, Inc., 951 Pershing Drive, Silver Spring, Maryland 20910.

FEP Guidelines, published by the Bureau of Business Practices, 24 Rope Ferry Road, Waterford, Connecticut 06386.

Human Resource Management, published by the Graduate School of Business, University of Michigan, Ann Arbor, Michigan 48109.

Human Resources Planning, published by the Human Resources Planning Society, PO Box 2553, Grand Central Station, New York, New York 10017.

Industrial and Labor Relations Review, New York State School of Labor and Industrial Relations, Cornell University, Ithaca, New York. Opinions and reports of studies on labor legislation, collective bargaining, and related subjects.

Industrial Medicine and Surgery, Industrial Medicine Publishing Company, 605 North Michigan Avenue, Chicago, Illinois. Emphasizes health programs in industry, with reports on health hazards, occupational diseases, handicapped workers, medical services, and related subjects.

Industrial Relations, Institute of Industrial Relations, University of California, Berkeley and Los Angeles, California. Ideas and opinions as well as reports of research.

Journal of the American Society of Training Directors, official publication of the American Society of Training Directors, 2020 University Avenue, Madison, Wisconsin. Broad coverage of the personnel field, with a special emphasis on training problems.

Journal of Applied Psychology, American Psychological Association, 1313 16th Street N.W., Washington, D.C. All phases of applied psychology, with numerous reports of personnel research.

Journal of Personnel Administration and Industrial Relations, Personnel Research Publishers, Washington, D.C. Reports original studies and theoretical analyses in all phases of industrial relations.

Labor Law Journal, Commerce Clearing House, Inc., 214 N. Michigan Avenue,

Chicago, Illinois. Generally presents nonlegalistic discussions of legal phases of industrial relations.

Management Record, The Conference Board, 247 Park Avenue, New York, New York. Numerous reports of both experience and research, surveys conducted by the National Industrial Conference Board staff, and digests of symposia.

Management Review, American Management Association, 330 W. 42nd Street, New York, New York. General coverage of all phases of management.

Monthly Labor Review, Bureau of Labor Statistics, U.S. Department of Labor, Washington, D.C. Summaries of staff studies on industrial relations; statistical sections include continuing series on industrial disputes, employment, payrolls, and cost of living.

Personnel, American Management Association, 135 W. 50th Street, New York, New York. Broad interest in entire field of industrial relations, with numerous reports of surveys, studies, and experience.

Personnel Administrator, published by the American Society for Personnel Administration (ASPA), 606 Washington Street, Alexandria, Virginia 20221. Information on taking the ASPA's examinations for the purpose of becoming a certified personnel administrator can be obtained by writing to the ASPA.

Personnel Journal, published at *Personnel Journal,* 866 W. 18th Street, Costa Mesa, California. Covers a broad spectrum of topics in personnel and labor relations.

Personnel Management, formerly the *Journal of the Institute of Personnel Management,* Institute of Personnel Management, Management House, 80 Fetter Lane, London, England. Theory and practice in both personnel management and labor relations.

Personnel Psychology, PO Box 6965, College Station, Durham, North Carolina. Emphasizes reports on research in psychological aspects of personnel and industrial relations.

Public Personnel Quarterly, published by the International Personnel Management Association, 1859 K Street N.W., Washington, D.C.

Studies in Personnel Policy, National Industrial Conference Board, 247 Park Avenue, New York, New York. Mainly compares experience and evaluations of programs, with frequent surveys of policy and practice.

U.S. Small Business Administration (SBA), P.O. Box 15434, Fort Worth, Texas 76119.

II. Personnel Information Services

Title: BNA Policy and Practice Series—
  Personnel Management
Address: Bureau of National Affairs, Inc.,
  1231 25th Street, N.W., Washington, D.C.
  20037
Title: Commerce Clearing House:
  —Human Resources Management Series
  —Ideas and Trends in Personnel
  —Employment Relations
  —Compensation
  —Equal Employment Opportunity
  —Personnel Practices/Communications

Address: Commerce Clearing House, Inc.,
  4025 W. Peterson Avenue, Chicago, Illinois
  60646
Title: Prentice-Hall:
  Personnel Management
  a) Policies and Practices
  b) Communications
  Industrial Relations Guide
Address: Prentice-Hall, Inc., Englewood
  Cliffs, New Jersey 07632

III. State Labor Departments and Human Rights Commissions*

Alabama:
Department of Industrial
 Relations
Industrial Relations
 Building
Montgomery, Alabama
 36130

Alaska:
Department of Labor
P.O. Box 1149
Juneau, Alaska 99811

Alaska State Commission
 for Human Rights
431 W. 7th Ave., Suite 105
Anchorage, Alaska 99501

Arizona:
Department of Labor
1601 West Jefferson
 Street
P.O. Box 19070
Phoenix, Arizona 85005

Arizona Civil Rights
 Division
1275 W. Washington
Phoenix, Arizona 85007

Arkansas:
Department of Labor
1022 High Street
Little Rock, Arkansas
 72202

California:
Department of Industrial
 Relations
525 Golden Gate Avenue
P.O. Box 603
San Francisco, Calif.
 94101

Department of Fair
 Employment and
 Housing
1201 I Street
Sacramento, Calif. 95814

Colorado:
Department of Labor and
 Employment
251 East 12th Avenue
Denver, Colorado 80203

Colorado Civil Rights
 Commission
State Services Building
1525 Sherman Street
Denver, Colorado 80203

Connecticut:
State Board of Labor
 Relations
2000 Folly Brook
 Boulevard
Wethersfield, Conn. 06109

Commission on Human
 Rights and
 Opportunities
90 Washington Street
Hartford, Conn. 06115

Delaware:
Department of Labor and
 Industrial Relations
820 N. French Street
Wilmington, Del. 19801
(Includes
 Antidiscrimination
 Section)

District of Columbia:
D.C. Department of
 Employment Services
500 C Street, N.W.
Washington, D.C. 20001

Commission on Human
 Rights
1424 K Street, N.W.
Washington, D.C. 20004

Florida:
Industrial Relations
 Commission
Berkeley Building

2562 Executive Center
 Circle East
Tallahassee, Florida
 32301

Commission on Human
 Relations
Montgomery Building
2562 Executive Center
 Circle East
Tallahassee, Florida
 32301

Georgia:
Department of Labor
State Labor Building
254 Washington Street,
 S.W.
Atlanta, Georgia 30334

Guam:
Department of Labor
Government of Guam
Box 23548, GMF
Guam, M.I. 96921

Hawaii:
Department of Labor and
 Industrial Relations
825 Mililani Street
Honolulu, Hawaii 96813

Idaho:
Department of Labor and
 Industrial Services
Industrial
 Administration
 Building
317 Main Street
Boise, Idaho 83720

Commission on Human
 Rights
Statehouse
Boise, Idaho 83720

Illinois:
Department of Labor

910 South Michigan
Avenue
Chicago, Illinois 60605

Department of Human
Rights
32 West Randolph Street
Chicago, Illinois 60601

Indiana:
Division of Labor
Room 1013
Indiana State Office
Building
100 N. Senate Avenue
Indianapolis, Indiana
46204

Civil Rights Commission
311 West Washington
Street
Indianapolis, Indiana
46204

Iowa:
Bureau of Labor
307 East 7th Street
Des Moines, Iowa 50319

Civil Rights Commission
8th Floor
Colony Building
507 Tenth Street
Des Moines, Iowa 50319

Kansas:
Department of Human
Resources
Division of Labor
Management and
Labor Standards
512 West 6th Street
Topeka, Kansas 66603

Commission on Civil
Rights
535 Kansas Avenue,
5th Floor
Topeka, Kansas 60603

Kentucky:
Department of Labor
U.S. 127, South
Frankfort, Kentucky
40601

Commission on Human
Rights

823 Capital Plaza Tower
Frankfort, Kentucky
40601

Louisiana:
Department of Labor
1045 Natural Resources
Building
P.O. Box 44063
Baton Rouge, La. 70804

Maine:
Bureau of Labor
Standards
7th Floor
State Office Building
Augusta, Maine 04333

Human Rights
Commission
State House—Station 51
Augusta, Maine 04333

Maryland:
Division of Labor and
Industry
203 East Baltimore Street
Baltimore, Maryland
21202

Commission on Human
Relations
20 East Franklin Street
Baltimore, Maryland
21202

Massachusetts:
Department of Labor and
Industries
State Office Building
100 Cambridge Street
Boston, Massachusetts
02202

Commission Against
Discrimination
1 Ashburton Place
Suite 601
Boston, Massachusetts
02108

Michigan:
Department of Labor
Leonard Plaza Building
309 N. Washington
P.O. Box 30015
Lansing, Michigan 48909

Department of Civil
Rights
Billie Farnum Building
125 W. Allegan Street
Lansing, Michigan 48913

Minnesota:
Department of Labor and
Industry
444 Lafayette Road
St. Paul, Minnesota 55101

Department of Human
Rights
5th Floor, Bremer Tower
7th Place and Minnesota
St.
St. Paul, Minnesota 55101

Mississippi:
Employment Security
Commission
1520 West Capital
P.O. Box 1699
Jackson, Mississippi
39205

Missouri:
Department of Labor and
Industrial Relations
1904 Missouri Boulevard
P.O. Box 599
Jefferson City, Mo. 65102

Commission on Human
Rights
204 Metro Drive
Jefferson City, Mo. 65102

Montana:
Department of Labor and
Industry
Capital Station
Helena, Montana 59620

Human Rights
Commission
23 South Last Chance
Gulch
Helena, Montana 59620

Nebraska:
Department of Labor
550 S. 16th Street
Box 94600
State House Station
Lincoln, Nebraska 68509

Equal Opportunity
Commission
301 Centennial Mall,
South
P.O. Box 94934
Lincoln, Nebraska 68509

Nevada:
State Labor Commission
Capitol Complex
505 East King Street
Carson City, Nevada
89710

Equal Rights Commission
1515 E. Tropicana
Las Vegas, Nevada 89158

New Hampshire:
Department of Labor
19 Pillsbury Street
Concord, N.H. 03301

Commission for Human
Rights
61 South Spring Street
Concord, N.H. 03301

New Jersey:
Department of Labor
CN 110
Trenton, New Jersey
08625

Division on Civil Rights
1100 Raymond Boulevard
Newark, New Jersey
07102

New Mexico:
State Labor and
Industrial Commission
509 Camino de Los
Marquez
Santa Fe, New Mexico
87501

Human Rights
Commission
303 Bataan Memorial
Bldg.
Santa Fe, New Mexico
87503

New York:
Department of Labor
State Campus
Albany, New York 12240

Division of Human Rights
Two World Trade Center
New York, N.Y. 10047

North Carolina:
Department of Labor
Labor Building
4 W. Edenton Street
Raleigh, N.C. 27601

North Dakota:
Department of Labor
State Capitol
Bismarck, North Dakota
58505

Ohio:
Department of Industrial
Relations
2323 W. 5th Avenue
Columbus, Ohio 43216

Civil Rights Commission
220 Parsons Avenue
Columbus, Ohio 43215

Oklahoma:
Department of Labor
State Capitol Building
Suite 118
Oklahoma City, Okla.
73105

Human Rights
Commission
Room G11
Jim Thorpe Building
P.O. Box 52945
Oklahoma City, Okla.
73152

Oregon:
Bureau of Labor and
Industries
State Office Building
1400 S.W. Fifth Avenue
Portland, Oregon 97201
(Includes Civil Rights
Division)

Pennsylvania:
Department of Labor and
Industry
1700 Labor and Industry
Building
Harrisburg, Pa. 17120

Human Relations
Commission
101 South Second Street
Suite 300, P.O. Box 3145
Harrisburg, Pa. 17105

Puerto Rico:
Department of Labor
505 Munoz Rivera Avenue
Hato Rey, Puerto Rico
00918
(Includes
Antidiscrimination
Unit)

Rhode Island:
Department of Labor
220 Elmwood Avenue
Providence, R.I. 02907

Commission for Human
Rights
334 Westminster Mall
Providence, R.I. 02903

South Carolina:
Department of Labor
3600 Forest Drive
P.O. Box 11329
Columbia, S.C. 29211

Human Affairs
Commission
Post Office Drawer 11300
Columbia, S.C. 29211

South Dakota:
Department of Labor
Capitol Complex
700 Illinois North
Pierre, South Dakota
57501

Commission on Human
Rights
State Capitol Building
Pierre, South Dakota
57501

Tennessee:
Department of Labor
501 Union Building
Nashville, Tennessee
37219

Commission for Human
Development
208 Tennessee Building

535 Church Street
Nashville, Tennessee
37219

Texas:
Texas Commission on
Human Rights
P.O. Box 13493
Capitol Station
Austin, Texas 78711

Department of Labor and
Standards
P.O. Box 12157
Capitol Station
Austin, Texas 78711

Utah:
Industrial Commission
560 South 300 East
Salt Lake City, Utah
84111

Antidiscrimination
Division
560 South 300 East
Salt Lake City, Utah
84111

Vermont:
Department of Labor and
Industry
State Office Building
Montpelier, Vermont
05602

Virginia:
Department of Labor and
Industry
205 N. 4th Street
P.O. Box 12064
Richmond, Virginia 23214

Virgin Islands:
Department of Labor
P.O. Box 890
Christiansted
St. Croix, V.I. 00820

Washington:
Department of Labor and
Industries
General Administration
Bldg.
Olympia, Washington
98504

Human Rights
Commission
402 Evergreen Plaza
Building
FJ-41
Olympia, Washington
98504

West Virginia:
Department of Labor
Capitol Complex
1900 Washington Street,
East
Charleston, W.Va. 25305

Human Rights
Commission
215 Professional Building
1036 Quarrier Street
Charleston, W.Va. 25301

Wisconsin:
Department of Industry,
Labor, and Human
Relations
201 East Washington
Ave.
P.O. Box 7946
Madison, Wisconsin
53707

Equal Rights Division
P.O. Box 7903
Madison, Wisconsin
53707

Wyoming:
Department of Labor and
Statistics
Hathaway Building
Cheyenne, Wyoming
82002

Fair Employment
Practices Commission
Hathaway Building,
Cheyenne, Wyoming
82002

IV. EEOC Offices*

Albuquerque:
505 Marquette, N.W.
Suite 1515
New Mexico 87101

Atlanta:
75 Piedmont Avenue,
N.E.
10th Floor
Georgia 30303

Baltimore:
711 West 40th Street
Suite 210
Maryland 21211

Birmingham:
2121 Eighth Avenue,
North
Alabama 35203

Boston:
150 Causeway Street
Suite 1000
Massachusetts 02114

Buffalo:
One West Genesee Street
Room 320
New York 14202

Charlotte:
1301 East Morehead
North Carolina 28204

Chicago:
536 South Clark Street
Room 234
Illinois 60605

Cincinnati:
550 Main Street
Room 7019
Ohio 45202

Cleveland:
1365 Ontario Street
Room 602
Ohio 44114

Dallas:
1900 Pacific
13th Floor
Texas 75201

Dayton:
200 West Second Street
Room 608
Ohio 45402

Denver:
1513 Stout Street
6th Floor
Colorado 80202

Detroit:
660 Woodward Avenue
Suite 600
Michigan 48226

El Paso:
2211 East Missouri,
Room E-235
Texas 79903

Fresno:
1313 P Street
Suite 103
California 93721

Greensboro:
324 West Market Street
Room 132
North Carolina 27402

Greenville:
7 North Laurens Street
Suite 507
South Carolina 29602

Houston:
2320 LaBranch
Room 1101
Texas 77004

Indianapolis:
46 East Ohio Street
Room 456
Indiana 46204

Jackson:
100 West Capitol Street
Suite 721
Mississippi 39201

Kansas City:
1150 Grand
1st Floor
Missouri 64106

Little Rock:
700 West Capitol
Arkansas 72201

Los Angeles:
3255 Wilshire Boulevard
9th Floor
California 90010

Louisville:
600 Jefferson Street
Kentucky 40202

Memphis:
1407 Union Avenue
Suite 502
Tennessee 38104

Miami:
300 Biscayne Boulevard
Way
Suite 414
Florida 33131

Milwaukee:
342 North Water Street
Room 612
Wisconsin 53202

Minneapolis:
12 South Sixth Street
Minnesota 55402

Nashville:
404 James Robertson
Pkwy.
Suite 1822
Tennessee 37219

Newark:
744 Broad Street
Room 502
New Jersey 07102

New Orleans:
600 South Street
Louisiana 70130

New York:
90 Church Street
Room 1301
New York 10007

*Reprinted by permission from *Law of the Workplace, Rights of Employers and Employees* by James W. Hunt, pp. 136–37, copyright © 1984 by The Bureau of National Affairs, Inc., Washington, D.C. 20037.

Norfolk:
200 Granby Mall
Room 412
Virginia 23510

Oakland:
1515 Clay Street
Room 640
California 94612

Oklahoma City:
50 Penn Place
Suite 1430
Oklahoma 73118

Philadelphia:
127 North Fourth Street,
Suite 200
Pennsylvania 19106

Phoenix:
201 North Central Avenue
Suite 1450
Arizona 85073

Pittsburgh:
1000 Liberty Avenue
Room 2038A
Pennsylvania 15222

Raleigh:
414 Fayetteville Street
North Carolina 27608

Richmond:
400 North Eighth Street
Room 6213
Virginia 23240

San Antonio:
727 East Durango
Suite B-601
Texas 78206

C

Career Management

Your Career Planning Activities

By actively managing your career, you'll do better than by not managing it. "Better" can be measured by any standard you choose—personal fulfillment, climbing to the top of the organization, happiness, or salary level. By planning and managing, you'll increase your chances of obtaining whatever you realistically identify as most important.

Exhibit C.1 outlines one strategy for getting into the organization of your choice. To obtain the most from this model, you should carefully follow each step.

Step 1: Conducting Personal Appraisal

This step involves taking a personal inventory of the following:

- Values
- Goals
- Skills

Personal Career Planning Activities   *Exhibit C.1*

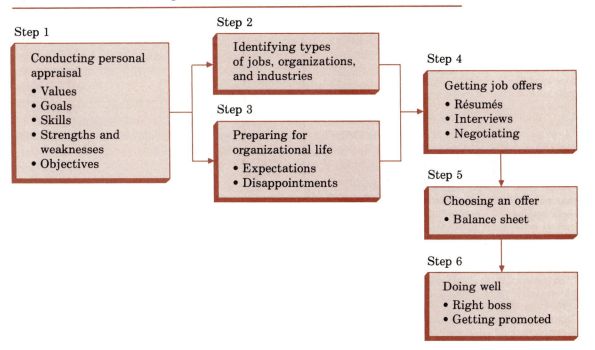

- Strengths and weaknesses
- Objectives

Do this step by completing the following exercise:

Goal Setting

Steps

1. List five goals for each of three categories: career, affiliations, and personal fulfillment.
2. Go back and rank them (1 = little importance, 5 = great importance). Which list has the most fours and fives?
3. Merge the three lists, ranking all fifteen goals in order of importance to you on the next sheet.
4. Select your top goal. Discuss this goal in relation to the following:
   a. Personal strengths and weaknesses
   b. Obstacles to prevent achieving the goal
   c. Strategies to circumvent obstacles
   d. Are the goals realistic, attainable, and measurable?
   e. What are the rewards for achieving the goal?
   f. Do you value these rewards?

Complete the form on pp. 716–717 for the top goal.

Career Goals (e.g., become president by age forty-five; become V.P. by age thirty-five)

1. _____

2. _____

3. _____

4. _____

5. _____

Affiliation/Interpersonal (e.g., family, friends, clubs, group members)

1. _____

2. _____

3. _____

4. _____

5. _____

Personal Fulfillment/Achievements (e.g., master the piano; run a marathon; get M.B.A. degree)

1. _____

2. _____

3. _____

4. _____

5. _____

Ranking Goals

1. _____

2. _____

3. _____

4. _____

5. _____

6. _____

7. _____

8. _____

9. _____

10. _____

11. _____

12. _____

13. _____

14. _____

15. _____

For your top goal, identify your:

Personal Strengths

1. _____

2. _____

3. _____

4. _____

5. _____

Personal Weaknesses

1. _____

2. _____

3. _____

4. _____

5. _____

Obstacles

1. _____

2. _____

3. _____

4. _____

5. _____

Strategies to Overcome

1. _____

2. _____

3. _____

4. _____

5. _____

_____

Rewards for Achieving the Goal (rank according to value)

1. _____

2. _____

3. _____

4. _____

5. _____

Indicators That You Have Achieved the Goal

1. _____

2. _____

3. _____

4. _____

5. _____

Steps to Achieve Goal   *Time Deadline*

1. _____

2. _____

3. _____

4. _____

5. _____

Step 2: Identifying Types of Jobs, Organizations, and Industries

Because the job or jobs you choose can have such an impact on your life, it is important to analyze carefully what you want for your first job and your first company. You may want to start by first identifying industries in which you may want to work.

For example, you may want to choose to work in an industry with great growth potential, such as the following:

- Banking
- Insurance
- Medical care
- Computer science, data processing
- Communications

Then within these industries, or any others, you next want to gather information on a particular company. Summer work experience, internships, and part-time work are valuable ways to gain exposure to new companies. Although some work experience may be boring to you, it sometimes helps if you consider them as learning experiences, ways of getting to know yourself better. Other sources of information are newspapers and professional magazines, school placement offices, libraries, direct mail, job-search firms, friends, and family.

Don't Exclude Nontraditional Jobs.   In thinking about the types of job, organizations, and industries in which you would like to work, think creatively. Consider jobs, organizations, and industries that you would label as nontraditional.

Many people hate their jobs because they dislike being closely supervised or confined to the same work area every day. Or they may feel they never have the satisfaction of seeing a finished product of their labor. Yet they see no escape.

There are actually numerous high-paying jobs (often $10 an hour and up) which permit great freedom of movement, require little supervision and offer lots of personal satisfaction. If you are skilled with your hands and you enjoy working with things, consider becoming any of the following: air-conditioning, refrigeration and heating mechanic; appliance serviceperson; television and radio service technician; business machine, computer, or industrial machinery serviceperson; truck or bus mechanic; vending machine mechanic.

Though most of these jobs are commonly thought of as men's work, the U.S. Department of Labor points out that they are equally suited to women. The Labor Department bases its opinion on the fact that the majority of repair occupations require relatively little physical strength and are performed indoors in warm surroundings. Most important, career-aptitude research indicates that the same high finger dexterity which allows women to excel at typing and factory assembly jobs also enables them to do very well at these highpay repair occupations.

Other research by the Department of Labor indicates that if you do learn one of these skills, you'll have plenty of job opportunities through the 1980's.[1]

Many other types of jobs can be considered, including self-employment and the more traditional entry-level jobs in larger organizations that are the first step in a series through promotions to senior management positions. Within larger organizations, these traditional paths are available in many functional areas such as personnel and across functional areas as described in the first part of this chapter. Also, a few job opportunities are in the relatively new field of internal corporate consulting.

Management consulting has long been a springboard to lofty corporate positions for men, and as far back as the late 1960s a handful of women also used it to move up in corporations. For instance, Mary C. Falvey, 40, who currently earns a salary estimated at well above $100,000 as vice-president of finance at Shaklee Corp. in San Francisco, joined the management consulting firm of McKinsey & Co. back in

1967. But only in the past four or five years have substantial numbers of women discovered consulting as a shortcut to corporate achievement, a demanding—but rewarding—way of bypassing lower managerial jobs.[2]

Step 3: Preparing for Organizational Life

It is one thing to know the type of jobs you might want and the type of industry or organization in which you want to work, but it's an entirely different thing to know the realities of living and working in an organization. Two qualities of organizational life, in almost any organization, that you should be aware of are (1) organizational expectations and (2) organizational disappointments.

Organizational Expectations.   Most organizations expect new employees to have certain characteristics:

- Competence to get a job done
- Ability to accept organizational realities
- Ability to generate and sell ideas
- Loyalty and commitment
- High personal integrity and strength
- Capacity to grow[3]

Organizational Disappointments.   Although organizations have high expectations of you, they may not always live up to their end of the bargain. What they do or don't do may bring you disappointments (**reality shock**). Here are several likely reasons why:

- *Low initial job challenge:* Although some findings have indicated the usefulness of giving new recruits a challenging initial job, many organizations continue to ease the new recruit into the organization. This is consistent with the organization's perception of the new recruit as a novice.

- *Low self-actualization and need satisfaction:* The new recruit may fail to experience the autonomy and challenge necessary to grow and to develop self-esteem and competency. Some researchers have suggested that an individual may actually lose competency of the job if not given the opportunity to advance in the direction of the growth and independence characteristic of mature adults.

- *The vanishing performance appraisal, or inability to determine what the real criteria are:* New recruits come on board with the expectation of receiving clear and unambiguous evaluations of their performance. In reality, new recruits report having little feedback on their performance, although their supervisors may claim the opposite.

- *Unrealistically high aspirations:* Most recruits have higher expectations of being able to use their skills and abilities than actually occur. The gap between an individual's skills and the skills actually used on the job is probably increased because of the manager's belief that the new recruit is not capable of assuming responsibility.

- *Inability to create challenge:* Although new recruits may not be given challenging assignments, they are also often incapable of creating their own challenge. They have been conditioned to receive well-defined projects from others. As a result, they find it more difficult to create challenge from an ill-defined or unstructured situation.

■ *Source of threat to the boss:* A new recruit's first boss plays a critical role for the recruit's future in the organization. This role tends to be negative, especially if the boss feels threatened. The threat may occur to the supervisor who is in a terminal position and can't go any further in the organization. The new recruit may be seen as a "comer" with a great deal more potential than the boss. In addition, the new recruit is probably younger and has different values and styles. As a result, the supervisor may not be very supportive of the new employee and may not provide many positive experiences.

■ *Amount of conflict and uncertainty in the organization:* New recruits think that rules and procedures, directions, and communications will be clear, crisp, and without conflict. The reality in many situations is just the opposite.[4]

Step 4: Getting Job Offers

Now that you've narrowed down (but not too much) the types of jobs, organizations, and industries you want and are prepared for organizational life, the next thing to do is get some job offers. Three aspects of getting job offers are as follows:

■ Résumé writing
■ Interviewing
■ Negotiating

Résumé Writing.   The **standard résumé** lists work experience from your current job or student status to those two years you spent delivering the daily paper (to show youthful vitality, industry, and responsibility for customers and money). Often it's a chronology of dates, titles, and responsibilities (whether they are previous jobs or positions held in school organizations).

Job Interviewing.   Step 1 has great value as preparation for job interviews. If you know yourself inside and out, you will find it easier to "sell" yourself to potential employers. Here are six suggestions for participating in job interviews:

■ "Sell" yourself to the recruiter with the same determination you would use in selling a product or service to a customer. The interview period is brief; yet a favorable impression of your appearance, sense of purpose, and clarity of self-expression will probably weigh more heavily with the recruiter than your transcript, your résumé, or your references.

■ Familiarize yourself ahead of time with the employer to be interviewed—know what the company does and what products or services it offers. Ask only pertinent questions during the interview, and suggest how your skills and abilities may benefit the organization.

■ Develop your ability to communicate, but do not come on too strong or be overly confident.

■ Cite academic achievements, especially if they appear to relate to the job area you are interested in. Remember that recruiting companies often view your college work as a preparatory period. Hence, cite your academic efforts as evidence that you can attain long-range goals and objectives.

■ Mention extracurricular activities that demonstrate your leadership or initiative.

■ Learn the art of interviewing by accepting as many interview opportunities as you can, even with organizations you think you may not prefer. Enroll in psychology and management courses where interviews are practiced by role playing.[5]

Negotiating.   An important topic that will surely arise in your interviewing is salary. How you handle this topic could make a substantial difference in how much you get paid. Here are a few tips on how to handle this aspect in your job search:

It's "dumb" for a job candidate to raise the question of salary early in the hiring process, says Pfizer divisional vice-president Max Hughes. And it is. Until the employer has had time to make up his or her mind to hire you, you aren't worth anything to the employer. To negotiate the highest possible salary, listen and ask questions so that you can identify the other person's needs and communicate how you can help meet them. It's best to delay the subject of salary until later in the interview. Loaded with information about your strengths, the employer should see you as a more valuable asset than when you began to talk. . . .

Inevitably, the employer who wants you on his or her team will ask, "What are your salary requirements?" Unlike some career consultants who encourage you to get the employer to name the first figure, executive recruiter Richard Irish, career consultant John Crystal, job-market analyst Richard Lathrop, and others say (and I agree) that you should name the first figure and make it high.[6]

Step 5: Choosing An Offer

Now that you have all the skills necessary to get several offers, equally necessary is to have the skills to choose one from among several offers. Although choosing the best offer may be more an art than a science to be taught and learned, one method that may help is the **career balance sheet.** On this you enter positive and negative aspects of given job offer. Enter aspects of each job offer with consideration for how they affect you personally and how they affect others—for example, your spouse, friends, or family. Although a job offer may have many positive aspects for you, it may have several negative aspects for others. You have as many sheets as you do job offers. A balance sheet helps you make your job choice because it requires you to organize and lay out job information in a systematic way.[7]

Step 6: Doing Well

Doing well involves getting what you want from the organization in which you are working. It means having things go your way. It may mean getting promoted, and it certainly means staying valuable and useful to the organization. As such, it requires that you know about the following:

■ Dealing with your boss
■ Getting promoted

The Right Boss.   People are more likely to develop strong leadership qualities if they work for a boss who has something to teach, who is on the move, and who is capable of taking others along. The preference for being on a winning team is a survival mechanism. People are less dependent and uncertain if they're allied with bosses who are strong leaders. Consequently, it pays to try to be in a position to select your boss. This is especially true for your first boss. You can enhance your chances of working for the boss of your choice by being an outstanding performer and by becoming a critical subordinate for your boss, but one who doesn't threaten the boss.[8]

Getting Promoted.   Getting promoted is much easier when you:

■ Have credibility with senior managers.

Managers with credibility can take greater risks and make more mistakes because they have the known ability to produce results. It's necessary to have credibility with superiors before developing it with subordinates. For example, a manager was brought in from the outside to run a division that designs aerospace equipment. He could barely get information he needed from headquarters—he had few connections and no clout. And when senior managers wanted answers, they went straight to his subordinates because the senior managers believed the subordinates had a better idea of what was going on. Without the support of top management, his subordinates thought little of him.[9]

■ Have a reputation as being an expert.

When a manager has the reputation of being an expert, others tend to defer to that manager on issues involving his or her expertise. This is important in large organizations where many people have only second-hand knowledge about one's professional competence.[10]

■ Are the first in the position.

A manager who is the first in a new position, takes risks, and succeeds is more likely to be rewarded than a manager who does something second. While excellent performance on routine tasks is usually valued, being innovative is a big plus.[11]

■ Know and use networks.

Knowing about and using networks can be critical to your job success. Essentially a **network** is a collection of friends and acquaintances, both inside and outside one's work place, that can be counted on for some kind of help. Networks can provide many kinds of help including information, services, support, and access.

Notes

1. Shirley Sloan Faber, *Family Weekly,* 18 Jan. 1981, p. 11.
2. "The Consulting Springboard,"*Business Week,* 17 Aug. 1981, pp. 101–4.
3. E. H. Schein, "How to Break in the College Graduate," *Harvard Business Review* (Mar./Apr. 1964):70; D. T. Hall and Associates, *Career Development in Organizations* (San Francisco: Jossey–Bass Publishers, 1986).
4. D. E. Berlew and D. T. Hall, "Some Determinants of Early Managerial Success," working paper 81-64 (Cambridge, Mass.: Sloan School of Management, MIT, 1964); R. A. Webber, "Career Problems of Young Managers," *California Management Review* (1976): 19–33.
5. J. H. Conley, J. M. Hueghi, and R. L. Minter, *Perspectives on Administrative Communication* (Dubuque, Iowa: Kendall/Hunt, 1976), p. 172; W. J. Morin, "The Four Interviewer Breeds: How to Tame Them," *New York Times Recruitment Survey,* 11 Oct. 1981, pp. 59, 62; J. T. Yenckel, "Careers: Facing the Interview," *Washington Post,* 20 Oct. 1981, sec. D, p. 5.
6. S. Chastain, "On the Job: The Winning Interview," in *Winning the Salary Game: Salary Negotiations for Women,* ed. D. Littman and C. Stegel (New York: Wiley, 1980).
7. I. Janis and D. Wheeler, "Thinking Clearly about Career Choices," *Psychology Today,* May 1978, pp. 67–76, 121–22.
8. "Managers Who Are No Longer Entrepreneurs," *Business Week,* 20 June 1980, pp. 74–82; J. J. Gabarro and J. P. Kotter, "Managing Your Boss," *Harvard Business Review* (Jan.–Feb. 1980): 92–100; B. Lehan Harragan, "Outwitting the Impossible Boss," *Savvy,* Dec. 1980, p. 22; M. Korda, "The Woman Who Wants to Succeed Ought to Appear to Be in Charge," *New York Times,* 4 Sept. 1977, pp. 1, 10; J. T. Yenckel, "Careers: Tell It to the Boss," *Washington Post,* 5 May 1981, sec. B, p. 5; "Guide to Careers," *Business Week,* 28 Mar. 1983, pp. 1–40.
9. "Living with the New Guidelines on Sexual Harassment," *People and Business,* July 1981, p. 3.
10. Ibid.
11. Ibid.

Index